THE ENDURING VISION

VOLUME ONE

THE ENDURING VISION

A HISTORY OF THE AMERICAN PEOPLE

Third Edition

Paul S. Boyer
University of Wisconsin, Madison

Clifford E. Clark, Jr.
Carleton College

Joseph F. Kett
University of Virginia

Neal Salisbury
Smith College

Harvard Sitkoff
University of New Hampshire

Nancy Woloch
Barnard College

D. C. Heath and Company
Lexington, Massachusetts   Toronto

Address editorial correspondence to:
D. C. Heath and Company
125 Spring Street
Lexington, MA 02173

Acquisitions: James Miller
Development: Sylvia Mallory
Editorial Production: Kathleen Deselle
Design: Henry Rachlin
Photo Research: Sharon Donahue, Bruce Carson, and Mary Lang
Art Editing: Gary Crespo
Production Coordination: Lisa Merrill and Dick Tonachel
Permissions: Margaret Roll

Published simultaneously in Canada.

Printed in the United States of America.

International Standard Book Number: 0-669-39772-5

Library of Congress Catalog Number: 94-74581

10 9 8 7 6 5 4 3 2 1

ABOUT THE AUTHORS

Paul S. Boyer, Merle Curti Professor of History at the University of Wisconsin, Madison, earned his Ph.D. from Harvard University. An editor of *Notable American Women, 1607–1950* (1971), he also coauthored *Salem Possessed: The Social Origins of Witchcraft* (1974), for which, with Stephen Nissenbaum, he received the John H. Dunning Prize of the American Historical Association. His other published works include *Urban Masses and Moral Order in America, 1820–1920* (1978), *By the Bomb's Early Light: American Thought and Culture at the Dawn of the Atomic Age* (1985), *When Time Shall Be No More: Prophecy Belief in Modern American Culture* (1992), and *Promises to Keep: The United States Since World War II* (1995). His articles and essays have appeared in *American Quarterly, The New Republic,* and other journals. He is an elected member of the American Antiquarian Society and the Society of American Historians.

Clifford E. Clark, Jr., M. A. & A. D. Hulings Professor of American Studies and professor of history at Carleton College, earned his Ph.D. from Harvard University. He has served as both the chair of the History Department and director of the American Studies program at Carleton. Clark is the author of *Henry Ward Beecher: Spokesman for a Middle-Class America* (1978), *The American Family Home, 1800–1960* (1986), and *The Intellectual and Cultural History of Anglo-America Since 1789* in the General History of the Americas. He also has edited and contributed to *Minnesota in a Century of Change: The State and Its People Since 1900* (1989). A past member of the Council of the American Studies Association, Clark is active in the fields of material culture studies and historic preservation, and he serves on the Northfield, Minnesota, Historical Preservation Commission.

Joseph F. Kett, professor of history at the University of Virginia, received his Ph.D. from Harvard University. His works include *The Formation of the American Medical Profession: The Role of Institutions, 1780–1860* (1968), *Rites of Passage: Adolescence in America, 1790–Present* (1977), *The Pursuit of Knowledge Under Difficulties: From Self-Improvement to Adult Education in America, 1750–1990* (1994), and *The Dictionary of Cultural Literacy* (1988), of which he is coauthor. A former History Department chair at Virginia, he also has participated on the Panel on Youth of the President's Science Advisory Committee, has served on the Board of Editors of the *History of Education Quarterly,* and is a past member of the Council of the American Studies Association.

Neal Salisbury, professor of history at Smith College, received his Ph.D. from the University of California, Los Angeles. The author of *Manitou and Providence: Indians, Europeans, and the Making of New England, 1500–1643* (1982) and *The Indians of New England: A Critical Bibliography* (1982), he also has contributed numerous articles to journals and edited collections, most recently to the forthcoming *Cambridge History of the Native Peoples of the Americas.* He has been awarded fellowships by the Smithsonian Institution, the National Endowment for the Humanities, the Charles Warren Center for Studies in American History at Harvard University, and the National Humanities Center. Formerly chair of the History Department at Smith, he is active in the fields of colonial and Native American history, has served on the editorial board of the journal *Ethnohistory,* and coedits a book series, Cambridge Studies in North American Indian History.

Harvard Sitkoff, professor of history at the University of New Hampshire, earned his Ph.D. from Columbia University. He is the author of *A New Deal for Blacks* (1978) and *The Struggle for Black Equality, 1954–1992* (1981, 1992), coeditor of *A History of Our Time* (1982, 1987, 1991), and editor of *Fifty Years Later: The New Deal Evaluated* (1985). A contributor to numerous edited collections, he also has published articles in many journals, among them *The American Quarterly, The Journal of American History, The Journal of Southern History,* and *The Wilson Quarterly.*

Nancy Woloch received her Ph.D. from Indiana University. She is the author of *Women and the American Experience* (1984, 1994, 1996), editor of *Early American Women: A Documentary History, 1600–1900* (1992), and coauthor, with Walter LaFeber and Richard Polenberg, of *The American Century: A History of the United States Since the 1890s* (1986, 1992). Her most recent book is *Muller v. Oregon: A Brief History with Documents* (1996). She teaches American history and American Studies at Barnard College, Columbia University.

PREFACE

Writing a textbook sometimes seems a labor of Sisyphus. It is not enough to push the rock uphill once; the job must be done over and over again, revising the book to keep it current with the best recent scholarship, responding to users' criticisms, rethinking our own conclusions, and all the while squirming under our editors' pleas that all the changes be made without lengthening the text.

Yet the rigors of this task are mitigated by the enthusiastic reception that our colleagues and students have given *The Enduring Vision* ever since its first edition in 1990. It is indeed a pleasure to realize that our efforts are producing a textbook from which hundreds of thousands of undergraduates are learning to think about the subtleties of American history, not merely memorizing facts, and with which historians with many different expectations find they can teach creatively. It was in the spirit of keeping such a diverse and warmly responsive audience satisfied that we prepared this Third Edition. We have tried to improve the readability, to give more attention to the peoples and cultures of the borderland communities in the South and West, and to continue weaving in the story of Americans' encounters with the natural environment. We hope that the results continue to please you.

One major change that will be of interest to instructors who may be rethinking the chronological divisions of the traditional two-semester survey course is D.C. Heath's decision to publish the twentieth-century chapters separately. Of course, the complete *Enduring Vision* is still available in two volumes. Volume One extends from the origins through Reconstruction (Chapters 1–16), and Volume Two, from Reconstruction to the present day (Chapters 16–33). The new twentieth-century version (Chapters 22–33, plus some material from Chapter 21) will serve the needs of those who teach a semester- or quarter-length course that begins with imperialism and the Spanish-American War and then takes up domestic developments with the Progressive Era.

Adopters' comments, as well as our own sense of the "rightness" of things, guided us in introducing these substantive changes in the Third Edition:

- Along with the origins of English colonization, Chapter 2 now discusses the beginnings of the Spanish, French, and Dutch colonies in North America; some of this material formerly appeared in Chapter 4.

- We have substantially overhauled Chapter 3: a new section, "The Spread of Slavery," combines coverage of the Caribbean colonies and the origin of Carolina; another new section, "The Middle Colonies," gives greater attention to this region's ethnic and religious pluralism; and the section "Rivals for North America" encompasses developments in the French and Spanish colonies. In keeping with our decision to give more attention to the borderlands, a new "Place in Time" essay focuses on Taos and the Pueblo revolt.

- Some condensation in Chapter 4 has made it possible to add a new subsection, "Colonial Farmers and the Environment," and to expand discussion of colonial women and of the French and Spanish colonies (particularly Louisiana).

- Chapter 5 now offers more British perspectives on the coming of the Revolution.

- Chapter 6 revises and extends the discussion of women in the new republic.

- In the chapters on antebellum America and the Civil War and Reconstruction, changes mainly involved compressing and streamlining some complex material. There is a new "Place in Time" essay in Chapter 11 on Frances Trollope's efforts to market popular culture in Cincinnati, new material on George Catlin's paintings of the American Indian, and—in line with recent scholarship—a new synthesis of the rise of the Republican party. The Civil War in the trans-Mississippi West also receives more attention.

- Users of the split version will find a new Prologue for Volume Two, tracing changes in attitudes toward the natural environment from the first years of settlement to the present.

- Chapter 17 offers more coverage of Mexican-American women.

- Chapter 18 now emphasizes the importance of coal as the cheap energy source that literally fueled American industrial expansion; it also expands the coverage of working women in the late nineteenth century and of the Homestead strike.

- Chapter 19's assessment of urban political bosses emphasizes how they exploited as well as helped immigrants.

- Chapter 20 offers new material on the "stem family" and on sports—racism in the boxing ring and the commercialization of sports at the turn of the century.

- Chapter 21 gives more analysis of populist ideology and of women's participation in the populist movement.

- Chapter 22 expands its discussion of Progressive Era social problems, such as drug and alcohol abuse, and of the origins and function of the Federal Reserve System.

- Chapter 23 now includes more material on the World War I combat experience and on the war's impact on the American economy and on progressivism.

- Chapter 24 more fully discusses revivalism and women's presence in both higher education and the workplace; and a new "Place in Time" essay explores the vibrancy and rich diversity of the Harlem Renaissance, as well as the bleaker realities of Harlem life in the 1920s.

- Chapter 25 also offers a new "Place in Time" profile, on Cimarron County, Oklahoma, bringing alive the human and ecological meaning of the Dust Bowl. The chapter features more discussion of depression-era economic thought, including Keynesianism.

- Chapter 26's analysis of the coming of World War II now includes a fuller treatment of isolationism's ideological roots.

- Chapter 27 provides updated coverage of the experience of blacks, Native Americans, and Chicanos during World War II, as well as of the Holocaust. A new "Place in Time" essay looks at life in wartime Honolulu.

- Chapter 29 gives more attention to nuclear-power plants and to the origins of the troubling nuclear-waste problem.

- Chapter 30 critically reexamines the Kennedy presidency in the light of recent scholarship.

- Chapter 31 offers an expanded discussion of the rise of the gay-power movement.

- Chapter 32's reorganized treatment of the Ford, Carter, and Reagan administrations smoothly synthesizes political, economic, social, and international developments. The inevitable compression of political coverage as these administrations recede has opened up opportunities for more synthesis of such trends as the revolution in mass marketing, mass entertainment, and the growing political clout of evangelical Christians.

- Chapter 33 analyzes the Clinton administration's first two years and offers a considered assessment of the major political shift represented by the Republican victory in the 1994 elections. A new "Place in Time" essay on contemporary Miami explores issues of cultural diversity and social conflict in a fascinating multiethnic American city.

- Throughout, we have updated bibliographies and suggestions for further reading.

Reflecting the best efforts of its authors and editors, this textbook also rests on the scholarly work of literally hundreds of historians over the years. We hope that you will find it helpful in making sense of America's unique historical experience, and in conveying your own research to your students.

Special Features

A range of useful study aids has been built into *The Enduring Vision*. Each chapter begins with a vignette of a person or an event that both swiftly draws the reader into the atmosphere and issues of the times and establishes the chapter's main themes. In every chapter a two-page, illustrated essay called "A Place in Time" delves into a single community's experiences. Tables and chronological charts on special topics occur regularly throughout the text, and each chapter closes with a Conclusion, a Chronology of pivotal events and developments, annotated For Further Reading recommendations for the student, and a lengthy Additional Bibliography. The Appendix provides statistical tables; handy reference lists; and the text of the Declaration of Independence, the Articles of Confederation, and the Constitution (with its amendments). The full-color design of *The Enduring Vision* features hundreds of photographs, paintings, and cartoons and almost 200 maps and graphs. Informative captions enrich the art program.

Supplementary Resources

An outstanding program of supplementary resources is available with this textbook. Included are:

- *Critical Reading: U.S. History and The Enduring Vision*, by Connie Cantrell

  This **all-new**, concise guide, developed for students by a reading specialist, offers a wealth of critical-reading exercises keyed to *The Enduring* Vision, Third Edition. Students will develop skills in such areas as previewing the text, discerning main arguments, identifying supporting material, and mastering other aspects of reading and studying history.

- *Student Guide with Map Exercises*, Third Edition, by Barbara Blumberg

  Keyed chapter-by-chapter to the textbook, the *Student Guide with Map Exercises,* available in one- and two-volume editions, provides an outline-summary of major topics and themes and includes several features guiding the student in chapter review and self-testing. Map exercises sharpen students' knowledge of and skills in understanding U.S. historical geography.

- *Reading and Writing American History: An Introduc-tion to the Historian's Craft*, by Peter Charles Hoffer and William W. Stueck

  This skills-based sourcebook, featuring discussions of the nature of historical inquiry, readings, and hands-on exercises, is available in two brief volumes to complement students' reading of their American history textbook.

- *Surveying the Land: Skills and Exercises in U.S. Historical Geography*, by Robert Grant

  This two-volume supplement strengthens students' understanding of U.S. geography and illuminates its shaping role in historical events. Comprising thirty-two units, *Surveying the Land* builds basic geographic literacy and develops map-reading proficiency through a blend of descriptive narrative and mapping exercises.

- *Getting the Most out of Your U.S. History Course: The History Student's Vade Mecum*, Third Edition, by Neil R. Stout

  With suggestions on reading the textbook, interpreting maps and graphs, taking lecture notes, preparing for exams, and more, the *Vade Mecum* is a convenient pocket-size handbook for beginning college students.

- *Enduring Voices Document Sets*, Third Edition, by James J. Lorence

  This one-of-a-kind, two-volume reader, organized to follow the chapter sequence of *The Enduring Vision,* presents discrete sets of primary sources, with each set built around a "problem" closely related to a major theme in the corresponding textbook chapter.

- *Regional Document Sets:*

  Document Sets for the South in U.S. History, by Richard Purday

  Document Sets for Texas and the Southwest in U.S. History, by J'Nell Pate

  Document Sets for California and the West in U.S. History, by Iris Engstrand

  These three unique collections of documents are designed to enhance students' understanding of regional history. They provide rich opportunities for students to work with primary sources and to explore matters of keen regional interest that are linked to larger questions in U.S. history.

- *Instructor's Guide*, Third Edition, by Robert Grant and James J. Lorence

  This indispensable instructor's resource provides introductory how-to essays and student handouts, followed by teaching suggestions and strategies tied to each chapter of *The Enduring Vision*, Third Edition. Also included are detailed guidelines for using the *Enduring Voices Document Sets* in the classroom.

- *Test Item File*, Third Edition, by Kenneth Blume

  This rich bank of identification, multiple-choice, essay, and map questions covers all the main topics and themes of *The Enduring Vision*. Questions suitable for midterm and final exams are included.

- *Computerized Testing* for IBM and Macintosh computers

  Available for Macintosh and IBM-compatible computers, this electronic test generator provides the same questions as the printed test bank, but in convenient electronic format.

- *The D. C. Heath U.S. History Transparency Set*, 1996 Edition

  Approximately 150 full-color maps and graphs are offered in this valuable two-volume collection of overhead-transparency acetates.

- *An American Portfolio* Videodisc

  This CAV-format disc for instructors provides thousands of still images of historic events, personages, and artifacts; twenty-seven minutes of full-motion historical video footage; and numerous historical maps showing change over time.

- *What Makes America Different?* Videodisc and Videotape

  This video features lively conversations among the authors of *The Enduring Vision* on the topic of what makes the American historical experience unique.

- Audiocassette for U.S. History

  This audio anthology of songs, speeches, and radio broadcasts affords students another link to important events from the nation's past.

An All-New CD-ROM Designed for Students

With this new edition comes the debut of a revolutionary concept in CD-ROMs—*EnVision: A Student Guide to U.S. History to Accompany The Enduring Vision*. EnVision, an all-new interactive study aid for students, offers extensive banks of documentary, map, and other resources; a large bank of self-tests with which students can review course material and prepare confidently for exams; and "big-picture" overviews of the main periods and themes of American history, presented by authors of *The Enduring Vision*. The full text of *The Enduring Vision*, Third Edition, is included as a handy reference. Students will learn history in a whole new, exciting way with this innovative resource, the ideal complement to *The Enduring Vision*.

In Conclusion—and with Thanks

In the supplements program as well as in the textbook, our goal has been to make teaching and learning American history enjoyable and stimulating. We would value any comments you and your students have as you navigate through your course using *The Enduring Vision* and its supplements; don't hesitate to write to us.

We wish to extend our sincere gratitude to the many people at D. C. Heath and Company who worked hand in hand with us as we planned and executed this revision. Senior editor James Miller and editorial director Sylvia Mallory—our editors now on all three editions of the textbook—ably coordinated all stages of the revision. Supplements developmental editor Pat Wakeley, production editor Kathleen Deselle, designer Henry Rachlin, photo editors Sharon Donahue, Bruce Carson, and Mary Lang, permissions editor Margaret Roll, and production coordinators Lisa Merrill and Dick Tonachel played crucial roles in the production and design of the textbook and its ancillary program. Marketing manager Kenneth Rust and marketing associate Alyssa Chung got the word out about the new edition in their usual thorough and timely fashion. We warmly thank them all.

We also owe a debt of gratitude to the many colleagues who provided reviews for this edition of *The Enduring Vision*: **Tyler Anbinder,** George Washington University; **Kevin Boyle,** University of Massachusetts, Amherst; **Diane Britton,** University of Toledo; **Gregory Bush,** University of Miami; **Brian Cannon,** Brigham Young University; **Kathleen Carter**, High Point University; **Paul Cunningham,** Catonsville Community College; **Christine Daniels,** Michigan State University; **Sam Elworthy**, Rutgers University; **Scott Garrett,** Paducah Community College; **Gregory Gordon,** College of Lake County; **John Jameson,** Kent State University; **Timothy Keirn,** California State University, Long Beach; **Gary Kornblith,** Oberlin College; **Virginia Laas,** Missouri Southern University; **Ralph Levering,** Davidson College; **Larry Menna,** State University of New York, Farmingdale; **Larry Peterson,** North Dakota State University; **William Robbins,** Oregon State University; **Yolanda Romero,** North Lake College; **Ronald Schlundt,** University of Maryland, European Division; **Sally Schwartz,** Marquette University; **Stanley Underdal,** San Jose State University; **Edward Weller,** San Jacinto College South; and **Gerald Wilson**, Duke University. Finally, we thank the countless others—instructors and students alike—who have taken the time to send in their thoughtful and constructive suggestions over the years. The book is much better for our having listened to them.

P. B.   N. S.
C. C.   H. S.
J. K.   N. W.

BRIEF CONTENTS

CONTENTS

4

COLONIAL SOCIETY COMES OF AGE, 1660–1750 92

6

THE FORGE OF NATIONHOOD, 1776–1788 162

7

LAUNCHING THE NEW REPUBLIC, 1789–1800 200

8

JEFFERSONIANISM AND
THE ERA OF GOOD FEELINGS 234

10

POLITICS, RELIGION, AND REFORM
IN THE AGE OF JACKSON 298

12

THE OLD SOUTH AND SLAVERY, 1800–1860 364

15

REFORGING THE UNION: CIVIL WAR, 1861–1865 460

16

THE CRISES OF RECONSTRUCTION, 1865–1877 498

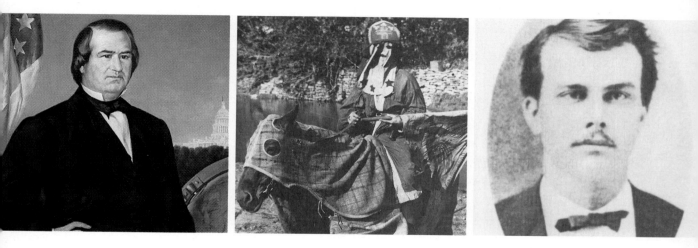

MAPS

CHARTS, GRAPHS, and TABLES

THE ENDURING VISION

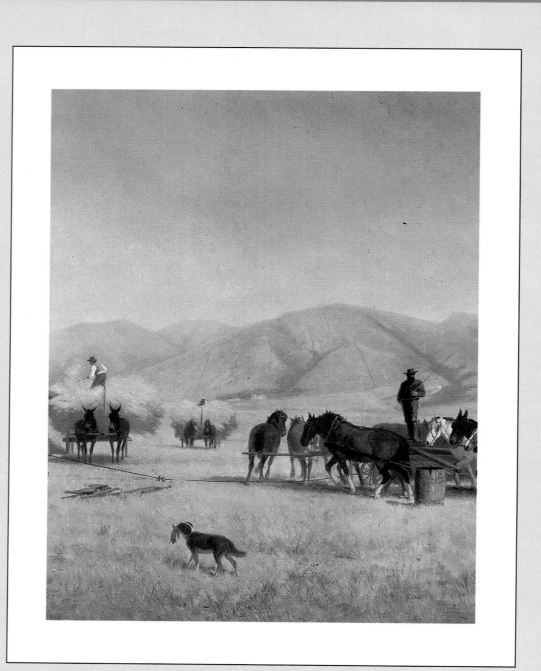

Harvest Time (detail)
by Carl William Hahn, 1875

ENDURING VISION, ENDURING LAND

This is the story of America and of the visions that Americans have shared. The first vision was of the land itself. For the Siberian adventurers who crossed the land bridge from Asia, for the Europeans who began to arrive in the sixteenth century, and for the later immigrants who poured in by the tens of millions, North America offered a haven for new beginnings. If life was hard elsewhere, it would be better here. And once here, the lure of the land continued. If times were tough in the East, they would be better in the West. New Englanders migrated to Ohio; Ohioans migrated to Kansas; Kansans migrated to California. For Africans the migration to America was forced and brutal. But after the Civil War, newly freed southern blacks embraced the vision and dreamed of new opportunities elsewhere:

> *I got my ticket,*
> *Leaving the thicket,*
> *And I'm a-heading for the Golden Shore!*

For most of American history, the vision of the land celebrated its beauty, its diversity, and its ability to provide sustenance and even wealth to those who exploited its fertility and its resources. But within this shared vision were deep-seated tensions. Whereas Native Americans regarded the land and other natural phenomena as spiritual forces to be feared and respected, many Europeans and their descendants considered nature a force to be conquered. The very abundance of America's natural resources led many to think of these resources as infinitely abundant and exploitable. In moving from one locale to another, some sought only to escape starvation or oppression, while others pursued wealth and power no matter the environmental consequences. Regardless of their motives and conditions, migrants often left behind a land bereft of

wild animals, its fertility depleted by intensive farming, its waters dammed and polluted or dried up altogether. If the land today remains part of the vision, it is only because we realize its vulnerability, rather than its immunity, to pollution and exploitation.

But the vision involves more than simply a love of the land. It also entails a commitment to an ongoing process: the process of creating a just social order. In pursuing this goal, Americans have sought to blend the best from their intellectual and cultural traditions with new, experimental social forms, a pattern often leading to bitter debates. Over thousands of years, Native Americans worked in this way to construct ideal social orders as they refined their relationships with one another and with the land around them. For the past five hundred years, immigrants from all over the world have pursued comparable ideals, both within their communities and in the nation at large.

Central to the American vision of the good society is the notion of individual freedom. To be sure, our commitment to freedom has frequently faltered in practice. The Puritans who sought freedom of worship for themselves often denied it to others. Southern whites who cheered the Declaration of Independence lived by the labor of black slaves. Many a wealthy employer conveniently forgot that economic exploitation can extinguish freedom as effectively as political tyranny or military force. And through much of our history, women—half the population—were relegated to second-class status. Yet the battered vision endured, prodding a sometimes reluctant nation to confront and explore its full meaning.

But freedom can be an empty and cheerless thing unless one is also part of a social group. The novelist O. E. Rölvaag, describing the emotions of a nineteenth-century Norwegian immigrant farm woman on the Great Plains, captured this feeling of social isolation:

> *A sense of desolation so profound settled upon her that she seemed unable to think at all. . . . She threw herself back in the grass and looked up into the heavens. But darkness and infinitude lay there, also—the sense of utter desolation still remained. . . . Suddenly, for the first time, she realized the full extent of her loneliness. . . .*

Thus the vision must also be one of community. Puritan leader John Winthrop, addressing a group of fellow immigrants aboard the *Arbella* on their way to America in 1630, eloquently summed up this dimension of the vision: "We must delight in each other, make others' conditions our own, rejoice together, mourn together, labor and suffer together: always having before our eyes our commission and community . . . as members of the same body."

The family, the town, the neighborhood, the church, the ethnic group, and the nation itself have been ways by which Americans have woven into their lives a web of social meaning. And *community* is not just a high-sounding abstraction; it has political implications. If we are not just a fragmented collection of self-absorbed individuals but also a *people,* what obligations do we owe each other? What limitations on our freedom are we willing to accept in order to be part of a social group? In struggling with tough questions like these, we have further defined our vision of America.

Finally, this vision is one of renewal and new beginnings. The story of America is part of the human story, and thus it has its dark and shameful passages as well as its bright moments of achievement. Arrogance, injustice, callous blindness to suffering, and national self-delusion have all figured in our history. But balancing the times when we lost our way are the moments when we found our bearings and returned to the hard task of defining what America at its best might truly be.

This, then, is the essence of the vision: a vision not of a foreordained national destiny unfolding effortlessly but of a laborious, often frustrating struggle to define what our common life as a people shall be. For all the failures and the wrong turns, it remains a vision rooted in hope, not despair. In 1980 Jesse de la Cruz, a Mexican-American woman who had fought for years to improve conditions for California's migrant workers, summed up the philosophy that kept her going: "Is America progressing toward the better? . . . We're the ones that are gonna do it. We have to keep on struggling. . . . With us, there's a saying: *La esperanza muere al último.* Hope dies last. You can't lose hope. If you lose hope, that's losing everything."

No sentiment could better sum up the enduring vision of American history.

◆

AN ANCIENT HERITAGE

"The land was ours before we were the land's." So begins the poem "The Gift Outright," which the aged Robert Frost read at President John F. Kennedy's inauguration in 1961. Frost's poem meditates on the interrelatedness of history, geography, and human consciousness. At first, wrote Frost, North American settlers merely possessed the land; but then, in a subtle spiritual process, they became possessed by it. Only by entering into this deep relationship with the land itself—"such as she was, such as she would become"—did their identity as a people fully take shape.

Frost's poem speaks of the encounter of English colonists with a strange new continent of mystery and promise; but of course, what the Europeans called the "New World" was in fact the homeland of the Native American peoples whose ancestors had been "possessed by" the land for at least fifteen thousand years. Native Americans had undergone an immensely long process of settling the continent, developing divergent cultures, discovering agriculture, and creating a rich spiritual life tightly interwoven with the physical environment that sustained them. We cannot fully comprehend the past five hundred years of American history without first understanding how, for thousands of years before then, Indians created the human habitats that non-natives and their descendants would occupy and transform.

To comprehend the American past, we first must know the American land itself. The patterns of weather; the undulations of valley, plain, and mountain; the shifting mosaic of sand, soil, and rock; the intricate network of rivers, streams, and lakes—these have profoundly influenced U.S. history. North America's fundamental physical characteristics have shaped human events from the earliest migrations from Asia to the later cycles of agricultural and industrial development, the rise of cities, the course of politics, and even the basic themes of American literature, art, and music. Geology, geography, and environment are among the fundamental building blocks of human history.

This prologue tells the story of the land itself: its geological origins; its reshaping by eons of lifting, sinking, erosion, and glaciation; the opportunities and limitations that it presents to human endeavor. It reminds us of the ultimate dependence of human beings on their environment.

It is sobering to begin the study of American history by contrasting the recent rise of a rich, complex human society on this continent with the awesomely slow pace by which the North American environment took form. Geologists trace the oldest known rocks on the continent back some 3 billion years when a single landmass, called Pangaea by geologists, encompassed

Volcanic Eruption, Hawaii

Formation of the Continents

After the break-up of the supercontinent of Pangaea, drifting land masses gradually formed today's continents.

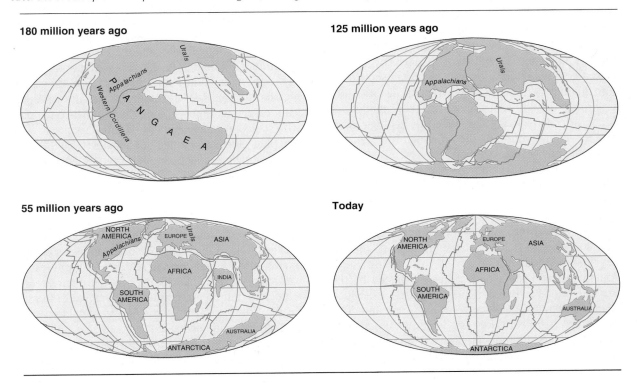

180 million years ago

125 million years ago

55 million years ago

Today

all the earth's dry surfaces. The rocky "floor" known as the Canadian Shield first became visible on the surface of what is now Canada during the earliest geologic era, the Precambrian, which ended 500 million years ago. Halfway between that remote age and the present, during the Paleozoic ("ancient life") era, forests covered much of what would eventually be the United States. From this organic matter, America's enormous coal reserves would be created, the largest yet discovered in the entire world. About 180 million years ago, during the Mesozoic ("middle life") era—the age of the dinosaurs—Pangaea began to break apart. By a process known as continental drift—which continues today at the rate of a few centimeters a year—today's continents were eventually formed. As a result, most plant and animal life in each of the earth's major landmasses—the Americas, Eurasia-Africa, Australia, and Antarctica—evolved in isolation from life in the others for 180 million years. As environmental historian Alfred W. Crosby puts it, "The ancestors of American buffalos, Eurasian cattle, and Australian kangaroos shambled and hopped down diverging paths of evolution." The overseas expansion of Europeans in the past five centuries has brought an abrupt end to that isolation, with some far-reaching consequences in North America that are noted in the chapters that follow.

So enormous a gulf of time separates the origins of North America from the beginning of human history that, if those 180 million years were compressed into the space of a single twenty-four-hour day, everything that has happened since the Indians' ancestors first migrated here would flash by in the last half-second before midnight, and the New World's history since Columbus would occupy about five-thousandths of a second. In considering the sweep of geologic time, one inevitably wonders how ephemeral human history itself may yet prove to be.

Many millions of years after North America's initial separation, violent movements of the earth's crust thrust up the Pacific Coastal, Sierra Nevada, and Cascade ranges on the continent's western edge. As the dinosaurs were dying out, toward the end of the Mesozoic some 65–70 million years ago, the vast, shallow sea that washed over much of west-central North America disappeared, having been replaced by the Rocky Mountains. By then, the decay and fossilization of plant and animal life were creating North America's once great petroleum deposits, which until a generation ago seemed almost limitless. Within the last 50 million years, volcanic eruptions raised the cones that now form the Hawaiian Islands, twenty-five hundred

miles southwest of California. Active Pacific-rim volcanoes and powerful earthquakes all over the continent dramatically demonstrate that the molding of the American landscape still continues.

Between 2 million and ten thousand years ago, four great glaciations left a tremendous imprint on the land. The Ice Age staggers the imagination. During periods of maximum glacial expansion, a carpet of ice as thick as thirteen thousand feet extended over most of Canada and crept southward into what is now New England, New York State, and much of the Midwest. As we shall see in Chapter 1, the first humans to inhabit North America—ancestors of American Indians—arrived as temperatures rose and the glaciers began their most recent, slow retreat northward. While the earth has been relatively stable during the last few thousand years, earthquakes in California and elsewhere remind us that the continents continue to drift and that the world as we know it is not static but in a state of steady change.

THE CONTINENT AND ITS REGIONS

As the glacial ice melted at last, raising the world's oceans to their present level, North America slowly warmed. The ensuing differences in climate, physical features, and organic life were the basis of America's extraordinary geographic diversity. Geographic diversity contributed, in turn, to the remarkable diversity of regional cultures that later emerged, first among American Indians and then among the non-native peoples who settled in America after Columbus's voyages. Geographic variety also made possible the United States' rise to political and economic preeminence in the modern world.

The West

With its severe climate and profuse wildlife, Alaska still evokes the land that ancient North America's earliest migrants discovered. Indeed, Alaska's far north resembles a world from which ice caps have just retreated— a treeless tundra of grasses, lichens, and stunted shrubs. This region, the Arctic, is a stark wilderness in winter, reborn in fleeting summers of colorful flowers and returning birds. In contrast, the subarctic of central Alaska and Canada is a heavily forested country known as taiga. Here rises North America's highest peak,

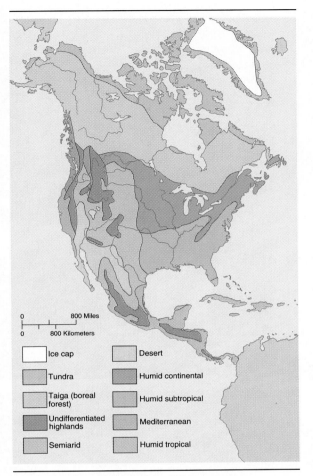

North American Climatic Regions

Ice cap
Tundra
Taiga (boreal forest)
Undifferentiated highlands
Semiarid
Desert
Humid continental
Humid subtropical
Mediterranean
Humid tropical

0   800 Miles

0   800 Kilometers

more uniformly temperate than anywhere else in North America. From Anchorage and the Alaska panhandle to a little south of San Francisco Bay, winters are cool, humid, and foggy, and the coast's dense forest cover includes the largest living organisms on earth, the giant sequoia (redwood) trees. Along the southern California coast, winds and currents generate a warmer, "Mediterranean" climate, and vegetation includes a heavy growth of shrubs and short trees, scattered stands of oak, and grasses able to endure prolonged seasonal drought.

The rugged Sierra Nevada, Cascade, and coastal ranges stretch the length of British Columbia, Washington, Oregon, and California. Their majestic peaks trap abundant Pacific Ocean moisture that gigantic clockwise air currents carry eastward. Between the ranges nestle flat, fertile valleys—California's Central Valley (formed by the San Joaquin and Sacramento rivers), Oregon's Willamette Valley, and the Puget

Mendenhall Glacier, Alaska

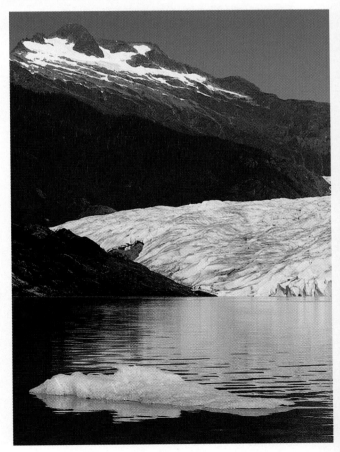

20,320-foot Mt. McKinley, or Denali. Average temperatures in the subarctic range from the fifties above zero in summer to well below zero in the long, dark winters, and the soil is permanently frozen except during summer surface thaws.

The expanse from Alaska's glacier-gouged and ruggedly mountainous Pacific shore southward to northern California forms the Pacific Northwest. Only a few natural harbors break the shoreline, but they include the magnificent anchorages of Puget Sound and San Francisco Bay. Offshore, cool currents and warm winds make possible rich coastal fisheries.

The Pacific coastal region is in some ways a world apart. Vegetation and animal life, isolated from the rest of the continent by mountains and deserts, include many species unfamiliar farther east. Warm, wet westerly winds blowing off the Pacific create a climate

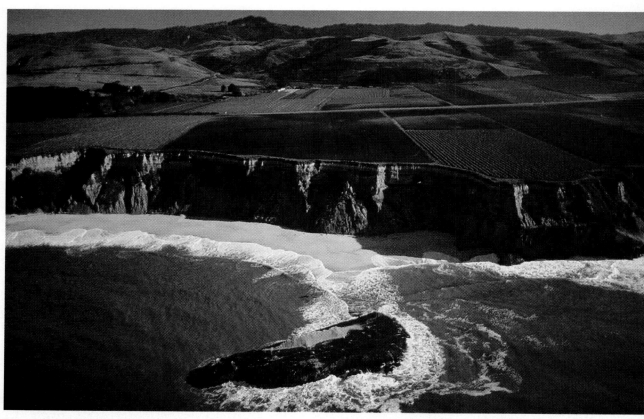

Coastal Farming, Northern California

Sound region in Washington—that have become major agricultural centers in recent times.

Well east of the Pacific coastal band lies the Great Basin, encompassing Nevada, western Utah, southern Idaho, and eastern Oregon. The few streams here have no outlet to the sea. Much of the Great Basin was once covered by an inland sea holding glacial meltwater, a remnant of which survives in Utah's Great Salt Lake. Today, however, the Great Basin is dry and severely eroded, a cold desert rich in minerals, imposing in its austere grandeur and lonely emptiness. North of the basin, the Columbia and Snake rivers, which drain the plateau country of Idaho and eastern Washington and Oregon, provide plentiful water for farming.

Western North America's "backbone" is the Rocky Mountains. In turn, the Rockies form part of the immense mountain system that reaches from Alaska to the Andes of South America. Elevations in the Rockies rise from a mile above sea level at Denver at the foot of the mountains to permanently snowcapped

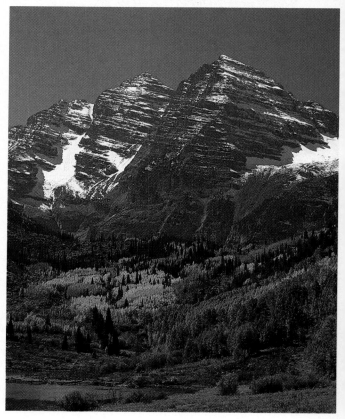

Maroon Bells of the Rocky Mountains, near Aspen, Colorado

peaks more than fourteen thousand feet above sea level. Beyond the front range of the Rockies lies the Continental Divide, the watershed separating the rivers flowing eastward into the Atlantic from those draining westward into the Pacific. The climate and vegetation of the Rocky Mountain high country resemble Arctic and subarctic types.

Arizona, southern Utah, western New Mexico, and southeastern California form America's southwestern desert. The climate is arid, searingly hot on summer days and cold on winter nights. Adapted to stringent environmental conditions, many plants and animals here could not survive elsewhere. Dust storms, cloudbursts, and flash floods have everywhere carved, abraded, and twisted the rocky landscape. Nature's fantastic sculpture appears on the most monumental scale in the Grand Canyon, where for 20 million years the Colorado River has been cutting down to Precambrian bedrock.

In the face of such tremendous natural forces, human activity might well seem paltry and transitory. Yet here the first crop cultivation began in what is now the

Lakes and Marshes in the Great Basin During the Last Ice Age

The Great Basin's extensive lakes and marshes during the last Ice Age contrast starkly with the diminished amount of surface water in the region today.

SOURCE: W. F. Ruddiman and H. E. Wright, Jr., eds. "North America and Adjacent Oceans During the Last Deglaciation." *The Geology of North America* K–3 (1987): 241.

continental United States. Indian peoples later modified their societies and cultures in order to establish elaborate irrigation systems. Such systems are maintained today by Pueblo Indian and Hispanic communities in the region.

The Heartland

North America's heartland comprises the area extending eastward from the Rockies to the Appalachians. This vast region forms one of the world's largest drainage systems. From it the Great Lakes empty into the North Atlantic through the St. Lawrence River, and the Mississippi-Missouri-Ohio river network flows southward into the Gulf of Mexico. Where the drainage system originates, at the northern and western reaches of the Great Lakes region, lie some of the world's richest deposits of iron and copper ore.

Bryce Canyon National Park, Utah, at sunset

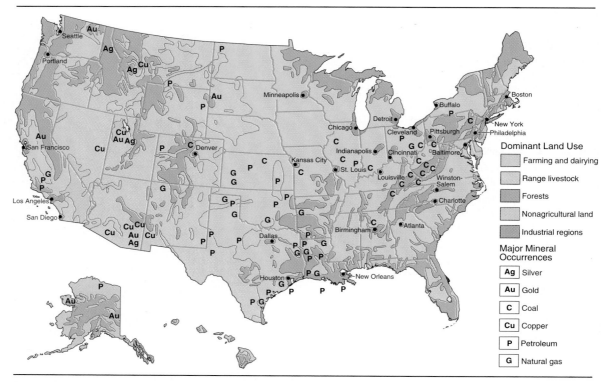

Present-Day U.S. Agriculture, Industry, and Resources

Confluence of the Mississippi and Ohio Rivers near Cairo, Illinois

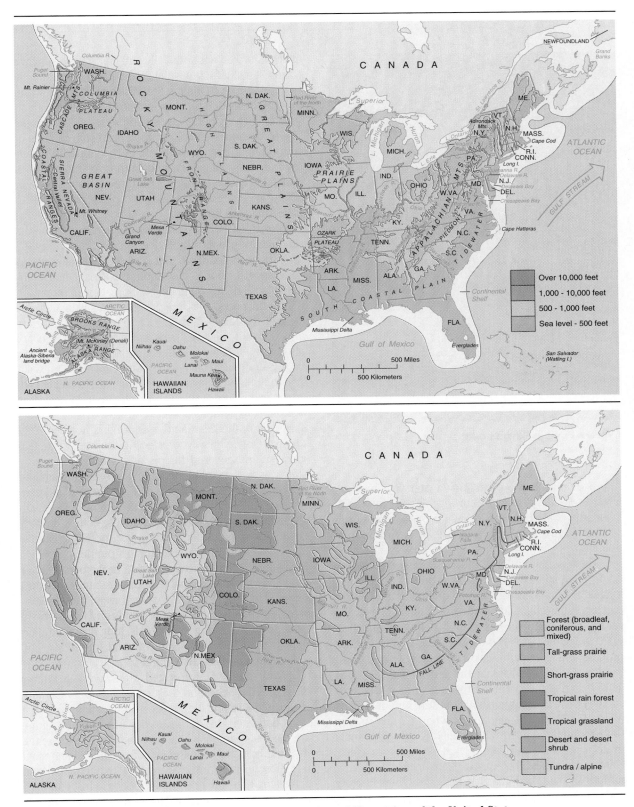

Above, **Physiographic Map of the United States** *Below,* **Natural Vegetation of the United States**

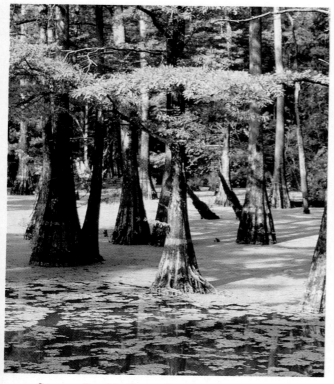

Cypress Pond in Bayou Country

In our own time, the heartland's waterways have offered a splendid means of carrying this mineral wealth to nearby coal-producing areas for processing but in so doing have spawned widespread environmental pollution.

The Mississippi—the "Father of Waters" to nearby Algonquian-speaking Indians, and one of the world's longest rivers—carries a prodigious volume of water and silt. It has changed course many times in geological history. The lower Mississippi (below the junction with the Ohio River) meanders constantly. In the process, the river deposits rich sediments throughout its broad, ancient floodplain. Indeed, the Missisippi has carried so much silt over the millennia that in its lower stretches, the river flows *above* the surrounding valley, which it catastrophically floods when its high banks (levees) are breached. Over millions of years, such riverborne sediment covered what was once the westward extension of the Appalachians in northern Mississippi and eastern Arkansas. Only the Ozark Plateau and Ouachita Mountains remain exposed, forming the hill country of southern Missouri, north-central Arkansas, and eastern Oklahoma. These uplands have

evolved into an economically and culturally distinctive region—beautiful but isolated and impoverished.

Below New Orleans the Mississippi empties into the Gulf of Mexico through an enormous delta with an intricate network of grassy swamps known as bayous. The Mississippi Delta offers good farm soil, capable of supporting a large population. Swarming with waterfowl, insects, alligators, and marine plants and animals, this environment has nurtured a distinctive way of life for the Indian, white, and black peoples who have inhabited it.

North of the Ohio and Missouri rivers, themselves products of glacial runoff, Ice Age glaciation molded the American heartland. Because the local terrain was generally flat prior to glaciation, the ice sheets distributed glacial debris quite evenly. Spread even farther by wind and rivers, this fine-ground glacial dust slowly created the fertile farm soil of the Midwest. Glaciers also dug out the five Great Lakes (Superior, Huron, Michigan, Ontario, and Erie), collectively the world's largest body of fresh water. Water flowing from Lake Erie to the lower elevation of Lake Ontario created Niagara Falls, comparable only to the Grand Canyon as testimony to nature's power.

Most of the heartland's eastern and northern sectors were once heavily forested. To the west thick, tall-grass prairie covered Illinois and parts of adjoining states, as well as much of the Missouri River basin and the middle Arkansas River basin (Oklahoma and central Texas). Beyond the Missouri the prairie gave way to short-grass steppe—the Great Plains, cold in winter, blazing hot in summer, and always dry. The great distances that separate the heartland's prairies and Great Plains from the moderating effects of the oceans have made this region's annual temperature range the most extreme in North America. As the traveler moves westward, elevations rise gradually, winds howl ceaselessly, trees grow only along streambeds, long droughts alternate with violent thunderstorms and tornadoes, and water and wood are ever scarcer.

Now much of this forested, grassy world is forever altered. The heartland has become open farming country. Gone are the flocks of migratory birds that once darkened the daytime skies of the plains; gone are the free-roaming bison. Forests now only fringe the heartland: in the lake country of northern Minnesota and Wisconsin, on Michigan's upper peninsula, and across the hilly uplands of the Appalachians, southern Indiana, and the Ozarks. The settlers who displaced the region's Indian inhabitants have done most of the plowing up of prairie grass and felling of trees since the

Bison on South Dakota Prairie

Grain Harvesting in America's Heartland

early nineteenth century. Destruction of the forest and grassy cover has made the Midwest both a "breadbasket" for the world market and, during intervals of drought, a "dust bowl."

The Atlantic Seaboard

The eastern edge of the heartland is marked by the ancient Appalachian Mountain chain, which over the course of 200 million years has been ground down to gentle ridges paralleling one another southwest to northeast. Between the ridges lie fertile valleys such as Virginia's Shenandoah. The Appalachian hill country's wealth is in thick timber and mineral beds—particularly the Paleozoic coal deposits—whose heavy exploitation since the nineteenth century has accelerated destructive soil erosion in this softly beautiful, mountainous land.

Descending gently from the Appalachians' eastern slope is the piedmont ("foot of the mountain"). In this broad, rolling upland extending from Alabama to Maryland, the rich red soil has been ravaged in modern times by excessive cotton and tobacco cultivation. The piedmont's modern piney-woods cover constitutes "secondary growth" replacing the sturdy hardwood trees that Native Americans and pioneering whites and blacks once knew. The northward extension of the piedmont from Pennsylvania to New England has

Cades Cove, Great Smoky Mountains; Tennessee Strip Mining
The impact of human hands is dramatically apparent in these two starkly contrasting Appalachian hill-country scenes.

Pemigewasset Wilderness, White Mountains, New Hampshire

Tidewater Wetlands, North Carolina

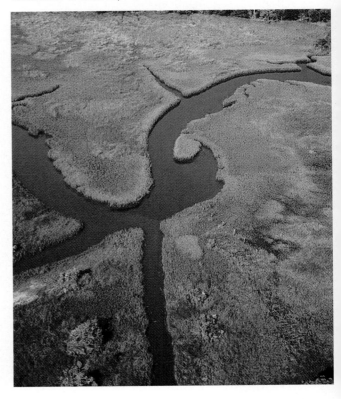

more broadleaf vegetation, a harsher winter climate, and (through the Hudson and Connecticut river valleys) somewhat better access to the piedmont itself. But unlike the piedmont, upstate New York and New England were shaped by glaciation: the terrain here comprises hills contoured by advancing and retreating ice, and numerous lakes scoured out by glaciers. Belts of debris remain, and in many places granite boulders shoulder their way up through the soil. Though picturesque, the land is the despair of anyone who has tried to plow it.

From southeastern Massachusetts and Rhode Island to south-central Alabama runs the fall line, the boundary between the relatively hard rock of the interior and the softer sediment of the coastal plain. Rivers crossing the fall line drop quickly to near sea level, thus making a series of rapids that block navigation upstream from the coast.

The character of the Atlantic coastal plain varies strikingly from south to north. In the extreme south, at the tip of the Florida peninsula, the climate and vegetation are subtropical. The southern coastal lands running north from Florida to Chesapeake Bay and the mouth of the Delaware River compose the tidewater region. This is a wide, rather flat lowland, heavily wooded with a mixture of broadleaf and coniferous

Oyster Men, Chesapeake Bay, Maryland

forests, ribboned with numerous small rivers, occasionally swampy, and often miserably hot and humid in summer. North of Delaware Bay, the coastal lowlands narrow and flatten to form the New Jersey Pine Barrens, Long Island, and Cape Cod—all of these created by the deposit of glacial debris. Here the climate is noticeably milder than in the interior. North of Massachusetts Bay, the land back of the immediate shoreline becomes increasingly mountainous.

Many large rivers drain into the Atlantic: the St. Lawrence, flowing out of the Great Lakes northeastward through eastern Canada; the Connecticut in New England; the Hudson, Delaware, Susquehanna, and Potomac in what are now the Middle Atlantic states; the Savannah in the South. Most of these originally carried glacial meltwater. The Susquehanna and the Potomac filled in the broad, shallow Chesapeake Bay, teeming with marine life and offering numerous anchorages for oceangoing ships.

North America's true eastern edge is not the coastline but the offshore continental shelf, whose relatively shallow waters extend as far as 250 miles into the Atlantic before plunging deeply. Along the rocky Cana-

dian and Maine coasts, where at the end of the Ice Age the rising ocean half covered glaciated mountains and valleys, oceangoing craft may find numerous small anchorages. South of Massachusetts Bay, the Atlantic shore and the Gulf of Mexico coastline form a shoreline of sandy beaches and long barrier islands paralleling the mainland. Tropical storms boiling up from the open seas regularly lash North America's Atlantic shores, and at all times brisk winds make coastal navigation treacherous.

Crossing the Atlantic east to west can daunt even skilled mariners, particularly those battling against powerful winds by sail. Here, on one of the world's stormiest seas, the mighty Gulf Stream current sweeps from southwest to northeast. Winds off the North American mainland also trend steadily eastward, and dangerous icebergs floating south from Greenland's waters threaten every ship. Little wonder that in 1620 the *Mayflower* Pilgrims' first impulse on landing was to sink to their knees in thanks to God for having transported them safely across "the vast and furious ocean." Many a vessel went to the bottom.

But for millennia, the Atlantic coastal region of North America offered a welcoming haven to settlers. For example, ten thousand years ago, ancient Indian hunters followed a warming climate eastward across the Appalachians to the coast. During the first millennium A.D., eastern peoples began adopting the Woodland culture and agriculture from the heartland. Offshore, well within their reach, lay such productive fishing grounds as the Grand Banks and Cape Cod's

The Tip of Cape Cod, Massachusetts

coastal bays, where cool-water upwellings on the continental shelf had lured swarms of fish and crustaceans. "The abundance of sea-fish are almost beyond believing," wrote a breathless English settler in 1630, "and sure I should scarce have believed it, except I had seen it with my own eyes."

◆

A LEGACY AND A CHALLENGE

At least three thousand miles of open sea separates North America from Europe and Africa; and Asia, except for the subarctic region where Alaska and Siberia once joined, lies even more distant.

A lingering sense of isolation stimulated European-descended Americans' hopes of keeping "Old World" problems away from the pristine "New World," just as North America's fertile soil, extensive forests, and rich mineral resources long conjured up visions of limitless wealth. But population growth, intensive agriculture, industrialization, urbanization, and a hunger for consumer goods have stretched to the limits the American land's ability to maintain a modern society without irreversible ecological damage. And only in the twentieth century have Americans learned that global transportation networks and instantaneous communication make isolation impossible. At last, as ecologist Aldo Leopold put it, they have begun discovering that the earth's people "are only fellow voyagers in the odyssey of evolution." And that lesson has been hard learned. "It required 19 centuries to define decent man-to-man conduct and the process is only half-done," Leopold admonished; "it may take as long to evolve a code of decency for man-to-land conduct."

It is in evolving such a code, however, that the Native American legacy may yet prove most enduring. Interacting constantly with their physical environments, Indians considered themselves spiritually related to the land and all living beings that shared it. In recapturing a sense that the land—its life-sustaining bounty and its soul-sustaining beauty—is itself of inestimable value and not merely a means to the end of material growth, future American generations may reestablish a sense of historical and cultural continuity with their Native American precursors. Thereby they can truly be possessed by their land instead of simply being its possessors.

CHRONOLOGY

c. 3,000,000,000 B.C.	Formation of oldest known rocks in present-day North America.
c. 500,000,000 B.C.	Precambrian era ends; Paleozoic era begins. Earliest forms of animal life appear.
c. 250,000,000 B.C.	Supercontinent of Pangaea forms.
c. 225,000,000 B.C.	Paleozoic era ends; Mesozoic era begins. First dinosaurs appear.
c. 210,000,000 B.C.	Appalachian Mountains emerge.
c. 180,000,000 B.C.	Pangaea begins to break up.
c. 65,000,000 B.C.	Mesozoic era ends; Cenozoic era begins. Dinosaurs become extinct. Rocky Mountains form.

Trilobite from Mesozoic era

c. 50,000,000 B.C.	Hawaiian Islands emerge.
c. 20,000,000 B.C.	Grand Canyon begins to form.
c. 5,000,000 B.C.	Earliest human ancestors appear in Africa.
c. 2,000,000 B.C.	Ice Age begins.
c. 300,000–100,000 B.C.	Humans spread throughout Eastern Hemisphere.
c. 120,000 B.C.	Wisconsin glaciation begins.
c. 40,000–15,000 B.C.	Ancestors of Native Americans cross Alaska-Siberian land bridge.
c. 10,000 B.C.	Ice Age ends. Wisconsin glaciation retreats from North America. Native Americans begin to spread throughout Western Hemisphere.
A.D. 1492	Christopher Columbus's first voyage to the Western Hemisphere.

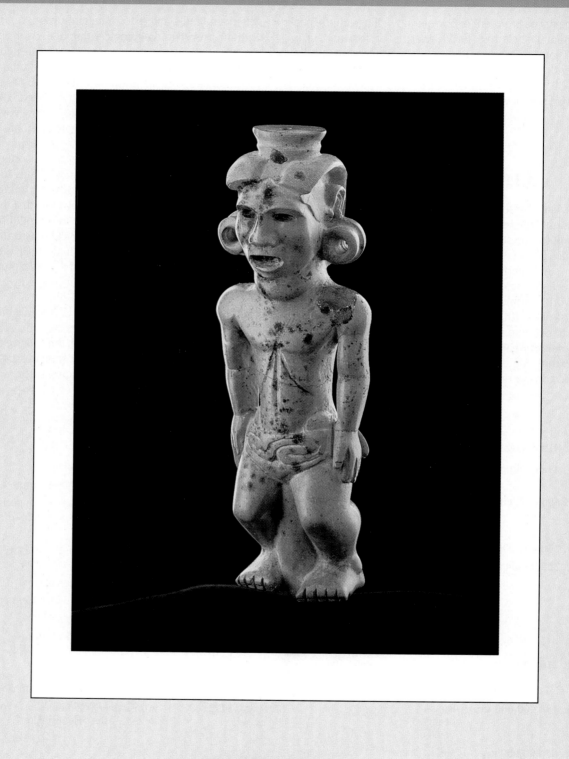

Adena Stone Effigy Pipe
c. 400–100 B.C.

AMERICA BEGINS

Hiawatha had known the depths of despair. For years his people, the group of Indian nations known as the Iroquois, had been beset by a destructive, seemingly endless cycle of violence and revenge. Families, villages, and nations fought one another, and neighboring Indians attacked relentlessly. When Hiawatha tried to restore peace among his own Onondaga people, an evil sorcerer who opposed peace caused the deaths of his seven beloved daughters. Grief-stricken and angry, Hiawatha wandered alone into the forest. After several days he reached the shore of a lake, where he experienced a series of visions. First he saw a flock of wild ducks suddenly fly up from the lake, taking the water with them. Hiawatha walked onto the dry lake bed, gathering and stringing the beautiful purple and white shells that lay there. He saw the shells, called wampum, as symbolic "words" of condolence that, when properly presented, would soothe grief, no matter how intense. Then he met a holy man named Deganawidah ("the Peacemaker"), who presented him the beads and spoke the appropriate words, one to dry his weeping eyes, another to open his ears to the words of peace and reason, a third to clear his throat so that he himself could once again speak peacefully and reasonably. Deganawidah and Hiawatha then took the wampum to the five Iroquois nations. To each they introduced the ritual of condolence as a new message of peace. The Iroquois subsequently submerged their differences and created a council of chiefs and a confederacy, based on the condolence ritual. Thus was born the powerful League of the Iroquois.

Although it is an oral tradition couched in the language of supernatural religion, the story of Hiawatha and Deganawidah depicts a concrete event in American history. Archaeological evidence at Iroquois sites corroborates the sequence of bloody warfare followed by peace and dates the league's origins at some time between the late fourteenth and the mid-fifteenth century. As with all of American history before the arrival of Europeans and their system of writing, archaeological evidence and oral traditions, examined critically, are our principal sources of knowledge about the past. In this case the story refers to an event of importance not only for pre-Columbian history but for the period of European contact with Native Americans as well. For the Iroquois Confederacy was a significant diplomatic and military force throughout the colonial period and has inspired and intrigued many non-Indians down to the present, despite the fact that it was established prior to, and entirely independently of, the Europeans' arrival.

The founding of the League of the Iroquois marked just one moment in a long history that began more than ten thousand years before Christopher Columbus's first voyage. Over that time an indigenous American history unfolded, utterly separate from that of the Eastern Hemisphere.

1

Some native peoples eked out their existences in precarious environments, whereas others enjoyed affluence and prosperity; some lived in small bands, whereas others lived in large cities; some believed that the first humans came from the sky, whereas others maintained that they originated underground. Wherever and however they lived and whatever they believed, native peoples together made North America a human habitat and gave it a history.

THE FIRST AMERICANS

Like the slow but relentless shaping of the planet itself, the origins of the human species extend back to the mists of prehistoric time. More than 5 million years ago, direct human ancestors evolved in the temperate grasslands of Africa. Between three hundred thousand and one hundred thousand years ago, humans began migrating through much of the Old World. During the last glaciation, which geologists term Wisconsin, hunting bands pursuing large game animals moved from Central Asia into Siberia. Between forty thousand and fifteen thousand years ago, some of these bands began crossing the broad land bridge then connecting Siberia to Alaska. In so doing, they became the first Americans.

Most Native Americans are descended from these earliest migrants. A few, however, trace their lineage to later arrivals. About nine thousand years ago, Athapaskan-speaking peoples crossed the land bridge and spread over much of northern and western Canada and southern and central Alaska. Some of them later migrated southward to form the Apaches and Navajos in the Southwest, as well as smaller groups elsewhere. Eskimos and Aleuts began crossing the Bering Sea—which had submerged the land bridge—from Siberia between five thousand and four thousand years ago, and the Hawaiian Islands remained uninhabited until after A.D. 300.

The Peopling of North America

About 10,000 B.C. the Ice Age was nearing its end. Melting glaciers had opened up an ice-free corridor leading from Alaska to the northern Plains. Bands of hunters moved through this corridor, and others probably trav-

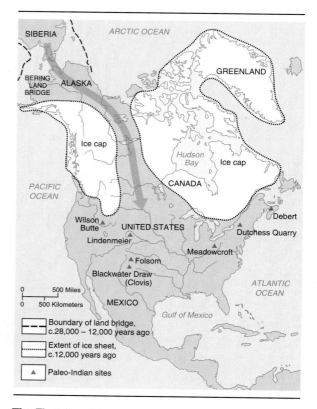

The First Americans

The arrow shows the "ice corridor" through which most ancestors of Native Americans passed before dispersing throughout the Western Hemisphere.

SOURCE: Dean R. Snow, *The Archaeology of North America* (New York: Chelsea House Publishers, 1989).

eled south along the Pacific coast by boat. As they emerged from the glacier-covered north, they discovered a hunter's paradise. Giant mammoths, mastodons, horses, camels, bison, caribou, and moose, as well as smaller species, roamed the continent innocent of the ways of human predators. So bountiful and accommodating was this new environment that the Paleo-Indians, as archaeologists call these hunters, fanned out and proliferated with astonishing speed. By 9000 B.C. descendants of the first Americans had dispersed throughout the Western Hemisphere.

Most Paleo-Indians dwelled in bands of about fifteen to fifty people. The men hunted; the women prepared the food and cared for the children. Members of a band lived together during the spring and summer and split into smaller groups of one or two families for the fall and winter. Although they moved constantly, they generally remained within informally defined

A Folsom Point
The Folsom point is the most common of the Paleo-Indian fluted spear points. This point is shown just as it was found, imbedded between two ribs of the extinct Bison taylori.

boundaries. An exception occurred when they traveled to favored quarries to obtain jasper or flint for making tools and spear points. At such sites they encountered other bands, with whom they traded, intermarried, and participated in religious ceremonies.

Even before leaving Alaska the Paleo-Indians had developed distinctly American ways. Their most characteristic innovation was their "fluted" points, so-called for their shape, which permitted fitting them on spears. Although fluted points have been found throughout the Western Hemisphere, none has been uncovered in Siberia. Around 9000 B.C. many of the big-game species such as the mammoths and mastodons became extinct. The effectiveness of the Paleo-Indian hunters may have contributed to this demise, but the animals were also doomed by the warming climate, which brought ecological changes that undermined the food chain on which they depended. In other words, the replacement of the big-game mammals by humans marked part of a larger

process of ecological change associated with the end of the Ice Age.

Archaic Societies

The warming of the earth's atmosphere continued until about 4000 B.C., with far-reaching effects on the North American continent. Sea levels rose, flooding shallow offshore areas, and glacial runoff in the interior filled the Great Lakes, the Mississippi River basin, and other waterways. As the glaciers receded northward, so did the arctic and subarctic environments that had previously extended far into what are now the "lower 48" states of the United States. Treeless plains and evergreen forests gave way to deciduous forests in the East, grassland prairies on the Plains, and desert in much of the West. An immense range of flora and fauna, both on land and in the waters, came to characterize the American landscape. We are familiar with many of these same plants and animals today.

Just as the Paleo-Indians had flourished in settings south of the glaciers, so their descendants now prospered in the abundance and diversity of their new environments. Instead of focusing most of their food gathering energy on big game, these Archaic peoples, as archaeologists term native North Americans from c. 8000 B.C. to 1500 B.C., lived off wide varieties of smaller mammals, fish, and wild plants. As they used the resources of their environments more efficiently, their communities required less land area and could

Archaic Hunting Aid
This duck decoy was made 2,000 to 3,000 years ago by a hunter living at Lovelock Cave in the Humboldt Basin of west-central Nevada.

support larger populations. Although the size of populations and territories of hunting-gathering bands in the Great Basin and Southwest changed little from Paleo-Indian times, people in parts of the East and Midwest now resided in villages with larger populations for all or most of the year. For example, a year-round village that flourished near Kampsville, Illinois, from 3900 to 2800 B.C., supported 100 to 150 people. It could do so because the residents knew how and when to procure fish and mussels from local lakes, in addition to the deer and other mammals, birds, nuts, and seeds available in the surrounding area.

Archaic peoples diversified other aspects of their lives as well. Besides using many more varieties of stone, they utilized bone, shell, copper, horn, ivory, asphalt, clay, and leather to make such objects as tools, weapons, utensils, and ornaments. Although many of these materials were available locally, the Native Americans obtained others through exchanges, both with neighbors and through long-distance trade networks. Archaeological evidence gives some indication of the extent and importance of this long-distance trade. Obsidian (a glassy black volcanic rock) from the Yellowstone region, copper from the Great Lakes, and marine shells from the coasts appear at sites hundreds and even thousands of miles from their points of origin. Archaic peoples, as well as Indians who encountered Europeans several millenia later, thought that such minerals contained supernatural power. A few large sites, among them Indian Knoll in western Kentucky, which dates to 2500–2000 B.C., served as major centers of interregional trade.

Trade networks were routes not only for materials but also for ideas about their uses. By means of these pathways, the techniques developed in one locale for making material objects, procuring food, or utilizing the medicinal properties of plants were carried to other areas, transcending the narrow boundaries of community, language, and ethnicity. Out of such diffusions of ideas arose regional cultural patterns (see below). Trade also served to spread religious beliefs, as exemplified in ideas and practices relating to death. Human burials became more elaborate during the Archaic era as Native Americans in many regions buried the dead with their personal possessions as well as with objects fashioned from obsidian, copper, shell, and other highly valued substances. They often sprinkled the flexed corpses with bright red hematite, a source of iron, so that they resembled a baby at birth. Ideas of death as a kind of rebirth remained widespread in North America at the time Europeans began arriving many centuries later.

Archaic Americans did not distinguish among themselves on the basis of class or rank, or centralize political power in the hands of one person or a few individuals. However, the growing complexity of their diets and of their technologies led them to sharpen many of the distinctions between women's and men's roles. Men took responsibility for fishing as well as hunting, whereas women harvested and prepared the products of wild plants, including the grinding and milling of seeds. Men and women each made the tools needed for their tasks. In general, men's activities entailed travel, and women's activities kept them close to the village, where they bore and raised children. These role distinctions are apparent in the burials at Indian Knoll, where tools relating to hunting, fishing, woodworking, and leatherworking were usually buried with men and those relating to nut cracking and seed grinding with women. Yet gender-specific distinctions by no means applied to all activities, for objects used by shamans, or religious healers, were distributed equally between male and female graves.

THE INDIANS' CONTINENT

By 1500 B.C. Indians in parts of North America were shaping new ways of life and new institutions, transcending the Archaic cultures developed over the preceding millennia. Most post-Archaic Americans remained in small bands consisting of a few families and continued to rely on combinations of hunting, fishing, and gathering. But others developed more specialized methods of food production and more actively shaped their environments to their own needs. In the Southwest, the Southeast, and the Northeast the advent of agriculture and of large centers of trade and population marked a radical departure from Archaic patterns and from the foraging way of life still followed by Indians in other regions.

Despite the discrepancies emerging among native societies, the ties between them grew strong. Trade networks carrying goods and ideas over geographic distances and across linguistic, ethnic, and cultural divides continued to proliferate. In this way the bow and arrow and ceramic pottery spread throughout the Americas, from the smallest bands to the largest cities.

Culture Areas of Native Americans and Locations of Selected Tribes, A.D. 1500
*"Culture area" is a convention enabling archaeologists and anthropologists to generalize
about regional patterns among pre-Columbian Native American cultures.*

And Indians virtually everywhere retained their preferences for seasonal food procurement and for living in communities based on kinship, often abandoning or resisting more centralized systems that proved unworkable or oppressive.

The Northern and Western Perimeters

In western Alaska, where the first Americans had arrived thousands of years earlier, the post-Archaic period marked the beginning of a new, arctic way of life.

The Eskimos and Aleuts had brought highly sophisticated tools and weapons from their Siberian homeland. Combining ivory, bone, and other materials, they fashioned harpoons and spears for the pursuit of sea mammals and—in the case of the Eskimos—caribou. Through their continued contacts with Siberia, the Eskimos were making and using the first bows and arrows, the first ceramic pottery, and the first pit houses (structures set partially below ground level) in the Americas by 1500 B.C. As they perfected their ways of living in the cold tundra regions of the far north, many

Eskimos spread across upper Canada to the shores of Labrador, western Newfoundland, and Greenland.

Long before the arrival of Columbus, the Eskimos made contact with Europeans and used some of their material goods. From about A.D. 1, a few iron tools were reaching western Alaska by way of Russia and Siberia. However, they were too few in number to affect Eskimo culture in any substantial way. Contacts with Europeans were more direct and sustained in areas of Greenland, Newfoundland, and Labrador, where Norse people from Scandinavia attempted to colonize, beginning in the late tenth century A.D. The Norse exchanged metal goods for ivory with the Eskimos and with the Beothuk Indians near their settlement in Newfoundland. But peaceful trade gave way to hostile encounters. By the eleventh century the native peoples' resistance to the newcomers' colonizing ambitions led the Norse to withdraw from Vinland, as they called Newfoundland. As a Norse leader, dying after losing a battle with some natives, put it, "There is fat around my belly! We have won a fine and fruitful country, but will hardly be allowed to enjoy it." Several more centuries would pass before Europeans would enjoy, at the expense of native peoples, the fruits of a "New World."

Along the Pacific coast, from Alaska to southern California, improvements in the production and storage of certain key foods enabled Indians to develop more settled ways of life. On the Northwest coast, from the Alaskan panhandle to northern California, and in the Columbia Plateau, natives devoted brief periods of each year to catching salmon and other spawning fish. After drying the fish, the Northwest Coast Indians stored it in quantities sufficient to last the year round. As a result, their seasonal movements gave way to a settled lifestyle in permanent villages consisting of cedar-plank houses. Plateau Indians constructed villages with pit houses where they ate salmon through the summer. They left the villages in spring and fall for hunting and gathering.

By A.D. 1 many villages on the Northwest coast numbered several hundred people. Trade and warfare with interior groups strengthened the power of chiefs and other leading figures, whose families were distinguished from those of commoners by their wealth and prestige. These leading families proclaimed their status most conspicuously in elaborate totem poles depicting supernatural beings supposedly linked to their ancestors and in potlatches, ceremonies in which they gave away or destroyed much of their material wealth. From

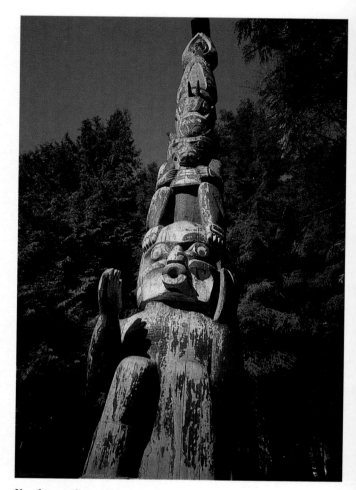

Northwest Coast Totem Pole
The most famous form of artistic expression among Northwest Coast Indians, totem poles served various purposes. Some advertised the genealogy and accomplishments of a clan, family, or individual. Others celebrated a successful potlatch. A few seem to have been intended to ridicule an enemy or simply to express the maker's whimsy and skill.

the time of the earliest contacts, Europeans were awestruck by the artistic and architectural achievements of the Northwest Coast Indians. "What must astonish most," wrote a French explorer in 1791, "is to see painting everywhere, everywhere sculpture, among a nation of hunters."

At about the same time as native peoples in the Northwest, Indians on the coast and in the interior valleys of what is now California became more settled. Residing in villages of about one hundred people, each established near large oak groves, they devoted extensive time and effort to processing acorns. After the fall harvest, the Indians ground the acorns into meal, leached them of their bitter tannic acid, and then roasted, boiled, or baked the nuts prior to eating or storing them. In the face of intense competition for acorns, native Californians defined territorial boundaries more rigidly than elsewhere in pre-Columbian North America and combined several villages under the leadership of a single chief. The chiefs conducted trade, diplomacy, and religious ceremonies with neighboring groups and, when necessary, led their people in battle. Along with the resources of game, fish, and plants available to them, acorns enabled the Indians of California to prosper. As a Spanish friar arriving in California from Mexico in 1770 wrote, "This land exceeds all the preceding territory in fertility and abundance of things necessary for sustenance."

The end of the Archaic period is less noticeable in the Great Basin than almost anywhere else in North America. This region's warm, dry climate was almost as forbidding to humans as that of the frigid Arctic. Foraging bands continued to move over the area, depending primarily on hunting small mammals and harvesting seeds and piñon (pine) nuts. Little change occurred until about the fourteenth or fifteenth century A.D., when Paiute, Ute, and Shoshone Indians fanned over the Great Basin from their homeland in southeastern California, absorbing or displacing the earlier inhabitants. Although the newcomers' way of life was essentially the same as that of the older groups, their more efficient seed processing enabled them to support larger populations, which in turn occupied ever-larger territories.

The Hawaiian Islands were not part of indigenous North America but rather of Oceania. By 3000 B.C. the Austronesian peoples of Australia, New Guinea, and nearby smaller islands had developed agriculture and crafted pottery, tools and other objects of stone and shell, and giant outrigger canoes for voyaging on the high seas. About 1600 B.C. some Austronesians began settling the formerly uninhabited islands of the south Pacific, but only in the fourth century A.D. did voyagers from the Marquesas Islands reach Hawaii, the northern extremity of Polynesia.

For the next four hundred years, these first Hawaiians lived in self-sufficient communities, cultivating sweet potatoes, yams, and taro (whose starchy root they made into a fermented paste) and exploiting a rich variety of fish and shellfish. Each community dis-

A Hawaiian Chief
This portrait was drawn by a member of Captain James Cook's expedition in 1778.

tinguished sharply between commoners and chiefs. The latter included a paramount chief as well as various lesser rulers who could prove kinship with him. As in parts of North America, Hawaiian chiefs collected food and craft goods from subordinate communities and allies. Unlike their counterparts in North America, these chiefs occasionally waged war for territorial conquest and the subjugation of other peoples.

When Europeans began arriving in Hawaii in the late eighteenth century, the islands numbered about four hundred thousand people, with communities averaging about two hundred individuals each. Thereafter European diseases had effects similar to those on the mainland: within half a century the native population plummeted to 130,000 and by 1890 to 40,000.

The Southwest

Although the peoples of the Northwest coast and California cultivated tobacco, they never farmed food-bearing plants. With their abundant food sources, they had little incentive to hazard the additional risks that agriculture would have entailed, especially in California, with its dry summers. However, elsewhere in North America agriculture became central to Indian life. In the arid Southwest, natives concentrated much of their communities' energy on irrigation in order to feed themselves by farming. In the humid Eastern Woodlands, on the other hand, plant cultivation came more easily. But in both regions, the advent of agriculture was a long, slow process that never entirely displaced other food-procuring activities.

Farming began in the Western Hemisphere about 5000 B.C.—just as agriculture was being introduced to Europe from southwestern Asia—when Indians living in the Tehuacán Valley of central Mexico experimentally planted the seeds of certain wild plants they customarily harvested. Among these were squash, maize (corn), and eventually beans. Slowly, the techniques of plant domestication spread in all directions. The earliest North American evidence is at Bat Cave in western New Mexico, where archaeologists have found maize and squash remains dating to about 3500 B.C. Yet for thousands of years more, farming remained only a minor activity for hunter-gatherers in both Mexico and the Southwest. Substantial changes in southwestern life began only after 400 B.C., when the introduction (probably from Mexico) of a more drought-resistant strain of maize enabled the inhabitants to move from the highlands to the drier lowlands. In the centuries that followed, populations rose throughout the region, and native culture was transformed. The two most influential new cultural traditions were the Hohokam and the Anasazi.

The Hohokam emerged during the third century B.C. when ancestors of the Pima and Papago Indians began farming in the Gila River and Salt River valleys of southern Arizona. Hohokam peoples built elaborate canal systems for irrigation that enabled them to harvest two crops per year, an astonishing achievement in such an arid environment. To construct and maintain their canals, the Hohokam people needed large, coordinated work forces. They built permanent villages, usually consisting of several hundred people. Although many such villages remained independent, others joined confederations in which several towns were linked by canals. The central village in each confederation coordinated labor, trade, and religious and political life for all the communities connected to it.

Essentially a local creation, Hohokam culture nevertheless drew extensively on materials and ideas from outside the Southwest. From about the sixth century A.D., the large villages had ball courts and platform mounds like those found throughout Mexico at the time. As in Mexico, ball games were major public events in Hohokam villages. Although no evidence of their rules survives, they probably resembled the Mexican game, in which play was rough, players could not use their hands, and the losers sacrificed some of their material possessions. Mexican influence was also apparent in the creations of Hohokam artists, who worked in clay, stone, turquoise, and shell. Archaeologists have unearthed such artifacts as rubber balls, macaw feathers, and copper bells among the Mexican items found at Hohokam sites. Artists used seashells from California in pottery, as backing for turquoise mosaics, and as material for intricate etchings.

Among the last southwesterners to make farming the focus of their subsistence were a people known as the Anasazi, a Navajo term meaning "ancient ones." Their culture originated in the Four Corners area where Arizona, New Mexico, Colorado, and Utah meet. By the sixth century A.D., the Anasazi people were only beginning to harvest beans, live in permanent villages with pit houses, make pottery (although they had crafted elaborately coiled baskets for centuries), use the bow and arrow, and domesticate turkeys—practices already adopted by most of their southwestern neighbors. Yet over the next six centuries, these ancestors of the modern Pueblo Indians expanded over a wide region and became the most powerful people in the region. And while they traded with Indians in Mexico, California, and elsewhere, the Anasazis borrowed little in the way of artistic or cultural ideas. Instead their neighbors borrowed from them.

One of the distinguishing characteristics of Anasazi culture was its architecture. Early Anasazi houses were round, with walls of stone slabs or clay plaster and domed roofs of logs and mud, supported by four central posts. They also featured underground storage cists, ventilator shafts, and small holes in the floor known as *sipapus*. The Anasazis and modern Pueblos maintain that the first humans reached the earth from underground, following a long and tortuous journey through several underworlds. Symbolizing this journey, the sipapu was a sacred place in each family's house. As village populations increased after the sixth century, often reaching one hundred or more houses, the Anasazis shifted to above-ground, rectangular apartments. However, they retained the form of the pit house in their *kivas*, round, partly underground structures in which the men held religious ceremonies. To this day Anasazi-style apartments and kivas are central features of Pueblo Indian architecture in the Southwest.

(top left) **Anasazi Cliffside Balcony House with Kiva, Mesa Verde, Colorado**
Some Anasazi peoples, most notably those at Mesa Verde in southwestern Colorado, built their villages in cliffside caves.

(bottom left) **Pueblo Bonito, Chaco Canyon**
Pueblo Bonito illustrates the richness and grand scale of Anasazi architecture.

These roads were perfectly straight; their builders even carved out stairs or footholds in the sides of steep cliffs rather than go around them. The largest of the villages, Pueblo Bonito, had about 1,200 inhabitants and was the home of two Great Kivas, each about fifty feet in diameter. People traveled from the outlying towns to Chaco Canyon for religious rituals. In addition, the canyon was the center of a turquoise industry that manufactured beads for trade with Mexico, and its pueblos supplied the outliers with food in times of drought. The ability of canyon residents to grow enough vegetables and other crops to feed themselves and others lay in their system of controlling rainwater runoff through small dams, terraces, and other devices.

From the beginning of the tenth century to the middle of the twelfth, during an unusually wet period in the Southwest, the Anasazis expanded over much of what is today northern New Mexico and Arizona. The population of some villages grew to more than a thousand. In Chaco Canyon in present-day northwestern New Mexico, a cluster of twelve villages forged a powerful confederation numbering about fifteen thousand people. A system of roads radiated out of the canyon to satellite pueblos located as far as sixty-five miles away.

The classic Anasazi culture, as manifested at Chaco Canyon, Mesa Verde in southwestern Colorado, Canyon de Chelly in northeastern Arizona, and other sites, came to an end in the twelfth and thirteenth centuries. Although Chaco Canyon's somewhat earlier collapse may have been triggered by a cutoff of its turquoise trade with Mexico, the overriding cause of the Anasazi demise was drought. Suddenly, the amount of available farmland was drastically reduced for a population that had grown rapidly during the preceding centuries. The great Anasazi centers were abandoned as the inhabitants dispersed. Most formed new pueblos on or near the upper Rio Grande, whereas others moved south to establish the Zuni and Hopi pueblos. Descendants of the Anasazis still inhabit many of these pueblos. Other large agricultural communities, such as those of the Hohokam, also dispersed when drought came. With farming peoples now clustered in the few areas with enough water, the drier lands of the Southwest attracted the foraging Apaches and Navajos, whose arrival at the end of the fourteenth century ended their long migration from northwestern Canada.

The Eastern Woodlands

Whereas the Hohokam and Anasazi peoples built large villages and created centralized or confederated political systems as a consequence of deciding to farm for most of their food, natives on the Northwest coast and in California enlarged and consolidated their societies in the absence of agriculture. Nonfarming Indians in much of the Eastern Woodlands—that vast stretch of land from the Mississippi Valley to the Atlantic Ocean—likewise experimented with village life and political centralization without farming. But after doing so, they developed an extraordinarily productive agriculture.

In 1200 B.C. about five thousand people had concentrated in a single village at Poverty Point on the Mississippi River in Louisiana. The village was flanked by two large mounds and surrounded by six concentric embankments, the outermost of which spanned more than half a mile in diameter. During the spring and autumn equinoxes, a person standing on the larger mound could watch the sun rise directly over the village center. As with similar communities of the period in Mexico, solar observations were the basis for religious beliefs as well as for a calendar. Poverty Point also lay at the center of a much larger political and economic unit. The settlement imported large quantities of quartz, copper, obsidian, crystal, and other sacred materials from throughout eastern North America and then redistributed them to nearby communities. These communities almost certainly supplied some of the labor for the earthworks. Although

Poverty Point was built by local inhabitants, its general design and organization suggest the influence of the Olmec peoples of Mexico. For reasons that are unclear, Poverty Point flourished for only about three centuries and then declined. Nevertheless, it foreshadowed later developments in the Mississippi Valley.

A different kind of mound-building culture, called Adena, emerged in the Ohio Valley in the fifth century B.C. Adena villages were smaller than Poverty Point, rarely exceeding four hundred inhabitants. But Adena people spread over a wide area and built hundreds of mounds, most of them containing graves. The largest, Grave Creek Mound in West Virginia, was 240 feet in diameter, 70 feet high, and contained 72,000 tons of soil. The treatment of Adena dead varied widely, indicating differences in social or political status. Some corpses were cremated, others were placed in round clay basins, and still others were given elaborate tombs. Some burials contained just a few utilitarian grave goods, whereas others had many more goods and a greater variety, including pipes and other finely crafted objects.

The Adena mounds constituted the heart of a religious movement whose adherents were diffused over much of the Northeast. Although many Adena burial practices, such as the inclusion of grave goods and the spreading of red hematite on some corpses, were familiar in the Northeast, the burial rituals themselves and many of the manufactured objects were new. Many of these objects were distributed throughout the Northeast via trade networks during the period in which Adena culture flourished.

During the first century B.C., Adena culture evolved into a more complex and widespread culture known as Hopewell. Hopewell ceremonial centers were even larger and more elaborate than their Adena predecessors. They proliferated not only in the Ohio Valley but also in the Illinois River valley. Some centers contained two or three dozen mounds within enclosures of several square miles. The variety and quantity of goods buried with members of the elite were also greater. The people surrounded some corpses with thousands of freshwater pearls or copper ornaments or with sheets of mica, quartz, or other sacred substances. Hopewell artisans fashioned a wide variety of effigies, ornaments, and jewelry, which their owners wore to their graves. The raw materials for these objects originated in locales throughout America east of the Rockies. Through trade networks Hopewell influence spread over much of the Eastern Woodlands—to

Great Serpent Mound, Ohio

This well-known mound, built for religious ceremonies rather than for burials, depicts a 1,254-foot-long snake devouring an egg or a frog.

Poverty Point, Louisiana

This perspective sketch shows the large mound located just outside the concentric rings, as well as a smaller mound in the upper right. The earthworks symbolized Poverty Point's importance as a regional center for trade and religious ceremonies.

communities as far away as Wisconsin, Missouri, Florida, and New York. Some of these, such as Marksville in Louisiana, emulated the Ohio centers in almost every detail, but others were more selective, imitating Hopewell mounds, copper work, or pottery. Although the great Hopewell centers of the Ohio and Illinois valleys were abandoned in the fifth century A.D. for reasons that are unclear, they had an enormous influence on subsequent developments in eastern North America.

Remarkably, the people who created the sophisticated Hopewell culture were hunter-gatherers rather than farmers. Archaic Indians in Kentucky and Missouri had cultivated small amounts of squash as early as 2500 B.C., and maize first appeared in eastern North America by 300 B.C. But agriculture became a dietary mainstay for Woodlands people only between the seventh and twelfth centuries A.D., as women moved beyond gathering and minor cultivating activities to become the major producers of food.

Mississippian Engraved Shell
Engraved conch shells, often with highly abstract designs, were among the goods traded by Mississippian peoples in the Southeast.

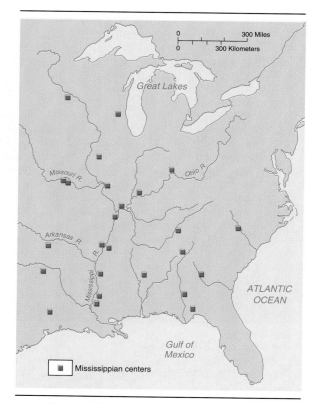

Major Mississippian Centers
SOURCE: Jay A. Levenson, ed., *Art in the Age of Exploration: Circa 1492* (New Haven, Conn.: Yale University Press, 1991).

The first full-time farmers in the East were Indians living on the floodplains of the Mississippi River and its major tributaries. They developed a new culture, called Mississippian, that incorporated elements of Hopewell culture and ideas from Mexico into their indigenous traditions. The volume of Mississippian craft production and long-distance trade dwarfed those of Adena and Hopewell cultures. At the same time, Mississippian towns, numbering hundreds or even thousands of people, were built around open plazas like those of central Mexico. Large platform mounds stood next to the plazas, topped by sumptuous religious temples and the residences of chiefs and other elites. Religious ceremonies focused on the worship of the sun as the source of agricultural fertility. The people considered chiefs to be related to the sun. When a chief died, his wives and servants were killed so that they could accompany him to the afterlife. Largely in connection with their religious and funeral rituals, Mississippian artists produced highly sophisticated work in clay, stone, shell, copper, wood, and other materials.

Many Mississippian centers were built not by local natives but by outsiders seeking to combine farming and riverborne trade. Local natives often were coerced into bringing corn and goods to a new center and pay-

ing homage to its chief. By the tenth century most Mississippian centers were part of even larger systems, based on trade and on shared religious beliefs and dominated by a single "super-center." The most powerful such system centered around Cahokia (see "A Place in Time"), located near modern St. Louis.

For two and a half centuries, Cahokia reigned supreme in the American heartland. Beginning in the thirteenth century, however, Cahokia and its allied centers began to experience shortages of food and other resources. Soon they were challenged militarily by neighboring peoples and, as a result, the inhabitants fled to the countryside. By the fifteenth century, Indians in the central Mississippi Valley were living (like their Archaic forebears) in small villages linked by reciprocity rather than coercion. Similar developments led to the decline of some temple-mound centers in the Southeast, but in this region new centers arose to take their place. Thus the decline of Etowah in northwestern Georgia near the end of the fourteenth century was followed by the rise of Coosa nearby. But Coosa and the other remaining centers were abandoned after 1500 as a result of European diseases.

The demise of Mississippian culture, like that of the Hopewell, ended a trend toward political centralization among Indians in eastern North America. In spite of their decline, however, the Mississippians profoundly affected native culture in the East. They spread new strains of maize and beans, along with many of the techniques and tools to cultivate these crops, enabling women to weave agriculture into the fabric of village life among the Iroquois and other Indians throughout the region. Only in portions of northern New England and the upper Great Lakes was the growing season for maize (one hundred frost-free days) generally too short for it to be a reliable crop. Some eastern Indians, searching for new farmlands, took the new ways to the river valleys of the plains, where they interacted peacefully with the region's hunting peoples.

Indian hands tended eastern North America's lands with skill and care. Over much of the region, great expanses of hardwood trees formed open, park-like tracts, free of underbrush (which the Indians had systematically burned) but rich with grass and berry bushes that attracted a profusion of game. The Woodland peoples' "slash-and-burn" method of land management was environmentally sound and economically productive. Men cleared the land by burning underbrush and destroying the larger trees' bark. Then, amid the leafless deadwood, women planted corn, beans, and pumpkins in soil enriched by ash. After several years of abundant harvests, yields declined, and the Indians moved on to a new site to repeat the process. Soon groundcover reclaimed the abandoned clearing, restoring fertility naturally, and the Indians could return.

The Indians rotated their crops to prevent soil depletion and diversified their food-producing activities (fishing, hunting, and gathering wild plants, as well as farming) to avoid dependence on a single food source. Later Europeans, importing a system in which land was divided into individual plots and valued according to the wealth it yielded, ignored and even belittled strategies that would have allowed natural resources to renew themselves.

By A.D. 1500 the North American continent presented a remarkable variety of human cultures, societies, and historical experiences. As they had for thousands of years, small, mobile hunting bands peopled the Arctic, Subarctic, Great Basin, and much of the Plains. More stable societies, based on fishing or gathering, predominated along the Pacific coast, whereas village-based agriculture was typical in the Eastern Woodlands and the river valleys of the Southwest and Plains. Finally, Mississippian urban centers still prevailed in portions of the Southeast.

Despite the vast differences among Native Americans, much bound them together. Trade facilitated the exchange not only of goods but of new ideas, techniques, and beliefs. Thus the bow and arrow, ceramic pottery, and certain beliefs and rituals surrounding the burial of the dead came to characterize Indians everywhere. Indians also shared a preference for the independent, kin-based communities that generally had characterized indigenous North America, a preference that probably was reinforced by the failure of such highly centralized systems as Cahokia and the Anasazi centers during the thirteenth century.

◆

NEW WORLD PEOPLES ON THE EVE OF EUROPEAN CONTACT

In 1492 the entire Western Hemisphere had a population of about 75 million. Native Americans clustered most thickly in Mexico and Central America, the Caribbean islands, and Peru. But North America was not an empty wasteland. In 1492 between 7 million and 10 million Indians lived north of present-day Mexico, unevenly distributed. Sparse populations of nomads inhabited the Great Basin, the high plains, and the northern forests. Fairly dense concentrations, however, thrived along the Pacific coast, in the Southwest and Southeast, in the Mississippi Valley, and along the Atlantic coast. All these peoples grouped themselves in several hundred nations and tribes, speaking many diverse languages and dialects. But the most important Indian social groups were the family, the village, and—in many societies—the clan. Within these spheres Native Americans fed themselves, reared their children, and interacted with one another and with the spiritual forces surrounding them.

Family and Community

Kinship cemented all Indian societies together. Ties to cousins, aunts, and uncles created complex patterns of social obligation. So did membership in clans—the large networks of kin groups who reckoned their

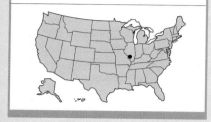

Cahokia in 1200

Artist's Rendering of Cahokia

This contemporary painting conveys Cahokia's grand scale. Not until the late eighteenth century did another North American city (Philadelphia) surpass the population of Cahokia, ca. 1200.

Between the tenth and thirteenth centuries, a city of about 20,000 people flourished near the confluence of the Mississippi and Missouri rivers. Called Cahokia, it filled more than 6 square miles and contained more than 120 earthworks. At its center a four-terraced structure called Monk's Mound covered 15 acres (more than the Great Pyramids of Egypt) and rose 100 feet at its highest point. Surrounding the city, a 125-square-mile metropolitan area encompassed 10 large towns and more than 50 farming villages. In addition, Cahokia dominated a vast network of commercial and political alliances extending over much of the American heartland.

Cahokia's beginnings lay in the seventh century A.D., as Native Americans in the East were shifting to farming as their primary means of procuring food. In search of better soil, several small villages moved to the low floodplain extending eastward from the Mississippi around what is now the Illinois side of greater St. Louis. Around A.D. 900 these villages began their transformation into a city with the construction of several mounds. Within another two centuries, a stockade enclosed Monk's Mound and numerous other public structures, and most of the city's residents lived on the outside.

Cahokia was ideally situated for a position of preeminence in mid-America. Its fertile land yielded surplus agricultural crops, which the women harvested, and the river provided rich supplies of fish and mussels. Game and wild plants abounded in nearby uplands. The city had ready access not only to the Mississippi and Missouri rivers but to the Ohio and Illinois, where Adena and Hopewell peoples had previously developed extensive trade networks based on shared religious beliefs. Cahokia and other Mississippian societies drew on Hopewell beliefs and new ideas from Mexico as they erected even more complex political, economic, and religious institutions. By the twelfth century, some scholars believe, Cahokia was the capital of a potential nation-state.

Archaeology provides evidence of what Cahokians made and left in the ground as well as clues to their social structure, trade networks, and beliefs. Work gangs dug the soil for the mounds with shovels made of wood and stone and then carried the dirt in baskets to construction sites, often more than half a mile away. Much of this backbreaking labor undoubtedly was drawn from neighboring towns, which also contributed agricultural surpluses to feed specialized artisans and elites in the city. The artisans produced pottery, shell beads, copper ornaments, clothing, stone tools, and a range of other goods. The raw materials for these objects were brought to Cahokia from locations all over eastern and central North America as tribute—payment by Indian societies dependent on Cahokia—or in return for the finished products. The coordination of labor, trade, and other activities also required a sizable class of managers or overseers. Atop all these were the political and religious leaders, whose overpowering roles are confirmed by French accounts, recorded in the eighteenth century, of a similar society among the Natchez Indians of the lower Mississippi River.

Archaeologists also find evidence of social ranking at Cahokia in the treatment of the dead. Most people were buried in mass graves outside the city, but more prestigious commoners were placed in ridgetop mounds, and those of highest status in conical mounds. In the single most remarkable mound, an adult male was laid out on a platform of twenty thousand beads, made from shells originating in the Gulf of Mexico. He was surrounded by bushels of mica from the Appalachians, a sheet of rolled copper from Lake Superior, and quivers of arrows from communities throughout the Mississippi Valley. This extraordinary man did not go to his grave alone. An adjacent pit contained the bodies of fifty young females in

Sandstone Tablet Depicting Birdman

their late teens and early twenties; another held the remains of four men whose heads and hands were cut off; and a third included three men and three women. French authors describe how, when a Natchez ruler died, his wife, servants, guards, and others personally attached to him were killed so that they could accompany him in the afterlife. The people called this ruler the Great Sun to denote his position as earthly representative of the sun, the central focus of Mississippian religion. This and burials like it at Cahokia appear to be based on similar beliefs.

By 1200 Cahokia had reached its peak. During the century that followed, it declined in size and power, while other centers in the Southeast and Midwest surpassed it. Although the causes of this decline are not certain, the archaeological evidence provides clues. First, neighboring communities were having increasing difficulty producing enough crops to feed themselves and the many Cahokians who did not grow their own food. Second, the city's demands for fuel and construction materials was seriously reducing the supply of wood in and around Cahokia. This depletion of the forests also deprived residents of the animals and wild plants on which they depended for food. Third, the strengthening of the stockade surrounding central Cahokia suggests that the elites were facing a military challenge from inside or outside the city, or both. Finally, the trade networks that formerly brought tribute to Cahokia and carried away the city's finished products had collapsed. Taken together, these trends indicate that a combination of environmental factors and resistance to centralized authority probably led to Cahokia's downfall. By the time the French explorer La Salle passed through in 1682, Cahokia was a small village of Illinois Indians who, like other native peoples of the region, had abandoned Mississippian religious and political systems for the autonomous villages of their ancestors.

Stone Spud
A spud was used in ceremonies as a symbol of authority.

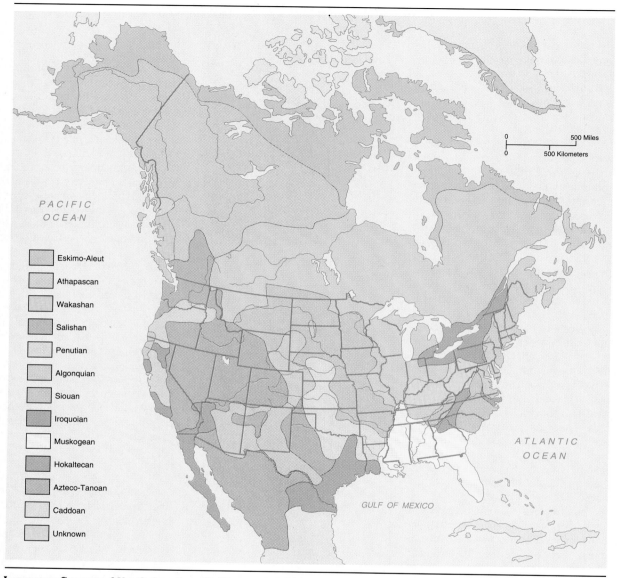

Language Groups of North American Indians, A.D. 1500

*The several hundred languages spoken by North American native peoples in A.D. 1500 were
derived from just a dozen basic language groups.*

SOURCE: Dean Snow, *The Archaeology of North America: American Indians and Their Origins* (London:
Thames and Hudson, Ltd., 1976).

descent from a common ancestor who embodied the
admired qualities of some animal. Depending on the
culture, clan membership could descend from either
the mother or the father. Clans linked widely scattered
groups within a tribe. Several different clans usually
dwelled together in a single Indian village.

Kinship bonds counted for much more in Indian
society than did the nuclear families that married couples and their children formed. Indians did not necessarily expect spouses to be bound together forever, but
kinship lasted for life. Thus Native Americans could accept the divorce of a married couple without feeling a

threat to the social order. Customs regulating marriages varied considerably, but strict rules always prevailed. In most cultures young people married in their teens, after winning social acceptance as adults and (generally) after a period of sexual experimentation. Sometimes male leaders took more than one wife, but nuclear families never stood alone. Instead, strong ties of residence and deference bound each couple to one or both sets of parents, producing what social scientists call extended families.

Kinship was also the basis for armed conflict. Indian societies typically considered homicide a matter to be resolved by the extended families of the victim and the perpetrator. If the perpetrator's family offered a gift that the victim's family considered appropriate, the question was settled. If not, the victim's kin might seek to avenge the killing by armed retaliation. If necessary, chiefs and other leaders intervened to resolve disputes between families within the same band, village, or tribe. But disputes between members of different groups could escalate into war. Densely populated societies that competed for scarce resources, as on the Northwest and California coasts, and centralized societies that attempted to dominate trade networks through coercion, such as Hopewell and Mississippian, experienced frequent and intense intergroup warfare. Some scholars believe that the warfare among the Iroquois in Hiawatha's time was a symptom of the political instability accompanying the collapse of a Mississippian center in the upper Ohio valley. Still, warfare remained a low-level affair in most of North America. An exasperated New England officer, writing of his effort to obtain Indian allies in the early seventeenth century, described a battle between two Indian groups as "more for pastime than to conquer and subdue enemies." He concluded that "they might fight seven years and not kill seven men."

Women did the cultivating among most agricultural Indians outside the Southwest. For Indian women, field work easily meshed with child care, as did such other tasks as preparing animal hides and gathering wild vegetation. Men did jobs that took them away from the women and children: hunting, fishing, trading, negotiating, and fighting. With women producing the greater share of the food supply, these communities accorded women more power than did European societies. Among the Iroquois of upstate New York, for example, the women collectively owned the fields, distributed food, and played a weighty role in

Chumash Baskets
California Indians, including the Chumash, gathered, prepared, and stored acorns and other foods in baskets crafted by specialized weavers.

tribal councils. In New England, women sometimes served as *sachems*, or chiefs.

In the Southwest, wresting a living from the severe environment demanded concentrated effort, but the native peoples succeeded remarkably well. The population was comparatively dense: a hundred thousand people may have lived in the pueblos in the early sixteenth century, and intensive cultivation also supported large river-valley settlements. As in the rest of North America, extended families formed the foundation of southwestern village life in both the pueblos and the river valleys.

Southwestern patterns of property ownership and gender roles differed, not only from those of Native Americans elsewhere but also among local cultures. Unlike Indians in other regions, here men and women shared agricultural labor. River-valley peoples of the Southwest owned land privately and passed it through the male line, and men dominated decision making. In pueblo society (which in this respect resembled societies in the Northeast and Southeast), land was communally owned, and women played an influential role in community affairs. A pueblo woman could end a marriage simply by tossing her husband's belongings out the door and sending him back to his kinfolk. Moreover, clan membership passed in the mother's line. Yet pueblo communities depended on secret male societies to perform the rituals that would secure the gods' blessing and ensure life-giving rain. More than with other Indians, pueblo society strictly subordinated the individual to the group and demanded rigorous cooperation.

Indian Religion and Social Values

Most Indians explained the origin and destiny of the human race in myths told by storytellers during religious ceremonies. In the beginning, said the Iroquois, was the sky world of unchanging perfection. From it fell a beautiful pregnant woman, whom the birds saved from plunging into the limitless ocean. On the back of a tortoise who rose from the sea, birds created the earth's soil, in which the woman planted seeds carried during her fall. From these seeds sprang all nature; from her womb, the human race.

Native American religions revolved around the conviction that all nature was alive, pulsating with a spiritual power—*manitou*, in the Algonquian languages, *orenda* in the Iroquoian, *wakan* in the Siouan. A mysterious, awe-inspiring force that could affect human life for both good and evil, such power united all nature in an unbroken web. Manitou encompassed "every thing which they cannot comprehend," wrote the Puritan leader Roger Williams, one of the few Europeans who genuinely tried to understand the northeastern Indians' spiritual world. Their belief in supernatural power led most Native Americans to seek constantly to conciliate all the spiritual forces in nature: living things, rocks and water, sun and moon, even ghosts and witches. For example, Indians were careful to pray to the spirits of the animals they hunted, justifying the killing of just enough game to sustain themselves. To Native Americans, humanity was only one link in the great chain of living nature. The Judeo-Christian view that God had given humanity domination over nature was very strange to them.

Indians had many ways of gaining access to spiritual power. One was through dreaming: most Native Americans took very seriously the visions that came to them in sleep. Some also sought access to the supernatural by artificially altering their consciousness through difficult physical ordeals. Young men in many societies commonly endured a traumatic rite of passage before gaining recognition as adults. Such a rite often involved a "vision quest"—going alone into a forest or up a mountain, fasting, and awaiting the mystical experience in which an animal spirit would reveal

itself as a protective guide and offer a glimpse of the future. Girls went through comparable rituals at the onset of menstruation to initiate them into the spiritual world from which female reproductive power flowed. Moreover, entire communities often practiced collective power-seeking rituals such as the Sun Dance, performed by Indians of the Plains and Great Basin (see Chapter 17).

Although on occasion all Indians tried to communicate directly with the spiritual world, they normally relied on shamans for help in understanding the unseen. The shamans were healers who used both medicinal plants and magical chants, but their role in Indian society went further. They interpreted dreams, guided vision quests, invoked war or peace spirits, and figured prominently in community councils. Chiefs had to maintain respectful relations with their people's shamans, who by the sixteenth century were organized into priesthoods in some societies in the Southeast and Southwest.

Even as they grew larger and more complex, Indian societies maintained the strong sense of interdependence forged over thousands of years by Paleo-Indians and their successors. As a result, they demanded a strong degree of conformity and close cooperation. From early childhood Indians learned to be accommodating and reserved—slow to reveal their own feelings before they could sense others'. Although few Native American peoples favored physical punishment in child rearing, Indian parents punished psychologically, by shaming. Throughout life the fear of becoming an isolated social outcast (a status that could mean death) forced individual Indians to maintain strict self-control. Communities took decisions by consensus, and leaders articulated slowly emerging agreements in memorable, persuasive, often passionate oratory. Shamans and chiefs therefore had to be dramatic orators. Noted John Smith, they spoke in public "with vehemency and so great passions that they sweat till they drop and are so out of breath they scarce can speak."

Because Indians highly valued consensus building in everyday life, their leaders' authority depended primarily on the respect that they invoked rather than what they could demand by compulsion. Distributing gifts was central to establishing and maintaining leadership within a Native American community, as a French observer in early seventeenth-century Canada clearly understood: "For the savages have that noble quality, that they give liberally, casting at the feet of him whom they will honor the present that they give him. But it is with hope to receive some reciprocal kindness, which is a kind of contract, which we call . . . 'I give thee, to the end thou shouldst give me.' "

Thus for Indians, trade was not merely an economic activity by which they acquired useful goods. It was also a means of ensuring goodwill with other peoples and of building their own prestige. European visitors almost always found Native Americans eager to barter. For many centuries, trade among the Indians had spanned the continent. The Hurons of southern Ontario and the Pueblo Indians of the Southwest produced large agricultural surpluses for trade, and southwestern turquoise found its way to Mexico and the Great Plains. Flint and other tool-making materials, salt, dyes, furs, exotic minerals and shells, and (in hard times) food and seeds were major objects of trade. So was tobacco, which Indians regarded primarily as a ceremonial drug, its fragrant smoke symbolizing the union of heaven and earth. Native Americans eagerly assimilated into their own way of life the new goods that European traders offered. Metal tools they valued for their practical, labor-saving benefits, and dyed cloth and glass objects quickly took on symbolic, prestige-enhancing qualities.

"They love not to be encumbered with too many utensils," remarked an early-seventeenth-century English visitor. Rather, prestige counted for everything in Native American societies. If Indians did accumulate possessions, it was primarily with the aim of giving them away, to win prestige. The most spectacular example of such gift-exchanging rituals was the Pacific Northwest potlatch ceremony. When a northwestern community's social hierarchy was shaken, an aspiring new leader would invite his neighbors to a potlatch, at which he would give away or destroy most of what he owned, all the while chanting about his own greatness and taunting his rivals. Those who received were expected later to give away even more. He who could give away the most gained the highest prestige and accumulated the greatest number of people obligated to him.

Scholars have used the word *reciprocity* to characterize Native American religious and social values. Reciprocity involved mutual give-and-take, but its aim was not to confer equality. Instead, societies based on reciprocity tried to maintain equilibrium and interdependence between individuals of unequal power and prestige. In their religious thinking, too, Indians applied the concept of reciprocity, in viewing nature as a web of interdependent spiritual powers into which humans had to fit. And in social organization, the Indians' principle of reciprocity required that communities be places of face-to-face, lifelong interaction. Trade and gift giving solidified such reciprocal bonds. The Indians' faith in social reciprocity also underlay their idea of property rights. They believed that the people of one area might agree to share with others the right to use the land for different but complementary purposes: hunting, gathering, farming, trapping, or traveling. The notion (then emerging in Europe) that property ownership conferred perpetual and exclusive control of land was alien to Indians.

But Native American society was hardly a simple, noncompetitive world. All Indian cultures possessed a strong sense of order. Custom, the demands of social conformity, and the rigors of nature strictly regulated life, and the people's everyday affairs mingled with the spiritual world at every turn. Nature and the supernatural world could sometimes be frightening. For example, Indians feared ghosts and believed that nonconformists could invoke evil spirits by witchcraft—the most dreaded crime in Indian cultures. Much in Indian religions involved placating the evil spirits that caused sickness and death. The pueblo peoples, whose existence depended on rainfall, expressed their gratitude by performing frequent rituals. And even in the Southwest, where stress on cooperation minimized competition, Indian life had an intensely competitive side. Individuals and communities eagerly strove to show physical prowess in ritualized games like lacrosse, and some bet enthusiastically on the outcome. "They are so bewitched with these . . . games, that they will lose sometimes all they have," said an Englishman of the Massachusett Indians about 1630. Such games served not only as recreation but also as a means of acquiring prestige.

The breakdown of order in Indian communities could bring fearful consequences: accusations of witchcraft, demands for revenge against wrongdoers, war against enemies. Going to war or exacting personal revenge was a ritualized way of restoring order that had broken down. A captured male could expect death after prolonged torture. Indian men learned from early childhood to inflict (and to bear) physical pain out of loyalty to kin and neighbors; they knew that they must withstand torture without flinching and death without fear. Endurance was central to Indian life.

CONCLUSION

Well before the first Siberian hunters crossed the Bering land bridge, geographic isolation and ecological variety had been the Americas' most striking characteristics. Isolation made possible Native Americans' social and cultural development untouched by alien influences and lethal epidemics. (The effects of Norse colonization were minimized because they were brief, involved few people, and above all because the Norse did not carry the epidemic diseases brought by later colonizers.) Meanwhile, great climatic and geographic variations among North American regions helped ensure that native cultures—all shaped significantly by their natural environments—would be extremely diverse.

When Europeans "discovered" America in 1492, they did not, as they thought, enter an unchanging world of simple savages. Instead, for thousands of years, native cultures and societies had transformed the North American continent into a human habitat. Indians had tapped the secrets of the land and the environment so as to be able to sustain themselves and flourish in almost every ecological zone. Over the millennia they learned the properties, uses, and values of plants, animals, soils, rocks, and other minerals, as well as the cycles of months, seasons, and years. And the Indians transformed the landscape, as evidenced by their hunting camps, villages, and cornfields and by the web of roads and trails connecting them to one another. But for Indians, these discoveries and accomplishments were not the basis for pride in their ability to conquer nature. Rather, they saw themselves as participants in a natural and supernatural order that pervaded the universe, and their attitudes, as expressed in their religious practices, were ones of gratitude and constant concern lest they violate that order.

These beliefs did not necessarily make all Indians careful conservationists. Plains hunters, stampeding herds of bison (an essential food source) over cliffs, often killed more animals than they could eat. There is evidence, moreover, that eastern Indians may sometimes have lost control of their fires and burned more land than intended. But the depletion of species in such cases was only temporary; Indians did not act consistently enough to prevent their renewal. However, other Indian actions were more consistent and hence more consequential. One reason for the decline of the great Anasazi centers in the Southwest and of the Mississippian center of Cahokia was the excessive demands placed on their environments by large concentrations of people. In these instances, Indians seemed to have learned the obvious lessons and abandoned destructive ways of life.

After 1500 a new attitude toward the land made itself felt in North America. "A people come from under the world, to take their world from them"—thus an early-seventeenth-century Virginia Indian characterized the English invaders of his homeland. Indeed, the modern society that since the seventeenth century has arisen on the Indians' ancient continent bears little resemblance to the world that the Native Americans once knew.

CHRONOLOGY

c. 5,000,000 B.C	Earliest human ancestors appear in Africa.
c. 2,000,000 B.C.	Ice Age begins.
c. 300,000–100,000 B.C.	Humans spread throughout Eastern Hemisphere.
c. 120,000 B.C.	Wisconsin glaciation begins.
c. 40,000–15,000 B.C.	Ancestors of Native Americans cross Alaska-Siberian land bridge.
c. 10,000 B.C.	Ice Age ends. Wisconsin glaciation retreats from North America.
c. 10,000–9000 B.C.	Paleo-Indians spread throughout Western Hemisphere.
c. 9000 B.C.	Extinction of big-game mammals.
c. 8000 B.C.	Archaic era begins.
c. 7000 B.C.	Athapaskan-speaking peoples arrive in North America.
c. 5000 B.C.	First domesticated plants grown in Western Hemisphere.
c. 3500 B.C.	First domesticated plants grown in North America.
c. 3000–2000 B.C.	Inuit and Aleut peoples arrive in North America.

c. 1500 B.C.	Archaic era ends.
	Bow and arrow and ceramic pottery introduced in North America.
c. 1200 B.C.	Poverty Point flourishes in Louisiana.
c. 400–100 B.C.	Adena culture flourishes in Ohio Valley.
c. 250 B.C.	Hohokam culture begins in Southwest.
c. 100 B.C.	Anasazi culture begins in Southwest.
c. 100 B.C.–A.D. 600	Hopewell culture thrives in Midwest.

c. A.D. 300	First people arrive at Hawaiian Islands.
c. A.D. 700	Mississippian culture begins.
c. A.D. 900	Stockade and first mounds built at Cahokia.
	Anasazi expansion begins.
c. A.D. 1000–1100	Norse settlement of Vinland flourishes on Newfoundland.
c. A.D. 1150	Anasazi peoples disperse to form pueblos.
c. A.D. 1200–1300	Cahokia declines.
c. A.D. 1400	League of the Iroquois formed.
A.D. 1492	Christopher Columbus begins permanent European colonization of Western Hemisphere.

Hopewell
Claw
Artifact

FOR FURTHER READING

John Bierhorst, *The Mythology of North America* (1985). An excellent introduction to Native American mythology, organized regionally.

Brian Fagan, *Ancient North America: The Archaeology of a Continent* (1991). An informative, comprehensive introduction to the continent's history before Europeans' arrival.

Åke Hultkrantz, *The Religions of the American Indians* (1979). A stimulating discussion by the leading scholar on the subject.

Gwyn Jones, *The Norse Atlantic Saga*, rev. ed. (1986). A single volume combining recent scholarship on Norse, Eskimos, and Indians with translations of the most important sagas.

Alvin M. Josephy, Jr., *America in 1492: The World of the Indian Peoples Before the Arrival of Columbus* (1992). Outstanding essays on life in the Western Hemisphere on the eve of European contact.

William C. Sturtevant, gen. ed., *Handbook of North American Indians* (20 vols. projected, 1978–   ). A partially completed reference work providing basic information on the history and culture of virtually every known native society, as well as surveys of regional archaeology and essays on topics of special interest.

ADDITIONAL BIBLIOGRAPHY

History and Anthropology

Harold E. Driver, *Indians of North America,* 2d ed. (1969); Charles Hudson, *The Southeastern Indians* (1976); Alvin Josephy, Jr., *The Indian Heritage of America,* 2d ed. (1991); Alice B. Kehoe, *North American Indians: A Comprehensive Account,* 2d ed. (1992); Eleanor Burke Leacock and Nancy Oestrich Lurie, eds., *North American Indians in Historical Perspective* (1971); Richard J. Perry, *Western Apache Heritage: People of the Mountain Corridor* (1991); Helen C. Rountree, *The Powhatan Indians: Their Traditional Culture* (1); Wilcomb E. Washburn, *The Indian in America* (1975).

Archaeology

Brian M. Fagan, *The Great Journey: The Peopling of Ancient America* (1987); Stuart J. Fiedel, *Prehistory of the Americas,* 2d ed. (1992); Melvin Fowler, *The Cahokia Atlas: A Historical Atlas of Cahokia Archaeology* (1989); Kendrick Frazier, *People of Chaco: A Canyon and Its Culture* (1986); Patricia Galloway, ed., *The Southeastern Ceremonial Complex: Artifacts and Analysis* (1989); Jesse Jennings, ed., *Ancient North Americans* (1983); Patrick Vinton Kirch, *Feathered Gods and Fishhooks: An Introduction to Hawaiian Archaeology and Prehistory* (1985); Lynda Norene Shaffer, *Native Americans Before 1492: The Moundbuilding Centers of the Eastern Woodlands* (1992); Stuart Struever and Felicia Antonelli Holton, *Koster: Americans in Search of Their Prehistoric Past* (1980).

Religion and World View

Paul Radin, *The Trickster: A Study in American Indian Mythology* (1972); Elisabeth Tooker, ed., *Native North American Spirituality of the Eastern Woodlands* (1979); Velerio Valeri, *Kingship and Sacrifice: Ritual and Society in Ancient Hawaii* (1985); Christopher Vecsey, *Imagine Ourselves Richly: Mythic Narratives of North American Indians* (1988); Ray A. Williamson, *Living the Sky: The Cosmos of the American Indian* (1987); Paul Zolbrod, *Diné bahane': The Navajo Creation Story* (1984).

Demography

David E. Stannard, *American Holocaust: The Conquest of the New World* (1992) and *Before the Horror: The Population of Hawai'i on the Eve of Western Contact* (1989); Russell Thornton, *American Indian Holocaust and Survival: A Population History Since 1492* (1987).

**Bartholomew Gosnold Trading with the Indians
at Martha's Vineyard, Massachusetts** *(detail)*
by Theodore De Bry, 1634

2

Transatlantic Encounters and Colonial Beginnings
1492–1630

A t ten o'clock on a moonlit night, the tense crew spotted a glimmering light. Then at two the next morning came the shout "Land! Land!" At daybreak they entered a shallow lagoon. The captain, Christopher Columbus (inset), rowed ashore, the royal flag fluttering in the breeze. "And, all having rendered thanks to the Lord, kneeling on the ground, embracing it with tears of joy for the immeasurable mercy of having reached it, [he] rose and gave this island the name San Salvador." The date was October 12, 1492. The place was a tiny tropical island less than four hundred miles southeast of present-day Florida.

Besides his crew, the only witnesses to Columbus's landing were a band of Taíno Indians peeking from the jungle as he claimed for his queen the island that they called Guanahaní. Soon curiosity overcame their fears. Gesturing and smiling, the Taínos walked down to the beach, where the newcomers quickly noticed the cigars they offered and the gold pendants in their noses.

The voyagers learned to savor the islanders' tobacco and to trade for golden ornaments as they sailed on among the West Indies, searching for the emperor of China's capital city. Although Columbus had found no potentates, he sensed that fabulous wealth lay within his grasp. He was sure that he had reached Asia—the Indies. Two months later, bringing with him some "Indians" and various souvenirs, he sailed home to tell of "a land to be desired and, once seen, never to be left."

Perhaps some Taínos would have agreed with the astonished Canadian Indian who saw his first shaggily bearded white man in 1632: "O, what an ugly man! Is it possible that any woman would look with favor on such a man?" Later Indians' accounts of their first sightings of Europeans also speak of wonder at seeing white-sailed "canoes" descending as from the sky and of fascination with the strangers' "magic"—their guns, gunpowder, durable metal pots and tools, and glass beads. Because the strangers were seldom prepared to survive unaided, the hospitable native people had ample opportunity to make themselves useful.

But the potential for deep misunderstanding was already present. From his first day in the New World, Columbus thought like a benevolent colonial master. "They should be good servants and of quick intelligence, ... and I believe that they would easily be made Christians, for it appeared to me that they had no creed." The Europeans would soon realize that Native Americans were neither gullible fools nor humble servants. Disillusioned, the newcomers would begin to see the Indians as lazy and deceitful "savages." Meanwhile, the Native Americans found much of the Europeans' "magic"—which included their diseases as well as their material goods— very destructive. In much of what is now Latin

America, the coming of the Europeans quickly turned into conquest. In the future United States and Canada, European mastery would come more slowly. More than one hundred years would pass before truly self-sustaining colonies were established. Nevertheless, from the moment of Columbus's landing on October 12, 1492, the American continents became the stage for the encounter of Native American, European, and African peoples.

AFRICAN AND EUROPEAN PEOPLES

The Eastern Hemisphere gave birth to the human race. For several million years, early humans went forth in waves from Africa's warm grasslands to people the globe. Then, as in the Americas, a great range of societies arose over a span of at least five thousand years before 1492. Stretching from West Africa and Europe to Siberia and Polynesia, complex networks of peaceful or aggressive interactions, cultural influences, and long-range trade linked many of these societies. Many Asian, African, and European peoples lived in hunter-gatherer or agricultural communities. But throughout the Eastern Hemisphere—as also in Mexico and Peru—there existed powerful states with armed forces, bureaucracies, religious institutions, proud aristocracies, and toiling common people.

West Africa and Its Peoples

For almost five thousand years, the vast, barren Sahara Desert has lain between much of Africa and the rest of the world. In addition, West Africa was effectively isolated from the land to its north by the prevailing Atlantic winds, which could bring old-fashioned sailing ships south but hampered them from returning north. Moreover, the yellow fever rampant in the West African rain-forest coastline helped ward off outside intruders. If contracted in youth, yellow fever could be survived with lifelong immunity, but it generally killed adult newcomers lacking such defenses.

Nevertheless, between the formidable Sahara and the forbidding coast, a broad swath of grassland (savanna) offered a hospitable shelter. By about 3000 B.C., people here were growing grain and herding livestock. Late in the first millennium B.C., when knowledge of

iron metallurgy reached the grasslands, the region's people began carrying their culture outward, eventually leaving their imprint on almost all of sub-Saharan Africa. By the sixteenth century, sub-Saharan Africa, twice the size of the United States, had a population of perhaps 20 million.

Despite its seeming isolation, West Africa looked northward. Camel caravans crossed the Sahara, and an important trade in gold and salt developed with North Africa's Mediterranean coast. From A.D. 600 to 1600, there arose in the grassland a series of West African empires—Ghana, Mali, and Songhai—that imposed tribute on their subject populations and taxed the merchant communities at the southern end of the caravan routes. Islam spread into West Africa from its Middle Eastern birthplace, and by the late eleventh century, the grassland empires became at least nominally Muslim. Their rulers kept records in Arabic and irregularly enforced Islamic law, but it was their wealth that made them famous throughout the Islamic world. By 1492 the last of the great West African empires, Songhai, stood at the height of its glory, with a bureaucracy and a vigorous army dominating much of the interior. Songhai's major city, Timbuktu, boasted flourishing markets and a famous Islamic university.

Compared with the grassland empires, coastal West Africa was relatively insignificant. In Senegambia at Africa's westernmost bulge, several small Islamic states took root. Infestation by the tsetse fly, the carrier of sleeping sickness, kept livestock-herding peoples out of Guinea's coastal forests, but many small states arose here, too, during the first millennium A.D. Among these was Benin, where artisans had been fashioning magnificent ironwork for centuries.

Then in the fifteenth century, Guinea's population rose. Foreign demands for gold that Africans panned from streams or dug from the earth touched off the spurt. Grassland warriors and merchants poured into Guinea and Senegambia, seeking new opportunities and on occasion founding or expanding the region's tiny states. Similarly thirsting for fresh opportunities were the Portuguese, who in the mid-fifteenth century used new maritime techniques to sail up and down West Africa's coast in search of gold and slaves.

West African political leaders differed sharply in the amounts and kinds of political power they wielded. Grassland emperors claimed semigodlike status, which they only thinly disguised when they adopted Islam. Rulers of smaller kingdoms depended largely on their ability to persuade, to conform to custom, and

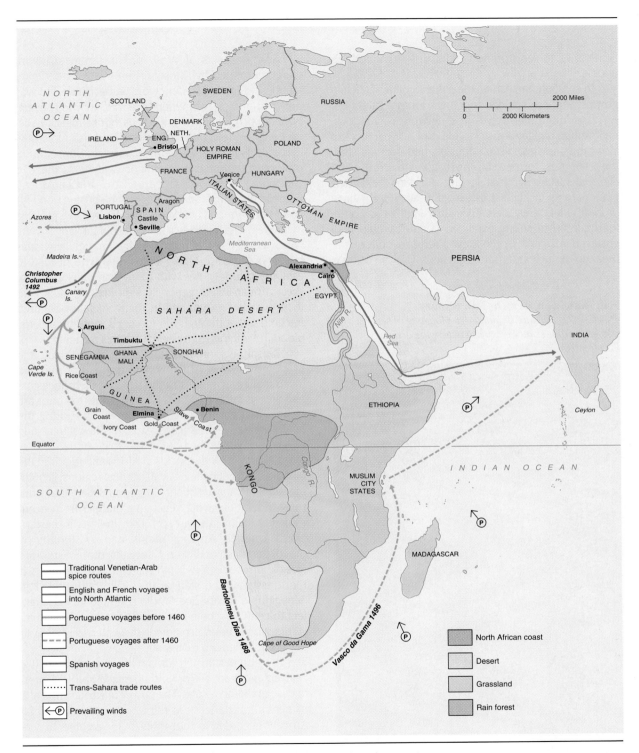

Europe, Africa, and the Near East in 1492

In 1492 Europeans had little knowledge of the outside world apart from the Mediterranean basin and Africa's west coast. Since the Azores, the Canary Islands, and the Cape Verde Islands had been explored recently in the eastern Atlantic, many Europeans were not surprised when Columbus encountered new islands farther west in 1492.

sometimes to redistribute wealth justly among their people.

In sub-Saharan Africa, the cohesiveness of kinship groups knitted society together. From childhood, Africans found themselves in a network of interlocking, mutual obligations to kinfolk. Not just parents but also aunts, uncles, distant cousins, and persons sharing clan ties formed an African's kin group and claimed his or her first loyalty. Africans held their grandparents in highest esteem and accorded village or clan elders great deference. In centuries to come, the tradition of strong extended families would help enslaved Africans in the New World to endure the breakup of nuclear families by sale.

Mali Horseman, c. 13th–14th century

This terra-cotta figure originated in Mali, one of several powerful empires in West Africa before the arrival of Europeans.

Some aspects of West African family structure were interpreted by Christian Europeans as demeaning to women and evidence of "barbarism." One was polygyny, the custom whereby a man married several wives and maintained numerous households. A second was bridewealth, a prospective husband's payment to his bride's kin before marriage. Christian Europeans interpreted both practices as demeaning to women and evidence of "barbarism." But an African man did not "buy" a wife; in effect, he posted bond for good behavior and acknowledged the relative prestige of his own and his bride's kin groups. Marrying several wives could cost a man heavily, so polygyny was largely confined to higher-status men who needed to establish marriage ties with more than one kin group. West African wives generally kept lifelong links with their own kin group, and in many societies children traced descent through the mother's, not the father's, bloodline. All this buttressed women's standing.

Kinship also informed attitudes toward land and property. To West Africans, kin groups not only enjoyed inalienable rights to the soil that their ancestors had always cultivated but also had a duty to honor ancestors and earth spirits by properly cultivating the land. Like Native Americans, Africans did not treat land as a commodity to be bought and sold.

Cultivation was difficult in Africa and required the labor of both genders. As in all tropical regions, scorching sunlight and frequent downpours prevented humus (slowly decaying vegetative matter) from accumulating in the African soil. Like Indians in eastern North America, Africans maintained soil fertility by practicing slash-and-burn tillage. In the coastal rain forests, Africans grew root crops, primarily yams. On the grasslands the staff of life was grain, which in Senegambia meant rice. In the seventeenth and eighteenth centuries, both rice and its Senegambian cultivators would be transplanted (the latter as slaves) to the North American mainland.

Religion permeated African life. West African, like Native American, religions recognized spiritual presences pervading nature. The power of earth spirits and of agricultural ancestors reinforced the esteem that Africans accorded to cultivators. In the eighteenth century, Europeans got an authentic glimpse of African religion from Olaudah Equiano, a West African who eventually managed to buy his freedom from slavery:

The natives believe that there is one Creator of all things, and that he lives in the sun, [and] . . . that he governs events. . . . Some . . . believe in the transmigration of souls [reincarnation] to some degree. Those spirits, who are not transmigrated, such as their dear friends or relations, they believe always attend them, and guard them from the bad spirits of their foes. For this reason, they always, before eating . . . put some small portion of the meat and pour some of their drink, on the ground for them; and they often make oblations [offerings] of the blood of beasts or fowls at their graves.

Magic and the placating of spiritual powers were important in West African life, and, as with Native Americans, the responsibility for maintaining contact with the spirit world fell to shamans. Africans explained misfortunes in terms of witchcraft, much as did Indians and Europeans. But African religion differed from other traditions in its focus on ancestor worship, in which departed forebears were venerated as spiritual guardians.

Africa's magnificent artistic traditions were also steeped in religion. The ivory, cast-iron, and wood sculpture of West Africa, whose bold design would help mold the twentieth-century Western world's modern art, was used in ceremonies reenacting creation myths and honoring spirits. A strong moralistic streak ran through African folk tales. Oral reciters transmitted these stories in dramatic public presentations with ritual masks, dance, and music of a highly complex rhythmic structure now appreciated as one of the foundations of jazz.

Much in traditional African culture seemed to clash with the great monotheistic religions, Islam and Christianity. Among Africans, Islam appealed primarily to merchants trading with Muslim North Africa and the Middle East and to the grassland rulers eager to consolidate their power. Even these ambitious emperors were incompletely Islamicized—some learned with dismay that Islam limited them to four wives. By the sixteenth century, Islam had only begun to affect the daily lives of grassland cultivators and artisans. Christianity, arriving in West Africa with the Portuguese in the fifteenth and sixteenth centuries, demanded that Africans break even more radically with their traditional culture, but until the nineteenth century had little impact.

European Culture and Society

When Columbus landed on San Salvador in 1492, Europe was approaching the height of a mighty cultural revival, the Renaissance. Contemporary intellectuals and poets believed that their age was witnessing a return to the standards of ancient Greek and Roman civilization. After a century-long economic recession, money had accumulated to pay for magnificent architecture, and wealthy patrons commissioned master painters and sculptors to create works glowing with idealized human beauty. Renaissance scholars strove to reconcile ancient philosophy with Christian faith, to explore the mysteries of nature, to map the world, and to explain the motions of the heavens.

But European society was quivering with tension. The era's artistic and intellectual creativity was partly inspired by intense social and spiritual stress, as Renaissance Europeans groped for stability by glorifying order, hierarchy, and beauty. A concern for power and rank ("degree") dominated European life between the fifteenth and seventeenth centuries. William Shakespeare (1564–1616), who expressed Renaissance values with incomparable eloquence, wrote:

> *The heavens themselves, the planets and this*
> *center [earth]*
> *Observe degree, priority, and place . . .*
> *Take but degree away, untune that string,*
> *And hark, what discord follows!*

Gender, wealth, inherited position, and political power affected every European's status, and few lived outside the reach of some political authority's claim to tax and impose laws upon them. But this order was shaky. Conflicts between states, between religions, and between rich and poor constantly threatened the balance. A few late-medieval and sixteenth-century revolts had democratic overtones, but the authorities mercilessly suppressed these uprisings. To most Europeans, especially elites, democracy in practice meant mob rule and the destruction of social distinctions. All the more eagerly, then, did they cling to visions of order and hierarchy.

At the top of the European hierarchy were kings, in the process of consolidating their power as heads of nation-states. (A handful of republics existed, the most important of which were the aristocratic city-states of Venice and Florence.) Lacking broad support, kings often waged wars with mercenary armies that cost mountains of money. The kings' forces spread disease and misery everywhere; they were "an unchristian, cursed tribe whose trade consists of gouging, pillaging, burning, murdering, gambling, drinking, whoring, blaspheming, willfully killing husbands and fathers, persecuting peasants . . . , stripping fields, and demanding tribute," a German chronicler wrote in 1531.

Rule by a woman frightened sixteenth-century people, especially in England, where Mary I and then Elizabeth I reigned for half a century (1553–1558 and 1558–1603, respectively). Not only did Europeans consider governance a male responsibility, but they also knew that a queen's marriage would ultimately transfer the crown to either a foreign dynasty or some domestic noble family. In this dangerous situation, Mary blundered repeatedly and saved the day only by dying soon. Elizabeth I, however, took her nation's interests to heart. Remaining the unmarried "virgin queen," she artfully managed Parliament, which represented the nation's landowning upper class and merchants. Parliament flooded her with advice, usually trying to push her further than she thought it prudent to go in dealing with political and religious issues. But by cleverly managing patronage—the distribution of royal favors and political offices—and by choosing shrewd advisers, Elizabeth remained in control of the nation's intricate political system and guided England through a perilous half-century.

As Elizabeth demonstrated, monarchs' power depended on gaining the cooperation of the upper classes, usually by consulting such representative institutions as Parliament. The men who dominated these institutions generally saw officeholding as a form of property owning and a legitimate way to improve their fortunes. No monarch could ride roughshod over such men, and by defending their own liberties, they were also preserving the principle of limited government against encroaching despotism.

All was not well with the upper classes, however, especially in England. To maintain status, they were expected to spend freely even if they could not afford to. Among the titled nobility, or aristocracy, only the eldest son inherited estates; younger sons normally had to fend for themselves in a world of shrinking opportunities. A stagnant economy also pinched many among the gentry—the "respectable" landowners without titles who traditionally lived without doing manual labor and played a prominent role in local government and Parliament.

At the bottom of the social heap toiled the ordinary people. In the overwhelmingly rural Europe of the times, peasants composed between 70 percent and 80 percent of the population. Peasants ranged from a few prosperous families with large holdings, such as the English yeomen, to landless laborers who barely

scraped by on odd jobs. Taxes, rents, and other dues to landlords and Catholic church officials were heavy, and poor harvests or war drove even well-to-do peasants to starvation.

Conditions among the peasants were made even worse by a sharp rise in population. After the plague epidemic known as the Black Death killed approximately one-third of Europe's people in the late fourteenth century, the population remained low for another half-century. But as the fear of mass death subsided and Europeans resumed having large families, the number of people increased dramatically, from about 55 million in 1450 to almost 100 million by 1600. But without corresponding improvements in technology and agriculture, output did not rise to meet growing demand. Northern European and English peasant families cultivated wheat or rye, barley, and oats on long strips scattered through their village's three or more fields; one field lay fallow every third year to restore fertility. Yields were pitifully low. Families had to cooperate in plowing, sowing, and harvesting, as well as in grazing their livestock on the fallow field and the jointly owned "commons," or pastureland and forest. With new land at a premium, the commons were a tempting prize for landlords, especially the English gentry, to "enclose"—that is, to convert to private property. Peasants who had no *written* title to their land were especially vulnerable, but yeomen with strong titles often kept their land, and a few even profited by enclosing.

European towns were numerous but small, typically with several thousand inhabitants each. A great metropolis like London, whose population ballooned from fifty-five thousand in 1550 to two hundred thousand in 1600, was quite exceptional. But all towns were dirty and disease-ridden, and townspeople lived close-packed with their neighbors.

Unappealing as sixteenth-century towns might seem today, ambitious (or desperate) men and women of the time viewed them as growing, dynamic centers of opportunity. Immigration from the countryside—rather than an excess of urban births over deaths—accounted for towns' expansion. Most of the displaced country people who flocked into towns remained at the bottom of the social order, however, as servants or laborers who often failed to accumulate enough money to marry and live independently. Manufacturing took place in household workshops, where subordinate workers were dependent on an artisan master. Successful artisans and merchants formed guilds to control employment, prices, and the sale of goods. Dominated by the richest citizens, urban governments enforced social conformity by "sumptuary laws" that forbade dressing inappropriately to one's social rank.

The consequences of rapid population growth were particularly acute in England, where the number of people doubled from about 2.5 million in 1500 to 5 million in 1620. In parts of the countryside, landowners united to divide the commons among themselves, raise sheep, and grow rich selling wool. But with textile-manufacturing technology largely unchanged, per capita output and real household income among textile workers fell. In effect, more workers competed for fewer jobs in the face of diminishing European markets for English cloth and rapidly rising prices for food. Enclosures aggravated unemployment, forcing large numbers of people to wander the countryside in search of work and so making England's population highly mobile. To the upper and middle classes, these poor "vagabonds" seemed to threaten law and order. To control them, Parliament passed "Poor Laws" that ordered vagrants whipped and sent home, where hardpressed taxpayers maintained them on relief.

Thus the hopes and ambitions that drew thousands into towns usually gave way to frustration. Some in England blamed the well-to-do, whom they charged with raising prices, goading the poor to revolt, and giving too little to charity. But others, such as the writer Thomas Nashe, spread the blame more widely:

> *From the rich to the poor . . . there is ambition, or swelling above their states [proper place in society]; the rich citizen swells against the pride of the prodigal courtier; the prodigal courtier swells against the wealth of the citizen. One company swells against another. . . . The ancients [elderly], they oppose themselves against the younger, and suppress them and keep them down all that they may. The young men, they call [the elderly] dotards, and swell and rage. . . .*

Conservative moralists like Nashe condemned "overreaching" (individuals' attempts to rise in society) and stoutly upheld the values of old-fashioned social reciprocity. As in America and Africa, traditional society in Europe rested on maintaining long-term, reciprocal relationships. But because its aim was the smooth functioning of social relationships between individuals of unequal status, European reciprocity required the upper classes to act with self-restraint and

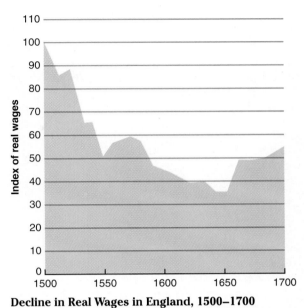

Decline in Real Wages in England, 1500–1700
This index of real wages, which measures the drop in purchasing power due to inflation and declining wages, indicates that as the Great Migration began around 1630, living standards for English workers had suffered a steady reduction of about 60 percent since the base year, 1500.

SOURCE: E. H. Phelps Brown and S. V. Hopkins, "Builders' Wage-Rates, Prices and Population: Some Further Evidence," *Economica*, XXVI (1959): 18–38; adapted from D. C. North and R. P. Thomas, *The Rise of the Western World: A New Economic History* (Cambridge: Cambridge University Press, 1973), 111.

dignity, and the lower classes to show deference to their "betters." It also demanded strict economic regulation to ensure that sellers charged a "just price"— one that covered costs and allowed the seller a "reasonable" living standard but that barred him from taking advantage of buyers' and borrowers' misfortunes or of shortages to make "excessive" profits.

Yet for several centuries Europeans had been compromising the ideals of traditional economic behavior. "In the Name of God and of Profit," thirteenth-century Italian merchants had written on their ledgers. By the sixteenth century, nothing could stop the charging of interest on borrowed money or sellers' price increases in response to demand. New forms of business organization slowly spread in the commercial world— especially the impersonal joint-stock company with many investors (see below), the ancestor of the modern corporation. Demand rose for capital investment,

The Banker and His Wife, *by Quentin Metsys, 1514*
Despite religious admonitions against excessive material gain, some sixteenth-century Europeans sought to reconcile profit with piety. In this portrait, a banker weighs gold coins to ensure their accurate value as his wife, watching him, holds a prayer book.

and so did the supply of accumulated wealth. Slowly a new economic outlook took form that justified both the unimpeded acquisition of wealth and unregulated economic competition, and insisted that individuals owed one another nothing but the money necessary to settle each market transaction. This new outlook, the central value system of capitalism or the "market economy," was the opposite of traditional demands for the strict regulation of economic activity to ensure social reciprocity and maintain "just prices."

Sixteenth- and seventeenth-century Europeans therefore held conflicting attitudes toward economic enterprise and social change, and their ambivalence remained unresolved. In Europe itself and in transplanted Europeans' colonial communities, a restless desire for fresh opportunity kept life simmering with competitive tension. But those who prospered still sought the security and prestige provided by traditional social distinctions, whereas the poor longed for the age-old values that they hoped would restrain irresponsible greed. Almost all intellectuals and clergymen defended traditional standards. When Europeans violated these standards, they did so with a

bad conscience. Thus ideal and reality remained far apart.

Fundamental change in European society could also be seen in the growing importance of the nuclear family. The tradition of broad kinship networks did survive in the sense that nuclear families prudently tried to retain the goodwill of distant relatives, but these networks seldom overruled the male head of each nuclear family. In a common cliché of the age, the nuclear family was a "little commonwealth." The father's government within the family was supposed to mirror God's rule over Creation and kings' lordship over their subjects. Even grown sons and daughters regularly knelt for their father's blessing. The ideal, according to a German writer, was that "wives should obey their husbands and not seek to dominate them; they must manage the home efficiently. Husbands . . . should treat their wives with consideration and occasionally close an eye to their faults." In practice, the father's domination often had to make room for the wife's responsibility in managing family affairs and helping to run the farm or the workshop. And repeated male complaints (such as that of an English author in 1622) about wives "who think themselves every way as good as their husbands, and no way inferior to them," suggested that male domination had its limits.

Europeans and Their God

"In the beginning God created the heaven and the earth. . . . And God said, Let us make man in our image . . . and let them have dominion . . . over all the earth. . . . So God created man in his own image, . . . male and female he created them." Sixteenth-century Europeans firmly believed in this biblical explanation of the origins of the world and its peoples. Christianity, to which the vast majority of Europeans adhered, taught that Jesus Christ, God's Son, had redeemed sinners by suffering crucifixion and rising from the dead. Equally vivid was their belief in the devil, Satan, whom God had hurled from heaven soon after the Creation and who ceaselessly lured people to damnation by tempting them to do evil. The non-Christian European minority encompassed small Jewish communities and Muslims in the Balkans and in Spain. But all Europe's population—Christians, Jews, and Muslims—worshiped a single supreme being, based on the God of the Old Testament.

Although Christianity had sunk deep roots into Europeans' consciousness by the sixteenth century, many also retained beliefs that originated outside the Christian tradition. Virtually all Europeans feared witches, and many thought that individuals could manipulate nature by invoking unseen spiritual powers—that is, by magic. Many also looked to astrology, which insisted that a person's fate depended on the conjunction of various planets and stars. Everyone envisioned nature as a "chain of being" infused by God with life and tingling with spiritual forces. Deeply embedded in European folklore, such supernaturalism also marked the "high culture" of educated Europeans. Indeed, the sixteenth-century European "mentality" had more in common with Indian and African mind sets than any of these traditional belief systems have with more modern world views.

The Catholic church, based in Rome, taught that Christ's sacrifice was repeated every time a priest said Mass, and that divine grace flowed to sinners through the sacraments that consecrated priests alone could administer—above all, baptism, confession, and the Eucharist (communion). The Church was a huge network of clergymen, set apart from laypeople by the fact that they did not marry. At the top was the pope, the "vicar (representative) of Christ," whose authority reached everywhere in Europe but Russia, Greece, and the Balkan Peninsula.

The papacy wielded awesome spiritual power. Fifteenth- and early-sixteenth-century popes claimed the authority to dispense extra blessings, or "indulgences," to repentant sinners in return for such "good works" as donating money to the Church. Indulgences promised time off from future punishment in purgatory, where souls atoned for sins they had already confessed and been forgiven. (Hell, from which there was no escape, awaited those who died unforgiven.) Given people's anxieties over "sinful" behavior, indulgences were enormously popular. The jingle of one successful indulgence seller in early-sixteenth-century Germany promised that

As soon as the coin in the cash box rings,
The soul from purgatory's fire springs.

But the sale of indulgences provoked charges that the materialism and corruption infecting economic life had spread to the Church. In 1517 the German friar Martin Luther (1483–1546) attacked the practice. When the papacy tried to silence him, Luther broadened his criticism to encompass the Mass, purgatory, priests, and the pope. Luther's revolt initiated the Protestant Reformation, which changed Christianity forever.

To Luther, indulgence selling and similar examples of clerical corruption were evil not just because they bilked people. The Church, he charged, also wronged people by giving them false confidence that they could "earn" salvation by doing good works. His own agonizing search for salvation had convinced Luther that God alone chose whom to save from damnation and that believers could trust only God's love. "I did not love a just and angry God, but rather hated and murmured against him," recalled Luther. "Night and day I pondered until I saw the connection between the justice of God and the [New Testament] statement that 'the just shall live [be saved] by faith.' . . . Thereupon I felt myself to be reborn and to have gone through open doors into paradise." Luther's spiritual struggle and experience of being "reborn" constituted a classic conversion experience—the heart of Protestant religion as it soon would be preached and practiced in northern Europe and North America.

A religious prophet of genius, Luther was socially conservative and politically naive. His assault on the Church's abuses won a fervent following among the German public, but Luther and his followers could carry out their program only with the aid of the German princes and city-states. Protestantism* thus had to allow civil governments' broad control over reformed religion. Luther's dream of rallying all Christendom around God's Word soon crumbled.

Protestant reformers could not even agree on what God's Word really meant. Thus Luther and the great French reformer John Calvin (1509–1564) interpreted salvation quite differently. Calvin insisted on the stark doctrine of predestination, in which an omnipotent God "predestined" most sinful humans to hell, saving only a few to exemplify his grace. And Calvinists and Lutherans, as the followers of the two Reformation leaders came to be called, were equally horrified by more radical Protestants such as the Anabaptists, who appealed strongly to women and common people with their criticisms of the rich and powerful and sought to restrict baptism to "converted" adults. Most Anabaptists were pacifists, and some renounced private property and lived communally. Judging the Anabaptists a threat to the social order, governments and mainstream churches persecuted them.

Still another disappointment for Protestants was the Catholic church's remarkable resilience. Catholic

---

*The word *Protestant* comes from the *protest* of Luther's princely supporters against Holy Roman Emperor Charles V's anti-Lutheran policies.

John Calvin, *by Hans Holbein the Younger,*
Sixteenth Century
Calvin was trained as a classical scholar before his reli-
gious conversion. He brought to Protestant theology
a scholar's erudition, a lawyer's appreciation of the
importance of God's sovereignty over Creation, and
a religious zealot's intense faith.

reform had begun in Spain even before Luther's revolt, and soon the papacy vigorously attacked corruption and combated Protestant viewpoints on major religious issues. The popes also sponsored a new religious order fervently committed to the papacy: the Jesuits, whose members would distinguish themselves for centuries as missionaries and royal advisers. This Catholic revival, the Counter-Reformation, brought into existence the modern Roman Catholic church.

The Reformation era left four major legacies. First, it created almost all the major Christian traditions that would eventually take root in American soil: Protestantism, Catholicism, and many radical Protestant impulses that would flower into dozens of denominations and visionary groups striving for human per-

fection. Second, Protestantism placed a high value on reading. Luther's own conversion had sprung from his long study of the Bible, and Protestants demanded that God's Word be translated from Latin into spoken languages and read carefully by believers. The new faith was spread best by the newly invented printing press; wherever Protestantism became established, basic education and religious indoctrination followed. Third, Protestantism denied that God had endowed priests with special powers. Instead, Luther claimed, the church was a "priesthood of all believers." Protestant reformers insisted that laypeople take responsibility for their own spiritual and moral conditions. Finally, the Reformation and Counter-Reformation reinforced a new crusading spirit in Europe, recently bolstered by Spain's fifteenth-century expulsions of Muslims and of Jews who refused to become Christians. Coinciding with the emergence of nation-states and overseas expansion, this spirit frequently gave Europeans a justification for assuming themselves superior to the non-Christian peoples of the Americas and Africa and for seizing their land, resources, and labor.

Along with its innovations, the Reformation had a conservative side. It created a yearning in many people for the simplicity and purity of the ancient Christian church. Protestantism condemned the replacement of traditional reciprocity by marketplace values and, more than Catholicism, questioned the pursuit of excessive wealth. In a world of troubling change, it could forge individuals of strong moral determination and equip them with the fortitude to survive and prosper. Protestantism's greatest appeal was to all those — ordinary individuals, merchants, and aristocrats alike—who brooded over their chances for salvation and valued the steady performance of duty.

Those in all camps who hoped that Christian concord would overcome religious quarrels were sadly disillusioned. Religious warfare consumed much of western and central Europe from the mid-sixteenth to the mid-seventeenth century, and international rivalries in western Europe, particularly between Catholic Spain and Protestant England, assumed a religious dimension. In England the crown itself was heavily entangled in domestic religious strife. King Henry VIII (ruled 1509–1547) wanted a legitimate male heir to ensure political stability. But his queen, Catherine of Aragon, failed to bear a son, and so Henry asked the pope to annul his marriage. After the pope denied Henry's request, the king had Parliament, in a series of acts in 1533–1534, dissolve his marriage and proclaim

Major Religions in Europe, c. 1560
Sixteenth-century Europe teemed with religious change and conflict.

him "supreme head" of the Church of England (or Anglican church). He then used his new position to seize vast tracts of land owned by Catholic monastic orders and to sell them to members of the gentry as a means of raising revenue.

The Rise of Puritanism in England

Religion remained a source of trouble in England for well over a century after Henry's break with Rome. His sale of monastic lands created a vested interest against returning to the old order. But Henry never quite decided whether he was a Protestant. Under Edward VI (ruled 1547–1553), the church veered sharply toward Protestantism; then Mary I tried to restore Catholicism, in part by burning several hundred Protestants at the stake.

The reign of Elizabeth I marked a crucial watershed. After "Bloody Mary," most English people were ready to become Protestant; *how* Protestant was the divisive question. A militant but minority Calvinist movement called Puritanism had arisen. Puritans demanded a wholesale "purification" of the Church of England from "popish [Catholic] abuses." As Calvinists, they affirmed salvation by predestination, denied Christ's presence in the Eucharist, and believed that a learned sermon was the heart of true worship. They wished to free each congregation and its minister from outside interference by bishops and encouraged lay members (nonclergy) to participate in parish affairs. Puritans also objected to certain ceremonies and practices inherited from Catholicism, such as the Mass, elaborate church decoration, kneeling, and the use of priestly vestments or communion rails—the latter two implying that the clergy were separate from, and superior to, their congregations.

Insisting that it was not sufficient for a person to lead an outwardly moral life, Puritans argued that Christians must forge a commitment to serve God through a special act of spiritual rebirth termed the *conversion experience*. At this moment of being "reborn," a soul confronted the horrifying truth of its own unworthiness and felt the transcending power of God's saving grace. Through a process known as sanctification, the new convert was cemented to God as a "saint," or member of the "elect." Whereas membership in the Church of England was automatic for anyone born in England, only saints could join Puritan congregations.

For many Puritans, the conversion process was understandably a tortuous one. Poverty, loneliness, and fear so pervaded England that no one could avoid feeling anxious over the future. Chronic unemployment and low wages constantly tempted the hard-pressed to become petty cheats. Even honest individuals had difficulty showing charity, because they found life so insecure. Unable to make a decent living, many had to fight the impulse to desert their families and the urge to drown their sorrows in drink. Because the faltering economy forced half of all men and women to delay marriage until after age twenty-five, young adults had to battle temptation through much of their lives. In such desperate times, it was natural for many to doubt that they could set the example expected of saints.

In preparing for spiritual rebirth, Puritans struggled to master their own wills, to internalize a highly idealistic code of ethics, and to forge the inner strength to survive in a world of economic and moral chaos. By the time of his or her redemption, a Puritan had undergone a radical personality transformation that replaced doubt with certainty. This reorientation of character produced the Puritans' strong sense of purpose, willingness to sacrifice, and ironclad discipline. The conversion experience molded individuals like the Puritan military and political leader Oliver Cromwell, who felt that, because he had conquered himself, he could conquer any enemy.

The severe self-discipline and righteousness demanded of Puritans appealed to certain elements of English society more than others. The new religion attracted only a few from the titled nobility, with their inherited wealth and privileges, and from the desperate poor, whose lives were consumed by the quest for physical survival. Puritanism's primary appeal lay instead among the small but growing number of people between the extremes of English society—landowning gentry, university-educated clergymen and intellectuals, merchants, shopkeepers, artisans, and yeoman farmers. Self-discipline had become central to both the secular and spiritual dimensions of these people's lives. From their ranks, and particularly from the farmers, artisans, and clergymen, would later come the settlers of New England (see Chapter 3).

Elizabeth distrusted Puritan militancy but also, after 1570, when the pope declared her a heretic and urged Catholics to overthrow her, she regarded English Catholics as potential traitors. She and her advisers gradually forged a strong Church of England that satisfied most Protestants in matters of belief and practice.

By courting influential Puritans and embracing militant anti-Catholicism, Elizabeth maintained most Puritans' loyalty. But religious tensions resurfaced in England after her death.

James I (ruled 1603–1625), the founder of England's Stuart dynasty, bitterly opposed Puritan efforts to eliminate the office of bishop. The monarchy's right to name bishops greatly strengthened its power because bishops composed about a quarter of the House of Lords, the upper chamber of Parliament, which at the time had a strong voice in enacting laws. Bishops also controlled the clergy and thus could silence ministers whose sermons or writings criticized government policies. James made it clear that he saw Puritan attacks on bishops as a direct threat to himself when he snapped, "No bishop, no king."

Under Elizabeth, most Puritans had come to expect that they would eventually tansform the Church of England into independent congregations of "saints." But James's position undermined that hope, leading many Puritans to become *Separatists* who insisted

that saints had to separate themselves from the corrupt state church. During James's reign, some Separatists moved to Calvinist Holland, and a few of these led the founding of Plymouth Plantation in New England (see below). *Non-Separatists,* in contrast, believed that the Church of England could be reformed from within. Some of them would lead the later colonization of Massachusetts Bay and Connecticut (see Chapter 3).

After Charles I became king in 1625, Anglican authorities undertook a systematic campaign to eliminate Puritan influence within the church. With the king's backing, bishops insisted that services be conducted according to the Book of Common Prayer, which prescribed rituals similar to Catholic practices, and they dismissed Puritan ministers who refused to perform these "High Church" rites. Church courts, which judged cases involving religious law, harassed the Puritan laity with fines or excommunication.

The Puritan's spiritual discontent was reinforced by England's poor economic situation. Between 1550 and 1650, wages fell by half. Bad harvests and depressions plagued England. A 30 percent rise in population from 1590 to 1640 spawned massive unemployment. When economic crisis and the outbreak of the Thirty Years' War on the European continent prevented Germany from importing large amounts of English cloth after 1618, a deep recession gripped England's weaving industry, taking a severe toll on the heavily Puritan southeastern counties. For Puritans, these problems contributed to England's spiritual and moral malaise. Dwindling economic opportunities made leading a godly life difficult for many. One Puritan minister wrote that everyone in England was tempted "to pluck his means, as it were, out of his neighbor's throat." Such conditions led many Puritans to consider migrating to New England after 1629 (see Chapter 3).

EUROPEAN EXPANSION

Europeans' outward thrust began centuries before Columbus's first voyage in 1492. In the tenth century, Norse voyagers from Scandinavia had reached North America (see Chapter 1). They established a settlement in Newfoundland and may have explored the New England coast. But the Norse soon abandoned and eventually almost forgot America, and the direction of European expansion changed. A series of crusading armies after 1096 struggled (ultimately in vain) to wrest Palestine from Muslim control. A brisk trade with the Middle East began in these years as Europeans sold cloth and bought silks and the spices they needed to preserve food and spark up a monotonous diet. Some thirteenth-century merchants such as Marco Polo even traveled overland to East Asia to buy directly from the Chinese. By the fourteenth and fifteenth centuries, the highly profitable spice and silk trade had enriched well-placed Italian merchants despite the era's generally depressed economic conditions. With their personal fortunes, the merchants financed the cultural flowering of the early Renaissance as well as the consolidation of domestic power and overseas expansion by the European monarchs.

Seaborne Expansion

Around 1460 a century of depression and population stagnation ended in Europe. An era of renewed economic and population growth opened. As Europeans competed for commercial advantage, they projected their power overseas.

Important changes in maritime technology occurred at this dawn of European expansion. In the early fifteenth century, shipbuilders and mariners along Europe's stormy Atlantic coast added the triangular Arab sail to the heavy cargo ships they used for voyaging between England and the Mediterranean. They created a more maneuverable vessel, the caravel, that could sail against the wind. Sailors also mastered the compass and astrolabe, by which they got their bearings on the open sea. Without this "maritime revolution," European exploration would have been impossible.

Renaissance scholars' search for more accurate readings of ancient texts forced fifteenth-century Europeans to look at their world with new eyes. The great ancient Greek authority on geography was Ptolemy, but Renaissance scholars had to correct his data when they tried to draw accurate maps. Thus Renaissance "new learning" combined with older Arabic and European advances in mathematics to sharpen Europeans' geographic sense.

The impetus to explore new worlds first arose in impoverished Portugal. Here zeal for continuing the struggle against the Muslims who were slowly being driven out of Spain and Portugal combined with an anxious search for new markets. Prince Henry "the Navigator" of Portugal (1394–1460) embodied both urges. Henry encouraged Portuguese seamen to pilot the new caravels farther down the African coast, searching for weak spots in Muslim defenses and for

An Astrolabe
A device for calculating the position and altitude of the sun, stars, and planets, the astrolabe was one of the world's oldest scientific instruments. It was known to the ancient Greeks and perfected by the medieval Arabs. Ocean navigators found it indispensable. This brass English astrolabe, dating to 1326, may be the oldest such European instrument extant.

opportunities to trade profitably. At the time of his death, the Portuguese had established a profitable slaving station at Arguin, and by the late fifteenth century, they had penetrated south of the equator. In 1488 Bartolomeu Días reached the Cape of Good Hope at Africa's southern tip. The Portuguese king John II seized the opportunity to open up direct contact with India, circumventing the Arabs and Venetians. In 1498 Vasco da Gama led a Portuguese fleet around the Cape of Good Hope and on to India.

Ultimately the Portuguese failed to destroy traditional Venetian-Arab commercial links, although for a century they remained an imperial presence in the Indian Ocean and present-day Indonesia. Already, however, they had brought Europeans face-to-face with black Africans.

The "New Slavery" and Racism

Slavery was well established in fifteenth-century West Africa, as elsewhere. The grassland emperors, as well as individual families, depended on slaves. But most slaves or their children were absorbed into African families over time. The eighteenth-century West African Olaudah Equiano, who had suffered enslavement by the British, explained the fate of war captives in his native society:

> *How different was their condition from that of the slaves in the West Indies! With us they do no more work than other members of the community, even their master. Their food, clothing, and lodging, were nearly the same as [free people's], except that they were not permitted to eat with those who were born free. . . . Some of these slaves even have slaves under them, as their own property, and for their own use.*

Outsiders—first Muslims then Europeans—turned African slavery into an intercontinental business and tore slaves from their native societies. One fifteenth-century Italian who witnessed Portuguese and Muslim slave trading noted that the Arabs "also have many Berber horses, which they trade, and take to the Land of the Blacks, exchanging them with the rulers for slaves. Ten or fifteen slaves are given for one of these horses, according to their quality. . . . These slaves are brought to the market town of Hoden; there they are divided. . . . [Some] are taken . . . and sold to the Portuguese leaseholders [of Arguin]. As a result every year the Portuguese carry away from [Arguin] a thousand slaves."

Equiano's eighteenth-century testimony starkly captures slaves' experience in earlier centuries too. Brought on a European slave ship, he wrote:

> *I was now persuaded that I had got into a world of bad spirits, and that they were going to kill me. Their complexions differing so much from ours, their long hair, and the languages they spoke . . . united to confirm me in this belief. . . . Quite overpowered with shock and horror, I . . . fainted. When I recovered a little, I found some black people around me, who I believed were some of those who brought me on board, and had been receiving their pay. . . . I asked them if we were not to be eaten by those white men. . . . They told me I was not. [But] soon after this the blacks who had brought me on board went off, and left me abandoned to despair. . . . I found some of my own nation [and] inquired . . . what was to be done with us? They gave me to understand that we were to be carried to these white people's country to work for them. I then was a*

> *little revived . . . but still I feared I should be put to death, the white people looked, as I thought, so savage. . . .*

The Portuguese found slave trading lucrative and kept out competitors until about 1600. Although in 1482 they built an outpost, Elmina, on West Africa's Gold Coast, they exploited existing African commercial and social patterns. Often Portuguese merchants traded slaves and local products to other Africans for gold. The local African kingdoms were too strong for the Portuguese to attack, and black rulers traded—or chose not to trade—according to their own self-interest.

West African societies changed with the coming of Portuguese slavers. In Guinea and Senegambia, which supplied the bulk of sixteenth-century slaves, small kingdoms expanded to "service" the trade. Some of their rulers became comparatively rich. Farther south, in present-day Angola, the kings of Kongo used the slave trade to consolidate their power and voluntarily adopted Christianity. Kongo flourished until the late sixteenth century, when attackers from the interior destroyed it.

The slave-trading African kings and their communities used the trade as a way of disposing of "undesirables," including slaves whom they already owned, lawbreakers, and persons accused of witchcraft. But most slaves were simply victims of raids or wars. Muslim and European slave trading greatly stimulated conflicts among African communities.

Although European societies had used slaves since the time of ancient Greece and Rome, there were ominous differences in the European slavery that arose once the Portuguese began voyaging to West Africa. First, the new slave trade was a high-volume business that expanded steadily. Between 1500 and 1600, perhaps 250,000 African slaves would land in the Western Hemisphere, and 50,000 would die en route. Another 200,000 would arrive between 1601 and 1621. Before the Atlantic slave trade finally ended in the nineteenth century, nearly 12 million Africans would be shipped in terrible conditions across the sea. Slavery on this scale had been unknown to Europeans since the collapse of the Roman Empire. Second, African slaves were treated exceptionally harshly. In medieval Europe slaves had primarily performed domestic service, but by 1450 the Portuguese and Spanish created large slave-labor plantations on their Atlantic and Mediterranean islands. These plantations produced sugar for European markets, using capital supplied by Italian investors to buy African slaves who toiled until death. In short, the African slaves owned by Europeans were destined for exhausting, mindless labor. By 1600 the "new slavery" had become a brutal link in a commerce that ultimately would encompass all major Western nations.

Finally, race became the explicit basis of the "new slavery." Africans' blackness and their alien religion dehumanized them in European eyes. As their racial prejudice hardened, Europeans justified enslaving blacks with increasing ease. From the fifteenth century onward, European Christianity made few attempts to soften slavery's rigors, and race defined a slave. Because the victims of the "new slavery" were physically distinctive as well as culturally alien, slavery became a lifelong, hereditary, and despised status.

Europeans Reach America

Europeans' varying motivations for expanding their horizons converged in the fascinating, contradictory figure of Christopher Columbus (1451–1506), the son of a weaver from the Italian port of Genoa. Columbus's maritime experience, self-taught geographical learning, and keen imagination led him to conclude that Asia could be reached by sailing westward across the Atlantic. By the early 1480s this idea obsessed him. Religious fervor led Columbus to dream of carrying Christianity around the globe and liberating Jerusalem from Muslim rule, but he also burned with ambition to win wealth and glory.

Columbus would not be the first European to venture far out into the Atlantic. Besides the early Norse, fifteenth-century English fishermen may already have sailed as far west as the Grand Banks and even the North American coast. But Columbus was unique in the persistence with which he hawked his "enterprise of the Indies" around the royal courts of western Europe. John II of Portugal showed interest until Días's discovery of the Cape of Good Hope promised a surer way to India. Finally, in 1492, hoping to break a threatened Portuguese monopoly on direct trade with Asia, the rulers of newly united Spain—Queen Isabella of Castile and King Ferdinand of Aragon—accepted Columbus's offer. Picking up the westward-blowing trade winds at the Canary Islands, Columbus's three small ships reached San Salvador within a month.

Columbus's success derived in part from a gigantic miscalculation. The West Indies lay about where he expected to find Japan, for he had combined Marco Polo's overestimate of Asia's eastward thrust with Ptolemy's underestimate of the earth's circumference. Another ancient Greek mathematician's calculation was close to the true circumference, and this figure was generally accepted by knowledgeable fifteenth-century Europeans; hence the skepticism that Columbus had aroused.

Word of Columbus's discovery caught Europeans' imaginations. It also induced Isabella and John II in 1494 to sign the Treaty of Tordesillas, which divided all future discoveries between Castile and Portugal. Meanwhile, Isabella had sent Columbus back to explore further, and he established a colony on Hispaniola, the Caribbean island today occupied by Haiti and the Dominican Republic. Columbus proved a poor administrator, and after his last voyages (1498–1502), he was shunted aside. He died an embittered man, convinced that he had reached the threshold of Asia, only to be cheated of his rightful rewards.

England's Henry VII (ruled 1485–1509) ignored Castile's and Portugal's claims of exclusive rights to new discoveries. In 1497 he sent an Italian navigator known in England as John Cabot westward into the Atlantic, tacking against the eastward winds of these latitudes. Cabot claimed for England Nova Scotia, Newfoundland, and the rich Grand Banks fisheries. Like Columbus, Cabot thought that he had reached Asia.

The more Columbus and others explored, the more apparent it became (to everyone except himself) that a vast landmass blocked the route to Asia. In 1500 the Portuguese claimed Brazil, and other voyages soon revealed a continuous coastline from the Caribbean to Brazil. In 1507 this landmass got its name when a publisher brought out a collection of voyagers' tales. One of the chroniclers was an Italian named Amerigo Vespucci. With a shrewd marketing touch, the publisher devised a catchy name for the new continent: America.

Getting past America and reaching Asia remained the early explorers' primary aim. In 1513 the Spaniard Vasco Núñez de Balboa chanced upon the Pacific Ocean when he crossed the narrow isthmus of Panama. Then in 1519 the Portuguese Ferdinand Magellan, sailing under the Castilian flag, began a voyage around the world by way of the stormy Magellan Straits at South America's southern tip. In an incredible feat of endurance, he crossed the Pacific to the Philippines, only to die fighting with local natives. One of his five ships and fifteen emaciated sailors finally returned to Spain in 1522, the first people to have sailed around the world. But Europeans hoped for easier access to East

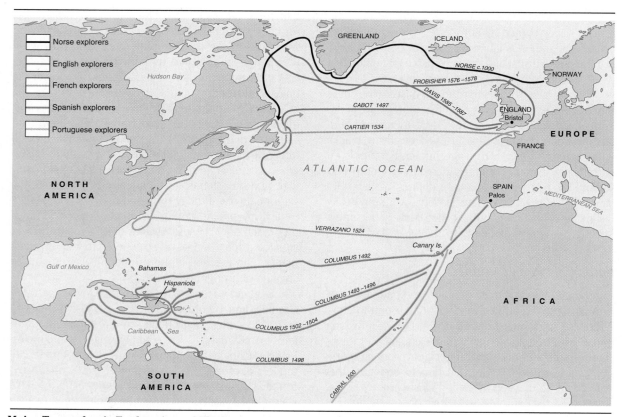

Major Transatlantic Explorations, 1000–1587

Following Columbus's 1492 voyage, Spain's rivals soon began laying claim to parts of the New World based on the voyages of Cabot for England, Cabral for Portugal, and Verrazano for France. Later English and French exploration focused on finding a passage to Asia around or through Canada.

Asia's fabled wealth. The French king Francis I accepted the challenge of finding a "northwest passage" to Asia. In 1524 he dispatched the Italian navigator Giovanni da Verrazano, who explored the North American coast from the Carolinas to Newfoundland. In three subsequent voyages between 1534 and 1542 the French explorer Jacques Cartier carefully probed the coasts of Newfoundland, Quebec, and Nova Scotia and ascended the St. Lawrence as far as present-day Montreal. Although encountering large numbers of Native Americans, Verrazano and Cartier found no gold and no northwest passage.

The Conquerors

Columbus was America's first slave trader and the first of the Spanish conquerors, or *conquistadores.* At his struggling colony on Hispaniola, he began exporting Indian slaves and created *encomiendas*—grants for the right to extract labor and other tribute from the Indians of a designated district. Other *conquistadores* would soon transplant this practice to the American mainland.

From the beginning *encomiendas* harshly exploited the native people, who died in droves from overwork, malnutrition, and disease. Then Portuguese slavers stepped in, supplying shiploads of Africans to replace the perishing Indians. Spanish friars who came to Hispaniola to convert the Indians quickly sent back grim reports of Indian exploitation; and King Ferdinand (who had made money by selling *encomiendas*) felt sufficiently shocked to attempt to forbid the practice. No one, however, worried about the African slaves' fate.

Spanish Map of the Antilles, 1519
This map offers a rare glimpse of Spain's initial stronghold in the Caribbean islands, center-
ing on what is now Haiti. The decorative figures are Africans, imported to replace Indian la-
bor lost to disease and harsh treatment.

Soon Spanish settlers were fanning out through the Caribbean in search of Indian slaves and gold. In 1519 the restless nobleman Hernán Cortés (1485–1547) led a small band of followers to the Mexican coast. Destroying his boats and gathering Indian allies, he marched inland over towering mountain passes to conquer Mexico.

Spaniards had dreamed of a prize such as Mexico ever since they reached America. Mexico was rich: an impressive civilization had been evolving there for three thousand years, culminating in the mighty Aztec Empire. It was exotic: the priests and soldiers who dominated the empire raided neighboring peoples to seize victims for grisly human sacrifices. And Mexico was highly organized. The three hundred thousand inhabitants of the capital, Tenochtitlán, enjoyed fresh water supplied by means of elaborate engineering works; their urban society was highly stratified; and artisans produced a profusion of finely crafted pottery as well as stone, copper, silver, and gold implements. "We were amazed and said that it was like the enchantments they tell of [in stories], and some of our soldiers even asked whether the things that we saw were not a dream?" recalled one of Cortés's soldiers of his first glimpse of Tenochtitlán's pyramids, lakes, and causeways. Certainly the golden gifts that the Aztecs offered in the vain hope of buying off the invaders were no dream. "They picked up the gold and fingered it like monkeys," recalled an Indian. "Their bodies swelled with greed, and their hunger was ravenous. They hungered like pigs for that gold."

Cortés attacked and swiftly prevailed. He owed his astonishing victories partly to firearms and horses, which terrified the Aztecs, and partly to initial Aztec

Cortés's Entrance into Veracruz, *c. 1550*
The ancient Mexicans called Veracruz the "Place of Precious Stones." Mexican Lienzo de Tlaxcala's pictorial description shows Cortés transporting cannons on his march through Mexico.

suppositions that the Spanish were the white, bearded gods whose return ancient legends had foretold. His success also resulted from his boldness and cunning, the Aztec emperor Moctezuma's fears, epidemics among the Indians, and the revolt of the Aztecs' subject peoples. By 1521 Cortés had overthrown the Aztecs and begun to build Mexico City on the ruins of Tenochtitlán. Soon the last Aztec emperor suffered defeat and execution, and within twenty years Central America lay at the Spaniards' feet. New Spain was born.

During the rest of the sixteenth century, other *conquistadores* and officials consolidated a great Hispanic empire stretching from New Spain (Mexico) to Chile. Subduing Native Americans and enriching themselves never troubled the *conquistadores'* consciences. Before a battle a herald would read the *requerimiento,* a proclamation in Spanish demanding the Indians' conversion to Christianity and blaming them for bloodshed if they resisted. From the beginning, however, the Spanish church and government worried that the *conquistadores* were becoming too powerful and abusive. The monarchs sent over hundreds of bureaucrats to govern in the hierarchical European manner and to defend Indian rights. Armies of Spanish friars established missions among the Indians, sometimes lessening the native people's suffering, other times increasing it, and often clashing with civilian authorities. The whole system was too cumbersome. "I obey, but I do not fulfill" became a standard bureaucratic dodge.

The human cost of the conquest was enormous. Mourned a vanquished Aztec:

> *Broken spears lie in the roads;*
> *We have torn our hair in our grief.*
> *The houses are roofless now . . .*
> *And the walls are splattered with gore . . .*
> *We have pounded our hands in despair*
> *Against the adobe walls.*

When Cortés landed in 1519, central Mexico's population had been about 25 million. By 1600 it had shrunk to between 1 million and 2 million. Peru and other regions experienced similar devastation. America had witnessed the greatest demographic disaster in world history.

Warfare, forced labor, starvation, and mass slaughter accounted for some of the catastrophe, but the greatest killers were microbes. Native Americans lacked antibodies to European and African infections—above all, the deadly, highly communicable smallpox. From the first years of contact, frightful epidemics decimated Indian communities. In the West Indian islands, the entire native population perished within fifty years, and devastation from disease facilitated the colonization of mainland North America. "The people began to die very fast, and many in a short space," an Englishman later remarked, adding that the deaths invariably occurred after Europeans had visited an Indian village. From early in the sixteenth century, raging epidemics of smallpox and other alien maladies scourged the defenseless Indians. Whole villages perished at once, with no one left to bury the dead. Up to 90 percent of the native population in some areas was lost.

Yet the "Columbian exchange"—the biological encounter of the Old and New Worlds—was not limited to deadly germs. In addition to diseases, sixteenth-century Europeans brought horses, cattle, sheep, swine, chickens, wheat and other grains, coffee, sugar cane, numerous fruits and garden vegetables, and an astonishing variety of weeds to America. In the next century, African slaves carried rice and yams with them across the Atlantic. The list of American gifts to the Eastern Hemisphere was equally impressive: corn, many varieties of beans, white and sweet potatoes, the tropical root crop manioc, tomatoes, squash, pumpkins, peanuts, vanilla, cacao, avocados, pineapples, chilis, tobacco, and turkeys. Often several centuries passed before new plants became widely accepted across the ocean; for example, many Europeans suspected that potatoes and tomatoes were either poisons or aphrodisiacs until the nineteenth century, and Indians at first had to be forced to grow wheat. European weeds and domestic animals drastically altered many environments in the Western Hemisphere, especially in North America, overwhelming indigenous plantlife and thereby driving away wild animals who fed on those plants. In this way, colonists' ways of life impinged directly on the lives of native peoples. Settlers' crops, intensively cultivated on lands never replenished by lying fallow, often exhausted American soil. But the worldwide exchange of food products also enriched human diets and later made possible enormous population growth.

Another dimension of the transatlantic encounters was the mixing of peoples. Throughout the sixteenth century, between one hundred thousand and three hundred thousand Spaniards immigrated, 90 percent of them male. Particularly in towns, a racially blended people emerged as these men married Indian women, giving rise to the large *mestizo* (mixed Spanish-Indian) population of Mexico and other Latin American countries. *Métis*, as the French termed people of both Indian and European descent, would appear in lesser proportions in the French and English colonies of North America. Throughout the Americas, particularly in plantation colonies, European men fathered *mulatto* children with African women, most of them slaves, and African-Indian unions occurred in nearly all regions. But the context for these population transfers and mixtures was the massive migrations of Europeans and enslaved Africans and the wholesale extermination of Native Americans through disease and violence.

The Americas supplied seemingly limitless wealth for Spain. Not only did some Spaniards grow rich from West Indian sugar plantations and Mexican sheep and cattle ranches, but immense quantities of silver crossed the Atlantic after rich mines in Mexico and Peru began producing in the 1540s. A robust trade between America and Spain grew up, which Castilian officials tried to regulate. Spain took in far more American silver than its economy could absorb, setting off inflation that eventually engulfed all Europe. Bent on dominating Europe, the Spanish kings needed ever more American silver to pay their armies. Several times they went bankrupt, and their efforts to squeeze more taxes from their subjects provoked in the 1560s the revolt of Spain's rich Netherlands provinces—modern Belgium, Holland, and Luxembourg. In the end, gaining access to American wealth cost Spain dearly.

The bloody history of Spain's American conquests and efforts to dominate Europe helped spin the "Black Legend"—Protestant Europeans' vision of a tyrannical, fanatically Catholic Spain intent on conquering everything in sight. Ironically, much of the Black Legend's lurid picture of American horrors derived from the writings of a devout Spanish friar, Bartolomé de Las Casas (1474–1566), who had repented his own participation (as a layman) in the subjugation of Hispaniola. By the end of the sixteenth century, Las Casas's noble hopes of justice for the Indians lay in ruins. The Spanish church became increasingly bureaucratic, intolerant, and restrictive. All this fueled the Black Legend. As Spain's struggle to reconquer the Netherlands and to dominate France spilled ominously near their homeland, Protestant Britons shuddered. But they also looked for opportunities across the Atlantic with which to strike back at Spain—and to enrich themselves.

FOOTHOLDS IN NORTH AMERICA

As early as 1510, the flow of wealth from the New World to Spain attracted swarms of Europeans. For the rest of the century, Europeans grew familiar with the North American coast through exploratory voyages, fishing expeditions, a small-scale fur trade, and piracy and smuggling. But except for a Spanish base at St.

Augustine, Florida, their attempts to plant colonies failed. These failures did not stem from lack of effort. Would-be conquerors and colonizers tried many times to establish the presence of Spain, France, or England on North American soil. But they predicated their efforts on unrealistic expectations of fabulous wealth and pliant natives.

As the seventeenth century dawned, the ravaging of Indian populations owing to disease, and the rise of English, French, and Dutch power finally made colonization possible. By 1614 Spain, England, France, and the Netherlands had established secure North American bases. Within another decade, each colony developed a distinct economic orientation, and patterns of Indian relations and geographic expansion. The first quarter of the seventeenth century marked the formative period of North America's modern history.

New Spain's Northern Frontier

The Spanish had built their American empire by subduing the Aztec and other Indian states, whose riches had attracted the invaders like a magnet. The dream of more such finds drew would-be *conquistadores* to the borderlands north of Mexico. "As it was his object to find another treasure like that . . . of Peru," a witness wrote of one such man, Hernando de Soto, he "would not be content with good lands nor pearls."

The earliest of these invaders was Juan Ponce de León, the conqueror of Puerto Rico, who in 1512–1513 and again in 1521 trudged through Florida in search of gold and slaves. His quest ended in death in an Indian skirmish. The most astonishing early expedition began in Florida in 1527. After provoking several attacks by Apalachee Indians, the three hundred explorers were separated into several parties. All were thought to have perished until eight years later, when four survivors, led by Alvar Nuñez Cabeza de Vaca and including the African slave Estevanico, arrived in northern Mexico. They had sailed to the Texas coast, where they were shipwrecked. They then walked west to New Mexico and turned south, living among many different Indian groups. They arrived in Mexico in 1536. Cabeza de Vaca's account of their journey is the most compelling European literary work on North America before permanent colonization.

Cabeza de Vaca provided direct inspiration for the two most formidable attempts at Spanish conquest. De Soto and his party in 1539–1543 blundered

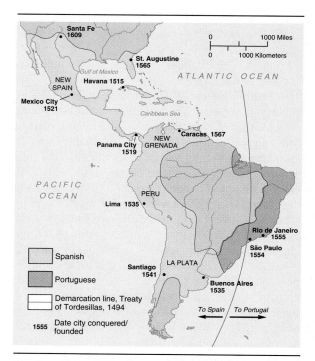

The Spanish and Portuguese Empires, 1610
By 1610 Spain dominated Latin America, including Portugal's possessions. Having devoted its energies to exploiting Mexico and the Caribbean, Spain had not yet expanded into what is now the United States, aside from establishing outposts in Florida and New Mexico.

from Tampa Bay to the Appalachians to southern Texas. Scouring the land for gold, de Soto harried the Indians mercilessly. "Think, then," an Indian chief appealed to him vainly,

> what must be the effect on me and mine, of the sight of you and your people, whom we have at no time seen, astride the fierce brutes, your horses, entering with such speed and fury into my country, that we had no tidings of your coming—things so absolutely new, as to strike awe and terror into our hearts.

Although de Soto died without finding gold or conquering any Indians, his and other expeditions caused epidemics that destroyed most of the remaining Mississippian societies. By the time Europeans returned to the southeastern interior late in the seventeenth century, only the Natchez on the lower Mississippi River still inhabited their sumptuous temple-mound center and remained under the rule of a Great Sun. Depopulated groups like the Cherokees and Creeks had adopted the less centralized village life of other eastern Indians.

As de Soto roamed the Southeast, some Spanish officials in Mexico were drawn by rumors that the fabled Seven Golden Cities of Cíbola lay to the north. In 1538 they launched an expedition, guided by Estevanico, to find them. Estevanico was killed by Zuni Indians, but the Spanish were certain that the Zunis' pueblo was one of the golden cities. In 1540–1542, Francisco Vásquez de Coronado led a massive expedition bent on conquest. Coronado plundered several pueblos and roamed from the Grand Canyon to Kansas before returning to Mexico, finding no gold but embittering many Native Americans. Other expeditions, along the California coast and up the Colorado River, likewise proved fruitless.

For several decades after these failed ventures, Spain's principal interest north of Mexico and the Caribbean lay in establishing strategic bases to keep out French and English intruders. In 1565 Spain established the first successful European settlement in North America, a powerful fortress at St. Augustine, Florida. Despite efforts to strengthen Florida and to build forts linking it to Mexico, St. Augustine remained only a military stronghold and a base for a chain of re-

ligious missions extending north to Chesapeake Bay. Rejecting missionary efforts to reorder their lives, the Indians rebelled and forced the closing of all the missions before 1600.

Franciscan missionaries renewed their efforts in Florida in the early seventeenth century and secured the nominal allegiance of about 16,000 Guale and Timucuan Indians. But epidemics in the 1610s killed about half the converts.

Meanwhile, in the 1580s, Spanish friars had returned to the southwestern pueblo country, preaching Christianity and scouting the area's potential wealth. Encouraged by their reports, in 1598 Juan de Oñate led five hundred Spaniards, mestizos, Mexican Indians, and African slaves into the upper Rio Grande Valley, where he proclaimed the royal colony of New Mexico, distributed *encomiendas,* and demanded tribute from the pueblo-dwelling Indians.

The new colony barely survived. The Spanish government replaced Oñate in 1606 because of mismanagement and excessive brutality toward the Indians. His successor founded Santa Fe in 1610, but many colonists established ranches nearer the pueblos in order to exploit Indian labor. New Mexico survived primarily through the efforts of Franciscan missionaries. By 1630 they had converted about 20,000 Indians (contrary to their claim of 500,000) and established more than 50 missions in the Rio Grande Valley and westward 250 miles to the Hopi villages in Arizona.

Indian View of Spanish Colonizers
This pictograph—a painting or drawing on rock—was sketched in the early colonial period in Cañon del Muerto, Arizona.

France: Initial Failures and Canadian Success

In 1534 Jacques Cartier of France, searching for the northwest passage, identified the St. Lawrence River as one of North America's two primary avenues of entry. After 1600 this river would become the center of French colonization. (The other such avenue, used by the French in later years, was the Mississippi River.) Before finally planting permanent American colonies, however, France experienced more than a half-century of failure.

France made the first attempt at European colonization in North America in 1541, when Cartier led ten ships carrying four hundred soldiers, three hundred sailors, and a few women to the St. Lawrence Valley. Cartier had already alienated many Indians along the St. Lawrence during two previous expeditions, and his construction of a fortified settlement on Indian land cut off all possibility of native support. Over the next two years, the French suffered heavy casualties from Indian attacks and from scurvy (for which the Indians could have shown them a cure) before abandoning the colony.

The failed French expedition seemed to verify the Spanish opinion, voiced by the cardinal of Seville, that "this whole coast as far [south] as Florida is utterly unproductive." The next French effort at colonization came in 1562, when French Huguenots (Calvinists) briefly established a base in what is now South Carolina. In 1564 the Huguenots founded a settlement near modern-day Jacksonville, Florida, which the Spanish destroyed a year later, massacring all 132 male defenders. These failures, along with a civil war between French Catholics and Huguenots, temporarily discouraged the French from further attempts at colonization.

Meanwhile, French and other European fishers were working the plenteous Grand Banks fisheries of the North Atlantic. Going ashore to dry their fish, some

European Settlements in Eastern North America, 1565–1625

Except for St. Augustine, Florida, and Santa Fe, New Mexico, all European settlements founded before 1607 were abandoned by 1625. Despite the migration of ten thousand Europeans to North America's Atlantic coast by 1625, the total number of Spanish, English, French, and Dutch on the continent was then about eighteen hundred, of whom two-thirds lived in Virginia. For French and Spanish settlement in the late colonial period, see the map on p. 118.

Battle of Lake Champlain, 1609

French soldiers and their Indian allies attack a band of Mohawk Iroquois. In this decisive battle, the French escalated the intensity of warfare in the Northeast with their introduction of firearms.

French sailors bartered with coastal Indians for skins of the beaver, a species almost extinct in Europe. By the late sixteenth century, as European demand for beaver hats skyrocketed, a French-dominated fur trade blossomed. Before the end of the century, French traders were returning annually to sites from Newfoundland to Maine and along the lower St. Lawrence.

Unlike explorers such as de Soto and colonizers such as those at Roanoke, the traders recognized the importance of reciprocity in dealing with the Indians. Consequently, they were generally more successful. In exchange for pelts, they traded metal tools such as axes and knives, cloth, and glass beads. Seen by the Europeans as "trinkets," glass beads to the Indians had the same supernatural power as quartz, mica, and other sacred substances obtained via trade networks for thousands of years. By the next century specialized factories in Europe would be producing both cloth and glass for the "Indian trade."

Between 1598 and 1604, a series of government-sponsored French fur-trading outposts appeared in Acadia (modern-day Nova Scotia). But only in 1608 did the first enduring French settlement on Canadian soil begin, founded by Samuel de Champlain at Quebec, far up the St. Lawrence River. Champlain wintered there with twenty-eight men, of whom twenty died.

Shrewdly understanding how to keep his settlement going, Champlain the next year joined nearby Indians in a battle with some Mohawk Iroquois at Lake Champlain. Using guns to defeat the dreaded Mohawks, the French secured the allegiance of several Indian nations, including the powerful Hurons. Through the latter, the French gained access to the thick beaver pelts of the Canadian interior and pledged to protect their Indian allies from the Iroquois. These economic and diplomatic arrangements defined the course of New France's history for the rest of the seventeenth century.

The Enterprising Dutch

By 1588 the independence of the northern, Dutch-speaking part of Spain's rebellious Netherlands provinces was secure, although the southern Netherlands—modern Belgium and Luxembourg—would remain under Spanish rule until 1713. The Dutch Republic was one of the seventeenth century's great powers. Mighty at sea, the Hollanders built an empire stretching from Brazil to West Africa to what is now Indonesia. North America was for them a relatively minor sphere of activity. Even so, the Dutch played a key role in colonizing the continent.

As early as 1609, the Dutch East India Company had become interested in North America when Henry Hudson sailed up the broad, deep river that today bears his name. The next year Dutch ships were sailing up the Hudson to trade with Indians. Among the most eager customers of the Dutch were Mohawk Iroquois,

New Amsterdam
After the Dutch "purchase" of Manhattan Island, the fortified settlement of New Amsterdam grew only slowly, as this view from 1651 (the earliest known depiction) clearly shows. Except for the tip, the island remained farmland or forest. Corn brought by canoe-paddling Indians also helped feed the settlement. Note the windmill, where grain was ground.

smarting from their defeat by the French the year before. In 1614 a Dutch trading company built Fort Nassau near what would become Albany, and established the colony of New Netherland. In 1625 the Dutch erected another fort on an island at the mouth of the Hudson. The colony's director-general, Peter Minuit, bought the island from local Indians in 1626 and began a second settlement there. The Dutch named the island Manhattan and the settlement New Amsterdam.

New Netherlanders lived by the fur trade. Through the Mohawks, they relied on the Iroquois Confederacy, much as the French depended on the Hurons. To stimulate a flow of furs to New Netherland, in the 1620s Dutch traders obtained from the Indians of Long Island Sound large quantities of wampun (tiny seashells traditionally denoting spiritual power, which Native Americans had long traded throughout the continent's interior) and used it to buy beaver pelts inland. Backed respectively by the French and the Dutch, Hurons and Iroquois became embroiled in an ever-deepening contest to control the movement of goods between Europeans and Indians.

Elizabethan England and the Wider World

In 1558, when Elizabeth I became queen, England was a minor power and stood on the sidelines as Spain and France grappled for supremacy in Europe. England's initial claims to North America had by now receded, although hundreds of English fishing vessels voyaged annually to North American shores and to the Grand Banks. The English remained preoccupied with chart-

ing the direction of their religious Reformation and coping with domestic instability.

This instability, however, helped propel Elizabethan expansion. Shipping its unemployed poor overseas seemed a good solution to England's economic woes. "Surplus" English people transplanted to the colonies across the ocean might not only provide raw markets for English cloth but also produce valuable export commodities. And the gentry of England's West Country (the southwestern peninsula jutting out into the Atlantic) itched for action. They were restless men, used to the sea, linked by family ties and Puritan sympathies, and frustrated by customs that limited the amount of family property inherited by younger sons. Francis Drake, John Hawkins, Humphrey Gilbert, and Walter Raleigh all fit this description and stood ready to lead England's overseas adventure.

But Spain blocked the way. When Elizabeth came to the throne, England and Spain were enjoying friendly relations. With the queen's support, Hawkins in the early 1560s made a tidy fortune raiding the Guinea coast for slaves and selling them legally to the Spanish; and Elizabeth stood by as the Spanish wiped out France's Florida colony in 1564. But the English worried about Spain's intervention in France's civil wars and its determined effort to crush the Netherlands revolt, as well as about the pope's call for Elizabeth's overthrow. Furthermore, by now the English had no incentive to trade legally with Spanish America: in 1568 the Spanish authorities in Mexico had chased Hawkins and Drake from the Caribbean. Secretly, Elizabeth stepped up her aid to Calvinist rebels in France and the Netherlands, and to "sea dogs" like Hawkins and Drake—from whose voyages she took a share of the plunder. In the 1570s she encouraged merchants to invest in Atlantic-oriented ventures.

Meanwhile, England's position in Ireland was deteriorating. As early as 1565, English troops fought to impose Tudor rule throughout the island. The conflict intensified when the pope and the Spanish began directly aiding Irish Catholics' resistance to the English. In the ensuing war that ground on through the 1580s, the English drove the Irish clans out of their strongholds, especially in northern Ireland, or Ulster, and established their own settlements ("plantations") of English and Scottish Protestant settlers. Since Irish resistance did not depend on fortified cities or large armies, English commanders had to develop new tactics to subdue the mobile, armed Irish people, who could easily disappear into bogs and forests. The English practiced total war to break the rebellious population's spirit, inflicting starvation and mass slaughter by destroying villages in the winter.

Elizabeth's generals justified these atrocities by claiming that the Irish were "savages." Ireland thus furnished precedents for strategies that the English later employed against North American Indians, whose customs, religion, and method of fighting likewise seemed to absolve the English from guilt in waging exceptionally cruel warfare. Fighting in Ireland and settling fellow citizens there, English colonizers such as Gilbert and Raleigh gained practical experience that they later applied in America.

England had two objectives in the Western Hemisphere in the 1570s. The first was to find the northwest passage to Asia and if possible to discover gold on the way; the second, in Drake's words, was to "singe the king of Spain's beard" by raiding Spanish fleets and ports from Spain to the West Indies. The search for the northwest passage only led to such embarrassments as explorer Martin Frobisher's return from the Canadian Arctic with a shipload of "fool's gold." However, privateering raids on the Spanish were both spectacularly successful and profitable for Drake's and Hawkins's financial backers, including merchants, gentry, government leaders, and Elizabeth herself. The most breathtaking enterprise was Drake's voyage around the world (1577–1580) in quest of sites for colonies. During this voyage he sailed up the California coast and entered Drake's Bay, north of San Francisco.

Now deadly rivals, Spain and England sought to plant strategic bases against each other. In 1572 the Spanish tried to fortify a Jesuit mission on the Chesapeake Bay. They failed, largely because Powhatan Indians resisted. Securing a royal patent (charter) to start an English colony in Newfoundland, Gilbert took five ships there in 1583 but drowned on his return voyage. In 1584 Gilbert's half-brother Raleigh acquired the patent. Raleigh dispatched Arthur Barlowe to explore the coast farther south, closer to the Spanish—the region that the English had already named Virginia in honor of their virgin queen. Barlowe returned singing the praises of Roanoke Island, but the colony Raleigh established there proved to be the costliest failure yet in England's brief imperial history (see "A Place in Time").

In 1588 England won a spectacular naval victory over the Armada, a huge invasion fleet sent into the English Channel by Spain's Philip II. This famous victory preserved England's independence and demonstrated that the kingdom could repel attacks although it had little offensive military might. The war churned on as before. In 1595 Drake and Hawkins died fighting in the Caribbean. Raleigh wasted his political influence and physical health in fruitless quests for the legendary gilded king ("El Dorado") in South America. England, France, and the Netherlands formed an alliance to dismember the Spanish Empire, but the French backed out. Only the Netherlanders' naval assaults on Spanish and Portuguese* outposts around the world had devastating effects. England made no further moves to carve out American colonies until after 1600.

Yet overseas expansion still lured individual Englishmen. To sustain public interest in the New World, in 1589 and again in 1601 Richard Hakluyt published monumental collections of explorers' accounts, *The Principal Navigations, Voyages, and Discoveries of the English Nation.* But neither the English crown nor Parliament would agree to spend money on colonies, and Roanoke's failure had proved that private fortunes were inadequate to finance successful settlements. Only joint-stock companies—business corporations that would amass capital through sales of stock to the public—could raise funds for American settlement. Such stock offerings produced large sums, but with limited risk for each investor. England's government henceforth would leave colonization to the private initiative of individuals or business groups and would

---

*Between 1580 and 1640, Portugal and its colonies were united with Spain.

spend no substantial sums on any colonies until the eighteenth century.

The Beginnings of English Colonization: Virginia

The hopes of would-be colonial investors rose after 1600 as Anglo-Spanish relations took a new turn. Elizabeth died in 1603, and her cousin, the king of Scotland, ascended the English throne as James I. The cautious and peace-loving king signed a truce with Spain in 1604. Seriously alarmed by Dutch naval victories, the Spanish considered England the lesser danger. The new Spanish king, Philip III, therefore conceded what his predecessors had always refused: a free hand to another power in part of the Americas. Spain renounced its claims to Virginia; England could now colonize unmolested.

On April 10, 1606, James I granted a charter authorizing overlapping grants of land in Virginia to two separate joint-stock companies, one based in London and the other in Plymouth. The Virginia Company of Plymouth received a grant extending south from modern Maine to the Potomac River, and the Virginia Company of London's lands ran north from Cape Fear to the Hudson River. The colonists would be business employees, not citizens of a separate political jurisdiction, and the stockholders of each company would regulate

their behavior. Both companies dispatched colonists in 1607.

The Virginia Company of Plymouth sent 120 men to Sagadahoc, at the mouth of the Kennebec River. Half left in 1608 after alienating the Abenaki Indians and enduring a hard Maine winter, and the rest went back to England a year later with Raleigh Gilbert (Humphrey's son) when he returned home to collect an inheritance. Soon thereafter the company disbanded.

The Virginia Company of London barely avoided a similar failure. Its first expedition included many members of the gentry, most of whom expected riches to fall into their laps. They chose a site on the James River in May 1607 and named it Jamestown. Discipline quickly fell apart after the discovery of iron pyrite sparked a fool's gold rush, and, as at Roanoke, the colonists neglected to plant crops. When relief ships arrived in January 1608 with reinforcements, only 38 survivors remained out of 105 immigrants.

Short of workers who could farm, fish, hunt, and do carpentry, Virginia also needed effective leadership on the council directing its affairs. The council's first president hoarded supplies, and its second was lazy and indecisive. In September 1608 the councilors turned to a brash soldier of fortune whose eagerness to settle arguments with his fists had landed him in irons for most of the 1607 voyage: the magnificent braggart Captain John Smith.

Artifacts from Early Virginia

This double-edged sword (shown with fragments of its guard and pommel) and elaborate pipe tamper (featuring a man wearing armor and smoking a pipe) were unearthed at Flowerdew Hundred, an early English settlement near present-day Hopewell, Virginia, and date from the first half of the seventeenth century.

Only twenty-eight years old and of yeoman origin, Smith had experience fighting Spaniards and Turks that prepared him well to assume control in Virginia. Organizing all but the sick in work gangs, he ensured sufficient food and housing for winter. Applying lessons learned in his soldiering days, he laid down rules for maintaining sanitation and hygiene to limit disease. Above all, he brought order through military discipline. During the winter of 1608–1609, Virginia lost just a dozen men out of two hundred.

Smith also became the colony's best diplomat. After local Native Americans captured him in late 1607, Smith displayed such courage that Powhatan, the leader of the nearby Powhatan Confederacy, arranged an elaborate reconciliation ceremony in which his daughter, Pocahontas, "saved" Smith's life during a mock execution. Smith maintained satisfactory relations with the Powhatan Confederacy in part through his personality, but he also employed calculated demonstrations of English military strength to mask the settlers' actual weakness.

John Smith prevented Virginia from disintegrating as Sagadahoc had. But when he returned to England in 1609 after being wounded in a gunpowder explosion, discipline again crumbled. Expecting the Indians to provide them with corn, the colonists had not laid away sufficient food for the winter. Consequently, relations with the Powhatans deteriorated. A survivor of the winter wrote:

> So lamentable was our scarcity, that we were constrained to eat dogs, cats, rats, snakes, toadstools, horsehides, and what not; one man out of the misery endured, killing his wife powdered her up [with flour] to eat her, for which he was burned. Many besides fed on the corpses of dead men, . . . and indeed so miserable was our estate that the happiest day that some of them hoped to see was when the Indians had killed a mare, they wishing whilst she was boiling that Sir Thomas Smythe [Treasurer of the Virginia Company] was upon her back in the kettle.

Of the five hundred residents at Jamestown in September 1609, about four hundred died by May 1610. But an influx of new recruits, coupled with the imposition of military rule, enabled Virginia to win the first Anglo-Powhatan War (1610–1614). By 1611 the colony had already expanded forty miles beyond Jamestown, to modern-day Richmond. The English population remained small, however, just 380 in 1616, and it had yet to produce anything of value for the stockholders.

Tobacco emerged as Virginia's economic salvation. John Rolfe, an Englishman who married Pocahontas after the war, spent several years perfecting a salable variety of tobacco and began planting it in Virginia. By 1619 the product commanded high prices, and that year Virginia exported large amounts of the crop. Thereafter the Virginia Company poured supplies and settlers into the colony.

To attract labor and capital, the company awarded fifty-acre grants ("headrights") to anyone paying his or her own passage or the transit of a laborer. By paying the passage of their indentured servants, some enterprising planters accumulated sizable tracts of land. Despite the uncertainty of life in Virginia, thousands of single young men and a few hundred women calculated that uncertainty was preferable to continued unemployment and poverty in England. In return for their passage, the servants worked for a fixed term, usually four to seven years. The Virginia Company also abandoned military rule and provided for an assembly to be elected by the "inhabitants" (apparently meaning only the planters). Although the assembly's actions were subject to the company's veto, its establishment in 1619 did mark the beginnings of representative government in North America.

By 1622 Virginia still faced three serious problems. First, local officials systematically defrauded the shareholders by embezzling treasury funds, overcharging for supplies, and using company laborers to work their own tobacco fields. They profited, but the company sank deep into debt. Second, the colony's population suffered from an exceptionally high death rate. The majority of fatalities stemmed from malnutrition owing to the poor diets of the servants, or from salt poisoning, typhus, or dysentery, contracted when the settlers drank the salty, polluted water from the lower James River. Most of the 3,500 immigrants entering Virginia from 1618 to 1622 died within three years. Finally, relations with the Powhatans steadily worsened after Pocahontas died in England in 1617, and Powhatan a year later. Leadership passed to Opechancanough, who at first sought to accommodate the English. But relentless expansion led to Indian discontent and to the rise of a powerful shaman, Nemattenew, who urged the Powhatans to resist the English to the death. After some settlers killed Nemattenew, the Indians launched a surprise attack in 1622 that killed 347 of the 1,240 colonists. With much of their livestock destroyed, spring planting prevented, and disease spreading through cramped fortresses, hundreds more colonists died in the ensuing months.

Roanoke, 1584–1590

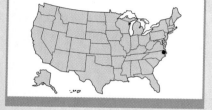

"We found the people most gentle, loving, and faithful, void of all guile and treason, and such as live after the manner of the golden age. . . . The earth bringeth forth all things in abundance, as at the first creation, without toil or labor." Arthur Barlowe, who wrote these glowing words in 1584 after returning to England from Roanoke Island, on the coast of North Carolina, thought that he had found a paradise. To be sure, the Algonquian-speaking Roanoke Indians seemed (to Barlowe) to fight cruel and bloody wars that had left them "marvelously wasted" and the country "desolate." (He was unaware of the prior impact of Spanish-induced epidemics and wars.) But this was all the more reason that they should welcome English protection. To establish friendly reciprocity, the Roanokes' chief, Winginia, immediately offered to trade.

He beckoned us to come and sit by him, and being set he made all signs of joy and welcome, striking on his head and breast and afterwards on ours to show that we were all one, smiling and making show the best he could of all love and familiarity. After he had made a long speech unto us, we presented him with divers [various] things, which he received very joyfully and thankfully.

Sir Walter Raleigh (1552?–1618),
by an unknown artist
Raleigh was the foremost advocate of colonization at the English court.

Shortly thereafter Barlowe returned home, taking two kidnapped Roanokes to impress them with the wealth and size of England, teach them the English language, and publicize their venture.

The voyagers had been sent by Sir Walter Raleigh, who dreamed of founding an American colony where English, Indians, and even Africans liberated from Spanish slavery could live together productively. Barlowe reported just what Raleigh wanted to hear. Raleigh persuaded Queen Elizabeth to dispatch ships and a company of soldiers to launch a colony at Roanoke, accompanied by painter John White and scientist Thomas Harriot.

At first all went well. Harriot carefully studied native culture, and White captured the Indians' life in paintings of extraordinary delicacy. Native Americans eagerly traded and shared their corn—which they grew with amazing ease: "Their country corn," Barlowe had already reported, "groweth three times in five months. . . . They cast the corn into the ground, breaking a little of the soft turf with a wooden matlock, or pickax. . . . They have also beans very fair of divers colors and wonderful plenty. Some growing naturally and some in their gardens. . . . " Given such abundance and native hospitality, the English wondered why they should work at all.

So the English refused to try growing their own food, expecting the Indians to feed them. By the first winter, they had outlived their welcome. Fearing that the Roanokes were about to attack them, the English killed Winginia in June 1586. When Raleigh's friend Drake arrived soon after with a shipload of Africans whom he had rescued from the Spanish and planned to settle at Roanoke, most of the English were ready to quit. Casually abandoning the blacks, the English sailed back across the Atlantic.

Raleigh did not give up yet. He sent another expedition in the summer of 1586 commanded by Richard Grenville, who left 15 men at Roanoke before hurrying off to fight the Spanish. In 1587 Raleigh dispatched White back to Roanoke with 110 settlers and their last Indian friend, Manteo, whom the English baptized and proclaimed "lord" of the local Indians. White found no trace of the little English garrison. Leaving the settlers (including his newborn granddaughter), he went home to bring more supplies.

But Spain's attack in the English Channel intervened. Drake and every other English seaman were needed to help repel the Armada of 1588. Not until 1590 could White return to Roanoke—and found only rusty armor, moldy books, and the word *CROATOAN* cut into a post. What had happened to the "lost colony"? Were the settlers killed by Indians? Did they starve or die in a hurricane or drown attempting to join the friendly Indians at Cape Hatteras? One theory is that they were absorbed into the Lumbee Indians of North Carolina; another, that they moved closer to Chesapeake Bay, only to be wiped out by the Powhatan Confederacy when the next English settlement was planted at Jamestown, in 1607. Historians will probably never know with certainty.

Roanoke's brief history illustrated several stubborn realities about early European experiences in North America. First, even a large-scale, well-financed colonizing effort could fail, given the settlers' unpreparedness for the American environment. Second, colonists did not bring enough provisions for the first winter and consistently disdained growing their own food. Although some early English settlers were curious and open-minded about the Indians' way of life, all assumed that the natives would submit to their authority and feed them while they looked for gold—a sure recipe for trouble. Third, colonizing attempts would have to be self-financing: financially strapped monarchs like Elizabeth I would not throw good money after bad into America. Fourth, conflict with the Spanish hung menacingly over every European attempt to gain a foothold in North America.

(Below) **A Carolina Indian Mother and Child;** *(Bottom)* **A Carolina Indian Warrior in Body Paint**

(Below) **Carolina Indians Fishing,** *by John White, 1585*
Using canoes, weirs, nets, and spears, coastal Indians depended on fishing as an important source of their food.

After the Virginia Company sent more men, Governor Francis Wyatt reorganized the settlers and took the offensive during the second Anglo-Powhatan War (1622–1632). Using tactics developed during the Irish war, Wyatt inflicted widespread starvation by destroying food supplies, conducted winter campaigns to drive Indians from their homes when they would suffer most, and fought (according to John Smith) as if he had "just cause to destroy them by all means possible." By 1625 the English had effectively won the war, and the Indians had lost their best chance of driving out the intruders.

The clash left the Virginia Company bankrupt and James I concerned over complaints against its officers. After receiving a report critical of the company's management, James revoked its charter in 1624 and Virginia became a royal colony. Only about five hundred colonists now lived in Virginia, including a handful of Africans who had been brought in since 1619.* So the roots from which Virginia's Anglo-American and African-American peoples later grew were fragile indeed.

The Origins of New England: Plymouth Plantation

Still another colonial venture was begun in the early seventeenth century by the English who settled New England. In 1614 the ever-enterprising John Smith, exploring its coast, gave New England its name. "Who," he asked, "can but approve this most excellent place, both for health and fertility?" An admirer of Cortés, Smith planned to conquer its "goodly, strong, and well-proportioned [Indian] people" and establish an English colony there. But his hopes came to naught. As for the region's native peoples, a terrible epidemic devastated the coastal tribes by about 90 percent in 1616–1618. Later visitors found the ground littered with the "bones and skulls" of the unburied dead, and acres of overgrown cornfields.

Against this tragic backdrop, in 1620 the Virginia Company of London gave a patent to some London merchants headed by Thomas Weston for a settlement. Weston sent over 24 families (a total of 102 people) in a small, leaky ship called the *Mayflower*. The colonists promised to send lumber, furs, and fish back to Weston in England for seven years, after which they would own the tract.

The expedition's leaders—but only half its members—belonged to a small religious community from the town of Scrooby in northern England. The group was made up of Separatist Puritans who had withdrawn from the Church of England and fled to the Netherlands to practice their religion freely. But fearing that their children were assimilating into Dutch culture, they decided to immigrate to America under Weston's sponsorship.

In November 1620 the *Mayflower* landed at Plymouth Bay, outside the bounds of Virginia. Knowing that they had no legal right to be there, the expedition's leaders insisted that all the adult males in the group (including Non-Separatists) sign the Mayflower Compact before they landed. By this document they constituted themselves a "civil body politic"—that is, a civil government—under James I's sovereignty and established the colony of Plymouth Plantation.

Weakened by their journey and unprepared for winter, half the Pilgrims, as they came to be known, died within four months of landing. Those still alive in the spring of 1621 owed much to the aid of two English-speaking Indians. One was Squanto, a local Patuxet Indian who had been taken to Spain as a slave some years earlier, escaped to England, and made himself useful to potential colonizers. Returning, he learned that most of the two thousand Patuxets had perished in the recent epidemic. The other friendly Indian, an Abenaki from Maine named Samoset, had experience trading with the English. To prevent the Pilgrims from stealing their food, the Indians taught the newcomers how to grow corn. The alliance that Squanto and Samoset arranged between Plymouth and local Wampanoag Indians headed by chief Massasoit united two weak parties. But with their firearms the colonists became the dominant partner, forcing the Indians to acknowledge English sovereignty. The Pilgrims' first harvest of 1621 was marked by a ceremony cementing the relationship, "at which time . . . we exercised our arms, many of the Indians coming amongst us, . . . some 90 men, whom for three days we entertained and feasted." This ceremony was the basis for Thanksgiving, a holiday established in the nineteenth century.

Plymouth's relations with the Native Americans worsened, however. News of the Virginia massacre of 1622 hastened the colony's militarization under the leadership of a professional soldier, Miles Standish, who threatened Plymouth's Indian "allies" with its monopoly of firepower. For although Massasoit remained

---

*Whether or not these first Africans were—or remained—slaves is unknown. The emergence of Virginia's African-American population will be traced in Chapter 3.

Early Plymouth Colony
After barely surviving their first winter, the settlers ensured their future by building simple houses and using Indian techniques to grow corn.

fur and wampum trade in New England. By the time Plymouth finally freed itself of obligations, the settlement had grown to several hundred people on Cape Cod and in the southeastern corner of present-day Massachusetts.

loyal, many other Indians were offended by the colonists' conduct.

Relations with Native Americans also enabled Plymouth to become economically self-sufficient. Systematically cheated by their English sponsors, after seven years the colonists had sunk so deeply into debt that they faced fifteen years' additional labor to free themselves. Fishing failed to be profitable, but some farmers, having turned from communal farming to individually owned plots, produced corn surpluses, which they traded to Abenakis in Maine for furs. In 1627 Plymouth agreed with the Dutch to divide the

At first an almost insignificant group, the Pilgrims were only one of several small English bands that immigrated to New England in the 1620s. Their importance was twofold. First, they would help inspire the later American vision of sturdy, self-reliant, God-fearing folk crossing the Atlantic to govern themselves freely. Second, they foreshadowed the methods that later generations of European-Americans would use to gain mastery over Indians. In both respects, the Pilgrims were the vanguard of a massive, voluntary migration of Puritans to New England in the 1630s.

CONCLUSION

The founding of colonies in North America occurred as part of the process by which Europe haltingly entered a new, "modern" era. Commercial capitalism, nation-states, and post-medieval Christianity all emerged during the sixteenth century. But they did not entirely displace economies based on subsistence and reciprocity, local communities rooted in centuries-old customs, and widespread beliefs in supernatural forces independent of the Christian God. Expansion and colonization strengthened the "modern" forces by providing new fields for investment and profit, and new foundations for national power. The overseas ventures also enabled European leaders and ideologues to portray Native

Americans and Africans as "savages" whose cultures and customs "civilized" Europeans should avoid at all cost.

The displacement of Indians and the enslavement of Africans underlined the early history of European settlement in America. Despite devastation by disease, however, Native Americans yielded only slowly to foreign incursions. As for Africans, even the horrors of the Atlantic slave trade did not strip them entirely of their heritage, which they later nurtured into a distinctive African-American culture.

During the first third of the seventeenth century, the general outlines of European land claims in North America emerged, as did the basic elements of the various colonies' economic life. In New Mexico and Florida, Spain advanced as far north as seemed worthwhile to protect their Mexican and Caribbean conquests. Virginia's victory over the Indians there strengthened the English position in the Chesapeake, where tobacco had become the principal commercial crop. Here and in the fragile Plymouth colony, English settlers depended primarily on farming. New France and New Netherland existed mainly to trade in furs. To one degree or another, all these enterprises depended for their success or security on maintaining stable relations with at least some Native Americans.

Given the thousands of lives lost and the fortunes wasted, the first tiny European outposts in North America may seem a minor achievement. By the 1630s they were just beginning to take on an air of permanence, leading discontented Europeans to imagine that new societies could be created across the Atlantic free from Europe's inherited problems or without painful labor. These dreamers seldom dared to cross the ocean, and those who did generally lost their illusions—or their lives—when faced with the rigors of a strange environment. The transplantation of Europeans into North America was hardly a story of inevitable triumph.

CHRONOLOGY

c. 600–1600	Rise of the great West African empires.
c. 1000	Norse establish a small settlement at Vinland (Newfoundland).
1096	European Crusades begin in Middle East.
1271–1295	Marco Polo travels to East Asia.
c. 1400–1600	Renaissance era—first in Italy, then elsewhere in Europe.
1440	Portuguese slave trade in West Africa begins.
1488	Bartolomeu Días reaches the Cape of Good Hope.
1492	Christopher Columbus lands at San Salvador.
1497	John Cabot reaches Nova Scotia and Newfoundland.
1512–1521	Juan Ponce de León explores Florida.
1513	Vasco Núñez de Balboa views the Pacific Ocean.
1517	Protestant Reformation begins in Germany.
1519	Ferdinand Magellan embarks on round-the-world voyage.
	Hernán Cortés begins conquest of Aztec empire.
1524	Giovanni da Verrazano explores the Atlantic coast of North America.
1534	Church of England breaks from Roman Catholic church.
1534–1542	Jacques Cartier explores eastern Canada for France.
1539–1543	de Soto explores the southeastern United States.
1540–1542	Francisco Vásquez de Coronado explores the southwestern United States.

1558	Elizabeth I becomes queen of England.
1565	St. Augustine founded by Spanish.
1565–1580s	English attempt to subdue Ireland.
1577	Francis Drake circumnavigates the globe.
1578	Humphrey Gilbert secures a patent to establish an English colony in Newfoundland.
1584–1587	Roanoke colony explored and founded.
1588	English defeat the Spanish Armada.
1598	New Mexico colony founded.
1603	James I becomes king of England.
1607	English found colonies at Jamestown and Sagadahoc.
1608	Samuel de Champlain founds Quebec.
1609	Henry Hudson explores the Hudson River for the Dutch Republic.
1610–1614	First Anglo-Powhatan War.
1614	New Netherland colony founded.
1619	Large exports of tobacco from Virginia begin.
	First Africans arrive in Virginia.
1620	Mayflower Compact signed; Plymouth Plantation founded.
1622–1632	Second Anglo-Powhatan War.
1624	James I revokes Virginia Company's charter.

Elizabeth I

FOR FURTHER READING

J. F. A. Ajayi and Michael Crowder, eds., *History of West Africa*, vol. I (1972). A comprehensive collection of essays covering the period prior to 1800.

Robert J. Berkhofer, Jr., *The White Man's Indian: Images of the American Indian from Columbus to the Present* (1978). A penetrating analysis of the shaping of European and American attitudes, ideologies, and policies toward Native Americans.

Carl Bridenbaugh, *Vexed and Troubled Englishmen, 1590–1642* (1968). A highly readable account of England at the outset of the colonial era.

Alfred W. Crosby, Jr., *Ecological Imperialism: The Biological Expansion of Europe, 900–1900* (1986). An outstanding discussion of the environmental and medical history of European overseas colonization.

D. W. Meinig, *The Shaping of America, vol. I: Atlantic America, 1492–1800* (1986). A geographer's engrossing study of Euro-

peans' encounter with North America and the rise of colonial society.

J. H. Parry, *The Age of Reconnaissance* (1963). A comprehensive analysis of European exploration and the rise of European overseas empires from the fifteenth to the seventeenth century.

David B. Quinn, *North America from Earliest Discoveries to First Settlements: The Norse Voyages to 1612* (1977). A thorough, learned account of European exploration, based on a wide range of scholarship.

Kirkpatrick Sale, *The Conquest of Paradise: Christopher Columbus and the Columbian Legacy* (1990). A polemical but informed critique of Columbus and his role in opening the Americas to European exploitation.

Eric Wolf, *Europe and the People Without History* (1982). An anthropologist's sweeping view of the causes and consequences of Europe's worldwide expansion.

ADDITIONAL BIBLIOGRAPHY

Africa and Slavery

Philip Curtin, *The Atlantic Slave Trade: A Census* (1969) and *Economic Change in Precolonial Africa: Senegambia in the Era of the Slave Trade* (1975); David Brion Davis, *The Problem of Slavery in Western Culture* (1966); Winthrop D. Jordan, *White over Black: American Attitudes Toward the Negro, 1550–1812* (1968); Paul E. Lovejoy, *Transformations in Slavery: A History of Slavery in Africa* (1983); Patrick Manning, *Slavery and African Life: Occidental, Oriental, and African Slave Trades* (1990); Roland Oliver and Anthony Atmore, *The African Middle Ages, 1400–1800* (1981); Walter Rodney, *A History of the Upper Guinea Coast, 1545–1800* (1970); John Thornton, *Africa and Africans in the Making of the Atlantic World, 1400–1680* (1992); Jon Vogt, *Portuguese Rule on the Gold Coast, 1469–1682* (1979).

Europe

Fernand Braudel, *The Mediterranean and the Mediterranean World in the Age of Philip II*, 2d ed. (1966; English trans., 1972) and *Civilization and Capitalism, 15th–18th Centuries* (3 vols., 1979; English trans., 1981); Peter Burke, *Popular Culture in Early Modern Europe* (1978); Patrick Collinson, *The Elizabethan Puritan Movement* (1967); Natalie Z. Davis, *Society and Culture in Early Modern France* (1975); Ralph Davis, *Rise of the Atlantic Economies* (1973); J. H. Elliott, *Imperial Spain, 1479–1716* (1963); Christopher Hill, *Society and Puritanism in Pre-Revolutionary England*, 2d ed. (1967); Peter Laslett, *The World We Have Lost: England Before the Industrial Age*, 3d ed. (1984); Stephen Ozment, *The Age of Reform, 1250–1550* (1980); Simon Schama, *An Embarrassment of Riches: Dutch Culture in the Golden Age* (1987); Lawrence Stone, *The Crisis of the English Aristocracy, 1558–1641*, abridged ed. (1965); Penry Williams, *The Tudor Regime* (1979); Keith Wrightson, *English Society, 1580–1680* (1982).

European Expansion and Colonization

Kenneth R. Andrews, *Trade, Plunder, and Settlement: Maritime Enterprise and the Genesis of the British Empire, 1480–1630* (1984); Nicholas P. Canny, *The Elizabethan Conquest of Ireland: A Pattern Established, 1565–1576* (1976); Alfred W. Crosby, Jr., *The Columbian Exchange: Biological and Cultural Consequences of 1492* (1972); W. J. Eccles, *France in America*, rev. ed. (1990); J. H. Elliott, *The Old World and the New, 1492–1650* (1970); Lewis Hanke, *The Spanish Struggle for Justice in the Conquest of America* (1965); Karen Ordahl Kupperman, *Roanoke: The Abandoned Colony* (1984); James Lockhart and Stuart B. Schwartz, *Early Latin America: A History of Colonial Spanish America and Brazil* (1983); William H. McNeill, *Plagues and Peoples* (1976); J. H. Parry, *The Establishment of the European Hegemony: Trade and Expansion in the Age of Renaissance* (1966); William D. Phillips, Jr., and Carla Rahn Phillips, *The Worlds of Christopher Columbus* (1992); Oliver Rink, *Holland on the Hudson: An Economic and Social History of Dutch New York* (1986); Carol O. Sauer, *Sixteenth Century North America* (1971); Marcel Trudel, *The Beginnings of New France, 1524–1663* (1973); David J. Weber, *The Spanish Frontier in North America* (1992).

Native Americans

James Axtell, *After Columbus: Essays in the Ethnohistory of Colonial North America* (1988); Charles Hudson and Carmen C. Tesser, eds., *The Forgotten Centuries: Indians and Europeans in the American South, 1521–1704* (1994); Francis Jennings, *The Invasion of America: Indians, Colonialism, and the Cant of Conquest* (1975); Calvin Martin, *Keepers of the Game: Indian-Animal Relationships and the Fur Trade* (1978); Daniel K. Richter, *The Ordeal of the Longhouse: The Peoples of the Iroquois League in the Era of European Colonization* (1992); Helen C. Rountree, *Pocahontas's People: The Powhatan Indians of Virginia Through Four Centuries* (1990); Neal Salisbury, *Manitou and Providence: Indians, Europeans, and the Making of New En-gland, 1500–1643* (1982); Russell Thornton, *American Indian Holocaust and Survival: A Population History Since 1492* (1987); Bruce G. Trigger, *Natives and Newcomers: Canada's "Heroic Age" Reconsidered* (1985); J. Leitch Wright, Jr., *The Only Land They Knew: The Tragic Story of the American Indians in the Old South* (1981).

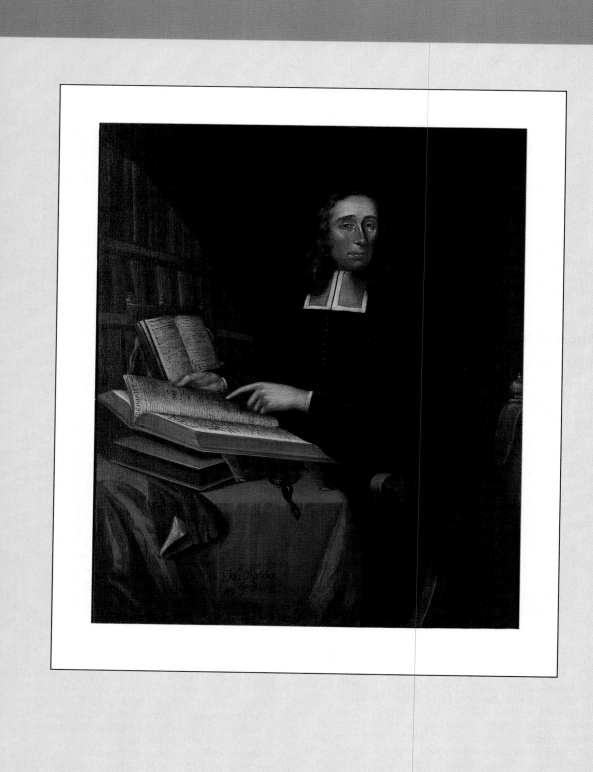

Increase Mather
by John Vander Spriett, 1688

EXPANSION AND DIVERSITY: THE RISE OF COLONIAL AMERICA

On the West Indian island of Barbados in 1692, a widowed Englishwoman named Sarah Horbin counted up her relatives to see who might deserve bequests of property in case her only son—a sailor being held for ransom in a North African prison—died. Through her kinsman John Seabury of Barbados, she had kept in contact with a dozen Seabury cousins in Massachusetts. She had also remained in touch with several Virginia relatives in the Empereur family and with a kinsman of her husband's, Andrew Rouse, who lived in the frontier zone between Virginia and Florida then simply called Carolina.

Sarah Horbin and her far-flung clan were part of a great migration of English, Dutch, French, Spanish, Irish, Scottish, and German women and men who built new communities in North America and the Caribbean during the seventeenth century. By 1700 there were more than 250,000 people of European birth or parentage, most of them English, within the modern-day United States. The vast exodus provided North America with its first large wave of immigrant settlers.

The Europeans were joined by a second movement of peoples during the seventeenth century—that of some three hundred thousand West Africans, mostly to the West Indies. But whereas Europeans might at least hope to realize economic opportunity or religious freedom, Africans and their progeny would be the property of others for as long as they lived. Although statistically improbable, it is possible to imagine that in the locales inhabited by Sarah Horbin and her kin in Massachusetts, Virginia, and Carolina was a parallel set of relatives, this one originating along the west coast of Africa between Senegambia and Angola. The vast majority of Africans taken to the Caribbean and North America during the seventeenth century went to the sugar plantations of Sarah Horbin's neighbors in Barbados and elsewhere in the West Indies; a small but distinct minority, to the mainland plantation colonies of the Southeast; and a scattered few to other regions.

These two vast migrations were possible only because of a third demographic upheaval, the depopulation and uprooting of Native Americans. Having begun in the sixteenth century, the process continued in the seventeenth, primarily as a result of epidemic diseases but also because of warfare and other factors arising from the European invasion of Indian lands. Although many native populations partly recovered, it is likely that about 1 million Indians died as a result of contact with Europeans by 1700. Sarah Horbin and her various kin settled not in wildernesses but in lands long inhabited and worked by Native Americans.

Although dominated by English immigrants, the wealth and vitality of the English colonies at the end of the seventeenth century resulted from the unequal encounter of peoples from three continents.

THE NEW ENGLAND WAY

In the late 1620s, as England's religious and political environment grew threatening and the economy worsened, many Puritans became interested in colonizing New England. Separatist Puritans (the "Pilgrims") had established Plymouth in 1620, and a few hundred others had drifted into the region over the next decade. But not until 1630 did large-scale migration begin. Building communities based on religious ideals, this larger, more formidable group of Puritans founded America's first utopian, or ideal, society.

A City upon a Hill

In 1628 several Puritan merchants obtained a charter to settle north of Plymouth colony between the Charles and Merrimack rivers. Organizing as the Massachusetts Bay Company, they took advantage of a gap in their charter and agreed in 1629 to move the seat of their colony's government to New England. Like Plymouth, Massachusetts Bay would be self-governed rather than controlled from England by stockholders, proprietors, or the crown.

After four hundred Puritans arrived at Salem, Massachusetts, in 1629, the company in 1630 sent out its "great fleet" of eleven ships and seven hundred passengers under Governor John Winthrop. In midvoyage Winthrop delivered a lay sermon titled "A Model of Christian Charity," describing the colony as a utopian alternative to old England.

John Winthrop
During the passage to America, Winthrop urged his shipmates to build a society about which "men shall say of succeeding plantations: 'The Lord make it like that of New England.'"

Winthrop boldly announced that "we shall be as a city upon a hill, the eyes of all people are upon us." The settlers would build a godly community whose compelling example would shame England into repenting. The English government would then truly reform the church, and a revival of piety would create a nation of saints.

Winthrop denounced the self-destructive economic jealousy that bred class hatred. God intended that "in all times some must be rich and some poor," the governor explained, in order that the saints could display virtue appropriate to their station in life. The rich had an obligation to show charity and mercy; those less wealthy should live out their faith in God's will by demonstrating patience and fortitude. God expected the state's rulers to keep the greedy among the rich from exploiting the needy and to prevent the lazy among the poor from burdening their fellow citizens.

In outlining a divine plan in which all people, rich and poor, depended on one another, Winthrop's sermon expressed a conservative European's understanding of social reciprocity (see Chapter 2) and voiced the Puritans' deep dismay with the economic forces battering—and changing—English society. Winthrop wanted charity to moderate the drive for profit, so that goods would be exchanged, wages set, and interest calculated in a manner that would allow a decent life for all. He expected the rich to serve God with their money, giving generously in time of need, and the less

The Great English Migration, 1630–1660
During the great transatlantic English migration, the present-day United States received just one-third of English immigrants. The West Indies attracted twice as many colonists as went to the Chesapeake, and over four times as many as settled in New England.

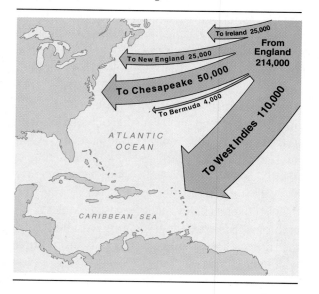

fortunate to sacrifice their time to serve in church, government, or the military.

Winthrop's shipboard sermon exemplified the main difference between New England's settlement and English colonization elsewhere. Other colonists would display the acquisitive impulses transforming England, but in New England, as one minister put it, "Religion and profit [would] jump together." While hoping for prosperity, Puritans believed there were limits to legitimate commercial behavior. They thought that moral self-restraint—or if need be, the government—should prevent merchants from taking advantage of shortages to squeeze out "excessive" profits. Above all, they hoped to turn religious idealism into a renewed sense of community. "It is a great thing," wrote an early New Englander, "to be a foundation stone in such a spiritual building." Massachusetts Bay would not be an extension of England but an alternative to it.

Winthrop and the great fleet arrived in June 1630 at Boston harbor, and by fall six towns had sprung up in the city's modern limits. During the unusually severe first winter, 30 percent of Winthrop's party died, and an additional 10 percent went home in the spring. By mid-1631, however, thirteen hundred new settlers had landed, and more were on the way. The worst was over. The colony would never suffer another starving time. In contrast to early Virginia, Massachusetts Bay attracted disciplined, motivated men and women of modest means who established the colony on a firm basis within a year.

Settlers and Natives

Also in contrast to the settlement of Virginia, the colonization of New England began with little sustained resistance from Native Americans, whose numbers were drastically reduced by the ravages of disease. After one epidemic killed about 90 percent of New England's coastal Indians between 1616 and 1618 (see Chapter 2), a second inflicted comparable casualties on Indians throughout the Northeast in 1633–1634. Having dwindled from twenty thousand in 1600 to a few dozen survivors by the mid-1630s, the Massachuset Indians sold most of their land to the English. During the 1640s Massachusetts Bay passed laws prohibiting them from practicing their own religion and encouraging missionaries to convert them to Christianity. Beginning in 1651 they surrendered much of their independence and moved into "praying towns" like Natick, a reserva-

tion established by the colony. In the praying towns Puritan missionary John Eliot hoped to teach the Native Americans Christianity and English ways.

The expansion of English settlement farther inland, however, aroused Indian resistance. As settlers moved into the Connecticut River Valley, beginning in 1633, friction developed with the Pequots, who controlled the trade in furs and wampum with New Netherland. After tensions escalated into violence, the English in 1637 took decisive action. Having gained the support of the Mohegan and Narragansett Indians, they waged a ruthless campaign, using tactics similar to those devised by the English to break Irish resistance during the 1570s (see Chapter 2). In a predawn attack English troops surrounded and set fire to a Pequot village at Mystic, Connecticut, and then cut down all who tried to escape. Several hundred Pequots, mostly women and children, were killed. Although their Narragansett allies protested that "it is too furious, and slays too many men," the Puritans found in the grisly massacre a cause for celebration. Wrote Plymouth's Governor William Bradford,

> It was a fearful sight to see them [the Pequots] thus frying in the fire and the streams of blood quenching the same, and horrible was the stink and scent thereof; but the victory seemed a sweet sacrifice, and they [the English] gave the praise to God, who had wrought so wonderfully for them, thus to enclose their enemies in their hands and give them so speedy a victory over so proud and insulting an enemy.

By late 1637 Pequot resistance was crushed, with surviving Pequots being taken by pro-English Indians as captives or by the English as slaves. English settlement of the new colonies of Connecticut and New Haven could now proceed unimpeded.

The Development of a Puritan Orthodoxy

As Non-Separatists, Massachusetts Puritans considered themselves spiritual members of the Church of England, but they created a system of self-governing congregations (congregationalism) that completely ignored the authority of Anglican bishops. (Except for the Separatists of Plymouth and Rhode Island, most New England Puritans were Non-Separatists.) More than any other person, the Reverend John Cotton shaped American congregationalism. This clergyman's prestige was so great that, according to a fellow

Two Sketches of an Early Plymouth Meetinghouse *(above);* **Interior of the "Old Ship Church," Hingham, Massachusetts** *(left)*
One early New Englander boasted that his community's meetinghouse had been erected "by our own vote, framed by our own hammers and saws, and by our own hands set in the convenientest place for us all." Hingham's First Parish Meeting House (1681, left) was built by ship carpenters. They simply constructed a ship's keel in reverse for the interior roof.

minister, Massachusetts settlers "could hardly believe that God would suffer Mr. Cotton to err."

Cotton's plan for governing the New England church placed control of each congregation squarely in the hands of the male saints (church members). By majority vote these men chose their minister, elected a board of "elders" to handle finances, decided who else deserved recognition as saints, and otherwise ran the church. In contrast, in a typical English parish, a powerful gentry family would select a new pastor (subject to a bishop's formal approval), and all other important decisions would be made by the parish council, or vestry, which was virtually always composed of wealthy landlords. New England congregationalism thus allowed for far more broad-based control of the church than did Anglicanism.

New England congregationalism fused elements of separating and nonseparating Puritanism. Congregational churches followed the Separatist tradition by allowing only saints to take communion and baptize their children, but as in Non-Separatist practice, they obliged all adults to attend services and pay set rates (or tithes) for their support. New England thus had a state-sponsored, or "established," church, whose relationship to civil government was symbolized by the fact that a single building—called a meetinghouse rather than a church—was used for both religious services and town business.

This "New England Way" also diverged from English practices by setting higher standards for identifying the elect. English Puritans usually accepted as saints those who could correctly profess the faith, had repented their sins, and lived free of scandal. Massachusetts Puritans, however, insisted that candidates for membership provide a soul-baring "relation," or account, of their conversion before the congregation.

English Puritans strongly criticized the conversion relation as an unnecessary barrier to membership that would intimidate humble saints who were hesitant to reveal their spiritual travails in public. Many early Puritans shared the reluctance of Jonathan Fairbanks, who refused to give a public profession of grace before the church in Dedham, Massachusetts, for several years, until the faithful persuaded him with many "loving conferences." The conversion relation would emerge as the New England Way's most vulnerable point and a major cause of its eventual demise.

New Englanders, like most European Protestants, could scarcely imagine conversion without literacy. Young people read the Bible to feel the quickening of God's grace, and saints often recorded their lapses and spiritual insights in diaries. In 1647 Massachusetts Bay enacted the Old Deluder Act, ordering every town of fifty or more households to appoint one teacher to whom all children could come for instruction, and every town of at least one hundred households to maintain a grammar school. The law's name derived from its declaration that "one chief project of that old deluder, Satan, [is] to keep men from knowledge of the Scriptures" by encouraging ignorance. By 1671 most other Puritan colonies enacted similar laws, which represented New England's first step toward public education. But none of these laws required school attendance, and boys were more likely to be taught reading and especially writing than were girls.

However diligent laypeople might be in reading the Bible and indoctrinating their children, clergymen had responsibility for leading saints to repentance and stimulating piety. The minister's role was to stir his parishioners' faith with direct, logical, and moving sermons understandable by average listeners, not just by a well-educated elite. The Puritans' preference for this "plain style" of preaching did not contradict their desire for a highly educated clergy, for ministers also had to uphold orthodoxy and be alert for signs of heresy. To produce learned ministers, Massachusetts founded Harvard College in 1636.

Harvard not only trained ministers but also offered instruction in the arts and sciences. Freshmen entered Harvard as young teenagers after demonstrating an ability to write and speak Latin and a knowledge of Greek grammar. Harvard offered a single curriculum emphasizing classical languages, logic, philosophy, and divinity. From 1642 to 1671, the college produced 201 graduates, including 111 ministers. Harvard's alumni made New England the only part of England's overseas empire to possess a college-educated elite during the seventeenth century, and they ensured that the New England Way would not falter for lack of properly trained clergy.

Dissenting Puritans

The values articulated by Winthrop, Cotton, and other New England leaders reinforced social order and religious conformity. Without order and conformity, the leaders feared, divisiveness among Puritans over questions such as church-state relations, church membership, economic individualism, and the role of women would lead to a splintering of the colonists and their failure in the eyes of God. Despite the leaders' efforts, some Puritans entertained quite radical ideas and insisted on expressing them.

Among the first to challenge the New England Way was Roger Williams, who arrived in 1631. Williams was one of those rare individuals who stir controversy without making personal enemies. Radiating the joy of serving God, he quickly became one of the most respected and popular figures in Massachusetts. But Williams questioned the legal basis of congregationalism. Once he began to insist that church and state be entirely separate, the Massachusetts Bay government moved to silence him.

Puritans agreed that the church must be free of state control, and they opposed theocracy (government run by clergy). However, they believed that a holy commonwealth required cooperation between church and state. Williams took a different stance, arguing that civil government should remain absolutely uninvolved with religious matters, whether blasphemy (cursing God), failure to pay tithes, refusal to attend worship, or swearing oaths on the Bible in court. He derived this position from the sixteenth-century Anabaptist tradition (see Chapter 2), which held that the elect must limit their association with society's sinners to protect God's church from contamination. Williams opposed any kind of compulsory church service or interference with private religious beliefs, not because he felt that all religions deserved equal respect (for he did not) but because he feared that the state would corrupt the church and its saints.

Believing that the very purpose of founding Massachusetts Bay was to protect true religion and prevent heresy, the political authorities declared Williams's opinions subversive and banished him in 1635. At his friend Winthrop's suggestion, he went south with four companions to a place that he called Providence, which he purchased from the Narragansett Indians. At Williams's invitation, a steady stream of dissenters drifted to the group of settlements near Providence on Narragansett Bay, which in 1647 joined to form Rhode Island colony. (Orthodox Puritans scorned the place as "Rogues Island.") True to Williams's ideals, Rhode Island was the only New England colony to practice religious toleration. Growing slowly, the colony's four towns had eight hundred settlers by 1650.

A second major challenge to the New England Way came from Anne Hutchinson, whom Winthrop described as "a woman of haughty and fierce carriage, of a nimble wit and active spirit." The controversy surrounding Hutchinson was especially ironic since her ideas derived from the much-respected John Cotton's theology. Cotton insisted that true congregationalism required the saints to be entirely free of religious or political control by anyone who had not undergone a conversion experience. His refusal to give any authority or power over religion to the nonelect applied even to those who led upright, blameless lives—until they had been reborn spiritually.

Anne Hutchinson extended Cotton's main point—that the saints must be free from interference by the nonelect—into a broad attack on clerical authority. Dissatisfied with her own minister, she charged that he was not among the elect, and asserted that the saints in his congregation could ignore his views. She eventually alleged that all the colony's ministers except John Cotton and her brother-in-law John Wheelwright had not been saved and so lacked authority over saints like herself.

By casting doubt on the clergy's spiritual state, Hutchinson undermined its authority over laypersons. Critics charged that her beliefs would delude individuals into imagining that they were accountable to no one but themselves. They branded her followers Antinomians, meaning those opposed to the rule of law. Hutchinson bore the additional liability of being a woman who stepped outside her prescribed role by voicing her criticisms at public meetings attended by

men. The authorities would have prosecuted Hutchinson had she been a man, but her gender made her an even more dangerous foe.

By 1636 Massachusetts Bay split into two camps. Hutchinson's supporters included Boston merchants (like her husband) who disliked the government's economic restrictions on their business; young men chafing against the rigid control of church elders; and most women, protesting their second-class status in church affairs. In 1636 the Antinomians were strong enough to have their candidate elected governor, but they suffered defeat with Winthrop's return to office in 1637.

The victorious Winthrop brought Hutchinson to trial for heresy before the Massachusetts Bay legislature (the General Court). While John Cotton watched nervously, the legislators peppered her with questions. Hutchinson's knowledge of Scripture was so superior to that of her interrogators, however, that she would have been acquitted had she not claimed to have communicated directly with the Holy Spirit. Like virtually all Christians, orthodox Puritans believed that God had ceased to make known matters of faith by personal revelation since New Testament times. Thus Hutchinson's own words were sufficient to condemn her.

The General Court banished the leading Antinomians from the colony, and some of the others voluntarily followed them to Rhode Island, New Hampshire, or back to England. The largest group, led by Hutchinson, settled in Rhode Island. After her husband died, Hutchinson moved to New Netherland, where in 1643 she was killed in that colony's war with local Indians (see below).

Antinomianism's defeat was followed by new restrictions on women's independence and on equality within those Puritan congregations that had previously acted more evenhandedly on matters of gender. Increasingly, women were prohibited from assuming the kind of public religious roles claimed by Hutchinson, and even required to relate their conversion experiences in private to their ministers rather than publicly before their congregations.

The most fundamental threat to Winthrop's city upon a hill was that the people would abandon the ideal of a close-knit community to pursue self-interest. Although most Puritans welcomed the chance to found villages dedicated to stability, self-discipline, and a sense of mutual obligation, a large minority had come to America to find prosperity and social mobility. The most visibly ambitious colonists were merchants, whose activities fueled New England's economy but whose way of life challenged its ideals.

Merchants fit uneasily into a religious utopia that idealized social reciprocity and equated financial shrewdness with greed. They also clashed repeatedly with government leaders, who were trying to regulate prices so that consumers would not suffer from the chronic shortage of manufactured goods that afflicted New England.

In 1635, when the Massachusetts General Court forbade the sale of any item above 5 percent of its cost, Robert Keayne of Boston and other merchants objected. These men argued that they had to sell some goods at higher rates in order to offset their losses from other sales, shipwrecked cargoes, and inflation. In 1639, after selling nails at 25 percent to 33 percent above cost, Keayne was fined heavily in court and was forced to make a humiliating apology before his congregation.

Though a pious Puritan whose annual profits averaged just 5 percent, Keayne symbolized the dangerous possibility that a headlong rush for profits would lead New Englanders to forget that they were their brothers' keepers. "Worldly gain was not the end design of the people of *New-England*," warned the Reverend John Higginson, "but *Religion*." Controversies like the one involving Keayne were part of a struggle for New England's soul. At stake was the Puritans' ability and desire insulate their city upon a hill from a market economy that, they feared, would strangle the spirit of community within a harsh new world of frantic competition.

Power to the Saints

To preserve the New England Way, the Puritans evolved political and religious institutions with far more popular participation than those in England. Unlike the Virginia Company of London, the Massachusetts Bay Company established its headquarters in America (see above). Massachusetts did not require voters or officeholders to own property but bestowed full citizenship on every adult male accepted as a saint. By 1641 about 55 percent of the colony's twenty-three hundred men could vote. By contrast, English property requirements allowed fewer than 30 percent of adult males to vote.

In 1634, after public protest that the governor and council held too much power, each town gained the option of sending two delegates to the General Court.

In 1644 the General Court became a bicameral (two-chamber) lawmaking body when the towns' deputies separated from the Governor's Council to form the House of Representatives.

In 1639 the new towns of Hartford, Windsor, and Wethersfield adopted a government, designed by Thomas Hooker, called the Fundamental Orders of Connecticut. Hooker modeled his government after that of Massachusetts Bay, except that voting and officeholding were opened to all adult male landowners.

The southwestern portion of modern-day Connecticut remained outside this agreement. Under John Davenport, a minister who felt that both Massachusetts Bay and Connecticut allowed too much moral laxness, this region set the strictest standards for verifying sainthood and based its laws most closely upon Old Testament examples. In 1643 the eight towns of this area united as the colony of New Haven.

England's basic unit of local government was the county court. Its members, the justices of the peace, not only decided legal cases as judges but also performed administrative tasks and assessed taxes. Gaining office by royal appointment rather than election, English justices were always members of the gentry selected because of their wealth and political connections. By contrast, New England's county courts functioned primarily as courts of law, and the vital unit of local administration was the town meeting. Town meetings decentralized authority over political and economic decisions to a degree unknown in either England or its other overseas colonies.

New England legislatures established a town by awarding a grant of land to several dozen heads of families. These men then laid out the settlement, organized its church, distributed land among themselves, set local tax rates, and made local laws. Each town determined its own qualifications for voting and holding office in the town meeting, although custom dictated that all male taxpayers (including non-saints) be allowed to participate. The meeting could exclude anyone from settling in town, and it could grant the right of sharing in any future land distributions to newcomers, whose children would inherit this privilege.

Community Life

The local economy and environment left their stamp on New England towns. Of these communities the seaports often seemed least tight-knit because of their transient population, whereas towns in Plymouth

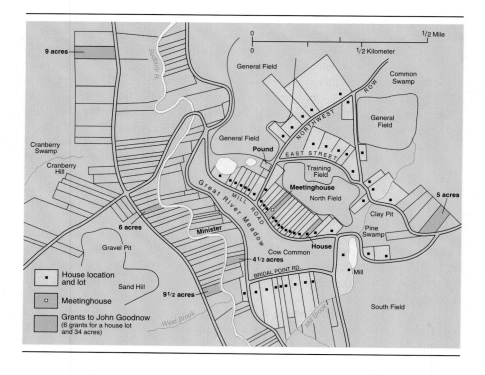

Land Divisions in Sudbury, Massachusetts, 1639–1656

Like other first-generation settlers, John Goodnow lived on a small house lot near the meetinghouse. He pastured his livestock on "common" fields owned by the town and grew crops on thirty-four acres in five separate locations at a distance from his house.

SOURCE: Sumner Chilton Powell, *Puritan Village: The Formation of a New England Town* (Middletown, Conn.: Wesleyan University Press, 1963). Reprinted by permission.

colony tended to be little more than a few stores, a mill, and a meetinghouse serving farmers dwelling over a wide distance. Nevertheless, towns in Massachusetts, Connecticut, and what would become New Hampshire (part of Massachusetts until 1679) were broadly uniform, since most were farm communities resembling traditional English villages.

The founders usually granted each family a one-acre house lot (just enough for a vegetable garden) within a half-mile of the meetinghouse. The town meeting also gave each household strips of land or small fields farther out for its crops and livestock. Often an individual owned several parcels of land in different locations and had the right to graze a few extra animals on the town "commons."

Few aspects of early New England life are more revealing than the first generation's attempt in many, but not all, towns to keep settlement tightly clustered by granting families no more land than they needed to support themselves. Dedham's forty-six founders, for example, received 128,000 acres from Massachusetts Bay in 1636 yet gave themselves just 3,000 acres by 1656, or about 65 acres per family. The rest remained in trust for future generations.

With families clustered within a mile of one another, New England towns' physical settings were conducive to traditional reciprocity. In some parts of England, meanwhile, this mode of land division was coming to seem inefficient as farmers tried to produce a greater surplus for sale by consolidating their landholdings. Reinforcing New England's sense of local community were the town meetings, in which all property-owning males participated, and the congregations, whose Sunday services everyone attended whether or not they were members. The region's generally compact system of settlement forced people to interact with each other and also established an atmosphere of mutual watchfulness that promoted godly order.

Puritan Families

To the Puritans, society's foundation rested not upon the individual but upon the "little commonwealth"— the nuclear family. *"Well ordered families,"* declared minister Cotton Mather in 1699, "naturally produce a *Good Order* in other *Societies.*" In a proper Puritan family, the wife, children, and servants dutifully obeyed

Seventeenth-Century Fashions
Made of heavy oxhide in the mid-1640s, this English coat was owned by Mass-achusetts Bay governor George Leverett. The woman's shoe was fashioned in England or New England around 1650. Stylish English men and women alike wore high beaver hats beginning in the early 1600s. In 1634 the Massachusetts General Court restricted the right to wear them to people holding property valued at two hundred pounds or more.

the husband. According to John Winthrop, a "true wife" thought of herself "in subjection to her husband's authority."

New Englanders defined matrimony as a contract subject to state regulation rather than a religious sacrament and so were married by justices of the peace instead of ministers. As a civil institution, a marriage could be dissolved by the courts in cases of desertion, bigamy, adultery, or physical cruelty. By permitting divorce, Puritans diverged radically from practices in England, where Anglican authorities rarely annulled marriages and civil divorces required a special act of Parliament. Still, New Englanders saw divorce as a remedy fit only for extremely wronged spouses, such as the Plymouth woman who discovered that her husband was simultaneously married to women in Boston, Barbados, and England. Massachusetts courts allowed just twenty-seven divorces from 1639 to 1692.

Because Puritans believed that healthy families were crucial to the community's welfare, they intervened whenever they discovered truly serious problems in a household. The courts disciplined unruly youngsters, disobedient servants, disrespectful wives, and violent or irresponsible husbands whose behavior

seemed dangerous or unusually disruptive to a family. Churches also censured, and sometimes expelled, spouses who did not maintain domestic tranquillity. Negligent parents, one minister declared, "not only wrong each other, but they provoke God by breaking his law."

Although New England wives enjoyed significant legal protections against spousal violence and nonsupport and also had more freedom than their English counterparts to escape a failed marriage, they suffered the same legal disabilities as all Englishwomen. English common law allowed a wife no property rights independently of her husband unless he consented to a special prenuptial agreement giving her control over any property that she already owned. Only if a husband had no other heirs or wrote a will awarding his widow full control over their possessions could she claim rights over household property, although the law reserved lifetime use of a third of the estate for her support.

In contrast to England, New England benefited from a remarkably benign disease environment. Although settlements were compact, minimal travel occurred between towns, especially in the winter, when people were most susceptible to infection. Furthermore, easy access to land allowed families an adequate diet, which improved resistance to disease and lowered death rates associated with childbirth.

Consequently, New Englanders lived long and raised large families. Life expectancy for men reached 65, and women lived nearly that long. More than 80 percent of all infants survived long enough to get married. The 58 men and women who founded Andover, Massachusetts, for example, had 247 children; by the fourth generation, the families of their descendants numbered 2,000 (including spouses who married in from other families). Despite the relatively small size and short duration of the Puritan exodus to New England (just 20,000 immigrants landed from 1630 to 1642, after which few newcomers arrived), the fact that about 70 percent of all settlers came as members of family groups soon resulted in a population evenly divided between males and females. This balance permitted rapid population growth without heavy immigration.

Most immigrants had little or no capital; instead they relied on the labor of their large, healthy families to sustain them and secure their futures. Male heads of households managed the family's scattered crops and livestock, conducted most of its business transactions, and represented it in town government. Besides bearing, nursing, and rearing children, wives had charge of most labor in the house, barn, and garden. In addition, they contributed to their communities by assisting at childbirths and aiding the poor and vulnerable, especially women living alone.

Lacking any legal right to share in town land divisions until they became their fathers' heirs, the founding generation's sons depended on their parents to provide them with acreage for a farm. Parents encouraged sons to delay marriage and work for them in return for a bequest of land at a later date. Young males often stayed at home to till their fathers' fields until their late twenties, when they finally received their own land. Because the average family raised three or four boys to adulthood, parents could depend on thirty to forty years of work if their sons delayed marriage until about age twenty-six.

Keeping sons dependent also ensured that the family line would continue in the hands of capable, experienced men. While daughters performed equally vital labor, their future lay with another family—the one into which they would marry. Being young, with many childbearing years ahead of them, enhanced their value to that family. Thus first-generation women, on average, were only 21 when they married.

Families with more sons and daughters enjoyed a labor surplus that allowed them to send their children to work as apprentices or hired hands for others. However, this system of family labor was inefficient for two reasons. First, the available supply of labor could not expand in times of great demand. Second, parents were reluctant to force their own children to work as hard as strangers. Nevertheless, family labor was the only system that most New Englanders could afford.

Saddled with the burdens of a short growing season, rocky soil salted with gravel, and a system of land distribution in which farmers cultivated widely scattered strips, the colonists managed to feed large families and keep ahead of their debts, but few became wealthy from farming. Seeking greater fortunes than agriculture offered, some seventeenth-century New Englanders turned lumbering, fishing, fur trading, shipbuilding, and rum distilling into major industries employing perhaps a fifth of all adults full-time and offering seasonal work to many natives and settlers alike. As its economy became more diversified, New England prospered. But in the process, its inhabitants grew more worldly, only to discover that fewer and fewer of their children were emerging as saints.

The Demise of the Puritan Errand

As New Englanders struggled to make a living and curb dissent, England fell into chaos. Charles I's efforts to impose taxes without Parliament's consent sparked a civil war in 1642. Alienated by years of religious harassment, Puritans gained control of the revolt, beheaded Charles in 1649, and eventually replaced the king with "Lord High Protector" Oliver Cromwell. After Cromwell's death, a provisional English government recalled the Stuarts and in 1660 crowned Charles II king.

The Stuart restoration doomed Puritanism in England. High Church Anglicans ruthlessly expelled Puritan ministers from their parishes and passed harsh laws forbidding Separatists from establishing churches and schools. One English saint summed up Puritan disillusionment: "God has spit in our face." The Restoration also left American Puritans without a mission. A generation of New England ministers had inspired their congregations to hope that their example would shame England into establishing a truly reformed church. However, having conquered a wilderness and built their city upon a hill, New Englanders discovered after 1660 that the eyes of the world were no longer fixed on them.

Simultaneously with the demise of English Puritanism, an internal crisis gripped the New England Way. The turmoil stemmed from the failure of the founding generation's children to declare themselves saints. The first generation believed that they had accepted a holy contract, or covenant, with God, which obliged them to establish a scripturally ordained church and charge their descendants with its preservation. In return for upholding this New England Way, God would make the city upon a hill prosper and shield it from corruption.

Relatively few second-generation Puritans, on the other hand, were willing to join the elect by making the required conversion relation before their congregation. By 1650, for example, fewer than half the adults in John Winthrop's congregation were saints. The principal reason was the second generation's reluctance to subject themselves to a grilling before relatives and friends. All children who matured in Puritan towns must have witnessed at least one person suffer an ordeal like that of Sarah Fiske. For more than a year, Fiske answered petty charges of speaking uncharitably about her relatives—especially her husband, Phineas—and then was admitted to the Wenham, Massachusetts, church only after publicly denouncing herself as worse "than any toad."

Because Puritan churches baptized only babies born to saints, the unwillingness of the second generation to submit to the conversion relation confronted their parents with the prospect that their own grandchildren would remain unbaptized unless standards for church membership were loosened. In 1662 a convention of clergy and laity devised a compromise known as the Half-Way Covenant, which permitted the children of all baptized members, including nonsaints, to receive baptism. This covenant allowed the founders' descendants to transmit church membership to their children, but it left these offspring "halfway" members who could not take communion or vote in church affairs. When forced to choose between a church system founded on a pure membership of the elect and one that embraced the entire community, New Englanders, after bitter struggles in many congregations, sacrificed purity for community.

The Half-Way Covenant signaled the end of the New England Way. The elect had been unable to bring up a new generation of saints whose religious fervor equaled their own. Most adults chose to remain in "halfway" status for life, and the saints became a shrinking minority as the third and fourth generations matured. Sainthood tended to flow in certain families, and by the 1700s there were more women among the elect than men in most congregations. But since women could not vote in church affairs, religious authority stayed in male hands. Nevertheless, ministers publicly recognized women's role in upholding piety and the church itself.

Expansion and Native Americans

As the settlers grew and prospered, the Native Americans declined. Although Indians began to recover from the initial epidemics by midcentury, the settlers brought new diseases such as diphtheria, measles, and tuberculosis, as well as new outbreaks of smallpox, that took heavy tolls. New England's Indian population had been reduced from 125,000 in 1600 to 10,000 in 1675.

Native Americans felt the English presence in other ways. The fur trade, which initially benefited interior natives, became a burden after midcentury. Once Indians began hunting for trade instead of just for their own subsistence needs, they quickly depleted the beavers and other fur-bearing animals of the region. And because English traders customarily advanced trade goods on credit to Indian hunters before the hunting season, the lack of pelts pushed many natives into debt. In this situation traders such as John Pynchon of Springfield, Massachusetts, began taking Indian land as collateral and selling it to settlers.

Elsewhere, English townsmen, eager to expand their agricultural output and provide land for their sons, voted themselves much larger amounts of land after 1660 and insisted that their scattered parcels be consolidated. For example, Dedham, Massachusetts, which distributed only three thousand acres from 1636 to 1656, allocated five times as much in the next dozen years. Rather than continue living closely together, many farmers built homes on their outlying tracts, thereby coming into closer proximity to native settlements and the Indians' hunting, gathering, and fishing areas.

Colonizing New England, 1620–1674
Puritan expansion reached its maximum extent in the seventeenth century just before King Philip's War, which erupted as a result of the pressure of white expansion on Indian communities. Frontier expansion did not resume in New England until after 1715.

SOURCE: Frederick Merk, *History of the Westward Movement.* Copyright © 1979 by Lois Bannister Merk. Reprinted by permission of Alfred A. Knopf, Inc.

As the settlements expanded, they put new pressures on the natives and the land alike. As early as 1642, Miantonomi, a Narragansett sachem (chief), warned other New England Indians:

These English having gotten our land, they with scythes cut down the grass, and with axes fell the trees; their cows and horses eat the grass, and their hogs spoil our clam banks, and we shall all be starved.

Within a generation, Miantonomi's fears were being borne out. By clearing away extensive stands of trees for fields and for use as fuel and building material, colonial farmers inadvertently altered an entire ecosystem. Deer were no longer attracted, and the wild plants upon which the Indians depended for food and medicine could not grow. The soil became drier and flooding more frequent in the face of this deforestation. The settlers also introduced domestic livestock, which, according to English custom, ran wild. Pigs damaged Indian cornfields (until the natives adopted the alien practice of fences) and shellfish gathering sites. English cattle and horses quickly devoured native grasses, which the settlers then replaced with English varieties.

With the native religious leaders, and their practices, powerless to halt the alarming decline of Indian population, land, and food sources, many Indians became demoralized. In their despair some turned to alcohol, increasingly available during the 1660s despite colonial efforts to suppress its sale to Native Americans. Interpreting the crisis as one of belief, others joined those Indians who had already converted to Christianity. By 1675 Puritan missionaries had established about thirty praying towns in eastern Massachusetts and Plymouth and on the islands of Martha's Vineyard and Nantucket. Supervised by missionaries, each praying town nevertheless had its own Native American magistrate, usually a sachem, and many praying congregations had Indian preachers. Although the missionaries struggled to convert the Indians to "civilization," by which they meant English culture and life-styles as well as to Christianity, most praying Indians integrated the new faith with their native cultural identities. This practice reinforced the hostility of most settlers, who believed that all Indians were irrevocably "savage" and heathen.

Anglo-Indian conflict became acute during the 1670s because of pressure imposed on unwilling Indians to sell their land and to accept missionaries and the legal authority of colonial courts. Tension ran especially high in the Plymouth colony, where the English had engulfed the Wampanoags and forced a number of humiliating concessions on their leader Metacom, or "King Philip," the son of Massasoit, the Pilgrims' onetime ally.

In 1675 Plymouth hanged three Wampanoags for killing a Christian Indian and threatened to arrest Metacom. A minor incident in which several Wampanoags were shot while burglarizing a farmhouse led to a steady escalation of violence; and Metacom soon organized about two-thirds of the Native Americans, including perhaps a third of all Christian Indians, into a military alliance. "But little remains of my ancestor's domain, I am resolved not to see the day when I have no country," Metacom declared as he and his followers ignited the conflict known as King Philip's War.

Metacom's forces—unlike the Indian combatants in the Pequot War, few of whom had fought with guns—were as well armed as the colonists. The Indians attacked 52 of New England's 90 towns (of which 12 were entirely destroyed), burned 1,200 houses, slaughtered 8,000 head of cattle, and killed 600 colonists.

The tide turned against Metacom in 1676 after the Mohawk Indians of New York and many Christian Indians joined the English against him. English militiamen destroyed their enemies' food supplies and sold hundreds of captives into slavery, including Metacom's wife and child. "It must have been as bitter as death to him," wrote Puritan clergyman Cotton Mather, "to lose his wife and only son, for the Indians are marvellously fond and affectionate toward their children." Perhaps three thousand Indians starved or fell in battle, including Metacom himself, and many more fled to New York and Canada.

King Philip's War reduced southern New England's Indian population by almost 40 percent and eliminated overt resistance to white expansion. It also deepened English hostility toward Native Americans, even the Christian Indians who fought Philip. In Massachusetts ten praying towns were disbanded and all Indians restricted to the remaining four; all Indian courts were dismantled; and "guardians" were appointed to supervise the reservations. "There is a cloud, a dark cloud upon the work of the Gospel among the poor Indians," mourned John Eliot. In the face of poverty and discrimination, remaining Indians managed to maintain their communities and cultural identities. To make up for the loss of traditional sources of sustenance, many worked as seamen or indentured servants, served in England's wars against the French in Canada, or made and sold baskets and other wares.

Economics, Gender, and Satan in Salem

In the three decades after the Half-Way Covenant's adoption in 1662, New Englanders endured an endless stream of sermons called jeremiads (after ancient Israel's prophet Jeremiah), in which the clergy berated them for failing to preserve the idealism of the region's founding generation. The ministers most bitterly complained about their parishioners' increasing tendency to forget, as one minister emphasized in 1663, "that New-England is originally a plantation of Religion, not a plantation of trade." The jeremiads indicted New Englanders for becoming more worldly and more individualistic, even blaming them for calamities like King Philip's War and the Dominion of New England (see Chapter 4), saying that God caused these as punishments or tests of his wayward saints.

In attacking the colonists' behavior, the clergy recognized that social and economic changes were undermining the New England Way. The dispersal of settlers away from town centers, besides putting pressure on Native Americans, generated friction between the townspeople settled near the meetinghouse, who usually dominated politics, and the "outlivers," whose distance from the town center generally limited their influence over town affairs. By the late seventeenth century, moreover, the region's occupational structure had become more complex, especially in its several port cities, and the distribution of wealth was growing more uneven. These developments undermined the spirit of community by sowing jealousy and creating the anxiety that a small minority might be profiting at the majority's expense. At the same time, New England's rising involvement in international trade led many individuals—in both cities and the countryside—to act more competitively, aggressively, and impersonally toward one another. John Winthrop's vision of a religiously oriented community sustained by a sense of reciprocity and charity was giving way to a world increasingly like the materialistic, acquisitive society that the original immigrants had fled in England.

Nowhere in New England did these trends have more disturbing effects than in Salem, Massachusetts, which grew rapidly after 1660 to become the region's second largest port. Trade made Salem prosperous but also destroyed the relatively equal society of humble fishermen and farmers that had once existed. A sharp distinction emerged between the port's residents—especially its rich merchants—and outlying farmers. Prior to 1661 the richest 10 percent of Salem residents owned 21 percent of the town's property, but by 1681 the richest tenth possessed 62 percent of all wealth.

Salem's farmers lost not only social standing to the merchants but also political power. Before 1665 twice as many farmers as merchants had held the town meeting's highest offices, but thereafter, merchant officeholders outnumbered those who were farmers by six to one. Salem became highly vulnerable to internal conflict between its prosperous merchants and its agricultural folk.

About six miles west of Salem's meetinghouse lay the precinct of Salem Village (now Danvers), an economically stagnant district whose residents resented Salem Town's political domination. The village was divided between supporters of the Porter and Putnam families. Well connected with the merchant elite, the Porters enjoyed political prestige in Salem Town and lived in the village's eastern section, whose residents farmed richer soils and benefited somewhat from Salem Town's prosperity. In contrast, most Putnams lived in Salem Village's less fertile western half, had little chance to share in Salem Town's commercial expansion, and had lost the political influence that they once held in town. The Porter-Putnam rivalry mirrored the tensions between Salem's urban and rural dwellers.

In late 1691 several Salem Village girls encouraged an African slave woman, Tituba, to tell fortunes and talk about sorcery. When the girls later began behaving strangely, villagers assumed that they were victims of witchcraft. Pressed to identify their tormenters, the girls named two local white women and Tituba.

So far the incident was not unusual. Until the late seventeenth century, belief in witchcraft was very strong at all levels of European and American society. Witches were people (nearly always women) whose pride, envy, discontent, or greed supposedly led them to sign a pact with the devil. Thereafter they allegedly used *maleficium* (the devil's supernatural power of evil) to torment neighbors and others by causing illness, destroying property, or—as with the girls in Salem Village—inhabiting or "possessing" their victims' bodies and minds. Apart from *maleficium*, wit-

nesses usually claimed that witches displayed aggressive, unfeminine behavior. And a disproportionate number of the 342 accused witches in New England were women who had either no living sons or no living brothers. As a result, they had inherited, or stood to inherit in the future, property beyond the one-third of a husband's estate normally bequeathed to widows. In other words, most witches were assertive women who had, once had, or soon might have more economic power and independence than many men. For New Englanders, who felt the need to limit both female independence and economic individualism, witches symbolized the dangers awaiting those who disregarded such limits. In most witchcraft accusations in New England, there was only one defendent and the case never went to trial. The few exceptions to this rule were tried with little fanfare. Events in Salem Village, on the other hand, led to a colonywide panic.

By April 1692 the girls had denounced two prosperous farm wives long considered saints in the local church, and they had identified the village's former minister as a wizard (male witch). Fears of witchcraft soon overrode doubts about the girls' credibility and led local judges to sweep aside normal procedural safeguards. Specifically the judges ignored the law's ban on "spectral evidence"—testimony that a spirit resembling the accused had been seen tormenting a victim. Thereafter accusations multiplied until the jails overflowed with accused witches.

The pattern of hysteria in Salem Village reflected that community's internal divisions. Most charges came from the village's troubled western division, especially from Putnam family members, who lodged 46 of the 141 formal indictments. With two exceptions, those named as witches lived outside the village's western half; they primarily included people connected economically or by marriage to the Porters—though no Porters were themselves named as witches—and several members of wealthy Salem Town families.

Anxieties concerning gender and age also influenced who became victims. Two-thirds of all accusers were "possessed" girls or young women aged eleven to twenty, and more than half had lost one or more parents in conflicts between Indians and settlers in Maine. They and other survivors had fled to Massachusetts, where most were now servants in other families' households. They most frequently named as witches middle-aged wives and widows—women

The Geography of Witchcraft: Salem Village, 1692

Geographic patterns of witchcraft testimony mirrored tensions within Salem Village. Accused witches and their defenders lived mostly in the village's eastern division or in Salem Town, whereas their accusers overwhelmingly resided in the village's western sector.

SOURCE: Adapted from Paul Boyer and Stephen Nissenbaum, *Salem Possessed: The Social Origins of Witchcraft* (Cambridge, Mass.: Harvard University Press, 1974).

who had avoided the poverty and uncertainty they themselves faced. At the same time, the "possessed" accusers gained momentary power and prominence by voicing the anxieties and hostilities of many others in their community and by virtually dictating the course of events in and around Salem for several months.

The number of persons facing trial multiplied quickly. Those found guilty desperately tried to stave off death by implicating others. As the pandemonium spread beyond Salem, fear dissolved ties of friendship and family. A minister heard himself condemned by his own granddaughter. A seven-year-old girl helped send her mother to the gallows. A wife and daughter facing death testified against their own husband and father. Fifty persons saved themselves by confessing. Twenty others who would neither disgrace their own name nor betray the guiltless went to their graves. Shortly before she was hanged, a victim of the

Petition of Mary Easty, 1690 *(Detail)*
In her petition Easty swore that "I know not the least thing of witchcraft."

witch hunters named Mary Easty begged the court to come to its senses: "I petition your honors not for my own life, for I know I must die . . . [but] if it be possible, that no more innocent blood be shed."

By late 1692 most Massachusetts ministers had come to doubt that justice was being done. They objected that spectral evidence, which was crucial in most convictions, lacked legal credibility because the devil could manipulate it. New Englanders, concluded Increase Mather, a leading clergyman, had fallen victim to a deadly game of "blind man's buffet" set up by Satan and were "hotly and madly, mauling one another in the dark." Backed by the clergy (and alarmed by an accusation against his wife), Governor William Phips forbade any further imprisonments for witchcraft in October—by which time over a hundred individuals were in jail and twice that many stood accused—and shortly thereafter he suspended all trials. Phips ended the terror in early 1693 by pardoning all those convicted or suspected of witchcraft.

The witchcraft hysteria reflected profound anxieties over social change in New England. The underlying causes for this tension were evident in the antagonism of Salem Village's communally oriented farmers toward the competitive, individualistic, and impersonal way of life represented by Salem Town. In this clash of values, the rural villagers assumed the symbolic role of purging their city upon a hill of its commercial witches, only to leave the landscape desecrated by their gallows.

By the last years of the seventeenth century, the New England Way had lost its relevance for the generation reaching maturity. Eighteenth-century New Englanders would be far less willing to accept society's right to restrict their personal behavior and economic freedom. True to their Puritan roots, the people would retain strong religious convictions and an extraordinary capacity for perseverance. Out of these roots now grew the traits of ingenuity, shrewdness, and a sharp eye for opportunity, on which New Englanders would build a thriving international commerce—and later an industrial revolution.

Throughout the seventeenth century, as New England moved away from its roots, the Chesapeake colony to the south also underwent a radical transformation that gave it a new prominence. But the differences between the two regions remained as great as ever.

CHESAPEAKE SOCIETY

Virginia's survival was no longer at stake when James I took control of the colony in 1624 from the bankrupt Virginia Company. The company had built a colony but destroyed itself in the process. Charles I and his successors refused to spend any significant amount of money on Virginia, even for the governors whom they appointed—whose salaries instead came from local taxes.

Royal indifference worked to the colonial elite's advantage by minimizing outside interference. Virginia's leading planters experimented with various systems of local administration and succeeded in forcing reluctant governors to cooperate with their legislature. The environment and the dominant regional crop—tobacco—determined the colonists' destiny. Similar forces shaped life in Maryland and northeastern North Carolina, which, with Virginia, evolved a common Chesapeake culture.

State and Church in Virginia

King James I disliked representative government and planned to rule Virginia through a governor of his own choosing, who would appoint and dismiss advisers to a newly created council. But Virginians petitioned repeatedly that their elected assembly be revived. In 1628 the new king, Charles I, grudgingly relented, but only to induce the assembly to lay a tax on tobacco exports that would transfer the cost of the colony's government from the crown to Virginia's taxpayers.

After 1630 the need for additional taxes led royal governors to call regular assemblies. The small number of elected representatives, or burgesses, initially met as a single body with the council to pass laws. During the 1650s the legislature split into two chambers—the House of Burgesses and the Governor's Council, whose members held lifetime appointments. Later other royal colonies all established bicameral legislatures like Virginia's.

Local government varied widely during Virginia's first quarter-century. All individuals who commanded the militia, enforced the law, or held courts were appointed to office rather than elected. After experimenting with various institutions of local administration, in 1634 Virginia's settlers adopted England's county-court system. The courts' members, or justices of the peace, acted as judges; they also set local tax rates, paid county officials, and saw to the construction and maintenance of roads, bridges, and public buildings. As in England, this system was undemocratic, for the justices and the sheriffs, who administered the counties during the courts' recesses, gained office by the royal governor's appointment instead of by citizens' votes. Everywhere south of New England, unelected county courts would become the basic unit of local government by 1710.

In contrast to Puritan New England, Virginia had as its established church the Church of England. First instituted in 1618, Anglican vestries governed each parish. The six vestrymen handled all church finances, determined who was deserving of poor relief, and investigated complaints against the minister. The taxpayers, who were legally obliged to pay fixed rates to the Anglican church, elected vestries until 1662, when the assembly made them self-perpetuating and independent of the voters.

Because few counties supported more than one parish, many residents could not conveniently attend services. A chronic shortage of clergymen left many communities without functioning congregations. In 1662 just ten ministers served Virginia's forty-five parishes. Compared to New Englanders, Chesapeake dwellers felt religion's influence lightly.

Virginia's First Families

Virginia encountered great difficulty in developing a social elite able and willing to provide disinterested public service. The gentry sent by the Virginia Company to supervise its affairs were rarely suited for a frontier society. By 1630 all but a few of these gentlemen had either died or returned to England.

The next cycle of leaders were primarily middle class in origins, but over time they acquired great wealth. Some had built large estates by defrauding Virginia Company stockholders. Others were rough-hewn gamblers who risked all on tobacco and won big. From 1630 to 1660, these individuals dominated Virginia's council and became even richer through land grants, tax exemptions, and public salaries. Because they had few or no children to assume their place in society, however, their influence died with them.

From 1660 to 1675, a third cycle of immigrants, who generally arrived after 1645, assumed political

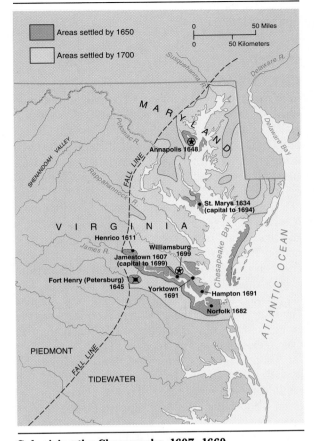

Colonizing the Chesapeake, 1607–1660
The native-settler frontier moved slowly westward until after Indian defeat in the Third Anglo-Powhatan War (1644–1646). By 1700, when the European and African population had reached 110,000, newcomers had spread virtually throughout the tidewater.

power. Principally members of English merchant families engaged in trade with Virginia, they had become planters. They usually emigrated with wealth, education, and burning ambition. By 1670 they controlled the council. Most of them profited from "public" service by obtaining huge land grants.

Unlike their predecessors, this group bequeathed their wealth and power to future generations, later known as the First Families of Virginia. Among them were the Burwell, Byrd, Carter, Harrison, Lee, Ludwell, Randolph, and Taylor families. The First Families would dominate Virginia politics for two centuries, and four of the first five American presidents would be descended from them.

Maryland

Until 1632 successful English colonization had resulted from the ventures of joint-stock companies, but afterward the crown repeatedly made presents of the Virginia Company's forfeited territory to reward English politicians. Overseas settlement thereafter resulted from grants of crown land to proprietors, who assumed the responsibility for peopling, governing, and defending their colonies.

In 1632 the first such grant went to Lord Baltimore (Cecilius Calvert) for a large tract of land north of the Potomac River and east of Chesapeake Bay, which he named Maryland in honor of England's Queen Henrietta Maria. Lord Baltimore also secured freedom from royal taxation, the power to appoint all sheriffs and judges, and the privilege of creating a local nobility. The only checks on the proprietor's power were the crown's control of war and trade and the requirement that an elected assembly approve all laws.

With Charles I's agreement, Lord Baltimore intended to create an overseas refuge for English Catholics, who constituted about 2 percent of England's population. Although English Catholics were rarely molested and many (like the Calverts) were very wealthy, they could not worship in public, had to pay tithes to the Anglican church, and could not hold political office.

In making Maryland a Catholic haven, Baltimore had to avoid antagonizing English Protestants. He sought to accomplish this by transplanting to the Chesapeake the old English institution of the manor—an estate on which a lord could maintain private law courts and employ as his chaplain a Catholic priest. Local Catholics could then come to the manor to hear Mass and receive the sacraments privately. Baltimore adapted Virginia's headright system (see Chapter 2) by offering wealthy English Catholic aristocrats large land grants on condition that they bring settlers at their own cost. Anyone transporting five adults (a requirement raised to twenty by 1640) received a two-thousand-acre manor. Baltimore hoped that this arrangement would allow Catholics to survive and prosper in Maryland while making it unnecessary to pass any special laws alarming to Protestants.

Maryland's initial colonization proceeded quite smoothly. In 1634 the first two hundred settlers landed.

Maryland was the first colony spared a starving time, thanks to the Calvert family's careful study of Virginia's early history. The new colony's success showed that English overseas expansion had come of age. Baltimore, however, stayed in England, governing as an absentee proprietor, and few Catholic settlers went to Maryland. From the outset, Protestants formed the majority of the population. Maryland became a society of independent landowners because land prices were low and few settlers consequently were willing to become tenants on the manors. These conditions doomed the Calvert family's dream of creating on the Chesapeake a manorial system of mostly Catholic lords collecting rents. By 1675 all of Maryland's sixty nonproprietary manors had evolved into plantations.

There was little religious tension in Maryland in the colony's first years, but the situation worsened over time. The Protestant majority dominated the colonial assembly's elective lower house, but many Catholics (including several Calvert relatives) became large landowners, held high public office in the colony, and dominated the appointive upper house. Serious religious problems first emerged in 1642, when Catholics and Protestants in the capital at St. Mary's argued over use of the city's chapel, which the two groups had shared until then. As antagonisms intensified, Baltimore drafted the Act for Religious Toleration, which the assembly passed in 1649. Baltimore hoped that the statute would reinforce the Catholic minority's legal rights, but the law also reflected his consistent support for freedom of conscience. The toleration act was America's first law affirming liberty of worship. However, it did not protect non-Christians, nor did it separate church and state, since it empowered the government to punish religious offenses such as blasphemy.

The toleration act did not secure religious peace. In 1654 the Protestant majority barred Catholics from voting, ousted Governor William Stone (himself a Protestant), and repealed the toleration act. In 1655 Stone raised an army of both faiths to regain the government but was defeated at the Battle of the Severn River. The victors imprisoned Stone and hanged three Catholic leaders. Catholics in Maryland actually experienced more trouble than did their counterparts during the English Civil War, in which Catholics were seldom molested by the victorious Puritans.

Maryland remained in Protestant hands until 1658. Ironically, Lord Baltimore resumed control by order of the Puritan authorities then ruling England. Even so, the Calverts encountered enormous obstacles in governing Maryland during the next four decades because of Protestant resistance to any political influence by Catholics.

Tobacco Shapes a Way of Life

Compared to colonists in New England's compact towns (where five hundred people often lived within a mile of the meetinghouse), Chesapeake residents had few neighbors. A typical community comprised about two dozen families in an area of twenty-five square miles, or about six persons per square mile. Friendship networks seldom extended beyond a three-mile walk from one's farm and rarely included more than twenty adults. Many, if not most, Chesapeake inhabitants lived in a constricted world much like that of Robert Boone, a Maryland farmer described by an Annapolis paper as having died at age seventy-nine "on the same Plantation where he was born in 1680, from which he never went 30 Miles in his Life."

The isolated folk in Virginia and Maryland and in the unorganized settlements of what would become North Carolina shared a way of life shaped by one overriding fact: their future depended on the price of tobacco. Tobacco had dominated Chesapeake agriculture since 1618, when demand for the crop exploded and prices spiraled to dizzying levels. The boom ended in 1629 after prices sank a stunning 97 percent, from a high of 36 pence per pound to a penny. After stabilizing near 2.4 pence, tobacco rarely again fetched more than 10 percent of its former high.

Despite its plunge, tobacco stayed profitable as long as it sold for over two pence per pound *and* was cultivated on fertile soil near navigable water. The plant grew best on level ground with good internal drainage, so-called light soil, which was usually found beside rivers. Locating a farm along Chesapeake Bay or the region's web of rivers also minimized transportation costs by permitting tobacco to be loaded on ships at wharves near one's home. Perhaps 80 percent of all Chesapeake homes lay within a half-mile of a riverbank, and most within just six hundred feet of the shoreline.

From such waterfront bases, wealthy planters built wharves that served not only as depots for tobacco exports but also as distribution centers for imported goods. The planters' control of both export and import commerce stunted the growth of towns and the

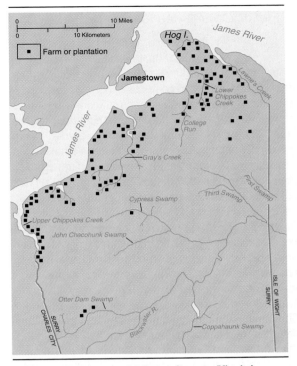

Pattern of Settlement in Surry County, Virginia, 1620–1660

Unlike the New England colonists, whose settlements were usually nucleated around a town center (see the map of Sudbury, Massachusetts, on page 60), the Chesapeake population distributed itself thinly along the banks of rivers and creeks.

SOURCE: Thad W. Tate and David Ammerman, eds., *The Chesapeake in the Seventeenth Century* (Chapel Hill: University of North Carolina Press, 1979). Published for the Institute of Early American History and Culture. Reprinted by permission.

emergence of a powerful merchant class. Urbanization therefore proceeded slowly in the Chesapeake, even in a capital like Maryland's St. Mary's, which as late as 1678 was still a mere hamlet of thirty scattered houses.

Although the tobacco crash left small producers struggling to support themselves, cultivating the "weed" could generate a large income for anyone with a sizable work force. Tobacco thus sustained a sharp demand for labor that lured about 110,000 English to the Chesapeake from 1630 to 1700. Ninety percent of these immigrants were indentured servants. Men were more valued as field hands than women, so 80 percent of servants were males, usually in their twenties.

Mortality, Gender, and Kinship

So few women immigrated to the Chesapeake in the early years of colonization that barely a third of all male servants could find brides before 1650. Furthermore, marriage occurred relatively late, because most inhabitants immigrated as servants whose indentures forbade them to wed before completing their term of labor. Their own scarcity gave women a great advantage in negotiating favorable marriages. Female indentured servants often found prosperous planters to be their suitors and to buy their remaining time of service.

Death ravaged seventeenth-century Chesapeake society mercilessly and left domestic life exceptionally fragile. Before 1650 the greatest killers were diseases contracted from contaminated water: typhoid, dysentery, and salt poisoning. After 1650 malaria became endemic as sailors, arriving from Africa, along with a few Africans, carried it into the marshy lowlands, where the disease was spread rapidly by mosquito bites. Life expectancy in the 1600s was about forty-eight for men and forty-four for women—slightly less than in England but nearly twenty years less than in New England. Servants died at horrifying rates, with perhaps 40 percent going to their graves within six years of arrival, and 70 percent by age forty-nine. Such high death rates severely crippled family life. Half of all people married in Charles County, Maryland, during the late 1600s became widows or widowers within seven years. The typical Maryland family saw half of its four children die in childhood.

Chesapeake women who lost their husbands tended to enjoy greater property rights than widows elsewhere. To ensure that their own children would inherit the family estate in the event that their widows remarried, Chesapeake men often wrote wills giving their wives perpetual and complete control of their estates. A widow in such circumstances gained economic independence yet still faced enormous pressure to marry a man who could produce income by farming her fields.

The prevalence of early death produced complex households in which stepparents might raise children with two or three different surnames. Mary Keeble of Middlesex County, Virginia, bore seven children before being widowed at age 29, whereupon she immediately married Robert Beverley, a prominent planter. Mary died in 1678 at age 41 after having five children by Beverley, who then married Katherine Hone, a

widow with one child. Upon Beverley's death in 1687, Katherine quickly wed Christopher Robinson, who had just lost his wife and needed a mother for his four children. Christopher and Katherine's household included children named Keeble, Beverley, Hone, and Robinson. This tangled chain of six marriages among seven people eventually produced twenty-five children who lived at least part of their lives with one or more stepparents.

The combination of predominantly male immigration and devastating death rates notably retarded population growth. Although the Chesapeake had received perhaps 110,000 English immigrants between 1630 and 1700, its white population stood at just 69,000 in 1700. By contrast, a benign disease environment and a more balanced gender ratio among the 25,000 immigrants to New England during the 1600s allowed that region's white population to climb to 91,000 by 1700.

The Chesapeake's dismal demographic history began improving in the late seventeenth century. By then resistance acquired from childhood immunities allowed native-born residents to survive into their fifties, or ten years longer than immigrants. As the number of families slowly rose, the ratio of men to women became more equal, since half of all children were girls. By 1690 an almost even division existed between the genders. Thereafter, the white population grew primarily through an excess of births over deaths rather than through immigration, so that by 1720 the Chesapeake was primarily a native-born society.

Tobacco's Troubles

The massive importation of servants into the seventeenth-century Chesapeake widened the gap between rich and poor. Taking advantage of the headright system, a few planters built up large landholdings and then earned substantial incomes from their servants' labor. The servants' lot was harsh. Most were poorly fed, clothed, and housed. The exploitation of Chesapeake labor was unequaled anywhere in the English-speaking world outside the West Indies.

Servants faced a bleak future when their indentures ended. Having received no pay, they entered into freedom without savings. Virginia obliged masters to provide a new suit of clothes and a year's supply of corn to a freed servant. Maryland required these items plus a hoe and an ax and gave the right to claim fifty

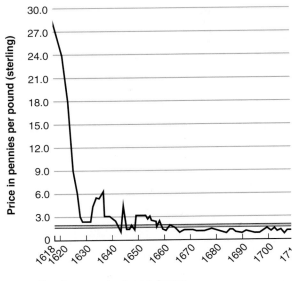

═══ Break-even price for producers

Tobacco Prices, 1618–1710

Even after its great plunge in the 1620s, tobacco remained profitable until about 1660, when its price fell below the break-even point—the income needed to support a family or pay off a farm mortgage.

SOURCE: Russell R. Menard, "The Chesapeake Economy, 1618–1720: An Interpretation" (unpublished paper presented at the Johns Hopkins University Seminar on the Atlantic Community, November 20, 1973) and "Farm Prices of Maryland Tobacco, 1659–1710," *Maryland Historical Magazine*, LVIII (Spring 1973): 85.

acres whenever an individual could pay to have the land surveyed and deeded.

Maryland's policy of reserving fifty acres for former servants permitted many of its so-called freedmen to become landowners. Two-thirds of all Chesapeake servants went to Virginia, however, where no such entitlement existed. After 1650 Virginia speculators monopolized most of the light soil along riverbanks so essential for a profitable farm, and freedmen found land ever more unaffordable. Upward mobility was possible, but few achieved it.

After 1660 upward mobility almost vanished from the Chesapeake as the price of tobacco fell far below profitable levels, to a penny a pound. So began a depression lasting over fifty years. Despite their own tobacco losses, large planters earned other income from rents, interest on loans, some shopkeeping, and government fees.

Most landowners held on by offsetting tobacco losses with small sales of corn and cattle to the West Indies. A typical family nevertheless inhabited a shack barely twenty feet by sixteen feet and owned no more property than Adam Head of Maryland possessed when he died in 1698: three mattresses without bedsteads, a chest and barrel that served as table and chair, two pots, a kettle, "a parcell of old pewter," a gun, and some books. Most tobacco farmers lacked furniture, lived on mush or stew because they had just one pot, and slept on the ground—often on a pile of rags. Having fled poverty in England or the Caribbean for the promise of a better life, they found utter destitution in the Chesapeake.

Servants who completed their indentures after 1660 fared even worse, for the depression slashed wages well below the level needed to build savings and in this way placed landownership beyond their means. Lacking capital, those living as tenants could not afford to breed cattle for the West Indies, and they had little corn to sell after meeting their own needs. Ex-servants formed a frustrated and embittered underclass that seemed destined to remain landless and poor.

Bacon's Rebellion

By the 1670s these bleak conditions trapped most Virginia landowners in a losing battle against poverty and left the colony's freedmen verging on despair. Both groups were capable of striking out in blind rage if an opportunity presented itself to stave off economic disaster. In 1676 this human powder keg exploded in violence that left hundreds of Indians dead, dozens of plantations looted, and Virginia's capital, Jamestown, burned. The person who lit the match was Nathaniel Bacon, a wealthy, well-educated young Englishman who had immigrated to Virginia in 1674 and established a plantation. He was a bold man and an inspiring speaker, and Governor William Berkeley, a distant relative, had immediately appointed him to the council.

Virginia had been free of serious conflict with Native Americans since the Third Anglo-Powhatan War (1644–1646). During that struggle, forces under Opechancanough, then nearly a century old but able to direct battles from a litter, killed five hundred of the colony's eight thousand whites before meeting defeat. By 1653 tribes encircled by English settlement began agreeing to remain within boundaries set by the government—in effect, on reservations. White settlement then expanded north to the Potomac River, and by 1675 Virginia's four thousand Indians were greatly outnumbered by forty thousand whites.

As in New England, tensions flared between natives struggling against depopulation and nearby settlers bent on altering the landscape. In Virginia tensions ran particularly high because Governor Berkeley and a few friends held a fur-trade monopoly that profited from friendly relations with some of the frontier Indians. As a result, settler resentments against the governor became fused with those against Indians. In June 1675 a dispute between some Doeg Indians and a Virginia farmer escalated until a force of Virginia and Maryland militia pursuing the Doegs murdered fourteen friendly Susquehannocks and then executed five of their chiefs during a peace conference. The violence was now unstoppable.

Governor Berkeley proposed defending the panic-stricken frontier with an expensive chain of forts linked by patrols. Stung by low tobacco prices and taxes that took almost a quarter of their yearly incomes, small farmers preferred the less costly solution of waging a war of extermination. Despite orders from Berkeley not to retaliate, three hundred settlers elected Bacon to lead them against nearby Indians in April 1676. Bacon's expedition found only peaceful Indians but massacred them anyway.

When he returned in June 1676, Bacon sought authority to wage war "against all Indians in generall." Bacon's newfound popularity forced the governor to grant his demand. The legislature voted a program designed to appeal to both hard-pressed taxpayers and ex-servants desperate for land. The assembly defined as enemies any Indians who left their villages without English permission (even if they did so out of fear of attack by Bacon), and declared their lands forfeited. Bacon's troops were free to plunder all "enemies" of their furs, guns, wampum, and corn harvests and also to keep Indian prisoners as slaves. The assembly's incentives for enlisting were directed at land-bound buccaneers eager to get rich quickly by seizing land and enslaving any Indians who fell into their clutches.

But Berkeley soon had second thoughts about letting Bacon's thirteen hundred men continue their frontier slaughter and called them back. The governor's order spared more Indians from attack, leading Bacon's

Virginia Indian, c. 1645
At the time that this contemporary sketch was made, Virginia's white settlers and Indians were embroiled in the Third Anglo-Powhatan War.

men to rebel and march on Jamestown. Forcing Berkeley to flee across Chesapeake Bay, the rebels burned Jamestown, offered freedom to any Berkeley supporters' servants or slaves who joined the rebels, and then looted their enemies' plantations. At the very moment of triumph, however, Bacon died of dysentery in late 1676, and his followers dispersed.

The tortured course of Bacon's Rebellion revealed a society under deep internal stress. The revolt began as an effort to displace escalating tensions within white society onto local Indians. Because social success in Virginia depended on accumulating land and labor, farmers and landless ex-servants alike responded enthusiastically to the prospect of taking Indian lands, stealing their furs, wampum, and harvests, and enslaving prisoners. So easily did the insurrection disintegrate into an excuse for settlers of all classes to plunder other whites, however, that it appears that the rebels were driven by economic opportunism as well as by racism. Bacon's Rebellion was an outburst of long pent-up frustrations by marginal taxpayers and ex-servants, driven to desperation by the tobacco depression, as well as by wealthier planters excluded from Berkeley's circle of favorites.

Slavery

Bacon's Rebellion exposed the crackling tensions underlying class relations among Chesapeake whites. This social instability derived in large part from the massive importation of indentured servants, who later became free agents in an economy that offered them little but poverty while their former masters seemingly prospered. But even before Bacon's Rebellion, the acute potential for class conflict was diminishing as Chesapeake planters gradually substituted black slaves for white servants.

Racial slavery developed in three stages in the Chesapeake. Africans first began appearing from 1619 to 1640. Although Anglo-Virginians carefully distinguished blacks from whites in official documents—in a manner that seems to show a tendency to discriminate according to race—they did not assume that every African sold was a slave rather than a servant destined for eventual freedom. The same was true for Indians captured in the colony's wars. Some Africans gained their freedom, and a few, mostly on Virginia's eastern shore, had their own tobacco farms. During the second phase, spanning the years 1640–1660, unmistakable evidence survives that growing numbers of blacks and some Indians were treated as slaves and that their children inherited that status, in contrast to white indentured servants, who had fixed terms of service. In the final phase, after 1660, whites officially recognized slavery and regulated it by law. Maryland first defined slavery as a lifelong, inheritable, racial status in 1661. Virginia followed suit in 1670. By 1705 strict legal codes defined the place of slaves in society and set standards of racial etiquette. By then free blacks had all but disappeared from the Chesapeake. Although this period saw slavery mature into a legal system, many of the specific practices enacted into law were evolving into custom before 1660.

Slavery was never considered a status appropriate for any European or any Christian. Although the English could have enslaved enemies such as the Irish and Spanish, they always reserved this complete denial of human rights for nonwhites. The English embarked on slavery as an "unthinking decision," one in which they unconsciously acted on the basis of a profoundly negative, emotional response to nonwhites, assuming that they were inferior to themselves—and so uniquely suited for slavery.

As late as 1660, fewer than a thousand slaves lived in Virginia and Maryland. The number in bondage first became truly significant in the 1680s, when the Chesapeake's slave population (by now almost entirely black, owing to Indian decline) almost tripled, rising from forty-five hundred to about twelve thousand. By 1700 nearly twenty thousand slaves resided in the region, and they made up 22 percent of the inhabitants. Even so, indentured servants still composed half of all unfree laborers in 1700.

Having been made possible by racism, slavery replaced indentured servitude for economic reasons. First, it became more difficult to import indentured servants as the seventeenth century advanced, because a gradual decline in England's population

Tobacco Label

The slave's central role in growing tobacco and serving his white master (here enjoying a smoke) is depicted.

Kositzky's Beſt Virginia *LONDON.*

between 1650 and 1700 reduced the number of people willing to emigrate overseas. As England's population decreased, labor became more valuable at home, and wages rose by about 50 percent. Second, before 1690 the Royal African Company, which held a monopoly on selling slaves to the English colonies, shipped nearly all its cargoes to the West Indies, a situation that left few blacks available for sale to the Chesapeake. During the 1690s this monopoly was broken, and rival companies soon expanded the supply of slaves. Large shipments of Africans then began reaching the Chesapeake.

The emergence of slavery relaxed the economic strains within white society that had helped precipitate Bacon's Rebellion. Gradually after 1690, nonslaveowning whites came to see themselves as sharing a common interest with upper-class planters in maintaining social control over a black race regarded as alien and threatening. Slavery's establishment as the principal form of labor in the Chesapeake was part of a larger trend among England's plantation colonies, one that began in the Caribbean and spread to the new mainland colony of Carolina.

THE SPREAD OF SLAVERY: THE CARIBBEAN AND CAROLINA

Simultaneously with the expansion of European colonization in mainland North America, a second wave of settlement swept the West Indies. Between 1630 and 1642 almost 60 percent of the seventy thousand English who emigrated went to the Caribbean or to the Western Atlantic provisioning base at Bermuda.

The English West Indies strongly influenced English North America. The Caribbean islands became the major market for New England's surplus foodstuffs, dried fish, and lumber. In the 1640s the English West Indians began adapting their economy to large-scale slave labor and devising a code of social conduct for nonwhites. In this way, the West Indies pioneered techniques of racial control that would later appear in the mainland colonies' plantation societies.

After 1660 a large outmigration of English islanders added significantly to English North America's population. Most of the migrants went to the Chesapeake and to Carolina, thereby introducing the habits

and prejudices of plantation slaveholding, as well as some slaves, to the mainland colonies. By 1710, the population of Carolina, like that of the Caribbean colonies, was predominantly black and enslaved.

The Chaotic Caribbean

In the sixteenth century, Spain claimed all the Caribbean, but the Spanish eventually concentrated on holding the four largest islands: Hispaniola, Puerto Rico, Cuba, and Jamaica. Successful English and French colonies appeared in the Caribbean only after Spain and the Dutch Republic went to war in 1621. Gambling that the Dutch would distract Spain from launching attacks against isolated outposts, English freebooters began seizing islands vacated by the Spanish. St. Kitts (St. Christopher) was first in 1624, and by 1640 the English had established nearly twenty communities from the Bahamas to the waters off Nicaragua. Spanish troops soon destroyed most of these fledgling settlements but left the English entrenched on St. Kitts, Barbados, Montserrat, Nevis, and Antigua. Later, in 1655, Jamaica also fell to an English force. Similarly, the French seized several islands in the Antilles and the western half of Hispaniola, which they called St. Domingue.

Born of war, England's West Indian colonies matured in turmoil. Between 1640 and 1713 every major island but Barbados suffered at least one invasion by Carib Indians, Spaniards, French, or Dutch. After 1680 pirates from the Bahamas menaced English shipping until the Royal Navy exterminated them during the 1720s. Seven slave revolts rocked the English islands prior to 1713, and they left a bitter legacy of racial hatred on the crowded West Indies.

Life in the Caribbean went on amid the constant violence inflicted on Catholic by Protestant, slave by master, and humans by nature. Of the seventy-four settlers who founded Barbados in 1627, only six remained alive just eleven years later. A bubonic-plague epidemic killed an estimated one-third of the islanders from 1647 to 1649. Up to five thousand militiamen (every sixth Englishman in the Caribbean) perished while fighting to capture Jamaica from Spain in the 1650s. Hundreds regularly lost their lives in hurricanes. In 1692 an earthquake killed almost seven thousand Jamaicans out of a population of forty thousand. Malaria and yellow fever never ceased their slaughter. Immigrants usually died less than twenty years after arriving, at about thirty-eight years of age.

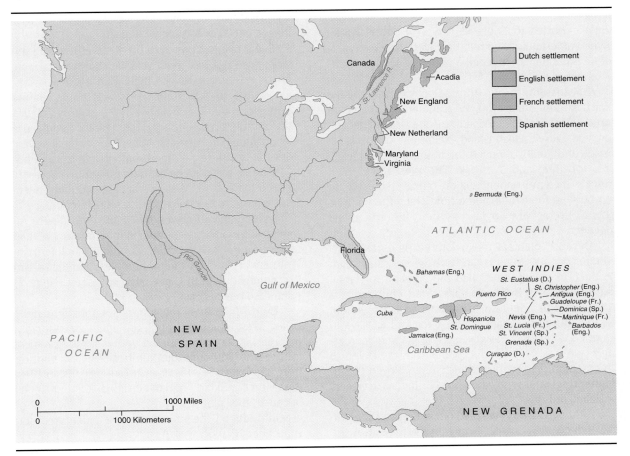

The Caribbean Colonies, 1660

Aside from Jamaica, England's sugar colonies were clustered in the eastern Caribbean's Leeward Islands. Lying within easy reach of seaborne attack, every English island but Barbados was the scene of major fighting.

Sugar and Slaves

As in the Chesapeake, a strong demand for tobacco led the first English settlers in the Caribbean to cultivate that plant almost exclusively. Although low prices inhibited upward mobility, through the 1630s the English West Indies remained a society with a large percentage of independent landowners, an overwhelmingly white population, and no extreme inequality of wealth.

During the early 1640s an alternative to tobacco appeared that rapidly revolutionized the islands' economy and society. Dutch merchants familiar with Portuguese methods of sugar production in Brazil began encouraging English planters to raise and process sugar cane, which the Dutch would then market.

Sugar could make a settler fabulously wealthy because European demand for the new sweetener was virtually unquenchable. But sugar manufacture was also a complex process that required grinding, boiling, refining, and (for rum) distilling the cane immediately after cutting—before it lost its sweetness—and therefore was a very costly venture. Besides a large labor force, a sugar producer needed a mill, several caldrons, a still, and a number of outbuildings. Growing sugar required more capital than ordinary tobacco farmers possessed or could borrow as long as tobacco prices stayed low. Aggressively buying land, a few sugar planters on Barbados closed off opportunity to small farmers by bidding up real-estate prices about 1,000 percent from 1643 to 1650. By 1680 a mere 7 percent of property owners held over half the agricultural acreage on Barbados, which grew 60 percent of the sugar exported to England. A typical sugar planter owned an estate of two hundred acres, whereas most white Barbadians scratched a pitiful living from farms of ten acres or less.

Because the profit from sugar vastly exceeded that from any other crop, West Indian planters soon turned all available acreage into cane fields. They deforested every English island except mountainous Jamaica and greatly reduced the amount of land available for grain and livestock. The West Indies then quickly became dependent on outside sources for lumber and foodstuffs, and a flourishing market thus opened up for New England farmers, fishermen, and loggers.

Because planters needed three times as many workers per acre to raise cane as tobacco, rising sugar production greatly multiplied the demand for labor. Before 1640 West Indians had imported white servants who signed an indenture, or contract, to work without pay for four to six years in return for free passage to America. After 1640, however, sugar planters increasingly purchased enslaved Africans from the Dutch to do common field work and instead employed the indentured servants who came from Britain as overseers or skilled artisans.

Although slavery had died out in England after the eleventh century, English immigrants to the Caribbean quickly copied the example set there by Spanish slaveowners. On Barbados, for example, English newcomers imposed slavery on both blacks and Indians immediately after settling on that island in 1627. The Barbadian government in 1636 condemned every black brought there to life-

long bondage. All other English islanders likewise plunged into slaveowning with gusto.

Sugar planters preferred black slaves to white servants because slaves could be driven harder and maintained less expensively. Unlike European servants, who wilted in the tropics, Africans could endure Caribbean conditions, because they had grown up in a hot, humid climate. Indentured servants could use their contracts to demand decent food, clothes, and housing; but slaves, as mere property, had no rights, and masters could spend the bare minimum necessary to keep them alive. Most servants ended their indentures after four years, just as they were becoming efficient workers, but slaves toiled on until death. Although slaves initially cost two to four times more than servants, they proved a more economical long-term investment. In this way the profit motive and the racism that emerged with the "new slavery" (see Chapter 2) reinforced one another.

By 1670 the sugar revolution had transformed the British West Indies into a predominantly slave society. In 1713 blacks outnumbered whites by a margin of four to one. Although the number of blacks shot up from approximately 40,000 in 1670 to 130,000 in 1713, the white population remained stable at about 33,000 because the planters' preference for slave labor greatly reduced the importation of indentured servants after 1670.

African Slaves Making Sugar

This drawing, published in 1665, shows slaves feeding sugar cane into a cattle-driven mill, which turns it into juice. Other slaves then boil the liquid.

Declining demand for white labor in the West Indies diverted the flow of English immigration from the islands to mainland North America and so contributed to population growth there. Furthermore, because the expansion of West Indian sugar plantations priced land beyond the reach of most whites, perhaps thirty thousand people left the islands from 1655 to 1700. Most whites who quit the West Indies also migrated to the mainland colonies—especially Carolina.

West Indian Society

At the bottom of Caribbean society were the slaves, who lived under a ruthless system of racial control imposed by the islands' European minority through laws known as slave codes. In 1661 Barbados passed the first comprehensive slave code, which served as a model for all colonies in the Caribbean and several on the North American mainland. The Barbados code professed to guarantee decent treatment for slaves (as did certain laws protecting indentured servants), but it failed to define an adequate diet or shelter, aside from requiring masters to furnish each woman with a dress and every man with a pair of pants and a hat. In effect, the code allowed owners to let their slaves run almost naked, house them in rickety shacks, and work them to exhaustion. Moreover, the Barbados code stripped slaves of all legal rights protected under English law. Unlike white servants, slaves could not be tried by juries. The law gave slaves no guarantee of a fair legal hearing and did not even forbid testimony obtained by torture.

In this way, West Indian governments allowed masters almost complete control over their human property. Their laws purposefully placed no limits on how or why a master could punish a slave. As a result, slaves suffered vicious beatings and whippings. If a master killed a slave, he could not be punished unless a jury determined that he acted intentionally, and even then he could only be fined, not jailed or executed. The slave codes effectively legalized assault, battery, manslaughter, and murder.

Slave codes, moreover, left those in bondage defenseless against *all* whites, not just their masters. Slaves could not testify in court against free people. Barbados allowed any ordinary white who caught a slave at large without a pass to give him a "moderate whipping," which could include beatings of up to fifty lashes.

Finally, slave codes attempted to terrorize those in bondage into obedience through cruel and extreme punishments. Judges could order ears sliced off for theft of food, have slaves torn limb from limb for allegedly poisoning masters, and sentence rebels to be burned alive. Heads or other body parts of executed slaves often dangled gruesomely in public places to generate an atmosphere of dread.

Mortality among blacks was especially frightful, even by Caribbean standards. Sugar production required arduous labor, but it was so profitable that planters had little incentive to keep their slaves healthy; they could well afford to replace those killed by overwork. Slaves usually arrived on the islands as men and women in their early twenties, and within ten years most were dead of exhaustion and abuse. So rapidly did the planters wear out field hands that, although they imported 264,000 Africans to the English West Indies before 1700, the slave population stood at just 100,000 in that year.

Despite these appalling conditions, enslaved Africans did what they could to maintain a semblance of normal existence. They were more likely than island whites to start families, since the ratio of male to female slaves neared equality by 1670. (Still, a staggering mortality rate among slave spouses cut most marriages short, and half or more of all slave children died before age five.) In their daily lives, slaves retained much of their native heritage. African music survived in work songs and ceremonial dances and chants, including the mournful laments in which newly arrived Africans grieved over their fate. Very few converted to Christianity; most clung to faith in ancestral spirits, and some committed suicide in the belief that their ghosts would return home. They also re-created African family structures, as well as marriage and funeral customs. In the end the islands' black culture displayed a stronger African imprint than did the African-American way of life that emerged on the North American mainland.

Among white islanders, family cohesion was weak. Because about 80 percent of servants were male, most English settlers led wild lives as bachelors. Not until after 1700 did a sufficient number of white women inhabit the islands to give all white men the option of marriage. Even then high death rates robbed most children of at least one parent well before they reached maturity.

Organized religion withered in the English Caribbean. The majority of churches had no minister, and aside from the small Jewish minority, most whites rarely attended services. English islanders spent far more time in taverns drinking rum (popularly known as Old Kill-Devil) than in church. According to an old Caribbean joke, upon founding a new settlement, the Spanish first constructed a church, the Dutch first built a fort, and the English immediately set up a barroom. If drinking habits on Bermuda in the 1620s were typical, the average English islander consumed well over a gallon of distilled liquor each month.

English residents demonstrated little sense of community. The rich generally hired overseers to manage their estates and retired in luxury to England. The poor left in droves for other colonies. In sum, the English Caribbean was a society of materialistic fortune seekers trying to get rich quickly before death overtook them, and of slaves being worked to death.

The West Indian colonies were the first of England's overseas possessions to evolve into plantation societies. The most extreme examples of labor exploitation, racial subordination, and social stratification could indeed be found in these Caribbean colonies, but a similar pattern of development also characterized English settlements in Chesapeake Bay and in the coastal region known as Carolina.

Carolina: The First Restoration Colony

During the 1650s settlers from New England and the English West Indies established several struggling, unauthorized little outposts along the swampy coast between Virginia and Spanish Florida. In 1663 King Charles II (who had assumed the throne when the Stuart monarchy was restored in 1660) bestowed this unpromising coast on several English supporters, making it the first of several Restoration colonies. The grateful proprietors named their colony Carolina in honor of Charles (*Carolus* in Latin).

Carolina grew haltingly at first. The proprietors organized the existing settlements in the northern part of their domain as a separate district and established a bicameral legislative body for it. Then in 1669 one of the proprietors, Anthony Ashley Cooper, speeded up settlement by offering immigrants fifty-acre land grants for every family member, indentured servant, or slave they brought in. Cooper's action marked a turning point. In 1670 settlement of southern Carolina began when two hundred Barbadian and English settlers landed near modern-day Charleston, "in the very chops of the Spanish." Here, in the settlement they called Charles Town, they formed the colony's nu-

cleus, with their own bicameral legislature distinct from that of the northern district.

Cooper and his secretary—John Locke, later acclaimed as one of the great philosophers of the age—devised an intricate plan for Carolina's settlement and government. Their Fundamental Constitutions of Carolina attempted to ensure the colony's stability by decreeing that political power and social rank should accurately reflect settlers' landed wealth. Thus they invented three orders of nobility, with "proprietors" on top, "landgraves" in the middle, and "caciques" at the bottom. Together this elite would hold two-fifths of all land, make laws through a Council of Nobles, and dispense justice through manorial law courts. Ordinary Carolinians with smaller landholdings were expected to defer to nobility, although they would enjoy religious toleration and the benefits of English common law.

The reality of Carolina's early settlement bore small resemblance to Locke's scheme. New arrivals who could get all the land they needed saw little reason to obey pseudofeudal lords and all but ignored most of the plans drawn up for them across the Atlantic.

Until the 1680s most settlers were small landowners from Barbados or the mainland colonies, along with some French Huguenots. Southern Carolinians raised livestock and exported deerskins and Indian slaves (see below), and colonists in northern Carolina exported tobacco, lumber, and pitch, giving local people the name tarheels. These activities did not at first produce enough profit to warrant maintaining many slaves, and so self-sufficient white families predominated in the area.

But Carolina had not been created so that settlers could merely eke out a marginal existence. Like the first Virginians, southern Carolinians sought a staple crop that could make them rich. By the early 1690s, they found it—rice. The grain was introduced by slaves from Senegambia, where it constituted the basic foodstuff. Because rice, like sugar, enormously enriched a few men with capital to invest in costly dams, dikes, and slaves, it remade southern Carolina into a society resembling that of the West Indies. By earning annual profits of 25 percent, rice planters within a generation became the only colonial elite whose wealth rivaled that of the Caribbean sugar planters.

The Carolina rice planters' huge profits had to be reaped at someone's expense, however. No matter how inhumanly they might be driven, indentured English servants simply could not survive in humid rice paddies swarming with malaria-bearing mosquitoes.

Tuscarora Resistance, 1711
Defending their homeland against an influx of settlers, the Tuscaroras captured Baron Christoph von Graffenried, leader of the Swiss community at New Bern. Graffenried drew this sketch, which depicts him being held along with an English trader, John Lawson, and an African slave. Lawson was later executed.

The planters' solution was to import an ever-growing force of African slaves, who possessed two major advantages for masters. First, perhaps 15 percent of the Africans taken to Carolina had cultivated rice in their homeland, and their expertise was vital in teaching whites how to raise the unfamiliar crop. Second, many Africans had developed partial immunity to malaria, the infectious and deadly disease transmitted by mosquito bites, which was endemic to coastal regions of West Africa and which African-born slaves (and infected slave ships' crews) carried to the New World. (Tragically, the antibody that helps ward off malaria also tends to produce the sickle-cell trait, a hereditary genetic condition often fatal to those children who inherit it.) These two advantages made possible commercial rice production in Carolina. A great demand for black slave labor resulted, for a typical rice planter farming 130 acres needed sixty-five slaves. The proportion of slaves in southern Carolina's population spurted from 17 percent in 1680 to 67 percent in 1720. Carolina was Britain's sole mainland colony with a black majority.

Rice thrived only within a forty-mile-wide coastal strip extending from Cape Fear to present-day Georgia. The hot, humid, marshy lowlands quickly became infested with malaria. Carolinians grimly joked that the rice belt was a paradise in spring, an inferno in summer, and a hospital in the wet, chilly fall. In the worst months, planters' families usually escaped to the relatively cool and more healthful climate of Charles Town and let overseers supervise their harvests.

As long as Europeans outnumbered Africans, race relations could be somewhat relaxed. But as a black majority emerged and swelled, whites increasingly relied on force and fear to control their slaves, adopting many of the galling restrictions and gruesome punishments imposed on slaves in Barbados. Bondage in the mainland colony was becoming as cruel and harsh as in the West Indies.

White Carolinians' attitudes toward Native Americans likewise hardened into exploitation and violence. In the 1670s traders in southern Carolina armed nearby Indians and encouraged them to raid Spanish missions in Florida. These allies captured unarmed Guale, Apalachee, and Timucua Indians at the missions and traded them, along with deerskins, to the Carolinians for guns and other European goods. The English then sold the enslaved Indians, mostly to planters in the West Indies. By the mid-1680s the Carolinians had extended the trade inland through alliances with the Yamasees (Guale Indians who had fled the inadequate protection of the Spanish in Florida) and the Creeks, a powerful confederacy centered in what is now western Georgia and northern Alabama. For three decades these Indians terrorized the Spanish and other Indians in the region with their slave raids. No statistical records of Carolina's Indian slave trade survive, but a recent study estimates that the number of Native Americans enslaved was in the tens of thousands. Once shipped to the West Indies, most died quickly because they lacked immunities to both European and tropical diseases.

Conflict came to northern Carolina in 1711 when the Tuscarora Indians, provoked by white encroachments on their land and by several instances of whites kidnapping Indians as slaves, destroyed New Bern, a frontier settlement of seven hundred Swiss immigrants. Northern Carolina enlisted the aid of southern Carolina and its well-armed Indian allies. By 1713, with a thousand of their people killed or enslaved (about one-fifth of the total population), the Tuscaroras surrendered. Nearly half the survivors eventually migrated to New York, where they became the Sixth Nation of the Iroquois Confederacy.

Having helped defeat the Tuscaroras, Carolina's Indian allies resented a growing number of incidents of cheating, violence, and enslavement perpetrated by English traders, and encroachments on their land by settlers. In 1715 the Yamasees, who were most seriously affected by these incidents, led a coordinated series of attacks on English trading houses and settlements. Only by enlisting the aid of the Cherokee Indians, and allowing four hundred slaves to bear arms, could the colony crush the uprising. Yamasees not killed or captured were driven back to Florida or to the Creek nation.

The first two generations of white settlers and black slaves had cleared the unhealthy coastal regions and developed Carolina's profitable exports. With help from Indian allies, they had extinguished resistance from hostile Native Americans. In realizing these formidable accomplishments, they had received little aid from the faraway proprietors, whose main activities had been grabbing land for themselves, vetoing laws passed by the assemblies, and appointing unpopular governors. Carolinians came to regard the proprietors as indifferent even to their defense. After southern Carolinians overthrew proprietary rule in 1719 (Carolina's fourth major rebellion), the British monarchy intervened and by 1729 created two royal colonies, North Carolina and South Carolina.

THE MIDDLE COLONIES

Between the Chesapeake and New England, a third mainland colonial region, the middle colonies, emerged slowly at first. New Netherland and New Sweden were small commercial outposts, although the Dutch colony began to grow and flourish at midcentury. But in 1664, England seized New Netherland from the Dutch, and in 1681 King Charles II authorized a new colony where New Sweden had stood. These actions resulted in three additional Restoration colonies—New York, New Jersey, and Pennsylvania. By the end of the seventeenth century, the middle colonies composed North America's fastest-growing region.

Precursors: New Netherland and New Sweden

New Netherland became North America's first multiethnic society. Barely half the settlers were Dutch; most of the rest were Germans, French, Scandinavians, and Africans, free as well as enslaved. In 1643 the population included Protestants, Catholics, Jews, and Muslims, and eighteen European and African languages were spoken. But religion counted for little (in 1642 the colony had seventeen taverns but not one place of worship), and the settlers' get-rich-quick attitude had long sapped company profits as private individuals persisted in trading illegally in furs. In 1639 the company bowed to the inevitable and legalized private fur trading.

Privatization led to a rapid influx of guns into the hands of New Netherland's Iroquois allies, giving them a distinct advantage over other natives. As overhunting depleted local supplies of beaver skins and as smallpox epidemics took their toll, the Iroquois encroached on pro-French rival Indians in a quest for pelts and for captives, who could be adopted into Iroquois families to replace the dead. After 1648 the Iroquois, in a series of bloody "beaver wars," dispersed the Hurons and other French allies, incorporating many members of these nations into their own ranks. Then they attacked the French settlements along the St. Lawrence. "They come like foxes, they attack like lions, they disappear like birds," wrote a French Jesuit of the Iroquois.

Although the Dutch allied successfully with the Iroquois, their relations with their nearer Indian neighbors were the worst of any Europeans. With its greedy settlers and military weakness, New Netherland had largely itself to blame. In 1643 all-out war erupted when Dutch forces massacred previously friendly Algonquian-speaking Indians and by 1645 the Dutch could temporarily prevail only with English help and by inflicting terrible atrocities. But the fighting had cut New Netherland's Indian population from sixteen hundred to seven hundred.

Another European challenger dangerously distracted the Dutch in their war with the Algonquians. In 1638 Sweden had planted a small fur-trading colony in the lower Delaware Valley. Trading with the

Delaware (or Lenni Lenape) Indians, New Sweden diverted many furs from New Netherland. Annoyed, in 1655 the Dutch colony's governor, Peter Stuyvesant, marched his militia against New Sweden. The four hundred residents of the rival colony peacefully accepted Dutch annexation. But New Netherland paid dearly for the victory. The Algonquians attacked during the militia's absence, this time destroying many scattered settlements and forcing Stuyvesant to ransom Dutch captives.

Tiny though they were, the Dutch and Swedish colonies were historically significant. New Netherland had attained a population of 9,000 and featured a wealthy, thriving port city by the time it came under English rule in 1664. Even short-lived New Sweden left a mark—the log cabin, that durable symbol of the American frontier, which Finnish settlers in the Swedish colony first introduced to the continent. Above all, the two colonies bequeathed an environment characterized by ethnic and religious diversity that would continue in England's "middle colonies."

English Conquests: New York and the Jerseys

Like Carolina, the English colonies of New York and New Jersey had their origins in the speculative enterprise of Restoration courtiers close to King Charles II. Here too upper-class proprietors hoped to create a hierarchical society in which they could profit from settlers' rents. These plans for the most part failed in New Jersey, as in Carolina. Only in New York did they come close to success.

In 1664, waging war against the Dutch Republic, Charles II dispatched a naval force to conquer New Netherland. Weakened by clashes with local Indians, Dutch governor Peter Stuyvesant and four hundred poorly armed civilians surrendered peacefully. Nearly all the Dutch (including Stuyvesant himself) remained in the colony on generous terms.

Charles II made his brother James, Duke of York, proprietor of the new province and renamed it New York. When the duke became King James II in 1685, he proclaimed New York a royal colony. Immigration from New England, Britain, and France boosted the population from nine thousand in 1664 to twenty thousand in 1700, of whom just 44 percent were descended from the original New Netherlanders.

New York's governors rewarded their most influential political supporters, both Dutch and English, with large land grants. By 1703 five families held approximately 1.75 million acres (about half the area

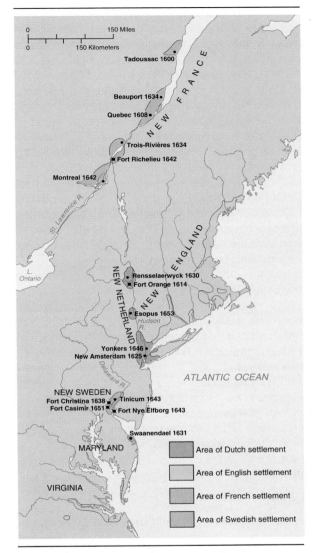

The Riverine Colonies of New France, New Netherland, and New Sweden, c. 1650
So that they could easily buy furs trapped by Indians farther inland, England's imperial rivals located their colonies along major river routes to the interior. The French settled along the St. Lawrence, the Dutch along the Hudson, and the Swedes along the Delaware.

east of the Hudson River and south of Albany), which they withheld from sale in hope of creating manors with numerous rent-paying tenants. Earning an enormous income from their rents over the next half-century, the New York *patroons* (the Dutch name for manor lords) by 1750 formed a landed elite second only in wealth to the Carolina rice planters.

Ambitious plans likewise collided with American realities in New Jersey, which also was carved out of New Netherland. Immediately after the Dutch province's conquest in 1664, the Duke of York awarded New Jersey to a group of proprietors headed by William Penn, John Lord Berkeley, and Sir Philip Carteret. The area at the time was inhabited by about four thousand Delaware Indians and a few hundred Dutch and Swedes. From the beginning the New Jersey proprietors had difficulty controlling their province. By 1672 several thousand New Englanders had settled along the Atlantic shore. After the quarrelsome Puritans renounced allegiance to them, Berkeley and Carteret sold the region to a group of even more contentious religious dissenters, called Quakers, who split the territory into the two colonies of West Jersey (1676) and East Jersey (1682).

East Jersey's new proprietors, a group of mostly Scottish Quakers, could no more successfully work with the local Puritans than had Berkeley and Carteret, and West Jersey's English Quakers squabbled constantly among themselves. The Jerseys' Quakers, Anglicans, Puritans, Scottish Presbyterians, Dutch Calvinists, and Swedish Lutherans got along poorly with each other and even worse with the proprietors. The governments collapsed between 1698 and 1701 as mobs disrupted the courts. In 1702 the disillusioned proprietors finally surrendered their political powers to the crown, which proclaimed New Jersey a royal province.

Quaker Pennsylvania

The noblest attempt to carry out European-born concepts of justice and stability in founding a colony began in 1681. That year Charles II paid off a huge debt by making a supporter's son, William Penn, the proprietor of the last unallocated tract of American territory at the king's disposal. Penn (1644–1718) had two aims in developing his colony. First, he was a Quaker and wanted to launch a "holy experiment" based on the teachings of the radical English preacher George Fox. Second, "though I desire to extend religious freedom," he explained, "yet I want some recompense for my trouble."

Quakers in late-seventeenth-century England stood well beyond the fringe of respectability. They appealed strongly to men and women at the bottom of the economic ladder, and they challenged the conventional foundation of the social order. George Fox, the

The New York Manors and Land Grants
Between 1684 and 1703, English governors awarded most of the best land east of the Hudson River as manors to prominent politicians—the majority of them Dutch—whose heirs became the wealthiest elite in the rural northern colonies.

movement's originator, had received his inspiration while wandering civil war–torn England's byways and searching for spiritual meaning among distressed common people. Tried on one occasion for blasphemy, he warned the judge to "tremble at the word

Abraham Wendell, *by an unknown artist, c. 1737*
The well-to-do Albany patroon *Abraham Wendell is shown standing before his land, stream, and mill.*

of the Lord" and was ridiculed as a "quaker." Fox's followers called themselves the Society of Friends, but the name Quaker stuck. They were among the most radical of the many religious sects born in England during the 1640s and 1650s.

The core of Fox's theology was his belief that the Holy Spirit or "Inner Light" could inspire every soul. Mainstream Christians, by contrast, found any such claim of special communication with God highly suspicious, as Anne Hutchinson's banishment from Massachusetts Bay colony in 1637 had revealed. Although trusting direct inspiration, Quakers also took great pains to ensure that individual opinions would not be mistaken for God's will. They felt confident that they understood Inner Light only after having reached near-unanimous agreement through intensive and searching discussion led by "Public Friends"—ordinary laypeople. In their simple religious services ("meetings"), Quakers sat silently until the Inner Light prompted one of them to speak.

Some of their beliefs led English Quakers to behave in ways that seemed disrespectful to government and the social elite and so aroused fierce hostil-

ity. For example, insisting that individuals deserved recognition for their spiritual state rather than their wealth or family status, Quakers refused to tip their hats to their social betters. For the same reason, they would not use the pronoun *you* (customarily employed when commoners spoke to members of the gentry), instead addressing everyone *thee* and *thou* as a token of equality. By wearing their hats in court, moreover, Quakers appeared to mock the state's authority; and by taking literally Scripture's ban on swearing oaths, they seemed to place themselves above the law. The Friends' refusal to bear arms appeared unpatriotic and cowardly to many. Finally, Quakers accorded women unprecedented equality. The Inner Light, Fox insisted, could "speak in the female as well as the male." A number of fiery Quaker proselytizers were women, including Mary Dyer, a former Antinomian who was exiled to Rhode Island. She helped organize Quaker groups there, and eventually was condemned for sedition and hanged in Massachusetts in 1660.

Not all Quakers came from the bottom of society. The movement's emphasis on quiet introspection and its refusal to adopt a formal creed also attracted well-educated and well-to-do individuals disillusioned by the quarreling of rival faiths. The possessor of a great fortune, William Penn was hardly a typical Friend, but there were significant numbers of merchants among the estimated sixty thousand Quakers in the British Isles in the early 1680s. Moreover, the industriousness that the Society of Friends encouraged in its members ensured that many humble Quakers were already accumulating money and property.

Quakers in England faced intense pressure to conform to the established church, but they throve on persecution. The courts severely fined those absent from Anglican services. Constables commonly collected fines by seizing Quakers' farm tools, equipment, or livestock and by destroying their looms or workbenches. Between 1660 and 1685, fifteen thousand Quakers were jailed, and many others suffered public whippings or facial disfigurements. Through all this adversity, they won a reputation for industriousness, even in prison. Jailed in 1669, William Penn found his fellow Quaker inmates busily engaged at crafts like weaving and spinning and absorbed in prayer during their work breaks. "The jail by that means became a meeting-house and a work-house," Penn proudly wrote, "for *they would not be idle anywhere.*"

Much care lay behind the Quaker migration to Pennsylvania that began in 1681, and it resulted in the most successful initial transplantation of Europeans in any North American colony. Penn sent an advance party to the Delaware Valley, where about five thousand Delaware Indians and one thousand Swedes and Dutch already lived. After an agonizing voyage in which one-third of the passengers died, Penn arrived in 1682. Choosing a site for the capital, he named it Philadelphia—the "City of Brotherly Love." By 1687 some eight thousand settlers had joined Penn across the Atlantic. Most were Quakers from the British Isles, but they also included Presbyterians, Baptists, Anglicans, and Catholics, as well as Lutherans and radical sectarians from Germany—all attracted by Pennsylvania's religious toleration. Because most Quakers immigrated in family groups rather than as single males, a high birthrate resulted, and the population grew rapidly. In 1698 a Quaker reported that in Pennsylvania one seldom met "any young Married Woman but hath a Child in her belly, or one upon her lap."

As planned by its founder, Pennsylvania offered Friends the freedom not only to live diligently but also to make laws according to their ideals. Having experienced persecution, Penn hated intolerance and arbitrary government. Thus in drafting the colony's Frame of Government (constitution), he proposed "to leave myself and my successors [as proprietor] no power of doing mischief, that the will of One man may not hinder the good of the whole company." After wavering between authoritarian and more democratic plans, Penn finally opted for a system with a strong executive branch (a governor and governor's council) and granted the lower legislative chamber (the assembly) only limited powers. Friends, forming the majority of the colony's population, dominated this elected assembly. Penn named Quakers and their supporters as governor, judges, and sheriffs. Hardly a democrat, he feared "the ambitions of the populace which shakes the Constitution," and he intended to check "the rabble" as much as possible. Because he also insisted on the orderly disposition of property and hoped to avoid unseemly wrangling, he carefully oversaw land sales in the colony. To prevent haphazard growth and social turmoil in Philadelphia, Penn designed the city with a grid plan, laying out the streets at right angles and reserving small areas for parks.

Good planning ensured that Pennsylvania suffered no initial "starving time." The colony was also fortunate in experiencing no large-scale wars for seventy years. Partly this resulted from the reduced Native American population in the Delaware Valley. To the Indians, Penn expressed a wish "to live together as Neighbours and Friends," and he tried to buy land fairly from them.

Pennsylvania seemed an ideal colony—intelligently organized, well financed, tolerant, open to all industrious settlers, and largely at peace with the Indians. Rich, level lands and a lengthy growing season produced bumper crops. Sharp West Indian demand for its grain quickly generated widespread prosperity and by 1700 made Philadelphia a major port.

But like other attempts to base new American societies on preconceived plans or lofty ideals, Penn's "peaceable kingdom" soon bogged down in human bickering. In 1684 the founder returned to England to resolve boundary disputes with adjacent Maryland, and in his absence (until 1699) the settlers quarreled incessantly. Although Penn spent much money on his colony, an opposition party attacked his efforts to monopolize foreign trade and to make each landowner pay him a small annual fee. Bitter struggles between Penn's supporters in the governor's council and opponents in the assembly deadlocked the government. From 1686 to 1688, the legislature passed no laws and the council once ordered the lower house's speaker arrested. Penn's brief return to Pennsylvania from 1699 to 1701 helped little, but just before he sailed home, he made the legislature a unicameral (one-chamber) assembly and allowed it to initiate measures.

In addition, religious conflict shook Pennsylvania during the 1690s, when George Keith, a college-educated Public Friend, urged Quakers to adopt a formal creed. This would have changed the democratically functioning Quaker sect—in which the humblest member had equal authority in interpreting the Inner Light—into a more traditional church dominated by an educated clergy. The majority of Quakers rejected Keith's views in 1692, whereupon he joined the Church of England, taking some Quakers with him. Keith's departure began a major decline in the Quaker share of Pennsylvania's population. The proportion fell further once Quakers ceased immigrating in large numbers after 1710.

William Penn met his strongest opposition in the counties on the lower Delaware River, where the best lands had been taken up by Swedes and Dutch. In 1704 these counties gained the right to elect their own legislature, but Penn continued to name their governor. Although the new colony of Delaware's separation temporarily strengthened the proprietor's party in what remained of Pennsylvania, by then the founder's dream of a harmonious society was dashed.

William Penn's Map of Philadelphia, *c. 1681;*
Portrait of Penn, *by Francis Place*
Central to William Penn's master plan for Philadelphia was the idea that each residence should stand in the middle of its plot, encircled by gardens and orchards. This pastel portrait is thought to be the most accurate likeness of Penn extant.

Sadness darkened Penn's last years. Having sunk a fortune into Pennsylvania, he later spent some months in a debtor's prison and died in debt. Long before, he had despaired at having to battle with the legislature's politicians, bent on economic and political advantage. As early as 1685, he begged them, "For the love of God, me, and the poor country, be not so governmentish; so noisy and open in your disaffection."

Despite Penn's anguish, his colony was a solid success. It and the other middle colonies soon demonstrated that British America could benefit by encouraging pluralism. New York and New Jersey successfully integrated New Netherland's Swedish and Dutch population; and Pennsylvania, New Jersey, and Delaware refused to require residents to pay support for any official church. Meanwhile, England's European rivals, France and Spain, were also extending their claims in North America.

RIVALS FOR NORTH AMERICA

In marked contrast to England's compact settlements, France and Spain had established far-flung inland networks of fortified trading posts and missions. To offset the English colonists' superiority in numbers, France and Spain enlisted Native Americans as trading partners and military allies, and the two Catholic nations

had far more success than English Protestants in converting Indians to Christianity. By 1720 missionaries, fur traders, soldiers, and merchants—and relatively few farmers—had spread French and Spanish influence through two-thirds of the present-day United States.

England's rivals exercised varying degrees of control in developing their American colonies. Louis XIV's France, the supreme power in late-seventeenth-century Europe, poured in state resources, whereas Spain, then in deep decay, made little attempt to influence North American affairs from afar. In both cases, local officials and settlers assumed the primary burden for extending imperial control.

France Claims a Continent

France's King Louis XIV (reigned 1661–1715) sought to subordinate his American colony to French interests. His principal adviser, Jean-Baptiste Colbert, was a forceful proponent of the doctrine of *mercantilism* (see Chapter 4), according to which colonies should provide their home country with raw materials it lacked and with markets for its manufactured goods. In this way, the nation would not have to depend on rival countries for trade. Accordingly, Colbert and Louis hoped that New France could increase its output of furs, ship agricultural surpluses to France's new sugar-producing colonies in the West Indies, and export

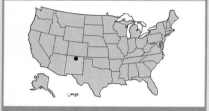

Taos Pueblo, New Mexico, in 1680

Since 1675 Native American leaders from many New Mexico pueblos had gathered regularly at Taos to plan the overthrow of Spanish rule. Hostile to the Spanish from the time of their arrival, Taos had become the center of a wider movement after Popé, a religious leader of San Juan Pueblo, fled there to avoid persecution by the Spanish.

In August 1680 Popé and his cohorts were ready to act. On the morning of August 10, some Taos Indians and their Apache allies attacked the homes of the seventy Spanish colonists residing near Taos and killed all but two. Then, with Indians from neighboring pueblos, they proceeded south and joined a massive siege of New Mexico's capital, Santa Fe. Thus began the Pueblo Revolt of 1680, the most significant event in the history of the colonial Southwest.

Taos's leading role in the revolt is not surprising, for it had long been a meeting-place for Native Americans from near and far and a center of anti-Spanish resistance. Before the Spanish arrived, Taos was a major center of trade between the farming Pueblo Indians and buffalo-hunting Apaches to the north and east. An early Spanish expedition reported some Apaches returning from Taos, "where they sell meat, hides, tallow, suet, and salt in exchange for cotton, blankets, pottery, maize, and some small green stones [turquoise]."

After establishing New Mexico in 1598, the Spanish collected corn as tribute from the pueblos. As a result, Pueblo Indians could no longer send their surplus crops to Taos and other trade centers for exchange with the Apaches. Having come to depend on corn, Apaches now raided pueblos for the grain. When Taos resisted colonial rule in 1602, Spanish troops waged a punitive raid on the pueblo. Four years later, Taos, two other trade centers, and several Apache bands urged the other pueblos to join them in overthrowing the Spanish. But most of the pueblos, fearing the Apaches, responded by strengthening their ties to the Spanish.

For the next seven decades, the Taos Indians struggled to retain their independence from the Spanish. On two occasions they destroyed Franciscan missions in their pueblo, only to watch as the churches were rebuilt under the protection of Span-

Diego de Vargas
Leader of the Spanish reconquest of New Mexico.

ish soldiers. The Taos also maintained their ties with the Apaches. In 1640 some Taos fled to live near friendly Apaches in Kansas, where they remained until Spanish troops forcibly returned them home in 1662. Meanwhile, the Spanish raided Taos and another pueblo where some Apaches lived, slaying all Apache men and enslaving Apache women and children.

For more than half a century, most of the other pueblos tried to accommodate Spanish rule and Catholicism. But during the 1660s they grew disillusioned. For several consecutive years their crops withered under the effects of sustained drought. Drought-induced starvation plus deadly epidemic diseases sent their population plummeting from about 80,000 in 1598 to just 17,000 in the 1670s. Riding horses stolen from the Spanish, Apaches inflicted more damage than ever in their raids. Reeling under the effects of these catastrophes, Christian Indians returned to traditional Pueblo beliefs and ceremonies in hopes of restoring the spiritual balance that had brought ample rainfall, good health, and

Taos Pueblo, North House Block, 1880

peace before the Spanish arrived. Seeking to suppress Pueblo religion as "witchcraft" and "idolatry," missionaries entered sacred, underground kivas, destroyed religious objects, and publicly whipped native religious leaders and their followers.

Matters came to a head in 1675 when Governor Juan Francisco Treviño ordered soldiers to sack the kivas and to arrest the religious leaders. Three leaders were sent to the gallows, a fourth hanged himself, and forty-three others—including Popé— were whipped, jailed, and sentenced to be sold as slaves. In response, armed warriors from several pueblos converged on Santa Fe and demanded the prisoners' release. With most of his soldiers off fighting the Apaches, Governor Treviño complied.

Despite this concession, there was now no cooling of Pueblo resentment against the Spanish. Besides Popé and his Taos host, El Saca, the leaders gathered at Taos included Luis Tupatú, Antonio Mala-

cate, and others whose Christian names signified that earlier they had been baptized. Some were of mixed Pueblo-Spanish ancestry, and one leader, Domingo Naranjo, combined Pueblo, Mexican Indian, and African ancestors. They and many of their followers had attempted to reconcile conversion to Christianity and subjection to Spanish rule with their identities as Indians. But the natives' deteriorating conditions and the cruel intolerance of the Spanish turned them against Catholicism. At each pueblo, rebels destroyed the churches and religious paraphernalia and killed those missionaries who did not escape. Then they "plunge[d] into the rivers and wash[ed] themselves with amole," a native root, in order to undo their baptisms. As a follower later testified, Popé also called on the Indians "to break and enlarge their cultivated fields, saying now they were as they had been in ancient times, free from the labor they had per-

formed for the religious and the Spaniards." In rejecting Christianity and the Spanish, Pueblo Indians from throughout New Mexico did what many Taos had urged them to do for decades.

The siege of Santa Fe led to the expulsion of the Spanish from New Mexico for twelve years. By the time Diego de Vargas, leading the Spanish reconquest, reached Taos in September 1692, most pueblos had already resubmitted to Spanish rule. Suspicious as always of Spanish intentions, the Taos retreated to the mountains until Vargas consented to pardon them. Once returned to their community, ninety-six of them agreed to be baptized, and two leaders told Vargas of a new plot against him. Nevertheless, many Taos people continued to resent the Spanish, and in 1696 they joined Indians from several other villages in an abortive uprising. Thereafter suspicions of the Spanish lingered, but Taos did not again attempt to overthrow them.

timber for those colonies and for the French navy. To begin realizing these goals, they revoked the charter of the private New France Company in 1663 and placed the colony under royal direction. They then sought to stifle the Iroquois threat to New France's economy and to encourage French immigration to Canada.

For more than half a century, and especially since the "beaver wars," the Iroquois had limited New France's productivity by intercepting convoys of beaver pelts from the interior. After assuming control of the colony, the royal government sent fifteen hundred soldiers (most of whom eventually became settlers) to stop Iroquois interference with the French fur trade. In 1666 these troops marched into present-day New York, panicking the local Mohawks into fleeing without a fight. Sobered by the burning of four villages well stocked with winter food, the Iroquois Confederacy made a peace that lasted until 1680. Subsequently, New France enormously expanded its North American fur exports.

Meanwhile, the French crown energetically built up New France's population by dispatching about six hundred settlers each year. About half were indentured servants who received land after three years' work and could marry among the "king's girls," female orphans shipped over with dowries.

But many French male immigrants quickly spurned farming in the St. Lawrence Valley, instead swarming westward in search of furs. By 1670 one-fifth of them were *coureurs de bois*—independent traders unconstrained by government authority or dubious pasts. Living and intermarrying with the Indians, the *coureurs* built for France an empire based on alliances with Canadian and Great Lakes Indians from whom the French exchanged furs for European goods, including guns to use against the Iroquois and other rivals.

Alarmed by the rapid expansion of England's colonies, France then boldly sought to contain the English, as well as to prevent Spain from linking Florida with New Mexico, by dominating the North American heartland. As early as 1672, fur trader Louis Jolliet and Jesuit missionary Jacques Marquette became the first Europeans known to have reached the upper Mississippi River (near modern Prairie du Chien, Wisconsin); they later paddled twelve hundred miles downstream, to the Mississippi's junction with the Arkansas River. Ten years later, the Sieur de La Salle, an ambitious upper-class adventurer, descended the entire Mis-

sissippi to the Gulf of Mexico. When he reached the delta, La Salle formally claimed all the Mississippi basin—half the territory of the present-day continental United States—for Louis XIV, in whose honor he named the territory Louisiana.

Having asserted title to this vast empire, the French began settling the southern gateway into it. In 1698 the first colonizers arrived near the mouth of the Mississippi. A year later, the French erected a fort near present-day Biloxi, Mississippi. In 1702 they occupied what is now Mobile, Alabama, as a fur-trading station.

The Spanish Borderlands

English and French expansion did not go unnoticed by the Spanish. They grew alarmed when La Salle temporarily occupied an outpost near modern-day Houston from 1685 to 1687. To defend their borderland holdings, Spanish authorities in Mexico proclaimed the province of Texas (or Tejas) in 1691. But no permanent Spanish settlements appeared there until 1716 (see Chapter 4).

Spanish preoccupation with New Mexico was a primary reason for this neglect of Texas. By 1680 about 2,300 Europeans—many of them scattered on isolated *ranchos* (ranches)—and 17,000 Pueblo Indians lived in New Mexico's Rio Grande Valley, compared with 80,000 natives in 1598 when the Spanish arrived. That year a Pueblo religious leader named Popé led a revolt, culminating nearly a century of grievances and sparked by Spanish efforts to outlaw the rituals central to the Pueblo peoples' way of life (see "A Place in Time"). The Indians killed 400 colonists (including most priests), captured Santa Fe, and drove the survivors south to El Paso. The Pueblo peoples held New Mexico until 1692, and their resistance continued to threaten Spanish rule until the end of the century.

In Florida, an even older colony than New Mexico, the Spanish fared no better. Before 1680 the colony faced periodic rebellions from Guale, Timucua, and Apalachee Indians protesting forced labor and the religious discipline imposed by Franciscan missionaries. Beginning in the 1680s, Creek and other slave raiders allied to Carolina added to the effects of recurrent diseases in reducing the number of Indians in Florida. When a new round of warfare erupted in Europe at the end of the decade, Spain was ill prepared to defend its beleaguered North American colonies.

CONCLUSION

In less than a century, from 1630 to 1715, European colonization transformed the map of North America. From a series of scattered settlements, Europeans now laid claim to most of the area composing the present-day United States east of the Rocky Mountains. A casual look at a map based on European claims as of 1715 would suggest that France and Spain were the dominant powers, for together they surrounded the seaboard-clinging English by land, from Florida to the Mississippi Valley to Canada. But the demographic and economic reality was quite different. By 1700 the European population of England's North American colonies was about 250,000, compared with 15,000 for the French holdings and 4,500 for the Spanish.

Within the English colonies, several distinct regions had emerged. The southern colonies, emulating the English West Indies, concentrated primarily on the specialized production of plantation crops using slave labor. New England's Puritanism had grown less utopian and more wordly as the inhabitants gradually reconciled their religious views with the realities of a commercial economy. In between New England and the South, the middle colonies, with their ethnic and religious pluralism, embraced the market economy with less hesitation. During the first half of the eighteenth century, these diverse, rapidly expanding colonial regions would be effectively integrated into the first empire in history rooted in commercial capitalism.

CHRONOLOGY

1627	English establish Barbados.
1630	John Winthrop, "A Model of Christian Charity." Massachusetts Bay colony founded.
1630–1660	The great English migration to North America.
1633	First English settlements in Connecticut.
1634	Cecilius Calvert (Lord Baltimore) founds proprietary colony of Maryland.
1635	Roger Williams banished from Massachusetts Bay; founds Providence, Rhode Island, in 1636.
1636	Harvard College established.
1637	Anne Hutchinson tried by Massachusetts Bay colony and banished to Rhode Island. Fequot War.
1638	New Sweden established.
1639	Fundamental Orders of Connecticut.
1640s	Large-scale slave-labor system takes hold in the West Indies.
1642	English Civil War begins.
1643	New Haven colony founded.
1644	Williams obtains permission to establish a legal government in Rhode Island.
1644–1646	Third Anglo-Powhatan War in Virginia.
1649	Maryland's Act for Religious Toleration. King Charles I beheaded. Five Nations Iroquois disperse Hurons.

1651	First New England "praying town" established at Natick, Massachusetts.
1653	First Indian reservation established in Virginia.
1655	New Netherland annexes New Sweden.
1660	Charles II becomes king of England.
1661	Barbados government creates first comprehensive slave code. Maryland defines slavery as a lifelong, inheritable racial status.
1662	Half-Way Covenant drafted.
1663	Carolina founded as English colony. New France made a royal colony.
1664	English conquer the Dutch colony of New Netherland, which becomes the English colony of New York. New Jersey established.
1670	Settlement of southern Carolina begins. Virginia defines slavery as a lifelong, inheritable racial status.
1672	Louis Jolliet and Jacques Marquette explore the Mississippi River.
1675–1676	King Philip's War in New England.
1676	Bacon's Rebellion in Virginia. Quakers organize the colony of West Jersey.
1680–1692	Pueblo revolt in New Mexico.
1681	William Penn founds the Pennsylvania colony.

1682   Quakers organize the colony of East Jersey.

The Sieur de La Salle descends the Mississippi River to the Gulf of Mexico and claims the Mississippi basin for France.

Sieur de La Salle

1690s   Collapse of the Royal African Company's monopoly on selling slaves to the English colonies; large shipments of Africans begin reaching the Chesapeake.

1691   Spain establishes province of Texas.

1692–1693   Salem witchcraft trials.

1698   French begin settlements near the mouth of the Mississippi River.

1711–1713   Tuscarora War in Carolina.

1715–1716   Yamasee War in Carolina.

FOR FURTHER READING

Paul Boyer and Stephen Nissenbaum, *Salem Possessed: The Social Origins of Witchcraft* (1974). A study of the witchcraft episode as the expression of social conflict in one New England community.

William Cronon, *Changes in the Land: Indians, Colonists, and the Ecology of New England* (1983). A pioneering study of the interactions of Native Americans and European settlers with the New England environment.

W. J. Eccles, *France in America,* rev. ed. (1991). An interpretive overview of French colonization in North America and the Caribbean by a distinguished scholar.

Jack P. Greene, *Pursuits of Happiness: The Social Development of Early Modern British Colonies and the Formation of American Culture* (1988). A brilliant synthesis of the colonial history of British America.

Winthrop D. Jordan, *The White Man's Burden: Historical Origins of Racism in the United States* (1974). A brief yet definitive analysis of racism's origins.

Carol F. Karlsen, *The Devil in the Shape of a Woman: Witchcraft in Colonial New England* (1987). An examination of the relationship between witchcraft episodes and gender in New England society.

Edmund S. Morgan, *American Slavery, American Freedom: The Ordeal of Colonial Virginia* (1975). The most penetrating analysis yet written on the origins of southern slavery.

Alan Simpson, *Puritanism in Old and New England* (1955). A good brief introduction to Puritanism.

David J. Weber, *The Spanish Frontier in North America* (1992). A masterful synthesis of Spanish colonial history north of the Caribbean and Mexico.

ADDITIONAL BIBLIOGRAPHY

Early New England

David Grayson Allen, *In English Ways: The Movement of Societies and the Transferral of English Local Law and Custom* (1981); Virginia DeJohn Anderson, *New England's Generation: The Great Migration and the Formation of Society and Culture in the Seventeenth Century* (1991); James Axtell, *The School upon a Hill: Education and Society in Colonial New England* (1974); Bernard Bailyn, *The New England Merchants in the Seventeenth Century* (1955); Emery Battis, *Saints and Sectaries: Anne Hutchinson and the Antinomian Controversy in the Massachusetts Bay Colony* (1962); Sacvan Bercovitch, *The Puritan Origins of the American Self* (1975); Charles L. Cohen, *God's Caress: The Psychology of Puritan Religious Experience* (1986); David Cressy, *Coming Over: Migration and Communication Between England and New England in the Seventeenth Century* (1987); Andrew Delbanco, *The Puritan Ordeal* (1989); John Demos, *A Little Commonwealth: Family Life in Plymouth Colony* (1970), *Entertaining Satan: Witchcraft and the Culture of Early New England* (1982), and *The Unredeemed Captive: A Family Story from Early America* (1994); Stephen Foster, *Their Solitary Way: The Puritan Social Ethic in the First Century of Settlement in New* *England* (1971); Richard Godbeer, *The Devil's Dominion: Magic and Religion in Early New England* (1992); Philip Greven, *Four Generations: Population, Land, and Family in Colonial Andover, Massachusetts* (1970); Philip F. Gura, *A Glimpse of Sion's Glory: Puritan Radicalism in New England, 1620–1660* (1984); David D. Hall, *Worlds of Wonder, Days of Judgment: Popular Religious Belief in Early New England* (1990); Stephen Innes, *Labor in a New Land: Economy and Society in Seventeenth-Century Springfield* (1983); David Thomas Konig, *Law and Society in Puritan Massachusetts, 1629–1692* (1979); Kenneth A. Lockridge, *A New England Town: The First Hundred Years: Dedham, Massachusetts, 1636–1736* (1970); John F. Martin, *Profits in the Wilderness: Entrepreneurship and the Founding of New England Towns in the Seventeenth Century* (1991); Edmund S. Morgan, *The Puritan Dilemma: The Story of John Winthrop* (1958); Carla Gardina Pestana, *Quakers and the Baptists in Colonial Massachusetts* (1991); Darrett B. Rutman, *Winthrop's Boston: A Portrait of a Puritan Town, 1630–1649* (1965); Laurel Thatcher Ulrich, *Good Wives: Image and Reality in the Lives of Women in the Northern New England, 1650–1750* (1982).

The Southern Colonies

Timothy H. Breen and Stephen Innes, *"Myne Own Ground":
Race and Freedom on Virginia's Eastern Shore, 1640–1676*
(1980); Lois Green Carr et al., *Colonial Chesapeake Society*
(1988) and *Robert Cole's World: Agriculture and Society in Early
Maryland* (1990); Carville Earle, *The Evolution of a Tidewater
Settlement Pattern: All Hallow's Parish, Maryland, 1650–1783*
(1975); Ivor Noël Hume, *Martin's Hundred*, rev. ed. (1991);
David W. Jordan, *Foundations of Representative Government in
Maryland* (1988); Daniel C. Littlefield, *Rice and Slavery: Ethnicity and the Slave Trade in Colonial South Carolina* (1981); Glo-
ria L. Main, *Tobacco Colony: Life in Early Maryland, 1650–1720*
(1982); James R. Perry, *Formation of a Society on Virginia's Eastern Shore, 1615–1655* (1990); Darret B. Rutman and Anita S. Rutman, *A Place in Time: Middlesex County, Virginia, 1650–1750*
(1984); Thad Tate and David Ammerman, eds., *The Chesapeake
in the Seventeenth Century: Essays on Anglo-American Society*
(1979); Wilcomb E. Washburn, *The Governor and the Rebel: A
History of Bacon's Rebellion in Virginia* (1957); Robert Weir,
Colonial South Carolina: A History (1983); Peter H. Wood, *Black
Majority: Negroes in Colonial South Carolina from 1670
Through the Stono Rebellion* (1974).

The West Indies

Hilary M. Beckles, *White Servitude and Black Slavery in Barba-
dos, 1627–1715* (1989); Philip P. Boucher, *Cannibal Encounters:
Europeans and Island Caribs, 1492–1763* (1992); Carl Briden-
baugh and Roberta Bridenbaugh, *No Peace Beyond the Line:
The English in the Caribbean, 1624–1690* (1972); Richard S.
Dunn, *Sugar and Slaves: The Rise of the Planter Class in the
English West Indies, 1624–1713* (1972); Richard B. Sheridan,
*Sugar and Slavery: An Economic History of the British West In-
dies, 1623–1775* (1973).

The Middle Colonies

Thomas J. Archdeacon, *New York City, 1664–1710: Conquest
and Change* (1976); Richard S. Dunn and Mary Maples Dunn,
eds., *The World of William Penn* (1986); Joyce D. Goodfriend,
*Before the Melting Pot: Society and Culture in Colonial New
York City, 1664–1730* (1991); Barry Levy, *Quakers and the Amer-
ican Family: British Settlement in the Delaware Valley* (1988);
Donna Merwick, *Possessing Albany, 1630–1710: The Dutch and
English Experiences* (1990); Gary B. Nash, *Quakers and Politics:
Pennsylvania, 1681–1726* (1968); Robert C. Ritchie, *The Duke's
Province: A Study of New York Politics and Society, 1664–1691*
(1977); Oliver A. Rink, *Holland on the Hudson: An Economic
and Social History of Dutch New York* (1986).

French and Spanish Colonies

Donald E. Chipman, *Spanish Texas, 1519–1821* (1992); Louise
Dechêne, *Habitants and Merchants in Seventeenth-Century
Montreal* (1992); W. J. Eccles, *Canada Under Louis XIV,
1663–1701* (1964); Ramón A. Gutiérrez, *When Jesus Came, the
Corn Mothers Went Away: Marriage, Sexuality, and Power in
New Mexico, 1500–1846* (1991); Richard Colebrook Harris, *The
Seigneurial System in Early Canada* (1966).

Indian-European Relations

James Axtell, *The Invasion Within: The Contest of Cultures in
Colonial North America* (1985); Jack D. Forbes, *Apache,
Navaho, and Spaniard* (1960); Francis Jennings, *The Invasion
of America: Indians, Colonialism, and the Cant of Conquest*
(1975); Elizabeth A. H. John, *Storms Brewed in Other Men's
Worlds: The Confrontation of Indians, Spanish, and French in
the Southwest, 1540–1795* (1975); Douglas Edward Leach, *Flint-
lock and Tomahawk: New England in King Philip's War* (1958);
James H. Merrell, *The Indians' New World: Catawbas and Their
Neighbors from European Contact Through the Era of Removal*
(1989); Daniel K. Richter, *The Ordeal of the Longhouse: The
Peoples of the Iroquois League in the Era of European Colonization* (1992); Helen C. Rountree, *Pocahontas's People: The
Powhatan Indians of Virginia Through Four Centuries* (1990);
Neal Salisbury, *Manitou and Providence: Indians, Europeans,
and the Making of New England, 1500–1643* (1982); Richard
White, *The Middle Ground: Indians, Empires, and Republics in
the Great Lakes Region, 1650–1815* (1991).

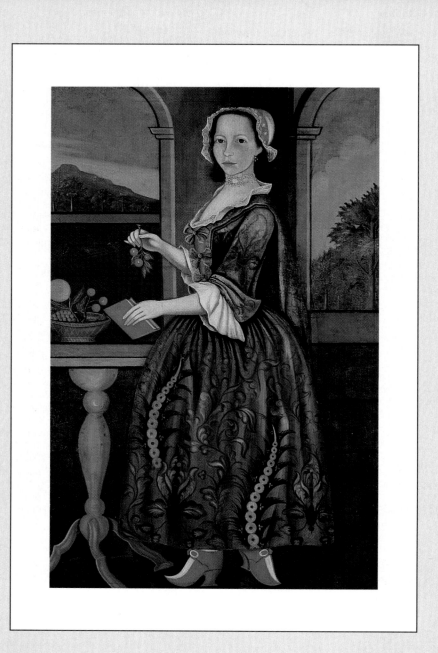

Mrs. Harme Gansevoort (Magdalena Bouw)
by Pieter Vanderlyn, c. 1740

COLONIAL SOCIETY COMES OF AGE
1660–1750

Alexander Garden was furious with the young Anglican minister George Whitefield (inset). Just over from England, Whitefield was stating publicly that Garden's ministers were unsaved and endangering their parishioners' souls. Garden, as the bishop of London's commissary (representative) in Charles Town, South Carolina, was responsible for the Church of England's well-being in the southern British colonies. He thought that he had plenty to contend with already— most pressingly, the numbing indifference of most of his flock—and did not appreciate this impudent outsider's accusations. With Whitefield's descent on the colonies like a hurricane, Garden sensed that 1740 would not be a good year for established religion.

Calling Whitefield in for an interview and demanding that he explain his repeated attacks, Garden got more than he bargained for. Whitefield claimed that Garden "was as ignorant as the rest" of the local clergy because he failed to teach the central Calvinist doctrine of salvation by predestination (see Chapter 2). And Whitefield threatened to speak out against the commissary if Garden refused to condemn dancing and other public entertainments. Garden shot back that Whitefield would be suspended if he preached in any church in the province—to which Whitefield retorted that he would treat such an action as he would an order from the pope. The meeting ended with Garden shouting, "Get out of my house!"

Garden got Whitefield out of his house but not out of his hair. The two men carried their dispute to the public. Garden accused Whitefield of jeopardizing the stability of colonial society. Whitefield accused the Anglican clergy of abandoning Calvinist doctrine in favor of the cold heresy of reason. An extraordinary orator, Whitefield stirred his listeners' passions, calling forth an "enthusiasm" for religion that undermined traditional order and deference. He inspired members of congregations to think themselves as good as, if not superior to, their ministers; wives, to question their husbands' piety; children, to claim divine grace that their parents did not feel; and common people, including slaves and subjugated Indians, to insist that they were the equal of anyone else.

That was Whitefield's greatest crime— to be heard throughout America. He became the first national figure in North America, traveling thousands of miles to spread his critique of the established religious order. Everywhere he went, the people poured out by the thousands to listen and feel, to sense individually the overwhelming power of a direct connection with God.

Sweeping through British North America in the 1740s, Whitefield encountered a vibrant society, a rapidly growing economy, and the beginnings of a richly diverse culture. By 1750 the colonies could claim the world's largest concentration of overseas Europeans; besides those of English stock, significant numbers descended from German, Irish, Scottish, Dutch, and French settlers. North America was also the enforced home of a burgeoning African population, by now slowly becoming both English-speaking and Christian. Geographically, however, the people remained isolated from one another.

Whitefield found it quicker to make the hazardous, disease-ravaged transatlantic voyage than to go overland from New England to Georgia.

A generation of imperial crisis and war with the French from 1685 to 1713 had forged among Anglo-America's whites a strong sense of shared allegiance to the English crown and of deeply felt Protestant heritage. Then, during an era of peace between 1713 and 1744, British Americans' provincialism faced the dual challenge of two vital yet conflicting European cultural currents. The first of these was the Enlightenment—the dissemination among the educated public of faith in reason rooted in an appreciation of natural science—which found its foremost American exponent in Benjamin Franklin. The second current was the religious revival pulsing across Protestant Europe in the 1730s and 1740s, one of whose greatest prophets was George Whitefield. That Franklin and Whitefield became the first two Anglo-American public figures to win fame not only throughout the colonies but also in the entire Western world testifies to America's active participation in the culture of the age.

The peace and prosperity that characterized mid-eighteenth-century British North America would have astonished seventeenth-century colonists, clinging to their uncertain footholds on the edge of the transatlantic wilderness. But even though by 1740 life was becoming reasonably stable and secure, especially for upper-class Anglo-Americans, the Great Awakening let loose spiritual and social tremors that jolted colonial self-confidence. Alexander Garden's nervousness was hardly unreasonable.

RESTORATION AND REBELLION

Although the English had established colonies as early as 1607, with the founding of Virginia, England made no serious effort to weld its colonies into a coherent empire until King Charles II (ruled 1660–1685) assumed the throne. Charles's ascension, marking the "restoration" of the Stuart monarchy in England, ended two decades of civil war and experimentation with re-

publican rule. Almost immediately, English authorities undertook a concerted policy that sought to expand the nation's overseas trade at the expense of its rivals and to subordinate its colonies to English commercial interests and political authority. Efforts to tighten royal control over the colonies ended in 1689 after the "Glorious Revolution" in England forced King James II into exile.

Stuart Policies

After the Restoration, Parliament passed laws collectively known as the Navigation Acts designed to benefit England's commercial interests. Expanding upon a 1651 law, the Navigation Acts of 1660 and 1663 barred colonial merchants from exporting such commodities

The Restoration Colonies
England's Restoration colonies were carved out of the claims or earlier colonial territory of rival European powers. Spain claimed the territory chartered as Carolina in 1663. Out of England's takeover of Dutch New Netherland in 1664 came the colonies of New York, East Jersey, West Jersey, Pennsylvania, and Delaware.

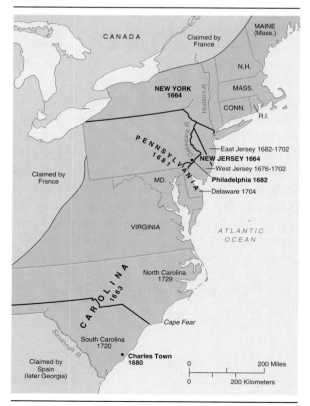

as sugar and tobacco anywhere except to England, and from importing goods in non-English ships. The act of 1672 provided administrative machinery to enforce these rules. The Restoration also set in motion a new wave of colony building that gave England control of the North American coast from Maine to South Carolina (see Chapter 3).

English domestic politics figured prominently in the Restoration government's plans for America. Charles II had clamoring supporters to reward. The Navigation Acts favored powerful commercial interests in England. The king entrusted the creation of the new colonies to important English politicians— the proprietors who organized settlement, oversaw governance (subject to loose control from London), and expected to profit handsomely. But, as earlier in Maryland, their plans collided with the colonists' determination to better themselves.

One of the Restoration's least effective initiatives was an effort to strengthen the Church of England in North America. Lamenting the sorry state of religious affairs in the Chesapeake, an Anglican minister in Maryland in 1660 described that colony as a "Sodom of uncleaness [sic] & a Pest house of iniquity." But because educated English clergy resisted taking American parishes, the reform of American Anglicanism never got very far. Neither did royal attempts to reorganize New England and to impose Anglicanism on its recalcitrant Puritans.

Royal Centralization

As the sons of a king executed by Parliament, the last two Stuart monarchs disliked representative government. Charles II called Parliament into session rarely after 1674, and not at all from 1681 until his death in 1685. James II (ruled 1685–1688) hoped to reign as an "absolute" monarch like France's Louis XIV, who never had to face a national parliament. Not surprisingly, neither English king had much sympathy for the American colonial assemblies.

Royal intentions of extending direct political control to North America first became evident in New York. The proprietor, Charles II's brother James, the Duke of York, considered elected assemblies "of dangerous consequence" and forbade legislatures to meet from 1664 to 1682. He relented from 1682 to 1686 but thereafter called none. Meanwhile, Charles showed a clear preference for naming high-ranking army men as colonial governors. Despite their new civilian status,

these governors were the militia's commanders in chief, and their background made them well suited to crushing civilian dissent with armed force. From 1660 to 1685, Charles appointed former army officers to about 90 percent of all gubernatorial positions, thereby compromising the time-honored English tradition of holding the military strictly accountable to civilian authority. By 1680 such "governors general" ruled 60 percent of all American colonists. James II later continued this policy.

Ever resentful of outside meddling, New Englanders proved most stubborn in defending self-government and resisting Stuart policies. As early as 1661, the Massachusetts assembly politely but firmly declared its citizens exempt from all laws and royal decrees from England except for a declaration of war. The colony ignored the Navigation Acts and continued welcoming Dutch traders. "The New England men break through and . . . trade to any place that their interest lead them," claimed Virginia's governor William Berkeley.

Soon Charles II targeted Massachusetts for special punishment. In 1679 he carved out of its territory a new royal colony, New Hampshire. Then in 1684 he declared Massachusetts itself a royal colony and revoked its charter, the very foundation of the Puritan city upon a hill. Puritan minister Increase Mather responded by openly calling on colonists to resist even to the point of martyrdom.

Royal centralization in America culminated after James II ascended to the throne. In 1686 the new king consolidated Massachusetts, New Hampshire, Connecticut, Rhode Island, and Plymouth into a single administrative unit, the Dominion of New England. He added New York and the Jerseys in 1688. With this bold stroke, all legislatures in these colonies ceased to exist, and still another former army officer, Sir Edmund Andros, became the governor of the Dominion of New England, at Boston.

Massachusetts burned with hatred for the new governor. By "Exercise of an arbitrary Government," preached Salem's minister, "ye wicked walked on Every Side & ye Vilest of men ware [sic] exalted." Andros was indeed arbitrary. He suppressed the legislature, limited towns to a single annual meeting, and jailed prominent citizens to crush protests. Furthermore, Andros hit a raw nerve by forcing a Boston Puritan congregation to share its meetinghouse with an Anglican minister, and he strictly enforced the Navigation Acts. "You have no more privileges left you,"

Andros reportedly told a group of outraged colonists, "than not to be sold for slaves." Other than his soldiers and a handful of recently arrived Anglican immigrants, however, Andros had no base of support in Massachusetts.

Tensions also ran high in New York, where Catholics held high political and military posts under the Duke of York's rule. By 1688 citizens feared that these Catholic officials would betray the colony to France. When Andros's local deputy, Captain Francis Nicholson, allowed the harbor's forts to deteriorate and reacted skeptically to rumors of Indian hostility, New Yorkers suspected the worst.

The Glorious Revolution in England and America

New England Puritans' fury at Andros's forcing them to tolerate Anglicanism was matched by English Protestants' growing worries about the Stuarts' predilection for Catholicism. The Duke of York became a Catholic in 1676, and Charles II converted on his deathbed. Both rulers violated Parliament's laws by issuing decrees that allowed Catholics to hold high office and worship openly. When seven Anglican bishops denounced one such edict in 1688, James II tried them as state enemies. English Protestants' fears that they would have to accept Catholicism intensified after both kings expressed their preference for allying with France just as Louis XIV was launching new persecutions of that country's Protestants in 1685.

The English tolerated James II's Catholicism only because his heirs, his daughters Mary and Anne, had remained Anglican. Then in 1688 James's wife bore a son, who would be raised—and might someday reign—as a Catholic. Aghast at the thought of a Catholic monarchy, some English politicians asked Mary and her husband, William of Orange (the Dutch Republic's leader) to intervene. When William and Mary led a small army to England in November 1688, most royal troops defected to them, and James II fled to France.

This bloodless revolution of 1688, also called the Glorious Revolution, created a "limited monarchy" as defined by England's Bill of Rights of 1689. The crown promised to summon Parliament annually, sign all its bills, and respect traditional civil liberties. The Glorious Revolution's vindication of limited representative government burned deeply into the English political consciousness, and Anglo-Americans never forgot it. Anglo-Americans not only came to share English

King William and Queen Mary
This plate, made in England in about 1700, depicts the monarchs who assumed the throne after the Glorious Revolution.

Protestants' pride in the Glorious Revolution but also struck their own blows for liberty. Soon Massachusetts, New York, and Maryland all rose up against local representatives of the Stuart regime.

News that England's Protestant leaders had risen up against James II electrified New Englanders. On April 18, well before confirmation of the English revolt's success, Boston's militia arrested Andros and his councilors. (The governor tried to flee in women's clothing but was caught after an alert guard spotted a "lady" in army boots.) The "sensible Gentlemen" of Massachusetts—the old political leaders—acted in the name of William and Mary, risking their necks should James return to power in England. Massachusetts and every other New England colony swiftly resumed self-government.

William and Mary would have preferred continuing the Dominion, but in the face of single-minded colonial determination to break it up, they wisely desisted. They gave official consent to dismantling the Dominion and restored to the citizens of Connecticut and Rhode Island the right of electing their own governors. However, they kept Massachusetts a royal colony, and, though allowing the province to absorb Plymouth and Maine, refused to let it regain New Hampshire.

In other respects, too, Massachusetts won only a partial victory. Despite Increase Mather's lobbying in London, the new royal charter of 1691 reserved to the crown the right of appointing the governor. Moreover, property ownership, not church membership, became the criterion for voting. Worst of all, the Puritan colony had to tolerate Anglicans, who were proliferating in the port towns. In a society trembling at divine displeasure over its ungodliness (see Chapter 3), this was indeed bitter medicine to swallow.

New York's counterpart of the anti-Stuart uprising was Leisler's Rebellion. Emboldened by news of Boston's April 18 coup and startled by rumors that Andros's deputy Nicholson had threatened to burn New York, the city's militia—consisting mainly of Dutch and other non-English artisans and shopkeepers—seized the harbor's main fort on May 31, 1689. With his authority strangled, Nicholson sailed for England. Captain Jacob Leisler of the militia took over command of the colony, repaired its run-down defenses, and called elections for an assembly. When English troops arrived at New York in 1691 and Leisler denied them entry to key forts for fear that their commander was loyal to James II, a skirmish resulted, and Leisler was arrested.

"Hott brain'd" Leisler unwittingly had set his own downfall in motion. He had jailed many elite New Yorkers for questioning his authority, only to find that his former enemies had gained the new governor's ear and persuaded him to charge Leisler with treason for firing on royal troops. In the face of popular outrage, a packed jury found Leisler and his son-in-law, Jacob Milborne, guilty. Both men went to the gallows insisting that they were dying "for the king and queen and the Protestant religion."

Quickly wresting control of the council and legal system, Leisler's enemies used the courts to plunder their opponents' estates. Their rampage ceased in 1695, when Parliament reversed Leisler's and Milborne's convictions and ordered them reburied with full honors. Leislerians and their opponents fought ruthlessly to defeat each other; but not until most of their leaders had died, in about 1720, did Jacob Leisler's vengeful ghost cease stalking New York.

News of England's Glorious Revolution heartened Maryland's Protestant majority, which had long chafed under Catholic rule. Hoping to prevent a repetition of religion-tinged uprisings that had flared in 1676 and 1681, Lord Baltimore sent a messenger from England in early 1689 to command Maryland's obedience to William and Mary. But the courier died en route. The colony's Protestants widely began to fear that their proprietor was a traitor who supported James II.

Soon John Coode, a leader of the 1681 revolt, and three others organized the Protestant Association to secure Maryland for William and Mary. These conspirators seem to have been motivated far more by their exclusion from high public office than by religion, for three of the four had Catholic wives. Coode's group seized the capital in July 1689, removed all Catholics from office, and requested that the crown take over the colony. They got their wish. Maryland became a royal province in 1691, and in 1692 it made the Church of England the established religion. Catholics, who composed less than one-fourth of the population, lost the right to vote and thereafter could worship only in private. Maryland stayed in royal hands until 1715, when the fourth Lord Baltimore joined the Church of England and regained his proprietorship.

The revolutionary events of 1688–1689 decisively changed the colonies' political climate by reestablishing legislative government and ensuring religious freedom for Protestants. Dismantling the Dominion of New England and directing governors to call annual assemblies, William and Mary allowed colonial elites to reassert control over local affairs and encouraged American political leaders to identify their interests with England. A foundation was thus laid for an empire based on voluntary allegiance rather than submission to raw power imposed from faraway London. The crowning of William and Mary opened a new era in which Americans drew rising confidence from their relationship to the English throne. "As long as they reign," wrote a Bostonian who helped topple Andros, "New England is secure."

A Generation of War

The Revolution of 1688 ushered in a quarter-century of warfare that convulsed both Europe and the colonies. In 1689 England joined a general European coalition against France's Louis XIV, who supported James II's claim to the English crown. The resulting War of the League of Augsburg (which Anglo-Americans called King William's War) was the first struggle to embroil the colonies in European rivalries.

With the outbreak of King William's War, New Yorkers and Yankees launched a two-pronged invasion of Canada (New France) in 1690, with one prong aimed at Montreal and the second at Quebec. Lack of supplies caused the Anglo-American expedition marching on Montreal to disintegrate in the New York wilderness. Meanwhile, their strength sapped by smallpox, half-rations, and insufficient ammunition, two thousand Massachusetts militiamen eventually abandoned a lengthy siege of Quebec. The war then took the form of cruel but inconclusive border raids against civilians on both sides, carried out by English and French troops and their Indian allies.

Already weary from a new wave of wars with pro-French Indians in the Ohio Valley, the Five Nations of the Iroquois bore the bloodiest fighting in King William's War. Standing almost alone against their foes, the Five Nations faced overwhelming odds. Not only did their English allies meet with little success intercepting enemy war parties, but the French had enlisted virtually all other Indians from Maine to the Great Lakes as combatants. In 1691 every Mohawk and Oneida war chief died in battle; by 1696 French armies had destroyed the villages of every Iroquois nation but the Cayugas and Oneidas.

Although the Anglo-French war ended in 1697, the Iroquois staggered under Algonquian invasions until 1700. By then one-quarter of the Five Nations' 2,000 warriors had been killed or taken prisoner, or had fled to Canada. The total Iroquois population declined 20 percent over twelve years, from 8,600 to 7,000. (By comparison, fewer than 900 English and Dutch, and perhaps no more than 400 French, died during the same period.)

By 1700 Iroquois society was divided into three factions—pro-English, pro-French, and neutralists. Under the impact of war, the neutralists succeeded in defining a new direction for Iroquois diplomacy. In the "Grand Settlement" of 1701, the Five Nations of the Iroquois made peace with France and its Indian allies in exchange for access to western furs while redefining their British alliance to exclude military cooperation. Skillful negotiations brought the exhausted Iroquois far more success than had war by allowing them to keep control of their lands, rebuild their decimated population, and gain recognition as holding the balance of power in the Northeast.

In 1702 European war again erupted when England fought France and Spain in the War of the Spanish Succession, called Queen Anne's War by England's American colonists. This conflict taught Anglo-Americans painful lessons about their military weakness. French and Indian raiders from Canada destroyed several towns in Massachusetts and Maine. The Spanish invaded southern Carolina and nearly took Charles Town in 1706. Enemy warships captured many colonial vessels and landed looting parties along the Atlantic coast. Colonial sieges of Quebec and St. Augustine ended as expensive failures.

English forces had more success than those of the colonies, seizing the Hudson Bay region, as well as Newfoundland and Acadia (henceforth called Nova Scotia). Although Britain kept these gains in the peace of 1713, the French and Indian hold on the continent's interior remained unbroken.

The most important consequence of the colonial wars for Anglo-Americans was political, not military. The wars instilled in them a profound sense of dependence on Great Britain. The clashes with France vividly reminded Americans of the loyalty they owed William and Mary for ousting James II, who the colonists believed would have persecuted Protestants and ruled despotically. Anglo-Americans also came to recognize their own military weakness and the extent to which their shipping needed the Royal Navy's protection. Even as a new generation of English colonists matured, war was thus reinforcing their sense of British identity by buttressing their loyalty to the crown.

A MATURING COLONIAL ECONOMY AND SOCIETY

Britons who visited mid-eighteenth-century America were generally impressed at the sight of a sophisticated society and widespread economic prosperity. "The nobleness of the town," wrote an English naval officer after first viewing New York in 1756, "surprized me more than the fertile appearance of the country. I had no idea of finding a place in America, consisting of near 2,000 houses, elegantly built of brick, raised on an eminence and the streets paved and spacious, . . . but such is this city that very few in England can rival it in its show." Seven years later, when issuing orders for demobilizing royal troops stationed in the colonies, General Jeffrey Amherst advised his regimental commanders to discourage their men from returning to the British Isles to be mustered out because "I would much rather they would take their Discharges in this country, where they can get their Livelyhood by working Easier than at Home."

The prosperity and social development that European visitors recorded, as well as the underlying rapid population growth and wide expansion of frontier settlement, were relatively new. By 1750 the colonies' brisk economic growth had been underway for fifty to seventy-five years, depending on the region. Throughout the first half of the eighteenth century, colonial exports climbed steadily and allowed Anglo-Americans to enjoy a relatively high standard of living because of protections established by Parliament.

British Economic Policy Toward America

Between 1651 and 1733, Parliament enacted a series of laws governing commerce between the British Isles and the overseas colonies. Historians label the rules of trade set forth in these laws the "navigation system," and they use the word *mercantilism* to describe the assumptions on which these laws rested. Both the navigation system and mercantilist thinking remained vigorously alive from the late seventeenth to the late eighteenth century, and they deeply affected North America's relationship with Great Britain.

Mercantilism was not a carefully elaborated economic theory. Rather, the word refers to European policy makers' aim of guaranteeing prosperity by making their own country as self-sufficient as possible—by eliminating dependence on foreign suppliers, damaging foreign competitors' commercial interests, and increasing their nation's net stock of gold and silver by selling more abroad than they bought. Mercantilist policies generally had the additional effect of favoring special interests such as chartered companies and merchants' guilds. Mercantilism was the antithesis of a competitive free-market system, which received its first great theoretical defense in Scottish economist Adam Smith's *The Wealth of Nations*, published in 1776. Until that revolutionary year, mercantilist thinking would dominate British economic policy almost unchallenged.

Parliament enacted England's first Navigation Act in 1651 to undercut the Dutch Republic's economic preponderance. Dutch shippers and merchants then controlled oceanic trade and probably owned three-quarters of northern Europe's commercial vessels; few English could compete with the well-financed and experienced Dutch traders. By the Navigation Acts, Parliament sought to exclude the Dutch from English trade and thereby to force England to build up its own merchant marine. Immediately after the Stuart restoration in 1660, Parliament reiterated these rules and also began protecting English manufactures from foreign competition. By 1750 a long series of Navigation Acts were in force, affecting the colonial economy in four major ways.

First, the laws limited all imperial trade to *British* ships, defined as those with British ownership and whose crews were three-quarters British. For purposes of this legislation, Parliament classified all colonists, including slaves, as British. When Parliament began strictly to enforce this requirement in the late seventeenth century, American colonists and some elements of the English business community alike objected, because the Dutch offered better prices, credit, and merchandise. After 1700, however, when Britain's merchant marine became equal to its Dutch competitors, this cause for complaint evaporated.

This new shipping restriction not only contributed to Great Britain's rise as Europe's foremost shipping nation but also laid the foundations for an American merchant marine. By the 1750s one-third of all imperial vessels were American-owned, mostly by merchants in New England and the middle colonies. The swift growth of this merchant marine diversified the northern colonial economy and made it more self-sufficient. The expansion of colonial shipping in turn hastened urbanization by creating a need for centralized docks, warehouses, and repair shops in America. By 1770 Philadelphia was the British Empire's second-largest port, after London, and New York City was not far behind. Shipbuilding emerged as a major colonial industry in these years, and by 1770 one-third of the "British" merchant marine was actually American-built.

The second major way in which the Navigation Acts affected the colonies lay in their barring the export of certain "enumerated goods" to foreign nations unless these items first passed through England or Scotland. The mainland's chief "controlled" items were tobacco, rice, furs, indigo (a Carolina plant that produced a blue dye), and naval stores (masts, hemp, tar, and turpentine). Parliament never restricted grain, livestock, fish, lumber, or rum, which altogether made up 60 percent of colonial exports. Furthermore, American exporters of tobacco and rice—the chief commodities affected by enumeration—had their burdens reduced by two significant concessions. First, Parliament gave Americans a monopoly over the British market by excluding foreign tobacco, even though this hurt the British consumers. (Rice planters enjoyed a natural monopoly because they had no competitors.) Second, Parliament tried to minimize the added cost of landing tobacco and rice in Britain (where customs officials collected duties on both) by refunding these duties on all tobacco and rice that the colonists later shipped to other countries. About 85 percent of all American tobacco and rice was eventually reexported and sold outside the British Empire.

The navigation system's third impact on the colonies was to encourage economic diversification in America. Parliament used British tax money to pay modest bounties to Americans producing such items as silk, iron, dyes, hemp, and lumber, which Britain would otherwise have had to import from other countries, and it raised the price of commercial rivals' imports by imposing protective tariffs on them.

On the surface, the trade laws' fourth consequence for the colonies was negative: they forbade Americans from competing with British manufacturers. In practice, however, this prohibition had little effect, for it banned only *large-scale* manufacturing of certain products, most notably clothing; colonial tailors, hatters, and housewives could continue to make any item of dress in their households or small shops. Manufactured by low-paid labor, British clothing imports to America generally undersold whatever the colonists could have produced at their higher labor costs. For this reason, Americans failed to establish a profitable clothing industry until after 1820. The colonists were free to produce iron, however, and by 1770 they had built 250 ironworks employing thirty thousand men, a work force larger than the entire population of Georgia or of any provincial city. At the American Iron Company's complex of eleven forges and furnaces near Ringwood, New Jersey, five hundred workers manned eleven furnaces that annually consumed eight square miles of timber as fuel. By 1770 British North America produced more iron than England and Wales, and only Sweden and Russia exceeded the colonies' output.

Colonial complaints against the navigation system raged in the late seventeenth century but rarely were heard after 1700. The trade regulation primarily burdened tobacco and rice exporters, whose income nevertheless was reduced by less than 3 percent. The commercial laws did increase the cost of non-British merchandise imported into the colonies, but seldom by enough to encourage smuggling (except in the case of tea from India and molasses from the French Caribbean). Anglo-American commerce provided mu-

tual advantages for Britain and its colonies, and when Americans lost their trading rights in 1783, their commerce declined greatly. Although Parliament intended the laws to benefit only Britain, the navigation system had far from crippled the provincial economy. Rather, British North America's economy grew at a per capita rate of 0.6 percent annually from 1650 to 1770, a pace twice that of Britain.

A Burgeoning, Diversifying Population

In 1751 Pennsylvania businessman, publicist, and scientist Benjamin Franklin (1706–1790) wrote in an essay, *Observations Concerning the Increase of Mankind and the Peopling of the Colonies*, that "people increase in proportion to the number of marriages, and that is greater in proportion to the ease and convenience of supporting a family. When families can be easily supported, more persons marry, and earlier in life." Cities, he noted, retarded such growth: they were unhealthy and contained many people too poor to marry and rear families. But British America, with its small cities and great expanses of rural space, clearly seemed destined to grow and flourish. Estimating the colonies' population at 1 million, Franklin calculated that this number would double every twenty-five years. He exulted, "What an accession of power to the British empire!" Franklin knew whereof he spoke: he was the tenth child among seventeen siblings. He estimated colonial growth trends with amazing precision, and modern research has confirmed his reasoning about the factors driving population change in his era.

After 1700, when life expectancy and family size in the South rose to levels typical of the North, British North America's growth rate far outpaced Great Britain's. Colonial women had an average of eight children and forty-two grandchildren; British women at the time typically bore five infants and had fifteen grandchildren. The ratio of England's population to that of the mainland colonies plummeted from 20 to 1 (1700) to 3 to 1 (1775).

Fully half of all colonial women bore more than eight children. This exceptionally high birthrate produced families like that of New Jersey resident Daniel Robbins, described in the *New England Weekly Journal* in 1733. By the time Robbins was 66, his wife had 13 children, of whom 11 had married and borne 62 offspring of their own. None of the Robbins's descendants had yet died, and more grandchildren were on the way. "Thus it appears," the *Weekly Journal* declared, "that said Daniel Robbins has successfully kept and fulfilled that great and necessary Commandment of *Multiply, be Fruitful,* and *Replenish the Earth.*" Such remarkable fertility was responsible for two-thirds of colonial population growth after 1700.

In the eighteenth century, immigration continued to contribute significantly to colonial population growth, although it became less important than natural increase. In the forty years after Queen Anne's War, the colonies absorbed 350,000 newcomers, 40 percent of them (140,000) African-born slaves who had survived a sea crossing of sickening brutality. All but a few enslaved immigrants originated along the west coast of Africa between Senegambia and Angola. Whereas most planters made few distinctions as to Africans' backgrounds, many in South Carolina expressly sought slaves from Gambia and nearby regions for their rice-growing experience.

Conditions aboard slave ships were appalling by any standard. Olaudah Equiano was an enslaved Ibo from the area that today is Nigeria. Equiano, who eventually became free, Christian, and an abolitionist, recalled being put aboard a Barbados-bound ship in 1756:

> *I was soon put down under the decks, and there I received such salutation in my nostrils as I had never experienced in my life; so that, with the loathsomeness of the stench, and crying together, I became so sick and low that I was not able to eat, nor had I the least desire to taste any thing. . . . On my refusing to eat, one of them [white men] held me fast by the hands, and laid me across I think the windlass while the other flogged me severely. . . . Could I have got over the nettings, I would have jumped over the side, but I could not.*

The approximately 210,000 whites who immigrated during these years included a sharply reduced share from England compared to the seventeenth century. Whereas between 1630 and 1700 an average

Architect's Plan of a Slave Ship
This plan graphically depicts the crowded, unsanitary conditions under which slaves were transported across the Atlantic.

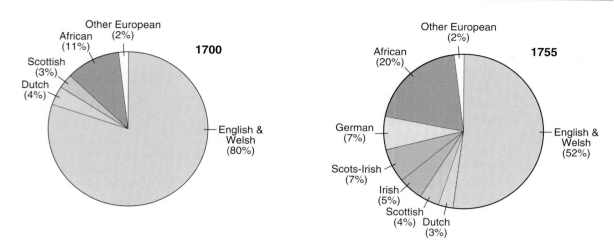

Distribution of Non-Indian Nationalities Within the British Mainland Colonies, 1700–1755

The impact of heavy immigration from 1720 to 1755 can be seen in the reduction of the English and Welsh stock from four-fifths of all colonists to a slight majority; in the doubling of the African-American population; and in the sudden influx of Germans and Irish, who together composed a fifth of all Anglo-Americans by 1755. For a more detailed breakdown of African origins, see the map on page 109.

SOURCE: Thomas L. Purvis, "The European Ancestry of the United States Population," *William & Mary Quarterly*, LXI (1984): 85–101.

of 2,000 English settlers landed annually (constituting 90 percent of all European immigrants), after 1713 the English contribution dropped to about 500 a year. Rising employment and higher wages in eighteenth-century England simply made voluntary immigration to America far less attractive than before. But economic hardship elsewhere in the British Isles and northern Europe supplied a steady stream of immigrants, and their coming ensured that white North Americans were growing more ethnically diverse.

The largest European contingent comprised 100,000 newcomers from Ireland, two-thirds of them "Scots-Irish" descendants of sixteenth-century Scottish Presbyterians who had settled in northern Ireland. After 1718 Scots-Irish fled to America to escape rack renting (frequent increases in farm rents), and they commonly came as complete families. In contrast, 90 percent of all Catholic Irish immigrants arrived as unmarried male indentured servants. Rarely able to find Catholic wives, they generally abandoned their faith to marry Protestant women.

Meanwhile, from Germany came a wave of 65,000 settlers, most of them refugees from terrible economic conditions in the Rhine Valley. Wartime devastation had compounded the misery of Rhenish peasants, many of whom were squeezed onto plots of land too small to feed a family. One-third of these people financed their voyage as "redemptioners"—that is, they had sold themselves or their children as indentured servants.

Most Germans were either Lutherans or Calvinists. But a significant minority belonged to small, pacifist religious sects that desired above all to be left alone.

Overwhelmingly, the eighteenth-century immigrants were poor. Those who became indentured servants had to give one to four years of work to an urban or rural master, who might well exploit them cruelly. Servants could be sold or rented out, beaten, granted minimal legal protection, kept from marrying, and sexually harassed; and attempted escape usually meant an extension of their service. But at the end of their term, most managed to collect "freedom dues," which could help them to marry and acquire land.

Few immigrants settled permanently in those parts of North America where land was relatively scarce and expensive—New England, New Jersey, lower New York, and the southern tidewater. New Englanders in particular did not welcome people who might become public charges: "these confounded Irish will eat us all up," snorted one Bostonian. Philadelphia became the immigrants' primary port of entry. So many foreigners went to Pennsylvania that by 1755 the English accounted for only one-third of that colony's population; the rest were mostly Germans, and Scots-Irish.

Rising numbers of immigrants also traveled to the piedmont region, stretching along the eastern slope of the Appalachians. A significant German community developed in upper New York, and thousands of other

Immigration and Frontier Expansion, to 1755

A sharp rise in the importance of African slaves made much of the southern tidewater a predominantly black region. Immigrants from Germany, Ireland, and Scotland tended to settle in the piedmont. A significant Jewish population emerged in the seaports.

Germans as well as Scots-Irish fanned southward from Pennsylvania into western Maryland. Many more from Germany and Ireland arrived in the second-most popular gateway to eighteenth-century America, Charles Town, whence they moved on to settle the Carolina piedmont. There they raised grain, livestock, and to-

bacco, generally without slaves. After 1750 both streams of immigration merged with an outpouring of Anglo-Americans from the Chesapeake in the rolling, fertile hills of western North Carolina. In 1713 few Anglo-Americans had lived more than fifty miles from the sea, but by 1750 one-third of all colonists resided in the piedmont.

English-descended colonists did not relish the influx of so many foreigners. Franklin spoke for many when he asked in his 1751 essay on population,

> *why should the Palatine boors [Germans] be suffered to swarm into our settlements, and, by herding together, establish their language and manners, to the exclusion of ours? Why should Pennsylvania, founded by the English, become a colony of aliens, who will shortly be so numerous as to Germanize us instead of us Anglicizing them, and will never adopt our language or customs any more than they can acquire our complexion?*

In the same ungenerous spirit, Franklin objected to the slave trade largely because it would increase America's black population at the expense of industrious whites.

On another occasion, Franklin suggested that the colonists send rattlesnakes to Britain in return for the convict laborers dumped on American shores. Deportation of lawbreakers to America had been common enough in the seventeenth century, and between 1718 and 1783, some thirty thousand convicts arrived. A few were murderers; most were thieves; some were guilty of the most trivial offenses, like a young Londoner who "got intoxicated with liquor, and in that condition attempted to snatch a handkerchief from the body of a person in the street to him unknown. . . ." Convicts were sold as servants on arrival. Relatively few continued to commit crimes in America, and some managed eventually to establish themselves as backcountry farmers. But like many contemporary Americans, colonists seldom wished to absorb the victims of other nations' social problems.

Eighteenth-Century Living Standards

Propelled by a tenfold increase in the volume of exports, colonial living standards in general rose dramatically in the years from 1700 to 1770. Nowhere was Americans' newfound prosperity more evident than in the Chesapeake, which in the late seventeenth century had been a region of impoverished tenants battered by depressed tobacco prices. Not only did tobacco exports triple from 1713 to 1774, but prices slowly crept upward, in large part owing to a 75 percent reduction in marketing costs. The Chesapeake economy further benefited from sharply higher exports of wheat and corn, which by 1770 equaled 25 percent of tobacco sales. Thus within three generations of Bacon's Rebellion, the Chesapeake had ceased to be a region locked in pervasive poverty.

Poverty was the lot mainly of slaves and of a small underclass of whites attempting to farm marginal-quality soil. At the same time, a landholding small-planter element arose, so large that perhaps 30 percent of all white families owned slaves. Atop Chesapeake society, moreover, an elite of wealthy large landowners and slavemasters flourished after about 1700.

Living standards were highest in the mid-Atlantic, spanning the area from New York south to Delaware. In 1770 per capita wealth here exceeded the colonial average by 40 percent. These colonies' striking prosperity owed much to rich soils, a long-term climatic warming that lengthened the growing season after 1700, and brisk demand for livestock, wheat, and corn in the West Indies and (to a lesser extent) southern Europe.

Of all colonial regions, New England prospered least. Though hardly poor, Yankees were on average only half as wealthy as colonists elsewhere. Plagued by mediocre soil and a short growing season, New Englanders had to import grain to feed themselves. Yankees sent two-thirds of their livestock, lumber, and fish exports to the West Indies, and although their cattle raising remained profitable, a long-term decline in lumber prices stung the local economy. By the 1750s most New England towns had become overpopulated, bursting with more young men than could acquire enough land to support a family. In subsequent decades only migration to the frontier—to Vermont, Maine, Nova Scotia, Pennsylvania, and upper New York—would ease the pressure.

Many New Englanders survived economically by turning to the sea. By 1700 the Yankee merchant marine and fishing industry were the largest in the colonies, providing employment for every seventh man. This prosperity came at a heavy cost, however, for the sea was cruel and took perhaps every fifth sailor to a watery grave. For this reason, the balcony on a ship captain's home from which his wife could watch for her husband's return to harbor became known as the widow's walk.

Taken as a whole, the American colonies by the mid-eighteenth century enjoyed a standard of living that greatly exceeded that of Scotland or Ireland and approximated that of England and Wales. Steady overseas demand for colonial products spawned a prosperity that enabled Americans to consume a huge volume of British products. Consequently, the share of British exports sold to the colonies spurted from just 5 percent in 1700 to almost 40 percent by 1760. "You may depend upon it," remarked Pennsylvania judge William Allen in commenting on prospects for self-improvement, "this is one of the best poor man's countries in the world."

Rural Men and Women

Although the benefits of rising living standards were widespread, the colonial population enjoyed these advantages unevenly. With few exceptions—Benjamin Franklin is the best known—true affluence was reserved for those born wealthy. For the rest, personal success was limited and came only through hard work, if at all.

Because the vast majority of landowners had just enough acreage for a working farm, they could not provide their children with land of their own when they married. Moreover, since couples typically started having children in their mid-20s, had their last babies sometime after 40, and lived past 60, all but their youngest children would be approaching middle age before receiving any inheritance. Even children who obtained inheritances before turning 30 rarely got more than a sixth or seventh of their parents' estate, because most families wrote wills that divided property evenly—or almost so—among all daughters and sons. A young male had to build savings to buy farm equipment by working (from about age 16 to 23) as a field hand for his father or neighbors. Because mortgages usually required down payments of 33 percent, a young husband normally supported his growing family by renting a farm from the local gentry until his early or mid-30s.

Landownership came quickest to those farmers who could find seasonal or part-time work. Some learned a craft like carpentry that earned money year-round. Many more trapped furs, gathered honey and beeswax, or made cider, shingles, turpentine, or wampum. Whenever possible, farmers found winter-time jobs draining meadows, clearing fields, or fencing

Women's Work
Rural women were responsible for most household and garden tasks. This print, dating to 1780, shows young women tending onions in Wethersfield, Connecticut.

land for wealthier landowners who did not own slaves or indentured servants. Such nonagricultural work might gain an industrious farmer half again of his total income from selling crops and livestock.

Families worked off mortgages slowly because the long-term cash income from a farm (6 percent) about equaled the interest on borrowed money (5–8 percent). After making a down payment of one-third, a husband and wife generally satisfied the next third upon inheriting shares of their deceased parents' estates. They paid off the final third when their children reached their teens and the family could thus expand farm output with two or three full-time workers. Only by their late 50s, just as their youngest offspring got ready to leave home, could most colonial parents hope to free themselves of debt.

In general, the more isolated a community or the less productive its farmland, the more self-sufficiency

and bartering its people practiced, although only the remotest settlements were completely self-sufficient. Almost all rural families depended heavily on wives' and daughters' production. Women contributed to their household's financial success by manufacturing items that the family would otherwise have had to purchase. Besides cooking, cleaning, and washing, wives preserved food, boiled soap, made clothing, and tended the garden, dairy, orchard, poultry house, and pigsty. Women often sold dairy products to neighbors or export merchants, spun yarn into cloth for tailors, knitted various garments for sale, and even vended their own hair for wigs. A farm family's ability to feed itself and its animals was worth about half of its cash income (a luxury that few European tenants had), and women did no less than men in meeting this end.

Legally, however, colonial American women found themselves constrained (see Chapter 3). A woman's single most autonomous decision was her choice of a husband. Once married, she lost control of her dowry (unless she was a New Yorker subject to old Dutch custom, which allowed her somewhat more authority). Still, widows controlled between 8 and 10 percent of all property in eighteenth-century Anglo-America, and some—among them Eliza Pinckney of South Carolina, a prominent political leader and the mother of two Revolutionary-era leaders—owned and managed several large estates.

Colonial Farmers and the Environment

The rapid expansion of English settlement hastened the transformation of the environment east of the Appalachians. Whereas the earliest colonists farmed land already cleared and cultivated by Native Americans, eighteenth-century settlers usually first had to remove trees from their plots. Despite the labor involved, farmers and planters, especially those using slave labor, preferred the most heavily forested areas, where the soil was most fertile. In New England farmers also had to clear innumerable heavy rocks—debris from the last Ice Age—with which they then built walls around their fields. And colonists everywhere used timber to construct their houses, barns, and fences and to provide fuel for heating and cooking. Farmers and planters also sold firewood to the inhabitants of colonial cities and towns. Only six years after Georgia's founding, a colonist noted that there was "no more firewood in Savannah; . . . it must be bought from the plantations for which reason fire-wood is already right expensive."

In removing the trees (deforestation), farmers drove away bears, panthers, wild turkeys, and other forest animals while attracting grass- and seed-eating rabbits, mice, and possums. By removing protection from winds and, in summer, from the sun, deforestation also produced warmer summers and colder winters, so that it actually reinforced the demand for wood as fuel. By hastening the runoff of spring waters, it led both to heavier flooding and drier streambeds in most areas and, where water could not escape, to more extensive swamps. In turn, less stable temperatures and water levels, along with impediments created by mills and by the floating of timbers downstream, rapidly reduced the number of fish in colonial waters. Writing in 1766, naturalist John Bartram noted that fish "abounded formerly when the Indians lived much on them & was very numerous," but that "now there is not the 100th or perhaps the 1000th [portion of] fish to be found."

Deforestation dried and hardened the soil, but colonists' crops had even more drastic effects. Native Americans, recognizing the soil-depleting effects of intensive cultivation, rotated their crops regularly so that fields could lie fallow (unplanted) and thereby be replenished with vital nutrients. But many colonial farmers either did not have enough land to leave some unplanted or were unwilling to sacrifice short-term profits for possible long-term benefits. As early as 1637, one New England farmer discovered that his soil "after five or six years [of planting corn] grows barren beyond belief and puts on the face of winter in the time of summer." Chesapeake planters' tobacco yields declined after only three or four years in the same plot. Like farmers elsewhere, they used animal manure to fertilize their food crops but not their tobacco, fearing that manure would spoil the taste for consumers. As Chesapeake tobacco growers moved inland to hillier areas, away from rivers and streams, they also contributed to increased soil erosion. By 1750, to remain productive, many Chesapeake farmers were shifting their crop from tobacco to wheat.

Because they confronted a more serious shortage of land and resources, well-to-do Europeans were already turning their attention to conservation and "scientific" farming. But most colonists ignored such techniques, either because they could not afford to implement them or because they believed that American land, including that still held by Indians, would sustain them and future generations indefinitely.

The Urban Paradox

The cities were colonial America's economic paradox. They shipped the livestock, grain, and lumber that enriched the countryside but were caught in a downward spiral of declining opportunity.

After 1740 economic success proved ever more elusive for the 4 percent of colonists who lived in cities. Poverty escalated rapidly in the three major seaports of Philadelphia, New York, and Boston. Debilitating ocean voyages left many immigrants too weak to work, and every incoming ship from Europe carried numerous widows and orphans. Moreover, the cities' poor rolls always bulged with the survivors of mariners lost at sea, as well as with unskilled, landless men, women (often widowed), and children from the countryside. High population density and poor sanitation in urban locales allowed contagious diseases to run rampant, so that half of all city children died before age twenty-one and urban adults lived ten years less on average than country folk.

Even the able-bodied found cities economically treacherous. Early-eighteenth-century urban artisans typically trained apprentices and employed them as journeymen for many years until the latter opened their own shops. After 1750, however, more and more employers kept their labor force only as long as business was brisk, and released workers when sales slowed; in 1751 a shrewd Benjamin Franklin recommended this practice as an intelligent way to use expensive labor. Recessions hit more frequently after 1720 and created longer spells of unemployment. As urban populations ballooned, wages correspondingly tended to shrink, and the cost of rents, food, and firewood shot up.

Urban poverty grew from insignificance before 1700 into a major problem in the mid-eighteenth century. By 1730 Boston could no longer shelter its destitute in the almshouse built in 1685, and by 1741 the town had declared every sixth citizen too poor to pay taxes. Not until 1736 did New York need a poorhouse (for just forty people), but by 1772, 4 percent of its residents (over eight hundred people) required public assistance to survive. The number of Philadelphia families listed as poor on tax rolls jumped from 3 percent in 1720 to 11 percent by 1760.

Wealth, on the other hand, remained highly concentrated in eighteenth-century colonial cities. For example, New York's wealthiest 10 percent owned about 45 percent of the property throughout the eighteenth century. Similar patterns existed in Boston and Philadelphia. Set alongside the growth of a poor underclass in these cities, such statistics underscored the polarization of status and wealth in urban America on the eve of the Revolution.

Economic frustration disposed townspeople to turn to violence to defend their interests. Before 1710 few serious disorders disrupted Boston, but between that year and 1750, the city experienced five major riots, aimed at closing a public market operated by wealthy merchants, stopping the navy from drafting sailors, or halting wartime profiteering. However, colonists used force only as a last resort to curb public nuisances. They usually achieved their goals through intimidation or property damage, after which they disbanded and let the law resume its course.

Most southern cities were little more than large towns. Charles Town, however, became North America's fourth-largest city. South Carolina's capital offered gracious living to the wealthy planters who flocked to their townhouses during the months of worst heat and insect infestation on their plantations. But shanties on the city's outskirts sheltered a growing crowd of destitute whites. The colony encouraged whites to immigrate in hopes of reducing blacks' numerical preponderance, but some European newcomers could not reach frontier farms or find any work except as ill-paid roustabouts. Like their counterparts in northern port cities, Charles Town's poor whites competed for work with urban slaves whose masters rented out their labor, and racial tensions simmered.

Although middle-class women in cities and large towns performed somewhat less manual drudgery than their country cousins, they nonetheless managed complex households that often included servants, slaves, apprentices, and other nonfamily members. While raising poultry and vegetables as well as sewing and knitting, urban wives purchased their cloth and most of their food in daily trips to public markets. Many had one or more household servants, usually young single women or widows, to help with cooking, cleaning, and laundering—tasks that required more attention than in the country because of higher urban standards of cleanliness and appearance. Wives also worked in family businesses located (unlike in modern times) in owners' homes.

Less affluent wives and widows housed boarders rather than servants, and many spun and wove cloth in their homes for local merchants. But especially in Boston, where conditions were the grimmest, many widows with children had to look to the community for relief. Whereas their Puritan forebears had deemed it one's Christian duty to care for poor dependents, affluent Bostonians turned an increasingly wary eye toward the needy. Preaching in 1752, the city's leading minister, Charles Chauncy, lamented "the Swarms of Children, of both Sexes, that are continually strolling and playing about the Streets of our Metropolis, cloathed in Rags, and brought up in Idleness and Ignorance," and another clergyman warned that charity for widows and their children was money "worse than Lost."

Slavery's Wages

From 1713 to 1754, five times as many slaves poured onto mainland North America as in all the preceding years. The proportion of blacks in the colonies doubled, rising from 11 percent at the beginning of the century to 20 percent by midcentury. Slavery was primarily a southern institution, but 15 percent of its victims lived north of Maryland, mostly in New York and New Jersey. By 1750 every seventh New Yorker was a slave.

Because West Indian and Brazilian slave buyers outbid the mainland colonists, a mere 5 percent of transported Africans were ever sold within the present-day United States. Unable to buy as many male field hands as they needed, mainland masters had no choice but to accept numerous female workers, and they protected their investments by maintaining the slaves' health. These factors promoted family formation and increased life expectancy far beyond the levels in the Caribbean, where family life was unstable and high death rates resulted from overwork and disease (see Chapter 3). On the mainland by 1750, the rate of natural increase for blacks almost equaled that for whites, and in some areas American-born slaves outnumbered those born in Africa.

For slaves, the economic progress achieved in colonial America by about 1750 meant primarily that masters could usually afford to keep them healthy. Rarely, however, did masters choose to make their human chattels comfortable. A visitor to a Virginia plantation from Poland (where most peasants lived in dire poverty) gave this impression of slaves' quality of life:

We entered some Negroes huts—for their habitations cannot be called houses. They are far more miserable than the poorest of the cottages of our peasants. The husband and wife sleep on a miserable bed, the children on the floor . . . a little kitchen furniture amid this misery . . . a teakettle and cups . . . five or six hens, each with ten or fifteen chickens, walked there. That is the only pleasure allowed to the negroes.

To maintain slaves, masters normally spent just 40 percent of the amount paid for the upkeep of indentured servants. Whereas white servants ate two hundred pounds of beef or pork yearly, most slaves consumed only fifty pounds of meat. The value of the beer and hard cider given to a typical servant alone equaled the expense of feeding and clothing the average slave. Masters usually provided adult slaves with eight quarts of corn and a pound of pork each week but expected them to grow their own vegetables, forage for wild fruits, and perhaps raise poultry.

Blacks as a Percentage of the Total Population in the British Colonies, 1650–1770

Wide differences developed in the racial composition of Britain's American colonies. By the mid-eighteenth century, the Caribbean sugar islands were almost 90 percent black, whereas the mainland colonies north of Maryland had become about 95 percent white. By 1750 slaves composed almost 40 percent of all mainland colonists south of Pennsylvania.

SOURCE: Robert W. Fogel and Stanley L. Engerman, *Time on the Cross* (Boston: Little, Brown, 1974), 21.

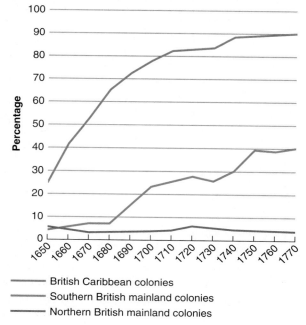

— British Caribbean colonies
— Southern British mainland colonies
— Northern British mainland colonies

Slaves worked for a far longer portion of their lives than whites. Slave children went to the fields as part-time helpers soon after reaching seven years and began working full-time between eleven and fourteen. Whereas most white women worked in their homes, barns, and gardens, female slaves routinely tended tobacco or rice crops, even when pregnant, and often worked outdoors in winter. Most slaves toiled until they died, although those who survived to their sixties rarely performed hard labor.

The rigors of bondage did not, however, crush its victims' spirits. Slaves proved resourceful at maximizing opportunities within a harsh, confining system. For example, some slaves accumulated small amounts of property by establishing exclusive rights over their gardens and poultry, and a few sold food to their masters. In 1769, for example, Thomas Jefferson made several purchases like the following:

gave negro for watermelon	7 pence
paid Fanny for 6 chickens	2 shillings
paid Cato for 1 doz eggs	3 pence

House slaves widely insisted on being tipped by guests for shining shoes and stabling horses. They sometimes sought presents aggressively on holidays, as a startled New Jersey tutor on a Virginia plantation discovered in 1774 when slaves demanding gifts of cash roused him from bed early Christmas morning.

In the South Carolina and Georgia rice country, slaves working under the highly favorable task system had control of about half their waking hours. Under tasking, each slave spent some hours caring for a quarter-acre—usually a half-day—after which his or her duties ended. By 1750 this system permitted certain slaves to keep hogs and sell surplus vegetables in Charles Town. A remarkable but atypical slave named Sampson earned enough money in his off-hours to hire another to work his own task, and became free in 1728.

But the independence of South Carolina's slaves and the fact that they constituted a majority of the colony's population aroused planters' fears that they were losing control of "their" blacks. For example, a 1735 law, noting that many Africans wore "clothes much above the condition of slaves," imposed a dress code limiting slaves' apparel to fabrics worth less than ten shillings per yard and even prohibited their wearing the cast-off clothes of their owners. Of even greater concern were gatherings of large numbers of blacks uncontrolled by whites. In 1721 Charles Town enacted a 9:00 P.M. curfew for blacks, while South Carolina's

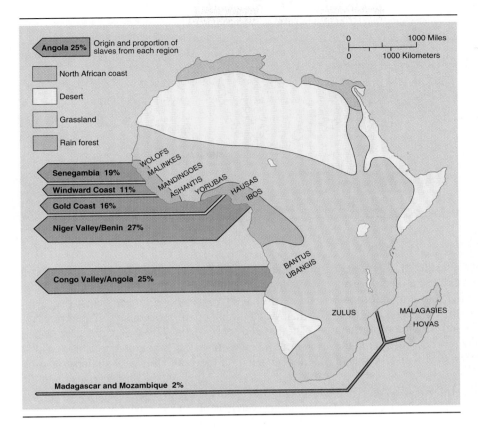

Legend:

Angola 25% — Origin and proportion of slaves from each region

North African coast

Desert

Grassland

Rain forest

0 — 1000 Miles
0 — 1000 Kilometers

WOLOFS
MALINKES
MANDINGOES
ASHANTIS
YORUBAS
HAUSAS
IBOS

Senegambia 19%
Windward Coast 11%
Gold Coast 16%
Niger Valley/Benin 27%

BANTUS
UBANGIS

Congo Valley/Angola 25%

ZULUS
MALAGASIES
HOVAS

Madagascar and Mozambique 2%

African Origins of North American Slaves, 1690–1807

Virtually all slaves brought to English North America came from West Africa, between Senegambia and Angola. Most were captured or bought inland and marched to the coast, where they were sold to African merchants who in turn sold them to European slave traders.

assembly placed all local slave patrols under the colonial militia. Slaves responded to the colony's vigilance and harsher punishments with increased instances of arson, theft, flight, and violence.

Tensions erupted in 1739 when South Carolina was rocked by a powerful slave uprising, the Stono Rebellion. It began when twenty slaves robbed guns and ammunition from a store twenty miles from Charles Town, at the Stono River Bridge. Marching under a makeshift flag and crying "Liberty!" they collected eighty men and headed for Spanish Florida, a well-known refuge for runaways (see "A Place in Time"). Along the way they burned seven plantations and killed twenty whites, but they spared a Scottish innkeeper who "was a good Man and kind to his slaves." Within a day mounted militia surrounded the slaves by a riverbank, cut them down mercilessly, and spiked a rebel head on every milepost between that spot and Charles Town. Disturbances elsewhere in the colony required more than a month to suppress, with insurgents generally "put to the most cruel Death." Thereafter white apprehension ran high, expressed in

a new slave code that would remain essentially in force until the Civil War. The code kept South Carolina slaves under constant surveillance. Furthermore, it threatened masters with fines for not disciplining slaves and required legislative approval for manumission (freeing of individual slaves). The Stono Rebellion thus speeded South Carolina's emergence as a rigid, racist, and fear-ridden society.

By midcentury slaves made up 20 percent of New York City's population and formed a majority in Charles Town and Savannah. City life offered slaves advantages, most notably the chance for those with skills to hire themselves out and keep part of their wages. By 1770 one-tenth of Savannah's slaves lived in rented rooms away from their owners. Though still in bondage, these blacks forced urban whites to allow them a substantial measure of personal freedom. But although city life afforded slaves greater freedom of association than the plantation did, it did not extend to them the opportunities being realized by their owners. In 1712 rebellious slaves in New York City killed nine whites in a calculated attack. As a result thirteen slaves

John Potter and His Family
*The Potters of Matunuck,
Rhode Island, relax at tea. In
commissioning a portrait depicting themselves at leisure
and attended by a black slave,
the Potters proclaimed their
elite status.*

were hanged, one was starved to death, three were
burned at the stake, and one was broken on the wheel.
Six others committed suicide to avoid similar tortures.
In 1741 a wave of thefts and fires attributed to New
York slaves led to the torture and hanging of thirteen
slaves and four whites (alleged accomplices), the
burning of an additional thirteen slaves, and the sale of
seventy more to the West Indies.

The Rise of the Colonial Elites

"A man who has money here, no matter how he came
by it, he is everything, and wanting [lacking] that he's
a mere nothing, let his conduct be ever so irreproach-
able." Thus a Rhode Islander in 1748 described how
colonial Americans defined high status. But once having achieved wealth, a man was expected by his contemporaries to behave with an appropriate degree of
responsibility, to display dignity and generosity, and to
be a community leader. His wife must be a skillful
household manager and, in the presence of men, a refined yet deferring hostess. In short, they were to act
like a "gentleman" and a "lady."*

Before 1700 the colonies' class structure was less
readily apparent, because the rural elite's more limited
resources were spent buying land, servants, or slaves
instead of luxuries. In 1715 a traveler visiting one of
Virginia's richest planters, Robert Beverley, noticed
that his host owned "nothing in or about his house but
just what is necessary, . . . [such as] good beds but no

---

*In the eighteenth century, the words *gentleman* and *lady* referred to
individuals who not only conformed to socially accepted standards
of behavior but also belonged to the upper class, or *gentry*.

curtains and instead of cane chairs he hath stools
made of wood."

After 1720 well-to-do colonists began displaying
their wealth more openly, particularly in their housing.
The greater gentry—the richest 2 percent, who held
about 15 percent of all property—constructed residences such as the Low House, New Jersey's most
splendid home in 1741, and the Shirley mansion in Virginia. The lesser gentry, or second-wealthiest 2 to 10
percent, who held about 25 percent of all property, typically lived in a more modest fieldstone dwelling such
as Pennsylvania's Lincoln homestead or a wood-frame
house such as Whitehall in Rhode Island. In contrast,
middle-class farmers commonly inhabited one-story
wooden buildings with four small rooms and a loft.

Colonial gentlemen and ladies also exhibited their
wealth after 1720 by living in imitation of the European
"grand style." They wore costly English fashions, drove
carriages instead of wagons, and bought expensive
chinaware, books, furniture, and musical instruments.
They pursued a gracious life by studying foreign languages, learning formal dances, and cultivating polite
manners. In sports men's preference shifted to horse
racing (on which they bet avidly) and away from cock-
fighting, a less elegant diversion. A few young colonial
males even got an English education. By midcentury
the elite's taste for consumer goods was spreading to
the middle class and helping to fuel a "consumer revolution" in the British Empire.

For Chesapeake gentlemen, debt was a problem
even if they lived virtuously. Tobacco planters were
perpetually short of cash and in debt to British merchants who bought their crops and sold them imported goods on credit at high prices. Noted the Mary-

land assembly in 1697, "The trade of this province ebbs and flows according to the rise or fall of tobacco in the market of England." Planters could respond only in two ways. First, they could strive for as much self-sufficiency as possible on their estates—for example, by training their slaves to manufacture glass, bricks, tools, nails, and carriages. Second, they could diversify away from the region's tobacco monoculture (dependence on a single staple crop) by growing wheat or cutting timber. Self-sufficiency and diversification became more widely accepted objectives as the eighteenth century wore on, and after 1750 respected landowners like George Washington and Thomas Jefferson strongly advocated them.

Elites and Colonial Politics

Colonial gentlemen not only monopolized wealth but also dominated politics. Governors invariably appointed members of the greater gentry to sit on their councils and as judges on the highest courts. Most representatives elected to the legislatures' lower houses (assemblies) also ranked among the wealthiest 2 percent, as did majors and colonels in the militia. In contrast, members of the lesser gentry sat less often in the legislature, but they commonly served as justices of the peace on the county courts and as militia officers up to captain.

Colonial America's only high-ranking elected officeholders were the members of the legislature's lower house. But outside New England (where any voter could hold office), legal requirements barred 80 percent of white men from running for the assembly, most often by specifying that a candidate must own a minimum of a thousand acres. (Farms then averaged 180 acres in the South and 120 acres in the mid-Atlantic colonies.) Even had there been no such property qualifications, however, few ordinary citizens could have afforded the high costs of elective office. Assemblymen received only living expenses, which might not fully cover the cost of staying at their province's capital, much less compensate a farmer or an artisan for his absence from farm or shop for six to ten weeks a year. Even members of the gentry grumbled about legislative duty, many of them viewing high office as "a sort of tax on them to serve the public at their own Expense besides the neglect of their business," according to Governor Lewis Morris of New Jersey.

For these reasons, political leadership fell to certain wealthy families with a tradition of public service.

Nine families, for example, provided one-third of Virginia's royal councilors during the century after 1680. John Adams, a rising young Massachusetts politician, estimated that most towns in his colony chose their legislators from among just three or four families.

The colonies set liberal qualifications for male voters, but all provinces excluded women, blacks (free as well as slaves), and Indians from elections. In seven colonies voters had to own land (usually forty to fifty acres), and the rest demanded that an elector have enough property to furnish a house and work a farm with his own tools. About 40 percent of free men could not meet these requirements, but nearly all of these were indentured servants, single sons still living with parents, or young men just beginning family life. Most white males in British North America would vote by age forty, whereas two-thirds of all men in England and nine-tenths in Ireland could not and would never vote.

In rural areas voter participation was low unless a vital issue was at stake. The difficulties of voting limited the average rural turnout to about 45 percent. (This rate of participation was, however, better than in typical U.S. elections today, apart from those for president.) Most governors called elections according to no set pattern, so that elections might lapse for years and suddenly be held on very short notice. Voters in isolated areas thus often had no knowledge of an upcoming contest. The fact that all polling took place at the county seat discouraged many electors from traveling long distances over poor roads to vote. In several colonies voters had to state their choice publicly, often face-to-face with the candidates. This procedure naturally inhibited participation on the part of those who might dissent. Finally, the absence of political parties also played a role in the turnout: no institutional means existed to stimulate popular interest in politics and to mobilize voters in support of candidates. Office seekers nominated themselves and usually ran on their reputation rather than issues that might spur public interest.

In view of these factors, indifference toward politics was not uncommon by the mid-eighteenth century. For example, to avoid paying legislators' expenses at the capital, numerous Massachusetts towns refused to choose assemblymen; in 1763, 64 of 168 towns held no elections. Thirty percent of men elected to South Carolina's assembly neglected to take their seats from 1731 to 1760, including a majority of those chosen in 1747 and 1749. Apathy would have been even greater

Charles County, Maryland, Courthouse and Ordinary
In the Chesapeake colonies, community life usually centered on the county courthouse and a few other buildings on a cleared parcel. On election days, voters were treated to drinks in the nearby ordinary (tavern) by candidates before proceeding to the courthouse and voting orally and publicly.

had candidates not freely plied voters with alcohol. This "swilling the planters with bumbo" was most popular among Virginians: George Washington dispensed almost two quarts of liquor for each voter at the courthouse when first elected to the assembly in 1758. Such practices helped the elite in most eighteenth-century colonies build up a tradition of community leadership that would serve them well in the years of revolutionary crisis after 1763.

Only in the major seaports did a truly competitive political life flourish. Voter turnout was relatively high

in the cities because of greater population density, better communications, and the use of secret ballots (except in New York). Furthermore, the cities' acute economic difficulties stimulated political participation among urban voters, ever hopeful that the government might ease their problems. In politics as in economics, cities were an exception to the general pattern for Anglo-America.

The most significant political development after 1700 was the rise of the assembly as the preponderant force in American government. Except in Connecticut and Rhode Island (where voters elected their governor), the crown or the proprietors in England chose each colony's governor, who except in Massachusetts in turn named a council, or upper house of the legislature. Thus the assembly became the vehicle through which members of the gentry asserted their own interests. Until 1689 governors and councils took the initiative in drafting laws, and the assemblies rather passively followed their lead; but thereafter, the assemblies assumed a more central role in politics.

Colonial leaders argued that their legislatures should exercise the same rights as those won by Parliament in its seventeenth-century struggle with royal authority. Indeed, Americans saw their assemblies as miniature Houses of Commons, and they assumed that governors possessed only those powers exercised by the British crown. Since Parliament had won supremacy over the monarchy through the Bill of Rights in 1689, colonials felt that their governors had strictly limited powers and should defer to the assemblies in cases of disagreement.

The lower houses steadily asserted their prestige and authority by refusing to permit outside meddling in their proceedings, taking firm control over taxes and budgets, and especially by keeping a tight rein on executive salaries. Although governors had considerable powers (including the right to veto acts, call or dismiss assembly sessions at will, and schedule elections anytime), they were vulnerable to legislatures' financial pressure because they received no salary from British sources and relied on the assemblies for income. Only through this "power of the purse" could assemblies force governors to sign laws opposed by the crown.

Moreover, because the British government had little interest in eighteenth-century colonial politics, the assemblies could seize considerable power at the governors' expense. The Board of Trade, which Parliament established in 1696, was charged with monitoring American developments and advising the crown on colonial affairs. But aside from its first decade and a vigorous period from 1748 to 1753, the board's small, inefficient staff lacked the vision and energy to provide the strong support needed by embattled governors wrestling to maintain royal authority. The board could have easily frustrated the assemblies' rise to power by persuading the crown to disallow objectionable colonial laws signed by the governors; but of 8,563 acts sent from the mainland between 1696 and 1776, the board had just 469 disapproved. The Board of Trade's ineffectiveness left a vacuum in royal policy that allowed the colonies to become self-governing in most respects except for trade regulation, restrictions on printing money, and declaring war. This autonomy, reinforced by self-assertive assemblies, would haunt British authorities when they attempted to exercise more direct rule after 1763 (see Chapter 5).

Thus during the first half of the eighteenth century, many colonists flourished and some grew wealthy. At the same time, however, class distinctions became more sharply etched. But British North America had no centuries-old institutions to bolster aristocratic privilege: no hereditary nobility, powerful bureaucracy, standing army, or royal court. Even the Anglican church was weak, lacking American bishops. Despite the absence of such institutions, its hold on colonial wealth, along with social expectations, largely sufficed to ensure that the American upper class would dominate public life in the colonies.

COMPETING FOR A CONTINENT

The first half of the eighteenth century witnessed the rapid transformation of North America as Europeans competed among themselves in expanding their territorial claims, engaging in more intensive trade and warfare alike with Native Americans, and opening up new areas for settlement by colonists. Native Americans welcomed some of these new developments and resisted others, depending on how they thought their livelihoods would be affected.

France and Native Americans

With the conclusion of the War of Spanish Succession in 1713, France aggressively resumed expanding and strengthening its North American empire, particularly the colony of Louisiana. Founded in 1718, New Orleans soon became the colony's capital and port. Louisiana's staunchest Indian allies were the Choctaws, through whom the French hoped to counter both the rapidly expanding influence of Carolina's traders and the weakening presence of the Spanish in the Southeast. But inroads by the persistent Carolinians led the Choctaws by the 1730s to become bitterly divided into pro-English and pro-French factions.

In no time Louisiana acquired a foul reputation, and few French immigrated there willingly. To boost its population, the government sent paupers and criminals there, recruited German refugees, and encouraged large-scale slave imports. By 1732 two-thirds of

Intercultural Trade in Colonial Louisiana
Alexandre de Batz, a French visitor in 1735, depicted an important dimension of Louisiana's economy in this drawing of Indians from several nations gathering to trade near New Orleans. Trade goods, including cured skins, kegs of fat, and bear oil, are lined up in the foreground.

lower Louisiana's fifty-eight hundred people were slaves. Life was dismal, even for whites. A thoroughly corrupt government ran the colony. With Louisiana's sluggish export economy failing to sustain them, settlers and slaves found other means of survival. Like the Indians, they hunted, fished, gathered wild plants, and cultivated gardens. In 1727 a priest described how some free settlers eventually prospered: "A man with his wife or partner clears a little ground, builds himself a house on four piles, covers it with sheets of bark, and plants corn and rice for his provisions; the next year he raises a little more for food, and has also a field of tobacco; if at last he succeeds in having three or four Negroes, then he is out of difficulties."

But many red, white, and black Louisianans depended on exchanges with one another in order to be "out of difficulties." Indians provided corn, bear oil, tallow (for candles), and above all deerskins to European merchants in return for blankets, kettles, axes, chickens, hogs, guns, and alcohol. Indians from west of the Mississippi brought horses and cattle, usually stolen from Spanish ranches in Texas. Familiar with cattle from their homelands, West African slaves managed many of Louisiana's herds, and some became rustlers and illicit traders of beef.

With Canada and Louisiana secure, the French sought to counter growing British influence in and around the Ohio Valley. After the valley was largely emptied of natives during wars with the Iroquois in the seventeenth century, the Iroquois' adoption of neutrality in 1701 (see Chapter 3) encouraged Indian refugees to settle there. Nations such as the Kickapoos and Mascoutens returned from the upper Great Lakes, while others, among them Shawnees and Delawares, arrived from the east to escape English encroachments. Hoping to secure commercial and diplomatic ties with these natives, the French expanded their trade activities. Detroit and several other French posts ballooned into sizable villages housing Indians, French, and mixed-ancestry *métis*. But with English traders increasingly active in the region, most Indians preferred a more independent course.

Although the French generally were more successful among Indians than the English, by no means did they enjoy universal success. The Carolina-supported Chickasaws frequently attacked the French and their native allies on the Mississippi River. Although ultimately unsuccessful, the Fox Indians led a long effort

Huron (Wyandotte) Woman
Her cloth dress, glass beads, and iron hoe reflect the influence of French trade on this woman and other Indians of the Great Lakes–Ohio region in the eighteenth century.

to prevent French traders from making direct contact with Sioux Indians to the west. And the French in 1729–1730 brutally suppressed the Natchez Indians, the last of the Mississippian peoples, in order to open up land in Louisiana for tobacco and sugar production.

By 1744 French fur traders had explored as far west as North Dakota and Colorado and were buying beaver pelts and Indian slaves on the Great Plains. At the instigation of these traders and their British competitors, trade goods, including guns, spread to Native Americans throughout central Canada and then to the Plains. Meanwhile, Indians in the Great Basin and southern Plains were acquiring horses, thousands of which had been left behind by the Spanish when they fled New Mexico during the Pueblo Revolt of 1680. Adopting the horse and gun, Indians such as the Lakota Sioux and Comanches moved to the Plains and built a new, highly mobile way of life based on the pursuit of buffalo.

Only at widely scattered places between Louisiana and Canada did the French attempt to settle, most notably in modern-day Missouri and Illinois. By 1750 France had an immense domain, but one that depended on often precarious relations with nearby Native Americans.

Native Americans and British Expansion

As in the seventeenth century, the rapid expansion of colonial settlement was made possible by the depopulation and dislocation of Native Americans. Epidemic diseases, environmental changes, war, and political pressures on Indians to cede land and to emigrate all combined to open up new lands for the immigrants. Pennsylvania, where William Penn's idealism was rapidly waning, coerced the Delaware Indians into selling more than fifty thousand acres between 1729 and 1734. In 1735 the colony's leaders (William Penn's sons and his former secretary) produced a patently fraudulent treaty in which the Delawares allegedly had agreed in 1686 to sell their land as far west as a man could walk in a day and a half. The colony then blazed a trail and hired three men to walk west as fast as they could. The men covered nearly sixty miles, meaning that the Delawares, in what became known as the Walking Purchase, had to cede an additional twelve hundred square miles of land. Despite the protests of Delaware elders who had been alive in 1686 and remembered no such treaty, the Delawares were forced to move under Iroquois supervision. The proprietors then sold these lands to settlers and speculators at a large profit. Within a generation the Delawares' former lands were among the most productive in the British Empire.

In helping to remove the Delawares from Pennsylvania, the Iroquois sought to accommodate the English while consolidating their own power. Late in the seventeenth century, the Iroquois had agreed with several colonies, from Maryland to Massachusetts, to relocate Indians whose lands were sought by colonists. Under these agreements, known collectively as the Covenant Chain, Indians were moved to areas of what are now New York and Pennsylvania on the periphery of the Iroquois' own homeland, where they could serve as buffers against English expansion. The removal of the Delawares marked Pennsylvania's entry

into the Covenant Chain. In so grouping other Native Americans around them and in incorporating the Tuscaroras as the sixth nation of their confederacy (see Chapter 3), the Iroquois established a center of Native American power distinct from, but cooperative with, the British.

Indians elsewhere along the frontier of settlement likewise confronted pressures from settlers on one side and from the Iroquois on the other. Typical of these were the Catawbas of the Carolina piedmont. After the defeat of the Yamasees (whose cause the Catawbas supported) in 1716, Carolina settlers moved uncomfortably close to some Catawba villages, provoking the kind of environmental upheavals experienced earlier by Indians in New England and other settled regions (see Chapter 3). Most Catawbas abandoned these villages to join more remote Catawbas who engaged in the deerskin trade. Having escaped the settlers, the Catawbas, however, faced rising conflict with the Iroquois, who, after making peace with the Indian allies of New France in 1701, looked south when launching raids for captives to adopt into their ranks. To counter the Iroquois, whose alliances with most of the northern colonies left them well armed, the Catawbas turned to South Carolina. By ceding land and helping defend that colony against outside Indians, the Catawbas received guns, food, and clothing. Their relationship with the English allowed the Catawbas the security they needed to strengthen their traditional institutions. However, the growing gap in numbers between them and the settlers, and their competition with the settlers for resources, made the Indians vulnerable and dependent.

British Settlement in the South: Georgia

Parliament's chartering of the colony of Georgia in 1732 represented a new expansionist thrust. Parliament intended Georgia as a refuge where bankrupt debtors (who typically rotted in English jails until they repaid their debts) could settle, their presence protecting South Carolina against attacks from Spanish Florida to the south. Meanwhile, the new colony's sponsors hoped that Georgia would flourish by exporting expensive commodities like wine and silk. Parliament even spent money to ensure the success of the colony, which became the only North American province besides Nova Scotia in which the British government actually invested funds.

Under tough-minded James Oglethorpe (1696–1785), who dominated the provincial board of trustees, Georgia took shape slowly during its first decade. Oglethorpe founded the port of entry, Savannah, in 1733, and by 1740 a small contingent of 2,800 colonists had settled in the colony. Almost half the immigrants came from Germany, Switzerland, and Scotland, and most had their overseas passage paid by the government. A small number of Jews were among the early settlers. Georgia thus began as the least English of all the colonies. In 1740 Oglethorpe led a massive assault on Florida (see "A Place in Time"). Although failing to seize St. Augustine, he led 650 men in repelling 3,000 Spanish troops and refugee South Carolina slaves who counterattacked Georgia in 1742. When peace returned in 1744, Georgia's survival was assured.

Oglethorpe hated slavery and tried to ban it from Georgia. "They live like cattle," he wrote to the trustees after viewing Charles Town's slave market. "If we allow slaves, we act against the very principles by which we associated together, which was to relieve the distressed." Slavery, he thought, degraded blacks, made whites lazy, and presented a terrible risk. South Carolina's Stono Rebellion of 1739 particularly alarmed him. Oglethorpe worried that wherever whites relied on a slave labor force, they courted slave revolts, which the Spanish could then exploit. But most of all, he recognized that slavery undermined the economic position of poor whites like those he sought to settle in Georgia.

At Oglethorpe's insistence, Parliament made Georgia the only colony where slavery was forbidden. He also pushed through a requirement that landholdings be no larger than 500 acres. These mea-sures were aimed at keeping rural Georgia populated by white, independent farmer-soldiers, ready to leap to the colony's defense and uncorrupted by the urge to speculate in real estate or build up slave-labor plantations.

But Oglethorpe's well-intentioned plans failed completely. Few debtors arrived because Parliament set impossibly stringent conditions for their release from prison. Limitations on settlers' rights to sell or enlarge their holdings, as well as the ban on slavery, also kept settlement low. Raising exotic export crops proved impractical; as in South Carolina, only rice yielded a profit. Oglethorpe struggled against economic reality for a decade and then gave up. In 1750 the trustees finally legalized slavery, and other restrictions on the market for land also fell by the wayside. As a result, Georgia boomed. The population rose from four thousand residents in 1750 (including up to a thousand hitherto illegal slaves) to twenty-three thousand inhabitants in 1770, 45 percent of them blacks.

Georgia's settlement completed British colonization of the Atlantic seaboard. Having held Georgia against Spain and pushed the frontier west 150 miles, British expansion virtually halted after 1750. Anglo-Americans would not settle beyond the Appalachians until the 1760s. Nevertheless, the colonial population continued to grow rapidly, doubling every twenty-six years—almost exactly what Franklin had predicted in 1751. Had this rate continued, the U.S. population to-

James Oglethorpe and the Indians
In 1734 Oglethorpe visited London with Creek Indians who had sold him land. Here the Creeks meet with Englishmen who have invested in the Georgia colony.

Yuchi Ceremony, 1736
A German visitor to Georgia drew this watercolor, which he titled A Festival. *The guns hanging inside the shelter were probably acquired from English traders in South Carolina.*

day would number around 850 million, second only to China's.

Spain's Struggles

While endeavoring to maintain its empire in the face of Native American, French, and British adversaries, Spain spread its language and culture over much of North America, especially in the Southwest.

Seeking to repopulate New Mexico with settlers after the Pueblo Revolt (see Chapter 3), Spain gave land grants of approximately twenty-six square miles wherever ten or more families founded a town. Strong fortifications arose to protect against Indian attacks, now coming primarily from the Apaches. As in the early New England towns, the settlers built homes on small lots around the church plaza, farmed separate fields nearby, grazed livestock at a distance, and shared a community woodlot and pasture.

The livestock-raising *ranchos,* radiating out for many miles from little clusters of houses, monopolized vast tracts along the Rio Grande and blocked further town settlement. On the *ranchos* mounted cattle and sheep herders *(vaqueros)* created the way of life later associated with the American cowboy—featuring lariat and roping skills, cattle drives, roundups, and livestock brandings.

By 1750 the population of New Mexico numbered just 3,800 Spanish, half of them in four towns, and

8,400 Pueblos (an astonishing 50 percent reduction since 1680). Most Pueblos were integrated into New Mexico society and, although many had converted to Catholicism, they also practiced their traditional religion. On the colony's borders, the Navajos and Apaches, whose raids once menaced Spanish and Pueblos alike, had made peace with New Mexico in order to gain its support against even more fearsome raids by armed and mounted Utes from the north and Comanches from the east.

Spain established Texas in order to counter growing French influence among the Comanches and other Native Americans on the southern Plains. Colonization began in 1716, when Spaniards established four missions and a small garrison. The most flourishing of these was San Antonio de Valero, where friars constructed a fortified mission building later famous as the Alamo. But the Indians of Texas preferred trading with the French to farming, Christianity, and the ineffective protection of the Spanish. Lack of security also deterred Hispanic settlement, so that by 1760 only 1,200 Spaniards faced periodic raids by French, Comanches, and other Indians.

Spain's position in Florida was equally precarious. After 1715 the neutrality of the Creeks enabled the Spanish to compete with the English and French in the southeastern deerskin trade, though with limited effectiveness, and to sponsor Indian counterraids into Carolina. In addition, the Spanish offered freedom to any

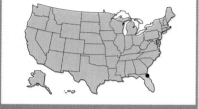

Mose, Florida, in 1740

The Spanish presence in Florida was always tenuous and, after English colonists established Charles Town in Carolina in 1670, vulnerable to outside attack. During the eighteenth century Spain retained its hold in Florida by enlisting the support of Native Americans and Africans alienated by the English. In particular, by promising freedom to slaves who fled from Carolina to Florida and converted to Catholicism, the Spanish bolstered their population and defenses. The black community of Mose, established near St. Augustine in 1738, vividly demonstrated the importance of these immigrants.

Blacks had lived in Florida since the founding of St. Augustine in 1565. In 1683, after Indians armed by Carolina began attacking and capturing Florida mission Indians for sale into slavery, the Spanish colony formed a black militia unit. In 1686 fifty-three blacks and Indians conducted a counterraid into Carolina and returned with, among other prizes, thirteen of the governor's slaves. In subsequent diplomatic negotiations between the two colonies, Florida's governor, Diego de Quiroga, refused English demands that he return the blacks, instead giving them wage-paying jobs. Soon other Carolina slaves were making their way to Florida. Spain's King Charles II ruled in 1693 that all arriving slaves should be given their freedom, "so that by their example and my liberality others will do the same."

With Spain deliberately encouraging Carolina slaves to escape to Florida, the numbers rose further, especially during the Yamasee War (1715–1716), when the English were nearly crushed by a massive uprising of Indians. In 1726 a former South Carolina slave, Francisco Menéndez, was appointed to command a militia unit consisting of his fellow Carolinians to defend against an expected English invasion. The Spanish built a fortified village for Menéndez's men and their families in 1738 and called it Gracia Real de Santa Teresa de Mose, usually shortened to Mose, an Indian name for the location.

Mose was strategically placed just two miles north of St. Augustine, so that its residents served as both sentries and a buffer for the capital. Spanish and English documents, along with recent archaeological excavations, reveal that it had sturdy earthen walls "lined round with prickly royal" (a thorny plant) and was surrounded by a moat. A stone fort was the most prominent structure inside the walls. Outside the fort the one hundred residents planted fields and gathered shellfish from the banks of a nearby saltwater stream. In a letter to the Spanish king, Florida's governor, Manuel de Montiano, praised Menéndez for having "distinguished himself in the establishment and cultivation of Mose, . . . [and] doing all he could so that the rest of his subjects, following his example, would apply themselves and learn good customs."

For its residents Mose symbolized their new status as freed men and women. Most had been born in West Africa and then enslaved and carried to Carolina. After escaping they had lived among friendly Indians who helped them make their way to the Spanish colony. Mose was their own community, their first since being taken from Africa. In agreeing to live there, they understood the price they might have to pay. Writing to the king in 1738, they declared themselves "the most cruel enemies of the English," who were ready to shed

English Map of St. Augustine and Mose, 1762
Mose is indicated as "Negroe Fort"; "Indian Town" is a settlement of pro-Spanish Indians.

now, after twelve years of assimilation in the capital city, seemed a mark of second-class citizenship.

In 1763 Spain ceded Florida to Britain in the Treaty of Paris (see Chapter 5). Spanish authorities evacuated the people of Mose and allotted them homesteads in Matanzas, Cuba. But the meager provisions given the blacks proved inadequate, and many, including Francisco Menéndez, soon moved to Havana. In 1783 another Treaty of Paris returned Florida to Spain (see Chapter 6), and the following year, a new Florida governor resumed the policy of granting freedom to escaped slaves. Hearing the news and recalling Florida's earlier reputation, hundreds of slaves responded. But now Spain proceeded more cautiously with the slaveholders' government to Florida's north; in 1790 U.S. Secretary of State Thomas Jefferson persuaded the Spanish to rescind the policy of granting freedom to escaped slaves. In 1819 the United States annexed Florida, and in 1845 it joined the Union as a slave state.

Ft. Mose Watercolor
Artist's reconstruction of Mose, based on archaeological and documentary evidence.

Puerto Rican Sergeant,
Seventeenth Century
This free black sergeant belonged to a Spanish militia unit in Puerto Rico, similar to the one based at Mose.

their "last drop of blood in defense of the Great Crown of Spain and the Holy Faith."

The importance of Florida's free blacks and their town was demonstrated in 1740 when Georgia's governor, James Oglethorpe, led a massive force of Georgia and South Carolina troops, Indian allies, and seven warships in an invasion of Florida. The English captured Mose in May after all its residents were evacuated, but Menéndez's militia and other troops recaptured the town a month later in a fierce battle that helped Oglethorpe decide to withdraw. (The British called the battle Bloody Mose.) But English destruction of the town and the Spanish crown's refusal to fund its rebuilding led Mose's residents to move into St. Augustine. For twelve years they lived among the Spanish as laborers, seamen, and hunters and in other capacities. In 1752 a new governor had Mose rebuilt and ordered the blacks to return to their former town despite their express "desire to live in complete liberty." To reside in the town, which they once had cherished as a symbol of their freedom,

English-owned slaves who escaped and made their way to Florida (see "A Place in Time").

The Spanish saw Georgia's founding in 1733 as a bold new threat to Florida, and planned, but then cancelled, an all-out invasion in 1737. When war broke out between England and Spain in 1739, the two sides attempted invasions of one another without success. Even though Spain had resisted the English, its reputa-

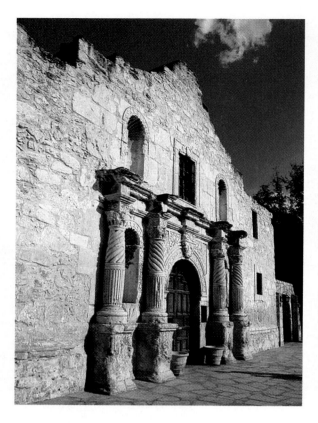

The Alamo

As the center of Franciscan missionary efforts in Texas, this church was a critical bulwark for Spain on its fragile northern frontier. It later became the symbol of Texan independence from Mexico (see Chapter 13).

French and Spanish Occupation of North America, to 1750

French fur traders became entrenched along the Great Lakes and upper Mississippi River between 1666 and 1700, after which they built many settlements in territory claimed by Spain along the Gulf of Mexico. Spanish colonization was concentrated in Florida, central Texas, and the Rio Grande Valley.

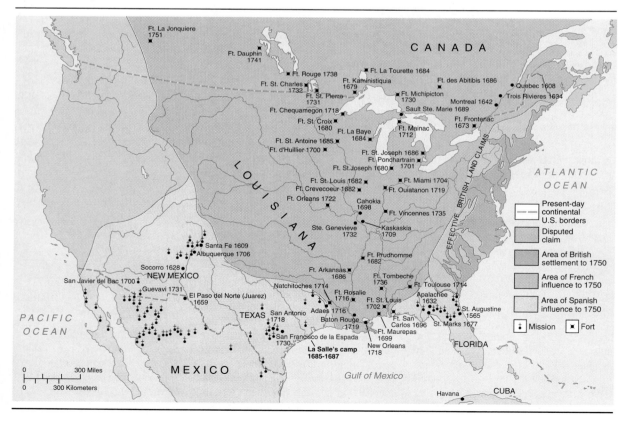

tion as "the sick man of Europe" clearly applied equally in North America.

By the mid-eighteenth century, Spain controlled much of the Southeast and Southwest, while France exercised influence in the Mississippi, Ohio, and Missouri River valleys, as well as around the Great Lakes and in Canada. Both empires, spread thin, depended heavily on Indian goodwill or acquiescence. In contrast, British North America was compact, densely populated by non-Indians, and aggressively expansionist.

ENLIGHTENMENT AND AWAKENING

Anglo-America was probably the world's most literate society in the eighteenth century. Perhaps 90 percent of New England's adult white male population and 40 percent of the women could write well enough to sign documents, thanks to the region's traditional support for primary education. Among white males elsewhere in the colonies, the literacy rate varied from about 35 percent to more than 50 percent. (In England, by contrast, no more than one-third of all males could read and write.) But how readily most of these people could (or would) read a book or write a letter was another matter. Ordinary Americans' reading fare at best encompassed only a few well-thumbed books: an almanac, a psalter, and the Bible. They inhabited a world of oral culture, in which ideas and information passed through the spoken word—a conversation with neighbors, an exchange of pleasantries with the local gentleman, a hot debate at the town meeting, a sermon by the minister. When uttered with feeling and sincerity, spoken words could move them with tremendous force.

However, members of the gentry, well-to-do merchants, educated ministers, and some self-improving artisans and farmers also lived in the world of print culture. Though costly, books, newspapers, and writing paper could open up eighteenth-century European civilization to reading men and women. And a rich, exciting world it was. Great advances in natural science seemed to explain the laws of nature; human intelligence appeared poised to triumph over ignorance and prejudice; life itself looked as if it would at last become pleasant. For those who had the time to read and think, an age of optimism and progress had dawned: the Enlightenment. Upper-class Americans could not resist its charms and could be powerfully moved by the promise of its written words.

The Enlightenment in America

Anglo-American intellectuals like the self-taught scientist Benjamin Franklin drew their inspiration from Enlightenment ideals, which combined confidence in human reason with skepticism toward beliefs not founded on science or strict logic. One source of Enlightenment thought lay in the writings of English physicist Sir Isaac Newton (1642–1727), who in 1687 explained how universal gravitation ruled the universe. Newton's work captured Europe's imagination by demonstrating the harmony of natural laws and stimulated others to search for rational principles in medicine, law, psychology, and government.

In the second quarter of the eighteenth century, no American more fully embodied the Enlightenment spirit than Franklin. Born in Boston in 1706, Franklin migrated to Philadelphia at age seventeen. He brought along skill as a printer, considerable ambition, and insatiable intellectual curiosity. In 1727 he gathered a small group of young men, mostly aspiring artisans like himself, into a club called the Junto, whose members pledged themselves to debate highbrow questions and to collect useful information for their "mutual improvement."

In moving to Philadelphia, Franklin put himself in the right place at the right time, for the city was growing much more rapidly than Boston and was attracting English and Scottish merchants who shared Franklin's zest for learning. These men nudged Franklin's career along by lending him books and securing him printing contracts. In 1732 Franklin began to publish *Poor Richard's Almanack*, a collection of maxims and proverbs that made him famous. By age forty-two Franklin had earned enough money to retire and devote himself to science and community service.

These dual goals—science and community benefit—were intimately related in Franklin's mind, for he believed that all true science would be useful in the sense of making everyone's life more comfortable. For example, experimenting with a kite, Franklin demonstrated in 1752 that lightning was electricity, a discovery that led to the useful lightning rod. Building on his Junto activities, Franklin organized the American Philosophical Society in 1743 to encourage "all philosophical experiments that let light into the nature of things, tend to increase the power of man over matter, and multiply the conveniences and pleasures of life." By 1769 this society had blossomed into an inter-colonial network of amateur scientists.

Franklin left his mark on Philadelphia in other ways. He established its first volunteer fire company—complete with engine—in 1736, inspired the creation of a circulating library that held America's finest collection of scientific books, and in 1740 helped to found an academy that became the College of Philadelphia (now the University of Pennsylvania). From this institution sprang the colonies' first medical school in 1765.

Although several southern plantation owners, including Thomas Jefferson, ardently championed progress through science, the Enlightenment's primary centers in America were the seaboard cities, where the latest books and ideas from Europe circulated and gentlemen and self-improving artisans met in small societies to investigate nature. In the eyes of many of these individuals, the ideal was the Royal Society in London, the foremost learned society in the English-speaking world. Franklin and Cotton Mather became members of the Royal Society. In this respect, the Enlightenment, at least initially, strengthened the ties between colonial and British elites. Although confident that science would benefit everyone, the Enlightenment's followers envisioned progress as gradual and proceeding from the top down. They trusted reason far more than they trusted the common people, whose judgment, especially on religious matters, seemed too easily deranged.

Just as Newton inspired the scientific bent of Enlightenment intellectuals, English philosopher John Locke's *Essay Concerning Human Understanding* (1690) led many to embrace "reasonable" or "rational" religion. Locke contended that ideas, including religion, are not inborn but are acquired by toilsome investigation of and reflection upon experience. To most Enlightenment intellectuals, the best argument for the existence of God seemingly could be derived through study of the harmony and order of nature, which pointed to a rational Creator. Some individuals carried this argument a step further by insisting that where the Bible conflicted with reason, one should follow the dictates of reason rather than the Bible. Those, such as Franklin and Jefferson, who took the argument furthest were called Deists. Deists concluded that God, having created a perfect universe, did not miraculously intervene in its workings but rather left it alone to operate according to natural laws.

Americans influenced by the Enlightenment usually described themselves as Christians and attended church. But they feared Christianity's excesses, particularly as indulged in by fanatics who persecuted others in religion's name, and by "enthusiasts" who claimed miraculous visions and direct mandates from God. Mindful of Locke's caution that a human can never be *absolutely* certain of anything but his or her own existence, they distrusted zealots. Typically, Franklin contributed money to most of the churches in Philadelphia but thought that religion's value lay in its encouragement of virtue and morality rather than in theological hair splitting.

Prior to 1740 colonial intellectuals usually associated fanaticism and bigotry with the bygone days of the early Puritans, and they looked on their own time as an era of progressive reasonableness. But a series of religious revivals known as the Great Awakening would soon shatter their complacency.

The Great Awakening

Viewing the world as orderly and predictable, rationalists were inclined to a sense of smug self-satisfaction. Franklin took the occasion of writing his will in 1750 to thank God for giving him "such a mind, with moderate passions" and "such a competency of this world's goods as might make a reasonable mind easy." But many Americans lacked a comfortable competency of worldly goods and lived neither orderly nor predictable lives. For example, in 1737 and 1738 an epidemic of diphtheria, a contagious throat disease, killed every tenth child under sixteen from New Hampshire to Pennsylvania. Such an event starkly reminded the colonists of the fragility of earthly life and turned their thoughts to religion.

A quickening of religious fervor began at scattered places in the colonies in the mid-1730s. Then in the 1740s, an outpouring of passionate Christian revivalism swept all of British North America. This "Great Awakening" cut across lines of class, status, and education. Even many elites found themselves caught up in it, realizing the inadequacy of reason alone to move their hearts. Above all, the Great Awakening represented an unleashing of anxiety and longing among ordinary people living in a world of oral culture—anxiety about sin, and longing for salvation. And the answers that they received were conveyed through the spoken word. Some preachers of the Great Awakening were themselves ntellectuals, comfortable amid the books and ideas of the print culture. But for all, religion was primarily a matter of emotional commitment.

In contrast to rationalists, who stressed the human potential for betterment, the ministers who roused their congregations into outbursts of religious fervor during the Great Awakening's revivals depicted the emptiness of material comfort, the utter corruption of human nature, the fury of divine wrath, and the need for immediate repentance. Although he was a brilliant thinker, well aware of contemporary philosophy and science, the Congregationalist Jonathan Edwards, who led a revival at Northampton, Massachusetts, in 1735, drove home this message with breathtaking clarity. "The God that holds you over the pit of Hell, much as one holds a spider or other loathsome insect over the fire, abhors you," Edwards intoned in one of his famous sermons, "Sinners in the Hands of an Angry God." "His wrath toward you burns like fire; He looks upon you as worthy of nothing else but to be cast into the fire."

Even before Edwards's Northampton revival, two men in central New Jersey—the Presbyterian minister William Tennent and the Dutch Reformed minister Theodore Frelinghuysen—had stimulated conversions in prayer meetings called the Refreshings. But the event that brought these isolated threads of revival together was the arrival in 1739 of the charismatic George Whitefield, an English clergyman who had been stoking the fires of revival in the Anglican church. So overpowering was Whitefield's presence that some joked that he could make crowds swoon simply by uttering "Mesopotamia." Crowds exceeding twenty thousand could hear his booming voice clearly, and many wept at his eloquence.

Whitefield's American tour inspired thousands to seek salvation. Most converts were young adults in their late twenties. In Connecticut alone, the number joining churches jumped from 630 in 1740 to 3,217 in 1741, and within four years of Whitefield's arrival, every fifth man and woman under forty-five had been "born again."

Whitefield's allure was so mighty that he even awed potential critics. Hearing him preach in Philadelphia, Benjamin Franklin first vowed to contribute nothing to the collection but gradually melted. So admirably did Whitefield conclude his sermon, Franklin recalled, "that I empty'd my Pocket wholly into the Collector's Dish, Gold and all." But divisions over the revivals quickly developed in Whitefield's wake and were widened by the tactics of some of his more extreme followers. For example, after leaving Boston in October 1740, Whitefield invited Gilbert Tennent (William's son) to follow "in order to blow up the divine flame lately kindled there." Denouncing Boston's established clergymen as "dead Drones" and lashing out at aristocratic fashion, Tennent built a following among the city's poor and downtrodden. So did another firebrand,

the Congregationalist James Davenport, who once preached to his Southold, New York, congregation for twenty-four hours.

Exposing colonial society's social divisions, Tennent and Davenport corroded support for the revivals among established ministers and officials. Increasingly, the lines hardened between the revivalists, known as New Lights, and the rationalist clergy, or Old Lights, who dominated the Anglican, Presbyterian, and Congregational churches. In 1740 Gilbert Tennent published *The Danger of an Unconverted Ministry,* which hinted that most Presbyterian ministers lacked saving grace and hence were bound for hell, and urged their parishioners to abandon them for the New Lights. By thus sowing the seeds of doubt about individual ministers, Tennent was undermining one of the foundations of social order, for if the people could not trust their own ministers, whom could they trust?

Old Light rationalists fired back. In 1742 Charles Chauncy, a well-known Boston Congregationalist, condemned the revival as an epidemic of the "enthusiasm" that Enlightened intellectuals so loathed. Chauncy particularly blasted those enthusiasts who mistook the ravings of their overheated imaginations for direct communications from God. He even provided a kind of checklist for spotting enthusiasts: look for "a certain wildness" in their eyes, the "quakings and tremblings" of their limbs, and foaming at the mouth, Chauncy suggested. Put simply, the revival had unleashed "a sort of madness."

The Great Awakening opened unprecedented splits in American Protestantism. In 1741 New and Old Light Presbyterians formed rival branches that did not reunite until 1758, when the revivalists emerged victorious. The Anglicans lost many members to New Light preachers, especially to Presbyterians and Baptists. Congregationalists splintered so badly that within twenty years of 1740, New Lights had seceded from one-third of all churches and formed separate parishes.

In Massachusetts and Connecticut, where the Congregational church was established by law, the secession of New Light parishes provoked bitter conflict. To force New Lights into paying tithes to their former church, Old Lights repeatedly denied new parishes legal status. Connecticut passed repressive laws forbidding revivalists to preach or perform marriages, and the colony expelled many New Lights from the legislature. In Connecticut's Windham County, an extra story had to be added to the jail to hold all the New Lights arrested for not paying tithes. Elisha Paine, a revivalist imprisoned at Windham for illegal preaching, continued giving sermons from his cell and drew such crowds that

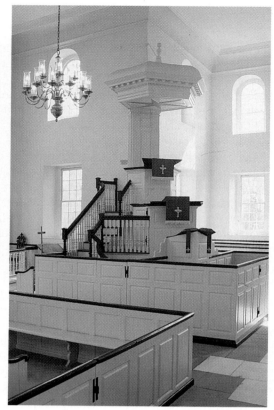

Baptist Meetinghouse and Anglican Church Interiors, Eighteenth-Century Virginia
The New Light Baptist structure (above) reflects the members' poverty as well as their preference for equality, simplicity, and intimacy in their services. The Old Light Anglican church (right) expresses an emphasis on hierarchy, formality, and distance among members. In particular, compare the relationship of minister to congregation in each church.

his followers built bleachers nearby to hear him. Paine and his fellow victims generated widespread sympathy for the New Lights, who finally won control of Connecticut's assembly in 1759.

Although New Lights made steady gains until the 1770s, the Great Awakening peaked in 1742. The revival then crested everywhere but in Virginia, where its high point came after 1755 with an upsurge of conversions by Baptists, who also suffered legal harassment.

For all the commotion it raised at the time, the Great Awakening's long-term effects exceeded its immediate impact. First, the revival started the decline in the influence of Quakers (who were not significantly affected by the Great Awakening), Anglicans, and Congregationalists. As these churches' importance waned, the number of Presbyterians and Baptists increased after 1740, and that of Methodists (pro-revival offshoots of Anglicanism) rose after 1770. Ever since the late 1700s, these three churches have dominated American Protestantism. Second, the Great Awakening stimulated the founding of new colleges, for existing colleges were scarred in their opponents' eyes by their affiliations with either Old or New Lights. In 1746 New Light Presbyterians established the College of New Jersey (Princeton). Then followed King's College

(Columbia) for Anglicans in 1754, the College of Rhode Island (Brown) for Baptists in 1764, Queen's College (Rutgers) for Dutch Reformed in 1766, and Dartmouth College for Congregationalists in 1769. Third, the revival went beyond the ranks of white society to draw many African-Americans and Native Americans to Protestantism for the first time. The revivals' oral and communal dimensions, along with their emphasis on piety over intellectual learning as the key to God's grace, enabled some members of both these groups to combine aspects of their traditional cultures with Protestant Christianity. The Great Awakening marked the real emergence of black Protestantism, which was almost nonexistent before 1740. New Lights reached out to slaves, some of whom joined white churches and even preached at revival meetings. Conversions came slowly, but by 1790 many blacks were Christians. Meanwhile, a few New Light preachers became missionaries to Indians still residing in the colonies. Among their converts were some Indians who had previously rejected Protestant missionaries. A few Christian Indians, such as Samson Occom, a Mohegan born in Connecticut, became widely known as preachers themselves. Despite these breakthroughs, blacks and

Reverend Samson Occom, Mohegan Indian Preacher

Born in a wigwam in Connecticut, Occom converted to Christianity under the influence of the Great Awakening and preached to other Native Americans. But he grew disillusioned with the treatment of his people by whites and, after the American Revolution, joined an exodus of Indians from New England to upstate New York.

Indians still faced considerable discrimination in colonial churches, even among New Lights.

The Great Awakening also gave added prominence to women in colonial religion. For several decades ministers had singled out women—who constituted the majority of church members—as embodying the Christian ideal of piety. Now some New Light churches, mostly Baptist and Congregationalist, began to grant women the right to speak and vote in church meetings. And like Anne Hutchinson a century earlier, some women moved from leading women's prayer and discussion groups to presiding over meetings that included men. One such woman, Sarah Osborn of New-

port, Rhode Island, conducted "private praying Societies Male and female" that included black slaves in her home. In 1770 Osborn and her followers won a bitter fight over their congregation's choice of a new minister. While most assertive women were prevented by detractors from exercising as much power as Osborn, none was persecuted as Hutchinson had been in Puritan New England.

Finally the revivals had the unintended effect of fostering religious toleration by blurring theological differences among New Lights. Although an Anglican who helped found Methodism, George Whitefield preached with Presbyterians such as Gilbert Tennent and Congregationalists like Jonathan Edwards. By emphasizing inner experience over doctrinal and institutional fine points, revivalism helped to prepare Americans to accept denominational pluralism, which emerged after the Revolution as the best means of accommodating religious diversity.

Historians have disagreed over whether the Great Awakening had political as well as religious effects. Although Tennent and Davenport called the poor "God's people" and flayed the wealthy, they never advocated a social revolution, and the Awakening did not produce any distinct political ideology. Yet by empowering ordinary people to criticize those in authority, the revivals laid some of the groundwork for political revolutionaries a generation later, who would contend that royal government in America had grown corrupt and unworthy of obedience.

CONCLUSION

The aura of sanctified purpose around George Whitefield and his religious revival lingered even after his death in Boston in 1770. In September 1775 a ragtag army of American rebels, marching through Massachusetts, paused on their way to attack the British stronghold at Quebec. Hoping to win a blessing for their risky venture, they broke open a tomb and prayed over a holy man's remains. The corpse was George Whitefield's.

By the 1750s the British mainland colonies had taken on the look of mature societies. For fifty years their population and wealth had been rising impressively. The mainland provinces were more populous than Scotland and almost one-third the size of England. White colonists' standard of living far ex-

ceeded those of Scotland and Ireland and equaled that of England. Literacy had spread widely in the northern colonies, and by 1766 Anglo-America had more institutions of higher learning than England, Scotland, and Ireland together. A self-confident Anglo-American upper class had garnered expertise in law, trade, finance, and politics.

Together Britain and its colonies had become a far more formidable presence in North America than their French and Spanish rivals. But after France was vanquished and Spain further weakened in the Seven Years' War (1756–1763), latent tensions in the colonies' relations with Britain developed into irreconcilable differences.

CHRONOLOGY

1651–1733	Parliament creates the navigation system to regulate British imperial commerce.
1660	Restoration of the Stuart dynasty to English throne.
1685	Duke of York becomes King James II of England.
1686–1689	Dominion of New England.
1688	Glorious Revolution in England; James II deposed.
1689	William and Mary ascend to English throne. Protestant Association seizes power in Maryland. Leisler's Rebellion in New York.
1689–1697	King William's War (in Europe, War of the League of Augsburg).
1690	John Locke, *Essay Concerning Human Understanding.*
1698	French begin settlements near the mouth of the Mississippi River.
1701	Iroquois adopt neutrality policy toward European powers.
1702–1713	Queen Anne's War (in Europe, War of the Spanish Succession).

1716	San Antonio founded.
1718	New Orleans founded.
1729–1730	French war on Natchez Indians in Louisiana.
1732	Georgia colony chartered. Benjamin Franklin begins publishing *Poor Richard's Almanack.*
1734	"Walking Purchase" of Delaware Indians in Pennsylvania.
1735	Jonathan Edwards leads revival in Northampton, Massachusetts.
1736	Benjamin Franklin establishes first American fire company, at Philadelphia.
1739	Great Awakening begins. Stono Rebellion in South Carolina.
1739–1744	Anglo-Spanish War.
1743	Benjamin Franklin founds American Philosophical Society.
1750	Slavery legalized in Georgia.

Jonathan Edwards

FOR FURTHER READING

Bernard Bailyn, *The Peopling of British North America: An Introduction* (1986). A brief interpretive overview of the causes and effects of European immigration to British North America.

Bernard Bailyn and Philip D. Morgan, eds., *Strangers Within the Realm: Cultural Margins of the First British Empire* (1991). Essays by leading historians examine the interplay of ethnicity and empire occurring in North America, the Caribbean, Scotland, and Ireland.

Richard L. Bushman, *From Puritan to Yankee: Character and the Social Order in Connecticut, 1690–1765* (1967). The best examination of social and cultural transformation in any eighteenth-century colony.

Rhys Isaac, *The Transformation of Virginia, 1740–1790* (1982). Pulitzer Prize–winning study of class relationships, race relations, and folkways during the Great Awakening and American Revolution.

John J. McCusker and Russell R. Menard, *The Economy of British America, 1607–1789,* rev. ed. (1991). A comprehensive discussion of the colonial economy in light of current scholarship.

James H. Merrell, *The Indians' New World: Catawbas and Their Neighbors from European Contact Through the Era of Removal* (1989). A pathbreaking examination, with broad implications for understanding the Native American past, of the interaction between South Carolina colonists and Catawba Indians.

Gary B. Nash, *The Urban Crucible: The Northern Seaports and the Origins of the American Revolution,* abridged ed. (1986). A study of social, economic, and political change in Boston, New York, and Philadelphia during the eighteenth century.

Timothy Silver, *A New Face on the Countryside: Indians, Colonists, and Slaves in South Atlantic Forests, 1500–1800* (1990). A highly readable discussion of the interactions of humans and their environment in one region.

Peter H. Wood, *Black Majority: Negroes in Colonial South Carolina from 1670 Through the Stono Rebellion* (1974). An engrossing study of slavery, racism, and African-American life in the Lower South.

ADDITIONAL BIBLIOGRAPHY

Rebellion and Imperial Warfare

Lois Green Carr and David W. Jordan, *Maryland's Revolution of Government, 1689–1692* (1974); Richard R. Johnson, *Adjustment to Empire: The New England Colonies, 1675–1715* (1981); David

S. Lovejoy, *The Glorious Revolution in America, 1660–1692* (1972); Stephen Saunders Webb, *The Governors General: The English Army and the Definition of the Empire, 1569–1681* (1979).

British Colonial Society and Economy

Ida Altman and James Horn, eds., *"To Make America": European Emigration in the Early Modern Period* (1991); Richard L. Bushman, *The Refinement of America: People, Houses, Cities* (1992); Karen Calvert, *Children in the House: The Material Culture of Early Childhood, 1600–1800* (1992); James Deetz, *In Small Things Forgotten: The Archaeology of Early American Life* (1977); A. Roger Ekirch, *Bound for America: The Transportation of British Convicts to the Colonies, 1718–1775* (1987); Joyce D. Goodfriend, *Before the Melting Pot: Society and Culture in Colonial New York City, 1664–1730* (1991); Christine Leigh Heyrman, *Commerce and Culture: The Maritime Communities of Colonial Massachusetts, 1690–1750* (1984); Stephen Innes, ed., *Work and Labor in Early America* (1988); Sung Bok Kim, *Landlord and Tenant in Colonial New York: Manorial Society, 1664–1775* (1978); Michael Kammen, *Empire and Interest: The American Colonies and the Politics of Mercantilism* (1970); Allan Kulikoff, *Tobacco and Slaves: The Development of Southern Cultures in the Chesapeake, 1680–1800* (1986); James T. Lemon, *The Best Poor Man's Country: A Geographical Study of Early Southeastern Pennsylvania* (1972); Barry Levy, *Quakers and the American Family: British Settlement in the Delaware Valley* (1988); James Leyburn, *The Scotch-Irish: A Social History* (1989); Peter C. Mancall, *Valley of Opportunity: Economic Culture Along the Upper Susquehanna, 1700–1800* (1991); Marcus Rediker, *Between the Devil and Deep Blue Sea: Merchant Seamen, Pirates, and the Anglo-American Maritime World, 1700–1750* (1989); Sharon V. Salinger, *"To Serve Well and Faithfully": Labor and Indentured Servants in Pennsylvania, 1682–1800* (1987); Marylynn Salmon, *Women and the Law of Property in Early America* (1986); Beverly Smaby, *The Transformation of Moravian Bethelem: From Communal Mission to Family Economy* (1988); Daniel Blake Smith, *Inside the Great House: Family Life in Eighteenth-Century Chesapeake Society* (1980); Phinizy Spalding, *Oglethorpe in America* (1977); Laurel Thatcher Ulrich, *Good Wives: Image and Reality in the Lives of Women in Northern New England, 1650–1763* (1982).

Blacks and Slavery

Ira Berlin, "Time, Space, and the Evolution of Afro-American Society in British Mainland North America," *American Historical Review* 85 (1980): 44–78; Philip D. Curtin, *The Atlantic Slave Trade: A Census* (1969); Winthrop D. Jordan, *White over Black: American Attitudes Toward the Negro, 1550–1812* (1968); Jane Landers, "Gracia Real de Santa Teresa de Mose: A Free Black Town in Spanish Colonial Florida," *American Historical Review* 95 (1990): 9–30; Edgar J. McManus, *Black Bondage in the North* (1973); Edmund S. Morgan, *American Slavery, American Freedom: The Ordeal of Colonial Virginia* (1975); Gerald W. Mullin, *Flight and Rebellion: Slave Resistance in Eighteenth-Century Virginia* (1972); William D. Piersen, *Black Yankees: The Development of an Afro-American Subculture in Eighteenth-Century New England* (1988); Mechal Sobel, *The World They Made Together: Black and White Values in Eighteenth-Century Virginia* (1987).

Native Americans

Richard Aquila, *The Iroquois Restoration: Iroquois Diplomacy on the Colonial Frontier, 1701–1754* (1983); James Axtell, *The Invasion Within: The Contest of Cultures in Colonial North America* (1985); Gregory Evans Dowd, *A Spirited Resistance: The North American Indian Struggle for Unity, 1745–1815* (1992); Tom Hatley, *The Dividing Paths: Cherokees and South Carolinians Through the Era of Revolution* (1993); Preston Holder, *The Hoe and the Horse on the Plains: A Study of Cultural Development Among North American Indians* (1970); Elizabeth A. H. John, *Storms Brewed in Other Men's Worlds: The Confrontations of Indians, Spanish, and French in the Southwest, 1540–1795* (1975); Michael N. McConnell, *A Country Between: The Upper Ohio Valley and Its Peoples, 1724–1774* (1992); Daniel K. Richter, *The Ordeal of the Longhouse: The Peoples of the Iroquois League in the Era of European Colonization* (1992); Daniel H. Usner, Jr., *Indians, Settlers, and Slaves in a Frontier Exchange Economy: The Lower Mississippi Valley Before 1783* (1992); Richard White, *The Middle Ground: Indians, Empires and Republics in the Great Lakes Region, 1650–1815* (1991); Peter H. Wood et al., eds., *Powhatan's Mantle: Indians in the Colonial Southeast* (1989); J. Leitch Wright, Jr., *The Only Land They Knew: The Tragic Story of the American Indians in the Old South* (1981).

French and Spanish Colonies

J. M. Bumsted, *The Peoples of Canada: A Pre-Confederation History* (1992); Donald E. Chipman, *Spanish Texas, 1519–1821* (1992); W. J. Eccles, *France in America*, rev. ed. (1991); Ramon A. Gutiérrez, *When Jesus Came, the Corn Mothers Went Away: Marriage, Sexuality, and Power in New Mexico, 1500–1846* (1991); Richard Colebrook Harris, *The Seigneurial System in Early Canada* (1966); Gerald E. Poyo and Gilberto M. Hinojosa, eds., *Tejano Origins in Eighteenth-Century San Antonio* (1991); David J. Weber, *The Spanish Frontier in North America* (1992).

The Enlightenment, Religion, and Politics

Bernard Bailyn, *The Origins of American Politics* (1968); Patricia Bonomi, *A Factious People: Politics and Society in Colonial New York* (1971) and *Under the Cope of Heaven: Religion, Society, and Politics in Colonial America* (1986); Richard D. Brown, *Knowledge Is Power: The Diffusion of Information in Early America, 1700–1865* (1991); Jon Butler, *Awash in a Sea of Faith: Christianizing the American People* (1990); Edwin S. Guastad, *The Great Awakening in New England* (1957); Jack P. Greene, *The Quest for Power: The Lower Houses of Assembly in the Southern Royal Colonies, 1689–1776* (1963); Frank Lambert, *"Pedlar in Divinity": George Whitefield and the Transatlantic Revivals* (1994); Kenneth A. Lockridge, *The Diary and Life of William Byrd II of Virginia* (1988) and *On the Sources of Patriarchal Rage: The Commonplace Books of William Byrd and Thomas Jefferson and the Gendering of Power in the Eighteenth Century* (1992); Sally Schwartz, *A Mixed Multitude: The Struggle for Toleration in Colonial Pennsylvania* (1987); Harry S. Stout, *The New England Soul: Preaching and Religious Culture in Colonial New England* (1988); Charles S. Sydnor, *American Revolutionaries in the Making: Political Practices in Washington's Virginia* (1965); Michael Warner, *The Letters of the Republic: Publication and the Public Sphere in Eighteenth-Century America* (1990); Marilyn J. Westerkamp, *Triumph of the Laity: Scots-Irish Piety and the Great Awakening, 1625–1760* (1988); Esmond Wright, *Franklin of Philadelphia* (1986).

Captain and Mrs. John Purves *(detail)*
by Henry Benbridge, 1775

THE ROAD TO REVOLUTION
1744–1776

In 1769 Benjamin Franklin (inset) was an agent for several American colonial assemblies and living in London, where he obtained an anonymous English pamphlet entitled *Good Humour*. Franklin bristled at the unknown author's charges that the colonists' recent opposition to parliamentary taxes represented *"a posture of hostility* against Great Britain." "There was no Posture of Hostility in America," Franklin angrily scribbled in the margin, "but Britain put herself in a Posture of Hostility against America."

As Franklin wrote those words, a constitutional crisis gripped the British Empire and was markedly affecting Britain's relationship with its overseas colonies. The conflict between Britain and the American colonies arose suddenly after 1763, when Parliament attempted to reorganize its suddenly enlarged empire by tightening control over economic and political affairs in the colonies. Long accustomed to benefiting economically from the empire while legislating for themselves, colonists resisted this unexpected effort to centralize decision making in London. Leaders like Franklin interpreted Britain's clampdown as calculated antagonism, intended to deprive the colonists of their prosperity and their relative independence.

As telling as they were, Franklin's words represented only one of many perspectives on unfolding events. For other colonists, the conflict was more than a constitutional crisis. In the port cities, crowds of poor and working people engaged in direct, often violent demonstrations against British authority. Sometimes they acted in concert with elite radicals; at other times, in defiance. Settlers in the remote "backcountry" of several colonies invoked the language and ideas of urban radicals when resisting the monopolies of large landowners and the policies of colonial governments dominated by seaboard elites.

These movements reflected social-economic tensions within the colonies and the emergence of distinctly nonelite views on the crisis. By the same token, the growing participation of women in colonial resistance brought to the fore yet another perspective on the crisis. Moreover, colonial protests did not arise in a vacuum but rather drew from ideas and opposition movements in Britain and elsewhere in Europe.

Taken as a whole, colonial resistance involved many kinds of people with many outlooks. It arose most immediately from a constitutional crisis within the British Empire, but it also reflected deep democratic stirrings in America and in the north Atlantic world generally. These stirrings would erupt in the American Revolution, beginning in 1776, and then in the French Revolution, which began in 1789.

Despite their apprehension over parliamentary taxes, colonial politicians usually expressed their opposition peacefully from 1763 to 1775, through such tactics as legislative resolutions and commercial boycotts. Few lost their lives during the twelve years prior to the battles at Lexington and Concord, the first military clashes of the Revolution, and all of those killed were American civilians rather than royal officials or soldiers. Even after fighting broke out, some colonists agonized for more than a year over whether to sever their political relationship with England—which even native-born Americans sometimes referred to affectionately as "home." Of all the world's colonial peoples, none became rebels more reluctantly than did Anglo-Americans in 1776.

◆

IMPERIAL WARFARE

Between 1713, when Queen Anne's War ended, and the early 1740s, the American colonies enjoyed a generation of peace, punctuated only by a brief war with Spain fought in Georgia from 1739 to 1742. But the war with Spain was symptomatic of renewed tensions between England on one hand and France and Spain on the other for overseas empire. That conflict merged with a second one in central Europe between Austria and Prussia, leading to an international war known as the War of the Austrian Succession (1740–1748). After a "diplomatic revolution" in which Austria dropped its alliance with Britain for one with France, leading Britain to align with Prussia, the conflict resumed as the Seven Years' War (1756–1763). In both wars the Anglo-French conflict was fought not in Europe but on the high seas; in India (where the two powers competed for influence among local rulers); and in North America. Although these conflicts originated in rivalries among the great powers of Europe, few colonists doubted that King George's War was also *their war,* or that their prosperity depended on a British victory in the Seven Years' War.

Yet these wars produced an ironically mixed effect. On one hand, they fused the bonds between the British and the Anglo-Americans. Fighting side by side, shedding their blood in the same cause, the British and the American colonists came to rely on each other as rarely before. At the same time, the conclusion of each war planted the seeds first of misunderstanding, then of suspicion, and finally of hostility between the two former compatriots.

King George's War

King George's War largely followed the pattern of earlier conflicts under William and Mary and Queen Anne (see Chapter 3). Few battles involved more than six hundred men, and most of the skirmishes consisted of raids and counterattacks in the Northeast, in which many civilians were killed and others captured, especially by French and Indians attacking New England frontier towns. Although prisoners were exchanged at the end of each conflict, some captives, particularly women and children, elected to remain with the French or Indians.

King George's War produced just one major engagement. In 1745 almost four thousand New Englanders under William Pepperell of Maine assaulted the French bastion of Louisbourg on the northern tip of Nova Scotia, which guarded the entrance to the St. Lawrence River. Unable to bring artillery with them, the New Englanders obtained siege guns by storming the enemy's outer batteries and then captured ammunition from several unsuspecting French supply ships that sailed into their clutches. For almost seven weeks they shelled Louisbourg, lobbing in nine thousand cannonballs and six hundred bombs until every building was either crumbling or on fire. On June 17, 1745, Pepperell took the fortress and almost 1,500 prisoners, at a loss of only 167 of his troops.

The colonists did not enjoy the fruits of victory for long. After three more years of inconclusive warfare, Britain and France signed the Treaty of Aix-la-Chapelle in 1748, exchanging Louisbourg for a British outpost in India that the French had taken during the war. The memory of how their stunning achievement at Louisbourg went for naught would rankle the colonists for a decade.

A Fragile Peace

King George's War had failed to establish either Britain or France as the dominant power in North America, and each side soon began preparations for another war. Although there were many points of contention between the two powers, it was the Ohio Valley that became the tinderbox for conflict.

For more than half a century, the region had attracted refugee Indians—Delawares from Pennsylvania, Shawnees returning to their homeland from Pennsylvania and South Carolina, and others driven there by colonial expansion and fur-trade rivalries (see Chapter 4). Even some Iroquois, eager for new trading opportunities, had moved to the area, where they became known as Mingos. Initially welcomed as trade partners and bulwarks against English expansion, these Indians increasingly irritated the French by their independence, in particular the willingness of some to deal with Pennsylvania traders and even to fight against the

"Join or Die," 1754
Benjamin Franklin published this well-known cartoon just before the Albany Congress convened. The snake symbolized the colonies' considerable divisions—a disunity that political leaders would have to struggle against in years to come.

French in King George's War. The French derided these Indians as "republicans" for their defiance of all outside authority—French, English, and Iroquois.

For the next decade and a half, the "republican" Indians sought to balance the English and French against each other while the two powers grew ever less patient with the Indians' neutrality. After the war Virginia pressured some Iroquois leaders into ceding land occupied by Delawares so that the colony's agents could build a fortified trading post at the junction of the Allegheny and Monongahela rivers—the site of modern Pittsburgh. As a result the Delawares and other "republican" Indians began to fear that the English were the greater threat to their independence.

By 1752 the Ohio Valley was the subject of competing claims by Virginia, Pennsylvania, France, and the Iroquois, as well as by the Indians who actually lived there. The next year the French began building a chain of forts in order to recapture control of trade with the Indians from Virginians and Pennsylvanians. Virginia retaliated by sending a twenty-one-year-old surveyor and speculator, George Washington, to demand that the French abandon their forts on the Alleghany River, but the French refused. Returning in 1754 with three hundred colonial militiamen and one hundred British regulars, Washington found the French already constructing Fort Duquesne at the juncture of the rivers. After killing and seizing members of a small French force, Washington's men built a crude defensive position about sixty miles southeast called Fort

Necessity. The French retaliated swiftly and effectively. On July 4, 1754, after losing one-fourth of his men in a daylong battle, Washington surrendered Fort Necessity to an enemy force four times larger than his own and led the survivors home.

Sensing the need to resolve differences among themselves and to restore the confidence of the Indians in the face of an almost certain response by France, delegates from seven colonies north of Virginia gathered in mid-1754 at Albany, New York, to lay plans for their mutual defense. By showering the wavering Iroquois with thirty wagonloads of presents, the colonists kept them neutral for the moment. (But virtually all Indians in Ohio itself now supported the French.) The delegates then endorsed a proposal for a colonial confederation, the so-called Albany Plan of Union, largely based on the ideas of Pennsylvania's Franklin and Massachusetts's Thomas Hutchinson. The plan called for a "Grand Council" representing all the colonial assemblies, with a crown-appointed "president general" as its executive officer. The Grand Council would devise policies regarding military defense and Indian affairs, and if necessary, it could demand funds from the colonies according to an agreed-upon formula. Although it provided a precedent for later American unity, the Albany Plan came to nothing, primarily because no colonial legislature would surrender the least control over its powers of taxation, even to fellow Americans and in the face of grave mutual danger.

The Seven Years' War in America

Although France and Britain remained at peace in Europe until 1756, Washington's action at Fort Necessity created a virtual state of war in North America. In response, nearly eight thousand colonists enlisted during 1755 to attack French strongholds menacing New York and Nova Scotia. That same year, British general Edward Braddock and a thousand regular troops arrived in North America to take Fort Duquesne.

Stiff-necked and scornful of colonial soldiers, Braddock expected his disciplined British regulars to make short work of the enemy and only dimly perceived the strength and resourcefulness of the forces gathering against him. Washington's failure in the Ohio Valley and Braddock's arrogance had lost them all Indian support. On July 9, 1755, about 850 French, Canadians, and Indians ambushed Braddock's force of 2,200 Britons and Virginians nine miles east of Fort Duquesne. Riddled by three hours of steady fire from

The Seven Years' War in America

After experiencing major defeats early in the war, Anglo-American forces turned the tide against the French by taking Fort Duquesne in late 1757 and Louisbourg in 1758. After Canada fell in 1760, the fighting shifted to Spain's Caribbean colonies.

an unseen foe, Braddock's troops retreated. Nine hdred regular and provincial soldiers died in Braddock's defeat, including the general himself, compared to just twenty-three on the French side.

Following this engagement, Indian raids convulsed Pennsylvania, Maryland, Virginia, and even parts of New Jersey—all colonies that had escaped attack in previous wars. Meanwhile, neither of two Anglo-American armies that marched against the French fortresses at Niagara and Crown Point in New York

reached its objective in 1755. The only successful British expedition that year was undertaken by two thousand New En-glanders who seized two French forts near Nova Scotia. This campaign was memorable less for its military significance than for its tragic aftermath. Following the takeover of the French forts, the governor of Nova Scotia ordered the troops to drive thousands of local French-Canadian civilians, the Acadians, from their homes—often with nothing more than they could carry in their arms—and to burn their

New British Fort, 1759
After the French abandoned Crown Point on Lake Champlain, British troops occupied it and built a greatly expanded fortress. This watercolor was painted by a British officer.

villages. This cruel expulsion stemmed from the Acadians' refusal to promise not to bear arms for France. Almost 5 percent of Canada's population was eventually deported in this way to the British colonies, especially Maryland and Pennsylvania. But facing poverty and intense anti-French, anti-Catholic prejudice, most Acadians moved on to Louisiana. There they became known as Cajuns.

Although Anglo-Americans outnumbered French forces twenty to one, the French commander in chief, Louis Joseph Montcalm, maintained the offensive in 1756 and 1757. A daring and resourceful general, Montcalm benefited from large numbers of French regulars in Canada, overwhelming Indian support (including even that of the Iroquois), and the mobilization of nearly every able-bodied Canadian into a militia that fought with the courage of desperate men. In contrast, the American colonies balked at providing many troops and frequently sent poorly trained men who had been enlisted for only a few months. "I would rather have no Troops," wrote a despairing British colonel in 1757, "than to be at the Trouble & expence to form them, & when they could begin to be able to perform their Duty, be oblig'd to disband them."

Confronted by the numerically superior but disorganized Anglo-Americans, the French seized Fort Oswego on Lake Ontario in 1756 and took Fort William Henry on Lake George in 1757. By now the French threatened central New York and western New England. In Europe, too, the war was going badly for Britain, which by 1757 seemed to be facing defeat on all fronts.

In this dark hour, two developments turned the tide for the British. First, the Iroquois and most Ohio Indians, sensing that the French were gaining too decisive an advantage, agreed at a treaty conference at Easton, Pennsylvania, in 1758 to abandon their support of the French. Their subsequent withdrawal from Fort Duquesne enabled the British to capture it and other French forts. Although some Indians stayed out of the fighting, others actively joined the British cause.

The second decisive development occurred when one of the British ministers, William Pitt, took control of military affairs in the royal cabinet and reversed the downward course. Imaginative and single-minded in his conception of Britain's imperial destiny, Pitt saw himself as the man of the hour. "I know," he declared, "that I can save this country and that no one else can." True to his word, Pitt reinvigorated British patriotism throughout the empire. By the war's end, he was the colonists' most popular hero, the symbol of what Americans and the English could accomplish when united.

Hard pressed in Europe by France and its allies (which included Spain after 1761), Pitt preferred not to send large numbers of British regulars to America. Fewer than four thousand British troops arrived on the mainland from mid-1757 until New France's defeat. Rather, Pitt believed that the key to crushing New France lay in the mobilization of colonial soldiers. To encourage the colonies to assume the military burden, he promised that if they raised the necessary men, Parliament would bear most of the cost of fighting the war.

Pitt's offer to free Americans from the war's financial burdens generated unprecedented support. The colonies organized twenty-one thousand troops in 1758, more soldiers than the crown sent to the mainland during the entire war, and raised an equal number in 1759. The resulting offensive under General Jeffery Amherst captured Fort Duquesne and Louisbourg by late 1758 and drove the French from northern New York the next year. In September 1759 Quebec fell after General James Wolfe defeated Montcalm on the Plains of Abraham outside that city, where both commanders died in battle. French resistance ended in 1760, when Montreal surrendered.

France ceded all its territories on the North American mainland by the Treaty of Paris of 1763, which officially ended the Seven Years' War in both America and Europe. France gave Britain all of its lands east of the Mississippi and transferred title to its claims west of that river to Spain, which also gained New Orleans. In return for Cuba, which a British expedition had taken over in 1762, Spain ceded Florida to Britain. Spain's vast American empire thus remained intact, but France's formerly extensive holdings were reduced to a few tiny fishing islands off Newfoundland and several thriving sugar isl in the West Indies. Britain reigned supreme in eastern North America.

George III, *Studio of A. Ramsay, c. 1767*
Although unsure of himself and emotionally little more than a boy upon his accession to the English throne, George III possessed a deep moral sense and a fierce determination to rule as well as to reign.

IMPERIAL REORGANIZATION

Following the Seven Years' War, Britain sought to finance its greatly expanded empire through a series of revenue measures imposed on Britons and colonists alike, and to exercise more direct control over its colonies. Opposition movements arose in both Britain and its colonies in mainland North America, from Massachusetts to Georgia, to protest not only the new measures' economic costs but what many people regarded as a dangerous extension of tyrannical power. In America this confrontation quickly escalated into a principled conflict over the colonies' relationship with Parliament in Britain.

These measures coincided with the beginning of the reign of George III (ruled 1760–1820), who ascended to the throne at age twenty-two. In contrast to his immediate predecessors, George I and George II, who had been largely content to let veteran politicians in Parliament run the country, the new king distrusted the British political establishment. He was determined to have a strong influence on government policy, but he wished to reign as a constitutional monarch who cooperated with Parliament and worked through prime ministers. However, neither his experience, his temperament, nor his philosophy suited George III to the formidable task of selecting satisfactory prime ministers to oversee the passage of imperial laws. Frequent clashes of personality and policy prompted the king to make abrupt changes in leadership at the very time when British government was trying to implement a massive reorganization of the empire. George's first prime minister, his friend and former tutor Lord Bute, lasted only from 1760 to 1763. Then in quick succession came the ministry of George Grenville from 1763 to 1765, that of the Marquis of Rockingham in 1766, the ministry of the ailing William Pitt in 1766, and a period

of uncertain leadership that ended only in 1770, with the appointment of the ministry led by Frederick, Lord North.

Friction Among Allies

An extraordinary coalition of Britons, colonists, and Native Americans had achieved the victory over France in North America. But the return of peace brought deep-seated tensions among these allies back to the surface.

In England, public opinion assumed that credit for the victory belonged to the professional soldiers

European Powers in the New World Before 1754 and in 1763
The Treaty of Paris (1763) divided France's North American empire between Britain and Spain. Hoping to prevent unnecessary violence between whites and Indians, Britain forbade any new white settlements west of the Appalachians' crest in the Proclamation of 1763.

Disputed claim

British territory

Danish territory

French territory

Spanish territory

Russian territory

Title not established

Before 1754

Proclamation line of 1763

In 1763

sent over from Britain. In fact, however, two of every five regulars who served had enlisted in America. Benjamin Franklin once complained that, although the force that captured two French forts on Nova Scotia's border in 1755 comprised two thousand Massachusetts troops and fewer than three hundred British regulars, "yet it could not be discovered by the Account . . . published in the London Gazette, that there was a single New England man concern'd in the Affair."

Although realizing that the newly formed colonial units would not perform as well as veteran regiments, Pitt had nevertheless placed the American enlistees in charge of vital support roles: forming the reserve force in battle, performing essential supply functions, and holding frontier forts. This plan had the advantage of freeing the greatest number of British regulars for combat against the highly trained French. But British officers in America regularly complained about the quality of colonial troops, not only their inability to fight but also their tendency to return home—even in the midst of campaigns—when their terms were up or when they were not paid on time. For their part, colonial soldiers complained of British officers who, as one put it, contemptuously treated their troops "but little better than slaves."

Tensions between British officers and colonial civilians also flared, with officers complaining about colonists' unwillingness to provide food and shelter and colonists resenting the officers' arrogant manners. One general groused that South Carolina planters were "extremely pleased to have Soldiers to protect their Plantations but will feel no inconveniences for them." Quakers in the Pennsylvania assembly, acting from their pacifist convictions, refused to vote funds to support the war effort, while assemblies in New York and Massachusetts opposed the quartering of British troops on their soil as an encroachment on their English liberties. English authorities regarded such actions as affronts to the king's prerogative and as stifling Britain's efforts to defend its territories.

Pitt's promise to reimburse the colonial assemblies for their military expenses also angered many Britons, who concluded that the colonists were escaping scot-free from the war's financial burden. The colonies had already profited enormously from the war, as military contracts and spending by British troops brought an influx of British currency into the hands of farmers, artisans, and merchants. Some colonial merchants, moreover, had continued their illicit trade with the French West Indies during the conflict,

so that they were not only violating the Navigation Acts but trading with the enemy. Meanwhile, Britain's national debt had nearly doubled during the war, from £72 million to over £132 million. At a time when the total debt of all the colonies collectively amounted to £2 million, the interest charges alone on the British debt came to more than £4 million a year. This debt was assumed by landowners through a land tax and, increasingly, by ordinary consumers through excise duties on a wide variety of items, including beer, tea, salt, and bread.

But many colonists felt equally burdened. Those who profited during the war spent their additional incomes on goods imported from Britain, the annual value of which doubled during the war's brief duration. Along with a parallel movement in Britain, the consumption of tea, wine, mass-produced textiles, ceramics, and metalware by members of the middle class was fueling Britain's economy, particularly its manufacturing sector. And it was transforming the habits and tastes of thousands of people who previously had made or purchased locally nearly everything they consumed. But the wartime boom in the colonies ended as abruptly as it had begun when peace returned in 1760. To maintain their new middle-class lifestyles, colonists went into debt. British creditors obliged their American merchant customers by extending the usual period for remitting payments from six months to a year. Nevertheless, many recently prosperous colonists suddenly found themselves overloaded with debts and in many cases bankrupt. As colonial indebtedness to Britain grew, some Americans began to suspect the British of deliberately plotting to "enslave" the colonies.

Victory over the French did not end the British need for revenue, for the settlement of the war spurred new Anglo-Indian conflicts that drove the British debt even higher. With the French vanquished, Ohio and Great Lakes Indians recognized that they could no longer play the two imperial rivals off against one another. Their fears that the British would treat them as subjects rather than allies were confirmed when General Amherst decided to cut expenses by refusing to distribute food, ammunition, and other gifts. Moreover, squatters from the colonies were moving onto Indian lands in some areas and harassing the occupants, and many Indians feared that the British occupation was intended to support these incursions.

As tensions mounted, a Delaware religious prophet named Neolin attracted a large following by calling for a complete repudiation by Indians of European culture, material goods, and alliances. Meanwhile, other Native Americans hoped that the French would return so they could once again balance the two powers against each other. Political leaders such as Pontiac, an Ottawa Indian, drew on these sentiments to forge an explicitly anti-British movement. During the spring and summer of 1763, they sacked eight British forts near the Great Lakes and besieged two others at Pittsburgh and Detroit. But over the next three years, shortages of food and ammunition, a smallpox epidemic (triggered when British officers at Fort Pitt distributed deliberately infected blankets at a peace parley), and a recognition that the French would not return led the Indians to make peace with Britain. Although word of the uprising spread to Indians in the Southeast and Mississippi Valley, the effective diplomacy of British agent John Stuart prevented violence from erupting in these areas.

Despite the uprising's failure, the Native Americans had not been decisively defeated. Hoping to conciliate the Indians and end the frontier fighting, the British government issued the Proclamation of 1763, by which it asserted direct control of land transactions, settlement, trade, and other activities of non-Indians west of the Appalachian crest. The government's goal was to restore order to the process of colonial expansion by replacing the authority of the various (and often competing) colonies with that of the crown. The proclamation recognized existing Indian land titles everywhere west of the "proclamation line" until such time as tribal governments agreed to cede their land through treaties. Although calming Indian fears, the proclamation angered the colonies by subordinating their western claims to imperial authority and by slowing expansion.

The uprising was also a factor in the British government's decision that ten thousand British soldiers should remain in North America to occupy the new western territories and to intimidate the Indian, French, and Spanish inhabitants. The British expected to spend £220,000 annually to maintain these troops, but the actual expense soared to nearly twice that figure. With the £20,000 needed to establish civil governments in Canada and Florida factored in, the burden of maintaining control over Britain's newly acquired territories would reach almost half a million pounds a year, fully 6 percent of Britain's peacetime budget. Britons considered it perfectly reasonable for the colonists to help offset this expense, which the colonists, however, saw as none of their responsibility. Although the troops would help to offset the colonies' unfavorable balance of payments with Britain, they appeared to many Americans as a "standing army" that in peacetime could only threaten their liberty. With the French menace to their security removed, increasing numbers of colonists saw westward expansion onto Indian lands as a way to prosperity, and they viewed British troops, enforcing the Proclamation of 1763, as hindering rather than enhancing that expansion.

The Writs of Assistance

Even before the Seven Years' War was over, British attempts to halt American merchants from trading with the enemy in the French West Indies produced a crackdown on smuggling. In 1760 the royal governor of Massachusetts authorized revenue officers to employ a document called a writ of assistance to seize illegally imported goods. The writ was a general search warrant that permitted customs officials to enter any ships or buildings where smuggled goods might be hidden. Because the document required no evidence of probable cause for suspicion, most English legal authorities considered it unconstitutional. The writ of assistance also threatened the traditional respect accorded the privacy of a family's place of residence, since most merchants conducted business from their homes. The writ allowed a customs agent to ransack a merchant's house in search of illegal goods, even if there was no evidence of lawbreaking.

Writs of assistance proved a powerful weapon against smuggling. In quick reaction to the writs, merchants in Boston, virtually the smuggling capital of the colonies, hired lawyer James Otis to challenge the constitutionality of these warrants. Arguing his case before the Massachusetts supreme court in 1761, Otis proclaimed that "an act against the Constitution is void"—even one passed by Parliament. But the court, heavily influenced by the opinion of Chief Justice Thomas Hutchinson, who noted the continuing use of identical writs in England, ruled against the Boston merchants.

Despite having lost the case, Otis had expressed with absolute clarity the fundamental conception of many, both in Britain and in the colonies, of Parliament's role under the British constitution. The British constitution was not a written document but a collection of customs and accepted principles that guaranteed certain rights to all citizens. Most British politicians assumed that Parliament's laws were themselves part of the constitution and hence that Parliament could alter the constitution at will. Like other colonists, Otis contended that Parliament possessed no authority to violate any of the traditional "rights of Englishmen," and he asserted that there were limits "beyond which if Parliaments go, their Acts bind not."

The Sugar Act

In 1764, just three years after Otis's court challenge, Parliament passed the Sugar Act with the goal of raising £100,000, a sum that would offset one-fifth of the military expenses in North America. Its enactment triggered a new round of tension between Britain and the colonies, for the Sugar Act ended Britain's long-standing policy of exempting colonial trade from revenue-raising measures. The Navigation Acts had not been designed to bring money into the British treasury but rather to benefit the imperial economy indirectly, by stimulating trade and protecting English manufacturers from foreign competition. The taxes that Parliament levied on colonial products entering Britain were paid by English importers who passed them on to consumers; they were not taxes paid by American producers. So little revenue did the Navigation Acts bring in (just £1,800 in 1763) that they did not even pay for the cost of their own enforcement, which came to about £8,000.

The Sugar Act amended the old Molasses Act of 1733, which had taxed all foreign molasses entering British America at 6 pence per gallon. Parliament had never intended this law to raise revenue but rather to serve as a protective tariff excluding French West Indian molasses from entering British North America, where colonists distilled it into rum. But colonists simply continued to import the cheaper French molasses, bribing customs officials into taking 1½ pence per gallon to look the other way when it was unloaded. Aware of the widespread bribery, Parliament assumed, erroneously, that rum drinkers could stomach a 3 pence duty per gallon.

New taxes were not the only feature of the Sugar Act objectionable to American merchants. The act also stipulated that colonists could export lumber, iron, skins, hides, whalebone, logwood, and many other commodities to foreign countries only if the shipments landed first in Britain. Previously, American ships had taken these products directly to the Netherlands or the German states, where captains purchased local goods and then sailed straight back to the colonies. By channeling this trade through Britain, Parliament hoped that colonial shippers would purchase more *imperial* wares for the American market and buy fewer goods from foreign competitors. Moreover, by slapping a heavy tax on the formerly thriving American business of carrying duty-free Portuguese wine from Madeira and the Azores to the colonists, the law also aimed to increase English merchants' sales of European wine. By interfering with a profitable trade developed through American enterprise, the Sugar Act had the perverse effect of creating a new category of smuggling where none had existed before, because many colonial merchants ultimately ignored the law, which in their view senselessly sacrificed their interests.

The Sugar Act also vastly complicated the requirements for shipping colonial goods. A captain now had to fill out a confusing series of documents to certify his trade as legal, and the absence of any of them left his entire cargo liable to seizure. Moreover, the Sugar Act defined oceanic commerce so broadly that much of the trade between colonies, never before regulated, became subject to complex rules for compliance. The law's petty regulations made it virtually impossible for many colonial shippers to avoid committing technical violations of the Sugar Act, even if they traded in the only manner possible under local circumstances.

Finally, the Sugar Act disregarded many traditional English protections for a fair trial. First, the law allowed customs officials to transfer smuggling cases from the colonial courts, in which juries decided the outcome, to vice-admiralty courts, where a judge alone gave the verdict. Because the Sugar Act (until 1768) awarded vice-admiralty judges 5 percent of any confiscated cargo, judges had a financial incentive to find defendants guilty. Second, until 1767 the law did not permit defendants to be tried where their offense allegedly had taken place (usually their home province) but required all cases to be heard in the vice-admiralty court at Halifax, Nova Scotia. Third, the law reversed normal courtroom procedures, which presumed innocence until guilt was proved, by requiring the defendant to disprove the prosecution's charge.

The Sugar Act was no idle threat. British prime minister George Grenville ordered the navy to enforce the measure, and it did so vigorously. A Boston resident complained in 1764 that "no vessel hardly comes in or goes out but they find some pretense to seize and detain her." That same year, Pennsylvania's chief justice reported that customs officers were extorting fees from small boats carrying lumber across the Delaware River to Philadelphia from New Jersey and seemed likely "to destroy this little River-trade."

Rather than pay the 3 pence tax, Americans continued smuggling molasses until 1766. Then, to discourage smuggling, Britain lowered the duty to 1 penny—less than the customary bribe American shippers paid to get their cargoes past inspectors. The law thereafter raised about £30,000 annually in revenue until 1775.

Colonial opponents hesitated to denounce the Sugar Act as unconstitutional, for it seemingly only amended the Molasses Act. Although nine provincial legislatures protested that in passing the Sugar Act, Parliament had abused its authority to regulate trade, seven of these objected on narrow grounds—either to its economic consequences for distillers or to its denial of traditional guarantees of a fair trial. Thus opposition to the Sugar Act remained fragmented and ineffective. The law's burden fell overwhelmingly on Massachusetts, New York, and Pennsylvania; other provinces had little interest in resisting a measure that did not affect them directly. In the end, the Sugar Act's immediate impact was minor. Soon a far more controversial issue would overshadow it—the Stamp Act.

The Stamp Act

The revenue raised by the Sugar Act did little to ease Britain's financial crisis. The national debt continued to rise, and the British public groaned under the weight of the second-highest tax rates in Europe. Particularly irritating to Britons was the fact that by 1765 their rates averaged 26 shillings per person, whereas the colonial tax burden varied from ½ to 1½ shillings per inhabitant, or barely 2 percent to 6 percent of the British rate. Well aware of how lightly the colonists were taxed, Grenville thought that fairness demanded a larger contribution to the empire's expenses in North America.

To force the colonists to pay their share of imperial expenses, Parliament passed the Stamp Act in March 1765. The law obliged Americans to purchase and use special stamped (watermarked) paper for newspapers, customs documents, various licenses, college diplomas, and numerous legal forms necessary for recovering debts, buying land, and making wills. As with the Sugar Act, any violators would face prosecution in vice-admiralty courts, without juries.

The prime minister projected yearly revenues of £60,000 to £100,000, which would offset 12 percent to 20 percent of North American military expenses. Unlike the Sugar Act, which was an *external* tax—one levied on imports as they entered the colonies—the Stamp Act was an *internal* tax, or a duty levied directly on property, goods, and government services in the colonies. Whereas external taxes were intended to regulate trade and fell mainly on merchants and ship captains, internal taxes were designed to raise revenue

Tax Stamps
Under the Stamp Act, all legal and commercial documents had to bear tax stamps such as the one shown here in close-up.

for the crown and had far wider effects. In the case of the Stamp Act, anyone who made a will, transferred property, borrowed money, or bought playing cards or newspapers would pay the tax.

To Grenville and most of his supporters in Britain, the new tax seemed a small price for the benefits of the empire, especially since Britons had been paying a similar tax since 1695. Nevertheless, some in England, most notably William Pitt, objected in principle to Britain's levying an internal tax on the colonies. They emphasized that the colonists had never been subject to British revenue bills and noted that they taxed themselves through their own elected assemblies.

Grenville and his followers agreed with Pitt that Parliament could not tax any British subjects unless they enjoyed representation in that body. But, they contended, Americans *were* represented in Parliament, even if no one in the colonies actually elected any members. Americans, the prime minister claimed, shared the same status as the majority of British adult males, who either lacked sufficient property to vote or lived in large cities like Sheffield, Manchester, and Birmingham—some more populous than the entire colony of Georgia in the mid-1760s—which had no seats in Parliament. Such people were considered to be "virtually" represented in Parliament. The theory of virtual representation held that every member of Parliament stood above the narrow interests of his constituents and considered the welfare of *all* subjects when deciding issues. By definition, then, no Briton was represented by any particular individual in the House of Commons, but rather all imperial subjects, including Americans, could depend on each member of Parliament to protect their well-being.

Grenville and his supporters also denied that the colonists were entitled to any exemption from British taxation because they elected their own assemblies. These legislative bodies were allegedly no different from English or Scottish town councils, whose local powers to pass laws and taxes did not nullify Parliament's authority over them. Accordingly, colonial assemblies were an adaptation to unique American circumstances and possessed no more power than Parliament allowed them to exercise. But Grenville's position clashed directly with the stance of many colonists who had been arguing for several decades that their assemblies exercised legislative powers equivalent to those of the House of Commons in Britain (see Chapter 4).

The Colonial Perspective

To many colonists the Stamp Act seemed to force them either to confront the issue of parliamentary taxation head-on or surrender any claim to meaningful rights of self-government. However much they might admire and respect Parliament, few colonists imagined that it represented them. American spokesmen accepted the theory of virtual representation as valid for England and Scotland, but they denied that it could be extended to inhabitants of the colonies. In their view, unless a lawmaker shared the interests of his constituents, he would have no personal stake in opposing bills contrary to their welfare.

To many colonists Parliament's passage of the Stamp Act demonstrated both its indifference to their interests and the shallowness of the theory of virtual representation. Colonial agents in London had lobbied against passage of the law, and provincial legislatures had sent petitions—carefully worded statements of principle—warning against passage, but all to no avail. Parliament had dismissed the petitions without a hearing. Parliament "must have thought us Americans all a parcel of Apes and very tame Apes too," concluded Christopher Gadsden of South Carolina, "or they would have never ventured on such a hateful, baneful experiment."

Although the colonists rejected Parliament's claim to tax them, they did concede that it possessed *limited* powers of legislation. For example, they be-

lieved that Parliament could standardize legal procedures throughout the realm to permit every British subject equal access to royal justice. The colonists also accepted the practical necessity for Parliament to regulate the empire's trade, even if their commerce was inconvenienced in the process.

Anglo-Americans considered the essential obligation of British allegiance to be loyalty to the crown, and their one unequivocal duty to be helping to defend the empire in wartime. The colonists insisted that they enjoyed a substantial measure of self-governance similar to that of Ireland, whose Parliament alone could tax its people but could not interfere with laws, like the Navigation Acts, passed by the British Parliament. In a speech before the Boston town meeting opposing the Sugar Act, James Otis expressed Americans' basic argument: "that by [the British] Constitution, every man in the dominions is a free man: that no parts of His Majesty's dominions can be taxed without consent: that every part has a right to be represented in the supreme or some subordinate legislature." In essence, the colonists assumed that the empire was a loose federation in which their legislatures possessed considerable autonomy, rather than an extended nation governed directly from London.

Resisting the Stamp Act

Unlike the Sugar Act, the Stamp Act generated a political storm that rumbled through all the colonies in 1765. Nearly every rank in society was caught up in the tempest—unskilled workers, artisans, small farmers, planters, and merchants; blacks as well as whites; women as well as men. Before the protest was over, upper-class community leaders had assumed direction of the colonial resistance movement.

In late May, Patrick Henry, a twenty-nine-year-old Virginia lawyer with a talent for fiery oratory, dramatically conveyed the rising spirit of resistance. Henry persuaded the Virginia House of Burgesses to adopt several strongly worded resolutions denying Parliament's power to tax the colonies, and in the debate over the resolutions, the Speaker of the House cut him off just short of his uttering a treasonous wish that "some good American would stand up for his country"—presumably by assassinating the British tyrant responsible. Rather garbled accounts of Henry's resolutions electrified other Americans, and by the year's end, eight other colonial legislatures took a firm stand against British taxation.

Stamp Act Protest
A Boston crowd burns bundles of the special watermarked paper intended for use as stamps.

Meanwhile, grass-roots resistance to the law was taking shape. In Boston by late summer, a group of mostly middle-class artisans, shopkeepers, and businessmen joined together as the Loyal Nine to fight the Stamp Act. They recognized that the stamp distributors, who alone could accept money for watermarked paper, were the law's weak link. If the public could pressure them into resigning before taxes became due on November 1, the Stamp Act would become inoperable. The Loyal Nine would propel Boston to the forefront of resistance.

It was no accident that Boston set the pace in opposing Parliament. Bostonians lived primarily by trade and distilling, and in 1765 they were not living well. No other port suffered so much from the Sugar Act's trade restrictions. The law burdened rum producers with a heavy tax on molasses, dried up a flourishing business of importing Portuguese wines, and prohibited the direct export of many New England products to prof-

itable overseas markets. The city, moreover, was still struggling to recover from a great fire in 1760 that had burned 176 warehouses and left every tenth family homeless.

Widespread economic distress produced an explosive situation in Boston. A large segment of its population blamed British policies for the town's hard times. The situation was unusually dangerous because Bostonians were accustomed to forming large crowds to engage in pointed but symbolic political expression. The high point of each year was November 5, Guy Fawkes Day, when thousands gathered to commemorate the failure of a Catholic plot in England in 1605 to blow up Parliament and kill King James I. On that day each year, crowds from the North End and the South End customarily burned gigantic effigies of the pope as well as of local political leaders and other elite figures, and generally satirized the behavior of the "better sort." High spirits sometimes overflowed into violent confrontations in which the two crowds battled each other with fists, stones, and barrel staves. In August 1765 the Loyal Nine oversaw a truce between the two groups that united them under a South End shoemaker named Ebenezer MacIntosh.

The morning of August 14 found a likeness of Boston's stamp distributor, Andrew Oliver, swinging from a tree guarded by a menacing crowd. Oliver apparently did not realize that the Loyal Nine were warning him to resign immediately, so at dusk MacIntosh and several hundred shouting followers demolished a new building of Oliver's at the dock. Thereafter, the Loyal Nine withdrew and the crowd continued on its own. The men surged toward Oliver's house, where they ceremoniously beheaded his effigy and "stamped" it to pieces, an exercise designed in part to give him time to flee to safety. The crowd then shattered the windows of his home, smashed his furniture, and even tore out the paneling. When Lieutenant Governor Thomas Hutchinson and the sheriff tried to disperse the crowd, they were driven off under a barrage of rocks. Surveying his devastated home the next morning, Oliver announced his resignation.

Bitterness against the Stamp Act unleashed spontaneous, contagious violence. Twelve days after the first Boston riot, Bostonians demolished the elegant home of Thomas Hutchinson. This attack occurred in part because smugglers held grudges against Hutchinson for certain decisions he had given as chief justice and also because many financially pinched citizens saw him as a symbol of the royal policies crippling Boston's already troubled economy and their own livelihoods. In their view, wealthy officials "rioted in luxury," with homes and fancy furnishings that cost hundreds of times the annual incomes of most Boston working men. Others lashed out in reaction to Hutchinson's efforts to stop the destruction of his brother-in-law Andrew Oliver's house. Ironically, Hutchinson privately opposed the Stamp Act.

Violence nearly got completely out of hand in Newport, Rhode Island. As in Boston, a working-class crowd organized by merchants quickly assumed a life of its own, but in this case the mob turned on the merchants themselves. After the rowdies burned the effigies and sacked the homes of three stamp distributors, an English seaman named John Webber assumed leadership. Webber threatened to destroy the merchants' homes and warehouses unless they paid a large sum, and publicly humiliated the sheriff. One of the deposed stamp masters—who was also the colony's attorney general—ended Webber's threats by clapping him in jail.

Meanwhile, groups similar to the Loyal Nine but calling themselves Sons of Liberty began forming throughout the colonies. The Sons of Liberty directed their violence against property and invariably left avenues of escape for their victims. No one was killed or tarred and feathered, although some stamp distributors had their pride deeply wounded.

After Webber's rampage and the frenzied assault on Hutchinson's mansion, the leaders of the Sons of Liberty sought to prevent more such incidents, lest they alienate elite opponents of the tax. They directed public demonstrations with firm discipline and sometimes used military formations to maneuver hundreds of protesters like a small army. Especially fearful that a royal soldier or revenue officer might be shot or killed, the Sons of Liberty forbade their followers to carry weapons, even when facing armed adversaries. Realizing the value of martyrs, they resolved that the only lives lost over the issue of British taxation would come from their own ranks.

In October 1765 representatives of nine colonial assemblies met in New York City in the so-called Stamp Act Congress. The session was remarkable for the colonies' agreement on and bold articulation of the general principle that Parliament lacked authority to levy taxes outside Great Britain and to deny any person a jury trial. Only once before had a truly intercolonial meeting taken place—the Albany Congress, in 1754—

and, as we have seen, its plea for unity had fallen on deaf ears. In 1765 the colonial response was entirely different. "The Ministry never imagined we could or would so generally unite in opposition to their measures," wrote a Connecticut delegate to the congress, "nor I confess till I saw the Experiment made did I."

By late 1765 most stamp distributors had resigned or fled, and, without the watermarked paper required by law, most royal customs officials and court officers were refusing to perform their duties. In response, legislators compelled the reluctant officials to resume operation by threatening to withhold their pay. At the same time, merchants obtained sailing clearances by insisting that they would sue if cargoes spoiled while delayed in port. By late December the courts and harbors of almost every colony were again functioning.

Thus the colonial upper class assumed control of the public outcry against the Stamp Act. Respectable gentlemen moved to keep an explosive situation from getting out of hand by taking over leadership of local Sons of Liberty groups, by coordinating protest through the Stamp Act Congress, and by having colonial legislatures restore normal business. Colonial leaders feared that chaos was about to break out, particularly if British troops landed to enforce the Stamp Act. An influential Pennsylvanian, John Dickinson, summed up how colonial elites envisioned the dire consequences of revolutionary turmoil: "a multitude of Commonwealths, Crimes, and Calamities, Centuries of mutual jealousies, Hatreds, Wars of Devastation, till at last the exhausted provinces shall sink into savagery under the yoke of some fortunate Conqueror."

Such extreme consequences did not come to pass, though the Stamp Act remained in effect. To force its repeal, New York's merchants agreed on October 31, 1765, to boycott all British goods, and businessmen in other cities soon followed their example. Because American colonists purchased about 40 percent of England's manufactures, this nonimportation strategy put the English economy in danger of recession. The colonial boycotts consequently triggered panic within England's business community, whose members descended on Parliament to warn that the Stamp Act's continuation would stimulate a wave of bankruptcies, massive unemployment, and political unrest.

For reasons unconnected with the Stamp Act, George Grenville had fallen from George III's favor in mid-1765 and had been succeeded by the Marquis of Rockingham. The new prime minister hesitated to advocate repeal because the overwhelming majority within the House of Commons was outraged at colonial defiance of the law. Then in January 1766 William Pitt, a steadfast opponent of the Stamp Act, boldly denounced all efforts to tax the colonies, declaring, "I rejoice that America has resisted." Parliamentary support for repeal thereafter grew, though only as a matter of practicality, not as a surrender of principle. In March 1766 Parliament revoked the Stamp Act, but only in conjunction with passage of the Declaratory Act, which affirmed parliamentary power to legislate for the colonies "in all cases whatsoever."

Because the Declaratory Act was written in general language, Americans interpreted its meaning to their advantage. Most colonial political leaders recognized that the law was modeled after an earlier statute of 1719 regarding Ireland, which was considered exempt from British taxation. The measure therefore seemed no more than a parliamentary exercise in saving face to compensate for the Stamp Act's repeal, and Americans ignored it. The House of Commons, however, intended that the colonists take the Declaratory Act literally to mean that they could not claim exemption from *any* parliamentary statute, including a tax law. The Stamp Act crisis thus ended in a fundamental disagreement between Britain and America over the colonists' political rights.

Although the Stamp Act crisis had not resolved the underlying philosophical differences between Britain and America, most colonists eagerly put the events of 1765 behind them, and they showered both king and Parliament with loyal statements of gratitude for the Stamp Act's repeal. The Sons of Liberty disbanded. Anglo-Americans manifestly still possessed a deep emotional loyalty to "Old England" and concluded with relief that their active resistance to the law had slapped Britain's leaders back to their senses. Nevertheless, the crisis led many to ponder British policies and actions more deeply than ever before.

Ideology, Religion, and Resistance

The Stamp Act and the conflicts that arose around it revealed a chasm between England and its colonies that startled Anglo-Americans. For the first time, some sensed a sinister quality to the imperial relationship that they previously had taken for granted and valued. In their efforts to grasp the significance of their new perceptions, a number of educated colonists turned to the works of philosophers, historians, and political writers. Many more, both educated and uneducated, looked to religion.

By the 1760s the colonists already were widely familiar with the political writings of European Enlightenment thinkers, particularly John Locke (see Chapter 4). Locke argued that humanity originated in a state of nature in which people enjoyed the "natural rights" of life, liberty, and property. Thereafter, people entered into a "social contract" in order to form governments that would protect those rights. A government that encroached on natural rights, then, broke its contract with the people. In such cases, people could resist their government, although Locke cautioned against outright rebellion except in the most extreme cases. To many colonial readers, Locke's concept of natural rights appeared to justify opposition to arbitrary legislation by Parliament.

Among the most widely read authors in the colonies were a group of English political writers known as oppositionists. According to John Trenchard, Thomas Gordon, and others belonging to this group, Parliament—consisting of the freely elected representatives of the people—formed the foundation of England's unique political liberties and protected those liberties against the inherent corruption and tyranny of executive power. But since 1720, the oppositionists argued, prime ministers had exploited the treasury's vast resources to provide pensions, contracts, and profitable offices to politicians or had bought elections by bribing voters in small boroughs. Most members of Parliament, in their view, no longer represented the true interests of their constituents; rather, they had sold their souls for financial gain and joined in a "conspiracy against liberty." Often referring to themselves as the "country party," these oppositionists feared that a power-hungry "court party" of nonelected officials close to the king was using a corrupted Parliament to gain absolute power for themselves.

During the 1760s and 1770s, a group of English radicals, most notably Joseph Priestley and James Burgh, drew on both Enlightenment and oppositionist authors to fashion a wide-ranging critique of English government and a new way of thinking about politics. At the heart of all political relationships, they argued, a struggle raged between the aggressive extension of artificial *power,* as represented by corrupt governments, and the natural *liberty* of the people. To protect their liberty, a free people had to avoid moral corruption in their own lives and resist the encroachments of power, or tyranny. Above all, they had to remain alert for "designs" or "conspiracies" against liberty wherever they might appear.

Influenced by such ideas, a number of colonists detected a diabolical conspiracy behind British policy during the Stamp Act crisis. John Adams referred to the actions of Massachusetts lieutenant governor Thomas Hutchinson as "serpentine wiles," and James Otis characterized a group of pro-British Rhode Islanders as a "little, dirty, drinking, drabbing, contaminated knot of thieves, beggars, and transports . . . made up of Turks, Jews, and other infidels, with a few renegade Christians and Catholics." Joseph Warren of Massachusetts noted that the act not unreasonably "induced some to imagine that the minister designed by this to force the colonies into a rebellion, and from thence to take occasion to treat them with severity, and, by military power, to reduce them to servitude." Over the next decade, a proliferation of pamphlets denounced British efforts to "enslave" the colonies through excessive taxation and the imposition of officials, judges, and a standing army directed from London. In such assaults on liberty and natural rights, some Americans found principled reasons for opposing British policies and actions.

Many colonists also followed the lead of Massachusetts assemblyman Samuel Adams, who expressed hope that America would become a "Christian Sparta." By linking religion and ancient history, Adams was combining two of colonial leaders' most potent rhetorical appeals in rallying public protest. Almost every eighteenth-century American had been steeped in Protestantism since childhood; and all whose education had gone beyond the basics had imbibed Greek and Latin learning, as well as seventeenth-century English literature. All these hallowed traditions, Americans believed, confirmed the legitimacy of their cause. "Having been initiated in youth, in the doctrines of civil liberty, as they were taught by such men as Plato . . . [and] Cicero . . . among the ancients; and such as . . . Milton [and] Locke . . . among the moderns," wrote the minister Jonathan Mayhew, "[and] having earlier still learnt from the holy scriptures, that wise, brave, and virtuous men were always friends of liberty . . . I would not, I cannot now, relinquish the fair object of my youthful affections, LIBERTY. . . ."

Recalling in later years the inspiring debate over the Stamp Act that he had witnessed in Virginia's House of Burgesses in 1765, Thomas Jefferson said of Patrick Henry that "he appeared to me to speak as Homer wrote." Jefferson was a typical educated man

of his day in revering the ancient republics of Greece and Rome for their supposedly stern, virtuous devotion to liberty. The pamphlets, speeches, and public declarations that gentlemen like Jefferson and Dickinson wrote resounded with quotations from the ancient classics. These allusions served as constant reminders to upper-class Americans of the righteous dignity of their cause. But appeals to ordinary Americans had to draw upon deeper wellsprings of belief. Significantly, the power of Henry's oratory also reflected his ability (unique among Virginia political leaders) to evoke the colonists' religious fervor, which the Great Awakening had stirred.

Beginning with the Stamp Act protest, New England's clergymen mounted their pulpits and summoned their flocks to stand up for God and liberty. "A just regard to our liberties . . . is so far from being

A Patriot View of British Officials, 1766

This Boston editorial cartoon depicts Lord Bute (left) and another British official as enslaved to the devil.

displeasing to God that it would be ingratitude to him who has given them to us to . . . tamely give them up," exhorted one minister. "We are bound in conscience to stand fast in the liberty with which Christ has made us free." Not quite so quickly, but in the end with equally heartfelt intensity, Baptist and other dissenting preachers took up the cause. Only Anglican ministers, whose church was headed by the king, tried to stay neutral or opposed the protest; and many pacifist Quakers kept out of the fray. But to most American Protestant clergymen, memories of battling for the Lord in the old Calvinist tradition proved too powerful to resist.

Voicing such a message, "the black regiment" of clergymen in their dignified gowns exerted an enormous influence on public opinion. Far more Americans heard sermons than had access to newspapers or pamphlets, and ministers always got a respectful hearing at town meetings. Community leaders' proclamations of days of "fasting and public humiliation"—in colonial America, a familiar means of focusing public attention on an issue and invoking divine aid—inspired sermons on the theme of God's sending the people woes only to strengthen and sustain them until victory. Even Virginia gentlemen not notable for their piety felt moved by such proclamations and ordered their families to comply. Moreover, protest leaders' calls for boycotting British luxuries meshed neatly with traditional pulpit warnings against frivolity and wastefulness. Few ordinary Americans escaped the unceasing public reminders that community solidarity against British tyranny and "corruption" meant rejecting sin and obeying God.

The ebbing of the Stamp Act crisis momentarily took the urgency out of such extreme views. But the alarm that Britain's actions raised in the minds of many colonists was not easily put to rest. After a hiatus of two years, it was clear that British and American views of the colonies' place in the empire remained as far apart as ever.

ERA OF ANGLO-AMERICAN CRISIS

From 1767 to 1773, Parliament pursued a confrontational policy that gradually corroded Americans' trust of Britain. The British government's actions in these years created a climate of fear and alienation that left most colonists convinced that the Stamp Act had not been an isolated mistake but part of a deliberate design to undermine colonial self-governance. In this they were joined by growing numbers in Britain who questioned policies that were economically costly and actions that seemed to threaten Britons and colonists alike.

The Quartering Act

In August 1766, in a move arising out of British politics, George III dismissed the Rockingham government and summoned William Pitt to form a cabinet. An opponent of taxing the colonies, Pitt had the potential to repair the Stamp Act's damage, for no man was more respected in America. Pitt's health collapsed in March 1767 however, and effective leadership passed to his chancellor of the exchequer (or treasurer) Charles Townshend.

Just as Townshend took office, a conflict arose with the New York legislature over the Quartering Act of 1765. This law ordered colonial legislatures to pay for certain goods needed by soldiers stationed within their respective borders. The necessary items were relatively inexpensive barracks supplies such as candles, windowpanes, mattress straw, polish, and a small liquor ration. The Quartering Act applied only to troops in settled areas, not on the frontier. It did not force citizens to accept soldiers in private homes or require legislatures to build new barracks. Just five colonies fell under its provisions, and four of these generally complied.

Despite its seemingly petty stipulations, the law aroused resentment, for it constituted an *indirect* tax; that is, although it did not (like the Stamp Act) empower royal officials to collect money directly from the colonists, it obligated particular assemblies to raise a stated amount of revenue by whatever means they considered appropriate. The act fell lightly or not at all on most colonies; but New York, where more soldiers were stationed than in any other province, found compliance very burdensome and refused to grant any supplies.

New York's resistance to indirect taxation produced a torrent of anti-American feeling in the House of Commons, whose members remained bitter at having had to withdraw the Stamp Act. Townshend responded by drafting the New York Suspending Act, which threatened to nullify all laws passed by the colony after October 1, 1767, if the assembly still refused to vote the supplies. By the time that George III signed the measure in June, however, New York had already appropriated the necessary funds.

Although New York's retreat averted further confrontation, the conflict over the Quartering Act revealed the full extent of anticolonial sentiment in the House of Commons. The incident demonstrated that British leaders would not hesitate to defend Parliament's sovereignty through the most drastic of all steps: by interfering with American claims to self-governance. What Townshend and others did not realize was that such a course of action would soon undermine a loyal people's political allegiance.

The Townshend Duties

The new wave of British resentment toward the colonies coincided with an outpouring of British frustration over the government's failure to cut taxes from wartime levels. Discontent raged among the landed gentry, whose members took advantage of their domination of the House of Commons to slash their own taxes by 25 percent in 1767. This move cost the government £500,000 and prompted Townshend to propose laws that would tax imports entering America and increase colonial customs revenue.

Townshend sought to tax the colonists by exploiting an oversight in their arguments against the Stamp Act. In confronting the Stamp Act, Americans had emphasized their opposition to *internal* taxes, but had said little about Parliament's right to tax imports as they entered the colonies. Townshend and other British leaders chose to interpret this silence as evidence that the colonists accepted Britain's right to tax their trade—to impose *external* taxes. Yet not all British politicians were so mistaken. "They will laugh at you," predicted a now wiser George Grenville, "for your distinctions about regulations of trade." Brushing aside Grenville's warnings, Parliament passed Townshend's Revenue Act of 1767 (popularly called the Townshend duties) in June and July 1767. The new law taxed glass, paint, lead, paper, and tea imported into the colonies.

On the surface, Townshend's contention that the Americans would submit to this external tax on imports was convincing, for the colonists had long accepted Parliament's right to regulate their overseas trade and had in principle acknowledged taxation as a legitimate form of regulation. Even the Sugar Act had not primarily aroused opposition in the colonies be-

cause it imposed taxes; rather, Americans had protested the law because it instituted impractical regulations for conducting trade and violated traditional guarantees of a fair trial.

Townshend's Revenue Act differed significantly from what Americans had long seen as a legitimate way of regulating trade through taxation. To the colonists, charging a duty was a lawful way for British authorities to control trade only if that duty excluded foreign goods by making them prohibitively expensive to consumers. The Revenue Act of 1767, however, set moderate rates that did not price goods out of the colonial market; clearly, its purpose was to collect money for the treasury. Thus from the colonial standpoint, Townshend's duties were taxes just like the Stamp Act duties.

Although Townshend had introduced the Revenue Act in response to the government's budgetary problems, he had an ulterior motive for establishing an American source of revenue. Traditionally, royal governors had depended on colonial legislatures to vote their salaries; for their part, the legislatures had often refused to allocate these salaries until governors had signed certain bills to which they were opposed. Through the Revenue Act, Townshend hoped to establish a fund that would pay the salaries of governors and other royal officials in America, thus freeing them from the assemblies' control. In effect, by stripping the assemblies of their most potent weapon, the power of the purse, the Revenue Act threatened to tip the balance of constitutional power away from elected colonial representatives and toward unelected royal officials.

In reality the Revenue Act would never yield anything like the income that Townshend anticipated. Of the various items taxed, only tea produced any significant revenue—£20,000 of the £37,000 that the law was expected to yield. And because the measure would serve its purpose only if British tea were affordable to colonial consumers (who could easily smuggle Dutch tea), Townshend eliminated £60,000 worth of import fees paid on East Indian tea entering Britain before transhipment to America. On balance, the Revenue Act *worsened* the British treasury's deficit by £23,000. By 1767 Britain's financial difficulties were more an excuse for, than the driving force behind, political demands to tax the colonies. From Parliament's standpoint, the conflict with America was becoming a test of national will over the *principle* of taxation.

The Colonists' Reaction

Parliament gave the colonists little time to plan resistance against the Townshend duties. Americans only learned of the Revenue Act shortly before it went into operation, and they hesitated over the appropriate response. The strong-arm tactics that sent stamp tax collectors into panicky flight would not work against the Townshend duties, which the navy could easily collect offshore, safe from any Sons of Liberty.

Resistance to the Revenue Act remained weak until December 1767, when John Dickinson published twelve essays entitled *Letters from a Farmer in Pennsylvania*. The son of a Maryland planter and himself the owner of a large country estate in Delaware, Dickinson was actually a highly successful Philadelphia lawyer. But with most colonists living on farms, his title suggested that his sentiments lay with those of ordinary people. The essays, which appeared in nearly every colonial newspaper, emphasized that, although Parliament could regulate trade by voting duties capable of providing small amounts of "incidental revenue," it had no right to tax commerce for the single purpose of raising revenue. In other words, the legality of any external tax depended on its intent. No tax designed to produce revenue could be considered constitutional unless a people's elected representatives voted for it. Dickinson said nothing that the colonists had not stated or implied during the Stamp Act crisis. Rather, his contribution lay in persuading Americans that the many arguments that they had marshaled against the Stamp Act also applied to the Revenue Act.

Soon after publication of Dickinson's *Letters*, James Otis, the Boston lawyer famed for his arguments in the writs-of-assistance case, chaired a Boston town meeting that asked the Massachusetts legislature to oppose the Townshend duties. In response, the assembly in early 1768 called on Samuel Adams to draft a "circular letter" to every other legislature. Harvard-educated yet possessing a flair for the push-and-shove of local politics, Adams had helped organize the Sons of Liberty in Boston in 1765. Adams's circular letter forthrightly condemned both taxation without representation and the threat to self-governance posed by Parliament's making governors and other royal officials financially independent of the legislatures. Nonetheless, the document acknowledged Parliament as the "supreme legislative Power over the whole Empire," and it advocated no illegal activities.

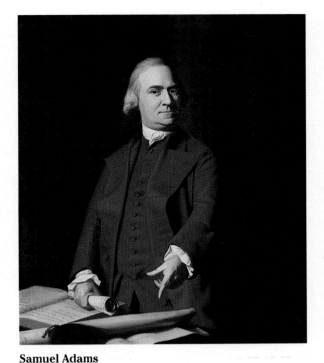

Samuel Adams
A central player in the drive for American liberty, Adams wrote in 1774 that "I wish for a permanent union with the mother country, but only in terms of liberty and truth. No advantage that can accrue to America from such a union, can compensate for the loss of liberty."

Virginia's assembly warmly approved Adams's eloquent message and sent out a more strongly worded circular letter of its own, urging all colonies to oppose imperial policies that would "have an immediate tendency to enslave them." But most colonial legislatures reacted indifferently to these letters. In fact, resistance to the Revenue Act might have disintegrated in time had the British government not overreacted to the circular letters.

Indeed, parliamentary leaders regarded even the mild Massachusetts letter as "little better than an incentive to Rebellion." Disorganized by Townshend's sudden death in 1767, the king's Privy Council directed Lord Hillsborough, first appointee to the new post of secretary of state for the colonies, to express the government's displeasure. Hillsborough flatly told the Massachusetts assembly to disown its letter, forbade all overseas assemblies to endorse it, and commanded royal governors to dissolve any colonial legislature that violated his instructions. George III later commented that he never met "a man of less judgment than Lord

The Alternative of Williamsburg, *by Philip Dawe, 1775*
In this cartoon, armed patriots in Williamsburg, Virginia,
obtain a merchant's written agreement not to import British
goods. The "alternative" is the containers of tar and feath-
ers hanging in the background.

Hillsborough." A wiser man might have tried to divide the colonists by appealing to their sense of British patriotism, but Hillsborough had chosen a course guaranteed to unite them in anger.

To protest Hillsborough's crude bullying, many legislatures previously indifferent to the Massachusetts circular letter now adopted it enthusiastically. The Massachusetts House of Representatives voted 92–17 not to recall its letter. The number 92 immediately acquired symbolic significance for Americans; colonial politicians on more than one occasion drank 92 toasts in tipsy salutes to Massachusetts's action. In obedience to Hillsborough, royal governors responded by dismissing legislatures in Massachusetts and elsewhere. These moves played directly into the hands of Samuel Adams, James Otis, and John Dickinson, who wished to ignite widespread opposition to the Townshend duties.

Although increasingly outraged over the Revenue Act, the colonists still needed some effective means of

pressuring Parliament for its repeal. One approach, nonimportation, seemed especially promising because it offered an alternative to violence and would distress Britain's economy. In August 1768 Boston's merchants therefore adopted a nonimportation agreement, and the tactic slowly spread southward. "Save your money, and you save your country!" became the watchword of the Sons of Liberty, who began reorganizing after two years of inactivity. Not all colonists supported nonimportation, however. Its effectiveness ultimately depended on the compliance of merchants, whose livelihood relied, in turn, on buying and selling imports. In several major communities, including Philadelphia and Baltimore, merchants continued buying British goods until early 1769, and Charles Town (Charleston), South Carolina, did not cut off its purchases until July 1769. Far from complete, the boycott probably kept out no more than 40 percent of all imports from Britain.

"Wilkes and Liberty"

The exclusion of 40 percent of imports seriously affected many people in Britain and thus heightened pressure there, too, for repeal of the Townshend duties. Hardest hit were merchants and artisans dealing in consumer goods. Their protests formed part of a larger movement that arose during the 1760s in opposition to the domestic and foreign policies of George III and a Parliament dominated by wealthy landowners. The leader of this movement was John Wilkes, a fiery London editor and member of Parliament who had first gained notoriety in 1763, when his newspaper regularly and irreverently denounced George III's policies. The government had finally arrested Wilkes for seditious libel, but to great popular acclaim, he had won his case in court. The government, however, had succeeded in shutting down his newspaper and in persuading members of the House of Commons to deny Wilkes his seat. After again offending the government with a publication, Wilkes had fled to Paris.

Wilkes returned to England in 1768, defying a warrant for his arrest, and ran again for Parliament. By this time the Townshend acts and other government policies were stirring up widespread protests. Merchants and artisans in London, Bristol, and other cities demanded the dismissal of the "obnoxious" ministers who were "ruining our manufactories by invidiously imposing and establishing the most impolitic and unconstitutional taxations and regulations on your Majesty's colonies." They were joined by (nonvoting) weavers, coal heavers, seamen, and other workers who protested low wages and high prices that stemmed in part from government policies. All these people rallied around the cry, "Wilkes and liberty!"

After he again was elected to Parliament, Wilkes was arrested. The next day, twenty to forty thousand angry "Wilkesites" massed on St. George's Fields, outside the prison where he was being held. When members of the crowd began throwing stones, soldiers and police responded with gunfire, killing eleven protesters. The "massacre of St. George's Fields" had given the movement some martyrs. Wilkes and an associate were elected to the seat twice more and were both times denied their seats by other legislators. Meanwhile, the imprisoned Wilkes was besieged by outpourings of popular support, from the colonies as well as from Britain. Some Virginians sent him tobacco, and the South Carolina assembly voted to contribute £1,500 to help defray his debts. He maintained a regular correspondence with the Boston Sons of Liberty and, upon his release in April 1770, was hailed in a massive Boston celebration as "the illustrious martyr to Liberty."

Wilkes's cause sharpened the political thinking of government opponents in Britain and the colonies alike. Thousands of voters in English cities and towns signed petitions to Parliament protesting its refusal to seat Wilkes as an affront to the electorate's will. Like the colonists, they regarded the theory of "virtual representation" in Parliament as a sham. Fearing arbitrary government actions, some of them formed a Society of the Supporters of the Bill of Rights "to defend and maintain the legal, constitutional liberty of the subject." And while more "respectable" opponents of the government such as William Pitt and Edmund Burke disdained Wilkes for courting the "mob," his movement emboldened them to speak more forcefully against the government, especially on its policies toward the colonies. For the colonists themselves, Wilkes and his following made clear that Parliament and the government represented a small if powerful minority whose authority could be legitimately questioned.

Women and Colonial Resistance

The tactical value of nonimportation was not restricted to damaging Britain's economy. It also hinged on colonists convincing the British—and one another—that all Americans were determined to sustain resistance, and on demonstrating that the American cause rested on the foundations of impeccable morality and sensible moderation. In this respect, the nonimportation movement provided a unique opportunity for women to join the protest against unconstitutional laws.

The enlistment of women in the colonial protest movement unfolded slowly. Calling themselves the Daughters of Liberty, upper-class female patriots had played a minor part in defeating the Stamp Act. Some had attended political rallies during the Stamp Act crisis, and others had reinforced colonial resolve by turning a cold shoulder to men unwilling to resist Grenville's tax.

In contrast, women assumed a highly visible role during the Townshend crisis. To protest the Revenue Act's tax on tea, more than three hundred "mistresses of families" in Boston denounced the consumption of the beverage in early 1770. In some ways, such nonconsumption was a more effective tactic than nonimportation, for although a minority of merchants might ignore nonimportation on the basis of principle or financial interest, a refusal by colonists to consume imports would chill merchants' economic incentive to continue bringing in English products.

Nonconsumption agreements therefore soon became popular and were extended to include English manufactures (mostly clothing) as well as tea. Again women played a vital role, because the boycott would fail unless the colonists replaced British imports with apparel of their own making. Responding to leaders' pleas that they expand domestic cloth production, women of all social ranks, even those who customarily did not weave their own fabric or sew their own clothing, organized spinning bees. These events attracted intense publicity as evidence of American determination to fight parliamentary taxation. The colonial cause, noted a New York woman, had enlisted "a fighting army of amazons . . . armed with spinning wheels."

Spinning bees not only helped undermine the masculine prejudice that women had no place in public life but also endowed spinning and weaving, previously considered routine household tasks, with special political virtue. "Women might recover to this country the full and free enjoyment of all our rights, properties and privileges," exclaimed the Reverend John Cleaveland of Ipswich, Massachusetts, in 1769; he then added with more than usual honesty that this "is more than the men have been able to do."

Spinning bees, combined with female support for boycotting tea, dramatically demonstrated American determination. Colonial leaders were waging a battle

Mr. and Mrs. Thomas Mifflin,
by John Singleton Copley, 1773
The Mifflins were prominent Philadelphians. Thomas, a
merchant in his early years, sat in the Pennsylvania assem-
bly and the First Continental Congress and was later an of-
ficer in the Continental Army. An ardent supporter of the
American cause, Sarah Morris Mifflin here demonstrates
her patriotism by spinning her own thread.

to convince public opinion in Britain that their society
would stand firm in opposing unconstitutional taxes.
Only if the British people believed that Americans—
male and female alike—were truly united would they
accept repeal of the Townshend duties. Female participation in symbolic protests forced the British public to
appreciate the depth of colonial commitment to maintaining the nonimportation agreements.

Customs Racketeering

Besides taxing colonial imports, Townshend sought to
increase revenues through closer British surveillance
of colonial trade. At the same time as he submitted his

Revenue Act of 1767, he introduced legislation creating
the American Board of Customs Commissioners,
whose members would strictly enforce the Navigation
Acts. This law raised the number of port officials,
funded the construction of a colonial coast guard, and
provided money for secret informers. In the face of lax
enforcement, including widespread bribery of customs officials by colonial shippers and merchants,
Towshend wanted the board to bring honesty, efficiency, and more revenue to overseas customs operations. But the law quickly drew protests because of the
ways it was enforced and because it assumed those
accused to be guilty until they could prove otherwise.

The new legal provisions awarded an informer
one-third of the value of all goods and ships appropriated through a conviction of smuggling. The fact that
fines could be tripled under certain circumstances provided an even greater incentive to seize illegal cargoes.
Smuggling cases were heard in vice-admiralty courts,
moreover, where the probability of conviction was extremely high.

Revenue agents commonly filed charges for technical violations of the Sugar Act, even when no evidence existed of intent to conduct illegal trade. They
most often exploited the provision that declared any
cargo illegal unless it had been loaded or unloaded
with a customs officer's written authorization. Many
vessels transporting lumber or tobacco found it impossible to comply, because they typically picked up these
items piecemeal at a succession of small wharves far
from a customhouse. Even a captain who threw rotting provisions overboard while at sea could be found
guilty of illegally unloading. One common device by
which customs officials created opportunities for
seizures was to accommodate local circumstances by
bending the rules for a time and then suddenly to enforce the letter of the law.

Customs commissioners also fanned angry passions by invading the traditional rights of sailors. Long-
standing maritime custom allowed a ship's crew to
supplement their incomes by making small sales between ports. Anything stored in a sailor's chest was
considered private property that did not have to be
listed as cargo on the captain's manifest and so was exempt from the regulations of the Navigation Acts. After
1767, however, revenue agents began treating such belongings as cargo, thus establishing an excuse to seize
the entire ship. Under this new policy, crewmen saw
their trunks ruthlessly broken open by arrogant inspectors and then lost trading stock worth several months'

wages because it was not listed on the captain's loading papers.

The commissioners thus embarked on a program of "customs racketeering" that constituted little more than a system of legalized piracy. The board's program fed an upsurge in popular violence. Above all, customs commissioners' use of informers provoked retaliation. The *Pennsylvania Journal* in 1769 scorned these agents as "dogs of prey, thirsting after the fortunes of worthy and wealthy men." By betraying the trust of employers, and sometimes of friends, informers aroused wild hatred in their victims and were roughly handled whenever found. Nearly all instances of tarring and feathering in these years were acts of private revenge against informers rather than acts of political reprisal.

Sailors developed deep hatred for customs officers who had seized their property, and eagerly awaited chances to get even. Not surprisingly, after 1767 inspectors fell increasingly victim to riots dominated by vengeful seamen. By enforcing the letter of the law, commissioners created a superheated climate that made such riots and assaults inevitable.

Nowhere were customs agents and informers more detested than in Boston, where in June 1768 citizens finally retaliated against their tormentors. The occasion was the seizure, on a technicality, of the colonial merchant John Hancock's sloop *Liberty*. A crowd tried to prevent the towing of Hancock's ship and then began assaulting customs agents. Growing to several hundred as it surged through the streets, the mob drove all revenue inspectors from Boston.

Hancock, reportedly North America's richest merchant and a leading opponent of British taxation, had become a chief target of the customs commissioners. In 1768 the commissioners used a perjured statement from a customs inspector to seize the *Liberty* for allegedly avoiding £700 in duties on Madeira wine worth £3,000. By then requesting the payment of triple charges on the wine, they made Hancock liable for a total fine of £9,000, an amount almost thirteen times greater than the taxes supposedly evaded.

Hancock's case forced Americans to reevaluate their former acceptance of the principle that Parliament had limited authority to pass laws for them. Prior to 1768 colonial leaders had single-mindedly denied Britain's power to tax them, without considering that freedoms of equal importance might also be jeopardized by other kinds of legislation. But by 1770 many argued that measures like the Sugar Act and the act

creating the American Board of Customs Commissioners seriously endangered property rights and civil liberties. They expanded their opposition from a rejection of taxation without representation to a more broadly based rejection of legislation without representation. By 1774 there would emerge a new consensus that Parliament possessed no lawmaking authority over the colonies except the right to regulate imperial commerce through statutes like the old Navigation Acts.

By 1770 the British government, aware of its customs officers' excesses, began reforming the service. The smuggling charges against Hancock were finally dropped because the prosecution feared that Hancock would appeal a conviction to England, where honest officials would take action against the persons responsible for violating his rights. But although the abuses largely ended by the early 1770s, the damage had been done. Townshend's American Board of Customs Commissioners contributed enormously to the colonists' growing suspicion of British motives and their progressive alienation from England.

Repeal of the Townshend Duties

In January 1770 Lord North became prime minister. Although described as a "great, heavy, booby-looking man" and noted for occasionally sleeping through debates in the House of Commons, North had ability and would retain his office until 1782. North favored eliminating most of the Townshend duties to prevent the American commercial boycott from widening, but to underscore British authority, he insisted on retaining the tax on tea. Parliament agreed, and in April 1770, giving in for the second time in three years to colonial pressure, it repealed most of the Townshend duties.

Parliament's partial repeal produced a dilemma for American politicians. They considered it intolerable that taxes remained on tea, the most profitable item for the royal treasury. Colonial leaders were unsure whether they should press on with the nonimportation agreement until they achieved total victory, or whether it would suffice to maintain a selective boycott of tea. When the nonimportation movement collapsed in July 1770, colonists resisted external taxation by voluntary agreements not to drink British tea. Through nonconsumption they succeeded in limiting revenue from tea to about one-sixth the level originally expected. This amount was far too little to pay the salaries of royal governors as Townshend had intended.

Yet American leaders took little satisfaction in having forced Parliament to compromise. The tea duty remained as a galling reminder that Parliament refused to retreat from the broadest possible interpretation of the Declaratory Act. Thus although the crisis passed in 1770, its legacy lingered long afterward. The tax on tea acted like a festering sore that slowly poisoned relations between Britain and its colonies. The Townshend crisis had begun the gradual process by which a loyal people lost all sense of allegiance to their king and country.

The Boston Massacre

As another consequence of the violence stirred up by the customs commissioners, a force of seventeen hundred British troops landed in Boston during the six weeks after October 1, 1768. Regarding the troops as a "standing army" that threatened their liberty, as well as a financial burden, Bostonians resented the soldiers' presence.

Boston rapidly took on the atmosphere of an occupied city and crackled with tension as armed sentries and resentful civilians traded insults. The mainly Protestant townspeople found it especially galling that many soldiers were Irish Catholics and a few, mostly drummers, were blacks. The majority of enlisted men, moreover, were free to seek employment following the morning muster.

Often agreeing to work for less than local laborers, they generated fierce hostility in a community plagued by persistently high unemployment.

Still, Bostonians endured their first winter as a garrison town without undue trouble and saw half the British troops sail home in mid-1769. Relations between the remaining soldiers and the city's poorer civilians then abruptly worsened. The deep-seated resentment against all who upheld British authority suddenly boiled over on February 22, 1770, when an unpopular customs informer fired bird shot at several children bombarding his house with rocks and killed an eleven-year-old German boy. While elite Bostonians had disdained the unruly exchanges between soldiers and crowds, the horror at a child's death momentarily united the community. "My Eyes never beheld such a funeral," wrote John Adams. "A vast Number of Boys walked before the Coffin, a vast Number of Women and Men after it. . . . This Shews there are many more Lives to spend if wanted in the Service of their country."

Although the army had played no part in the shooting, it became a natural target for popular frustration and rage. A week after the boy's funeral, ten-

The Boston Massacre, 1770,
Engraving by Paul Revere Shortly after this incident, one Bostonian observed that "unless there is some great alteration in the state of things, the era of the independence of the colonies is much nearer than I once thought it, or now wish it."

sions between troops and Boston civilians erupted at the guardpost protecting the customs office. When an officer tried to disperse a crowd led by Crispus Attucks, a seaman of African and Native American descent, his men endured a steady barrage of flying objects and dares to shoot. One soldier finally did fire, after having been knocked down by a block of ice, and the others pulled their triggers without orders. Their uneven volley hit eleven persons, five of whom, including Attucks, died.

The shock that followed the March 5 bloodshed marked the emotional high point of the Townshend crisis. Royal authorities in Massachusetts tried to defuse the situation in Boston by isolating all British soldiers on a fortified island in the harbor, and Governor Thomas Hutchinson promised that the soldiers who had fired would be tried. Patriot leader John Adams, an opponent of crowd actions, served as their attorney. Adams intended not only to demonstrate Americans' commitment to impartial justice but also "to lay before [the people of Boston], the Law as it stood, that they might be apprized of the Dangers . . . which must arise from intemperate heats and irregular commotions." All but two of the soldiers were acquitted, and the ones found guilty suffered only a branding on their thumbs.

Burning hatreds produced by an intolerable situation underlay the "Boston Massacre," as it came to be called in conscious recollection of the "St. George's Fields Massacre" of Wilkesites in London two years earlier. The shooting of unarmed American civilians by British soldiers, and the light punishment given the soldiers, forced the colonists to confront the stark possibility that the British government was bent on coercing and suppressing them through naked force.

The Committees of Correspondence

Although Lord North's government virtually ignored the colonies from mid-1770 to 1772, the brief truce ended on June 9, 1772, when the customs schooner *Gaspee* ran aground near Providence, Rhode Island. One of the last revenue cutters to engage in customs racketeering by plundering cargoes for technical violations of the Sugar Act, the *Gaspee* had acquired an odious reputation among Rhode Islanders. Its crew had frequently landed to steal fruit, unfenced livestock, and firewood, and the captain was said to be "more imperious and haughty than the Grand Turk himself." Now helplessly stuck in the mud, the *Gaspee* presented a tempting target for local inhabitants. That night, more than one hundred disguised men burned it to the waterline.

The British government dispatched a commission to look into the attack, with instructions to send all suspects to England for trial. The investigators failed to identify any raiders and came back empty-handed. Nevertheless, colonists were alarmed that the ministry intended to dispense with another essential civil liberty, an accused citizen's right to be tried by a local jury.

In the fall of 1772, meanwhile, Lord North's ministry was preparing to implement Townshend's goal of paying the royal governors' salaries out of customs revenue. The colonists had always viewed this intention to free the governors from legislative domination as a fundamental threat to representative government. In response, Samuel Adams persuaded Boston's town meeting to request that every Massachusetts community appoint persons responsible for exchanging information and coordinating measures to defend colonial rights. Of approximately 260 towns, about half immediately established "committees of correspondence," and most others did so within a year. From Massachusetts the idea spread throughout New England.

The committees of correspondence were the colonists' first attempt to maintain close and continuing political cooperation over a wide area. By linking almost every interior community to Boston through a network of dedicated activists, the system allowed Adams to conduct a campaign of political education for all of Massachusetts, and increasingly for all New England. Adams sent out messages for each town's local committee to read at its own town meeting, which would then debate the issues and adopt a formal resolution. Forcing tens of thousands of citizens to consider evidence that their rights were in danger, the system committed them to take a personal stand by voting.

Adams's most successful venture in whipping up public alarm came in June 1773, when he publicized certain letters of Massachusetts governor Thomas Hutchinson that Benjamin Franklin had obtained. Massachusetts town meetings discovered through the letters that their own chief executive had advocated "an abridgement of what are called English liberties" and "a great restraint of natural liberty." The publication of the Hutchinson correspondence confirmed American suspicions that a plot was afoot to destroy basic freedoms.

Meanwhile, in reaction to the *Gaspee* commission's instructions, Patrick Henry, Thomas Jefferson, and Richard Henry Lee proposed in March 1773 that

Virginia establish colony-level committees of correspondence. Within a year every province but Pennsylvania had followed its example. By early 1774 colonial leaders were linked by a communications web for the first time since 1766.

In contrast to the brief, intense Stamp Act crisis, the dissatisfaction spawned by the Townshend duties and the American Board of Customs Commissioners persisted and gradually poisoned relations between Britain and America. In 1765 feelings of loyalty and affection toward Britain had remained strong in America and thus had helped disguise the depth of the division over the constitutional issue of taxation. By 1773, however, colonial allegiance was becoming conditional and could no longer be assumed.

Frontier Tensions

Although most of the conflicts between colonists and British officials took place in the eastern seaports, tensions along the frontier contributed to a continuing sense of crisis among natives, settlers, and colonial authorities. These stresses were rooted in the rapid growth of both the colonial population and the economy. This growth had spurred the migration of people and capital to the Appalachian frontier, where colonists and their governments sought access to Indian land. Land pressures and the lack of adequate revenue from the colonies left the British government utterly helpless in enforcing the Proclamation of 1763. Speculators such as George Washington sought western land because "any person who . . . neglects the present opportunity of hunting out good Lands will never regain it." Settlers, traders, hunters, and thieves also trespassed on Indian land, and a growing number of instances of violence by colonists toward Indians were going unpunished. In the meantime, the British government was unable to maintain garrisons at many of its forts, to enforce violations of laws and treaties, and to provide gifts to its native allies. Under such pressure, Britain and the Iroquois agreed in the Treaty of Fort Stanwix (1768) to grant land along the Ohio River that was occupied by the Shawnees, Delawares, and Cherokees to the government of Pennsylvania and Virginia. The Shawnees now assumed leadership of the "republican" Indians who, along with the Cherokees, sensed that no policy of appeasement could stop colonial expansion.

The Treaty of Fort Stanwix resolved the conflicting claims of Pennsylvania and Virginia in Ohio at the Indians' expense. But other frontier disputes led directly to

conflict among the colonists themselves. Settlers moving west in Massachusetts in the early 1760s found their titles challenged by some of New York's powerful landlords. When two of the landlords threatened tenants with eviction in 1766, the New Englanders made common cause with the tenants in an armed uprising, calling themselves Sons of Liberty after the Stamp Act protestors. In 1769, in what is now Vermont, settlers from New Hamsphire also came into conflict with New York. After four years of guerrilla warfare, the New Hampshire settlers, calling themselves the Green Mountain Boys, established an independent government. Unrecognized at the time, it eventually became the government of Vermont. A third group of New England settlers, from Connecticut, settled in the Wyoming Valley of Pennsylvania, where they clashed in 1774 with Pennsylvanians claiming title to the same land.

Expansion also provoked conflicts between frontier settlers and their colonial governments. In North Carolina a group known as the Regulators aimed to redress the grievances of settlers living in the colony's western regions. The westerners, underrepresented in the colonial assembly, had found themselves exploited by dishonest, self-serving officeholders appointed by eastern politicians. The Regulator movement climaxed on May 16, 1771, at the battle of Alamance Creek. Leading an army of perhaps thirteen hundred easternmilitiamen, North Carolina's royal governor defeated about twenty-five hundred Regulators in a clash that produced almost three hundred casualties. Although the Regulator uprising then disintegrated, it crippled the colony's subsequent ability to resist British authority.

An armed Regulator movement also arose in South Carolina, in this case to counter the government's unwillingness to prosecute bandits who were terrorizing the settlers. But the South Carolina government did not dispatch its militia to the frontier for fear that the colony's restive slave population might use the occasion to revolt. Instead it conceded to the principal demands of the Regulators by establishing four new judicial circuits and allowing jury trials in the newly settled areas.

Although not directly related to one another, these frontier episodes all reflect the tensions generated by a rising land-hungry population and its willingness to defy established authorities and resort to violence. As tensions mounted between colonists and British authorities in older settled areas, the frontier dweller's anxious mood spread.

◆

TOWARD INDEPENDENCE

Although the British Empire remained superficially tranquil in early 1773, it had resolved none of its underlying constitutional problems. To a large degree, Americans ignored the continued taxation of tea because of a widespread expectation that Lord North would eventually have the duty repealed. Parliament suddenly blasted this unrealistic hope when it passed the Tea Act in 1773. This measure set off a chain reaction that started with the Boston Tea Party in late 1773 and was followed by Parliament's attempt to retaliate through the Coercive Acts in 1774, the First Continental Congress in September 1774, the outbreak of fighting in April 1775, and the colonists' declaration of their independence in July 1776.

The Tea Act

Colonial smuggling and nonconsumption had taken a heavy toll on Britain's East India Company, which enjoyed a legal monopoly on importing tea into the British Empire. By 1773, with tons of tea rotting in its warehouses, the East India Company was teetering on the brink of bankruptcy. But Lord North could not let the company fail. Not only did it pay substantial duties on the tea it imported into Britain, but it also provided huge indirect savings for the government by maintaining British authority in India at its own expense.

If the company could only control the colonial market, North reasoned, its chances for returning to profitability would greatly increase. Americans supposedly consumed more than a million pounds of tea each year, but by 1773 they were purchasing just one-quarter of it from the company. In May 1773, to save the beleaguered East India Company from financial ruin, Parliament passed the Tea Act, which eliminated all remaining import duties on tea entering England and thus lowered the selling price to consumers. (Ironically, the same saving could have been accomplished by repealing the Townshend tax, which would have ended colonial objections to the company's tea and produced enormous goodwill toward the British government.) To lower the price further, the Tea Act also permitted the company to sell its tea directly to consumers rather than through wholesalers.

These two concessions reduced the cost of East India Company tea in the colonies well below the price of all smuggled competition. Parliament expected simple economic self-interest to overcome American scruples about buying taxed tea. With the resulting revenue, the British government would finally be able to achieve Townshend's goal of making the royal governors independent of colonial assemblies by paying their salaries.

But the Tea Act alarmed many Americans, above all because they saw in it a menace to colonial representative government. By making taxed tea competitive in price with smuggled tea, the law in all likelihood would raise revenue, which the British government would use to pay royal governors. The law thus threatened to corrupt Americans into accepting the principle of parliamentary taxation by taking advantage of their weakness for a frivolous luxury. Quickly, therefore, the committees of correspondence decided to resist the importation of tea, though without violence and without the destruction of private property. Either by pressuring the company's agents to refuse acceptance or by intercepting the ships at sea and ordering them home, the committees would keep East India Company cargoes from being landed. In Philadelphia an anonymous "Committee for Tarring and Feathering" warned harbor pilots not to guide any ships carrying tea into port.

In Boston, however, this strategy failed. On November 28, 1773, the first ship came under the jurisdiction of the customhouse, to which duties would have to be paid on its cargo within twenty days. Otherwise, the cargo would be seized from the captain and the tea claimed by the company's agents (who included two of Governor Hutchinson's sons) and placed on sale. When Samuel Adams, John Hancock, and other leading citizens repeatedly asked the customs officers to issue a special clearance for the ship's departure, they found themselves blocked by the governor's refusal to compromise.

On the evening of December 16, Samuel Adams convened a meeting in Old South Church. He informed the five thousand citizens of Hutchinson's insistence upon landing the tea, told them that the grace period would expire in a few hours, and announced that "this meeting can do no more to save the country." About fifty young men disguised as Indians then yelled a few war whoops and headed for the wharf, followed by most of the crowd.

The disciplined band assaulted no one and damaged nothing but the hated cargo. Thousands lined the waterfront to see them heave forty-five tons of tea overboard. For almost an hour, the onlookers stood silently transfixed, as if at a religious service, while they peered through the crisp, cold air of a moonlit night. The only sounds were the steady chop of hatchets breaking open wooden chests and the soft splash of tea on the water. When their work was finished, the participants left quietly, and the town lapsed into a profound hush—"never more still and calm," according to one observer.

The Coercive Acts

Boston's "Tea Party" inflamed the British. Lord North fumed that only "New England fanatics" could imagine themselves oppressed by inexpensive tea. A Welsh member of Parliament drew wild applause by declaring that "the town of Boston ought to be knocked about by the ears, and destroy'd." In vain did the great parliamentary orator Edmund Burke plead for the one action that could end the crisis. "Leave America . . . to tax herself. . . . Leave the Americans as they anciently stood. . . ." The British government, however, swiftly asserted its authority by enacting four Coercive Acts that, together with the unrelated Quebec Act, became known to many colonists as the "Intolerable Acts."

The first of the Coercive Acts, the Boston Port Bill, became law on April 1, 1774. It ordered the navy to close Boston harbor unless the Privy Council certified

by June 1 that the town had arranged to pay for the ruined tea. Lord North's cabinet deliberately imposed this impossibly short deadline in order to ensure the harbor's closing, which would lead to serious economic distress. The government therefore refused to let a group of London merchants post bond for the necessary £9,000.

The second Coercive Act, the Massachusetts Government Act, had actually been under consideration before the Boston Tea Party. This law revoked the Massachusetts charter and restructured the government to make it less democratic. The colony's upper house would no longer be elected annually by the assembly but appointed for life by the crown. The governor gained absolute control over the naming of all judges and sheriffs. Jurymen, previously elected, were now appointed by sheriffs. Finally, the new charter forbade communities to hold more than one town meeting a year without the governor's permission. These changes brought Massachusetts into line with other royal colonies, but the colonists interpreted them as evidence of hostility toward representative government.

The final two Coercive Acts—the Administration of Justice Act and a new Quartering Act—rubbed salt into the wounds. The first of these permitted any person charged with murder while enforcing royal authority in Massachusetts (such as the British soldiers

"Boston Cannonaded"
In this pro-resistance cartoon, Britain's ministers harass and force tea down the throat of America, depicted as an innocent woman. Note that one minister carries a copy of the (Boston) Port Bill (1774) that forced the closing of the city's harbor.

indicted for the Boston Massacre) to be tried in England or in other colonies. The second went beyond the Quartering Act of 1766 by allowing the governor to requisition *empty* private buildings for housing troops. These measures, along with the appointment of General Thomas Gage, Britain's military commander in North America, as the new governor of Massachusetts, struck New Englanders as proof of a plan to place them under a military despotism.

Americans learned of the Quebec Act along with the previous four statutes and associated it with them. Intended to cement loyalty to Britain among conquered French-Canadian Catholics, the law established Roman Catholicism as Quebec's official religion. This provision alarmed Protestant Anglo-Americans, who widely associated Catholicism with arbitrary government. Furthermore, the Quebec Act gave Canada's governors sweeping powers but established no legislature. It also permitted property disputes (but not criminal cases) to be decided by French law, which did not use juries. Additionally, the law extended Quebec's territorial claims south to the Ohio River and west to the Mississippi, a vast area populated by Native Americans and some French. Although covered by the Proclamation of 1763, the region was claimed by several colonies.

The "Intolerable Acts" convinced New Englanders that the crown was plotting to corrode traditional English liberties throughout North America. Many believed that after starving Boston into submission, the governor of Massachusetts would appoint corrupt sheriffs and judges to crush political dissent through rigged trials. The Quartering Act would repress any resistance by forcing troops on an unwilling population. The Administration of Justice Act, which the colonists cynically called the Murder Act, would encourage massacres by preventing local juries from convicting soldiers who killed civilians. Once resistance in Massachusetts had been smashed, the Quebec Act would serve as a blueprint for extinguishing representative government throughout the colonies. Parliament would revoke every colony's charter and introduce a government like Quebec's. Elected assemblies, freedom of religion for Protestants, and jury trials would all disappear.

Intended by Parliament simply to punish Massachusetts—and particularly that rotten apple in the barrel, Boston—the acts instead pushed most colonies to the brink of revolution. Repeal of these laws became, in effect, the colonists' nonnegotiable demand. Of the twenty-seven reasons justifying the break with Britain that the Americans cited in their 1776 Declaration of Independence, six concerned these statutes.

Virginia's response was particularly important because that colony could provide more military manpower than any other. Sentiment for active resistance first solidified in the Virginia assembly, whose members returned to their counties and enlisted the local gentry in the cause of firmly opposing the offensive laws. As the upper class quickly pulled together, the leading planters undertook a program of political education for the colony's ordinary citizens, who up to that point had been apathetic about the Anglo-American confrontation. On public occasions such as court days and militia musters, the gentry spoke repeatedly of the need to support Massachusetts, persuading voters to commit themselves to resistance by signing petitions against the Coercive Acts. Within two years the gentry had mobilized Virginia's free population overwhelmingly against Parliament, and it was clear that if war broke out, the British Army would face united resistance not only in New England but also in Virginia.

The First Continental Congress

In response to the "Intolerable Acts," the extralegal committees of correspondence of every colony but Georgia sent delegates to a Continental Congress in Philadelphia. Among those in attendance when the Congress assembled on September 5, 1774, were the colonies' most prominent politicians: Samuel and John Adams of Massachusetts; John Jay of New York; Joseph Galloway and John Dickinson of Pennsylvania; and Patrick Henry, Richard Henry Lee, and George Washington of Virginia. The fifty-six delegates had come together to find a way of defending American rights short of war, and in interminable dinner parties and cloakroom chatter, they took one another's measure.

The First Continental Congress opened by endorsing a set of extreme statements of principle called the Suffolk Resolves that recently had placed Massachusetts in a state of passive rebellion. Adopted by delegates at a convention of Massachusetts towns just as the Continental Congress was getting under way, the resolves declared that the colonies owed no obedience to any of the Coercive Acts, that a provisional government should collect all taxes until the former Massachusetts charter was restored, and that defensive measures should be taken in the event of an attack by royal troops. The Continental Congress also voted to boycott all British goods after December 1 and to cease exporting almost all goods to Britain and its West Indian possessions after September 1775 unless a reconciliation had been accomplished. This agreement, the Continental Association, would be enforced by locally elected committees of "observation" or "safety," whose members in effect were usurping control of American trade from the royal customs service.

Such bold defiances were not to the liking of all delegates. Jay, Dickinson, Galloway, and other moderates who dominated the middle-colony contingent most feared the internal turmoil that would surely accompany a head-on confrontation with Britain. These "trimmers" (John Adams's scornful phrase) vainly opposed nonimportation and tried unsuccessfully to win endorsement of Galloway's plan for a "Grand Council," an American legislature that would share with Parliament the authority to tax and govern the colonies.

Finally, however, the delegates summarized their principles and demands in a petition to the king. This document conceded to Parliament the power to regulate colonial commerce, but it argued that all previous parliamentary efforts to impose taxes, enforce laws through admiralty courts, suspend assemblies, and unilaterally revoke charters were unconstitutional. By addressing the king rather than Parliament, Congress was imploring George III to end the crisis by dismissing those ministers responsible for passing the Coercive Acts.

The Fighting Begins

Most Americans hoped that their resistance would jolt Parliament into renouncing all authority over the colonies except trade regulation. But a minority of the colonial elite took alarm, and bonds between men formerly united in outlook sometimes snapped. John Adams's onetime friend Jonathan Sewall, for example, charged that the Congress had made the "breach with the parent state a thousand times more irreparable than it was before." Fearing that Congress was enthroning "their *High Mightinesses,* the MOB," he and like-minded Americans fell back on their loyalty to the

Battle of Lexington
James Pike, a Massachusetts militiaman, recorded the clash at Lexington on his powder horn: The other side shows British "regulars, the aggressors," assaulting "provincials defending" a Liberty Tree.

king. In England meanwhile, George III sniffed rebellion in the Congress's actions. His instincts, and those of American loyalists, were correct. A revolution was indeed brewing.

To solidify their defiance, the American resistance leaders coerced waverers and loyalists (or "Tories," as they were often called). Thus the elected committees that Congress had created to enforce the Continental Association often turned themselves into vigilantes, compelling merchants who still traded with Britain to burn their imports and make public apologies, browbeating clergymen who preached pro-British sermons, and pressuring Americans to adopt simpler diets and dress in order to relieve their dependence on British imports. Additionally, in colony after colony, the committees took on government functions by organizing volunteer military companies and extralegal legislatures. By the spring of 1775, colonial patriots had established provincial "congresses" that paralleled and rivaled the existing colonial assemblies headed by royal governors.

The uneasy calm was first broken in April 1775, in Massachusetts. There as elsewhere, citizens had prepared for the worst by collecting arms and organizing extralegal militia units (locally known as minutemen) whose members could respond instantly to an emergency. The British government ordered Massachusetts governor Gage to quell the "rude rabble" by arresting the principal patriot leaders. Aware that most of these had already fled Boston, Gage instead sent 700 British soldiers on April 19, 1775, to seize military supplies that the colonists had stored at Concord. Two couriers, William Dawes and Paul Revere, quickly alerted nearby towns of the British troops' movements and target. At Lexington about seventy minutemen hastily drawn up on the town green attempted to oppose the soldiers. After a confused skirmish in which eight minutemen died and a single redcoat was wounded, the British pushed on to Concord. There they found few munitions but encountered a growing swarm of armed Yankees (see "A Place in Time"). When some minutemen mistakenly became convinced that the town was being burned, they exchanged fire with the British regulars and touched off a running battle that continued most of the sixteen miles back to Boston. By day's end the redcoats had lost 273 men, and they had gained some respect for Yankee courage.

These engagements awakened the countryside, and by the evening of April 20, some twenty thousand New Englanders were besieging the British garrison in Boston. On May 10 the Green Mountain Boys, led by Ethan Allen, overran Fort Ticonderoga on Lake Champlain, partly with the intent of using its captured cannon in the siege of Boston. That same day, the Second Continental Congress convened in Philadelphia. Most delegates still opposed independence and at Dickinson's urging agreed to send a "loyal message" to George III. Dickinson composed what became known as the Olive Branch Petition; excessively polite, it nonetheless presented three demands: a cease-fire at Boston, repeal of the Coercive Acts, and negotiations to establish guarantees of American rights. Events quickly overtook this effort at reconciliation. The Olive Branch Petition reached London at the same time as news of a battle fought just outside Boston on June 17. In this engagement British troops attacked colonists entrenched on Breed's Hill and Bunker Hill. Although successfully dislodging the Americans, the British suffered 1,154 casualties out of 2,200 men, compared to a loss of 311 Yankees. After Bunker Hill the British public wanted retaliation, not reconciliation, and on August 23 the king proclaimed New England in a state of rebellion. In December Parliament declared all the colonists rebellious and made their ships subject to seizure.

The Failure of Reconciliation

Despite the turn of events, most Americans clung to hopes of reconciliation. Even John Adams, who believed in the inevitability of separation, described himself as "fond of reconciliation, if we could reasonably entertain Hopes of it on a constitutional basis." Yet the same Americans who pleaded for peace passed measures that Britain could only construe as rebellious. Before the delegates to the Continental Congress even heard about the Battle of Bunker Hill, they voted to establish an "American continental army" and appointed George Washington its commander.

Still, most Americans resisted independence, partly because they clung to the notion that evil ministers rather than the king were forcing unconstitutional measures on them and partly because they expected that saner heads would rise to power in Britain. On both counts they were wrong. The Americans exaggerated the influence of Pitt, Burke, Wilkes (who finally took his seat in Parliament in 1774), and their other friends in Britain. For example, when Burke proposed in March 1775 that Parliament acknowledge the colonists' right to raise and dispose of taxes, he was voted down by a thumping majority in Parliament. Lord North's sole counterproposal was to allow the colonists to tax themselves, but on condition that they collect whatever sum Parliament ordered. This concession amounted to no more than involuntary self-taxation.

The Americans' sentimental attachment to the king, the last emotional barrier to their accepting independence, finally crumbled in January 1776 with the publication of Thomas Paine's *Common Sense*. A failed corsetmaker and schoolmaster, Paine immigrated to the colonies from England late in 1774 with a letter of introduction from Benjamin Franklin, a penchant for radical politics, and a gift for writing plain and pungent prose that anyone could understand.

Paine told Americans what they had been unable to bring themselves to say: kingship was an institution rooted in superstition, dangerous to liberty, and inappropriate to Americans. The king was "the royal brute" and a "hardened, sullen-tempered Pharaoh." Whereas previous writers had maintained that an English conspiracy against American liberty was being directed by certain corrupt politicians, Paine argued that such a conspiracy was rooted in the very institutions of monarchy and empire. Moreover, he argued, America had no economic need for the British connection. As he put it, "The commerce by which she [America] hath enriched herself are the necessaries of life, and will always have a market while eating is the custom in Europe." In addition, he pointed out, the events of the preceding six months

Concord, Massachusetts, in 1775

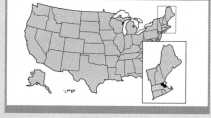

About 2 A.M. on April 19, 1775, the alarm bell in Concord, Massachusetts, started to ring furiously. Normally, it summoned men to turn out with fire buckets, but on this night drowsy citizens (including the town's minister, Reverend William Emerson) ambled toward the town square clutching muskets. Concord's minutemen were gathering to oppose 750 British troops marching to seize arms and ammunition stored in their town. Concord's mobilization on that chilly spring night was sure evidence that the colonies were teetering on the brink of revolution.

Until recently, the citizens had been loyal British subjects. Like other rural New Englanders, they had been indifferent to the British Empire's political crisis until they had debated Boston's circular letter of November 20, 1772. Thereafter, Concord's town meeting endorsed a steady flow of correspondence from Boston denouncing unconstitutional parliamentary laws. In June 1774, 80 percent of Concord's men signed a strongly worded pledge to boycott British goods until the Coercive Acts were repealed. By March 6, 1775, all but three men in town had sworn to uphold the Continental Congress against Massachusetts's royal governor, General Thomas Gage. Within the brief span of thirty months, Concord had shed its apathy and become united in resisting the Coercive Acts.

As dawn approached, the townspeople hid bullets and gunflints throughout their houses, concealed gunpowder in the woods, and buried cannon and muskets. Fifteen-year-old Milicent Barrett, the granddaughter of the minutemen's colonel, supervised teenage girls in the manufacture of cartridges. Reinforcements for Concord's 150 minutemen arrived from nearby towns. Word came that the British had opened fire on Lexington's minutemen, but no one knew if blood had been shed.

At daybreak Captain David Brown marched his company toward Lexington and promptly ran into the British. Sizing up the situation, Brown swung back to Concord with drums beating and fifes squealing. "We had grand music," Corporal Amos Barrett later recalled. Badly outnumbered, Colonel James Barrett evacuated the town center and took up position on high ground overlooking the Concord River bridge to await reinforcements.

After posting a guard at the bridge, just out of the minutemen's range, the British scoured the town for military equipment. Much of what little remained behind was saved by the town's women, who outwitted redcoats sent to search their homes. Mrs. Amos Wood tricked an officer who correctly suspected the presence of hidden ammunition into believing that a locked room sheltered panic-stricken women. "I forbid anyone entering this room," commanded the chivalrous Englishman. Hannah Barnes bluffed a search party out of entering a room that contained a chest filled with money needed to buy additional military supplies.

The British regulars dumped five hundred pounds of bullets into a pond, destroyed sixty barrels of flour, and found two cannon. They also accidentally set fire to the courthouse and a blacksmith shop, which they saved before serious damage

"The White Cockade"
Fifer Luther Blanchard and drummer Francis Barker played this martial tune shortly before the skirmish near the bridge.

A View of the Town of Concord, 1775, *by Ralph Earl*

resulted. But the minutemen on the ridge became enraged by the rising smoke.

"Will you let them burn the town down?" screamed hotheaded Lieutenant Joseph Hosmer at Colonel Barrett. Now commanding four hundred men, Barrett decided to reenter the town and led his men toward the hundred redcoats guarding the bridge. The British withdrew across the river and fired several warning shots. One round wounded Luther Blanchard, a fifer who had been merrily playing a marching tune. Suddenly, smoke billowed from the British ranks and musketballs whistled across the water. Captain Isaac Davis and Private Abner Hosmer, volunteers from nearby Acton, fell dead. "For God's sake, fire," shouted Captain Jonathan Buttrick to his Concord company, which shot a volley at the British that killed three soldiers and wounded nine others.

The skirmish lasted only two or three minutes. The British withdrew to the town center. The minutemen crossed the river but then broke ranks and milled about in confusion. Both sides kept their distance

until noon, when the British started to march back to Boston.

The British delay in leaving Concord allowed hundreds of minutemen to arrive from neighboring towns. At Meriam's Corner, these reinforcements began harassing the redcoats in a running battle that continued for sixteen miles. "Every man," recalled Private Thaddeus Blood, "was his own commander." By day's end almost three hundred royal troops were killed, wounded, or missing, and eighty colonists lay dead or injured.

Concord citizens escaped the day with slight losses: four men wounded, none dead. The war, however, had barely begun, and during the coming months, Concord sent off every able-bodied man between the ages of eighteen and forty to serve in the army. After the war the fight at the bridge assumed mythic dimensions for Americans, who celebrated the patriots who dared death at "the rude bridge that arched the flood" and "fired the shot heard 'round the world." But Concord citizens were too familiar with the events to romanticize

British Looters
A colonial cartoonist caught the red-coats in a looting spree during their retreat from Concord.

them. In 1792 they unemotionally tore up the historic bridge and built a more convenient crossing several hundred yards downriver.

157b

had made independence a reality. Finally, Paine linked America's awakening nationalism with the sense of religious mission felt by many in New England and elsewhere when he proclaimed, "We have it in our power to begin the world over again. A situation, similar to the present, hath not happened since the days of Noah until now." America, in Paine's view, would be not only a new nation but a new *kind* of nation, a model society founded on new principles and unburdened by the oppressive beliefs and institutions of the European past.

Printed in both English and German, *Common Sense* sold more than one hundred thousand copies within three months, equal to one for every fourth or fifth adult male. The Connecticut Gazette described it as "a landflood that sweeps all before it." By the spring of 1776, Paine's pamphlet had dissolved lingering allegiance to George III and removed the last psychological barrier to independence.

Independence at Last

John Adams described the movement toward independence as a coach drawn by thirteen horses, which could not reach its destination any faster than the slowest ones were willing to run. New England was already in rebellion, and Rhode Island declared itself independent in May 1776. The middle colonies hesitated to support revolution because they feared, correctly, that the war would largely be fought over control of Philadelphia and New York. Following the news in April that North Carolina's congressional delegates were authorized to vote for independence, the South began pressing for separation. Virginia's extralegal legislature soon instructed its delegates at the Second Continental Congress to propose independence, which Richard Henry Lee did on June 7. Formally adopting Lee's resolution on July 2, Congress created the United States of America.

The task of drafting a statement to justify the colonies' separation from England fell to Virginia delegate Thomas Jefferson. Congress reviewed his manuscript on July 3 and approved it the next day. The Declaration of Independence never mentioned Parliament by name—even though the central point of dispute since 1765 had been Parliament's legislative powers—because Congress was unwilling to imply, even indirectly, that it held any authority over America. Jefferson instead followed Paine and focused on the king, citing George III's "repeated injuries and usurpations" against the colonies. And he drew on a familiar line of thinking when he added that the king's actions had as their "direct object the establishment of an absolute tyranny over these states."

Also like Paine, Jefferson elevated the colonists' grievances from a dispute over English freedoms to a struggle of universal dimensions. In the tradition of Locke and other Enlightenment figures, Jefferson argued that the English government had violated its contract with the colonists, thereby giving them the right to replace it with a government of their own design. His eloquent emphasis on the equality of all individuals and their natural entitlement to justice, liberty, and self-fulfillment expressed the Enlightenment's deepest longing for a government that would rest on neither legal privilege nor the exploitation of the majority by the few.

Jefferson addressed the Declaration of Independence as much to Americans uncertain about the wisdom of independence as to world opinion, for he wanted to convince his fellow citizens that social and political progress could no longer be accomplished within the British Empire. The declaration never claimed that perfect justice and equal opportunity existed in the United States; rather, it challenged the Revolutionary generation and all who later inherited the nation to bring this ideal closer to reality.

CONCLUSION

The most moving section of the Declaration of Independence's original draft was directed to the people of England, whom Jefferson regretfully reminded that "we might have been a free and great people together." Congress eliminated these words, which expressed the feelings of most Americans all too well, for in a civil war it is never wise to dwell on the matter of shedding common blood. Throughout the long imperial crisis, Americans had repeatedly pursued the goal of reestablishing the empire as it had functioned before 1763, when colonial trade was protected and encouraged—not taxed and plundered—by the Navigation Acts, and when colonial assemblies had exercised exclusive power over taxation and internal legislation. These reluctant revolutionaries now had to face the might of Europe's greatest imperial power and win their independence on the battlefield. They also had to decide to what degree they would implement the idealistic vision evoked in Jefferson's declaration. Neither task would prove simple or easy.

CHRONOLOGY

1744–1748 King George's War (in Europe, the War of Austrian Succession, 1740–1748).

1754–1760 Seven Years' War (in Europe, 1756–1763).

1760 George III becomes king of Great Britain.
Massachusetts controversy over writs of assistance.

1763–1766 Indian uprising in Ohio Valley and Great Lakes.

1763 Proclamation of 1763.

1764 Sugar Act.

1765 Stamp Act.
First Quartering Act.
Loyal Nine formed in Boston to oppose the Stamp Act.
Sons of Liberty band together throughout the colonies.
Stamp Act Congress.
Colonists begin boycott of British goods.

1766 Stamp Act repealed.
Declaratory Act.

1767 New York Suspending Act.
Revenue Act (Townshend duties).

Commemorative Teapot, 1766

John Dickinson, *Letters from a Farmer in Pennsylvania.*
American Board of Customs Commissioners created.

1768 Massachusetts "circular letter."
Boston merchants adopt the colonies' first nonimportation agreement.
John Hancock's ship *Liberty* seized by Boston customs commissioner.
British troops arrive in Boston.
First Treaty of Fort Stanwix.
John Wilkes elected to Parliament; arrested.
St. George's Fields Massacre in London.

1770 Townshend duties, except tea tax, repealed.
Boston Massacre.

1771 Battle of Alamance Creek in North Carolina.

1772 *Gaspee* incident in Rhode Island.
Committees of correspondence begin in Masschusetts and rapidly spread.

1773 Tea Act.
Boston Tea Party.

1774 Coercive Acts.
Quebec Act.
First Continental Congress meets in Philadelphia and adopts Suffolk Resolves.
Continental Association.

1775 Battles of Lexington and Concord.
Second Continental Congress meets.
Olive Branch Petition.
Battles at Breed's Hill and Bunker Hill.

1776 Thomas Paine, *Common Sense.*
Declaration of Independence.

FOR FURTHER READING

Bernard Bailyn, *The Ideological Origins of the American Revolution* (1967). Pulitzer Prize–winning examination of the political heritage that shaped colonial resistance to British authority.

Edward Countryman, *The American Revolution* (1985). An outstanding introduction to the Revolution and its background.

Robert A. Gross, *The Minutemen and Their World* (1976). An eloquent and evocative examination of Concord, Massachusetts, in the Revolutionary era.

Pauline Maier, *From Resistance to Revolution: Colonial Radicals and the Development of American Opposition to Britain, 1765–1776* (1972). An insightful, definitive examination of how colonial leaders strove to force the repeal of unconstitutional laws with a minimum use of violence.

Robert Middlekauff, *The Glorious Cause: The American Revolution, 1763–1789* (1982). A judicious, learned, and highly readable narrative of the events leading to Independence.

Edmund S. Morgan and Helen M. Morgan, *The Stamp Act Crisis: Prologue to Revolution*, rev. ed. (1963). The most penetrating, and now classic, analysis of colonial constitutional principles regarding the limits on Parliament's taxing power.

Robert R. Palmer, *The Age of the Democratic Revolution: Vol. I, The Challenge* (1959). Bancroft Prize–winning examination of the American Revolution in comparison to events in England, Ireland, and France.

Gordon S. Wood, *The Radicalism of the American Revolution* (1991). A sweeping account of the Revolution's long-range impact on American society.

ADDITIONAL BIBLIOGRAPHY

The Military Background

Fred Anderson, *A People's Army: Massachusetts Soldiers and Society in the Seven Years' War* (1984); Sylvia R. Frey, *The British Soldier in America: A Social History of Military Life in the Colonial Period* (1981); John Shy, *Toward Lexington: The Role of the British Army in the Coming of the America Revolution* (1965); Ian K. Steele, *Betrayals: Fort William Henry and the "Massacre"* (1990).

Native Americans and the Frontier

David H. Corkran, *The Creek Frontier, 1540–1783* (1967); Gregory Evans Dowd, *A Spirited Resistance: The North American Indian Struggle for Unity, 1745–1815* (1992); Tom Hatley, *The Dividing Paths: Cherokees and South Carolinians Through the Era of Revolution* (1993); Dorothy V. Jones, *License for Empire: Colonialism by Treaty in Early America* (1982); Francis Jennings, *Empire of Fortune: Crowns, Colonies and Tribes in the Seven Years' War in America* (1988); Michael N. McConnell, *A Country Between: The Upper Ohio Valley and Its Peoples, 1724–1774* (1992); Richard White, *The Middle Ground: Indians, Empires, and Republics in the Great Lakes Region, 1650–1815* (1991).

Taxing and Regulating Trade

Thomas C. Barrow, *Trade and Empire: The British Customs Service in Colonial America* (1967); Oliver M. Dickerson, *The Navigation Acts and the American Revolution* (1951); Michael Kammen, *Empire and Interest: The American Colonies and the Politics of Mercantilism* (1970); John W. Tyler, *Smugglers and Patriots: Boston Merchants and the Advent of the American Revolution* (1986); Carol Ubbelohde, *The Vice-Admiralty Courts and the American Revolution* (1960).

Constitutional Issues

Richard L. Bushman, *King and People in Provincial Massachusetts* (1985); Jack P. Greene, *Peripheries and Center: Constitutional Development in the Extended Politics of the British Empire and the United States, 1607–1788* (1987); Jerrilyn G. Marston, *King and Congress* (1987); Edmund S. Morgan, *Inventing the People: The Rise of Popular Sovereignty in England and America* (1988); John G. A. Pocock, *Three British Revolutions: 1641, 1688, 1776* (1980); Jack R. Pole, *Political Representation in England and the Origins of the American Republic* (1966); John P. Reid, *Constitutional History of the American Revolution: The Authority of Rights* (1986), *Constitutional History of the American Revolution: The Power to Tax* (1987).

Religious Influences

Ruth H. Bloch, *Visionary Republic: Millennial Themes in American Thought, 1756–1800* (1985); Patricia U. Bonomi, *Under the Cope of Heaven: Religion, Society, and Politics in Colonial America* (1986); Jack P. Greene and William G. McLoughlin, *Preachers and Politicians: Two Essays on the Origin of the American Revolution* (1977); Nathan O. Hatch, *The Sacred Cause of Liberty: Republican Thought and the Millennium in Revolutionary New England* (1977).

Resistance

David Ammerman, *In the Common Cause: American Response to the Coercive Acts of 1774* (1974); Michael Bellesiles, *Revolutionary Outlaws: Ethan Allen and the Struggle for Independence* (1993); John L. Brooke, *The Heart of the Commonwealth: Society and Political Culture in Worcester County, Massachusetts, 1713–1861* (1989); Richard D. Brown, *Revolutionary Politics in Massachusetts: The Boston Committees of Correspondence and the Towns, 1772–1774* (1970); Marc Egnal, *A Mighty Empire: The Origins of the American Revolution* (1988); Jay Fleigelman, *Prodigals and Pilgrims: The American Revolution Against Patriarchal Authority, 1750–1800* (1982); Michael G. Kammen, *A Rope of Sand: The Colonial Agents, British Politics, and the American Revolution* (1968); Benjamin W. Labaree, *The Boston Tea Party* (1964); Edmund S. Morgan and Helen M. Morgan, *The Stamp Act Crisis: Prologue to Revolution*, rev. ed. (1963); Gary B.

Nash, *The Urban Crucible: The Northern Seaports and the Origins of the American Revolution,* abridged ed. (1986); Mary Beth Norton, *Liberty's Daughters: The Revolutionary Experience of American Women, 1750–1800* (1980); John Sainsbury, *Disaffected Patriots: London Supporters of Revolutionary America, 1769–1782* (1987); Peter Shaw, *American Patriots and the Rituals of Revolution* (1981); Neil R. Stout, *The Perfect Crisis: The Beginnings of the Revolutionary War* (1976); Peter D. G. Thomas, *The Townshend Duties Crisis: The Second Phase of the American Revolution, 1767–1773* (1987); Robert W. Tucker and David C. Hendrickson, *The Fall of the First British Empire: Origins of the War of American Independence* (1982); Hiller B. Zobel, *The Boston Massacre* (1970).

Biographies

Bernard Bailyn, *The Ordeal of Thomas Hutchinson* (1974); Richard R. Beeman, *Patrick Henry: A Biography* (1974); Milton E. Flower, *John Dickinson: Conservative Revolutionary* (1983); Eric Foner, *Tom Paine and Revolutionary America* (1976); Pauline Maier, *The Old Revolutionaries: Political Lives in the Age of Samuel Adams* (1980); Dumas Malone, *Jefferson the Virginian* (1948).

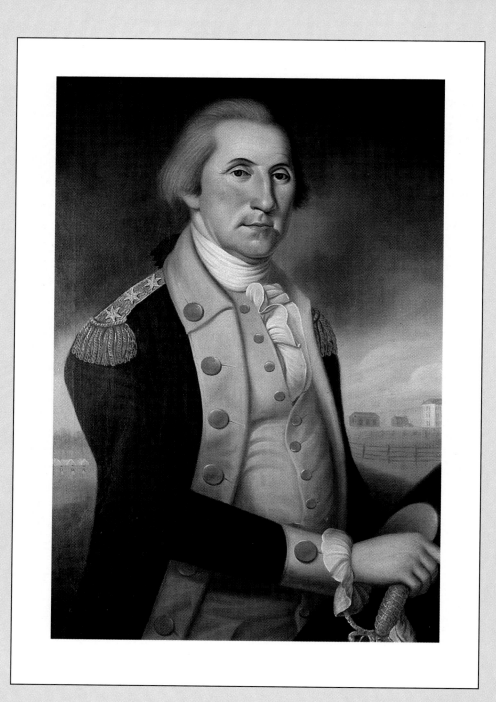

George Washington [1777]
by Charles Peale Polk, c. 1792–1793

THE FORGE OF NATIONHOOD
1776–1788

In November 1775 General George Washington ordered Colonel Henry Knox (inset) to bring the British artillery recently captured at Fort Ticonderoga to the siege of Boston. Washington knew firsthand of the difficulties of wilderness travel, especially in the winter, and he must have wondered if this city-bred officer was up to the task. Only twenty-five years old and a Boston bookseller with little experience in the woods, Knox was nevertheless the army's senior artillerist, largely because he had read several books on the subject while business in his store was dull.

Knox and his men built crude sleds to haul their fifty-nine cannons through dense forest covered by two feet of snow. On good days they moved these sixty tons of artillery about seven miles. On two very bad ones, they shivered for hours in freezing water while retrieving guns that had fallen through the ice at river crossings. As their oxen grew weak from overexertion and poor feed, the men had to throw their own backs into pulling the cannons across New York's frozen landscape. On reaching the Berkshire Mountains in western Massachusetts, their pace slowed to a crawl as they trudged uphill through snow-clogged passes. Forty days and three hundred miles after leaving Ticonderoga, Knox and his exhausted New Yorkers reported to Washington in late January 1776. The Boston bookseller had more than proved himself: he had accomplished one of the Revolution's great feats of endurance.

The guns from Ticonderoga placed the outnumbered British in a hopeless position and forced them to evacuate Boston on March 17, 1776. A lifelong friendship formed between Washington and Knox. Knox served on the Virginian's staff throughout the war and accepted his request to be the nation's first secretary of war in 1789.

Friendships like the one between Washington and Knox were almost as revolutionary as the war that produced them. Because inhabitants of different colonies had little opportunity to become acquainted before 1775, their outlooks had remained narrowly confined within the borders of their provinces. This localism was well entrenched at the start of the war. George Washington at first described New Englanders as "an exceeding dirty and nasty people." Yankee soldiers irritated troops from distant colonies such as Virginia with smug assumptions of superiority expressed in their popular marching song "Chester," whose rousing lyrics rang out:

Let tyrants shake their iron rod,
and slavery clank her galling chains.
We fear them not, we trust in God.
New England's *God forever reigns.*

The Revolution gave northerners and southerners their first real chance to learn what they had in common, and they soon developed mutual admiration. George Washington, who in the war's early days dismissed New England officers as "the most indifferent kind of people I ever saw," changed his mind after meeting men like Henry Knox.

In July 1776 the thirteen colonies had out of desperation declared independence and established a new nation. But only as a result of the collective hardships experienced during eight years of terrible fighting did the inhabitants of the thirteen states cease to see themselves simply as military allies and begin to accept each other as fellow citizens.

The return of peace in 1783 left Americans with a false sense of security. Major problems remained unsolved and ignored, particularly the power and authority of the national government relative to that of the states. With the ratification of the Constitution, the United States arrived at a resolution of this fundamental question, thereby completing the process whereby thirteen colonies became a single nation.

◆

AMERICA'S FIRST CIVIL WAR

The Revolution was both a collective struggle that marched a sizable portion of the American people against Britain and a civil war between inhabitants of North America. Eventually, it would degenerate into a brothers' war of the worst kind, conducted without restraint, mutual respect, or compassion. From a military standpoint, the Revolution's outcome depended not only on the ability of the supporters of independence, called the patriots, or Whigs, to wear down the British army but also on the rebels' success in suppressing fellow North Americans' opposition to independence.

A British View of the Loyalists

This British cartoon depicts Americans as "savage" Indian warriors massacring helpless loyalists. It is also critical of Prime Minister Lord Shelburne for failing to protect the loyalists.

Loyalists and Other British Sympathizers

As late as January 1776, most colonists still hoped that declaring independence from Britain would not be necessary. Not surprisingly, when separation came six months later, many Americans remained unconvinced that it was justified. About 20 percent of all whites either opposed the rebellion actively or refused to support the Continental Congress unless threatened with fines or imprisonment. Although these internal enemies of the Revolution called themselves loyalists, they were "Tories" to their Whig foes. Whigs remarked, but only half in jest, that "a tory was a thing with a head in England, a body in America, and a neck that needed stretching."

Loyalists avowed many of the same political values as did the patriots. Like the rebels, they usually opposed Parliament's claim to tax the colonies. Many loyalists thus found themselves fighting for a cause with which they did not entirely agree, and as a result many of them would change sides during the war. Most doubtless shared the apprehension expressed in 1775 by the Reverend Jonathan Boucher, a well-known Maryland loyalist, who preached with two loaded pistols lying on his pulpit cushion: "For my part I equally dread a Victory by either side."

Loyalists disagreed, however, with the patriots' insistence that only independence could preserve the colonists' constitutional rights. The loyalists denounced separation as an illegal act certain to ignite an unnecessary war. Above all, they retained a profound reverence for the crown and deeply believed that if they failed to defend their king, they would sacrifice their personal honor.

The most important factor in determining loyalist strength in any area was the degree to which prominent local Whigs had successfully convinced the mass of voters that representative government was endangered by the king and Parliament. Town leaders in New England, the Virginia gentry, and the rice planters of South Carolina's seacoast all vigorously pursued a program of political education and popular mobilization from 1772 to 1776. Repeatedly explaining the issues at public meetings, these elites shook the mass of citizens from their apathy and persuaded the overwhelming majority in favor of resistance. As a result, probably no more than 5 percent of whites in these areas were committed loyalists in 1776. Where the leading families acted indecisively, however, their communities remained divided when the fighting began. Because the gentry of New York and New Jersey were especially reluctant to declare their allegiance to either side, the proportion of loyalists was highest there. Those two states eventually furnished about half of the twenty-one thousand Americans who fought in loyalist military units.

The next most significant factor influencing loyalist military strength was the geographic distribution of recent British immigrants, who closely identified with their homeland, not America, and overwhelmingly opposed independence. Among these newcomers were thousands of British soldiers who had served in the Seven Years' War and then remained in the colonies, usually in New York, where they could obtain land grants of two hundred acres. Furthermore, more than 125,000 English, Scots, and Irish landed from 1763 to 1775—the greatest number of Britons to arrive during any dozen years of the colonial era. Major centers of loyalist sympathy existed wherever large concentrations of such British-born people lived. In New York, Georgia, and the backcountry of North and South Carolina, where the native-born Britons were heavily concentrated, the proportion of loyalists among whites probably ranged from 25 percent to 40 percent in 1776. In wartime the British army organized many Tory units comprising immigrants from the British Isles, including the Loyal Highland Emigrants, the North Carolina Highlanders, and the Volunteers of Ireland. After the war foreign-born loyalists composed a majority of those compensated by the British for property losses during the Revolution—including

three-quarters of all such claimants from the Carolinas and Georgia.

Other minorities supported the British cause, not out of loyalty to the crown but from a perception that an independent American republic would pose the greater threat to their own liberty and independence. A small number of German, Dutch, and French religious congregations that resisted use of the English language felt indebted to the British government for their religious freedom and doubted that their rights would be as safe in an independent nation dominated by Anglo-Americans. Yet on balance, these ethnic and religious minorities provided few loyalists. The great majority of German colonists in Pennsylvania, Maryland, and Virginia, for example, had embraced emergent American republicanism by 1776 and would overwhelmingly support the Revolutionary cause.

Canada's French Catholics composed the most significant white minority to hold pro-British sympathies. Although the British had conquered them in the Seven Years' War, the Quebec Act of 1774 guaranteed their religious freedom and their continued use of French civil law. Remembering that the American colonists had denounced this measure and demanded its repeal, French Catholics worried that their privileges would disappear if they were absorbed into an independent Protestant America.

Canadian anxieties intensified in mid-1775, when the Continental Congress ordered Continental forces to "free" Canada from British tyranny unless this action was "disagreeable" to the French population. In reality, Congress cared little what the French-Canadians thought, for Congress believed that a conquest of Canada was essential to block a British invasion from the north. In 1775 Continental armies (one of them led by Benedict Arnold, a fervent patriot who later turned traitor) marched into Canada and attacked Quebec but suffered defeat on December 31, 1775. French Catholics emerged from the shock of invasion more loyal to the crown than ever before. The rebels never even attempted to win over three other mainland colonies—Nova Scotia and East and West Florida—whose small populations of mainly recent immigrants were firmly dominated by British military authorities.

The British cause would also draw significant wartime support from nonwhites. As a deeply alienated group within society, slaves quickly realized that the Revolution was not intended to benefit them. In 1766, when a group of African-American slaves, inspired by the protests against the Stamp Act, had marched through Charles Town, South Carolina, shouting "Liberty!" they had faced arrest for inciting a rebellion. By 1775 it was the British who most often offered liberty to enslaved African-Americans. For example, in 1775 Lord Dunmore, governor of Virginia, promised freedom to any slave who enlisted in the cause of restoring royal authority. About eight hundred blacks joined him before he fled the colony. Meanwhile, hundreds of South Carolina slaves had escaped and taken refuge on British ships in Charles Town's harbor. During the war at least twenty thousand American slaves ran away to sign on as laborers or soldiers in the Royal Army. Among the Whig slaveholders who saw many of his slaves escape to British protection was Thomas Jefferson.

Although the Native American population was divided, most supported the British. Indians along the frontier recognized the danger to their homelands posed by expansion-minded Anglo-Americans. As had been the case since midcentury, tensions ran especially high in the Ohio Country. There, Shawnees, Delawares, Mingos, and other Indians continued to bristle at white incursions, as did the Cherokees to the south. Native Americans in the upper Great Lakes, after the uprising of 1763 (see Chapter 5), had developed good rapport with British agents in the former French forts and were solidly in the British camp. The Iroquois and Creek confederacies, whose neutrality had been a source of strength until the French defeat in 1760, were now divided. The Creeks' allegiance reflected each village's earlier trade ties with either Britain or Spain (the latter leaned toward the colonists' cause). Most Iroquois followed the lead of the English-educated Mohawk chief Joseph Brant in supporting Britain. Only the Oneidas and Tuscaroras, influenced by Congregationalist missionary Samuel Kirkland, sided with the rebels. Native Americans in upper New England and the Canadian maritime provinces and in the Illinois and Wabash valleys initially took an anti-British stand because of earlier ties with the French, though many of them became alienated from the colonists during the war. Most of the dwindling number of Indians living in the established colonies favored the rebellion.

Toward loyalists collectively, Whigs reserved an intense hatred, far greater than their antipathy toward the British army, and loyalists responded with equal venom. Each side saw its cause as so sacred that opposition by a fellow American was an unforgivable act of betrayal. The worst atrocities committed during the war were inflicted by Americans upon each other.

The Opposing Sides

Britain entered the war with two major advantages. First, in 1776 the 11 million inhabitants of the British Isles greatly outnumbered the 2.5 million colonists, one-third of whom were either slaves or loyalists. Second, Britain possessed the world's largest navy and one of its best professional armies. Nevertheless, the royal military establishment grew during the war years to a degree that strained Britain's resources. The army more than doubled from 48,000 to 111,000 men, not only in North America but also in the British Isles and the West Indies. To meet its manpower needs, the British government had to raise the recruiting bonuses paid to get men to enlist, lower physical requirements, widen age limits, and sometimes enroll soldiers forcibly. But even these measures failed to provide the required numbers. Without hiring 30,000 German mercenaries known as Hessians and later enlisting 21,000 loyalists, Britain could not have met its manpower needs.

Despite its smaller population, the new nation mobilized its people more effectively than did Britain. By the end of the war, the rebels had enlisted or drafted into the Continental Army or the state militias perhaps half of all free males from age sixteen to forty-five—about 220,000 troops—compared to the 162,000 Britons, loyalists, and Hessians who served in the British army.

Britain's ability to crush the rebellion was further weakened by the decline in its seapower that had resulted from peacetime budget cuts after 1763. Midway through the war, half of the Royal Navy's ships sat in dry dock awaiting major repairs. Although the navy expanded rapidly from 18,000 to 111,000 sailors, it lost 42,000 men to desertion and 20,000 to disease or wounds. In addition, Britain's merchant marine suffered mightily from raids by the numerous American privateers newly outfitted from the colonies' thriving merchant marine. During the war rebel privateers and the fledgling U.S. Navy would capture over 2,000 British merchant vessels and 16,000 crewmen.

Britain could ill afford these losses, for it faced a colossal task in trying to supply its troops in America. Although at one time or another the British army controlled all the major American cities, British soldiers ventured into the agricultural hinterland only at their peril and hence could not easily round up supplies. In fact, almost all the food consumed by the army, a third

**Woodcut from "A New Touch on the Times. . . . By a
Daughter of Liberty, Living in Marblehead," 1779**
*Americans on the home front as well as in the front lines
experienced stunning wartime hardships. This illustration of
a female partisan holding a musket accompanied a poem
by Molly Gutridge, whose theme was women's sacrifice and
suffering in a seaport economy upset by war.*

of a ton per soldier per year, had to be imported from
Britain. Seriously overextended, the navy barely kept
the army supplied and never effectively blockaded
American ports.

Mindful of the enormous strain that the war imposed, British leaders faced serious problems maintaining their people's support for the conflict. The war
more than doubled the national debt, thereby adding
further to the burdens of a people already paying
record taxes. The politically influential landed gentry
could not be expected to vote against their pocketbooks forever.

The United States faced different but no less severe wartime problems. First, one-fifth of its free population openly favored the British. Second, although the
state militias sometimes performed well in hit-and-run

guerrilla skirmishes and were also effective in intimidating loyalists and in requisitioning war supplies, they
lacked the training to fight pitched battles. Congress
recognized that independence would never be secured
if the United States relied on guerrilla tactics, avoided
major battles, and allowed the British to occupy all major population centers. Moreover, because European
powers would interpret U.S dependence on guerrilla
warfare as evidence that Americans could not drive out
the British army, that strategy would doom efforts by
the Continental Congress to gain foreign loans and
diplomatic recognition.

The Continental Army thus had to fight in the standard European fashion of the times. Professional eighteenth-century armies relied on expert movements of
mass formations. Victory often depended on rapid maneuvers to crush an enemy's undefended flank or rear.
Attackers needed exceptional skill in close-order drill
in order to fall on an enemy before the enemy could reform and return fire. Because muskets had a range of
under one hundred yards, armies in battle were never
far apart. Battles usually occurred in open country with
space for maneuver. The troops advanced within musket range of each other, stood upright without cover,
and fired volleys at one another until one line weakened from its casualties. Discipline, training, and nerve
were essential if soldiers were to stay in ranks while
comrades fell beside them. The stronger side then attacked at a quick walk with bayonets drawn and drove
off its opponents.

In 1775 Britain possessed a well-trained army with
a strong tradition of discipline and bravery under fire.
In contrast, the Continental Army had neither an inspi-
rational heritage nor many experienced officers or
sergeants who might turn raw recruits into crack units.
Consequently, the Americans experienced a succession of heartbreaking defeats in the war's early years.
Yet to win the war, the Continentals did not have to destroy the British army but only prolong the rebellion
until Britain's taxpayers lost patience with the struggle.
Until then, American victory would hinge heavily on
the ability of one man to keep his army fighting despite
defeat. He was George Washington.

George Washington

Few generals ever looked and acted the role as much
as Washington. He spoke with authority and com-
ported himself with dignity. At six feet two inches, he
stood a half-foot taller than the average man of his day.

Powerfully built, athletic, and hardened by a rugged outdoor life, he was one of the war's few generals whose presence on the battlefield could inspire troops to heroism.

Washington's military experience began at age twenty-two, when he had taken command of a Virginia regiment raised to resist French claims in the Ohio Valley (see Chapter 5). He had lost his first battle to a force vastly outnumbering his own. A year later, at Braddock's defeat, he had placed himself at the point of greatest danger and had two horses killed under him, besides having his hat shot off and his coat ripped by five bullets. Washington's early military experience—his mistakes and lost battles—taught him lessons that he might not have learned from easy, glorious victories. He discovered the dangers of overcon-

fidence and the need for determination in the face of defeat. He also learned much about American soldiers, especially that they performed best when led by example and treated with respect.

With Virginia's borders safe from attack in 1758, Washington had resigned his commission and become a tobacco planter. He had sat in the Virginia House of Burgesses, where his influence had grown, not because he thrust himself into every issue but because others respected him and sought his opinion. Having emerged as an early, though not outspoken, opponent of parliamentary taxation, he had also sat in the Continental Congress. In the eyes of the many who valued his advice and remembered his military experience, Washington was the logical choice to head the Continental Army.

The Battle of Princeton (1777), *by James Peale, c. 1790*
In the battle's first phase, fought south of the town, the American advance guard clashed with redcoats who were en route to Trenton, where they planned to link up with Lord Cornwallis. The British had the upper hand until George Washington and the main Continental force arrived, attacked, and drove them off.

War in Earnest

Henry Knox's successful transport of artillery from Ticonderoga to Boston prompted the British to evacuate Boston in March 1776 and to move on to New York, which they wished to seize and use as a base for conquering New England. Under two brothers—General William Howe and Admiral Richard, Lord Howe—130 warships carrying 32,000 royal troops landed near New York harbor in the summer of 1776. Defending New York, America's second-largest city, were 18,000 poorly trained soldiers under George Washington.

On August 27, 15,000 of William Howe's men nearly overwhelmed the 10,500 troops whom Washington had stationed on Long Island, just across a river from New York City. Inflicting over 1,000 casualties while losing fewer than 400 men, the British were on the verge of annihilating the Americans. But Washington executed a masterful night evacuation to New York City, saving 9,500 soldiers and most of his artillery from certain capture. He himself was the last American to board a boat.

By the third week of September 1776, the Continental Army around New York included more than 16,000 men fit to bear arms. Over the next three months, the British killed or took prisoner one-quarter of these troops and drove the survivors into headlong retreat across New Jersey. By early December, when Washington crossed the Delaware River from New Jersey into Pennsylvania, he had fewer than 7,000 troops fit for duty. Thomas Paine accurately described these demoralizing days as "the times that try men's souls."

With the British in striking distance of Philadelphia, Washington decided to seize the offensive before the morale of his army and country collapsed completely. On Christmas night, 1776, he led his troops back into New Jersey and attacked a Hessian garrison at Trenton, where he captured 918 Germans and lost only 4 Continentals. Washington then attacked 1,200 British at Princeton on January 3, 1777, and killed or took captive one-third of them while sustaining only 40 casualties.

These American victories at Trenton and Princeton had several important consequences. At a moment when defeat seemed inevitable, they boosted civilian and military morale. In addition, by checking the British offensive, they frustrated Howe's plans to pacify New Jersey by persuading inhabitants opposed to or skeptical of independence to rally to the British cause. Although nearly 5,000 New Jerseyans with loyalist sympathies swore allegiance to the crown late in 1776, Washington's victories forced the British early in 1777 to remove virtually all their New Jersey garrisons to New York, while Washington established winter quarters at Morristown, New Jersey, only twenty-five miles from New York City.

As long as they had enjoyed the support of the redcoats, New Jersey's loyalists had plundered local Whigs. Now stripped of British protection, the loyalists fell prey to the rebel militia, who drove thousands of loyalists into British-held New York, where many joined the Royal Army. Although some loyalists formed guerrilla bands and raided their former neighbors, New Jersey loyalism never recovered from the blow it received when the British evacuated the state early in 1777. The state militia became a relentless police force dedicated to rooting out political dissent. The militia disarmed known loyalists, jailed their leaders, and kept a constant watch on suspected Tories. Ironically, the British themselves contributed to the undermining of New Jersey loyalism, for prior to the Battle of Trenton, British commanders had failed to prevent an orgy of looting by their troops that damaged loyalists and Whigs equally. Surrounded by armed enemies and facing constant danger of arrest, most loyalists who remained in the state bowed to the inevitable and swore allegiance to the Continental Congress; more than a few ex-loyalists themselves joined the rebel militia.

The same process was eventually repeated following British invasions of New York in 1777, Georgia in 1778, and the Carolinas in 1779. Upon regaining the upper hand, Whig militias ruthlessly pursued loyalists aiding the redcoats, forced many to flee, and coerced most into renouncing the crown.

Not all loyalists shifted sides, however. The war drove perhaps one of every six loyalists into exile in Canada, Britain, or the West Indies. Twenty percent of all New Yorkers may have left the United States by 1784. When the British evacuated Savannah in 1782, 15 percent of all whites in Georgia accompanied them. Most of those who departed were evidently British immigrants. Whether loyalists changed sides or became political refugees, loyalism declined as a force during the war. By 1782 few active loyalists remained outside British lines.

The War in the North, 1776–1779
Following the British evacuation of Boston, the war shifted to New York City, which the British held from 1776 to 1783. In 1777 Britain's success in taking Philadelphia was offset by defeat in upstate New York. The hard-fought battle of Monmouth Court House, New Jersey, ended the northern campaigns in 1778.

The Turning Point

Shortly after the battles of Trenton and Princeton, the Marquis de Lafayette, a young French aristocrat, joined Washington's staff. Lafayette was twenty years old, highly idealistic, very brave, and infectiously optimistic. Given Lafayette's close connections with the French court, his presence in America indicated that the French king, Louis XVI, might recognize U.S. independence and perhaps declare war on Britain. Before recognizing the United States, however, Louis wanted proof that the Americans could win a major battle, a feat they had not yet accomplished.

Louis did not have to wait long. In the summer of 1777, the British planned a two-pronged assault intended to crush American resistance in New York State and thereby isolate New England. Pushing off from Montreal, a force of regulars and their Iroquois allies, marching under Lieutenant Colonel Barry St. Leger, would proceed south along Lake Ontario and invade central New York from Fort Oswego in the west, while General John Burgoyne would lead the main British force south from Quebec through eastern New York and link up with St. Leger near Albany.

The British would have faced a formidable task under any circumstances; but to complicate matters, General William Howe, the British commander in chief in North America, chose to launch a *second* major campaign in the summer of 1777, which was aimed at the American capital, Philadelphia. Howe intended to draw the Continentals south to the defense of their capital, defeat them in battle, and then use Philadelphia as a base for building loyalist support in the mid-Atlantic region. Howe's fateful decision to move against Philadelphia meant that neither he nor the modest force that he had left behind in New York City under General Henry Clinton could decisively aid St. Leger or Burgoyne if their invasion of New York misfired.

Unfortunately for Howe, nothing went according to plan in New York. St. Leger's force of 1,900 British and Iroquois advanced a hundred miles and halted to besiege 750 New York Continentals at Fort Stanwix. Unable to take the post after three weeks, St. Leger retreated in late August 1777.

Meanwhile, on July 6 Burgoyne's 8,300 British and Hessians had taken Fort Ticonderoga, about a hundred miles north of Albany. But by now Burgoyne's supply lines were overstretched, and a force that he dispatched to seize supplies at Bennington, Vermont, was repulsed with heavy losses. Along with the 900 troops that Burgoyne had detached to garrison Fort Ticonderoga, his losses in Vermont depleted his army and gave General Horatio Gates time to collect nearly 17,000 American troops for an attack. Gates fought two indecisive battles near Saratoga in the fall, inflicting another 1,200 casualties on Burgoyne. Surrounded and hopelessly outnumbered, Burgoyne's 5,800 troops honorably laid down their arms on October 17, 1777.

The diplomatic impact of the Battle of Saratoga rivaled its military significance and made it the war's turning point. Early in December 1777, news of the battle reached France, where Benjamin Franklin had recently arrived as the U.S. ambassador. Although one of America's wealthiest, wisest, and most sophisticated men, Franklin shrewdly captured the French imagination by appearing in a fur cap and playing the part of an innocent backwoods philosopher. Turning himself into the French court's latest fad, Franklin won widespread French sympathy for the United States. Then with the victory at Saratoga, France became convinced that the Americans could win the war and thus deserved diplomatic recognition.

In February 1778 France therefore formally recognized the United States. Four months later, it went to war with Britain. Spain declared war on Britain in 1779, but as an ally of France, not the United States, and the Dutch Republic joined them in the last days of 1780. Now facing a coalition of enemies, Britain had no allies.

The American allies soon made their presence felt. Between 1779 and 1781, Spanish troops based in Louisiana drove the British from West Florida, effectively preventing Britain from taking the Mississippi Valley. Beginning in 1781, French troops also contributed to rebel victories. Moreover, Britain sent thousands of soldiers to Ireland and the West Indies to guard against French invasion, thus reducing the manpower available to fight in the United States. The French and Spanish navies, which together approximately equaled the British fleet, won several large battles, denied Britain control of the sea, and punctured the Royal Navy's blockade.

The Continentals Mature

While Gates and Burgoyne maneuvered in upstate New York, Howe landed 18,000 troops near Philadelphia in late August. With Washington at their head and Lafayette at his side, 16,000 Continentals paraded through the imperiled city on August 24, 1777. "They marched twelve deep," John Adams wrote to his wife Abigail, "and yet took up above two hours in passing by." Adams noted that the troops were well armed and uniformed but that they did not keep their heads straight or wear their hats cocked properly—in short, they still had not acquired "quite the air of soldiers." They would pay a fearful price for their lack of training when they met Howe's professionals.

The two armies collided on September 11, 1777, at Brandywine Creek, Pennsylvania. In the face of superior British discipline, not only did most Continental units crumble but Congress soon fled Philadelphia in panic, enabling Howe to occupy the city. Howe again defeated Washington at Germantown on October 4. In one month's bloody fighting, 20 percent of the Continentals were killed, wounded, or captured.

In early December 1777, 11,000 tentless American survivors huddled around campfires at Whitemarsh, Pennsylvania. Short on rations and chilled to the bone from marching into a wall of sleet, they took a full week to walk to their winter quarters fourteen miles away. A fourth of them had worn out at least one shoe, and on days when the roads froze, they suffered horribly on the ice-covered ridges. Washington later remembered that "you might have tracked the army from White Marsh to Valley Forge by the blood of their feet."

While the British army rested comfortably eighteen miles away in Philadelphia, the Continentals stumbled around the bleak hills of Valley Forge, building crude huts. Despite some lapses in morale and discipline, the troops somehow preserved a sense of humor, which they occasionally demonstrated by joining together in a thousand voices to squawk like crows watching a cornfield. Underlying these squawks was real hunger: James Varnum reported on December 20 that his Connecticut and Rhode Island troops had gone the two previous days without meat and three days without bread.

The army slowly regained its strength but still lacked training. The Continentals had forced Burgoyne to surrender more by their overwhelming numbers than by their skill. Indeed, when Washington's men had met Howe's forces on equal terms, they lost badly. The Americans mainly lacked the ability to march as compact units and maneuver quickly. Regiments often straggled single-file into battle and then wasted precious time forming to attack, and few troops were expert in bayonet drill.

The Continental Army's ill-trained recruits received a desperately needed boost in February 1778, when the German soldier of fortune Friedrich von Steuben arrived at Valley Forge. The short, squat Steuben did not look like a soldier, but this earthy German instinctively liked Americans and became immensely popular. He had a talent for motivating men (sometimes by staging humorous tantrums featuring a barrage of German, English, and French swearing);

but more important, he possessed administrative genius. In a mere four months, General Steuben almost single-handedly turned the army into a formidable fighting force.

General Henry Clinton, now British commander in chief, evacuated Philadelphia in mid-1778 and marched to New York. The Continental Army got its first opportunity to demonstrate Steuben's training when it caught up with Clinton's rear guard at Monmouth Court House, New Jersey, on June 28, 1778. Although the Americans initially faltered, General Washington re-formed them along a strong defensive position. Clinton ordered his best units against Washington's line, only to see them thrown back at bayonet point. The battle raged for six hours in one-hundred-degree heat until Clinton broke off contact. Expecting to renew the fight at daybreak, the Americans slept on their arms, but Clinton's army slipped away before then. The British would never again win easily, except when they faced more militiamen than Continentals.

The Battle of Monmouth ended the contest for the North. Clinton occupied New York, which the Royal Navy made safe from attack. Washington kept his army nearby to watch Clinton. Meanwhile, the Whig militia hunted down the last few Tory guerrillas and extinguished loyalism.

Friedrich von Steuben
The Prussian-born Steuben arrived in the United States in December 1777. Although the government and the army alike felt deep disillusionment over the value of foreign officers at that time, the talented Steuben overcame this disability and was appointed the Continental Army's major-general in 1778.

Frontier Campaigns

A different kind of war developed west of the Appalachians and along the western borders of New York and Pennsylvania. The numbers engaged in these frontier skirmishes were relatively small, but the fighting was fierce and the stakes—for the new nation, for the British, and for Indians in the region—were high. In 1776 few Anglo-Americans had a clear notion of the western boundaries of the new nation; by 1783, when the Peace of Paris concluded the war, the new nation was able to assert its claim to the Mississippi River as

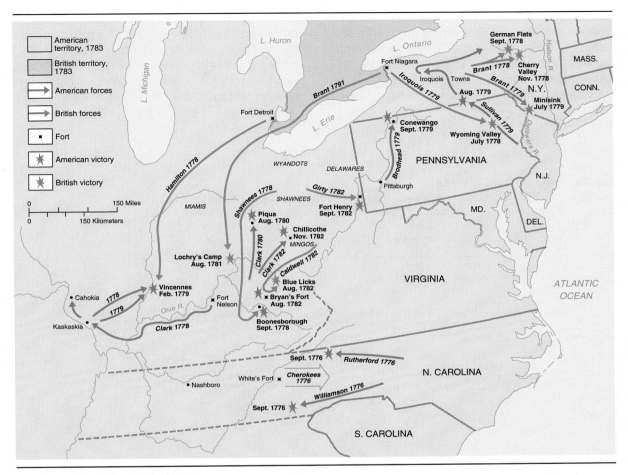

The War in the West, 1776–1779

George Rogers Clark's victory at Vincennes in 1779 gave the United States effective control of the Ohio Valley. Carolina militiamen drove attacking Cherokees far back into the Appalachians in 1776. In retaliation for their raids on New York and Pennsylvania, John Sullivan inflicted widespread starvation on the Iroquois by burning their villages and winter food supplies in 1779.

its western border. So although the frontier campaigns did not determine the outcome of the war, they had a significant impact on the future shape of the United States.

Frontier fighting erupted first in the South, where Cherokees began attacking settlers from Virginia to Georgia in 1776. After suffering heavy losses, the southern colonies recovered and organized retaliatory expeditions. Within a year these expeditions had burned most Cherokee towns, forcing the Cherokees to sign treaties that ceded most of their land in South Carolina and substantial tracts in North Carolina and Tennessee.

Elsewhere the intense fighting lasted longer. Natives and settlers fought for two years in Kentucky with neither side gaining a clear advantage. Then in June 1778 British troops moved into the areas settled by French farmers in what are now Illinois and Indiana. To counter these movements, Colonel George Rogers Clark led 175 Kentucky militiamen north of the Ohio River. After capturing and losing the French community of Vincennes on the Wabash River, Clark retook the settlement for good in February 1779. With the British unable to offer assistance, the Indians were vulnerable. In May, John Bowman led a second

Kentucky unit in a campaign that destroyed most Shawnee villages, and in August a move northward from Pittsburgh by Daniel Brodhead inflicted similar damage on the Delawares and the Seneca Iroquois. Although these raids depleted their populations and food supplies, most Ohio Indians resisted the Americans until the war's end.

In the East meanwhile, pro-British Iroquois, led by the gifted Mohawk leader Joseph Brant, devastated the Pennsylvania and New York frontiers in 1778. They killed 340 Pennsylvania militia at Wyoming, Pennsylvania, and probably slew an equal number in their other raids. In 1779 the U.S. general John Sullivan retaliated by invading the Iroquois country with 3,700

The War in the South, 1778–1781

By 1780 Britain held the South's major cities, Charles Town and Savannah, but could not establish control over the backcountry because of resistance from Nathanael Greene's Continentals. By invading Virginia, Lord Cornwallis placed himself within striking distance of Washington's U.S. and French forces, a decision that rapidly led to the British surrender at Yorktown in October 1781.

Continentals and several hundred Tuscaroras and Oneidas. Sullivan fought just one battle, near present-day Elmira, New York, in which his artillery routed Brant's warriors. After he burned two dozen Indian villages and destroyed a million bushels of corn, most Iroquois fled without food into Canada. Untold hundreds starved during the next winter, when more than sixty inches of snow fell.

In 1780 Brant's thousand warriors fell upon the Tuscaroras and Oneidas and then laid waste to Pennsylvania and New York for two years. But this final whirlwind of Iroquois fury masked reality: Sullivan's campaign had destroyed the Iroquois peoples' heartland; their population had declined by about one-third during the eight-year war.

American Foot Soldiers, Yorktown Campaign,
by Jean-Baptiste-Antoine DeVerger, 1781

Victory in the South

After 1778, as Britain formulated a new strategy that reflected changed circumstances, the war's focus shifted to the South. With the entry of France and Spain into the war, the conflict had acquired international dimensions; Britain was suddenly locked in a struggle that raged from India to Gibraltar to the West Indies and the American mainland. By securing ports in the South, the British would acquire the flexibility to move their forces back and forth between the West Indies and the United States as necessity dictated. In addition, the South looked like a relatively easy target. General Henry Clinton recalled that in 1778 a British force of 3,500 troops had taken Savannah, Georgia, without great difficulty, and he expected that a renewed invasion of the South would tap a huge reservoir of loyalist support. In sum, the British plan was to seize key southern ports and, with the aid of loyalist militiamen, move back toward the North, pacifying one region after another.

The plan unfolded smoothly at first. Sailing from New York with 9,000 troops, Clinton forced the surrender of Charles Town, South Carolina, and its 3,400-man garrison on May 12, 1780. Clinton then returned to New York with a third of his army, leaving mopping-up operations in the South to Lord Charles Cornwallis, now in command of British forces in that region. However, the British quickly found that there were fewer loyalists than they had expected. The Carolinas and Georgia did contain a sizable loyalist population, whose members enlisted by the thousands in royal militia units. Most were British immigrants, and Scots were especially prominent. But southern loyalism had

suffered a serious blow in 1776, when the Cherokees had attacked the Carolina frontier and killed residents indiscriminately. Numerous Tories had switched sides, joining the rebel militia to defend their homes. After the British capture of Charles Town, the loyalist militia, embittered by countless instances of harsh treatment under patriot rule, lost little time in taking revenge. Patriots struck back whenever possible. So began an escalating cycle of revenge, retribution, and retaliation that engulfed the Lower South through 1782.

This southern war became intensely personal. Individuals often chose sides not for political reasons but to avenge an outrage perpetrated by the other. For example, Thomas Sumter and Andrew Pickens, South Carolina's two foremost rebel guerrillas, both took up arms after Tories plundered their plantations in 1780. And when another South Carolinian, the Tory William Cunningham, learned that his brother had been whipped to death by patriot militiamen, he grimly walked sixty miles to find and to kill the officer responsible. Afterward, while leading loyalist guerrillas, Cunningham earned the nickname Bloody Bill.

But the southern conflict was not all personal feuds and guerrilla warfare. After the capture of Charles Town, Congress sent General Horatio Gates to take command in the South. With only a small force of Continentals at his disposal, however, Gates had to rely on poorly trained militiamen. In August 1780 Cornwallis inflicted a crushing defeat on Gates at Camden, South Carolina. Fleeing after firing a single volley, Gates's militia left his badly outnumbered Continentals to be overrun. Camden was the worst rebel defeat of the war.

Washington and Congress responded by relieving Gates of command and sending General Nathanael Greene to confront Cornwallis. Greene subsequently fought three major battles between March and September 1781, and he lost all of them. "We fight, get beat, rise, and fight again," he wrote back to Washington. Still, Greene won the campaign, for he gave the Whig militia the protection they needed to hunt down loyalists, stretched British supply lines until they began to snap, and sapped Cornwallis's strength by inflicting much heavier casualties than the British general could afford. Greene's dogged resistance forced Cornwallis to leave the Carolina backcountry in American hands and to lead his battered troops into Virginia.

Secure in New York City, Clinton wanted Cornwallis to return to Charles Town and renew his Carolina campaign; but Cornwallis had a mind of his own and established a new base at Yorktown, Virginia, near the coast. From Yorktown Cornwallis hoped to fan out into Virginia and Pennsylvania, but he never got the chance. Cornwallis's undoing began on August 30, 1781, when a French fleet from the West Indies, commanded by Admiral De Grasse, dropped anchor off the Virginia coast and landed troops near Yorktown. Soon Lafayette joined them, leading a small force of Continentals. Meanwhile, Washington made enough feints at New York City to prevent Clinton from coming to Cornwallis's aid and then moved his army south to tighten the noose around the British. Trapped in Yorktown, Cornwallis's 6,000 British stood off 8,800 Americans and 7,800 French for three weeks. They finally surrendered with military honors on October 19, 1781.

The Peace of Paris

"Oh God!" Lord North exclaimed upon hearing of Yorktown, "It's all over." Indeed, Cornwallis's surrender drained the will of England's overtaxed people to fight and forced the government to commence peace negotiations. John Adams, Benjamin Franklin, and John Jay were America's principal diplomats at the peace talks in Paris, which began in June 1782.

Military realities largely influenced the terms of the peace. Britain recognized American independence and stipulated the evacuation of all royal troops from U.S. soil. Although the vast majority of Americans lived in the thirteen states clustered near the eastern seaboard, the British had little choice but to award the United States all lands east of the Mississippi, for by 1783 twenty thousand Anglo-Americans lived west of the Appalachians, and Clark's victories had given Americans control of the Northwest. The treaty also gave the United States important fishing rights off the Grand Banks of Canada.

On the whole, the settlement was highly favorable to the United States, but it did not resolve all disputes. In a separate treaty, Britain transferred East and West Florida back to Spain, but the boundaries designated by this treaty were ambiguous. Spain interpreted the treaty to mean that it regained the same Florida territory that it had ceded to Britain in 1763. But Britain's treaty with the United States named the thirty-first parallel as the Floridas' northern border, well south of the area claimed by Spain. Spain and the United States would dispute the northern boundary of Florida until 1795.

The Peace of Paris also planted the seeds of several future disputes between Britain and the United States. Although the United States promised to urge the state legislatures to compensate loyalists for their property losses and agreed that no legal bars would prevent British creditors from collecting prewar debts, several state governments later refused to pay back loyalists and erected barriers against British creditors. In response, the British failed to honor their treaty pledge to return slaves confiscated by their troops.

Notably missing in the Peace of Paris was any reference to the Native Americans, most of whom had supported the British in order to avert the alternative—an independent American republic that would be no friend to Indian interests. In effect the treaty left the native peoples to deal with this new republic on their own, without any provision for their status or treatment. Not surprisingly, many Native Americans did not acknowledge the new nation's claims to sovereignty over their territory.

The Peace of Paris ratified American independence, but winning independence had exacted a heavy price. At least 5 percent of all free white males aged sixteen to forty-five died in the war. If the present-day U.S. population fought a war with comparable casualties, 2.5 million people would be killed. Only the Civil War produced a higher ratio of casualties to the nation's population. Furthermore, although the war secured American independence, it did not settle two important issues: what kind of society America was to become and what sort of government the new nation would possess. Yet the war had a profound impact on both questions.

REVOLUTIONARY SOCIETY

Two forces shaped the social effects of the Revolution: first, the principles articulated in the Declaration of Independence; and second, the dislocations caused by the war itself. These factors combined to change relationships between members of different classes, races, and genders momentously.

Egalitarianism

Between 1700 and 1760, social relations between elites and the common people had grown more formal, distant, and restrained. Members of the colonial gentry had emphasized their social position by living far beyond the means of ordinary families. By the late 1760s, however, many in the upper classes began wearing homespun rather than imported English clothes in support of the boycott of British goods and subsequently watched their popularity soar. When the First Families of Virginia organized minutemen companies in 1775, they threw away their expensive militia uniforms and dressed in homespun hunting shirts; then even the poorest farmer would not be too embarrassed to enlist because of his humble appearance. By 1776 some of the more visible distinctions of wealth had been noticeably reduced.

Then came war, which accelerated the erosion of class differences by forcing the gentry, who held officers' rank, to show respect to the ordinary folk serving as privates. Indeed, the soldiers demanded to be treated with consideration, especially in light of the ringing words of the Declaration of Independence, "All men are created equal." The soldiers would follow commands, but not if they were addressed as inferiors. General Steuben reported to a European army officer, "You say to your soldier, 'Do this,' and he doeth it, but I am obliged to say 'This is the reason why you ought to do that,' and he does it."

The best officers realized this fact immediately. Some, among them General Israel Putnam of Connecticut, went out of their way to show that they felt no superiority to their troops. While inspecting a regiment digging fortifications around Boston in 1776, Putnam saw a large stone nearby and told a noncommissioned officer to throw it onto the outer wall. The individual protested, "Sir, I am a corporal." "Oh," replied Putnam,

"I ask your pardon, sir." The general then dismounted his horse and hurled the rock himself, to the immense delight of the troops working there.

A majority of men of military age were exposed to treatment of this sort in the course of the war. Soldiers came to expect that their worth as individuals would be recognized by their officers, at least within the limits of the army. After these common soldiers returned to civilian life, they retained a sense of self-esteem and insisted on respectful treatment. As these feelings of personal pride gradually translated into political behavior and beliefs, candidates took care not to scorn the common people. The war thus subtly but fundamentally democratized Americans' political assumptions.

The gentry's sense of social rank also diminished as they met men who rose through ability rather than through advantages of wealth or family. The war produced numerous examples like James Purvis, the illiterate son of a nonslaveowning Virginia farmer, who joined the First Virginia Regiment as a private in 1775, soon rose to sergeant, and then taught himself to read and write so that he could perform an officer's duties. Captain Purvis fought through the entire war and impressed his well-born officers as "an uneducated man, but of sterling worth." As elites saw more and more middle-class farmers and even artisans performing responsibilities previously thought to be above their station in life, they developed a new appreciation that a person's merit was not always related to his wealth.

This new emphasis on equality did not extend to propertyless males, women, and nonwhites, but it undermined the tendency to believe that wealth or distinguished family background conferred a special claim to public office. "One should consider himself as good a man as another," declared the *New Jersey Gazette* in 1780, "and not be brow beaten or intimidated by riches or supposed superiority." After the war a fraternal organization of veteran Continental Army officers, the Society of the Cincinnati, evoked widespread alarm because its charter gave membership to sons and their descendants who, it was feared, might evolve into a hereditary aristocracy.

In short, Revolutionary-generation Americans came to insist that virtue and sacrifice defined a citizen's worth independently of his wealth. Voters widely began to view members of the "natural aristocracy"— those who had demonstrated fitness for government service by personal accomplishments—as the ideal candidates for political office. This natural aristocracy

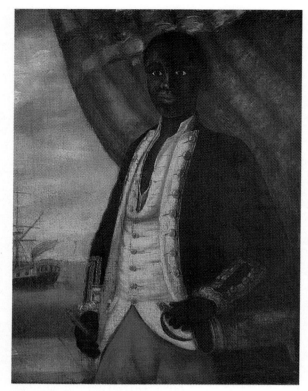

Revolutionary War Sailor,
by an unknown artist, c. 1780

had room for a few self-made men such as Benjamin Franklin, as well as for those, like Jefferson and John Hancock, born into wealth. Voters still elected the wealthy to office, but not if they flaunted their money. And members of the gentry increasingly acted like the "harmless aristocrats" of Virginia described by Judge St. George Tucker, who "never failed to pull off their hats to a poor man whom they met, and generally appeared to me to shake hands with every man in a Court-yard or a Church-yard."

A Revolution for Black Americans

The wartime situation of African-Americans contradicted the ideals of equality and justice for which Americans were fighting. About five hundred thousand black persons—20 percent of the total population—inhabited the United States in 1776, of whom all but about twenty-five thousand lived in bondage. Even those who were free could not vote, lived under curfews and other galling restrictions, and lacked the guarantees of equal justice held by the poorest white

criminal. Free blacks could expect no more than grudging toleration, and few slaves ever gained their freedom.

Although the United States was a "white man's country" in 1776, the war opened some opportunities to African-Americans. Amid the confusion of war, some slaves, among them Jehu Grant of Rhode Island, ran off and posed as freemen. Grant later recalled his excitement "when I saw liberty poles and the people all engaged for the support of freedom, and I could not but like and be pleased with such a thing." Black men also made their way into the Continental Army. Even though the army late in 1775 forbade the enlistment of any African-Americans, black soldiers were already fighting in units during the siege of Boston, and the ban on black enlistments started to collapse in 1777. All states but Georgia and South Carolina eventually recruited black soldiers.

In contrast to the twenty thousand who joined British forces, approximately five thousand African-Americans served in the Continental forces, most from the North. The majority were slaves serving with their masters' consent, usually in integrated units. In 1781 a German mercenary described Rhode Island's black regiment as "the most neatly dressed, the best under arms, and the most precise in its maneuvers."

For the most part, these wartime opportunities for African-Americans grew out of the army's need for manpower rather than a white commitment to equal justice. In fact, until the mid-eighteenth century, few in the Western world had criticized slavery at all. Like disease and sin, slavery was considered part of the natural order. But in the decade before the Revolution, American opposition to slavery had swelled. The first American prohibition against slaveowning came from the annual leadership conference (known as the yearly meeting) of the New England Quakers in 1770. The yearly meetings of New York and Philadelphia Quakers followed suit in 1776, and by 1779 Quaker slaveowners had freed 80 percent of their slaves.

Although the Quakers aimed mainly to abolish slaveholding within their own ranks, the Declaration of Independence's broad assertion of natural rights and human equality spurred a more general attack on the institution of slavery. Between 1777 and 1784, Vermont, Pennsylvania, Massachusetts, Rhode Island, and Connecticut ended slavery. New York did so in 1799, and New Jersey in 1804. New Hampshire, unmoved by petitions like that written in 1779 by Portsmouth slaves demanding liberty "to dispose of our lives, freedom, and property," never freed its slaves; but by 1810 there were none in the state.

The movement against slavery reflected the Enlightenment's emphasis on gradual change, initiated by leaders who carefully primed public opinion. The Revolutionary generation, rather than advocating slavery's immediate abolition, favored steps that would weaken the institution and in this way bring about its eventual demise. Most state abolition laws provided for gradual emancipation, typically declaring all children born of a slave woman after a certain date—often July 4—free. (Such individuals still had to work, without pay, for their mother's master for up to twenty-eight years.) Furthermore, the Revolution's leaders did not press for decisive action against slavery in the South, out of fear that widespread southern emancipation would either bankrupt or end the Union. They argued that the United States, already deeply in debt as a result of the war, could not finance immediate abolition in the South, and any attempt to do so without compensation would drive that region into secession. "Great as the evil is," observed Virginia's James Madison in 1787, "a dismemberment of the union would be worse."

Yet even in the South, slavery worried the consciences of some Whigs. When one of his slaves ran off to join the British and later was recaptured, Madison concluded that it would be hypocritical to punish the runaway "merely for coveting that liberty for which we have paid the price of so much blood." Still, Madison did not free the slave, and no state south of Pennsylvania abolished slavery. Nevertheless, every state but North Carolina passed laws making it possible for masters to manumit (set free) slaves without posting large sums of money as bond for their good behavior. By 1790 the number of free blacks in Virginia and Maryland had risen from about four thousand in 1775 to nearly twenty-one thousand, or about 5 percent of all African-Americans there.

These "free persons of color" faced the future as destitute, second-class citizens. Most had purchased their freedom by spending their small cash savings earned in off-hours and were past their physical prime. Once free, they found whites reluctant to hire them or to pay equal wages. Black ship carpenters in Charleston (formerly Charles Town), South Carolina, for example, earned one-third less than their white coworkers in 1783. Under such circumstances, most free blacks remained poor laborers or tenant farmers. However, even under such extreme disadvantages,

Phillis Wheatley, African-American Poet
Though a slave, Wheatley was the best-known poet in America at the time of the Revolution. Some of her poems linked the liberty sought by the colonists with a plea for the liberty of slaves. Despite her fame, Wheatley died in poverty in 1784.

some free blacks became landowners or skilled artisans. One who achieved considerable fame was Benjamin Banneker of Maryland, a self-taught mathematician and astronomer. Later, in 1789, he served on the commission that designed Washington, D.C., and after 1791 he published a series of almanacs.

Free blacks relied on one another for help. Self-help among African-Americans largely flowed through religious channels. Because many white congregations spurned them and because racially separate churches provided mutual support, self-pride, and a sense of accomplishment, free blacks began founding their own Baptist and Methodist congregations after the Revolution. In 1787 black Methodists in Philadelphia started the congregation that by 1816 would become the African Methodist Episcopal church. Black churches, a great source of inner strength and community cohesion for African-Americans ever since, had their origins in the Revolutionary period.

Most states granted important civil rights to free blacks during and after the Revolution. Free blacks

Sarah Livingston Jay and Her Children,
by James Sharpless, 1798
Jay was not only the devoted mother pictured here but a shrewd political observer who was married to the politician, diplomat, and chief justice John Jay.

had not participated in colonial elections, but those who were male and met the property qualification gained this privilege everywhere by the 1780s. Most northern states repealed or stopped enforcing curfews or other colonial laws restricting their freedom of movement. These same states generally changed their laws to guarantee free blacks equal treatment in court hearings.

The Revolution neither ended slavery nor brought equality to free blacks, but it did begin a process by which slavery eventually could be extinguished. In half the nation, human bondage had been outlawed and white southerners increasingly viewed slavery as a necessary evil—an attitude that implicitly recognized its immorality. Slavery had begun to crack, and free blacks had made some gains. But this shift proved short-lived, as events in the 1790s squelched the move toward egalitarianism.

Women in the New Republic

"To be adept in the art of Government is a prerogative to which your sex lay almost exclusive claim," wrote Abigail Adams to her husband John in 1776. She was one of the era's shrewdest political commentators and her husband's political confidante and best friend, but she had no public role. Indeed, for most women and almost all men in the 1780s, a woman's duty was to maintain her household and raise her children.

Apart from the fact that some states eased women's difficulties in obtaining divorces, the Revolution did not significantly affect the legal position of women. Women did not gain any new political rights, although New Jersey's 1776 constitution did not exclude white female property holders from voting, which they did in significant numbers until barred (along with free blacks) in 1807. The assumption that women were naturally dependent—either as children subordinate to their parents or as wives to their husbands—continued to dominate discussions of the female role. Nevertheless, the Revolutionary War and contemporary ideological currents emphasizing liberty and equality were significant for white American women.

Women's support of colonial resistance before Independence (see Chapter 5) broadened into an even wider range of support activities during the war. Female "camp followers," many of them soldiers' wives, served military units on both sides by cooking and laundering and by nursing the wounded. A few women, by disguising themselves as men, even joined in the fighting. Many more women remained at home, where they managed families, households, farms, and businesses on their own. After her civilian husband was seized by loyalists and turned over to the British on Long Island, Mary Silliman of Fairfield, Connecticut, tended to her four children (and bore a fifth), oversaw several servants and slaves, ran a commercial farm that had to be evacuated when the British attacked Fairfield, and launched appeals for her husband's release. Despite often enormous struggles, such experiences boosted women's confidence in their abilities to think and act on matters traditionally reserved for men.

As with African-Americans, the Revolutionary era witnessed the beginnings of a challenge to traditional attitudes toward women. American republicans increasingly recognized the right of a woman to choose her husband—a striking departure from the tradition whereby marriages were approved or even arranged by fathers. Thus in 1790, on the occasion of his daughter's marriage, Jefferson wrote to a friend that, following "the usage of my country, I scrupulously suppressed my wishes, [so] that my daughter might indulge her sentiments freely." Outside elite circles, such independence was apparent even before the Revolution. Especially in the Northeast, daughters increasingly got pregnant by prospective husbands, thus forcing their fathers to consent to their marrying in order to avoid a public scandal. For example, Mary Brown's father objected to her wedding John Chamberlain in Hallowell, Maine, in May 1792. In December he finally consented and the couple wed, just two days before their daughter's birth. By becoming pregnant, northeastern woman also secured for themselves economic support in a region where an exodus of young, unmarried men left a growing number of women single.

White women also had fewer children overall than their mothers and grandmothers. In Sturbridge, Massachusetts, women in the mid-eighteenth century averaged nearly nine children per marriage, compared with just six in the first decade of the nineteenth century. Whereas 40 percent of Quaker women had nine or more children before 1770, only 14 percent bore that many thereafter. Such statistics testify to declining farm sizes and urbanization, both of which were incentives for having fewer children. But they also indicate that women were finding some relief from the near-constant state of pregnancy and nursing that consumed their forebears.

As women's roles expanded, so too did republican notions of male-female relations. "I object to the word 'obey' in the marriage-service," wrote a female author calling herself Matrimonial Republican, "because it is a general word, without limitations or definition." "The obedience between man and wife," she continued, "is, or ought to be mutual." Lack of mutuality was one reason for a rising number of divorce petitions from women, from fewer than 14 per year in Connecticut before the Revolution, to 45 in 1795. A few women also challenged the sexual double standard that allowed men to indulge in extramarital affairs while their female partners, single or married, were condemned. Writing in 1784, an author calling herself Daphne pointed out how a woman whose illicit affair was exposed was "forever deprive[d] . . . of all that renders life valuable," while "the base [male] betrayer is suffered to triumph in the success of his unmanly

arts, and to pass unpunished even by a frown." Daphne called on her "sister Americans" to "stand by and support the dignity of our own sex" by publicly condemning seducers rather than their victims.

Gradually, the subordination of women, which once was taken for granted, became the subject of debate. In the essay "On the Equality of the Sexes," written in 1779 and published in 1790, Massachusetts essayist and poet Judith Sargent Murray contended that the genders had equal intellectual ability and deserved equal education. "We can only reason from what we know," she wrote, "and if an opportunity of acquiring knowledge hath been denied us, the inferiority of our sex cannot fairly be deduced from there." Murray hoped that "sensible and informed" women would improve their minds rather than rush into marriage (as she had at eighteen), and would instill republican ideals in their children.

Like many of her contemporaries, Murray supported "republican motherhood." Republicans emphasized the importance of educating women in the values of liberty and independence in order to strengthen virtue in the new nation. It was the duty of women to inculcate these values in their sons as well as their daughters. Even so conservative a man as John Adams reminded his daughter that she was part of "a young generation, coming up in America . . . [and] will be responsible for a great share of the duty and opportunity of educating a rising family, from whom much will be expected." After 1780 the urban upper class founded numerous private schools, or academies, for girls, and these provided to American women their first widespread opportunity for advanced education. Massachusetts also established an important precedent in 1789, when it forbade any town to exclude girls from its elementary schools.

Although the great struggle for female political equality would not begin until the nineteenth century, the frequent Revolutionary-era assertions that women were intellectually and morally men's peers provoked scattered calls late in the eighteenth century for political equality. In 1793 Priscilla Mason, a young woman graduating from one of the female academies, blamed "*Man*, despotic man" for shutting women out of the church, the courts, and government. In her salutatory oration, she urged that a women's senate be established by Congress to evoke "all that is human—all that is *divine* in the soul of woman."

Priscilla Mason had pointed out a fundamental limitation to republican egalitarianism: besides being a virtuous wife and mother, there was little a woman could *do* with her education.

Native Americans and the Revolution

For Native Americans, the consequences of the United States' triumph over Britain were less certain. Whereas Revolutionary ideology held out at least an abstract hope for blacks, women, and others seeking equal rights and status in American society, it made no provision for the many Indians who sought to maintain some degree of political and cultural independence. Moreover, in an overwhelmingly agrarian society like the United States, the Revolution's implicit promise of equal economic opportunity for all citizens set the stage for territorial expansion beyond the areas already settled, thereby threatening Indian landholdings. Even where Indians retained land, the influx of settlers posed dangers to them in the form of deadly diseases, farming practices inimical to Indian subsistence (see Chapter 3), and alcohol. Indians were all the more vulnerable because, during the three decades encompassed by the Seven Years' War and the Revolution (1754–1783), the native population east of the Mississippi had declined by about half, and many Indian communities had been uprooted.

In the face of these uncertainties, Native Americans continued their efforts to incorporate the most useful aspects of European culture into their own. From the beginning of the colonial period, Indians had selectively adopted European-made goods of cloth, metal, glass, and other materials into their lives. But Native Americans did not give up their older ways altogether; rather, their clothing, tools, weapons, utensils, and other material goods combined elements of the old and the new. Indians, especially those no longer resisting American expansion, also selectively participated in the American economy by working occasionally for wages or by selling food, crafts, or other products. This interweaving of the new with the traditional characterized Indian communities up and down the newly independent states, such as the Seneca Iroquois town of Jenuchshadago (see "A Place in Time"). Even Indians west of the settled areas, who hoped to avert the takeover of their lands by the new republic, looked to the British in Canada or the Spanish in Florida for trade as well as for diplomatic and military support.

Native Americans, then, did not remain stubbornly rooted in traditional ways, nor did most of them resist participation in a larger world dominated by Europeans or Euro-Americans. But they did insist on retaining control of their communities and their ways of life. As a group of Iroquois bluntly told an Anglo-American missionary in 1745, "We are Indians and do not wish to be transformed into white men. The English are our Brethren, but we never promised to become what they are." In the Revolution's aftermath, it remained unclear whether the new nation would accommodate Native Americans on such terms.

The Revolution and Social Change

The American Revolution left the overall distribution of wealth in the nation unchanged. Because the 3 percent of Americans who fled abroad as loyalists represented a cross section of society, their departure left the new nation's class structure unaltered. Loyalists' confiscated estates tended to be bought up by equally well-to-do Whig gentlemen. Overall, the American upper class seems to have owned about as much of the national wealth in 1783 as it did in 1776.

In short, the Revolution did not obliterate social distinctions nor even challenge most of them. Class distinctions, racial injustice, and the subordination of women persisted into the nineteenth century. In particular, the institution of slavery survived intact in the South, where the vast majority of slaves lived. Yet the Revolutionary era set in motion significant social changes. Increasingly, the members of the gentry had to earn respect by demonstrating their competence and by treating the common people with dignity. The Revolution dealt slavery a decisive blow in the North, greatly enlarged the free-black population, and awarded free people of color important political rights. Although the momentous era did not bring women political equality, it placed new issues pertaining to the relations between the genders on the agenda of national debate. And inevitably, the social changes wrought by the Revolution shaped the new nation's momentous political debates.

FORGING NEW GOVERNMENTS

Americans had drawn many political conclusions from the imperial crisis of the 1760s, including the conviction that without vigilance by the people, governments would become despotic. But before the Declaration of

Independence was written, few Americans had given much thought to forming governments of their own. Although guiding and inspiring the rebels, the Continental Congress lacked the sovereign powers usually associated with governments, including the authority to impose taxes.

During the war years, rebels quickly recognized the need to establish government institutions to sustain the war effort and to buttress the United States' claim to independent nationhood. But the task of forging a government would prove arduous, in part because of the inevitable upheavals of war. In addition, the state governments that Americans formed after the Declaration of Independence reflected two different and often conflicting impulses: on one hand, the traditional ideas and practices that had guided Anglo-Americans for much of the eighteenth century; on the other, the republican ideals that found a receptive audience in America in the 1760s and early 1770s.

"Can America be happy under a government of her own?" asked Thomas Paine in 1776. He answered his own question: "as happy as she pleases: she hath a blank sheet to write upon."

Tradition and Change

In establishing the Revolutionary state governments, patriots relied heavily on ideas about government inherited from the colonial experience. For example, most Whigs took for granted the value of bicameral legislatures. As we have seen, the colonial legislatures in the royal provinces had consisted of two houses: an elected lower chamber (or assembly) and an upper chamber (or council) appointed by the governor or chosen by the assembly. These two-part legislatures resembled Parliament's division into the House of Commons and House of Lords and symbolized the assumption that a government should give separate representation to aristocrats and common people.

Despite the Revolution's democratic tendencies, few questioned the long-standing practice of setting property requirements for voters and elected officials. In the prevailing view, only the ownership of property, especially land, made it possible for voters to think and act independently. Whereas tenant farmers and hired laborers might sell their votes or vote against their best judgment to avoid displeasing their landlords or employers, property holders could express their opinions freely. The association be-

tween property and citizenship was so deeply ingrained that even radicals such as Samuel Adams opposed allowing all males—much less women—to vote and hold office.

The notion that elected representatives should exercise independent judgment in leading the people rather than simply carry out the popular will also survived from the colonial period and restricted the democratization of politics. Although Americans today take political parties for granted, the idea of parties as necessary instruments for identifying and mobilizing public opinion was alien to the eighteenth-century political temper, which equated parties with "factions"—selfish groups that advanced their own interests at the expense of the public good. In general, candidates for office did not present voters with a clear choice between policies calculated to benefit rival interest groups; instead, they campaigned on the basis of their personal reputations and fitness for office. As a result, voters did not know where office seekers stood on specific issues and hence found it hard to influence government actions.

Another colonial practice that persisted into the 1770s and 1780s was the equal (or nearly equal) division of legislative seats among all counties or towns, regardless of differences in population. Inasmuch as representation had never before been apportioned according to population, a minority of voters normally elected a majority of assemblymen. Additionally, many offices that later would become elective—such as sheriffs and justices of county courts—were appointive in the eighteenth century.

In sum, the colonial experience provided no precedent for a democratization of the United States during the Revolutionary era. Yet without intending to extend political participation, political elites found themselves pulled in a democratic direction by the logic of the imperial crisis of the 1760s and 1770s. The colonial assemblies, the most democratic parts of colonial government, had led the fight against British policy during Americans' ideological clash with England, whereas the executive branch of colonial governments, filled by royal governors and their appointees, had repeatedly locked horns with the assemblies. Colonists entered the Revolution dreading executive officeholders and convinced that even elected governors could no more be trusted with power than could monarchs. Recent history seemed to confirm the message hammered home by British "country party" ideology (see Chapter 5) that those in

Jenuchshadago, Pennsylvania, in the 1780s

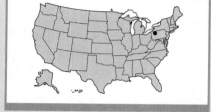

In the Revolution's aftermath, hundreds of new settlements sprang up west of the old colonial frontier. The best known of these settlements were inhabited by white pioneers who had streamed across the Appalachians in search of new lands and new opportunities. Many Native Americans in the West also took up new settlements—not to realize hopes and dreams but to regroup in the wake of a disastrous war in which they had lost family members and friends, homes, and land. Such was the case for the two hundred or three hundred Senecas who gathered during the early 1780s at the old town of Jenuchshadago, also known as Cornplanter's Town (after the name of their *sachem,* or chief), on the west bank of the Allegheny River just south of the New York–Pennsylvania boundary.

The Senecas and the other four original members of the Iroquois Confederacy had developed a rich culture and a sophisticated political and military organization that served them well as Dutch, French, and English moved in around them to trade, settle, and extend their empires. Seneca life had changed drastically after the mid-eighteenth century, when the movement of English colonists into the Ohio Valley upset the balance of power that had maintained peace between Indians and Europeans and between Britain and France. During the Revolution the Senecas, like most Iroquois, had sided with the British in hopes of restraining the settlers' westward push. In 1779 U.S. forces had raided Iroquois country and systematically burned every Seneca village, field, and fruit grove. After the war most Iroquois had moved to British Canada, prepared to continue the fight against the United States. But the Senecas, as the westernmost of the Iroquois, were less familiar than other Iroquois with the British, and most had declined to move.

The Senecas of Jenuchshadago were a demoralized people in the 1780s. During the recent war the symbol of Iroquois unity—the confederacy's central council fire at Onondaga—had been allowed to die out for the first time since the Confederacy's formation about four centuries earlier, owing to differences among the Iroquois people over which side to support. Thereafter Iroquois had fought one another. At the war's end the Senecas who remained in their homeland had been re-

Ki-In-Twog-Ky (Cornplanter), *1796*

Seneca reservations

LAKE ONTARIO

TUSCARORA RESERVATION

Black Rock
Buffalo

Genesee R.

Canandaigua L.

Cayuga L.

Seneca L.

LAKE ERIE

Salamanca
Cold Spring
Genesingunta
Warren
Jenuchshadago

Olean
Ceres

Genesee R.

Susquehanna R.

Meadville

Oil City
Ft.
Franklin

Allegheny R.

0   40 Miles
0   40 Kilometers

Seneca Reservations, 1790

Pressured after the American Revolution to give up most of their land, the Senecas now lived in a few widely separated villages.

SOURCE: *The Death and Rebirth of the Seneca* by Anthony F. C. Wallace. Copyright © 1969 by Anthony F. C. Wallace. Reprinted by permission of Alfred A. Knopf, Inc.

Seneca Cradleboard

viled for abandoning the Confederacy by fellow Iroquois who moved to Canada. These and other Indians had called for continuing the war against the United States. The authority and prestige of Cornplanter and other sachems had been undermined when they accepted bribes for agreeing to additional cessions of land. On several occasions white interlopers had killed innocent Indians, including two of Cornplanter's relatives.

Repudiated by all those around them, the Senecas also had been diminished as a people. Only eighteen hundred of a prewar population of four thousand survived, scattered in small villages on widely separated tracts of land. Beyond those who had died in combat, many had perished from starvation in the winter following the U.S. raids and from smallpox epidemics in the winters of 1776–1777 and 1781–1782. The effects of liquor aggravated their health problems. Indians who hunted, logged, or worked in other capacities for whites were paid in the unfamiliar medium of cash but found little to spend it on except liquor. Many Senecas drank to excess, and some died from alcohol-induced illness or violence linked to alcoholism.

Despite their sufferings and the tenuousness of their situation, the people of Jenuchshadago survived, and so did many of their cultural traditions. The isolation of the town, located as it was on a narrow strip of land between steep cliffs and the river, helped shield residents from many of the more destructive outside influences that undermined native cultures elsewhere after the Revolution. The fertile floodplain enabled the women to reap bountiful harvests of corn, beans, and squash, the Senecas' dietary mainstays for about a thousand years. The men and boys hunted bears, deer, elk, and turkeys. At sites downriver the people returned annually for maple sugaring and spearfishing. And along the riverbank and clifftops grew medicinal herbs whose efficacy brought fame to the healers of Jenuchshadago among the Senecas.

The community itself also nurtured aspects of traditional culture. Between the river and the village lay Jenuchshadago's burial ground, now used with greater frequency than ever. In the middle of town was the ceremonial center where the Indians each year burned a white dog as part of the traditional midwinter ceremony. Nearby stood Cornplanter's house and the two or three dozen other dwellings in the village. Although they no longer lived in multifamily longhouses as many had before the war, the people of Jenuchshadago had reconstituted some of the most important components of a traditional Iroquois community.

The continuity in their ways of life, institutions, and ceremonies was the basis for Seneca survival during the difficult period after the Revolution. Yet many remained uncertain at the end of the 1780s on the question of religion, for the cumulative destruction of the war and its aftermath implied that traditional religion had failed. In their spiritual torment some found the message of American missionaries attractive, but others sought to escape through alcohol. Among the residents of Jenuchshadago was Cornplanter's young half-brother, Handsome Lake. After a bout with alcoholism and severe illness, Handsome Lake would emerge in 1799 to lead a revival among the Senecas that would accommodate traditional religion to the Indians' new circumstances.

power tended to become either corrupt or dictatorial. Consequently, Revolutionary statesmen proclaimed the need to strengthen legislatures at the governors' expense.

Despite their preference for vesting power in popularly elected legislatures, Revolutionary leaders described themselves as republicans rather than democrats. Although used interchangeably today, these words had different connotations in the eighteenth century. At worst, democracy suggested mob rule; at best, it implied the concentration of power in the hands of an uneducated multitude. In contrast, republicanism presumed that government would be entrusted to capable leaders, elected for their superior talents and wisdom. For most republicans, the ideal government would delicately balance the interests of different classes to prevent any one group from gaining absolute power. Some, including John Adams, thought that a republic could include a hereditary aristocracy or even a monarchy as part of this balance, but most thought otherwise. Having blasted one king in the Declaration of Independence, most political leaders had no desire to enthrone another. Still, their rejection of hereditary aristocracy and monarchy posed a problem for republicans as they set about drafting state constitutions: how to maintain balance in government amid pervasive distrust of executive power.

Reconstituting the States

The state governments that Americans constructed during the Revolution reflected a struggle between more radical, democratic elements and elites who would minimize popular participation. In keeping with colonial practice, eleven of the thirteen states maintained bicameral legislatures. In all but a few states, the great majority of officeholders, at both the state and the county level, were still appointed rather than elected. The most radical constitution, Pennsylvania's, attempted to ensure that election districts would be roughly equal in population, so that a minority of voters could not elect a majority of legislators. Nine of the thirteen states reduced property requirements for voting, but none abolished such qualifications entirely, and most of the reductions were modest.

Yet the persistence of these conservative features should not obscure the pathbreaking components of the state constitutions. Above all, they were *written* documents whose adoption usually required popular

ratification and which could be changed only if the people voted to amend them. In short, Americans jettisoned the British conception of a constitution as a body of customary arrangements and practices, insisting instead that constitutions were written compacts that defined and limited the powers of rulers. Moreover, as a final check on government power, the revolutionary constitutions spelled out citizens' fundamental rights. By 1784 all state constitutions included explicit bills of rights that outlined certain freedoms beyond government control. In sum, governments were no longer to serve as the final judge of the constitutionality of their activities.

The earliest of those new state constitutions severely limited executive power in particular. In most states the governor became an elected official, and elections themselves occurred far more frequently. Prior to 1776 colonial elections, typically called at the governor's pleasure, most often took place every three or four years. In contrast, after 1776 each state scheduled annual elections except South Carolina, which held them every two years. In most states the power of appointments was transferred from the governor to the legislature. Legislatures usually appointed judges and could reduce their salaries or impeach them (try them for wrongdoing). By relieving governors of most appointive powers, denying them the right to veto laws, and making them subject to impeachment, the constitutions turned governors into figureheads who simply chaired an executive council that made militia appointments and supervised financial business. (Pennsylvania actually eliminated the office of governor altogether.)

As the new state constitutions weakened the executive branch and vested more power in the legislatures, they also made the legislatures, especially the upper chambers, more responsive to the will of the people. Nowhere could the governor appoint the upper chamber. Eight constitutions written before 1780 allowed voters to select both houses of the legislature, one (Maryland) used a popularly chosen "electoral college" for its upper house, and the remaining "senates" were filled by vote of their assemblies. Pennsylvania and Georgia abolished the upper house and substituted a single-chamber (unicameral) legislature. Americans' assault on the executive branch and their enhancement of legislative authority reflected their bitter memories of royal governors who had acted arbitrarily to prorogue (dismiss) assemblies and control government through their power of appointment, and it underscored the influence of "country-party" ideologues, who had warned that republics' undoing began with executive usurpation of authority.

In the first flush of revolutionary enthusiasm, elites had to content themselves with state governments dominated by popularly elected legislatures. Gradually, however, wealthier landowners, bankers, merchants, and lawyers reasserted their desires for centralized authority and the political prerogatives of wealth. In Massachusetts an elite-dominated convention in 1780 pushed through a constitution stipulating stiff property qualifications for voting and holding office, state senate districts that were apportioned according to property values, and a governor with considerable powers in making appointments and vetoing legislative measures. The Massachusetts constitution signaled a general trend. Georgia and Pennsylvania substituted bicameral for unicameral legislatures by 1790. Other states raised property qualifications for members of the upper chamber in a bid to encourage the "senatorial element" and to make room for men of "Wisdom, remarkable integrity, or that Weight which arises from property."

The elites' deference to the principle of balanced government revealed a central feature of their thought. Gradations among social classes and restrictions on the expression of popular will troubled them far less than the prospect of tyranny by those in power. But elites also believed that social divisions, if deep-seated and permanent, could jeopardize republican liberty. Although more committed to liberty than to equality, some republican leaders attempted to implement major social changes through legislation by the new state governments. In Virginia, for example, between 1776 and 1780, Thomas Jefferson drafted a series of bills to promote greater equality. In October 1776 he persuaded the Virginia legislature to abolish entails, legal requirements that prevented an heir and all his descendants from selling or dividing an estate. Although entails were easy to break through special laws—Jefferson himself had escaped from the restrictions of one—he hoped that their elimination would strip wealthy families of the opportunity to amass land continuously and become an overbearing aristocracy. Through Jefferson's efforts, Virginia also ended primogeniture, the legal requirement that the eldest son inherit all a family's property in the absence of a will. Thereby, Jefferson hoped to ensure a continuous division of wealth. By 1791 no state provided for primogeniture, and just two allowed entails.

These years also witnessed the end of state-established churches in most of the country. New England, whose religious climate was the nation's most conservative, resisted this reform, and the Congregational church continued to collect tithes (church taxes) until 1817 in New Hampshire, 1818 in Connecticut, and 1833 in Massachusetts. But in every state where colonial taxpayers had supported the Anglican church, such support was abolished by 1786. Thomas Jefferson best expressed the ideal behind disestablishment in his Statute for Religious Freedom (1786), whose preamble resounded with a defense of religious freedom at all times and places. "Truth is great," proclaimed Jefferson, "and will prevail if left to itself."

The American Revolution, wrote Thomas Paine in 1782, was intended to ring in "a new era and give a new turn to human affairs." This was an ambitious declaration and seemed to conflict with elites' tendency to borrow from the past institutions such as state senates and property requirements for voting. Paine's point was not that the unique features of some constitutions, such as the termination of primogeniture and the disestablishment of the Anglican church, outweighed the traditional elements of the constitutions. Instead, he was expressing the republican ideal that *all* political institutions now were being judged by the standard of whether they served the public good rather than the interests of the powerful few. More than any single innovation of the era, it was this new way of thinking that made American politics revolutionary.

The Articles of Confederation

As with their revolt against Britain and their early state constitutions, Americans' first national government reflected widespread fears of centralized authority and its potential for corruption. In 1776 John Dickinson, who had stayed in Congress despite having refused to sign the Declaration of Independence, drafted a proposal for a national government, which he called the Articles of Confederation. Congress adopted a weakened version of the Articles and sent it to the states for ratification in 1777.

The Articles explicitly reserved to each state "its sovereignty, freedom and independence" and established a form of government in which Americans were citizens of their own states first and of the United States second. As John Adams later explained, the Whigs of 1776 never thought of "consolidating this vast Continent under one national Government" but instead

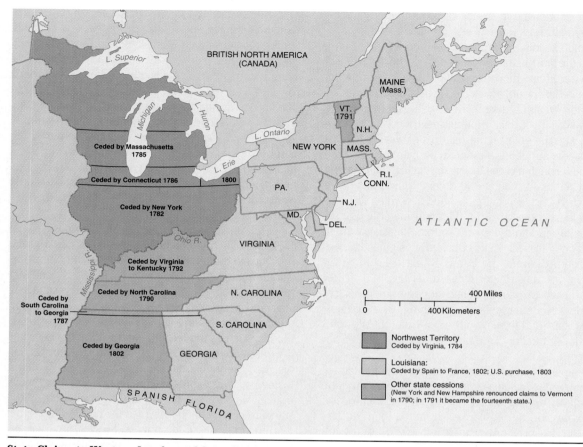

State Claims to Western Lands, and State Cessions to the Federal Government, 1782–1802

Eastern states' surrender of land claims paved the way for new state governments in the West. Georgia was the last state to cede its western lands, in 1802.

erected "a Confederacy of States, each of which must have a separate government."

Under the Articles, the national government consisted of a single-chamber national Congress, elected by the state legislatures, in which each state had only one vote. Congress could request funds from the states but could enact no tax of its own without every state's approval, nor could it regulate interstate or overseas commerce. The Articles did not provide for an executive branch. Rather, congressional committees oversaw financial, diplomatic, and military affairs. Nor was there a judicial system by which the national government could compel allegiance to its laws.

The Articles would not become operational until approved by all thirteen state legislatures. Twelve states

agreed to the new government by 1779, but Maryland delayed, refusing to sign until all states claiming lands north of the Ohio River turned these territories over to the United States. Maryland lawmakers wanted to keep Virginia and New York from expanding to such a degree that they would dominate the new nation. Beginning in 1781, northwestern claims by individual states were abandoned, and the Articles finally became law in March 1781.

With the Confederation in place, the United States had taken a critical step in defining the role of national sovereignty in relation to the sovereignty of the individual states. Whereas the Continental Congress had directed most of the war effort without defined powers, the nation now had a formal government. Nevertheless, the Whigs' misgivings left the Confederation government severely limited in important respects.

Finance and Trade Under the Confederation

Perhaps the greatest challenge facing the Confederation was putting the nation on a sound financial footing. Winning the war cost the nation's six hundred thousand taxpayers a staggering $160 million, a sum that exceeded by 2,400 percent the taxes raised to pay for the Seven Years' War. To finance the War for Independence, which cost far more than could be immediately collected through taxation, the government borrowed funds from abroad and printed its own paper money, called Continentals. Lack of public faith in the government destroyed 98 percent of the value of the Continentals from 1776 to 1781, an inflationary disaster that gave rise to the expression "not worth a Continental."

Faced with a desperate financial situation, Congress turned to a wealthy, self-made Philadelphia merchant, Robert Morris, who in 1781 became the nation's superintendent of finance. Morris proposed that the states authorize the collection of a national import duty of 5 percent to finance the congressional budget and to guarantee interest payments on the war debt. Because the Articles stipulated that every state had to approve the levying of national taxes, the import duty failed to pass in 1782 when Rhode Island alone rejected it.

Hoping to panic the country into creating a regular source of national revenue, Morris and New York congressman Alexander Hamilton then engineered a dangerous gamble known later as the Newburgh Conspiracy. In 1783 the two men secretly persuaded some army officers, then encamped at Newburgh, New York, to threaten a coup d'etat unless the treasury obtained the taxation authority needed to raise their pay, which was months in arrears. But George Washington, learning of the conspiracy before it was carried out, ended the plot by delivering a speech that appealed to his officers' honor and left them unwilling to proceed. Although Morris may never have intended that a coup actually occur, his willingness to take such a risk demonstrated the new nation's perilous financial straits and the vulnerability of its political institutions.

When peace came in 1783, Morris found it impossible to secure adequate funding for the United States. That year, Congress sent another tax measure to the states, but once again a single legislature, this time New York's, blocked it. From then on, the states steadily decreased their contributions to Congress. By the late 1780s, the states had fallen behind nearly 80 percent in providing the funds that Congress requested to operate the government and honor the national debt.

Nor did the Confederation succeed in prying trade concessions from Britain. Before Independence, almost 60 percent of northern exports had gone to the West Indies, and New England's maritime community had employed approximately 15 percent of all adult males. After Independence, however, Britain quickly slapped strict limitations on U.S. commerce. The new republic's ships lost all rights to carry cargoes to the West Indies and faced high customs fees for landing products in Great Britain. For the most part, American foodstuffs, lumber, and tobacco were welcome in Britain only if they arrived in British ships. Because half of all U.S. exports went to Great Britain or its West Indian colonies, these restrictions allowed British shippers to increase their share of the Atlantic trade at American expense. The loss of this trade contributed mightily to an economic depression that gripped the nation beginning in 1784.

The Confederation and the West

Another formidable challenge confronting the Confederation was the postwar settlement and administration of western lands. Settlers and speculators were determined to possess these lands, and Native Americans were just as determined to keep them out. At the same time, Britain and Spain sought to contain the new nation's territorial expansion.

After the states surrendered claims to more than 160 million acres north of the Ohio River, Congress established uniform procedures for surveying this land in the Ordinance of 1785. The law established as the basic unit of settlement a township six miles square. Every township would be subdivided into thirty-six sections of 640 acres each, one of which would be reserved as a source of income for schools. Subsequently, in the Northwest Ordinance of 1787, Congress defined the steps for the creation and admission of new states. This law designated the area north of the Ohio River as the Northwest Territory and provided for its later division into states. It forbade slavery while the region remained a territory, although the citizens could legalize the institution after statehood (as Illinois almost did in 1824).

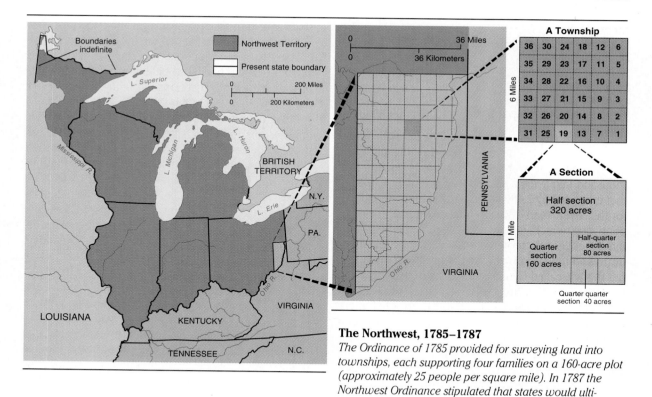

The Northwest, 1785–1787
The Ordinance of 1785 provided for surveying land into townships, each supporting four families on a 160-acre plot (approximately 25 people per square mile). In 1787 the Northwest Ordinance stipulated that states would ultimately be created in the region

The Northwest Ordinance outlined three stages for admitting states into the Union. First, during the initial years of settlement, Congress would appoint a territorial governor and judges. Second, as soon as five thousand adult males lived in a territory, the people would write a temporary constitution and elect a legislature that would pass the territory's laws. Third, when the total population reached sixty thousand, the settlers would write a state constitution, which Congress would have to approve before granting statehood.

The Ordinance of 1785 and the Northwest Ordinance became the Confederation's major contributions to American life. These laws set the basic principles for surveying the frontier, allowed territorial government at an early stage of settlement, and provided reasonable standards for obtaining statehood. Both measures served as models for organizing territories later acquired west of the Mississippi River. The Northwest Ordinance also established a significant precedent for banning slavery from certain territories. But because Indians, determined to keep out white

settlers, controlled virtually the entire region north of the Ohio River, the Confederation's ordinances respecting the Northwest had no immediate effect.

The Northwest Territory seemed to offer enough rich land to guarantee future citizens landownership for centuries. This fact satisfied American republican sentiment, which placed great importance upon opening the West for settlement out of fears that the rapidly growing U.S. population would quickly exhaust the land east of the Appalachians and so create a large class of tenants and poor laborers who would lack the property needed to vote. By poisoning politics through class conflict, such a development would undermine the equality that republicans thought essential for a healthy nation. In the anticipated westward push by whites, Thomas Jefferson and other republican thinkers hoped to avoid conflict with the northwestern Indians by assimilating them into white society. However, since Native Americans had no desire to abandon their own cultures, republican anxieties over preserving economic opportunity by giving white settlers access to western lands made war inevitable.

Joseph Brant, *by Wilhelm von Moll Berczy, c. 1800*
In the 1780s several Indian leaders—among them Brant (a Mohawk), Blue Jacket (a Shawnee), and Little Turtle (a Miami)—worked to create a northwestern Indian confederation that would strengthen Native American resolve not to bargain with land-hungry whites.

At postwar treaty negotiations, Native Americans repeatedly heard U.S. commissioners scornfully declare, "You are a subdued people . . . we claim the country by conquest." Under threats of continued warfare, some Indian leaders initially gave in. The Iroquois, who had suffered heavily during the war, lost about half their land in New York and Pennsylvania in the second Treaty of Fort Stanwix (1784). In the treaties of Fort McIntosh (1785) and Fort Finney (1786), the Delawares and Shawnees, respectively, were obliged to recognize American sovereignty over their lands. But most Indians reacted with outrage and repudiated these treaties on the grounds that their negotiators lacked the authority to give up their nations' lands.

The Indians' resistance also stemmed from their confidence that the British—still a presence in the West—would provide the arms and ammunition they needed to defy the United States. Britain had refused to abandon seven forts on the nation's northwestern frontier, officially because several state legislatures had blocked the collection of prewar debts owed British merchants and had also refused to compensate loyalists for wartime property losses. In April 1784, however, well before Britain knew about the violation of these provisions of the peace treaty, its colonial office had secretly ordered the governor of Canada to hold those forts. With Indian support, Britain hoped eventually to reestablish its claim to the Northwest Territory.

The Mohawk Joseph Brant emerged as the initial inspiration behind Indian resistance to white encroachments. Courageous in battle, skillful in diplomacy, and highly educated (he had translated the Bible into Iroquois), Brant became a minor celebrity when he visited King George at London in 1785. At British-held Fort Detroit in 1786, he helped organize the northwestern Indians into a military alliance to exclude white settlers north of the Ohio River. But Brant and his Mohawks, who had relocated beyond American reach in Canada, could not win support from Iroquois such as the Senecas of Jenuchshadago, who had chosen to remain in New York. John Sullivan's campaign of 1779 had left the Six Nations unwilling to risk another such invasion.

The Confederation confronted similar problems in the Southeast, where Spain and its Indian allies took steps to prevent American settlers from encroaching on their lands. The Spanish found a brilliant ally in the Creek leader Alexander McGillivray. In a series of fraudulent treaties, two Creeks had surrendered extensive territory to Georgia that McGillivray intended to regain. Patiently holding back his followers for three years, McGillivray negotiated a secret treaty with Spain that promised the Creeks weapons so that they could protect themselves "from the Bears and other fierce Animals." When McGillivray finally unleashed his forces in 1786, he assaulted only occupants on the disputed lands and wisely offered a cease-fire after winning his objective. Eager to avoid voting taxes for a costly war, Georgia politicians let him keep the land.

Spain also sought to prevent American infiltration by denying western settlers permission to ship their crops down the Mississippi River to New Orleans. Having negotiated a separate treaty with Britain (see above), Spain had not signed the Peace of Paris, by which Britain promised the United States export rights down the Mississippi, and in 1784 the Spanish closed New Orleans to Anglo-American commerce.

To negotiate trading privileges at New Orleans, the United States sent John Jay to Spain. Jay failed to win concessions, but he returned with a treaty that opened up valuable Spanish markets to eastern merchants and renounced Spanish claims to disputed southwestern lands—at the cost, however, of relinquishing American export rights through New Orleans for twenty years. Although Congress rejected this Jay-Gardoqui Treaty in 1786, the treaty infuriated westerners and southerners, whose interests seemed to have been sacrificed to benefit northern commerce.

Shays's Rebellion

Without an outbreak of violence in Massachusetts late in 1786, the Confederation might have tottered on indefinitely. The depression that had begun in 1784 struck especially hard in Massachusetts after the state lost its best market, the British West Indies. To worsen matters, the state legislature voted early in 1786 to pay off its Revolutionary debt in three years. This ill-considered policy necessitated a huge tax hike. Meanwhile, the state's unfavorable balance of payments with Britain had produced a shortage of specie (gold and silver coin) because British creditors refused any other currency. Fearing a flood of worthless paper notes, Massachusetts bankers and merchants insisted that they, too, be paid in specie, while the state mandated the same for payment of taxes. At the bottom of this cycle of debt were thousands of small family farmers who rarely handled hard currency. As with small farmers throughout America, those in Massachusetts were accustomed to paying each other and local creditors in goods such as grain and wool and sometimes with a service such as shoeing a horse or helping to build a barn. Creditors allowed debts from local customers to run for months and years at a time. The notion of immediately paying all debts and taxes owed in hard currency was not only alien to but impossible for many.

The plight of Massachusetts farmers was especially severe in the western counties, where agriculture was least profitable. Farmers held public meetings, as they had more than a decade earlier, to discuss "the Suppressing of tyrannical government." This time, however, they meant the Massachusetts government rather than the British. Late in 1786 farmer and former Revolutionary War officer Daniel Shays led some two thousand angry men in an attempt to shut down the courts in three of these western counties, and thereby stop sheriffs' auctions for unpaid taxes and prevent foreclosures on farm mortgages. Although routed by state troops after several skirmishes, sympathizers of Shays won control of the Massachusetts legislature in 1787, cut taxes, and secured a pardon for their leader.

Shays's supporters had limited objectives, were dispersed with relatively little bloodshed, and never seriously posed the danger of anarchy. But his uprising, and similar but less militant movements in other states, symbolized for critics of the weak national government the Republic's fragility under the Confederation. By threatening to seize weapons from a federal arsenal at Springfield, Massachusetts, the Shaysites unintentionally enabled nationalists to argue that the United States had become vulnerable to "mobocracy." At the same time, rumors were flying that the Spanish had offered export rights at New Orleans to westerners if they would secede from the Union. Nationalists sowed fears that the United States was on the verge of coming apart.

Not everyone shared these apprehensions. In contrast to New England, the mid-Atlantic and southern states were emerging from the depression, thanks to rising tobacco and food exports to Europe. Taxpayers in these sections, moreover, were paying off war debts easily. Furthermore, the regions' numerous small farming families, living in relatively isolated communities and trading largely with neighbors, were in quiet times widely indifferent to national politics. But the minority of people intensely dissatisfied with the Confederation was growing. Urban artisans, for example, hoped for a stronger national government that would impose a uniformly high tariff and thereby protect them from foreign competition. Merchants and shippers wanted a government powerful enough to secure trading privileges for them, and land speculators and western settlers preferred a government capable of pursuing a more activist policy against the Indians. To these groups were now added economic and political elites who saw in Shays's Rebellion a sign of worse things to come.

Shortly before the outbreak of the rebellion, delegates from five states had assembled at Annapolis, Maryland. They had intended to discuss means of promoting interstate commerce but instead called for a general convention to propose amendments to the Articles of Confederation. Accepting their suggestion, Congress asked the states to appoint delegations to meet in Philadelphia.

The Philadelphia Convention

In May 1787 fifty-five delegates from every state but Rhode Island began gathering at the Pennsylvania State House in Philadelphia, later known as Independence Hall. Among them were figures with an established reputation like George Washington, Benjamin Franklin, John Dickinson, and Robert Morris, as well as talented newcomers such as Alexander Hamilton and James Madison. Most were wealthy and in their thirties or forties, and nineteen owned slaves. More than half had legal training.

The convention immediately closed its sessions to the press and the public, kept no *official* journal, and even appointed chaperones to accompany the aged and talkative Franklin to dinner parties lest he disclose details of what was happening. Although these measures opened the members of the convention to the charge of acting undemocratically and conspiratorially, the delegates thought secrecy essential to ensure themselves freedom of debate without fear of criticism from home.

The delegates shared a "continental" or "nationalist" perspective, instilled through their extended involvement with the national government. Thirty-nine had sat in Congress, where they had seen the Articles' defects firsthand. In the postwar years, they had become convinced that unless the national government were freed from the state legislatures' control, the country would fall victim to foreign aggression or simply disintegrate.

The convention faced two basic issues. The first was whether to tinker with the Articles, as the state legislatures had formally instructed the delegates to do, or to scrap the Articles and draw up an entirely new frame of government. The second fundamental question was how to balance the conflicting interests of large and small states. James Madison of Virginia, who had entered Congress in 1780 at twenty-nine, proposed an answer to each issue. Despite his youth and almost frail build, Madison commanded enormous respect for his profound knowledge of history and the passionate intensity that he brought to debates.

Madison's Virginia Plan, introduced by his fellow Virginian Edmund Randolph in late May, boldly called for the establishment of a national government rather than a federation of states. Madison's blueprint gave Congress virtually unrestricted rights of legislation and taxation, the power to veto any state law, and authority to use military force against the states. As delegate Charles Pinckney of South Carolina immediately saw, the Virginia Plan was designed "to abolish the State Govern[men]ts altogether." The Virginia Plan specified a bicameral legislature and fixed representation in both houses of Congress proportionally to each state's population. The voters would elect the lower house, which would then choose delegates to the upper chamber from nominations submitted by the legislatures. Both houses would jointly name the country's president and judges.

Madison's scheme aroused immediate opposition, however, especially his call for state representation

The Assembly Room in Independence Hall
Much history was made in this room. The Declaration of Independence was signed here in 1776, and the constitutional-convention delegates met in this chamber in 1787.

James Madison

Although one of the Philadelphia Convention's youngest delegates, Madison of Virginia was among its most politically astute. He played a central role in the Constitution's adoption.

according to population—a provision highly favorable to his own Virginia. On June 15 William Paterson of New Jersey offered a counterproposal, the so-called New Jersey Plan, which recommended a single-chamber congress in which each state had an equal vote, just as under the Articles.

Despite their differences over representation, Paterson's and Madison's proposals alike would have strengthened the national government at the states' expense. No less than Madison, Paterson wished to empower Congress to raise taxes, regulate interstate commerce, and use military force against the states. The New Jersey Plan, in fact, was the first to define congressional laws and treaties as the "supreme law of the land"; it would also have established courts to force reluctant states to accept these measures.

The New Jersey Plan was highly significant because it exposed the convention's great stumbling block: the question of representation. The Virginia Plan would have given the four largest states a majority in both houses. The New Jersey Plan would have al-

lowed the seven smallest states, which included just 25 percent of all Americans, to control Congress. By July 2 the convention had arrived "at a full stop," as Roger Sherman of Connecticut noted. To end the impasse, the delegates assigned a member from each state to a "grand committee" dedicated to compromise. The panel adopted a proposal offered earlier by the Connecticut delegation: an equal vote for each state in the upper house and proportional voting in the lower house. Madison and the Virginians doggedly fought this so-called Connecticut Compromise, but they were voted down on July 17. The convention overcame the remaining hurdles rather easily in the next two months.

As finally approved on September 17, 1787, the Constitution of the United States was an extraordinary document, and not merely because it successfully reconciled the conflicting interests of the large and small states. Out of hard bargaining among different states' representatives emerged the Constitution's delicate balance between the desire of nearly all delegates for a stronger national government and their fear that governments tended to grow despotic. The Constitution augmented national authority in several ways. Although it did not incorporate Madison's proposal to give Congress a veto over state laws, it vested in Congress the authority to lay and collect taxes, to regulate interstate commerce, and to conduct diplomacy. States could no longer coin money, interfere with contracts and debts, or tax interstate commerce. All acts and treaties of the United States became "the supreme law of the land." All state officials had to swear to uphold the Constitution, even against acts of their own states. The national government could use military force against any state.

These provisions added up to a complete abandonment of the principle on which the Articles of Confederation had rested: that the United States was a federation of independent republics known as states, with all authority concentrated in their legislatures. Yet still concerned about too centralized a federal system, the Constitution's framers devised two ways to restrain the power of the new national government. First, they established three distinct branches—executive, legislative, and judicial—within the national government; and second, they designed a system of checks and balances to prevent any one branch from dominating the other two. The framers systematically applied to the national government the principle of a *functional* separation of powers, an idea that had been evolving in the states since about 1780. In the bicameral Congress, states' equal representation in the Senate was offset by the proportional representation, by population, in the House; and each chamber could block hasty measures demanded by the other. Furthermore, where the state constitutions had deliberately weakened the executive, the Constitution gave the president the power to veto acts of Congress; but to prevent capricious use of the veto, Congress could override the president by a two-thirds majority in each house. The president could conduct diplomacy, but only the Senate could ratify treaties. The president named his cabinet, but only with Senate approval. The president and all his appointees could be removed from office by a joint vote of Congress, but only for "high crimes," not for political disagreements.

To further ensure the independence of each branch, the Constitution provided that the members of one branch would not choose those of another, except for judges, whose independence was protected by lifetime appointment. For example, the president was to be selected by an electoral college, whose members the states would select as their legislatures saw fit. The state legislatures also elected the members of the Senate, whereas the election of delegates to the House of Representatives was achieved by popular vote.

In addition to checks and balances, the founders improvised a novel form of federalism—that being a system of shared power and dual lawmaking by the national and state governments—in order to place limits on central authority. Not only did the state legislatures have a key role in electing the president and senators, but the Constitution could be amended by the votes of three-fourths of the state legislatures. Thus, the convention devised a form of government that differed significantly from Madison's plan to establish a "consolidated" national government entirely independent of, and superior to, the states.

A key assumption behind federalism was that the national government would limit its activities to foreign affairs, national defense, regulating interstate commerce, and coining money. Most other political matters were left to the states. Regarding slavery in particular, each state retained full authority.

The dilemma confronting the Philadelphia convention revolved around whether slaves should be considered persons or property. For most purposes, the southern states regarded slaves as the property of their owners. But given that slaves constituted substantial proportions of southern populations, these states' delegates wished to count them as persons when it came to determining representation in the House of Representatives. Northern delegates hailed from states that were abolishing slavery, and hesitated to give southern states a political advantage by allowing them to count people who had no civil or political rights. But as property owners themselves, northern delegates were even more hesitant to question southern planters' notions of property rights, no matter what form the property took. Accordingly, they agreed to allow three-fifths of all slaves to be counted for congressional representation. The Constitution also forbade any state's people to prevent the return of runaway slaves to another state. The Constitution did limit slavery to the extent of permitting Congress to ban the importation of slaves after 1808, and by not repudiating Congress's earlier ban on slavery in the Northwest Territory.

Although leaving much authority to the states, the Constitution established a national government clearly superior to the states in several spheres, and it utterly abandoned the notion of a federation of virtually independent states. Having thus strengthened national authority, the convention had to face the issue of ratification. For two reasons, it seemed unwise to submit the Constitution to state legislatures for ratification. First, the framers realized that the state legislatures would reject the Constitution, which shrank their power relative to the national government. Second, most of the framers repudiated the idea—implicit in ratification by existing state legislatures—that the states composed the foundation of the new government. The opening words of the Constitution—"We the People of the United States"—underlined the delegates' growing conviction that the government had to be based on the consent of the American people themselves, "the fountain of all power" in Madison's words.

In the end, the Philadelphia Convention provided for the Constitution's ratification by special state conventions composed of delegates elected by the people. Approval by only nine such conventions would put the new government in operation. Because any state refusing to ratify the Constitution would remain under the Articles, the possibility existed that the country might divide into two nations.

Under the Constitution the framers expected the nation's "natural aristocracy" to continue exercising political leadership; but did they also intend to rein in the democratic currents set in motion by the Revolution? In one respect they did, by curtailing what most nationalists considered the excessive power of popularly elected legislatures. But the Constitution made no attempt to control faction and disorder by suppressing liberty—a "remedy," wrote Madison, that would be "worse than the disease." The framers did provide for one crucial democratic element in the new government, the House of Representatives. Equally important, the Constitution recognized the American people as the ultimate source of political legitimacy. Moreover, by making the Constitution flexible and amendable (though not easily amendable) and by dividing political power among competing branches of government, the framers made it possible for the national government to be slowly democratized in ways unforeseen in 1787, without turning into a tyranny of ideologues or temporary majorities. Madison eloquently expressed the founders' intention of controlling the dangers inherent in any society:

If men were angels, no government would be necessary. If angels were to govern men, neither external nor internal controls on government would be necessary. In framing a government which is to be administered by men over men, the great difficulty lies in this: You must first enable the government to control the governed; and in the next place, oblige it to control itself. A dependence on the people is no doubt the primary control on the government; but experience has taught mankind the necessity of external precautions.

Ratification

The Constitution's supporters began the campaign for ratification without significant national support. Most Americans had expected that the Philadelphia Convention would offer only limited amendments to the Articles. A majority therefore hesitated to adopt the radical restructuring of government that had been proposed. Undaunted, the Constitution's friends moved decisively to marshal political support. In a clever stroke, they called themselves Federalists, a term that implied that the Constitution balanced the relationship between the national and state governments and thereby

lessened the opposition of those hostile to a centralization of national authority.

The Constitution's opponents commonly became known as Antifederalists. This negative-sounding title probably hurt them, for it did not convey the crux of their argument against the Constitution—that it was not "federalist" at all since it failed to balance the power of the national and state governments. Indeed, many Antifederalists doubted whether any such balance was possible. In their view, either the national or the state governments would dominate the Republic; no even division of power could be achieved. By augmenting national authority, Antifederalists maintained, the Constitution would ultimately doom the states.

The Antifederalist arguments reflected a deep-seated Anglo-American suspicion of concentrated power, expressed from the time of the Stamp Act crisis (see Chapter 5) through the War of Independence and during the framing of the first state constitutions and the Articles of Confederation. Unquestionably, the Constitution gave the national government unprecedented authority in an age when almost all writers on politics taught that the sole means of preventing despotism was to restrain the power of government officials. Compared to a national government, which inevitably would be distant from the people in an era when news traveled slowly, the state governments struck Antifederalists as far more responsive to the popular will. "The vast Continent of America cannot be long subjected to a Democracy if consolidated into one Government. You might as well attempt to rule Hell by Prayer," wrote a New England Antifederalist. True, the framers had devised a system of checks and balances to guard against tyranny, but no one could be certain that the untried scheme would work. For all its checks and balances, in addition, the Constitution nowhere contained ironclad guarantees that the new government would protect the liberties of individuals or the states. The absence of a bill of rights made an Antifederalist of Madison's nationalist ally and fellow Virginian, George Mason, the author of the first such state bill in 1776.

Although the Antifederalists advanced some formidable arguments, they confronted a number of disadvantages in publicizing their cause. While Antifederalist ranks included prominent political figures, among them Patrick Henry and Richard Henry Lee, the Federalists claimed most of the country's

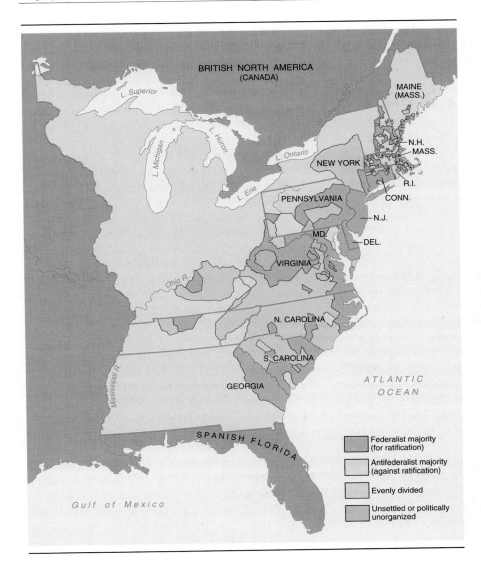

Federalist and Antifederalist Strongholds, 1787–1790
Federalists drew their primary backing from densely populated areas along major transportation routes, where trade, mobility, and frequent contact with people in other states encouraged a nationalistic identity. Antifederalist support came from interior regions where geographic isolation bred a localistic perspective. However, some frontier regions, among them Georgia and western Virginia, voted for a strong central government that would push back the Indians or the Spanish.

Map labels: BRITISH NORTH AMERICA (CANADA), L. Superior, L. Michigan, L. Huron, L. Ontario, L. Erie, St. Lawrence R., MAINE (MASS.), N.H., MASS., R.I., CONN., NEW YORK, PENNSYLVANIA, N.J., DEL., MD., VIRGINIA, Ohio R., N. CAROLINA, S. CAROLINA, GEORGIA, ATLANTIC OCEAN, SPANISH FLORIDA, Gulf of Mexico, Mississippi R., Missouri R.

Legend:
- Federalist majority (for ratification)
- Antifederalist majority (against ratification)
- Evenly divided
- Unsettled or politically unorganized

wealthiest and most honored men. And no Antifederalist had the stature of George Washington or Benjamin Franklin. Moreover, most American newspapers were pro-Constitution and did not hesitate to bias their reporting in favor of the Federalist cause. Finally, as state and local leaders, the Antifederalists lacked their opponents' contacts and experience at the national level, acquired through service in the officer corps of the Continental Army or in Congress.

The Federalists' advantages in funds and political organizing proved decisive. The Antifederalists failed to create a sense of urgency among their supporters, as-

suming incorrectly that a large majority would rally to them. Only one-quarter of the voters turned out to elect delegates to the state ratifying conventions, however, and most had been mobilized by Federalists.

Federalist delegates prevailed in eight conventions between December 1787 and May 1788, in all cases except one by margins of at least two-thirds. Such lopsided votes reflected the Federalists' organizational skills and aggressiveness rather than the degree of popular support for the Constitution. Advocates of the new plan of government did indeed ram through approval in some states "before it can be digested or deliberately considered," in the words of a Pennsylvania Antifederalist. Only Rhode Island and North Carolina rejected the Constitution and thus refused to join the new United States.

But unless Virginia and New York ratified, the new government would not be workable. In both states (and elsewhere) antifederalist sentiment ran high among small farmers, who saw the Constitution as a scheme favoring city dwellers and monied interests. Prominent political leaders in these two states called for refusing ratification, including New York governor George Clinton and Virginia's Richard Henry Lee, George Mason, Patrick Henry, and future president James Monroe.

The Constitution became the law of the land on June 21, 1788, when the ninth state, New Hampshire, ratified by the close vote of 57–47. At that moment debate was still under way in the Virginia convention. The Federalists won crucial support from the representatives of the Alleghany counties—modern West Virginia—who wanted a strong national government capable of ending Indian raids across the Ohio River. Western Virginians' votes, combined with James Madison's logic and the growing support for the Constitution among tidewater planters, proved too much for Henry's spellbinding oratory. On June 25 the Virginia delegates ratified by a narrow 53 percent majority.

The struggle was even closer and more hotly contested in New York. Antifederalists had solid control of the state convention and would probably have voted down the Constitution, but then news arrived of New Hampshire's and Virginia's ratification. The Federalist forces, led by Alexander Hamilton and John Jay, began hinting strongly that if the convention voted to reject, pro-Federalist New York City would secede from the state and join the Union alone, leaving upstate New York a landlocked enclave. When a number of Antifederalist delegates took alarm at this threat and switched sides, New York ratified on July 26, by a 30–27 vote.

So the Antifederalists went down in defeat, and they did not survive as a political movement. Yet they left an important legacy. At their insistence, the Virginia, New York, and Massachusetts conventions ratified the Constitution with the accompanying request that the new charter be amended to include a bill of rights protecting Americans' basic freedoms. So widespread was the public demand for a bill of rights that it became an inevitable item on the new government's agenda, even as the states were choosing members of Congress and as presidential electors were unanimously designating George Washington president of the United States.

Antifederalists' objections in New York also stimulated a response in the form of one of the greatest works of political analysis ever written: *The Federalist,* a series of eighty-five newspaper essays penned by Alexander Hamilton, James Madison, and John Jay. *The Federalist* papers probably had little or no influence on the voting in the New York State convention. Rather, their importance lay in providing a glimpse of the framers' intentions in designing the Constitution, and thus powerfully shaping the American philosophy of government. The Constitution, insisted *The Federalist*'s authors, had a twofold purpose: first, to defend the minority's rights against majority tyranny; and second, to prevent a stubborn minority from blocking well-considered measures that the majority believed necessary for the national interest. Critics, argued *The Federalist,* had no reason to fear that the Constitution would allow a single economic or regional interest to dominate. In the most profound essay in the series, *Federalist* No. 10, Madison rejected the Antifederalist argument that establishing a republic for a nation as large as the United States would unleash a chaotic contest for power and ultimately leave the majority exploited by a minority. "Extend the sphere," Madison insisted, "and . . . you make it less probable that a majority of the whole will have a common motive to invade the rights of other citizens, . . . [or will be able to] act in unison with each other." The country's very size and diversity would theoretically neutralize the attempts of factions to manipulate unwise laws through Congress.

Madison's analysis was far too optimistic, however. As the Antifederalists predicted, the Constitution afforded enormous scope for special interests to influence the government. The great challenge for Madison's generation would be how to maintain a government that would provide equal benefits to all but at the same time accord special privileges to none.

CONCLUSION

The entry of North Carolina into the Union in late 1789 and of Rhode Island in May 1790 marked the final triumph of the nationalism born of the War for Independence. The devastating eight-year conflict swept up half of all men of military age and made casualties of one-fifth of these. Never before had such a large part of the population been called on to make sacrifices in a common cause of this magnitude.

The collective experience of fighting together as countrymen made many veterans self-consciously American. After several years in the army, General Nathanael Greene of Rhode Island condemned the "prejudices" of those with "local attachments." "I feel the cause and not the place," Greene said; "I would as soon go to Virginia [to fight] as stay here [New England]." The distractions of peace almost allowed this sentiment to evaporate, but the Constitution offered the firmest proof that a growing number of Americans now felt comfortable viewing themselves as a common people rather than citizens of allied states.

CHRONOLOGY

1770   Yearly meeting of New England Quakers prohibits slaveowning—first American ban on slaveholding.

1775   Virginia governor Lord Dunmore promises freedom to any slave assisting in the restoration of royal authority.

1776   British troops evacuate Boston.

British defeat American forces under George Washington in fighting around New York City.

American victory in Battle of Trenton.

Cherokees attack North Carolina frontier.

1777   American victory in Battle of Princeton.

British general John Burgoyne surrenders at Saratoga.

Battle of Brandywine Creek; British occupy Philadelphia.

British general William Howe defeats Washington at Battle of Germantown.

Congress approves Articles of Confederation.

1778   France formally recognizes the United States.

France declares war on Britain.

Philadelphia evacuated by British general Henry Clinton; Battle of Monmouth Court House (New Jersey).

British occupy Savannah.

Joseph Brant leads Iroquois attacks in western Pennsylvania and New York.

1779   Spain declares war on Britain.

George Rogers Clark's recapture of Vincennes.

John Sullivan leads U.S. raids in Iroquois country.

Judith Murray writes "On the Equality of the Sexes" (published 1790).

George Rogers Clark

1780   British seize Charles Town.

Dutch Republic declares war on Britain.

1781   Articles of Confederation become law.

Battle of Yorktown; British general Charles Cornwallis surrenders.

1782   British evacuate Savannah.

Paris peace negotiations begin.

Rhode Island rejects national import duty.

1783   Peace of Paris.

Newburgh Conspiracy.

Treaty of Augusta.

1784   Spain closes New Orleans to American trade.

Economic depression begins.

Second Treaty of Fort Stanwix.

1785	Ordinance of 1785.
	Treaty of Fort McIntosh.
1786	Congress rejects Jay-Gardoqui Treaty.
	Treaty of Fort Finney.
	Joseph Brant organizes Indian resistance to U.S. expansion.
	Virginia adopts Thomas Jefferson's Statute for Religious Freedom.

1786–1787	Shays's Rebellion in Massachusetts.
1787	Northwest Ordinance.
	Philadelphia Convention; federal Constitution signed.
1788	Alexander Hamilton, James Madison, and John Jay, *The Federalist.*
	Federal Constitution becomes law.

FOR FURTHER READING

Edward Countryman, *The American Revolution* (1985). An excellent introduction to developments from the Revolution through ratification of the Constitution.

Jack P. Greene, ed., *The American Revolution: Its Character and Limits* (1987). Leading scholars' analysis of how Americans dealt with the problem of applying their political ideals to an imperfect society without endangering the nation's survival.

Robert Middlekauff, *The Glorious Cause: The American Revolution, 1763–1789* (1982). A comprehensive account of military and political developments through the Philadelphia Convention.

Mary Beth Norton, *Liberty's Daughters: The Revolutionary Experience of American Women, 1750–1800* (1980). A wide-ranging study of changes in the lives and roles of women during the Revolutionary era.

Benjamin Quarles, *The Negro in the American Revolution* (1961). An authoritative study of blacks' role in the Revolution and its consequences for them.

Charles Royster, *A Revolutionary People at War: The Continental Army and American Character* (1980). An illuminating analysis of how Revolutionary Americans created and fought in an army.

Gordon Wood, *The Creation of the American Republic, 1776–1787* (1969). Comprehensive treatment of the evolution of American political thought from the first state governments to the Philadelphia Convention.

ADDITIONAL BIBLIOGRAPHY

The Military Struggle

Richard Buel, Jr., *Dear Liberty: Connecticut's Mobilization for the Revolutionary War* (1980); Robert M. Calhoon, *The Loyalists in Revolutionary America, 1760–1781* (1973); E. Wayne Carp, *To Starve the Army at Pleasure: Continental Army Administration and American Political Culture, 1775–1783* (1984); Jonathan R. Dull, *A Diplomatic History of the American Revolution* (1985); Barbara Graymont, *The Iroquois in the American Revolution* (1972); Don Higginbotham, *The War of American Independence: Military Attitudes, Policies, and Practice, 1763–1789* (1983); Ronald Hoffman and Peter J. Albert, eds., *Arms and Independence: The Military Character of the American Revolution* (1984); Ronald Hoffman and Thad W. Tate, eds., *An Uncivil War: The Southern Backcountry During the American Revolution* (1985); James O'Donnell, *Southern Indians in the American Revolution* (1973); Steven Rosswurm, *Arms, Country, and Class: The Philadelphia Militia and the "Lower Sort" in the Era of the American Revolution* (1987); John Shy, *A People Numerous and Armed: Reflections on the Military Struggle for American Independence* (1976); Paul H. Smith, *Loyalists and Redcoats: A Study in British Revolutionary Policy* (1964); Jack M. Sosin, *The Revolutionary Frontier, 1763–1783* (1967).

Revolutionary Society

Ira Berlin and Ronald Hoffman, eds., *Slavery and Freedom in the Age of the American Revolution* (1983); Joy Day Buel and Richard Buel, Jr., *The Way of Duty: A Woman and Her Family in Revolutionary America* (1984); Jeffrey J. Crow and Larry E. Tise, *The Southern Experience in the American Revolution* (1978); Sylvia R. Frey, *Water from the Rock: Black Resistance in a Revolutionary Age* (1991); Ronald Hoffman and Peter J. Albert, eds., *Women in the Age of the American Revolution* (1989); Rhys Isaac, *The Transformation of Virginia, 1740–1790* (1982); Michael Kammen, *A Season of Youth: The American Revolution and the Historical Imagination* (1978); Linda K. Kerber, *Women of the Republic: Intellect and Ideology in Revolutionary America* (1980); Duncan J. MacLeod, *Slavery, Race, and the American Revolution* (1974); Jackson Turner Main, *The Social Structure of Revolutionary America* (1965); Gary B. Nash, *Race and Revolution* (1990); Gary B. Nash and Jean R. Soderlund, *Freedom by Degrees: Emancipation in Pennsylvania and Its Aftermath* (1991); Anthony F. C. Wallace, *The Death and Rebirth of the Seneca* (1969); Gordon S. Wood, *The Radicalism of the American Revolution* (1992).

Politics and Constitutionalism

Willi Paul Adams, *The First American Constitutions: Republican Ideology and the Making of the State Constitutions in the Revolutionary Era* (1980); Richard Beeman et al., eds., *Beyond Confederation: Origins of the Constitution and American National Identity* (1987); Herman Belz et al., eds., *To Form a More Perfect Union: The Critical Ideas of the Constitution* (1992); John L. Brooke, *The Heart of the Commonwealth: Society and Political Culture in Worcester County, Massachusetts, 1713–1861* (1989); Robert A. Gross, ed., *In Debt to Shays: The Bicentennial of an Agrarian Rebellion* (1993); Van Beck Hall, *Politics Without*

Parties: Massachusetts, 1780–1791 (1972); Donald S. Lutz, *Origins of American Constitutionalism* (1988); Forrest McDonald, *E Pluribus Unum: The Formation of the American Republic, 1776–1790* (1965) and *Novus Ordo Seclorum: The Intellectual Origins of the Constitution* (1985); Jackson T. Main, *The Antifederalists: Critics of the Constitution, 1781–1788* (1961) and *Political Parties Before the Constitution* (1973); Cathy D. Matson and Peter S. Onuf, *Union of Interests: Political and Economic Thought in Revolutionary America* (1990); Anne M. Ousterhout, *A State Divided: Opposition in Pennsylvania to the American Revolution* (1987); J. G. A. Pocock, *The Machiavellian Moment: Florentine Political Thought and the Atlantic Republican Tradition* (1975); Jack N. Rakove, *The Beginnings of National Politics: An Interpretive History of the Continental Congress* (1979); Norman K. Risjord, *Chesapeake Politics, 1781–1800* (1978); David P. Szatmary, *Shays' Rebellion: The Making of an Agrarian Insurrection* (1980).

Biographies

James T. Flexner, *Washington: The Indispensable Man* (1974); Isabel Thompson Kelsay, *Joseph Brant, 1743–1807: Man of Two Worlds* (1984); Ralph Ketcham, *Benjamin Franklin* (1966) and *James Madison: A Biography* (1971); Dumas Malone, *Jefferson and the Rights of Man* (1951); Sheila L. Skemp, *William Franklin: Son of a Patriot, Servant of a King* (1990).

Silk Embroidery
Rachel Breck Hooker, Early Nineteenth Century

7

LAUNCHING THE NEW REPUBLIC
1789–1800

Early in 1789 a mysterious stranger from New Orleans named André Fagot appeared in Nashville, Tennessee. Fagot was officially there to talk business with local merchants, but in reality he was a Spanish agent sent to stir up discontent. For years, westerners had agonized over the American government's failure to win Spanish permission for them to export crops through New Orleans (inset), without which their settlements would never flourish. Fagot made westerners a tempting offer—unrestricted export privileges at New Orleans, which promised to ensure them prosperity. But in return, they would have to request that Spain annex Tennessee to its Louisiana colony.

Fagot found many local residents willing to discuss becoming Spanish subjects. One of his more enthusiastic contacts was a young lawyer recently arrived from the Carolinas. Aware that poor communities could support only poor lawyers, the Carolinian was drawn irresistibly to the plot. Learning that Spain would give valuable land grants in the lower Mississippi Valley to anyone who renounced U.S. citizenship, the lawyer began visiting Spanish Louisiana regularly to investigate settling there. Fagot probably placed little reliance on this brash conspirator, who had a wild temper and a reputation for gambling and drinking. In 1789 he seemed just another frontier opportunist. But in little more than a quarter-century, the Nashville lawyer would become the country's most popular hero and the symbol of American nationalism. He was Andrew Jackson.

The fact that even Jackson could talk secession to Spanish agents underscores the fragility of the United States in 1789, one year after the Constitution's ratification. North Carolina (which controlled Tennessee territory) and Rhode Island had not yet joined the Union. Westerners appeared to be abandoning the new government. The United States faced the prospect that foreign powers would slice off western territory. The nation could conceivably have disintegrated into several smaller republics, much as Latin America would splinter into numerous nations after rebelling against Spain in the early nineteenth century.

Few incoming American presidents have confronted as many grave problems as did George Washington in 1789. The West might well have separated from the Union. Indians and frontier whites fought endlessly. Foreign restrictions on U.S. exports threatened the nation's economy. The treasury was bankrupt, and the government's credit in shambles.

Some of the most serious obstacles facing the United States in 1789 were overcome by the time Washington's second administration ended in 1797, but only at the price of unleashing fiercely emotional party divisions among citizens. By 1798 a sense of crisis gripped the nation. The party in power resorted to political repression. Fearing that a fair election might be impossible and that the national government was slipping into despotism, the opposing party desperately tried to justify the right of state legislatures to veto federal laws. In the election of 1800, each side damned the other in increasingly irresponsible rhetoric. Only when the election had been settled—by the narrowest of margins—could it be said that the United States had managed to avoid dissolution and preserve civil liberties for its citizens.

THE FRAGILE NEW NATION

By 1789 six years had elapsed since Britain had recognized U.S. independence, but for many Americans peace had brought problems rather than prosperity. Restrictions on export markets endangered the livelihoods of innumerable farmers, sailors, and merchants. Foreign efforts to prevent Americans from settling the frontier frustrated influential land speculators and toiling pioneers. The Confederation's default on the national debt had injured tens of thousands of Revolutionary creditors from all levels of society by delaying their compensation, and even after 1788 there was no guarantee that the new government would honor their claims fully. All these conditions had helped convince prominent Americans that a new constitution and a new government were desperately needed. But Antifederalists had not disappeared from public life, and supporters of the new government faced enormous pressure to succeed.

In the first two decades under the Constitution, it proved impossible for the government to devise policies that would provide equal benefits throughout the land. The different regions' interests varied greatly and often conflicted. Other fissures also became apparent in American society: among blacks, Indians, and whites; between emerging capitalists and wage-earning workers; above all, among citizens who interpreted the republican ideology of the Revolutionary years in different ways.

Regional and ideological conflicts would split the new nation's Congress, first into factions and then into hostile parties—just what the Constitution's framers had hoped to avoid. And political polarization would also bring into focus something else that few members of the Philadelphia Convention had favored: a rising demand for a *democratic* republic.

The West and the South

Most U.S. territory from the Appalachians to the Mississippi River belonged to those peoples whom the Declaration of Independence had condemned as "merciless Indian savages." Divided into more than eighty tribes and numbering perhaps 150,000 people in 1789, these Native Americans were struggling to preserve their way of life. During the Revolutionary War, patriot forces had dealt the Iroquois and Cherokees a punishing series of blows. But most Indians, although bloodied, continued to resist threats to their land. Tribes in the Ohio Valley formed a defensive confederacy in 1786 (see Chapter 6). The powerful southeastern nations refused to acknowledge American rule. Great Britain openly backed Indian resistance in the Northwest, and Spain armed the southeastern Native Americans. As the Constitution took effect, the federal government faced the prospect of having to force Britain and Spain to abandon the Indians and then of negotiating land purchases from them.

Confronting the inland Indians were approximately two hundred thousand settlers who had established homesteads on the frontier. Although their ranks included some well-to-do planters and merchants, most families found life exceedingly harsh. Above all, frontier settlers were isolated and vulnerable. By 1786 a succession of Indian war parties spread death, destruction, and anxiety from Pennsylvania to Georgia. In Kentucky alone, where just 74,000 settlers lived in 1790, more than 1,500 pioneers were killed or captured in Indian raids from 1784 to 1790—a casualty rate twice as high as that of the Revolutionary War. Frontier people retaliated ruthlessly. "The people of Kentucky," wrote an army officer trying to end the fighting, "will carry on private expeditions against the Indians and kill them whenever they meet them, and I do not believe there is a jury in all Kentucky [that] will punish a man for it."

Whites could conquer the Indians only by mustering overwhelming military force and threatening entire tribes with starvation by ravaging their villages and stocks of winter food. Such large-scale operations lay beyond the capability of poorly equipped, ill-trained frontier militia. This fact became obvious in 1786, when a lack of supplies forced 1,200 Kentuckians marching under George Rogers Clark against the Indians of the Great Lakes region to abandon their campaign. If Clark, who had prevailed against enormous odds during the Revolution, found himself thus overwhelmed, clearly only federal forces could defeat the Indians. But in 1789 the U.S. Army's total strength was 672 soldiers, less than half the number of warriors that the northwestern Indian confederation could raise. Little wonder that the weakness of the U.S. government caused many frontier folk to despair—and to decide that the United States had forfeited their loyalty. Clark spoke for untold Kentuckians in 1788 when he declared that "no property or person is safe under a government so weak as that of the United States."

Nevertheless, militia raids across the Ohio River did force the Miamis, Shawnees, and Delawares gradually to evacuate southern Indiana and Ohio. These Indians' withdrawal northward, toward the Great Lakes, tempted whites to make their first settlements in what is now Ohio. In the spring of 1788, about fifty New Englanders sailed down the Ohio River in a bullet-proof barge named the *Mayflower* and founded the town of Marietta. That same year, some Pennsylvanians and New Jerseyites established a second community north of the Ohio, on the site of modern-day Cincinnati. By then the contest for the Ohio Valley was nearing a decisive stage.

Westerners felt a special bitterness toward the British. The recent enemy's continued occupation of seven forts on American soil seemed the mainspring of the unceasing border fighting. Royal diplomats justified this violation of the Peace of Paris by citing certain states' failure to compensate loyalists for confiscated property and to honor prewar debts owed by U.S. citizens. But these complaints served only as pretexts for retarding American expansion westward until Britain could sponsor an Indian buffer state south of the Great Lakes and possibly annex the region to Canada. Meanwhile, the lingering British presence in the Northwest allowed Canadian fur traders to maintain a brisk business there.

Having failed to prevent American settlers from occupying territory it claimed in the Southeast, Spain sought to win the newcomers' allegiance by offering them citizenship. Noting that Congress under the Articles of Confederation seemed ready to accept the permanent closing of New Orleans in return for Spanish concessions elsewhere (see Chapter 6), many westerners began talking openly of secession. "I am decidedly of the opinion," wrote Kentucky's attorney general in 1787, "that this western country will in a few years Revolt from the Union and endeavor to erect an Independent Government." In 1788 Tennessee conspirators boldly advertised their flirtation with Spain by

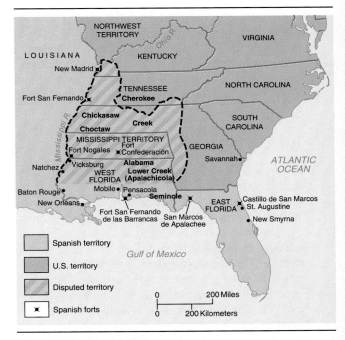

Disputed Territorial Claims, Spain and the United States, 1783–1796
The two nations' claims to lands east of the Mississippi and north of the thirty-first parallel were a principal point of contention until the Treaty of San Lorenzo was ratified in 1796.

naming a large district along the Cumberland River after Spain's governor in New Orleans. Most westerners who accepted Spanish favors and gold meant only to pocket badly needed cash in return for vague promises of goodwill. The episode showed, however, that leading citizens were susceptible to foreign manipulation and subversion. As young Andrew Jackson concluded in 1789, making some arrangements with the Spanish seemed "the only immediate way to obtain peace with the Savage [Indians]."

Meanwhile, southerners watched the deterioration of Anglo-American fortunes in the West with concern. Many southern citizens had acquired a personal stake in trans-Appalachian affairs because Virginia and North Carolina had rewarded Revolutionary soldiers with western land. Whether these veterans intended to move west themselves or to profit by selling their rights to others, all wanted to see the western territories prosper. Hoping to make a quick fortune in land speculation, southern planters (including George Washington) had borrowed heavily to buy frontier real estate; but uncertainty about the West's future made them worry that land prices would crash. By 1789 a potent combination of small farmers and landed gentry in the South had become enraged at foreign barriers to frontier expansion and eagerly supported politicians, among them Thomas Jefferson and James Madison, who advocated strong measures against the British and Spanish.

Regional Economies

The frustrations of southern planter-speculators were compounded by the failure of their principal crops, tobacco and rice, to return to prewar export levels. Whereas nearly two-thirds of the mainland colonies' exports originated in the South in 1770, less than half the new nation's exports were produced by southern states in 1790. In an effort to stay afloat, many Chesapeake tobacco growers shifted to wheat, and others expanded their production of hemp. But these changes had little effect on the region as a whole. The South's failure to recover its export base, along with barriers to westward expansion, contributed to nagging uncertainties about its future.

In the mid-Atlantic region, particularly Pennsylvania and New York, agricultural production benefited from a steady demand for foodstuffs and by 1788 had largely recovered from the Revolution's ravages. As famine stalked Europe, American farmers in the Delaware and Hudson River valleys prospered from climbing export prices.

New Englanders were not so fortunate. A short growing season and poor soil kept yields so low, even in the best of times, that farmers barely produced enough grain for local consumption. New Englanders also faced both high taxes to repay the money borrowed to finance the Revolution and a tightening of credit that spawned countless lawsuits against debtors. These problems had sparked Shays's Rebellion in 1786 and still defied solution. Whereas most southern states had largely eliminated their war debts and the Middle Atlantic states had made great progress in managing theirs, New England taxpayers remained under a crushing obligation. Economic depression only aggravated the region's chronic overpopulation. Young New England men continued migrating to the frontier or to the cities, and their discontent and restless mobility loosened the bonds of parental authority and left many women without marriage prospects.

British restrictions against trading with the West Indies (see Chapter 6) fell especially hard on New England. Resourceful captains took cargoes to the French West Indies, Scandinavia, and even China. Some even smuggled foodstuffs to the British West Indies under the very nose of the Royal Navy. Nevertheless, by 1791 discriminatory British treatment had reduced the number of seamen in the Massachusetts cod and whale fisheries by 42 percent compared to the 1770s. Recognizing that Great Britain could not be forced to grant trade concessions, New England's leaders preferred to solve the problem through peaceful accommodation, an approach entirely opposite to western and southern preferences for direct confrontation with Britain—even at the risk of war.

Entrepreneurs, Artisans, and Wage Earners

After 1783, through the enterprise of an ambitious, aggressive class of businessmen, the northern economy became less dependent on farming. Most of these individuals had begun as merchants, and they now used their profits to invest in factories, ships, government bonds, and banks (see "A Place in Time"). These men believed that the United States would gain strength if Americans balanced agriculture with banking, manufacturing, and commerce, and they wanted to limit American dependence on imported British manufactures. They also insisted that the nation needed a healthy merchant marine standing ready to augment U.S. naval forces in wartime.

Such entrepreneurs stimulated a flurry of innovative business ventures that pointed toward the future. The country's first private banks were founded in the 1780s in Philadelphia, Boston, and New York. Philadelphia merchants created the Pennsylvania Society for the Encouragement of Manufactures and the Useful Arts in 1787. This organization promoted the immigration of English artisans familiar with the latest industrial technology, including Samuel Slater (see Chapter 9), a pioneer of American industrialization who helped establish a cotton-spinning mill at Pawtucket, Rhode Island, in 1793. In 1791 investors from New York and Philadelphia started the Society for the Encouragement of Useful Manufactures, which attempted to demonstrate the potential of large-scale industrial enterprises by building a factory town at Paterson, New Jersey. That same year, New York merchants and insurance underwriters organized America's first formal association for trading government bonds, out of which the New York Stock Exchange evolved.

Certificate of the "New York Mechanick Society"
In the face of changing times and narrowing opportunity, many urban artisans organized societies to set wages and working hours.

Many of these early enterprises ended in financial ruin, however, because they proved premature or unrealistic. Not a few of their promoters shared the fate of Philadelphia businessman Robert Morris, who had signed both the Declaration of Independence and Constitution yet would spend three years in a debtors' prison after 1798. But the vision of these men was ultimately vindicated, for as often happens, failure preceded success: in the nineteenth century, the United States gradually became an industrial society.

Yet in 1789 the northeastern cities remained overwhelmingly preindustrial, without large factories. Half the urban work force consisted of "mechanics," whose ranks included both master artisans and journeymen. Mechanics manufactured goods by hand, typically in workshops where the master and his family employed a few journeymen or apprentices. Journeymen changed jobs frequently; those hired in Samuel Ashton's Philadelphia cabinet shop, for example, stayed an average of just six months between 1795 and 1803. Moreover, well-to-do artisan households, as well as professional and upper-class families, employed numerous servants. And masters and other employers could draw upon the growing ranks of low-paid day workers, who included most free blacks and many orphans, widows, and drifters.

Mechanics tended to follow in their fathers' occupational footsteps. They lived in close-knit neighborhoods with others who practiced their trade and with whom they enjoyed such traditional pastimes as drinking, marching, and "mobbing." Their wives and daughters often helped in the shop but rarely sought outside employment unless widowed or orphaned. Despite their industriousness and thrift, mechanics faced stiff competition from British manufacturers, who increasingly used labor-saving machinery and unskilled, low-paid labor. Consequently, American mechanics were disposed to support political leaders willing to raise the price of imported British goods through a national tariff. Most mechanics had supported the Constitution, hoping that it would create a strong and assertive national government.

A few artisans succeeded in adapting techniques of large-scale production to their crafts. The textile-finishing, printing, furniture-making, and construction trades most successfully exploited new technology or unskilled wage labor; they offered many opportunities for master artisans to establish flourishing family businesses. But most mechanics were either reluctant to abandon traditional household-oriented shops for an impersonal factory system or else could not modernize for lack of credit, which was scarce and expensive. Many artisans thus found opportunity shrinking, and they responded by organizing societies to set wages and working hours. Over the long run, the artisan community would contract as the mechanics themselves became wage earners working for entrepreneurial industrialists; but in the 1790s these trends were only beginning to emerge.

In 1789 virtually all politically conscious Americans—entrepreneurs and merchants, urban mechanics and frontier settlers, nationalists and Antifederalists, northerners and southerners—expressed their hopes for the nation's future in terms of republican ideals. These lofty goals of selfless service to the general good had helped community leaders rally the public behind them in resisting British encroachments since the 1760s. Republican ideology had guided the men who hammered out state constitutions and the new federal Constitution, and it had also helped Antifederalists state their case against the Constitution. Now in the 1790s, how to interpret republican ideals, with their abiding distrust of government power, became a nagging question in the cut-and-thrust of everyday politics. Most Americans thought that they knew what republican virtue meant, and most tended to condemn rivals' views as the road to corruption. Noting in *The Federalist* the numerous divergent meanings of the word

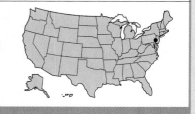
From 1790 to 1800, Philadelphia was the United States' capital, largest city, main financial market, and intellectual and scientific center. Home to forty-four thousand people in 1790, by 1800 Philadelphia almost doubled its population. This growth occurred despite a series of frightful yellow-fever epidemics, which cost thousands of lives and sent wealthier residents (including President Washington and the entire federal government) fleeing each summer while the disease raged. A constant stream of country people and foreign immigrants poured in, and large numbers of Germans, French, Irish, and Scots kept Philadelphia's population diverse.

The dynamism and diversity of Philadelphia's economy made for a society consisting of several distinct layers.

The City or Port of Philadelphia on the River Delaware from Kensington,
by William Birch, 1800
This engraving illustrates Philadelphia's remarkable growth in little more than a century. From the large elm under which William Penn was said to have first negotiated with the Delaware Indians (see Chapter 4), it looks across the Delaware River to the busiest port in North America.

205a

The richest 10 percent of Philadelphians owned about half the city's wealth. This upper crust included old Quaker merchant families, recent wartime profiteers, and hustling new entrepreneurs. Philadelphia was still a preindustrial city entirely dependent on foreign trade for its existence, and most of its wealthiest men made their fortunes in commerce.

Philadelphia's economic environment was treacherous, however. Given rapidly changing market conditions, merchants had to be ever ready to act decisively. They repeatedly gambled everything in hopes of developing new overseas markets for Delaware Valley foodstuffs or of expanding the sphere within which they could retail European-made imports. But overseas trade was the most nerve-wracking of all Philadelphia businesses. From 1785 to 1791, bankruptcies reduced the number of trading firms from 514 to 440. Of the sixty-five wealthiest traders operating in 1779, only nine were still in business seventeen years later. The survivors were calculating, daring, and grasping.

In 1776, into this competitive commercial world came the half-blind French immigrant Stephen Girard. Relying on a quick mind and a scrappy, abrasive personality, Girard struggled for years just to avoid bankruptcy. But he exemplified the traits necessary for commercial success in Philadelphia—a determination to conduct his business personally (even when laid up with a painful head wound) and a willingness to take chances. "Since I have not as much as I desire, it seems necessary for me to take some risks or remain always poor." By 1795 he ranked high among the city's wealthiest individuals.

Girard's phenomenal success stemmed from his refusal to imitate conservative businessmen, who demonstrated a "prudence that will risk nothing." He and his fellow entrepreneurs helped propel Philadelphia into the industrial age. They provided two essential elements that would transform the city's economy—capital amassed from foreign trade, and a

Absalom Jones,
by Raphael Peale, 1810
Born a slave, Jones was allowed to study and work for pay; eventually he bought his freedom. He became a businessman, co-founder of the African Methodist Episcopal Church, and a stalwart in Philadelphia's free-black community.

readiness to take chances by investing in manufacturing.

Amid the shifting sands of precarious commerce and embryonic industrial capitalism, the wealthier families in the 1790s helped a flourishing, cultured city continue to prosper. The well-to-do could even afford to send their daughters to the Young Ladies' Academy, founded in 1787 by Dr. Benjamin Rush. "The patriot—the hero—the legislator," Dr. Rush grandly proclaimed, "would find the sweetest reward for their toils, in the approbation of their wives"—and how better could young women bestow this approval than by being educated themselves? Among the subjects that they studied was bookkeeping.

Most Philadelphians belonged to artisan families practicing such trades as carpentry, bricklaying, tailoring, and leatherworking. These crafts supplied the city's elite with elegant imitations of the latest European styles in dress, furniture, and housing. The better endowed artisans, along with small merchants and

professional men, lived fairly comfortably, if not opulently.

Such was not the case for the thousands of Philadelphians known to those in the upper and middle ranks as the lower sort. Employed as porters, woodcutters, washer-women, dock workers, seamen, and in dozens of other occupations, the "lower sort" provided vital services but led lives of uncertainty. When they had work at all, it was temporary and low paying. They had higher rates of illness and death than other Philadelphians because of their poor diets and living conditions and their inability to afford smallpox immunizations. Many received relief and charity or spent time in the almshouse, workhouse, or jail. Among the "lower sort" in 1790 were 1,840 African-Americans, all but 301 of whom were free. (Pennsylvania had enacted gradual emancipation in 1780.) Whereas some slaves had been trained in a skilled trade such as blacksmithing, young free men of color found themselves excluded from crafts and relegated to menial work. Still, free blacks strove to improve their lot: this largest free black community in North America maintained seven schools and three churches, all of which were segregated.

Philadelphia's bustling commerce and unequal distribution of wealth produced social strain. Journeymen printers and leatherworkers, for example, organized and struck in a vain attempt to avoid becoming permanent wage earners. Yet the "lower sort" largely avoided politics, and the city's most notable political pressure group of the 1790s did not promote class conflict. In this organization, Philadelphia's Democratic Society, artisan masters rubbed shoulders with members of the professional elite like Dr. Rush and famed scientist David Rittenhouse—and with entrepreneur Stephen Girard. What united these republican enthusiasts were a conviction that individuals of talent and ambition ought not be held back by special interests, an admiration for revolutionary France, and a determination to preserve the liberty so hard won in the American Revolution.

republican, James Madison had concluded that "no satisfactory one would ever be found."

◆

CONSTITUTIONAL GOVERNMENT TAKES SHAPE

Traveling slowly over the nation's miserable roads, the men entrusted with launching the federal experiment began assembling in New York, the new national capital, in March 1789. Because so few members were on hand, Congress opened its session a month late. George Washington did not arrive until April 23 and only took his oath of office a week later.

The slowness of these first halting steps, however, disguised the seriousness of the tasks at hand. The country's elected leaders had to make far-reaching decisions on several critical questions left unresolved by the Constitution's framers. For example, the Constitution gave the president no formal responsibility for preparing a legislative agenda, although it allowed him wide discretion by directing him to make periodic reports on the state of the Union and by permitting him to recommend matters for Congress's consideration. The Philadelphia Convention likewise had not specified whether cabinet officers would be accountable to Congress or to the president. Nor did the Constitution say how the federal court system should be structured. Finally, widespread distrust of any government unrestrained by a bill of rights required that Congress prepare amendments for the states' consideration, but the exact scope and character of these amendments remained to be determined. "We are in a wilderness," wrote James Madison, "without a footstep to guide us."

Consequently, even though the Constitution had been ratified as the supreme law of the land, its framers' intentions might still have been reversed. The First Congress could easily have weakened presidential authority, limited access to federal courts, or passed amendments resurrecting features of the Articles of Confederation. Antifederalists conceivably could have convoked another constitutional convention, ostensibly to prepare a bill of rights but actually to rewrite the entire Constitution. In 1789 the nation's future remained unsettled in these, as in many other, regards.

Defining the Presidency

No office in the new government aroused more suspicion than the presidency. Many feared that the president's powers could make him a virtual king. Public apprehension remained in check only because of George Washington's reputation for honesty. Washington tried to calm fears of unlimited executive power.

The Constitution mentioned the executive departments only in passing, required the president to obtain the Senate's approval for his nominees to head these bureaus, and made all executive personnel liable to impeachment. Otherwise, Congress was free to determine the organization and accountability of what became known as the cabinet. The first cabinet, established by Congress, consisted of four departments, headed by the secretaries of state, treasury, and war and by the attorney general. Vice President John Adams's tie-breaking vote defeated a proposal that would have forbidden the president from dismissing cabinet officers without Senate approval. This outcome reinforced the president's authority to make and carry out policy; it also separated the powers of the executive and legislative branches beyond what the Constitution required, and so made the president a more equal partner with Congress.

President Washington suggested few laws to Congress. Rarely did he speak out against opponents of government policy, and generally he limited his public statements to matters of foreign relations and military affairs. He deferred to congressional decisions concerning domestic policy whenever possible and cast only two vetoes during his eight-year tenure (1789–1797).

Washington tried to reassure the public that he was above favoritism and conflicts of interest. Believing himself duty-bound to seek advice from a wide range of opinions, he balanced his cabinet with southerners and northeasterners. When Secretary of State Thomas Jefferson opposed certain policies of Secretary of the Treasury Alexander Hamilton, Washington implored Jefferson not to leave his post, even though the president supported Hamilton.

"He is polite with dignity, affable without familiarity, distant without haughtiness, grave without austerity, modest, wise, and good." So Abigail Adams, the wife of the vice president, described Washington. Once the government had settled into Philadelphia (the nation's capital from 1790 to 1800), the president enjoyed the private company of wealthy citizens, but he felt truly comfortable only at his Virginia estate, Mount Vernon, or on the Pennsylvania farm he rented. More than any other national leader, Washington sincerely strove to understand the aspirations of the two groups that dominated American society—northeastern merchants and entrepreneurs, and southern planters. Like most republican leaders, he believed that the proper role for ordinary citizens was not to set policy through elections but rather to choose well-educated, politically sophisticated men who would make laws in the people's best interest, though independently of direct popular influence.

The president endured rather than enjoyed the pomp of office. Suffering from a variety of ailments that grew as the years passed, Washington longed to escape the presidency. Only with difficulty was he persuaded to accept reelection in 1792. He dreaded dying while in office and thus setting the precedent for a lifetime presidency. With great anxiety he realized that "the preservation of the sacred fire of liberty and the destiny of the republican model of government are . . . *deeply,* perhaps *finally,* staked on the experiment entrusted to the hands of the American people." Should he contribute to that experiment's failure, he feared, his name would live only as an "awful monument."

National Justice and the Bill of Rights

The Constitution merely authorized Congress to establish federal courts below the level of the Supreme Court; it had offered no guidance as to how the judicial system should be structured. And although the Constitution specifically barred the federal government from committing such abuses as passing ex post facto laws* and bills of attainder,[†] the absence of a comprehensive bill of rights had led several delegates at Philadelphia to refuse to sign the Constitution and had been a major point of attack by Antifederalists. The task of filling in these gaps fell to the First Congress.

In 1789 many citizens feared that the new federal courts would ride roughshod over local customs. Every state had gradually devised a unique, time-honored blend of judicial procedures appropriate to local cir-

---

*Ex post facto law: a law criminalizing previously legal actions and punishing those who have been engaging in such actions.

[†]Bill of attainder: a legislative act proclaiming a person's guilt and stipulating punishment without a judicial trial.

cumstances. Any attempt to force states to abandon their legal heritage would have produced strong counterdemands that federal justice be narrowly restricted. Bowing to such sentiments, Congress might have drastically curtailed the scope and power of the federal judiciary or limited the federal judicial system to the Supreme Court. Congress might also have forbidden federal judges to accept cases from the states on a range of subjects (as permitted by Article III, Section 2). Such actions by Congress would have tipped the balance of power in the new nation to the states.

But when it passed the Judiciary Act of 1789, which created the federal-court system, Congress did not seek to hobble the national judiciary. Yet the act managed to quiet popular apprehensions by establishing in each state a federal district court that operated according to local procedures. As the Constitution stipulated, the Supreme Court exercised final jurisdiction. Congress had struck a reasonable compromise that respected state traditions while offering wide access to federal justice.

Behind the movement for a bill of rights lay Americans' long-standing fear that a strong central government would lead to tyranny. Many Antifederalists believed that the best defense against tyranny would be to strengthen the powers of state governments at the expense of the federal government, but many more Americans wanted simply to guarantee basic personal liberties. James Madison, who had been elected to the House of Representatives, battled fiercely to keep the Constitution's opponents from undermining the powers essential for a firm national government. It was Madison who played the leading role in drafting the ten amendments that became known as the Bill of Rights when ratified by the states in December 1791.

Madison insisted that the first eight amendments guarantee personal liberties, not strip the national government of any necessary authority. The First Amendment guaranteed the most fundamental freedoms of expression—religion, speech, press, and political activity—against federal interference. The Second Amendment ensured that each state could form its own citizen militia. Like the Third Amendment, it sought to protect citizens from what eighteenth-century Britons and Americans alike considered the most sinister embodiment of tyrannical power: standing armies. The Fourth through Eighth amendments limited the police powers of the state by guaranteeing individuals' fair treatment in legal and judicial proceedings. The Ninth and Tenth amendments reserved to the people or to the states powers not allocated to the federal government under the Constitution, but Madison headed off proposals to limit federal power more explicitly. In general, the Bill of Rights imposed no serious check on the framers' nationalist objectives.

Once the Bill of Rights was in place, the federal judiciary moved decisively to establish its authority. In 1793, in *Chisholm* v. *Georgia,* the Supreme Court ruled that a state could be sued in federal courts by nonresidents. In 1796 the Court declared its right to determine the constitutionality of congressional statutes in *Hylton* v. *United States* and to strike down state laws in *Ware* v. *Hylton.* But Congress decided that the Court had encroached too far on states' authority in *Chisholm,* and in 1794 it voted to overturn this decision through a constitutional amendment. Ratified in 1798, the Eleventh Amendment revised Article III, Section 2, so that private citizens could no longer undermine states' financial autonomy by using federal courts to sue another state's government in civil cases and claim money from that state's treasury. The defeat of *Chisholm* stands as one of the handful of instances in American history whereby the Supreme Court was subsequently overruled by a constitutional amendment.

By endorsing the Eleventh Amendment, Congress expressed its recognition that federal power could threaten vital local interests. Such awareness had been growing since the early 1790s, rupturing the nationalist coalition that had written the Constitution, secured its ratification, and dominated the First Congress. A dramatic sign of this split was James Madison's shift from nationalist to critic of excessive federal power in 1790–1791. Up to this time, Madison and most of his fellow nationalists had not thought very deeply about how federal power should be used. The chief exception was Alexander Hamilton, whose bold program alienated many like-minded nationalists by demonstrating that federal policies could be shaped to reward special interests.

◆

NATIONAL ECONOMIC POLICY AND ITS CONSEQUENCES

Realizing that war would jeopardize national survival, Washington concentrated his attention on diplomacy and military affairs. His reluctance to become involved with pending legislation enabled his energetic secretary of the treasury, Alexander Hamilton, to set the administration's domestic priorities. Hamilton quickly emerged as the country's most imaginative and dynamic statesman by formulating a sweeping program for national economic development. But Hamilton's agenda proved deeply divisive.

Hamilton and His Objectives

Born in the West Indies in 1755, Hamilton had sailed to New York in 1772 to enroll at King's College (now Columbia University), where he had emerged as a passionate defender of American rights. He had entered the Continental Army in 1775, distinguished himself in battle several times, and won the nickname the Little Lion.

During his four years on Washington's staff, Hamilton developed an exceptionally close relationship with his commander in chief. Hamilton's mother had been the mistress of a Scottish merchant who had abandoned her and their children when Alexander was about ten. For Hamilton, Washington helped fill the emotional void created by his own father's desertion. At the same time, for the childless Washington, Hamilton became almost a son. Hamilton thus gained extraordinary influence over Washington, who despite misgivings frequently supported the younger man's policies.

Hamilton formulated his financial proposals to strengthen the nation against foreign enemies and also to lessen the threat of disunion. In his mind, the most immediate danger concerned national security: the possibility of war with Great Britain, Spain, or both. The Republic could finance a full-scale war only by borrowing heavily, but because Congress under the Articles of Confederation had failed to redeem or pay interest on the Revolutionary debt, the nation's credit had been seriously weakened abroad and at home. The country's economy also seemed unequal to fighting a major European power. War with Britain would mean a blockade, which would strangle commerce and stop the importation of necessary manufactured goods. French assistance had overcome this danger during the Revolution; but France's navy had declined greatly since 1783 (while the British navy had vastly improved). Moreover, growing political instability in France was transforming America's wartime ally into an uncertain friend. Unless the United States achieved self-sufficiency in the manufacture of vital industrial products and maintained a strong merchant marine ready for combat, Hamilton reasoned, its chances of surviving a second war with Britain appeared slim.

Hamilton also feared that the Union might disintegrate because of Americans' tendency to think first of their local loyalties and interests. Born outside the thirteen colonies, he felt little personal identification with his adopted state, New York, or any other American locale. Instead, his six years in the Continental Army produced a burning nationalistic faith. For him, the Constitution's adoption had been a close victory of national over state authority. Now he worried that the states might reassert power over the new government. If this happened, he doubted whether the nation could prevent ruinous trade discrimination between states, deter foreign aggression, and avoid civil war.

Both his wartime experiences and his view of human nature forged Hamilton's political beliefs. An enthusiastic young patriot who had fought bravely during the Revolution's darkest hours, Hamilton had grown profoundly disillusioned by civilian profiteering. Like many disappointed idealists, he became a cynic who believed that few could live up to his own standards. Thus, he came to share the conviction of many other nationalists that the Republic's population (like the rest of humanity) would never show limitless self-sacrifice and virtue. Hamilton concluded that the federal government's survival depended on building support among politically influential citizens through a straightforward appeal to their financial interests. Private ambitions would then serve the national welfare.

Charming and brilliant, vain and handsome, a notorious womanizer, and thirsting for fame and power, Hamilton himself exemplified the worldly citizen whose fortunes he hoped to link to the Republic's future. But to the growing ranks of his opponents, Hamilton would embody the dark forces luring the Republic to its doom—a man who, Jefferson wrote, believed in "the necessity of either force or corruption to govern men."

Report on the Public Credit

Seeking guidance on how to restore the nation's credit worthiness, in 1789 Congress directed the Treasury Department to evaluate the status of the Revolutionary debt. Hamilton seized the opportunity to devise policies that would at once strengthen the country's credit, enable it to defer paying its debt, and entice a key sector of the upper class to place their prestige and capital at its service. Congress received his Report on the Pub-

Continental Currency

lic Credit in January 1790. The report listed $54 million in U.S. debt: $42 million owed to Americans, and the rest to foreigners. Hamilton estimated that on top of the national debt, the states had debts of $25 million, an amount that included several million dollars that the United States had promised to reimburse, such as Virginia's expenses in defending settlements in the Ohio Valley.

Hamilton's first major recommendation was that the federal government support the national debt by "funding" it—that is, raising the $54 million needed to honor the debt by selling an equal sum in new securities. Purchasers of these securities would choose from several combinations of federal "stock" and western lands. Those who wished could retain their original bonds and earn 4 percent interest. All of the options would reduce interest payments on the debt from the full 6 percent set by the Confederation Congress. Hamilton knew that creditors would not object to this reduction because their investments would now be more valuable and more secure.

Second, the report proposed that the federal government pay off the state debts remaining from the Revolution. Such obligations would be funded along with the national debt in the manner described above.

Hamilton argued that the continued failure of certain states to honor their obligations would undermine U.S. credit in overseas markets. Although this reasoning contained a kernel of truth, it masked his most important motive. He saw the federal assumption of state debts as a chance for the national government to win the gratitude and loyalty of state creditors by honoring their claims before the remaining states could pay

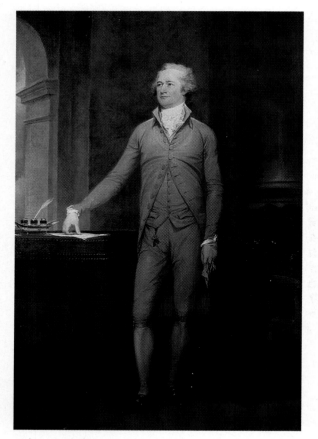

Alexander Hamilton, *by John Trumbull, 1792*
Hamilton's self-confident pride clearly shines through in this portrait, painted at the height of his influence in the Washington administration.

them. Since legislatures awash in debt wanted to avoid piling more taxes on the voters, they would accept any relief, regardless of Hamilton's actual intentions.

Hamilton exhorted the government to use the money earned by selling federal lands in the West to pay off the $12 million owed to Europeans as quickly as possible. The Treasury could easily accumulate the interest owed on the remaining $42 million by collecting customs duties on imports and excise taxes on whiskey distillers. In addition, Hamilton proposed that money owed to American citizens should be made a permanent debt. That is, he urged that the government *not* attempt to repay the $42 million principal but instead keep paying interest to people wishing to hold bonds as an investment. If Hamilton's recommendation were adopted, the only burden on the taxpayers

would be the small annual cost of interest. It would then be possible to uphold the national credit at minimal expense, without ever having to pay off the debt itself.

Hamilton advocated a perpetual debt above all as a lasting means of uniting the economic fortunes of the nation's creditors to the United States. In an age when financial investments were notoriously risky, the federal government would protect the savings of wealthy bond holders through conservative policies but still offer an interest rate competitive with the Bank of England's. The guarantee of future interest payments would act as the explicit link uniting the interests of the moneyed class with those of the government. Few other investments would entail so little risk.

Hamilton's Report on the Public Credit provoked immediate controversy. Although no one in Congress doubted that its provisions would fully restore the country's fiscal reputation, many objected that those least deserving of reward would gain the most. The original owners of more than three-fifths of the debt certificates issued by the Continental Congress (ranging from George Washington to Revolutionary patriots of modest means) had long before sold theirs at a loss, many out of dire financial necessity. Foreseeing Hamilton's intentions, wealthy speculators, on the other hand, had by then accumulated large holdings at the expense of unsuspecting original owners. Now these astute speculators stood to reap huge gains, even collecting interest that had fallen due before they had purchased the certificates. "That the case of those who parted with their securities from necessity is a hard one, cannot be denied," Hamilton admitted. But making exceptions would be even worse.

To Hamilton's surprise, Madison—his longtime colleague and initially a supporter of the plan— emerged as one of the chief opponents of reimbursing current holders at face value. Sensing opposition to the plan in his home state of Virginia, Madison now tried but failed to obtain compensation for original owners who had sold their certificates. Congress rejected his suggestions primarily because some members feared that they would weaken the nation's credit. Hamilton's policy was defensible, but it generated widespread resentment because it rewarded rich profiteers while ignoring the wartime sacrifices of ordinary citizens.

Opposition to assuming the state debts also ran high. Only Massachusetts, Connecticut, and South Carolina had failed to make effective provisions for paying their creditors. Understandably, the issue stirred the fiercest indignation in the South, which except for South Carolina had extinguished 83 percent of its debt. To allow residents of the laggard states to escape heavy taxes while others had liquidated theirs at great expense seemed to reward irresponsibility. Many Virginians, among them Madison, opposed Hamilton not only for reasons of high principle but also because of their state's self-interest. South Carolina became the sole southern state that supported Hamilton's policies.

Southern hostility almost defeated assumption. In the end, however, Hamilton managed to save his proposal by exploiting the strong desire among Virginians to relocate the national capital in their region. Virginians expected that moving the capital would make their state the crossroads of the country and thus help preserve its position as the nation's largest, most influential state. In return for the northern votes necessary to transfer the capital to the Potomac River, Hamilton secured enough Virginians' support to win the battle for assumption. Yet the debate over state debts alienated most southerners by confirming their suspicions that other regions monopolized the benefits of a stronger union.

Congressional enactment of the Report on the Public Credit dramatically reversed the nation's fiscal standing. Thereafter, Europeans grew so enthusiastic for U.S. bonds that by 1792 some securities were selling at 10 percent above face value.

Reports on the Bank and Manufactures

In December 1790 the secretary of the treasury presented Congress with a second message, the Report on a National Bank. Having managed to restore full faith in greatly undervalued certificates, Hamilton in effect had significantly expanded the stock of capital available for investment. He intended to direct that money toward projects that would diversify the national economy through a federally chartered bank.

The proposed bank would raise $10 million through a public stock offering. The Treasury would hold one-fifth of the stock and name one-fifth of the directors, but four-fifths of the control would fall to private hands. Private investors could purchase shares by paying for three-quarters of their value in government bonds. In this way, the bank would capture a significant portion of the recently funded debt and make it available for loans; it would also receive a substantial and steady flow of interest payments from the Trea-

sury. Anyone buying shares under these circumstances had little chance of losing money and was positioned to profit handsomely.

Hamilton argued that the Bank of the United States would cost the taxpayers nothing and greatly benefit the nation. It would provide a safe place for the federal government to deposit tax revenues, make inexpensive loans to the government when taxes fell short, and help relieve the scarcity of hard cash by issuing paper notes that would circulate as money. Furthermore, it would possess authority to regulate the business practices of state banks. Above all, the bank would provide much needed credit to expand the economy.

Finally, Hamilton called for American economic self-sufficiency. He admired the "prodigious effect" on Great Britain's national wealth that the recent expansion of factories had stimulated in that nation, and he wanted to encourage similar industrialization in the United States. His Report on Manufactures of December 1791 advocated protective tariffs on foreign imports to foster domestic manufacturing, which in turn would both attract immigrants and create national wealth. Elsewhere the secretary called for assisting the merchant marine against British trade restrictions by reducing duties on goods imported into the United States on American ships and by offering subsidies (called bounties) for fishermen and whalers. These measures would also indirectly protect the national bank's loans to industrialists and shippers.

Hamilton's Challenge to Limited Government

In the eyes of many of the new government's supporters, Hamilton's plan to establish a permanent national debt violated the principle of equality among citizens; it seemed to favor the interests of public creditors over those of other Americans. Hamilton's critics also denounced his proposal for a national bank, interpreting it as a dangerous scheme that would give a small, elite group special power to influence the government.

The bank issue drew Thomas Jefferson into the ranks of Hamilton's opponents. It was almost an article of faith among Revolutionary-generation Americans like Madison and Jefferson that the Bank of England had undermined the integrity of government in Britain. Shareholders of the new Bank of the United States could just as easily become the tools of unscrupulous politicians. If significant numbers in

Congress also owned bank stock, they would likely vote in support of the bank even at the cost of the national good. To Jefferson, the bank was "a machine for the corruption of the legislature [Congress]." Representative John Taylor of Virginia predicted that its vast wealth would enable the bank to take over the country, which would thereafter, he quipped, be known as the United States of the Bank.

Opponents' strongest argument against the bank was their claim of its unconstitutionality. The Constitution gave Congress no specific authorization to issue charters of incorporation; indeed the constitutional convention had rejected a proposal giving Congress just such power. Unless Congress adhered to a "strict interpretation" of the Constitution, critics argued, the central government might oppress the states and trample individual liberties, just as Parliament had done to the colonies. Strictly limiting the powers of the government seemed the surest way of preventing the United States from degenerating into a corrupt despotism, as Britain had.

Congress approved the bank by only a thin margin. Doubtful of the bank's constitutionality, Washington turned for advice to both Jefferson and Hamilton. Jefferson distrusted banking and did not want to extend government power beyond the letter of the Constitution. "To take a single step beyond the boundaries thus specifically drawn around the powers of Congress is to take possession of a boundless field of power no longer susceptible of any definition," warned Jefferson. Hamilton fought back, urging Washington to sign the bill. Because Congress could enact all measures "necessary and proper" (Article I, Section 8), Hamilton contended that the only unconstitutional activities were those actually *forbidden* to the national government. In the end, the president accepted Hamilton's cogent argument for a "loose interpretation" of the Constitution. In February 1791 the Bank of the United States obtained a charter guaranteeing its existence for twenty years. Washington's acceptance of the principle of loose interpretation was the first victory for those advocating an active, assertive national government.

Madison and Jefferson also strongly opposed Hamilton's proposal to encourage industry through protective tariffs on foreign manufactures. They viewed such protectionism as an unfair subsidy promoting uncompetitive industries that would founder without government support. Moreover, tariffs doubly injured the majority of citizens, first by imposing heavy import taxes that were passed on to consumers and then by reducing the incentive for American manufacturers to produce goods at a lower cost than imports. Together these results unjustifiably raised prices. The only beneficiaries would be those shielded from overseas competition and institutions, like the bank, that lent them money. Fearing that American cities might develop a dangerous class of dependent and politically volatile poor people, Jefferson and Madison saw industrialization as a potential menace to the Republic's stability.

Congress ultimately refused to approve a high protective tariff. Nevertheless, Hamilton succeeded in setting higher duties on goods imported into the United States by British vessels than on items carried by American ships. As a result, the tonnage of such goods carried by the American merchant marine more than tripled from 1789 to 1793. Congress also approved subsidies for New England's beleaguered whale and cod fisheries in 1792.

Hamilton's Legacy

Hamilton's attempt to erect a base of political support by appealing to economic self-interest proved highly successful. His arrangements for rescuing the nation's credit provided enormous gains for the speculators, merchants, and other "monied men" of the port cities who by 1790 held most of the Revolutionary debt. As holders of bank stock, these same groups had yet another reason to use their prestige on behalf of national authority. Assumption of the state debts liberated taxpayers from a crushing burden in New England, New Jersey, and South Carolina. Hamilton's efforts to promote industry, commerce, and shipping struck a responsive chord among the Northeast's budding entrepreneurs and hard-pressed artisans.

Those attracted to Hamilton's policies called themselves Federalists, in large part to imply (incorrectly) that their opponents had formerly been Antifederalists. Despite the Federalists' effort to associate themselves with the Constitution, they actually favored a "consolidated" (centralized) national government instead of a truly federal system with substantial powers left to the states. Federalists dominated public opinion in New England, New Jersey, and South Carolina besides enjoying considerable support in Pennsylvania and New York.

However, Hamilton's program sowed dissension in sections of the country where Federalist economic policies provided few benefits. Resentment ran high among those who felt that the government appeared to be rewarding special interests. This situation appeared a perversion of the common understanding that the Constitution had been ratified to bring equal advantages to all Americans. Southern reaction to Hamilton's program, for example, was overwhelmingly negative. Few southerners (aside from some wealthy Charleston merchants) had retained Revolutionary certificates until 1789. By that date only South Carolina of all the southern states had any significant remaining Revolutionary debt. The Bank of the United States had few southern stockholders, and it allocated very little capital for loans there.

Hamilton's plans for commercial expansion and industrial development likewise seemed irrelevant to the interests of the West, where agriculture promised to be exceptionally profitable if only the right to export through New Orleans would be guaranteed. In Pennsylvania and New York, too, the uneven impact of Hamiltonian policies generated dissatisfaction. Resentment against a national economic program whose main beneficiaries seemed to be eastern "monied men" and Yankees who refused to pay their debts gradually united westerners, southerners, and many individuals in the mid-Atlantic region into a political coalition that challenged the Federalists for control of the government and called for a return to the "true principles" of republicanism.

The Whiskey Rebellion

Hamilton's financial program not only sparked an angry political debate in Congress but also helped ignite a civil insurrection called the Whiskey Rebellion. Severely testing the federal government's authority, this insurrection was the young republic's first serious crisis.

To augment the national government's revenue from import duties, Hamilton had recommended an excise tax on domestically produced whiskey. He insisted that his proposal would distribute the expense of financing the national debt evenly across the United States. He even alleged that the country's morals would improve if higher prices induced Americans to drink less liquor, a contention enthusiastically endorsed by Philadelphia's College of Physicians.

Though Congress complied with Hamilton's request in March 1791, many members doubted that Americans (who on average annually imbibed six gallons of hard liquor per adult) would submit tamely to sobriety. James Jackson of Georgia, for example, warned the administration that his constituents "have long been in the habit of getting drunk and that they will get drunk in defiance of a dozen colleges or all the excise duties which Congress might be weak or wicked enough to pass."

The accuracy of Jackson's prophecy became apparent in September 1791, when a crowd tarred and feathered an excise agent near Pittsburgh. Western Pennsylvanians found the new tax especially burdensome. Unable to ship their crops to world markets through Spanish New Orleans, most farmers had grown accustomed to distilling their rye or corn into alcohol, which could be carried across the Appalachians at a fraction of the price charged for bulky grain. Hamilton's excise equaled 25 percent of whiskey's retail value, enough to wipe out a frontier farmer's profit.

The law furthermore specified that all trials concerning tax evasion be conducted in federal courts. Any western Pennsylvanian indicted for noncompliance thus had to travel three hundred miles to Philadelphia. Not only would the accused then face a jury of unsympathetic easterners, but he would have to bear the cost of a long journey and lost earnings while at court, in addition to fines and other court penalties if found guilty. Consequently, western Pennsylvanians had justifiable reasons for complaining that local circumstances made the whiskey tax excessively burdensome.

Moreover, Treasury officials rarely enforced the law rigorously outside western Pennsylvania. An especially diligent excise inspector lived near Pittsburgh. His efforts to collect the tax increasingly enraged local residents and in time touched off massive resistance.

Initially, most residents preferred to protest the tax peacefully, through mass meetings and petitions to Congress. Only a frustrated minority resorted to violence, not only attacking federal revenue officers but even turning on their own neighbors, destroying property and occasionally pinning down farmers with rifle fire for hours. Despite such tactics, popular opposition to the whiskey tax became increasingly militant.

In a scene reminiscent of colonial protests against Britain, large-scale resistance erupted in July 1794.

One hundred men attacked a U.S. marshal serving sixty delinquent taxpayers with summonses to appear in court at Philadelphia. A crowd of five hundred burned the chief revenue officer's house after a shootout with federal soldiers assigned to protect him. Roving bands torched buildings, assaulted tax collectors, chased government supporters from the region, and flew a flag symbolizing an independent country that they hoped to create from six western counties.

The frontier turmoil played directly into the Washington administration's hands. Echoing British denunciation of colonial protests, Hamilton blasted the rebellion as simple lawlessness, in particular because Congress had reduced the tax rate per gallon in 1792 and just recently had voted to allow state judges in western Pennsylvania to hear trials. Washington concluded that failure to respond strongly to the uprising would encourage similar outbreaks in other frontier areas where lax enforcement had allowed distillers to escape paying taxes.

Washington accordingly summoned 12,900 militiamen from Pennsylvania, Maryland, Virginia, and New Jersey to march west under his command. Opposition evaporated once the troops reached the Appalachians, and the president left Hamilton in charge of making arrests. Of about 150 suspects seized, Hamilton sent twenty in irons to Philadelphia. Two men received death sentences, but Washington eventually pardoned them both, noting that one was a "simpleton" and the other "insane."

The Whiskey Rebellion was a milestone in determining limits on public opposition to federal policies. In the early 1790s, many Americans still assumed that it was legitimate to protest unpopular laws using the same tactics with which they had blocked parliamentary measures like the Stamp Act. Indeed, western Pennsylvanians had justified their resistance with exactly such reasoning. Before 1794 the question of how far the people might go in resisting federal laws remained unresolved because, as Washington declared, "We had given no testimony to the world of being able or willing to support our government and laws." But by firmly suppressing the first major challenge to national authority, Washington served notice that if citizens wished to change the law, they could do so only through constitutional procedures—by making their dissatisfaction known to their elected representatives and if necessary by electing new representatives.

◆

THE UNITED STATES IN A HOSTILE WORLD

By 1793 disagreements over foreign affairs had emerged as the primary source of friction in American public life. The political divisions created by Hamilton's financial program hardened into ideologically oriented factions that argued vehemently over whether the country's foreign policy should be pro-French or pro-British.

The United States faced a particularly hostile international environment in the 1790s. European powers restricted American trade, supported Indian raids on the frontier, strengthened and expanded their North American empires, and maintained military garrisons on U.S. soil. Because the new nation's economic well-being depended heavily on exports, foreign-policy issues loomed large in national politics. Disputes over foreign relations would poison public life from 1793 to 1815.

Foreign Powers and Native Americans in the West

The most serious perils to the nation's future rose from British, Spanish, and Native American efforts to resist U.S. expansion farther westward.

Spain's efforts were a facet of its larger attempt to counter potential rivals for North American territory— Russia and Britain on the Pacific; Britain and the United States in the Mississippi Valley. In the 1740s, Russian traders in Siberia had crossed the Bering Sea and had begun trading with Alaskan natives for sea-otter pelts, frequently using brutal force and spreading deadly diseases in the process. Meanwhile, Britain was searching for the "Northwest Passage," a route that would link the Canadian interior with the Pacific. Sensing twin threats to its previously unchallenged monopoly in the north Pacific, Spain boldly expanded its empire northward from Mexico by establishing "New California," a long stretch of coast from San Diego to Sonoma (north of San Francisco), beginning in 1769. Efforts to encourage large-scale Hispanic immigration to New California failed, so that the colony was sustained primarily by its religious missions. Spanish colonists' spreading of epidemic and venereal diseases among coastal Californian natives precipitated a decline in the Indians' numbers

Spanish Settlements in New California, 1784
While the United States was struggling to establish its independence, Spain was extending its empire northward along the Pacific coast.

Consulting with the Senate as the Constitution required, President Washington nevertheless tried to keep tight control of foreign policy. Realizing that he could not quickly resolve the complex western problem, he pursued a course of patient diplomacy that was intended "to preserve the country in peace if I can, and to be prepared for war if I cannot." The prospect of peace improved in 1789 when Spain unexpectedly opened New Orleans to American commerce, although exports remained subject to a 15 percent duty that westerners bitterly resented. Still, secessionist sentiment gradually subsided.

Washington now moved to weaken Spanish influence in the West by neutralizing Spain's most important ally, the Creek Indians. The Creeks numbered more than twenty thousand, including perhaps five thousand warriors, and they bore a fierce hostility toward Georgian settlers, whom they called *Ecunnaunuxulgee*, or "the greedy people who want our lands." In 1790 the Creek leader Alexander McGillivray

Stimafachki of the Koasati Creeks,
by John Trumbull, 1790
This portrait was sketched during the U.S.–Creek conference that resulted in the Treaty of New York.

from about 72,000 in 1770 to about 18,000 by 1830. Survivors who did not escape were placed in missions, where priests sought to Christianize and "civilize" them by imposing rigid disciplinary measures and putting them to work in vineyards and in other enterprises. Meanwhile, Spain strengthened its position in the Southwest by making peace with the Comanches, Navajos, and most of the Apache nations that had previously threatened its settlements.

Revitalized by its far western successes, Spain, along with Britain and the Native Americans, constituted a formidable barrier to U.S. aims in the Mississippi Valley.

In the early years of Washington's administration, Spanish officials commonly bribed numerous well-known political figures in Tennessee and Kentucky, among them a former general on Washington's staff, James Wilkinson, whose unscrupulous intrigues would continue well past 1800. Thomas Scott, a congressman from western Pennsylvania, meanwhile schemed with the British. Between 1791 and 1796, the federal government anxiously admitted Vermont, Kentucky, and Tennessee to the Union, partly in the hope of strengthening their sometimes flickering loyalty to the United States.

signed the Treaty of New York with the United States. The treaty permitted American settlers to occupy lands in the Georgia piedmont fought over since 1786, but in other respects preserved Creek territory against U.S. expansion. Washington insisted that Georgia restore to the Creeks' allies, the Chickasaws and Choctaws, the vast area along the Mississippi River known as the Yazoo Tract, which Georgia claimed and had begun selling off to white land speculators.

Hoping to conclude a similar agreement with Great Britain's Indian allies, the United States sent an envoy to the Great Lakes tribes in 1790. The Miamis responded by burning a captured American to death. Late that same year, the president's first effort to force peace through military action failed when General Josiah Harmar abandoned his march against the Miamis after the loss of nearly two hundred of his soldiers. A second campaign ended in disaster on November 4, 1791, when Indians killed nine hundred men out of a force of fourteen hundred led by General Arthur St. Clair.

While employing military force, the Washington administration, led by Secretary of War Henry Knox, also sought to pacify the Indians through a benevolent policy similar to that proclaimed by the British in 1763 (see Chapter 5). Alarmed by the chaos on the frontier, where trespassers invaded Indian lands and the native peoples rejected U.S. claims to sovereignty, the government formally recognized Indian title as secure and inalienable except by the "free consent" of the Indians themselves. To reinforce this policy, Congress passed laws prohibiting trespassing on Indian lands, punishing crimes committed there by non-Indians, outlawing alcohol, and regulating trade. In addition, the administration sought to encourage Indians to leave off their "savage" ways and become "civilized," by which it meant above all abandoning communal landownership and seasonal migrations for hunting, gathering, and fishing. By adopting private property and a strictly agricultural way of life, Knox and others thought, Indians would find a niche for themselves in American society while making much additional land available for non-Indians.

Knox recognized that his "civilization" policy would have limited appeal. Although most Indians were receptive to European material goods, they were unwilling to give up their traditional ways entirely and assimilate into an alien culture. And most whites were averse to integrating Native Americans into their society. Accordingly, the United States continued to pressure most Native Americans to sell their lands and move farther west.

With many Indians opposed to abandoning both their lands and their cultures, and with St. Clair's defeat in 1791, Washington's frontier policy lay in a shambles. Not only had two military expeditions suffered defeat in the Northwest Territory, but in 1792 the Spanish had persuaded the Creeks to renounce their treaty with the federal government and to resume hostilities. Ultimately, the damage done to U.S. prestige by these setbacks convinced many Americans that the combined strength of Britain, Spain, and the Native Americans could be counterbalanced only by an alliance with France.

France and Factional Politics

One of the most momentous events in history, the French Revolution began in 1789 with the meeting (for the first time in almost two centuries) of France's legislative assembly, the Estates General. Americans remained fundamentally sympathetic to the revolutionary cause as the French abolished nobles' privileges, wrote a constitution, and bravely repelled invading armies from Austria and Prussia. France became a republic early in 1793; it then proclaimed a war of all peoples against all kings, in which it assumed that the United States would eagerly enlist.

Enthusiasm for a pro-French foreign policy raged in the South and on the frontier, in particular after France went to war against Spain and Great Britain in 1793. Increasingly, western settlers and southern speculators in frontier lands hoped for a decisive French victory in Europe that, they reasoned, would leave Britain and Spain militarily too exhausted to continue meddling in the West. The United States could then insist on free navigation of the Mississippi, force the evacuation of British garrisons, and end both nations' support of Indian resistance.

Moreover, a slave uprising in France's Caribbean colony of Saint Domingue (later renamed Haiti), in which the British became involved, soon generated passionate anti-British sentiment in the South. White southerners grew alarmed for the future of slavery and their own lives as thousands of terrified French planters fled to the United States from Saint Domingue with accounts of how British invaders in 1793 had supported the rebellious slaves. The blacks had fought with determination and inflicted heavy casualties on the French. Southern whites concluded that the British had intentionally sparked a bloodbath on the island and worried that a British-inspired race war would engulf the South as well. Anti-British hysteria even began to undermine South Carolina's loyalty to Federalist policies.

After 1790 American reactions to the French Revolution diverged sharply in the North and the South, in large measure for economic reasons. In the North merchants' growing antagonism toward France reflected not only their conservatism but also their strong awareness that good relations with Britain were essential for their region's prosperity. Virtually all the nation's merchant marine operated from northern ports, and by far the largest share of U.S. foreign trade was with Great Britain. Merchants, shippers, and ordinary sailors in New England, Philadelphia, and New York feared that an alliance with France would provoke British retaliation against this valuable commerce, and they argued that the United States could win valuable concessions by demonstrating friendly intentions toward Great Britain. Indeed, important members of Parliament, including Prime Minister William Pitt the Younger, seemed to favor liberalizing trade with the United States.

Southerners had no such reasons to favor Britain. Southern spokesmen like Jefferson and Madison viewed Americans' reliance on British commerce as a menace to national self-determination and wished to divert most U.S. trade to France. Jefferson and Madison repeatedly demanded that British imports be reduced through the imposition of discriminatory duties on cargoes shipped from England and Scotland in British vessels. Their recommendations gravely threatened ties with Britain, which sold more manufactured goods to the United States than to any other country. In the heat of the debate, Federalist opponents of a discriminatory tariff warned that the English would not stand by while a weak French ally pushed them into depression. If Congress adopted this program of trade retaliation, Hamilton predicted in 1792, "there would be, in less than six months, an open war between the United States and Great Britain."

After declaring war on Britain and Spain in 1793, France actively tried to embroil the United States in the conflict. The French dispatched Edmond Genet as minister to the United States with orders to mobilize republican sentiment in support of France, enlist American mercenaries to conquer Spanish territories and attack British shipping, and strengthen the treaty of alliance between the two nations. Much to the French government's disgust, however, President Washington issued a proclamation of American neutrality on April 22.

Meanwhile, Citizen Genet (as he was known in French Revolutionary style) had arrived on April 8. He found no shortage of southern volunteers for his American Foreign Legion despite America's official neutrality. Making generals of George Rogers Clark of Kentucky and Elisha Clarke of Georgia, Genet directed them to seize the Spanish garrisons at New Orleans and St. Augustine. Clark openly defied Washington's Neutrality Proclamation by advertising for recruits for his mission in Kentucky newspapers; Clarke began drilling three hundred troops on the Florida border. But the French failed to provide adequate funds for either campaign. And as for the American recruits, although all were willing to fight for France, few were willing to fight for free, and so both expeditions eventually disintegrated in 1794 for lack of French money to supply them.

However, Genet did not need funds to outfit privateers, whose crews were paid from captured plunder. By the summer of 1793, almost a thousand Americans were at sea in a dozen ships flying the French flag. These privateers seized more than eighty British vessels and towed them to U.S. ports, where French consuls sold the ships and cargoes at auction.

The British Crisis

Even though the Washington administration swiftly closed the nation's harbors to Genet's buccaneers and requested the French ambassador's recall, his exploits provoked an Anglo-American crisis. George III's ministers decided that only a massive show of force would deter further American aggression. Accordingly, on November 6, 1793, the Privy Council issued secret orders confiscating any foreign ships trading with French islands in the Caribbean. The council purposely delayed publishing these instructions until after most American ships carrying winter provisions to the Caribbean left port, so that their captains would not know that they were sailing into a war zone. The Royal Navy then seized more than 250 American vessels, a high price for Genet's troublemaking.

Meanwhile, the U.S. merchant marine was suffering a second galling indignity—the drafting of its crewmen into the Royal Navy. Thousands of British sailors, including numerous naval deserters, had previously fled to U.S. ships, where they hoped to find an easier life than under the tough, poorly paying British system. In late 1793 British naval officers began routinely inspecting American crews for British subjects, whom they then impressed (forcibly enlisted) as the king's sailors. Overzealous commanders sometimes broke royal orders by taking U.S. citizens, and in any case the British did not recognize former subjects' right to adopt American citizenship. Impressment scratched a raw nerve in most Americans, who recognized that their government's willingness to defend its citizens from such contemptuous abuse was a critical test of national character.

Next the British boldly challenged the United States for control of the West. In February 1794 Canada's royal governor delivered an inflammatory speech at an Indian council, denying U.S. claims north of the Ohio River and urging his listeners to destroy every white settlement in the Northwest. Soon British troops were building an eighth garrison on U.S. soil, Fort Miami, near present-day Toledo, Ohio. Meanwhile, the Spanish encroached further upon territory owned by the United States by building Fort San Fernando in 1794 at what is now Memphis, Tennessee.

Hoping to halt the drift toward war, Washington launched a desperate diplomatic initiative in 1794. He sent Chief Justice John Jay to Great Britain, dispatched Thomas Pinckney to Spain, and authorized General Anthony Wayne to negotiate a treaty with the Indians of the Ohio Valley.

Having twice defeated federal armies, the Indians scoffed at Washington's peace offer. But the tide turned as "Mad Anthony" Wayne led three thousand regulars and Kentucky militiamen deep into the Indian homeland and ruthlessly razed every village within his reach. On August 20, 1794, his troops routed a thousand Indians at the Battle of Fallen Timbers just

two miles from British Fort Miami. Wayne's army marched past the post in a provocative victory parade and then built an imposing stronghold to challenge British authority in the Northwest, appropriately named Fort Defiance. Indian morale plummeted. In August 1795 Wayne compelled twelve northeastern tribes to sign the Treaty of Greenville, which opened most of modern-day Ohio to white settlement and ended Indian hostilities for sixteen years.

Wayne's success allowed John Jay to win a major diplomatic victory in London: a British promise to withdraw troops from American soil. He also managed to gain access to West Indian markets for small American ships, but only by bargaining away U.S. rights to load cargoes of sugar, molasses, and coffee from the Caribbean. On other points, Jay found the British unyielding. Aside from fellow Federalists, few Americans could interpret Jay's Treaty as preserving peace with honor.

Jay's Treaty left Britain free not only to violate American neutrality but also to ruin a profitable commerce by restricting U.S. trade with French ports during wartime. Many opponents, moreover, passionately decried Jay's failure to end impressment and predicted that Great Britain would thereafter force even more Americans into the Royal Navy. And southerners re-

Negotiating the Treaty of Greenville

In this detail of a contemporary painting believed to have been done by a member of General Wayne's staff, Chief Little Turtle of the Miamis speaks to Wayne, who stands with one hand behind his back.

sented that Jay had not achieved their long-sought goal of compensation for slaves taken away by the British army during the Revolution. As the Federalist-dominated Senate ratified the treaty by a one-vote margin in 1795, Jay nervously joked that he could find his way across the country by the fires of rallies burning him in effigy.

Despite its unpopularity, Jay's Treaty probably represented the most that a weak, politically divided United States could have extracted from mighty Britain. Although enormously unpopular, the treaty was one of the Washington administration's major accomplishments. First, it defused an explosive crisis with Great Britain before war became inevitable. Second, it ended a twelve-year British occupation of U.S. territory. Third, the treaty provided for the settlement, by arbitration, of the claims of British merchants who were owed American debts from before 1776, and it also arranged for U.S. citizens' compensation for property seized by the Royal Navy in 1793 and 1794 (though these accounts were not finally settled until 1804).

Although the Senate rejected the provision granting limited trading rights with the West Indies in return for a British monopoly over certain commodities, Jay's Treaty played a critical role in stimulating an enormous expansion of American trade. British governors in the West Indies used the treaty's ratification as an excuse to proclaim their harbors open to U.S. ships. Other British officials permitted Americans to develop a thriving commerce with India, even though this trade infringed on the East India Company's monopoly. Within a few years after 1795, American exports to the British Empire shot up 300 percent.

On the heels of Jay's Treaty came an unqualified diplomatic triumph engineered by Thomas Pinckney. Ratified in 1796, the Treaty of San Lorenzo with Spain (also called Pinckney's Treaty) won westerners the right of unrestricted, duty-free access to world markets via the Mississippi River. Spain also promised to recognize the thirty-first parallel as the United States' southern boundary, to dismantle all fortifications on American soil, and to discourage Indian attacks against western settlers.

By 1796 the Washington administration thus had successfully defended the country's territorial integrity, restored peace to the frontier, opened the Mississippi for western exports, made it possible for northeastern shippers to regain British markets, and kept the nation out of a dangerous European war. As the popular outcry over Jay's Treaty demonstrated, however, the na-

tion's foreign policy had left Americans much more deeply divided in 1796 than they had been in 1789.

BATTLING FOR THE NATION'S SOUL

Besides distrusting centralized executive authority, colonial and Revolutionary Americans feared organized political parties. Labeling parties "factions," Americans (and many Britons) assumed that such groups were formed by corrupt conspirators operating against the liberties of the people. Neither the Constitution nor *The Federalist* had envisioned political parties, and none existed in 1789 when Washington became president. By the end of his second term, however, politically conscious Americans had split into two hostile parties, Federalists and Republicans.

The unfolding struggle transcended the economic and sectional differences so evident in earlier disputes about Hamiltonian finance and the possibility of war with Britain. After 1796 a battle raged over the very future of representative government, culminating in the election of 1800, whose outcome would determine whether the nation's political elite could accommodate demands from ordinary citizens for a more active and influential role in determining government policy. No issue was more important or hotly argued than the matter of officeholders' accountability to their constituents.

Ideological Confrontation

By the mid-1790s the French Revolution had led many Americans to reassess their political values. American attitudes toward events in France divided sharply after that nation's revolutionary regime turned radical in 1793–1794, sending thousands of "counterrevolutionaries" to the guillotine. The polarization of American opinion assumed a strongly, though not completely, regional dimension.

For northern Federalists, revolutionary France became an abomination—"an open hell," thundered Massachusetts Federalist Fisher Ames, "still ringing with agonies and blasphemies, still smoking with sufferings and crimes." New England was the United States' most conservative, religiously oriented region, and most of its people came to detest the French

The Republican Court, *by Daniel Huntington Federalists emphasized the dignity of the national government by staging sumptuous balls and formal receptions. Administration critics saw these affairs as an effort to emulate European court life. Washington, although mindful of upholding presidential dignity, found public functions tedious, and his stiff formality often masked his personal discomfort.*

government's disregard for civil rights and its attempt to substitute the adoration of Reason for the worship of God. Middle Atlantic businessmen, who were perhaps less religious than New Englanders but hardly less conservative, condemned French leaders as evil radicals who incited the poor against the rich. A minority of well-off northern merchants and professional men, however, continued to look favorably upon the French Revolution, primarily out of loyalty to deeply felt republican principles.

Federalists trembled at the thought of guillotines and "mob rule" looming in the United States' future. Memories of Shays's Rebellion and the Whiskey Rebellion reinforced their fears. So did the tendency of artisans in Philadelphia and New York to bandy the French revolutionary slogan "Liberty, Equality, Fraternity" and to admire pro-French political leaders such as Jefferson. Moreover, Citizen Genet had openly encouraged vocal opposition to the Washington administration until the faction in the French government that he represented fell from power—and even more troubling, he had found hundreds of Americans willing to fight for France. Federalists worried that all of this was just the tip of an iceberg.

By the mid-1790s Federalist leaders had concluded that it was unwise and perhaps dangerous to involve the public too deeply in politics. The people, they believed, were not evil-minded but simply undependable and could easily fall prey to a rabble rouser such as Genet. As Senator George Cabot of Massachusetts put it, "The many do not think at all." For Federalists, democracy meant "government by the passions of the multitude," though they also felt that the people, if properly led, could stand as a powerful (but passive) bulwark against anarchy. Indeed, they *did* trust ordinary property owners to judge a candidate's personal fitness for high office. Federalists consequently argued that citizens need not be presented with choices over policy during elections; instead, voters ought to choose candidates according to their personal merits. Thus they favored a representative government, in which elected officials would rule in the people's name but would be independent of direct popular influence.

Preserving order, the Federalists maintained, required demonstrating the dignity of the government and forging a close, visible relationship between the government and the upper class. Such a spectacle would not only reassure citizens that their future was in competent hands but also set high standards that few radicals could meet. As early as 1789, Vice President John Adams had tried to give the president and

George Washington, *by James Sharples, 1795*

other high officials such royal-sounding titles as "His High Mightiness." (Adams had failed amid much ridicule, including being lampooned as "His Rotundity.") During the 1790s government officials continued to dramatize their social distance from average citizens. Members of Congress and the cabinet dressed in high fashion, traveled in expensive coaches, appeared with retinues of servants, and attended endless formal dinners and balls, which served as grand opportunities for the upper class to flaunt its wealth. Federalists insisted that they ruled *of* and *for* the people, but they took pains to symbolize that their government was not *by* the people.

The Federalists aimed to limit public office to wise and virtuous men who would vigilantly protect liberty. This objective was consistent with eighteenth-century fears that corruption and unchecked passion would undermine society, for in republican theory a "virtuous" government need not be directly responsible to public opinion. If (as many assumed) democracy meant "mob rule," then political virtue and direct democracy were incompatible. The Federalists' profound suspicion of the common people therefore was deeply rooted not only in old-fashioned social reciprocity (see Chapter 2) and in conservative colonial

political traditions but also in republican ideology itself.

A very different understanding of republican ideology influenced Jefferson, Madison, and others alienated by Federalist measures. Although some critics of the administration surfaced in New England and the Middle Atlantic states, opposition ran particularly high in the South. Indeed, the southern interpretation of republicanism stressed the corruption inherent in a powerful government dominated by a highly visible few, and white southerners widely insisted that liberty would be safe only if power were diffused among virtuous, independent citizens. With their own labor force consisting of enslaved blacks rather than of free white wage workers, southern elites feared popular participation in politics far less than their northern counterparts. Furthermore, few southern planters were strongly religious, and many had absorbed the Enlightenment's faith that the free flow of ideas would inevitably ensure progress. They also felt confident of their ability to lead (and be elected by) the smaller farmers. Consequently, many white southerners felt exhilarated by the events unfolding in France; they saw the French as fellow republicans, carrying on a work of universal revolution that would replace hereditary privilege with liberty, equality, and brotherhood. Unlike northern Federalists, nervous about urban mobs, southern planters faced the future with optimism and viewed attempts to inhibit widespread political participation as unworthy of educated gentlemen.

Self-interest, too, drove men like Jefferson and Madison to rouse ordinary citizens' concerns about civic affairs. Political apathy was widespread in the early 1790s, a situation that favored the Federalists by making it unlikely that they would be criticized for passing unwise laws. If, however, the Federalists could be held accountable to the public, they would think twice before enacting measures opposed by the majority; or if they persisted in advocating misguided policies, they would ultimately be removed from office. Such reasoning led Jefferson, a wealthy landowner and large slaveholder, to say, "I am not among those who fear the people; they and not the rich, are our dependence for continued freedom."

Organized efforts to turn public opinion against the Federalists had begun in October 1791 with the publication of the nation's first opposition newspaper, the *National Gazette*. Then in 1793–1794, popular dissatisfaction with the government's policies led to the formation of dozens of Democratic (or Republican) societies, primarily in seaboard cities but also in the rural South and in frontier towns. Their memberships ranged from planters and merchants to artisans and sailors. Conspicuously absent were clergymen, the poor, and nonwhites.

Sharply critical of the Federalists, the societies spread dissatisfaction with the Washington administration's policies. Because many of the clubs arose during Genet's ministry, and because all of them also acclaimed revolutionary France, Federalists assumed (wrongly) that their members were acting as foreign agents. Federalists interpreted their emotional appeals to ordinary people as demagoguery and denounced the societies' followers as "democrats, mobocrats, & all other kinds of rats."

The Federalists feared that the societies would grow into revolutionary organizations. Washington privately warned that "if [the clubs] were not counteracted (not by prosecutions, the ready way to make them grow stronger) or did not fall into disesteem . . . they would shake the government to its foundation." During the Whiskey Rebellion, the president publicly denounced "certain self-created societies." So great was his prestige that the societies temporarily broke up. But by attacking them, Washington had at last ended his nonpartisan stance and identified himself unmistakably with the Federalists. The censure would cost him dearly.

The Republican Party

Neither Jefferson nor Madison belonged to a Democratic society. However, these private clubs helped publicize administration critics' views, and they initiated into political activity numerous voters who would later support Jefferson's and Madison's Republican party. Ironically, Madison had earlier been one of the most outspoken opponents of political parties.

In the early 1790s, politically active Americans believed that deliberately organizing a political faction or party was a corrupt, subversive action. The Constitution's framers had neither wanted nor planned for political parties, and in *The Federalist* No. 10, Madison had claimed that the Constitution would prevent the rise of national political factions. Republican ideology commonly assumed that factions or parties would fill Congress with politicians of little ability and less integrity, pursuing selfish goals at the expense of national welfare. Good citizens, it was assumed, would

shun partisan scheming. These ideals, however, began to waver as controversy mounted over Hamilton's program and foreign policy. President Washington still tried to set an example of impartial leadership by seeking advice from both camps. (He did not know that in their partisan zeal both Hamilton and Jefferson maintained indiscreet contacts with British and French diplomats, respectively.) But Jefferson finally resigned from the cabinet in 1793, and thereafter even the president could not halt the widening political split. Each side saw itself as the guardian of republican virtue and attacked the other as an illegitimate "cabal" (faction).

In 1794 party development reached a decisive stage. Shortly after Washington had openly identified himself with Federalist policies, followers of Jefferson who called themselves Republicans* successfully attacked the Federalists' "pro-British" leanings in many local elections and won a slight majority in the House of Representatives. The election signaled the Republicans' transformation from a faction of officeholders to a broad-based party capable of coordinating local political campaigns throughout the nation.

Federalists and Republicans alike used the press to mold public opinion in the 1790s. In this decade American journalism came of age as the number of newspapers multiplied from 92 to 242, mostly in New England and the Middle Atlantic states. By 1800 newspapers had perhaps 140,000 paid subscribers (about one-fifth of the eligible voters), and their secondhand readership probably exceeded 300,000. Newspapers of both camps were libelous and irresponsible. They cheapened the quality of public discussion through incessant fear mongering and character assassination. Republicans stood accused of plotting a reign of terror and of wishing to turn the nation over to France. Federalists faced charges of favoring a hereditary aristocracy and even of planning to establish an American dynasty by marrying off John Adams's daughter to George III. Such tactics whipped up mutual distrust and made political debate emotional and subjective. Nevertheless, the newspaper warfare stimulated many citizens to become politically active, even if for the wrong reasons.

Behind the inflammatory rhetoric, the Republicans' central charge was that the Federalists had evolved into a faction bent on enriching wealthy citi-

---

*Jefferson and Madison preferred the party name *Republican* rather than the radical-sounding *Democratic*.

zens at the taxpayers' expense. In 1794 a Republican writer claimed that Federalist policies would create "a privileged order of men . . . who shall enjoy the honors, the emoluments, and the patronage of government, without contributing a farthing to its support." Although almost every Republican leader, too, was well born, Republicans asserted that the Federalists planned to recreate the atmosphere of a European court through highly publicized state dinners, formal balls, and other dazzling entertainments. The Republicans erred in claiming that their opponents were scheming to introduce legal privilege, aristocracy, and monarchy. But they correctly identified the Federalists' fundamental assumption: that citizens' worth could be measured in terms of their money.

Republican charges that the president secretly supported alleged Federalist plots to establish a monarchy enraged Washington. "By God," Jefferson reported him swearing, "he [the president] would rather be in his grave than in his present situation . . . he had rather be on his farm than to be made *emperor of the world.*" Furthermore, the president took alarm at the stormy debate over Jay's Treaty, and he dreaded the nation's polarization into hostile factions. Republicans' abuse sharply stung him. "As for you, sir," sneered Thomas Paine in a pamphlet, "treacherous in private friendship . . . and a hypocrite in public life, the world will be puzzled to decide whether you are an apostate or an impostor, whether you have abandoned good principles or ever had any." Lonely and surrounded by mediocre advisers after Hamilton's return to private life, Washington decided in the spring of 1796 to retire after two terms. Four years earlier, Madison had drafted the president's parting message to the nation; but now Washington called on Hamilton to give a sharp political twist to his Farewell Address.

The heart of Washington's message was a vigorous condemnation of political parties. Partisan alignments, he insisted, endangered the republic's survival, especially if they became entangled in disputes over foreign policy. Washington warned that the country's safety depended on citizens' avoiding "excessive partiality for one nation and excessive dislike of another." Otherwise, independent-minded "real patriots" would be overwhelmed by demagogues championing foreign causes and paid by foreign governments. Aside from scrupulously fulfilling its existing treaty obligations and maintaining its foreign commerce, the United States must avoid "political connection" with Europe and its wars. If the United States gathered its strength under "an efficient government," it could defy any foreign challenge; but if it became sucked into Europe's quarrels, violence, and corruption, then the republican experiment was doomed. Washington and Hamilton had skillfully turned the central argument of republicanism against their Republican critics. They had also evoked a vision of America virtuously isolated from foreign intrigue and power politics, which would remain a potent inspiration until the twentieth century.

Washington left the presidency in 1797 and died in 1799. Like many later presidents, he went out amid a barrage of criticism. During his brief retirement, the nation's political division into Republicans and Federalists hardened. Each party consolidated its hold over particular states and groups of voters, leaving the electorate almost equally divided.

The Election of 1796

As the election of 1796 approached, the Republicans cultivated a large, loyal body of voters. Their efforts to marshal support marked the first time since the Revolution that the political elite had effectively mobilized ordinary Americans to take an interest in public affairs. The Republicans' constituency included the Democratic societies, workingmen's clubs, and immigrant-aid associations.

Immigrants became a prime target for Republican recruiters. During the 1790s the United States absorbed perhaps twenty thousand French refugees from Saint Domingue and more than sixty thousand Irish, including some conspirators exiled for plotting against British rule. Although potential immigrant voters were few—composing less than 2 percent of the electorate—the Irish in particular could exert crucial influence in Pennsylvania and New York, where public opinion was closely divided and a few hundred immigrant voters could tip the balance away from the Federalists. In short, Irish immigrants could provide the Republicans with a winning margin in the two states, and the Republicans' pro-French and anti-British rhetoric ensured enthusiastic Irish support.

In 1796 the presidential candidates were Vice President John Adams, supported by the Federalists, and the Republicans' Jefferson. Republicans expected to win as many southern electoral votes and congressional seats as the Federalists counted on in New England, New Jersey, and South Carolina. The crucial

Adams Family Farm; John Adams, *by Gilbert Stuart, 1826 (Detail)*
The Adamses hailed from Quincy, Massachusetts. John Adams was born in the house at the right; his son, John Quincy Adams, in the saltbox at the left. Soon after the elder Adams's death, John Quincy Adams, himself now president, commissioned a final portrait; this gentle and distinguished canvas was the result.

"swing" states were Pennsylvania and New York, where the Republicans tried mightily to tip the balance by wooing the large immigrant (particularly Irish) vote. In the end, however, the Republicans took Pennsylvania but not New York, and so Jefferson lost the presidency by just three electoral votes. The Federalists narrowly regained control of the House and maintained their firm grip on the Senate. But by a political fluke possible under the Constitution at the time, Jefferson became vice president.*

The new president exemplified both the strengths and the weaknesses of an intellectual. His brilliance, insight, and idealism have rarely been equaled among American presidents. Like most intellectuals, however, Adams was more comfortable with ideas than with people, more theoretical than practical, and rather inflexible. He inspired trust and often admiration but could not command personal loyalty. His wisdom and historical vision were drowned out in highly emotional political debate. Adams's rational, reserved personality was likewise ill suited to inspiring the

*The Constitution then stipulated that the presidential candidate with the second-highest electoral vote would become vice president. This was one example of the Constitution's failure to provide for political partisanship.

electorate, and he ultimately proved unable to unify the country.

The French Crisis

Adams was initially fortunate, however, that French provocations produced a sharp backlash against the Republicans. The French interpreted Jay's Treaty as an American attempt to assist the British in their war against France. On learning of Jefferson's defeat, the French ordered the seizure of American ships carrying goods to British ports; and within a year the French had plundered more than three hundred vessels. The French government rubbed in its contempt for the United States by directing that every American captured on a British naval ship (even those involuntarily impressed) should be hanged.

Hoping to avoid war, Adams sent a peace commission to Paris. But the French foreign minister, Charles de Talleyrand, refused to meet the delegation, instead promising through three unnamed agents ("X, Y, and Z") that talks could begin after he received $250,000 and France obtained a loan of $12 million. This barefaced demand for a bribe became known as the XYZ Affair. Americans reacted to it with outrage.

"Millions for defense, not one cent for tribute" became the nation's battle cry as the 1798 congressional elections began.

The XYZ Affair discredited the Republicans' foreign policy views, but the party's leaders compounded the damage by refusing to condemn French aggression and opposing Adams's call for defensive measures. The Republicans tried to excuse French behavior, whereas the Federalists rode a wave of militant patriotism. In the 1798 elections, Jefferson's supporters were routed almost everywhere, even in the South.

Congress responded to the XYZ Affair by arming fifty-four ships to protect American commerce. The new warships were at once put to use in what has become known as the Quasi-War—an undeclared Franco-American naval conflict in the Caribbean from 1798 to 1800, during which U.S. forces seized ninety-three French privateers at the loss of just one vessel. The British navy meanwhile extended the protection of its convoys to America's merchant marine. By early 1799 the French were a nuisance but no longer a serious threat at sea.

Despite the president's misgivings, the Federalists in Congress tripled the regular army to ten thousand men in 1798, with an automatic expansion of land forces to fifty thousand in case of war. But the risk of a land war with the French was minimal. In reality, the Federalists primarily wanted a military force ready in the event of a civil war, for the crisis had produced near-hysteria about conspiracies that were being hatched by French and Irish malcontents flooding into the United States.

Federalists were well aware that the French legation was not only engaged in espionage but also making treasonous suggestions to prominent persons. The government knew, for example, that in 1796 General Victor Collot had traveled from Pittsburgh to New Orleans under orders to investigate the prospects for establishing a pro-French, independent nation west of the mountains, and also that he had examined strategic locations to which rebellious frontier dwellers might rally. The State Department heard in 1798 that France had created in the West "a party of mad Americans ready to join with them at a given Signal."

The Alien and Sedition Acts

The Federalists, moreover, insisted that the likelihood of open war with France required stringent legislation to protect national security. In 1798 the Federalist-dominated Congress accordingly passed four measures known collectively as the Alien and Sedition Acts. Adams neither requested nor particularly wanted these laws, but he deferred to Federalist congressional leaders and signed them.

The least controversial of the four laws, the Alien Enemies Act, was designed to prevent wartime spying or sabotage. This measure outlined procedures for determining whether the citizens of a hostile country posed a threat to the United States; if so, they were to be deported or jailed. The law established fundamental principles for protecting national security and respecting the rights of enemy citizens. It was to operate only if Congress declared war and so was not used until the War of 1812 (see Chapter 8).

Second, the Alien Friends Act was a peacetime statute enforceable until June 25, 1800. It authorized the president to expel any foreign residents whose activities he considered dangerous. The law did not require proof of guilt, on the assumption that spies would hide or destroy evidence of their crime. Republicans maintained that the law's real purpose was to deport prominent immigrants critical of Federalist policies.

Republicans also denounced the third law, the Naturalization Act. This measure increased the residency requirement for U.S. citizenship from five to fourteen years (the last five continuously in one state), with the purpose of reducing Irish voting.

Finally came the Sedition Act, the only one of these measures enforceable against U.S. citizens. Although its alleged purpose was to distinguish between free speech and attempts at encouraging others to violate federal laws or to overthrow the government, the act nevertheless defined criminal activity so broadly that it blurred any real distinction between sedition and legitimate political discussion. Thus it forbade an individual or group "to oppose any measure or measures of the United States"—wording that could be interpreted to ban any criticism of the party in power. Another clause made it illegal to speak, write, or print any statement about the president that would bring him "into contempt or disrepute." Under such restrictions, for example, a newspaper editor might face imprisonment for disapproving of an action by Adams or his cabinet members. The Federalist *Gazette of the United States* expressed the twisted logic of the Sedition Act perfectly: "It is patriotism to write in favor of our government—it is sedition to write against it."

Sedition cases were heard by juries, which could decide if the defendant had really intended to stir up rebellion or was merely expressing political dissent. But whatever way one looked at it, the Sedition Act interfered with free speech. Ingeniously, the Federalists wrote the law to expire in 1801 (so that it could not be turned against them if they lost the next election) and to leave them free meanwhile to heap abuse on the *vice* president, Jefferson.

Federalist enforcement of the first of the repressive new laws, the Alien Friends Act, produced mixed results. The president signed a deportation order for French agent Collot, who escaped capture. No expulsions were actually carried out under the law, although two of Collot's assistants and several dozen other French sailed home before they could be forcibly removed from the country.

The real target of Federalist repression was the U.S. opposition press. Four of the five largest Republican newspapers were charged with sedition just as the election of 1800 was getting under way. The attorney general used the Alien Friends Act to threaten an Irish journalist, John Daly Burk, with expulsion (Burk went underground instead). Scottish editor Thomas Callender was on the verge of being deported when he suddenly qualified for citizenship. Now unable to expel Callender, the government tried him for sedition before an all-Federalist jury, which sent him to prison for criticizing the president.

Federalist leaders never intended to fill the jails with Republican martyrs. Rather, they wanted to use a small number of highly visible prosecutions to intimidate most journalists and candidates into keeping quiet during the election of 1800. The attorney general charged seventeen persons with sedition and won ten convictions. Among the victims was the Republican congressman Matthew Lyon of Vermont ("Ragged Matt, the democrat," to the Federalists), who spent four months in prison for publishing a blast against Adams.

Vocal criticism of Federalist repression erupted only in Virginia and Kentucky. During the summer of 1798, militia commanders in these states mustered their regiments, not to drill but to hear speeches demanding that the federal government respect the Bill of Rights. Entire units then signed petitions denouncing the Alien and Sedition Acts. The symbolic implications of these protests were sobering. Young men stepped forward to sign petitions on drumheads with a pen in one hand and a gun in the other, as older officers who had fought in the Continental Army looked on approvingly. It was not hard to imagine Kentucky rifles being

substituted for quill pens as the men who had led one revolution took up arms again.

Ten years earlier, opponents of the Constitution had warned that giving the national government extensive powers would eventually endanger freedom. By 1798 their prediction had come true. Shocked Republicans realized that because the Federalists controlled all three branches of the government, neither the Bill of Rights nor the system of checks and balances protected individual liberties. In this context, the doctrine of states' rights was advanced as a means of preventing the national government from violating basic freedoms.

Madison and Jefferson anonymously wrote two manifestos on states' rights that the assemblies of Virginia and Kentucky officially endorsed in 1798. Madison's Virginia Resolutions and Jefferson's Kentucky Resolutions declared that the state legislatures had never surrendered their right to judge the constitutionality of federal actions and that they retained an authority called interposition, which enabled them to protect the liberties of their citizens. A set of Kentucky Resolutions adopted in November 1799 added that objectionable federal laws might be "nullified" by the states. The terms *interposition* and *nullification* were not defined, but the intention was obviously to prevent residents from being tried for breaking an unconstitutional law. The Virginia and Kentucky legislatures must have understood that interposition would ultimately challenge the jurisdiction of federal courts and perhaps require that state militia march into a federal courtroom to halt proceedings at bayonet point.

Although no other states endorsed these resolutions (most in fact expressed disapproval), their passage demonstrated the great potential for violence in the late 1790s. So did a minor insurrection called the Fries Rebellion, which broke out in 1799 when crowds of Pennsylvania German farmers released prisoners jailed for refusing to pay taxes needed to fund the national army's expansion. Fortunately, the disturbance collapsed just as federal cavalry arrived, and the only casualties were several head of rebellious cattle shot by trigger-happy soldiers.

The nation's leaders increasingly acted as if a crisis were imminent. Vice President Jefferson hinted that events might push the southern states into secession from the Union. The normally sensible President Adams hid guns in his home. After passing through Richmond and learning that state officials were purchasing thousands of muskets for the militia, an alarmed Supreme Court justice wrote in January 1799 that "the General Assembly of Virginia are pursuing steps which will lead directly to civil war." A tense atmosphere hung over the Republic as the election of 1800 neared.

The Election of 1800

In the election the Republicans rallied around Jefferson for president and the wily New York politician Aaron Burr for vice president. The Federalists meanwhile became mired in wrangling between Adams and the extreme "High Federalists" who looked to Alexander Hamilton for guidance. That the nation survived the election of 1800 without a civil war or the disregard of voters' wishes owed much to the good sense of the more moderate leaders of both parties. Thus Jefferson and Madison discouraged radicalism that might provoke intervention by the national army, while Adams rejected High Federalist demands that he ensure victory by deliberately sparking an insurrection or asking Congress to declare war on France.

"Nothing but an open war can save us" argued Adams's High Federalist secretary of the treasury. But when the president suddenly discovered the French willing to seek peace in 1799, he proposed a special diplomatic mission. "Surprise, indignation, grief & disgust followed each other in quick succession," said a Federalist senator on hearing the news. Adams obtained Senate approval for his envoys only by threatening to resign and so make Jefferson president, an action that he later described with justifiable pride as "the most disinterested . . . in my whole life." The High Federalists were so outraged that they tried unsuccessfully to dump Adams. Hamilton denounced him as a fool, but this ill-considered maneuver rallied most New Englanders around their stubborn, upright president.

Adams's negotiations with France did not achieve a settlement until 1801, but the expectation that normal—and perhaps friendly—relations with the French would resume prevented the Federalists from exploiting charges of Republican sympathy for the enemy. Without the immediate threat of war, moreover, voters grew resentful that in merely two years, taxes had soared 33 percent to support an army that had done nothing except chase terrified Pennsylvania farmers. As the danger of war receded, voters gave the Federalists less credit for standing up to France and more blame for ballooning the national debt by $10 million.

Two years after their triumph in the 1798 elections, support for the Federalists had eroded sharply. High Federalists who had hoped for war spitefully withheld the backing that Adams needed to win. The Republicans meanwhile redoubled their efforts to elect Jefferson. They were especially successful in mobilizing voters in Philadelphia and New York, where artisans, farmers, and some entrepreneurs were ready to forsake the Federalists, whom they saw as defenders of entrenched privilege and upstart wealth. As a result, popular interest in politics rose sharply. Voter turnouts in 1800 leaped to more than double those of 1788, rising from about 15 percent to almost 40 percent, and in hotly contested Pennsylvania and New York more than half the eligible voters participated.

Playing on their opponent's reputation as a religious free thinker, the Federalists forged a case against Jefferson that came down to urging citizens to vote for "GOD—AND A RELIGIOUS PRESIDENT; or impiously declare for JEFFERSON—AND NO GOD!!!" But this ploy did not prevent thousands of deeply religious Baptists, Methodists, and other dissenters from voting Republican. Nor did voters know that Adams was scarcely more conventional in his religious views than Jefferson.

Adams lost the presidency by just 8 electoral votes out of 138. He would have won if his party had not lost control of New York's state senate, which chose the electors, after a narrow defeat in New York City. Unexpectedly, Jefferson and his running mate Burr also carried South Carolina because their backers made lavish promises of political favors to that state's legislators.

Although Adams lost, Jefferson's election was not assured. Because all 73 Republican electors voted for both their party's nominees, the electoral college deadlocked in a Jefferson-Burr tie.* The choice of president devolved upon the House of Representatives, where thirty-five ballots over six days produced no result. Finally, Delaware's only representative, a Federalist, abandoned Burr and gave Jefferson the presidency by history's narrowest margin.

---

*The Twelfth Amendment (ratified in 1804) eliminated the possibility of such problems. It stipulated that electors vote for presidential and vice-presidential candidates as a pair; no longer would the runner-up in the presidential contest become vice president.

DEFERRING EQUALITY

The election of 1800 did not make the United States more democratic. Rather, it prevented rigidly antidemocratic prejudices from blocking future political liberalization. The Republican victory also repudiated the Federalist willingness, so evident in Hamilton's plans, to create a base of support for the government through special-interest legislation. Such self-serving goals led critics like Madison to condemn the Federalists for "substituting the motive of private interest for public duty." After 1800 government policies would be judged by Jefferson's standard of "equal rights for all, special privileges for none."

But not all Americans won equal rights. Women and African-Americans took almost no part in politics, and few people felt that they should. As for the Native Americans, the nation's diplomatic gains came largely at their expense. Moreover, in the Republic's early years, white Americans lost much of the idealism that Revolutionary ideology had inspired, and they began to assume that racial minorities could never be more than second-class citizens at best.

Indians in the New Republic

By 1795 eastern Indians had suffered severe reductions in population and territory. Innumerable deaths had resulted from battle, famine, exposure to the elements during flight from enemies, and disease. From 1775 to 1795, the Cherokees declined from 16,000 to 10,000 and the Iroquois fell from about 9,000 to 4,000. Meanwhile, in the quarter-century before 1800, Indians forfeited more land than the area inhabited by whites in 1775. Settlers crowded Indians onto reservations (often illegally), liquor dealers and criminals trespassed on Indian lands, and government agents and missionaries pressured Native Americans to give up their communal lands and traditional cultures.

In the face of such losses and pressures, many Indians became demoralized. Unable to strike back at whites, Indians often consumed enormous quantities of whiskey and inflicted violence on one another. The situation among the Iroquois was all too typical. "The Indians of the Six Nations," wrote a federal offi-

Sauk Chief, *c. 1805*
This portrait probably depicts Wa Pawni Ha, a seventeen-year-old leader of the Sauk nation.

cial in 1796, "have become given to indolence, drunkenness, and thefts, and have taken to killing each other."

The Indians' predicament spawned a profound social and moral crisis within tribes threatened by the settlers' expansion. Among those most afflicted were the Seneca Iroquois. But beginning in 1799, a Seneca prophet, Handsome Lake, led his people in one of the most resourceful efforts to resolve this crisis. Overcoming his own problems with liquor, he sought to end alcoholism among Indians by appealing to their religious traditions. Even more radically, he welcomed Quaker missionaries and federal aid earmarked for teaching Euro-American agricultural methods to Iroquois men, who had to look for new livelihoods after the loss of most of their lands and the demise of the fur trade. More traditional Indians rejected the notion that Indian men should work like white farmers; said one, only "squaws and hedgehogs are made to scratch the ground." But many Iroquois men welcomed the change. It was the women who resisted most, because they stood to lose their collective ownership of farmland, their control of the food supply, and their place in tribal councils. Women who did not accept Handsome Lake's and the Quakers' urging to exchange farming for housewifery found themselves ac-

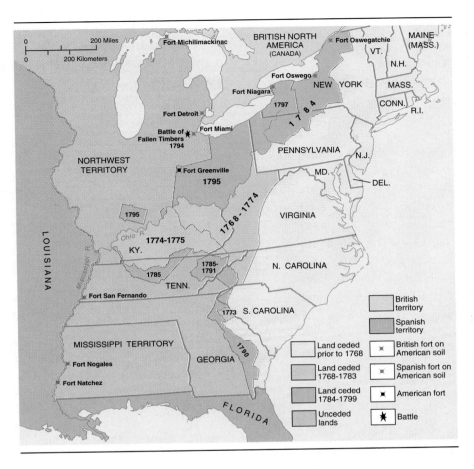

Indian Land Cessions, 1768–1799

Between 1768 and 1775, western Indians sold off vast territories, mostly hunting grounds in mountainous regions. The upheavals of the Revolutionary War, followed by conflicts with U.S. military forces from 1784 to 1799, led to large cessions of inhabited Indian lands.

cused of witchcraft, and some were killed. As a result of such conflicts between traditional and new ways, cultural change among the Senecas and other tribes proceeded slowly.

Redefining the Color Line

The Republic's first years marked the high tide of African-Americans' Revolutionary era success in bettering their lot. Although racism had not disappeared, Jefferson's eloquent words "all men are created equal" had awakened many whites' consciences. By 1790, 8 percent of all African-Americans enjoyed freedom—many having purchased liberty or earned it through wartime service. Ten years later, 11 percent controlled their own fate. Various state reforms meanwhile attempted to improve slaves' conditions. In 1791, for example, the North Carolina legislature declared that the former "distinction of criminality between the murder

of a white person and one who is equally an human creature, but merely of a different complexion, is disgraceful to humanity" and authorized the execution of whites who murdered slaves. By 1794 most states had outlawed the Atlantic slave trade.

Hesitant measures to ensure free blacks' legal equality also appeared in the 1780s and early 1790s. Most states dropped restrictions on their freedom of movement and protected their property. Of the sixteen states in the Union by 1796, all but three either permitted free blacks to vote or made no specific attempt to exclude them. But by then a countertrend was reversing many of the Revolutionary era advances for free blacks. Before the 1790s ended, abolitionist sentiment ebbed, slavery became more entrenched, and whites demonstrated unmistakable reluctance to accept even free blacks as fellow citizens.

Federal law led the way in restricting blacks' rights. When Congress established procedures for

State	Total Number of Free Blacks	Free Blacks as a Percentage of Total Black Population		
Massachusetts	7,378	100%		
Vermont	557	100%		
New Hampshire	855	99%		
Rhode Island	3,304	90%		
Pennsylvania	14,564	89%		
Connecticut	5,300	85%		
Delaware	8,268	57%		
New York	10,374	33%		
New Jersey	4,402	26%		
Maryland	19,587	16%		
Virginia	20,124	6%		
North Carolina	7,043	5%		
South Carolina	3,185	2%		
Georgia	1,019	2%		
Kentucky	741	2%		
Tennessee	309	2%		
UNITED STATES	108,395*	11%		

Number and Percentage of Free Blacks, by State, 1800

Within a generation of the Declaration of Independence, a large free black population emerged that included every ninth African-American. In the North, only in New Jersey and New York did most blacks remain slaves. Almost half of all free blacks lived in the South. Every sixth black in Maryland was free by 1800.

SOURCE: U.S. Bureau of the Census.

* Total includes figures from the District of Columbia, Mississippi Territory, and Northwest Territory. These areas are not shown on the chart.

naturalizing aliens in 1790, it limited eligibility to foreign whites. The federal militia law of 1792 required whites to enroll in local units but allowed states to exclude free blacks, an option that state governments increasingly chose. The navy and the marine corps forbade nonwhite enlistments in 1798. Delaware stripped free blacks of the vote in 1792, and by 1807 Maryland, Kentucky, and New Jersey had followed suit. Free blacks continued to vote and serve in integrated militia organizations in many localities after 1800 (including the slave states of North Carolina and Tennessee), but the number of places that treated them as the political equals of whites dropped sharply in the early 1800s.

An especially revealing indication of changing racial attitudes occurred in 1793, when Congress enacted the Fugitive Slave Law. This law required judges to award possession of a runaway slave upon any formal request by a master or his representative. Accused runaways not only were denied a jury trial but also were sometimes refused permission to present evidence of their freedom. Slaves' legal status as property

disqualified them from claiming these constitutional privileges, of course, but the Fugitive Slave Law denied *free* blacks the legal protections that the Bill of Rights guaranteed them as citizens. Congress nevertheless passed this measure without serious opposition. The law marked a striking departure from the atmosphere of the 1780s, when state governments had invariably given whites and free blacks the same legal privileges. By 1793 white Americans clearly found it easy to forget that the Constitution had not limited citizenship to their race, and fewer of them felt honor-bound to protect black rights.

The bloody slave revolt on Saint Domingue notably undermined the trend toward abolition and reinforced the kind of fears that spawned racism. Reports of the slaughter of French slaveowners made white Americans more reluctant to criticize slavery in the United States and helped transform the image of blacks from that of victims of injustice to one of a potential menace. In August 1800 smoldering southern white fears were kindled when a slave insurrection broke out near Virginia's capital, Richmond. Having

Slave Artifacts

These objects, uncovered at the site of slave quarters on a large plantation, were used by African-Americans after the day's work was finished. They include part of a fiddle bow, a fragment of a writing slate, pencils, a penknife, dominoes, marbles, and a jew's harp.

secretly assembled weapons, more than a thousand slaves planned to march on Richmond. State militiamen, called out by Governor James Monroe, swiftly put down the conspiracy and executed some thirty-five slaves, including the leader, Gabriel Prosser. "I have nothing more to offer than what General Washington would have had to offer, had he been taken by the British officers and put to trial by them," said one rebel before his execution. "I have ventured my life in endeavoring to obtain the liberty of my countrymen, and I am a willing sacrifice to their cause."

Gabriel's Rebellion confirmed whites' anxieties that Saint Domingue's terrifying experience could be replayed on American soil. For years thereafter, isolated uprisings occurred, and rumors persisted that a massive revolt was brewing. Antislavery sentiment diminished quickly. By 1810 abolitionists ceased to exert political influence, and not until the 1830s would the antislavery movement recover from the damage inflicted by the Saint Domingue revolt.

A different kind of development would also strengthen slavery. During the 1790s demand in the British textile industry stimulated the cultivation of cotton in coastal South Carolina and Georgia. The soil and climate were ideal for growing long-staple cotton, a variety whose fibers could be separated easily from its seed by squeezing it through rollers. In the South's upland and interior regions, however, the only cotton that would thrive was the short-staple variety, whose seed stuck so tenaciously to the fibers that rollers crushed the seeds and ruined the fibers. It was as if southerners had discovered gold only to find that they could not mine it. But in 1793 a Connecticut Yankee, Eli Whitney, rescued the South by inventing a cotton gin that successfully separated the fibers of short-staple cotton from the seed. Quickly copied and improved upon by others, Whitney's invention removed a major obstacle to the spread of cotton cultivation. It gave a new lease on life to plantation slavery and undermined the doubts of those who considered slavery economically outmoded.

By the time Thomas Jefferson assumed the presidency in 1801, free blacks had suffered a subtle erosion of their substantial political gains since 1776, and slaves were no closer to freedom. Two vignettes poignantly communicate the plight of African-Americans. By arrangement with her late husband, Martha Washington freed the family's slaves in 1800, a year after George died. But many of the freed blacks remained impoverished and dependent on the Washington estate because Virginia law prohibited the education of blacks and otherwise denied them the opportunities to realize their freedom. Meanwhile, across the Potomac, work was proceeding on the new national capital that would bear the first president's name. Enslaved blacks performed most of the labor. African-Americans were manifestly losing ground.

CONCLUSION

The United States had survived the perils of birth. First George Washington had steered the country through the initial uncertain years under the new Constitution. But even before his retirement, an outbreak of bitter political strife led to the formation of distinct political parties and threatened the unity of the still fragile new nation. Then a peaceful transfer of power, unprecedented in history, occurred when the Federalists allowed Thomas Jefferson to become president. By 1801 the dangers of civil war and national disintegration had abated, though they had not vanished. Ideological hatreds remained strong, and the West's allegiance to the Union was by no means assured. Racial tensions were growing, not diminishing. It remained to be seen whether Jefferson's liberal version of republicanism could serve as a better philosophy of government than the Federalists' conservative republicanism.

CHRONOLOGY

1787   Pennsylvania Society for the Encouragement of Manufactures and the Useful Arts established.

1789   First Congress convenes in New York.

George Washington sworn in as first president.

Judiciary Act of 1789.

French Revolution begins.

Inaugural Commemorative Mug

1790   Alexander Hamilton submits his Report on the Public Credit and Report on a National Bank to Congress.

Treaty of New York.

1791   Bank of the United States is granted a twenty-year charter.

Vermont admitted to the Union.

Bill of Rights ratified.

Slave uprising begins in French colony of Saint Domingue.

Society for the Encouragement of Useful Manufactures founded.

Hamilton submits his Report on Manufactures to Congress.

1792   Washington reelected president.

Kentucky admitted to the Union.

1793   Fugitive Slave Law.

Chisholm v. *Georgia.*

Large-scale exodus of French planters from Saint Domingue to the United States.

France declares war on Britain and Spain.

Washington's Neutrality Proclamation.

Citizen Genet arrives in United States.

Democratic societies established.

1794   Whiskey Rebellion in western Pennsylvania.

A Contemporary Cartoon, "The Exciseman"

1794   General Anthony Wayne's forces rout Indians in the Battle of Fallen Timbers.

1795   Treaty of Greenville.

Jay's Treaty with Britain ratified.

1796   *Hylton* v. *United States.*

Ware v. *Hylton.*

Tennessee admitted to the Union.

Treaty of San Lorenzo (Pinckney's Treaty) ratified.

Washington's Farewell Address.

John Adams elected president.

1798   XYZ Affair.

Alien and Sedition Acts.

Eleventh Amendment to the Constitution ratified.

1798–1799   Virginia and Kentucky Resolutions.

1798–1800   United States fights Quasi-War with France.

1799   Fries Rebellion in Pennsylvania.

1800   Gabriel's Rebellion in Virginia.

Thomas Jefferson elected president.

For Further Reading

Joyce Appleby, *Capitalism and a New Social Order: The Republican Vision of the 1790s* (1984). A brief, penetrating analysis of Jeffersonian ideology.

Stanley Elkins and Eric McKitrick, *The Age of Federalism: The Early American Republic, 1788–1800* (1993). A magisterial account of politics and diplomacy through the election of 1800.

Richard Hofstadter, *The Idea of a Party System: The Rise of Legitimate Opposition in the United States, 1780–1840* (1969). A classic account of how and why America's founders, originally fearing political parties, came to embrace them.

Drew R. McCoy, *The Elusive Republic: Political Economy in Jeffersonian America* (1980). An insightful portrayal of the influence of economic considerations on early national political thought.

James M. Smith, *Freedom's Fetters: The Alien and Sedition Laws and American Civil Liberties,* rev. ed. (1966). The most comprehensive study of the country's first great crisis in civil rights.

Laurel Thatcher Ulrich, *A Midwife's Tale: The Life of Martha Ballard, Based on Her Diary, 1785–1812* (1990). A Pulitzer Prize–winning study of a woman's life in rural America.

Anthony F. C. Wallace, *The Death and Rebirth of the Seneca* (1969). An anthropologist's masterful account of the Senecas' devastation during the Revolution and their remarkable cultural recovery afterward.

Additional Bibliography

Early National Society

Ira Berlin, *Slaves Without Masters: The Free Negro in the Antebellum South* (1974); James Essig, *Bonds of Wickedness: American Evangelicals Against Slavery, 1770–1808* (1982); Alfred N. Hunt, *Haiti's Influence on Antebellum America* (1989); Robert McColley, *Slavery and Jeffersonian Virginia* (1964); Gary B. Nash, *Forging Freedom: The Formation of Philadelphia's Black Community, 1720–1840* (1990) and *Race and Revolution* (1991); Curtis P. Nettles, *The Emergence of a National Economy, 1775–1815* (1962); Howard B. Rock, *Artisans of the New Republic: The Tradesmen of New York City in the Age of Jefferson* (1979); George C. Rogers, Jr., *Charleston in the Age of the Pinckneys* (1969); Bernard W. Sheehan, *Seeds of Extinction: Jeffersonian Philanthropy and the American Indian* (1973); Billy G. Smith, *The "Lower Sort": Philadelphia's Laboring People, 1750–1800* (1990); Charles G. Steffen, *The Mechanics of Baltimore: Workers and Politics in the Age of Revolution, 1763–1812* (1984); Alan Taylor, *Liberty Men and Great Proprietors: The Revolutionary Settlement on the Maine Frontier, 1760–1820* (1990); Shane White, *Somewhat More Independent: The End of Slavery in New York City, 1770–1810* (1991).

Diplomatic, Military, and Western Affairs

Harry Ammon, *The Genet Mission* (1973); Colin G. Calloway, *Crown and Calumet: British-Indian Relations, 1783–1815* (1987); Alexander DeConde, *Entangling Alliance: Politics and Diplomacy Under George Washington* (1958), Gregory Evans Dowd, *A Spirited Resistance: The North American Indian Struggle for Unity, 1745–1815* (1992); Felix Gilbert, *To the Farewell Address: Ideas of Early American Foreign Policy* (1961); Reginald Horsman, *The Frontier in the Formative Years, 1783–1815* (1970); Richard H. Kohn, *Eagle and Sword: The Federalists and the Creation of the Military Establishment in America, 1783–1802* (1975); Daniel G. Lang, *Foreign Policy in the Early Republic: The Law of Nations and the Balance of Power* (1985); Bradford Perkins, *The First Rapprochement: England and the United States, 1795–1805* (1955); Charles R. Ritcheson, *Aftermath of Revolution: British Policy Toward the United States, 1783–1795* (1969); Thomas P. Slaughter, *The Whiskey Rebellion: Frontier Epilogue to the American Revolution* (1986); Wiley Sword, *President Washington's Indian War: The Struggle for the Old Northwest, 1790–1795* (1985); Mary K. B. Tachau, *Federal Courts in the Early Republic: Kentucky, 1789–1816* (1978); Richard White, *The Middle Ground: Indians, Empires, and Republics in the Great Lakes Region, 1650–1815* (1991); J. Leitch Wright, *Britain and the American Frontier, 1783–1815* (1975).

Politics

Lance Banning, *The Jeffersonian Persuasion: Evolution of a Party Ideology* (1978); Richard Beeman, *The Old Dominion and the New Nation, 1788–1801* (1972); Rudolph M. Bell, *Party and Faction in American Politics: The House of Representatives, 1789–1801* (1974); Richard Buel, Jr., *Securing the Revolution: Ideology in American Politics, 1789–1815* (1972); E. James Ferguson, *The Power of the Purse: A History of American Public Finance, 1776–1790* (1961); Paul Goodman, *The Democratic Republicans of Massachusetts* (1964); John F. Hoadley, *Origins of American Political Parties, 1789–1803* (1986); Ralph Ketcham, *Presidents Above Party: The First American Presidency, 1789–1829* (1984); John C. Miller, *The Federalist Era, 1789–1801* (1960); Peter S. Onuf, ed., *Jeffersonian Legacies* (1993); Thomas L. Pangle, *The Spirit of Modern Republicanism: The Moral Vision of the American Founders and the Followers of Locke* (1988); Lisle A. Rose, *Prologue to Democracy: The Federalists in the South, 1789–1800* (1968); Robert A. Rutland, *The Birth of the Bill of Rights, 1776–1791* (1955); Bernard Schwartz, *The Great Rights of Mankind* (1977); Donald H. Stewart, *The Opposition Press of the Federalist Period* (1969); Gerald Strouzh, *Alexander Hamilton and the Idea of Republican Government* (1970); Alfred F. Young, *The Democratic Republicans of New York: The Origins, 1763–1797* (1967); John Zvesper, *Political Philosophy and Rhetoric: A Study of the Origins of American Party Politics* (1977).

Biographies

Jacob E. Cooke, *Alexander Hamilton* (1982); Marcus Cunliffe, *George Washington: Man and Monument* (1958); John Mack Faragher, *Daniel Boone: The Life and Legend of an American Pioneer* (1992); John Ferling, *John Adams: A Life* (1992); Ralph Ketcham, *James Madison: A Biography* (1971); Forrest McDonald, *Alexander Hamilton: A Biography* (1979); Dumas Malone, *Jefferson and the Ordeal of Liberty* (1962); Richard B. Morris, *John Jay: The Nation and the Court* (1967); Merrill Peterson, *Thomas Jefferson and the New Nation: A Biography* (1970); Peter Shaw, *The Character of John Adams* (1976).

Portrait of Samuel Chester Reid
by John Wesley Jarvis, 1815

JEFFERSONIANISM AND THE ERA OF GOOD FEELINGS

Arriving at a diplomatic reception in 1803, the British minister to the United States, Anthony Merry, was aghast to find the American president, Thomas Jefferson, "ACTUALLY STANDING IN SLIPPERS DOWN AT THE HEELS." Such "utter slovenliness and indifference to appearances," Merry concluded, could only be "intended as an insult, not to me personally, but to the sovereign I represented." In fact, Jefferson intended no insult. He never paid much attention to his dress and believed that pomp and fanfare had gotten out of hand in the administrations of George Washington and John Adams. Jefferson's casual dress, including his penchant for wearing slippers on public occasions, reflected both his personal preference and his desire to restore "republican simplicity" to the American government. That same desire led Jefferson to walk to his inaugural and then back to his boardinghouse, and later to substitute written messages for personal appearances before Congress.

The appearance of the new capital, Washington (inset), reinforced Merry's impression of Americans' shabbiness. Designed for the traffic of London and the elegance of Versailles, Washington possessed neither in 1800. It could boast of two public buildings of note, the president's mansion and the Capitol, both unfinished and separated by a mile and a half of swampy terrain. The best that could be said for the place, a British visitor observed, was that the partridges nesting around the Capitol's wall provided excellent shooting.

Washington's spare arrangements mirrored conditions in the young nation. In 1800 the two most populous states, Virginia and Pennsylvania, contained fewer than fourteen inhabitants per square mile. At a time when London reported more than a million inhabitants and Paris more than half a million, no American city held even seventy thousand people. The poor quality or utter lack of roads forced Americans to live very isolated from each other. Stagecoaches running between Baltimore and Washington, for example, had to pass through a virtually trackless forest. To get to Washington from Monticello, his home in Virginia, President Jefferson had to cross five rivers that lacked bridges.

This isolation ensured that the political horizons of most Americans were limited by the physical boundaries of their own towns or villages. Republicans and Federalists clashed venomously in Washington, but in many rural areas, neither party aroused intense support. The outgoing president, John Adams, had not seen himself as the leader of a political party. The incoming president, Thomas Jefferson, did play the role of party leader and in this respect was a more modern figure than Adams. But neither Jefferson's Republicans nor the rival Federalists had any effective grass roots organization. However sharp the clashes between Republicans and Federalists in Washington, national issues only occasionally concerned ordinary Americans. Women, slaves, and the propertyless were legally barred from voting, and even those citizens who were eligible to vote often found national issues remote and uninteresting. Few voters ever laid eyes on a president. Jefferson, for example, had not been in New England since 1784, and he never did venture west of the Appalachian Mountains or south of Virginia.

Despite its deeply ingrained localism, America was to experience the most extraordinary national events between 1800 and 1820. In swift succession, the United States would double its land area; survive a bizarre scheme by a former vice president to divide the Union; stop all its trade with Europe in an effort to avoid war, and then go to war anyway and nearly lose; conclude a peace more favorable than it had a right to expect; and almost disintegrate in a battle over statehood for Missouri while simultaneously profiting from European power concessions that would extend its territorial claims from the Atlantic to the Pacific.

The intrusion of so dizzying a sequence of events upon a society known for its sleepy provinciality was not altogether accidental. Because communications were poor, the age proved congenial to adventurers like Jefferson's vice president, Aaron Burr, who hatched wild conspiracies with the hope of succeeding before his plans became common knowledge. Furthermore, the strength of local attachments among the common people somewhat insulated leaders like Jefferson and his successor, James Madison, from their constituents. This insulation, in turn, enabled Jefferson and Madison to view politics on a grand scale. In their eyes, politics was more a process for transforming philosophical ideas into realities than for accommodating the special needs of diverse groups.

America's newness also contributed to the philosophical or ideological cast of its politics. Because there had never before been a transfer of political power from a defeated party to a victorious party, no one was sure how the Republicans would behave in office or what would become of the Federalists. The absence of precedents that might have quietly settled certain issues meant that seemingly minor questions such as replacement of Federalist

officeholders became occasions for major philosophical clashes between the Republicans and the Federalists. In sum, one of the tasks that faced Jefferson and Madison was to devise and gain popular acceptance of ground rules to guide the operations of republican government.

◆

THE AGE OF JEFFERSON

Although basically a dispassionate man, Thomas Jefferson aroused deep emotions in others. His admirers saw him as a vigilant defender of popular liberty, an aristocrat who trusted the people. His detractors, pointing to his doubts about some Christian doctrines and to his early defense of the French Revolution, portrayed him as an infidel and a frenzied radical. Jefferson had so many facets that it was hard not to misunderstand him. Trained in law, he spent much of his prepresidential life in public office—as governor of Virginia, secretary of state under Washington, and vice president under John Adams. His interests included the violin, architecture, languages, and science. He designed his own mansion, Monticello, in Virginia; studied Latin, Greek, French, Italian, Anglo-Saxon, and several Native American languages; and served for nearly twenty years as president of the American Philosophical Society, the nation's first and foremost scientific organization. He viewed himself as a stronger friend of equality than either Washington or Adams; yet he owned more than two hundred slaves.

History convinced Jefferson that republics collapsed from within, not from without. Hostile neighbors notwithstanding, the real threat to freedom was posed by governments that progressively undermined popular liberty. Taxes, standing armies, and corrupt officials had made governments the masters, rather than the servants, of the people. Anyone who doubted this lesson of history needed only to look at the French Revolution; Jefferson had greeted it with hope and then watched in dismay as Napoleon Bonaparte assumed despotic power in 1799.

To prevent the United States from sinking into tyranny, Jefferson advocated that state governments retain considerable authority. He reasoned that in a vast republic marked by strong local attachments, state

The World of Thomas Jefferson at Monticello
*Jefferson spent much of his adult life building and remodeling Monticello, his "simple and elegant"
Virginia mansion, and he died there on July 4, 1826, fifty years to the day after the signing of the
Declaration of Independence. Preferring the useful to the showy, he omitted the grand staircase ev-
ident in other mansions, designed the house to appear smaller than it actually was, and filled it with
labor-saving gadgets.*

governments were more immediately responsive to
the popular will than was the government in Washington. He also believed that popular liberty required popular virtue. For republican theorists like Jefferson,
virtue consisted of a disposition to place the public
good ahead of one's private interests and to exercise
vigilance to keep governments from growing out of
control. To Jefferson, the most vigilant and virtuous
people were educated farmers, who were accustomed
to act and think with sturdy independence. The least
vigilant were the inhabitants of cities. Jefferson regarded cities as breeding grounds for mobs and as
menaces to liberty. When the people "get piled upon
one another in large cities, as in Europe," he wrote,
"they will become corrupt as in Europe."

Despite his deep philosophical beliefs, Jefferson
was not impractical. Of all the charges leveled at him
by contemporaries, the most inaccurate was that he
was a dreamy philosopher incapable of governing.
"What is practicable," he wrote, "must often control
pure theory." He studied science not because he liked
to ponder abstract puzzles but because he believed that
every scientific advance would increase human happiness. All true knowledge was useful knowledge. This
practical cast of mind revealed itself both in his inven-

tions—he designed an improved plow and a gadget for
duplicating letters—and in his presidential agenda.

Jefferson's "Revolution"

Jefferson described his election as a revolution, but the
revolution he sought was to restore the country to the
liberty and tranquillity it had known before Alexander
Hamilton's economic program and John Adams's
Alien and Sedition Acts: to reverse the drift into despotism that he had detected during the 1790s. One alarming sign of this drift was the growth of the national debt
by $10 million under the Federalists. Jefferson and his
secretary of the treasury, the Swiss-born Albert Gallatin, objected to the debt on both political and economic grounds. Hamilton had argued that by giving
creditors a financial stake in the health of the federal
government, a national debt would strengthen that
government. Jefferson and Gallatin disagreed. Merely
to pay the interest on the debt, there would have to be
taxes, which Jefferson and Gallatin opposed for many
of the same reasons that they opposed the debt. Taxes
would suck money from industrious farmers, the backbone of the Republic, and put it in the hands of
wealthy creditors, parasites who lived off interest

Explosion of the *Intrepid*
In September 1804 the American fireship Intrepid, *loaded with powder and intending to penetrate Tripoli harbor and explode enemy ships, blew up before reaching its target, killing Captain Richard Somers and his crew. Seven months earlier, commanded by Lieutenant Stephen Decatur, the* Intrepid *had destroyed the American frigate* Philadelphia, *which had fallen into Tripolitan hands. Britain's Lord Nelson reportedly described Decatur's exploit as "the most bold and daring act of the age."*

payments. Increased tax revenues might also tempt the government to create a standing army, always a threat to liberty.

Jefferson and Gallatin induced Congress to repeal most internal taxes, and they slashed expenditures by closing some embassies overseas and reducing the army. The navy was a different matter. In 1801 Jefferson ordered a naval squadron into action in the Mediterranean against the so-called Tripolitan (or Barbary) pirates of North Africa. For centuries, the Muslim rulers of Tripoli, Morocco, Tunis, and Algiers had solved their own budgetary problems by engaging in piracy and extorting tribute in exchange for protection; seamen whom they captured were held for ransom or sold into slavery. Most European powers handed over the fees demanded, but Jefferson calculated that going to war would be cheaper than paying high tribute to maintain peace. Although suffering its share of reverses during the ensuing fighting, the United States did not come away empty-handed. In 1805 it was able to conclude a peace treaty with Tripoli for roughly half the price that it had been paying annually for protection.

Jefferson was not a pacifist and would continue to use the navy to gain respect for the American flag, but he and Gallatin placed economy ahead of military preparedness. Gallatin calculated that the nation could be freed of debt in sixteen years if administrations held the

line on expenditures. In Europe, the Peace of Amiens (1802) brought a temporary halt to the hostilities between Britain and France that had threatened American shipping in the 1790s, and buoyed Jefferson's confidence that minimal military preparedness was a sound policy. The Peace of Amiens, he wrote, "removes the only danger we have to fear. We can now proceed without risks in demolishing useless structures of expense, lightening the burdens of our constituents, and fortifying the principles of free government." This may have been wishful thinking, but it rested on a sound economic calculation, for the vast territory of the United States could never be secured from attack without astronomical expense.

Jefferson and the Judiciary

In his inaugural address, Jefferson reminded Americans that their agreements were more basic than their disagreements. "We have called by different name brothers of the same principle," he proclaimed. "We are all republicans; we are all federalists." He was enough of a realist to know that the political conflict would not evaporate, but he sincerely hoped to allay fear of the Republican party and to draw moderate Federalists over to his side. There was a chance of success. He and John Adams had once been friends. The two shared many views, and each was suspicious of Hamilton. But the eventual reconciliation between Adams and Jefferson (they renewed their friendship after Jefferson's presidency), and more generally between Federalists and Republicans, would not occur during Jefferson's administration, largely because of bitter feelings over the composition and control of the judiciary.

In theory, Jefferson believed that talent and virtue rather than political affiliation were the primary qualifications for judgeships. In theory, Federalists believed the same, but they rarely had detected either talent or virtue among Republicans, and in 1800 not a single Republican sat on the federal judiciary. For Republicans, the crowning blow was the Federalist-sponsored Judiciary Act, passed on February 27, 1801. On the surface, this law had a nonpartisan purpose. By creating sixteen new federal judgeships, the act promised to relieve Supreme Court justices of the burden of riding far from Washington to hear cases. But the act contained several features that struck Jefferson as objectionable, including a provision to reduce the number of justices on the Supreme Court from six to five. This provision threatened both to strip Jefferson of his first opportunity to appoint a justice and to perpetuate Federalist domination of the judiciary.

Recalling the federal courts' zealousness in enforcing the Alien and Sedition Acts, and dismayed by the absence of Republicans on the federal judiciary, Jefferson saw in the Judiciary Act of 1801 a confirmation of his fears that the Federalists were retreating into the judiciary as a stronghold, "and from that battery all the works of Republicanism are to be beaten down and erased." Any lingering doubts Jefferson might have had about Federalist intentions were swept away by the actions of outgoing president John Adams during his last days in office. Between December 12, 1800, the day on which Adams's defeat in the election became clear, and March 4, 1801, the date of Jefferson's inauguration, Adams appointed several last-minute, or "midnight," judges. All federal judges appointed by Adams under provisions of the Judiciary Act were prominent Federalists. Some had been defeated for office during the election of 1800. One had captained a loyalist regiment during the Revolution, and three were brothers or brothers-in-law of John Marshall, the Federalist chief justice who was also the reputed author of the Judiciary Act of 1801.

Some radical Jeffersonians believed that judges should be elected, but Jefferson himself had no quarrel with the practice of appointing judges to serve during "good behavior" (normally for life); indeed, he

thought that an independent judiciary was vital to the success of republican government. But the Federalists seemed to be turning the judiciary into an arm of their party, and in defiance of the popular will. Ironically, it was not the midnight appointments that Adams actually made but one that he left unfinished that stiffened Jefferson's resolve to seek repeal of the Judiciary Act. On his last day in office, Adams appointed an obscure Federalist, William Marbury, as justice of the peace in the District of Columbia but then failed to deliver Marbury's commission before midnight. With Jefferson in office, the new secretary of state, James Madison, refused to release the commission. Marbury petitioned the Supreme Court for a writ of mandamus,* ordering Madison to make the delivery. Chief Justice Marshall then called on Madison to show cause why he should not be compelled to hand over the commission. Although the Supreme Court did not decide the case of *Marbury* v. *Madison* until 1803, Jefferson detected in Marshall's maneuvers the early signs of still another Federalist scheme to use the judiciary to advance partisan interests, and in 1802 he won congressional repeal of the Judiciary Act. The Federalists were in despair. The Constitution, moaned Federalist senator Gouverneur Morris, "is dead. It is dead."

As John Marshall would soon demonstrate, however, the Federalist judiciary was alive and brimming with energy. Like Jefferson, Marshall was a Virginian, but he was the son of an ordinary farmer, not an aristocrat. Marshall's service in the Continental Army during the Revolution had instilled in him (as in Alexander Hamilton) a burning attachment to the Union rather than to any state, and in the 1790s he had embraced the Federalist party. In 1803 Marshall's long-awaited decision in *Marbury* v. *Madison* came down. From the perspective of constitutional history, Marshall's decision would have immense significance, for in it he declared an act of Congress unconstitutional. Specifically, he denied Marbury's petition for a writ of mandamus (to force Madison to deliver his commission) on grounds that Congress had exceeded its constitutional authority when, in the Judiciary Act of 1789, it had granted the Court the authority to issue such a writ. This was the first time the Court declared an act of Congress unconstitutional. It would not do so again until 1857, but the justices had set an important precedent.

*Mandamus: an order from a higher court commanding that a specified action be taken.

John Marshall, *by Chester Harding*
In his three decades as chief justice of the Supreme
Court, Marshall greatly strengthened the power of both
the Court and the national government, each of which
he thought vital to preserving the intrinsic rights of life,
liberty, and property.

Marshall's decision, however, had a different significance for Jefferson. Along with most mainstream
Republicans, Jefferson thought that the courts did
have a right to engage in judicial review (that is, to declare legislative acts unconstitutional). As far as judicial review went, Jefferson merely held that courts
had no *exclusive* right of review; other branches of the
government should also have the right to review the
constitutionality of measures before them. Since Marshall's decision in *Marbury* did not assert that courts
alone could declare laws unconstitutional, Jefferson

had no quarrel with the principle of judicial review as
Marshall advanced it. What infuriated Jefferson was
that Marshall used part of his decision to lecture Madison on his moral duty (as opposed to his legal obligation) to have delivered the commission to Marbury.
This gratuitous lecture—really a lecture to Jefferson
as Madison's superior—struck Jefferson as another
example of Federalist partisanship with respect to the
judiciary.

While the *Marbury* decision was brewing, the Republicans had already taken the offensive against the
judiciary by moving to impeach (charge with wrongdoing) two Federalist judges, John Pickering of the
New Hampshire District Court and Samuel Chase of
the U.S. Supreme Court. The particulars of the two
cases differed. Pickering was an insane alcoholic who
behaved in a bizarre manner in court. In one case, he
decided against the prosecution before hearing any of
its witnesses and then taunted the district attorney that
even if he could present forty thousand witnesses,
"they will not alter the decree." Chase, a notoriously
partisan Federalist, had rigorously enforced the Sedition Act of 1798 and had jailed several Republican editors, including one whom Jefferson had befriended. To
Republicans, Chase was the devil incarnate; all of
them knew that Chase's name formed the correct ending of a popular ditty:

Cursed of thy father, scum of all that's base,
Thy sight is odious, and thy name is . . .

Despite these differing details, the two cases
raised the same issue. The Constitution provided that
federal judges could be removed solely by impeachment, which could be considered only in cases of
"Treason, Bribery and other high Crimes and Misdemeanors." Was impeachment an appropriate way to
get rid of judges who were insane or excessively partisan? Despite misgivings among Federalists and
some Republicans about charging an obviously insane man with crimes and misdemeanors, the Senate
voted to convict Pickering on March 12, 1804. That
same day, the House of Representatives voted to indict
Chase. John Randolph, one of Jefferson's supporters
in Congress, so completely botched the prosecution of
Chase that he failed to obtain the necessary two-thirds
majority for conviction on any of the charges. But
even if Randolph had done a competent job, Chase
might still have gained acquittal, because moderate
Republicans were coming to doubt whether im-

peachment was a solution to the issue of judicial partisanship.

Chase's acquittal ended Jefferson's skirmishes with the judiciary. Although his radical followers continued to attack the principles of judicial review and an appointed judiciary as undemocratic, Jefferson objected to neither. He merely challenged Federalist use of judicial power for political goals. Yet there was always a gray area between law and politics. Federalists did not necessarily see a conflict between protecting the Constitution and advancing their party's cause. Nor did they use their control of the federal judiciary to undo Jefferson's "revolution" of 1800. The Marshall court, for example, upheld the constitutionality of the repeal of the Judiciary Act of 1801. For his part, Jefferson never proposed to impeach Marshall. In supporting the impeachments of Pickering and Chase, Jefferson was trying to make the judiciary more responsive to the popular will by challenging a pair of judges whose behavior had been outrageous. No other federal judge would be impeached for more than fifty years.

The Louisiana Purchase

Jefferson's goal of avoiding foreign entanglements would remain beyond reach as long as European powers had large landholdings in North America. In 1800 Spain, a weak and declining power, controlled East and West Florida as well as the vast Louisiana Territory. The latter alone was equal in size to the United States at that time. In the Treaty of San Ildefonso (October 1, 1800), Spain ceded the Louisiana Territory to France, which was fast emerging under Napoleon Bonaparte as the world's foremost military power. It took six months for news of the treaty to reach Jefferson and Madison but only a few minutes for them to grasp its significance.

Jefferson had long dreamed of an "empire of liberty" extending across North America and even into South America, an empire to be gained not by military conquest but by the inevitable expansion of the free and virtuous American people. An enfeebled Spain constituted no real obstacle to this expansion. As long as Louisiana had belonged to Spain, time was on the side of the United States. But Bonaparte's capacity for mischief was boundless. What if Bonaparte and the British reached an agreement that gave England a free hand in the Mediterranean and France a license to ex-

pand into North America? Then the United States would be sandwiched between the British in Canada and the French in Louisiana. What if Britain refused to cooperate with France? In that case, Britain might use its naval power to seize Louisiana before the French took control, thereby trapping the United States between British forces in the South and West as well as in the North and West.

Although Americans feared these two possibilities, Bonaparte actually had a different goal. During the 1790s he had dreamed of a French empire in the Middle East, but his defeat by the British fleet at the Battle of the Nile in 1798 had blasted this dream. Now Bonaparte devised a plan for a new French empire, this one bordering the Caribbean and the Gulf of Mexico. The fulcrum of the empire was to be the Caribbean island of Santo Domingo (today comprising Haiti and the Dominican Republic). He wanted to use Louisiana not as a base from which to threaten the United States but as a breadbasket for an essentially Caribbean empire. His immediate task was to subdue Santo Domingo, where a bloody slave revolution in the 1790s had resulted by 1800 in the takeover of the government by the black statesman Toussaint L'Ouverture (see Chapter 7). Bonaparte dispatched an army to reassert French control and to reestablish slavery, but yellow fever and fierce resistance on the part of former slaves combined to destroy the army.

As a slaveholder himself, Jefferson tacitly approved Bonaparte's attempted reconquest of Santo Domingo; as a nationalist, he continued to fear a French presence in Louisiana. This fear intensified in October 1802, when the Spanish colonial administrator in New Orleans issued an order prohibiting the deposit of American produce in New Orleans for transshipment to foreign lands. Because American farmers west of the Appalachians depended on New Orleans as a port for the cash crops that they shipped down the Mississippi River, the order was a major provocation to Americans. The order had in fact originated in Spain, but most Americans assumed that it had come from Bonaparte, who, although he now owned Louisiana, had not yet taken possession of it. An alarmed Jefferson wrote to a friend that "the day that France takes possession of N. Orleans . . . we must marry ourselves to the British fleet and nation."

The combination of France's failure to subdue Santo Domingo and the termination of American rights

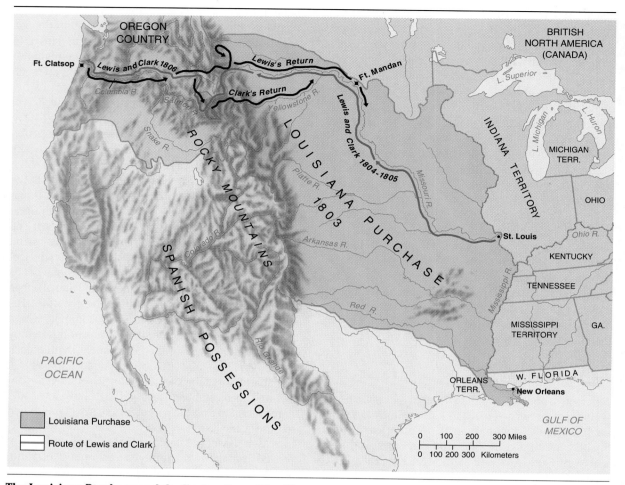

The Louisiana Purchase and the Exploration of the West
The explorations of Lewis and Clark demonstrated the vast extent of the area purchased from France.

to deposit produce in New Orleans stimulated two crucial decisions, one by Jefferson and the other by Bonaparte, that ultimately resulted in the United States' purchase of Louisiana. First, Jefferson nominated James Monroe and Robert R. Livingston to negotiate with France for the purchase of New Orleans and as much of the Floridas as possible. (Because West Florida had repeatedly changed hands between France, Britain, and Spain, no one was sure who owned it.) Meanwhile, Bonaparte, mindful of his military failure in Santo Domingo and of American opposition to French control of Louisiana, had concluded that his projected Caribbean empire was not worth the cost. In addition,

he planned to recommence the war in Europe and needed cash. Accordingly, he decided to sell *all* of Louisiana. After some haggling between the American commissioners and Bonaparte's minister, Talleyrand, a price of $15 million was settled upon. (One-fourth of the total represented an agreement by the United States to pay French debts owed to American citizens.) For this sum the United States gained an immense, uncharted territory west of the Mississippi River. No one knew its exact size; Talleyrand merely observed that the bargain was noble. But the purchase virtually doubled the area of the United States at a cost, omitting interest, of 13½¢ an acre.

Because Jefferson's commissioners had exceeded their instructions, however, the president had doubts about the constitutionality of the purchase. No provision of the Constitution explicitly gave the government authority to acquire new territory or to incorporate it into the Union. Jefferson therefore drafted a constitutional amendment that authorized the acquisition of territory and prohibited the American settlement of Louisiana for an indefinite period. Fearing that an immediate and headlong rush to settle the area would lead to the destruction of the Native Americans and to an orgy of land speculation, Jefferson wanted to control development so that Americans could advance "compactly as we multiply." Few Republicans, however, shared Jefferson's constitutional reservations, and the president himself soon began to worry that ratification of an amendment would take too long and that Bonaparte might in the meantime change his mind about selling Louisiana. Consequently, he quietly dropped the amendment and submitted the treaty to the Senate, where it was quickly ratified.

It is easy to make too much of Jefferson's dilemma over Louisiana. He was wedded to strict construction of the Constitution, believing that the Constitution should be interpreted according to its letter. But he was also committed to the principle of establishing an "empire of liberty." Doubling the size of the Republic would guarantee land for American farmers, the backbone of the Republic and the true guardians of liberty. Like the principle of states' rights to which Jefferson also subscribed, strict construction was not an end in itself but a means to promote republican liberty. If that end could be achieved by some way other than strict construction, so be it. In addition, Jefferson was alert to practical considerations. Most Federalists opposed the Louisiana Purchase on the grounds that it would decrease the relative importance of their strongholds on the eastern seaboard. As the leader of the Republican party, Jefferson saw no reason to hand the Federalists an issue by dallying over ratification of the treaty.

The Lewis and Clark Expedition

Louisiana dazzled Jefferson's imagination. Here was an immense territory about which Americans knew virtually nothing. No one was sure of its western boundary. A case could be made for the Pacific Ocean, but Jefferson was content to claim that Louisiana extended at least to the mountains west of the Missis-

sippi. No one, however, was certain of the exact location of these mountains, because few Americans had ever seen them. Jefferson himself had never been more than fifty miles west of his home in Virginia. Thus the Louisiana Purchase was both a bargain and a surprise package.

Even before the acquisition of Louisiana, Jefferson had planned an exploratory expedition; picked its leader, his personal secretary and fellow Virginian Lieutenant Meriwether Lewis; and sent him to Philadelphia for a crash course in sciences such as zoology, astronomy, and botany that were relevant to exploration. Jefferson instructed Lewis to trace the Missouri River to its source, cross the western highlands, and follow the best water route to the Pacific. In requesting congressional funding for the expedition, Jefferson stressed the commercial possibilities that it might uncover; along the line of the Missouri and beyond, the Indians' trade in pelts might be diverted from Canada to the south. But the advance of scientific knowledge probably had a higher priority for Jefferson. His specific instructions to Lewis focused on the need to obtain accurate measurements of latitude and longitude; to gather information about Native American languages and customs; and to learn about climate, plants, birds, reptiles, insects, and volcanoes.

Setting forth from St. Louis in May 1804, Lewis, his second-in-command William Clark, and about fifty others followed the Missouri River and then the Snake and Columbia rivers. In the Dakota country, Lewis and Clark hired a French-Canadian fur trader, Toussaint Charbonneau, as a guide and interpreter. Slow-witted and inclined to panic in crises, Charbonneau proved a mixed blessing, but his wife, Sacajawea, who accompanied him on the trip, made up for his failings. A Shoshone and probably no more than sixteen years old in 1804, Sacajawea had been stolen by a rival tribe and then claimed by Charbonneau, perhaps in settlement for a gambling debt. When first encountered by Lewis and Clark, she had just given birth to a son; indeed, her infant's presence helped to reassure Native American tribes of the expedition's peaceful intent. Additionally, Sacajawea showed Lewis and Clark how to forage for wild artichokes and other plants, often their only food, by digging into the dens where rodents stored them. Clutching her baby, she rescued most of the expedition's scientific instruments after a storm capsized one of its boats on the Missouri River.

William Clark and Meriwether Lewis, *by Charles Willson Peale Clark, the brother of the famed Indian fighter George Rogers Clark, fought at the Battle of Fallen Timbers. He later became the governor of Missouri and an outspoken advocate of the interests of the Native Americans, whom he had opposed in his youth. Lewis grew up near Jefferson's Virginia home and later served as his personal secretary.*

Plains Pipe Bowl
Instructed by Jefferson to acquaint themselves with the Indians' "ordinary occupations in the arts," Lewis and Clark collected this Lakota sacred pipe, whose red stone symbolized the flesh and blood of all people and whose smoke represented the breath that carries prayers to the Creator. Considering pipes sacred objects, Indians used them to seal contracts and treaties and to perform ceremonial healing.

The group finally reached the Pacific Ocean in November 1805 and then returned to St. Louis, but not before collecting a mass of scientific information, including the disturbing fact that more than three hundred miles of mountains separated the Missouri from the Columbia. It also produced a sprinkling of tall tales, many of which Jefferson believed, about gigantic Indians, soil too rich to grow trees, and a mountain composed of salt. Jefferson's political opponents railed that he would soon be reporting the discovery of a molasses-filled lake. For all the ridicule, the expedition stimulated rather than dampened interest in the West.

The Election of 1804

Jefferson's acquisition of Louisiana left the Federalists dispirited and without a popular national issue. As the election of 1804 approached, the main threat to Jefferson was not the Federalist party but his own vice president, Aaron Burr. In 1800 Burr had tried to take advantage of a tie in the electoral college to gain the

The Election of 1804

Candidates	Parties	Electoral Vote
THOMAS JEFFERSON	Democratic-Republican	162
Charles C. Pinckney	Federalist	14

presidency, a betrayal in the eyes of most Republicans, who assumed that he had been nominated for the vice presidency. Although the adoption in 1804 of the Twelfth Amendment, which required separate and distinct ballots in the electoral college for the presidency and vice presidency, put an end to the possibility of an electoral tie for the presidency, it did not put an end to Burr. Between 1801 and 1804, Burr entered into enough intrigues with the Federalists to convince the Republicans that it would be unsafe to renominate him for the vice presidency. The Republicans in Congress rudely dumped Burr in favor of George Clinton. Without a hope of success, the Federalists nominated Charles C. Pinckney and Rufus King and then watched their candidates go down in complete and crushing defeat in the election. The Federalists carried only two states, failing to hold even Massachusetts. Jefferson's overwhelming victory brought his first term to a fitting close; between 1801 and 1804, the United States had doubled its territory, taken steps to pay off its debt, and remained at peace. In short, Jefferson basked in the sun of success.

THE GATHERING STORM

The sky was not cloudless for long. In gaining control of Louisiana, the United States had benefited from the preoccupation of European powers with their own struggles. The nation would again benefit from this preoccupation between 1814 and 1823. But between 1803 and 1814, the renewal of the Napoleonic wars in Europe turned the United States into a pawn in a chess game played by others and helped to make Jefferson's second term far less successful than his first. In fact, the very success of his first administration contained the germs of problems that would plague his second term. As long as the two parties could compete on a more or less even basis, as in the election of 1800,

leaders within each party could demand unity as a prerequisite for victory. But as the Federalist opposition weakened, unity among Republicans became less important, and they increasingly fell victim to internal squabbles.

Jefferson's Coalition Fragments

For the moment, the election of 1804 eliminated the Federalists as a force in national politics. More troubling to Republicans than Federalist opposition was factionalism within their own party, much of it the product of the inventive and perverse mind of Aaron Burr. Burr suffered a string of reverses in 1804. After being denied renomination as vice president, he entered into a series of intrigues with a faction of despairing and extreme (or "High") Federalists in New England. Led by Senator Timothy Pickering of Massachusetts, these High Federalists plotted to sever the Union by forming a pro-British "Northern Confederacy," composed of Nova Scotia (part of British-owned Canada), New England, New York, and even Pennsylvania. Although most Federalists disdained the plot, Pickering and others settled on Burr as their leader and helped him gain the Federalist nomination for the governorship of New York. Alexander Hamilton, who had thwarted Burr's plans for the presidency in 1800 by throwing his weight behind Jefferson, now foiled Burr a second time by allowing the publication of his "despicable opinion" of Burr. Defeated by a Republican in the election for New York's governor, Burr challenged Hamilton to a duel and mortally wounded him at Weehawken, New Jersey, on July 11, 1804.

Under indictment in two states for his murder of Hamilton, Burr, still vice president, now hatched a scheme so bold that it gained momentum initially because his political opponents seriously doubted that even Burr was capable of such machinations. He allied himself with the unsavory general James Wilkinson, the military governor of the Louisiana Territory. Wilkinson had been on Spain's payroll intermittently as a secret agent since the 1780s. Together, Burr and Wilkinson conspired to separate the western states into an independent confederacy south of the Ohio River. In addition, Wilkinson had long entertained the idea of an American conquest of Mexico, and Burr now added West Florida as a possible target. They presented these ideas to westerners as having the covert support of the administration, to the British as a way to attack Spanish-owned Mexico and West Florida, and to the Spanish (removing Mexico and West Florida as targets) as a way to divide up the United States.

Jefferson, who described Burr as a crooked gun that never shot straight, let the plot germinate for more than a year before taking action. By the fall of 1806, Burr and about sixty followers had left their staging ground, an island in the upper Ohio River, and were making their way down the Ohio and Mississippi rivers to join Wilkinson at Natchez. But Wilkinson was not there to greet Burr and his several boatloads of conspirators. Recognizing that Jefferson was now moving against Burr and that the British were uninterested in supporting the plot, Wilkinson wrote to Jefferson to report the conspiracy and then took refuge in New Orleans, where he proclaimed himself the most loyal of the president's followers.

A few weeks later, in October 1806, Jefferson officially denounced the conspiracy. Now Burr panicked. He tried to escape to West Florida but was intercepted; brought back to Richmond, he was put on trial for treason. Chief Justice Marshall presided at the trial and charged the jury that the prosecution had to prove not merely that Burr had treasonable intentions but also that he had committed treasonable acts, a virtually impossible task inasmuch as the conspiracy had fallen apart before Burr accomplished what he had planned. Jefferson was furious, but Marshall was merely following the clear wording of the Constitution, which deliberately made treason difficult to prove. The jury returned a verdict of "not proved," which Marshall entered as "not guilty." Still under indictment for his murder of Hamilton, Burr fled to Europe, where he tried to interest Napoleon in making peace with Britain as a prelude to a proposed Anglo-French invasion of the United States and Mexico. He returned to the United States in 1812 and, in keeping with his reputation as a womanizer, fathered two illegitimate children in his seventies and was divorced for adultery at eighty. Perhaps the most puzzling man in American history, he died in 1836.

Jefferson and the Quids

Besides the Burr conspiracy, Jefferson faced a challenge from a group of Republicans known as the Quids,* who were led by the president's fellow Vir-

---

*Quid: a name taken from the Latin *tertium quid,* or "third thing"; roughly, a dissenter.

ginian John Randolph. A man of abounding eccentricities and acidic wit, Randolph stood squarely in the tradition of the "country" ideology of the 1770s, the set of beliefs that celebrated the honest wisdom of the farmer against the corruption of rulers and "court" hangers-on and that warned against the tendency of all governments to encroach on liberty. Jefferson had started out with the same beliefs but had gradually recognized their limitations. Country ideology was a stance for those out of power, an ideology of opposition rather than governance. In gaining political power, Jefferson had learned to compromise. Randolph, in contrast, remained frozen in an earlier time period. He denounced every change as a decline from the purity of 1776 and once said that he would throw all politicians to the dogs if he had less respect for dogs.

After serving in the House of Representatives between 1801 and 1805, Randolph turned on Jefferson. First, he blasted Jefferson for backing a compromise in the Yazoo land scandal. In 1795 the Georgia legislature had sold the huge "Yazoo" tract (35 million acres comprising most of present-day Alabama and Mississippi) for a fraction of its value to four land companies that had bribed virtually the entire legislature. Responding to public outrage, the next legislature canceled the sale, but not before many investors had purchased land. The scandal posed a moral challenge for Jefferson because some of the purchasers, knowing nothing of the bribery, had bought the land in good faith. It presented a political challenge, too, because some of the buyers were northerners whom Jefferson hoped to woo to the Republican party. In 1803 a federal commission awarded 5 million acres to Yazoo investors as a compromise. For Randolph, the compromise was itself a scandal—further evidence of the decay of republican virtue.

Randolph next collided with Jefferson over the president's request for a congressional appropriation to purchase East and West Florida from Spain. Characteristically, Randolph raged less at the idea of obtaining the Floridas than at Jefferson's apparent act of deception in requesting money for extraordinary diplomatic expenses without officially informing Congress of the real object of the expenditures. In fact, Jefferson had privately informed members of Congress, including Randolph, of his plans for the purchase; but to Randolph, it all seemed like another betrayal of virtue.

The Suppression of American Trade

Burr's acquittal and Randolph's taunts shattered the aura of invincibility that had surrounded Jefferson after the Louisiana Purchase and the election of 1804. Now foreign affairs began to pose an even sharper challenge to his administration. In 1803 the Peace of Amiens collapsed. Britain and France resumed their war. As a neutral, the United States prospered at Britain's expense. American vessels carried sugar and coffee from French and Spanish colonies in the Caribbean to Europe. This trade not only provided Napoleon with supplies but also drove down the price of sugar and coffee from the British West Indies by adding to the glut of these commodities on the world markets. Understandably, the British concluded that American prosperity was the cause of Britain's economic difficulties.

The basis of the American prosperity was the re-export trade—an American adaptation to the British Rule of 1756, which stated that trade closed in time of peace could not be opened in time of war. For example, in peacetime, France usually restricted to French ships the transportation of products such as sugar from the French West Indies. According to the Rule of 1756, the ships of a neutral country such as the United States could not replace French ships as carriers now that the war between France and Britain made French vessels fair game for the British navy. The American response to the Rule of 1756 was the "broken voyage." American vessels would carry produce from the Spanish and French West Indies to an American port, unload it and pass it through customs, then reload it and reexport it to Europe as *American* produce. Between 1795 and 1805, the British tolerated broken voyages but thereafter charted a new course. Seeking now to strangle French commerce as well as to defeat Napoleon's armies, Britain pursued total war against France. A sign of the new policy was a British court's decision in the 1805 *Essex* case declaring broken voyages illegal.

The British followed the *Essex* decision in May 1806 with the first of several trade regulations known as Orders in Council, which established a blockade of French-controlled ports on the continent of Europe. Napoleon responded with his so-called Continental System, a series of counterproclamations that ships obeying British regulations would be subject to seizure by France. In effect, this Anglo-French war of decrees outlawed virtually all U.S. trade: if an American ship complied with British regulations, it became a French target, and vice versa.

Both Britain and France seized American ships, but British seizures were far more humiliating to Americans. France was a weaker naval power than Britain; much of the French fleet had been destroyed by the British at the Battle of Trafalgar in October 1805. Accordingly, most of France's seizures of American ships occurred in European ports where American ships had been lured by Napoleon's often inconsistent enforcement of his Continental System. In contrast, British warships hovered just beyond the American coast. Off New York, for example, the Royal Navy stopped and searched virtually every American vessel. At times, U.S. ships had to line up a few miles from the American coast to be searched by the Royal Navy.

Impressment

On top of these provocations, the British added that of impressment. At issue was the seizure from American merchant ships, and the subsequent pressing into service, of purported British sailors who had deserted from the Royal Navy.

British sailors had good reason to be discontented with the navy. Aside from the fact that discipline on the Royal Navy's "floating hells" was often brutal, wages were much lower than on American ships. The pay of an able-bodied seaman on a British ship was only around seven dollars a month, compared to twenty-five to thirty-five dollars a month on American ships. As a result, at a time when war intensified Britain's need for sailors, the Royal Navy suffered a high rate of desertion to U.S. ships; for example, in 1807 the American frigate *Constitution* carried a crew of 419 men, of whom 149 were British subjects.

Impressed sailors led harrowing lives that included frequent escapes and recaptures. One seaman suffered impressment on eleven separate occasions; another, on the verge of his third recapture, drowned himself rather than spend another day in the Royal Navy. The British practice of impressment was not only cruel to individuals but galling to American pride, because many deserters from the Royal Navy had acquired American naturalization papers and become American citizens. The British impressed these men anyway on the principle that once a Briton, always a Briton. At times, the British also impressed American-born citizens, despite documentation proving their

American birth. Between 1803 and 1812, the British impressed over six thousand American citizens. Although impressment did less damage to the American economy than the seizure of ships, it was more humiliating.

Any doubts Americans had about British arrogance evaporated in June 1807 when a British warship, HMS *Leopard,* patrolling off Hampton Roads, Virginia, attacked an unsuspecting American frigate, USS *Chesapeake,* and forced it to surrender. The British then boarded the vessel and seized four supposed deserters. One, a genuine deserter, was later hanged; the other three were former Britons, now American citizens, who had "deserted" only from impressment. Even the British had never before asserted their right to seize deserters off government ships. The so-called *Chesapeake* Affair enraged the country. Jefferson remarked that he had not seen so belligerent a spirit in America since 1775. Yet while making some preparations for war, the president sought peace—first by conducting fruitless negotiations with Britain to gain redress for the *Chesapeake* outrage, and second by steering the Embargo Act through Congress in December 1807.

The Embargo Act

By far the most controversial legislation of either of Jefferson's administrations, the Embargo Act prohibited vessels from leaving American ports for foreign ports. Technically, it prohibited only exports, but its practical effect was to stop imports as well, for few foreign ships would venture into American ports if they had to leave without cargo. Amazed by the boldness of the act, a British newspaper described the embargo as "little

short of an absolute secession from the rest of the civilized world."

Jefferson advocated the embargo as a means of "peaceable coercion." By restricting French and British (especially British) trade with the United States, he hoped to pressure both nations into respecting American neutrality. But the embargo did not have the effect that Jefferson intended. Although British sales to the United States dropped 50 percent between 1807 and 1808, the British quickly found new markets in South America, where rebellions against Spanish rule had flared up, and in Spain itself, where a revolt against Napoleon had opened trade to British shipping. Furthermore, the Embargo Act itself contained some loopholes. For example, it allowed American ships blown off course to put in at European ports if necessary; suddenly, many captains were reporting that adverse winds had forced them across the Atlantic. Treating the embargo as a joke, Napoleon seized whatever American ships he could lay hands on and then informed the United States that he was only helping to enforce the embargo. The British were less amused, but the embargo confirmed their view that Jefferson was an ineffectual philosopher, an impotent challenger compared with Napoleon.

The harshest effects of the embargo were felt not in Europe but in the United States. Some thirty thousand American seamen found themselves out of work. Merchants stumbled into bankruptcy by the hundreds, and jails swelled with debtors. A New York City newspaper ruefully noted that the only activity still flourishing in the city was prosecution for debt. Farmers, too, were devastated. Unable to export their produce or sell

The Embargo Act
This nasty lampoon of the Embargo Act portrays the tiny Madison, left, parroting Jefferson's policy. Here Madison is made to say: "France wants an embargo & must have it," an expression of the widespread view that the embargo favored the French at America's expense.

it at a decent price to hard-pressed urban dwellers, many farmers could not earn enough cash to pay their debts. In desperation, one farmer in Schoharie County, New York, sold his cattle, horses, and farm implements, worth eight hundred dollars before the embargo, for fifty-five dollars. Speculators who had purchased land expecting to sell it later at a higher price also took a beating, because cash-starved farmers stopped buying land. "I live and that is all," wrote one New York speculator. "I am doing no business, cannot sell anybody property, nor collect any money."

The embargo fell hardest on New England and particularly on Massachusetts, which in 1807 had twice the ship tonnage per capita of any other state and more than a third of the entire nation's ship tonnage in foreign trade. For a state so dependent on foreign trade, the embargo was a calamity. Wits reversed the letters of *embargo* to form the phrase "O grab me."

The picture was not entirely bleak. The embargo forced a diversion of merchants' capital into manufacturing. In short, unable to export produce, Americans began to make products. Before 1808 the United States had only fifteen mills for fashioning cotton into textiles; by the end of 1809, an additional eighty-seven mills had been constructed. But none of this comforted merchants already ruined or mariners driven to soup kitchens. Nor could New Englanders forget that the source of their misery was a policy initiated by one of the "Virginia lordlings," "Mad Tom" Jefferson, who knew little about New England and who had a dogmatic loathing of cities, the very foundations of New England's prosperity. A Massachusetts poet wrote:

> Our ships all in motion once whitened the ocean,
> They sailed and returned with a cargo;
> Now doomed to decay they have fallen a prey
> To Jefferson, worms, and embargo.

The Election of 1808

Even before the Embargo Act, Jefferson had announced that he would not be a candidate for reelection. With his blessing, the Republican congressional caucus nominated James Madison and George Clinton for the presidency and vice presidency, whereas the Federalists countered with Charles C. Pinckney and Rufus King, the same ticket that had made a negligible showing in 1804. In 1808 the Federalists staged a modest comeback, gaining twenty-four congressional seats. Still, Madison won 122 of 175 electoral votes for

The Election of 1808

Candidates	Parties	Electoral Vote
JAMES MADISON	Democratic-Republican	122
Charles C. Pinckney	Federalist	47
George Clinton	Democratic-Republican	6

president, and the Republicans retained comfortable majorities in both houses of Congress.

Several factors contributed to the Federalists' revival in 1808. First, the embargo gave them the national issue that they had long lacked. Also, younger Federalists, represented by men like Harrison Gray Otis of Massachusetts and Robert G. Harper of South Carolina, were making their influence felt. Old-time Federalists, expecting the voters to defer naturally to gentlemen, had refused to campaign actively for votes, and they judged it disgraceful that their Republican opponents treated voters to barbecues and staged mass meetings. The younger Federalists, on the other hand, deliberately imitated the vote-winning techniques that had proved successful for the Republicans.

The Failure of Peaceable Coercion

To some contemporaries, the diminutive "Little Jemmy" Madison (he was only five feet, four inches tall) seemed a weak and shadowy figure alongside the commanding presence of Jefferson. But in fact, Madison brought to the presidency an intelligence and a capacity for systematic thought that matched Jefferson's. Like Jefferson, Madison believed that American liberty had to rest on the virtue of the people and that that virtue was critically tied to the growth and prosperity of agriculture. More clearly than Jefferson, Madison also recognized that agricultural prosperity depended on the vitality of American trade, for Americans would continue to enter farming only if they could get their crops to market. In particular, the British West Indies, dependent on the United States for much of their lumber and grain, struck Madison as a natural trading partner for the United States. Britain alone could not fully supply the West Indies. Therefore, if the United States embargoed its own trade with the West Indies, Madison reasoned, the British would be forced to their knees before Americans could suffer severe losses from the embargo. Britain, he wrote, was "more vulnerable in her commerce than in her armies."

The problem was that the American embargo was coercing no one. Increased trade between Canada and the West Indies after 1808 made a shambles of Madison's plan to pressure Britain by blocking American trade to the West Indies. On March 1, 1809, Congress repealed the Embargo Act and substituted the weaker, although face-saving, Non-Intercourse Act. This act opened American trade to all nations except Britain and France and authorized the president to restore trade with either nation if it ceased to violate neutral rights. But the act failed to persuade the British or the French to respect American shipping. Grasping at straws, Madison then negotiated an agreement with David Erskine, the British minister in Washington, to reopen American trade in return for a British promise to revoke its Orders in Council. That same day, June 10, 1809, some six hundred American ships sailed for Britain. But Erskine had acted without orders. British Foreign Secretary George Canning disavowed the Erskine agreement as soon as he got wind of it, and Madison was forced to reembargo trade with Britain.

Madison called Canning's policy a "mixture of fraud and folly," but Canning thought that he was pursuing a level-headed course of action and had trouble understanding American belligerence. Canning and most British statesmen saw the world as containing a few great powers like Britain and France and innumerable small and weak powers. When great powers waged war against each other, there were no neutrals. Weak nations such as the United States should logically seek the protection of a great power. Since Britain was a natural trading partner for the United States, Americans should recognize, the reasoning went, that their best interests would be served by peacefully submitting to dependency on Britain. The problem was that Jefferson and Madison refused to accept this British conception of power relationships. In their view, the United States, however weak its military, was a nation founded on majestic principles that made it morally superior to Europe. The outgrowth of vanity and ambition, Europe's wars were of no concern to Americans. Jefferson wrote of France and England: "The one is a den of robbers and the other of pirates."

As an economic boom swept across Britain in 1809, the failure of the American policy of peaceable coercion was becoming obvious. Nor was that policy having a noticeable impact on France. Holding the same view of international power relations as the British, Napoleon tried to manipulate the United States into a collision course with Britain. Confronted by implacable hostility from Britain and France, Congress continued to drift. In May 1810 it substituted Macon's Bill No. 2 for the Non-Intercourse Act. The Macon legislation reopened trade with Britain and France and then offered a clumsy bribe to each: if either Britain or France repealed its restrictions on neutral shipping, the United States would halt all commerce with the other. Jumping at the opportunity presented by Macon's Bill No. 2, Napoleon promised to repeal his edicts against American trade. Madison snapped at the bait and proclaimed non-intercourse against Britain. But Napoleon had no intention of respecting American neutrality. His plan all along had been to trick the Americans into a posture of hostility toward Britain, and he continued to seize American ships spotted in French-controlled ports. Peaceable coercion had become a fiasco.

The Push into War

Madison soon found himself faced not only by a hostile Britain and France but by militants within his own party who demanded more aggressive policies. Most of these men were southerners and westerners. Coming from regions where honor was a sacred word, they were infuriated by insults to the American flag. In addition, when an economic recession struck the South and West between 1808 and 1810, South Carolina's John C. Calhoun and others realized that British policies were wrecking the economies of their regions. Consequently, a war spirit began to pulsate in the veins of several young congressmen elected in 1810. Drawn mainly from the South and West, these hotbloods formed a cohesive group, dubbed the "war hawks," in the House of Representatives. Their leader was a thirty-four-year-old Kentuckian, Henry Clay, who preferred war to the "putrescent pool of ignominious peace." With the support of the other war hawks, such as Calhoun, Richard M. Johnson of Kentucky, and William R. King of North Carolina—all of them future vice presidents—Clay was elected to the speakership of the House over the aging Nathaniel Macon, the author of Macon's Bill No. 2.

Tecumseh and the Prophet

Voicing a more emotional and pugnacious nationalism than Jefferson and Madison, the war hawks called for the expulsion of the British from Canada and the Spanish from the Floridas. Their demands merged with western settlers' fears that the British in Canada were actively recruiting the Indians to halt the march of American settlement. These fears, groundless but plausible, became intense when the Shawnee chief Tecumseh and his half-brother the Prophet sought to unite several tribes in Ohio and the Indiana territory against American settlers. Demoralized by the continu-

Tenskwatawa, the Prophet

In periods of crisis, the Native American cultures often gave rise to prophets—religious revivalists of sorts—such as Tecumseh's brother Tenskwatawa. Known to non-Indians as the Prophet, Tenskwatawa tried to revive traditional Indian values and customs such as the common ownership of land and the wearing of animal skins and furs. His religious program blended with Tecumseh's political program to unite the western tribes.

ing loss of Native American lands to the whites and by the ravages of Native American society by alcoholism, Tecumseh and the Prophet (himself a reformed alcoholic) tried to unify their people and revive traditional Native American virtues. Both men believed that the Indians had to purge themselves of liquor and other corrupting messengers of white civilization as part of this revival. For example, to express his rejection of the whites' ways, Tecumseh long refused to learn English.

The aspirations of these Shawnee leaders set them on a collision course with Governor William Henry Harrison of the Indiana Territory. A wily bargainer, Harrison had purchased much of central and western Indiana from the Miami and the Delaware Indians in the Treaty of Fort Wayne (1809) for the paltry sum of ten thousand dollars. When Tecumseh's Shawnee people had refused to sign the treaty, however, Harrison began to regard the brilliant and charismatic Native American leader as an enemy.

With white settlers in Indiana convinced that Tecumseh's effort to unite the Indians was a scheme inspired by the British, Harrison gathered an army in September 1811 and marched against a Shawnee encampment, the Prophet's Town, at the junction of the Wabash and Tippecanoe rivers. Then in November the Shawnees, led by the Prophet (Tecumseh was off recruiting Creek Indians), attacked Harrison. In the ensuing Battle of Tippecanoe, the Shawnees were beaten, the Prophet's Town was destroyed, and the Prophet was discredited in Tecumseh's eyes for his premature attack. Ironically, the Battle of Tippecanoe, which made Harrison a national hero, accomplished precisely what it had been designed to prevent. Never before a British agent, Tecumseh now joined with the British.

Congress Votes for War

By the spring of 1812, President Madison had reached the decision that war with Britain was inevitable. On June 1 he sent his war message to Congress. Meanwhile, an economic depression struck Britain, partly because the American policy of restricting trade with that country had finally started to work. Under pressure from its merchants, Britain repealed the Orders in Council on June 23, but by then Congress, unaware that the British were contemplating repeal of the orders, had passed the declaration of war. It was still possible, of course, for Madison to revoke the declaration now that the maritime issue had been partly settled.

The British cabinet believed that he would do so. What the British failed to comprehend, however, was how much more belligerent American political leaders, particularly Republicans, had become between 1810 and 1812.

Although both war hawks and westerners had contributed to this hostile mood, neither held the key to the vote in favor of war. The war hawks composed a minority within the Republican party; the West was still too sparsely settled to have many representatives in Congress. Rather, the votes of Republicans in populous states like Pennsylvania, Maryland, and Virginia were the main force propelling the war declaration through Congress. Most opposition to war came from Federalist strongholds in Massachusetts, Connecticut, and New York. Because Federalists were so much stronger in the Northeast than elsewhere, congressional opposition to war revealed a sectional as well as a party split. In general, however, southern Federalists opposed the war declaration, whereas northern Republicans supported it. In other words, the vote for war followed party lines more closely than sectional lines. Much like James Madison himself, the typical Republican advocate of war had not wanted war in 1810 nor even in 1811 but had been led by the accumulation of grievances to demand it in 1812.

The Causes of the War

In his war message, Madison listed impressment, the continued presence of British ships in American waters, and British violations of neutral rights as grievances that justified war. But none of these complaints was new. Taken together, they do not fully explain why Americans went to war in 1812 rather than earlier—for example, in 1807 after the *Chesapeake* affair. Madison also listed British incitement of the Indians as a stimulus for war. This grievance of recent origin contributed to war feeling in the West. "The War on the Wabash," a Kentucky newspaper proclaimed, "is purely British. The British scalping knife has filled many habitations both in this state as well as in the Indiana Territory with widows and orphans." But the West had too few American inhabitants to account for the nation's being propelled into war. A more important underlying cause was the economic recession that affected the South and West after 1808—and the conviction, held by John C. Calhoun and others, that British policy was damaging America's economy. Finally, the fact that Madison rather than Jefferson was president in 1812 was of ma-

jor importance. Jefferson had believed that the only motive behind British seizures of American ships was Britain's desire to block American trade with Napoleon. Hence Jefferson had concluded that time was on America's side; the seizures would stop as soon as the war in Europe ceased. In contrast, Madison had become persuaded that Britain's real motive was to strangle American trade once and for all and thereby eliminate the United States as a trading rival. War or no war in Europe, Madison saw Britain as a menace to America. In his war message, he stated flatly that Britain was meddling with American trade not because that trade interfered with Britain's "belligerent rights" but because it "frustrated the monopoly which she covets for her own commerce and navigation."

THE WAR OF 1812

The popular American war slogan in June 1812 was "Free Trade and Sailors' Rights," and maritime issues had indeed been the centerpiece of Madison's war message. Yet Americans marched rather than sailed to war; they aimed at Canada, not at the British fleet. There were several reasons for this strategy. First, the growth of Canadian exports to the West Indies after 1808 had convinced Madison that Canada was not a snowbound wasteland but a key prop of the British Empire, an indispensable component of Britain's designs to strangle American trade. Moreover, an attack on Canada seemed a practical tactic. Between 1800 and 1812, the Republicans had consistently preferred economy to preparedness. They had shrunk the national debt from $83 million to $27.5 million, and as a result the American navy contained only six frigates, three sloops of war, and a number of smaller vessels, including gunboats. A brainchild of Jefferson, the gunboats were little more than floating gun docks designed for harbor defense. They often sank when they ventured out to sea and at times could not even hold anchor in harbors. When a hurricane blew one gunboat eight miles inland onto a cornfield, the Federalists mordantly toasted it as the finest ship "upon earth."

Unable to challenge Britain at sea, Americans looked north to Canada as a practical objective. Few Americans expected a prolonged or difficult struggle. The United States outstripped Canada in everything: 25 to 1 in population, 9 to 1 in militia, 7 to 5 in regular army soldiers. Furthermore, not only were the best British troops in Europe fighting Napoleon but three out of every five settlers in Canada were Americans from New York, Pennsylvania, and Connecticut. These settlers, now technically Canadians, had been lured north by cheap land but feared the British more than they feared their kin on the American side. To Jefferson, the conquest of Canada seemed "a mere matter of marching."

Expectations of an easy victory, however, rested on a much shakier foundation than many Americans realized. First, the British had an invaluable ally in the Native Americans, who proved to be terrifying as well as tough warriors. Although not the only ones to commit atrocities, the Indians struck fear in beholders by dangling scalps from their belts. The British quickly learned to play on this fear, in some cases forcing Americans to surrender by hinting that the Indians might be uncontrollable in battle. Second, most American generals were aged and incompetent, and one of the only good ones, Andrew Jackson, was long denied a federal commission, on political grounds. And the American state militias were filled with Sunday soldiers who "hollered for water half the time, and whiskey the other. . . ." Their lack of training aside, few militiamen really understood the goals of the war. In fact, outside Congress, there simply was not much blood lust in 1812. In New England, where opposition to the war was widespread, the people had little stomach for an invasion of Canada. (The loyal minority in New England, however, did provide the army with more regiments than either the middle states or the South.) President Madison was able to raise only 10,000 one-year volunteers out of the 50,000 authorized by Congress. In Kentucky, the home of the prominent war hawk Henry Clay, only 400 answered the first call for volunteers. This lukewarm response in all sections indicates not only that most people viewed Canada as remote but also that national political issues did not necessarily penetrate deeply into American society in 1812. Local attachments remained stronger than national ones.

The military campaigns of the war developed in two broad phases. From the summer of 1812 to the spring of 1814, the Americans assumed the offensive position, launching a succession of poorly coordinated and generally unsuccessful attacks on Canada. From the spring of 1814 into early 1815, the British took the offensive and achieved some spectacular victories while losing key battles.

On to Canada

Whereas some Americans wanted to commence the war with an attack on Montreal, the ardor of western politicians dictated that the opening offensive occur in the West. In July 1812 sixty-year-old General William Hull led an American army from Detroit into Canada, but the ingenious Tecumseh cut his supply line. Hull then retreated to Detroit. Unnerved by the sight of Tecumseh and by the hint of the British commander, General Isaac Brock, that "the numerous body of Indians who have attached themselves to my troops will be beyond my control the moment the contest commences," Hull surrendered two thousand men to thirteen hundred British and Native American troops.

Now the British concentrated their strength against a mixed force of regulars and New York militia menacing Canada north of Niagara Falls. While the American regulars marched into Canada, the New York militiamen, contending that they had volunteered only to protect their homes, not to invade Canada, refused to cross their state line. As the militia looked on from the American side, a detachment of American regulars was crushed by the British at the Battle of Queenston (October 13, 1812). Again the daunting Indian presence proved decisive. Winfield Scott, later to become a candidate for the presidency of the United States, negotiated the American surrender as Mohawk Indians were attacking his men. The third American offensive of 1812 never got off the ground. The sixty-two-year-old general Henry Dearborn was to have moved on Montreal via Lake Champlain. He had advanced twenty miles north of Plattsburgh by November 19, when the militia refused to go any farther. Thus Dearborn returned to Plattsburgh.

Under General William Henry Harrison, the Americans renewed their offensive in 1813 and tried to retake Detroit. A succession of reverses convinced Harrison that offensive operations were futile as long as the British controlled Lake Erie. During the winter of 1812–1813, Captain Oliver H. Perry constructed a little fleet of vessels out of green wood, cannon captured in a raid on York (Toronto), and supplies dragged across the snow from Pittsburgh to his headquarters at Presqu'ile (Erie). Perry encountered and destroyed a British squadron at Put-in-Bay on the western end of Lake Erie on September 10, 1813, reporting, "We have met the enemy, and they are ours." Losing control of Lake Erie, the British pulled back from Detroit, but Harrison overtook and defeated a combined British and Indian force at the Battle of the Thames on October 5. Tecumseh, now a legend among the whites, died in the battle; Colonel Richard Johnson's claim, never proved, to have killed Tecumseh later contributed to Johnson's election as vice president of the United States.

The Naval War

Even before their victory at Put-in-Bay, Americans had achieved sensational successes on the high seas. Republican tightfistedness had not altogether succeeded in starving the United States Navy. However small, the navy had entered the war with three of the largest and fastest frigates afloat—the *Constitution*, the *United States*, and the *President*. On August 19, 1812, the *Constitution* destroyed HMS *Guerrière* in the mid-Atlantic and on December 29 wrecked HMS *Java* off Brazil. But U.S. victories had more psychological than strategic value. Although they gave Americans something to cheer, the British clamped a blockade on the American coast, starting with Delaware Bay and Chesapeake Bay in the fall of 1812 and extending to New York in the spring of 1813 and to New England in the spring of 1814. The *United States* was now corked in the bottle of New York harbor, the *President* in New Haven, and the *Constitution* in Boston. Nor did Perry's victory on Lake Erie and Harrison's at the Battle of the Thames

hasten the conquest of Canada. Efforts to invade Canada in the Niagara area and to gain control of Lake Ontario failed.

The British Offensive

Britain's military fortunes crested in the spring of 1814. After his disastrous invasion of Russia in 1812 and a series of defeats in 1813, France's Napoleon abdicated as emperor in April 1814, and Britain began to move regulars from Europe to North America. The British quickly found, however, that earlier defeats had toughened the Americans, who were now fighting to defend their homes rather than to invade Canada. The first sign of trouble for the British came on the Niagara front in July 1814, when attacking redcoats were stopped by fierce American resistance at the battles of Chippewa (July 5) and Lundy's Lane (July 25).

The main British thrust came not on the Niagara front but down Lake Champlain. At the head of ten thousand British veterans, the largest and best-equipped British army ever sent to North America, General Sir George Prevost advanced south via the lake at the end of August and reached Plattsburgh on September 6. Prevost's plan was to split the New England states from the rest of the country. At Plattsburgh, however, he encountered a well-entrenched American army. Resolving that he had to control the

The *Constitution* Ranging Alongside the *Guerrière*, *by Michael Felice Corne, 1812 (Detail)*
The Constitution *won more battles than any other early American frigate. Its most famous victory was over H.M.S.* Guerrière *in August 1812. Known affectionately as Old Ironsides, it was saved from demolition in 1830 by the poet Oliver Wendell Holmes, became a schoolship for the U.S. Naval Academy, was nearly confiscated by the fledgling Confederate navy in 1861, and today survives as a naval relic in Boston harbor.*

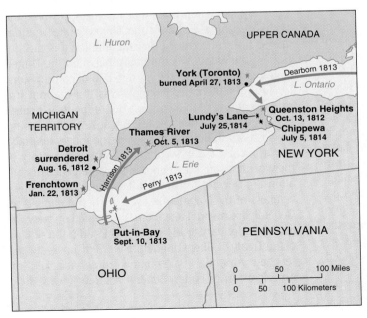

Major Battles of the War of 1812

Most of the war's major engagements occurred on or near the United States' northern frontier; but the Royal Navy blockaded the entire Atlantic coast, and the British army penetrated as far south as Washington and New Orleans.

Dolley Madison, *by Gilbert Stuart, 1804*
As the attractive young wife of Secretary of State James Madison, Dolley Madison acted virtually as the nation's First Lady during the administration of Jefferson, a widower. Friendly, tactful, and blessed with an unfailing memory for names and events, she added to her reputation as an elegant hostess after her husband became president.

lake before attacking Plattsburgh, Prevost called up his fleet, but an American naval squadron under Captain Thomas Macdonough defeated the British squadron on September 11. Dispirited, Prevost abandoned the campaign.

Ironically, the British achieved a far more spectacular success in an operation originally designed merely as a diversion from their main thrust down Lake Champlain. In 1814 a British army sailed from Bermuda for Chesapeake Bay, landed near Washington, and on August 24 met a larger American force, composed mainly of militia, at Bladensburg, Maryland. The Battle of Bladensburg quickly became the "Bladensburg races" as the American militia fled, almost without firing a shot. The British then descended on Washington. Madison, who had witnessed the Bladensburg fiasco, escaped into the Virginia hills. His wife, Dolley, pausing only long enough to load her sil-

ver, a bed, and a portrait of George Washington onto her carriage, hastened to join her husband, while British troops ate the supper prepared for the Madisons at the presidential mansion. Then they burned the mansion along with other public buildings in Washington. A few weeks later, the British attacked Baltimore, but after failing to crack its defenses, they broke off the operation.

The Treaty of Ghent

In August 1814 negotiations to end the war commenced between British and American commissioners at Ghent, Belgium. The British appeared to command a strong position. Having frustrated American designs on Canada, they stood poised for their Lake Champlain initiative. In reality, however, their position was not as strong as it appeared and would grow weaker as negotiations progressed.

With Napoleon's abdication as emperor, Britain's primary goal had become a favorable and lasting peace in Europe; the British had little to gain from prolonging a minor war in America. Mindful of their superior military position, they demanded territorial concessions from the United States. The American naval victory at Plattsburgh, however, brought home to Britain the fact that after two years of fighting, the British controlled neither the Great Lakes nor Lake Champlain. Similarly, the spectacular raid on Washington had no strategic significance, and so the British gave way on the issue of territorial concessions. The final treaty, signed on Christmas Eve 1814, restored the status quo ante bellum*: the United States neither gained nor lost territory. Several additional issues, including the fixing of a boundary between the United States and Canada, were referred to joint commissions for future settlement. Nothing was done about impressment, but with Napoleon out of the way, neutral rights became a dead issue. Because there was no longer a war in Europe, there were no longer neutrals.

Ironically, the most dramatic American victory of the war came after the conclusion of the peace negotiations. In December 1814 a British army, composed of veterans of the Napoleonic wars and commanded by General Sir Edward Pakenham, descended on New Orleans. On January 8, 1815, two weeks after the signing of the Treaty of Ghent but before word of the treaty had reached America, Pakenham's force attacked an American army under General Andrew ("Old Hick-

---

*Status quo ante bellum: Latin for the state of affairs before the war.

The Election of 1812

Candidates	Parties	Electoral Vote
JAMES MADISON	Democratic-Republican	128
DeWitt Clinton	Federalist	89

Peace Medal
Bearing the president's portrait, peace medals such as this were given as gifts to Native Americans in the Old Northwest during the War of 1812. At the same time, the British were wooing the Indians with silver medals bearing the image of George III.

ory") Jackson. Already a legend for his ferocity as an Indian fighter, Jackson inspired little fear among the British, who advanced into battle far too confidently, but he did strike enough terror in his own men to prevent another American rout. In an hour of gruesome carnage, Jackson's troops shredded the line of advancing redcoats, killing Pakenham and inflicting more than two thousand casualties while losing only thirteen Americans.

The Hartford Convention

Because the Treaty of Ghent had already concluded the war, the Battle of New Orleans had little significance for diplomats. Indirectly, however, it had an impact on domestic politics by eroding Federalist strength.

The comeback that the Federalists had made in the election of 1808 had continued into the 1812 campaign. Buoyed by hostility to the war in the Northeast, the Federalists had thrown their support behind DeWitt Clinton, an antiwar Republican. Although Madison won the electoral vote 128 to 89, Clinton carried all of New England except Vermont, as well as New York and New Jersey. American military setbacks in the war intensified Federalist disdain for the new Madison administration. Indeed, from their bastions in New England (see "A Place in Time"), Federalists saw a nation misruled for over a decade by Republican bunglers.

Jefferson's attack on the judiciary had seemed to threaten the rule of law. His purchase of Louisiana, a measure of doubtful constitutionality, had enhanced Republican strength and reduced the relative importance of Federalist New England in the Union. The Embargo Act had severely damaged New England's commerce. Now "Mr. Madison's War" was bringing fresh misery to New England in the form of the British blockade. A few Federalists began to talk of New England's secession from the Union. Most, however, rejected the idea, believing that they would soon benefit from popular disfavor with the war and spring back into power.

In late 1814 a Federalist convention met in Hartford, Connecticut. Although some advocates of secession were present, moderates took control and passed a series of resolutions summarizing New England's grievances. At the root of these grievances lay the belief that New England was becoming a permanent minority in a nation dominated by southern Republicans who failed to understand New England's commercial interests. Accordingly, the convention proposed to amend the Constitution to abolish the three-fifths clause (which gave the South a disproportionate share of votes in Congress by allowing it to count slaves as a basis of representation), to require a two-thirds vote of Congress to declare war and to admit new states into the Union, to limit the president to a single term, to prohibit the election of two successive presidents from the same state, and to bar embargoes lasting more than sixty days. As bold as these proposals were, their timing was disastrous for the Federalists. News of the Treaty of Ghent and of Jackson's victory at New Orleans dashed the Federalists' hopes of gaining broad popular support. The goal of the Hartford Convention had been to assert states' rights rather than disunion, but to many the proceedings smelled of a traitorous plot. The restoration of peace, moreover, stripped the Federalists of the primary grievance that had fueled the convention. In the election of 1816, Republican James Monroe, Madison's hand-picked successor, swept the nation over negligible Federalist opposition. He would

Bulfinch's Boston

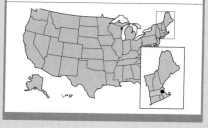

During the first quarter of the nineteenth century, Boston shed its quaint colonial-era character and was transformed into a bustling commercial and cultural hub and one of the most important towns in the independent nation. Formerly a community dotted with frame houses and boxy brick residences—most with gardens and orchards—Boston became a prosperous seaport in the Republic's early years. Stately brick homes with heavy oak doors and multipaned windows sprang up in many quarters, giving whole neighborhoods a newly formal air. These were the residences of the town's elite, many of whom, after the Revolution, had risen to new heights of prosperity.

Success in maritime industry underlay Boston's metamorphosis. Shipping, cod fishing, whaling, and trade in sea-otter pelts (obtained in the Pacific Northwest, and especially prized in China) thrived in the port town. Graceful sailing ships bobbed gently in the harbor, blending into a riot of masts. Bostonians going about their daily business on the waterfront passed wharf after wharf lined with the brick warehouses and countinghouses that had sprouted to manage Bostonians' widening sea trade. In the mid-1790s eighty humming quays gave the harborfront streets a distinctively commercial flavor.

A highly profitable commerce with the East Indies, China, and Europe, along with shipping to ports in the Indies and elsewhere in the United States, fueled the furious seaside activity. Boston merchants and sea captains built substantial fortunes from their shipping and fishing ventures; some voyages realized profits of more than $100,000, a huge take for the times. The spices, teas, silks, and fine porcelain they brought home were eagerly sought by their fellow elites.

New England cotton manufacturers benefited handsomely too after the Revolution. Savvy Yankees began to turn a former home industry into a large-scale business operation that supplied the duck and canvas for the harbor's panorama of sails. The fledgling American navy also needed sails; those for the *Constitution* had to be made in an old grain storehouse because no other town structure was long enough.

Even before the imposition of the embargo that stifled these lucrative enterprises, Boston, the home of many of President Thomas Jefferson's most bitter Federalist critics, among them George Cabot and Harrison Gray Otis, was a thorn in Jefferson's side. A Federalist elite ran the city, dominating its politics and culture as well as its maritime economy. Composing the elite were not only the merchants upon whom the town's commercial prosperity rested but also the lawyers who controlled its judicial offices, as well as men who had made a fortune in real estate. These uppercrust Bostonians supported the town's cultural institutions, such as the Boston Athenaeum, the nation's largest private library; the American Academy of Arts and Sciences; and Harvard College in nearby Cambridge. Austere and even frigid in their manners, Boston's Federalist leaders were a study in contrast to friendly, backslapping Virginia squires.

Following a grand tour of Europe, the architect Charles Bulfinch, in love with the classical style that he had seen in ancient Roman ruins, designed the majestic Massachusetts State House (completed in 1798) and the gracious mansions on Beacon Hill from which Boston's Federalists

Charles Bulfinch,
by Mather Brown, 1786
Bulfinch learned about architecture as a boy by browsing in the well-stocked architectural library of his maternal grandfather, the wealthy Charles Apthorp. In the 1780s Bulfinch's interest was further stimulated by his visits to Rome, Florence, and London and by the encouragement of Thomas Jefferson.

looked down upon "their" prosperous city. Bulfinch did more than cater to the elite; the scion of colonial aristocrats, he was part of the elite and served as Boston's police chief. The vast majority of Bostonians, of course, shared none of the privileges and splendor enjoyed by Bulfinch and others of the elite; artisans, mariners, and laborers looked up to Beacon Hill, not down from it. Yet even when Jefferson's Republicans began to score victories in Massachusetts, Boston stayed solidly Federalist.

How could the Federalists retain their political control for so long? Part of the answer is that Boston artisans and laborers remembered how the elite families had supported the Revolution and the Constitution. In addition, the Federalist elite profited from the attitude still prevailing among the common people that social superiors deserved respect and even obedience. Historians call this attitude deference, and there was a lot of it in Boston. To secure deference, the elite paid careful attention to dress. Powdered wigs, lace ruffles, silk stockings, and gold canes were all part of a carefully fashioned image that members of the elite projected when they walked the streets. This attention to image was important, especially among elite

Massachusetts State House
Like Jefferson, Bulfinch admired the classical style of ancient Greece and Rome. But Bulfinch was less inclined than Jefferson to copy ancient buildings literally. Bulfinch's design for the Massachusetts State House reflects the symmetry of neoclassicism; unlike Jefferson's plan for the Virginia Capitol, it is not based on any particular Roman structure.

families like the Cabots and the Lowells, recent arrivals to Boston who had made their fortunes during and after the Revolution. If deference showed any sign of weakening, the Boston elite could and did fall back on its control of elections. Until 1822, for example, Boston Brahmins beat back efforts to establish decentralized polling places. All Bostonians voted in Faneuil Hall under the eyes of the elite, and only after presenting evidence of property owning.

Bulfinch advised young men against becoming architects, for he believed that few new buildings would be constructed in Boston. His attitude reflected the fact that Boston's population had grown by only 10 percent between 1743 and 1790. Immigrants avoided stuffy Federalist Boston. Adventurers and radicals found New York and Philadelphia more congenial. Yet even as Bulfinch designed his stately mansions, the city was changing. Its population rose from 18,000 in 1790 to nearly 34,000 in 1810, and to 58,000 in 1826. By the 1820s the city had become too large and diverse to follow the leadership of a single elite. By the late 1820s, new political alignments had shattered Federalist domination of Boston's politics.

The Tea Party, *by Henry Sargent, c. 1821*
Bulfinch's Federalist patrons craved elegant interiors and could afford wall-to-wall carpeting. Tea parties like this unified as well as entertained Boston's elite.

The Election of 1816

Candidates	Parties	Electoral Vote
JAMES MONROE	Democratic-Republican	183
Rufus King	Federalist	34

The Election of 1820

Candidates	Parties	Electoral Vote
JAMES MONROE	Democratic-Republican	231
John Quincy Adams	Independent Republican	1

win reelection in 1820 with only a single dissenting electoral vote. As a force in national politics, the Federalists were finished.

THE AWAKENING OF AMERICAN NATIONALISM

The United States emerged from the War of 1812 bruised but intact. In its first major war since the Revolution, the American republic had demonstrated not only that it could fight on even terms against a major power but also that republics could fight wars without turning themselves into despotisms. The war produced more than its share of symbols of American nationalism. Whitewash cleared the smoke damage to the

presidential mansion; thereafter, it became known as the White House. The British attack on Fort McHenry, guarding Baltimore, prompted a young observer, Francis Scott Key, to compose "The Star-Spangled Banner." The Battle of New Orleans boosted Andrew Jackson onto the stage of national politics and became a source of legends about why the Americans had won the battle. It appears to most scholars today that the British lost because Pakenham's men, advancing within range of Jackson's riflemen and cannon, unaccountably paused and became sitting ducks. But in the wake of the battle, Americans spun a different tale. The legend arose that Jackson owed his victory not to Pakenham's blundering tactics but to hawk-eyed Kentucky frontiersmen whose rifles picked off the British with unerring accuracy. In fact, many frontiersmen in Jackson's army had not carried rifles; even if they had, gunpowder smoke would have obscured the enemy. But none of this mattered at the time. Just as Americans preferred militia to professional soldiers, they chose to believe that their greatest victory of the war was the handiwork of mere amateurs.

Madison's Nationalism and the Era of Good Feelings

The War of 1812 had three major political consequences. First, it eliminated the Federalists as a national political force. Second, it went a long way toward convincing the Republicans that the nation was strong and resilient, capable of fighting a war while maintaining the liberty of its people. The third consequence was an outgrowth of the first two. With the Federalists tainted by disloyalty and with fears about the fragility of republics fading, Republicans increas-

Manuscript for "The Star-Spangled Banner" *(Detail)*

O say can you see, ~~through~~ by the dawn's early light,
what so proudly we hail'd at the twilight's last gleaming,
Whose broad stripes & bright stars through the perilous fight
O'er the ramparts we watch'd, were so gallantly streaming?
And the rocket's red glare, the bomb bursting in air,
Gave proof through the night that our flag was still there,
O say does that star spangled banner yet wave
O'er the land of the free & the home of the brave?

ingly embraced some doctrines long associated with the Federalists. In a message to Congress in December 1815, Madison called for federal support for internal improvements, tariff protection for the new industries that had sprung up during the embargo, and the creation of a new national bank. (The charter of the first Bank of the United States had expired in 1811.) In Congress another Republican, Henry Clay of Kentucky, proposed similar measures, which he called the American System, with the aim of making the young nation economically self-sufficient and free from dependency on Europe. In 1816 Congress chartered the Second Bank of the United States and enacted a moderate tariff. Federal support for internal improvements proved to be a thornier problem. Madison favored federal aid in principle but believed that a constitutional amendment was necessary to authorize it. Accordingly, he vetoed an internal-improvements bill passed in 1817.

As Republicans adopted positions that they had once disdained, an "Era of Good Feelings" dawned on American politics. A Boston newspaper, impressed by the warm reception accorded President Monroe while touring New England, coined the phrase in 1817. It has stuck as a description of Monroe's two administrations, from 1816 to 1824. Compared with Jefferson and Madison, Monroe was neither brilliant, polished, nor wealthy, but he keenly desired to heal the political divisions that a stronger intellect and personality might have inflamed. The phrase "Era of Good Feelings" reflects not only the war's elimination of some divisive issues but also Monroe's conscious effort to avoid political controversies. But the good feelings were paper-thin. Madison's 1817 veto of the internal-improvements bill revealed the persistence of disagreements about the role of the federal government under the Constitution. Furthermore, the embargo, the War of 1812, and the continuation of slavery had aroused sectional animosities that a journalist's phrase about good feelings could not dispel. Not surprisingly, the postwar consensus began to unravel almost as soon as Americans recognized its existence.

John Marshall and the Supreme Court

Jefferson's old antagonist John Marshall continued to preside over the Supreme Court during the Monroe administrations and in 1819 issued two opinions that stunned Republicans. The first case, *Dartmouth College* v. *Woodward,* centered on the question of whether New Hampshire could transform a private corporation, Dartmouth College, into a state university.

Marshall concluded that the college's original charter, granted to its trustees by George III in 1769, was a contract. Since the Constitution specifically forbade states to interfere with contracts, New Hampshire's effort to turn Dartmouth into a state university was unconstitutional. The implications of Marshall's ruling were far-reaching. Charters or acts of incorporation provided their beneficiaries with various legal privileges and were sought by businesses as well as by colleges. In effect, Marshall said that once a state had chartered a college or business, it surrendered both its power to alter the charter and, in large measure, its authority to regulate the beneficiary.

A few weeks later, the chief justice handed down an even more momentous decision in the case of *McCulloch* v. *Maryland.* The issue here was whether the state of Maryland had the power to tax a national corporation, specifically the Baltimore branch of the Second Bank of the United States. The bank was a national corporation, chartered by Congress, but most of the stockholders were private citizens who reaped whatever profits the bank made. Speaking for a unanimous Court, Marshall ignored these private features of the bank and concentrated instead on two issues. First, did Congress have the power to charter a national bank? Nothing in the Constitution, Marshall conceded, explicitly granted this power. But the Constitution did authorize Congress to lay and collect taxes, to regulate interstate commerce, and to declare war. Surely these enumerated powers, he reasoned, implied a power to charter a bank. Marshall was clearly engaging in a broad, or "loose," rather than strict, construction (interpretation) of the Constitution. The second issue was whether a state could tax an agency of the federal government that lay within its borders. Marshall argued that any power of the national government, express or implied, was supreme within its sphere. States could not interfere with the exercise of federal powers. A tax by Maryland on the Baltimore branch was such an interference and hence was plainly unconstitutional.

Marshall's decision in the *McCulloch* case dismayed many Republicans. Although Madison and Monroe had supported the establishment of the Second Bank of the United States, the bank had made itself unpopular by tightening its loan policies during the summer of 1818. This contraction of credit triggered a severe depression, the Panic of 1819, that gave rise to considerable distress throughout the country, especially among western farmers. At a time when the bank was widely blamed for the panic, Marshall's ruling stirred controversy by placing the bank beyond the regulatory power of any state government. His decision, indeed, was as much an attack on state sovereignty as it was a defense of the bank. The Constitution, Marshall argued, was the creation not of state governments but of the people of *all* the states and thus was more fundamental than state laws. His reasoning assailed the Republican theory, best expressed in the Virginia and Kentucky resolutions of 1798–1799, that the Union was essentially a compact among states. Republicans had continued to view state governments as more immediately responsive to the people's will than was the federal government and to regard the compact theory of the Union as a guarantor of popular liberty. As Republicans saw it, Marshall's *McCulloch* decision, along with his decision in the *Dartmouth College* case, stripped state governments of the power to impose the will of their people upon corporations.

The Missouri Compromise

The fragility of the Era of Good Feelings again became apparent in the prolonged controversy between 1819 and 1821 over the territory of Missouri. In February 1819 the House of Representatives was considering a bill to admit Missouri as a slave state. James Tallmadge, Jr., a New York Republican, offered an amendment that prohibited the further introduction of slaves into Missouri and provided for the emancipation, at age twenty-five, of all slave offspring born after Missouri's admission as a state. Following bitter debate, the House approved the bill with Tallmadge's amendment. The Senate, after an equally rancorous debate, struck the amendment from the Missouri bill. In each chamber the vote on the Tallmadge amendment followed sectional lines, with the South virtually unanimously opposed to the provisions regarding slavery and the North predominantly in support. "This momentous question," Jefferson worried, "like a fire bell in the night, awakened and filled me with terror."

American politics had long been torn by sectional conflict, and slavery had at times figured in this discord, notably in the debate at the Constitutional Convention over the three-fifths clause. Yet prior to 1819, slavery had not been the primary factor in sectional division. Issues like Alexander Hamilton's economic program and the Jay Treaty had done more than slavery to polarize the country along sectional lines. During the 1790s Jefferson's main fear had been that Federalist economic policies were favoring northern

commercial development at the expense of southern agriculture. After 1800 Federalist opposition to the Louisiana Purchase and to the War of 1812 grew mainly out of concern that the now dominant Republicans were sacrificing New England's political and commercial interests to those of the South and West. The Hartford Convention of 1814 had been a reaction not so much to the spread of slavery as to the decline of New England's political influence.

For various reasons, the Missouri question thrust slavery into the center of this long-standing sectional conflict. In 1819 the Union had eleven free and eleven slave states. The admission of Missouri as a slave state would upset this balance to the advantage of the South. Noting that every president since John Adams had been a Virginian, Federalists portrayed the admission of Missouri as part of a conspiracy to perpetuate the rule of Virginia slaveholders. Republicans countered by pointing to the relatively sudden emergence in the House of Representatives of a vocal antislavery block, which included many northern Federalists, and to the growing number of Federalist-dominated societies in the North that promoted the manumission (freeing) of slaves. In response to these developments, some Republicans began to view all efforts to restrict slavery as part of a plot by the Federalists to divide northern and southern Republicans and thus regain political power. In sum, by 1819 the slavery issue had become intertwined with the prevailing distrust between the parties and between the sections.

Virtually every issue that was to wrack the Union during the next forty years was present in the controversy over Missouri: southern charges that the North was conspiring to destroy the Union and to end slavery; accusations by northerners that southerners were conspiring to extend the institution. For a while, leaders doubted that the Union would survive the crisis. House Speaker Henry Clay wrote that the words *civil war* and *disunion* were commonly uttered, almost without emotion. But a series of congressional agreements in 1820 and 1821, known collectively as the Missouri Compromise, resolved the crisis.

The first of these agreements involved the balance between slave states and free states. At the same time that Congress was considering statehood for Missouri, Maine was seeking admission as a free state. In 1820 Congress agreed to admit Maine as a free state, to pave the way for Missouri's admission as a slave state, and to prohibit slavery in the remainder of the Louisiana Purchase territory north of 36° 30′ (the

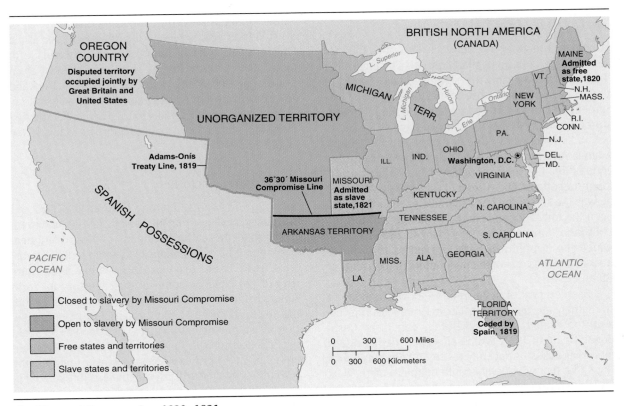

The Missouri Compromise, 1820–1821

The Missouri Compromise temporarily quelled controversy over slavery by admitting Maine as a free state and Missouri as a slave state, and by prohibiting slavery in the remainder of the Louisiana Purchase north of 36° 30'.

southern boundary of Missouri). But compromise did not come easily. The components of the eventual compromise passed by close and ominously sectional votes. Additionally, no sooner had the compromise been forged than it nearly fell apart. As a prelude to statehood, Missourians drafted a constitution that prohibited free blacks from entering their territory. This provision raised a thorny question, for some eastern states recognized free people of color as citizens, who, as such, were protected from discrimination by the federal Constitution, which clearly stated that "Citizens of each State shall be entitled to all Privileges and Immunities of Citizens in the several States." Balking at Missourians' exclusion of free blacks, antislavery northerners barred Missouri's admission into the Union until 1821, when Henry Clay engineered a new agreement. This second Missouri Compromise prohibited Missouri from discriminating against citizens

of other states but left open the issue of whether free blacks were citizens.

The Missouri Compromise was widely viewed as a southern victory. The South had gained admission of Missouri, whose acceptance of slavery was controversial, while conceding to the North the admission of Maine, whose rejection of slavery inspired no controversy at all. Yet the South had conceded to freedom a vast block of territory north of 36° 30'. Although much of this territory was unorganized Indian country that some viewed as unfit for white habitation, it would not remain a wilderness for long. Also, the Missouri Compromise reinforced the principle, originally set down by the Northwest Ordinance of 1787, that Congress had the right to prohibit slavery in some territories. Southerners had implicitly accepted the argument that slaves were not like other forms of property that could be moved from place to place at will.

Foreign Policy Under Monroe

American foreign policy between 1816 and 1824 reflected more consensus than conflict. The end of the Napoleonic Wars and the signing of the Treaty of Ghent had removed most of the foreign-policy disagreements between Federalists and Republicans. Moreover, Monroe was fortunate to have as his secretary of state an extraordinary diplomat, John Quincy Adams. An austere and scholarly man whose library equaled his house in monetary value, Adams was a tough negotiator and a fervent nationalist. Although he was the son of the last Federalist president, he had been the only Federalist in the Senate to support the Louisiana Purchase. He later backed the embargo, joined the Republican party, served as minister to Russia, and was one of the negotiators of the Treaty of Ghent.

As secretary of state, Adams moved quickly to strengthen the peace with Great Britain. During his term the United States and Britain signed the Rush-Bagot Treaty of 1817, which effectively demilitarized the Great Lakes by severely restricting the number of ships that the two powers could maintain there. Next the British-American Convention of 1818 fixed the boundary between the United States and Canada from the Lake of the Woods west to the Rockies and restored to Americans the same fishing rights off Newfoundland that they had enjoyed before the War of 1812. As a result of these two agreements, for the first time since independence, the United States had a secure border with British-controlled Canada and could turn its attention southward and westward.

Adams's dealings with the Spanish, who still owned East Florida and claimed West Florida, were also successful. It had never been clear whether the Louisiana Purchase included West Florida. Acting as if it did, the United States in 1812 had simply added a slice of West Florida to the state of Louisiana and another slice to the Mississippi Territory. In 1818 Andrew Jackson, the American military commander in the South, seizing upon the pretext that Florida was both a base for Seminole Indian raids into American soil and a refuge for fugitive slaves, invaded East Florida, hanged two British subjects, and captured Spanish forts. Jackson had acted without explicit orders, but Adams supported the raid, guessing correctly that it would panic the Spanish into further concessions. In 1819 Spain agreed to the Adams-Onís (or Transcontinental) Treaty. By its terms, Spain ceded East Florida

to the United States, renounced its claims to all of West Florida, and agreed to a southern border of the United States west of the Mississippi that ran north along the Sabine River (separating Texas from Louisiana) and then westward along the Red and Arkansas rivers to the Rocky Mountains, finally following the forty-second parallel to the Pacific. For the first time, the United States had a legitimate claim to the Pacific coast.

The Monroe Doctrine

John Quincy Adams had long believed that God and nature had ordained that the United States would eventually span the entire continent of North America. Throughout his negotiations leading up to the Adams-Onís Treaty, he made it clear to Spain that if the Spanish did not concede some of their territory in North America, the United States might seize all of it, including Texas and even Mexico. Americans were fast acquiring a reputation as an aggressive people. Yet Spain was concerned with larger issues than American encroachment. Its primary objective was to suppress the revolutions against Spanish rule that had broken out in South America. To accomplish this goal, Spain sought support from the European monarchs who had organized the Holy Alliance in 1815. The brainchild of the tsar of Russia, the Holy Alliance aimed to quash revolutions everywhere in the name of Christian principles, and by 1822 its members talked of helping Spain suppress the South American revolutions. But Britain refused to join the Holy Alliance; British foreign minister George Canning proposed that the United States and Britain issue a joint statement opposing any European interference in South America while pledging that neither would annex any part of Spain's old empire in the New World.

While sharing Canning's opposition to European intervention in the New World, Adams preferred that the United States make a declaration of policy on its own rather than "come in as a cock-boat in the wake of the British man-of-war." Specifically, Adams rejected Canning's insistence on a joint Anglo-American pledge never to annex any part of Spain's former territories, for Adams wanted to keep the United States' freedom to annex Texas or Cuba, should their inhabitants one day "solicit a union with us."

This was the background of the Monroe Doctrine, as President Monroe's message to Congress on December 2, 1823, later came to be called. The message, largely written by Adams, announced three key principles: that unless American interests were involved, the United States' policy was to abstain from European wars; that the "American continents" were not "subjects for future colonization by any European power"; and that the United States would construe any attempt at European colonization in the New World as an "unfriendly act."

Europeans widely derided the Monroe Doctrine as a mere unilateral pronouncement by the United States. Fear of the British navy, not the Monroe Doctrine, prevented the Holy Alliance from intervening in South America. With hindsight, however, the Europeans would have taken the doctrine more seriously, for it had important implications. First, by pledging itself not to interfere in European wars, the United States was excluding the possibility that it would support revolutionary movements in Europe. For example, Adams opposed the United States' recognition of Greek patriots, who were then fighting against Turkish domination. Second, by keeping open its options to annex territory in the Americas, the United States was using the Monroe Doctrine to claim a preeminent position in the New World.

CONCLUSION

Although the diplomatic achievements of John Quincy Adams and James Monroe were formidable, the greatest accomplishment of the early Republic's leaders was to fashion a workable body of political institutions and customs to govern the young nation. The framers of the Constitution had not anticipated the rise of political parties, and when Jefferson took office in 1801, it was unclear how a victorious party would behave. The range of possibilities was great. Some feared that the Republicans would amend the Constitution to ensure their political ascendancy. One reason why Jefferson's early actions against the judiciary had terrified Federalists was that they viewed his maneuverings as part of a larger plan to destroy them.

As it turned out, Jefferson did not destroy the Federalists; they destroyed themselves. Until the embargo, they failed to come up with a popular national issue, and then they rode opposition to the embargo and to the War of 1812 for too long. When the war ended, a surge of national pride swept the Federalists aside. The election of 1800 had generated anxiety bordering on hysteria; that of 1820 produced yawns. Indeed, the nation was almost too peaceful. Federalist collapse and the embrace by the Republicans of former Federalist policies like the tariff and national banking blurred divisions once sharp.

James Monroe's reelection in 1820 marked the high point of the Republican surge. Even as Republicans congratulated themselves on the emergence of an era of apparent good feelings, the signs of future divisions were growing. The furor over the Missouri Compromise shattered sectional harmony. Subtle changes were starting to occur in American society—changes that would create new political issues and divisions by 1830.

CHRONOLOGY

1800–1801	John Adams's midnight appointments.
1801	Thomas Jefferson's inauguration.
1802	Repeal of the Judiciary Act of 1801. Yazoo land compromise. American right of deposit at New Orleans revoked.
1803	*Marbury* v. *Madison.* Conclusion of the Louisiana Purchase.
1804	Judge John Pickering convicted by the Senate. Impeachment of Justice Samuel Chase. Aaron Burr kills Alexander Hamilton in a duel. Jefferson elected to a second term.
1804–1806	Lewis and Clark expedition.
1805	Start of the Burr conspiracy. Chase acquitted by the Senate. *Essex* case.

1806	British government issues the first Order in Council.
1807	Burr acquitted of treason. *Chesapeake* Affair. Embargo Act passed.
1808	James Madison elected president.
1809	Non-Intercourse Act passed; Embargo Act repealed.
1810	Macon's Bill No. 2.
1811	Battle of Tippecanoe.
1812	Orders in Council revoked. United States declares war on Britain. Madison reelected to a second term. General William Hull surrenders at Detroit. USS *Constitution* defeats HMS *Guerrière*. Battle of Queenston.
1813	Battle of Lake Erie (Put-in-Bay). Battle of the Thames.
1814	Battles of Chippewa and Lundy's Lane. Battle of Bladensburg.

James Madison

1814   British burn Washington, D.C.

Captain Thomas Macdonough's naval victory at the Battle of Plattsburgh.

Hartford Convention.

Treaty of Ghent signed.

1815	Battle of New Orleans.
1816	James Monroe elected president. Second Bank of the United States chartered.
1817	Rush-Bagot Treaty.
1818	British-American Convention of 1818. Andrew Jackson invades East Florida.
1819	Adams-Onís (Transcontinental) Treaty. *Dartmouth College* v. *Woodward*. *McCulloch* v. *Maryland*.
1820	Monroe reelected to a second term.
1820–1821	Missouri Compromise.
1823	Monroe Doctrine.

FOR FURTHER READING

Henry Adams, *History of the United States During the Administrations of Jefferson and Madison,* 9 vols. (1889–1891). A classic study by the great-grandson of John Adams.

Drew R. McCoy, *The Last of the Fathers: James Madison and the Republican Legacy* (1989). The best recent book on Madison.

Forrest McDonald, *The Presidency of Thomas Jefferson* (1976). A lively overview.

Dumas Malone, *Jefferson and His Time,* vols. 4 and 5 (1970, 1974). An extremely comprehensive biography.

Merrill Peterson, *Thomas Jefferson and the New Nation: A Biography* (1970). The best one-volume biography of Jefferson.

Marshall Smelser, *The Democratic Republic, 1801–1815* (1968). A thorough general work.

J. C. A. Stagg, *Mr. Madison's War: Politics, Diplomacy and Warfare in the Early Republic* (1983). An important reinterpretation of the causes of the War of 1812.

G. Edward White, *The Marshall Court and Cultural Change, 1815–1835* (1991). A seminal reinterpretation of the Supreme Court under John Marshall.

ADDITIONAL BIBLIOGRAPHY

Political Ideologies

Joyce Appleby, *Capitalism and a New Social Order: The Republican Vision of the 1790s* (1984); Lance Banning, *The Jeffersonian Persuasion: Evolution of a Party Ideology* (1978); Drew McCoy, *The Elusive Republic: Political Economy in Jeffersonian America* (1980); Steven Watts, *The Republic Reborn* (1987).

Political Parties

James Banner, *To the Hartford Convention: The Federalists and the Origins of Party Politics in the Early Republic, 1789–1815* (1967); Noble E. Cunningham, *The Jeffersonian Republicans and Power: Party Operations, 1801–1809* (1963); David Hackett Fischer, *The Revolution of American Conservatism: The Federalist Party in the Era of Jeffersonian Democracy* (1965); Ronald P. Formisano, *The Transformation of Political Culture: Massachusetts Parties, 1790s–1840s* (1983); Robert M. Johnstone, Jr., *Jefferson and the Presidency: Leadership in the Young Republic* (1978); Linda K. Kerber, *Federalists in Dissent: Imagery and Ideology in Jeffersonian America* (1970); Shaw Livermore, *The Twilight of Federalism: The Disintegration of the Federalist*

Party, 1815–1830 (1962); Alan Taylor, *Liberty Men and Great Proprietors: The Revolutionary Settlement on the Maine Frontier* (1990); James S. Young, *The Washington Community: 1800–1828* (1966).

Political Leaders

Thomas P. Abernethy, *The Burr Conspiracy* (1954); Robert Dawidoff, *The Education of John Randolph* (1979); Milton Lomask, *Aaron Burr,* 2 vols. (1979, 1982); Samuel Eliot Morison, *Harrison Gray Otis, 1765–1848: The Urbane Federalist* (1962); Robert Shalhope, *John Taylor of Caroline: Pastoral Republican* (1978).

Law and the Judiciary

Leonard Baker, *John Marshall: A Life in Law* (1974); Albert J. Beveridge, *John Marshall,* 4 vols. (1916–1919); Richard E. Ellis, *The Jeffersonian Crisis: Courts and Politics in the Young Republic* (1971); Charles G. Haines, *The Role of the Supreme Court in American Government and Politics, 1789–1835* (1944); Peter C. Hoffer and N. E. H. Hull, *Impeachment in America, 1635–1805* (1984); Morton J. Horwitz, *The Transformation of American Law, 1780–1860* (1977).

The War of 1812 and Its Prologue

Pierre Berton, *The Invasion of Canada* (1980); Roger H. Brown, *The Republic in Peril* (1964); A. L. Burtt, *The United States, Great Britain, and British North America* (1940); Harry L. Coles, *The War of 1812* (1965); Donald R. Hickey, *The War of 1812: A Forgotten Conflict* (1989); Reginald Horsman, *The Causes of the War of 1812* (1962); Bradford Perkins, *Prologue to War: England and the United States, 1805–1812* (1961); Julius W. Pratt, *Expansionists of 1812* (1925); Burton Spivak, *Jefferson's English Crisis: Commerce, Embargo, and the Republican Revolution* (1979).

Nationalism and Sectionalism

Harry Ammon, Jr., *James Monroe: The Quest for National Identity* (1971); George Dangerfield, *The Awakening of American Nationalism, 1815–1828* (1965) and *The Era of Good Feelings* (1952); Don E. Fehrenbacher, *The South and Three Sectional Crises* (1980); Glover Moore, *The Missouri Compromise, 1819–1821* (1953); Donald L. Robinson, *Slavery in the Structure of American Politics, 1765–1820* (1971).

John Quincy Adams and the Monroe Doctrine

Samuel F. Bemis, *John Quincy Adams and the Foundations of American Foreign Policy* (1949); Walter LaFeber, ed., *John Quincy Adams and the American Continental Empire* (1965); Ernest R. May, *The Making of the Monroe Doctrine* (1975); Dexter Perkins, *Hands Off: A History of the Monroe Doctrine* (1951) and *The Monroe Doctrine, 1823–1826* (1927).

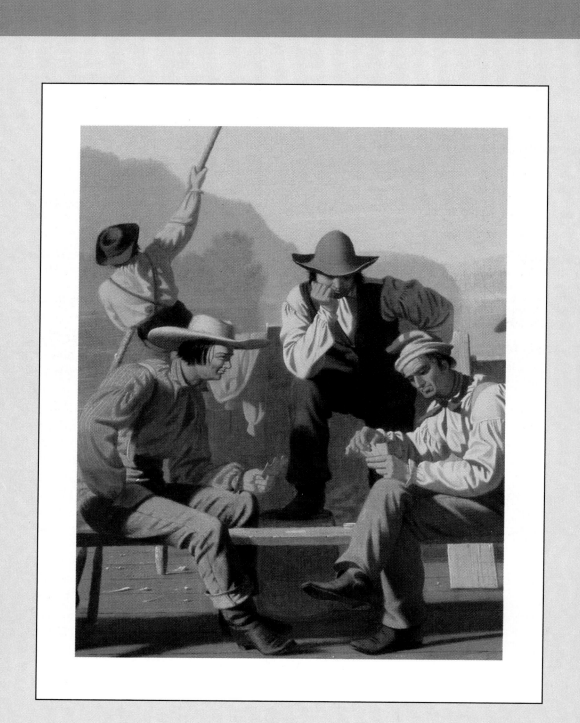

Raftsmen Playing Cards *(detail)*
by George Caleb Bingham, 1847

THE TRANSFORMATION OF AMERICAN SOCIETY 1815–1840

In 1835 William Kirkland and his wife, Caroline, left the private school that they had run in Geneva, New York, and moved to Detroit, in the Michigan Territory. William's plan was simple. He and Caroline would teach in Detroit long enough to earn money to invest in land. Detroit was being flooded by immigrants from the East who, as Caroline wrote, "came to buy land,— not to clear and plough, but as men buy a lottery ticket or dig for gold—in the hope of unreasonable and unearned profits." Although William intended to found a settlement in the wilderness rather than merely to buy and sell land, he, too, hoped to get rich in the West.

Reared in cultivated refinement in New York City and educated at excellent Quaker schools, Caroline had her own notions about the West. The novels and travelers' accounts that she had read projected conflicting but invariably rosy images of the frontier: the West was a land of boundless treasure, a vast garden eager to yield the fruits of its soil, and a romantic wilderness through which one could easily drive a carriage on a moonlit night.

After serving for a year as the principal of a school for young women in Detroit, William acquired thirteen hundred acres of land in Livingston County, sixty miles northwest of Detroit, and laid out his settlement around the village of Pinckney. But life in Pinckney failed to live up to the Kirklands' expectations. Instead of a quaintly romantic cottage, Caroline found herself forced to live in a tiny log cabin, far too small for her fancy eastern furniture. Equally disconcerting to the Kirklands was westerners' attitude toward others' possessions. Frontier people thought that they had a right to borrow anything that Caroline owned, with no more than a blunt declaration that "you've got plenty." "For my own part," Caroline related, "I have lent my broom, my thread, my tape, my spoons, my cat, my thimble, my scissors, my shawl, my shoes; and have been asked for my combs and brushes: and my husband, for his shaving apparatus and his pantaloons."

Other surprises were in store for the Kirklands. Accustomed to servants, Caroline found that even poor western girls refused to hire themselves out permanently as household help. As William noted, occasionally a poor girl would enter service long enough to earn money for a new dress, "but never as a regular calling, or with an acknowledgement of inferior station." Yet the Kirklands gradually realized that the peculiarities of westerners sprang not from selfishness or laziness but from an underlying belief in equality. For example, westerners' penchant for borrowing arose from their attitude that frontier men and women had to share and share alike, or go under.

Caroline turned her experiences in Michigan to good advantage by writing a fictionalized account of them, *A New Home—Who'll Follow?* (1839). Justly hailed as the first realistic account of western life, *A New Home* established Caroline's literary reputation, which she continued to build after she and William returned to New York in 1843.

Between 1815 and 1840, many Americans like the Kirklands ventured into the West and had their visions of easy living punctured by the harsh realities of the frontier. Even those who remained in the East had to adjust—to the successive waves of economic and social change that swept the nation after the conclusion of the War of 1812. For westerners and easterners alike, improvements in transportation (the so-called transportation revolution) were spearheaded by the completion in 1825 of the Erie Canal. This "revolution" both stimulated interregional trade and migration and encouraged an unprecedented development of towns and cities. The new urban dwellers, in turn, formed a market not only for agricultural produce but also for the products of the industries springing up in New England and the major northeastern cities.

Viewed superficially, these changes did not greatly affect the way most Americans lived. Whether in 1815 or 1840, the majority of Americans dwelled outside of cities, practiced agriculture for a living, and traveled on foot or by horse. Yet this surface impression of continuity is misleading, because by 1840 many farmers had moved to the West. The nature of farming had also changed, as farmers increasingly raised crops for sale in distant markets rather than merely for their families' consumption. Although most Americans still depended on agriculture, by 1840 alternatives to farming abounded. The rise of such alternatives, in turn, affected some of the most basic social relationships: between parents and children, and between wives and husbands.

WESTWARD EXPANSION AND THE GROWTH OF THE MARKET ECONOMY

The spark that ignited these changes was the spread of Americans across the Appalachian Mountains. In 1790 the vast majority of the people resided east of the

mountains and within a few hundred miles of the Atlantic Ocean. But by 1840 one-third lived between the Appalachians and the Mississippi River. In this area, known at the time as the West, settlers were buffeted by a succession of unexpected social and economic forces.

The Sweep West

This outward thrust of the population occurred in a series of bursts. The first began even before the 1790s and was reflected in the admission of four new states into the Union between 1791 and 1803: Vermont, Kentucky, Tennessee, and Ohio. Then, after an interlude of over ten years that saw the admission of only one new state, Louisiana, six states entered the Union between 1816 and 1821: Indiana, Mississippi, Illinois, Alabama, Maine, and Missouri. Even as Indiana and Illinois were gaining statehood, settlers were pouring farther west into Michigan. Ohio's population jumped from 45,000 in 1800 to 581,000 by 1820 and 1,519,000 by 1840; Michigan's, from 5,000 in 1810 to 212,000 by 1840.

An adventuring spirit carried Americans far beyond the Mississippi. On an exploring expedition in the Southwest in 1806, Zebulon Pike sighted the Colorado peak that was later named after him. The Lewis and Clark expedition whetted interest in the Far West. In 1811 a New York merchant, John Jacob Astor, founded the fur-trading post of Astoria at the mouth of the Columbia River in the Oregon Country. In the 1820s and 1830s, fur traders also operated along the Missouri River from St. Louis to the Rocky Mountains and beyond. At first, whites relied on the Native Americans to bring them furs, but during the 1820s white trappers or "mountain men"—among them, Kit Carson, Jedediah Smith, and the mulatto Jim Beckwourth—gathered furs on their own while performing astounding feats of survival in harsh surroundings.

Jedediah Smith was representative of these men. Born in the Susquehanna Valley of New York in 1799, Smith moved west with his family to Pennsylvania and Illinois and in 1822 signed on with an expedition bound for the upper Missouri River. In the course of this and subsequent explorations, he was almost killed by a grizzly bear in the Black Hills of South Dakota, learned from the Native Americans to trap beaver and shoot buffalo, crossed the Mojave Desert into California, explored California's San Joaquin Valley, and hiked back across the Sierras and the primeval Great Basin to the Great Salt Lake, a trip so forbidding that even the Native Americans avoided it.

The Mountain Men
Rocky Mountain trappers or "mountain men" were among the most colorful and individualistic of nineteenth-century Americans. Entrepreneurs who trapped beavers for their pelts (which were used until the 1830s to make hats), the mountain men were also hunters, explorers, and adventurers who lived "a wild Robin Hood kind of life" with "little fear of God and none at all of the Devil."

Their exploits popularized in biographies, the mountain men became legends in their own day. They were, however, atypical migrants. For most pioneer settlers, the West meant the area between the Appalachians and the Mississippi River, the region today known as the Midwest, and before 1840 very few ventured into the Far West. In contrast to Jedediah Smith, whose unquenchable thirst for adventure led to his death at the hands of Comanches in 1831, most pioneers sought stability and security. The newspaper reports, pamphlets, and letters home that told easterners what to expect in the West usually stressed that western living was bountiful rather than harsh or even risky. A legislator in the Missouri Territory wrote in 1816 that in the states west of the Appalachians, "there neither is, nor, in the nature of things, can there ever be, any thing like poverty there. All is ease, tranquility and comfort."

Western Society and Customs

In their desire for stability, pioneers usually migrated as families rather than as individuals. Because they needed to get their crops to market, most settlers be-
tween 1790 and 1820 clustered near the navigable rivers of the West, especially the magnificent water system created by the Ohio and Mississippi rivers. Only with the spread of canals in the 1820s and 1830s, and later of railroads, did westerners feel free to venture far from rivers. In addition, westerners often clustered with people who hailed from the same region back east. For instance, in 1836 a group of farmers from nearby towns met at Castleton, Vermont, listened to a minister intone from the Bible, "And Moses sent them to spy out the land of Canaan," and soon established the town of Vermontville in Michigan. Other migrants to the West were less organized than these latter-day descendants of the Puritans, but most hoped to settle among familiar faces in the West. Finding southerners already well entrenched in Indiana, for example, New Englanders tended to prefer Michigan.

Far from seeking isolation, most westerners craved sociability. Even before there were towns and cities in the West, farm families joined with their neighbors in group sports and festivities. Men met for games that, with a few exceptions like marbles (popular among all ages), were tests of strength or agility. These included wrestling, lifting weights, pole jumping

**Merrymaking at
a Wayside Inn,**
*by Pavel Svinin
Country inns served as social
centers for rural neighborhoods
as well as stopping places for
travelers. Although this painting
evokes rustic charm, guests at
inns complained of the stale
odor of rum, pie crusts that
tasted like leather, cheese that
defied digestion, and a lack of
privacy that made them look
forward to the crack of the
coachman's whip and another
day on the road.*

(for distance rather than height), and a variant of the modern hammer toss. Some of these games were brutal. In gander pulling, horseback riders competed to pull the head off a gander whose neck had been stripped of feathers and greased. Women usually combined work and play in quilting and sewing parties, carpet tackings, and even chicken and goose pluckings. Social activities brought the genders together. Group corn huskings usually ended with dances; and in a variety of "hoedowns" and "frolics," even westerners who in theory might disapprove of dancing promenaded to singing and a fiddler's tune.

Within western families, there was usually a clear division of labor between men and women. Men performed most of the heaviest labor such as cutting down trees and plowing fields, but women had many chores. Women usually rose first in the morning, because their work included milking the cows as well as preparing breakfast. Women also fashioned the coverlets that warmed beds in unheated rooms, and prior to the spread of factory-made clothing in the 1830s, they made shirts, coats, pants, and dresses on home spinning wheels for family use. They often helped butcher hogs. They knew that the best way to bleed a hog was to slit its throat while it was still alive, and after the bleeding, they were adept at scooping out the innards,

washing the heart and liver, and hanging them to dry. There was nothing dainty about the work of pioneer women.

Most western sports and customs had been transplanted from the East. Gander pulling, for example, had been a popular pastime in Virginia before it made its way to the frontier. Yet the West had a character of its own. Before 1830 few westerners could afford elegant living. Cowpaths did double duty as sidewalks in country towns. The West contained no more than a sprinkling of elegant mansions. Even in the wealthy cotton-growing regions of Alabama and Mississippi, most planters lived in rough conditions prior to 1830. Their relative lack of refinement made westerners easy targets for easterners' contemptuous jibes. Criticisms of the West as a land of half-savage yokels tended, in turn, to give rise to counterassertions by westerners that they lived in a land of honest democracy and that the East was soft and decadent. The exchange of insults fostered a regional identity among westerners that further shaped their behavior. Priding themselves on their simple manners, westerners were often not only hostile to the East but also intolerant of those westerners who had pretensions to gentility. On one occasion, a traveler who hung up a blanket in a tavern to cover his bed from public gaze had it promptly ripped down. On another, a woman who improvised a screen behind which to retire in a crowded room was dismissed as "stuck up." And a politician who rode to a public meeting in a buggy instead of on horseback lost votes.

The Federal Government and the West

Of the various causes of expansion to the Mississippi from 1790 to 1840, the one that operated most generally and uniformly throughout the period was the growing strength of the federal government. Even before the Constitution's ratification, several states had ceded their western land claims to the national government, thereby creating the bountiful public domain. The Land Ordinance of 1785 had set forth plans for surveying and selling parcels of this public treasure to settlers. The Northwest Ordinance of 1787 provided for the orderly transformation of western territories into states. The Louisiana Purchase of 1803 brought the entire Mississippi River under American control, and the Transcontinental Treaty of 1819 wiped out the last vestiges of Spanish power east of the Mississippi. The federal government directly stimulated settlement of its expanding landholdings by inducing soldiers to enlist during the War of 1812 in return for promises of land after the war. With 6 million acres allotted to these so-called military bounties, many former soldiers pulled up roots and tried farming in the West. To facilitate westward migration, Congress authorized funds in 1816 for continued construction of the National Road, a highway begun in 1811 that reached Wheeling, Virginia, on the Ohio River, in 1818 and Vandalia, Illinois, by 1838. Soon the road was thronged with settlers. "Old America seems to be breaking up," a traveler on the National Road wrote in 1817. "We are seldom out of sight, as we travel on this grand track towards the Ohio, of family groups before and behind us."

Although whites gained innumerable advantages from having a more powerful national government behind them, the rising strength of that government brought misery to the Indians. Virtually all the foreign-policy successes during the Jefferson, Madison, and Monroe administrations worked to the Native Americans' disadvantage. Both the Louisiana Purchase and the Transcontinental Treaty stripped them of Spanish protection. In the wake of the Louisiana Purchase, Lewis and Clark bluntly told the Indians that they must "shut their ears to the counsels of bad birds" and listen henceforth only to the Great Father in Washington. The

outcome of the War of 1812 also worked against the Native Americans; indeed, the Indians were the only real losers of the war. Early in the negotiations leading to the Treaty of Ghent, the British had insisted on the creation of an Indian buffer state in the Old Northwest, between the United States and Canada. But after the American victory at the Battle of Plattsburgh, the British dropped the demand and essentially abandoned the Indians to the Americans.

The Removal of the Indians

As white settlers poured into the West, they found in their path sizable pockets of Indians, particularly in the South. The Cherokees, Creeks, Choctaws, Chickasaws, and Seminoles—whom non–Native Americans collectively called the Five Civilized Tribes—occupied large parts of Tennessee, Georgia, Alabama, Mississippi, and Florida. Years of commercial dealings and intermarriage with non-Indians had created in all these tribes an influential minority of mixed-bloods, who had heeded the call of white missionaries to embrace Christianity and agriculture. Among the Cherokees, for example, not only was agriculture practiced, but some Native Americans built looms and gristmills and even owned slaves. One of their chiefs, Sequoyah, devised a written form of the Cherokee language, whereas other Cherokees published their own newspaper, the *Cherokee Phoenix*.

In whites' eyes, these were extraordinary accomplishments, and the federal government welcomed them as signs of advancing "civilization" among the Indians. But "civilizing" the Native Americans did not always work to the federal government's advantage. Although some assimilated mixed-bloods willingly sold tribal lands to the government and moved west, others, recognizing that their prosperity depended on commercial dealings with whites, resisted removal. In addition, within the "civilized" tribes, the majority of Indians were full-bloods. Although some full-bloods willingly moved west, most were keen to retain their ancestral lands in the East and were contemptuous both of whites and of mixed-bloods who bartered away tribal land to whites. When the Creek mixed-blood chief William McIntosh sold to the government all Creek lands in Georgia and two-thirds of Creek lands in Alabama in the Treaty of Indian Springs (1825), other Creeks executed him.

As whites' demands for Native American lands reached the boiling point during the 1820s, the traditional policy of negotiating treaties piecemeal with the Indians came under fire. Andrew Jackson embodied the whites' new militancy. Jackson was one of the first prominent government officials to recognize that the balance of power between Native Americans and whites had shifted drastically since the American Revolution. His victory over the Creeks at the Battle of Horseshoe Bend in 1814 had convinced him that the Indians were much weaker than whites often realized. And because they were weakening, Jackson could see no justification for continuing "the farce of treating with the Indian tribes." The Indians were not independent nations, Jackson argued, but were subject to the laws of whatever state they resided in.

When Jackson became president in 1829, he promptly instituted a more coercive removal policy. His policy reflected not only his disdain for the Indians but also his conviction that, as long as the Indians stayed in the East, the "real" Indians who still retained their "savage" ways would be exploited by mercenary whites and self-serving mixed-bloods. In 1830 he secured from a divided Congress passage of the Indian Removal Act, which granted the president funds and authority to remove Native Americans by force if necessary. By then, Georgia and other states were putting overwhelming pressure on the Indians. Resolutions pushed through the Georgia legislature provided that after 1830 Native Americans could not be parties to or witnesses in legal cases involving whites. By the late 1820s, the Creeks in Georgia and Alabama started to move west. In 1836 the Georgia militia attacked Creeks still in the state, and when starving Creeks raided white settlements for food, federal troops finished the job begun by the militia. In 1836 fifteen thousand Creek Indians, most of the Creek nation, were removed—many in chains and handcuffs—and resettled west of the Mississippi.

A similar fate befell the other "civilized" tribes of the South. Treaties signed in 1830 and 1832 achieved the removal of the Choctaws from Mississippi and the Chickasaws from northern Alabama and northern Mississippi. The visiting Frenchman Alexis de Tocqueville witnessed the arrival of the Choctaws, including "the wounded, the sick, newborn babies, and the old men on the point of death," at Memphis on the Mississippi. "I saw them embark to cross the great river, and the sight will never fade from my memory. Neither sob nor complaint rose from that silent assembly. Their afflictions were of long standing, and they felt them to be irremediable." Most Seminoles were removed from

Political Cartoon of Jackson and Native Americans
This cartoon, which depicts Native Americans as children or dolls subject to father Andrew Jackson, was intended as a satire on Jackson's policy of forcibly removing the Indians to reservations. The painting in the upper right corner pointedly depicts the goddess Liberty trampling a tyrant.

Florida, but only after a bitter war between 1835 and 1842 that cost the federal government $20 million.

The Cherokees, the most assimilated of the southern tribes, tried legal resistance to removal, but to no avail. In 1827 the Cherokees proclaimed themselves an independent republic within Georgia. When the Georgia legislature subsequently passed laws extending the state's jurisdiction over this "nation," the Cherokees petitioned the U.S. Supreme Court for an injunction to halt the execution of Georgia's legislation. In the case of *Cherokee Nation* v. *Georgia* (1831), Chief Justice John Marshall ruled that the Cherokees were neither a state nor a foreign nation and hence lacked standing to bring suit. But Marshall acknowledged that prolonged occupancy gave the Cherokees a right to their land, and a year later, he clarified the Cherokees' legal

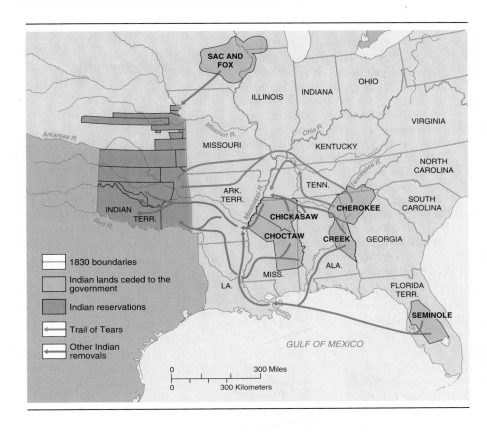

The Removal of the Native Americans to the West, 1820–1840
The so-called Trail of Tears, followed by the Cherokees, was one of several routes along which various tribes migrated on their forced removal to reservations west of the Mississippi.

position in *Worcester* v. *Georgia,* by holding that they were a "domestic dependent nation" entitled to federal protection from molestation by Georgia.

But Marshall's decision had little impact. Jackson ignored it, reportedly sneering, "John Marshall has made his decision; now let him enforce it." The Cherokees themselves were divided into a majority antiremoval faction and a minority proremoval faction. Federal agents persuaded a proremoval chief to sign the Treaty of New Echota (1835), which ceded all Cherokee land to the United States for $5.6 million and free transportation west. Most Cherokees denounced the treaty, and on June 22, 1839, a party of Cherokees took revenge by murdering its three principal signers, including a former *Cherokee Phoenix* editor. But the Cherokees' fate had already been sealed. Between 1835 and 1838, bands of Cherokees straggled west to the Mississippi along the so-called Trail of Tears. Unlike the Creeks, the Cherokees policed their own removal, but this fact did not lessen their physical and spiritual sufferings. Between 2,000 and 4,000 of the 16,000 migrating Cherokees died (see "A Place in Time").

Indians living in the Northwest Territory fared no better. A series of treaties extinguished their land titles, and most moved west of the Mississippi. The removal of the northwestern Indians was notable for two uprisings. The first, led by Red Bird, a Winnebago chief, began in 1827 but was quickly crushed. The second was led by a Sac and Fox chief, Black Hawk, who resisted removal until 1831 and then moved his people west of the Mississippi, only to return the following year. In June 1832 federal troops and Illinois militia furiously attacked his band and virtually annihilated Black Hawk's followers as they tried to recross the Mississippi into Iowa. Black Hawk's downfall induced the other Old Northwest tribes to cede their lands. Between 1832 and 1837, the United States acquired nearly 190 million acres of Indian land in the Northwest for $70 million in gifts and annuities.

The Agricultural Boom

In pushing Indians from the path of white settlers, the federal government was responding to whites' demands for land and more land. Depleted soil and overcrowding had long driven eastern farmers west, but after the War of 1812, a new incentive—the bounding prices of agricultural commodities such as wheat, corn, and cotton—pulled settlers westward in search

Tahlequah, Indian Territory

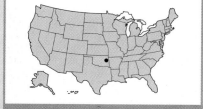

The sufferings of the southeastern Indian tribes along the Trail of Tears did not end when the Cherokees, Choctaws, Creeks, Chickasaws, and other nations arrived in the Indian Territory that is now Oklahoma. Most of the tribes found that the federal government failed to deliver fully on promises of supplies and that white merchants, who had contracted to feed the Native Americans until they could raise their own crops, often cheated them. At times, white contractors bought up Indian claims for corn rations for cash, which the Indians then spent on whiskey. One white agent reported seeing two thousand drunken Creeks, more than 10 percent of the entire tribe, on a single day in 1837.

Yet left to their own devices, the southeastern Indians were thriving in their new western home by the 1840s. In addition to establishing farms and small

Chief John Ross,
by John Rubens Smith, 1841
After becoming the principal chief of the eastern Cherokees in 1828, Ross, who was only one-eighth Cherokee himself, emerged as a leading opponent of Jackson's Indian-removal policy.

Cherokee Hunter,
by Baroness Hyde de Neuville, 1820
On the eve of their removal to the West, the Cherokees and the other southeastern tribes had increasingly abandoned their traditional hunting, fishing, and gathering for agriculture and trade.

factories, the Native Americans developed a passion for education. With the aid of white missionaries, they built elementary schools and academies. They operated printing presses that turned out schoolbooks, hymnals, and catechisms in the Creek, Choctaw, and Cherokee languages as well as in English. Some historians have concluded that the Native Americans' school system was the best west of the Mississippi in the 1840s. As white Americans trekked to Texas and California during that decade, moreover, they came to depend on the food and other supplies that they purchased from the transplanted southeastern Indians.

With prosperity, the tribes gradually overcame their internal political divisions. Rival Cherokee factions, for example, united in 1839 and established a government seat at Tahlequah, a village in present-day eastern Oklahoma, near the Illinois River. But the "civilized" tribes continued to suffer from raids by the nomadic prairie Indians such as the Osages and Comanches. In June 1843 Tahlequah became the scene of a most extraordinary

273a

Tahlequah Council, 1843,
by John Mix Stanley
The seventeen-tribe council of the summer of 1843 was intended to establish friendly ties between the Cherokee exiles and the Indian Territory's Plains peoples.

council of tribes. Some four thousand delegates from seventeen Indian nations, including the seven-foot-tall Osage leader Black Dog and the son of Tecumseh, crowded into Tahlequah to hear the presiding Cherokee chief, John Ross, proclaim: "By peace our condition has been improved in the pursuits of civilized life. We should, therefore, extend the hand of peace from tribe to tribe, till peace is established between every nation of red men within the reach of our voice." In addition to destroying a thousand gallons of whiskey, the council agreed on a compact that provided for punishment of offenders from one tribe who raided another tribe.

No Indian council, however, could remove the source of intertribal raiding: the steady shrinkage of the nomadic Indians' hunting grounds caused by the relentless advance of white settlement and by the very prosperity of the "civilized" Indians. Reduced to near starvation, the Osages and Comanches continued to raid the settled tribes' livestock until these nomads themselves were forced onto reservations.

Choctaw Girls
These young Choctaws, members of one of the Five Civilized Tribes, were photographed in the Oklahoma Indian Territory.

273b

of better farmland. Several factors accounted for the skyrocketing farm prices. First, Britain and France, exhausted by the Napoleonic Wars, were importing wheat and corn from America, and the United States had swiftly captured former British markets in the West Indies and former Spanish markets in South America. In addition, the beginnings of industrialization in New England even before the war combined with the westward migration of New England farmers to create a demand in the eastern United States for western foodstuffs. So as domestic and foreign demand intensified, commodity prices rose between 1815 and 1819. The West's splendid river systems made it possible for farmers in Ohio to ship wheat and corn down the Ohio River to the Mississippi and then down the Mississippi to New Orleans. There wheat and corn were either sold or transshipped to the East, the West Indies, South America, or Europe. Just as government policies made farming in the West possible, high prices for foodstuffs made it attractive.

As the prospect of raising wheat and corn pulled farmers toward the Old Northwest, Eli Whitney's invention of the cotton gin in 1793 (see Chapter 7) cleared the path for settlement of the Old Southwest, particularly the states of Alabama and Mississippi on the Gulf of Mexico. After the War of 1812, the explosive thrust of small farmers and planters from the seaboard South into the Old Southwest resembled a gold rush. By 1817 "Alabama fever" gripped the South; settlers bid the price of good land up to thirty dollars to fifty dollars an acre. By 1820 Alabama and Mississippi produced half of the nation's cotton. Stimulated by the seemingly bottomless demand of the British textile industry for raw cotton, cotton production tripled between 1816 and 1826, and the story was only beginning. Between 1831 and 1836, the value of cotton exports rose 300 percent. Accounting for less than a quarter of all American exports between 1802 and 1807, cotton composed just over half by 1830, and nearly two-thirds by 1836.

The Rise of the Market Economy

To farmers, the high prices of agricultural commodities between 1815 and 1819 appeared an unmixed blessing. Most planned to grow enough food to feed their families (called subsistence agriculture) *and* a cash crop like wheat or cotton to sell in local or distant markets (called commercial agriculture, or the "market economy"). Farming for markets was not new;

many farmers had done so during the colonial era. What was new after the War of 1812 was the extent to which farmers entered the market economy. High crop prices tempted many former subsistence farmers into the commercial economy. Often these individuals had little experience with commercial dealings and little idea of what they were getting into. Commercial agriculture exposed farmers to innumerable new risks. First, cash crops like wheat and cotton were sold to people whom the farmers themselves frequently never met, in places that they never saw. Second, farmers had no control over the fluctuations of distant markets. Furthermore, there was inevitably an interval, often a long one, between harvesting a cash crop and selling it. To sustain themselves during the interval, farmers had to borrow money. Thus commercial agriculture forced farmers into short-term debt in the hope of long-term profit.

The debt was frequently worse than most had expected. In the first place, many western farmers had to borrow money to buy their land. The roots of this indebtedness for land lay, in turn, in the federal government's inability to devise an effective policy for transferring the public domain directly into the hands of small farmers.

Federal Land Policy

Partisan and sectional pressures buffeted federal land policy like a kite in a March wind. The result was a succession of land laws passed between 1796 and 1820, each of which sought to undo the damage caused by its predecessors.

At the root of early federal land policy lay a preference for the orderly settlement of the public domain. To this end, the Ordinance of 1785 divided public lands into townships of six miles square each and then subdivided each township into one-mile-square lots (usually called sections) of 640 acres. The architects of the ordinance did not expect that ordinary farmers could afford to purchase 640-acre sections; rather, they assumed that farmers who shared ties based on religion or region of origin would band together to purchase sections. This outcome would ensure that compatible settlers would live on adjoining lots in what amounted to rural neighborhoods, and it would make the task of government much easier than if settlers were to live in isolation on widely scattered homesteads.

Political developments in the 1790s undermined the expectations of the ordinance's framers. Because their political bases lay in the East, the Federalists were reluctant to encourage headlong settlement of the West, but at the same time they were eager to raise revenue for the federal government from land sales. They reconciled these goals—retarding actual settlement while gaining revenue—by encouraging the sale of huge tracts of land to wealthy speculators who did not intend to farm the land but instead planned to hold it until its value rose, and then sell off parcels to farmers. In the 1790s land speculators swarmed through the area east of the Appalachians. The Holland Land Company, for example, composed mainly of Dutch investors, bought up much of western New York and western Pennsylvania. A federal land law passed in 1796 reflected Federalist aims by maintaining the minimum purchase at 640 acres at a minimum price of two dollars an acre, and by allowing only a year for complete payment.

Believing that the small farmer was the backbone of the Republic, and fully aware of Republican political strength in the West, Thomas Jefferson and the Republicans took a different tack. Starting in 1800, federal land laws increasingly reflected the Republicans' desire to ease the transfer of the public domain to farmers. Accordingly, the land law of 1800 dropped the minimum purchase to 320 acres and allowed up to four years for full payment but kept the minimum purchase price at $2.00 an acre. In 1804 the minimum purchase came down to 160 acres, in 1820 to 80 acres, and in 1832 to 40 acres. The minimum price also declined from $2.00 an acre in 1800 to $1.64 in 1804 and to $1.25 in 1820.

Although the government steadily liberalized its land policy, speculators always remained one step ahead of Congress. Long before 1832, speculators were selling 40-acre lots to farmers. Farmers actually preferred these small lots (and rarely bought more than 160 acres), because the "farm" they purchased typically was a forest. A new landowner could clear no more than ten to twelve acres of trees a year. But small lots carried a price. All land in the public domain was sold at auction, usually for much more than the two-dollar minimum. With agricultural prices soaring, speculators assumed that land would continue to rise in value and accordingly were willing to bid high on new land, which they resold to farmers at hefty prices.

The growing availability of credit after the War of 1812 fed speculation. The chartering of the Second Bank of the United States in 1816 had the dual effect of increasing the amount of money in circulation and

stimulating the chartering of private banks within states (state banks). The circulation of all banks grew from $45 million in bank notes in 1812 to $100 million in 1817. The stockholders and directors of these banks viewed them less as a sound investment for their capital (many directors actually had very little capital when they started state banks) than as agencies that could lend them money for land speculation. Secretary of the Treasury William H. Crawford observed in 1820 that banks had been incorporated "not because there was capital seeking investment, not because the places where they were established had commerce and manufacturers which required their fostering aid; but because men without active capital wanted the means of obtaining loans, which their standing in the community would not command from banks or individuals having real capital and established credit." In short, banks were founded so that they could lend their directors money for personal investment in land speculation. The result was an orgy of land speculation between 1815 and 1819. In 1819 sales of public land were over 1,000 percent greater than the average in 1800–1814.

The Speculator and the Squatter

Nevertheless, most of the public domain eventually found its way into the hands of small farmers. Because speculators gained nothing by holding land for prolonged periods, they were only too happy to sell it when the price was right. In addition, a familiar frontier type, the squatter, exerted a restraining influence on the speculator.

Even before the creation of the public domain, squatters had helped themselves to western land; George Washington himself had been unable to drive squatters off lands that he owned in the West. Squatters were an independent and proud lot, scornful of their fellow citizens, who were "softened by Ease, enervated by Affluence and Luxurious Plenty, & unaccustomed to Fatigues, Hardships, Difficulties or dangers." Disdaining land speculators above all, squatters formed claims associations to police land auctions and prevented speculators from bidding up the price of land. Squatters also pressured Congress to allow them "preemption" rights—that is, the right to purchase at the minimum price land that they had already settled on and improved. Seeking to undo the pernicious effects of its own laws, Congress responded by passing special preemption laws for squatters in specific areas and finally, in 1841, acknowledged a general right of preemption.

But preemption laws were of no use to farmers who arrived after speculators had already bought up land. Having spent their small savings on livestock, seed, and tools, these settlers then had to buy land from speculators on credit at vicious interest rates that ranged as high as 40 percent. Saddled by steep indebtedness, many western farmers had no choice but to skimp on subsistence crops while expanding cash crops in the hope of paying off their creditors. Farmers in these years were not merely entering the market economy; they were lunging into it.

Countless farmers who had carried basically conservative expectations to the West and who had hoped to establish self-sufficient farms in a land of abundance quickly became economic adventurers. Wanting land that they could call their own, but forced to raise cash crops in a hurry, many farmers worked their acreage to exhaustion and thus had to keep moving in search of new land. The phrase "the moving frontier" refers not only to the obvious fact that with each passing decade the line of settlement shifted farther west but also to the fact that the same people kept moving. The experience of Abraham Lincoln's parents, who migrated from the East through several farms in Kentucky and then to Indiana, was representative of the westward trek.

The Panic of 1819

In 1819 the land boom collapsed like a house of cards, the victim of a financial panic. The state banks' loose practices contributed mightily to the panic. Like the Bank of the United States, these banks issued their own bank notes. In the absence of any national system of paper money, these notes served as a circulating medium. A bank note was just a piece of paper with a printed promise from the bank's directors to pay the bearer ("redeem") on demand a certain amount of specie (gold or silver coinage). State banks had long emitted far more bank notes than they could redeem, and these notes had fueled the economic boom after 1815. With credit so readily available, farmers borrowed money to buy more land and to plant more crops, confident that they could repay their loans when they sold their crops. After 1817, however, the combination of bumper crops in Europe and a business recession in Britain trimmed the foreign demand for U.S. wheat, flour, and cotton—at the

very time when American farmers were becoming more dependent on agricultural exports to pay their debts.

In reaction to the overemission of state bank notes, the Bank of the United States, in the summer of 1818, began to insist that state banks redeem in specie their notes that were held by the Bank of the United States. Because the Bank of the United States had more branches than any state bank, notes of state banks were often presented by their holders to branches of the Bank of the United States for redemption. Whenever the Bank of the United States redeemed a state bank note in specie, it became a creditor of the state bank. In turn, to pay their debts to the Bank of the United States, the state banks had no choice but to force farmers and land speculators to repay loans. The result was a general curtailment of credit throughout the nation, but particularly in the West.

The biggest losers were the land speculators, who had bought huge tracts with the expectation that prices would rise but now found prices tumbling. Land that had once sold for as much as $69 an acre dropped to $2 an acre. Land prices fell, in turn, because the credit squeeze drove down the market prices of staples like wheat, corn, cotton, and tobacco. Cotton, which sold for 32¢ a pound in 1818, sank as low as 17¢ a pound in 1820. Since farmers could not get much cash for their crops, they could not pay the debts that they had incurred to buy land. Since speculators could not collect money owed them by farmers, the value of land that they still held for sale collapsed.

The significance of the panic lay not only in the economic damage it did but also in the conclusions that many Americans drew from it. First, the panic left a bitter taste about banks, particularly the Bank of the United States, which was widely blamed for the hard times. In addition, the panic dramatized the vulnerability of American factories to cheap foreign competition (a vulnerability evident even before the economic downturn) and thereby stimulated demands for the protection of domestic industries. These demands would lead to the passage of higher tariffs in 1824 and 1828. Finally, plummeting prices for cash crops demonstrated how much farmers were coming to depend on distant markets. In effect, it took a severe business reverse to show farmers the extent to which they had become entrepreneurs. The fall in the prices of cash crops intensified the search for better forms of transportation to reach those faraway markets. If the cost of transporting crops could be cut, farmers could keep a larger share of the value of their crops and thereby adjust to falling prices.

The Transportation Revolution: Steamboats, Canals, and Railroads

Most forms of transportation available to Americans in 1820 had severe drawbacks. The great rivers west of the Appalachians ran primarily from north to south and hence could not by themselves connect western farmers with eastern markets. The National Road, with its crushed-stone surface, was a well-built highway that advanced farther west each year. In addition, between 1815 and 1825, several northern states chartered private companies to build toll roads (turnpikes). But roads could not solve the nation's transportation problems. Aside from the fact that horse-drawn wagons could carry only limited produce, roads were expensive to maintain. After 1825 investment in turnpikes slackened, and the interest of both public and private investors shifted toward the development of waterways.

In 1807 Robert R. Livingston and Robert Fulton successfully introduced a steamboat popularly known as the *Clermont* on the Hudson River. Livingston and Fulton soon gained a monopoly from the New York legislature to run a ferry service on the Hudson between New York and New Jersey. So spectacular were their profits that rival entrepreneurs secured a license from Congress to operate a competing ferry service and thereby challenged the Livingston-Fulton monopoly. A long court battle followed. Finally, in 1824 the U.S. Supreme Court decided against the monopoly in the famous case of *Gibbons* v. *Ogden*. Speaking for a unanimous Court, Chief Justice John Marshall ruled that commerce included not merely the exchange of products but navigation as well. This was an important finding, because the Constitution clearly empowered Congress to regulate commerce "among the several States." In the event of a conflict between state and congressional regulation of commerce, Marshall continued, the congressional power must prevail. Thus Marshall upheld the competitors (who had a license from Congress) and effectively broke the Livingston-Fulton monopoly. In the wake of Marshall's decision, state efforts to establish monopolies over river trade quickly collapsed. The number of steamboats operating on western rivers jumped from 17 in 1817 to 69 in 1820 and to 727 by 1855.

Interior of a Flatboat,
by Charles-Alexandre Lesueur, 1826
Not all flatboats that carried produce and pioneers on American rivers were floating rafts. Many had roomy interiors that accommodated whole families, provisions, and even barn animals.

Prior to the introduction of steamboats on the Mississippi, flatboats (often just rafts) carried produce downriver. Since they were unable to navigate upstream, the flatboats were broken up and sold for firewood in New Orleans. The return voyage was made either by foot or horse through Indian country, or by sailing vessels from New Orleans to Philadelphia or New York and then by foot or horse across the Appalachians to the West. Keelboats—similar to flatboats but moved by a rudder—could make the upstream voyage, though at a snail's pace. It took a keelboat three or four months to complete the 1,350-mile journey from New Orleans to Louisville. In contrast, steamboats could travel upstream at a relatively fast speed. As early as 1817, a steamboat made the trip in twenty-five days. Moreover, although the English had developed steam-propulsion technology in the eighteenth century, between 1820 and 1840 Americans discovered many practical techniques for increasing the effectiveness of steamboats. The gradual introduction of long, shallow hulls made steamboats suitable for use in shallow water (particularly the stretch of the Mississippi-Ohio river system from Louisville to Pittsburgh). The result was an extension of the navigation season; hot, dry summer weather that lowered water levels no longer forced steamboats out of service.

Erie Canal, *by John William Hill, 1831 Construction of the Erie Canal was a remarkable feat—all the more so because the United States did not possess a single school of engineering at the time. The project's heroes were lawyers and merchants who taught themselves engineering, and brawny workmen, often Irish immigrants, who hacked a waterway through the forests and valleys of New York.*

Steamboats became more ornate as well as more practical. To compete for passengers, they began to offer luxurious cabins and lounges (called saloons). The saloon of the *Eclipse,* a Mississippi steamboat, was the length of a football field and featured skylights, chandeliers, a ceiling crisscrossed by Gothic arches, and mahogany furniture covered with velvet. Such "elegance bordering on magnificence" helped to reassure westerners that whatever easterners might say, they were not savage backwoods people but polished and urbane citizens. Yet most steamboat passengers only glimpsed this elegance. Saloons were reserved for the small minority who booked "cabin" passage. The majority of travelers purchased "deck" passage, which entitled them to sleep on a cotton bale if they were lucky enough to find one, on the floor if they were not.

Whether cabin or deck passengers, all steamboat travelers confronted the hazards of this mode of navigation. Fires were common—not surprisingly, in view of the fact that steamboats needed huge furnaces and often carried combustible cargoes like oil and hay. Collisions claimed many lives. The worst, occurring in 1837 on the Mississippi, killed several hundred Creek Indians who were being transported by steamer to reservations in the West. Submerged snags often cracked the fragile hulls of fast-moving steamers: British novelist Charles Dickens described the Mississippi above Cairo, Illinois, as "an enormous ditch . . . choked and obstructed everywhere by huge logs and whole forest trees." Moreover, because little was

known about the reaction of metals under stress, boiler explosions destroyed many steamboats, not to mention their passengers. So common were such explosions that one company introduced a line of steamboats on the Hudson River that, for safety's sake, carried the passengers in tow on a barge.

Once steamboats had demonstrated the feasibility of upriver navigation, popular enthusiasm for internal improvements shifted away from turnpikes and toward canals. As late as 1816, the United States had only a hundred miles of canals. Not only did Americans know little about building canals in these early years, but the capital required to construct them was mind-boggling. Even Thomas Jefferson dismissed the idea of canals as "little short of madness." However, the invention of the steamboat, the abundance of western settlers desperate for access to markets, and the natural endowment of the Great Lakes combined to make the lure of canals irresistible. Canals offered the prospect of connecting the superb Mississippi-Ohio river system with the Great Lakes, and the Great Lakes with eastern markets.

The construction of the Erie Canal was the first major canal project. Started by New York State in 1817, the canal at its completion stretched for 363 miles between Albany and Buffalo. The Erie Canal was ten times longer than any previous American canal and by far the longest in the Western world. More than a waterway, it was a capstone of the sometimes fragile Era of Good Feelings, a symbol of American ingenuity and peaceful progress. As part of the celebration of its completion in 1825, a procession of American steam-boats formed a perfect circle of salute around two British warships anchored in New York Harbor. The British responded by striking up "Yankee Doodle," to which the Americans replied with "God Save the King." Through the Erie Canal, New York City was linked by inland waterways (the Hudson River, the canal itself, and Lake Erie) all the way to Ohio.

Major Rivers, Roads, and Canals, 1825–1860

Railroads and canals increasingly tied the economy of the Midwest to that of the Northeast.

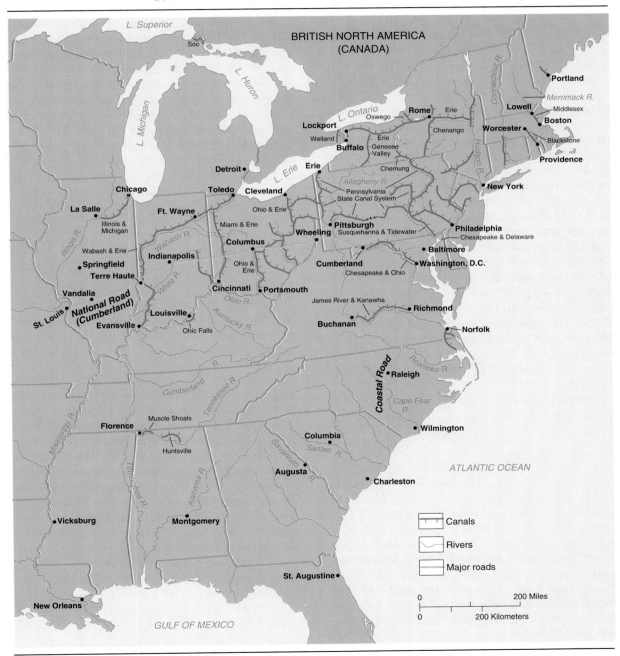

In New England the Blackstone Canal (1824–1828) created a water highway between Worcester, Massachusetts, and the Narragansett Bay in Rhode Island. By 1834 the Main Line (or Pennsylvania) Canal connected eastern Pennsylvania with Pittsburgh. The Main Line Canal was an even more remarkable feat of engineering than the Erie because it crossed the Allegheny Mountains with the aid of a railroad. Canal boats on this system had to be built in collapsible sections; they were disassembled upon reaching the mountains and then carried up one side and down the other on cable cars. As these canals spread like fingers from east to west, a similar system of canals was under construction from west to east. By 1836 the Ohio and Erie Canal stretched from Portsmouth on the Ohio River to Cleveland on Lake Erie. From Lake Erie, packets and steamboats could carry produce to the Erie Canal and on to Albany and New York City. In 1836, 365,000 bushels of western wheat entered the milling city of Rochester on the Erie Canal and left as 369,000 barrels of flour bound for eastern New York.

The canal boom drastically cut shipping costs. In 1817, just before construction began on the Erie Canal, the cost of transporting wheat from Buffalo to New York City was three times the market value of wheat in New York City, whereas the transportation costs for corn and oats over the same route were, respectively, six and twelve times their market value in New York City. Average freight charges between Buffalo and New York City dropped from 19¢ a ton per mile in 1817 to less than 2¢ a ton per mile in 1830. Throughout the nation, canals reduced shipping costs from 20¢ to 30¢ a ton per mile before 1815 to 2¢ to 3¢ a ton per mile by the 1830s.

When another economic depression hit in the late 1830s, various states found themselves overcommitted to costly canal projects and ultimately scrapped many. Yet even as the canal boom was ending, railroads were spreading. In 1825 the world's first railroad devoted to general transportation began operation in England, and by 1840 some three thousand miles of track had been laid in America, about the same as the total canal mileage in 1840. During the 1830s, investment in American railroads actually exceeded that in canals. Cities like Baltimore and Boston, which lacked major inland waterway connections, turned to railroads to enlarge their share of the western market. The Baltimore and Ohio Railroad, chartered in 1828, took business away from the Chesapeake and Ohio Canal farther south. Blocked by its Berkshire Mountains from

building a canal to the Erie, Massachusetts chartered the Boston and Worcester Railroad in 1831 and the Western Railroad (from Worcester to Albany) in 1833.

Faster, cheaper to build, and able to reach more places, railroads had obvious advantages over canals and also contributed to the growth of communities that were remote from waterways. But railroads' potential was only slowly realized. Most early railroads ran between cities in the East rather than from east to west and carried more passengers than freight. Not until 1849 did freight revenues exceed passenger revenues, and not until 1850 was the East Coast connected by rail to the Great Lakes.

Several factors explain the relatively slow spread of interregional railroads. Unlike canals, which were built directly by state governments, most railroads were constructed by private corporations seeking quick profits. To minimize their original investment, railroad companies commonly resorted to cost-cutting measures such as covering wooden rails with iron bars. As a result, although relatively cheap to build, American railroads needed constant repairs and were even more vulnerable than canals to economic fluctuations. In contrast, although expensive to construct, canals needed relatively little maintenance and were kept in operation for decades after railroads appeared. Moreover, it remained cheaper to ship bulky commodities such as iron ore, coal, and nonperishable agricultural produce by canal.

The Growth of the Cities

The transportation revolution contributed to the rapid growth of towns and cities. In 1820 only 6.1 percent of the population lived in places of 2,500 or more inhabitants, and only two cities, New York and Philadelphia, had more than 100,000 people. Four of the ten largest cities in the United States in 1820 had fewer than 15,000 inhabitants. The next forty years witnessed, in relative terms, the most rapid urbanization in American history. By 1860 nearly 20 percent of the population lived in places of 2,500 or more. New York City's population rose from 124,000 in 1820 to 800,000 in 1860. By 1860 there were eight American cities larger than the largest city in 1820. An even more revealing change was the transformation of sleepy villages of a few hundred into thriving towns of several thousand. In 1820 only 56 incorporated towns could boast between 2,500 and 10,000 inhabitants; by 1850 there were over 350 such towns. The Erie Canal transformed

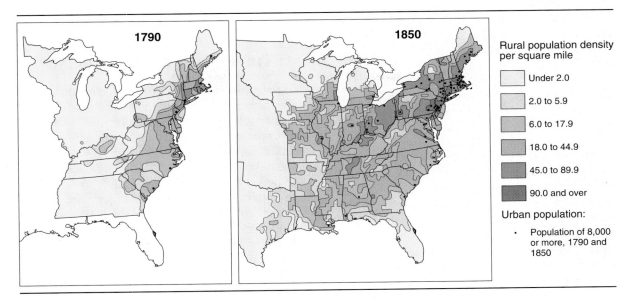

Population Distribution, 1790 and 1850
By 1850 high population density characterized parts of the Midwest as well as the Northeast.
SOURCE: *1900 Census of Population, Statistical Atlas,* plates 2 and 8.

Rochester, New York, for example, from a village of a few hundred people in 1817 to a thriving town of 9,000 by 1830.

City and town growth occurred with dramatic suddenness, especially in the West. Pittsburgh, Cincinnati, and St. Louis were little more than villages in 1800. The War of 1812 stimulated the growth of Pittsburgh, whose iron forges provided shot and weapons for American soldiers, and Cincinnati, which became a staging ground for attacks on the British in the Old Northwest. Meanwhile, St. Louis acquired some importance as a fur-trading center. Then between 1815 and 1819, the agricultural boom and the introduction of the steamboat transformed all three places from outposts with transient populations of hunters, traders, and soldiers into bustling cities. Cincinnati's population, for example, nearly quadrupled between 1810 and 1820 and doubled in the 1820s.

With the exception of Lexington, Kentucky, whose lack of access to water forced it into relative stagnation after 1820, all the prominent western cities were river ports: Pittsburgh, Cincinnati, and Louisville on the Ohio; St. Louis and New Orleans on the Mississippi. Except for Pittsburgh, all were essentially commercial hubs rather than manufacturing centers and were flooded by individuals extremely eager to make money. In 1819 land speculators in St. Louis were bidding as much as a thousand dollars an acre for lots that had sold for thirty dollars an acre in 1815. Waterfronts endowed with natural beauty were swiftly overrun by stores and docks. "Louis Ville, by nature is beautiful," a visitor wrote, "but the handy Work of *Man* has instead of improving destroy'd the works of Nature and made it a detestable place."

The transportation revolution acted like a fickle god, selecting some cities for growth while sentencing others to relative decline. Just as the steamboat had elevated the river cities over land-locked Lexington, the completion of the Erie Canal shifted the center of western economic activity toward the Great Lakes. The result was a gradual decline in the importance of river cities and a rise between 1830 and 1860 in the importance of lake cities such as Buffalo, Cleveland, Detroit, Chicago, and Milwaukee. In 1830 nearly 75 percent of all western city dwellers lived in the river ports of New Orleans, Louisville, Cincinnati, and Pittsburgh, but by 1840 the proportion had dropped to 20 percent.

The growth of cities and towns was spurred initially by the transportation revolution and the development of interregional trade. Urban expansion received an added boost from the rise of manufacturing between 1815 and 1840.

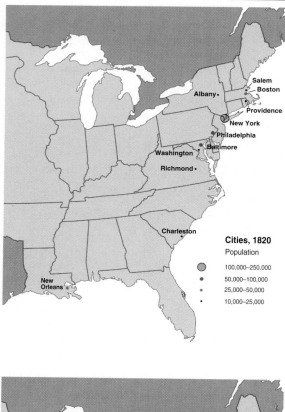

Cities, 1820
Population

○ 100,000–250,000

● 50,000–100,000

· 25,000–50,000

· 10,000–25,000

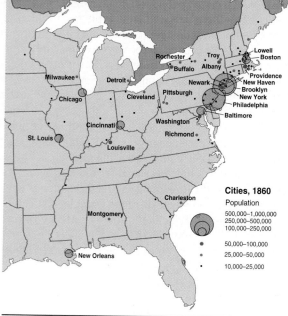

Cities, 1860
Population

500,000–1,000,000
250,000–500,000
100,000–250,000

● 50,000–100,000

· 25,000–50,000

· 10,000–25,000

American Cities, 1820 and 1860

In 1820 most cities were seaports. By 1860, however, cities dotted the nation's interior and included San Francisco on the West Coast. This change occurred in large measure because of the transportation revolution.

SOURCE: *Statistical Abstract of the United States.*

THE RISE OF MANUFACTURING

Today we customarily equate the word *manufacturing* with industrialization—that is, with large factories, machinery, and mass production. But the literal meaning of *manufacturing* is "making by hand." During the colonial era, most products were made by hand, either in households or in the workshops of skilled artisans. The period between 1815 and 1860 marked a transition from colonial to modern manufacturing. Household, or "cottage," industries declined, whereas large factories and power-driven machinery came to dominate the production of cotton textiles. But small shops were still responsible for a great deal of manufacturing. As late as 1860, the average manufacturing establishment contained only eight workers.

Few Americans believed in 1860 that they lived in an industrial society; most continued to think of the United States as a nation of farmers and small producers. This self-image, however, was misleading. By 1850 the 20 percent of the labor force engaged in manufacturing produced about 30 percent of the national output. Furthermore, industrialization was starting to affect many crafts besides textile making.

Industrialization was not a single occurrence, a kind of tidal wave that washed away traditional forms of manufacturing. Rather, it was a gradual process with several distinct stages. First, the tasks involved in making a product were subdivided, so that instead of making a whole product, each worker made only a part. Next, workers were gathered into factories with rooms devoted to specialized operations performed by hand or by simple machines. Finally, power-driven machinery replaced fabrication by hand. These three stages arrived quickly and almost simultaneously in New England's cotton textile industry, but many crafts—including the making of shoes, hats, guns, trunks, and saddles—experienced at least the first two stages before 1860. Many variations of this pattern appeared between 1815 and 1860. In some crafts, task subdivision and simple machinery were introduced without the creation of large factories. In others, like shoe manufacturing, the subdivision of tasks and the emergence of large factories occurred before the introduction of power-driven machinery. Because industrialization occurred gradually and unevenly, people did not always realize that hand fabrication by skilled artisans was becoming obsolete and that machines would soon tumble artisans from their pedestals.

Causes of Industrialization

A host of factors stimulated industrialization. The Embargo Act of 1807 persuaded merchants barred from foreign trade to redirect their capital into factories. The War of 1812 sparked support for protective tariffs to end American economic dependence on Europe; particularly in the 1820s, tariffs reduced imports of English cloth and contributed to the 15.4 percent average annual rise in American cloth products between 1815 and 1833. Improvements in transportation made it possible for manufacturers to sell finished products in distant markets and provided an incentive to increase production. In addition, a popular preference for factory-made rather than home-made products developed wherever the transportation revolution reached. Household production declined not only in cities but in rural areas along canals and railroads and never gained a secure footing in the West. The more farmers went into the business of selling as well as raising crops, the more they were inclined to buy articles like shoes and clothes rather than make them.

Immigration was also vital. Five million people migrated from Europe to the United States between 1790 and 1860, most of them to pursue economic opportunity. The majority were German or Irish, but the smaller number of British immigrants played the key role in launching industrialization. In Britain industrialization was a generation ahead of the United States, and by 1790 Britain had a class of artisans who understood the workings of machines. For example, Samuel Slater, who immigrated to the United States in 1789, had learned the "mystery" of textile production in England. Although British laws forbade emigration by skilled "mechanics," Slater disguised himself and brought his knowledge of machines to eager Americans.

Although Britain had a head start in developing the technology relevant to industrialization, Americans made contributions of their own. Unlike Britain, America had no craft organizations (called guilds) that tied artisans to a single trade. As a result, American artisans freely experimented with machines outside their craft. In the 1790s wagon maker Oliver Evans of Delaware, for example, built an automated flour mill that required only a single supervisor to look on as the grain poured in from one side and was discharged from the other as flour. In addition, the relatively high wages paid to American workers gave manufacturers an incentive to find substitutes for expensive hand labor in order to make products as quickly and cheaply as possible. After inventing the cotton gin, Eli Whitney in 1798 filled a government contract for ten thousand muskets by using unskilled workers to make identical parts that could be interchanged from musket to musket. The idea of interchangeable parts actually originated in Europe, but the United States led all nations in applying the idea in factories—so much so that it came to be called the American system of manufacturing.

New England Industrializes

New England became America's first industrial region. The gradual strangulation of American trade by Britain's Orders in Council, Napoleon's Continental System, and Jefferson's embargo hit New England more severely than regions less dependent on European trade. Incentives were thus provided for New England's merchants to invest in manufacturing. In addition, New England's rivers were numerous, swift-flowing, and ideally suited to provide water power for mills. At the same time, the region's soil, thin and rocky in many places, forced young men off the land and into the westward flow of migration, leaving villages and towns with a surplus of young women. The textile mills that multiplied in New England after 1815 depended on the labor of the sisters who had stayed at home while their brothers headed west or moved to the cities.

Within New England the main innovation came in the manufacture of cotton textiles. In 1790 Samuel Slater arrived in Pawtucket, Rhode Island, and established there the first permanent American mill for spinning cotton into yarn through the use of the spinning frame invented by the Englishman Richard Arkwright. Starting with nine workers, Slater had a hundred by 1800 and constructed other mills around Rhode Island and Massachusetts. Slater's mills performed only two of the many operations needed to turn raw cotton into clothing: carding, or fashioning broad laps of cotton into fine strands or slivers, and spinning these strands into yarn. The actual weaving of yarn Slater contracted out to women working in their homes. This "putting-out" system reinforced rather than challenged the traditional position of household, or "cottage," industry.

The incorporation in 1813 of the Boston Manufacturing Company by a group of merchant capitalists called the Boston Associates began a new chapter in the relationship between factories and cottage industries. Starting with a capital stock of $400,000 (more than ten times the stock of a typical Rhode Island mill), the Boston Manufacturing Company in quick succession established cotton textile factories in the Massachusetts towns of Waltham on the Charles River and Lowell on the Merrimack. By 1836 the Boston Associates had a total investment of $6.2 million in eight companies employing more than six thousand workers.

Size was not the only factor that distinguished these new mills from Slater's. In contrast to Slater's mills, the Waltham and Lowell factories produced finished products and thus challenged the cottage industries that Slater's system had sustained. Additionally, the Waltham and Lowell mills upset the traditional ordering of New England society to a degree that Slater never contemplated. Slater had sought to preserve tradition by hiring entire families to work in his mill complexes, just as entire families had traditionally worked on farms. He hired men to raise crops on nearby land owned by the factory and their wives and children to tend the machines inside. Under this arrangement, children were never out of parental sight for long. In contrast, 80 percent of the workers in the mills operated by the Boston Manufacturing Company were unmarried women between the ages of fifteen and thirty, who had been lured from New England's farms by the promise of factory work. Mary Paul, a Vermont teenager, settled her doubts about leaving home for work in Lowell by concluding that "I . . . must work where I can get more pay." Although these young women often wrote home, they rarely saw their parents. In place of traditional family discipline, the Waltham and Lowell operatives, as the mill workers were called, experienced new kinds of restraints. The Boston capitalists who financed the mills did not personally oversee them; rather, they delegated oversight to managers, who imposed their own forms of discipline on the work force. Operatives had to live either in boardinghouses built by the factory owners or in licensed private dwellings. Company regulations required operatives to attend church on the Sabbath, to observe a 10:00 P.M. curfew, and to accept what one minister called the "moral police of the corporations." At least initially, most young female operatives submitted without complaint to the "moral police."

Mill Girls
New England's humming textile mills were a magnet for untold numbers of independence-seeking young women in antebellum America.

A major reason why the corporations enforced high moral standards was to give the mills a good reputation so that New England farm girls would continue to be attracted into factory work. Yet mill conditions were far from attractive. To prevent the threads from snapping, the factories had to be kept humid. To create this condition, overseers nailed the windows shut and sprayed the air with water. Operatives also had to contend with flying dust and the deafening roar of the machines. Then keener competition and a worsening economy in the late 1830s led the mill owners to reduce wages and speed up work schedules. Such conditions were common in nineteenth-century factories, but in Lowell and Waltham they were intensified by the basic impersonality of the system. Each of the major groups that contributed to the system lived in a self-

mechanics' lien laws	enlarged shop	factory	interchangeable parts 330
Erie Canal	putting out system	Lowell System	central shop
the Bowery	Brer Rabbit	Nat Turner	pine barrens
city central unions	Boston Associates	Eli Whitney	yeoman farmer
Joseph Smith	Brigham Young	Mormons	
camp meeting	Charles G. Finney	Amer. Bible Society	Methodists
circuit rider	Francis Asbury	anxious bench	Second Awakening 304-305
Henry Clay	Removal Act of 1830	Worcester v. Georgia	Maysville Road veto 304
Burned-over District	veto of Bank of US	Tecumseh	spoils system 304
rotation in office	Nullification	John C. Calhoun 312	S. Car. Expos. & Protest
Andrew Jackson	Martin Van Buren	Specie Circular - 313	Whigs
Wm. H. Harrison	J. Q. Adams	"corrupt bargain" - 302	

1. Analyze carefully the parallels and contrasts between the Federalists and Whigs and the Democratic-Republicans (1790s/early 1800s) and the Democrats (1820s-30s). In addition to examining their policies, deal with their underlying assumptions about society and the role of government.

2. Compare/contrast the economic systems of the North and the South.

3. Explain how some historians contend that the institution of slavery and policies and attitudes toward Native Americans were built on paternalism.

4. Present an "argument" that the religion was a profound influence upon US society in the first half of the 19th century.

5. Describe major factors which stimulated economic change and explain how economic change produced widespread change in the US after 1815.

contained world. The Boston Associates raised capital but rarely visited the factories. Their agents, all men, gave orders to the operatives, mainly women. Some 800 Lowell mill women quit work in 1834 to protest a reduction in wages. Two years later, there was another "turnout," this time involving 1,500 to 2,000 women. These were the largest strikes in American history to that date, noteworthy as strikes not only of employees against employers but also of women against men.

Manufacturing in New York City and Philadelphia

With their large size, reliance on female labor, and dependence on machinery, the Lowell and Waltham textile mills were the most conspicuous examples of industrialization before 1840. In contrast to such planned factory towns, cities like New York and Philadelphia during the 1820s and 1830s witnessed an industrialization that lacked even the appearance of orderliness, depended far less on machinery and on female workers, occurred in small firms as well as in large ones, and encompassed a greater range of products, including shoes, saddles, tools, rope, hats, and gloves.

Although diverging from the Lowell-Waltham model, the factories of New York and Philadelphia exposed workers to some of the same forces encountered by New England mill girls. By expanding the market for manufactures, the transportation revolution had turned some urban artisans, auctioneers, and merchants into aggressive merchandisers who scoured the country for orders. As a result, by 1835 New York City's ready-made clothing industry, for example, was supplying cheap dungarees and shirts to western farmers and even southern slaves; in the 1840s it was providing expensive suits for well-to-do customers. In turn, the possibility of reaching distant markets intensified competition and spurred entrepreneurs to slash the cost of their products by increasing output, cutting wages, or both. In New England the Boston Associates had responded by introducing machines, but New York City lacked an easily harnessable source of water power, and before 1840 few machines existed that could speed up the fabrication of products like shoes. Thus factory owners in cities like New York and Philadelphia had to use different tactics to increase their share of the marketplace: they hired large numbers of unskilled or semiskilled workers, many of them women, and paid them low wages to perform simple, specialized hand operations like

stitching cloth and soling shoes. In place of the colonial artisan who had fabricated the whole shoe on demand for a customer, such unskilled or semiskilled laborers no longer made whole shoes and rarely even saw a customer.

This subdivision of tasks (without the use of machines) characterized a great deal of industrialization before 1840 and occurred in a variety of work settings. In the boot and shoe industry that developed after 1820 in eastern Massachusetts, especially at Lynn, workers were gradually gathered into large factories to perform specialized operations in different rooms. In metropolises like New York and Philadelphia, the pattern was a little different. Here, although some large factories appeared in nearly all crafts, much of the subdivision of tasks took place in small shops, garrets, or homes. Because of the population density in these cities, it was unnecessary to gather workers into large factories. Middlemen could simply subcontract tasks out to widows, immigrants, and others who would fashion parts of shoes or saddles or dresses anywhere that light would enter. "We have been in some fifty cellars in different parts of the city," a New York *Tribune* reporter wrote in 1845, "each inhabited by a shoe-maker and his family. The floor is made of rough plank laid loosely down, and the ceiling is not quite so high as a tall man. The walls are dark and damp and . . . the miserable room is lighted only by a shallow sash partly projecting above the surface of the grounds and by the little light that struggles from the steep and rotting stairs. In this apartment often lives the man and his work bench, the wife, and five or six children of all ages; and perhaps a palsied grandfather and grandmother and often both. . . . Here they work, here they cook, they eat, they sleep, they pray. . . ."

In further contrast to places like Lowell and Waltham, which had not even existed in the eighteenth century, New York and Philadelphia were home to artisans with proud craft traditions and independence. Those with a highly marketable skill like cutting leather or clothing continued to earn good wages. Others grew rich by turning themselves into entrepreneurs who spent less time making products than taking trips to obtain orders and who then hired workers to fill the orders. Thus industrialization did not reduce all artisans to misery. But many artisans, even though skilled, found themselves on the downslope. Increasingly faced with factory competition, they could either eke out a living as independent artisans by working longer hours and skimping on food or other necessaries, or enter factories at low wages as semiskilled or unskilled workers.

In the late 1820s, skilled artisans in New York, Philadelphia, and other cities began to form trade unions and "workingmen's" political parties to protect their interests. Disdaining association with unskilled workers, most of these groups initially sought to restore privileges and working conditions that artisans had once enjoyed rather than to act as leaders of unskilled workers. But the steady deterioration of working conditions in the early 1830s tended to throw skilled and unskilled workers into the same boat. When coal heavers in Philadelphia struck for a ten-hour day in 1835, they were quickly joined by carpenters, cigar makers, shoemakers, leather workers, and other artisans in the United States' first general strike.

The emergence of organized worker protest underscored the mixed blessings of economic development. Although some benefited from the new commercial and industrial economy, others found their economic position deteriorating. By the 1830s many Americans wondered whether their nation was truly a land of equality.

EQUALITY AND INEQUALITY

Observers of antebellum (pre–Civil War) America sensed changes sweeping the country but had trouble describing them or agreeing on their direction. Some insisted that wealth was "universally diffused." Others, like the New York merchant Philip Hone, portrayed an unhappy society marked by extremes of "costly luxury" and "squalid misery."

One of the most astute of these observers was the French nobleman Alexis de Tocqueville, who spent nine months in America in 1831–1832. Although Tocqueville filled his private journals with references to inequality, in his two-volume *Democracy in America* (1835, 1840) he cited the "general equality of condition among the people" as the fundamental shaping force of American society. Inclined to view everything in comparative terms, Tocqueville, while certainly recognizing inequality, thought that wealth was more evenly distributed in the United States than in France and that, regardless of an individual's wealth, Americans believed that one person was as good as another. American servants insisted on being called the "help" and viewed as neighbors invited to assist in running a

household rather than as permanent menials. Similarly, whereas in France merchants were disdained by the titled nobility, in America merchants thought themselves equal to anyone.

Historians continue to argue about the meaning and extent of equality in antebellum America, but by using refined techniques of measurement they have drawn a more detailed portrait of antebellum society than the profile sketched by contemporaries. The following discussion applies mainly to northern society. We examine the South, whose "peculiar institution" of slavery created a distinctive social structure and set of social relationships, in Chapter 12.

Growing Inequality: The Rich and the Poor

The gap between the rich and the poor, which had increased during the late eighteenth century, widened further during the first half of the nineteenth century. Although Americans portrayed them as oases of equality, farm areas contained a good deal of inequality. In 1850 the poorest 40 percent of native-born farmers owned less than one hundred dollars worth of property, whereas the richest 30 percent to 40 percent of farmers owned three-fourths or more of the total farm property. But the truly striking inequalities developed in the cities, where a small fraction of the people owned a huge share of urban wealth. In Boston, for example, the richest 10 percent of the population owned a little over half of the city's real estate and personal property in 1771. By 1833 the richest 4 percent owned 59 percent of the wealth, and by 1848 nearly two-thirds of the wealth. By 1848, 81 percent of Boston's population owned only 4 percent of its wealth. In New York City, the richest 4 percent owned nearly half the wealth in 1828 and more than two-thirds by 1845. These statistics are representative of trends that affected all major cities.

Although commentators celebrated the self-made American who rose "from rags to riches," few individuals actually accumulated their wealth in this way. The vast majority of those who became extremely rich started out with considerable wealth. Fewer than five of every hundred wealthy individuals started poor, and close to ninety of every hundred started rich. The old-fashioned way to make money was to inherit it, marry into more, and then invest wisely. There were just enough instances of fabulously successful poor boys like John Jacob Astor, who built a fur-trading empire,

View of St. Louis, *by Leon Pomarede, 1832*
When the trans-Mississippi fur trade declined in the 1830s, the steamboats plying the Mississippi and Missouri rivers became the key to St. Louis's expansion. With under 5,000 inhabitants in 1820, the city contained 100,000 by the 1850s. Population growth drove up the value of choice lots and contributed to the widening distance between social classes.

to sustain popular belief in the rags-to-riches myth, but not enough to turn that myth into a reality.

Their splendid residences as well as their wealth set the rich apart. The urban rich built imposing mansions clustered in neighborhoods. In 1828 over half of the 500 wealthiest families in New York City lived on only 8 of the city's more than 250 streets. During the early 1830s, half of Boston's wealthy families lived on but 8 of its 325 streets. Social clubs also separated the rich from others. The Philadelphia Club, founded in 1834, was a stronghold for proper Philadelphians. By the late 1820s, New York City had a club so exclusive that it was called just The Club. Tocqueville noted that in America "the wealthiest and most enlightened live

among themselves." Yet Tocqueville was also struck by how the rich feigned respect for equality when they moved about in public. They rode in ordinary rather than sumptuous carriages, brushed elbows easily with the less privileged, and avoided the conspicuous display of wealth that marked their private lives.

At the opposite end of the social ladder were the poor. By today's standards, most antebellum Americans were poor: they lived "close to the margin" of poverty, depended heavily on their children's labor to meet expenses, had little money to spend on medical care or recreation, and were subject to unemployment, not just during general economic downturns but from month to month, even in times of prosperity.

Freezing weather, for instance, could temporarily throw day laborers, factory workers, and boatmen out of work. In 1850 an estimated three out of eight males over the age of twenty owned little more than their clothing and the cash in their pockets.

In evaluating economic status, it is important to recognize that statistics on the distribution of wealth to some extent mask the fact that the accumulation of property takes place over an entire lifetime and increases with age. With its extraordinarily high birthrate, antebellum America was overwhelmingly a nation of young people with little property; not all of them would remain propertyless as they grew older.

Also keep in mind that when antebellum Americans themselves spoke of poverty, they were not thinking of the condition of hardship that affected most people. Instead, they were referring to a state of dependency, a total inability to fend for oneself, that affected *some* people. They often called this dependency *pauperism*. The absence of health insurance and old-age pensions condemned many infirm and aged people to pauperism. Widows whose children had left home might also have a hard time avoiding pauperism. Contemporaries usually classified all such people as the "deserving" poor and contrasted them with the "undeserving" poor—such as indolent loafers and drunkards whose poverty was self-willed. Most moralists claimed that America was happily free of a permanent class of paupers. They assumed that since pauperism resulted either from circumstances beyond anyone's control, such as old age and disease, or from voluntary decisions to squander money on liquor, it could not afflict entire groups generation after generation.

This assumption was comforting but also misleading, because a class of people who could not escape poverty was emerging in the major cities during the first half of the nineteenth century. One source of this class was immigration. As early as 1801, a New York newspaper called attention to boatloads of immigrants with large families, without money or health, and *"expiring from the want of sustenance."* The arrival of huge numbers of Irish immigrants during the 1840s and 1850s made a bad situation worse. The Irish were among the poorest immigrants ever to arrive in America. Fleeing famine in Ireland, they found even worse conditions in noxious slums like New York's infamous Five Points district. Starting with the conversion of a brewery into housing for hundreds of people

in 1837, the Five Points became probably the worst slum in America.

The Irish were not only poor but, as Catholics, also belonged to a church despised by the Protestant majority. In short, they were different and had little claim on the kindly impulses of most Protestants. But even the Protestant poor came in for rough treatment in the years between 1815 and 1840. The more Americans convinced themselves that success was within everyone's grasp, the less they accepted the traditional doctrine that poverty was ordained by God, and the more they were inclined to hold the poor responsible for their own poverty. Ironically, even as many Americans blamed the poor for being poor, they practiced discrimination that kept some groups mired in enduring poverty. Nowhere was this more true than in the case of northern free blacks.

Free Blacks in the North

Prejudice against blacks was deeply ingrained in white society throughout the nation. Although slavery had largely disappeared in the North by 1820, laws penalized blacks in many ways. One form of discrimination was to restrict the blacks' right to vote. In New York State, for example, a constitutional revision of 1821 eliminated property requirements for white voters but kept them for blacks. Rhode Island banned blacks from voting in 1822; Pennsylvania did so in 1837. Throughout the half-century after 1800, blacks could vote on equal terms with whites in only one of the nation's major cities, Boston. Efforts were made to bar free blacks from migrating to other states and cities. Missouri's original constitution authorized the state legislature to prevent blacks from entering the state "under any pretext whatsoever." Free blacks were often barred from public conveyances and facilities and were either excluded from public schools in major cities or forced into segregated schools. Segregation was the rule in northern jails, almshouses, and hospitals. But of all restrictions on free blacks, the most damaging was the social pressure that forced them into the least skilled and lowest-paying occupations throughout the northern cities. Recollecting his youthful days in Providence, Rhode Island, in the early 1830s, the free black William J. Brown wrote: "To drive carriages, carry a market basket after the boss, and brush his boots, or saw wood and run errands was as high as a colored man could rise." Although a few free blacks became successful entrepreneurs and grew moder-

DANCING FOR EELS, 1820 CATHARINE MARKET.

Dancing for Eels, Catharine Market, 1820
Expressive dancing was part of African-American street festivals in the eighteenth-century cities. Fearing that such street dancing perpetuated white stereotypes of blacks, antislavery whites and black leaders tried to suppress it after 1800, but black dancing survived in dance cellars in New York City's Five Points slum. As this sketch indicates, blacks sometimes danced in public for applause, "a bunch of eels" or other fish, and perhaps money. The black at the left is "patting juba," which meant keeping time by hand clapping or by beating hands against legs. "Juba" also became the nickname of William Henry Lane. After seeing Lane perform in 1842 in a Five Points cellar, the novelist Charles Dickens labeled him "the greatest dancer known."

ately wealthy, urban free blacks were only half as likely as city dwellers in general to own real estate.

The "Middling Classes"

The majority of antebellum Americans lived neither in splendid wealth nor in grinding poverty. Most belonged to what men and women of the time called the middling classes. Even though the wealthy owned an increasing proportion of all wealth, most people's standard of living rose between 1800 and 1860, particularly between 1840 and 1860, when per capita income grew at an annual rate of around 1.5 percent.

Americans applied the term *middling classes* to farmers and artisans, whose ideal was self-employ-

ment. Commentators viewed them as steady and dependable, the nation's sturdy "producers." Yet life in the middle was unpredictable, filled with jagged ups and downs. Words like *farmer* and *artisan* were often misleading, for they gave a greater impression of steadiness and stability than was really the case. For example, Asa G. Sheldon, born in Massachusetts in 1788, described himself in his autobiography as a farmer, offered advice on growing corn and cranberries, and gave speeches about the glories of farming. Although Sheldon undoubtedly knew a great deal about farming, he actually spent very little time tilling the soil. In 1812 he began to transport hops from New England to brewers in New York City, and he soon extended this business to Philadelphia and Baltimore. He invested his profits in land, but rather than farm the land, he made money selling its timber. When a business setback forced him to sell his property, he was soon back in operation "through the disinterested kindness of friends," who lent him money with which he purchased carts and oxen. These he used to get contracts for filling in swamps in Boston and for clearing and grading land for railroads. From all this and from the backbreaking labor of the Irish immigrants he hired to do the shoveling, Sheldon the "farmer" grew prosperous. But his prosperity in fact owed little to farming.

The increasingly commercial and industrial economy of antebellum America created opportunities for success and forced individuals like Sheldon to adapt. Not everyone, though, had an opportunity for success. Had it not been for the intervention of wealthy friends, Sheldon would have ended up in a poorhouse. Many lacked kindly friends with money to lend. Some, like Sheldon, rose. Others, like Allan Melville, father of novelist Herman Melville, slipped down the slope. An enterprising import merchant, Allan Melville had an abounding faith in his nation, in "our national Eagle, 'with an eye that never winks and a wing that never tires,' " and in the inevitable triumph of honesty and prudence. The Melvilles lived comfortably in Albany and New York City, but in the late 1820s, Melville's business, never robust, sagged. By 1830 he was begging his father for a loan of $500, proclaiming that "I am destitute of resources and without a shilling—without immediate assistance I know not what will become of me." He got the $500 plus an additional $3,000, but the downward spiral continued. In 1832 he died, broken in spirit and nearly insane.

The case of artisans also illustrates the perils of life in the middling classes. During the colonial period, artisans had formed a proud and cohesive group whose members often attained the goal of self-employment. They owned their own tools, made their own products on order from customers, boarded their apprentices and journeymen in their homes, and passed their skills on to their children. By 1850, in contrast, artisans had entered a new world of economic relationships. This was true even of a craft like carpentry that did not experience any industrial or technological change. Town and city growth in the wake of the transportation revolution created a demand for housing. Some carpenters, usually those with access to capital, became contractors who took orders for more houses than they could build themselves and who then hired large numbers of journeymen to do the construction work. Likewise, as we have seen, in the early industrialization of shoe manufacturing during the 1820s, some shoemakers spent less time crafting shoes than making trips to obtain orders for their products, then hired workers to fashion parts of shoes. In effect, the old class of artisans was splitting into two new groupings. On one side were artisans who had become entrepreneurs; on the other, journeymen with little prospect of self-employment.

An additional characteristic of the middling classes (one that they shared with the poor) was a high degree of transiency, or "spatial mobility." Farmers who cultivated land intensively in order to raise a cash crop and so get out of debt exhausted their land quickly and had to move on. Artisans displaced from skilled jobs by machines found that much unskilled work was seasonal and that they had to move from job to job to survive. Canal workers and boatmen had to secure new work when waterways froze. Even for city dwellers, to shift jobs often meant changing residences, for the cities were spreading out at a much faster rate than was public transportation. Some idea of the degree of transiency can be gained from a survey made by the Boston police on Saturday, September 6, 1851. At a time when Boston's population was 145,000, the survey showed that from 6:30 A.M. to 7:30 P.M., 41,729 people entered the city and 42,313 left.

The multiplying risks and opportunities that confronted Americans both widened the gap between social classes and increased the psychological burdens on individuals. Commercial and industrial growth also placed pressure on such basic social relationships as

those between lawyers and their clients, ministers and their parishioners, and children and their parents.

THE REVOLUTION IN SOCIAL RELATIONSHIPS

Following the War of 1812, the growth of interregional trade, commercial agriculture, and manufacturing disrupted many traditional social relationships and forged new ones. Two broad generalizations encompass these changes. First, Americans questioned authority to an unprecedented degree. In 1775 they had rebelled against their king. Now, it seemed, they were rebelling as well against their lawyers, physicians, ministers, and even their parents. An attitude of individualism sprouted and took firm root in antebellum America. Once *individualism* had meant nothing more than selfishness, but now Americans used the word to signify positive qualities: self-reliance and the conviction that each person was the best judge of his or her own true interests. Ordinary Americans might still agree with the opinions of their leaders, but only after they had thought matters through on their own. Those with superior wealth, education, or social position could no longer expect the automatic deference of the common people.

Second, even as Americans widely proclaimed themselves a nation of self-reliant individualists and questioned the traditional basis of authority, they sought to construct new foundations for authority. For example, among middle-class women, the idea developed that they possessed a "separate sphere" of authority in the home. In addition, individuals increasingly joined with others in these years to form voluntary associations through which they might influence the direction that their society would take.

The Attack on the Professions

The first phase in this alteration of social relationships was the erosion of traditional forms of authority. In the swiftly changing antebellum society, claims to social superiority were questioned as never before. The statesman Harrison Gray Otis put it in a nutshell in 1836: "Everywhere the disposition is found among those who live in the valleys to ask those who live on the hills, 'How came we here and you there?' "

Intense criticism of lawyers, physicians, and ministers exemplified this assault on authority. As far back as the 1780s, Benjamin Austin, a radical Boston artisan, had complained that lawyers needlessly prolonged and confused court cases so that they could charge high fees. Between 1800 and 1840, a wave of religious revivals known as the Second Great Awakening (see Chapter 10) sparked new attacks on the professions. Some revivalists blasted the clergy for creating complicated theologies that ordinary men and women could not comprehend, for drinking expensive wines, and for fleecing the people. One religious revivalist, Elias Smith, extended the criticism to physicians, whom he accused of inventing Latin and Greek names for diseases in order to disguise their own ignorance of how to cure them.

Attacks on the learned professions peaked between 1820 and 1850. In medicine a movement arose under the leadership of Samuel Thomson, a farmer's son with little formal education, to eliminate all barriers to entry into the medical profession. Thomson believed that anyone could understand the principles of medicine and become a physician. His crusade was remarkably successful. By 1845 every state had repealed laws that required licenses and education to practice medicine. Meanwhile, attacks on lawyers sharpened, and relations between ministers and their parishioners grew tense and acrimonious. In colonial New England, ministers had usually served a single parish for life, but by the 1830s a rapid turnover of ministers was becoming the norm as finicky parishioners commonly dismissed clergymen whose theology displeased them. Ministers themselves were becoming more ambitious—more inclined to leave small, poor congregations for large, wealthy ones.

The increasing commercialization of the economy contributed both to the growing number of professionals and to the attacks on them. The rise of the market economy intensified the demand for lawyers and physicians; the number of medical schools, for example, grew from one in 1765 to twenty in 1830 and sixty-five in 1860. Like so many other antebellum Americans, these freshly minted lawyers and doctors often were transients without deep roots in the towns that they served and without convincing claims to social superiority. Describing lawyers and physicians, a contemporary observer wrote: "Men dropped down into their places as from clouds. Nobody knew who or what they were, except as they claimed, or as a surface view of their character indicated." A horse doctor one day

would the next day hang up his sign as "Physician and Surgeon" and "fire at random a box of his pills into your bowels, with a vague chance of hitting some disease unknown to him, but with a better prospect of killing the patient, whom or whose administrator he charged some ten dollars a trial for his marksmanship."

The questioning of authority was particularly sharp on the frontier. Here, to eastern and foreign visitors, it seemed that every man they met was a "judge," "general," "colonel," or "squire." In a society in which everyone was new, such titles were easily adopted but just as easily challenged. Where neither law nor custom sanctioned claims of superiority, would-be gentlemen substituted an exaggerated sense of personal honor. Obsessed with their fragile status, many of these "gentlemen" reacted testily to the slightest insult. Dueling became a widespread frontier practice. At a Kentucky militia parade in 1819, a colonel's dog jogged onto the field and sat at his master's knee. Enraged by this breach of military decorum, the regiment's general ran the dog through with his dress sword. A week later, general and colonel met with pistols at ten paces. The colonel was killed; the general, crippled for life.

The Challenge to Family Authority

In contrast to the public, philosophical attacks on the learned professions, children engaged in a quiet questioning of parental authority. Economic change created new opportunities that forced young people to choose between staying at home to help their parents and venturing out on their own. Writing to her parents in Vermont shortly before taking a job in a Lowell textile mill, eighteen-year-old Sally Rice quickly got to the point: "I must of course have something of my own before many more years have passed over my head and where is that something coming from if I go home and earn nothing. You may think me unkind but how can you blame me if I want to stay here. I have but one life to live and I want to enjoy myself as I can while I live."

A similar desire for independence propelled young men to leave home at earlier ages than in the past and to strike out on their own. Although the great migration to the West was primarily a movement of entire families, movement from farms to towns and cities within regions was frequently spearheaded by restless and single young people. Two young men in Virginia put it succinctly: "All the promise of life seemed to us to be at the other end of the rainbow—somewhere else—anywhere else but on the farm. . . . And so all our youthful plans had as their chief object the getting away from the farm."

Antebellum Americans also widely wished to be free of close parental supervision, and their changing attitudes influenced courtship and marriage. Many young people who no longer depended on their parents for land insisted on privacy in courting and wanted to decide for themselves when to marry. Increasingly, too, romantic love between the partners rather than parental preferences determined decisions to marry. Whereas seventeenth-century Puritans had advised young people to choose marriage partners whom they *could* love, by the early 1800s, young men and women viewed romantic love as the indispensable basis for a successful marriage. "In affairs of love," a young lawyer in Maine wrote, "young peoples hearts are generally much wiser than old peoples heads."

One sign of young people's growing control over courtship and marriage was the declining likelihood that the young women of a family would marry in their exact birth order. Traditionally, fathers had wanted their daughters to marry in the order of their birth, to avoid planting the suspicion that there was something wrong with one or more of them. Toward the end of the eighteenth century, however, the practice ceased to be customary, as daughters were making their own marital decisions. Another mark of the times was the growing number of long engagements. Having made the decision to marry, some young women were reluctant to tie the knot, fearing that marriage would snuff out their independence. For example, Caroline and William Kirkland were engaged for seven years before their marriage in 1828. Equally striking was the increasing number of young women who chose not to marry. Catharine Beecher, the daughter of the prominent minister Lyman Beecher, broke off her engagement to a young man during the 1820s, despite her father's pressure to marry him. She later renewed the engagement, but after her fiancé's death in a shipwreck, she remained single for the rest of her life.

Thus young people lived more and more in a world of their own. Not surprisingly, moralists reacted with alarm and flooded the country with books of advice to youth such as William Alcott's *The Young Man's Guide*, which went through thirty-one editions between 1833 and 1858. The number of such advice books sold in antebellum America was truly vast, but to an amazing extent, they all said the same thing. They did not advise young men and women to return to farms, and they assumed that parents had little control over them. Rather, their authors exhorted youths to develop habitual rectitude, self-control, and "character." It was an age not just of the self-made adult but also of the self-made youth.

Wives, Husbands

Another class of advice books pouring from the antebellum presses counseled wives and husbands on their rights and duties. These were a sign that relations between spouses, too, were changing. Young men and women who, as teenagers, had grown accustomed to making decisions on their own were more likely than their ancestors to approach wedlock as a compact between equals. Of course, wives remained unequal to their husbands in many tangible ways, the most obvious being the continuation into the 1830s of the traditional legal rule that married women could not own property. But relations between wives and husbands were changing during the 1820s and 1830s toward a form of equality.

One source of the change was the rise of a potent ideology known as the doctrine of separate spheres. Traditionally, women had been viewed as subordinate to men in all spheres of life. Now middle-class men and women developed a kind of separate-but-equal doctrine that portrayed men as superior in making money and governing the world and women as superior for their moral influence on family members. One of the most important duties assigned to the sphere of women was the raising of children. During the eighteenth century, ministers had addressed sermons to fathers to remind them of their duty to govern the family, but by the 1830s child-rearing manuals increasingly appealed to mothers rather than fathers. "How entire and perfect is this dominion over the unformed character of your infant," the popular writer Lydia Sigourney proclaimed in her *Letters to Mothers* (1838). Advice books instructed mothers to discipline their children by loving them and withdrawing affection when they misbehaved rather than by using corporal punishment. A whipped child might become more obedient but would remain sullen and bitter. In contrast, the gentler methods advised in manuals promised to penetrate to the child's heart, to make the child want to do the right thing.

The idea of a separate women's sphere blended with a related image of the family and the home as secluded refuges from a society marked by commotion and disorder. The popular culture of the 1830s and 1840s painted an alluring portrait of the pleasures of "spirit of unrest" and the feverish pace of American life. He wrote of the ideal home: "There should be something to love. There must be nooks about it, where one would love to linger; windows, where one can enjoy the quiet landscape at his leisure; cozy rooms, where all fireside joys are invited to dwell."

As a prophet, Downing deserves high marks, because one of the motives that has impelled many Americans to flee cities for suburbs in the twentieth century has been the desire to achieve ownership of a single-family residence. However, in the 1820s and 1830s, this ideal was beyond the reach of most people—not just blacks, immigrants, and sweatshop workers, but much of the middle class as well. In the countryside, although middle-class farmers still managed productive households, these were anything but tranquil: wives milked cows and bled hogs, and children fetched wood, drove cows to pasture, and chased blackbirds from cornfields. In the cities, middle-class families often had to sacrifice their privacy by taking in boarders to supplement family income.

Still, the doctrine of separate spheres for men and women, and the image of the home as a calming refuge from a harsh world, were powerful ideals, and virtually the only ones projected in antebellum magazines. Although they were ideals rather than descriptions of reality, they did intersect with the real world at *some* points. For example, the decline of cottage industries and the rising number of urban families headed by merchants, lawyers, or brokers (all of whom worked away from their homes) gave married women more time to spend on child rearing. Above all, even if they could not afford to live in a Downing-designed house, married women found that they could use the doctrine of separate spheres and the image of the home as a refuge to gain new power within their families. A subtle implication of the doctrine of separate spheres was that women should have control not only over the discipline of children but also over the more fundamental issue of the number of children that they would bear.

In 1800 the United States had one of the highest birthrates ever recorded. The average American woman bore 7.04 children. It is safe to say that married women had become pregnant as often as possible. In the prevailing farm economy, children were valuable for carrying out essential tasks and, as time passed, for relieving aging parents of the burden of heavy farm labor. Most parents had assumed that the more children, the better. However, the spread of a commercial economy raised troublesome questions about

Ingersell Family in 1818
This watercolor of a Maine family captures the large size of antebellum families and the importance they attached to children. The parents point toward the infant Peggy. But childhood was short. Five-year-old Solomon on the bottom left is dressed as a child, but his older brothers to his left, respectively twelve and nine, are clothed as adults, and Eli grips a paper scroll rather than Solomon's butterfly.

home life through songs like "Home, Sweet Home" and poems such as Henry Wadsworth Longfellow's "The Children's Hour" and Clement Moore's "A Visit from St. Nicholas." The publication of Moore's poem coincided with the growing popularity of Christmas as a holiday season in which family members gathered to exchange warm affection. Even the physical appearance of houses changed as architects offered new designs for the ideal home. The prominent architect Andrew Jackson Downing published plans for peaceful single-family homes that he hoped would offset the children's economic value. Unlike a farmer, a merchant or lawyer could not send his children to work at the age of seven or eight. The average woman, who had borne 7.04 children in 1800, was bearing only 5.02 by 1850, and 3.98 by 1900. The birthrate remained high among blacks and among many immigrant groups, but it slumped drastically among native-born whites, particularly in towns and cities. The birthrate also declined in rural areas, but more sharply in rural villages than on farms, and more sharply in the East, where land was scarce, than in the West, where abundant land created continued incentives for parents to have many children.

For the most part, the decline in the birthrate was accomplished by abstinence from sexual intercourse, by *coitus interruptus* (withdrawal of the penis before ejaculation), or by abortion. By the 1840s such abortionists as New York City's notorious Madame Restell advertised remedies for "female irregularities," a common euphemism for unwanted pregnancies. There were no foolproof birth-control devices, and as much misinformation as information circulated about the techniques of birth control. Nonetheless, interest in birth-control devices was intensifying. In 1832 Charles Knowlton, a Massachusetts physician, described the procedure for vaginal douching in his book *Fruits of Philosophy*. Although Knowlton was frequently prosecuted and once jailed for obscenity, efforts to suppress his ideas only resulted in their being publicized even more. By 1865 popular tracts had familiarized Americans with a wide range of birth-control methods, including the rubber condom and the vaginal diaphragm. Whatever the method, the decision to limit family size was usually reached jointly by wives and husbands. Economic and ideological considerations blended together. Husbands could note that the economic value of children was declining; wives, that having fewer children would give them more time to nurture each one and thereby carry out the duties of the woman's sphere.

Supporters of the ideal of separate spheres did not advocate full legal equality for women. Indeed, the idea of separate spheres was an explicit *alternative* to legal equality. But the concept did enhance women's power within marriage by justifying their demands for influence over such vital issues as child rearing and the frequency of pregnancies. In addition, it allowed some women a measure of independence from the home. For example, it sanctioned Catharine Beecher's travels to lecture women on better ways to raise children and manage their households.

Horizontal Allegiances and the Rise of Voluntary Associations

As some forms of authority, such as that of parents over their children and of husbands over their wives, were weakening, Americans devised new ways through which individuals could extend their influence over others. The pre–Civil War period witnessed the widespread substitution of *horizontal* allegiances for *vertical* allegiances. An example of vertical allegiance is found in the traditional patriarchal family, wherein a wife and children looked up to the father for leadership. Another example occurs in the small eighteenth-century workshop, where apprentices and journeymen took direction from the master craftsman and even lived in the craftsman's house, subject to his authority. Common to these examples is the idea of authority flowing from the top down. In a vertical allegiance, people in a subordinate position identify their best interests with the interests of their superiors rather than with those of other individuals in the same subordinate position.

When social relationships began to assume a horizontal form, several new patterns emerged. Although the older kind of vertical relationships did not disappear, they became less important in people's lives. Relationships now arose that linked those in a similar position. For example, in large textile mills during the 1830s, many operatives discovered that they had more in common with each other than with their managers and overseers. Similarly, wives were increasingly inclined to form associations that bound them with other married women. Young men formed associations with other young men. None of these associations was intended to overthrow traditional authority. Many of them in fact professed to strengthen the family or community. But all represented the substitution of new allegiances for old ones.

A sign of the change can be seen in the large number of voluntary associations formed in the 1820s and 1830s. These were associations that arose apart from government and sought to accomplish some goal of value to their members. Tocqueville observed that in France the government stood at the head of every enterprise but that in America "you will be sure to find an association."

At the most basic level, the voluntary associations encouraged sociability. As transients and newcomers flocked into towns and cities, they tended to join with others who shared similar characteristics, experiences, or interests. Gender was the basis of many voluntary societies. Of twenty-six religious and charitable associations in Utica, New York, in 1832, for instance, one-third were exclusively for women. Race was still another basis for voluntary associations. Although their names did not indicate it, Boston's Thompson Literary and Debating Society, its Philomathean Adelphic Union for the Promotion of Literature and Science, and New York City's Phoenix Society were all organizations for free blacks.

Promoting sociability was not the only benefit of voluntary associations. These associations also allowed their members to assert their influence at a time when traditional forms of authority were weakening. For example, voluntary associations proved compatible with the idea that women had a separate sphere. As long as a woman could argue that her activities were in the best interests of the home, she could escape the kitchen long enough to join maternal associations (where mothers exchanged ideas about child rearing), temperance associations (where they promoted absti-

nence from alcoholic beverages), and moral-reform societies. These latter societies, which multiplied in the 1830s and 1840s, combated prostitution.

Temperance and moral-reform societies had a dual purpose. They sought to suppress well-known vices *and* to enhance women's power over men. Temperance advocates assumed that intemperance was a male vice. Moral reformers attributed the prevalence of prostitution to the lustfulness of men who, unable to control their passions, exploited poor and vulnerable girls. While exhorting prostitutes to give up their line of work, moral reformers also tried to shame brothel patrons into chastity by publishing their names in newspapers. Just as strikes in Lowell in the 1830s were a form of collective action by working women, temperance and moral-reform societies represented collective action by middle-class women to increase their influence in society. Here, as elsewhere, the tendency of the times was to forge new forms of horizontal allegiance between like-minded Americans.

CONCLUSION

Alexis de Tocqueville described the United States of the 1830s as remarkable not for "the marvellous grandeur of some undertakings" but for the "innumerable multitude of small ones." In fact, a number of grand enterprises *were* undertaken between 1815 and 1840, among them the construction of the Erie Canal and the establishment of the Lowell mills. But Tocqueville was basically correct. The distinguishing feature of the period was the amount of small to medium-size enterprises that Americans embarked upon: commercial farms of modest proportions, railroads that ran for a few hundred miles, manufacturing companies that employed five to ten workers.

The changes of the period were modest in comparison to those that would come in the late nineteenth century, when industrial firms routinely employed hundreds of workers and railroads spanned the continent. Nevertheless, to antebellum Americans, it seemed as if the world of their ancestors was breaking apart. In 1800 no human or machine had been able to sustain motion at more than ten miles an hour. The railroads changed that. In 1800 it had been natural to assume that the limits of trade were set by the limits of rivers.

Canals changed that. Everywhere traditional assumptions about what was "natural" were being challenged.

As traditional assumptions eroded, new ones took their place. Ties to village leaders and even to parents weakened, but new bonds with the like-minded and with age peers emerged. Individualism became a major force in the sense that a widening circle of Americans insisted on the right to shape their own economic destinies. "No man in America is contented to be poor," a magazine proclaimed, "or expects to continue so." Yet Americans did not desire isolation from each other. Voluntary associations based on the personal preferences of their members, rather than on custom, proliferated. A host of advice books aimed at young people, wives, and husbands tried to teach Americans how to play the new roles thrust upon them by economic and social change. The marriage manual was as much a part of antebellum America as the Erie Canal or the Boston Manufacturing Company.

The social transformations of 1815 to 1840 not only changed the private lives of Americans but also brought a host of new political issues to the fore, as we shall see in Chapter 10.

CHRONOLOGY

1790 Samuel Slater opens his first Rhode Island mill for the production of cotton yarn.

1793 Eli Whitney invents the cotton gin.

Eli Whitney

1807 Robert R. Livingston and Robert Fulton introduce the steamboat *Clermont* on the Hudson River.

1811 Construction of the National Road begins at Cumberland, Maryland.

1813 Incorporation of the Boston Manufacturing Company.

1816 Second Bank of the United States chartered.

1817 Erie Canal started.

1819 Economic panic, ushering in four-year depression.

1820–1850 Growth of female moral-reform societies.

1820s Expansion of New England textile mills.

1824 *Gibbons* v. *Ogden*.

1825 Completion of the Erie Canal.

1828 Baltimore and Ohio Railroad chartered.

1830 Indian Removal Act passed by Congress.

1831 *Cherokee Nation* v. *Georgia*.
Alexis de Tocqueville begins visit to the United States to study American penitentiaries.

1832 *Worcester* v. *Georgia*.

1834 First strike at the Lowell mills.

1837 Economic panic begins a depression that lasts until 1843.

1840 System of production by interchangeable parts perfected.

FOR FURTHER READING

Rowland Berthoff, *An Unsettled People: Social Order and Disorder in American History* (1971). A stimulating interpretation of American social history.

Ray A. Billington, *Westward Expansion: A History of the American Frontier* (1949). The standard study of westward movement and settlement.

Carl Degler, *At Odds: Women and the Family in America from the Revolution to the Present* (1980). A fine overview of the economic and social experiences of American women.

Harry N. Scheiber, *The Ohio Canal Era: A Case Study of Government and the Economy, 1820–1861* (1969). An analysis that speaks volumes about economic growth in the early republic.

Sean Wilentz, *Chants Democratic: New York City and the Rise of the American Working Class, 1788–1850* (1983). A stimulating synthesis of economic, social, and political history.

ADDITIONAL BIBLIOGRAPHY

Agriculture and the Westward Movement

Charles Danhof, *Change in Agriculture: The Northern United States, 1820–1870* (1969); Robert Feller, *The Public Lands in Jacksonian Politics* (1984); Paul W. Gates, *The Farmer's Age: Agriculture, 1815–1860* (1960); William H. Goetzmann, *Explorations and Empire: The Explorer and the Scientist in the Winning of the American West* (1966); Hildegard B. Johnson, *Order Upon the Land* (1976); Malcolm Rohrbough, *The Land Office Business: The Settlement and Administration of American Public Lands, 1789–1837* (1968); Michael Williams, *Americans and Their Forests* (1989).

Indians

Robert F. Berkhofer, Jr., *The White Man's Indian: Images of the American Indian from Columbus to the Present* (1979); John R. Finger, *The Eastern Band of Cherokees, 1819–1900* (1984); Michael D. Green, *The Politics of Indian Removal: Creek Government and Society in Crisis* (1982); Joseph Herring, *The Enduring Indians of Kansas* (1990); William G. McLoughlin, *Cherokee Renascence in the New Republic* (1987); Roy H. Pearce, *The Savages of America* (1965); Richard Slotkin, *Regeneration Through Violence: The Mythology of the American Frontier, 1600–1860* (1973); Wilcomb E. Washburn, *The Indian in*

America (1975); J. Leitch Wright, Jr., *Creeks and Seminoles* (1986).

The Transportation Revolution

Albert Fishlow, *American Railroads and the Transformation of the Ante-Bellum Economy* (1965); Robert W. Fogel, *Railroads and American Economic Growth: Essays in Econometric History* (1964); Carter Goodrich, *Government Promotion of American Canals and Railroads, 1800–1890* (1960); Erik F. Haites, James Mak, and Gary M. Walton, *Western River Transportation: The Era of Early Internal Development, 1800–1860* (1975); Harry N. Scheiber, *The Ohio Canal Era: A Case Study of Government and the Economy, 1820–1861* (1969); R. E. Shaw, *Erie Water West* (1966); George R. Taylor, *The Transportation Revolution, 1815–1860* (1951).

Communities

Jeffrey S. Adler, *Yankee Merchants and the Making of the Urban West* (1991); Stuart Blumin, *The Urban Threshold: Growth and Change in a Nineteenth-Century American Community* (1976); Don H. Doyle, *The Social Order of a Frontier Community: Jacksonville, Illinois, 1825–1870* (1978); Clyde Griffen and Sally Griffen, *Natives and Newcomers: The Ordering of Opportunity in Mid-Nineteenth-Century Poughkeepsie* (1978); David Hamer, *New Towns in the New World* (1990); Paul Johnson, *A Shopkeeper's Millennium: Society and Revivals in Rochester, New York, 1815–1837* (1978); Steven J. Ross, *Workers on the Edge: Work, Leisure, and Politics in Industrializing Cincinnati, 1788–1890* (1985); Richard C. Wade, *The Urban Frontier* (1964); Anthony F. C. Wallace, *Rockdale: The Growth of an American Village in the Early Industrial Revolution* (1977).

Immigrants

Rowland Berthoff, *British Immigrants in Industrial America* (1953); Kathleen N. Conzen, *Immigrant Milwaukee, 1836–1860* (1976); Jay P. Dolan, *The Immigrant Church: New York's Irish and German Catholics, 1815–1860* (1975); Oscar Handlin, *Boston's Immigrants: A Study in Acculturation*, rev. ed. (1959); Marcus L. Hansen, *The Atlantic Migration, 1607–1860* (1940); Philip Taylor, *The Distant Magnet: European Emigration to the United States of America* (1971); Carl Wittke, *The Irish in America* (1956).

Technology

Siegfried Giedion, *Mechanization Takes Command* (1948); H. J. Habakkuk, *American and British Technology in the Nineteenth Century* (1962); Otto Mayr and Robert C. Post, eds., *Yankee Enterprise: The Rise of the American System of Manufactures* (1981); Merritt R. Smith, *Harpers Ferry Armory and the New Technology* (1977).

Manufacturing and Economic Growth

W. Elliot Brownlee, *Dynamics of Ascent* (1974); Stuart Bruchey, *The Roots of American Economic Growth, 1607–1861* (1965); Christopher Clark, *The Roots of Rural Capitalism: Western Massachusetts, 1780–1860* (1990); Thomas C. Cochran, *Frontiers of Change: Early Industrialism in America* (1981); Alan Dawley, *Class and Community: The Industrial Revolution in Lynn* (1976); Thomas Dublin, *Women at Work: The Transformation of Work and Community in Lowell, Massachusetts, 1826–1860* (1979); Bruce Laurie, *Working People of Philadelphia, 1800–1850* (1980); Judith A. McGaw, *Most Wonderful Machine: Mechanization and Social Change in Berkshire Paper Making, 1815–1885* (1987); Douglass North, *The Economic Growth of the United States, 1790–1860* (1961); Ronald Schultz, *The Republic of Labor: Philadelphia Artisans and the Politics of Class, 1720–1830* (1993); Peter Temin, *The Jacksonian Economy* (1969); Barbara Tucker, *Samuel Slater and the Origins of the American Textile Industry, 1790–1860* (1984).

Rich and Poor

Elizabeth Blackmar, *Manhattan for Rent, 1785–1850* (1989); Leonard P. Curry, *The Free Black in Urban America, 1800–1850* (1981); Paul A. Gilje, *The Road to Mobocracy: Popular Disorder in New York City, 1763–1834* (1987); Peter Knights, *The Plain People of Boston, 1830–1860* (1971); Edward Pessen, *Riches, Class, and Power Before the Civil War* (1973); Stephan Thernstrom, *Poverty and Progress* (1964).

Professions

Daniel H. Calhoun, *Professional Lives in America: Structure and Aspiration, 1750–1850* (1965); Donald M. Scott, *From Office to Profession: The New England Ministry, 1750–1850* (1978); Richard Shryock, *Medical Licensing in America, 1650–1965* (1967); William B. Skelton, *An American Profession of Arms: The Army Officer Corps, 1784–1861* (1993).

Women and the Family

Jeanne Boydston, *Home and Work* (1990); Nancy F. Cott, *The Bonds of Womanhood: 'Woman's Sphere' in New England, 1780–1835* (1977); Suzanne Lebsock, *The Free Women of Petersburg: Status and Culture in a Southern Town, 1784–1860* (1984); James C. Mohr, *Abortion in America: The Origins and Evolution of National Policy, 1800–1900* (1978); Glenda Riley, *Women and Indians on the Frontier, 1825–1915* (1984); Ellen K. Rothman, *Hands and Hearts: A History of Courtship in America* (1987); Mary Ryan, *Cradle of the Middle Class: The Family in Oneida County, New York, 1790–1865* (1981); Kathryn K. Sklar, *Catharine Beecher: A Study in American Domesticity* (1973); Christine Stansell, *City of Women: Sex and Class in New York, 1789–1860* (1986); Gwendolyn Wright, *Building the Dream: A Social History of Housing in America* (1981).

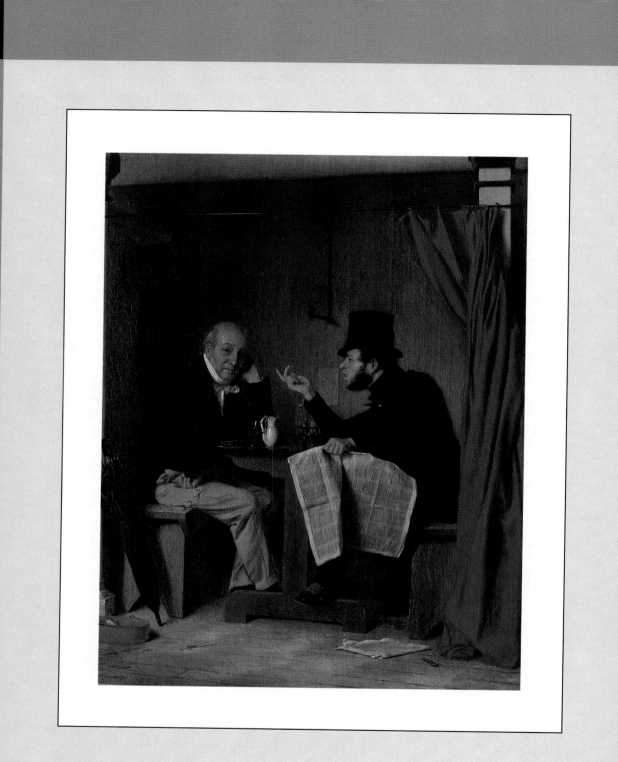

Politics in an Oyster House
by Richard Caton Woodville, 1848

POLITICS, RELIGION, AND REFORM IN THE AGE OF JACKSON

In 1824 the Marquis de Lafayette (inset), former major general in the Continental Army and a Revolutionary War hero, accepted the invitation of President James Monroe and Congress and revisited the United States. For thirteen months as "the Nation's Guest," Lafayette traveled to every state and received a welcome that fluctuated between warm and tumultuous. There seemed no limits to what Americans would do to show their admiration for this "greatest man in the world." "There were," one contemporary wrote, *"La Fayette* boots—*La Fayette* hats— *La Fayette* wine—and *La Fayette* everything." In New York City, some fervid patriots tried to unhitch the horses from Lafayette's carriage and pull it up Broadway themselves.

Lafayette had contributed mightily to the Revolution's success. Americans venerated him as a living embodiment of the entire Revolutionary generation fast passing from the scene. The majority of Americans alive in 1824 had been born since George Washington's death in 1799. John Adams and Thomas Jefferson survived, but they were along in years. Both would die on July 4, 1826, fifty years to the day after the signing of the Declaration of Independence. Seizing on Washington's remark that he loved Lafayette "as my own son," Americans toasted the Frenchman as a cherished member of the family of Revolutionary heroes. In Charleston the toast ran: "WASHINGTON, our Common Father—*you* his favorite *son*"; in New Jersey, "LA FAYETTE, a living monument of greatness, virtue, and faithfulness still exists—a second Washington is now among us."

The festive rituals surrounding Lafayette's visit symbolized Americans' conviction that they had remained true to their heritage of republican liberty. The embers of conflict between Federalists and Republicans that once had seemed to threaten the Republic's stability had cooled; the Era of Good Feelings still reigned over American politics in 1824. Yet even as Americans were turning Lafayette's visit into an affirmation of their ties to the Founders, those ties were fraying in the face of new challenges. Westward migration, growing economic individualism, and increasing sectional conflict over slavery shaped politics mightily between 1824 and 1840. The impact of economic and social change shattered old assumptions and contributed to a vigorous new brand of politics.

This transformation led to the birth of a second American party system, in which two new parties, the Democrats and the Whigs, replaced the Republicans and the Federalists. More was at work here than a change of names. The new parties took advantage of the transportation revolution to spread their messages to the farthest corners of the nation and to arouse voters in all sections. The new parties' leaders were more effective than their predecessors at organizing grass roots support, more eager to make government responsive to the popular will, and more likely to enjoy politics and welcome conflict as a way to sustain interest in political issues.

Not all Americans looked to politics as the pathway to their goals. Some, in fact, viewed politics as suited only to scoundrels and could identify with the sentiments of the Detroit workingman who wrote in 1832 that he "did not vote. I'll [have] none of sin." Despairing of politics, many men and women became active in reform movements pursuing various goals, among them the abolition of slavery, the suppression of the liquor trade, improved public education, and equality for women. Strongly held religious beliefs impelled reformers into these causes, while simultaneously increasing their distrust of politics. Yet even reformers hostile to politics gradually found that the success of their reforms depended on their ability to influence the political process.

During the 1820s and 1830s, the political and reform agendas of Americans diverged increasingly from those of the Founders. The Founders had feared popular participation in politics, enjoyed their wine and rum, left an ambiguous legacy on slavery, and displayed only occasional interest in women's rights. Yet even as Americans shifted their political and social priorities, they continued to venerate the Founders, who in death meant even more than in life. Histories of the United States, biographies of Revolutionary patriots, and torchlight parades that bore portraits of Washington and Jefferson alongside those of Andrew Jackson all helped to reassure the men and women of the young nation that they were remaining loyal to their republican heritage.

THE TRANSFORMATION OF AMERICAN POLITICS, 1824–1832

In 1824 Andrew Jackson and Martin Van Buren, who would lead the Democratic party in the 1830s, and John Quincy Adams and Henry Clay, who would help to guide the rival National Republican (or Whig) party in the 1830s, all belonged to the same political party—the Republican party of Thomas Jefferson. Yet by 1824 the Republican party was coming apart at the seams under pressures generated by industrialization in New England, the spread of cotton cultivation in the South,

and westward expansion. These forces sparked issues that would become the basis for the new political division between Democrats and Whigs. In general, those Republicans (augmented by a few former Federalists) who retained Jefferson's suspicion of a strong federal government and preference for states' rights became Democrats; those Republicans (along with many former Federalists) who believed that the national government should actively encourage economic development became Whigs.

Regardless of which path a politician chose, all leaders in the 1820s and 1830s had to adapt to the rising democratic idea of politics as a forum for the expression of the will of the common people rather than as an activity that gentlemen conducted for the people. Gentlemen could still be elected to office, but their success now depended less on their education or wealth than on their ability to identify and follow the will of the majority. Americans still looked up to their political leaders, but the leaders could no longer look down on the people.

Democratic Ferment

The process by which politics gradually became more democratic took several forms. In one state after another, the requirement, common in the eighteenth century, that voters own property was scaled down to a stipulation that voters merely pay poll taxes. Maryland, South Carolina, Massachusetts, Connecticut, and New York all liberalized their suffrage laws for white voters between the 1790s and 1821, and none of the eight new states admitted between 1796 and 1821 required voters to own property. Moreover, written ballots replaced the old custom of voting aloud (called *viva voce* or "stand up" voting), which had enabled social superiors to influence their inferiors at the polls. Many appointive offices became elective. Although the electoral college remained in place, the practice of allowing state legislatures to choose presidential electors gave way to the selection of electors by popular vote. In 1800, rather than voting for Thomas Jefferson or John Adams, most Americans could do no more than vote for the men who would vote for the men who would vote for Jefferson or Adams. By 1824, however, legislatures chose electors in only six states, and by 1832 in only one (South Carolina).

Nothing did more to undermine the old barriers to the people's expression of their will than a fierce tug-of-war between the Republicans and the Federalists in the 1790s and early 1800s. Because party survival depended on the ability to win elections, political parties had to court voters. First the Republicans and then the Federalists learned to woo voters by staging grand barbecues at which men from Massachusetts to Maryland washed down free clams and oysters with free beer and whiskey. Wherever one party was in the minority, it sought to increase the number of eligible voters in order to turn itself into the majority party. In the South, where the Republicans were strong, they showed little interest in increasing the size of the electorate; but in the North, they built a following by advocating expanded suffrage. Federalists played the same game when it suited them; the initiator of suffrage reform in Maryland, for example, was an aristocratic Federalist.

The democratization of politics developed at an uneven pace, however. As late as 1820, the Republican and Federalist parties continued to be organized from the top down. To nominate candidates, for example, both parties relied on the caucus, a meeting of party members in the legislature, rather than on popularly elected nominating conventions. Moreover, few party leaders rushed to embrace the *principle* of universal white manhood suffrage. Even the newly admitted western states tried at first to imitate the suffrage restrictions of the East and abandoned them only when it became clear that in a region where nearly everyone's land title was in dispute, to require property ownership for voting merely invited fraud. Nor did the democratization of politics necessarily draw more voters to the polls. Waning competition between the Republicans and the Federalists between 1816 and 1824 deprived voters of clear choices and turned national politics into a boring spectacle.

Yet no one could mistake the tendency of the times: to oppose the people or democracy had become a formula for political suicide. The people, a Federalist moaned, "have become too saucy and are really beginning to fancy themselves equal to their betters." Whatever their convictions, politicians learned to adjust.

The Election of 1824

Partially submerged political tensions surfaced in the election of 1824 and inflicted sudden death on the Era of Good Feelings. Even before the election, President Monroe's Republican coalition was cracking under pressure from its rival sectional components. In 1824 five candidates, all Republicans, ended up vying for the presidency. John Quincy Adams emerged as New En-gland's favorite. South Carolina's brilliant John C. Calhoun contended with Georgia's William Crawford, an old-school Jeffersonian, for southern support. Out of the West marched Henry Clay of Kentucky, ambitious, crafty, and confident that his American System of protective tariffs and federally supported internal improvements would endear him to the manufacturing regions of the East as well as to the New West.

Clay's belief that he was holding a solid block of western states was punctured by the rise of a fifth candidate, Andrew Jackson of Tennessee. At first, none of the other candidates took Jackson seriously. But he was popular on the frontier and in the South and stunned his rivals by gaining the support of opponents of the American System from Pennsylvania and other northern states.

Although the Republican congressional caucus chose Crawford as the party's official candidate early in 1824, the caucus could no longer unify the party. Three-fourths of the Republicans in Congress had refused to attend the caucus. Crawford's already diminished prospects evaporated when he suffered a paralyzing stroke. Impressed by Jackson's support, Calhoun withdrew from the race and ran unopposed

The Election of 1824

Candidates	Parties	Electoral Vote	Popular Vote	Percentage of Popular Vote
JOHN QUINCY ADAMS	Democratic-Republican	84	108,740	30.5
Andrew Jackson	Democratic-Republican	99	153,544	43.1
William H. Crawford	Democratic-Republican	41	46,618	13.1
Henry Clay	Democratic-Republican	37	47,136	13.2

for the vice presidency. In the election, Jackson won more popular and electoral votes than any other candidate (Adams, Crawford, and Clay) but failed to gain a majority, as required by the Constitution. Thus the election was thrown into the House of Representatives, whose members had to choose from the three top candidates—Jackson, Adams, and Crawford. Hoping to forge an alliance between the West and Northeast in a future bid for the presidency, Clay gave his support to Adams. Clay's action secured the presidency for Adams, but when Adams promptly appointed Clay his secretary of state, Jackson's supporters raged that a "corrupt bargain" had cheated Jackson of the presidency. Although there is no evidence that Adams had traded Clay's support for an explicit agreement to appoint Clay his secretary of state (an office from which Jefferson, Madison, Monroe, and Adams himself had risen to the presidency), the allegation of a corrupt bargain was widely believed. It formed a cloud that hung over Adams's presidency.

John Quincy Adams as President

Adams's appointment of Clay as his secretary of state was the first of several clumsy miscalculations that cloaked his presidency in controversy. Basically, Adams failed to understand the changing political climate. In his first annual message to Congress in December 1825, the president made a series of proposals that might have won acclaim in 1815 but that only antagonized interests that had grown more powerful and alert in the ensuing decade. He proposed, for example, a program of federal support for internal improvements, an idea that had gained support from Republicans like Henry Clay, the architect of the American System, after the War of 1812. Between 1819 and 1825, however, opponents of the American System had multiplied. Strict Jeffersonians (often called Old Republicans), among them the Virginian John Randolph, had consistently attacked federal aid for internal improvements as unconstitutional, but they were no longer the mainstays of the opposition. Adams's call for federal support for improvements came within a few months of New York's completion of the Erie Canal. Because New York had built the canal with its own money, its senator, Martin Van Buren, opposed federal aid for internal improvements; such support would only enable other states to construct rival canals.

John Quincy Adams
This photo captures John Quincy Adams's austerity, determination, integrity, and respect for knowledge.

In addition, Adams infuriated southerners by proposing to send American delegates to a conference of newly independent Latin American nations in Panama. Southerners feared that U.S. attendance would imply recognition of Haiti, a black republic that had gained its independence from France through a slave revolution. Both the sharp debate over the Missouri Compromise in 1819–1820 and the discovery of a planned slave revolt in South Carolina in 1822 (organized by a free black, Denmark Vesey) had shaken southern slaveholders and generated hostility to Adams's proposal. If Adams had simply recognized that he was antagonizing important groups and responded by seeking new bases of support, he might have saved himself. But he clung to an increasingly obsolete notion of the president as a custodian of the public good who stayed aloof from factions and parties. Far from purging his political opponents, he appointed several to high office and thereby alienated even his friends. As late as 1829, he wrote blithely, "I have no wish to fortify myself by the support of any party whatever."

The Rise of Andrew Jackson

As Adams's popularity declined, Andrew Jackson's rose. Jackson's victory over the British in the Battle of New Orleans in 1815 had given him a national reputation. The fact that he was a Tennessee slaveholder, a renowned Indian fighter, and a militant advocate of Indian removal endeared Jackson to the South. Where Adams tried to uphold treaties between the federal government and the Indians that gave the Native Americans the option of staying in the East, Jackson urged that southerners be allowed a free hand in pushing the Indians further westward. Southerners praised Jackson's stance as a noble application of the Jeffersonian principle of states' rights and recognized that it would satisfy their hunger for land. Furthermore, as the only presidential candidate in the election of 1824 with no connection to the Monroe administration, Jackson was in an ideal position to capitalize on what John C. Calhoun called "a vague but widespread discontent" in the wake of the Panic of 1819 that left people with "a general mass of disaffection to the Government" and "looking out anywhere for a leader."

Jackson's supporters swiftly established committees throughout the country. Two years before the election of 1828, towns and villages across the United States buzzed with furious but unfocused political activity. With the exception of the few remaining Federalists, almost everyone called himself a Republican. Some Republicans were "Adams men," others were "Jackson men," and still others styled themselves "friends of Clay." Amid all the confusion, few realized that a new political system was being born. The man most alert to the signs of the times was Martin Van Buren, who was to become vice president during Jackson's second term and president upon Jackson's retirement.

Van Buren exemplified a new breed of politician. A tavernkeeper's son, he had started his political career in county politics and worked his way up to New York's governorship. In Albany he built a powerful political machine, the Albany Regency, composed mainly of men like himself from the lower and middling ranks. His arch rival in New York politics, De-Witt Clinton, was all that Van Buren was not—tall, handsome, aristocratic, and brilliant. But Van Buren

had a geniality that made ordinary people feel comfortable and an uncanny ability to sense in which direction the political winds were about to blow. Van Buren loved politics, which he viewed as a wonderful game; he was one of the first prominent American politicians to make personal friends from among his political enemies.

The election of 1824 convinced Van Buren of the need for renewed two-party competition. Without the discipline imposed by a strong opposition party, the Republicans in 1824 had splintered into sectional pieces. No candidate had secured an electoral majority, and the House of Representatives had decided the outcome amid charges of intrigue and corruption. It would be better, Van Buren concluded, to let all the shades of opinion in the nation be reduced to two. Then the parties would clash, and a clear popular winner would emerge. Jackson's strong showing in the election persuaded Van Buren that "Old Hickory" could lead a new political party. In the election of 1828, this party, which gradually became known as the Democratic party, put up Jackson for president and Calhoun for vice president. Its opponents, increasingly calling themselves the National Republicans, rallied behind Adams and his running mate, treasury secretary Richard Rush. Slowly but surely, the second American party system was taking shape.

The Election of 1828

The 1828 campaign was a vicious, mudslinging affair. The National Republicans attacked Jackson as a murderer (between duels and military executions, he was directly responsible for several men's deaths), a drunken gambler, and an adulterer. The adultery charge stemmed from the fact that in 1791 Jackson had married Rachel Robards, and each erroneously believing that her divorce from her first husband had become final. "Ought a convicted adulteress and her paramour husband," the Adams men taunted, "be placed in the highest office of this free and Christian land?" Jackson's supporters replied in kind. They accused Adams of wearing silk underwear, being rich, being in debt, and having gained favor with the tsar of Russia by trying to provide him with a beautiful American prostitute.

Although both sides engaged in mudslinging, Jackson's men had better aim. Charges by Adams's supporters that Jackson was an illiterate backwoodsman only added to Jackson's popular appeal by making him seem just like an ordinary citizen. Jackson's supporters portrayed the clash as one between "the *democracy* of the *country,* on the one hand, and a *lordly purse-proud aristocracy* on the other." Jackson, they said, was the common man incarnate—his mind unclouded by learning, his morals simple and true, his will fierce and resolute. In contrast, Jackson's men represented Adams as an aristocrat, a dry scholar whose learning obscured the truth, a man who could write but not fight. Much of this, of course, was wild exaggeration. Jackson was a wealthy planter, not a simple backwoodsman. But it was what people wanted to hear. Uncorrupt, natural, plain, Jackson was presented as the common man's image of his better self.

The election swept Jackson into office with more than twice the electoral vote of Adams. Yet the popular vote, much closer, made it clear that the people were not simply responding to the personalities or images of the candidates (though these factors dominated the campaign). The vote also reflected the strongly sectional bases of the new parties. The popular vote was close only in the middle states and the Northwest. Adams gained double Jackson's vote in New England; Jackson received double Adams's vote in the South, and nearly triple Adams's vote in the Southwest.

The Election of 1828

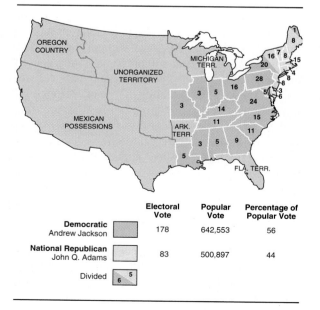

	Electoral Vote	Popular Vote	Percentage of Popular Vote
Democratic Andrew Jackson	178	642,553	56
National Republican John Q. Adams	83	500,897	44
Divided	5 6		

Jackson in Office

For all its fanfare, the campaign had revealed little about Jackson's stands on major issues. On such key questions as federal aid for internal improvements and the tariff, Jackson had sent out conflicting signals. In Tennessee he had aggressively pursued wealth and opposed legislation for the relief of debtors. Yet he understood the popular feelings that had carried him to the presidency and he would use the office to express the will of the majority.

His first policy on coming to office was to openly support the principle of "rotation in office"—the removal of officeholders of the rival party—which critics called the spoils system. Jackson did not invent this policy: many of his predecessors had employed it. Nor did he pursue it with unusual thoroughness, for he removed only about one-fifth of the federal officeholders whom he inherited from Adams. But Jackson defended removal on new and democratic grounds. The duties of officeholders were so plain and simple, he argued, that any intelligent man could perform them. By moving civil servants into and out of office at will, Jackson hoped not only to give as many individuals as possible a chance to work for the government but also to prevent the emergence of an elite bureaucracy that operated beyond the will of the people.

Although Jackson's policy toward the civil service ruffled feathers, it did not produce deep sectional or ideological division. But the issues of federal support for internal improvements and protective tariffs ignited sectional controversy. The South had fewer canals and roads than other sections and, in 1830, fewer plans to build them. Its main cash crop, cotton, was nonperishable and could be transported by rivers and the ocean. Accordingly, southerners were cool toward spending federal money for internal improvements. Jackson, whose firmest political base was in the South, became convinced that federal support for internal improvements was a lavish giveaway program prone to corruption. He also believed that such funding violated the principle that Congress could appropriate money only for objectives shared by *all* Americans, such as national defense, not for the objectives of particular sections or interests. Accordingly, in 1830 Jackson vetoed a bill to provide federal support for a road in Kentucky between Maysville and Lexington.

Coupled with the almost simultaneous passage of the Indian Removal Act (see Chapter 9), the Maysville

Road veto enhanced Jackson's popularity in the South. The tariff issue, however, sternly tested the South's allegiance to Jackson. In 1828, while John Quincy Adams was still in office, Jackson's supporters in Congress had contributed to the final passage of a bill that favored western agricultural interests by raising tariffs (import taxes) on imported hemp, wool, fur, flax, and liquor as well as New England manufacturing interests by raising the tariff on imported textiles. The South, which had few industries to protect from foreign competition, was left high and dry, for tariffs effectively raised the cost of manufactured goods for southerners. Jackson's followers had assumed that the support of the South could be taken for granted in the upcoming election and that embittered southerners would blame the Adams administration for this "Tariff of Abominations." In reality, Jackson rather than Adams would bear the brunt of the South's ire over the tariff.

Nullification

The tariff of 1828 laid the basis for a rift between Jackson and his vice president, John C. Calhoun, that was to shake the foundations of the Republic. Early in his career, Calhoun had been an ardent nationalist. He had entered Congress in 1811 as a "war hawk," supported the protectionist tariff of 1816, and dismissed strict construction of the Constitution as refined philosophical nonsense. During the late 1820s, however, Calhoun the nationalist gradually became Calhoun the states' rights sectionalist. The reasons for his shift were complex. He had supported the tariff of 1816 essentially as a measure conducive to national defense in the wake of the War of 1812. By encouraging fledgling industries, he had reasoned, the tariff would free the United States from dependence upon Britain and provide revenue for military preparedness. By 1826, however, few Americans perceived national defense as a priority. Furthermore, the infant industries of 1816 had grown into troublesome adolescents that demanded higher and higher tariffs.

There was also the matter of Calhoun's fierce ambition. He longed to be president. Jackson had stated that he would serve only one term, and as vice president, Calhoun assumed that he would succeed Jackson. To do so, however, he had to maintain the support of his native South Carolina and of the South in general. As the center of cotton production shifted to the Southwest—Alabama and Mississippi—South Carolina's economy declined during the 1820s, and South Carolinians largely blamed protective tariffs. Tariffs not only drove up the price of manufactured goods but also threatened to reduce the sale of British textile products in the United States. Such a reduction might eventually lower the British demand for southern cotton and cut cotton prices. The more New England industrialized, the clearer it became that tariff laws were pieces of sectional legislation. New Englanders like Massachusetts's eloquent Daniel Webster swung toward protectionism; southerners responded with militant hostility.

Calhoun followed the Virginia and Kentucky resolutions of 1798–1799 in viewing the Union as a compact by which the states had conferred limited and specified powers on the federal government. Although the Constitution did empower Congress to levy tariffs, Calhoun insisted that only tariffs that raised revenue for such common purposes as defense were constitutional. Set so high that it deterred foreign exporters from shipping their products to the United States, the tariff of 1828 could raise little revenue, and hence it failed to meet Calhoun's criterion of constitutionality: that federal laws benefit everyone *equally.* In 1828 Calhoun anonymously wrote the widely circulated *South Carolina Exposition and Protest,* in which he spelled out his argument that the tariff of 1828 was unconstitutional and that aggrieved states therefore had the right to nullify, or override, the law within their borders.

Vehement opposition to tariffs in the South, and especially in South Carolina, rested on more than economic considerations, however. Southerners feared that a federal government that passed tariff laws favoring one section over another might also pass laws meddling with slavery. Because Jackson himself was a slaveholder, the fear of federal interference with slavery was perhaps farfetched. But South Carolinians, long apprehensive of assaults on their crucial institution of slavery, had many reasons for concern. South Carolina was one of only two states in which blacks composed a majority of the population in 1830. Moreover, in 1831 a bloody slave revolt led by Nat Turner boiled up in Virginia. That same year, William Lloyd Garrison established *The Liberator,* an abolitionist newspaper. These developments were enough to convince many troubled South Carolinians that a line had to be drawn against tariffs and possible future interference with slavery.

Jackson Versus Calhoun

Like Calhoun, Jackson was strong-willed and proud. Unlike Calhoun, he was already president and the leader of a national party that included supporters in pro-tariff states like Pennsylvania (which had gone for Jackson in the election of 1828). Thus to retain key northern support while soothing the South, Jackson devised two policies.

The first was to distribute surplus federal revenue to the states. Tariff schedules kept some goods out of the United States but let many others in for a price. The price, in the form of duties on imports, became federal revenue. In these years before federal income taxes, tariffs were a major source of federal revenue. Jackson hoped that this revenue, fairly distributed among the states, would remove the taint of sectional injustice from the tariff and force the federal government to restrict its own expenditures. All of this was good Jeffersonianism. Second, Jackson hoped to ease tariffs down from the sky-high tariff of 1828.

Calhoun disliked the idea of distributing federal revenue to the states because he believed that such a policy could become an excuse to maintain tariffs forever. But he was loath to break openly with Jackson. Between 1828 and 1831, Calhoun muffled his protest, hoping that Jackson would lower the tariff and that he, Calhoun, would retain both Jackson's favor and his chances for the presidency. Congress did pass new, slightly reduced tariff rates in 1832, but these did not come close to satisfying South Carolinians.

Before passage of the tariff of 1832, however, two personal issues had ruptured relations between Calhoun and Jackson. In 1829 Jackson's secretary of war, John H. Eaton, married the widowed daughter of a Washington tavernkeeper. By her own account, Peggy O'Neale Timberlake was "frivolous, wayward, [and] passionate." While still married to a naval officer away on duty, Peggy had acquired the reputation of flirting with Eaton, who boarded at her father's tavern. After her husband's death and her marriage to Eaton, she and Eaton were snubbed socially by Calhoun's wife and by his friends in the cabinet. Jackson, who never forgot how his own wife had been wounded by slander during the campaign of 1828, not only befriended the Eatons but concluded that Calhoun had initiated the snubbing to discredit him and to advance Calhoun's own presidential aspirations.

To make matters worse, in 1830 Jackson received convincing documentation of his suspicion that in 1818, Calhoun, as secretary of war under President Monroe, had urged that Jackson be punished for his unauthorized raid into Spanish Florida. The revelation that Calhoun had tried to stab him in the back in 1818, combined with the snubbing of the Eatons, convinced Jackson that he had to "destroy [Calhoun] regardless of what injury it might do me or my administration." A symbolic confrontation occurred between Jackson and Calhoun at a Jefferson Day dinner in April 1830. Jackson proposed the toast, "Our Union: It must be preserved." Calhoun responded: "The Union next to Liberty the most dear. May we always remember that it can only be preserved by distributing equally the benefits and burdens of the Union."

The stage was now set for a direct clash between the president and his vice president over nullification. In 1831 Calhoun acknowledged his authorship of the *South Carolina Exposition and Protest.* In November 1832 a South Carolina convention nullified the tariffs of 1828 and 1832 and forbade the collection of customs duties within the state. Jackson reacted quickly. He despised nullification, calling it an "abominable doctrine" that would reduce the government to anarchy, and he berated the South Carolina nullifiers as "unprincipled men who would rather rule in hell, than be subordinate in heaven." Jackson even began to send arms to loyal Unionists in South Carolina, and in December 1832 he issued a proclamation that while promising South Carolinians further tariff reductions, lambasted nullification as itself unconstitutional. The Constitution, he emphasized, had established "a single nation," not a league of states.

The crisis eased in March 1833, when Jackson signed into law two measures—"the olive branch and the sword," in one historian's words. The olive branch was the tariff of 1833 (also called the Compromise Tariff), which provided for a gradual but significant lowering of duties between 1833 and 1842. The sword was the Force Bill, authorizing the president to use arms to collect customs duties in South Carolina. Although South Carolina did not abandon nullification in principle—in fact, it nullified the Force Bill—it construed the Compromise Tariff as a concession and rescinded its nullification of the tariffs of 1828 and 1832.

Like most of the accommodations by which the Union lurched from one sectional crisis to the next before the Civil War, the Compromise of 1833 grew out of a mixture of partisanship and statesmanship. The moving spirit behind the Compromise Tariff was Kentucky's senator Henry Clay, who had long favored high

Andrew Jackson, *by Thomas Sully, 1845*

John C. Calhoun, *by Charles Bird King, c. 1825 Jackson, defeated in the presidential election of 1824, won handily four years later. The magnetic Calhoun, Jackson's vice president, broke with Jackson over nullification and the Peggy Eaton affair and resigned the vice presidency in 1832.*

tariffs. A combination of motives brought Clay and the nullifiers together in favor of tariff reduction. Clay feared that without concessions to South Carolina on tariffs, the Force Bill would produce civil war. Furthermore, he was apprehensive that without compromise, the principle of protective tariffs would disappear under the wave of Jackson's immense popularity. In short, Clay would rather take responsibility for lowering tariffs than allow the initiative on tariff questions to pass to the Jacksonians. For their part, the nullifiers hated Jackson and defiantly toasted "Andrew Jackson: On the soil of South Carolina he received an humble birthplace. May he not find in it a traitor's grave!" Although recognizing that South Carolina had failed to gain support for nullification from other southern states and that they would have to bow to pressure, the nullifiers preferred that Clay, not Jackson, be the hero of the hour. So they supported Clay's Compromise Tariff. Everywhere Americans now hailed Clay as the Great Compromiser. Even Martin Van Buren frankly stated that Clay had "saved the country."

The Bank Veto

One reason Jackson signed Clay's compromise tariff into law was that he did not have strong convictions about an alternative. Inclined to react passionately to most issues, Jackson was relatively open-minded on the subject of tariffs. In sharp contrast, as a result of some disastrous financial speculations early in his career, Jackson was deeply suspicious of all banks, all paper money, and all exclusive monopolies. On each count, the Bank of the United States was a likely target.

In 1816 the Second Bank of the United States had received a twenty-year charter from Congress. As a creditor of state banks, the Bank of the United States could contract the lending capacity of the state banks whenever it chose by demanding that they redeem in specie (gold or silver coinage) their bank notes that were held by the Bank of the United States. Because most banks emitted more notes than they could redeem in specie, the Bank of the United States exerted an often healthy restraint on excessive lending by state banks.

Many aspects of the Bank of the United States, however, made it controversial. As we have seen, its decision to contract credit precipitated the Panic of 1819, for which it was widely blamed. Furthermore, at a time when privilege was coming under fire, the bank was undeniably a privileged institution. First, it was the official depository for federal revenue, a fact that greatly increased its capacity to lend money and that gave it a commanding position over all state banks. Second, although the federal government accorded it privileges not available to any other bank, the Bank of the United States was only remotely under the federal government's control. The bank's stockholders were private citizens—a "few monied capitalists," in Jackson's words. In addition, although chartered by Congress, the bank was located not in Washington but in Philadelphia; and the federal government allowed the bank's directors (a majority of whom were government appointees) considerable independence. Finally, the bank's president, the aristocratic Nicholas Biddle, viewed himself as a public servant whose duty was to keep the bank above politics.

In his first annual message to Congress in 1829, Jackson questioned "both the constitutionality and expediency" of the Bank of the United States. Strongly influenced by Henry Clay, Biddle resolved to seek recharter of the bank in 1832, four years before its existing charter expired. With his eyes on the presidential election of 1832, Clay sensed that a pro-bank stand would boost his own chances in the election. Although Biddle and Clay secured congressional approval to recharter, Jackson promptly vetoed the recharter bill. He denounced the bank as a private and privileged monopoly that drained the West of specie, was immune to taxation by states (as Chief Justice Marshall had established in his 1819 *McCulloch* v. *Maryland* decision), gathered inordinate power into

the hands of a few men, and made "the rich richer and the potent more powerful." Failing to persuade Congress to override Jackson's veto, Clay now pinned his hopes on gaining the presidency himself.

The Election of 1832

By 1832 Jackson's views on major issues were considerably clearer than in 1828. The Indian Removal Act, his vetoes of the Maysville Road Bill and the recharter of the Bank of the United States, his policy of distributing federal revenues, and his lowering of tariffs all marked him as a strong defender of states' rights. But at the same time, his vigorous response to nullification had established him as a staunch Unionist. States' rights and Unionism were compatible doctrines. Although he cherished the Union, Jackson believed that the states were far too diverse to accept strong, purposeful direction from the federal government. The safest course was to allow the states considerable freedom, so that they would remain contentedly within the Union and reject dangerous doctrines like nullification.

Despite earlier statements to the contrary, Jackson ran again, selecting Martin Van Buren, now clearly the heir apparent, as his running mate to replace Calhoun, who had resigned. Against Jackson the National Republicans put up Henry Clay. Clay's platform was his American System of protective tariffs, national banking, and federal support for internal improvements. The election of 1832, the first in which national nominating conventions chose the candidates, was more issue-oriented than the vicious campaign of 1828. But Jackson continued to benefit from his great personal popularity. He carried 219 electoral votes to Clay's 49 and even took pro-bank and pro-tariff Pennsylvania. Clay's economic nationalism made him popular in pro-tariff New England. But Clay could not topple

The Election of 1832

Candidates	Parties	Electoral Vote	Popular Vote	Percentage of Popular Vote
ANDREW JACKSON	Democratic	219	687,502	55.0
Henry Clay	National Republican	49	530,189	42.4
William Wirt	Anti-Masonic	7 }	33,108	2.6
John Floyd	National Republican	11 }		

Jackson's stronghold in the South, whereas Jackson chalked up support in the North and West as well as the South. Secure in office for another four years, Jackson was ready to finish the job of dismantling the Bank of the United States.

THE BANK CONTROVERSY AND THE SECOND PARTY SYSTEM

Coming late in Andrew Jackson's first term, the veto of the bank's recharter had relatively little impact on the election of 1832. However, between 1833 and 1840, banking became an issue that ignited extraordinary popular passion. In no period of American history have issues relating to banking generated keener public interest than during these seven years. Jackson's veto of recharter unleashed a tiger that threatened to devour all banks.

Why did banking so raise people's temperature? Part of the answer lay in the fact that the U.S. government did not issue paper currency of its own; there were no "official" dollar bills as we know them today. Paper money took the form of notes (promises to redeem in specie) emitted by private banks. As a consequence, private bankers had enormous influence over economic transactions and could easily be viewed by ordinary people as sinister. In addition, a basic issue lurked behind most of the banking debates of the 1830s. What sort of society would the United States become? If paper money circulated in abundance, businessmen and farmers could readily obtain loans to open factories or buy more land. Such an economy would be speculative in the sense that it would raise expectations for profit while posing risks. A sudden slump in the prices of industrial or agricultural products would leave businessmen and farmers mired in debt. Furthermore, a speculative economy would not benefit everyone equally. Factory owners would reap profits, but their employees would have to perform poorly paid and often unhealthy work. Would the United States be a nation that embraced swift economic development, even at the price of allowing some to get rich quickly off investments while others languished? Or would it be a nation characterized by more modest growth in traditional molds, but one anchored by "honest" manual work and frugality?

Before the answer to any of these questions was clear, the banking issue dramatically transformed American politics. It contributed mightily to the emergence of opposition to the Democrats and to the steady expansion of popular interest in politics.

The War on the Bank

Once reelected, Jackson could have allowed the bank to die a natural death when its charter ran out in 1836. But Jackson and several of his rabid followers viewed the bank as a kind of dragon that would grow new limbs as soon as old ones were cut off. As one radical Jacksonian put it, were the bank allowed to escape with a breath of life, "it will soon recover its wonted strength, its whole power to injure us, and all hope of its destruction must forever be renounced." When Biddle, anticipating further moves against the bank by Jackson, began to call in the bank's loans and contract credit during the winter of 1832–1833, Jacksonians saw their darkest fears confirmed. The bank, Jackson assured Van Buren, "is trying to kill me, but I will kill it." Accordingly, Jackson embarked on a controversial policy of removing federal deposits from the Bank of the United States and placing them in state banks.

Once in place, the policy of removing deposits only raised a new and even thornier issue. Those state banks that became the depositories for federal revenue could use that revenue as the basis for issuing more paper money and for extending more loans. In short, the removal policy enabled state banks to increase their lending capacity. But Jackson hated both paper money and a speculative economy in which capitalists routinely took out large loans. The policy of removal seemed a formula for producing exactly the kind of economy that Jackson wanted to abolish. Jackson recognized the danger and hoped to sharply limit the number of state banks that would become depositories for federal revenue. But as state banks increasingly clamored for the revenue, the number of state-bank depositories soon multiplied beyond Jackson's expectations. There were twenty-three by the end of 1833. Critics dubbed them "pet banks" because they were usually selected for their loyalty to the Democratic party. During the next few years, fueled by paper money from the pet banks and by an influx of foreign specie to purchase cotton and for investment in canal projects, the economy entered a heady expansion. Jackson could not stem the tide. In 1836, pressured by Congress, he reluctantly signed into law the Deposit

Jackson Versus the Bank

Andrew Jackson, aided by Martin Van Buren (center), attacks the Bank of the United States, which, like the many-headed serpent Hydra of Greek mythology, keeps sprouting new heads. The largest head belongs to Nicholas Biddle, the bank's president.

Act, which both increased the number of deposit banks and loosened federal control over them.

Jackson's policy of removing deposits deepened a split within his own Democratic party between advocates of soft money (paper) and those of hard money (gold or silver coinage, or specie). Both sides agreed that the Bank of the United States was evil, but for different reasons. Soft-money Democrats resented the bank's role in periodically contracting credit and restricting the lending activities of state banks; their hard-money counterparts disliked the bank because it sanctioned an economy based on paper money. Prior to the Panic of 1837, the soft-money position was more popular among Democrats outside Jackson's inner circle of advisers than within that circle. For example, western Democrats had long viewed the Bank of the United States' branch in Cincinnati as inadequate to supply their need for credit and favored an expansion of banking activity.

Aside from Jackson and a few other figures within the administration, the most articulate support for hard money came from a faction of the Democratic party in New York called the Locofocos. The Locofocos grew out of various "workingmen's" parties that had sprouted during the late 1820s in northern cities and that called for free public education, the abolition of imprisonment for debt, and a ten-hour workday. Most of these parties had collapsed within a few years, but in New York the "workies" had gradually been absorbed by the Democratic party. Once in the party, the workingmen were hard to keep in line. Composed of a mixture of intellectuals and small artisans and journey-men threatened by economic change, they worried about inflation, preferred to be paid in specie, and distrusted banks and paper money. In 1835 a faction of workingmen had broken away from Tammany Hall, the main Democratic party organization in New York City, and held a dissident meeting in a hall whose candles were illuminated by a newfangled invention, the "loco foco," or match. Thereafter, these radical workingmen were known as Locofocos.

The Rise of Whig Opposition

During Jackson's second term, the opposition National Republican party changed its name to the Whig party. More important, the opposition began to broaden its base in both the South and the North. Jackson's magnetic personality had swept him to victory in 1828 and 1832. But as the profile of Jackson's administration became more sharply delineated—as Jackson's vague Jeffersonianism of 1829 gave way to hard-and-fast positions against the Bank of the United States, federal aid for internal improvements, protective tariffs, and nullification—the opposition drew into its fold increasing numbers alienated by Jackson's policies.

Jackson's crushing of nullification, for example, led some of its southern supporters into the Whig party, not because the Whigs favored nullification but because they opposed Jackson. Jackson's war on the Bank of the United States produced the same result. His policy of removing deposits from the bank pleased some southerners but dismayed others who had been satisfied with the bank and who did not share westerners' mania for even cheaper and easier credit. Jackson's opposition to federal aid for internal improvements also alienated some southerners who feared that the South would languish behind the North unless it began to push ahead with improvements. Because so much southern capital was tied up in slavery, pro-improvement southerners looked to the federal government for aid, and when they were met with a cold shoulder, they drifted into the Whig party. None of this added up to an overturning of the Democratic party in the South; the South was still the Democrats' firmest base. But the Whigs were making significant inroads, particularly in southern market towns and among planters who had close ties to southern bankers and merchants.

Meanwhile, in the North, social reformers were infusing new vitality into the opposition to Jackson. These reformers wanted to improve American society by attacking the sale of liquor, opposing slavery, bettering public education, and elevating public morality. Most opponents of liquor (temperance reformers) and most public-school reformers gravitated to the Whigs. Whig philosophy was more compatible with the reformers' goals than with Democratic ideals. Where Democrats maintained that the government should not impose a uniform standard of conduct on a diverse society, the Whigs' commitment to Clay's American System implied an acceptance of active intervention by the government to change society. Reformers wanted the government to play a positive role specifically by suppressing the liquor trade and by establishing centralized systems of public education. Thus a shared sympathy for active government programs tended to unite Whigs and reformers.

Reformers also indirectly stimulated new support for the Whigs from native-born Protestant workers. The reformers, themselves almost all Protestants, widely distrusted immigrants, especially the Irish, who viewed drinking as a normal recreation and who, as Catholics, suspected (correctly) that the public schools favored by reformers would teach Protestant doctrines. The rise of reform agitation and its frequent association with the Whigs drove the Irish into the arms of the Democrats but, by the same token, gained support for the Whigs from many native-born Protestant workers who were contemptuous of the Irish.

No source of Whig strength, however, was more remarkable than Anti-Masonry, a protest movement against the secrecy and exclusiveness of the Masonic lodges, which had long provided prominent men with fraternal fellowship and exotic rituals. The spark that set off the Anti-Masonic crusade was the abduction and disappearance in 1826 of William Morgan, a stonemason in Genesee County, New York, who had threatened to expose Masonic secrets. Every effort to solve the mystery of Morgan's disappearance ran into a stone wall because local officials were themselves Masons seemingly bent on obstructing the investigation. Throughout the Northeast the public became increasingly aroused against the Masonic order, and rumors spread that Masonry was a powerful conspiracy of the rich to suppress popular liberty, a secret order of men who loathed Christianity, and an exclusive retreat for drunkards.

By 1836 the Whigs had become a national party with widespread appeal. In both the North and South, they attracted those with close ties to the market economy—commercial farmers, planters, merchants, and bankers. In the North they also gained support from reformers, evangelical clergymen (especially Presbyterians and Congregationalists), Anti-Masons, and manufacturers. In the South they appealed to some former nullificationists; Calhoun himself briefly became a Whig. Everywhere the Whigs assailed Jackson as an imperious dictator, "King Andrew I"; indeed, they had taken the name "Whigs" to associate their cause with that of the American patriots who had opposed King George III in 1776.

The Election of 1836

As the election of 1836 approached, the Whigs lacked only a national leader. Henry Clay came close, but he was scarred by many political battles and additionally could not shake his reputation as a man who spent his days at the gaming table and his nights in brothels. Unable to agree on a single candidate, the Whigs ran four sectional candidates: William Henry Harrison of Ohio in the Old Northwest, Hugh Lawson White of Tennessee and W. P. Mangum of North Carolina in the South, and Daniel Webster of Massachusetts in the East. The Whig strategy was to prevent Vice President Martin Van Buren, the Democratic candidate, from gaining the required majority of electoral votes. That

The Election of 1836

Candidates	Parties	Electoral Vote	Popular Vote	Percentage of Popular Vote
MARTIN VAN BUREN	Democratic	170	765,483	50.9
William H. Harrison	Whig	73		
Hugh L. White	Whig	26	739,79	49.1
Daniel Webster	Whig	14		
W. P. Mangum	Whig	11		

would force the election into the House of Representatives, where the Whigs thought that they had a chance to win.

Van Buren, whose star in the Democratic party had risen as Calhoun's had fallen, captured 170 electoral votes to 124 for the four Whigs combined. The Whig strategy obviously had backfired, but there were signs of trouble ahead for the Democrats. In the South the Whigs ran virtually even in the popular vote and captured Georgia and Tennessee. Even in the southern states held by Van Buren, the Democratic proportion of the popular vote was much smaller than in 1832; in North Carolina, for example, it dropped from 70 percent to 53 percent.

The Panic of 1837

Jackson left office in March 1837 in a sunburst of glory. Hailed as "the greatest man of his age," he returned to his Nashville home in a triumphant procession. But the public's mood quickly became less festive, for no sooner was Van Buren in office than a severe depression began.

The years 1835 and 1836 had witnessed a speculative boom fed by Jackson's policy of removing federal deposits from the Bank of the United States and placing them in state banks. In 1830 there were 329 banks in the nation with a total capital of $110 million. By 1835 the number of banks had increased to 704, with a total capital of $231 million. The value of bank notes in circulation grew from $61 million in 1830 to $149 million in 1837. Commodity prices rose an average of 13 percent a year in 1835 and 1836. Land sales skyrocketed. States made new commitments to build canals. Then in May 1837, prices began to tumble, and bank after bank suspended specie payments. After a short rally, the economy crashed again in 1839. The Bank of the United States, which had continued to operate as a

state bank with a Pennsylvania charter, failed. Nicholas Biddle himself was charged with fraud and theft. Banks throughout the nation once again suspended specie payments.

The ensuing depression was far more severe and prolonged than the economic downturn of 1819. Those lucky enough to find work saw their wage rates drop by roughly one-third between 1836 and 1842. In despair, many workers turned to the teachings of William Miller, a New England religious enthusiast whose reading of the Bible convinced him that the end of the world was imminent. Dressed in black coats and stovepipe hats, Miller's followers roamed urban sidewalks and rural villages in search of converts. Many Millerites sold their possessions and purchased white robes to ascend into heaven on October 22, 1843, the date on which Millerite leaders calculated the world would end. Ironically, by then the worst of the depression was over; but at its depths in the late 1830s and early 1840s, the economic slump fed the gloom that made poor people receptive to Miller's predictions.

The origins of the depression were both national and international. In July 1836 Jackson had issued a proclamation called the Specie Circular, which provided that after August 15 only specie was to be accepted in payment for public lands. The Specie Circular was one of Jackson's final affirmations of his belief that paper money encouraged people to embark on speculative, get-rich-quick schemes, sapped "public virtue," and robbed "honest labour of its earnings to make knaves rich, powerful and dangerous." He hoped that the Specie Circular would reverse the damaging effects of the Deposit Act of 1836, which he had signed reluctantly. The Specie Circular took the wind out of the speculative boom by making banks hesitant to issue more of the paper money that was fueling the boom, because western farmers eager to buy public lands would now demand that banks immediately redeem their paper in specie. Although the Specie Circular chilled bankers' confidence, it was not the sole or even the major reason for the depression. There were international causes as well, most notably the fact that in 1836, Britain, in an effort to restrain the outflow of British investment, checked the flow of specie from its shores to the United States.

The Search for Solutions

Van Buren came to office with a well-deserved reputation as a crafty politician; contemporaries called him the "sly fox" and the "little magician." Now he had to act decisively, for the depression was causing misery not only for ordinary citizens but for the Democratic party as well. Railing against "Martin Van Ruin," the Whigs in 1838 swept the governorship and most of the legislative seats in Van Buren's own New York.

To regain the political initiative, the president called for the creation of an Independent Treasury. Instead of depositing its revenue in state banks, the federal government would keep the revenue itself and thereby withhold public money from the grasp of business corporations. Introduced in Congress in 1837, the Independent Treasury Bill finally passed in 1840. With a flourish, Van Buren signed it into law on July 4, 1840; his supporters hailed it as America's second Declaration of Independence.

The establishment of the Independent Treasury reflected the basic Jacksonian suspicion of an alliance between the federal government and banking. From the moment that it was introduced, the Independent Treasury Bill promised not only to give the Democrats a clear national issue around which to rally but to get the federal government out of the banking business. But the Independent Treasury proposal failed to address the banking issue on the state level. Jackson's dismemberment of the Bank of the United States had not slowed the establishment of state banks, whose number by 1840 had grown to over nine hundred. Although holding charters from state governments, these banks were privately controlled institutions whose loans to businessmen and farmers fueled the kind of speculative economy that Jacksonians feared.

Whigs and Democrats differed sharply in their approach to the multiplication of state banks. Eager to encourage economic development, Whigs in New York and elsewhere introduced the idea of "free banking." Free banking allowed any group to start a bank as long as its members met general state requirements.

In the eyes of Whigs, Jackson's Specie Circular, not banks themselves, had caused the depression. In contrast, Democrats took a different view of both the causes of the depression and the value of state banks. Disillusioned by the collapse of the speculative boom of 1835–1836, a growing number of Democrats blamed the depression on banks and paper money and adopted the hard-money stance long favored by Jackson and his advisers. In Louisiana and Arkansas, Democrats successfully prohibited banks altogether. Elsewhere, Democrats imposed severe legislative restrictions on banks—for example, by banning the emission of paper money in small denominations. In sum, after 1837 the Democrats became an antibank, hard-money party.

The Election of 1840

Despite the depression, Van Buren gained his party's renomination. Avoiding their mistake of 1836, the Whigs settled on a single candidate, Ohio's William Henry Harrison, and ran former Virginia senator John Tyler as vice president. Harrison, sixty-seven years old and barely eking out a living on a farm, was picked because he had few enemies. Early in the campaign, the Democrats made a fatal mistake by ridiculing Harrison as "Old Granny," a man who desired only to spend his declining years in a log cabin sipping cider. Without knowing it, the Democrats had handed the Whigs the

The Election of 1840

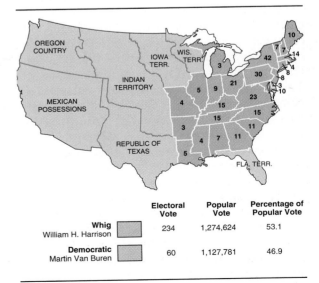

		Electoral Vote	Popular Vote	Percentage of Popular Vote
Whig William H. Harrison		234	1,274,624	53.1
Democratic Martin Van Buren		60	1,127,781	46.9

FEDERAL BANK WHIG MOTTO.

"WE STOOP TO CONQUER."

FEDERAL-ABOLITION-WHIG TRAP,
TO CATCH VOTERS IN.

The Federal-Abolition–Whig Trap

This Democratic cartoon from the 1840 campaign linked the Whigs to the discredited Federalists and to the unpopular abolitionists. An unwary voter, seeking a harmless sip of hard cider, is about to be entrapped by the log cabin, the campaign symbol of the Whig William Henry Harrison.

most famous campaign symbol in American history. The Whigs immediately reminded the public that Harrison had been a rugged frontiersman, the hero of the Battle of Tippecanoe, and a defender of all frontier people who lived in log cabins.

Refusing to publish a platform, the Whigs ran a "hurrah" campaign. They used log cabins for headquarters, sang log-cabin songs, gave out log-cabin cider, and called their newspaper the *Log Cabin.* For a slogan, they trumpeted "Tippecanoe and Tyler too." When not celebrating log cabins, they attacked Van Buren as a soft aristocrat who lived in "regal splendor." Whereas Harrison was content to drink hard cider from a plain mug, the Whigs observed, Van Buren had turned the White House into a palace fit for an oriental despot and drank fine wines from silver goblets while he watched people go hungry in the streets.

The election results gave Harrison a clear victory. Van Buren carried only seven states and failed even to hold his own New York. The depression would have made it difficult, if not impossible, for any Democrat to have triumphed in 1840, but Van Buren had other disabilities besides the economic collapse. Unlike Harrison and Jackson, he had no halo of military glory.

Moreover, Van Buren ran a surprisingly sluggish campaign. Prior to 1840 the Whigs had been slower than the Democrats to mobilize voters by new techniques. But in 1840 it was Van Buren who directed his campaign the old-fashioned way by writing encouraging letters to key supporters, whereas Harrison broke with tradition and went about the country (often on railroads) campaigning. Ironically, Van Buren, the master politician, was beaten at his own game.

The Second Party System Matures

In losing the presidency in 1840, Van Buren actually received 400,000 more popular votes than any previous presidential candidate. The total number of votes cast in presidential elections had risen from 1.2 million in 1828 to 1.5 million in 1836 to 2.4 million in 1840. The leap in the size of the popular vote between 1836 and 1840, 60 percent, is the greatest proportional jump between consecutive elections in American history. Neither lower suffrage requirements nor population growth was the main cause of this change. Rather, the spurt in the popular vote resulted from a jump in the percentage of eligible voters who *chose* to vote. In the three elections before 1840, the proportion of white males who voted had fluctuated between 55 percent and 58 percent; in 1840 it rose to 80 percent.

Both the depression and the frenzy of the log-cabin campaign had jolted previously indifferent voters into going to the polls. Yet voter turnouts stayed up even after prosperity returned in the 1840s. The second party system, which had been developing slowly since 1828, reached a high plateau in 1840 and remained there for more than a decade. What gave politicians their appeal in the eyes of ordinary people were not only their rousing campaign techniques but also the strong contrasts and simple choices that they could present. The gradual hardening of the line between the two parties stimulated enduring popular interest in politics.

No less than the tariff and banking issues, reform also aroused partisan passions by 1840. Yet many of the seeds of the reform movements that burst upon the national scene in the 1830s were initially sown in the field of religion rather than politics.

THE RISE OF POPULAR RELIGION

In *Democracy in America*, Alexis de Tocqueville pointed out an important difference between France and the United States. "In France I had almost always seen the spirit of religion and the spirit of freedom pursuing courses diametrically opposed to each other; but in America I found that they were intimately united, and that they reigned in common over the same country." From this assertion Tocqueville drew a startling conclusion: religion was "the foremost of the political institutions" of the United States.

In calling religion a political institution, Tocqueville did not mean that Americans gave special political privileges to any particular denomination. Rather, he was referring to the way in which religious impulses reinforced American democracy and liberty. Just as Americans demanded that politics be made accessible to the average person, they insisted that ministers preach doctrines that appealed to ordinary people. The most successful ministers were those who used plain words to move the heart, not those who tried to dazzle their listeners with theological complexities. Increasingly, too, Americans demanded theological

doctrines that put individuals in charge of their own religious destiny. They thrust aside the Calvinist doctrine that God had arbitrarily selected some people for salvation and others for damnation and substituted the belief that anyone could attain heaven.

Thus heaven as well as politics became democratized in these years. This harmony between religious and democratic impulses owed much to a series of religious revivals known as the Second Great Awakening.

The Second Great Awakening

The Second Great Awakening had begun in Connecticut during the 1790s and set ablaze one section of the nation after another during the following half-century. At first, educated Congregationalists and Presbyterians such as Yale University's president Timothy Dwight had dominated the revivals. But as they moved from Connecticut to frontier states like Tennessee and Kentucky, the revivals had undergone striking changes that were typified by the rise of camp meetings. Camp meetings were gigantic revivals in which members of several denominations gathered together in sprawling open-air camps for up to a week to hear revivalists proclaim that the Second Coming of Jesus was near and that the time for repentance was now. The most famous camp meeting had occurred at Cane Ridge, Kentucky, in August 1801, when a huge crowd had come together on a hillside to listen to thunderous sermons and to sing hymns and experience the influx of divine grace. One eyewitness vividly described the meeting:

> *At night, the whole scene was awfully sublime. The ranges of tents, the fires, reflecting light amidst the branches of the towering trees; the candles and lamps illuminating the encampment; hundreds moving to and fro, with lights or torches, like Gideon's army; the preaching, praying, singing, and shouting, all heard at once, rushing from different parts of the ground, like the sound of many waters, was enough to swallow up all the powers of contemplation.*

The Cane Ridge revival had been an episode of the larger Great Kentucky Revival of 1800–1801. Among the distinguishing features of these frontier revivals was the appearance of "exercises" in which men and women rolled around like logs, jerked their heads furiously (a phenomenon known simply as "the jerks"),

Methodist Camp Meeting
Frontier revivals occurred outdoors, lasted for days, and attracted an abundance of women and children as well as men.

and grunted like animals (the "barking exercise"). Observing the apparent pandemonium that had broken loose, critics had blasted the frontier frenzy for encouraging fleshly lust more than spirituality and complained that in revivals, "more souls were begot than saved." In fact, the early frontier revivals had challenged traditional religious customs. The most successful frontier revivalist preachers were not college graduates but ordinary farmers and artisans who had experienced powerful religious conversions and who had contempt for learned ministers with their dry expositions of doctrine.

No religious denomination had been more successful on the frontier than Methodists. With fewer than seventy thousand members in 1800, the Methodists had by 1844 become America's largest Protestant denomination, claiming a little over a million members. in contrast to New England Congregationalists and Presbyterians, Methodists emphasized that religion was primarily a matter of the heart rather than the head. Too, the frontier Methodists disdained a "settled" ministry—that is, ministers tied to fixed parishes. Instead, they preferred itinerant circuit riders—young, unmarried men—who moved on horseback from place to place and preached in houses, open fields, or wherever else listeners gathered.

Although the frontier revivals disrupted religious custom, they also worked to promote law, order, and a sense of morality on the frontier. Drunken rowdies who tried to invade camp meetings met their match in brawny itinerants like the Methodist Peter Cartwright. It was not only in camp meetings that Cartwright and his peers sought to raise the moral standard of the frontier. The basic unit of Methodist discipline on the frontier was the "class." When revivals broke up, the converted formed these tiny groups of twelve or so members who met weekly to provide mutual encouragement of both religion and morality. During these class meetings, Methodists chastised each other for drunkenness, fighting, fornication, gossiping, and even sharp business practices.

Eastern Revivals

By the 1820s the Second Great Awakening had begun to shift back to the East. The hottest revival fires blazed in an area of western New York known as the Burned-Over District. No longer a frontier, western New York teemed with descendants of Puritans who hungered for religious experience and with people drawn by the hope of wealth after the completion of the Erie Canal. At this time it was a fertile field of high expectations and bitter discontent.

The man who harnessed these anxieties to religion was Charles G. Finney. Finney began his career as a lawyer, but after a religious conversion in 1821, which he described as a "retainer from the Lord Jesus Christ to plead his cause," he became a Presbyterian minister and conducted revivals in towns along the canal like Rome and Utica. Although he also found time for trips to New York and Boston, his greatest "harvest" came in the thriving canal city of Rochester in 1830–1831.

The Rochester revival had several features that justify Finney's reputation as the "father of modern revivalism." First, it was a citywide revival in which all denominations participated. Finney was a pioneer of cooperation among Protestant denominations. In addition, in Rochester and elsewhere, Finney introduced devices for speeding conversions. Among these were the "anxious seat," a bench to which those ready for conversion were led so that they could be made objects of special prayer, and the "protracted meeting," which went on nightly for up to a week. Finney's emphasis on special revival techniques sharply distinguished him from eighteenth-century revivalists, including Jonathan Edwards. Whereas Edwards had portrayed revivals as the miraculous work of God, Finney made them out to be human creations. The divine spirit flowed in revivals, but humans made them happen. Finally, although a Presbyterian, Finney flatly rejected the Calvinist belief that humans had a natural and nearly irresistible inclination to sin (the doctrine of "human depravity"). Rather, he affirmed, sin was purely a voluntary act; no one *had* to sin. Men and women could will themselves out of sin just as readily as they had willed themselves into it. Indeed, he declared, it was theoretically possible for men and women to will themselves free of all sin—to live perfectly. Those who heard Finney and similar revivalists came away convinced that they had experienced the washing away of all past guilt and the beginning of a new life. "I have been born again," a young convert wrote. "I am three days old when I write this letter."

The assertions that people could live without sin ("perfectionism") and that revivals were human contrivances made Finney a controversial figure. Yet his ideas came to dominate "evangelical" Protestantism, forms of Protestantism that focused on the need for an emotional religious conversion. He was successful because he told people what they wanted to hear: that their destinies were in their own hands. A society that celebrated the "self-made" individual found plausible Finney's assertion that even in religion, people could make of themselves what they chose. Moreover, compared to most frontier revivalists, Finney had an unusually dignified style. Taken together, these factors gave him a potent appeal to merchants, lawyers, and small manufacturers in the towns and cities of the North. Finally, more than most revivalists, Finney recognized that without the mass participation of women, few revivals would have gotten off the ground. During the Second Great Awakening, female converts outnumbered male converts by about two to one. Finney encouraged women to give public testimonials of their religious experiences in church, and he often converted husbands by first converting their wives and daughters. After a visit by Finney, Melania Smith, the wife of a Rochester physician who had little time for religion, greeted her husband with a reminder of "the woe which is denounced against the families which call not on the Name of the Lord." Soon Dr. Smith heeded his wife's pleading and joined one of Rochester's Presbyterian churches.

Critics of Revivals: The Unitarians

Whereas some praised revivals for saving souls, others doubted that they produced permanent changes in behavior and condemned them for encouraging "such extravagant and incoherent expressions, and such enthusiastic fervor, as puts common sense and modesty to the blush."

One small but influential group of revival critics was the Unitarians. The basic doctrine of Unitarianism—that Jesus Christ was less than fully divine—had gained quiet acceptance among religious liberals during the eighteenth century. However, it was not until the early nineteenth century that Unitarianism emerged as a formal denomination with its own churches, ministry, and national organization. In New England in these years, hundreds of Congregational churches were torn apart by the withdrawal of socially prominent families who had embraced Unitarianism and by legal battles over which group—Congregationalists or Unitarians—could occupy church property. Although Unitarians won relatively few converts outside New England, their tendency to attract the wealthy and educated gave them influence beyond their numbers.

Unitarians criticized revivals as uncouth emotional exhibitions and argued that moral goodness should be cultivated by a gradual process of "character building," in which the individual learned to model his or her behavior on that of Jesus rather than by a sudden emotional conversion as in a revival. Yet Unitarians and revivalists shared the belief that human behavior could be changed for the better. Both rejected the Calvinist emphasis on innate human wickedness. William Ellery Channing, a Unitarian leader, claimed that Christianity had but one purpose: "the perfection of human nature, the elevation of men into nobler beings."

The Rise of Mormonism

The Unitarians' assertion that Jesus Christ was human rather than divine challenged a basic doctrine of orthodox Christianity. Yet Unitarianism proved far less controversial than another of the new denominations of the 1820s and 1830s, the Church of Jesus Christ of Latter-day Saints, or Mormons. Its founder, Joseph Smith, grew to manhood in one of those families that seemed in constant motion to and fro but never up. After moving his family nearly twenty times in ten years, Smith's

Mormon Migrants
Persecution of the Mormons raged in Missouri in the 1830s, and in 1838 the state's governor ordered the militia to kill the Mormons or drive them from the state. By 1839 most Mormons had left. Many resettled in Nauvoo, Illinois, only to migrate again to Deseret in the late 1840s.

ne'er-do-well father settled in Palmyra, New York, in the heart of the Burned-Over District. As a boy, Smith's imagination teemed with plans to find buried treasure, while his religious views were convulsed by the conflicting claims of the denominations that thrived in the region. "Some were contending for the Methodist faith, some for the Presbyterian, and some for the Baptists," Smith later wrote. He wondered who was right and who wrong, or whether they were "all wrong together."

The sort of perplexity that Smith experienced was widespread in the Burned-Over District, but his resolution of the confusion was unique. Smith claimed that an angel led him to a buried book of revelation and to special stones for use in translating it. He completed his translation of this Book of Mormon in 1827. The Book of Mormon tells the story of an ancient Hebrew prophet, Lehi, whose descendants came to America and created a prosperous civilization that looked forward to the appearance of Jesus as its savior. Jesus had actually appeared and performed miracles in the New World, the book claimed, but the American descendants of Lehi had departed from the Lord's ways and quarreled among themselves. God had cursed some with dark skin; these were the American Indians, who, when later discovered by Columbus, had forgotten their history.

Despite his astonishing claims, Smith quickly gathered followers. The appeal of Mormonism lay partly in its positioning of America at the center of Christian history and partly in Smith's assertion that he had discovered a new revelation. The idea of an additional revelation beyond the Bible appeared to some to resolve the turmoil created by the Protestant denominations' inability to agree on what the Bible said or meant.

Smith and his followers steadily moved west from New York to Ohio and Missouri. Then they migrated to Illinois, where they built a model city, Nauvoo, and a magnificent temple supported by thirty huge pillars. By moving to these areas, the Mormons hoped to draw closer to the Indians, whose conversion was one of their goals, and to escape persecution. Smith's claim to have received a new revelation virtually guaranteed a hostile reception for the Mormons wherever they went, because Smith had seemingly undermined the authority of the Bible, one of the two documents (the other being the Constitution) upon which the ideals of the American republic rested.

Smith added fuel to the fire when he reported in 1843 that he had received still another revelation, this one sanctioning the Mormon practice of having multiple wives, or polygyny. Although Smith did not publicly proclaim polygyny as a doctrine, its practice among Mormons was a poorly kept secret. Smith's self-image also intensified the controversy that boiled around Mormonism. He refused to view himself merely as the founder of another denomination; instead, he saw himself as a prophet of the kingdom of God and was called a "Second Mohammed." Mormonism would be to Christianity what Christianity had been to Judaism: an all-encompassing, higher form of religion. In 1844 he announced his candidacy for the presidency of the United States. But the state of Illinois was already moving against him. Charged with treason, he was jailed in Carthage, Illinois, and along with his brother, murdered there by a mob in June 1844.

Despite persecution, the Mormons won converts, not only in the United States but in the teeming slums of English factory cities from which Mormon agents brought thousands to America. In the thirty years after 1840, the number of Mormons grew from six thousand to two hundred thousand. After Smith's death a new leader, Brigham Young, led the main body of Mormons from Nauvoo to the Great Salt Lake Valley in Utah, which then was still under the control of Mexico. There Mormons established an independent republic, the state of Deseret. A thousand miles from Illinois, they prospered. Their isolation, combined with the firm control of Young, the "Old Boss," kept the rank and file in line. Polygyny, which Young officially proclaimed as a church doctrine, did not produce the hoped-for increase in Mormon numbers, but it did guarantee that

Mormons would remain a people apart from the mainstream of American society. Above all, the Mormons were industrious and deeply committed to the welfare of other Mormons. Cooperation among Mormons took several forms, not the least of which was the practice of devoting each Mormon's "surplus" production to public projects like irrigation. Mormons transformed the valley into a rich oasis. When Utah came under American control after the Mexican War, they dominated its government.

Although Mormonism is one of the few religions to have originated in the United States, the antebellum Mormons pushed against the currents of standard American religion and society. They rejected the Bible as the sole source of revelation, substituted polygyny for monogamy, and elevated economic cooperation above competitiveness. Mormonism appealed to the downtrodden and insecure rather than to the prosperous and secure. It offered the downcast an explicit alternative to dominant religious and social practices. In this respect, Mormonism mirrored the efforts of several religious communal societies whose members resolutely set themselves apart from society. In general, these religious communitarians were less numerous, controversial, and long-lasting than the Mormons, but one group among them, the Shakers, has continued to fascinate Americans.

The Shakers

The leader of the Shakers (who derived their name from a convulsive religious dance that was part of their ceremony) was Mother Ann Lee, the illiterate daughter of an English blacksmith. Lee had set sail for America in 1774, and her followers soon organized a tightly knit community in New Lebanon, New York. In this and in other communities, the Shakers proved themselves able artisans. Shaker furniture became renowned for its beauty and strength. But for all their achievements as artisans, the Shakers were fundamentally otherworldly and hostile to materialism. Lee insisted that her followers abstain from sexual intercourse, believed that the end of the world was imminent, and derived many of her doctrines from trances and heavenly visions that she claimed to have. Among these doctrines was her conviction that at the Second Coming, Jesus would take the form of a woman, herself.

Her teachings about the evils of sexual relations would quickly have doomed the Shakers to extinction had it not been for the spread of religious revivalism in

1790. Turning up at Cane Ridge and other revival sites, Shaker missionaries made off with converts whom the revivals had loosened from their traditional religious moorings. At their peak during the second quarter of the nineteenth century, the Shakers numbered about six thousand in eight states.

Shakers and Mormons chose to live apart from society. But the message of most evangelical Protestants, including Charles G. Finney, was that religion and economic individualism—a person's pursuit of wealth—were compatible. Most revivalists told people that getting ahead in the world was acceptable as long as they were honest, temperate, and bound by the dictates of their consciences. By encouraging assimilation into rather than retreat from society, evangelicalism provided a powerful stimulus to the manifold reform movements of the 1820s and 1830s.

◆

THE AGE OF REFORM

Despite rising popular interest in politics between 1824 and 1840, large numbers of people were excluded from politics. Women were not allowed to vote, and blacks generally suffered rather than benefited from the gradual liberalization of voting requirements. By 1860 most northern states denied free people of color the right to vote. Too, the political parties did not welcome the intrusion of controversial issues like slavery, nor did they show much interest in women's rights.

During the 1820s and 1830s, unprecedented numbers of men and women overcame these limits of political parties by joining organizations that aimed to improve society. Slavery's abolition, women's rights, temperance, better treatment of criminals and the insane, public education, and even the establishment of perfect, utopian communities were high on various reformers' agenda. Although they occasionally cooperated with political parties, especially the Whigs, reformers gave their loyalty to their causes, not to parties. Indeed, politics struck most reformers as a sorry spectacle that allowed a man like Andrew Jackson, a duelist who married a divorcee, to become president and that routinely rewarded persons who would sacrifice any principle for victory at the polls.

Reformers believed that they were on God's side on any issue. Religious revivalism contributed to their intense moralism. Virtually all prominent temperance reformers of the 1820s and 1830s, for example, had been inspired initially by revivals. But revivalism and reform were not always so intimately linked. Influential school reformers and women's rights advocates were frequently religious liberals either hostile or indifferent to revivals. And although some abolitionists owed their first flush of idealism to revivals, others did not, and almost all came to criticize the churches for condoning slavery. Yet even those reformers opposed to revivalism borrowed the evangelical preachers' language and psychology by portraying drunkenness, ignorance, and inequality as sins that called for immediate repentance and change.

Reform had a dark side. Reformers did not hesitate to coerce people into change by calling for the legal prohibition of liquor and for compulsory education. For criminals, they designed penitentiaries on highly repressive principles. While assailing intemperance with fury, they frequently ignored the slums and working conditions that stimulated drinking.

Although the reform movements appealed to those excluded from or repelled by politics, most lacked the political parties' national organizations. New England and those parts of the Midwest settled by New Englanders were hotbeds of reform. In contrast, southerners actively suppressed abolition, displayed only mild interest in temperance and education reform, ignored women's rights, and saw utopian communities as proof of the mental instability of northern reformers.

The War on Liquor

Agitation for temperance (either total abstinence from alcoholic beverages, or moderation in their use) intensified during the second quarter of the nineteenth century. Temperance reformers addressed a growing problem. The spread of the population across the Appalachians stimulated the production and consumption of alcohol. Before the transportation revolution, western farmers, unable to get their grain to markets, commonly distilled it into spirits. Annual per capita consumption of rum, whiskey, gin, and brandy rose until it exceeded seven gallons by 1830, nearly triple today's rate. By the late 1820s, the average adult male drank a half-pint of liquor a day. With some justification, reformers saw alcoholic excess as a male indulgence whose bitter consequences (spending wages on liquor instead of food) fell on women and children.

Politicians in a Country Bar,
by James Clooney, 1844
*The temperance movement did not
deter politicians from soliciting voters in taverns.*

Not surprisingly, millions of women would march behind the temperance banner during the nineteenth
century.

There had been agitation against intemperance
before 1825, but that year the Connecticut revivalist Lyman Beecher ushered in a new phase when, in six
widely acclaimed lectures, he thundered against all
use of alcohol. A year later, evangelical Protestants created the American Temperance Society, the first national temperance organization. By 1834 some five
thousand state and local temperance societies were
loosely affiliated with the American Temperance Society. Where as previous temperance supporters had advised moderation in the use of spirits, the American
Temperance Society followed Beecher in demanding
total abstinence. The society flooded the country with
tracts denouncing the "amazing evil" of strong drink
and urged churches to expel any members who condoned alcohol.

Among the main targets of the evangelical temperance reformers were moderate drinkers among the
laboring classes. In the small shops where a handful of
journeymen and apprentices worked informally, passing the jug every few hours was a time-honored way
to relieve fatigue and monotony. But with the rise of
large factories, new demands arose for a disciplined
work force. Factory owners with precise production
schedules to meet needed
orderly and steady workers.
Thus evangelical temperance
reformers quickly gained manufacturers' support. In East
Dudley, Massachusetts, for example, three factory owners refused to sell liquor in factory
stores, calculating that any profits from the sale would be more
than offset by lost working time and "the scenes of riot
and wickedness thus produced."

Workers showed little interest in temperance before the late 1830s. But after the Panic of 1837, a new
stage of temperance agitation sprang up in the form of
the Washington Temperance Societies. Starting in Baltimore in 1840, the Washingtonians were more likely
to be mechanics (workingmen) and laborers than
ministers and manufacturers. Many were reformed
drunkards, and most had concluded that their survival
in the harsh climate of depression depended on their
commitment to sobriety and frugality. For example,
Charles T. Woodman, a baker, had been forced by the
collapse of his business to flee Boston for Philadelphia
to escape his creditors. Like most Washingtonians,
Woodman blamed his ruin on the revival of his "old
habit" of drink. The forces dislocating workers in the
late 1830s were often far beyond their control. Part of
the appeal of temperance was that it lay *within* their
control. Take care of temperance, a Washingtonian assured a Baltimore audience, and the Lord would take
care of the economy.

For all their differences from earlier temperance
associations, the Washingtonians reflected the impact
of revivals even more than did the American Temperance Society. Viewing drinking as sinful, they held "experience meetings," in which members described their

"salvation" from liquor and their "regeneration" through abstinence (or "teetotalism"*). Their wives joined "Martha Washington" societies, in which they pledged to smell their husbands' breath each night and paraded with banners that read "Teetotal or No Husband." The Washingtonians spread farther and faster than any other antebellum temperance organization.

As temperance won new supporters, anti-alcohol crusaders gradually shifted their tactics from calls that individuals abstain to demands that cities and towns, and even states, ban all traffic in liquor. This shift from moral suasion to legal prohibition was controversial even within the movement. But by the late 1830s, prohibition was scoring victories. In 1838 Massachusetts prohibited the sale of distilled spirits in amounts less than fifteen gallons, thereby restricting small purchases by individual drinkers; in 1851 Maine banned the manufacture and sale of all intoxicating beverages. Controversial though these laws were, the temperance movement earned a measure of success. After rising steadily between 1800 and 1830, per capita consumption of distilled spirits began to fall during the 1830s. The rate of consumption during the 1840s was less than half that in the 1820s.

Public-School Reform

No less than temperance reformers, school reformers worked to encourage orderliness and thrift in the common people. Rural America's so-called district schools provided reformers with one of their main targets. One-room log or clapboard cabins containing pupils aged anywhere from three to twenty or more, the district schools taught farmers' children to read and count but little more. Those who attended the district schools never forgot their primitive conditions or harsh discipline: "the wood-pile in the yard, the open fireplace, the backless benches," and the floggings until "the youngster vomited or wet his breeches."

For all their drawbacks, the district schools enjoyed popular and financial support from rural parents. But reformers saw these schools in a different light, insisting that schools had to equip children for the emerging competitive and industrial economy. The most articulate and influential of the reformers, Horace Mann of Massachusetts, in 1837 became the first secretary of his state's newly created board of education,

and for the next decade, he promoted a sweeping transformation of public education. Mann's goals included shifting the burden of financial support for schools from parents to the state, grading the schools (that is, classifying pupils by age and attainment), extending the school term from two or three months to as many as ten months, introducing standardized textbooks, and compelling attendance. In place of loosely structured schools that were mere appendages of the family, Mann and other reformers advocated highly structured institutions that would occupy most of the child's time and energy.

School reformers hoped not only to combat ignorance but to spread uniform cultural values by exposing all children to identical experiences. Children would arrive at school at the same time and thereby learn punctuality. Graded schools that matched children against their age peers would stimulate the competitiveness needed in a rapidly industrializing society. Children would all read the same books and absorb such common sayings as "Idleness is the nest in which mischief lays its eggs." The McGuffey readers, which sold 50 million copies between 1836 and 1870, created a common curriculum and preached industry, honesty, sobriety, and patriotism.

Although school reform made few gains in the South (see Chapter 12), much of the North remodeled its schools along the lines advocated by Mann, and in 1852 Massachusetts passed the nation's first compulsory school law. Success did not come easily, however. Educational reformers faced challenges from farmers, who were satisfied with the informality of the district schools, and from urban Catholics led by New York City's Bishop John Hughes, who pointed out that the textbooks used in public schools contained anti-Catholic and anti-Irish barbs. And in both rural and urban areas, the laboring poor opposed compulsory education as a menace to parents dependent on their children's wages.

Yet school reformers prevailed, in part because their opponents, rural Protestants and urban Catholics, were incapable of cooperating with each other. In part, too, reformers succeeded by gaining influential allies. For example, their stress on free, tax-supported schools won the backing of the urban workingmen's parties that arose in the late 1820s; and their emphasis on punctuality appealed to manufacturers, who needed a disciplined work force. The new ideas also attracted reform-minded women, who recognized that the grading of schools would ease women's entry into

---

*Teetotal: coined by an English laborer at a temperance meeting in 1834, *teetotal* was merely an emphatic form of *total*.

teaching. People of the times widely believed that a woman could never control the assortment of three- to twenty-year-olds found in a one-room schoolhouse, but managing a class of eight- or nine-year-olds was a different matter. Catharine Beecher accurately predicted that school reform would render teaching a suitable profession for women. Women gradually did take the place of men in the classroom wherever school reform left its mark. By 1900 about 70 percent of the nation's schoolteachers were women.

School reform also appealed to native-born Americans alarmed by the swelling tide of immigration. The public school emerged as the favorite device by which reformers forged a common American culture out of an increasingly diverse society. "We must decompose and cleanse the impurities which rush into our midst" through the "one infallible filter—the SCHOOL."

School reformers were assimilationists in the sense that they hoped to use public education to give children common values through shared experiences. In one respect, however, these reformers wore blinders on the issue of assimilation, for few stressed the integration of black and white children. When black children were fortunate enough to get any schooling, it was usually in segregated schools. Black children who entered integrated public schools met with such virulent prejudice that black leaders in northern cities frequently preferred segregated schools.

Abolition

Antislavery sentiment among whites flourished in the Revolutionary era but declined in the early nineteenth century. The main antislavery organization founded between 1800 and 1830 was the American Colonization Society (1817), which displayed little moral outrage against slavery. The society proposed a plan for gradual emancipation, with compensation to the slaveowner, and the shipment of freed blacks to Africa. This proposal attracted support from some slaveholders in the Upper South who would never have dreamed of a general emancipation.

At its core, colonization was hard-hearted and softheaded. Colonizationists assumed that blacks were a degraded race that did not belong in American society, and they underestimated the growing dependence of the South's economy on slavery. Confronted by a soaring demand for cotton and other commodities, few southerners were willing to free their slaves, even if compensated. In any event, the American Coloniza-

tion Society never had enough funds to buy freedom for more than a fraction of slaves. Between 1820 and 1830, only 1,400 blacks migrated to Liberia, and most were already free. In striking contrast, the American slave population, fed by natural increase (the excess of births over deaths), rose from 1,191,000 in 1810 to more than 2,000,000 in 1830.

During the 1820s the main source of radical opposition to slavery was blacks themselves. Blacks had little enthusiasm for colonization. Most American blacks were native- rather than African-born. How, they asked, could they be sent back to a continent that they had never left? "We are *natives* of this country," a black pastor in New York proclaimed. "We only ask that we be treated as well as *foreigners.*" In opposition to colonization, blacks formed scores of abolition societies. In 1829 the Boston free black David Walker published an *Appeal* for a black rebellion to crush slavery.

Not all whites acquiesced to the continuance of slavery. In 1821 the Quaker Benjamin Lundy began a newspaper, the *Genius of Universal Emancipation,* and put forth proposals that no new slave states be admitted, that the internal slave trade be outlawed, that the three-fifths clause of the Constitution be repealed, and that Congress abolish slavery wherever it had the authority to do so. In 1828 Lundy hired a young New Englander, William Lloyd Garrison, as an assistant editor. Prematurely bald and with steel-rimmed glasses, and typically donning a black suit and black cravat, Garrison looked more like a schoolmaster than a rebel. But in 1831, when he launched his own newspaper, *The Liberator,* he quickly established himself as the most famous and controversial white abolitionist. "I am in earnest," Garrison wrote. "I will not equivocate—I will not excuse—I will not retreat a single inch—AND I WILL BE HEARD."

Garrison's battle cry was "immediate emancipation." In place of exiling blacks to Africa, he substituted the truly radical notion that blacks should enjoy civil (or legal) equality with whites. He greeted slaves as "a Man and a Brother," "a Woman and a Sister." Even Garrison, however, did not think that all slaves could be freed overnight. "Immediate emancipation" meant that all people had to realize that slavery was sinful and its continued existence intolerable.

Garrison quickly gained support from the growing number of black abolitionists. A black barber in Pittsburgh sent Garrison sixty dollars to help with *The Liberator.* Black agents sold subscriptions and three-fourths of *The Liberator*'s subscribers in the early

A is an Abolitionist—
A man who wants to free
The wretched slave—and give to all
An equal liberty.

B is a Brother with a skin
Of somewhat darker hue,
But in our Heavenly Father's sight,
He is as dear as you.

C is the Cotton-field, to which
This injured brother's driven,
When, as the white man's *slave*, he toils
From early morn till even.

D is the Driver, cold and stern,
Who follows, whip in hand,
To punish those who dare to rest,
Or disobey command.

The Antislavery Alphabet
Viewing children as morally pure and hence as natural opponents of slavery, abolitionists produced antislavery toys, games, and, as we see here, alphabet books.

years were black. The escaped slave Frederick Douglass and a remarkable freed slave who named herself Sojourner Truth proved eloquent lecturers against slavery. Douglass could rivet an audience with an opening line. "I appear before the immense assembly this evening as a thief and a robber," he gibed. "I stole this head, these limbs, this body from my master, and ran off with them."

Relations between black and white abolitionists were not always harmonious. White abolitionists called for legal equality for blacks but not necessarily for social equality. Not without racial prejudice, they preferred light- to dark-skinned Negroes and, Garrison excepted, were hesitant to admit blacks to antislavery societies. Yet the prejudices of white abolitionists were mild compared to those of most whites. A white man or woman could do few things less popular in the 1830s than become an abolitionist. Mobs, often including colonizationists, repeatedly attacked abolitionists. For example, a Boston mob, searching for a British abolitionist in 1835, found Garrison instead and dragged him through town on the end of a rope. An abolitionist editor, Elijah Lovejoy, was murdered by a mob in Alton, Illinois, in 1837.

Abolitionists drew on the language of revivals and described slavery as sin, but the Protestant churches did not rally behind abolition as strongly as behind temperance. Lyman Beecher roared against the evils of strong drink but whimpered about those of slavery and in 1834 tried to suppress abolitionists at Cincinnati's

Lane Theological Seminary. In response, Theodore Dwight Weld, an idealistic follower of Charles G. Finney, led a mass withdrawal of students. These "Lane rebels" formed the nucleus of abolitionist activity at the antislavery Oberlin College.

As if external hostility were not enough, abolitionists argued continually with each other. The American Anti-Slavery Society, founded in 1833, was the scene of several battles between Garrison and prominent New York and midwestern abolitionists such as the brothers Lewis and Arthur Tappan, Theodore Dwight Weld, and James G. Birney. One of the issues between the two sides was whether abolitionists should enter politics as a distinct party. In 1840 Garrison's opponents ran Birney for president on the ticket of the newly formed Liberty party. As for Garrison himself, he was increasingly rejecting *all* laws and governments, as well as political parties, as part of his doctrine of "nonresistance." In 1838 he and his followers had founded the New England Non-Resistance Society. The starting point of the doctrine was the fact that slavery depended on force. Garrison then added that all governments ultimately rested on force; even laws passed by elected legislatures needed police enforcement. Because Garrison viewed force as the opposite of Christian love, he concluded that Christians should refuse to vote, hold office, or have anything to do with government. It is a small wonder that many abolitionists thought of Garrison as extreme, or "ultra."

The second issue that divided the American Anti-Slavery Society concerned the role of women in the abolitionist movement. In 1837 Angelina and Sarah Grimké, daughters of a South Carolina slaveholder, embarked on an antislavery lecture tour of New England. Women had become deeply involved in antislavery societies during the 1830s, but always in female auxiliaries affiliated with those run by men. What made the Grimké sisters so controversial was that they drew mixed audiences of men and women to their lectures at a time when it was thought indelicate for women to speak before male audiences. Clergymen chastised the Grimké sisters for lecturing men rather than obeying them.

Such criticism backfired, however, because the Grimkés increasingly took up the cause of women's rights. In 1838 each wrote a classic of American feminism. Sarah produced her *Letters on the Condition of Women and the Equality of the Sexes,* and Angelina contributed her *Letters to Catharine E. Beecher* (Lyman Beecher's daughter and a militant opponent of female equality). Some abolitionists tried to dampen the feminist flames. The abolitionist poet John Greenleaf Whittier dismissed women's grievances as "paltry" compared to the "great and dreadful wrongs of the slave." Even Theodore Dwight Weld, who had married Angelina Grimké, wanted to subordinate women's rights to antislavery. But the fiery passions would not be extinguished. Garrison, welcoming the controversy, promptly espoused women's rights and urged that women be given positions equal to men in the American Anti-Slavery Society. In 1840 the election of a woman, Abby Kelley, to a previously all-male committee split the American Anti-Slavery Society wide open. A substantial minority of pro-feminist delegates left—some to join the Liberty party, others to follow Lewis Tappan into the new American and Foreign Anti-Slavery Society.

The disruption of the American Anti-Slavery Society did not greatly damage abolitionism. The national society had never had much control over the local societies that had grown swiftly during the mid-1830s. By 1840 there were more than fifteen hundred local societies, principally in Massachusetts, New York, and Ohio. By circulating abolitionist tracts, newspapers, and even chocolates with antislavery messages on their wrappers, these local societies kept the country ablaze with agitation.

One of the most disruptive abolitionist techniques was to flood Congress with petitions calling for an end to slavery in the District of Columbia. Congress had no time to consider all the petitions, but to refuse to address them meant depriving citizens of their right to have petitions heard. In 1836 southerners secured congressional adoption of the "gag rule," which automatically tabled abolitionist petitions and thus prevented discussion of them in Congress. Ex-president John Quincy Adams, then a representative from Massachusetts, led the struggle against the gag rule and finally secured its repeal in 1845. The debate over the gag rule subtly shifted the issue from the abolition of slavery to the constitutional rights of free expression and petitioning Congress. Members of Congress with little sympathy for abolitionists found themselves attacking the South for suppressing the right of petition. In a way, the gag-rule episode vindicated Garrison's tactic of stirring up emotions on the slavery issue. By holding passions over slavery at the boiling point, Garrison kept the South on the defensive. The less secure southerners felt, the more they were tempted into clumsy overreactions like the gag rule.

Women's Rights

The position of American women in the 1830s contained many contradictions. Women could not vote. If married, they had no right to own property (even inherited property) or to retain their own earnings. Yet the spread of reform movements provided women with unprecedented opportunities for public activity without challenging the prevailing belief that their proper sphere was the home. By suppressing liquor, for example, women could claim that they were transforming wretched homes into nurseries of happiness.

The argument that women were natural guardians of the family was double-edged. It justified reform activities on behalf of the family, but it undercut women's demands for legal equality. Let women attend to their sphere, the counterargument ran, and leave politics and finance to men. So deeply ingrained was sexual inequality, indeed, that most feminists did not start out intending to attack it. Instead, their experiences in other reform movements, notably abolition, led them to the issue of women's rights.

Among the early women's rights advocates who started their reform careers as abolitionists were the Grimké sisters, the Philadelphia Quaker Lucretia Mott, Lucy Stone, and Abby Kelley. Like abolition, the cause of women's rights revolved around the conviction that differences of race and gender were unimportant and incidental. "Men and women," Sarah Grimké wrote, "are CREATED EQUAL! They are both moral and accountable beings, and whatever is *right* for man to do,

Most newspapers ridiculed the Seneca Falls convention that Stanton and Mott organized to advance women's rights. More than three hundred people attended.

Lucretia Mott   **Elizabeth Cady Stanton**

is *right* for woman." The most articulate and aggressive advocates of women's rights, moreover, tended to gravitate to William Lloyd Garrison rather than to more moderate abolitionists. Garrison, himself a vigorous feminist, repeatedly stressed the peculiar degradation of women under slavery. The early issues of *The Liberator* contained a "Ladies' Department" headed by a picture of a kneeling slave woman imploring, "Am I Not a Woman and a Sister?" It was common knowledge that slave women were vulnerable to the sexual demands of white masters. Garrison denounced the South as a vast brothel and described slave women as "treated with more indelicacy and cruelty than cattle."

Although their involvement in abolition aroused advocates of women's rights, the discrimination they encountered within the abolition movement infuriated them and impelled them to make women's rights a separate cause. In the 1840s Lucy Stone became the first abolitionist to lecture solely on women's rights. When Lucretia Mott and other American women tried to be seated at the World's Anti-Slavery Convention in London in 1840, they were relegated to a screened-off section. The incident made a sharp impression not only on Mott but on Elizabeth Cady Stanton, who had elected to accompany her abolitionist husband to the meeting as a honeymoon trip. In 1848 Mott and Stanton organized a women's rights convention at Seneca Falls, New York, that proclaimed a Declaration of Sentiments. Modeled on the Declaration of Independence, the Seneca Falls Declaration began with the assertion that "all men and women are created equal." The convention passed twelve resolutions,

and only one, a call for the right of women to vote, failed to pass unanimously; but it did pass. Ironically, after the Civil War, the call for woman suffrage became the main demand of women's rights advocates for the rest of the century.

Although its crusaders were resourceful and energetic, women's rights had less impact than most other reforms. Temperance and school reform were far more popular, and abolitionism created more commotion. Women would not secure the right to vote throughout the nation until 1920, fifty-five years after the Thirteenth Amendment would abolish slavery. One reason for the relatively slow advance of women's rights was that piecemeal gains—such as married women securing the right to own property in several states by the Civil War—satisfied many women. The cause of women's rights also suffered from a close association with abolitionism, which was unpopular. In addition, the advance of feminism was slowed by the competition that it faced from the alternative ideal of domesticity. By sanctioning activities in reforms such as temperance and education, the cult of domesticity provided many women with worthwhile pursuits beyond the family. In this way, it blunted the edge of female demands for full equality.

Penitentiaries and Asylums

Reform efforts took shape during the 1820s to combat poverty, crime, and insanity by establishing highly regimented institutions, themselves products of striking new assumptions about the causes of deviancy.

Charlestown Jail
The military precision of prisoners' movements in the courtyard of the Charlestown (Massachusetts) jail reflected the belief of reformers that the character of wrongdoers would be reshaped by order and discipline.

In the colonial era, Americans had viewed poverty as neither the fault of its victims nor a sign of a defective social order. Rather, poverty was seen as a permanent condition of society, ordained by God to test Christians' humility and charity. Men and women thought of crime, too, as an enduring feature of society. Faced with punishment, individual criminals might mend their ways, but new lawbreakers would take their place. So ingrained were the defects of human nature that some would always choose the way of crime.

Several developments undermined these assumptions during the first half of the nineteenth century. Not only were poverty and crime rising, but in the swiftly growing cities, each was more visible than in the past. Alarmed legislators launched investigations into the causes of both indigence and crime, from which they concluded that deviant behavior often resulted from exposure to drunken fathers and broken homes. The failure of parental discipline, not the will of God or the wickedness of human nature, lay at the root of evil.

Few Americans would have reached these conclusions (or even undertaken the investigations that led to them) had it not been for their growing belief that the moral qualities of the individual were changeable rather than fixed. Both religious revivalists and reformers increasingly came to think that human nature could be altered by the right combination of moral influences. Most grasped the optimistic implications. "The study of the *causes* of crime," William Ellery Channing concluded, "may lead us to its *cure*."

To cure crime, reformers created substitutes for parental discipline, most notably the penitentiary. Penitentiaries were prisons marked by an unprecedented degree of order and discipline. Of course, colonial Americans had incarcerated criminal offenders, but jails had been used mainly to hold prisoners awaiting trial or to lock up debtors. For much of the eighteenth century, the threat of the gallows rather than of imprisonment had deterred wrongdoers. In contrast, nineteenth-century reformers believed that rightly managed, penitentiaries would bring about the sincere reformation of offenders.

To purge offenders' violent habits, reformers usually insisted on solitary confinement. Between 1819 and 1825, New York built penitentiaries at Auburn and Ossining (Sing Sing), in which prisoners were confined by night in small, windowless cells. By day they could work together but never speak and rarely even look at each other. Some reformers criticized this "Auburn system" for allowing too much contact and preferred the rival "Pennsylvania system," in which each prisoner spent all of his or her time in a single cell (each with a walled courtyard for exercise) and received no news or visits from the outside.

Antebellum America also witnessed a remarkable transformation in the treatment of poor people. The prevailing colonial practice of offering relief to the poor by supporting them in a household ("outdoor relief") gradually gave way to the construction of almshouses for the infirm poor and workhouses for the able-bodied poor ("indoor relief"). The argument for indoor relief was much the same as the argument for penitentiaries: plucking the poor from their demoralizing surroundings and exposing them to a highly regimented institution could change them

The most controversial of the antebellum experiments in communitarian utopianism, the Oneida community in New York State challenged conventional notions of religion, property, gender roles, marriage, sex, dress, and motherhood. Contemporaries dismissed its founder, John Humphrey Noyes, as a licentious crackpot, and Oneida as the "utopia of obscenity." Yet by the standards of utopian experiments, Oneida passed the test of time, achieved considerable economic prosperity, and continued to attract new members long after the collapse of less radical utopian experiments.

Little in Noyes's background—he had been born in 1811 into a well-connected Vermont family—marked him as an iconoclast. But Noyes came of age at a time when America was boiling over with radical religious doctrines that contained the seeds of still more unsettling social principles, and he possessed a penchant for carrying ideas to their logical conclusions, however extreme, and for leading his willing followers into uncharted regions of experience.

Converted in a Vermont revival in 1831, Noyes studied theology at Yale, where he came under the influence of Nathaniel W. Taylor, a theologian who pried Congregationalism from its Calvinist heritage by emphasizing that sin resulted from the individual's choice rather than from any divine plan. This interpretation left open the possibility that some people could achieve freedom from all sin—the doctrine of perfectionism. In 1834 Noyes startled his peers by asserting that he had achieved this perfect state. When, in response, the orthodox clergy revoked his license to preach, he announced that he would go on preaching just as they were free to go on sinning.

In the late 1830s Noyes began to gather disciples at Putney, Vermont, and to attack monogamous marriage. Because monogamy involved an exclusive attach-

Bag Bee
Communal work, shown here in the form of a "bee" (gathering) for making traveling bags, complemented Noyes's belief in the communal ownership of property.

ment to one person, Noyes viewed it as selfish and suited only to sinners. Soon he put his theory into practice by acknowledging his love for Mary Cragin, the wife of one of the Putney perfectionists, while Noyes's wife Harriet disclosed her own affection for Mary's husband. Noyes did not intend to divorce Harriet; rather, he proclaimed that among the perfect, all men would be married to all women and all women to all men—the doctrine of "complex marriage." When the Putney perfectionists recruited two young sisters from the village—one only fifteen years old—to their circle, the villagers exploded in outrage. Indicted for adultery with Mary Cragin, Noyes moved his little colony of the sinless to Oneida County in western New York in 1848.

To ordinary minds, Noyes was an advocate of free love. In reality, Noyes tied complex marriage to "male continence"; that is, men could engage in sexual intercourse with women, but they had to discipline themselves to withhold ejaculation (*coitus reservatus*). In this way, they not only practiced birth control but also demonstrated their perfect self-mastery. Like the Shakers, the Oneida community grew at first by attracting converts rather than by natural increase.

Consistent with Noyes's loathing of any form of proprietorship, whether of people or things, Oneidans renounced private property and practiced communism. But they accepted the profit motive in dealing with outsiders, the "worldlings." When an Oneidan invented an improved animal trap, the community marketed it through a Chicago dealer. In contrast to most other utopian communities, which cherished agriculture as a soothing alternative to the frenzied pace of industry, Oneidans fabricated and sold a wide array of products, including embroidered gentlemen's slippers, silk goods, mop handles, wheel spokes, and silverware. As the community prospered, its membership rose from under one hundred in 1849 to nearly three hundred by 1875.

Yet Noyes's unconventional ideas left their stamp even on work routines in Oneida's homes and factories. Although Noyes believed that women were less perfect than men, he mechanized domestic work wherever possible, insisted that males perform kitchen duties alongside

John Humphrey Noyes
Noyes possessed a magnetic attraction for women and commanded the unswerving loyalty of his female followers.

Harriet Holton
Having heard of Noyes's doctrine of perfection, Harriet Holton had rushed to hear him preach, judged his face to "shine like an angel's," and fallen in love.

women, and allowed women to work in the community's stores and factories. Indeed, Noyes bitterly criticized the idea of a separate sphere for women, with its exclusive assignment of females to household duties. Oneida women not only worked outside the home but *looked* as if they did. They preferred pantaloons to unwieldy hoop skirts and cut their hair short in an age when middle-class women enhanced their coiffures by purchasing false hair.

Obsessed by the dream of elevating all humanity to perfection, Noyes in 1867 launched Oneida on its boldest experiment: the breeding of a perfect race by means of "stirpiculture." Stirpiculture* necessitated modifying male continence to allow consummation, but Noyes continued to abhor free love. Although individuals could voice preferences for sexual mates and veto proposed candidates, the final decision was left to a committee of elders, headed by "Father" Noyes. Like most educated people of his day, Noyes believed that moral and spiritual as well as physical qualities would be transmitted to children (the doctrine of "acquired characteristics"), and accordingly, he saw to it that the "more perfect," usually the older members of the community, mated with

"less perfect" younger members—old men with young women, and young men with older women.

Noyes's influence over matings provoked dissent from Oneida's younger women, who faced criticism and even expulsion whenever they fell in love with men their own age and who suspected that stirpiculture too conveniently rationalized the lust of old men (including the ever prolific "Father" Noyes) for young women. Mounting outside criticism in the 1870s found the community weak and divided. In 1879 Noyes exiled himself to Canada to avoid prosecution (although local and state officials could not identify any law that he had broken); that same year, Oneidans renounced the doctrine of complex marriage. In 1881 they formally abandoned communism.

Oneida is more remarkable for its persistence than for its ultimate collapse. Despite the hostility of the clergy, Noyes usually maintained good relations with nearby worldlings, who found jobs in Oneida's factories. At the same time, the radical doctrines on which the experiment rested gave Oneida a degree of cohesion lacking at Brook Farm. By embracing a seemingly outlandish sexual doctrine, Oneidans, like Mormons, effectively burned their bridges to the world, and when they abandoned complex marriage, their unity dissolved.

---

*Stirpiculture: from the Latin *stirps*—a root or strain.

into virtuous, productive citizens. However lofty the motives behind workhouses and almshouses, the results were often abysmal. In 1833 a legislative committee found that the inmates of the Boston House of Industry were packed seven to a room and included unwed mothers, the sick, and the insane as well as the poor.

As for insane people, those living in a workhouse such as the Boston House of Industry were relatively well off, for many experienced even worse treatment by confinement in prisons. In 1841 an idealistic Unitarian schoolteacher, Dorothea Dix, was teaching a Sunday school class in a jail in East Cambridge, Massachusetts, and discovered there insane people kept in an unheated room. Dix pursued her investigation and visited jails and almshouses throughout the state. In 1843 she presented a memorial to the state legislature, which described the insane confined "in *cages, closets, cellars, stalls, pens! Chained, naked, beaten with rods, and lashed into obedience.*" With the support of Horace Mann and the Boston reformer Samuel G. Howe, she encouraged legislatures to build insane asylums, and by the time of the Civil War, twenty-eight states, four cities, and the federal government had constructed public mental institutions.

Penitentiaries, workhouses, and insane asylums all reflected the same optimistic belief that deviancy could be erased by resettling deviants in the right environment. But what was the "right" environment? In some aspects, the answer was clear-cut. Heated rooms were better than frigid ones, and sober parents preferable to drunkards. But reformers demanded much more than warm rooms and responsible parents. Reformers were convinced that the unfettered freedom and individualism of American society were themselves defects in the environment and that the poor, criminal, and insane needed extraordinary regimentation if they were to change. Prison inmates were to march around in lock step; in workhouses the poor, treated much like prisoners, were often forbidden to leave or receive visitors without permission. The idealism behind such institutions was genuine, but later generations would question reformers' underlying assumptions.

Utopian Communities

The belief that individuals could live perfectly, which tinged most antebellum reform movements, took its most extreme form in the experimental societies or "utopian" communities that flourished in these years. Although varying widely in their philosophies and arrangements, utopian communities had some common features. Their founders were intellectuals who designed their communities as alternatives to the prevailing competitive economy and as models whose success would inspire imitation. Unlike the Shakers and the Mormons, the utopians did not claim to have visions of God or visits from angels. Nor did they burn their bridges to society.

American interest in utopian communities first spurted during the 1820s. In 1825 British industrialist and philanthropist Robert Owen founded the New Harmony community in Indiana. Owen had already acquired a formidable reputation (and a fortune) from his management of cotton mills at New Lanark, Scotland. His innovations at New Lanark had substantially improved his workers' educational opportunities and living conditions and left him convinced that similar changes could transform the lives of working people everywhere. He saw the problem of the early industrial age as social rather than political. If social arrangements could be perfected, all vice and misery would disappear; human character was formed, "without exception," by people's surroundings or environment. The key to perfecting social arrangements lay, in turn, in the creation of small, planned communities—"Villages of Unity and Mutual Cooperation," each to contain a perfect balance of occupational, religious, and political groups.

Lured to the United States by cheap land and by Americans' receptivity to experiments, Owen confidently predicted that by 1827 the northern states would embrace the principles embodied in New Harmony. Unfortunately, by 1827 there was little left to embrace, for the community had quickly fallen apart. New Harmony had attracted more than its share of idlers and fanatics, and Owen had spent too much time on the road publicizing the community and not enough time managing it. He had clashed with clergymen, who still believed that Original Sin, not environment, shaped human character. Yet Owenism survived the wreckage of New Harmony. The ideas that human character was formed by environment and that cooperation was superior to competition had a potent impact on urban workers for the next half-century. Owen's ideas, for example, impelled workingmen's leaders to support educational reform during the late 1820s.

In the early 1830s, the utopian impulse weakened, only to revive amid the economic chaos of the late 1830s and 1840s. Appalled by the misery that came with economic depression, small bands of idealists gathered anew in experimental communities whose names—Hopedale, Fruitlands, Brook Farm—suggested idyllic retreats. Their founders' visions were fired by intense but unconventional forms of Christianity. Adin Ballou, a Universalist minister who founded Hopedale, near Milford, Massachusetts, described it as a "miniature Christian republic." Brook Farm, near Boston, was mainly the creation of a group of religious philosophers called transcendentalists. Most transcendentalists, including Ralph Waldo Emerson and George Ripley, had started as Unitarians but sought to revitalize Unitarianism—and indeed, all denominations—by proclaiming the infinite spiritual capacities of ordinary men and women.

Like other utopias, Brook Farm was both a retreat and a model. Convinced that the competitive commercial life of the cities was unnatural, philosophers welcomed the opportunity to engage in elevated discussions after a day perspiring in the cabbage patch. Although Brook Farm never had more than a hundred residents, it attracted several renowned writers. Emerson visited it, and novelist Nathaniel Hawthorne lived there for a period; Brook Farm's literary magazine, *The Dial,* became a forum for transcendentalist ideas about philosophy, art, and literature (also see Chapter 11).

Few utopias enjoyed success to match their ambition. Brook Farm disbanded in 1849; Hopedale, in 1853. In general, utopian communities were less durable and attracted fewer people than religious communities such as those of the Shakers and Mormons. In contrast to the religious communitarians, the utopians kept open their avenues to society and moved back and forth between their communities and antislavery or women's rights conventions. With the notable exception of the Oneida community (see "A Place in Time"), utopians neither sought nor attained the kind of grip on the allegiance of their members held by a Mother Ann Lee or a Joseph Smith.

Widely derided as fit only for eccentrics, the antebellum utopias nevertheless exemplified in extreme form the idealism and hopefulness that permeated nearly all reform in the Age of Jackson.

CONCLUSION

During the 1820s and 1830s, American society burst beyond its traditional physical and intellectual boundaries. Everywhere the old leadership provided by the Revolutionary generation gave way to new leaders born after 1775. Surrounded by weak foreign neighbors and at peace with the great powers of Europe, Americans, without much restraint from traditional or external threats, grappled with the implications of a changing society.

Political parties, religious revivals, and reform movements responded to social change in ways that were novel and inventive but never uniform. By reducing the innumerable interests and opinions that composed American society to two alternatives—the Democrats and the Whigs—the second party system gave direction to the conflicts that were created by economic and social change. Those excluded from politics or dismayed by the compromises into which politicians routinely entered turned to the churches and to reform movements as vehicles for change. Yet religion and reform were not simply alternatives to politics, for each intersected politics at scores of points. The closer one drew to 1840, the greater were the number of intersections. Temperance advocates began to demand legal prohibition of liquor; some abolitionists turned to the Liberty party; some feminists demanded the vote; utopians became political targets. Politics became a medium that even those antagonistic to politics had to understand.

CHRONOLOGY

1800–1801	Great Kentucky Revival.
1817	American Colonization Society founded.
1824	John Quincy Adams elected president by the House of Representatives.

1826	American Temperance Society organized.
1828	Andrew Jackson elected president.
	Congress passes the "Tariff of Abominations."
	John Calhoun anonymously writes *South*

1828	*Carolina Exposition and Protest.*
1830	Jackson's Maysville Road Bill veto.
	Indian Removal Act.
1830–1831	Charles G. Finney's Rochester revival.
1831	William Lloyd Garrison starts *The Liberator.*
1832	Jackson vetoes recharter of the Bank of the United States.
	Jackson reelected president.
	South Carolina Nullification Proclamation.
1833	Force Bill.
	Compromise Tariff.
	American Anti-Slavery Society founded.
	South Carolina nullifies the Force Bill.
1834	Whig party organized.
1836	Congress imposes the gag rule.
	Deposition Act.
	Specie Circular.
	Martin Van Buren elected president.
1837	Horace Mann becomes secretary of the Massachusetts Board of Education.

William Lloyd Garrison

1837	Economic depression sets in.
	Elijah Lovejoy murdered by proslavery mob.
	Grimké sisters set out on lecture tour of New England.
1838	Garrison's New England Non-Resistance Society founded.
	Publication of Sarah Grimké's *Letters on the Condition of Women and the Equality of the Sexes* and Angelina Grimké's *Letters to Catharine E. Beecher.*
1839	Depression deepens as the Bank of the United States fails.
1840	Independent Treasury Act passed.
	William Henry Harrison elected president.
	First Washington Temperance Society started.
1841	Dorothea Dix begins exposé of prison conditions.
	Brook Farm Community founded.
1848	Seneca Falls Convention.
	John Humphrey Noyes starts the Oneida Community.

Dorothea Dix

FOR FURTHER READING

Lee Benson, *The Concept of Jacksonian Democracy: New York as a Test Case* (1961). A major revisionist interpretation of the period.

William W. Freehling, *Prelude to Civil War* (1966). A major study of the nullification crisis.

Richard P. McCormick, *The Second American Party System: Party Formation in the Jacksonian Era* (1966). An influential work stressing the role of political leaders in shaping the second party system.

Edward Pessen, *Jacksonian America: Society, Personality, and Politics*, rev. ed. (1979). A comprehensive interpretation of the period that emphasizes the lack of real democracy in American society and politics.

Robert V. Remini, *Henry Clay: Statesman for the Union* (1991).

An important new biography of the leading Whig statesman of the period.

Arthur M. Schlesinger, Jr., *The Age of Jackson* (1945). A classic study, now dated in some of its interpretations but still highly readable.

Fred Somkin, *Unquiet Eagle: Memory and Desire in the Idea of American Freedom, 1815–1860* (1967). A penetrating study of American political values.

Ronald G. Walters, *American Reformers, 1815–1860* (1978). A balanced study that addresses the negative as well as positive aspects of nineteenth-century reform.

Chilton Williamson, *American Suffrage: From Property to Democracy, 1760–1860* (1960). The standard study of changing requirements for voting.

ADDITIONAL BIBLIOGRAPHY

Political Leaders

Donald B. Cole, *Martin Van Buren and the American Political System* (1984); James C. Curtis, *The Fox at Bay: Martin Van Buren and the Presidency, 1837–1841* (1970); Richard B. Latner, *The Presidency of Andrew Jackson: White House Politics, 1829–1837* (1979); John Niven, *Martin Van Buren and the Romantic Age* (1983); Merrill D. Peterson, *The Great Triumvirate: Webster, Clay*

and Calhoun (1987); Leonard L. Richards, *The Life and Times of Congressman John Quincy Adams* (1986); Major L. Wilson, *The Presidency of Martin Van Buren* (1984).

Political Parties

Jean H. Baker, *Affairs of Party: The Political Culture of Northern Democrats in the Mid-Nineteenth Century* (1983); Ronald P.

Formisano, *The Birth of Mass Political Parties, 1827–1861* (1971) and *The Transformation of American Political Culture: Massachusetts Parties, 1790s–1840s* (1983); Paul Goodman, *Towards a Christian Republic: Antimasonry and the Great Tradition in New England, 1826–1836* (1988); Daniel W. Howe, *The Political Culture of the American Whigs* (1980); Robert V. Remini, *The Election of Andrew Jackson* (1963); and *Andrew Jackson and the Course of American Empire* (1977); Harry L. Watson, *Jacksonian Politics and Community Conflict: The Emergence of the Second American Party System in Cumberland County, North Carolina* (1981); Sean Wilentz, *Chants Democratic: New York City and the Rise of the American Working Class, 1788–1850* (1983).

Banking and the Economy

Bray Hammond, *Banks and Politics in America from the Revolution to the Civil War* (1957); John M. McFaul, *The Politics of Jacksonian Finance* (1972); William G. Shade, *Banks or No Banks: The Money Question in Western Politics* (1972); James Roger Sharp, *The Jacksonians Versus the Banks: Politics in the United States After the Panic of 1837* (1970); Peter Temin, *The Jacksonian Economy* (1965).

Religious Revivals

Sydney E. Ahlstrom, *A Religious History of the American People*, 2 vols. (1975); Leonard J. Arrington, *The Mormon Experience* (1979) and *Brigham Young: American Moses* (1985); John Boles, *The Great Revival, 1787–1805* (1972); Whitney Cross, *The Burned-Over District* (1950); Nathan O. Hatch, *The Democratization of American Christianity* (1989); Donald G. Mathews, *Religion in the Old South* (1977); Stephen J. Stein, *The Shaker Experience in America* (1992).

Relationships Between Religion and Reform

Gilbert Barnes, *The Anti-Slavery Impulse* (1933); Clifford S. Griffin, *Their Brothers' Keepers: Moral Stewardship in the United States* (1960); Mary Ryan, *Cradle of the Middle Class: The Family in Oneida County, New York, 1790–1865* (1981); Timothy L. Smith, *Revivalism and Social Reform* (1957).

Temperance

Jed Dannenbaum, *Drink and Disorder: Temperance Reform in Cincinnati from the Washingtonian Revival to the WCTU* (1984); Ian Tyrrell, *Sobering Up: From Temperance to Prohibition in Antebellum America* (1979).

Educational Reform

Carl F. Kaestle, *Pillars of the Republic: Common Schools and American Society, 1780–1860* (1983); Carl F. Kaestle and Maris A. Vinovskis, *Education and Social Change in Nineteenth-Century Massachusetts* (1980); Michael B. Katz, *The Irony of Early School Reform* (1968); Stanley K. Schultz, *The Culture Factory: Boston Public Schools 1789–1860* (1973).

Abolitionists

Robert H. Abzug, *Passionate Liberator: Theodore Dwight Weld and the Dilemma of Reform* (1890); William Cheek and Aimee Lee Cheek, *John Mercer Langston and the Fight for Black Freedom, 1829–1865* (1989); David B. Davis, *The Problem of Slavery in the Age of Revolution, 1770–1823* (1975); Hugh Davis, *Joshua Leavitt: Evangelical Abolitionist* (1990); Lawrence J. Freidman, *Gregarious Saints: Self and Community in American Abolitionism, 1830–1870* (1982); Louis Gerteis, *Morality and Utility in American Antislavery Reform* (1987); Blanche Glassman Hersh, *The Slavery of Sex: Feminist Abolitionists in America* (1978); William McFeely, *Frederick Douglass* (1991); Jane A. Pease and William H. Pease, *They Who Would Be Free: Blacks' Search for Freedom, 1830–1861* (1974); Lewis Perry, *Radical Abolitionism: Anarchy and the Government of God in Antislavery Thought* (1973); Benjamin Quarles, *Black Abolitionists* (1969); Leonard L. Richards, *"Gentlemen of Property and Standing": Anti-Abolition Mobs in Jacksonian America* (1970); Ronald G. Walters, *The Antislavery Appeal: American Abolitionists After 1830* (1976); Bertram Wyatt-Brown, *Lewis Tappan and the Evangelical War Against Slavery* (1969).

Women's Rights

Lois Banner, *Elizabeth Cady Stanton* (1980); Barbara J. Berg, *The Remembered Gate—The Woman and the City, 1800–1860* (1978); Carl N. Degler, *At Odds: Women and the Family in America from the Revolution to the Present* (1980); Ellen C. DuBois, *Feminism and Suffrage: The Emergence of an Independent Women's Movement in America, 1848–1869* (1978); Lori D. Ginzberg, *Women and the Work of Benevolence* (1990); Elisabeth Griffith, *In Her Own Right: The Life of Elizabeth Cady Stanton* (1984); Gerda Lerner, *The Grimké Sisters from South Carolina: Rebels Against Slavery* (1967); Jean Fagan Yellin, *Women and Sisters: The Antislavery Feminists in American Culture* (1989).

Institutional Reformers

Gerald W. Grob, *Mental Institutions in America: Social Policy to 1875* (1973); W. David Lewis, *From Newgate to Dannemora: The Rise of the Penitentiary* (1965); Robert Mennel, *Thorns and Thistles* (1973); David Rothman, *The Discovery of the Asylum* (1971).

Utopian Communities

Michael Barkun, *Crucible of the Millennium* (1986); Arthur E. Bestor, *Backwoods Utopias: The Sectarian and Owenite Phases of Communitarian Utopianism in America, 1663–1829* (1950); Michael Fellman, *The Unbounded Frame: Freedom and Community in Nineteenth-Century America Utopianism* (1973); Lawrence Foster, *Women, Family, and Utopia* (1991); Carl J. Guarneri, *Utopian Alternative: Fourierism in Nineteenth-Century America* (1991); Carol Kolmerten, *Women in Utopia* (1990).

Chess Game
mid-1860s, hand-colored stereograph

11

LIFE, LEISURE, AND CULTURE
1840–1860

Americans, wrote Alexis de Tocqueville, "care but little for what has been, but they are haunted by visions of what will be." British novelist Charles Dickens remarked that while the watchword of the English was "All right," that of Americans was "Go ahead." Indeed, a belief in irreversible progress captivated Americans in the 1840s and 1850s. Each passing year seemed to offer new evidence for Thomas Jefferson's prediction that Europe "will have to lean on our shoulders and hobble along by our side."

Inventiveness and material betterment loomed large in American conceptions of progress. Agricultural innovations such as the McCormick reaper helped farmers produce a surplus of food despite a swiftly rising population. Americans could confidently brush aside the gloomy forecast of Britain's Thomas Malthus, who at the end of the eighteenth century had argued that a growing population would exhaust its food supply and suffer famine. During the two decades before the Civil War, material progress also affected transportation and industry. Railroads ribboned their way throughout the eastern United States. The widening use of steam power and the perfection of manufacturing on the principle of interchangeable parts contributed to lower commodity prices and a gradual rise in real wages. The evidence of prosperity lay not only in higher wages but in the multiplication of conveniences that transformed such daily activities as cooking, eating, and drinking.

American achievements in agriculture, industry, and transportation led to growing demands in these years that the United States throw off any lingering cultural dependence on Europe. Some contemporaries began to insist that Americans read books written by their compatriots, and others called for the development of a distinctiveAmerican literary and artistic style. No less than economic innovation, literary and artistic inventiveness made a mark on antebellum America. The period between 1820 and 1860 produced Washington Irving, the first American man of letters to gain fame throughout Europe; James Fenimore Cooper, the first American novelist to make a living continuously and exclusively by his writing; Henry Wadsworth Longfellow, the first nationally famous American poet; Edgar Allan Poe, the first and only American to invent a new literary genre, the detective story; and the Hudson River school of painting, the first native school of American painting. In 1820 a British critic had asked rhetorically, "In the four quarters of the Globe, who reads an American book?" By 1860 the answer was clear, for Europeans and Americans alike had learned to cherish Irving, Cooper, Ralph Waldo Emerson, Nathaniel Hawthorne, and other luminaries of what is often called the American Renaissance.

For the most part, antebellum Americans equated material, cultural, and moral progress. Samuel F. B. Morse, for example, expected that his invention of the telegraph in 1844 would not only speed communication but end war as well. Similar high expectations greeted other innovations. Advances in the technology of printing, a clergyman enthused in 1851, "multiply the word of God literally with every minute."

Yet progress had its darker side. Spread unevenly throughout the society, technological advances neither prevented nor ameliorated the depression of the late 1830s and early 1840s and had little positive impact on the poor. Periodic cholera epidemics reminded Americans that technology, in the shape of railroads and steamboats, could transport disease as well as food. Leading writers of the period, among them the philosopher and essayist Henry David Thoreau, questioned the easy assumption that material progress would stimulate moral progress. For the first time, widespread anxieties arose about the despoliation of the American landscape, and conscious efforts were launched to preserve enclaves of nature as parks and retreats safe from progress.

TECHNOLOGY AND ECONOMIC GROWTH

As evidence that they were a progressive people, Americans increasingly pointed to the march of "technology." The word *technology* was popularized after 1829 to describe how an understanding of scientific principles could be used to transform the practical conveniences of life. "We have invented more useful machines within twenty years," a Bostonian wrote in the 1830s, "than have been invented in all Europe." To those familiar with the progress of invention, *DeBow's Review* observed in 1846, "scarcely anything now will appear impossible."

Belief in the progressive effects of technology sprang from widely varying quarters. In 1836 the conservative Whig Daniel Webster contended that machines would advance civilization because they could perform the work of ten people without consuming food or clothing. At the other end of the political spectrum, a Lowell mill girl and labor organizer, Sarah Bagley, wrote in 1847: "It is emphatically the age of improvement. The arts and sciences have been more fully developed and the great mass of society are feeling its improvement." Practical science promised to make everyone's life more comfortable. The benefits of technology seemed to be democratic.

Woman at Singer Sewing Machine
Asked to repair a sewing machine that did not do continuous stitching, Isaac M. Singer invented one that did. Patented in 1851, the Singer machine quickly dominated the market. Although most early sewing machines were used in factories, some had made their way into households by 1860.

The technical innovations that transformed the quality of life in antebellum America included the steam engine, the cotton gin, the reaper, the use of interchangeable parts in manufacturing, the sewing machine, and most dazzling of all, the telegraph. Several of these innovations, including the steam engine and the principle of interchangeable parts, had originated in Europe. But Americans had a flair for investing in others' inventions and for perfecting their own, to the point where the inventions became profitable. Improvements in Eli Whitney's cotton gin between 1793 and 1860, for example, led to an eightfold increase in the amount of cotton that could be ginned in a day. Of course, technology did not benefit everyone. Improvements in the cotton gin served to rivet slavery firmly in place by making the South more dependent on cotton.

Technology also rendered many traditional skills obsolete and thereby undercut the position of artisans. But technology contributed to improvements in transportation and increases in productivity, which in turn lowered commodity prices and raised the living standards of a sizable body of free Americans between 1840 and 1860.

Agricultural Advancement

Before the Civil War, relatively few settlers ventured into the treeless and semiarid Great Plains that stretched west of Missouri, Iowa, and Minnesota. After 1830, however, settlement increasingly edged west of the woodlands of Ohio and Kentucky into parts of Indiana, Michigan, and Illinois, where flat grasslands (prairies) alternated with forests. Farmers had long assumed that the soil beneath forests was fertile, but some worried that the prairie's matted sod, which was difficult to break for planting, would no more sustain crops than trees.

Settlers who ventured into Indiana and Illinois were perplexed to discover treeless areas in otherwise humid regions, and only a few correctly guessed the reason: Native Americans regularly had set fire to undergrowth to hold back forests. But farmers quickly adapted to the new environment, in part because east of the Great Plains there were always some forested areas to afford ample timber for housing and fencing. Inventions also helped; in 1837 John Deere devised a steel-tipped plow that would cut in half the labor required to clear an acre of prairie.

Wheat became to midwestern farmers what cotton was to their southern counterparts. "The wheat crop is the great crop of the North-west, for exchange purposes," an agricultural journal noted in 1850. "It pays debts, buys groceries, clothing and lands, and answers more emphatically the purposes of trade among farmers than any other crop." Technological advances speeded the harvesting as well as the planting of wheat on the midwestern prairies. Using the traditional hand sickle consumed huge amounts of time and labor, all the more so because cut wheat had to be picked up and bound. Inventors in Europe had experimented since the eighteenth century with horse-drawn machines to replace sickles. But until Cyrus McCormick came on the scene, the absence of the right combination of technical skill and business enterprise had relegated mechanical reapers to the realm of tinkerers' dreams. In 1834 McCormick, a Virginian, patented a mechanical reaper that drew on but improved previous designs. Opening a factory in Chicago in 1847, McCormick manufactured reapers by mass production and introduced aggressive marketing techniques such as deferred payments and money-back guarantees. By harvesting grain seven times more rapidly than traditional methods, and with half the labor force, the reaper guaranteed the preeminence of wheat on the midwestern prairies of

He That Tilleth the Land Shall be Satisfied, c. 1850
This painting celebrates the American ideal of the family farm.

Illinois, Indiana, Iowa, and Missouri. McCormick sold 80,000 reapers by 1860, and this was only the beginning. During the Civil War, he made immense profits by selling more than 250,000 reapers.

Ironically, just as a Connecticut Yankee, Eli Whitney, had stimulated the foundation of the Old South's economy by his invention of the cotton gin, Cyrus McCormick, a proslavery southern Democrat, would help the North win the Civil War. Indeed, the North provided the main market for McCormick's reaper and for the models of his many competitors; the South, with its reliance on slave labor, had far less incentive to mechanize agriculture. The reaper would keep northern agricultural production high at a time when labor shortages caused by troop mobilization might otherwise have slashed production.

Although Americans proved resourceful at inventing and marketing machines to speed planting and harvesting, they farmed wastefully. With land abundant, farmers were more inclined to look for virgin soil than to improve "worn out" soil. But a movement for agricultural improvement in the form of more efficient use of the soil did develop before 1860, mainly in the East. Confronted by the superior fertility of western soil, easterners who did not move west or take jobs in factories increasingly experimented with new agricultural techniques. In Orange County, New York, for example, farmers fed their cows the best clover and bluegrass and emphasized cleanliness in the processing of dairy products. Through these practices, they produced a superior butter that commanded more than double the price of ordinary butter. Still other eastern farmers turned to the use of fertilizers to keep their wheat production competitive with that of the bountiful midwestern prairies. By fertilizing their fields with plaster left over from the construction of the James River Canal, Virginia wheat growers raised their average yield per acre to fifteen bushels by the 1850s, up from only six bushels in 1800. Similarly, during the 1840s American cotton planters began to import guano, left by the droppings of sea birds on islands off Peru, for use as a fertilizer. Fertilizers helped eastern cotton farmers close the gap created by the superior fertility of southwestern soil for cotton.

Technology and Industrial Progress

Although Americans had made several important technical innovations before 1820, the early growth of American manufacturing depended mainly on *imported* technology. Gradually, however, American industries gained a reputation abroad for their own innovations. As early as 1835, a British observer reported that a woolen mill in Lowell, Massachusetts, contained a remarkable number of labor-saving contrivances. In 1853 a small-arms factory in England reequipped itself with machine tools (machines that shaped metal products) manufactured by two firms in the backwoods of Vermont. Americans had relatively few reservations about investing in technology. After finishing a tour of American factories in 1854, a noted British engineer concluded that "wherever [machinery] can be introduced as a substitute for manual labor, it is universally and willingly resorted to."

During the 1840s and 1850s, American industries advanced toward perfecting manufacturing by the use of interchangeable parts. Eli Whitney had introduced this idea (often called the American system of manufacturing) to the United States in 1798, but in Whitney's day the manufacture of guns or other items by the use of interchangeable parts required a great deal of time-consuming hand filing before the parts could be fitted together. In the 1840s American factories immeasurably improved the quality of their machine tools and thereby eliminated much of the need for hand filing. As a result, it became possible to substitute parts that were made in one year for those fabricated in another. In 1853 a British commission investigating American technology looked on in amazement as the superintendent of the Springfield, Massachusetts, armory ordered rifles produced in ten consecutive years to be stripped and their parts reassembled at random.

The American system of manufacturing contained several distinctive advantages. Traditionally, damage to any part of a mechanical contrivance had rendered the whole useless, for no new part would fit. With the perfection of manufacturing by interchangeable parts, however, replacements could be ordered for damaged parts. In addition, the improved machine tools upon which the American system depended enabled entrepreneurs to push inventions swiftly into mass production. The likelihood that inventions would quickly enter production in turn attracted investors. By the 1850s Connecticut firms like Smith and Wesson were massproducing the revolving pistol, which Samuel Colt had invented in 1836. Sophisticated machine tools made it possible, a manufacturer wrote, to increase production "by confining a worker to one particular limb of a pistol until he had made two thousand." The sewing machine, invented in 1846 by Elias Howe, entered mass production only two years later.

Americans also displayed an eagerness to eliminate the constraints of time and space. An impatient people inhabiting a huge area, they seized enthusiastically on Samuel F. B. Morse's invention of the telegraph in 1844. "The advantages to be derived from the adoption of the Electric Telegraph," a British engineer noted in 1854, "have in no country been more promptly appreciated than in the United States. A system of communication that annihilates distance was felt to be of vital importance, both politically and commercially, in a country so vast, and having a population so widely scattered." The speed with which Americans formed telegraph companies and erected lines stunned the British. "No private interests can oppose the passage of a line through any property," the same British engineer wrote. "There are no committees, no counsel, no long array of witnesses and expensive hearings; compensation is made simply for damage done, the amount being assessed by a jury, and generally on a most moderate estimate. With a celerity that is surprising a company is formed, a line is built, and operations are commenced." Although telegraph lines usually transmitted political and commercial messages, some cities adapted them for reporting fires. By the early 1850s, Boston had an elaborate system of telegraph stations from which news of a blaze could be swiftly transmitted to fire companies throughout the city. Whatever their use, telegraph lines spread rapidly. By 1852 more than fifteen thousand miles of lines connected cities as distant as Quebec, New Orleans, and St. Louis.

The Railroad Boom

The same penchant for overcoming the natural limits imposed by time and space drove antebellum Americans to make an extraordinary investment in railroads. To an even greater degree than the telegraph, the railroad embodied progress through technology.

In 1790 even European royalty could travel no faster than fourteen miles an hour, and that only with frequent changes of horses. Yet by 1850 an ordinary American could travel on a train at three times that speed. The swift, comfortable transport that American railroads provided for the common man and woman dramatized the democratic promise of technology more vividly than any other technological innovation of the time.

In Europe railroads usually had several classes of travel. The common people were traditionally herded into crowded cars and seated on wooden benches or chairs. Only those who paid to travel first-class enjoyed a modicum of luxury. In contrast, in America there was only *one* class of railroad travel (except for blacks, who were often forced to sit separately). Furthermore, American inventors introduced a level of comfort that astonished Europeans. They experimented with adjustable upholstered seats that could be turned in whatever direction the train was traveling and that could be converted into couches at night. In effect, everyone could travel first-class. Americans, a Frenchman observed, had "a perfect passion for railroads" and loved them "as a lover loves his mistress."

Yet in the 1830s little about the railroads appeared lovable. The first trains were drawn by horses rather than by locomotives; a few actually used sails for power. Those with locomotives showered their passengers' clothing with sparks, for the riding cars were often open to the air. In the absence of brakes, passengers at times had to get out and pull trains to stops. Without means of illumination, trains rarely ran at night. Scheduling posed problems because the United States did not adopt standard time until 1883 (see Chapter 18); at noon in Boston, it was twelve minutes before noon in New York. Moreover, trains en route faced innumerable delays. Because most railroads owned only a single track, trains had to wait on sidings for other trains to pass. Since a train's whereabouts remained a mystery once it had left a station, such waits on the sidings could seem interminable.

Between 1840 and 1860, a stunning transformation occurred in the size of the rail network and in the power and convenience of trains. Railroad track increased from three thousand to thirty thousand miles. Passengers now traveled in flat-roofed coaches. Illumination by kerosene lamps made night travel possible. Locomotives gained in power to the point where they no longer had to be pulled uphill by horses or by stationary engines. Fifty thousand miles of telegraph wires enabled dispatchers to communicate with trains en route and to reduce delays.

Passengers nevertheless still confronted inconveniences. Sleeping accommodations remained crude and schedules erratic. Since individual railroads continued to use track of different gauges, frequent changes of train (eight between Charleston and Philadelphia in the 1850s) remained a necessity. Yet nothing could slow the advance of railroads or cure Americans' mania for them. By 1860 the United States had more track than the rest of the nations of the world combined.

Just as canals had spearheaded the first phase of the transportation revolution, railroads led the second

BRITISH NORTH AMERICA (CANADA)

Boston
Detroit
Pittsburgh
Chicago
New York
St. Joseph
Philadelphia
Cincinnati
Washington, D.C.
Louisville
Richmond
St. Louis
Nashville
Memphis
Charleston
Savannah
Jackson
Jacksonville
Houston
New Orleans

Railroads, 1850

Railroads built 1850 – 1860

0   500 Miles
0   500 Kilometers

Railroad Growth, 1850–1860
Rail ties between the East and the Midwest greatly increased during the railroad "boom" of the 1850s.

phase during the 1840s and 1850s. Canals were not abandoned; the Erie Canal, for example, did not reach its peak volume until 1880. But railroads, providing much faster transport and being less vulnerable to winter frosts, gradually overtook canals, first in passenger and then in freight traffic. By 1860 the value of goods transported by railroad greatly exceeded that carried by canals.

As late as 1860, few rail lines extended west of the Mississippi, but railroads had spread like spiderwebs east of the great river. The 1840s saw vigorous railroad construction in New England; by 1850 Massachusetts had half of the track that it would possess in 1950. Elsewhere to the east of the Mississippi, the railroad boom developed mainly in the 1850s, when twenty-two thousand miles of track were added to the nation's rail network. In the South railroads transformed places like Chattanooga and Atlanta into thriving commercial

hubs. The most important development of the 1850s, however, lay in the forging of rail lines between the East and the Midwest (or "Old Northwest"). The New York Central and the Erie railroads joined eastern New York to Buffalo; the Pennsylvania Railroad connected Philadelphia and Pittsburgh; and the Baltimore and Ohio linked Baltimore to Wheeling, Virginia (now West Virginia). Simultaneously, intense construction in Ohio, Indiana, and Illinois created trunk lines that joined each of these routes. By 1860 rail lines ran from Buffalo to Cleveland, Toledo, and Chicago; from Pittsburgh to Fort Wayne; and from Wheeling to Cincinnati and on to St. Louis.

The completion of rail links between the East and the Midwest rerouted much of the commerce of the nation's interior. Before the 1850s most of the agricultural surplus of the Upper Mississippi Valley had made its way down the river to New Orleans for transshipment to the East. Although a railroad between New Orleans and Cincinnati was finally completed in 1859, the earlier completion of the east-west trunk lines had already deflected the flow of grain, livestock, and dairy products directly to the East, bypassing the Mississippi Valley. Gradually, Chicago supplanted New Orleans as the nation's main interior commercial hub. In 1849 Chicago had virtually no rail service, but by 1860 eleven railroads radiated from it.

Too, the forging of east-west rail trunks dramatically stimulated the settlement and agricultural development of the Midwest. By 1860 Illinois, Indiana, and Wisconsin had replaced Pennsylvania, Ohio, and New York as the leading wheat-growing states. Although settlers usually arrived in advance of the railroads, the trains gave hot pursuit. Furthermore, by enabling midwestern farmers to speed their produce to the East, railroads greatly increased the value of their farms and thereby promoted additional settlement. By encouraging settlement, moreover, railroads indirectly stimulated the industrial development of the Midwest, because new settlers needed lumber for fences and houses, and mills to grind wheat into flour. Cities like Chicago, Davenport, Iowa, and Minneapolis grew not only as railroad hubs but as centers of lumber and flour trade.

Railroads also propelled the growth of small towns along their routes. The Illinois Central Railroad, which had more track than any other railroad in 1855, made money not only from its traffic but also from real-estate speculation. Purchasing land for stations along its route, the Illinois Central then laid out towns

The Express Train

Antebellum depictions of trains usually showed their smoke as harmless, cloudlike puffs, but this picture renders the real color more accurately and menacingly.

around the stations. The selection of Manteno, Illinois, as a stop of the Illinois Central, for example, transformed the site from a crossroads without a single house in 1854 into a bustling town of nearly a thousand in 1860, replete with hotels, lumberyards, grain elevators, and gristmills. (The Illinois Central even dictated the naming of streets. In the towns along its route, streets running east and west were always named after trees, and those running north and south were numbered. Soon one town looked much like the next.) By the Civil War, few thought of the railroad-linked Midwest as a frontier region or viewed its inhabitants as pioneers.

As the nation's first big business, the railroads transformed the conduct of business. During the early 1830s, railroads, like canals, depended on financial aid from state governments. With the onset of depression in the late 1830s, however, state governments scrapped overly ambitious railroad projects. Convinced that railroads burdened them with high taxes and blasted hopes, voters turned against state aid, and in the early 1840s, several states amended their constitutions to bar state funding for railroads and canals. The federal government took up some of the slack, but federal aid did not provide a major stimulus to railroads before 1860. Rather, part of the burden of finance passed to city and county governments in agricultural areas that wanted to attract railroads. Municipal governments, for example, often gave railroads rights-of-way, grants of land for stations, and public funds.

The dramatic expansion of the railroad network in the 1850s, however, strained the financing capacity of local governments and required a turn toward private investment, which had never been absent from the picture. Well aware of the economic benefits of railroads, individuals living near them had long purchased railroad securities issued by governments and had directly bought stock in railroads, often paying by contributing their labor to building the railroads. But the large railroads of the 1850s needed more capital than such small investors could generate. Gradually, the center of railroad financing shifted to New York City, and in fact, it was the railroad boom of the 1850s that helped make Wall Street the nation's greatest capital market. The securities of all the leading railroads were traded on the floor of the New York Stock Exchange during the 1850s. In addition, the growth of railroads turned New York City into the center of modern investment firms. The investment firms evaluated the securities of railroads in Toledo or Davenport or Chattanooga and then found purchasers for these securities in New York, Philadelphia, Paris, London, Amsterdam, and Hamburg. Controlling the flow of funds to railroads, the investment bankers began to exert influence over the railroads' internal affairs by supervising administrative reorganizations in times of trouble. A Wall Street analyst noted in 1851 that railroad men seeking financing "must remember that money is power, and that the [financier] can dictate to a great extent his own terms."

Rising Prosperity

Technological advances also improved the lives of consumers by bringing down the price of many commodities. For example, clocks that cost $50 to fabricate by hand in 1800 could be produced by machine for 50¢ by 1850. In addition, the widening use of steam power contributed to a 25 percent rise in the average worker's real income (actual purchasing power) between 1840 and 1860. Early–nineteenth-century factories, which had depended on water wheels to propel their machines, of necessity had to shut down when the rivers or streams that powered the wheels froze. With the spread of steam engines, however, factories could stay open longer and workers could increase their annual wages by working more hours. Cotton textile workers were among those who benefited: although their hourly wages showed little gain, their average annual wages rose from $163 in 1830 to $176 in 1849 to $201 by 1859.

The growth of towns and cities also contributed to an increase in average annual wages. Farmers experienced the same seasonal fluctuations as laborers in the early factories. In sparsely settled rural areas, the onset of winter traditionally brought hard times; as demand for agricultural labor slumped, few alternatives existed to take up the slack. "A year in some farming states such as Pennsylvania," a traveler commented in 1823, "is only of eight months duration, four months being lost to the laborer, who is turned away as a useless animal." In contrast, densely populated towns and cities offered more opportunities for year-round work. The urban dockworker thrown out of his job as a result of frozen waterways might find work as a hotel porter or an unskilled indoor laborer.

Towns and cities also provided women and children with new opportunities for paid work. (Women and children had long performed many vital tasks on farms, but rarely for pay.) The wages of children between the ages of ten and eighteen came to play an integral role in the nineteenth-century family economy. Family heads who earned more than $600 a year might have been able to afford the luxury of keeping their children in school, but most breadwinners were fortunate if they made $300 a year. Although the cost of many basic commodities fell between 1815 and 1860 (another consequence of the transportation revolution), most families lived close to the margin. Budgets of working-class families in New York City and Philadelphia during the early 1850s reveal annual expenditures of $500–$600, with more than 40 percent spent on food, 25–30 percent on rent, and most of the remainder on clothing and fuel. Such a family obviously could not survive on the annual wages of the average male head of the household. It needed the wages of the children and, at times, those of the wife as well.

Life in urban wage-earning families was not necessarily superior to life in farming communities. A farmer who owned land, livestock, and a house did not have to worry about paying rent or buying fuel for cooking and heating, and rarely ran short of food. Many Americans continued to aspire to farming as the best of all occupations. But to purchase, clear, and stock a farm involved a considerable capital outlay that could easily amount to five hundred dollars, and the effort promised no rewards for a few years. The majority of workers in agricultural areas did not own farms and were exposed to the seasonal fluctuations in demand for agricultural labor. In many respects, they were worse off than urban wage earners.

The economic advantages that attended living in cities help explain why so many Americans moved to urban areas during the first half of the nineteenth century. As a further attraction, during the 1840s and 1850s, cities also provided their residents with an unprecedented range of comforts and conveniences.

THE QUALITY OF LIFE

In addition to large-scale transformations in production, transportation, and income, the two decades before the Civil War witnessed subtle alterations in the quality of everyday life in the United States. Less visible and dramatic than those wrought by the railroad, these changes in everyday experiences occurred for the most part within the privacy of homes and affected such routine activities as eating, drinking, and washing. Technological improvements in these years made the daily home-life experiences of Americans far more comfortable. "Think of the numberless contrivances and inventions for our comfort and luxury which the last half dozen years have brought forth," the poet Walt Whitman exclaimed to his readers, and you will "bless your star that fate has cast your lot in the year of Our Lord 1857." Indeed, the patent office in Washington was flooded with sketches of reclining seats, sliding tables, beds convertible into chairs, lounges convertible into cradles, street-sweeping machines, and fly traps. Machine-made furniture began to transform the interiors of houses. Stoves revolutionized heating and cooking. By bringing fresh vegetables to city dwellers, railroads stimulated important changes in diet.

Despite all the talk of comfort and progress, however, many Americans experienced little improvement in the quality of their lives. Technological advances made it possible for the middle class to enjoy luxuries formerly reserved for the rich but often widened the distance between the middle class and the poor. At a time when the interiors of urban, middle-class homes were becoming increasingly lavish, the urban poor congregated in cramped and unsightly tenements. In addition, some aspects of life remained relatively unaffected by scientific and technical advances. Medical science, for example, made a few advances before 1860, but none that rivaled the astonishing changes wrought by the railroad and the telegraph.

The benefits rather than the limitations of progress, however, gripped the popular imagination. Few Americans accepted the possibility that progress could neglect such an important aspect of everyday life as health. Confronted by the failure of the medical profession to rival the achievements of Cyrus McCormick and Samuel F. B. Morse, Americans embraced popular health movements that sprang up outside the medical profession and promised to conquer disease by the precepts of diet and regimen.

Housing

During the early 1800s, urban dwellings had grown far more standardized. Builders had responded to the swift growth of cities by erecting quickly constructed row houses—uniform attached dwellings increasingly made of brick. Whereas city dwellers in the eighteenth century usually had lived in unattached frame houses of one or two stories, all of which looked different and faced in different directions, their nineteenth-century counterparts were more likely to inhabit row houses. Some praised the uniformity of row houses as democratic, but others condemned the structures as monotonous. "The great defect in the houses," an English visitor observed, "is their extreme uniformity—when you have seen one, you have seen all."

The average row house was narrow and long, fifteen to twenty feet across, thirty to forty feet from front to back. Most had open spaces in the rear for gardens, pigs, privies, and cisterns. Row houses were not all alike. In the nineteenth century, middle-class row houses were larger (3 to 3½ stories) than working-class row houses (2 to 2½ stories). Between 1830 and 1860, moreover, the interiors of middle-class row houses became more elaborate than those of common laborers. Such features as cast-iron balconies (especially popular in the South), elegant doors, curved staircases, carved columns between rooms, and rooms with fanciful, asymmetrical shapes distinguished the row houses of the middle class from those of the less fortunate. The most fashionable urban residences surrounded small parks ringed by iron fences and contained "Place" rather than "Street" in their addresses.

As land values rose in the early nineteenth century (as much as 750 percent in Manhattan between 1785 and 1815), renting rather than owning homes became more common. By 1815 more than half of the homes in the large cities were rented, usually by artisans, jour-

neymen, and day laborers. Soaring land values also led to the subdividing of many row houses for occupancy by several families or boarders. The worst of these subdivided houses were called tenements and became the usual habitats of Irish immigrants and free blacks.

In rural areas, the quality of housing depended on the date of settlement as much as on social class. In recently settled areas, the standard dwelling was a rude, one-room log cabin with floors made of split logs that allowed drafts to seep in, roofs that let in snow, crude chimneys made of sticks and clay, and windows covered by oiled paper or cloth. As rural communities matured, however, log cabins gave way to frame houses of two or more rooms with glass windows and better insulation. Most of these houses were built on a principle known as the balloon frame. Originally, *balloon frame* was a term used by traditional artisans to express their contempt for houses that appeared so flimsily constructed as to risk blowing away. In place of foot-thick heavy timbers that were laboriously fitted together, the balloon-frame house had a skeleton of thin sawed timbers nailed together in such a way that every strain ran against the grain of the wood. The strength of balloon-frame houses soon confounded their critics, whereas their simplicity and cheapness endeared them to western builders with neither the time nor the skill to cut heavy beams and fit them into each other.

Home Furniture

Furniture trends between 1840 and 1860 revealed the widening gap between the life-styles of the prosperous and those of the poor. Families in the middle and upper classes increasingly decorated their parlors with a style of furniture known as French antique or rococo. Rococo furniture reflected both the affluence and the formality of middle- and upper-class families. In such households, the ideal parlor required a seven-piece matched set: an armchair for the husband, a smaller and less expensive lady's chair for his wife, a sofa, and four parlor chairs for guests and children. Rococo furniture was by definition ornate. Upholstered chairs, for example, displayed intricate scrolls depicting vines, leaves, or flowers and had curved legs with ornamental feet (called cabriole legs). The heavily upholstered backs of sofas often contained designs of rose blossoms topped by carved medallions. Artisans framed hanging mirrors with intricately fashioned and gilded moldings that depicted birds, flowers, and even young

Family Group
This daguerreotype, taken about 1852, reveals the little things so important to etching a middle-class family's social status: curtains; a wall hanging; a piano with scrolled legs; a small desk with elegantly curved legs; a pet; ladies posed in nonproductive but "improving" activities (music, reading); and a young man seemingly staring into space—and perhaps pondering how to pay for it all.

women. The finished products frequently weighed so much that they threatened to tumble from the wall.

The highly ornamented rococo furniture marked its possessors as people of substantial wealth. At the same time, the rise of mass production in such furniture centers as Grand Rapids, Michigan, and Cincinnati brought the rococo style within the financial reach of the middle class and thereby helped close the gap between the truly wealthy (who often imported their furniture from France) and those who were merely well off. Unable to afford even mass-produced rococo pieces, however, the great majority of Americans had to be content with simpler furniture. Technological advances in the fabrication of furniture tended to level taste between the middle and upper classes while simultaneously marking those classes off from everyone else.

Heating, Cooking, and Diet

In the 1840s the transportation and industrial revolutions affected such basic household features as heating, cooking, and diet. As soon as the transportation revolution had opened distant markets, some iron foundries began to specialize in the production of cast-

iron stoves. In urban areas, stoves were rapidly displacing open hearths for both heating and cooking by the late 1840s.

Even though most of the heat from open hearths was lost up the chimney, country people continued to prefer them to stoves, partly because their labor in clearing the land had left them with an abundance of wood. Wood could be used in stoves, too, but only if laboriously chopped into small pieces. In contrast, city dwellers, who had to pay for wood, increasingly preferred coal-fired stoves. Before 1830 English and Welsh immigrants had taught Americans how to hew coal (that is, mine it with heavy instruments), and the discovery in eastern Pennsylvania of a superior variety of coal called anthracite guaranteed a steady supply.

Coal, however, had its drawbacks. A faulty coal-burning stove could fill a room with poisonous carbon monoxide, and coal left a dirty residue that fouled urban air and blackened the snow. But coal burned longer and hotter than wood and reduced the time and expense that urban families had traditionally devoted to acquiring fuel. Stoves were also superior to hearths for cooking. Householders could leave meals

Popping Corn
Popping kernels of corn by heating them, a skill that the colonists acquired from the Indians, was a popular pastime in antebellum homes.

unattended on stoves, and they no longer ran the danger of scorching their clothing while bending to reach into open flames. In addition, they could cook several dishes at once on a stove. In this way, stoves contributed to the growing variety of the American diet.

As more and more people congregated in towns and cities, and as transportation improved, urban markets for the sale of country produce multiplied. Into America's towns and cities railroads brought fresh vegetables, which in the eighteenth century had been absent even from lavish banquet tables. By 1860 Boston and St. Louis each had ten large public markets. Even small towns in the Midwest were likely to have public markets by the 1840s.

Despite the improvements brought about by the transportation revolution, personal diets were still subject to seasonal fluctuations. Only the rich could afford fruit out of season, for they alone could afford to buy sugar in sufficient quantities to preserve fruit. (The Florida and California citrus fruit industries still lay in the future.) Indeed, preserving almost any kind of food presented problems. Although Americans pioneered technical advances in the harvesting and storing of ice before 1840, home iceboxes were rare before 1860. One contemporary writer recommended that housewives bury meat in the snow to keep it from spoiling, but salt remained the most widely used preservative. One reason antebellum Americans ate more pork than beef was that salt affected the taste of pork less objectionably than it did the flavor of beef.

Water and Sanitation

Rural homes rarely had running water. Water was brought in from wells, springs, or cisterns; used; carried outside again; and dumped. During the early 1800s, the same had been true in cities, but with increasing population density, alarm rose about the threat to well water posed by leakage from outdoor privies. In response, some cities had constructed public waterworks. In 1823 Philadelphia had completed a system that brought water along aqueducts and through pipes from the Schuylkill and Delaware rivers to street hydrants. Visiting Philadelphia in 1842, Charles Dickens marveled that the city "is most bountifully provided with fresh water, which is showered and jerked about, and turned on, and poured off every where." During the 1840s and 1850s, several other major cities constructed similar waterworks. New York City completed the Croton aqueduct (which brought water into the city from reservoirs to the north) in the 1840s, and Cleveland, Detroit, Hartford, Louisville, and Cincinnati built waterworks during the 1850s. By 1860 sixty-eight public water systems operated in the United States.

Although these municipal water systems were among the most impressive engineering triumphs of the age, their impact is easily exaggerated. Many small cities like Rochester and Poughkeepsie, New York, had no waterworks in 1860. As late as 1862, Louisville had only 239 houses connected to its system. The 53,000 customers of New York City's system in 1856 only

The Beauties of Street Sprinkling, *by Thomas Worth, 1856 Street sprinklers controlled flying dust, but they also created slick surfaces that sent unwary pedestrians flying.*

composed less than a tenth of the city's population. Even with the establishment of waterworks, few houses had running water; the incoming water usually ended its journey at a street hydrant. As in rural areas, families had to carry water into and out of houses. Moreover, houses blessed with running water rarely possessed hot water. Before one could take a bath, water had to be heated on the stove or over the fireplace. Not surprisingly, people rarely bathed. A New England physician claimed in 1832 that not one in five of his patients took one bath a year. Fewer than fourteen hundred baths served New York City in 1855.

Because Americans bathed infrequently, their bodily odors undoubtedly were pungent, but so were smells of every sort. Even fashionable residential streets often contained stables backed by mounds of manure. Municipal sanitation departments were virtually nonexistent. Street cleaning was mainly the responsibility of private contractors, who gained a reputation for slackness in discharging their duties. To supplement the work of such undependable contractors, Americans relied on hogs, which they let roam freely and scavenge. (Scavenging hogs that turned down the wrong street often made tasty dinners for the poor.) The abundance of outdoor privies added to the stench. Flush toilets were rare outside of cities, and within cities provisions for sewerage lagged behind those for waterworks. With a population of 178,000 in 1860, Boston had only about five thousand flush toilets, a far higher ratio of toilets to people than most cities could report. Americans normally answered calls of nature by trips to outdoor privies, whose unpleasant smells they suppressed mainly by the application of shovelsful of dirt.

Comforts and conveniences later taken for granted were still rare in 1860. Conveniences like stoves and folding beds that made their way into the home, far from liberating women from housework, merely elevated the standards of housekeeping. In her widely popular *Treatise on Domestic Economy* (1841), Catharine Beecher used technological advances to justify her contention that women had a duty to make every house a "glorious temple" by utilizing space and other resources more efficiently. None of this, however, changes the fact that middle-class antebellum Americans increasingly boasted of how comfortable their lives were becoming and pointed to the steady improvement in wages, diet, and water supplies as tangible marks of betterment.

Disease and Health

Despite a slowly rising standard of living, Americans remained vulnerable to disease. Between 1793, when an outbreak of yellow fever had devastated Philadelphia, and 1918–1919, when an influenza epidemic killed more than half a million Americans (and at least 20 million people worldwide), epidemics posed a constant but unpredictable threat. In 1832–1833 the combined effects of cholera and yellow fever had killed perhaps a fifth of New Orleans's population. Cholera returned to the United States in 1849 and carried off 10 percent of St. Louis's population while dealing staggering blows to most other cities.

Although not the only threats to health, epidemic diseases were the most visible and feared dangers. With grim irony, the transportation revolution increased the peril from epidemics. The cholera epidemic of 1832 had the dubious distinction of being America's first national epidemic. Its course followed that of the transportation revolution. One route of the epidemic ran from New York City up the Hudson River, across the Erie Canal to Ohio, and down the Ohio River to the Mississippi and New Orleans; the other route followed shipping up and down the East Coast from New York City.

Each major antebellum epidemic of cholera or yellow fever intensified public calls for the establishment of municipal health boards, and by the 1850s most major cities had formed such agencies. However, so few powers did city governments give them that the boards could not even enforce the reporting of diseases. The inability of physicians to find a satisfactory explanation for epidemic diseases led to a general distrust of the medical profession and contributed to making public health a low-priority issue.

Prior to 1860 no one understood that tiny organisms called bacteria caused both cholera and yellow fever. Rather, rival camps of physicians battled furiously and publicly over the merits of the "contagion" theory versus those of the "miasm" theory. Insisting that cholera and yellow fever were transmitted by touch, contagionists called for vigorous measures to quarantine affected areas. In contrast, supporters of the miasm theory argued that poisonous gases (miasms) emitted by rotting vegetation or dead animals carried disease through the air. The miasm theory led logically to the conclusion that swamps should be drained and streets cleaned. Neither theory, however, was consistent with the evidence. Quarantines failed to check cholera and yellow fever (an argument against the contagionist theory), and many residents of filthy slums and stinking, low-lying areas contracted neither of the two diseases (a refutation of the miasm theory). Confronted by this inconclusive debate between medical experts, municipal leaders refused to delegate more than advisory powers to health boards dominated by physicians. After the worst epidemic in the city's history, a New Orleans editor stated in 1853 that it was "much safer to follow the common sense and unbiased opinion of the intelligent mass of the people than the opinions of medical men . . . based upon hypothetical theories."

Although most epidemic diseases baffled antebellum physicians, a basis for forward strides in surgery was laid during the 1840s by the discovery of anesthetics. Prior to 1840 young people often entertained themselves at parties by inhaling nitrous oxide, or "laughing gas," which produced sensations of giddiness and painlessness; and semicomical demonstrations of laughing gas became a form of popular entertainment. (Samuel Colt, the inventor of the revolver, had begun his career as a traveling exhibitor of laughing gas.) But nitrous oxide had to be carried around in bladders, which were difficult to handle, and in any case, few recognized its surgical possibilities. Then in 1842 Crawford Long, a Georgia physician who had attended laughing-gas frolics in his youth, employed sulfuric ether (an easily transportable liquid with the same properties as nitrous oxide) during a surgical operation. Long failed to follow up on his discovery, but four years later William T. G. Morton, a dentist, successfully employed sulfuric ether during an operation at Massachusetts General Hospital in Boston. Within a few years, ether came into wide use in American surgery.

The discovery of anesthesia improved the public image of surgeons, long viewed as brutes who hacked away at agonized patients. Furthermore, by making longer operations possible, anesthesia encouraged surgeons to take greater care than previously during surgery. Nevertheless, the failure of most surgeons to recognize the importance of clean hands and sterilized instruments partially offset the benefits of anesthesia before 1860. In 1843 Boston physician and poet Oliver Wendell Holmes, Sr., published an influential paper on how the failure of obstetricians to disinfect their hands often spread a disease called puerperal fever among mothers giving birth in hospitals. Still, the medical profession only gradually accepted the importance of disinfection. Operations remained as dangerous as the diseases or wounds that they tried to heal. The mortality rate for amputations hovered around 40 percent, and during the Civil War, 87 percent of soldiers who suffered abdominal wounds died from them.

Popular Health Movements

Doubtful of medicine and skeptical of the benefits of public health, antebellum Americans turned to a variety of therapies and regimens that promised to give them healthier and longer lives. One popular response to disease was hydropathy, or the "water cure," which filtered into the United States from Europe during the 1840s. By the mid-1850s the United States had twenty-seven hydropathic sanatoriums, which claimed to offer by cold baths and wet packs "an abundance of water of dewy softness and crystal transparency, to cleanse, renovate, and rejuvenate the disease-worn and dilapidated system." The water cure held a special attraction for well-off women, partly because hydropathics professed to relieve the pain associated with childbirth and menstruation and partly because hydropathic sanatoriums were congenial gathering places in which middle-class women could relax and exercise in private.

In contrast to the water cure, which necessitated the time and expense of a trip to a sanatorium, a health system that anyone could adopt was propounded by Sylvester Graham, a temperance reformer turned popular health advocate. Alarmed by the 1832 cholera epidemic, Graham counseled changes in diet and regimen as well as total abstinence from alcohol. Contending that Americans ate too much, he urged them to substitute vegetables, fruits, and coarse, whole-grain bread (called Graham bread) for meat and to abstain from spices, coffee, and tea as well as from alcohol. Soon Graham added sexual "excess" (by which he meant most sex) to his list of forbidden indulgences. Vegetables were preferable to meat, according to Graham, because they provoked less hunger. The food cravings of the "flesh-eater" were "greater and more imperious" than those of the vegetarian.

Many of Graham's most enthusiastic disciples were reformers. Grahamites had a special table at the Brook Farm community. Until forced out by outraged parents and hungry students, one of Graham's followers ran the student dining room at reformist Oberlin College. Much like Graham, reformers traced the evils of American society to the unnatural cravings of its people. Abolitionists, for example, contended that slavery intensified white men's lust and contributed to the violent behavior of white southerners. Similarly, Graham believed that eating meat stimulated lust and other aggressive impulses.

Yet Graham's doctrines attracted a broad audience that extended beyond the perimeters of the reform movements. Many towns and cities had boardinghouses whose tables were set according to his principles. His books sold well, and his public lectures were thronged. Like hydropathy, Grahamism addressed the popular desire for better health at a time when orthodox medicine seemed to do more damage than good. Graham used religious phrases that were familiar to churchgoers and then channeled those concepts toward nonreligious goals. Luxury was "sinful," disease resembled hell, and health was a kind of heaven on earth. In this way, he provided simple and familiar assurances to an audience as ignorant as he was of the true causes of disease.

Phrenology

The belief that each person was ultimately the master of his or her own destiny marked the popular antebellum health movements. A similar impulse underlay phrenology, the most popular of the scientific fads that swept antebellum America.

The creation of the Viennese physician Franz J. Gall, phrenology centered on the idea that the human mind was composed of thirty-seven distinct faculties, or "organs," each localized in a different part of the brain. Phrenologists thought that the degree of each organ's development determined the shape of the skull, so that they could accurately analyze an individual's character by examining the bumps and depressions of the skull.

Transported to the United States in the 1830s, phrenology first commanded serious attention from educated dabblers in science. In the 1840s it entered a new phase in the hands of the brothers Orson and Lorenzo Fowler. Orson Fowler originally intended to become a Protestant missionary. Instead, he became a missionary for phrenology and opened a publishing house in New York City (Fowlers and Wells) that marketed books on phrenology everywhere. When some critics argued that phrenology was godless because it eliminated the idea of the human soul, the Fowlers pointed to a huge organ called Veneration to establish that people were naturally religious. When others said that phrenology was pessimistic because a person presumably could not change the shape of his or her skull, the Fowlers retorted that every desirable organ could be improved by exercise. Lorenzo Fowler reported that several of his skull bumps had actually grown. Orson Fowler wrapped it all into a tidy slogan: "Self-Made, or Never-Made."

Drawing phrenological charts of oneself or one's friends became a parlor game of sorts during the 1840s and 1850s, but phrenology appealed to Americans less as a pastime than as a "practical" science. In a mobile and individualistic society where people routinely transacted business with strangers, phrenology promised to provide at a glance a quick assessment of others. Merchants used phrenological charts to pick suitable clerks, and young women induced their fiancés to undergo phrenological analyses before tying the knot. Before phrenology, a supporter declared, "the wisest of men had no means of deciding, with anything like certainty, the talents or character of a stranger."

Phrenology did not cure disease, but phrenologists had close ties to the popular health movement. Fowlers and Wells issued the *Water-Cure Journal* after 1848 and brought out Sylvester Graham's *Lectures on the Science of Human Life.* Orson Fowler filled his popular phrenological books with tips on the evils of coffee, tea, meat, spices, and sex that could have been plucked from Graham's writings. As a "science," phrenology sprang from the same impulse as the health movements—the belief that anyone could understand and obey the "laws" of life.

Unlike hydropathy, phrenology did not require any investment of money. Unlike Grahamism, it did not call for painful abstinence. Easily understood and practiced by the average person, and filled with the promise of universal betterment, phrenology was the ideal science for antebellum America. Just as Americans invented machines to better their lives, they were not above inventing "sciences" that promised human betterment.

DEMOCRATIC PASTIMES

Between 1830 and 1860 technology increasingly transformed leisure by making Americans more dependent on recreation that could be manufactured and sold. People purchased this commodity in the form of cheap newspapers and novels as well as affordable tickets to plays, museums, and lectures.

Just as the Boston Associates had daringly capitalized on new technology to produce textiles at Lowell and Waltham, imaginative entrepreneurs utilized technology to make and sell entertainment. Men like James Gordon Bennett, one of the founders of the penny press in America, and P. T. Barnum, the greatest showman of the nineteenth century, amassed fortunes by sensing what people wanted and then employing available technology to satisfy their desire. To a degree, indeed, these men induced the public to want what they had to sell. Barnum, for example, had a genius for using newspaper publicity to pique popular interest in curiosities that he was about to exhibit.

Bennett and Barnum thought of themselves as purveyors of democratic entertainment. They would sell their wares cheaply to anyone. Barnum's famous American museum in New York City catered to a wide variety of social classes that paid to view paintings, dwarfs, mammoth bones, and other attractions. By marketing the American Museum as family entertainment, Barnum helped break down barriers that had long divided the pastimes of husbands from those of their wives. Similarly, the racy news stories in Bennett's *New York Herald* provided its vast audience with a common stock of information and topics for conversation. In these ways, the impact of technology on amusement was democratic.

Technology also ignited the process by which individuals became spectators rather than the creators of their own amusements. Americans had long found ways to enjoy themselves. Even the gloomiest Puritans had indulged in games and sports. After 1830, however, the burden of providing entertainment began to shift from individuals to entrepreneurs who supplied ways to entertain the public.

Newspapers

In 1830 the typical American newspaper was a mere four pages long, with the front and back pages devoted almost wholly to advertisements. The second and third pages contained editorials, details of ship arrivals and of their cargoes, reprints of political speeches, and notices of political events. Few papers depended on their circulation for profit; even the most prominent papers had a daily circulation of only one thousand to two thousand. Rather, papers often relied on subsidies from political parties or factions. When a party gained power, it inserted paid political notices only in papers loyal to it. "Journalists," a contemporary wrote, "were usually little more than secretaries dependent upon cliques of politicians, merchants, brokers, and office seekers for their prosperity and bread."

As a result, newspapers could be profitable without being particularly popular. Because of their potential for profit, new papers were constantly being established. But most had limited appeal. The typical paper sold for six cents an issue at a time when the average daily wage was less than a dollar. Papers often seemed little more than published bulletin boards. Merely records of events, they typically lacked the exciting news stories and eye-catching illustrations that later generations would take for granted.

The 1830s witnessed the beginnings of a stunning transformation. Technological changes, most of which originated in Europe, vastly increased both the supply of paper (still made from rags) and the speed

Newspaper Boy, *by Edward Bannister, 1869*
Newsboys such as this one poignantly painted by the black artist Edward Bannister were a familiar sight on nineteenth-century street corners.

Cheapness was not the only feature of the penny papers. Dependent on circulation and advertising rather than on subsidies, the penny press revolutionized the marketing and format of papers. Where single copies of the six-cent papers were usually available only at the printer's office, newsboys hawked the penny papers on busy street corners. Moreover, the penny papers subordinated the recording of political and commercial events to human-interest stories of robberies, murders, rapes, and abandoned children. They dispatched reporters to police courts and printed transcripts of trials. As sociologist Michael Schudson observes, "The penny press invented the modern concept of 'news.'" Rather than merely recording events, the penny papers wove events into gripping stories. They invented not only news but also news reporting. Relying on party stalwarts to dispatch copies of speeches and platforms, and reprinting news items from other papers, the older six-cent papers did little, if any, reporting. In contrast, the penny papers employed their own correspondents and were the first papers to use the telegraph to speed news to readers.

Some penny papers were little more than scandal sheets, but the best, like Bennett's *New York Herald* and Horace Greeley's *New York Tribune* (1841), pioneered modern financial and political reporting. From its inception, the *Herald* contained a daily "money article" that substituted the analysis and interpretation of financial events for the dull recording of commercial facts. "The spirit, pith, and philosophy of commercial affairs is what men of business want," Bennett wrote. The relentless snooping of the *Tribune*'s Washington reporters outraged politicians. In 1848 *Tribune* correspondents were temporarily barred from the House floor for reporting that Representative Sawyer of Ohio ate his lunch (sausage and bread) each day in the House chamber, picked his teeth with a jackknife, and wiped his greasy hands on his pants and coat.

The Popular Novel

Like newspapers, novels became enormously popular between 1830 and 1860. Of course, novels had been read long before 1830, and some authors, among them the Scot Sir Walter Scott, had gained a wide following. But the cost of novels before 1830 had restricted their sales. Each of Scott's novels, for example, was issued in a three-volume set that retailed for as much as thirty dollars. During the 1830s and 1840s, the impact of the transportation revolution and technical

of printing presses. The substitution of steam-driven cylindrical presses for flatbed hand presses led to a tenfold increase in the number of printed pages that could be produced in an hour. Enterprising journalists, among them the Scottish-born James Gordon Bennett, grasped the implications of the new technology. Newspapers could now rely on vast circulation rather than on political subsidies to turn a profit. To gain circulation, journalists like Bennett slashed the price of newspapers. In 1833 the *New York Sun* became America's first penny newspaper, and Bennett's *New York Herald* followed in 1835. By June 1835 the combined daily circulation of New York's three penny papers reached 44,000; in contrast, before the dawn of the penny press in 1833, the city's eleven dailies had a combined daily circulation of only 26,500. Spearheaded by the penny papers, the combined daily circulation of newspapers throughout the nation rose from roughly 78,000 in 1830 to 300,000 by 1840. The number of weekly newspapers spurted from 65 in 1830 to 138 in 1840.

advances in printing brought down the price of novels. As canals and railroads opened crossroads stores to the latest fiction, publishers in New York and Philadelphia vied to deliver inexpensive novels to the shelves. By the 1840s cheap paperbacks that sold for as little as seven cents began to flood the market.

Those who did not purchase such fictional books could read serializations in newspapers that were devoted mainly to printing novels. The most successful of these story papers was the *New York Ledger*, which a young Scotch-Irish immigrant, Robert Bonner, started in the mid-1840s. Like James Gordon Bennett, the lord of the penny press, Bonner had a genius for identifying what the public wanted and for launching publicity extravaganzas. To herald the serialization of one novel, Bonner spent twenty thousand dollars and arranged the firing of a one-hundred-gun salute in City Hall Park. By 1860 the *Ledger* had an astonishing weekly circulation of four hundred thousand.

The most popular fiction on the market in the 1840s and 1850s was the sentimental novel, which sought to evoke feelings or emotions. The tribulations of orphans and the deaths of children filled the pages of these tearjerkers. In Susan Warner's *The Wide, Wide World* (first serialized in 1850), the heroine burst into tears on an average of every other page for two volumes. Sentimentalism was not confined to novels. The popular writer Lydia Sigourney wrote a poem on the death of a canary that had accidentally been starved to death.

Women contributed the main audience for sentimental novels. This genre was a kind of women's fiction, written by women about women and mainly for women. The most lucrative occupation open to women before the Civil War, writing often attracted those in desperate need of cash. Hard times had lured many renowned female novelists into the field. Susan Warner, for example, had been brought up in luxury and then tossed into poverty by the financial ruin of her father in the Panic of 1837. Mrs. E. D. E. N. Southworth, who gained fame and fortune from *The Hidden Hand* (first serialized in 1859) and other novels, turned to writing after a broken marriage left her supporting two children on a teacher's salary of $250 a year.

Women's fiction dealt with more than the flow of tears. A major theme in the novels of Susan Warner and Mrs. Southworth was that women could conquer any obstacle. Women's novels challenged the stereotype of the male as the trusty provider and of the female as the delicate dependent by portraying men as liars, drunken lechers, or vicious misers and depicting women as re-sourceful and strong-willed. In the typical plot, a female orphan or a spoiled rich girl thrown on hard times, or a dutiful daughter plagued by a drunken father, learned grittily to master every situation. The moral was clear. Women could overcome trials and make the world a better place. Few of the novelists were active feminists, but their writings provided a glimpse into the private feelings of their female readers.

The Theater

During the 1850s novelists like the Englishman Charles Dickens and the American Harriet Beecher Stowe, the author of *Uncle Tom's Cabin*, were as well known through dramatizations of their work as by sales of their books. Antebellum theaters were large (twenty-five hundred to four thousand seats in some cities) and crowded by all classes. With seats as cheap as twelve cents and rarely more than fifty cents, the typical theater audience included lawyers and merchants and their wives, artisans and clerks, sailors and noisy boys, and a sizable body of prostitutes. Prostitutes usually sat in the top gallery, called the third tier, "that dark, horrible, guilty" place. The presence of prostitutes in theaters was taken for granted; the only annoyance came when they left the third tier to solicit customers in the more expensive seats.

The prostitutes in attendance were not the only factor that made the antebellum theater vaguely disreputable. Theatrical audiences were notoriously rowdy. They showed their feelings by stamping their feet, whistling, hooting at villains, and throwing potatoes or garbage at the stage when they did not like the characters or the acting. Individual actors developed huge followings, and the public displayed at least as much interest in the actors as in the plays. In 1849 a long-running feud between the leading American actor, Edwin Forrest, and the popular British actor William Macready ended with a riot at New York City's Astor Place that left twenty people dead.

The Astor Place riot demonstrated the broad popularity of the theater. Forrest's supporters included a following of Irish workers who loathed the British and appealed to the "working men" to rally against the "aristocrat" Macready. Macready, who projected a more polished and intellectual image than Forrest, attracted the better-educated classes. Had not all classes patronized the theater, the deadly riot probably would never have occurred.

The plays themselves were as diverse as the audiences. Most often performed were melodramas, whose plots resembled those of sentimental novels. Vice was punished, virtue rewarded, and the heroine finally married the hero. Yet the single most popular dramatist was William Shakespeare. In 1835 audiences in Philadelphia witnessed sixty-five performances of Shakespeare's plays. Americans who may never have read a line of Shakespeare grew familiar with Othello, King Lear, Desdemona, and Shylock. Theatrical managers adapted Shakespeare to a popular audience. They highlighted the swordfights and assassinations, cut some speeches, omitted minor characters, and pruned words or references that might have offended the audience's sense of propriety. For example, they substituted *pottels* for *urinals* and quietly advanced Juliet's age at the time that she falls in love with Romeo from fourteen to eighteen. They occasionally changed sad endings to happy ones. The producers even arranged for short performances or demonstrations between acts of Shakespeare—and indeed, of every play. During such an interlude, the audience might have observed a brief impersonation of Tecumseh or Aaron Burr, jugglers and acrobats, a drummer beating twelve drums at once, or a three-year-old who weighed a hundred pounds.

Minstrel Shows

The Yankee or "Brother Jonathan" figure who served as a stock character in many antebellum plays helped audiences to form an image of the ideal American as rustic, clever, patriotic, and more than a match for city slickers and decadent European aristocrats. In a different way, the minstrel shows that Americans thronged to see in the 1840s and 1850s forged enduring stereotypes that buttressed white Americans' sense of superiority by diminishing black people.

Minstrel shows arose in northern cities in the 1840s, as blackfaced white men took to the stage to present an evening of songs, dances, and humorous sketches. Minstrelsy borrowed some authentic elements of African-American culture, especially dances characterized by the sliding, shuffling step of southern blacks, but most of the songs had origins in white culture. Such familiar American songs as Stephen Foster's "Camptown Races" and "Massa's in the Cold Ground," which first aired in minstrel shows, reflected white Americans' notions of how blacks sang more than it represented authentic black music. In addition, the images of blacks projected by minstrelsy both catered to and reinforced the prejudices of the working-class

Dan Bryant, the Minstrel
Bryant was one of many antebellum popularizers of black minstrelsy. One of the earliest known minstrelsy performances occurred in Boston in 1799, when the white man Gottlieb Graupner, reportedly made up as a black, sang and accompanied himself on the banjo.

whites who dominated the audience of minstrel shows. Minstrel troupes usually depicted blacks as stupid, clumsy, and obsessively musical and emphasized the Africanness of blacks by giving their characters names like the Ethiopian Serenaders and their acts titles like the Nubian Jungle Dance and the African Fling. At a time of intensifying political conflict over race, minstrel shows planted images and expectations about blacks' behavior through stock characters. These included Uncle Ned, the tattered, humble, and docile slave, and Zip Coon, the arrogant urban free black who paraded around in a high hat, long-tailed coat, and green vest and who lived off his girlfriends' money. Minstrels lampooned blacks who assumed public roles by portraying them as incompetent stump speakers who called Patrick Henry "Henry Patrick," referred to John Hancock as "Boobcock," and confused the word *statute* with *statue*.

By the 1850s major cities from New York to San Francisco had several minstrel theaters. Touring professional troupes and local amateur talent even brought minstrelsy to small towns and villages. Mark Twain later recalled how minstrelsy had burst upon Hannibal, Missouri, in the early 1840s as "a glad and stunning surprise." So popular was the craze that minstrels even visited the White House and entertained Presidents John Tyler, James K. Polk, Millard Fillmore, and Franklin Pierce.

P. T. Barnum

Like Frances Trollope (see "A Place in Time") but on a grander scale, P. T. Barnum understood how to turn the antebellum public's craving for entertainment into a profitable business. As a young man in his native Bethel, Connecticut, Barnum savored popular journalism by starting a newspaper, the *Herald of Freedom,* that assailed wrongdoing in high places. Throughout his life, he thought of himself as a public benefactor and pointed to his profits as proof that he gave people what they wanted. Yet honesty was never his strong suit. As a small-town grocer in Connecticut, he regularly cheated his customers on the principle that they were trying to cheat him. Barnum, in short, was a hustler raised in the land of the Puritans, a cynic and an idealist rolled into one.

After moving to New York City in 1834, Barnum started a new career as an entrepreneur of popular entertainment. His first venture exhibited a black woman, Joice Heth, whom Barnum billed as the 169-year-old former slave nurse of George Washington. Barnum neither knew nor cared how old Joice was (in fact, she was probably around 80); it was enough that people would pay to see her. Strictly speaking, he cheated the public, but he knew that many of his customers shared his doubts about Joice's age. Determined to expose Barnum's gimmick, some poked her to see whether she was really a machine rather than a person. He was playing a game with the public, and the public with him.

In 1841 Barnum purchased a run-down museum in New York City, rechristened it the American Museum, and opened a new chapter in the history of popular entertainment. The founders of most earlier museums had intended an educational purpose. They exhibited stuffed birds and animals, specimens of rock, and portraits. Most of these museums, however, had languished for want of public interest. Barnum, in contrast, made piquing public curiosity the main goal. To attract people, he added collections of curiosities and faked exhibits. Visitors to the American Museum could see ventriloquists, magicians, albinos, a five-year-old midget whom Barnum named General Tom Thumb and later took on a tour of Europe, and the "Feejee Mermaid," a shrunken oddity that Barnum billed as "positively asserted by its owner to have been taken alive in the Feejee Islands." By 1850 the American Museum had become the best-known museum in the nation and a model for popular museums in other cities.

Blessed with a genius for publicity, Barnum recognized that newspapers could invent as well as report news. One of his favorite tactics was to puff his exhibits by writing letters (under various names) to newspapers, in which he would hint that the scientific world was agog over some astonishing curiosity of nature that the public could soon see for itself at the American Museum. But Barnum's success rested on more than publicity. A staunch temperance advocate, he provided regular lectures at the American Museum on the evils of alcohol and soon gave the place a reputation as a center for safe family amusement. Finally, Barnum tapped the public's insatiable curiosity about natural wonders. In 1835 the editor of the *New York Sun* had boosted his circulation by claiming that a famous astronomer had discovered pelicans and winged men on the moon. At a time when each passing year brought new technological wonders, the public was ready to believe in anything, even the Feejee Mermaid.

THE QUEST FOR NATIONALITY IN LITERATURE AND ART

Sentimental novels, melodramas, minstrel shows, and the American Museum belonged to the world of popular culture. All these genres lacked the dignity and originality that would endear them to those seeking cultural expressions that would reflect the American national spirit and command respect abroad. The limits of the popular genres—with their frequent crudity and their interchangeable plots, characters, and themes—did not escape the notice of reflective observers. During the 1830s Ralph Waldo Emerson emerged as the most influential spokesman for those who sought a national literature and art.

"Our day of dependence, our long apprenticeship to the learning of other lands, draws to a close," Emerson announced in his address "The American Scholar"

Frances Trollope Invents Popular Culture in Cincinnati

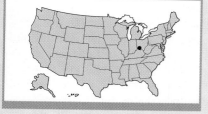

Words like *pioneer* and *frontier* still evoke images of a West of majestic forests and wide, rushing rivers, of buck-skin-clad settlers and Indians in loincloths. But in fact, throughout the early–nine-teenth-century westward migrations, cities were a colorful and vital part of the west-ern fabric.

Located on the Ohio River in a vast agricultural basin that spread from Ohio to parts of Kentucky and Indiana, Cincinnati was positioned astride the major east-west and north-south trade routes, and its growth was nothing short of remarkable. A mere village of 750 inhabitants in 1788, it had become the West's leading city and the nation's ninth-largest city by 1820. By 1850 its industrial and commercial output was exceeded only by that of New York and Philadelphia.

Early Cincinnatians developed an edginess about criticism, to which they re-sponded by crowning their city with one grand title after another: Queen of the West; Athens of the West; Wonder of the West; the Second Boston; and the Infant Hercules. Cincinnati's very success in at-tracting settlers aroused envy in the East, especially among journalists, who rou-tinely disparaged it as a pestilence-ridden haven of roughnecks, devoid of culture and refinement.

Already sensitive to these insults, Cincinnati dwellers, especially its fledgling

Republicans at Theatre
Snoring or chatting their way through a performance of Shakespeare's Hamlet, *these Americans display the boorish man-ners that so annoyed Frances Trollope.*

Frances Trollope,
by Auguste Hervieu, c. 1832
With the publication of Domestic Manners of the Americans *at the age of fifty-three, Frances Trollope began a new life as a writer of novels and travel books. She made enough money to over-come the financial catastrophes that overtook her husband and to keep her family together, and she communicated her self-discipline to her son Anthony, who became a famous novelist. Not surpris-ingly, her fictional heroines were as strong and aggressive as she herself.*

high society of merchants, professionals, and their spouses, found more cause to complain with the publication in 1832 of Frances Trollope's *The Domestic Manners of the Americans.* This account of the British-born Trollope's four-year residence in America, including two in Cincinnati, made Cincinnati famous as a symbol of American crassness and materialism. Wealthy men there, she related, spent their time spitting, talking about the price of produce and hogs (a leading hog-pack-ing center, Cincinnati acquired "Porkopo-lis" as another of its many nicknames), and spitting again. Excluded from all con-versation about business or politics, the city's society ladies were ignored even by their husbands and passed their hours evaluating each other's dresses down to the last pin.

The Domestic Manners of the Amer-icans would earn a small fortune for

Frances Trollope, and not a moment too soon. When she composed the book, she was in her early fifties, with four children and a husband in England who was on the verge of financial and nervous collapse. Accompanied by her son Henry and Henry's tutor, a French artist and political refugee named Auguste Hervieu, Trollope had arrived in Cincinnati in 1828 after a brief sojourn at Nashoba, an interracial utopian community in Tennessee. Nothing about her seemed quite right to Cincinnatians, who did not relish an intellectual woman, particularly one with utopian and abolitionist leanings and most especially a married woman who traveled without her husband but accompanied by a handsome Frenchman. But like the country boy P. T. Barnum in New York City, she was an outsider who recognized something that the locals missed: that urban resources could be marshaled to create new forms of popular entertainment.

Reasoning that Cincinnatians probably found the place as dull as she did and that they would pay to experience the weird and exotic, she soon grasped the commercial possibilities of one of the city's few cultural institutions, the Western Museum. Founded in 1819 to house western scientific collections, the museum had been sliding into financial ruin: Cincinnatians would not pay to look at stuffed birds and animal bones, even if western. Trollope and the museum's director, the French-born Joseph Dorfeuille, boldly conceived the idea of replacing the scientific exhibits with displays evoking mystery, dread, and romance.

With Hervieu's aid, she helped Dorfeuille to construct two such exhibits. The first, "The Invisible Girl," was housed in a room exotically decorated with wax figures drawn from characters in ancient Greek and Egyptian mythology. A mysterious voice rose from behind a machine-made cloud to answer questions (three to a customer) from the audience in a variety of known and unknown languages. The voice of this "Invisible Girl" was actually that of Trollope's son, Henry, who had studied Latin and Greek in England and who could fake or invent other languages. Most of the time the "girl" spoke gibberish, but customers considered her

a multilingual wonder. So successful was this show that the team of Trollope, Hervieu, and Dorfeuille quickly mounted another, "The Infernal Regions," a fancifully fearsome exhibit of hell with mechanical and wax figures depicting imps, snakes, demons, goblins, and the Evil One, and with the tension heightened by blackouts punctuated by "horrid groans" and "terrible shrieks." The view, one observer recorded, "is calculated to awaken serious but not unprofitable reflections." Such was the crush of visitors to the exhibit that an electrified fence had to be installed to deter them from touching the figures.

Trollope's next scheme was a "bazaar," a kind of nineteenth-century shopping mall rolled into a single building. Designed in the exotic Egyptian or "arabesque" style, the emporium boasted a coffeehouse, a bar, an art gallery, and sundry rooms devoted to selling jewelry, sculpture, and clothing. Unlike her other ventures, the bazaar failed dismally, partly because she ran out of (borrowed) money to construct it and partly because, in contrast to her silent partnership in the museum exhibits, her sponsorship of the bazaar was public knowledge. With additional backing someone else probably would have succeeded, for Trollope had grasped what Barnum would later discover: that there was a hungry market for popular culture as long as exhibits, whether mysterious or outlandish, were lifelike, made at least a pretense at edification, and did not remind Americans too much of America.

Trollope left the city after the collapse of her bazaar, sorry that she had ever entered it. But she had left her mark. Successful purveyors of popular culture not only in Cincinnati but also in the East would follow her formula. Painters, for example, found that, although Cincinnatians lacked interest in western landscapes, they would pay to see "panoramas." Popular artists accordingly painted football-field–long canvases that depicted such subjects as events in the life of Napoleon and that were gradually unrolled before their viewers. These "moving pictures" foreshadowed the newsreels of the twentieth century.

Compared to the paintings of the Hudson River school (see p. 357), popular art was notable for its lack of symbolism or abstraction. Popular cultural exhibits catered to their viewers' pretensions toward refinement by routinely drawing on classical, mythological, or European themes, but they also featured an obsession with the "authentic" and the lifelike that gave customers the feeling that they were part of the scene itself.

The Bazaar
Detractor's called it Trollope's Folly, but with its arabesque windows, Egyptian columns, and Moorish dome, Frances Trollope's Bazaar was splendid relief from Cincinnati's monotony. Its plans called for a basement housing a barroom and coffee house, a main floor for the bazaar itself, and a top floor with a ballroom and arched mosaics in the style of the Alhambra in Spain.

(1837). For too long, Emerson affirmed, Americans had deferred to European precedents in literature and learning. Now the time had come for the American people to trust themselves. Let "the single man plant himself indomitably on his instincts and there abide," and "the huge world will come round to him."

Contemporaries proclaimed "The American Scholar" an intellectual Declaration of Independence and praised Emerson for having "cut the cable" that still moored the United States to European thought. Yet Emerson's plea for cultural autonomy was hardly new; ever since the Revolution, Americans had been calling for cultural as well as political independence from Britain. In the 1780s Noah Webster, the famous compiler of textbooks and dictionaries that substituted phonetic American spellings for British spellings, had warned that basing American literature on European taste and manners was as foolish as constructing "a durable and stately edifice . . . upon the mouldering pillars of antiquity."

"The American Scholar" had an electrifying effect for several reasons. First, as Emerson recognized, the democratic spirit of the age had made Americans more self-reliant. Successful in their political and material lives, they no longer felt the need to defer to European standards. In addition, the dramatic impact of Emerson's address reflected his ability to adapt an international literary movement known as romanticism to American conditions. Originating in Europe in the second half of the eighteenth century, romanticism challenged the rival impulse known as classicism (or neoclassicism). Classicists described standards of beauty and taste as universal and decreed that the most desirable literary productions display elegance and polish. In contrast, romantics argued that each nation had to discover its own unique literary genius. They further insisted that great literature reflect not only national character but also the most profound emotions of the writer. Where classicists expected that all fine literature and art would conform to an identical standard of elegance, romantics sought individuality in literary and artistic expression.

As we have seen, during the 1830s the transcendentalist movement emerged as a challenge to Unitarianism, and in their literary work, Emerson and other transcendentalists evolved a uniquely American form of romanticism. Dismissing the prevailing idea that all knowledge came through the senses, transcendentalists argued instead that such basic conceptions as those of God and freedom were inborn. Knowledge re-

sembled sight—an instantaneous, direct perception of truth. Emerson concluded that learned people enjoyed no special advantages in the pursuit of truth. All persons could see the truth if only they would trust the promptings of their hearts. Applied to the United States, transcendentalist doctrine led to the exhilarating conclusion that a young, democratic society could produce as noble a literature and art as the more traditional societies of Europe. Although such a fledgling, democratic society might lack elegance and polish, it could draw upon the inexhaustible resources of the common people.

Literary Geography

Emerson's "The American Scholar" coincided with a flowering of distinctively American literature and art, often called the American Renaissance, that had been gaining momentum since the 1820s. By 1837 the American public had grown as familiar with native-born authors such as Washington Irving and James Fenimore Cooper as with such lions of the British literary world as Sir Walter Scott and Charles Dickens. Emerson did not initiate this outpouring of native talent, but he expressed its ideals and helped shape its direction.

Of all the regions of the United States, New England had the most fertile soil for literature. Its poets ranged from the urbane Henry Wadsworth Longfellow and polished Boston aristocrats like Oliver Wendell Holmes, Sr., and James Russell Lowell to the farm-born, self-taught Quaker John Greenleaf Whittier. Boston also became the home of George Bancroft, William Hickling Prescott, Francis Parkman, and John Lothrop Motley, the four most distinguished historians of the antebellum period. Twenty miles from Boston lay Concord, the home of Emerson, Nathaniel Hawthorne, the eccentric Henry David Thoreau, and the brilliant philosopher and critic Margaret Fuller. Not far from Concord lay Fruitlands, a utopian community where Louisa May Alcott, the author of *Little Women* (1868), passed part of her childhood under the sometimes dizzying influence of her unworldly father, Bronson Alcott. Farther to the west was Amherst, the residence of Emily Dickinson. Shy and reclusive, she lived out her entire fifty-six years on the same street ("I do not go from home," she stated with characteristic pithiness), where she wrote exquisite poems that examined, in her own words, every splinter in the groove of the brain. Dreading the corruption of her art

Louisa May Alcott, c. 1858
Raised in bleak if genteel poverty, Louisa May Alcott first gained recognition for her sketches of her experiences as a nurse in a military hospital during the Civil War. The publication of Little Women, *her largely autobiographical novel of New England family life, brought her fame and enough money to support herself and her sisters.*

by commercialism, she staunchly refused to publish her verse.

Most New Englanders did not share Emily Dickinson's horror of publicity. Nineteenth-century New England writers and publishers widely exported their region's culture. By the end of the century, schoolchildren throughout the nation were turning pages of Longfellow's *Evangeline* (1847) and *The Song of Hiawatha* (1855), Whittier's *Snow-Bound* (1866), and Lowell's antislavery *The Biglow Papers* (1848). What had begun as a regional culture became enshrined as a national culture, and for this reason alone, New England's literary renaissance deserves special recognition.

New England, however, always faced a challenge from New York, the home of Irving, Cooper, and later of Walt Whitman and Herman Melville. Even before

the flowering of American literature, New York had abounded with literary clubs, composed for the most part of wealthy young lawyers and merchants. It was in New York that the wealthy and gifted Irving had made his reputation with the publication of the comedic *Diedrich Knickerbocker's A History of New York* (1809). After serving in the War of 1812, Irving had left the United States for Europe and had not returned until 1832. Yet his *Sketch Book* (1820), which contained "Rip Van Winkle" and "The Legend of Sleepy Hollow," continued to endear him to Americans, who displayed a boastful pride in the literary accomplishments of their best-known writer.

The literary flowering affected all regions. Southerners such as William Gilmore Simms, the author of *The Yemassee* (1835), acquired reputations that spread beyond their native section. Although he did most of his writing in New York and Philadelphia, Edgar Allan Poe was a Virginian by upbringing and emotional identification. In the lower and westerly regions of the Old South, Augustus B. Longstreet and Johnson J. Hooper crafted humorous sketches that captured a kind of backcountry roguishness and rowdiness so extravagant that it became hilarious. Longstreet's *Georgia Scenes* (1835) described gander pulling, eye gouging, and other frontier pastimes. Hooper's *Some Adventures of Captain Simon Suggs* (1846) related how Suggs cheated his own father at cards to obtain a horse and how he went to a camp meeting to get religion and came away with the contents of the collection box instead.

Not all antebellum writers, however, have passed the test of time. Irving's writings now strike critics as examples of a comfortable second-ratedness. Although polished poets, neither Longfellow nor Whittier was notably innovative. Dickinson was a genius, but although born in 1830, she did most of her writing after 1860. In retrospect, regional humorists like Longstreet and Hooper are significant mainly because they foreshadowed a far greater humorist, Mark Twain.

Yet within the large circle of antebellum writers, the genius of seven individuals continues to shine: Cooper, Emerson, Thoreau, Whitman, Hawthorne, Melville, and Poe. Cooper and Emerson basked in public esteem in their day, but neither Hawthorne nor Poe gained the popular audience that each believed he deserved. The antebellum public largely ignored the remaining three—Thoreau, Whitman, and Melville. Creativity rather than popularity became the unifying characteristic of these seven writers. Each challenged existing literary conventions and created new ones. Cooper demonstrated the possibility of writing a novel using distinctively American literary themes. Emerson gave a new direction to an old literary form, the essay. Thoreau wrote about nature in a way that captured not only its beauty but its constant activity. By breaking with the conventions of rhyme and meter, Whitman breathed new vitality into poetry. As a writer of both short fiction and poetry, Poe went far to free literature from the insistence that it preach a moral and to establish the principle that fiction and poetry be judged by the pleasure that they imparted. Hawthorne and Melville turned the novel into a vehicle for exploring the depths of human psychology.

James Fenimore Cooper and the Stirrings of Literary Independence

Until well after 1800, British literature had dominated American literary taste. With the publication of *Waverley* (1814), a historical novel set in Britain in the 1740s, the star of Sir Walter Scott had begun its spectacular ascent on the American horizon. Americans had named more than a dozen towns Waverley; advertisements for subsequent novels by Scott had borne the simple caption, "By the author of *Waverley*."

Because he wrote historical novels under Scott's influence, James Fenimore Cooper, born in 1789, has often been called the American Scott. But this designation is misleading, for the enormously popular Cooper was remarkably creative in his own right. His most important innovation was to introduce the frontiersman Natty Bumppo ("Leatherstocking") as a fictional character. In *The Pioneers* (1823), Natty appears as an old man settled on the shores of Lake Otsego in upstate New York. Although Natty is a hunter, he blames the farmers for the wanton destruction of game and for turning the silent and majestic forests into deserts of tree stumps. As a spokesman for nature against the march of civilization, Natty immediately became a popular figure, and in subsequent novels such as *The Last of the Mohicans* (1826), *The Pathfinder* (1840), and *The Deerslayer* (1841), Cooper unfolded Natty's life for an appreciative reading public.

Cooper's success marked the first step in a process that saw Americans develop an imaginative literature of their own. They still read British novels, but they increasingly enjoyed American writers. In 1800

American authors accounted for a negligible proportion of the output of American publishers. By 1830, 40 percent of the books published in the United States were written by Americans; and by 1850, 75 percent.

Emerson, Thoreau, and Whitman

Emerson's advocacy of a national literature extended beyond his urgings in "The American Scholar." In writings of his own, he tried (not always successfully) to capture the brisk language of the common people of the United States. Furthermore, he encouraged younger American writers like Thoreau and Whitman. Whitman, extravagantly patriotic, contrasted sharply with Emerson and Thoreau, who often criticized the materialism and aggressiveness of their compatriots. The ideal of nationality in literature clearly did not always mean the uncritical celebration of Americans and American policies. But the uniquely American prose or poetry that flowed from the pens of these three writers did share a strong common feature: it emphasized the spontaneous and vivid expression of personal feelings over learned analysis, which the writers associated with European traditions.

Born in 1803, Emerson served briefly as a Unitarian minister. During the 1830s he carved out a new career for himself as a public lecturer. The topics of his addresses, most of which he published as essays, appeared to be broad and general: "Beauty," "Nature," "Power," "Representative Men," and "New England Reformers." But a unique pungency and vividness characterized his language. For example, in "The American Scholar," in which Emerson emphasized the importance of independent thought on the part of the true scholar, his language was striking: "Let him [the scholar] not quit his belief that a popgun is a popgun, though the ancient and honorable of the earth affirm it to be the crack of doom." Equally remarkable was Emerson's way of developing his subjects. A contemporary compared listening to Emerson to trying to see the sun in a fog; one could see light but never the sun itself. As a transcendentalist who believed that knowledge reflected the voice of God within every person and that truth was inborn and universal, Emerson never amassed evidence or presented systematic arguments to prove his contentions. Rather, he relied on a sequence of vivid and arresting though often unconnected assertions. The argument was hard to follow (one listener thought she might have better understood Emerson if she had stood on her head), but the overall effect dazzled the audience.

Emerson had a magnetic attraction for intellectually inclined young men and women who did not fit easily into American society. Henry David Thoreau, born in 1817 in Concord, Massachusetts, where Emerson took up residence during the 1830s, was representative of the younger Emersonians. Yet a crucial difference separated the two men. Adventurous in thought, Emerson was basically unadventurous in action. As contemplative as Emerson, Thoreau was more of a doer. At one point, Thoreau went to jail rather than pay his poll tax. This revenue, he knew, would support the war against Mexico, which he viewed as part of a southern conspiracy to extend slavery. The experience led Thoreau to write *Civil Disobedience* (1849), in which he defended the right to disobey unjust laws.

In the spring of 1845, Thoreau moved a few miles from Concord into the woods near Walden Pond. There he constructed a simple cabin on land owned by Emerson and spent the next two years providing for his wants away from civilization. Thoreau's stated purpose in retreating to Walden was to write a description (later published) of a canoe trip that he and his brother had taken down the Concord and Merrimack rivers in 1839. During his stay in the woods, however, he conceived and wrote a much more important book, *Walden* (1854). A contemporary described *Walden* as "the logbook of his woodland cruise," and indeed, Thoreau filled its pages with descriptions of hawks and wild pigeons, his invention of raisin bread, his trapping of the woodchucks that despoiled his vegetable garden, and his construction of a cabin for exactly $28.50. Few writers have matched Thoreau's ability to capture both the details and the cycles of nature and to give the reader the sensation of being present at the scene. But true to transcendentalism, Thoreau had a larger message. His woodland retreat taught him that he (and by implication, others) could satisfy material wants with only a few weeks' work each year and thereby leave more time for reexamining life's purpose. The problem with Americans, he said, was that they turned themselves into "mere machines" to acquire wealth without asking why. Thoreau bore the uncomfortable truth that material and moral progress were not as intimately related as Americans liked to think.

One of Ralph Waldo Emerson's qualities was an ability to sympathize with such dissimilar personalities

Walt Whitman
Whitman is today considered one of the major nineteenth-century poets, but in his day many derided his verse as indecent. In 1865 Whitman lost his job with the U.S. government when his superiors found out that he was the author of Leaves of Grass.

as Thoreau and Walt Whitman—the former eccentric, reclusive, and critical; the latter self-taught, outgoing, exuberant, and in love with virtually everything about America except slavery. Born in 1819, Whitman left school at eleven and became a printer's apprentice and later a journalist and editor for various newspapers in Brooklyn, Manhattan, and New Orleans. A familiar figure at Democratic party functions, he marched in the vanguard of party parades and put his pen to the service of the party's free-soil wing.

Journalism gave Whitman an intimate knowledge of ordinary Americans; the more he knew them, the more he liked them. His reading of Emerson nurtured his belief that America was to be the cradle of a new citizen in whom natural virtue would flourish unimpeded by European corruption, a man like Andrew Jackson, that "massive, yet most sweet and plain character." The threads of Whitman's early career came together in his major work, *Leaves of Grass*, a book of poems first published in 1855 and reissued with additions in subsequent years.

Leaves of Grass shattered most existing poetic conventions. Not only did Whitman write in free verse (that is, most of his poems had neither rhyme nor meter), but the poems were also lusty and blunt at a time when delicacy reigned in the literary world. Whitman wrote of "the scent of these armpits finer than prayer" and "winds whose soft-tickling genitals rub against me." No less remarkably, Whitman intruded himself into his poems, one of which he titled "Song of Walt Whitman" (and later retitled "Song of Myself"). Although Whitman thought well of himself, it was not egotism that propelled him to sing of himself. Rather, he viewed himself—crude, plain, self-taught, and passionately democratic—as the personification of the American people. He was

> *Comrade of raftsmen and coalmen, comrade*
> *of all who shake hands and welcome to*
> *drink and meat,*
> *A learner with the simplest, a teacher of the*
> *thoughtfullest.*

By 1860 Whitman had acquired a considerable reputation as a poet. Nevertheless, the original edition of *Leaves* (a run of only about eight hundred copies) was ignored or derided as a "heterogeneous mass of bombast, egotism, vulgarity, and nonsense." One reviewer suggested that it was the work of an escaped lunatic. Only Emerson and a few others reacted enthusiastically. Within two weeks of publication, Emerson, never having met Whitman, wrote: "I find it the most extraordinary piece of wit and wisdom that America has yet contributed." Emerson had long called for the appearance of "the poet of America" and knew in a flash that in Whitman, that poet had arrived.

Hawthorne, Melville, and Poe

In "The American Scholar," Emerson called upon American writers to create a democratic literature by comprehending "the near, the low, the common"— the everyday experiences of ordinary Americans. However exhilarating a message, Emerson's plea had a negligible impact on the major writers of fiction during the 1840s and 1850s—Nathaniel Hawthorne, Herman Melville, and Edgar Allan Poe. Hawthorne, for example, set *The Scarlet Letter* (1850) in New England's Puritan past, *The House of the Seven Gables* (1851) in a

mansion haunted not by ghosts but by memories of the past, and *The Marble Faun* (1859) in Rome. Poe set several of his short stories such as "The Murders in the Rue Morgue" (1841), "The Masque of the Red Death" (1842), and "The Cask of Amontillado" (1846) in Europe; as one critic has noted, "His art could have been produced as easily had he been born in Europe." Melville did draw materials and themes from his own experiences as a sailor and from the lore of the New England whaling industry, but for his novels *Typee* (1846), *Omoo* (1847), and *Mardi* (1849), he picked the exotic setting of islands in the South Seas; and for his masterpiece *Moby-Dick* (1851), the ill-fated whaler *Pequod*. If the only surviving documents from the 1840s and 1850s were its major novels, historians would face an impossible task in describing the appearance of antebellum American society.

The unusual settings favored by these three writers partly reflected their view that American life lacked the materials for great fiction. Hawthorne, for example, bemoaned the difficulty of writing about a country "where there is no shadow, no antiquity, no mystery, no picturesque and gloomy wrong, nor anything but a commonplace prosperity in broad and simple daylight, as is happily the case with my dear native land." In addition, psychology rather than society riveted the attention of these three writers; each probed the depths of the human mind rather than the intricacies of social relationships. Their preoccupation with analyzing the mental states of their characters grew out of their underlying pessimism about the human condition. Emerson, Whitman, and (to a degree) Thoreau optimistically believed that human conflicts could be resolved if only individuals followed the promptings of their better selves. In contrast, Hawthorne, Melville, and Poe saw individuals as bundles of conflicting forces that, even with the best intentions, might never be reconciled.

Their pessimism led them to create characters obsessed by pride, guilt, a desire for revenge, or a quest for perfection and then to set their stories along the byways of society, where they would be free to explore the complexities of human motivation without the jarring intrusion of everyday life. For example, in *The Scarlet Letter* Hawthorne turned to the Puritan past in order to examine the psychological and moral consequences of the adultery committed by Hester Prynne and the minister Arthur Dimmesdale. So completely did Hawthorne focus on the moral dilemmas of his central characters that he conveyed little sense of the social life of the Puritan village in which the novel is set. Melville, who dedicated *Moby-Dick* to Hawthorne, shared the latter's pessimism. In the novel's Captain Ahab, Melville created a frightening character whose relentless and futile pursuit of the white whale fails to fill the chasm in his soul and brings death to all of his mates save the narrator, Ishmael. Poe also channeled his pessimism into creative achievements of the first rank. In perhaps his finest short story, "The Fall of the House of Usher" (1839), he demonstrated an uncanny ability to weave the symbol of a crumbling mansion with the mental agony of a crumbling family.

Hawthorne, Melville, and Poe did not heed Emerson's call to write about the everyday experiences of their fellow Americans. Nor did they follow Cooper's lead by creating distinctively American heroes. Yet each contributed to an indisputably American literature. Ironically, their conviction that the lives of ordinary Americans provided inadequate materials for fiction led them to create a uniquely American fiction, one marked less by the description of the complex social relationships of ordinary life than by the analysis of moral dilemmas and psychological states. In this way, they unintentionally fulfilled a prediction made by Alexis de Tocqueville that writers in democratic nations, while rejecting many of the traditional sources of fiction, would explore the abstract and universal questions of human nature.

American Landscape Painting

American painters also sought to develop nationality in art between 1820 and 1860. Lacking a mythic past of the sort represented by the gods and goddesses of the ancient world that Europeans called upon, Americans subordinated history and figure painting to landscape painting. Yet just as Hawthorne had complained about the flat, commonplace character of American society, the painters of the Hudson River school recognized that the American landscape lacked the European landscape's "poetry of decay" in the form of ruined castles and crumbling temples. Like everything else in the United States, the landscape was fresh, relatively unencumbered by the human imprint. This fact posed a challenge to the Hudson River school painters.

The Hudson River school flourished from the 1820s to the 1870s. Numbering more than fifty painters, it is best represented by Thomas Cole, Asher Durand, and Frederic Church. All three men painted scenes of the region around the Hudson River, a waterway that Americans compared in majesty to the Rhine. But none was exclusively a landscapist. Some of Cole's most popular paintings were allegories, including *The Course of Empire*, a sequence of five canvases depicting the rise and fall of an ancient city and clearly implying that luxury doomed republican virtue. Nor did these artists paint only the Hudson. Church, a student of Cole and internationally the best known of the three, painted the Andes Mountains during an extended trip to South America in 1853. After the Civil War, the German-born Albert Bierstedt applied many Hudson River school techniques in his monumental canvases of the Rocky Mountains.

The works of Washington Irving and the opening of the Erie Canal had sparked artistic interest in the Hudson during the 1820s. After 1830 the writings of Emerson and Thoreau popularized a new view of nature. Intent on cultivating land, the pioneers of Kentucky and Ohio had deforested a vast area. One traveler complained that Americans would rather view a wheat field or a cabbage patch than a virgin forest. But Emerson, Thoreau, and landscape architects like Frederick Law Olmsted glorified nature; "in wildness is the preservation of the world," Thoreau wrote. Their outlook blended with growing popular fears that, as one contemporary expressed it in 1847, "The axe of civilization is busy with our old forests." As the "wild and picturesque haunts of the Red Man" became "the abodes of commerce and the seats of civilization," he concluded, "it behooves our artists to rescue from its grasp the little that is left before it is too late."

The Hudson River painters wanted to do more than preserve a passing wilderness. Their special contribution to American art was to emphasize emotional effect over accuracy. Cole's use of rich coloring, billowing clouds, massive gnarled trees, towering peaks, and deep chasms so heightened the dramatic impact of his paintings that the poet and editor William Cullen Bryant compared them to "acts of religion." Similar motifs marked Church's paintings of the Andes Mountains, which used erupting volcanoes and thunderstorms to evoke dread and a sense of majesty. Lacking the ruined castles and crumbling temples that dotted European landscapes, the Americans strove to capture the natural grandeur of their own landscape.

Like Cole, the painter George Catlin also tried to preserve a vanishing America. Observing a delegation of Indians passing through Philadelphia in 1824, Catlin

Rainmaking Among the Mandan, 1837–1839

**The Author Painting a Chief at
the Base of the Rocky Mountains, 1850**

Tchow-ee-put-o-kaw, 1834

*George Catlin's paintings preserved the faces, customs, and habitats of the Indian
tribes whose civilization was collapsing in the face of white advance.*

resolved on his life's work: to paint as many Native Americans as possible in their pure and "savage" state. Journeying up the Missouri River in 1832, he sketched at a feverish pace, and in 1837 he first exhibited his "Indian gallery" of 437 oil paintings and thousands of sketches of faces and customs from nearly fifty tribes.

Catlin's Indian paintings made him famous, but his romantic view of Indians as noble savages ("the Indian mind is a beautiful blank") was a double-edged sword. Catlin's admirers delighted in his portrayals of dignified Indians but shared his view that such noble creatures were "doomed" to oblivion by the march of progress.

While painters sought to preserve a passing America on canvas, landscape architects aimed at creating little enclaves of nature that might serve as sources of spiritual refreshment to harried city dwellers. Starting with the opening of Mount Auburn Cemetery near Boston in 1831, "rural" cemeteries with pastoral names such as "Harmony Grove" and "Greenwood" sprang up near major cities and quickly became tourist attractions, so much so that one orator described them as designed for the living rather than the dead. In 1858 New York City chose a plan drawn by Frederick Law Olmsted and Calvert Vaux for its proposed Central Park. Olmsted (who became the park's chief architect) and Vaux wanted the park to look as much like the countryside as possible, showing nothing of the surrounding city. A bordering line of trees screened out buildings, drainage pipes were dug to create lakes, and four sunken thoroughfares were cut across the park to carry traffic. The effect was to make Central Park an idealized version of nature, "picturesque" in that it would remind visitors of the landscapes that they had seen in pictures. Thus nature was made to mirror art.

The "Diffusion" of Knowledge

Just as Emerson contended that the democratizing spirit of his age would encourage Americans to discover their cultural identity, many of his contemporaries argued that in a democratic society, the educated had a duty to "diffuse" or spread enlightenment among the common people. Some hoped that inexpensive books and magazines would automatically bring fine literature to the masses. Reflecting on the declining cost of printed material, a clergyman concluded in 1841 that "genius sends its light into cottages." Many others, however, feared that the public would prefer the sensational penny-press fiction and the predictable sentimental novels to more elevating intellectual fare, and they pointed to the need for organized efforts to instruct and uplift American minds.

Advocates of systematic popular instruction turned not only to the public schools but also to lyceum lectures to popularize knowledge. The brainchild during the 1820s of Josiah Holbrook, an eccentric Connecticut inventor and educator, lyceums were essentially local organizations that sponsored public lectures. The topics and audiences of these lectures were diverse. In the winter of 1851–1852, for example, the lyceum in Belfast, Maine, sponsored lectures on astronomy, biology, physiology, geology, conversation, reading, the cultivation of memory, popular illusions concerning the Middle Ages, Iceland, the equality of the human condition, the true mission of women, and the domestic life of the Turks. Audiences usually included professional men, merchants, farmers, artisans, and a large number of middle-class women.

The lecturers were also a diverse lot. Prior to 1840 most were well-known locals who wished to show off their learning before admiring neighbors. But between 1840 and 1860, the spread of railroads contributed to the creation of a group of nationally known lecturers, a virtual road show of the American Renaissance. Emerson, for example, delivered some sixty lectures in Ohio alone between 1850 and 1867. Known in the 1830s as a radical and eccentric Yankee philosopher, he acquired a reputation throughout the North as a venerable sage by 1860. Another popular lecturer, the poet and world traveler Bayard Taylor, enthralled audiences everywhere with his descriptions of Arabia, Greece, Russia, and Japan. Taylor's frequent appearances in the garb of a cossack or an Arab (complete with scimitar) only heightened the effect. Tickets to lectures sold for as little as twelve cents, but so large were the crowds (up to two thousand) that some literary figures could command the then astounding fee of $125 per lecture. Most lecturers were content with more modest rewards; one stalwart of the lyceum circuit claimed that he did it for "F.A.M.E.—Fifty and My Expenses." Herman Melville, no more popular as a lecturer than as a novelist, pledged, "If they will pay expenses and give a reasonable fee, I am ready to lecture in Labrador or on the Isle of Desolation off Patagonia."

Railroads, the spread of public education, and lower costs for newspapers and books helped bring audiences and lecturers together. Newspapers, for example, announced the comings and goings of lecturers. Bayard Taylor began to receive invitations to lecture only after the public had read his published accounts of his travels. Originating in New England, lyceums expanded quickly across the northern states and made inroads into the South.

The spread of lyceums revealed a broad popular hunger for knowledge and refinement. By 1840 thirty-five hundred towns had lyceums. Yet 1840 was also the year of the log-cabin campaign, which blasted Martin Van Buren for displays of refinement as fully as Andrew Jackson's supporters had earlier gouged John Quincy Adams for being a man of learning. Americans clearly were of two minds on the subject of learning.

This ambivalence toward refined knowledge was nowhere sharper than in the West. Westerners often prided themselves on their rough ways. Western almanacs sprinkled stories of Davy Crockett and other unlettered western heroes among their weather predictions and planting advice, and some western writers fiercely resisted cultural penetration from the East. Yet the West was filled with eastern missionaries who were eager to dispel the notion that westerners were crude backwoods folk and who cultivated learning as well as Protestantism by building scores of colleges, academies, and lyceum halls. In 1800 there was only one college in what is now the Midwest; by 1850 there were nearly seventy, more than in any other region. "They drive schools along with them, as shepherds drive their flocks," clergyman Henry Ward Beecher observed of westerners. "They have herds of churches, academies, lyceums, and their religious and educational institutions go lowing along the western plains, as Jacob's herd lowed along the Syrian hills." Western newspapers sometimes railed at transplanted easterners for "namby-pamby, uptownish" lyceum lectures, but audiences still flocked to listen to emissaries of eastern refinement.

The movement to popularize knowledge bridged the cultural gap between classes but never closed it. Furthermore, the popularization of culture carried a hidden price tag. In bringing learning and art to the masses, creative thinkers had to soften their ideas. Lyceum lecturers, for example, usually avoided controversy. Even Emerson, whose early pronouncements on religion were extremely controversial, learned to pull his punches on the lyceum circuit. Although his epigrammatic style of presenting his ideas made him eminently quotable, his vagueness made it possible to quote him on both sides of most issues.

CONCLUSION

Hailed as progressive and democratic, technological advances transformed the lives of millions of Americans between 1840 and 1860. The introduction of the mechanical reaper increased wheat production and substantiated a federal official's contention in 1860 that "the ratio of increase of the principal agricultural products of the United States had more than kept pace with the increase of population." The gradual introduction of steam power reduced the vulnerability of factories to the vagaries of the weather, stretched out the employment season, and increased both productivity and annual income. The widespread introduction of coal-burning stoves not only warmed houses but, in conjunction with the spread of railroads, brought greater variety to the American diet. Technology also left an enduring mark on leisure pursuits. By bringing down the cost of printing, technical advances stimulated the rise of the penny press and the inexpensive novel, vastly increased the size of the reading public, and encouraged efforts to popularize knowledge.

Even dissenters usually directed their fire at technology's effects rather than at technology itself. Sylvester Graham wanted Americans to return to simpler lives, but he understood that vegetarianism depended on railroads to bring fresh produce into cities. The bright possibilities rather than the dark potential of technology impressed most antebellum Americans. Yet technology scarcely obliterated class and ethnic differences, nor did it quiet sectional strife. Even as the penny press and the telegraph spread throughout the nation, Americans were finding that speedier communication could not bridge their differences over slavery.

CHRONOLOGY

1820 Washington Irving, *The Sketch Book*.

Washington Irving

1823 Philadelphia completes the first urban water-supply system.
James Fenimore Cooper, *The Pioneers*.

1826 Josiah Holbrook introduces the idea for lyceums.
Cooper, *The Last of the Mohicans*.

1831 Mount Auburn Cemetery opens.

1832 A cholera epidemic strikes the United States.

1833 The *New York Sun*, the first penny newspaper, is established.

1834 Cyrus McCormick patents the mechanical reaper.

1835 James Gordon Bennett establishes the *New York Herald*.

1837 Ralph Waldo Emerson, "The American Scholar."

1841 P. T. Barnum opens the American Museum.

1842 Edgar Allan Poe, "The Murders in the Rue Morgue."

1844 Samuel F. B. Morse patents the telegraph.
The American Art Union is established.
Poe, "The Raven."

1846 W. T. G. Morton successfully uses anesthesia.

1849 Second major cholera epidemic.
Astor Place theater riot leaves twenty dead.

1850 Nathaniel Hawthorne, *The Scarlet Letter*.

Nathaniel Hawthorne

1851 Hawthorne, *The House of the Seven Gables*.
Herman Melville, *Moby-Dick*.
Erie Railroad completes its line to the West.

1852 Pennsylvania Railroad completes its line between Philadelphia and Pittsburgh.

1853 Ten small railroads are consolidated into the New York Central Railroad.

1854 Henry David Thoreau, *Walden*.

1855 Walt Whitman, *Leaves of Grass*.

1856 Pennsylvania Railroad completes Chicago link.
Illinois Central completed between Chicago and Cairo, Illinois.

1857 Baltimore–St. Louis rail service completed.

1858 Frederick Law Olmsted is appointed architect in chief for Central Park.

Frederick Law Olmsted

FOR FURTHER READING

Carl Bode, *The Anatomy of American Popular Culture, 1840–1861* (1959). A useful general survey.

Mary Kupiec Cayton, *Emerson's Emergence: Self and Society in the Transformation of New England, 1800–1845* (1989). A sensitive interpretation of the major figure in the American Renaissance.

Ann Douglas, *The Feminization of American Culture* (1977). An analysis of the role of the middle-class women and liberal ministers in the cultural sphere during the nineteenth century.

Siegfried Giedion, *Mechanization Takes Command* (1948). An interpretive overview of the impact of technology on Europe and America.

Barbara Novak, *Nature and Culture: American Landscape Painting, 1825–1875* (1982). An insightful study of the relationships between landscape painting and contemporary religious and philosophical currents.

Gwendolyn Wright, *Building the Dream: A Social History of Housing in America* (1981). An exploration of the ideologies and policies that have shaped American housing since Puritan times.

ADDITIONAL BIBLIOGRAPHY

Technology, Progress, and the Standard of Living

Ruth Schwartz Cowan, *More Work for Mother: The Ironies of Household Technology from the Open Hearth to the Microwave* (1983); Durand Echeverria, *Mirage in the West: A History of the French Image of American Society to 1815* (1957); H. J. Habakkuk, *American and British Technology in the Nineteenth Century* (1962); Dolores Hayden, *The Grand Domestic Revolution: A History of Feminist Designs for American Homes, Neighborhoods, and Cities* (1981); David A. Hounshell, *From the American System to Mass Production, 1800–1932* (1984); John F. Kasson, *Civilizing the Machine: Technology and Republican Values in America, 1776–1900* (1976); Jack Larkin, *Reshaping Everyday Life, 1790–1849* (1988); Susan Strasser, *Never Done: A History of American Housework* (1983).

Railroads

Eugene Alvarez, *Travel on Southern Antebellum Railroads, 1828–1860* (1974); Alfred D. Chandler, *The Visible Hand: The Managerial Revolution in American Business* (1977); Stewart H. Holbrook, *The Story of American Railroads* (1947); Edward C. Kirkland, *Men, Cities and Transportation: A Study in New England History, 1820–1900* (1948); Robert J. Parks, *Democracy's Railroads: Public Enterprise in Michigan* (1972); John F. Stover, *American Railroads* (1961).

Disease and Health

John D. Davies, *Phrenology: Fad and Science* (1955); John S. Haller, Jr., *American Medicine in Transition, 1840–1910* (1981); Stephen Nissenbaum, *Sex, Diet, and Debility in Jacksonian America: Sylvester Graham and Health Reform* (1980); Martin S. Pernick, *A Calculus of Suffering: Pain, Professionalism, and Anesthesia in Nineteenth-Century America* (1985); Charles Rosenberg, *The Cholera Years: The United States in 1832, 1849, and 1866* (1962); Paul Starr, *The Social Transformation of American Medicine* (1982).

Popular Culture

Richard D. Brown, *Knowledge Is Power: The Diffusion of Information in Early America, 1700–1865* (1989); Daniel A. Cohen, *Pillars of Salt, Monuments of Grace: New England Crime Literature and the Origins of American Popular Culture, 1674–1860* (1993); Ann Fabian, *Card Sharps, Dream Books, and Bucket Shops: Gambling in 19th-Century America* (1990); David Grimsted, *Melodrama Unveiled: American Theater and Culture, 1800–1850* (1968); Karen Halttunen, *Confidence Men and Painted Women: A Study in Middle-Class Culture in America, 1830–1870* (1982); Neil Harris, *Humbug: The Art of P. T. Barnum* (1973); Dan Schiller, *Objectivity and the News: The Public and the Rise of Commercial Journalism* (1981); Michael Schudson, *Discovering the News: A Social History of American Newspapers* (1978); Donald Scott, "The Popular Lecture," *Journal of American History* 66 (March 1980): 791–809; Robert C. Toll, *Blacking Up: The Minstrel Show in Nineteenth-Century America* (1974); Ronald J. Zboray, *A Fictive People: Antebellum Economic Development and the American Reading Public* (1993).

Literature

Nina Baym, *Woman's Fiction: A Guide to Novels by and About Women in America, 1820–1870* (1978); Vincent Buranelli, *Edgar Allan Poe* (1977); Mary Kupiec Cayton, *Emerson's Emergence: Self and Society in the Transformation of New England, 1800–1845* (1989); William Charvat, *The Profession of Authorship in America, 1800–1870* (edited by Matthew J. Bruccoli, 1968); David Levin, *History as Romantic Art: Bancroft, Prescott, Motley, and Parkman* (1963); Kenneth S. Lynn, *Mark Twain and Southwestern Humor* (1972); Lucy Maddox, *Removals: Nineteenth-Century American Literature and the Politics of Indian Affairs* (1991); James Mellow, *Nathaniel Hawthorne in His Time* (1980); Benjamin T. Spencer, *The Quest for Nationality: An American Literary Campaign* (1957); Tony Tanner, *The Reign of Wonder: Naiveté and Reality in American Literature* (1965); Larzer Ziff, *Literary Democracy: The Declaration of Cultural Independence in America* (1981).

Visual Arts

Elizabeth Barlow, *Frederick Law Olmsted's New York* (1972); Thomas Bender, *Toward an Urban Vision: Ideas and Institutions in Nineteenth-Century America* (1975); Albert Fein, *Frederick Law Olmsted and the Environmental Tradition* (1972); Neil Harris, *The Artist in American Society: The Formative Years, 1790–1860* (1966); Lee Clark Mitchell, *Witness to a Vanishing America* (1981); Raymond J. O'Brien, *Landscape and Scenery of the Lower Hudson Valley* (1981); Nancy Rash, *The Painting and Politics of George Caleb Bingham* (1991); Laura Wood Roper, *FLO: A Biography of Frederick Law Olmsted* (1973); Bryan J. Wolf, *Romantic Re-Vision: Culture and Consciousness in Nineteenth-Century American Painting and Literature* (1982).

**Charlotte Helen
and Her Faithful Nurse, Lydia**
1857

12

THE OLD SOUTH AND SLAVERY
1800–1860

During the winter of 1831–1832, an intense debate over the future of slavery galvanized Virginians. A slave insurrection led by Nat Turner in August 1831 aroused new anxieties, particularly among the nonslave-holding whites in the western part of the state. "What is to be done?" an editorial writer in the *Richmond Enquirer* queried. "Oh my God, I don't know, but something must be done." Plans for a gradual emancipation of slaves, one of them advanced

by Thomas Jefferson's grandson, leaped onto the state's political agenda. For a period, opponents of slavery held the initiative and protested against the institution with a fury that would have cheered antislavery northerners. Slavery, according to one Virginian, was "a mildew which has blighted in its course every region it has touched from the creation of the world." In the words of another, slavery "is ruinous to whites; retards improvements; roots out our industrious population; banishes the yeomanry from the country; and deprives the spinner, the weaver, the smith, the shoemaker, and the carpenter of employment and support." In the end, the advocates of emancipation were defeated, but only narrowly, and mainly because the state legislature was grossly malapportioned in favor of eastern slaveholders and against western nonslaveholders.

However narrow, the defeat of Virginia's emancipationists at the start of the 1830s marked a point of no return for the region known to history as the Old South. The Old South gradually took shape between the 1790s and 1860. As late as the American Revolution, *south* referred more to a direction than to a place. But by the 1850s, southerners were publishing books with titles like *Sociology for the South* and *Social Relations in Our Southern States* that took for granted the South's separate regional identity. The distinctive feature of the Old South was that it condoned slavery at a time when the institution had come under attack everywhere else in the civilized world. In 1775 slavery had known no sectional boundaries in America. However, by 1800 nearly every northern state had either abolished slavery or adopted a plan for the gradual emancipation of slaves within its borders, and Congress banned the importation of slaves in 1808. Thereafter, opposition to slavery intensified, not only in the United States, but in Europe and South America. Without too much exaggeration, Senator James Buchanan of Pennsylvania proclaimed in 1842, "All Christendom is leagued against the South upon the question of domestic slavery."

Virginians' debate over slavery in 1831–1832 underscored the internal divisions within Virginia and the South as a whole. In every southern state, nonslaveholding farmers, or yeomen, composed a majority of the white population throughout the antebellum period. Furthermore, among the states that would secede and in 1861 form the Confederate

States of America, there was a basic distinction between the Upper South (Virginia, North Carolina, Tennessee, and Arkansas) and the Lower, or Deep, South (South Carolina, Georgia, Florida, Alabama, Mississippi, Louisiana, and Texas). Socially and economically, the Upper South relied far less than the Lower South on slavery and on cotton. With varied agricultural economies based on the raising of wheat, tobacco, hemp, vegetables, and livestock, the states of the Upper South in many ways resembled the free states of the North. Politically, the Upper South approached secession far more reluctantly than the Lower South.

For all its internal variety, however, the Old South possessed strong bonds of unity that derived from slavery. The defense of slavery gradually united white opinion in the South. After reaching a climax in Virginia in 1831–1832, southern white opposition to slavery steadily weakened, and most whites came to dread the thought of a general emancipation of slaves. In the final analysis, the Upper and Lower Souths were merely parts of a single Old South, because slavery gave southern society such a distinctive cast. Although reminded by daily contact with whites of the contempt in which their race was held, blacks could do little to escape bondage. Slavery scarred all social relationships in the Old South: between blacks and whites, among whites, and even among blacks. Without slavery there never would have been an Old South.

KING COTTON

The traditional cash crops of the South declined in the late eighteenth century. That old standby tobacco, a crop notorious for depleting soil nutrients, depended on foreign markets that were essentially undependable, especially after independence stripped American trade of British protection. Tidewater Virginia, once the center of tobacco production, had dwindled economically to a shadow of its former self. North Carolina, whose soil had been depleted by tobacco, so languished that contemporaries called it the Rip Van Winkle of the Union. Rice provided the coastal region of South Carolina with a major cash crop, but it could not be grown inland. Cotton growing was also confined to seaboard areas. Indeed, in 1790 the South's population was concentrated in states bordering on the Atlantic. Three out of every four southerners lived in Maryland, Virginia, North Carolina, and South Carolina, and one out of every three in Virginia alone.

The contrast between the South of 1790 and that of 1850 was stunning. By 1850 only one out of every seven white southerners lived in Virginia. One out of every three white southerners lived in seven flourishing states (Alabama, Arkansas, Florida, Louisiana, Mississippi, Missouri, and Texas) admitted to the Union after 1800. What transformed the stagnant South of 1800 into the dynamic and bustling South of 1850? The answer, in a word, is cotton. The growth of the British textile industry in the late eighteenth

Value of Cotton Exports as a Percentage of All U.S. Exports, 1800–1860
By 1840 cotton accounted for more than half of all U.S. exports.

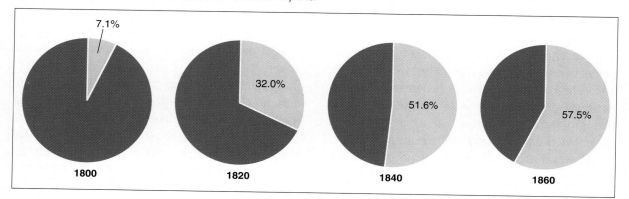

century had created a huge demand for cotton and provided a stimulus to the development of the cotton gin. The removal of the Indians (see Chapter 9) opened the way to the expansion of cotton production in new territories. Armed with cotton gins, settlers swept into Alabama and Mississippi after 1815. By 1860 Mississippi had become the leading cotton producer in the nation, and settlers had already pushed farther west, into east Texas. At its peak the cotton belt (or "Cotton Kingdom") stretched from South Carolina, Georgia, and northern Florida in the east through Alabama, Mississippi, central and western Tennessee, and Louisiana, and from there on to Arkansas and Texas.

The Lure of Cotton

To British traveler Basil Hall, it seemed that all southerners could talk about was cotton. "Every flow of wind from the shore wafted off the smell of that useful plant; at every dock or wharf we encountered it in huge piles or pyramids of bales, and our decks were soon choked with it. All day, and almost all night long, the captain, pilot, crew, and passengers were talking of nothing else." With its warm climate, wet springs and summers, and relatively dry autumns, the Lower South was especially suited to the cultivation of cotton. In contrast to the sugar industry, which thrived in southeastern Louisiana, cotton required neither expensive irrigation canals nor costly machinery. Sugar was a rich man's crop that demanded a considerable capital investment to grow and process. But cotton could be grown profitably on any scale. A cotton farmer did not even need to own a gin; commercial gins were available. Nor did a cotton farmer have to own slaves; in 1860, 35 percent to 50 percent of all farmers in the cotton belt owned no slaves. Cotton was profitable for anyone, even nonslaveholders, to grow; it promised to make poor men prosperous and rich men kings.

Although modest cotton cultivation did not require slaves, large-scale cotton growing and slavery grew together. As the southern slave population nearly doubled between 1810 and 1830, cotton employed three-fourths of all southern slaves. Owning slaves made it possible to harvest vast tracts of cotton speedily, a crucial advantage because a sudden rainstorm at harvest time could pelt cotton to the ground and soil it. Slaveholding also enabled planters to increase their cotton acreage and hence their profits.

Growth of Cotton Production and the Slave Population, 1790–1860
Cotton and slavery rose together in the Old South.

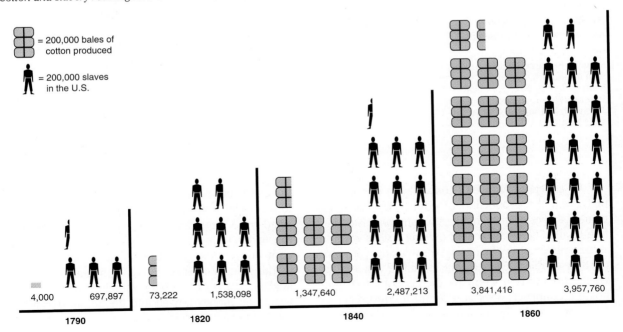

= 200,000 bales of cotton produced

= 200,000 slaves in the U.S.

| 4,000 | 697,897 | 73,222 | 1,538,098 | 1,347,640 | 2,487,213 | 3,841,416 | 3,957,760 |

| 1790 | 1820 | 1840 | 1860 |

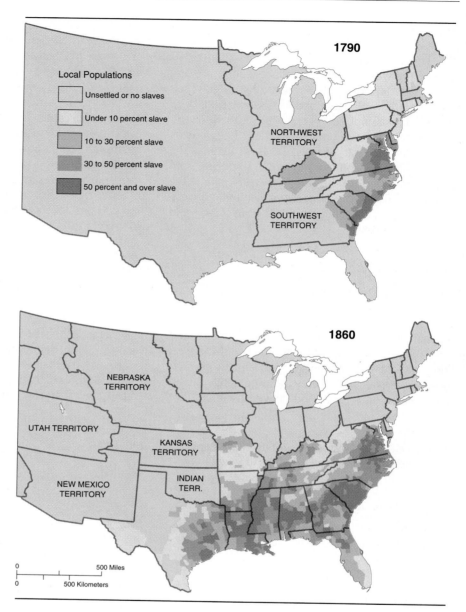

Distribution of Slaves, 1790 and 1860

In 1790 the majority of slaves resided along the southeastern seaboard. By 1860, however, slavery had spread throughout the South, and slaves were most heavily concentrated in the Deep South states.

SOURCE: Reprinted with permission of Alfred A. Knopf, Inc. from *Ordeal by Fire: The Civil War and Reconstruction* by James M. McPherson. Copyright 1982 by Alfred A. Knopf, Inc.

An added advantage of cotton lay in its compatibility with the production of corn. Corn could be planted earlier or later than cotton and harvested before or after. Since the cost of owning a slave was the same whether or not he or she was working, corn production enabled slaveholders to utilize slave labor when slaves were not employed on cotton. Nonslaveholding cotton growers also found it convenient to raise corn, and by 1860 the acreage devoted to corn in the Old South actually *exceeded* that devoted to cotton. Corn fed both families and the livestock that flourished in the South (in 1860 the region had two-thirds of the nation's hogs). From an economic standpoint, corn and cotton gave the South the best of both worlds. Fed by intense demands in Britain and New England, the price of cotton remained high, with the result that money flowed into the South. Because of southern self-sufficiency in growing corn and in raising

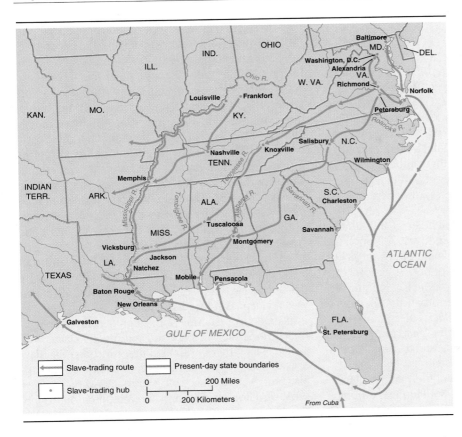

The Internal Slave Trade, 1810–1860

An internal slave trade developed after the slavetrade with Africa ended in 1808. With the growth of cotton production, farmers in the Upper South found it profitable to sell their slaves to planters in the Lower South.

hogs that thrived on the corn, money was not drained out of the region to pay for food produced in the North. In 1860 the twelve wealthiest counties in the United States were all in the South.

Ties Between the Lower and Upper South

Sugar and cotton were the main cash crops in the Lower South. The agriculture of the Upper South, founded on tobacco, hemp, wheat, and vegetables, depended far less than that of the Lower South on a few great cash crops. Yet the Upper South identified with the Lower South rather than with the agricultural regions of the free states. The reasons were social, political, and even psychological. Many settlers in states like Alabama and Mississippi had come from Upper South states like Virginia and North Carolina. All white southerners benefited from the three-fifths clause of the Constitution, which enabled them to count slaves as a basis for congressional representation. All southerners were stung by abolitionists' criti-

cisms of slavery, drawing no distinction between the Upper and Lower South. Importantly, too, economic ties linked the Upper and Lower South. The profitability of cotton and sugar in the Lower South increased the value of slaves throughout the South. Between 1790 and 1860, perhaps a million or more slaves were herded across state lines in the Old South. Roughly three-fourths of these slaves moved with their masters, whereas the remainder were sold as individuals. The sale of slaves from states with declining or stagnant plantation economies (Maryland, Virginia, and South Carolina) to those with booming economies (Alabama, Mississippi, Louisiana, Arkansas, and Texas) became a huge business. Arguing against a proposal for the gradual emancipation of slaves, Professor Thomas R. Dew of Virginia's College of William and Mary stated in 1832, "Virginia is, in fact, a *negro* raising State for other States; she produces enough for her own supply, and six thousand a year for sale." Without the sale of its slaves, Dew concluded, "Virginia will be a desert."

The North and South Diverge: Economic Patterns

The South had emerged from a slump in the last quarter of the eighteenth century to become a region of dynamic change between 1800 and 1860. But it had changed in ways that only widened the distance between it and the North. At a time when the North was rapidly urbanizing, the South remained predominantly rural. In 1820 the proportion of the southern population living in urban areas was about half that of New England and the mid-Atlantic states; by 1860 the proportion had dropped to a third.

One reason for the rural character of the South was that it contained very little industry. Although a third of the population of the United States in 1850 lived there, the South accounted for only 10 percent of the nation's manufacturing. The industrial output of the entire South in 1850 was less than that of New Hampshire and only one-third that of Massachusetts. Between 1840 and 1860, the South's share of the capital invested in American manufacturing actually *declined,* from 20 percent to 16 percent.

Yet the South had advocates of both industrialization and factories. A minority of southerners, among them editor J. D. B. De Bow of New Orleans, applauded industrialization as a way to revive the economies of older states such as Virginia and South Carolina, to retard migration to the Southwest, to reduce the South's dependency on northern manufactured products, and by proving that slavery had not transformed the South into a backwater, to quiet "the slanderous tongue of northern fanatics." Pleas for industrialization met with some success as a few large manufacturing companies took root. In South Carolina William Gregg, a prosperous Charleston jewelry merchant, zealously advocated industrialization after touring New England's textile mills in 1844. A year later, he started the Graniteville Manufacturing Company, which owned nine thousand spindles and three hundred looms by the late 1840s. Graniteville became a company town, with lumber mills, gristmills, and a machine shop as well as textile mills. In Richmond Joseph Reid Anderson guided the Tredegar Iron Works to success. By 1860 the Tredegar Works ranked fourth among the nation's largest producers of iron products, and during the Civil War, it contributed greatly to the Confederate cause. Farther southwest, Daniel Pratt constructed an industrial village near Montgomery, Alabama, in which he produced cotton textiles and ginned raw cotton.

These striking examples of industrial success in the Old South, however, do not change the general picture. Industrial output in the South ran somewhat behind that of the West and far behind that of New England and the Middle Atlantic states. Compared to factories in New England, New York, and Pennsylvania, those of the South were small; they produced mainly for nearby markets; and they were much more closely tied to agriculture. The leading northern industries turned hides into tanned leather and leather into shoes, or cotton into threads and threads into suits. In contrast, although the South had some textile and shoe factories, its leading industries were only a step removed from agriculture. They turned grain into flour, corn into meal, and trees into lumber.

If the South could develop some large and successful industries, why did it not develop more? Slavery did not in itself impede industrial growth, for slaves were widely employed in factories. In the Tredegar Iron Works, for example, Anderson overcame opposition from white workers and introduced slaves into skilled rolling-mill positions. Indirectly, however, slavery did undercut the enthusiasm of whites for industrialization. The prospect of industrial slavery troubled most slaveholders. Slaves who were hired out to factory masters in cities like New Orleans and Richmond could pass themselves off as free, and they often acted as if they were free by negotiating better working conditions and by shifting from factory to factory. The same objection applied to small rural workshops. Even rural factories drew slaves off the plantations, where discipline could be more easily enforced. A Virginia planter who rented his slaves to an iron manufacturer complained that they made money by working overtime and "got the habit of roaming about and *taking care of themselves.*"

White laborers, of course, could be employed in factories. William Gregg proved at Graniteville that supposedly unruly southern whites could be forged into a disciplined labor force. But any effort to introduce extensive industrialization faced a major problem: to raise capital for industrialization, planters would have had to sell their slaves. They had little incentive to do so. Cash crops like cotton and sugar were proven winners, whereas the benefits of industrialization remained remote and doubtful. Moreover, industrialization threatened to disrupt social relations, a southerner contended, by introducing "filthy, overcrowded, licentious factories" and by attracting antislavery white immigrants to the South. As long as southerners believed that an economy founded on

Port and City of New Orleans, *by Marie Adrien Persac, 1858*
The South's largest city, New Orleans was the main port of exit for cotton and Mississippi Valley produce. It was also a major entry port for immigrants, many of whom followed the Mississippi River north in order to avoid working in a slave society.

cash crops would remain profitable, they had little reason to leap into the uncertainties of industrialization.

The North and South Diverge: Education in a Cotton Economy

Compared to the antebellum North, the Old South made only meager provisions for public elementary schools. Flurries of enthusiasm for public education periodically swept the South, but without much effect. Southerners flatly rejected the idea of compulsory education, which was gaining ground in the North by the 1850s, and they were reluctant to tax property to support education. The idea of educating slaves in any kind of school became increasingly abhorrent to southern legislatures; indeed, lawmakers made it a crime even to teach slaves to read. Some public aid flowed to state universities and to schools for white paupers, but for most whites, the only available schools were private. As a result, white illiteracy, which

had been more extensive in the South than in the North during the eighteenth century, remained high in the South even as it declined in the North during the antebellum period. For example, nearly 60 percent of the North Carolinians who enlisted in the United States Army before the Civil War were illiterate. The comparable proportion for northern enlistees was less than 30 percent.

Various factors help explain why the South lagged behind the North in the field of public education. Because the Lower South's economy relied so heavily on cotton, state revenues rose and fell with the price of cotton, and so did legislative enthusiasm for education. In addition, the South's low population density made it difficult to provide public schools for all children. The idea of having a public school within walking distance of each child was appealing until one realized just how far each child would have to walk. But a low population density did not stop midwestern states from energetically promoting public education. The most probable reason for the South's failure to develop effective public schools was widespread indifference to the idea.

As was true of southern arguments in favor of industrialization, pro-education proclamations were bountiful, but these issued from a small segment of the leadership and often fell on deaf ears. Agricultural, self-sufficient, and independent, the middling and poor whites of the South remained unconvinced of the need for public education. They had little dependency on the printed word, few complex commercial transactions, and infrequent dealings with urban people. Even the large planters, some of whom did support public education, had a less intense commitment to it than did northern manufacturers. Whereas many northern businessmen accepted Horace Mann's argument that public schools would create a more orderly and alert work force, planters had no need for an educated white work force, for they already had a black one that they were determined to keep illiterate lest it acquire through books ideas about freedom.

Cotton and Southern Progress

Because the South diverged so sharply from the North, it is tempting to view the South as backward and lethargic, doomed to be bypassed by the more energetic northern states. Increasingly, northerners associated the spread of cities and factories with progress. Finding few cities and factories in the South, they concluded that the region was a stranger to progress as well. A northern journalist wrote of white southerners in the 1850s: "They work little, and that little, badly; they earn little, they sell little; they buy little, and they have little—very little—of the common comforts and consolations of civilized life."

Yet the white South did not lack progressive features. In 1840 per capita income in the white South was only slightly below the national average, and by 1860 it exceeded the national average. Although it is true that southerners made few contributions to technology to rival those of northerners, many southerners had a progressive zeal for agricultural improvement. The Virginian Edmund Ruffin, who allegedly touched off the Civil War by firing the first cannon on Fort Sumter in 1861 and committed suicide in despair at the South's defeat in 1865, was an enthusiastic supporter of crop rotation and of the use of fertilizer and an important figure in the history of scientific agriculture.

Rather than viewing the Old South as economically backward, it is better to see it merely as different. Cotton was a wonderful crop, and southerners could

hardly be blamed for making it their ruler. "No! You dare not make war upon cotton; no power on earth dares to make war upon it," a senator from South Carolina proclaimed in 1858. "Cotton is king."

SOCIAL RELATIONS IN THE WHITE SOUTH

Antislavery northerners often charged that slavery twisted the entire social structure of the South out of shape. By creating a permanent black underclass of bond servants, they alleged, slavery robbed lower-class whites of the incentive to work, reduced them to shiftless misery, and rendered the South a premodern throwback in an otherwise progressive age. Stung by northern allegations that slavery turned the white South into a region of rich planters and poor common folk, southerners retorted that the real center of white inequality was the North, where merchants and financiers paraded in fine silks and never soiled their hands with manual labor.

In reality, the white South was a curious mix of aristocratic and democratic, premodern and modern features. Although it contained considerable class inequality, property ownership was widespread. Rich planters occupied seats in state legislatures out of proportion to their numbers in the population, but they did not necessarily get their way, nor did their political agenda always differ from that of other whites. Practices like slaveholding and dueling not only survived but intensified in the Old South at a time when they were dying out elsewhere in the civilized world. Visitors to the South sometimes thought that they were traveling backward in time. "It seems as if everything had stopped growing, and was growing backwards," novelist Harriet Beecher Stowe wrote of the South. Yet like northerners, white southerners were restless, acquisitive, eager to make money, skillful at managing complex commercial enterprises, and when they chose, capable of becoming successful industrialists.

The Social Groups of the White South

Although all agricultural regions of the South contained slaveholders and nonslaveholders, there was considerable diversity within each group. Some slaveholders in every southern state owned vast estates, magnificent homes, and hundreds of slaves, but most lived more modestly. In 1860 one-quarter of all white families in the South owned slaves. Of these, nearly half owned fewer than five slaves, and nearly three-quarters had fewer than ten slaves. Only 12 percent owned twenty or more slaves, and only 1 percent had a hundred or more. Large slaveholders clearly were a minority within a minority. Nonslaveholders also formed a diverse group. Most were landowners whose farms drew on the labor of family members, but the South also contained nonslaveholding whites who squatted on land in the so-called pine barrens or piney woods and who scratched out a livelihood by raising livestock, hunting and fishing, and planting a few acres of corn, oats, or sweet potatoes.

Despite all the diversity, one might reasonably divide the South's social structure into four main groups—the planters, the small slaveholders, the yeomen (or family farmers), and the people of the pine barrens—although even this classification is a little arbitrary. Historians usually classify as planters those who owned twenty or more slaves, the minimum number considered necessary for specialized plantation agriculture. Yet in any group of twenty slaves, some were likely to be too old and others too young to work. Arguably, a planter needed more than twenty slaves to run a plantation. Similarly, those with fewer than twenty slaves are usually described as small slaveholders, but an obvious difference separated an individual who owned ten to nineteen slaves and one who owned fewer than five. The former was close to becoming a planter; the latter was only a step removed from a yeomen. A great deal depended on where one lived. In the low country and delta regions of the South, the planters dominated; most small slaveholders in these areas had dealings with the planters and looked to them for leadership. In the hilly upland regions, the yeomen were dominant, and small slaveholders tended to acquire their outlook.

Of course, many lawyers, physicians, merchants, and artisans, who did not fall into any of these four main groups, also made the Old South their home. But because the South was fundamentally rural and agricultural, those outside of agriculture usually identified their interests with one or another of the four agricultural groups. Rural artisans and merchants had innumerable dealings with the yeoman. Urban merchants and lawyers depended on the planters and absorbed their outlook on most issues. Similarly, slave traders relied on the plantation economy for their livelihood.

Nathan Bedford Forrest, the uneducated son of a humble Tennessee blacksmith, made a fortune as a slave trader in Natchez, Mississippi. When the Civil War broke out, Forrest enlisted in the Confederate army as a private and rose swiftly to become the South's greatest cavalry general. "That devil Forrest," the Yankees called him. Plantation slavery directed Forrest's allegiances as surely as it did those of planters like Jefferson Davis, the Confederacy's president.

Planters and Plantation Mistresses

With porticoed mansion and fields teeming with slaves, the plantation still stands at the center of the popular image of the Old South. This romanticized view, reinforced by novels and motion pictures like *Gone with the Wind,* is not entirely misleading, for the South contained plantations that travelers found "superb beyond description." Whether devoted to cotton, tobacco, rice, or sugar, the plantations were characterized by a high degree of division of labor. In the 1850s Bellmead, a tobacco plantation on Virginia's James River, was virtually an agricultural equivalent of a factory village. Its more than one hundred slaves were classified into the domestic staff (butlers, waiters, seamstresses, laundresses, maids, and gardeners), the pasture staff (shepherds, cowherds, and hog drivers), outdoor artisans (stonemasons and carpenters), indoor artisans (blacksmiths, carpenters, shoemakers, spinners, and weavers), and field hands. Such a division of labor was inconceivable without abundant slaves and land. Wade Hampton's cotton plantation near Columbia, South Carolina, encompassed twenty-four hundred acres. With such resources, it is not surprising that large plantations could generate incomes that contemporaries viewed as immense ($20,000–$30,000 a year).

During the first flush of settlement in the piedmont and trans-Appalachian South, in the eighteenth century, most well-off planters had been content to live in simple log cabins. In contrast, between 1810 and 1860, elite planters often vied with each other to build stately mansions. Some, like Lyman Hardy of Mississippi, hired architects. Hardy's "Auburn," built in 1812 near Natchez, featured Ionic columns and a portico thirty-one feet long and twelve feet deep. Others copied designs from books like Andrew Jackson Downing's *The Architecture of Country Houses* (1850), which sold sixteen thousand copies between 1850 and 1865.

However impressive, these were not typical planters. The wealth of most planters, especially in

Colonel and Mrs. James A. Whiteside, Son Charles and Servants,
by James A. Cameron, c. 1858–1859
*This portrait captures the patriarchy as well as the graciousness that whites associated with
the ideal plantation. Not only the slave waiter and nurse but the planter's wife appear over-
shadowed by the master's presence.*

states like Alabama and Mississippi, consisted primarily
in the value of their slaves rather than in such finery as
expensive furniture or silver plate. In monetary terms,
slaves were worth a great deal, as much as seventeen
hundred dollars for a field hand in the 1850s. Planters
could convert their wealth into cash for purchasing luxuries only by selling slaves. A planter who sold his
slaves ceased to be a planter and relinquished the
South's most prestigious social status. Not surprisingly,
most planters clung to large-scale slaveholding, even if
it meant scrimping on their life-styles. A northern journalist observed that in the Southwest, men worth millions lived as if they were not worth hundreds.

Planters had to worry constantly about profitability, for the fixed costs of operating plantations—including hiring overseers, housing and feeding slaves, and

maintaining cotton gins and other equipment—were
considerable. Their drive for profits led planters to
search constantly for more and better land, to organize
their slaves into specialized work gangs for maximum
efficiency, and to make their plantations self-sufficient
in food. Their quest for profits also impelled planters to
cultivate far-flung commercial connections. Like any
commodity, cotton went up and down in price. Sometimes the fluctuations were long term; more often, the
price fluctuated seasonally. In response to these rises
and falls, planters assigned their cotton to commercial
agents in cities. These agents held the cotton until the
price was right and extended credit to enable the
planters to pay their bills before the cotton was sold.
Thus indebtedness became part of the plantation economy. Persistent debt intensified the planters' quest for

more profits to escape from the burden of debt. Planters enjoyed neither repose nor security.

Plantation agriculture placed psychological strains as well as economic burdens on planters and their wives. Frequent moves disrupted circles of friends and relatives, all the more so because migration to the Southwest carried families into progressively less settled, more desolate areas. In 1850 those regions of the South with thriving plantation economies—notably Alabama, Mississippi, and southeastern Louisiana—had only recently emerged from the frontier stage.

For plantation women, migration to the Southwest often amounted to a fall from grace, for many of them had grown up in seaboard elegance, only to find themselves in isolated regions, surrounded by slaves, and bereft of the companionship of white social peers. "I am sad tonight, sickness preys on my frame," wrote a bride who moved to Mississippi in 1833. "I am alone and more than 150 miles from any near relative in the wild woods of an Indian nation." At times wives lacked even their husbands' companionship. Plantation agriculture kept men on the road, scouting new land for purchase, supervising outlying plantations, and transacting business in New Orleans or Memphis.

Planters and their wives found various ways to cope with their isolation from civilized society. Many spent long periods of time in cities and left the management of plantations to overseers. In 1850 fully one-half the planters in the Mississippi Delta were absentees living in or near Natchez or New Orleans rather than on their plantations. Yet in 1850 only 30 percent of planters with a hundred or more slaves employed white overseers; the majority managed their own estates. In response, many made plantation life more sociable by engaging in lavish hospitality. But hospitality imposed enormous burdens on plantation wives, who might have to entertain as many as fifteen people for breakfast and attend to the needs of visitors who stayed for days. Indeed, in the plantation economy, wives had even less leisure than their husbands. Aside from raising their own children and caring for guests, plantation mistresses supervised house slaves, made carpets and clothes, looked after outlying buildings like smokehouses and dairies, and planted garden fruits and vegetables. Plantation women were anything but the delicate idlers of legend. In the absence of their husbands or fathers, they frequently kept the plantation accounts.

Among the greatest sorrows of some plantation mistresses was the presence of the mulatto children, who stood as daily reminders of their husbands' infidelity. Mary Boykin Chesnut, an astute Charleston woman and famous diarist, commented, "Any lady is ready to tell you who is the father of all the mulatto children in everybody's household but her own. These, she seems to think, drop from clouds." Insisting on sexual purity for white women, southern men followed a looser standard for themselves. After the death of his wife, the brother of the famous abolitionist sisters Sarah and Angelina Grimké fathered three mulatto children. The gentlemanly code usually tolerated such transgressions as long as they were not paraded in public—but at times, even if they were. Richard M. Johnson of Kentucky, the man who allegedly killed Tecumseh during the War of 1812, was elected vice president of the United States in 1836 despite having lived openly for years with his black mistress.

The isolation, drudgery, and humiliation that planters' wives experienced turned very few against the system. When the Civil War came, they supported the Confederacy as enthusiastically as any group. However much they might hate living as white islands in a sea of slaves, they recognized no less than their husbands that their wealth and position depended on slavery.

The Small Slaveholders

In 1860, 88 percent of all slaveholders owned fewer than twenty slaves, and most of these possessed fewer than ten slaves. Some slaveowners were not even farmers: one out of every five was employed outside of agriculture, usually as a lawyer, physician, merchant, or artisan.

As a large and extremely diverse group, small slaveholders experienced conflicting loyalties and ambitions. In the upland regions, they absorbed the outlook of yeomen (nonslaveowning family farmers), the numerically dominant group. Typically, small upland slaveholders owned only a few slaves and rarely aspired to become large planters. In contrast, in the low country and delta regions, where planters formed the dominant group, small slaveholders often aspired to planter status. In these planter-dominated areas, someone with ten slaves could realistically look forward to the day when he would own thirty. The deltas were thus filled with ambitious and acquisitive individuals who linked success to owning more slaves. Whether one owned ten slaves or fifty, the logic of slaveholding was much the same. The investment in slaves could be justified only by setting them to work on profitable crops. Profitable crops demanded, in turn, more and better land. Much like the planters, the small slaveholder of the low country and delta areas were restless and footloose.

The social structure of the deltas was fluid but not infinitely so. Small slaveholders were usually younger than large slaveholders, and many hoped to become planters in their own right. But as the antebellum period wore on, a clear tendency developed toward the geographical segregation of the small slaveholders from the planters in the cotton belt. Small slaveholders led the initial push into the cotton belt in the 1810s and 1820s, whereas the large planters, reluctant to risk transporting their hundreds of slaves into the still turbulent new territory, remained in the seaboard South. Gradually, however, the large planters ventured into Alabama and Mississippi. Colonel Thomas Dabney, a planter originally from tidewater Virginia, made several scouting tours of the Southwest before moving his family and slaves to the region of Vicksburg, Mississippi, where he started a four-thousand-acre plantation. The small slaveholders already on the scene at first resented Dabney's genteel manners and misguided efforts to win friends. He showed up at house raisings to lend a hand, but the hands he lent were not his own, which remained gloved, but those of his slaves. The small slaveholders muttered about transplanted Virginia snobs. Dabney responded to complaints simply by buying up much of the best land in the region. In itself, this was no loss to the small slaveholders. They had been first on the scene, and it was their land that the Dabneys of the South purchased. Dabney and men like him quickly turned the whole region from Vicksburg to Natchez into one of large plantations. The small farmers took the proceeds from the sale of their land, bought

more slaves, and moved elsewhere to grow cotton. Small slaveholders gradually transformed the region from Vicksburg to Tuscaloosa, Alabama, into a belt of medium-size farms with a dozen or so slaves on each.

The Yeomen

Nonslaveholding family farmers, or yeomen, composed the largest single group of southern whites. Most were landowners. Landholding yeomen, because they owned no slaves of their own, frequently hired slaves at harvest time to help in the fields. In an area where the land was poor, like eastern Tennessee, the landowning yeomen were typically subsistence farmers, but most grew some crops for the market. Whether they engaged in subsistence or commercial agriculture, they controlled landholdings far more modest than those of the planters—more likely in the range of fifty to two hundred acres than five hundred or more acres. Yeomen could be found anywhere in the South, but they tended to congregate in the upland regions. In the seaboard South, they populated the piedmont region of Georgia, South Carolina, North Carolina, and Virginia; in the Southwest they usually lived in the hilly upcountry, far from the rich alluvial soil of the deltas. A minority of yeomen did not own land. Typically young, these men resided with and worked for landowners to whom they were related.

The leading characteristic of the yeomen was the value that they attached to self-sufficiency. As non-

Ye Southern Planter, *1838*
Although they aspired to be leisured gentlemen and live in mansions, most planters resided in modest dwellings and actively managed their estates.

slaveholders, they were not carried along by the same logic that impelled slaveholders to acquire more land and plant more cash crops. Although most yeomen raised cash crops, relative to planters, they devoted a higher proportion of their acreage to subsistence crops like corn, sweet potatoes, and oats than to cash crops. The ideal of the planters was profit with modest self-sufficiency; that of the yeomen, self-sufficiency with modest profit.

Yeomen dwelling in the low country and delta regions dominated by planters were often dismissed as "poor white trash." But in the upland areas, where they constituted the dominant group, the yeomen were highly respectable. There they coexisted peacefully with the slaveholders, who typically owned only a few slaves (large planters were rare in the upland areas). Both the small slaveholders and the yeomen were essentially family farmers. With or without the aid of a few slaves, fathers and sons cleared the land and plowed, planted, and hoed the fields. Wives and daughters planted and tended vegetable gardens, helped at harvest, occasionally cared for livestock, cooked, and made clothes for the family.

In contrast to the far-flung commercial transactions of the planters, who depended on distant commercial agents to market their crops, the economic transactions of yeomen usually occurred within the neighborhood of their farms. Yeomen often exchanged their cotton, wheat, or tobacco for goods and services from local artisans and merchants. In some areas they sold their surplus corn to the herdsmen and drovers who made a living in the South's upland regions by specializing in the raising of hogs. Along the French Broad River in eastern Tennessee, some twenty thousand to thirty thousand hogs were fattened for market each year; at peak season, a traveler would see a thousand hogs a mile. When driven to market, the hogs were quartered at night in huge stock stands, veritable hog "hotels," and fed with corn supplied by the local yeomen.

The People of the Pine Barrens

One of the most controversial groups in the Old South comprised independent whites of the wooded "pine barrens." In a region marked by slaveholding, widespread landownership, and agriculture, these people stood out as deviants. Composing about 10 percent of southern whites, they were neither slaveholders nor (as a rule) landowners nor primarily farmers.

Rather, they typically put up crude cabins, cleared a few acres of surrounding land (on which they usually squatted), planted some corn between tree stumps, and grazed hogs and cattle in the woods. Their simple diet—cornmeal and pork supplemented by fish and game—did not differ much from that of the yeomen or slaves. But their way of life was different. They did not raise cash crops, nor did they engage in the daily routine of orderly work that marked family farmers. With their ramshackle houses and handful of stump-strewn acres, they appeared to be lazy and shiftless.

Antislavery northerners cited the people of the pine barrens as proof that slavery degraded nonslaveholding whites. A southern defender of slavery, Daniel R. Hundley, summarized the antislavery argument: "Look at the Poor Whites of the South, . . . and behold the fruits of slavery." Then he attacked the argument. The pine barrens folk were poor, he conceded, but unlike the paupers of the northern cities, they could fend for themselves. Hundley's contention was well founded. The people of the pine barrens acquired a degree of self-sufficiency to which the South's climate and customs contributed. Mild winters made it possible to graze livestock in the woods for much of the year. Furthermore, the South retained the legal tradition (rapidly being dismantled in the antebellum North) of treating unfenced and unimproved land as available for public use. Despite complaints, the people of the pine barrens (along with many yeomen) hunted on land belonging to others as long as it was neither enclosed nor improved.

The economic independence of the pine barrens dwellers shaped their attitudes toward work. The men were reluctant to hire themselves out as farm laborers, and even when they did, they refused to perform "slave" tasks like caring for cattle and fetching wood and water. The women had similar attitudes. They might sew or quilt on hire, but they refused to become servants.

It is misleading to think of these people as victimized or oppressed. Many lived in the pine barrens out of choice. The grandson of a farmer who had migrated from Emanuel County, Georgia, to the Mississippi pine barrens explained his grandfather's motives in these words: "The truth is it looks like Emanuel County. The turpentine smell, the moan of the winds through the pine trees, and nobody within fifty miles of him, [were] too captivating . . . to be resisted, and he rested there."

Conflict and Consensus in the White South

Planters tangled with yeomen on several issues in the Old South. With their extensive economic dealings and need for credit, planters and their urban commercial allies inclined toward the Whig party, which was generally more sympathetic to banking and economic development. Cherishing their self-sufficiency, and economically independent, the yeomen tended to be Democrats.

The occasions for conflict between these groups were minimal, however, and an underlying political unity reigned in the South. Especially in the Lower South, each of the four main social groups—planters, small slaveholders, yeomen, and pine barrens people—tended to cluster in different regions. The delta areas that planters dominated contained relatively small numbers of yeomen. In other regions small slaveowners, families with ten to fifteen slaves, predominated. In the upland areas far from the deltas, the yeomen congregated. And the people of the pine barrens lived in a world of their own. There was more geographical intermingling of groups in the Upper South than in the Lower, but throughout the South each group attained a degree of independence from the others. With widespread landownership and relatively few factories, the Old South basically was not a place where whites worked for other whites, and this tended to minimize friction among whites.

In addition, the white South's political structure was sufficiently democratic to prevent any one social group from gaining exclusive control over politics. It is true that in both the Upper and the Lower South, the majority of state legislators were planters. Large planters, those with fifty or more slaves, were represented in legislatures far out of proportion to their numbers in the population. Yet these same planters owed their election to the popular vote. The white South was affected by the same democratic currents that swept northern politics between 1815 and 1860, and the newer states of the South had usually entered the Union with democratic constitutions that included universal white manhood suffrage—the right of all adult white males to vote.

Although yeomen often voted for planters, the nonslaveowners did not issue their elected representatives a blank check to govern as they pleased. During the 1830s and 1840s, Whig planters who favored banks faced intense and often successful opposition from Democratic yeomen. These yeomen blamed banks for the Panic of 1837 and pressured southern legislatures to restrict bank operations. On banking issues, nonslaveholders got their way often enough to nurture their belief that they ultimately controlled politics and that slaveholders could not block their goals.

Conflict over Slavery

Nevertheless, there was considerable potential for conflict between the slaveholders and nonslaveholders. The white carpenter who complained in 1849 that "unjust, oppressive, and degrading" competition from slave labor depressed his wages surely had a point. Between 1830 and 1860, slaveholders gained an increasing proportion of the South's wealth while declining as a proportion of its white population. The size of the slaveholding class shrank from 36 percent of the white population in 1831 to 31 percent in 1850 to 25 percent in 1860. A Louisiana editor warned in 1858 that "the present tendency of supply and demand is to concentrate all the slaves in the hands of the few, and thus excite the envy rather than cultivate the sympathy of the people." That same year, the governor of Florida proposed a law guaranteeing to each white person the ownership of at least one slave. Some southerners began to support the idea of Congress's reopening the African slave trade to increase the supply of slaves, bring down their price, and give more whites a stake in the institution.

As the debate over slavery in Virginia during 1831–1832 (see this chapter's introduction) attests, slaveholders had good reasons for uncertainty over the allegiance of nonslaveholders to the "peculiar institution" of slavery. The publication in 1857 of Hinton R. Helper's *The Impending Crisis of the South*, which called upon nonslaveholders to abolish slavery in their own interest, revealed the persistence of white opposition to slavery. On balance, however, slavery did not create profound and lasting divisions between the South's slaveholders and nonslaveholders. Although antagonism to slavery flourished in parts of Virginia up to 1860, proposals for emancipation dropped from the state's political agenda after 1832. In Kentucky, a state with a history of antislavery activity that dated back to the 1790s, calls for emancipation were revived in 1849 in a popular referendum. But the pro-emancipation forces went down to crushing defeat. Thereafter, the continuation of slavery ceased to be a political issue in Kentucky and elsewhere in the South.

The rise and fall of pro-emancipation sentiment in the South raises a key question. Since the majority of white southerners were nonslaveholders, why did they not attack the institution more consistently? To look ahead, why were so many of them to fight ferociously and die bravely during the Civil War in defense of an institution in which they appeared not to have had any real stake? There are various answers to these questions. First, some nonslaveholders hoped to become slaveholders. Second, most simply accepted the racist assumptions upon which slavery rested. Whether slaveholders or nonslaveholders, white southerners dreaded the likelihood that emancipation might encourage "impudent" blacks to entertain ideas of social equality with whites. Blacks might demand the right to sit next to whites in railroad cars and even make advances to white women. "Now suppose they [the slaves] was free," a white southerner told a northern journalist in the 1850s, "you see they'd all think themselves just as good as we; of course they would if they was free. Now just suppose you had a family of children, how would you like to hev a niggar steppin' up to your darter?" Slavery, in short, appealed to whites as a legal, time-honored, and foolproof way to enforce the social subordination of blacks. Finally, no one knew where the slaves, if freed, would go or what they would do. After 1830 a dwindling minority of northerners and southerners still dallied with the idea of colonizing freed blacks in Africa, but that alternative increasingly seemed unrealistic in a society where slaves numbered in the millions. Without colonization, southerners concluded, emancipation would produce a race war. In 1860 Georgia's governor sent a blunt message to his constituents, many of them nonslaveholders: "So soon as the slaves were at liberty thousands of them would leave the cotton and rice fields . . . and make their way to the healthier climate of the mountain region [where] we should have them plundering and stealing, robbing and killing." There was no mistaking the conclusion. Emancipation would not merely deprive slaveholders of their property, it would jeopardize the lives of nonslaveholders.

The Proslavery Argument

Between 1830 and 1860, as slaveholders and nonslaveholders closed ranks behind slavery, southern intellectuals constructed a defense of the institution as a positive good rather than a necessary evil. Some found defenses of slavery in the Bible, especially in St. Paul's order that servants obey their masters. Others, including the Virginian George F. Holmes, tried to establish slavery as both an ancient and a progressive institution by noting that the slave society of ancient Athens had produced Plato and Aristotle and that Roman slaveholders had laid the basis of Western civilization. Another Virginian, George Fitzhugh, turned the tables on antislavery northerners by contrasting the plight of northern "wage slaves"—white factory workers—with the conditions of black slaves in the South. Whereas northern mill owners discarded wage earners when they were too old or too sick to work, Fitzhugh argued, southern masters gave continuous care to their slave property, attending to their health, clothing, and discipline.

But as they sought to establish slavery's congruence with humanitarian and progressive impulses, southerners increasingly suppressed open discussion of slavery within the South. In the 1830s southerners seized and burned abolitionist literature mailed to the South. In Kentucky the abolitionist editor Cassius Marcellus Clay positioned two cannons and a powder keg to protect his press, but in 1845 a mob dismantled it anyway. By 1860 any southerner found with a copy of Helper's *The Impending Crisis* had every reason to fear for his life.

The rise of the proslavery argument coincided with a shift in the position of the southern churches on slavery. During the 1790s and early 1800s, some Protestant ministers had assailed slavery as immoral. By the 1830s, however, most members of the clergy had convinced themselves that slavery was not only compatible with Christianity but also necessary for the proper exercise of the Christian religion. Like the proslavery intellectuals, clergymen contended that slavery provided the opportunity to display Christian responsibility toward one's inferiors, and it helped blacks develop Christian virtues like humility and self-control. With this conclusion solidified, southerners increasingly attacked antislavery evangelicals in the North for disrupting the allegedly superior social arrangement of the South. In 1844 the Methodist Episcopal church split into northern and southern wings. In 1845 Baptists formed a separate Southern Convention. Even earlier, southerners and conservative northerners had combined in 1837 to drive the antislavery New School Presbyterians out of that denomination's

THE NEGRO IN HIS OWN COUNTRY.

THE NEGRO IN AMERICA.

Proslavery propagandists contrasted what they believed to be the black's African savagery with the blessings of civilization on an American plantation.

main body. All this added up to a profound irony. In 1800 southern evangelicals had been more critical of slavery than southerners as a whole. Yet the evangelicals effectively seceded from national church organizations long before the South seceded from the Union.

HONOR AND VIOLENCE IN THE OLD SOUTH

Almost everything about the Old South struck northern visitors as extreme. Although inequality certainly flourished in the North, no group in northern society was as deprived as the slaves. The Irish immigrants who arrived in the North in great waves in the 1840s often owned no property, but unlike the slaves, they were not in themselves a form of property. Not only did northerners find the gap between the races in the South extreme, but individual southerners seemed to run to extremes. One minute they were hospitable and gracious; the next, savagely violent. Abolitionists were not the only ones to view the Old South as a land of extremes. "The Americans of the South," Alexis de Tocqueville asserted, "are brave, comparatively ignorant, hospitable, generous, easy to irritate, violent in their resentments, without industry or the spirit of enterprise."

Violence in the White South

No one who lived in a southern community, a northern journalist noted in the 1850s, could fail to be impressed with "the frequency of fighting with deadly weapons." Throughout the colonial and antebellum periods, violence deeply colored the daily lives of white southerners. In the 1760s a minister described backcountry Virginians "biting one anothers Lips and Noses off, and gowging one another—that is, thrusting out anothers Eyes, and kicking one another on the Cods [genitals], to the Great damage of many a Poor Woman." In the 1840s a New York newspaper described a fight between two raftsmen on the Mississippi that started when one accidentally bumped the other into shallow water. When it was over, one raftsmen was dead; the other boasted, "I can lick a steamboat. My fingernails is related to a sawmill on my mother's side, . . . and the brass buttons on my coat have all been boiled in poison." Gouging out eyes became a specialty of sorts among poor whites. On one occasion, a South Carolina judge entered his court to find a plaintiff, a juror, and two witnesses all missing one eye. Stories of eye gougings and ear bitings lost nothing in the telling and became part of the folklore of the Old South. Mike Fink, a legendary southern fighter and hunter, boasted that he was so mean that in infancy, he refused his mother's milk and cried out for a bottle of whiskey. Yet beneath the folklore lay the reality of violence that gave the Old South a murder rate as much as ten times higher than that of the North.

The Code of Honor and Dueling

At the root of most violence in the white South lay intensified feelings of personal pride that themselves reflected the inescapable presence of slaves. Every day of their lives, white southerners saw slaves who were degraded, insulted, and powerless to resist. This experience had a searing impact on whites, for it encouraged them to react violently to even trivial insults in order to demonstrate that they had nothing in common with slaves. Among gentlemen this exaggerated pride took the form of a code of honor. In this context, honor can best be defined as an extraordinary sensitivity to one's reputation, a belief that one's self-esteem depends on the judgment of others. In the antebellum North, moralists celebrated a rival ideal, character—the quality that enabled an individual to behave in a steady fashion regardless of how others acted toward him or her. A person possessed of character acted out of the promptings of conscience. In contrast, in the honor culture of the Old South, the slightest insult, as long as it was perceived as intentional, could become the basis for a duel (see "A Place in Time").

Formalized by British and French officers during the Revolutionary War, dueling gained a secure niche in the Old South as a means by which gentlemen dealt with affronts to their honor. To outsiders, the incidents that sparked duels seemed so trivial as to be scarcely credible: a casual remark accidentally overheard, a harmless brushing against the side of someone at a public event, even a hostile glance. Yet dueling did not necessarily terminate in violence. Dueling constituted part of a complex code of etiquette that governed relations among gentlemen in the Old South and, like all forms of etiquette, called for a curious sort of self-restraint. Gentlemen viewed dueling as a refined alternative to the random violence of lower-class life. The code of dueling did not dictate that the insulted party leap at his antagonist's throat or draw his pistol at the perceived moment of insult. Rather, he was to remain cool, bide his time, settle on a choice of weapons, and agree to a meeting place. In the interval, negotiations between friends of the parties sought to clear up the "misunderstanding" that had evoked the challenge. In

this way, most confrontations ended peaceably rather than on the field of honor at dawn.

Although dueling was as much a way of settling disputes peaceably as of ending them violently, the ritual could easily terminate in a death or maiming. Dueling did not allow the resolution of grievances by the courts, a form of redress that would have guaranteed a peaceful outcome. As a way of settling personal disputes that involved honor, recourse to the law struck many southerners as cowardly and shameless. Andrew Jackson's mother told the future president, "The law affords no remedy that can satisfy the feelings of a true man."

In addition, dueling rested on the assumption that a gentleman could recognize another gentleman and hence would know when to respond to a challenge. Nothing in the code of dueling compelled a gentleman to duel someone beneath his status, because such a person's opinion of a gentleman hardly mattered. An insolent porter who insulted a gentleman might get a whipping but did not merit a challenge to a duel. Yet it was often difficult to determine who was a gentleman. The Old South teemed with pretentious, would-be gentlemen. A clerk in a country store in Arkansas in the 1850s found it remarkable that ordinary farmers who hung around the store talked of their honor and that the store's proprietor, a German Jew, kept a dueling pistol.

The Southern Evangelicals and White Values

With its emphasis on the personal redress of grievances and its inclination toward violence, the ideal of honor had a potential for conflict with the values preached by the southern evangelical churches, notably the Baptists, Methodists, and Presbyterians. These evangelical denominations were on the rise even before the Great Kentucky Revival of 1800–1801 and continued to grow in the wake of the revival. With just forty-eight thousand southern members in 1801, for example, the Methodists reported eighty thousand by 1807. All of the evangelical denominations stressed humility and self-restraint, virtues that stood in contrast to the entire culture of show and display that buttressed the extravagance and violence of the Old South.

Prior to 1830 most southern gentlemen looked down on the evangelicals as uncouth fanatics, and even after 1830 evangelical values scarcely dominated the South's white leadership. But evangelicals gradually shed their image as illiterate backwoods people by

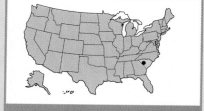

Edgefield District, South Carolina, in the Antebellum Era

L ocated on the western edge of South Carolina near the Georgia border, Edgefield District combined features of the aristocratic low country, to which it was linked by the Savannah River, and the yeoman-dominated upland regions of the Old South. Most Edgefield whites were small farmers or agricultural workers. In 1860 a majority did not own any slaves, and a sizable minority had no land. Yet the invention of the cotton gin had attracted wealthy low-country planters to Edgefield, and by 1860 the district had become the state's leading cotton producer. These planters formed the nucleus of the district's elite. By 1860 the wealthiest 10 percent of white heads of household in Edgefield controlled 57 percent of the district's real and personal property. Intermarriage strengthened ties within the elite. By the Civil War, the leading families, among them the Butlers, Bonhams, Brookses, Simkinses, and Pickenses, had intermarried.

Black slaves were the basis of upper-crust Edgefield's wealth. By 1860 slaves outnumbered whites by 50 percent in the district. The vast majority of Edgefield's black bond servants were field slaves. Almost all of those dwelling on the great plantations worked under the "gang" system, by which they were divided into a number of groups, each performing a specified amount of work. (The gang system stood in contrast to the "task" system, in which individual slaves carried out designated chores.) The plantations' "plow gangs" comprised strong young men and occasionally some women, whereas "hoe gangs" generally included elderly slaves and women. A small number of Edgefield's slaves were skilled artisans who did blacksmithing and carpentry on the district's omnipresent farms. Whether field hands or skilled artisans, most slaves lived with their families in simple, rude one-room cabins in close prox-

Pierce Mason Butler
A leading Edgefield politician, Butler was befriended early in his career by John Calhoun, who secured an army commission for him. Joining Calhoun in the early 1830s in support of nullification, Butler was elected governor of South Carolina in 1836. He led the Palmetto regiment in the Mexican War and was killed in action in 1847.

Francis Wilkinson Pickens
Pickens came to Edgefield to study and practice law. A relative of Calhoun, he favored nullification. Elected governor of South Carolina just before its secession from the Union in 1860, Pickens once said that "before a free people can be dragged into a war, it must be in defense of great national right as well as national honor."

Presentation Sword and Ceramic Jar

*Decorative arts in Edgefield ranged from this presentation sword owned by
P. M. Butler, which symbolized the valor and military honor associated with
the role of the southern planter class, to slave-made pottery such as this jar
produced in one of the district's ten or so clayworks. Wheel-thrown and
painted with alkaline glazes, the jar gets its distinctive appearance from
having been taken from the kiln while red-hot and then thrust into a pit of
pine needles.*

imity to the dwellings of other slaves. An Edgefield black born into slavery in 1852 recalled that the slaves "had houses of weatherboards, big enough for [a] chicken coop—man, wife, and chillun [live] dere."

Only one-quarter of Edgefield's whites owned twenty or more of such slaves in 1860. This elite minority accounted for possession of nearly two-thirds of the district's slaves. Using their slaves not only as agrarian workers but as collateral for loans, the great planters agreed with John C. Calhoun's northern-bred son-in-law Thomas Green Clemson—the owner of the Edgefield plantation called Canebreak—that "slaves are the most valuable property in the South, being the basis of the whole southern fabric." Yet despite the yawning gap between the wealth of the planters and the income of most other whites, class conflict did not convulse antebellum Edgefield's white society, which as a whole was tightly unified. Verbal assaults on "aristocrats" did sweep through the district from time to time, but lawyers (whom the people treated with suspicion because they did not work with their hands) rather than planters bore the brunt of these attacks.

Religion contributed mightily to this harmony reigning within Edgefield's white society. Indeed, religion was at the core of both family life and community life in the district and significantly molded the world view of the people. Although many churches dotted the countryside, so dispersed was Edgefield's population—the district contained only two incorporated towns—that ministers were limited. Thus devout Episcopalian planters and zealous Baptist yeomen farmers often found themselves sitting side by side listening to whatever traveling preacher had happened through their neighborhood. As a further boon to white solidarity, Edgefield's small farmers depended on the plantation lords to gin and market their cotton, and during the harvest they often rented slaves from the great planters. Nonslaveholding yeomen were likelier than small slaveowners to be dissatisfied with their lot in life, and many moved west into the states of Georgia, Alabama, Mississippi, and Louisiana rather than stay and complain about the rich. Nearly 60 percent of Edgefield's white heads of household in 1850 no longer resided in the district in 1860.

The code of honor further unified the whites. Like southern gentlemen elsewhere, Edgefield's male elite saw affronts to honor behind every bush. Two military officers once fought a duel because one questioned the other's chess moves. Louis Wigfall, an Edgefield planter who later served as a Confederate senator from Texas and who was rumored to be "half drunk all the time," posted signs denouncing as cowards those who refused to accept his innumerable challenges to duels. Yet however much the code of honor set individual against individual, it could unify a region. For example, in 1856 Preston Brooks, a U.S. congressman from Edgefield, brutally caned Massachusetts senator Charles Sumner on the Senate floor after Sumner had delivered an antislavery oration that dealt roughly with one of Brooks's relatives. As Representative Brooks later wrote to his constituents, it was not just the honor of a relative that he sought to defend. Rather, he had set himself up as a "sentinel" guarding the honor of every white South Carolinian against the slanderous tongues of northerners. By the mid-1850s growing attitudes like this were demonstrating that the battle lines clearly had been drawn between southerners and northerners. The time seemed to be fast approaching when, as Edgefield newspaper editor Arthur Simkins observed, southern planters' "rich blessings . . . inherited from a virtuous ancestry" would lead them to band together to strongly oppose "mobocratic tendencies in American society" flourishing in the Northeast's "larger cities and more populous manufacturing towns."

founding colleges like Randolph Macon (Methodist, 1830) and Wake Forest (Baptist, 1838) and by exhorting pious women, who composed two-thirds of the membership of evangelical churches, to make every home "a sanctuary, a resting place, a shadow from the heats, turmoils, and conflicts of life, and an effectual barrier against ambition, envy, jealousy, and selfishness." During the 1830s evangelical values and practices like revivalism began to penetrate even the Episcopal church, the denomination long preferred by the gentry.

Southern evangelicals rarely attacked honor as such, but they railed against dueling, brawling, intemperance, and gambling and, in the words of a Georgia woman, the *"Revenge, Ambition, Pride"* that undergirded these practices. By the 1860s the South contained many Christian gentlemen like the bible-quoting Presbyterian general Thomas J. "Stonewall" Jackson, fierce in a righteous war but a sworn opponent of strong drink, the gaming table, and the duel.

◆

LIFE UNDER SLAVERY

Slavery, the institution that lay at the root of the code of honor and other distinctive features of the Old South, has long inspired controversy among historians. Some have portrayed slavery as a benevolent institution in which blacks lived contentedly under kind masters; others, as a cruel and inhuman system that drove slaves into constant rebellion. Neither view is accurate, but both contain a germ of truth. There were kind masters who accepted the view expressed by a Baptist minister in 1854: "Give your servants that which is just and equal, knowing that you also have a Master in heaven." Moreover, some slaves developed genuine affection for their masters. Yet slavery was an inherently oppressive institution that forcefully appropriated the life and labor of one race for the material benefit of another. Despite professions to the contrary by apologists for slavery, the vast majority of slaveholders exploited the labor of blacks to earn a profit. Kind masters might complain about cruel overseers, but the masters hired and paid the overseers to get as much work as possible out of blacks. When the master of one plantation chastised his overseer for "barbarity," the latter replied, "Do you not remember what you told me the time you employed me that [if] I failed to make you good crops I

would have to leave?" Indeed, kindness was a double-edged sword, for the benevolent master came to expect grateful affection from his slaves and then interpreted that affection as loyalty to the institution of slavery. In fact, blacks felt little, if any, loyalty to slavery. When northern troops descended upon plantations during the Civil War, masters were dismayed to find many of their most trusted slaves deserting to Union lines.

Although the kindness or cruelty of masters made some difference to slaves, the most important determinants of their experiences under slavery depended on such impersonal factors as the kind of agriculture in which they were engaged, whether they resided in rural or urban areas, and whether they lived in the eighteenth or nineteenth century. The experiences of slaves working on cotton plantations in the 1830s differed drastically from those of slaves in 1700, for reasons unrelated to the kindness or brutality of masters.

The Maturing of the Plantation System

Slavery changed significantly between 1700 and 1830. In 1700 the typical slave was a young man in his twenties who had recently arrived aboard a slave ship from Africa or the Caribbean and worked in company with other recent arrivals on isolated small farms. Drawn from different African regions and cultures, few such slaves spoke the same language. Because commercial slave ships contained twice as many men as women, and because slaves were widely scattered, blacks had difficulty finding sexual partners and creating a semblance of family life. Furthermore, as a result of severe malnutrition, black women who had been brought to North America on slave ships bore relatively few children. Thus the slave trade had a devastating effect on natural increase among blacks. Without importations, the number of slaves in North America would have declined between 1710 and 1730.

In contrast, by 1830 the typical North American slave was as likely to be female as male, had been born in America, spoke a form of English that made possible communication with other slaves, and worked in the company of numerous other slaves on a plantation. The key to the change lay in the rise of plantation agriculture in the Chesapeake and South Carolina during the eighteenth century. Plantation slaves had an easier time finding mates than those on the remote farms of the early 1700s. As the ratio between slave men and women fell into balance, marriages occurred with increasing frequency between slaves on the same or nearby plantations. The native-born slave population rose after 1730 and soared after 1750. Importations of African slaves gradually declined after 1760, and Congress banned them in 1808.

Work and Discipline of Plantation Slaves

In 1850 the typical slave experience was to work on a large farm or plantation with at least ten fellow bond servants. Almost three-quarters of all slaves that year were owned by masters with ten or more slaves, and just over one-half lived in units of twenty or more slaves. To understand the daily existence of the typical antebellum slave, then, requires an examination of the work and discipline routines common on large-scale farming operations.

The day of antebellum plantation slaves usually began an hour before sunrise with the sounding of a horn or bell. After a sparse breakfast, slaves marched to the fields. A traveler in Mississippi described a procession of slaves on their way to work. "First came, led by an old driver carrying a whip, forty of the largest and strongest women I ever saw together; they were all in a simple uniform dress of bluish check stuff, the skirts reaching little below the knee; their legs and feet were bare; they carried themselves loftily, each having a hoe over the shoulder, and walking with a free, powerful swing." Then came the plow hands, "thirty strong, mostly men, but few of them women. . . . A lean and vigilant white overseer, on a brisk pony, brought up the rear."

As this account indicates, slave men and women worked side by side in the fields. Female slaves who did not labor in the fields scarcely idled their hours away. A former slave, John Curry, described how his mother milked cows, cared for the children whose mothers worked in the fields, cooked for field hands, did the ironing and washing for her master's household, and took care of her own seven children. Plantations never lacked tasks for slaves of either gender. As former slave Solomon Northup noted, "ploughing, planting, picking cotton, gathering the corn, and pulling and burning stalks, occupies the whole of the four seasons of the year. Drawing and cutting wood, pressing cotton, fattening and killing hogs, are but incidental labors." Regardless of the season, the slave's day stretched from dawn to dusk. Touring the South in the 1850s, Frederick Law Olmsted prided himself on rising early and riding late but added, "I always found the negroes in the field when I first looked out, and generally had to wait for the negroes to come from the field to have my horse fed when I stopped for the night." When darkness made field work impossible, slaves toted cotton bales to the ginhouse, gathered up wood for supper fires, and

Black Women and Men on a Trek Home, South Carolina
Much like northern factories, large plantations made it possible to impose discipline and order on their work force. Here black women loaded down with cotton join their men on the march home after a day in the fields.

fed the mules. Weary from their labors, they slept in log cabins on wooden planks. "The softest couches in the world," a former bondsman wryly observed, "are not to be found in the log mansions of a slave."

Although virtually all antebellum Americans worked long hours, no laboring group experienced the same combination of long hours and harsh discipline as did slave field hands. Northern factory workers did not have to put up with drivers who, like one described by Olmsted, walked among the slaves with a whip, "which he often cracked at them, sometimes allowing the lash to fall lightly upon their shoulders." The lash did not always fall lightly. The annals of American slavery contain stories of repulsive brutality. Pregnant slave women were sometimes forced to lie in depressions in the ground and endure whipping on their backs, a practice that supposedly protected the fetus while abusing the mother. The disciplining and punishment of slaves was often left to white overseers and black drivers rather than to masters. "Dat was de meanest devil dat ever lived on the Lord's green earth," a former Mississippi slave said of his driver. The barbaric discipline meted out by others twinged the conscience of many a master. But even masters who professed Christianity viewed the disciplining of slaves as a priority— indeed, as a Christian duty to ensure the slaves' proper "submissiveness." The black abolitionist Frederick Douglass, once a slave, recalled that his worst master had been converted at a Methodist camp meeting. "If religion had any effect on his character at all," Douglass related, "it made him more cruel and hateful in all his ways."

Despite the relentless, often brutal discipline, plantation agriculture gave a minority of slaves opportunities for advancement, not from slavery to freedom but from unskilled and exhausting field work to semi-skilled or skilled indoor work. Some slaves developed skills like blacksmithing and carpentry and learned to operate cotton gins. Others were trained as cooks, butlers, and dining-room attendants. These house slaves became legendary for their arrogant disdain of field hands and poor whites. The legend often distorted the reality, for house slaves were as subject to discipline as field slaves. "I liked the field work better than I did the house work," a female slave recalled. "We could talk and do anything we wanted to, just so we picked the cotton." Such sentiments were typical, but skilled slave artisans and house servants were greatly valued and treated accordingly; they occupied higher rungs than field hands on the social ladder of slavery.

The Slave Family

Masters thought of slaves as naturally promiscuous and flattered themselves into thinking that they alone held slave marriages together. Masters did have an incentive to encourage slave marriages in order to bring new slaves into the world and to discourage slaves from running away. Some masters baked wedding cakes for slaves and later arbitrated marital disputes. James Henry Hammond, the governor of South Carolina and a large slaveholder, noted in his diary how he "flogged Joe Goodwyn and ordered him to go back to his wife. Ditto Gabriel and Molly and ordered them to come together. Separated Moses and Anny finally."

Yet this picture of benevolent masters holding together naturally promiscuous slaves is misleading. The keenest challenge to the slave family came not from the slaves themselves but from slavery. The law provided neither recognition of nor protection for the slave family. Although some slaveholders were reluctant to break slave marriages by sale, such masters could neither bequeath this reluctance to their heirs nor avoid economic hardships that might force them to sell off slaves. The reality, one historian has calculated, was that on average, a slave would witness in a lifetime the sale of eleven family members.

Naturally, the commonplace buying and selling of slaves severely disrupted the slaves' attempts to create a stable family life. Poignant testimony to the effects of sale on slave families, and to the desire of slaves to remain near their families, was provided by an advertisement for a runaway slave in North Carolina in 1851. The advertisement described the fugitive as presumed to be "lurking in the neighborhood of E. D. Walker's, at Moore's Creek, who owns most of his relatives, or Nathan Bonham's who owns his mother; or, perhaps, near Fletcher Bell's, at Long Creek, who owns his father." Small wonder that a slave preacher pronounced a slave couple married "until death or *distance* do you part."

Aside from their disruption by sale, slave families experienced separations and degradations from other sources. The marriage of a slave woman gave her no protection against the sexual demands of a master nor, indeed, of any white. The slave children of white masters at times became targets of the wrath of white mistresses. Sarah Wilson, the daughter of a slave and her white master, remembered that as a child, she was "picked on" by her mistress until the master ordered his wife to let Sarah alone because she "got big, big

The Land of the Free and The Home of the Brave, *by Henry Byam Martin, 1833 White southerners could not escape the fact that much of the Western world loathed their "peculiar institution." In 1833, when a Canadian sketched this Charleston slave auction, Britain abolished slavery in the West Indies.*

blood in her." Slave women who worked in the fields usually were separated from their children by day; young sons and daughters often were cared for by the aged or by the mothers of other children. When slave women took husbands from nearby (rather than their own) plantations, the children usually stayed with the mother. Hannah Chapman remembered that her father tried to visit his family under cover of darkness "because he missed us and us longed for him." But if his master found him, "us would track him the nex' day by de blood stains."

Despite enormous obstacles, the relationships within slave families were often intimate and, where possible, long-lasting. In the absence of legal protection, slaves developed their own standards of family morality. A southern white woman observed that slaves "did not consider it wrong for a girl to have a child before she married, but afterwards were extremely severe upon anything like infidelity on her part." When given the opportunity, slaves sought to solemnize their marriages before clergymen. White clergymen who accompanied the Union army into Mississippi and Louisiana in the closing years of the Civil War conducted thousands of marriage rites for slaves who had long viewed themselves as married and who now desired a formal ceremony and registration.

Although slaves tried to solemnize their marriage vows in the same fashion as whites, the slave family did not merely copy the customs of white families. In white families, for example, the parent-child bond overrode all others; slaves, in contrast, emphasized ties between children and their grandparents, uncles, and aunts as well as parents. Such broad kinship ties

marked the West African cultures from which many slaves had originally been brought to America, and they were reinforced by the separations between children and one or both parents that routinely occurred under slavery. Frederick Douglass never knew his father and saw his mother infrequently, but he vividly remembered his grandmother, "a good nurse, and a capital hand at making nets for catching shad and herring." In addition, slaves often created "fictive" kin networks; in the absence of uncles and aunts, they simply named friends their uncles, aunts, brothers, or sisters. In effect, slaves invested non-kin relations with symbolic kin functions. In this way, they helped protect themselves against the involuntary disruption of family ties by forced sale and established a broader community of obligation. When plantation slaves greeted each other as "brudder," they were not making a statement about actual kinship but about obligations they felt for each other. Apologists for slavery liked to argue that a "community of interests" bound masters and slaves together. In truth, the real community of interests was the one that slaves developed among themselves in order to survive.

The Longevity, Diet, and Health of Slaves

In general, slaves in the United States reproduced faster and lived longer than slaves elsewhere in the Western Hemisphere. The evidence comes from a compelling statistic. In 1825, 36 percent of all slaves in the Western Hemisphere lived in the United States, whereas Brazil accounted for 31 percent. Yet of the 10 million to 12 million African slaves who had been imported to the New

World between the fifteenth and nineteenth centuries, only some 550,000 (about 5 percent) had come to North America, whereas 3.5 million (nearly 33 percent) had been taken to Brazil. Mortality had depleted the slave populations of Brazil and the Caribbean to a far greater extent than in North America.

Several factors account for the different rates between the United States on the one hand and Brazil and the Caribbean on the other. First, the gender ratio among slaves equalized more rapidly in North America, encouraging earlier and longer marriages and more children. Second, because growing corn and raising livestock were compatible with cotton cultivation, the Old South produced plenty of food. The normal ration for a slave was a peck of cornmeal and three to four pounds of fatty pork a week. Slaves often supplemented this nutritionally unbalanced diet with vegetables grown in small plots that masters allowed them to farm and with catfish and game. In the barren winter months, slaves ate less than in the summer; in this respect, however, they did not differ much from most whites.

As for disease, slaves had greater immunities to both malaria and yellow fever than did whites, but they suffered more from cholera, dysentery, and diarrhea. In the absence of privies, slaves usually relieved themselves behind bushes; urine and feces washed into the sources of drinking water and caused many diseases. Yet slaves developed some remedies that, though commonly ridiculed by whites, were effective against stomach ailments. For example, the slaves' belief that eating white clay would cure dysentery and diarrhea rested on a firm basis, for we know now that kaolin, an ingredient of white clay, is a remedy for these ailments.

Although slave remedies were often more effective than those of white physicians, slaves experienced higher mortality rates than whites. At any age, a slave faced a shorter life than a white, but most strikingly in infancy. Rates of infant mortality for slaves were at least twice those of whites. Between 1850 and 1860, fewer than two out of three black children survived to the age of ten. Whereas the worst mortality occurred on plantations in disease-ridden, low-lying areas, pregnant, overworked field hands often miscarried or gave birth to weakened infants even in healthier regions. Masters allowed pregnant women to rest, but rarely enough. "Labor is conducive to health," a Mississippi planter told a northern journalist; "a healthy woman will rear most children."

Slaves off Plantations

Although plantation agriculture gave some slaves, especially males, opportunities to acquire specialized skills, it imposed a good deal of supervision on them. The greatest opportunities for slaves were reserved for those who worked off plantations and farms, either as laborers in extractive industries like mining and lumbering or as artisans in towns and cities. Because the lucrative cotton growing attracted so many whites onto small farms, a perennial shortage of white labor plagued almost all the nonagricultural sectors of the southern economy. As a consequence, there was a steady demand for slaves to drive wagons, to work as stevedores (ship-cargo handlers) in port cities, to man river barges, and to perform various tasks in mining and lumbering. In 1860 lumbering employed sixteen thousand workers, most of them slaves who cut trees, hauled them to sawmills, and fashioned them into useful lumber. In sawmills black engineers fired and fixed the steam engines that provided power. In iron-ore ranges and ironworks, slaves not only served as laborers but occasionally supervised less skilled white workers. In addition, just as mill girls composed the labor force of the booming textile industry in New England, slave women and children worked in the South's fledgling textile mills.

Behind all of this were some basic, long-standing features of southern society. Even before the rise of cotton, the profitability of southern cash crops like rice and indigo had pulled white labor out of towns and cities and indirectly provided considerable scope for slaves to work as skilled artisans. In the eighteenth century, cities like Charleston and Savannah had a large class of highly skilled slave blacksmiths and carpenters. This tradition continued into the next century and affected both enslaved and free blacks. Whether slave or free, blacks generally found it easier to work in skilled occupations in southern cities than in northern cities during the antebellum period. Not only did tradition open up skilled crafts to blacks, but the South did not attract the same flow of immigrant labor to compete with blacks as did the North.

As a result, despite slavery's stranglehold on black society, some southern blacks had opportunities in cities that were denied to blacks in northern cities. For the most part, enslaved blacks who worked in factories or in extractive industries like lumbering and mining were not owned by their employers. Rather, they were hired out by their rural masters to urban employers. If conditions in factories or mines deteriorated to the point where slaves grew ill or died, rural masters would refuse to provide urban employers with more slaves. So it was in the interest of white supervisors to keep conditions of work for slaves off the plantations at a tolerable level. Watching the loading of a steamboat with cotton bales, Frederick Law Olmsted was amazed to see slaves sent to the top of the bank to roll the bales down to Irishmen who stowed them on the ship. Asking the reason for this arrangement, Olmsted was told, "The niggers are worth too much to be risked here; if the Paddies [Irish] are knocked overboard, or get their backs broke, nobody loses anything."

Life on the Margin: Free Blacks in the Old South

Free blacks were more likely than southern blacks in general to live in cities. In 1860 one-third of the free blacks in the Upper South and more than half in the Lower South were urban.

The relatively specialized economies of the cities provided free people of color with opportunities to become carpenters, coopers (barrel makers), barbers, and even small traders. A visitor to an antebellum southern market would find that most of the meat, fish, vegetables, and fruit had been prepared for sale by free blacks. Urban free blacks formed their own fraternal orders and churches; a church run by free blacks was often the largest house of worship in a southern city. In New Orleans free blacks had their own literary journals and opera. In Natchez a free black barber, William Tiler Johnson, invested the prof-

its of his shop in real estate, acquired stores that he rented out, purchased slaves and a plantation, and even hired a white overseer.

As Johnson's career suggests, some free blacks were highly successful. But free blacks were always vulnerable in southern society and became more so as the antebellum period wore on. Although free blacks continued to increase in absolute numbers (a little more than a quarter-million free people of color dwelled in the South in 1860), the rate of growth of the free black population slowed after 1810. Between 1790 and 1810, this population had more than tripled, to 108,265. The reason for the slowdown after 1810 was that fewer southern whites were setting slaves free. Until 1820 masters with doubts about the rightness of slavery frequently manumitted (freed) their black mistresses and mulatto children, and some set free their entire work forces. In the wake of the Nat Turner rebellion in 1831 (see below), laws restricting the liberties of free blacks were tightened. During the mid-1830s, for example, most southern states made it a felony to teach blacks to read and write. Every southern state forbade free blacks to enter that state, and in 1859 Arkansas ordered all free blacks to leave.

So although a free black culture flowered in cities like New Orleans and Natchez, that culture did not reflect the conditions under which most free blacks lived. Free blacks were tolerated in New Orleans, in part because there were not too many of them. A much higher percentage of blacks were free in the Upper South than in the Lower South. Furthermore, although a disproportionate number of free blacks lived in cities, the majority lived in rural areas, where whites lumped them together with slaves. Even a successful free black like William Tiler Johnson

Street Scene
Early New Orleans contained a large population of free blacks. Note the contrast here between the woman on the right wearing a slave collar and the well-dressed free black on the left.

could never dine or drink with whites. When Johnson attended the theater, he sat in the colored gallery.

The position of free blacks in the Old South contained many contradictions. So did their minds. As the offspring, or the descendants of offspring, of mixed liaisons, a disproportionate number of free blacks had light brown skin. Some of them were as color-conscious as whites and looked down on "darky" field hands and coal-black laborers. Yet as whites' discrimination against free people of color intensified during the late antebellum period, many free blacks realized that such a future as they had was as blacks, not as whites. Feelings of racial solidarity grew stronger among free blacks in the 1850s, and after the Civil War, the leaders of the freed slaves were usually blacks who had been free before the war.

Slave Resistance

The Old South contained the seeds of organized slave insurrections. In the delta areas of the Lower South,

Black Society in the Old South, c. 1860
Slaves greatly outnumbered free blacks in the Old South. Most slaves were owned by masters with ten or more slaves.

SOURCES: *Eighth Census of the United States, 1860: Population by Age, Sex, Race;* and Lewis C. Gray, *History of Agriculture in the Southern United States* (New York: Kelley, 1933).

Slaves in groups of 10 – 99 (60.5%)

Slaves in groups of 1 – 9 (24.1%)

Slaves in groups of 100 or more (9.4%)

Free (6%)

Free (6%)

Slaves (94%)

(For all states in which slavery was legal in 1860)

where blacks outnumbered whites, enslaved blacks experienced continuous forced labor on plantations and communicated their bitterness to each other in the slave quarters. Free blacks in the cities could have provided leadership for rebellions. Rumors of slave conspiracies flew around the southern white community, and all whites knew of the massive black insurrection that had destroyed French rule in Santo Domingo.

Yet only three organized rebellions occurred in the Old South, and taken together, they illustrate more the futility than the possibility of a slave insurrection. In 1800 Virginia slave Gabriel Prosser's planned slave uprising was betrayed by other slaves, and Prosser and his followers were executed. That same year, a South Carolina slave, Denmark Vesey, won fifteen hundred dollars in a lottery and bought his freedom. Purchasing a carpentry shop in Charleston and becoming a preacher at that city's African Methodist Episcopal church, Vesey built a cadre of dedicated black followers, including a slave of the governor of South Carolina and a black conjurer named Gullah Jack. In 1822 they devised a plan to attack Charleston and seize all the city's arms and ammunition, but they were betrayed by other slaves and executed.

The Nat Turner rebellion, which occurred in 1831 in Southampton County, Virginia, was the only one of the three slave insurrections to result in the death of whites. Gloomy and introspective by nature, Nat Turner taught himself to read and write in childhood and became a prodigious reader of the Bible. He gained recognition from slaves as a preacher of electrifying sermons delivered in woodland clearings or in the shacks where slaves gathered to hear "real preachin'." Soon he added a reputation for visions and prophecy; he told, for example, of seeing white and black angels warring in the sky. Yet for all his gifts—a white later said that Turner had "a mind capable of attaining anything"—Turner's life was one of onerous field work, punctuated by a sale that separated him from his wife and that reminded him that whites measured his value only in cash.

In 1831 Turner's conviction of the injustice of slavery, intensified by his reading of the Bible and by his own experiences, boiled over. Slaves who had long venerated him as a prophet now took him as their "general." In August he set out with a handful of slaves armed with axes and clubs. Gathering recruits as they moved from plantation to plantation, Turner and his followers killed all white men, women, and children they encountered. Before the rebellion was suppressed and Turner hanged, fifty-five whites had been slain, a number roughly equal to Turner's force at its peak strength.

Turner's rebellion stunned the South. In the widely circulated *Confessions of Nat Turner*, which Turner dictated to a white lawyer while awaiting execution, Turner's steadfast belief in the justice of his cause flashed again. When asked, "Do you not find yourself mistaken now?," Turner replied, "Was not Christ crucified?" In company with the earlier slave uprising in Santo Domingo, Turner's rebellion convinced white southerners of the ever-present threat of a slave insurrection. Yet neither the Turner rebellion nor the Prosser and Vesey plots ever had a chance of success. The latter two were conspiracies that never got off the ground. During the Turner rebellion, several slaves alerted their masters to the threat, less out of loyalty to slavery than from a correct assessment of Turner's chances. Despite constant fears of slave rebellion, the Old South experienced far less in the way of organized rebellion than did the Caribbean region and South America.

Why is this so? First, although slaves formed a majority in South Carolina and a few other states, they did not constitute a *large* majority in any state. Second, in contrast to the Caribbean, an area of absentee landlords and sparse white population, the white presence in the Old South was formidable, and the whites had all the guns and soldiers. The rumors of slave conspiracies that periodically swept the white South demonstrated to blacks the promptness with which whites could muster forces and mount slave patrols. Third, the development of family ties among slaves made them reluctant to risk death and leave their children parentless. Finally, blacks who ran away or plotted rebellions had no allies. Southern Indians routinely captured runaway slaves and exchanged them for rewards; some Indians even owned slaves.

Short of rebellion, slaves could try to escape to freedom in the North. Perhaps the most ingenious, Henry Brown, induced a friend to ship him from Richmond to Philadelphia in a box and won immediate fame as "Box" Brown. Some light mulattoes passed as whites. More often, fugitive slaves borrowed, stole, or forged passes from plantations or obtained papers describing them as free. Frederick Douglass borrowed a sailor's papers in making his escape from Baltimore to New York City in 1838. Some former slaves, among them Harriet Tubman and Josiah Henson, made repeated trips back to the South to help other slaves escape. These sundry methods of escape fed the legend of the "Underground Railroad," supposedly an organized network of safe houses owned by white abolitionists who spirited blacks to freedom. In reality, fugitive slaves owed very little to abolitionists. Some white sympathizers in border states did provide safe houses for blacks, but these houses were better known to watchful slave catchers than to most blacks.

Escape to freedom was a dream rather than an alternative for most blacks; out of millions of slaves, probably fewer than a thousand escaped to the North. Yet slaves often ran away from masters, not to escape to freedom but to visit spouses or avoid punishment. Most runaways remained in the South; indeed, some returned to former, kinder masters. During the eighteenth century, African slaves had often run away in groups to the interior and sought to create self-sufficient colonies or villages of the sort that they had known in Africa. But once the United States had acquired Florida, long a haven for runaways, few uninhabited places remained in the South to which slaves could escape.

Despite poor prospects for permanent escape, slaves could disappear for prolonged periods into the free black communities of southern cities. Because whites in the Old South depended so heavily on black labor, slaves enjoyed a fair degree of practical freedom to drive wagons to market and to come and go when they were off plantations. Slaves hired out or sent to a city might overstay their leave and even pass themselves off as free. The experience of slavery has sometimes been compared to the experience of prisoners in penitentiaries or on chain gangs, but the analogy is misleading. The supervision that slaves experienced was sometimes intense (for example, when working at harvest time under a driver), but often lax; it was irregular rather than consistent.

The fact that antebellum slaves frequently enjoyed some degree of practical freedom did not change the underlying oppressiveness of slavery. But it did give slaves a sense that they had certain rights on a day-to-day basis, and it helped to deflect slave resistance into forms that were essentially furtive rather than open and violent. Theft was so common that planters learned to keep their tools, smokehouses, closets, and trunks under lock and key. Overworked field hands might leave valuable tools out to rust, or

St. Catherine's Island, Georgia, Slave Quarters
Judged by their whitewashed exteriors, these slave cabins attached to a large cotton plantation belonged to the better class of slave housing, which did not differ much from the accommodations available to the white working class. Southern agricultural periodicals advised the regular white-washing of slave cabins as a health measure. But the quality of slave cabins varied and most fell below this standard.

feign illness, or simply refuse to work. As an institution, slavery was vulnerable to such tactics; unlike free laborers, slaves could not be fired for negligence or malingering. Frederick Law Olmsted found slaveholders in the 1850s afraid to inflict punishment on slaves "lest the slave should abscond, or take a sulky fit and not work, or poison some of the family, or set fire to the dwelling, or have recourse to any other mode of avenging himself."

Olmsted's reference to arson and poisoning reminds us that not all furtive resistance was peaceful. Arson and poisoning, both common in African culture as forms of vengeance, were widespread in the Old South, and the fear of each was even more so. Masters afflicted by dysentery and similar ailments never knew for sure that they had not been poisoned.

Arson, poisoning, work stoppages, and negligence were alternatives to violent rebellion. Yet these furtive forms of resistance differed from rebellion. The goal of rebellion was freedom from slavery. The goal of furtive resistance was to make slavery bearable. The kind of resistance that slaves usually practiced sought to establish customs and rules that would govern the conduct of masters as well as that of slaves without challenging the institution of slavery as such. Most slaves would have preferred freedom but settled for less. "White folks do as they please," an ex-slave said, "and the darkies do as they can."

THE EMERGENCE OF AFRICAN-AMERICAN CULTURE

A distinctive culture emerged among blacks in the slave quarters of antebellum plantations. This culture drew on both African and American sources, but it was more than a mixture of the two. Enslaved blacks gave a distinctive twist to the American as well as African components of their culture.

The Language of Slaves

Before slaves could develop a common culture, they had to be able to communicate with each other. During the colonial period, verbal communication among slaves had often been difficult, for most slaves had been born in Africa, which contained an abundance of cultures and languages. The captain of a slave ship noted in 1744,

> As for the languages of Gambia [in West Africa], they are so many and so different that the Natives on either Side of the River cannot understand each other; which, if rightly consider'd, is no small happiness to the Europeans who go thither to trade for slaves.

In the pens into which they were herded before shipment and on the slave ships themselves, however, Africans developed a "pidgin"—that is, a language that has no native speakers but in which people with different native languages can communicate. Pidgin is not unique to black people. When Tarzan announced, "Me Tarzan, you Jane," he was speaking English pidgin. Nor is English pidgin the only form of pidgin; slaves that were sent to South America developed Spanish and Portuguese pidgins.

Many of the early African-born slaves learned English pidgin poorly or not at all, but as American-born slaves came to compose an increasingly large proportion of all slaves, English pidgin took root. Indeed, it became the only language most slaves knew. Like all pidgins, this was a simplified language. Slaves usually dropped the verb *to be* (which had no equivalent in African tongues) and either ignored or confused genders. Instead of saying "Mary is in the cabin," they said, "Mary, he in cabin." To negate, they substituted *no* for *not,* saying, "He no wicked." English pidgin

Reed Basket, *1860*
A Florida slave artisan used traditional African skills in making this basket.

contained several African words. Some, like *banjo,* became part of standard English; others, like *goober* (peanut), became part of southern white slang. Although they picked up pidgin terms, whites ridiculed field hands' speech. Some slaves, particularly house servants and skilled artisans, learned to speak standard English but had no trouble understanding the pidgin of field hands. However strange pidgin sounded to some, it was indispensable for communication among slaves.

African-American Religion

The development of a common language marked the first step in the forging of African-American culture. No less important was the religion of the slaves.

Africa contained rich and diverse religious customs and beliefs. Some of the early slaves were Muslims; a few had acquired Christian beliefs either in Africa or in the New World. But the majority of the slaves transported from Africa were neither Muslims nor Christians but rather worshipers in one of many native African religions. Most of these religions, which whites lumped together as heathen, drew little distinction between the spiritual and material worlds. Any event or development, from a storm to an earthquake or an illness, was assumed to stem from supernatural forces. These forces were represented by God, by spirits that inhabited the woods and waters, and by the spirits of ancestors. In addition, the religions of West Africa, the region from which most American slaves originally came, attached special significance to water, which suggested life and hope.

The majority of the slaves brought to America in the seventeenth and eighteenth centuries were young men who may not have absorbed much of this religious heritage before their enslavement. In any case, Africans differed from each other in their specific beliefs and practices. For these reasons, African religions could never have unified blacks in America. Yet some Africans probably clung to their beliefs during the seventeenth and eighteenth centuries, a tendency made easier by the fact that whites undertook few efforts before the 1790s to convert slaves to Christianity. Furthermore, dimly remembered African beliefs such as the reverence for water may have predisposed slaves to accept Christianity when they were finally urged to do so, because water had a symbolic significance for Christians, too, in the sacrament of baptism. The Christianity preached to slaves by Methodist and Baptist revivalists during the late eighteenth and nineteenth centuries, moreover, resembled African religions in that Christianity also drew few distinctions between the sacred and the secular. Just as Africans believed that a crop-destroying drought or a plague resulted from supernatural forces, the early revivalists knew in their hearts that every drunkard who fell off his horse and every Sabbath-breaker struck by lightning had experienced a deliberate and direct punishment from God.

By the 1790s blacks formed about a quarter of the membership of the Methodist and Baptist denominations. Yet masters continued to fear that a Christianized slave would be a rebellious slave. Converted slaves in fact played a significant role in each of the three major slave rebellions in the Old South. The leaders of Gabriel Prosser's rebellion in 1800 used the Bible to prove that slaves, like the ancient Israelites, could prevail against overwhelming numbers. Denmark Vesey read the Bible, and most of the slaves executed for joining his conspiracy belonged to Charleston's African Methodist church. Nat Turner was both a preacher and a prophet.

Despite the "subversive" impact of Christianity on some slaves, however, these uprisings, particularly the Nat Turner rebellion, actually stimulated Protestant missionaries to intensify their efforts to convert slaves. Missionaries pointed to the self-taught Turner to prove

that slaves would hear about Christianity in any event and that organized efforts to convert blacks were the only way to ensure that slaves learned correct versions of Christianity, which emphasized obedience rather than rebellion. Georgia missionary and slaveholder Charles Colcock Jones reassuringly told white planters of the venerable black preacher who, upon receiving some abolitionist tracts in the mail, promptly turned them over to the white authorities for destruction. A Christian slave, the argument ran, would be a better slave rather than a bitter slave. For whites, the clincher was the split of the Methodists, Baptists, and Presbyterians into northern and southern wings by the mid-1840s. Now, they argued, it had finally become safe to convert slaves, for the churches had rid themselves of their antislavery wings. Between 1845 and 1860, the number of black Baptists doubled.

The experiences of Christianized blacks in the Old South illustrate many of the contradictions of life under slavery. Urban blacks often had their own churches, but in the rural South, where the great majority of blacks lived, slaves worshiped in the same churches as whites. Although the slaves sat in segregated sections, they heard the same sermons and sang the same hymns as whites. Some black preachers actually developed followings among whites, and Christian masters were sometimes disciplined by biracial churches for abusing Christian slaves in the same congregation. The churches were, in fact, the most interracial institutions in the Old South. Yet none of this meant that Christianity was an acceptable route to black liberation. Ministers went out of their way to remind slaves that spiritual equality was not the same as civil equality. The effort to convert slaves gained momentum only to the extent that it was becoming certain that Christianity would not change the basic inequality of southern society.

Although they listened to the same sermons as whites, slaves did not necessarily draw the same conclusions. It was impossible to Christianize the slaves without telling them about the Chosen People, the ancient Jews whom Moses led from captivity in Pharaoh's Egypt into the Promised Land of Israel. Inevitably, slaves drew parallels between their own condition and the Jews' captivity. Like the Jews, blacks concluded, they themselves were "de people of de Lord." If they kept the faith, then, like the Jews, they too would reach the Promised Land. The themes of the Chosen People and the Promised Land ran through the sacred songs, or "spirituals," that blacks sang, to the point where Moses and Jesus almost merged:

> *Gwine to write to Massa Jesus,*
> *To send some Valiant Soldier*
> *To turn back Pharaoh's army, Hallelu!*

A listener could interpret a phrase like "the Promised Land" in several ways; it could refer to Israel, to heaven, or to freedom. From the perspective of whites, the only permissible interpretations were Israel and heaven, but some blacks, like Denmark Vesey, thought of freedom as well. The ease with which slaves constructed alternative interpretations of the Bible also reflected the fact that many plantations contained black preachers, slaves trained by white ministers to spread Christianity among blacks. When in the presence of masters or white ministers, these black preachers usually just repeated the familiar biblical command, "Obey your master." Often, however, slaves met for services apart from whites, usually on Sunday evenings but during the week as well. Then the message changed. A black preacher in Texas related how his master would say "tell them niggers iffen they obeys the master they goes to Heaven." The minister quickly added, "I knowed there's something better for them, but I daren't tell them 'cept on the sly. That I done lots. I tells 'em iffen they keep praying, the Lord will set 'em free."

Some slaves privately interpreted Christianity as a religion of liberation from the oppression of slavery, but most recognized that their prospects for freedom were slight. On the whole, Christianity did not turn them into revolutionaries. Neither did it necessarily turn them into model slaves. It did, however, provide slaves with a view of slavery different from their masters' outlook. Where the masters argued that slavery was a benign and divinely ordained institution in blacks' best interests, Christianity told them that slavery was really an affliction, a terrible and unjust institution that God had allowed in order to test their faith. For having endured slavery, he would reward blacks. For having created it, he would punish masters.

Black Music and Dance

Compared to the prevailing cultural patterns among elite whites, the culture of blacks in the Old South was extremely expressive. In religious services, blacks shouted "Amen" and let their bodily movements reflect their feelings long after white religious observances, some of which had once been similarly expressive, had grown sober and sedate. Frederick Law Olmsted recorded how, during a slave service in New Orleans during the 1850s, parishioners "in indescribable expression of ecstasy" exclaimed every few moments: "Glory! oh yes! yes!—sweet Lord! sweet Lord!"

Slaves also expressed their feelings in music and dance. Drawing on their African musical heritage, which used hand clapping to mark rhythm, American slaves made rhythmical hand clapping—called patting juba—an indispensable accompaniment to dancing, because southern law forbade them to own "drums, horns, or other loud instruments, which may call together or give sign or notice to one another of their wicked designs and intentions." Slaves also played an African instrument, the banjo, and beat tin buckets as a substitute for drums. Whatever instrument they played, their music was tied to bodily movement. Sometimes slaves imitated white dances like the minuet, but in a way that ridiculed the high manners of their masters. More often, they expressed themselves in a dance African in origin, emphasizing shuffling steps and bodily contortions rather than the erect precision of whites' dances.

Whether at work or at prayer, slaves liked to sing. Work songs describing slave experiences usually consisted of a leader's chant and a choral response:

> *I love old Virginny*
> *So ho! boys! so ho!*
> *I love to shuck corn*
> *So ho! boys! so ho!*
> *Now's picking cotton time*
> *So ho! boys! so ho!*

Masters encouraged such songs, believing that singing induced the slaves to work harder and that the innocent content of most work songs proved that the slaves were happy. Recalling his own past, Frederick Douglass came closer to the truth when he observed that "slaves sing most when they are most unhappy. The songs of the slave represent the sorrows of his heart; and he is relieved by them, only as an aching heart is relieved by its tears."

Blacks also sang religious songs, later known as spirituals. The origin of spirituals is shrouded in obscurity, but it is clear that by 1820 blacks at camp meetings had improvised what one white described as "short scraps of disjointed affirmations, pledges, or prayers

The Banjo Lesson,
by Henry O. Tanner, c. 1893
Tanner, a black artist, captured African-Americans' rich musical traditions and close family bonds in this evocative painting. Africans brought the banza, or banjo, to the Americas. Crafted from gourds and animal hides, the instruments shown above were made and played by slaves.

lengthened out with long repetition choruses." As this description suggests, whites usually took a dim view of spirituals and tried to make slaves sing "good psalms and hymns" instead of "the extravagant and nonsensical chants, and catches, and hallelujah songs of their own composing." Indeed, when around whites, blacks often sang hymns like those of Isaac Watts and other great white evangelicals, but nothing could dampen slaves' enthusiasm for songs of their own making.

Spirituals reflected the potent emphasis that the slaves' religion put on deliverance from earthly travails. To a degree, the same was true of white hymns, but spirituals were more direct and concrete. Slaves sang, for example,

In that morning, true believers,
*   In that morning,*
We will sit aside of Jesus
*   In that morning,*
If you should go fore I go,
*   In that morning,*
You will sit aside of Jesus
*   In that morning,*
True believers, where your tickets
*   In that morning,*
Master Jesus got your tickets
*   In that morning.*

Another spiritual proclaimed, "We will soon be free, when the Lord will call us home."

CONCLUSION

The emergence of an African-American culture was one among many features that made the Old South distinctive. With its huge black population, lack of industries, and dispersed white population, the South seemed a world apart. Even while finding individual southerners agreeable, northerners increasingly recognized the differences between their region and the South in the antebellum years. Whether or not they believed that the federal government should tamper with slavery, northerners grew convinced that slavery had cut the South off from progress and had turned it into a region of "sterile land, and bankrupt estates."

Conversely, to most white southerners, the North, and especially the industrial Northeast, appeared to be the region that deviated from the march of progress. Southerners felt most Americans—indeed, most people throughout the world—practiced agriculture and that agriculture made the South a more comfortable place for millions than factories rendered the North. In reaction to northern assaults on slavery, southerners portrayed the institution as a time-honored and benevolent response to the natural inequality of the black and white races. Southerners pointed to the slaves' adequate nutrition, their embrace of evangelical Protestantism, the affection of some slaves for their masters, and even their work songs as evidence of the slaves' contentment.

In reality, few if any slaves accepted slavery. Although slaves rebelled infrequently and had little chance for permanent escape, they often engaged in covert resistance to their bondage. The slaves embraced Christianity, but they understood it differently from whites. Whereas Christianity taught whites the need to make slaves submissive, it taught slaves the gross injustice of human bondage.

CHRONOLOGY

1790s	Methodists and Baptists start to make major strides in converting slaves to Christianity.
1793	Eli Whitney invents the cotton gin.
1800	Gabriel Prosser leads a slave rebellion in Virginia.
1808	Congress prohibits external slave trade.
1812	Louisiana, the first state formed out of the Louisiana Purchase, is admitted to the Union.
1816–1819	Boom in cotton prices stimulates settlement of the Southwest.
1817	Mississippi enters the Union.
1819	Alabama enters the Union.
1819–1820	Missouri Compromise.
1822	Denmark Vesey's conspiracy is uncovered in South Carolina.
1831	William Lloyd Garrison starts *The Liberator*. Nat Turner leads a slave rebellion in Virginia.
1832	Virginia legislature narrowly defeats a proposal for gradual emancipation. Virginia's Thomas R. Dew writes an influential defense of slavery.
1835	Arkansas admitted to the Union.
1837	Economic panic begins, lowering cotton prices.
1844–1845	Methodist Episcopal and Baptist churches split into northern and southern wings over slavery.
1845	Florida and Texas admitted to the Union.
1849	Sugar production in Louisiana reaches its peak.
1849–1860	Period of high cotton prices.
1857	Hinton R. Helper, *The Impending Crisis of the South*.
1859	John Brown's raid on Harpers Ferry.
1860	South Carolina secedes from the Union.

FOR FURTHER READING

John B. Boles, *Black Southerners, 1619–1869* (1983). An excellent synthesis of scholarship on slavery.

Orville Vernon Burton, *In My Father's House Are Many Mansions: Family and Community in Edgefield, South Carolina* (1985). An extremely valuable study of the South Carolina upcountry.

Wilbur J. Cash, *The Mind of the South* (1941). A brilliant interpretation of southern history.

Bruce Collins, *White Society in the Antebellum South* (1985). A very good, brief synthesis of southern white society and culture.

William J. Cooper, *Liberty and Slavery: Southern Politics to 1860* (1983). A valuable synthesis and interpretation of recent scholarship on the antebellum South in national politics.

Clement Eaton, *The Growth of Southern Civilization, 1790–1860* (1961). A fine survey of social, economic, and political change.

Robert W. Fogel, *Without Consent or Contract: The Rise and Fall of American Slavery* (1989). A comprehensive reexamination of the slaves' productivity and welfare.

Robert W. Fogel and Stanley L. Engerman, *Time on the Cross: The Economics of American Negro Slavery* (1974). A controversial book that uses mathematical models to analyze the profitability of slavery.

Eugene D. Genovese, *Roll, Jordan, Roll: The World the Slaves Made* (1974). The most influential work on slavery in the Old South written during the last twenty years; a penetrating analysis of the paternalistic relationship between masters and slaves.

James Oakes, *The Ruling Race: A History of American Slaveholders* (1982). An important attack on the ideas of Eugene D. Genovese.

James Oakes, *Slavery and Freedom: An Interpretation of the Old South* (1990). A study stressing slavery's development in the context of liberal capitalism.

U. B. Phillips, *American Negro Slavery* (1918), and *Life and Labor in the Old South* (1929). Works marred by racial prejudice but containing a wealth of information about slavery and the plantation system.

Kenneth M. Stampp, *The Peculiar Institution: Slavery in the Ante-Bellum South* (1956). A standard account of the black experience under slavery.

ADDITIONAL BIBLIOGRAPHY

The Economic and Social Structure of the White South

William L. Barney, *The Road to Secession* (1972); Fred Bateman and Thomas Weiss, *A Deplorable Scarcity: The Failure of Industrialism in the Slave Economy* (1981); Orville V. Burton and Robert McMath, eds., *Class, Conflict, and Consensus* (1982); Mary B. Chesnut, *A Diary from Dixie* (edited by Ben Ames Williams, 1949); Blanche Henry Clark, *The Tennessee Yeoman, 1840–1860* (1942); Catherine G. Clinton, *The Plantation Mistress: Women's World in the Old South* (1982); Barbara J. Fields, *Slavery and Freedom on the Middle Ground: Maryland During the Nineteenth Century* (1985); Elizabeth Fox-Genovese, *Within the Plantation Household: Black and White Women of the Old South* (1988); Eugene Genovese, *The Political Economy of Slavery* (1965); Steven Hahn, *The Roots of Southern Populism: Yeomen Farmers and the Transformation of the Georgia Upcountry, 1850–1890* (1983); Daniel R. Hundley, *Social Relations in Our Southern States* (1860); Suzanne Lebsock, *The Free Women of Petersburg: Status Culture in a Southern Town, 1784–1860* (1984); Forrest McDonald and Grady McWhiney, "The Antebellum Southern Herdsman: A Reinterpretation," *Journal of Southern History* 41 (May 1975): 147–166; Frank L. Owsley, *Plain Folk of the Old South* (1949); Anne F. Scott, *The Southern Lady: From Pedestal to Politics, 1830–1930* (1970); Herbert Weaver, *Mississippi Farmers, 1850–1860* (1945); Ralph A. Wooster, *Politicians, Planters, and Plain Folk* (1975); Gavin Wright, *The Political Economy of the Cotton South* (1978).

The Values of the White South

David F. Allmendinger, Jr., *Ruffin: Family and Reform in the Old South* (1990); Edward L. Ayers, *Vengeance and Justice: Crime and Punishment in the Nineteenth-Century American South* (1984); David T. Bailey, *Shadow on the Church: Southwestern Evangelical Religion and the Issue of Slavery, 1783–1860* (1985); Dickson D. Bruce, *Violence and Culture in the Antebellum South* (1979); William J. Cooper, *The South and the Politics of Slavery, 1829–1856* (1978); James D. Essig, *The Bonds of Wickedness: American Evangelicals Against Slavery, 1770–1808* (1982); Drew G. Faust, *A Sacred Circle: The Dilemma of the Intellectual in the Old South, 1840–1860* (1977) and *James Henry Hammond and the Old South: A Design for Mastery* (1982); John Hope Franklin, *The Militant South* (1966); George M. Fredrickson, *The Black Image in the White Mind: The Debate on Afro-American Character and Destiny, 1817–1914* (1971) and *White Supremacy: A Comparative Study in American and South African History* (1981); Alison G. Freehling, *Drift Toward Dissolution: The Virginia Slavery Debate of 1831–1832* (1982); Elliott J. Gorn, " 'Gouge and Bite, Pull Hair and Scratch': The Social Significance of Fighting in the Southern Backcountry," *American Historical Review* XC (February 1985): 18–43; Michael Hindus, *Prison and Plantation: Crime, Justice, and Authority in Massachusetts and South Carolina, 1767–1878* (1980); John McCardell, *The Idea of a Southern Nation: Southern Nationalists and Southern Nationalism* (1979); Donald G. Mathews, *Religion in the Old South* (1977); Ronald Takaki, *A Pro-Slavery Crusade: The Agitation to Reopen the African Slave Trade* (1980); J. Mills Thornton, *Politics and Power in a Slave Society: Alabama, 1800–1860* (1978); Larry E. Tise, *Proslavery: A History of the Defense of Slavery in America, 1701–1840* (1987); Bertram Wyatt-Brown, *Southern Honor: Ethics and Behavior in the Old South* (1982).

Black Experience and Culture in the Old South

Ira Berlin, *Slaves Without Masters: The Free Negro in the Antebellum South* (1974); John Blassingame, *The Slave Community* (1972); Leonard P. Curry, *The Free Black in Urban America, 1800–1850: The Shadow of the Dream* (1981); Carl N. Degler, *Neither Black Nor White: Slavery and Race Relations in Brazil and the United States* (1971); Dena J. Epstein, *Sinful Tunes and Spirituals: Black Folk Music to the Civil War* (1977); Claudia D. Goldin, *Urban Slavery in the American South, 1820–1860*

(1976); Herbert G. Gutman, *The Black Family in Slavery and Freedom, 1759–1925* (1976); Vincent Harding, *There Is a River: The Black Struggle for Freedom in America* (1981); Jacqueline Jones, *Labor of Love, Labor of Sorrow: Black Women, Work, and the Family from Slavery to the Present* (1985); Lawrence W. Levine, *Black Culture and Black Consciousness: Afro-American Folk Thought from Slavery to Freedom* (1977); Stephen B. Oates, *The Fires of Jubilee* (1975); Leslie H. Owens, *This Species of Property: Slave Life and Slave Culture in the Old South* (1976); Albert J. Raboteau, *Slave Religion* (1978); George P. Rawick, *From Sundown to Sunup: The Making of a Black Community* (1972); Jon Michael Spencer, *Black Hymnody* (1992); Robert S. Starobin, *Industrial Slavery in the Old South* (1970); Michael Tadman, *Speculators and Slaves: Traders and Slaves in the Old South* (1989).

California Forty-Niner
c. 1850

IMMIGRATION, EXPANSION, AND SECTIONAL CONFLICT
1840–1848

Considering themselves uniquely civilized and progressive, many antebellum Americans found the idea that God had ordained the spread of their civilization over all of North America irresistible. "Americans regard this continent as their birthright," proclaimed Sam Houston, the first president of the independent republic of Texas, in 1847. Those whom Americans saw as less civilized, notably the Indians and the Mexicans, could rightfully be dispossessed of their land in order to make way for "our mighty march."

This was not idle talk. In less than a thousand days of feverish activity during the administration of President James K. Polk, the United States increased its land area by 50 percent. The nation not only annexed Texas and successfully negotiated with Britain to acquire that part of Oregon south of the forty-ninth parallel but also fought a war with Mexico that led to the acquisition of California and New Mexico. Americans justified these takeovers on some of the same grounds that they had used earlier to dispossess the Indians of their lands. South Carolina's John C. Calhoun boasted that nothing could prevent Americans, "an industrious and civilized race," from "passing into an uninhabited country where the power of the owners is not sufficient to keep them out." Some commentators even contended that expansion was a blessing in disguise for peoples whom Americans deemed less progressive than themselves. Calling in 1848 for the annexation of all of Mexico, a New York journalist argued that the acquisition of that territory would give "an entirely new character and new development to her population." Beyond expanding its physical boundaries, the United States swelled dramatically in population during the 1840s and 1850s, in part because of a spectacular rise in European immigration. The number of immigrants who entered the United States in these two decades alone exceeded the nation's entire population in 1790. European immigration soared during the mid-1840s, at the same time that the nation plunged into expansion.

Although antebellum immigration and territorial expansion had different sources, the two developments became closely linked. For example, as the penny press whipped up fervor for expansion among the urban immigrant masses, they increasingly championed efforts to push the national boundary to the Pacific Ocean. Most immigrants, moreover, supported the Democratic party, which embraced expansion far more enthusiastically than the rival Whig party. The immigrant vote helped to tip the election of 1844 to the Democrats and brought an ardent expansionist, James K. Polk, to the White House.

Beyond these direct connections between immigration and expansion, immigration indirectly stimulated expansion. New immigrants, particularly the Irish, crowded into cities and factory towns in search of work at a time when the post-1837 depression kept the wages of native-born workers low. Ugly outbursts of anti-immigrant feeling reflected the mounting tensions between the immigrant and native-born populations. A number of influential Democrats concluded that the best solution to the intensifying class and ethnic conflict lay in expanding the national boundaries, bringing more land under cultivation, and attracting immigrants to that land, in the process recapturing the ideal of America as a nation of self-sufficient farmers.

Moreover, Democrats advocated expansion as a means of reducing strife between the sections. Expansion into Oregon would gratify the North; expansion into Texas would please the South. Some influential Democrats even argued that Texas would become a kind of highway along which slaves and free blacks alike would wend their way over the horizon and into Mexico. In this way, the argument ran, expansion would gradually drive the sectionally divisive issue of race out of politics.

In reality, expansion brought sectional antagonism to the boiling point, split the Democratic party in the late 1840s, and set the nation on the path to the Civil War.

NEWCOMERS AND NATIVES

Between 1815 and 1860, 5 million European immigrants landed in the United States. Of these, 4.2 million arrived between 1840 and 1860; 3 million of them came in the single decade from 1845 to 1854. This ten-year period witnessed the largest immigration proportionate to the total population (then around 20 million) in American history. The Irish led the way as a source of immigration between 1840 and 1860, with the Germans running a close second. Smaller contingents continued to immigrate to the United States from England, Scotland, and Wales, and a growing number came from Norway, Sweden, Switzerland, and Holland. But by 1860 three-fourths of the 4.1 million foreign-born Americans were either Irish or German.

Expectations and Realities

A desire for religious freedom drew some immigrants to the United States. For example, when Mormon missionaries actively recruited converts in the slums of English factory towns, a number of English migrated to America. Many emigrants from Norway were Quakers fleeing persecution by the official Lutheran clergy. But a far larger number of Europeans sailed for America to better their economic condition. Their hope was fed by a continuous stream of travelers' accounts and letters from relatives describing America as a utopia for poor people. German peasants learned that they could purchase a large farm in America for the price of renting a small one in Germany. English men and women were told that enough good peaches and apples were left rotting in the orchards of Ohio to sink the British fleet.

Hoping for the best, emigrants often encountered the worst. Their problems began at ports of embarkation, where hucksters frequently sold them worthless tickets and where ships scheduled to leave in June might not sail until August. Countless emigrants spent precious savings in waterfront slums while awaiting departure. The ocean voyage itself proved terrifying; many emigrants had never set foot on a ship. Most sailed on cargo ships as steerage passengers, where, for six weeks or more, they endured quarters almost as crowded as on slave ships.

For many emigrants, the greatest shock came when they landed. "The folks aboard ship formed great plans for their future, all of which vanished quickly after landing," wrote a young German from Frankfurt in 1840. Immigrants quickly discovered that farming in America was a perilous prospect at best. Aside from lacking the capital to start a farm, most immigrants had to confront the fact that farming in the United States bore little resemblance to farming in Europe. European farmers valued the associations of their communities. Their social and cultural lives revolved around villages that were fringed by the fields that they worked. In contrast, as many immigrants quickly learned, American farmers lived in relative isolation. They might belong to rural neighborhoods in which farmers on widely scattered plots of land met occasionally at revivals or militia musters. But they lacked the compact village life of European farmers, and they possessed an individualistic psychology that led them to speculate in land and to move frequently.

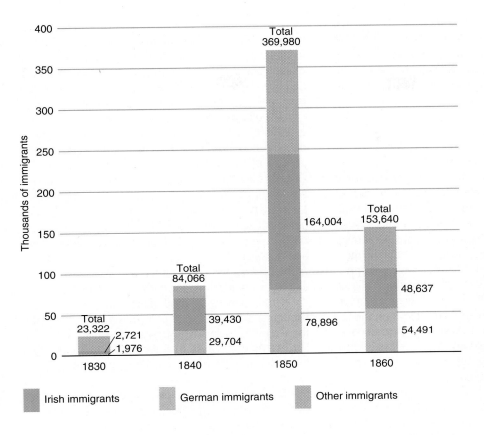

400
350
300
250
200
150
100
50
0

Thousands of immigrants

Total
369,980

Total
153,640

164,004

Total
84,066

48,637

Total
23,322

39,430

78,896

54,491

2,721

1,976

29,704

1830   1840   1850   1860

Irish immigrants   German immigrants   Other immigrants

German, Irish, and Total Immigration, 1830–1860
Irish and German immigrants led the more than tenfold growth of immigration between 1830 and 1860.
SOURCE: U.S. Bureau of the Census, *Historical Statistics of the United States, Colonial Times to 1970,* Bicentennial Edition (Washington, D.C., 1975).

Despite the shocks and dislocations caused by migration, certain patterns emerged in the distribution of immigrants within the United States. Initially shaped by trade routes, these patterns were then perpetuated by custom. Most of the Irish settlers before 1840 departed from Liverpool on sailing ships that carried English manufactures to eastern Canada and New England in return for timber. On arrival in America, few of these Irish had the capital to become farmers, and hence they crowded into the urban areas of New England, New York, Pennsylvania, and New Jersey, where they could more easily find jobs. In contrast, German emigrants usually left from continental ports on ships engaged in the cotton trade with New Orleans. However, deterred from settling in the South by the presence of slavery, the oppressive climate, and the lack of economic opportunity, the Germans congregated in the upper Mississippi and Ohio valleys, especially in Illinois, Ohio, Wisconsin, and Missouri. Geographical concentration also characterized most of the smaller groups of immigrants. More than half of the Norwegian immigrants, for example, settled in Wisconsin, where they typically became farmers.

Immigrants were usually less likely to pursue agriculture in the New World than in Europe. Both the Germans and, to an even greater degree, the Irish tended to concentrate in cities. By 1860 these two groups formed more than 60 percent of the population of St. Louis; nearly half the population of New York City, Chicago, Cincinnati, Milwaukee, Detroit, and San Francisco; and well over a third that of New Orleans, Baltimore, and Boston. These fast-growing cities created an intense demand for the labor of people with strong backs and a willingness to work for low wages. Irish construction gangs built the houses, new streets, and aqueducts that were changing the face of urban America and dug the canals and railroads that threaded together the rapidly developing cities. A popular song recounted the fate of the thousands of Irishmen who died of cholera contracted during the building of a canal in New Orleans:

Ten thousand Micks, they swung their picks,
To build the New Canal
But the choleray was stronger 'n they.
An' twice it killed them awl.

The cities provided the sort of community life that seemed lacking in farming settlements. Immigrant societies like the Friendly Sons of St. Patrick took root in cities and combined with associations like the Hibernian Society for the Relief of Emigrants from Ireland to welcome the newcomers.

The Germans

In the mid-nineteenth century, the Germans were an extremely diverse group. In 1860 Germany was not a nation-state like France or Britain, but a collection of principalities and small kingdoms. German immigrants thought of themselves as Bavarians, Westphalians, or Saxons rather than as Germans. Moreover, the German immigrants included Catholics, Protestants (usually Lutherans), and Jews as well as a sprinkling of freethinkers who denounced the ritual, clergy, and doctrines of all religions. Although few in number, these critics were vehement in their attacks on the established churches. A pious Milwaukee Lutheran complained in 1860 that he could not drink a glass of beer in a saloon "without being angered by anti-Christian remarks or raillery against preachers."

German immigrants came from a wide range of social classes and occupations. The majority had engaged in farming, but a sizable minority were professionals, artisans, and tradespeople. Heinrich Steinweg, an obscure piano maker from Lower Saxony, arrived in New York City in 1851, anglicized his name to Henry Steinway, and in 1853 opened the firm of Steinway and Sons, which quickly achieved international acclaim for the quality of its pianos. Levi Strauss, a Jewish tailor from Bavaria, migrated to the United States in 1847. Upon hearing of the discovery of gold in California in 1848, Strauss gathered rolls of cloth and sailed for San Francisco. When a miner told him of the need for durable work trousers, Strauss fashioned a pair of overalls from canvas. To meet a quickly skyrocketing demand, he opened a factory in San Francisco; his cheap overalls, later known as blue jeans or Levi's, made him rich and famous.

For all their differences, the Germans were bound together by their common language, which strongly induced recent immigrants to the United States to congregate in German neighborhoods. Even prosperous Germans bent on climbing the social ladder usually did so within German neighborhoods. Germans formed their own militia and fire companies, sponsored parochial schools in which German was the language of instruction, started German-language newspapers, and organized their own balls and singing groups. The range of voluntary associations among Germans was almost as broad as among native-born Americans.

Other factors beyond their common language brought unity to the German immigrants. Ironically, the Germans' diversity also promoted their solidarity. For example, because they were able to supply their own doctors, lawyers, teachers, journalists, merchants, artisans, and clergy, the Germans had little need to go outside their own neighborhoods. Moreover, economic self-sufficiency conspired with the strong bonds of their language to encourage a clannish psychology among the German immigrants. Although they admired the Germans' industriousness,

German Winter Gardens
A well-known beer hall on lower Manhattan's Bowery, the German Winter Gardens were famous for music and sociability.

native-born Americans resented their economic success and disdained their clannishness. German refugee Moritz Busch complained that "the great mass of Anglo-Americans" held the Germans in contempt. The Germans responded by becoming even more clannish. In turn, their psychological separateness made it difficult for the Germans to be as politically influential as the Irish immigrants.

The Irish

Between 1815 and 1860, Irish immigration to the United States passed through several stages. Irish soldiers who fought against the United States in the War of 1812 had returned to their homeland with reports that America was a paradise filled with fertile land and abundant game, a place where "all a man wanted was a gun and sufficient ammunition to be able to live like a prince." Among the Irish who subsequently emigrated between 1815 and the mid-1820s, Protestant small landowners and tradespeople in search of better economic opportunity predominated.

From the mid-1820s to the mid-1840s, the character of Irish immigration to the United States gradually changed. Increasingly, the immigrants were Catholics drawn from the poorer classes, many of them tenant farmers whom Protestant landowners had evicted as "superfluous." Protestant or Catholic, rich or poor, 800,000 to a million Irish immigrants entered the United States between 1815 and 1844. Then, between 1845 and the early 1850s, a blight destroyed every harvest of Ireland's potatoes, virtually the only food of the peasantry, and spawned one of the most gruesome famines in history. The Great Famine inflicted indescribable suffering on the Irish peasantry and killed perhaps a million people. One landlord characterized the surviving tenants on his estate as no more than "famished and ghastly skeletons." To escape the ravages of famine, 1.8 million Irish migrated to the United States in the decade after 1845.

Overwhelmingly poor and Catholic, the Irish usually entered the work force at or near the bottom. The popular image of Paddy with his pickax and Bridget the maid contained a good deal of truth. Irish men in the cities dug cellars and often lived in them; outside the cities, they dug canals and railroad beds. Irish women often became domestic servants. Compared to other immigrant women, a high proportion of Irish women entered the work force, if not as maids then often as textile workers. By the 1840s Irish women were displacing native-born women in the textile mills of Lowell and Waltham. Poverty drove Irish women to work at early ages, and the outdoor, all-season work performed by their husbands turned many of them into working widows. Winifred Rooney became a nursemaid at the age of seven and an errand girl at eleven. She then learned needlework, a skill that helped her support her family after her husband's early death. The high proportion of employed Irish women reflected more than their poverty. Compared to the predominantly male German immigrants, more than half of the Irish immigrants were women, most of whom were single adults. In both Ireland and America, the Irish usually married late, and many never married. For Irish women to become self-supporting was only natural.

The lot of most Irish people was harsh. One immigrant described the life of the average Irish laborer in America as "despicable, humiliating, [and] slavish"; there was "no love for him—no protection of life—[he] can be shot down, run through, kicked, cuffed, spat upon—and no redress, but a response of 'served the damn son of an Irish b___ right, damn him.' " Yet some Irish struggled up the social ladder. In Philadelphia, which had a more varied industrial base than Boston, Irish men made their way into iron foundries, where some became foremen and supervisors. Other Irish rose into the middle class by opening grocery and liquor stores.

The varied occupations pursued by Irish immigrants brought them into conflict with two quite different groups. The poorer Irish who dug canals and cellars, hauled cargo on the docks, washed laundry for others, and served white families competed directly with equally poor free blacks. This competition stirred up Irish animosity toward blacks and a hatred of abolitionists. At the same time, enough Irish men eventually secured skilled or semiskilled jobs that clashes with native-born white workers became unavoidable.

Anti-Catholicism, Nativism, and Labor Protest

The hostility of native-born whites toward the Irish often took the form of anti-Catholicism. Anti-Catholicism had been a strong, if latent, impulse among American Protestants since the early Puritan days. The surge of Irish immigration during the second quarter of the nineteenth century revived anti-Catholic fever. For example, in 1834 rumors circulated among Boston Protestants that a Catholic convent in nearby Charlestown contained dungeons and torture chambers. The mother superior turned away a

Defenders of the True Faith
This cartoon portrays the mob that attacked a Roman Catholic convent in Charlestown, Massachusetts, in 1834, as composed of bigoted ruffians who flatter themselves that their deed will live as a heroic act in the national memory.

delegation of officials demanding to inspect the convent. Soon the building lay in ashes, the victim of a Protestant mob. In 1835 Samuel F. B. Morse, the future inventor of the telegraph, warned that the despotic governments of Europe were systematically flooding the United States with Catholic immigrants as part of a conspiracy to destroy republican institutions. "We must first stop this leak in the ship," he wrote, "through which the muddy waters from without threaten to sink us." That same year, the combative evangelical Protestant Lyman Beecher issued *A Plea for the West*, a tract in which he warned faithful Protestants of an alleged Catholic conspiracy to send immigrants to the West in sufficient numbers to dominate the region. A year later, the publication of Maria Monk's best-selling *Awful Disclosures of the Hotel Dieu Nunnery in Montreal* rekindled anti-Catholic hysteria. Although Maria Monk was actually a prostitute who had never lived in a convent, she professed to be a former nun. In her book, she described how the mother superior forced nuns to submit to the lustful advances of priests who entered the convent by a subterranean passage.

As Catholic immigration swelled in the 1840s, Protestants mounted a political counterattack. It took the form of nativist (anti-immigrant) societies with names like the American Republicans and the United Order of Americans. Although usually started as secret or semi-secret fraternal orders, most of these societies developed political offshoots. One, the Order of the Star-Spangled Banner, would evolve by 1854 into the "Know-Nothing," or American, party and would become a major political force in the 1850s. During the 1840s, however, nativist parties enjoyed only brief moments in the sun. These occurred mainly during flare-ups over local issues, such as whether students in predominantly Catholic neighborhoods should be allowed to use the Catholic Douay rather than Protestant King James version of the Bible for the scriptural readings that began each school day. In 1844, for example, after the American Republican party (which opposed any concessions to Catholics) won some offices in Philadelphia elections, fiery Protestant orators mounted soapboxes to denounce "popery," and Protestant mobs descended on Catholic neighborhoods. Before the militia quelled these "Bible Riots," thirty buildings lay in charred ruins and at least sixteen people had been killed.

Nativism fed on an explosive mixture of fears and discontents. Protestants thought that their doctrine that each individual could interpret the Bible was more democratic than Catholicism, which made doctrine the province of the pope and bishops. In addition, at a time when the wages of native-born artisans and journeymen were being depressed by the subdivision of tasks and by the aftermath of the Panic of 1837 (see Chapter 10), many Protestant workers concluded that Catholic immigrants, often desperately poor and willing to work for anything, were threats to their jobs. In reaction, Protestant artisans joined nativist societies.

Nativist outbursts were not labor's only response to the wage cuts that accompanied the depression. Some agitators began to advocate land reform as a solution to workers' economic woes. Americans had long cherished the notion that a nation so blessed by abundant land as the United States need never give rise to a permanent class of factory "wage slaves." In 1844 the English-born radical George Henry Evans organized the National Reform Association and rallied supporters with the slogan "Vote Yourself a Farm." Evans advanced neo-Jeffersonian plans for the establishment of "rural republican townships," composed of 160-acre plots for workers. He quickly gained the backing of artisans who preferred such "agrarian" notions to a further advance of the industrial order that was undermining their position. Evans was also supported by a number of middle-class intellectuals, among them Horace Greeley, the editor of the *New York Tribune*.

Land reformers argued that workers' true interests could never be reconciled with an industrial order in which factory operatives sold their labor for wages. By engaging in wage labor, they said, workers abandoned any hope of achieving economic independence. These reformers most appealed to articulate and self-consciously radical workers, particularly artisans and small masters whose independence was being threatened by factories and who feared that American labor was "fast verging on the servile dependence" common in Europe. But land reform offered little to factory operatives and wage-earning journeymen who completely lacked economic independence. In an age when a horse cost the average worker three months' pay and most factory workers dreaded "the horrors of wilderness life," the idea of solving industrial problems by resettling workers on farms seemed a pipe dream.

The land reformers believed that only a fundamental restructuring of economic relations would improve the condition of workers. They therefore opposed strikes for short-term wage increases. In contrast, labor unions, less idealistic in their goals, were more sympathetic to strikes. Unions had flourished in a number of cities during the mid-1830s and then experienced a resurgence in the mid-1840s as the effects of the depression wore off. They appealed to several groups indifferent to land reform. For example, as refugees from an agricultural society, desperately poor Irish immigrants could more realistically hope to improve their status through unions and strikes rather than through farming. The most celebrated strike in the New York City area in the 1840s was organized by Irish dockworkers in Brooklyn. Women workers also unionized in the 1840s. In 1845 tailoresses and seamstresses organized the Ladies Industrial Association in New York City; their leader, Elizabeth Gray, proclaimed, "Too long have we been bound down by tyrant employers."

Agitation by labor unionists generated considerable commotion in the 1840s and resulted in a few victories for workers. In the landmark case of *Commonwealth* v. *Hunt* (1842), the Massachusetts Supreme Court ruled that labor unions, or "combinations," were not illegal monopolies that restrained trade. But because less than 1 percent of the work force belonged to a labor union during the 1840s, the impact of unions was sharply limited.

Although immigrant and native-born workers at times united to support land reform or unions, profound divisions along ethnic and religious lines split the antebellum working class. Even after labor had gained a modest victory in the *Commonwealth* v. *Hunt* decision, employers freely fired union agitators and replaced them with cheap immigrant labor. "Hundreds of honest laborers," a labor paper reported in 1848, "have been dismissed from employment in the manufactories of New England because they have been suspected of knowing their rights and daring to assert them." This kind of repression effectively blunted agitation for the ten-hour day (at a time when workers typically toiled for twelve to fourteen hours). The drive for a shorter workday had gained support in the 1840s from a number of organizations, among them the Lowell Female Reform Association.

During the 1830s and 1840s, tensions between native-born and immigrant workers inevitably became intertwined with the political divisions of the second party system.

Labor Protest and Immigrant Politics

Very few immigrants had ever cast a vote in an election prior to their arrival in America, and only a small fraction were refugees from political persecution. Political upheavals had erupted in Austria and several of the German states in the turbulent year of 1848 (the so-called Revolutions of 1848), but among the million German immigrants to the United States, only about ten thousand were political refugees, or "Forty-Eighters."

Once they had settled in the United States, however, many immigrants became politically active. They quickly found that urban political organizations, some of them dominated by earlier immigrants, would help them to find lodging and employment—in return for votes. Both the Irish and the Germans identified overwhelmingly with the Democratic party. An obituary of 1837 that described a New Yorker as a "warm-hearted Irishman and an unflinching Democrat" could have been written of millions of other Irish. Similarly, the Germans became stalwart supporters of the Democrats in cities like Milwaukee and St. Louis.

The immigrants' worries about staying financially afloat partly explain their widespread Democratic support. Andrew Jackson had given the Democratic party an antiprivilege and anti-aristocratic coloration, and most immigrants, especially the Irish, saw the Democrats as more sympathetic than the Whigs to the common people. Moreover, many Irish immigrants turned to the Democrats because antislavery was more closely identified in the North with the Whig party than with the Democratic party. The Irish loathed abolitionism out of fear that emancipated slaves would migrate north and compete with them for unskilled jobs.

Beyond these economic considerations, most Irish and German immigrants saw the Whigs as more of a threat than the Democrats to their moral and religious values. The Whigs' identification with temperance reform, for example, pushed the Irish and Germans toward the Democrats, for both immigrant groups had hearty traditions of drinking. The fact that some prominent temperance reformers were also leading anti-Catholics further strengthened the allegiance of Catholic immigrants to the anti-temperance Democrats. Public-school reform, a major Whig goal, also drew fire from immigrants. The Irish looked upon school reform as a menace to the Catholicism of their children; the Germans saw it as a threat to the integrity of their language and culture.

Liquor regulations and school laws were city or state concerns rather than federal responsibilities, but the two major parties proved adept at attracting voters who initially had been aroused by local issues. For example, nativists usually voted for Whigs rather than for the candidates of one of the overtly nativist parties like the American Republicans. The Democratic party that the immigrants so widely supported in their battles over local matters served them as a kind of school of broad, national principles. It taught them to venerate George Washington, to revere Thomas Jefferson and Andrew Jackson, and to view "monied capitalists" as parasites who would tremble when the people spoke. It introduced immigrants to Democratic newspapers, Democratic picnics, and Democratic parades. The Democrats, by identifying their party with all that they thought best about the United States, helped give immigrants a sense of themselves as Americans. By the same token, the Democratic party introduced immigrants to national issues. It redirected political loyalties that often had been forged on local issues into the arena of national politics. During the 1830s the party had persuaded immigrants that national measures like the Bank of the United States and the tariff, seemingly remote from their daily lives, were vital to them. Now during the 1840s, the Democrats would try to convince immigrants that national expansion advanced their interests.

◆

THE WEST AND BEYOND

As late as 1840, Americans who referred to the West still meant the area between the Appalachian Mountains and the Mississippi River or just beyond, a region that included much of the present-day Midwest. Beyond the states bordering the Mississippi lay an inhospitable region unlike any that the earlier settlers had ever known. Those who ventured west of Missouri encountered the Great Plains, a semiarid plateau with few trees. Winds sucked the moisture from the soil. Bands of nomadic Indians—including the Pawnees, Kiowas, and Sioux—roamed this territory and gained sustenance mainly from the buffalo. They ate its meat, wore its fur, and covered their dwellings with its hide. Aside from some well-watered sections of northern Missouri and eastern Kansas and Nebraska, the Great Plains presented would-be farmers with massive obstacles.

The formidable barrier of the Great Plains did not stop settlement of the West in the long run. Temporarily, however, it shifted public interest toward the verdant region lying beyond the Rockies, the Far West.

The Far West

With the Transcontinental (or Adams-Onís) Treaty of 1819, the United States had given up to Spain its claims to Texas west of the Sabine River. This had left Spain in undisputed possession not only of Texas but also of California and the vast territory of New Mexico. Combined, California and New Mexico included all of present-day California and New Mexico as well as modern Nevada, Utah, and Arizona, and parts of Wyoming and Colorado. Two years later, a series of revolts against Spanish rule had culminated in the independence of Mexico and in Mexico's takeover of all North American territory previously claimed by Spain. The Transcontinental Treaty also had provided for Spain's cessation to the United States of its claims to the country of Oregon north of the forty-second parallel (the northern boundary of California). Then in

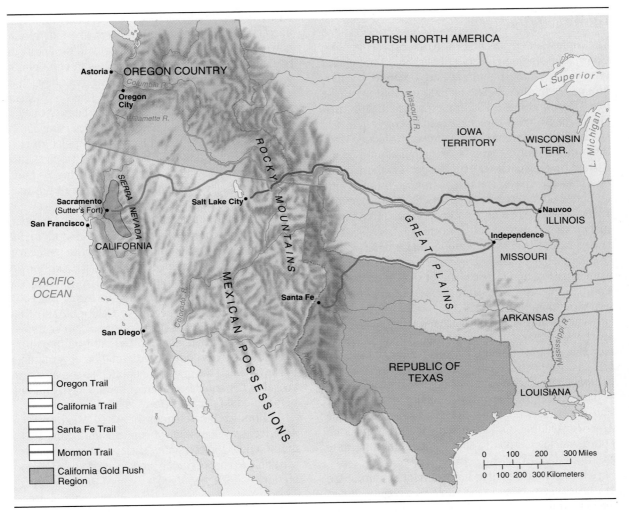

Trails to the West, 1840

By 1840 several trails carried pioneers from Missouri and Illinois to the West.

1824 and 1825, Russia abandoned its claims to Oregon south of 54°40′ (the southern boundary of Alaska). In 1827 the United States and Britain, each of which had claims to Oregon based on discovery and exploration, revived an agreement (originally signed in 1818) for joint occupation of the territory between 42° and 54°40′, a colossal area that contemporaries could describe no more precisely than the "North West Coast of America, Westward of the Stony [Rocky] Mountains" and that included all of modern Oregon, Washington, and Idaho as well as parts of present-day Wyoming, Montana, and Canada.

Collectively, Texas, New Mexico, California, and Oregon composed an area larger than Britain, France, and Germany combined. Such a vast region should have tempted any nation, but during the 1820s Mexico, Britain, and the United States viewed the Far West as a remote and shadowy frontier. By 1820 the American line of settlement had only reached Missouri, well over 2,000 miles (counting detours for mountains) from the West Coast. El Paso on the Rio Grande and Taos in New Mexico lay, respectively, 1,200 and 1,500 miles north of Mexico City. Britain, of course, was many thousands of miles from Oregon.

Far Western Trade

The earliest American and British outposts on the West Coast were trading centers established by merchants who had reached California and Oregon by sailing around South America and up the Pacific. Between the late 1790s and the 1820s, for example, Boston merchants had built a thriving exchange of coffee, tea, spices, cutlery, clothes, and hardware—indeed, anything that could be bought or manufactured in the eastern United States—for furs (especially those of sea otters), cattle, hides, and tallow (rendered from cattle fat and used for making soap and candles). Between 1826 and 1828 alone, Boston traders took more than 6 million cattle hides out of California; in the otherwise undeveloped California economy, these hides, called "California banknotes," served as the main medium of exchange. During the 1820s the British Hudson's Bay Company developed a similar trade in Oregon and northern California.

The California trade occasioned little friction with Mexico. Producing virtually no manufactured goods, Hispanic people born in California (called *californios*) were as eager to buy as the traders were to sell—so eager that they sometimes rowed out to the vessels laden with goods, thus sparing the traders the trip ashore. Those traders who did settle in California, like the American Thomas O. Larkin and the Swiss-born John Sutter, quickly learned to speak Spanish and became assimilated into Mexican culture.

Farther south, trading links developed during the 1820s between St. Louis and Santa Fe along the famed Santa Fe Trail. The Panic of 1819 left the American Midwest short of cash and its merchants burdened by unsold goods. Pulling themselves up from adversity, however, plucky midwesterners loaded wagon trains with tools, utensils, clothing, windowpanes, and household sundries each spring and rumbled westward to Santa Fe, where they traded their merchandise for mules and New Mexican silver. To a far greater extent than had Spain, Mexico welcomed this trade. Indeed, by the 1830s more than half the goods entering New Mexico by the Santa Fe Trail trickled into the mineral-rich interior provinces of Mexico such as Chihuahua and Sonora, with the result that the Mexican silver peso, which midwestern traders brought back with them, quickly became the principal medium of exchange in Missouri.

Some Americans ventured north from Santa Fe to trap beaver in what is today western Colorado and eastern Utah. The profitability of the beaver trade also encouraged merchants and trappers like the "mountain man" Jedidiah Smith (see Chapter 9) to venture directly from St. Louis into the Rockies in competition with both the Santa Fe traders and agents of the Hudson's Bay Company. On the Green River in Mexican territory, the St. Louis–based trader William Ashley in 1825 inaugurated an annual rendezvous or encampment where traders exchanged beaver pelts for supplies, thereby saving themselves the trip to St. Louis. With the aid of Ashley's encampments, the St. Louis traders gradually wrested the beaver trade from their competitors in Santa Fe.

For the most part, American traders and trappers operating on the northern Mexican frontier in the 1820s and 1830s posed more of a threat to the beaver than to Mexico's provinces. (If silk hats had not become fashionable in Europe in the mid-1830s, the beaver might have been hunted to extinction.) Not only did the Mexican people of California and New Mexico depend on the American trade for manufactured goods, but Mexican officials in both provinces relied on customs duties to support their governments. In New Mexico the government often had to await the arrival of the annual caravan of traders from St. Louis before it could pay its officials and soldiers.

Although the relations between Mexicans and Americans were mutually beneficial during the 1820s, the potential for conflict was never absent. Spanish-speaking, Roman Catholic, and accustomed to a more hierarchical society, the Mexicans formed a striking contrast to the largely Protestant, individualistic Americans. And although few American traders themselves became permanent residents of Mexico, many returned with glowing reports of the climate and fertility of Mexico's northern provinces. By the 1820s American settlers were already moving into eastern Texas. At the same time, the ties that bound the central government of Mexico to its northern frontier provinces were starting to fray.

Mexican Government in the Far West

Spain, and later Mexico, recognized that the key to controlling the frontier provinces lay in promoting their settlement by civilized Hispanic people—that is, by Spaniards, Mexicans, and Indians who had embraced Catholicism and agriculture. The mission had long been the key instrument of Spanish expansion on the frontier. By the early nineteenth century, missions

Mission San Gabriel, *by Ferdinand Deppe, 1832*
The San Gabriel Mission was founded in 1771 in southern California, partly with the intent of converting the local Indians, who are shown here settled in a thatched hut, to Catholicism. In 1781 the Spanish governor set out from this mission to found El Pueblo de Nuestra Señora la Reina de Los Angelos Porciúncula, now usually known simply as Los Angeles.

stretched up the California coast from San Diego to San Francisco and into the interior of New Mexico and Texas.

The Spanish mission combined political, economic, and religious goals—an arrangement alien to the American separation of church and state. The Franciscan priests who staffed the missions were paid government agents who endeavored to convert the Native Americans and to settle them on mission lands. By 1823 more than twenty thousand Indians lived on the lands of the twenty-one California missions. To protect the missions, the Spanish often constructed forts, or presidios, near them. San Francisco was the site of a mission and a presidio founded in 1776 and did not develop as a town until the 1830s.

Dealt a blow by the successful struggle for Mexican independence, Spain's system of missions and presidios declined in the late 1820s and 1830s. The Mexican government gradually "secularized" the missions by distributing their lands to ambitious government officials and private ranchers. Freed from the supervision of Franciscan priests, some former mission-dwelling Native Americans became forced laborers in white communities, but many returned to their nomadic ways and joined with Indians who had always resisted the missions. During the 1820s and 1830s, these "barbaric Indians"—notably, the Comanches, Apaches, Navajos, and Utes—terrorized the Mexican frontier by stealing livestock and carrying off Hispanic women and children. Apaches and Comanches attacked New

Watermelon Race
As Americans advanced into the Southwest, they became familiar with such colorful Mexican customs as the watermelon race shown here.

Mexico and Texas, and the Comanches swept into northern Mexico, striking within 150 miles of Mexico City. The legislature of the Mexican state of Chihuahua complained in 1846 that "we travel the roads at their [the Indians'] whim; we cultivate the land where they wish and in the amount that they wish."

Mexican policy was partly responsible for this up-surge in terrorism. With the secularization of the missions, Hispanic ranchers had turned some Native Americans into virtual slaves on ranches now bloated by the addition of former mission lands. In addition, Mexican frontier dwellers thought little of raiding Native American tribes for domestic servants. "To get Indian girls to work for you," a descendant of Hispanic settlers recalled, "all you had to do was organize a company against the Navahos or Utes or Apaches and kill all the men you could and bring captive the children." In short, the "barbaric Indians" had many scores to settle with the Mexicans.

Because the overofficered and corrupt Mexican army had little taste for frontier fighting, Mexican settlers on the frontier could not rely on the military for protection against the Indians. Consequently, few Mexicans ventured into the undeveloped, lawless territories. Few areas in the Western Hemisphere potentially so rich were so underpopulated. In 1836 New Mexico contained about 30,000 people of Hispanic culture; California, about 3,200; and Texas, 4,000. Far from their government in Mexico City,

which often seemed indifferent to their welfare, and dependent on American traders for the necessities of civilization, the Mexicans of the frontier provinces formed only a frail barrier against the advance of American settlement.

The American Settlement of Texas

Unlike the provinces of New Mexico and California, the Mexican state known as Coahuila-Texas lacked the natural protection of mountains and deserts. During the post-1815 cotton boom, small bands of southern farmers began to push across the Sabine River into eastern Texas in search of more land for cotton cultivation. In addition, after the Panic of 1819, many debt-ridden Americans in the Midwest and South found flight into Texas a convenient escape from creditors. By 1823 some three thousand Americans lived in eastern Texas. In 1824 the Mexican government began actively to encourage American colonization of Texas as a way to bring in manufactured goods (of which the Mexicans produced virtually none) and to gain protection against the Indians. Expecting that American settlers would live peacefully under Mexican rule, the Mexican government bestowed generous land grants on agents (known as *empresarios*) who contracted to bring Americans into Texas. The most successful of these *empresarios*, Stephen F. Austin, had attracted some three hundred American families to

Texas by 1825. Other *empresarios* followed suit, and by 1830 some seven thousand Americans lived in Texas, more than double the Mexican population dwelling there.

Although Mexico gained some advantages from the American immigration into Texas, the Americans proved a mixed blessing to the Mexican people. Some unscrupulous American traders, like the notorious Harlan Coffee, provoked the Indians to raid Mexican settlements and seize livestock to trade for American liquor and guns. Other American immigrants were roust-abouts who moved to Texas to escape debts and sheriffs. But even law-abiding Americans posed a problem. Unlike the relatively assimilated American traders in California, the settlers of Texas were farming families who dwelled in eastern Texas, apart from the Mexicans who had congregated in the western part of the state. Although naturalized as Mexican citizens, the American settlers distrusted the Mexicans and complained constantly about the creaking, erratic Mexican judicial system. Above all, Mexico had not bargained for the size and speed of the American immigration. The Amercans, reported Mexican general Manual Mier y Terán in 1828, had established farming communities before the Mexicans were even aware of their presence. Four years later, Mier y Terán ran a sword through his heart in despair over Mexico's inability to stem and control the American advance.

As early as 1826, an American *empresario*, Haden Edwards, led a revolt against Mexican rule, but Mexican forces, aided by Stephen F. Austin, quickly crushed the uprising. Although, like Austin, most Americans were still willing to live in Texas as naturalized Mexican citizens, during the early 1830s, the allegiance of the Americans to the Mexican government was severely eroded. In 1830 Mexico closed Texas to further immigration from the United States and, having emancipated its own slaves in 1829, forbade the introduction of more slaves to Texas. The latter measure struck directly at the Americans, many of whom were slaveholders. However, Mexico lacked the military might to enforce its decrees. Between 1830 and 1834, the number of Americans in Texas doubled. In 1834 Austin secured repeal of the 1830 prohibition on American immigration, and by 1835 an estimated one thousand Americans a month were crossing into Texas. In 1836 Texas contained some 30,000 white Americans, 5,000 black slaves, and 4,000 Mexicans.

As American immigration swelled, Mexican politics grew increasingly unstable. "The political charac-

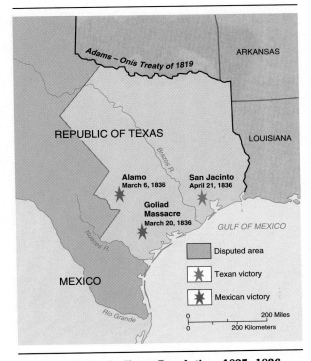

Major Battles in the Texas Revolution, 1835–1836
Sam Houston's victory at San Jacinto was the decisive action of the war and avenged the massacres at the Alamo and Goliad.

ter of this country," Austin wrote, "seems to partake of its geological features—all is volcanic." From its inception, the government of the Mexican republic had rested on a precarious balance between liberals (or federalists), who favored popular liberty and decentralized government, and conservative centralists, who sought to concentrate power in the hands of military and church officials in Mexico City. In 1834 Mexican president Antonio López de Santa Anna ousted leading liberals from his government and began to restrict the powers of the regimes in Coahuila-Texas and other Mexican states. His actions ignited a series of rebellions in the Mexican states, the most important of which became known as the Texas Revolution.

The Texas Revolution

Santa Anna's brutality in crushing most of the rebellions alarmed Austin and others. Austin initially had taken a moderate position. He hoped to cooperate with Mexican liberals to restore the Mexican Constitution of 1824 and to secure greater autonomy for Texas

Sam Houston
This photo shows Houston as a prosperous and successful elder statesman. But in his youth Houston had a reputation for wildness. In 1829 he resigned Tennessee's governorship and lived for three years among the Cherokees.

within Mexico. At the outset, he did not favor Texas's independence from Mexico. When Santa Anna invaded Texas in the fall of 1835, however, Austin cast his lot with the more radical Americans who wanted independence.

At first, Santa Anna's army met with success. In late February 1836, his force of 4,000 men laid siege to San Antonio, whose 200 Texan defenders retreated into an abandoned mission, the Alamo. After repelling repeated attacks and inflicting more than 1,500 casualties on Santa Anna's army, the remaining 187 Texans, including such famed frontiersmen as Davy Crockett and Jim Bowie, were wiped out to the last man on March 6. A few weeks later, Mexican troops massacred some 350 Texas prisoners at Goliad.

Even before these events, Texas delegates had met in a windswept shed in the village of Washington, Texas, and declared Texas independent of Mexico. The rebels by then had settled on a military leader, Sam Houston, for their president. A giant man who wore

leopard-skin vests, Houston retreated east to pick up recruits (mostly Americans who crossed the border to fight Santa Anna). Houston turned and surprised Santa Anna on a prairie near the San Jacinto River in April. Shouting "Remember the Alamo," Houston's army of eight hundred tore through the Mexican lines, killing nearly half of Santa Anna's men in fifteen minutes and taking Santa Anna himself prisoner. Houston then forced Santa Anna to sign a treaty (which the Mexican government never ratified) recognizing the independence of Texas.

American Settlements in California, New Mexico, and Oregon

California and New Mexico, both less accessible than Texas, exerted no more than a mild attraction for American settlers during the 1820s and 1830s. Only a few hundred Americans resided in New Mexico in 1840; that same year, California contained perhaps four hundred Americans. A contemporary observed that the Americans living in California and New Mexico during these years "are scattered throughout the whole Mexican population, and most of them have Spanish wives. . . . They live in every respect like the Spanish."

Yet the beginnings of change were already evident. California's Hispanic population generally welcomed American immigration as a way to encourage economic development. In addition, some Americans who settled in California before 1840 sent back highly favorable reports of the region to induce immigration. One story, tongue-in-cheek, told of a 250-year-old man who had to leave the region when he finally wanted to die. Such reports produced their intended effect. During the 1840s an ever-widening stream of Americans migrated to the interior Sacramento Valley, where they lived geographically and culturally apart from the Mexicans. For these land-hungry settlers, no sacrifice seemed too great if it led to California.

Oregon, with its abundant farmland, beckoned settlers from the Mississippi Valley. During the 1830s missionaries like the Methodist Jason Lee moved into Oregon's Willamette Valley, and by 1840 the area contained some five hundred Americans. Enthusiastic reports sent back by Lee piqued interest in Oregon. An orator in Missouri described Oregon as a "pioneer's paradise" where "the pigs are running around under the great acorn trees, round and fat and already cooked, with knives and forks sticking in them so that you can cut off a slice whenever you are hungry." Indeed, to some, Oregon seemed even more attractive than California. Oregon was already jointly occupied by Britain and the United States, and its prospects for eventual U.S. annexation appeared better than California's.

The Overland Trail

Whether bound for California or Oregon, the pioneers faced a four-month journey across terrain that was all the more terrifying because little was known about it. The eastern press teemed with horror stories, mostly fictitious, of Indian massacres. Assuming that they would have to fight their way across the plains, settlers prepared for the trip by buying enough guns for an army from merchants in the rival jump-off towns of Independence and St. Joseph, Missouri. In reality, the pioneers were more likely to shoot themselves or each other by accident than to be shot by the usually cooperative Indians, and much more likely to be scalped by the inflated prices charged by merchants in Independence or "St. Joe" than by the Native Americans.

Once embarked, the emigrants faced new hardships and hazards: kicks from mules, oxen that collapsed from thirst, overloaded wagons that broke down. Trails were difficult to follow—at least until they became littered by the debris of broken wagons

and by the bleached bones of oxen. After 1845 guidebooks helped emigrants to chart their course, but these often understated the distance across such formidable barriers as the Great Salt Desert. The Donner party, which set out from Illinois in 1846, lost so much time following the advice of one such book that its members became snowbound in the High Sierra and reached California only after its survivors had turned to cannibalism.

Emigrants responded to the challenges of the overland trail by cooperating closely with each other. Most set out in huge wagon trains rather than as individuals. Reflecting firmly entrenched traditions, husbands depended on their wives to pack and unpack the wagon each day, to milk the cows brought along to stock the new farms in the West, and to cook. Women, too, assisted with the childbirths that occurred on the trail at about the same frequency as in the nation as a whole. Men yoked and unyoked the oxen, drove the wagons and stock, and formed hunting parties.

Between 1840 and 1848, an estimated 11,500 emigrants followed an overland trail to Oregon, and some 2,700 reached California. These numbers were modest and concentrated in the years from 1844 to 1848. Yet even small numbers could make a huge difference in the Far West, for the British could not effectively settle Oregon at all, and the Mexican population in California was small and scattered. By 1845 California clung to Mexico by the thinnest of threads. The territory's Hispanic population, the californios, felt little allegiance to Mexico, which they contemptuously referred to as the "other shore." Nor did they feel any allegiance to the United States. Some californios wanted independence from Mexico; others looked to the day when California might

Conestoga Wagon
Originating in southeastern Pennsylvania around 1750, drawn by four or six horses or mules, and distinguished by its slanting gates and its cloth cover supported by bows of bent wood, the conestoga wagon served for a century as the ship of American inland commerce.

become a protectorate of Britain or perhaps even France. But these *californios*, with their shaky allegiances, now faced a growing number of American settlers whose political sympathies were not at all divided.

THE POLITICS OF EXPANSION

The major issue that arose as a by-product of westward expansion was whether the United States should annex the independent Texas republic. In the mid-1840s the Texas-annexation issue generated the kind of political passions that banking questions had ignited in the 1830s, and became entangled with equally unsettling issues relating to California, New Mexico, and Oregon. Between 1846 and 1848, a war with Mexico and a dramatic confrontation with Britain settled all these questions on terms favorable to the United States.

Yet at the start of the 1840s, western issues occupied no more than a tenuous position on the national political agenda. From 1840 to 1842, questions relating to economic recovery—notably, banking, the tariff, and internal improvements—dominated the attention of political leaders. Only after politicians failed to address the economic issues coherently did opportunistic leaders thrust issues relating to expansion to the top of the political agenda.

The Whig Ascendancy

The election of 1840 brought the Whig candidate William Henry Harrison to the presidency and installed Whig majorities in both houses of Congress. The Whigs had raced to power with a program, based on Henry Clay's American System, to stimulate economic recovery, and they had excellent prospects of success. They quickly repealed Van Buren's darling, the Independent Treasury. They then planned to substitute some kind of national "fiscal agent," which, like the defunct Bank of the United States, would be a private corporation chartered by Congress and charged with regulating the currency. The Whigs also favored a tariff, but with a twist. In the past, Whigs had supported a "protective" tariff, one set so high as to discourage the importation of goods that would compete with the products of American industries. Now the Whigs proposed a modification in the form of a "revenue" tariff, one high enough to provide "incidental"

protection for American industries but low enough to allow most foreign products to enter the United States. The duties collected on these imports would accrue to the federal government as revenue. The Whigs then planned to distribute this revenue to the states for internal improvements, a measure as popular among southern and western Whigs as the tariff was among northeastern Whigs.

The Whig agenda might have breezed into law had it not been for the untimely death of Harrison after only one month in office. With Harrison's demise, Vice President John Tyler, an upper-crust Virginian who had been put on the ticket in 1840 to strengthen the Whigs' appeal in the South, assumed the presidency. From virtually every angle, the new president proved a disaster for the Whigs.

A former Democrat, Tyler had broken with Jackson over nullification, but he continued to favor the Democratic philosophy of states' rights. As president, he repeatedly used the veto to shred his new party's program. In August 1841 a Whig bill to create a new national bank became the first casualty of Tyler's veto. Stunned, the Whig majority in Congress quickly passed a modified banking bill, only to see Tyler veto it as well.

Congressional Whigs fared little better on the issues of the tariff and the distribution of tariff revenues to the states. The Compromise Tariff of 1833 had provided for a gradual scaling down of tariff duties, until none was to exceed 20 percent by 1842. Amid the depression of the early 1840s, however, the provision for a 20 percent maximum tariff appeared too low to generate revenue. Without revenue, the Whigs would have no money to distribute among the states for internal improvements and no program with national appeal. In response, the Whig congressional majority passed two bills in the summer of 1842 that simultaneously postponed the final reduction of tariffs to 20 percent and ordered distribution to the states to proceed. Tyler promptly vetoed both bills. Tyler's mounting vetoes infuriated the Whig leadership. "Again has the imbecile, into whose hands accident has placed the power, vetoed a bill passed by a majority of those legally authorized to pass it," screamed the *Daily Richmond Whig*. Some Whigs talked of impeaching Tyler. Finally, in August, Tyler, needing revenue to run the government, signed a new bill that maintained some tariffs above 20 percent but abandoned distribution to the states.

Tyler's erratic course confounded and disrupted his party. By maintaining some tariffs above 20 percent, the tariff of 1842 satisfied northern manufacturers, but by abandoning distribution, it infuriated many southerners and westerners. Northern Whigs succeeded in passing the bill with the aid of many northern Democrats, particularly pro-tariff Pennsylvanians, whereas large numbers of Whigs in the Upper South and West opposed the tariff of 1842.

In the congressional elections of 1842, the Whigs paid a heavy price for failing to enact their program. Although retaining a slim majority in the Senate, they lost control of the House to the Democrats. Now the nation witnessed one party in control of the Senate, its rival in control of the House, and a president who appeared to belong to neither party.

Tyler and the Annexation of Texas

Although a political maverick disowned by his party, Tyler ardently desired a second term as president. Domestic issues offered him little hope of building a popular following, but foreign policy was another matter. In 1842 Tyler's secretary of state, Daniel Webster, concluded a treaty with Great Britain, represented by Lord Ashburton, that settled a long-festering dispute over the boundary between Maine and the Canadian province of New Brunswick. Awarding more than half of the disputed territory to the United States, the Webster-Ashburton Treaty was popular in the North. Tyler reasoned that if he could now arrange for the annexation of Texas, he would build a national following.

The issue of slavery, however, had long clouded every discussion of Texas. By the late 1830s antislavery northerners viewed proposals to annex Texas as part of an elaborate southern conspiracy to extend American territory south into Mexico, Cuba, and Central America, thus allowing for an unlimited number of new slave states while the British presence in Canada would limit the number of free states. In fact, some southerners talked openly of creating as many as four or five slave states out of the vast territory encompassed by Texas.

Nevertheless, in the summer of 1843, Tyler launched a propaganda campaign for Texas annexation. He justified his crusade by reporting that he had learned of certain British designs on Texas, which Americans, he argued, would be prudent to forestall. Tyler's campaign was fed by reports from his unofficial agent in London, Duff Green, a protégé of John C. Calhoun and a man whom John Quincy Adams contemptuously dismissed as an "ambassador of slavery." Green assured Tyler that as a prelude to undermining slavery in the United States, the British would pressure Mexico to recognize the independence of Texas in return for the abolition of slavery there. Calhoun, who became Tyler's secretary of state early in 1844, embroidered these reports with fanciful theories of British plans to use abolition as a way to destroy rice, sugar, and cotton production in the United States and gain for itself a monopoly on all three staples.

In the spring of 1844, Calhoun and Tyler submitted to the Senate for ratification a treaty, secretly drawn up, annexing Texas to the United States. Among the supporting documents accompanying the treaty was a letter from Calhoun to Richard Pakenham, the British foreign minister in Washington, that defended slavery as beneficial to blacks, the only way to protect them from "vice and pauperism." Antislavery northerners no longer had to look under the carpet for evidence that the impulse behind annexation lay in a desire to protect and extend slavery; now they needed only to read Calhoun's words. Both Martin Van Buren, the leading northern Democrat, and Henry Clay, the most powerful Whig, came out against immediate annexation, on grounds that annexation would provoke the kind of sectional conflict that each had sought to bury. By a vote of 35 to 16, the treaty went down to crushing defeat in the Senate. Decisive as it appeared, however, this vote only postponed the final decision on annexation to the upcoming election of 1844.

The Election of 1844

Tyler's ineptitude turned the presidential campaign into a free-for-all. The president hoped to succeed himself in the White House, but he lacked a base in either party. Testing the waters as an independent, he could not garner adequate support and was forced to drop out of the race.

Henry Clay had a secure grip on the Whig nomination. Martin Van Buren appeared to have an equally firm grasp on the Democratic nomination, but the issue of Texas annexation split his party. Trying to appease all shades of opinion within his party, Van Buren stated that he would abide by whatever Congress might decide on the annexation issue. Van Buren's attempt to evade the issue succeeded only in alienating

1844 Campaign Banner
Clay hoped to convince the public that the Whig programs of high tariffs and the distribution of tariff revenues would restore prosperity, here represented by a well-dressed farmer and his well-fed horse.

the modest number of northern annexationists, led by Michigan's former governor Lewis Cass, and the much larger group of southern annexationists. At the Democratic convention, Van Buren and Cass effectively blocked each other's nomination. The resulting deadlock was broken by the nomination of James K. Polk of Tennessee, the first "dark-horse" presidential nominee in American history.

Although little known outside the South, the slaveholding Polk was the favorite of southern Democrats, who accurately described him as the "bosom friend of [Andrew] Jackson, and a pure whole-hogged Democrat, the known enemy of banks and distribution." On the Texas issue, Polk supported immediate "reannexation," a curious turn of phrase that reflected Andrew Jackson's belief that Texas had been part of the Louisiana Purchase until unwisely ceded to Spain by the Transcontinental Treaty of 1819. Indeed, Polk followed Old Hickory's lead so often that he became known as Young Hickory.

Gibing "Who is James K. Polk?" the Whigs derided Polk's nomination. Polk himself marveled at his turn of fortune, for he had lost successive elections for the governorship of Tennessee. Yet he proved a wily campaign strategist. To satisfy pro-tariff Pennsylvania Democrats, Polk adjusted his position on the tariff to hold out some hope for protection. In addition, Polk and supporters like Senator Robert J. Walker of Mississippi managed to convince many northerners that the annexation of Texas would advance their interests. By foiling alleged British plans to abolitionize Texas,

Walker contended, annexation would make Texas a safe haven for slavery and draw both slaves and free blacks away from states bordering the North. Failure to annex, on the other hand, would prevent the westward dispersal of the South's slave population, intensify racial tensions in the existing slave states, and increase the chances of a race war that would spill over into the North. However farfetched, Walker's arguments played effectively on the racial phobias of many northerners and helped Polk detach annexation from Calhoun's narrow, pro-southern defense of it.

In contrast to the Democrats, who established a clear direction in their arguments, Clay kept muddying the waters. In the spring of 1844, he had opposed the annexation treaty. Then he sent conflicting messages to his followers throughout the summer of 1844, saying that he had nothing against annexation as long as it would not disrupt sectional harmony. Finally, in September 1844 he again came out against annexation. Clay's shifts on annexation alienated his southern supporters and prompted a small but influential body of northern antislavery Whigs to desert to the Liberty party, which had been organized in 1840. Devoted to the abolition of slavery by political action, the Liberty party nominated Ohio's James G. Birney for the presidency.

Annexation was not the sole issue of the campaign. The Whigs infuriated Catholic immigrant voters by nominating Theodore Frelinghuysen as Clay's running mate. A leading Presbyterian layman, Frelinghuysen gave "his head, his hand, and his heart" to temperance and an assortment of other Protestant causes. His presence on their ticket fixed the image of the Whigs as the orthodox Protestant party and roused the largely Catholic foreign-born voters to turn out in large numbers for the Democrats.

On the eve of the election in New York City, so many Irish marched to the courthouse to be qualified for voting that the windows had to be left open for people to get in and out. "Ireland has reconquered the country which England lost," an embittered Whig moaned. Polk won the electoral vote 170–105, but his margin in the popular vote was only 38,000 out of 2.6 million votes cast, and he lost his own state of Tennessee by 113 votes. In most states the two main parties contended with each other on close terms, a sign of the maturity of the second party system. A shift of 6,000 votes in New York, where the immigrant vote and Whig defections to the Liberty party hurt Clay, would have given Clay both the state and the presidency.

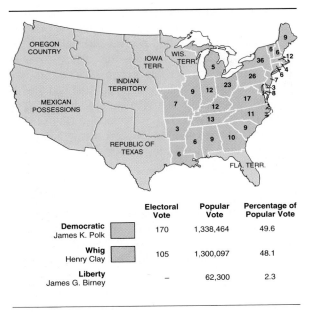

		Electoral Vote	Popular Vote	Percentage of Popular Vote
Democratic James K. Polk		170	1,338,464	49.6
Whig Henry Clay		105	1,300,097	48.1
Liberty James G. Birney		—	62,300	2.3

The Election of 1844

Manifest Destiny

The election of 1844 demonstrated one incontestable fact: the annexation of Texas had more national support than Clay had realized. The surging popular sentiment for expansion that made the underdog Polk rather than Clay the man of the hour reflected a growing conviction among the people that America's natural destiny was to expand into Texas and all the way to the Pacific Ocean.

Expansionists emphasized extending the "area of freedom" and talked of "repelling the contaminating proximity of monarchies upon the soil that we have consecrated to the rights of man." For contemporary young Americans like Walt Whitman, such restless expansionism knew few limits. "The more we reflect upon annexation as involving a part of Mexico, the more do doubts and obstacles resolve themselves away," Whitman wrote. "Then there is California, on the way to which lovely tract lies Santa Fe; how long a time will elapse before they shine as two new stars in our mighty firmament?"

Americans awaited only a phrase to capture this ebullient spirit of continentalism. In 1845 John L. O'Sullivan, a New York Democratic journalist, wrote of "our manifest destiny to overspread and to possess the whole of the continent which Providence has given us for the development of the great experiment of liberty and federated self-government entrusted to us."

Advocates of Manifest Destiny used lofty language and routinely invoked God and Nature to sanction expansion. Inasmuch as most proponents of Manifest Destiny were Democrats, many of whom supported the annexation of Texas, northern Whigs frequently dismissed Manifest Destiny as a smoke screen aimed at concealing the evil intent of expanding slavery. In reality, many advocates of Manifest Destiny were neither supporters of slavery nor zealous annexationists. Oregon and California loomed more prominently in their minds than Texas. For despite their flowery phrases, these expansionists rested their case on hard material calculations. Most blamed the post-1837 depression on the failure of the United States to acquire markets for its agricultural surplus and saw the acquisition of Oregon and California as solutions. A Missouri Democrat observed that "the ports of Asia are as convenient to Oregon as the ports of Europe are to the eastern slope of our confederacy, with an infinitely better ocean for navigation." An Alabama Democrat praised California's "safe and capacious harbors," which, he assured, "invite to their bosoms the rich commerce of the East."

Expansionists desired more than profitable trade routes, however. At the heart of their thinking lay an impulse to preserve the predominantly agricultural character of the American people and thereby to safeguard democracy. Most expansionists associated the industrialization that was transforming America with social stratification and class strife, and many saw the concentration of impoverished Irish immigrants in cities and factory towns as evidence of the common people's shrinking opportunities for economic advancement. After a tour of New England mill towns in 1842, John L. O'Sullivan warned Americans that should they fail to encourage alternatives to factories, the United States would sink to the level of Britain, a nation that the ardent Democratic expansionist James Gordon Bennett described as a land of "bloated wealth" and "terrible misery."

Most Democratic expansionists came to see the acquisition of new territory as a logical complement to their party's policies of low tariffs and opposition to centralized banking. Where tariffs and banks tended to "favor and foster the factory system," expansion would provide farmers with land and with access to foreign markets for their produce. As a consequence, Americans would continue to become farmers, and the foundations of the Republic would remain secure. The acquisition of California and Oregon would provide enough land and harbors to sustain not only the 20 million Americans of 1845 but the 100 million that some expansionists projected for 1900 and the 250 million that O'Sullivan predicted for 1945.

The expansionists' message, especially as delivered by the penny press in such newspapers as Bennett's *New York Herald*, made sense to the laboring poor of America's antebellum cities. The *Herald*, the nation's largest-selling newspaper in the 1840s, played upon the anxieties of its working-class readers by arguing relentlessly for the expulsion of the British from Oregon and for thwarting alleged British plans to abolitionize the United States. These readers, many of them fiercely antiblack, anti-British Irish immigrants, welcomed any efforts to open up economic opportunities for the common people. Most also favored the perpetuation of slavery, for the freeing of slaves would throw masses of blacks into the already intense competition for jobs.

The expansionists with whom these laboring-class readers sided drew ideas from Thomas Jefferson, John Quincy Adams, and other leaders of the early Republic who had proclaimed the American people's right to displace uncivilized or European people from the path of their westward movement. Early expansionists, however, had feared that overexpansion might create an ungovernable empire. Jefferson, for example, had proposed an indefinite restriction on the settlement of Louisiana. In contrast, the expansionists of the 1840s, citing the virtues of the telegraph and the railroad, believed that the problem of distance had been "literally annihilated." James Gordon Bennett claimed that the telegraph would render the whole nation as compact and homogeneous as New York City. Ironically, although many expansionists pointed with alarm to the negative effects of industrialization on society, their confidence in technology convinced them that the nation could expand with minimal risk to the people.

Polk and Oregon

The most immediate impact of the growing spirit of Manifest Destiny was to escalate the issue of Oregon. To soften northern criticism of the still-pending annexation of Texas, the Democrats had included in their platform for the election of 1844 the assertion that American title "to the whole of the Territory of Oregon is clear and unquestionable." Taken literally, the plat-

form committed the party to acquire the entire area between California and 54°40′, the southern boundary of Alaska. Since Polk had not yet been elected, the British could safely ignore this extraordinary claim for the moment, and in fact, the Oregon issue had aroused far less interest during the campaign than had the annexation of Texas. But in his inaugural address, Polk reasserted the "clear and unquestionable" claim to the "country of Oregon." If by this Polk meant all of Oregon, then the United States, which had never before claimed any part of Oregon north of the forty-ninth parallel, had executed an astounding and belligerent reversal of policy.

Polk's objectives in Oregon, however, were more subtle than his language. He knew that the United States could never obtain all of Oregon without a war with Britain, and he wanted to avoid that. He proposed to use the threat of hostilities to persuade the British to accept what they had repeatedly rejected in the past: a division of Oregon at the forty-ninth parallel. Such a division would give the United States both the excellent deep-water harbors of Puget Sound and the southern tip of British-controlled Vancouver Island. For their part, the British had long held out for a division along the Columbia River, which entered the Pacific Ocean far south of the forty-ninth parallel.

Polk's comments in his inaugural speech roused among westerners a furious interest in acquiring the whole territory. Mass meetings adopted such resolutions as "We are all for Oregon, and *all* Oregon in the West" and "The Whole or None!" Furthermore, each passing year brought new American settlers into Oregon. Even John Quincy Adams, who advocated neither the annexation of Texas nor the 54°40′ boundary for Oregon, believed that the American settlements in Oregon gave the United States a far more reasonable claim to the territory than mere exploration and discovery gave the British. The United States, not Britain, Adams contended, was the nation bound "to make the wilderness blossom as the rose, to establish laws, to increase, multiply, and subdue the earth," all "at the first behest of God Almighty."

In April 1846 Polk secured from Congress the termination of joint British-American occupation of Oregon and promptly gave Britain the required one-year's notice. With joint occupation abrogated, the British could either go to war over American claims to 54°40′ or negotiate. They chose to negotiate. Although the British raged against "that ill-regulated, overbearing, and aggressive spirit of American democ-

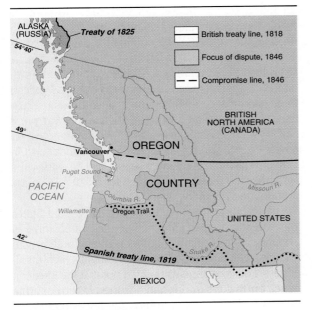

Legend:
British treaty line, 1818
Focus of dispute, 1846
Compromise line, 1846

ALASKA (RUSSIA)
Treaty of 1825
54°40'
49°
Vancouver
Puget Sound
PACIFIC OCEAN
Columbia R.
Willamette R.
Oregon Trail
42°
Spanish treaty line, 1819
BRITISH NORTH AMERICA (CANADA)
OREGON
COUNTRY
Missouri R.
Snake R.
UNITED STATES
MEXICO

Oregon Boundary Dispute
Although demanding that Britain cede the entire Oregon Territory south of 54°40', the United States settled for a compromise at the forty-ninth parallel.

racy," they had too many domestic and foreign problems to welcome a war over what Lord Aberdeen, the British foreign secretary, dismissed as "a few miles of pine swamp." The ensuing treaty provided for a division at the forty-ninth parallel, with some modifications. Britain retained all of Vancouver Island as well as navigation rights on the Columbia River. The Senate ratified the treaty (with the proviso that Britain's navigation rights on the Columbia were merely temporary) on June 15, 1846.

The Origins of the Mexican War

Even as Polk was challenging Britain over Oregon, the United States and Mexico moved steadily toward war. The impending conflict had both remote and immediate causes. One long-standing grievance lay in the failure of the Mexican government to pay some $2 million in debts owed to American citizens. In addition, bitter memories of the Alamo and of the Goliad massacre continued to arouse in Americans a loathing of Mexicans. Above all, the issue of Texas embroiled relations between the two nations. Mexico still hoped to regain Texas or at least to keep it independent of the United

States. Once in control of Texas, the Mexicans feared, the United States might seize other Mexican provinces, perhaps even Mexico itself, and treat the citizens of Mexico much as it had treated its slaves.

Unfortunately for Mexico, Polk's election boosted the strength of pro-annexation forces in the United States. The arguments that Polk and Senator Robert J. Walker had put forth during the election campaign of 1844 had persuaded many northerners of the national, rather than purely sectional, benefits of annexing Texas. Recognizing the growing popularity of annexation, both houses of Congress passed a resolution in February 1845 to annex Texas. Soon after taking office, Polk dispatched agents to the Texas republic to gain acceptance of annexation. Some Texans feared that annexation would provoke an invasion of Texas by Mexico, which had never formally recognized Texas's independence and which now served notice that it "would consider equivalent to a declaration of war against the Mexican Republic the passage of an act for an incorporation of Texas with the territory of the United States."

Confronted by Texan timidity and Mexican belligerence, Polk moved on two fronts. To sweeten the pot for the Texans, he supported their claim to the Rio Grande as the southern boundary of Texas. This claim ran counter to Mexico's view that the Nueces River, a hundred miles northeast of the Rio Grande, bounded Texas. The area between the Nueces and the Rio Grande was largely uninhabited, but the stakes were high. Although only a hundred miles southwest of the Nueces at its mouth on the Gulf of Mexico, the Rio Grande meandered west and then north for nearly two thousand miles and encircled a huge slice of territory, including part of New Mexico. The Texas that Polk proposed to annex thus encompassed far more land than the Texas that had gained independence from Mexico in 1836. Reassured by Polk's support, a Texas convention voted overwhelmingly on July 4, 1845, to accept annexation. In response to Mexican war preparations, Polk then made a second move, ordering American troops under General Zachary Taylor to the edge of the disputed territory. Taylor took up a position at Corpus Christi, a tiny Texas outpost situated just south of the Nueces and hence in territory still claimed by Mexico.

Never far from Polk's thoughts in his insistence on the Rio Grande boundary lay his desire for California and for its fine harbors of San Diego and San Francisco. In fact, Polk had entered the White House with the firm intention of extending American control over

California. By the summer of 1845, his followers were openly proclaiming that if Mexico went to war with the United States over Texas, "the road to California will be open to us." Then in October 1845, Polk received a dispatch from Thomas O. Larkin, the American consul at Monterey, California, that warned darkly of British designs on California but ended with the optimistic assurance that the Mexicans in California would prefer American to British rule. Larkin's message gave Polk the idea that California might be acquired by the same methods as Texas: revolution followed by annexation.

Visions of new territorial acquisitions were dancing merrily in Polk's mind when Texas accepted annexation in July 1845. With Taylor's troops at Corpus Christi, the next move belonged to Mexico. Unfortunately, Mexico had difficulty making any firm moves, for its politics had again slipped into turmoil with the ouster of Santa Anna by General José Herrera in December 1844. Herrera's own position in Mexican politics was shaky, and prodded by the British, he agreed to receive a delegation from the United States to reach an amicable settlement. Simultaneously, Polk, locked in a war of words with the British over Oregon, decided to give negotiations with Mexico a try. In November 1845 he sent an emissary, the Spanish-speaking John Slidell, to Mexico City. Slidell's final instructions were to gain Mexican recognition of the annexation of Texas, including the Rio Grande boundary, in return for the United States' assumption of all financial claims on the part of American citizens against the Mexican government. Polk also authorized Slidell to offer up to $25 million for New Mexico and California or, failing this, to offer $5 million for New Mexico alone.

By the time Slidell reached Mexico City on December 6, 1845, the threat of a military revolt led by General Mariano Paredes had pushed the Herrera government to the brink of collapse. Too weak to negotiate any concessions to the United States, Herrera refused to receive Slidell. In response to Mexico's refusal to negotiate, Polk now ordered Taylor to march from Corpus Christi southward to the north bank of the Rio Grande. Still viewing the Rio Grande as the key to the Far West, Polk hoped that Taylor's presence on the river would spur the Mexicans to attack. Mexican aggression, the president anticipated, would unify Americans and would quiet northerners who were suspiciously contrasting Polk's willingness to compromise on Oregon with his continuing belligerence toward Mexico. Polk had no intention of compromising

on the Texas boundary, but if it came to war, he wanted a united country behind him.

On May 9, 1846, Polk notified his cabinet that he could no longer await a Mexican attack and that he must send a war message to Congress. A few hours after the cabinet adjourned, news arrived that a Mexican force had crossed the Rio Grande and ambushed two companies of Taylor's troops. Now the prowar press had its martyrs. "American blood has been shed on American soil!" one of Polk's followers proclaimed. On May 11 Polk informed Congress that war "exists by the act of Mexico herself" and called for a $10 million appropriation to fight the war.

Polk's disarming assertion that the United States was already at war provoked furious opposition in Congress, where John C. Calhoun briefly united with antislavery Whigs to protest the president's high-handedness. Polk's opponents pointed out that the Mexican attack on Taylor's troops had occurred in territory that no previous administration had claimed as part of the United States. By announcing that war already existed, moreover, Polk seemed to be undercutting Congress's power to declare war and using a mere border incident as a pretext for plunging the nation into a general war to acquire more slave territory. The pro-Whig *New York Tribune* warned its readers that Polk was "precipitating you into a fathomless abyss of crime and calamity." Antislavery poet James Russell Lowell of Massachusetts wrote of the Polk Democrats:

> They just want this Californy
>   So's to lug new slave-states in
> To abuse ye, an' to scorn ye,
>   An' to plunder ye like sin.

But Polk had maneuvered the Whigs into a corner. Few Whigs could forget that the opposition of the Federalists to the War of 1812 had wrecked the Federalist party, and few wanted to appear unpatriotic by refusing to support Taylor's beleaguered troops. Swallowing their outrage, most Whigs backed appropriations for war against Mexico.

Throughout the negotiations with Britain over Oregon and with Mexico over Texas, Polk had demonstrated his ability to pursue his goals unflinchingly. A humorless, austere man who banned dancing and liquor at White House receptions, Polk inspired little personal warmth, even among his supporters. But he possessed clear objectives and a single-mindedness in their pursuit. At every point, he had encountered opposition on the home front: from Whigs who saw him as a reckless adventurer; from northerners of both parties opposed to any expansion of slavery; and from John C. Calhoun, who loathed Polk for his high-handedness and feared that a war with Britain would strip the South of its market for cotton. Yet Polk triumphed over all opposition, in part because of his opponents' fragmentation, in part because of expansion's popular appeal, and in part because of the weakness of his foreign antagonists. Reluctant to fight over Oregon, Britain chose to negotiate. Too weak to negotiate, Mexico chose to fight over territory that it had already lost (Texas) and for territories over which its hold was feeble (California and New Mexico).

The Mexican War

Most European observers expected Mexico to win the war. With a regular army four times the size of the American forces, Mexico had the added advantage of fighting on home ground. The United States, which had botched its one previous attempt to invade a foreign nation, Canada in 1812, now had to sustain offensive operations in an area remote from American settlements.

In contrast to the Europeans, expansionists in the United States hardly expected the Mexicans to fight at all. A leading Democrat confidently predicted that Mexico would offer only "a slight resistance to the North American race" because its mixed Spanish and Indian population had been degraded by "amalgamation." Newspaper publisher James Gordon Bennett proclaimed that the "imbecile" Mexicans were "as sure to melt away at the approach of [American] energy and enterprise as snow before a southern sun."

In fact, the Mexicans fought bravely and stubbornly, though with little success. In May 1846 Taylor, a sixty-two-year-old veteran of the War of 1812, defeated the Mexicans in two battles north of the Rio Grande and then crossed the river to defeat them again at Matamoros and to capture the major northern Mexican city of Monterrey in September. Taylor's victories touched off a wave of enthusiasm in the United States. Recruiting posters blared, "Here's to Old Zach! Glorious Times! Roast Beef, Ice Cream, and Three Months' Advance!" Already the Whigs were touting Taylor, "Old Rough and Ready," for the presidency in 1848.

After taking the supposedly impregnable Monterrey, however, Taylor, starved for supplies, granted the Mexicans an armistice by which he pledged not to pursue them for eight weeks. Eager to undercut Taylor's popularity, and judging him "wholly unqualified for the command he holds," Polk now stripped Taylor of half his men and assigned them to General Winfield Scott. Polk ordered Scott to prepare an amphibious assault on Vera Cruz, a city on the Gulf of Mexico far to the south, and to proceed overland to Mexico City. Before Scott could attack Vera Cruz, however, Taylor gained even greater fame. Seeking to win an easy victory over Taylor's depleted army, Santa Anna, who had made another of his many comebacks in Mexican politics, led an army of twenty thousand men north to dislodge Taylor. The two armies met at the Battle of Buena Vista, February 22–23, 1847. After a series of futile charges, Santa Anna's men, demoralized by the superior American artillery, retreated.

While Taylor was winning fame in northern Mexico, and before Scott had launched his attack on Vera Cruz, American forces farther north were dealing decisive blows to the remnants of Mexican rule in New Mexico and California. In the spring of 1846, Colonel Stephen Kearny marched an army from Fort Leavenworth, Kansas, toward Santa Fe. Like the pioneers on the Oregon Trail, Kearny's men faced immense natural obstacles as they marched over barren ground. Finally reaching New Mexico, Kearny took the territory by a combination of bluff, bluster, and perhaps bribery, without firing a shot. The Mexican governor, following his own advice that "it is better to be thought brave than to be so," fled at Kearny's approach. After suppressing a brief rebellion by Mexicans and Indians, Kearny sent a detachment of his army south into Mexico. There, having marched fifteen hundred miles from Fort Leavenworth, these troops joined Taylor in time for the Battle of Buena Vista.

Like New Mexico, California fell easily into American hands. In 1845 Polk had ordered Commodore John D. Sloat and his Pacific Squadron to occupy California's ports in the event of war with Mexico. To ensure victory, Polk also dispatched a courier overland with secret orders for one of the most colorful and important actors in the conquest of California, John C. Frémont. A Georgia-born adventurer, Frémont had married Jessie Benton, the daughter of the powerful senator Thomas Hart Benton of Missouri. Benton used his influence to have accounts of Frémont's explorations in the Northwest (mainly written by Jessie Benton Frémont) published as government documents. All of this earned glory for Frémont as "the Great Pathfinder." Finally overtaken by Polk's courier in

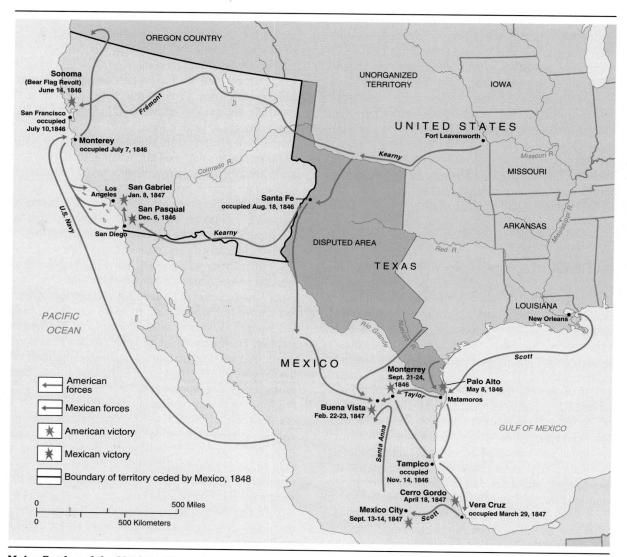

Major Battles of the Mexican War
The Mexican War's decisive campaign began with General Winfield Scott's capture of Vera Cruz and ended with his conquest of Mexico City.

Oregon, Frémont was instructed to proceed to California and to "watch over the interests of the United States." Interpreting his orders liberally, Frémont rounded up some American insurgents, seized the town of Sonoma, and proclaimed the independent "Bear Flag Republic" in June 1846. The combined efforts of Frémont, Sloat, his successor David Stockton, and Stephen Kearny (who arrived in California after capturing New Mexico) quickly established American control over California.

The final and most important campaign of the war saw the conquest of Mexico City itself. In March 1847 Winfield Scott landed near Vera Cruz at the head of twelve thousand men and quickly pounded the city into submission. Moving inland, Scott encountered Santa Anna at the seemingly impregnable pass of Cerro Gordo, but a young captain in Scott's command, Robert E. Lee, helped to find a trail that led around the Mexican flank to a small peak overlooking the pass. There Scott planted howitzers and, on April

18, stormed the pass and routed the Mexicans. Scott now moved directly on Mexico City. Taking the key fortresses of Churubusco and Chapultepec (where another young captain, Ulysses S. Grant, was cited for bravery), Scott took the city on September 13, 1847.

In virtually all these encounters on Mexican soil, the Mexicans were numerically superior. In the final assault on Mexico City, Scott commanded eleven thousand troops against Santa Anna's twenty-five thousand. But doom stalked the Mexican army. Hampered by Santa Anna's nearly unbroken string of military miscalculations, the Mexicans fell victim to the vastly superior American artillery and to the ability of the Americans to organize massive military movements. The "barbarians of the North" (as the Mexicans called the American soldiers) died like flies from yellow fever, and they carried into battle the agonies of venereal disease, which they picked up (and left) in every Mexican town they took. But the Americans benefited from the unprecedented quality of their weapons, supplies, and organization.

By the Treaty of Guadalupe Hidalgo (February 2, 1848), Mexico ceded Texas with the Rio Grande boundary, New Mexico, and California to the United States. In return, the United States assumed the claims of American citizens against the Mexican government and paid Mexico $15 million. Although the United States gained the present states of California, Nevada, New Mexico, Utah, most of Arizona, and parts of Colorado and Wyoming, some rabid expansionists in the Senate denounced the treaty because it failed to include all of Mexico. But the acquisition of California, with its excellent Pacific ports of San Diego and San Francisco, satisfied Polk. Few senators, moreover, wanted to annex the mixed Spanish and Indian population of Mexico. A writer in the *Democratic Review* expressed the prevailing view that "the annexation of the country [Mexico] to the United States would be a calamity," for it would incorporate into the United States "ignorant and indolent half-civilized Indians," not to mention "free negroes and mulattoes" left over from the British slave trade. In this way, the virulent racism of American leaders allowed the Mexicans to retain part of their nation. On March 10, 1848, the Senate ratified the treaty by a vote of 38 to 10.

The Mexican War in the Popular Mind

Occurring amid the rise of the penny press and the popular novel, the Mexican War became the most fully reported war that America had yet fought and the first conflict in which war correspondents were employed. The extensive coverage given to battlefield victories fueled the soaring nationalism and helped to submerge political divisions. "We are now all Whigs and all Democrats," an Indiana newspaper declared.

Romance as well as patriotism gripped the popular mind. Writers portrayed the war as evidence that the noble, chivalric streak in the American character could prevail over the grasping materialism of American society. To a generation fed on the historical novels of Sir Walter Scott, it seemed that the age of chivalry had returned. Innumerable popular war novels, with titles like *The Texan Ranger; or, The Maid of Matamoros,* mingled patriotism and romance by relating how American soldiers routed Mexican men only to fall in love with Mexican women.

The main beneficiary of the publicity swirling out of the war was Zachary Taylor. Taylor had the right combination of qualities to enchant a people in search of heroes. To those who danced to the hastily composed "Rough and Ready Polka" and the "General Taylor Quick Step," Taylor's military genius seemed equaled only by his democratic bearing and conspicuously ordinary manner. In contrast to the more soldierly Winfield Scott ("Old Fuss and Feathers"), Taylor went into battle wearing a straw hat and plain brown coat. To an idolizing public, even Taylor's short stature and inclination to corpulence became an advantage; some said that he resembled Napoleon.

The war made Taylor a military hero. The conflicts that spun out of the war would now boost his political career.

Intensifying Sectional Divisions

Despite the wartime patriotic enthusiasm, sectional conflict sharpened between 1846 and 1848. To a degree, this conflict intensified over issues unrelated to expansion. Many of the problems stemmed from Polk's uncompromising and literal-minded Jacksonianism.

Once in office, Polk not only had restored the Independent Treasury, a measure that dismayed the Whigs, but also had eroded the unity of his own party by pursuing Jacksonian policies on tariffs and internal improvements. The numerous northern Democrats who supported a modestly protective tariff had taken heart during the 1844 campaign from Polk's promise to combine a revenue tariff with a measure of protection. But Polk's administration, glutted with southerners, quickly abandoned any talk of protection. The tariff of 1846, fashioned by Robert J. Walker, who became

Patriotism and the Mexican War
U.S. soldiers commonly wore tall hats known as shako caps during the Mexican War. The caps were adorned with decorative plates showing the eagle spreading its wings, the symbol of Manifest Destiny. Inexpensive and mass-produced lithographs such as the one above, depicting the Battle of Sacramento, aroused patriotic support for the war.

Polk's secretary of the treasury, slashed all duties to the minimum necessary for revenue. Polk then disappointed western Democrats, thirsting for federal aid for internal improvements, by vetoing a law that they supported, the Rivers and Harbors Bill of 1846. To these western Dem-ocrats, this veto appeared to be another sign of the prosouthern tilt of Polk's presidency and did more to weaken western support for Polk than his abandonment of the fight for the 54°40′ boundary of Oregon.

Ultimately, however, sectional conflict over tariffs and internal improvements proved far less important than the battles generated by territorial expansion. Polk held true to his belief that expansion had provided an "additional guaranty for the preservation of the Union itself." Like most Jacksonian Democrats, he saw the bursting of the nation's boundaries as a way to disperse the population, weaken dangerous tendencies toward centralized government, and retain the agricultural and democratic character of the United States. In Polk's judgment, expansion would accomplish these

objectives whether the new territory acquired were slave or free. Focusing attention on slavery in the territories struck him as "not only unwise but wicked." The Missouri Compromise, prohibiting slavery north of 36°30′, impressed him as a simple and permanent solution to the problem of territorial slavery.

Yet many northerners were coming to see slavery in the territories as a profoundly disruptive issue that could not be resolved merely by extending the 36°30′ line to the Pacific. Some antislavery Whigs, especially those from abolitionist strongholds in New England and Ohio, opposed *any* extension of slavery, on moral grounds. But these Whigs, still a minority in their party, posed no immediate threat to Polk. A more damaging challenge emerged within Polk's own party: from a group of northern Democrats who, though not viewing slavery as morally evil, feared that extension of slavery into California and New Mexico (parts of each lay south of 36°30′) would deter free laborers from settling those territories. These Democrats argued that competition with slave labor clearly degraded free labor, that the westward extension of slavery would create a barrier to the westward migration of free labor, and that such a barrier would intensify the social problems already evident in the East: excessive concentration of population, labor protest, class strife, and social stratification.

The Wilmot Proviso

A young Democratic congressman from Pennsylvania, David Wilmot, became the spokesman for these disaffected northern Democrats. On a sizzling night in August 1846, he introduced an amendment to an appropriations bill for the upcoming negotiations with Mexico over Texas, New Mexico, and California. This amendment, known as the Wilmot Proviso, stipulated that slavery be prohibited in any territory acquired by the negotiations. Neither an abolitionist nor a critic of Polk on tariff policy, Wilmot spoke for those loyal Democrats who had supported the annexation of Texas on the assumption that Texas would be the last slave state. Wilmot's intention was not to split his party along sectional lines but to hold Polk to what Wilmot and other northern Democrats took as an implicit understanding: Texas for the slaveholders, California and New Mexico for free labor. With strong northern support, the proviso passed in the House but stalled in the Senate. Polk refused to endorse it, and most southern Democrats opposed any barrier to the expansion of slavery south of the Missouri Compromise line. Accepting the view that the westward extension of slavery would reduce the concentration of slaves in the older regions of the South and thus lessen the chances of a slave revolt, southern Democrats tried to put as much distance as possible between themselves and Wilmot.

The proviso raised unsettling constitutional issues. Calhoun and fellow southerners contended that since slaves were property, slaveholders enjoyed the Constitution's protection of property and could carry their slaves wherever they chose. This position led to the conclusion (drawn explicitly by Calhoun) that the Missouri Compromise of 1820, prohibiting slavery in the territories north of 36°30′, was unconstitutional. On the other side were many northerners who cited the Northwest Ordinance of 1787, the Missouri Compromise, and the Constitution itself, which gave Congress the power to "make all needful rules and regulations respecting the territory or other property belonging to the United States," as justification for congressional legislation over slavery in the territories. With the election of 1848 approaching, politicians of both sides, eager to hold their parties together and avert civil war, searched frantically for a middle ground.

The Election of 1848

Having asserted that their policies of national banking and high tariffs alone could pull the nation out of the depression, the Whigs had watched in dismay as prosperity returned under the Democrat Polk's program of an independent treasury and low tariffs. Never before had Clay's American System seemed so irrelevant. But the Wilmot Proviso gave the Whigs a political windfall, for, originating in the Democratic party, the proviso enabled the Whigs to portray themselves as the only dependable friends of the South.

These considerations inclined the majority of Whigs toward Zachary Taylor. As a Louisianian and large slaveholder, Taylor had an obvious appeal to the South. As a political newcomer who had never voted in a presidential election, he had no loyalty to Clay's American System. As a war hero, he might have a broad national appeal. Nominating Taylor, the Whigs presented him as an ideal man "without regard to creeds or principles" and ran him without any platform.

The Election of 1848

Candidates	Parties	Electoral Vote	Popular Vote	Percentage of Popular Vote
ZACHARY TAYLOR	Whig	163	1,360,967	47.4
Lewis Cass	Democratic	127	1,222,342	42.5
Martin Van Buren	Free-Soil		291,263	10.1

San Francisco in the Gold Rush

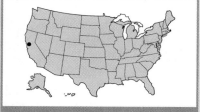

San Francisco became a favorite destination for newcomers in the gold rush. Its population spurted from 1,000 in 1849 to 50,000 in 1856. Few American towns had presented less likely prospects for growth. The Spanish had constructed a presidio and a mission on the site in 1776, and a small town, Yerba Buena, had sprung up around the mission. But when the United States took possession of Yerba Buena in July 1846, the town stretched for only a few streets in each direction and contained a mere 150 people who huddled amid its low mountains and fog-enshrouded sand hills. Arriving in the summer of 1846, a boatload of 200 Mormons more than doubled the population of Yerba Buena, which became San Francisco in 1847.

The gold rush transformed the town into "a pandemonium of a city" in the words of John Woodhouse Audubon, who became stranded there by Christmas 1849, on his way to the gold fields. San Francisco quickly emerged as the main supply depot for miners and prospectors in the interior. At first, virtually all commodities that passed through the city originated outside of California. Lumber came from Maine and Oregon, flour from Chile and Virginia, sugar from Hawaii, and manufactured goods from the eastern states and Britain. This reliance on imports shaped the town's occupational structure between 1849 and 1853. San Francisco's economy was so top-heavy with merchants and storekeepers that those willing to drive carts (draymen) or unload ships or build houses could command wages that elsewhere would have seemed unbelievable. A New England–born lawyer seriously considered giving up his practice to

Montgomery Street, San Francisco, 1850, *daguerreotype by Frederick Coombs*
In the view of historian William H. Goetzmann and art historian William N. Goetzmann, San Francisco was "the final living embodiment of Manifest Destiny, a golden dream city of great instant wealth."

become a drayman, for "they pay a man to drive a cart fifteen to twenty dollars a day," a generous wage at the time. By the mid-1850s the establishment of iron foundries and flour mills relieved the growing city's dependence on imports, but the supply of commodities remained uncertain, and commodity prices continued to gyrate crazily. Flour that cost $10 a barrel one month might jump to $19 the next. Real-estate prices also soared during the early rush, particularly near the waterfront. The city's economy was vulnerable to crashes as precipitous as its booms. A commercial panic in 1855 produced nearly two hundred bankruptcies and left close to $7 million in uncollectable debts.

The variety of San Francisco's population rivaled the volatility of its economy. Emigrants came from all around the world. By the 1850s the Irish outnumbered every other group of foreign-born immigrants. Many Irish were convicts who arrived by way of Australia, to which they had been exiled as punishment for their crimes. China, France, and Italy, nations that did not contribute many immigrants to other parts of the United States before 1860, all sent sizable contingents to San Francisco. Part of the city's tiny black population was also foreign-born. Richard Dalton, for example, came from the West Indies as a steward on a steamer and then labored on the ships that plied the Sacramento and San Joaquin rivers to Sacramento and Stockton. Indeed, no other U.S. city contained people from more parts of the world, and only two, St. Louis and Milwaukee, had a higher proportion of foreign-born residents in 1860. In addition, by the early 1850s, San Francisco contained six to ten times as many men as women.

In a city bursting with rival ethnic and racial groups and lacking the constraints imposed by family responsibilities, violence became a principal noncommercial activity. Audubon reported how the place teemed with men "more blasphemous, and with less regard for God and his commands than all I have ever seen on the Mississippi." A young clergyman wrote in 1851 that "most of our citizens if not all go armed" and confessed that he carried a harmless-looking cane, which "will be found to contain a sword

San Francisco Saloon, *by Frank Marryat*
Mexicans, Chinese, Yankees, and southerners drink together in an ornate San Francisco saloon in the booming gold-rush days.

two-and-a-half feet long." The city's small fledgling police force posed little challenge to criminals. For protection, some entrepreneurs organized disbanded soldiers into an extralegal force called the Hounds. Unfortunately, the Hounds soon terrorized the people whom they were supposed to protect. In response, in 1851 San Francisco's merchants organized the first of several Committees of Vigilance, which patrolled the streets, deported undesirables, and tried and hanged thieves and murderers.

The vigilantes turned out during subsequent outbursts of lawlessness. In 1855 a gambler named Charles Cora insulted the wife of William Richardson, a U.S. marshal. Richardson then insulted Cora's mistress, a prostitute. A crusading editor, William King, joined the fight on Richardson's side, and a political hack and longtime antagonist of King, James Casey, added his barbs to the fray. The outcome revealed much about law and order in early San Francisco. Richardson armed himself and sought out Cora in a saloon, only to be shot to death by Cora; Casey shot and killed King on a street. Vigilantes then seized Cora and Casey, tried them in secret, and hanged them.

These incidents underscore the city's religious and ethnic tensions as well as its atmosphere of easy violence. Richardson was a southerner and a Protestant, and his supporter King crusaded against the Catholic church. Although less than models of virtue, their opponents Cora and

Casey had been raised Catholic and resented attacks on the religion of their parents. Americans thought of the Far West as a land of opportunity where past antagonisms and traditions would be eradicated, but all the divisions of the larger society were reproduced in San Francisco. The major racial, regional, religious, and ethnic groups kept their distance from each other. Blacks were forced to sit in segregated parts of theaters and to attend segregated schools. Southern and New England Protestants worshiped at different churches. Emigrants from Europe also divided on the basis of language and nationality. German, Polish, Russian, and Anglo-American Jews each maintained separate religious congregations.

Regional and ethnic antagonisms even threatened at times to disrupt the harmony within the city's political parties. Transplanted southerners and Irish immigrants, for example, vied with each other for control of the Democratic party. But at election time, these groups laid aside their antagonisms and united against the rival parties. The Germans usually joined the Irish to ally with the Democrats, whereas the Whigs (and later the Republicans) drew support from former New Englanders, from temperance advocates, and from some immigrants who resented the brash and brawling Irish. In this way, party politics gave coherence to the city's divisions and provided a generally peaceful outlet for the populace's overheated tempers.

Because Wilmot was one of their own, the Democrats faced a greater challenge. They could not ignore the issue of slavery in the territories, but if they embraced the positions of either Wilmot or Calhoun, they would suffer an unmendable sectional fracture. With Polk declining to stand for reelection, the Democrats nominated Lewis Cass of Michigan, who solved their problem by evolving a doctrine of "squatter sovereignty," or popular sovereignty as it was later called. Cass argued that the issue of slavery in the territories should be kept out of Congress "and left to the people of the confederacy in their respective local governments." In other words, let the actual settlers in each territory decide the issue for themselves. Cass's position benefited from both its arresting simplicity and its vagueness. Was he saying that Congress had the power to prohibit slavery in the territories but, in the interests of sectional harmony, should leave the issue to each territory? Or did he mean that Congress lacked any power to legislate on slavery in the territories? As a further complication, the doctrine of squatter sovereignty did not establish a clear time frame for territorial action. Did the doctrine mean that the first territorial legislature could abolish slavery, or did it intend that the final decision on slavery had to await the moment of admission to the Union? In actuality, few Democrats wanted definitive answers to these questions. The very vagueness of squatter sovereignty added to its appeal, for Democrats north and south were free to interpret it to their own advantage to their constituents.

Although both parties tried to steer around the issue of slavery in the territories, neither one fully succeeded. A pro–Wilmot Proviso faction of the Democratic party in New York, called the Barnburners, broke away from the party. Proclaiming their dedication to "Free Trade, Free Labor, Free Speech, and Free Men," the Barnburners courted Liberty party abolitionists and antislavery "Conscience" Whigs, who were dismayed by their party's nomination of the slaveholding Taylor. In August 1844 Barnburners, Conscience Whigs, and former Liberty party adherents met in Buffalo, created the Free-Soil party, and nominated Martin Van Buren on a platform opposing any extension of slavery. Van Buren's motives in accepting this third-party nomination reflected both lingering bitterness at his rejection by the Democrats in 1844 (a defeat engineered largely by Lewis Cass) and alarm at the increasingly southern domination of the party under Polk.

The Whig candidate, Taylor, benefited from the opposition's alienation of key northern states over the tariff issue, from Democratic disunity over the Wilmot Proviso, and from his glowing military record. He captured a majority of the electoral votes in both the North and the South. Although failing to carry any state, the Free-Soil party ran well enough in the North to demonstrate the grass roots popularity of opposition to the extension of slavery. Defections to the Free-Soilers, for example, probably cost the Whigs the state of Ohio. Van Buren wrote that the new party had gained "more than we had any right to expect." Indeed, by showing that opposition to the spread of slavery had far greater popular appeal than the abolitionism of the old Liberty party, the Free-Soilers sent the Whig and Democratic parties a message that these parties would be unable to ignore in future elections.

The California Gold Rush

When Wilmot had first made public his proviso, the issue of slavery in the Far West was more abstract than practical, because Mexico had not yet ceded any territory and relatively few Americans resided in either California or New Mexico. Nine days before the signing of the Treaty of Guadalupe Hidalgo, however, an American carpenter discovered gold while constructing a sawmill in the foothills of California's Sierra Nevada range. A frantic gold rush was on within a few months. A San Francisco paper complained that "the whole country from San Francisco to Los Angeles, and from the shore to the base of the Sierra Nevada, resounds with the sordid cry to gold, GOLD, GOLD! while the field is left half-planted, the house half-built, and everything neglected but the manufacture of shovels and pickaxes." (Deprived of its staff, advertisers, and subscribers, the newspaper then suspended publication.) By December 1848 pamphlets with titles like *The Emigrant's Guide to the Gold Mines* had hit the streets of New York City. To speed the gold-rushers to their destination, builders constructed sleek clipper ships like Donald McKay's *Flying Cloud*, which made the eighteen-thousand-mile trip from New York to San Francisco around Cape Horn in a record eighty-nine days on its maiden voyage in 1851. But most gold-rushers traveled overland. Overland immigrants to California rose from 400 in 1848 to 25,000 in 1849 and to 44,000 in 1850 (see "A Place in Time").

With the gold rush, the issue of slavery in the Far West became practical as well as abstract, and immediate rather than remote. In 1849 gold attracted a hundred thousand newcomers to California, including Mexicans, free blacks, and slaves brought by planters from the South. White prospectors loathed the thought of competing with any of these groups and wanted to drive all of them out of the gold fields. Spawned by disputed claims and prejudice, violence mounted, and demands grew for a strong civilian government in California to replace the ineffective military government left over from the war. Polk began to fear that without a satisfactory congressional solution to the slavery issue, Californians might organize a government independent of the United States. The gold rush thus guaranteed that the question of slavery in the Mexican cession would be the first item on the agenda for Polk's successor and, indeed, for the nation.

CONCLUSION

By calling their destiny manifest, Americans of the 1840s implied that they had no other course than to annex Texas, seize California and New Mexico, and secure the lion's share of Oregon. Obstacles might arise, but most believed that barriers to expansion would melt away in the face of a dynamic and resolute people.

This image of expansion as inevitable had deep roots in the experiences and values of the American people. Fed by immigration, the population continued to grow dramatically; by 1850 the United States had nearly five times its population in 1800. The fate of Mexican rule in Texas was sealed as much by the overwhelming numerical superiority of the American settlers as by Sam Houston's brilliant victory at the Battle of San Jacinto. In addition, expansion rested on a sequence of propositions that seemed self-evident to many antebellum Americans: that a nation of farmers would never experience sustained misery; that given the chance, most Americans would rather work on farms than in factories; and that expansion would provide more land for farming, reduce the dangerous concentration of people in cities, and restore opportunity for all.

Beyond all the talk of inevitable expansion, however, Americans saw their society's divisions deepen in the 1840s, not only between native-born and immigrant people but also between northerners and southerners. Expansion proved so controversial that it split the Democratic party over the Wilmot Proviso, widened the gap between northern and southern Whigs, and spurred the emergence of the Free-Soil party. Victorious over Mexico and enriched by the discovery of gold in California, Americans counted the blessings of expansion in these years but began to fear its costs.

CHRONOLOGY

1818 The United States and Britain agree on joint occupation of Oregon for a ten-year period.

1819 Transcontinental (Adams-Onís) Treaty.

1821 Mexico gains independence from Spain.

1822 Stephen F. Austin founds the first American community in Texas.

Stephen F. Austin

1824–1825 Russia abandons its claims to Oregon south of 54°40′.

1826 Haden Edwards leads an abortive rebellion against Mexican rule in Texas.

1827 The United States and Britain renew their agreement on joint occupation of Oregon for an indefinite period.

1830 Mexico closes Texas to further American immigration.

1834 Antonio López de Santa Anna comes to power in Mexico.

1834   Austin secures repeal of the ban on American immigration into Texas.

1835   Santa Anna invades Texas.

1836   Texas declares its independence from Mexico.
Fall of the Alamo.
Goliad massacre.
Battle of San Jacinto.

1840   William Henry Harrison elected president.

1841   Harrison dies; John Tyler becomes president.
Tyler vetoes Whig National Banking Bill.

1842   Whigs abandon distribution.
Webster-Ashburton Treaty.

1843   Tyler launches campaign for Texas annexation.

1844   Philadelphia Bible Riots.
Senate rejects treaty annexing Texas.
James K. Polk elected president.

1845   Congress votes joint resolution to annex Texas.
Texas accepts annexation by the United States.
Mexico rejects Slidell mission.

1846   Congress ends the joint occupation of Oregon.
Zachary Taylor defeats the Mexicans in two battles north of the Rio Grande.
The United States declares war on Mexico.

1846   John C. Frémont proclaims the Bear Flag Republic in California.

Congress votes to accept a settlement of the Oregon boundary issue with Britain.
Walker Tariff (tariff of 1846).
Colonel Stephen Kearny occupies Santa Fe.
Wilmot Proviso introduced.
Taylor takes Monterrey.

1847   Taylor defeats Santa Anna at the Battle of Buena Vista.
Vera Cruz falls to Winfield Scott.
Mexico City falls to Scott.
Lewis Cass's principle of "squatter sovereignty."

1848   Gold discovered in California.
Treaty of Guadalupe Hidalgo signed.
Taylor elected president.

FOR FURTHER READING

Ray A. Billington, *The Far Western Frontier, 1830–1860* (1956). A comprehensive narrative of the settlement of the Far West.

William R. Brock, *Parties and Political Conscience: American Dilemmas, 1840–1850* (1979). An excellent interpretive study of the politics of the 1840s.

William H. Goetzmann, *When the Eagle Screamed: The Romantic Horizon in American Diplomacy, 1800–1860* (1966). A lively overview of antebellum expansionism.

Maldwyn A. Jones, *American Immigration* (1960). An excellent brief introduction to immigration.

Patricia Nelson Limerick, *Legacy of Conquest* (1987). A provocative interpretation of western history.

Charles G. Sellers, *James K. Polk: Continentalist, 1843–1846* (1966). An outstanding political biography.

Henry Nash Smith, *Virgin Land: The American West as Symbol and Myth* (1950). A classic study of westward expansion in the American mind.

ADDITIONAL BIBLIOGRAPHY

Immigration, Nativism, and Labor Protest

Tyler Anbinder, *Nativism and Slavery: The Northern Know Nothings and the Politics of the 1850s* (1992); Lee Benson, *The Concept of Jacksonian Democracy: New York as a Test Case* (1961); Ray A. Billington, *The Protestant Crusade, 1800–1860: A Study of the Origins of Nativism* (1938); R. A. Burchell, *The San Francisco Irish, 1848–1880* (1980); Kathleen Conzen, *Immigrant Milwau-*kee, *1836–1860* (1976); Hasia R. Diner, *Erin's Daughter in America* (1983); Oscar Handlin, *Boston's Immigrants,* rev. ed. (1969); Bruce Laurie, *Working People of Philadelphia, 1800–1850* (1980); Bruce Levine, *The Spirit of 1848: German Immigrants, Labor Conflict, and the Coming of the Civil War* (1992); Lawrence J. McCaffrey, *The Irish Diaspora in America* (1984); Kerby A. Miller, *Emigrants and Exiles: Ireland and the Irish*

Exodus to North America (1985); Norman Ware, *The Industrial Worker, 1840–1860* (1964); Sean Wilentz, *Chants Democratic: New York City and the Rise of the American Working Class, 1788–1850* (1984); Carl Wittke, *The Irish in America* (1956).

The Far West

John W. Caughey, *The California Gold Rush* (1975); Malcolm Clark, Jr., *Eden Seekers: The Settlement of Oregon, 1818–1862* (1981); Douglas H. Daniels, *Pioneer Urbanities: A Social and Cultural History of Black San Francisco* (1980); Arnoldo De Leon, *They Called Them Greasers: Anglo Attitudes Toward Mexicans in Texas, 1821–1900* (1983); John Mack Faragher, *Women and Men on the Overland Trail* (1979); William H. Goetzmann, *Exploration and Empire: The Explorer and the Scientist in the Winning of the American West* (1966); Neal Harlow, *California Conquered: War and Peace on the Pacific, 1846–1850* (1982); Theodore J. Karaminski, *Fur Trade and Exploration: Opening of the Far Northwest, 1821–1852* (1983); Frederick Merk, *History of the Westward Movement* (1978); Leonard Pitt, *The Decline of the Californios: A Social History of the Spanish-Speaking Californians, 1846–1890* (1966); Alfred Robinson, *Life in California* (1891); John I. Unruh, Jr., *The Plains Across: Overland Emigrants and the Trans-Mississippi West, 1840–1860* (1979); David J. Weber, *The Mexican Frontier, 1821–1846: The American Southwest Under Mexico* (1982).

The Politics and Diplomacy of Expansion

K. Jack Bauer, *The Mexican War, 1846–1848* (1974); Paul H. Bergeron, *The Presidency of James K. Polk* (1987); William C. Binkley, *The Texas Revolution* (1952); Gene M. Brack, *Mexico Views Manifest Destiny* (1976); Seymour Connor and Odie Faulk, *North America Divided: The Mexican War, 1846–1848* (1971); William J. Cooper, *Liberty and Slavery: Southern Politics to 1860* (1983); Bernard DeVoto, *The Year of Decision, 1846* (1943); Norman A. Graebner, *Empire on the Pacific: A Study in American Continental Expansion* (1955); Thomas R. Hietala, *Manifest Design: Anxious Aggrandizement in Late Jacksonian America* (1985); Reginald Horsman, *Race and Manifest Destiny: The Origins of American Racial Anglo-Saxonism* (1981); Robert W. Johannsen, *To the Halls of the Montezumas: The Mexican War in the American Imagination* (1985); Ernest McPherson Lander, Jr., *Reluctant Imperialist: Calhoun, the South Carolinian, and the Mexican War* (1980); Frederick Merk, *Slavery and the Annexation of Texas* (1972); David M. Pletcher, *The Diplomacy of Annexation: Texas, Oregon, and the Mexican War* (1973); Joseph G. Raybeck, *Free Soil: The Election of 1848* (1970); John H. Schroeder, *Mr. Polk's War: American Opposition and Dissent, 1846–1848* (1971); Charles G. Sellers, *James K. Polk: Jacksonian, 1795–1843* (1957); Joel H. Silbey, *The Shrine of Party: Congressional Voting Behaviour, 1841–1852* (1967); Otis A. Singletary, *The Mexican War* (1960).

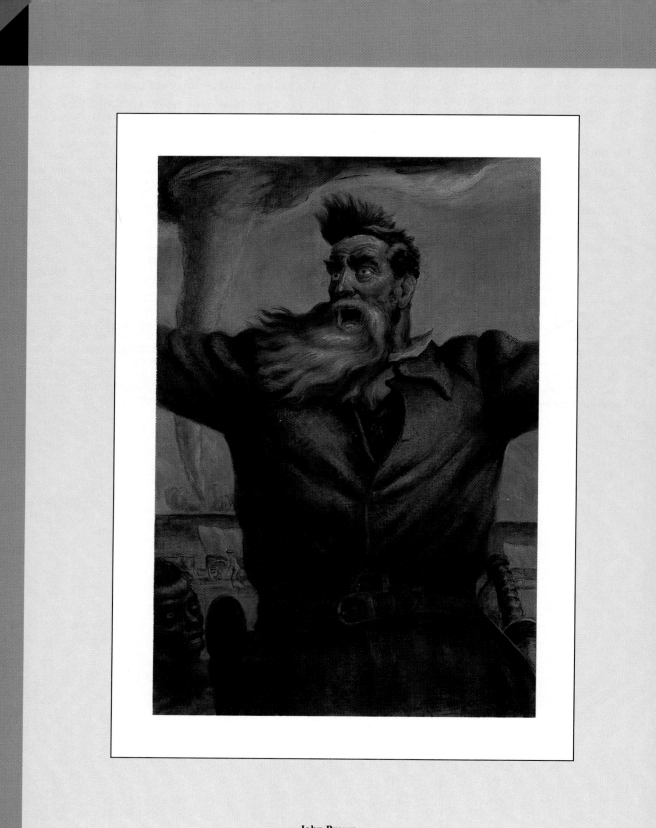

John Brown
by John Steuart Curry, 1939

FROM COMPROMISE TO SECESSION 1850–1861

Between December 1859 and February 1860, collisions between northerners and southerners in Congress produced a prolonged deadlock over the election of the Speaker of the House of Representatives. Tempers flared as never before. A South Carolinian observed that "the only persons who do not have a revolver and a knife are those who have two revolvers." Although the election of an obscure and inoffensive New Jersey congressman finally broke the deadlock, the tension and discord in Congress mirrored the division between the North and the South that would soon lead to the secession of the slave states from the Union.

Secession, a southern newspaper editor conceded in 1861, was a desperate measure. But, he quickly added, "We must recollect that we live in desperate times." A series of confrontations with the North over the status of slavery in the territories fed this growing sense of desperation in the South. Viewing the West as a boundless field of economic opportunity for themselves, northerners abhorred the idea of competing with slaves there for jobs and thus zealously resisted the westward advance of slavery. During the 1850s a growing number of northerners embraced the doctrine known as free soil, the belief that Congress had to prohibit slavery in all the territories. Free-soilers like New York's Republican senator William H. Seward and Illinois's senatorial candidate Abraham Lincoln did not call for the abolition of slavery in the southern states, but they did define the conflict between slavery and freedom as national in scope. In 1858 Seward spoke of an "irrepressible conflict" between slavery and freedom and predicted that either the wheat fields of the North would become slave or the cotton fields of the South free. Invoking the biblical warning that "a house divided against itself cannot stand," Lincoln made the same point in 1858: "I believe that this nation cannot exist permanently half slave and half free." In the eyes of these men, the only solution lay in a congressional prohibition of slavery in the territories.

The doctrine of free soil ultimately rested on an image of a good society as one in which free individuals worked to achieve economic self-sufficiency as landowning farmers, self-employed artisans, and small shopkeepers. Like free-soil northerners, white southerners valued economic independence, but they insisted that without slaves to do society's menial jobs, common white people could never attain economic self-sufficiency. By 1850 most southern whites had persuaded themselves that slavery was an institution that treated blacks humanely while enabling whites to enjoy comfortable lives.

These differing images of the good society made conflict over slavery in the territories virtually unavoidable. White southerners interpreted free-soil attacks on territorial slavery as slaps in their faces. Nothing infuriated them more than the idea that they could not take their property, slaves, anywhere that they chose. Increasingly, too, southerners viewed free-soilers' hostility as a thinly disguised attempt to corrode the foundations of slavery in both the territories and the South itself. When the abolitionist John Brown recklessly attempted to spark a southern slave insurrection in 1859, innumerable southerners concluded that only the extreme step of secession could safeguard the South against northern onslaughts. "Not only our property," a southern newspaper editor proclaimed in 1861, "but our honor, our lives and our all are involved."

THE COMPROMISE OF 1850

Ralph Waldo Emerson had predicted that an American victory in the Mexican War would be akin to swallowing arsenic, and his forecast proved disturbingly accurate. When the Treaty of Guadalupe Hidalgo was signed in 1848 to end the war, the United States contained an equal number (fifteen) of free and slave states. The vast territory ceded by Mexico (the Mexican cession) threatened to upset this balance in ways that few could have foreseen. Furthermore, all of the proposed solutions to the problem of slavery in the Mexican cession—a free-soil policy, extension of the Missouri Compromise line, and popular sovereignty—ensured controversy. The prospect of "Free Soilism, Wilmot Provisoism, and all such tomfoolery" horrified southerners. The idea of extending the Missouri Compromise line, 36°30', to the Pacific, which would allow slavery in New Mexico and southern California, antagonized northerners committed to free soil. (This second proposal simultaneously angered southern extremists, notably John C. Calhoun and his followers, by conceding to Congress the right to bar slavery in any of the territories.) The third solution, popular (or "squatter") sovereignty, which promised to ease the issue of slavery extension out of national politics by allowing each territory to decide the question for itself, offered the greatest hope for compromise. Yet popular sovereignty would appease neither those opposed in principle to the expansion of slavery nor those opposed to prohibitions on its expansion.

As statesmen fashioned their positions on slavery extension, the flow of events plunged the nation into a crisis. In the spring of 1849, the nonslaveholding Mor-

mons in Deseret drew up a constitution and sought admission to the Union. (The state of Deseret had been established by Brigham Young's followers on soil that had become part of the United States with the Treaty of Guadalupe Hidalgo.) Then in the fall of 1849, Californians, their numbers swollen by thousands of gold-rushers, framed a constitution that banned slavery, and in 1850 they petitioned for statehood. (From the standpoint of popular sovereignty, California had jumped the gun, for Congress had not yet recognized it as a territory.) To complicate matters, Texas, admitted as a slave state in 1845, laid claim to the eastern half of New Mexico, a region where the future of slaves remained in doubt.

By 1850 these territorial issues had become intertwined with two other concerns. Northern orators had long denounced slavery and the sale of slaves in the District of Columbia, within the shadow of the federal government. For their part, southerners had often complained that northerners were flouting the Fugitive Slave Act, which Congress had passed in 1793, and were actively frustrating slaveholders' efforts to catch runaways on northern soil and return them to the South. Any broad compromise between the sections would have to take into account northern demands for a restriction on slavery in the District of Columbia and southern insistence on a more effective fugitive-slave law.

Zachary Taylor at the Helm

Although elected president in 1848 without a platform, Zachary Taylor came to office with a clear position on the issue of slavery in the Mexican cession. A slaveholder himself, he took for granted the South's need to defend slavery. Taylor insisted that southerners would best protect slavery if they refrained from rekindling the issue of slavery in the territories. He rejected Calhoun's idea that the protection of slavery in the southern states ultimately depended on the expansion of slavery into the western territories. In Taylor's eyes, neither California nor New Mexico was suited to slavery; in 1849 he told a Pennsylvania audience that "the people of the North need have no apprehension of the further extension of slavery."

Although Taylor looked to the exclusion of slavery from California and New Mexico, his position differed from that embodied in the Wilmot Proviso, the free-soil measure proposed in 1846 by a northern Democrat. The proviso had insisted that *Congress* bar slavery in the territories ceded by Mexico. Taylor's plan, in contrast, left the decision to the states. Recognizing that most Californians opposed slavery in their state, Taylor had prompted California to bypass the territorial stage that normally preceded statehood, to draw up their constitution in 1849, and to apply directly for admission as a free state. The president strongly hinted that he expected New Mexico, where slavery had been abolished under Mexican rule, to do the same.

Taylor's strategy appeared to promise a quick, practical solution to the problem of slavery extension. It would give the North two new free states. At the same time, it would acknowledge a position upon which all southerners agreed: a *state* could bar or permit slavery as it chose. This conviction in fact served as the very foundation of the South's defense of slavery, its armor against all the onslaughts of the abolitionists. Nothing in the Constitution forbade a state to act one way or the other on slavery.

Despite its practical features, Taylor's plan dismayed southerners of both parties. Having gored the Democrats in 1848 as the party of the Wilmot Proviso, southern Whigs expected more from the president than a proposal that in effect yielded the proviso's goal—the banning of slavery in the Mexican cession. Many southerners, in addition, questioned Taylor's assumption that slavery could never take root in California or New Mexico. To one observer, who declared that the whole controversy over slavery in the Mexican cession "related to an imaginary negro in an impossible place," southerners pointed out that both areas already contained slaves and that slaves could be employed profitably in the mining of gold and silver. "California is by nature," a southerner proclaimed, "peculiarly a slaveholding State." Calhoun trembled at the thought of adding more free states. "If this scheme excluding slavery from California and New Mexico should be carried out—if we are to be reduced to a mere handful . . . wo, wo, I say to this Union." Disillusioned with Taylor, nine southern states agreed to send delegations to a southern convention that was scheduled to meet in Nashville in June 1850.

Henry Clay Proposes a Compromise

Taylor might have been able to contain mounting southern opposition if he had held a secure position in the Whig party. But the leading Whigs, among them Daniel Webster of Massachusetts and Kentucky's Henry Clay, each of whom had presidential aspirations, never reconciled themselves to Taylor, a political novice. Early in 1850 Clay boldly challenged Taylor's leadership by forging a set of compromise proposals to

Henry Clay
Eloquent but at the same time earthy, Clay was first elected to the Senate during Jefferson's administration. Subsequently, Clay himself made five unsuccessful bids for the presidency. A European visitor was struck by his penchant for chewing tobacco, drinking whiskey, putting his legs on the table, and spitting "like a regular Kentucky hog-driver."

resolve the range of contentious issues. Clay proposed (1) the admission of California as a free state; (2) the division of the remainder of the Mexican cession into two territories, New Mexico and Utah (formerly Deseret), without federal restrictions on slavery; (3) the settlement of the Texas–New Mexico boundary dispute on terms favorable to New Mexico; (4) as a pot-sweetener for Texas, an agreement that the federal government would assume the considerable public debt of Texas; (5) in the District of Columbia, the continuance of slavery but the abolition of the slave trade; and (6) a more effective fugitive-slave law.

Clay rolled all of these proposals into a single "omnibus" bill, which he hoped to steer through Congress. The debates over the omnibus during the late winter and early spring of 1850 witnessed the last major appearances on the public stage of Clay, Webster, and Calhoun, the trio of distinguished senators whose lives had mirrored every public event of note since the War of 1812. Clay played the role of the conciliator, as he had during the controversy over Missouri in 1820 and again during the nullification crisis in the early 1830s. He warned the South against the evils of secession and assured the North that nature would check the spread of slavery more effectively than a thousand Wilmot Provisos. Gaunt and gloomy, a dying Calhoun listened as another senator read his address, in which Calhoun summarized what he had been saying for years: the North's growing power, enhanced by protective tariffs and by the Missouri Compromise's exclusion of slaveholders from the northern part of the Louisiana Purchase, had created an imbalance between the sections. Only a decision by the North to treat the South as an equal could now save the Union. Three days later, Daniel Webster, who believed that slavery, "like the cotton-plant, is confined to certain parallels of climate," delivered his memorable "Seventh of March" speech. Speaking not "as a Massachusetts man, nor as a Northern man, but as an American," Webster chided the North for trying to "reenact the will of God" by legally excluding slavery from the Mexican cession and declared himself a forthright proponent of compromise.

However eloquent, the conciliatory voices of Clay and Webster made few converts. With every call for compromise, some northern or southern speaker would rise and inflame passions. The antislavery New York Whig William Seward, for example, enraged southerners by talking of a "higher law than the Constitution"—namely, the will of God against the extension of slavery. Clay's compromise became tied up in a congressional committee. To worsen matters, Clay, who at first had pretended that his proposals were in the spirit of Taylor's plan, broke openly with the president in May, and Taylor attacked Clay as a glory-hunter.

As the Union faced its worst crisis since 1789, a series of events in the summer of 1850 eased the way toward a resolution. When the Nashville convention assembled in June, extreme advocates of "southern rights," called the fire-eaters because of their recklessness, boldly made their presence felt. But talk of southern rights smelled suspiciously like a plot to disrupt the Union. "I would rather sit in council with the six thousand dead who have died of cholera in St. Louis," Senator Thomas Hart Benton of Missouri declared, "than go into convention with such a gang of scamps." Only nine of the fifteen slave states, most in the Lower South, sent delegates to the convention, and moderates took control and isolated the extremists. Then Zachary Taylor, after eating and drinking

too much at an Independence Day celebration, fell ill with gastroenteritis and died on July 9. His successor, Vice President Millard Fillmore of New York, quickly proved himself more favorable than Taylor to the Senate's compromise measure by appointing Daniel Webster as his secretary of state. Next, after the compromise suffered a devastating series of amendments in late July, Stephen A. Douglas of Illinois took over the floor leadership from the exhausted Clay. Recognizing that the compromise lacked majority support in Congress, Douglas jettisoned Clay's strategy by chopping the omnibus into a series of separate measures and seeking to secure passage of each bill individually. This ingenious tactic worked beautifully. By summer's end, in the Compromise of 1850, Congress had passed each component of Clay's plan: statehood for California; territorial status for Utah and New Mexico, allowing popular sovereignty; resolution of the Texas–New Mexico boundary disagreement; federal assumption of the Texas debt; abolition of the slave trade in the District of Columbia; and a new fugitive-slave law.

Assessing the Compromise

President Fillmore hailed the compromise as a "final settlement" of sectional divisions, and Clay's reputation for conciliation reached new heights. Yet the compromise did not bridge the underlying differences between the two sections. Far from leaping forward to save the Union, Congress had backed into the Compromise of 1850; the majority of congressmen in one or another section opposed virtually all of the specific bills that made up the compromise. Most southerners, for example, voted against the admission of California and the abolition of the slave trade in the District of Columbia; the majority of northerners opposed the Fugitive Slave Act and the organization of New Mexico and Utah without a forthright congressional prohibition of slavery. These measures passed only because the minority of congressmen who genuinely desired compromise combined with the majority in either the North or the South who favored each specific bill.

Each section both gained and lost from the Compromise of 1850. The North won California as a free state, New Mexico and Utah as likely future free states, a favorable settlement of the Texas–New Mexico boundary (most of the disputed area was awarded to New Mexico, a probable free state), and the abolition of the slave trade in the District of Columbia. The

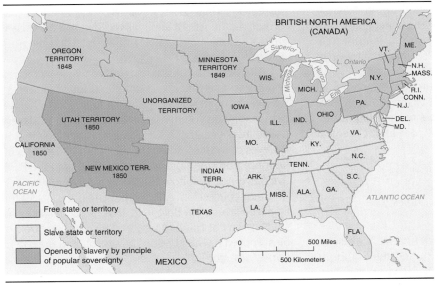

BRITISH NORTH AMERICA
(CANADA)

OREGON
TERRITORY
1848

MINNESOTA
TERRITORY
1849

WIS.

MICH.

UNORGANIZED
TERRITORY

IOWA

UTAH TERRITORY
1850

ILL.   IND.   OHIO

PA.

N.Y.

VT.   ME.

N.H.
MASS.
R.I.
CONN.
N.J.

CALIFORNIA
1850

MO.   KY.

VA.

DEL.
MD.

NEW MEXICO TERR.
1850

INDIAN
TERR.

TENN.

N.C.

ARK.   S.C.

PACIFIC
OCEAN

MISS.   ALA.   GA.

ATLANTIC OCEAN

LA.

TEXAS

FLA.

Free state or territory

Slave state or territory

Opened to slavery by principle
of popular sovereignty

MEXICO

0   500 Miles
0   500 Kilometers

The Compromise of 1850
The Compromise of 1850 admitted California as a free state. Utah and New Mexico were left open to slavery or freedom on the principle of popular sovereignty.

South's benefits were cloudier. By stipulating popular sovereignty for New Mexico and Utah, the compromise, to most southerners' relief, had buried the Wilmot Proviso's insistence that Congress formally prohibit slavery in these territories. But to southerners' dismay, the position of the free-soilers remained viable, for the compromise left open the question of whether Congress could prohibit slavery in territories outside of the Mexican cession.

Not surprisingly, southerners reacted ambivalently to the Compromise of 1850. In southern state elections during the fall of 1850 and in 1851, procompromise, or Unionist, candidates thrashed anticompromise candidates who talked of southern rights and secession. But even southern Unionists did not dismiss the possibility of secession. Unionists in Georgia, for example, forged the celebrated Georgia platform, which threatened secession if Congress either prohibited slavery in New Mexico or Utah or repealed the fugitive-slave law.

The one clear advantage gained by the South, a more stringent fugitive-slave law, quickly proved a mixed blessing. Because few slaves had been taken into the Mexican cession, the question of slavery there had a hypothetical quality. However, the issues raised by the new fugitive-slave law were far from hypothetical; the law authorized real southerners to pursue real fugitives on northern soil. Here was a concrete issue to which the average northerner, who may never have

seen a slave and who cared little about slavery a thousand miles away, would respond with fury.

Enforcement of the Fugitive Slave Act

Northern moderates accepted the Fugitive Slave Act as the price the North had to pay to save the Union. But the law contained a string of features distasteful to moderates and outrageous to staunchly antislavery northerners. It denied alleged fugitives the right of trial by jury, did not allow them to testify in their own behalf, permitted their return to slavery merely on the testimony of the claimant, and enabled court-appointed commissioners to collect ten dollars if they ruled for the slaveholder but only five dollars if they ruled for the fugitive. In authorizing federal marshals to raise posses to pursue fugitives on northern soil, the law threatened to turn the North into "one vast hunting ground." In addition, the law targeted not only recent runaways but also those who had fled the South *decades* earlier. For example, it allowed slave-catchers in 1851 to wrench a former slave from his family in Indiana and return him to the master from whom he had fled in 1832. Above all, the law brought home to northerners the uncomfortable truth that the continuation of slavery depended on their complicity. By legalizing the activities of slave-catchers on northern soil, the law reminded northerners that slavery was a national problem, not merely a peculiar southern institution.

Antislavery northerners assailed the law as the "vilest monument of infamy of the nineteenth century." "Let the President . . . drench our land of freedom in blood," proclaimed Ohio's Whig congressman Joshua Giddings, "but he will never make us obey that law." His support for the law turned Senator Daniel Webster of Massachusetts into a villain in the eyes of the very people who for years had revered him as the "godlike Daniel." The abolitionist poet John Greenleaf Whittier wrote of his fallen idol:

All else is gone; from those giant eyes
  The soul has fled:
When faith is lost, when honor dies,
  The man is dead.

Efforts to catch and return fugitive slaves inflamed feelings in both the North and the South. In 1854 a Boston mob, aroused by antislavery speeches, broke into a courthouse and killed a guard in an abortive effort to rescue the fugitive slave Anthony Burns. Determined to prove that the law could be enforced "even in Boston," President Franklin Pierce sent a detachment of federal troops to escort Burns to the harbor, where a ship carried him back to slavery. No witness would ever forget the scene. As five platoons of troops marched with Burns to the ship, some fifty thousand people lined the streets. As the procession passed, one Bostonian hung from his window a black coffin bearing the words "THE FUNERAL OF LIBERTY." Another draped an American flag upside down as a symbol that "my country is eternally disgraced by this day's proceedings." The Burns incident shattered the complacency of conservative supporters of the Compromise of 1850. "We went to bed one night old fashioned conservative Compromise Union Whigs," the textile manufacturer Amos A. Lawrence wrote, "and waked up stark mad Abolitionists." A Boston committee later successfully purchased Burns's freedom, but the fate of many fugitives was far less happy. One such unfortunate was Margaret Garner, who, about to be captured and sent back to Kentucky as a slave, slit her daughter's throat and tried to kill her other children rather than witness their return to slavery.

In response to the Fugitive Slave Act, vigilance committees sprang up in many northern communities to spirit endangered blacks to safety in Canada. As another ploy, lawyers used obstructive tactics to drag out legal proceedings and thus raise the slave-catchers' expenses. Then during the 1850s, nine northern states passed "personal-liberty laws." By such techniques as forbidding the use of state jails to incarcerate alleged fugitives, these laws aimed to bar state officials from enforcing the law.

The frequent cold stares, obstructive legal tactics, and occasional violence encountered by slaveholders who ventured north to capture runaway slaves helped demonstrate to southerners that opposition to slavery boiled just beneath the surface of northern opinion. In the eyes of most southerners, the South had gained little more from the Compromise of 1850 than the Fugitive Slave Act, and now doubts surrounded even that northern concession. After witnessing riots against the Fugitive Slave Act in Boston in 1854, a young Georgian studying law at Harvard wrote to his mother, "Do not be surprised if when I return home you find me *a confirmed disunionist.*"

Uncle Tom's Cabin

The publication in 1852 of Harriet Beecher Stowe's novel *Uncle Tom's Cabin* aroused wide northern sympathy for fugitive slaves. Stowe, the daughter of the famed evangelical Lyman Beecher and the younger sister of Catharine Beecher, the stalwart advocate of domesticity for women, greeted the Fugitive Slave Act with horror and outrage. In a memorable scene from the novel, she depicted the slave Eliza escaping to freedom, clutching her infant son while bounding across ice floes on the Ohio River. Yet Stowe targeted slavery itself more than merely the slave-catchers who served the institution. Much of her novel's power derives from its intimation that even good intentions cannot prevail against so evil an institution. Torn from his wife and children by sale and shipped on a steamer for the Lower South, the black slave Uncle Tom rescues little Eva, the daughter of kindly Augustine St. Clare, from drowning. In gratitude, St. Clare purchases Tom from a slave-trader and takes him into his home in New Orleans. But after St. Clare's death, his cruel widow sells Tom to the vicious (and northern-born) Simon Legree, who whips Tom to death. Stowe played effectively on the emotions of her audience by demonstrating to an age that revered family life how slavery tore the family apart.

Three hundred thousand copies of *Uncle Tom's Cabin* were sold in 1852, and 1.2 million by the summer of 1853. Dramatized versions, which added dogs to chase Eliza across the ice, eventually reached perhaps fifty times the number of people as the novel itself. As a play, *Uncle Tom's Cabin* enthralled working-portrayed only light-skinned blacks as aggressive and intelligent; she depicted dark-skinned blacks such as Uncle Tom as docile and submissive. In addition, some of the stage dramatizations softened the novel's antislavery message. In one version, which P. T. Barnum produced, Tom was rescued from Legree and returned happily as a slave to his original plantation.

Surgery on the plot, however, could not fully excise the antislavery message of *Uncle Tom's Cabin*. Though the novel hardly lived up to the prediction of a proslavery lawyer that it would convert 2 million people to abolitionism, it did push many waverers toward a more aggressively antisouthern and antislavery stance. Indeed, fear of its impact inspired a host of southerners to pen anti–Uncle Tom novels. As historian David Potter has concluded, the northern attitude toward slavery "was never quite the same after *Uncle Tom's Cabin*."

The Election of 1852

The issue of the enforcement of the Fugitive Slave Act fragmented the Whig party. The majority of northern Whigs, strongly supportive of free soil, had opposed the passage of the Fugitive Slave Act and now were leading defiance of the law. This vocal and potent northern free-soil wing put southern Whigs on the spot, for these southerners had long come before the southern electorate as the party best able to defend slavery within the Union.

The Whigs' nomination in 1852 of General Winfield Scott, the Mexican War hero, in place of the pro-compromise Millard Fillmore, widened the sectional split in their party. Although a Virginian, Scott had fallen under the influence of Senator William H. Seward of New York, a leader of the party's free-soil wing, and owed his nomination to northern votes. During the campaign Scott issued only a single, feeble endorsement of the Compromise of 1850, far less than southern Whigs needed if they were to brand the Democrats as the party of disunion and portray themselves as the party of both slavery and the Union.

The Democrats suffered from divisions of their own. In 1848 defectors from the Democratic party, led by Martin Van Buren, had formed the core of the Free-Soil party, which had gained over 10 percent of the popular vote. By 1852, however, most of the Free-Soilers of 1848, hungry for the spoils of office, returned to the Democratic party. As an idea rather than as a third party, free soil continued to win adherents between 1848 and 1852, but most converts to the idea of free

Harriet Beecher Stowe, *1853*
Although her direct knowledge of slavery had been gleaned during a single visit to a Kentucky plantation, Stowe did extensive research before writing Uncle Tom's Cabin. *By making the demonic Simon Legree a northerner and by portraying southerners as well meaning, she effectively indicted slavery as an institution.*

class audiences normally indifferent, if not hostile, to abolitionism. During one stage performance, a reviewer for a New York newspaper observed that the gallery was filled with men "in red woollen shirts, with countenances as hardy and rugged as the implements of industry employed by them in the pursuit of their vocations." Astonished by the silence that fell over these men at the point when Eliza escapes across the river, the reviewer turned to discover that many of them were in tears.

The impact of *Uncle Tom's Cabin* cannot be precisely measured. Although the novel stirred deep feelings, it reflected the prevailing stereotypes of blacks far more than it overturned commonly held views. Stowe

The Election of 1852

Candidates	Parties	Electoral Vote	Popular Vote	Percentage of Popular Vote
FRANKLIN PIERCE	Democratic	254	1,601,117	50.9
Winfield Scott	Whig	42	1,385,453	44.1
John P. Hale	Free-Soil		155,825	5.0

soil gravitated to the Whig rather than the Democratic party.

The Democratic convention began as a three-sided struggle among Lewis Cass of Michigan, James Buchanan of Pennsylvania, and Stephen A. Douglas of Illinois but ended with the nomination of a dark horse, Franklin Pierce of New Hampshire. Handsome, charming, and friendly, Pierce had served in Congress and in the Mexican War. But his appeal to the Democrats rested less on his political experience or his undistinguished war record (during a battle near Mexico City, he had passed out after having been thrown from his horse) than on his acceptability to all factions of the party. The "ultra men of the South," a friend of Pierce noted, "say they can cheerfully go for him and none, none say they cannot." In both the North and the South, the Democrats rallied not only behind the Compromise of 1850 but behind the idea of applying popular sovereignty to *all* the territories. In the most one-sided election since 1820, Pierce swept twenty-seven of the thirty-one states and won the electoral vote 254–42. The outcome was particularly galling for southern Whigs, who had soared to new heights four years previously. Compared to the 49.8 percent of the popular vote in the South won by Zachary Taylor in 1848, in 1852, Scott could claim only 35 percent of the southern vote. In state elections during 1852 and 1853, moreover, the Whigs were devastated in the South; one Whig stalwart lamented "the decisive breaking-up of our party."

◆

THE COLLAPSE OF THE SECOND PARTY SYSTEM

Franklin Pierce had the dubious distinction of being the last presidential candidate for eighty years to win the popular and electoral vote in both the North and the South. Not until 1932 did another president, Franklin D. Roosevelt, repeat this accomplishment.

Pierce was also the last president to hold office under the second party system—Whigs against Democrats. For two decades the Whigs and the Democrats had battled, often on even terms. Then, within the four years of Pierce's administration, the Whig party disintegrated. In its place two new parties, first the American (Know-Nothing) party, and then the Republican party, arose.

Unlike the Whig party, the Republican party was a purely sectional, northern party. Its support came from former northern Whigs and from discontented northern Democrats. The Democrats survived as a national party, but with a base so shrunken in the North that in 1856, the Republican party, although scarcely a year old, swept two-thirds of the free states.

For decades the second party system had kept the conflict over slavery in check by giving Americans other issues—banking, internal improvements, tariffs, and temperance—to argue about. By the 1850s the debate over slavery extension was pushing such issues into the background and exposing raw divisions in each party. Of the two parties, Whig and Democratic, the Whigs had the larger, more aggressive free-soil wing, and hence they were more vulnerable than the Democrats to disruption. When Stephen A. Douglas in 1854 put forth a proposal to organize the vast Nebraska territory without restrictions on slavery, he ignited a firestorm that consumed the Whig party.

The Kansas-Nebraska Act

Signed by President Pierce at the end of May 1854, the Kansas-Nebraska Act dealt a shattering blow to the already weakened second party system. Moreover, the law triggered a renewal of the sectional strife that many Americans believed the Compromise of 1850 had buried. The origins of the act lay in the seemingly uncontroversial advance of midwestern settlement. Farm families in Iowa and Missouri had long dreamed of establishing homesteads in the vast prairies to their west, and their congressional repre-

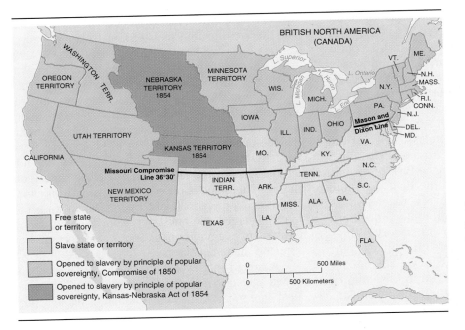

BRITISH NORTH AMERICA
(CANADA)

Free state or territory

Slave state or territory

Opened to slavery by principle of popular sovereignty, Compromise of 1850

Opened to slavery by principle of popular sovereignty, Kansas-Nebraska Act of 1854

0   500 Miles

0   500 Kilometers

The Kansas-Nebraska Act, 1854
Kansas and Nebraska lay within the Louisiana Purchase, north of 36°30', and hence were closed to slavery until Stephen A. Douglas introduced his bills in 1854.

sentatives had repeatedly introduced bills to organize the territory west of these states, so that Native American land titles could be extinguished and a basis for government provided. Too, since the mid-1840s, advocates of national expansion had looked to the day when a railroad would link the Midwest to the Pacific; and St. Louis, Milwaukee, and Chicago had vied to become the eastern end of the projected Pacific railroad.

In January 1854 Senator Stephen A. Douglas of Illinois proposed a bill to organize Nebraska as a territory. An ardent expansionist, Douglas had formed his political ideology in the heady atmosphere of Manifest Destiny during the 1840s. As early as the mid-1840s, he had embraced the ideas of a Pacific railroad and the organization of Nebraska as ways to guarantee a continuous line of settlement between the Midwest and the Pacific. Although he preferred a railroad from his hometown of Chicago to San Francisco, Douglas dwelled on the national benefits that would attend construction of a railroad from *anywhere* in the Midwest to the Pacific. Such a railroad would enhance the importance of the Midwest, which could then hold the balance of power between the older sections of the North and South and guide the nation toward unity rather than disruption. In addition, westward expansion through Nebraska with the aid of a railroad struck Douglas as an issue, comparable to Manifest Destiny, around which the

contending factions of the Democratic party would unite.

Douglas recognized two sources of potential conflict over his Nebraska bill. First, some southerners advocated a rival route for the Pacific railroad that would start at either New Orleans or Memphis. Second, Nebraska lay within the Louisiana Purchase and north of the Missouri Compromise line of 36°30', a region closed to slavery. Unless Douglas made some concessions, southerners would have little incentive to vote for his bill, because the organization of Nebraska would simultaneously create a potential free state and increase the chances for a northern, rather than a southern, railroad to the Pacific. As the floor manager of the Compromise of 1850 in the Senate, Douglas thought that he had an ideal concession to offer to the South. The Compromise of 1850 had applied the principle of popular sovereignty to New Mexico and Utah, territories outside of the Louisiana Purchase and hence unaffected by the Missouri Compromise. Why not assume, Douglas reasoned, that the Compromise of 1850 had taken the place of the Missouri Compromise *everywhere*? Believing that expansion rather than slavery was uppermost in the public's mind, Douglas hoped to avoid controversy over slavery by ignoring the Missouri Compromise. But he quickly came under pressure from southern congressmen, who wanted an explicit repudiation of the Missouri Compromise. Soon southerners forced Douglas to state publicly that the Nebraska bill "superseded" the Missouri Compromise and rendered it "void." Still under pressure, Douglas next agreed to a division of Nebraska into two territories: Nebraska to the west of Iowa, and Kansas to the west of Missouri. Because Missouri was a slave state, most congressmen assumed that the division aimed to secure Kansas for slavery and Nebraska for free soil.

The modifications of Douglas's original bill set off a storm of protest. Congress quickly tabled the Pacific railroad (which, in the turn of events, would not be built until after the Civil War) and focused on the issue of slavery extension. A group of "Independent Democratic" northern congressmen, composed of antislavery Whigs and free-soil Democrats, assailed the bill as "part and parcel of an atrocious plot" to violate the "sacred pledge" of the Missouri Compromise and to turn Kansas into a "dreary region of despotism, inhabited by masters and slaves." Their rage electrified southerners, many of whom initially had reacted indifferently to the Nebraska bill. Some southerners had opposed an explicit repeal of the Missouri Compromise from fear of stimulating sectional discord; others doubted that Kansas would attract many slaveholders. But the furious assault of antislavery northerners united the South behind the Kansas-Nebraska bill by turning the issue into one of sectional pride as much as slavery extension.

Despite the uproar, Douglas successfully guided the Kansas-Nebraska bill through the Senate, where it passed by a vote of 37 to 14. In the House of Representatives, where the bill passed by little more than a whisker, 113 to 100, the true dimensions of the conflict became apparent. Not a single northern Whig representative in the House voted for the bill, whereas the northern Democrats divided evenly, 44 to 44.

The Surge of Free Soil

Douglas obviously had miscalculated the reaction to his Kansas-Nebraska bill. Amid the clamor over the bill, he conceded that he could now travel to Chicago by the light of his own burning effigies. Yet Douglas was neither a fool nor a political novice. Rather, he was the victim of a political force, the surge of feeling for free soil, that exploded under his feet.

Support for free soil united northerners who could agree on little else. Many northern free-soilers were racists who opposed letting any blacks, free or slave, into the West. In 1851 and 1853, racist free-soil advocates in Iowa and Illinois secured the passage of laws prohibiting settlement by black people; and in Iowa, Michigan, and Wisconsin, free-soilers refused by overwhelming majorities to allow blacks to vote. In Oregon, after rejecting slavery by a three-to-one majority in 1857, voters excluded all blacks from the state by an eight-to-one majority. But laws excluding blacks from western settlement were not always enforced, and not all free-soilers were racist. Some rejected slavery on moral grounds and opposed blatantly racist legislation. However, as the abolitionist George W. Julian accurately observed, the antislavery convictions of many westerners were grounded on a "perfect, if not supreme" hatred of blacks.

Although split over the morality of slavery, free-soilers agreed that slavery impeded whites' progress. Most free-soilers accepted Abraham Lincoln's portrayal of the North as a society of upwardly mobile farmers, artisans, and small businessmen and subscribed to the doctrine of "free labor"—the idea that in America, any enterprising individual could escape the class of wage labor and attain self-employment. "The man who labored for another last year," Lincoln insisted, "this year labors for himself, and next year he will hire others to labor for him." Because a slave worked for nothing, the free-soil argument ran, no free laborer could compete with a slave. A territory might contain only a handful of slaves or none at all, but as long as Congress refused to prohibit slavery in the territories, the institution could gain a foothold. Then slavery would grow, and free labor would wither; competition with slave labor would either drive out free labor or deter free labor from entering. Wherever slavery appeared, a free-soiler proclaimed, "labor loses its dignity; industry sickens; education finds no schools; religion finds no churches, and the whole land of slavery is impoverished."

Furthermore, free-soilers flatly rejected the idea that slavery had natural limits. As long as slaves could enter a territory, they believed, slaveholders would find tasks for them. In 1851 a free-soiler warned that "slavery is as certain to invade New Mexico and Utah, as the sun is to rise." By 1854 free-soilers were predicting that once secure in Kansas, slavery would invade the Minnesota Territory.

One free-soiler articulated the growing suspicions of many when he branded the Kansas-Nebraska Act "a part of a continuous movement of slaveholders to advance slavery over the entire North." At every turn, the free-soilers contended, the spread of slavery depended on the complicity of politicians. At the heart of the free-soil argument lay the belief that southern planters, southern politicians, and their northern dupes like Stephen A. Douglas were conspiring to spread slavery. And rather than any single event, there emerged a *pattern* of events—the Fugitive Slave Act, the repeal of the Missouri Compromise, and the Kansas-Nebraska division—that convinced free-soilers that a diabolical Slave Power was spreading its tentacles like an octopus. "I voted for the compromise measures of 1850, with the exception of the fugitive slave law," wrote a Whig congressman from Massachusetts, "and had little sympathy with abolitionists, but the repeal of the Missouri Compromise, that most wanton and wicked act, so obviously designed to promote the extension of slavery, was too much to bear. I now advocate the freedom of Kansas under all circumstances and at all hazards, and the prohibition of slavery in all territories now free."

The Ebbing of Manifest Destiny

The Kansas-Nebraska Act strained Democratic harmony and embarrassed the Pierce administration. The hubbub over the law doomed Manifest Destiny, the issue that had unified the Democrats in the 1840s.

Pierce had come to office as a champion of Manifest Destiny. In 1853 his emissary James Gadsden concluded a treaty with Mexico for the purchase of a strip of land south of the Gila River (now southern Arizona and part of southern New Mexico), an acquisition favored by advocates of a southern railroad route to the Pacific. The fiercely negative reaction to the so-called Gadsden Purchase, however, pointed up the mounting suspicions of expansionist aims. Encountering stiff northern opposition, Gadsden's treaty gained Senate approval in 1854 only after an amendment slashed nine thousand square miles from the purchase. Clearly, the same sectional rivalries that were brewing conflict over the existing territory of Nebraska were threatening to engulf proposals to gain *new* territory.

Pierce encountered even more severe buffeting when he tried to acquire the island of Cuba. Even as Congress was wrestling with the Kansas-Nebraska bill, Mississippi's former senator John A. Quitman was planning a massive filibustering (unofficial) military expedition—to seize Cuba from Spain. Pierce himself wanted to purchase Cuba and may have encouraged

Quitman as a way to scare Spain into selling the island. However, northerners, aroused by the Kansas-Nebraska bill, increasingly viewed filibustering as another manifestation of the Slave Power's conspiracy to grab more territory for the "peculiar institution." Pierce, alarmed by northern reaction to the Kansas-Nebraska bill and by signs that Spain planned to defend the island militarily, forced Quitman to scuttle the planned expedition.

Pierce still hoped to purchase Cuba, but events quickly slipped out of his control. In October 1854 the American ambassadors to Great Britain, France, and Spain, two of them from the South, met in Belgium and issued the unofficial Ostend Manifesto, which called upon the United States to acquire Cuba by any necessary means, including force, and then to welcome the island "into that great family of states of which the Union is the Providential Nursery." Already beset by the storm over the Kansas-Nebraska Act, and faced by northern outrage at the threat of aggression against Spain, Pierce quickly repudiated the manifesto.

Despite the Pierce administration's opposition to the Ostend Manifesto, the idea of expansion into the Caribbean continued to attract southerners, including the Tennessee-born adventurer William Walker. Slightly built and so shy and unassuming that he usually spoke with his hands in his pockets, Walker seemed an unlikely soldier of fortune. Yet between 1854 and 1860, the year he was executed by a firing squad in Honduras, Walker led a succession of filibustering expeditions into Central America. Taking advantage of civil chaos in Nicaragua, he made himself the chief political force in that nation, reinstituted slavery there, and talked openly of making Nicaragua a U.S. colony. Southern expansionists also kept the acquisition of both Cuba and parts of Mexico at the top of their agenda and received some support from northern Democrats. As late as 1859, President James Buchanan, Pierce's successor, tried to persuade Congress to appropriate funds for the purchase of Cuba.

For all of the proclamations and intrigues that surrounded the movement for southern expansion in the 1850s, the expansionists' actual strength and goals remained open to question. Many planned filibustering expeditions never got off the ground. With few exceptions the adventurers were shady characters whom southern politicians might admire but upon whom they could never depend. Moreover, a sizable body of southerners did not support the idea of southward expansion. The largely Whig sugar planters in Louisiana, for example, opposed acquiring Cuba, on grounds that once Cuba was annexed, its sugar would enter the United States duty-free and compete with American sugar.

Still, southern expansionists created enough commotion to worry antislavery northerners that the South aspired to establish a Caribbean slave empire. Like a card in a poker game, the threat of expansion southward was all the more menacing for not being played. As long as the debate over the extension of slavery focused on territories in the continental United States, slavery's prospects for expansion were limited and, Kansas aside, seemed fairly dim. If parts of the Caribbean were added to the United States, however, all these calculations would have to change.

The Whigs Disintegrate

While straining Democratic unity, the Kansas-Nebraska Act wrecked the Whig party. In the law's immediate aftermath, most northern Whigs hoped to blame the Democrats for the act and to entice free-soil Democrats to their side. In the state and congressional elections of 1854, the Democrats were decisively defeated. But the Whig party failed to benefit from the backlash against the Democrats. However furious they felt at Douglas for initiating the act, free-soil Democrats could not forget that the southern Whigs had supported Douglas. In addition, the northern Whigs themselves were deeply divided between antislavery "Conscience" Whigs, led by Senator William Seward of New York, and conservatives, led by former president Millard Fillmore, who were convinced that the Whig party had to adhere at all costs to the Compromise of 1850 to maintain itself as a national party.

Divisions within the Whig party not only repelled antislavery Democrats from affiliating with it but also prompted many antislavery Whigs to look for an alternative party. By 1856 the new Republican party would become the home for most of these northern refugees from the traditional parties; but in 1854 and 1855, when the Republican party was only starting to organize, the American, or Know-Nothing, party emerged as the principal alternative to the established parties.

The Rise and Fall of the Know-Nothings

The Know-Nothings evolved out of a secret nativist organization, the Order of the Star-Spangled Banner, founded in 1850. (The party's popular name, Know-Nothing, derived from the standard response of its members to inquiries about its activities: "I know nothing.") One of many such societies that mushroomed in response to the unprecedented immigration of the 1840s, the Order of the Star-Spangled Banner had sought to rid the United States of immigrant and Catholic political influence by pressuring the existing parties to nominate and appoint only native-born Protestants to office, and by advocating an extension of the naturalization period before immigrants could vote.

Throughout the 1840s nativists usually voted Whig, but their allegiance to the Whigs started to buckle during Winfield Scott's campaign for the presidency in 1852. In an attempt to revitalize his party, which was badly split over slavery, Scott had courted the traditionally Democratic Catholic vote. But Scott's tactic backfired, for most Catholics voted for Franklin Pierce. Nativists, meanwhile, felt betrayed by their party, and, after Scott's defeat, many gravitated toward the Know-Nothings. The Kansas-Nebraska Act cemented their allegiance to the Know-Nothings, who in the North opposed both the extension of slavery and Catholicism. Indeed, an obsessive fear of conspiracies unified the Know-Nothings. Just as they denounced the pope for allegedly conspiring to subvert the American republic, they saw the evil influence of Slave Power everywhere.

The Know-Nothings' surge was truly stunning. In 1854 they captured the governorship, all the congressional seats, and almost all the seats in the state legislature in Massachusetts. Know-Nothings were sufficiently strong in the West to retard the emergence of the Republican party, and so strong in the East that they exploded any hopes that the Whigs had of capitalizing on hostility to the Kansas-Nebraska Act.

After rising spectacularly between 1853 and 1855, the star of Know-Nothingism nevertheless plummeted and gradually disappeared from the horizon after 1856. The Know-Nothings proved as vulnerable as the Whigs to sectional conflicts over slavery. Although primarily a force in the North, the Know-Nothings had a southern wing, composed mainly of former Whigs who loathed both the antislavery northerners who were abandoning the Whig party and the southern Democrats, whom they viewed as disunionist firebrands. In 1855 these southern Know-Nothings combined with northern conservatives to make acceptance of the Kansas-Nebraska Act part of the Know-Nothing platform, and thus they blurred the attraction of Know-Nothingism to those northern voters who were more antislavery than anti-Catholic. One such Whig refugee, Illinois congressman Abraham Lincoln, asked pointedly: "How can anyone who abhors the oppression of negroes be in favor of degrading classes of white people ?" "We began by declaring," Lincoln continued, "that 'all men are created equal.' We now practically read it 'all men are created equal except negroes.' When the Know-Nothings get control, it will read 'all men are created equal, except Negroes and foreigners and Catholics.' " Finally, even most Know-Nothings eventually came to conclude that, as one observer put it, "neither the Pope nor the foreigners ever can govern the country or endanger its liberties, but the slavebreeders and slavetraders *do* govern it, and threaten to put an end to all government but theirs." Consequently, the Know-Nothings proved vulnerable to the challenge posed by the emerging Republican party, which did not officially embrace nativism and which had no southern wing to blunt its antislavery message.

The Origins of the Republican Party

Born in the chaotic aftermath of the Kansas-Nebraska Act, the Republican party sprang up in several northern states in 1854 and 1855. With the Know-Nothings' demise after 1856, the Republicans would become the main opposition to the Democratic party, and they would win each presidential election from 1860 through 1880; but in 1855 it was unclear whether the Republicans had any future. While united by opposition to the Kansas-Nebraska Act, the party held various shades of opinion in uneasy balance. At one extreme were conservatives who merely wanted to restore the Missouri Compromise; at the other was a small faction of former Liberty party abolitionists; and the middle held a sizable body of free-soilers.

In addition to bridging these divisions, the Republicans confronted the task of building organizations on the state level, where the Know-Nothings were already well established. Politicians of the day knew that the voters' allegiances were often shaped by state issues, including temperance. Maine's passage of the nation's first statewide prohibition law in 1851 spurred calls elsewhere for liquor regulation. Linking support for temperance with anti-Catholicism and antislavery, the Know-Nothings were well positioned to answer these calls.

Frequently, the same voters who were antislavery were also pro-temperance and anti-Catholic. The common thread here was the belief that addiction to alcohol and submission to the pope were forms of enslavement that had to be eradicated. Intensely moralistic, such voters viewed the traditional parties as controlled by unprincipled hacks, and they began to search for a new party. In competing with the Know-Nothings on the state level, the Republicans faced a dilemma, created by the fact that both parties were targeting many of the same voters. The Republican leadership had clearer antislavery credentials than did the Know-Nothing leadership, but this fact alone did not guarantee that voters would respond more to antislavery than to anti-Catholicism or temperance. Thus, if the Republicans attacked the Know-Nothings for stressing anti-Catholicism over antislavery, they ran the risk of alienating the very voters whom they had to attract. If they conciliated the Know-Nothings, they might lose their own identity as a party.

Sometimes attacking, sometimes conciliating, the Republicans won some successes in state elections in 1855; but as popular ire against the Kansas-Nebraska Act cooled, they also suffered setbacks. Even at the start of 1856, they were organized in only half the northern states and lacked any national organization. The Republicans desperately needed a development that would make voters worry more about the Slave Power than about rum or Catholicism. No single occurrence did more to unite the party around its free-soil center, to intensify voters' antislavery feelings, and, consequently, to boost the Republicans' fortunes than the outbreak of violence in Kansas, which quickly gained for the territory the name Bleeding Kansas.

Bleeding Kansas

In the wake of the Kansas-Nebraska Act, Boston-based abolitionists had organized the New England Emigrant Aid Company to send antislavery settlers into Kansas. The abolitionists' aim was to stifle escalating efforts to turn Kansas into a slave state. But antislavery New Englanders arrived slowly in Kansas; the bulk of the territory's early settlers came from Missouri or elsewhere in the Midwest. Very few of these early settlers opposed slavery on moral grounds. Some, in fact, favored slavery; others wanted to keep all blacks, whether slave or free, out of Kansas. "I kem to Kansas to live in a free state," exclaimed a clergyman, "and I don't want niggers a-trampin' over my grave."

Despite most settlers' racist leanings and utter hatred of abolitionists, Kansas became a battleground between proslavery and antislavery forces. In March 1855 thousands of proslavery Missourian "border

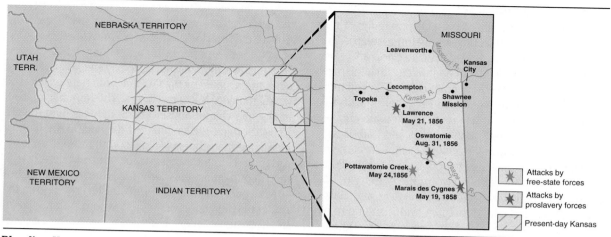

Bleeding Kansas
Kansas became a battleground between free-state and slave-state factions in the 1850s.

ruffians," led by Senator David R. Atchison, crossed into Kansas to vote illegally in the first election for a territorial legislature. Drawing and cocking their revolvers, they quickly silenced any judges who questioned their right to vote in Kansas. These proslavery advocates probably would have won an honest election, because they would have been supported by the votes both of slaveholders and of nonslaveholders horrified at rumors that abolitionists planned to use Kansas as a colony for fugitive slaves. But by stealing the election, the proslavery forces committed a grave tactical blunder. A cloud of fraudulence thereafter hung over the proslavery legislature subsequently established at Lecompton, Kansas. "There is not a proslavery man of my acquaintance in Kansas," wrote the wife of an antislavery farmer, "who does not acknowledge that the Bogus Legislature was the result of a gigantic and well planned fraud, that the elections were carried by an invading mob from Missouri." This legislature then further darkened its image by expelling several antislavery legislators and passing a succession of outrageous acts. These laws limited officeholding to individuals who would swear allegiance to slavery, punished the harboring of fugitive slaves by ten years' imprisonment, and made the circulation of abolitionist literature a capital offense.

The legislature's actions set off a chain reaction. Free-staters, including a small number of abolitionists and a much larger number of settlers enraged by the proceedings at Lecompton, organized a rival government at Topeka, Kansas, in the summer and fall of

1855. In response, the Lecompton government in May 1856 dispatched a posse to Lawrence, where free-staters, heeding the advice of antislavery minister Henry Ward Beecher that rifles would do more than Bibles to enforce morality in Kansas, had taken up arms and dubbed their guns "Beecher's Bibles." Riding under flags emblazoned "SOUTHERN RIGHTS" and "LET YANKEES TREMBLE AND ABOLITIONISTS FALL," the proslavery posse tore through the town like a hell-bent mob. Although the intruders did not kill anyone, they burned several buildings and destroyed two free-state printing presses—enough to earn their actions in the Republican press as "THE SACK OF LAWRENCE."

The next move belonged to John Brown. The son of a Connecticut abolitionist, Brown had drifted through business failures, bankruptcy, and even a charge of embezzlement, sustained only by his belief that God had ordained his misfortunes to test him. The sack of Lawrence convinced Brown that God now beckoned him, in the words of a neighbor, "to break the jaws of the wicked." In late May, Brown led seven men, including his four sons and his son-in-law, toward the Pottawatomie Creek near Lawrence. Setting upon five men associated with the Lecompton government, they shot one to death and hacked the others to pieces with broadswords. Brown's "Pottawatomie massacre" struck terror into the hearts of southerners and completed the transformation of "bleeding Kansas" into a battleground between the South and the North. A month after the massacre, a South Carolinian living in Kansas wrote to his sister:

I never lie down without taking the precaution to fasten my door and fix it in such a way that if it is forced open, it can be opened only wide enough for one person to come in at a time. I have my rifle, revolver, and old home-stocked pistol where I can lay my hand on them in an instant, besides a hatchet and an axe. I take this precaution to guard against the midnight attacks of the Abolitionists, who never make an attack in open daylight, and no Proslavery man knows when he is safe in this Ter[ritory.]

In Kansas popular sovereignty flunked its major test. Instead of quickly resolving the issue of slavery extension, popular sovereignty merely institutionalized the division over slavery by creating two rival governments, in Lecompton and Topeka. The Pierce administration then shot itself in the foot by denouncing the Topeka government and recognizing only its Lecompton rival. Pierce had forced northern Democrats into the awkward position of appearing to ally with the South in support of the fraudulently elected legislature at Lecompton. Nor did popular sovereignty keep the slavery issue out of national politics. On the day before the sack of Lawrence, Republican senator Charles Sumner of Massachusetts delivered a bombastic and wrathful speech, "The Crime Against Kansas," in which he verbally whipped most of the United States Senate for complicity in slavery and singled out Senator Andrew Butler of South Carolina for his choice of "the harlot, slavery" as his mistress and for the "loose expectoration" of his speech (a nasty reference to the aging Butler's tendency to drool). Sumner's oration stunned most senators. Douglas wondered aloud whether Sumner's real aim was "to provoke some of us to kick him as we would a dog in the street." Two days later a relative of Butler, Democratic representative Preston Brooks of South Carolina, strode into the Senate chamber, found Sumner at his desk, and struck him repeatedly with a cane. The hollow cane broke after five or six blows, but Sumner required stitches, experienced shock, and did not return to the Senate for three years. Brooks became an instant hero in the South, and the fragments of his cane were "begged as sacred relics." A new cane, presented to Brooks by the city of Charleston, bore the inscription "Hit him again."

Now "Bleeding Kansas" and "Bleeding Sumner" united the North. The sack of Lawrence, Pierce's recognition of the proslavery Lecompton government, and Brooks's actions seemed to clinch the Republican argument that an aggressive slaveocracy held white northerners in contempt. Abolitionists remained unpopular in northern opinion, but southerners were becoming even less popular than abolitionists. Northern migrants to Kansas coined a name reflecting their feelings toward southerners: "the pukes." Other northerners attacked the slaveholding migrants to Kansas as the "Missouri savages." By denouncing the Slave Power more than slavery itself, Republican propagandists sidestepped the issue of slavery's morality, which divided their followers, and focused on portraying southern planters as arrogant aristocrats and the natural enemies of the laboring people of the North.

The Election of 1856

The election of 1856 revealed the scope of the political realignments of the preceding few years. In this, its first presidential contest, the Republican party nominated John C. Frémont, the famed "pathfinder" who had played a key role in the conquest of California during the Mexican War. The Republicans then maneuvered the northern Know-Nothings into endorsing Frémont. The southern Know-Nothings picked the last Whig president, Millard Fillmore, as their candidate, and the Democrats dumped Pierce for the seasoned James Buchanan of Pennsylvania. A four-term congressman and long an aspirant to the presidency, Buchanan finally secured his party's nomination because he had the good luck to be out of the country (as minister to Great Britain) during the furor over the Kansas-Nebraska Act. As a signer of the Ostend Manifesto, he was popular in the South: virtually all of his close friends in Washington were southerners.

The campaign quickly turned into two separate races—Frémont versus Buchanan in the free states and Fillmore versus Buchanan in the slave states. In the North the candidates divided clearly over slavery extension; Frémont's platform called for a congressional prohibition of slavery in the territories, whereas Buchanan pledged congressional "non-interference." In the South Fillmore appealed to traditionally Whig voters and called for moderation in the face of secessionist threats. But by nominating a well-known moderate in Buchanan, the Democrats undercut some of Fillmore's appeal. Although Fillmore garnered more than 40 percent of the popular vote in ten of the slave states, he carried only Maryland. In the North Frémont outpolled Buchanan in the popular vote and won eleven of the sixteen free states; if Frémont had carried

The Election of 1856

Candidates	Parties	Electoral Vote	Popular Vote	Percentage of Popular Vote
JAMES BUCHANAN	Democratic	174	1,832,955	45.3
John C. Frémont	Republican	114	1,339,932	33.1
Millard Fillmore	American	8	871,731	21.6

Pennsylvania and either Illinois or Indiana, he would have won the election. As it turned out, Buchanan, the only truly national candidate in the race, secured the presidency.

The election yielded three clear conclusions. First, the American party was finished as a major national force. Having worked for the Republican Frémont, most northern Know-Nothings now joined that party, and in the wake of Fillmore's dismal showing in the South, southern Known-Nothings gave up on their party and sought new political affiliations. Second, although in existence scarcely more than a year, lacking any base in the South, and running a political novice, the Republican party did very well. A purely sectional party had come within reach of capturing the presidency. Finally, as long as the Democrats could unite behind a single national candidate, they would be hard to defeat. To achieve such unity, however, the Democrats would have to find more James Buchanans—"dough-face" moderates who would be acceptable to southerners and who would not drive even more northerners into Republican arms.

THE CRISIS OF THE UNION

No one ever accused James Buchanan of impulsiveness or fanaticism. Although he disapproved of slavery, he believed that his administration could neither restrict nor end the institution. In 1860 he would pronounce secession a grave wrong, but he would again affirm that his administration could not stop it. Understandably, contemporaries hailed his election as a victory for moderation. Yet his administration encountered a succession of controversies, first over the famed *Dred Scott* decision of the Supreme Court, then over the proslavery Lecompton constitution in Kansas, next following a raid by John Brown on Harpers Ferry,

Virginia, and finally concerning secession itself. Ironically, a man who sought to avoid controversy presided over one of the most controversy-ridden administrations in American history. Buchanan's problems arose less from his own actions than from the fact that the forces driving the nation apart were already spinning out of control by 1856. By the time of Buchanan's inauguration, southerners who looked north saw creeping abolitionism in the guise of free soil, whereas northerners who looked south saw an insatiable Slave Power. Once these images had taken hold in the minds of the American people, politicians like James Buchanan had little room to maneuver.

The Dred Scott Case

Pledged to congressional "non-interference" with slavery in the territories, Buchanan had long looked to the courts for a judicious and nonpartisan resolution of the vexatious issue of slavery extension. A case that appeared to promise such a solution had been winding its way through the courts for years; on March 6, 1857, two days after Buchanan's inauguration, the Supreme Court handed down its decision in *Dred Scott* v. *Sandford*.

Dred Scott, a slave, had been taken by his master during the 1830s from the slave state Missouri into Illinois and the Wisconsin Territory, areas respectively closed to slavery by the Northwest Ordinance of 1787 and by the Missouri Compromise. After his master's death, Scott sued for his freedom on the grounds of his residence in free territory. A jury sided with Scott and set him free. On appeal, however, the Missouri Supreme Court overturned the jury's decision in 1852 and returned Scott to slavery. Subsequently, Scott's new owner moved to New York while leaving Scott in Missouri, a turn of events that encouraged Scott to sue in the federal courts (which had jurisdiction over suits brought by citizens of one state against those of another). In 1856 the case finally reached the Supreme Court.

The Court faced two key issues. Did Scott's residence in free territory during the 1830s make him free? Next, regardless of the answer to this question, did Scott, again enslaved in Missouri, have a right to sue in the federal courts? The Court could have resolved the case on narrow grounds by answering the second question in the negative, but Buchanan wanted a far-reaching decision that would deal with the broad issue of slavery in the territories.

In the end, Buchanan got the broad ruling that he sought, but one so controversial that it settled little. In the most important of six separate majority opinions, Chief Justice Roger B. Taney, a seventy-nine-year-old Marylander whom Andrew Jackson had appointed to succeed John Marshall in 1835, began with the narrow conclusion that Scott, a slave, could not sue for his freedom. Then the thunder started. No black, whether a slave or a free person descended from a slave, could become a citizen of the United States, Taney continued. Next Taney whipped the thunderheads into a tornado. Even if Scott had been a legal plaintiff, Taney ruled, his residence in free territory years earlier did not make him free, because the Missouri Compromise, whose provisions prohibited slavery in the Wisconsin Territory, was *itself* unconstitutional. The compromise, declared Taney, violated the Fifth Amendment's protection of property (including slaves) from deprivation without due process of law.

Contrary to Buchanan's hopes, the decision touched off a new blast of controversy over slavery in the territories. The antislavery press flayed it as a "willful perversion" filled with "gross historical falsehoods." Taney's ruling gave Republicans more evidence that a fiendish Slave Power conspiracy gripped the nation. Although the Kansas-Nebraska Act had effectively repealed the Missouri Compromise, the Court's majority now rejected even the *principle* behind the compromise, the idea that Congress could prohibit slavery in the territories. Five of the six justices who rejected this principle were from slave states. The Slave Power, a northern paper bellowed, "has marched over and annihilated the boundaries of the states. We are now one great homogenous slaveholding community."

Like Stephen Douglas after the Kansas-Nebraska Act, President Buchanan now appeared as another northern dupe of the slaveocracy. Republicans restrained themselves from open defiance of the decision only by insisting that it did not bind the nation; Taney's comments on the constitutionality of the Missouri Compromise, they contended, amounted merely

to *obiter dicta*, opinions unnecessary to settling the case.

Reactions to the decision underscored the fact that by 1857 no "judicious" or nonpartisan solution to slavery extension was possible. Anyone who still doubted this needed only to read the fast-breaking news from Kansas.

The Lecompton Constitution

While the Supreme Court wrestled with the abstract issues raised by the expansion of slavery, Buchanan sought a concrete solution to the gnawing problem of Kansas, where the free-state government at Topeka and the officially recognized proslavery government at Lecompton viewed each other with profound distrust. Buchanan's plan for Kansas looked simple: an elected territorial convention would draw up a constitution that would either permit or prohibit slavery; Buchanan would submit the constitution to Congress; Congress would then admit Kansas as a state.

Unfortunately, no sooner had Buchanan devised his plan than it began to explode in his face. Popular sovereignty, the essence of Buchanan's plan, demanded fair play, a scarce quality in Kansas. The territory's history of fraudulent elections left both sides reluctant to commit their fortunes to the polls. An election for a constitutional convention took place in June 1857, but free-staters, by now a majority in Kansas, boycotted the election on grounds that the proslavery side would rig it. Dominated by proslavery delegates, a constitutional convention then met and drew up a frame of government, the Lecompton constitution, that protected the rights of those slaveholders already living in Kansas to their slave property and provided for a referendum in which voters could decide whether to allow in more slaves.

The Lecompton constitution created a dilemma for Buchanan. A supporter of popular sovereignty, he had gone on record in favor of letting the voters in Kansas decide the slavery issue. Now he was confronted by a constitution drawn up by a convention that had been elected by less than 10 percent of the eligible voters, by plans for a referendum that would not allow voters to remove slaves already in Kansas, and by the prospect that the proslavery side would conduct the referendum no more honestly than it had others. Yet Buchanan had compelling reasons to accept the Lecompton constitution as the basis for Kansas's admission as a state. The South, which had provided him

The Little Giant in the Character of Gladiator,
1858
Douglas and his supporters are shown as gladiators menacing President Buchanan and his administration's newspaper, the Washington Union, *for approving the Lecompton constitution.*

with 112 of his 174 electoral votes in 1856, supported the constitution. Buchanan knew, moreover, that only about two hundred slaves resided in Kansas, and he believed that the prospects for slavery in the remaining territories were slight. The contention over slavery in Kansas struck him as another example of how extremists could turn minor issues into major ones. To accept the constitution and speed the admission of Kansas as either a free state or a slave state seemed the best way to pull the rug from beneath the extremists and quiet the commotion in Kansas. Accordingly, in December 1857 Buchanan formally endorsed the Lecompton constitution.

Buchanan's decision provoked a bitter attack from Senator Stephen A. Douglas. What rankled Douglas and many others was that the Lecompton convention, having drawn up a constitution, then allowed voters to decide only whether more slaves could be brought into the territory. "I care not whether [slavery] is voted down or voted up," Douglas declared. But to refuse to allow a vote on the constitution itself, with its protection of existing slave property, smacked of a "system of trickery and jugglery to defeat the fair expression of the will of the people."

Even as Douglas broke with Buchanan, events in Kansas took a new turn. A few months after electing delegates to the convention that drew up the Lecompton constitution, Kansans had gone to the polls to elect a territorial legislature. So flagrant was the fraud in this election—one village with thirty eligible voters returned more than sixteen hundred proslavery votes—that the governor disallowed enough proslavery returns to give free-staters a majority in the legislature. After the drafting of the Lecompton constitution, this territorial legislature called for a referendum on the entire document. Whereas the Kansas constitutional convention's goal had been to restrict the choice of voters to the narrow issue of the future introduction of slaves, the territorial legislature sought a referendum that would allow Kansans to vote against the protection of existing slave property as well as the introduction of more slaves.

In December 1857 the referendum called earlier by the constitutional convention was held. Boycotted by free-staters, the constitution with slavery passed overwhelmingly. Two weeks later, in the election called by the territorial legislature, the proslavery side abstained, and the constitution went down to crushing defeat. Having already cast his lot with the Lecompton convention's election, Buchanan simply ignored this second election. But he could not ignore the obstacles that the division in Kansas created for his plan to bring Kansas into the Union under the Lecompton constitution. When he submitted the plan to Congress, a deadlock in the House forced him to accept a proposal for still another referendum. This time, Kansans were given the choice between accepting or rejecting the entire constitution, with the proviso that rejection would delay statehood. Despite the proviso, Kansans overwhelmingly voted down the constitution.

Not only had Buchanan failed to tranquilize Kansas, but he had alienated northerners in his own party. His support for the Lecompton constitution confirmed the suspicion of northern Democrats that the southern Slave Power pulled all the important strings in their party. Douglas became the hero of the hour for northern Democrats and even for some Republicans. "The bone and sinew of the Northern Democracy are with you," a New Yorker wrote to Douglas. Yet Douglas himself could take little comfort from the Lecompton fiasco, as his cherished formula of popular sovereignty increasingly looked like a prescription for civil strife rather than harmony.

The Lincoln-Douglas Debates

Despite the acclaim he gained in the North for his stand against the Lecompton constitution, Douglas faced a stiff challenge in Illinois for reelection to the United States Senate. Of his Republican opponent, Abraham Lincoln, Douglas said: "I shall have my hands full. He is the strong man of his party—full of wit, facts, dates—and the best stump speaker with his droll ways and dry jokes, in the West."

Physically as well as ideologically, the two men formed a striking contrast. Tall (6'4") and gangling, Lincoln once described himself as "a piece of floating driftwood." Energy, ambition, and a passion for self-education had carried him from the Kentucky log cabin where he was born in 1809 through a youth filled with odd occupations (farm laborer, surveyor, rail-splitter, flatboatman, and storekeeper) into law and politics in his adopted Illinois. There he had capitalized on westerners' support for internal improvements to gain election to Congress in 1846 as a Whig. Having opposed the Mexican War and the Kansas-Nebraska Act, he joined the Republican party in 1856.

Douglas was fully a foot shorter than the towering Lincoln. But his compact frame contained astonishing energy. Born in New England, Douglas appealed primarily to the small farmers of southern origin who populated the Illinois flatlands. To these and others, he was the "little giant," the personification of the Democratic party in the West. The campaign quickly became more than just another Senate race, for it pitted the Republican party's rising star against the Senate's leading Democrat and, thanks to the railroad and the telegraph, received unprecedented national attention.

Although some Republicans extolled Douglas's stand against the Lecompton constitution, to Lincoln nothing had changed. Douglas was still Douglas, the author of the infamous Kansas-Nebraska Act and a man who cared not whether slavery was voted up or down as long as the vote was honest. Opening his campaign with the "House Divided" speech ("this nation cannot exist permanently half slave and half free"), Lincoln reminded his Republican followers of the gulf that still separated his doctrine of free soil from Douglas's popular sovereignty. Douglas dismissed the house-divided doctrine as an invitation to secession. What mattered to him was not slavery, which he viewed as merely an extreme way to subordinate an allegedly inferior race, but

the continued expansion of white settlement. Like Lincoln, he wanted to keep slavery out of the path of white settlement. But unlike his longtime rival, Douglas believed that popular sovereignty was the surest way to attain this goal without disrupting the Union.

The high point of the campaign came in a series of seven debates held from August 21 to October 15, 1858. The idea for the debates was proposed by Lincoln, who hoped to gain by them public recognition, and accepted by Douglas, who viewed the encounters as a way of putting an end to Lincoln's practice of speaking in each Illinois town as soon as Douglas had left. The Lincoln-Douglas debates mixed political drama with the atmosphere of a festival. For the debate at Galesburg, for example, dozens of horse-drawn floats descended on the town from nearby farming communities. One bore thirty-two girls dressed in white, one for each state, and a thirty-third, who dressed in black with the label "Kansas" and carried a banner proclaiming "THEY WON'T LET ME IN."

Douglas used the debates to portray Lincoln as a virtual abolitionist and advocate of racial equality. Both charges were calculated to doom Lincoln in the eyes of the intensely racist Illinois voters. In response, Lincoln affirmed that Congress had no constitutional authority to abolish slavery in the South, and in one debate he asserted bluntly that "I am not, nor ever have been in favor of bringing about the social and political equality of the white, and black man." However, fending off charges of extremism was getting Lincoln nowhere; so in order to seize the initiative, he tried to maneuver Douglas into a corner.

In view of the *Dred Scott* decision, Lincoln asked in the debate at Freeport, could the people of a territory lawfully exclude slavery? In essence, Lincoln was asking Douglas to reconcile popular sovereignty with the *Dred Scott* decision. Lincoln had long contended that the Court's decision rendered popular sovereignty as thin as soup boiled from the shadow of a pigeon that had starved to death. If, as the Supreme Court's ruling affirmed, Congress had no authority to exclude slavery from a territory, then it seemingly followed that a territorial legislature created by Congress also lacked power to do so. To no one's surprise, Douglas replied that notwithstanding the *Dred Scott* decision, the voters of a territory *could* effectively exclude slavery simply by refusing to enact laws that gave legal protection to slave property.

Douglas's "Freeport doctrine" salvaged popular sovereignty but did nothing for his reputation among southerners, who preferred the guarantees of the *Dred*

Stephen A. Douglas
Douglas's politics were founded on his unflinching conviction that most Americans favored national expansion and would support popular sovereignty as the fastest and least controversial way to achieve it. Douglas's self-assurance blinded him to rising northern sentiment for free soil.

Abraham Lincoln
Clean-shaven at the time of his famous debates with Douglas, Lincoln would soon grow a beard to give himself a more distinguished appearance.

Scott decision to the uncertainties of popular sovereignty. Whereas Douglas's stand against the Lecompton constitution had already tattered his reputation in the South ("he is already dead there," Lincoln affirmed), his Freeport doctrine stiffened southern opposition to his presidential ambitions.

Lincoln faced the problem throughout the debates that free soil and popular sovereignty, although distinguishable in theory, had much the same practical impact. Neither Lincoln nor Douglas doubted that popular sovereignty, if fairly applied, would keep slavery out of the territories. In order to keep the initiative and sharpen their differences, Lincoln shifted in the closing debates toward attacks on slavery as "a moral, social, and political evil." He argued that Douglas's view of slavery as merely an eccentric and rather unsavory southern custom would dull the nation's conscience and facilitate the legalization of slavery everywhere. But Lincoln compromised his own position by rejecting both abolition and equality for blacks.

Neither man scored a clear victory in argument, and the senatorial election itself settled no major issues. Douglas's supporters captured a majority of the seats in the state legislature, which at the time was responsible for electing U.S. senators. But despite the racist leanings of most Illinois voters, Republican candidates for the state legislature won a slightly larger share of the popular vote than did their Democratic rivals. Moreover, in its larger significance, the contest solidified the sectional split in the national Democratic party and made Lincoln famous in the North and infamous in the South.

John Brown's Raid

Although Lincoln explicitly rejected abolitionism, he often spoke of free soil as a step toward the "ultimate extinction" of slavery in the South. Predictably, many southerners ignored the distinction between free soil and abolition and concluded that Republicans and abolitionists were inseparable components of an unholy alliance against slavery. Indeed, to many southerners, the entire North seemed locked in the grip of demented leaders bent on civil war. One of the South's more articulate defenders of slavery, for example, equated the doctrine of the abolitionists with those of "Socialists, of Free Love and Free Lands, Free Churches, Free Women and Free Negroes—of No-Marriage, No-Religion, No-Private Property, No-Law and No-Government."

No single event did more to rivet this image of the North in southerners' minds than the raid in 1859 on the federal arsenal at Harpers Ferry, Virginia, by John Brown, the brooding religious zealot responsible for the Pottawatomie massacre in Kansas three years earlier. At the head of twenty-one men, Brown seized the arsenal on October 16, 1859, in the hope of igniting a massive slave uprising, first in Virginia and then throughout the South. But Brown neglected to inform the slaves of his plans and even failed to provision his men with enough food to last a day. A detachment of federal troops, commanded by Lieutenant Colonel Robert E. Lee, quickly overpowered the raiders. Convicted of treason, Brown was hanged on December 2, 1859.

If this had been the whole story, southerners might have dismissed the raid as the act of an isolated lunatic. Captured correspondence, however, revealed that Brown, far from acting alone, had extensive ties to prominent northern abolitionists. These northerners had provided both moral and financial support for Brown's plan to invade Virginia, free the slaves, and "purge this land with blood." Any lingering southern doubts about the scope of the conspiracy vanished when parts of the North responded to Brown's execution with memorial services and tolling bells. Ralph Waldo Emerson exulted that Brown would "make the gallows as glorious as the cross," and William Lloyd Garrison proclaimed his support for "every slave insurrection at the South and in any slave country." Republicans, including Lincoln and Senator William Seward of New York, denounced Brown's raid, but southerners suspected that Brown's failure, rather than the deed itself, provoked the repudiation.

Although Brown had failed to start a slave insurrection, his abortive raid rekindled southern fears of slave uprisings. In the wake of Brown's raid and throughout 1860, rumors flew around the South of assorted slave plots to devastate the region. Vigilantes turned out to battle conspiracies that existed only in their own minds. For example, a horde of southern defenders mobilized to rout the thousands of abolitionists who were rumored to be conspiring to pillage northeastern Texas. In various other incidents, vigilantes rounded up thousands of slaves, whipped some into confessing to nonexistent plots, and then lynched them. The hysteria played into the hands of the southern-rights extremists known as the fire-eaters. Indeed, this faction actively encouraged the witch hunt by spreading tales of slave conspiracies in the press so that southern voters would turn to them as alone able to "stem the current of Abolition."

Although southern fears of slave insurrections proved unfounded, nothing calmed those apprehensions. Nor did it make any difference to southerners that Seward and Lincoln denounced Brown's raid. Most southerners interpreted the evidence linking Brown to abolitionists as just the tip of an iceberg and concluded that the abolitionists themselves were mere agents of the Republican party. Had not the Republicans repeatedly assailed slavery and sought unconstitutionally to bar its expansion? Had not Seward spoken of an "irrepressible conflict" between freedom and slavery? The incident at Harpers Ferry, declared resolutions passed by the Tennessee legislature, was "the natural fruit of this treasonable 'irrepressible conflict' doctrine put forth by the great head of the Black Republican party and echoed by his subordinates." In the

John Brown, *c. 1850*
*Brown ran to extremes of
kindness and brutality, sympathy and egotistic self-righteous-
ness, all threaded together by his
Calvinist religious beliefs. Convinced
of humans' utter dependency on God,
he was sure that God had destined him
to start a slave insurrection. Brown contracted for the production of one thousand
pikes like the one shown here, with which he
planned to arm the slaves.*

final analysis, southerners contended, John Brown, abolitionists, and Republicans all rested their case on the same premise: that slaves were somehow an illegitimate form of property and that the South deserved only scorn for its "peculiar institution."

The South Contemplates Secession

Convinced that they were menaced not only by the eccentric William Lloyd Garrisons of the North but also by the Republican party that had swept two-thirds of the northern states in the election of 1856, southerners increasingly spoke of secession from the United States as their only recourse. "The South must dissever itself," a South Carolinian insisted, "from the rotten Northern element."

Southerners reached this conclusion gradually, and often reluctantly. In 1850 few southerners could have conceived of transferring their political and emotional allegiances from the United States to some new nation. Relatively insulated from the main tide of immigration, southerners thought of themselves as the most American of Americans. The fire-eaters, many of whom ardently desired secession, by no means represented southern thought. But the events of the 1850s

brought a growing number of southerners to the conclusion that the North had deserted the true principles of the Union. Southerners interpreted northern resistance to the Fugitive Slave Act and to slavery in Kansas as either illegal or unconstitutional, and they viewed headline-grabbing phrases like "irrepressible conflict" and "a higher law" as virtual declarations of war on the South. In southerners' eyes, it was the North, not the South, that had grown peculiar.

This sense of the North's deviance tinged reports sent home by southern visitors to the North during the 1850s. A Mississippi planter could scarcely believe his eyes, for example, when he witnessed a group of northern free blacks refusing to surrender their seats to a party of white women. Abolitionist hecklers rankled southern lecturers in the North. When assured by their northern friends that such hostility to the South's institutions did not reflect the whole of northern opinion, southerners could only wonder why northerners kept electing Republicans to office. Southern visitors increasingly described their northern trips as ventures into "enemy territory" and "a totally different country."

In this context of fraying sectional ties, John Brown's raid had an electrifying effect on southern opinion. Thousands of southerners, a Richmond newspaper editor observed after the raid, "who, a month ago, scoffed at the idea of a dissolution of the Union as a madman's dream . . . now hold the opinion that its days are numbered, its glory perished." A pamphlet published in 1860 embodied in its title the growing conviction of southerners that *The South Alone Should Govern the South*.

Viewed as a practical tactic to secure concrete goals, secession did not make a great deal of sense. Some southerners contended that secession would make it easier for the South to acquire more territory for slavery in the Caribbean; yet the South was scarcely united in desiring additional slave territory in Mexico, Cuba, or Central America. States like Alabama, Mississippi, and Texas contained vast tracts of unsettled land that could be converted to cotton cultivation far more easily than the Caribbean. Other southerners continued to complain that the North blocked the access of slaveholders to territories in the continental United States. But it is unclear how secession would solve this problem. If the South were to secede, the remaining continental territories would belong exclusively to the North, which could then legislate for them as it chose. Nor would secession stop future John Browns from infiltrating the South to provoke slave insurrections.

Yet to dwell on the impracticality of secession as a choice for the South is to miss the point. Talk of secession was less a tactic with clear goals than an expression of the South's outrage at the irresponsible and unconstitutional course that southerners viewed the Republicans as taking in the North. It was not merely that Republican attacks on slavery sowed the seeds of slave uprisings. More fundamentally, southerners believed that the North was treating the South as its inferior—indeed, as no more than a slave. "Talk of Negro slavery," exclaimed southern proslavery philosopher George Fitzhugh, "is not half so humiliating and disgraceful as the slavery of the South to the North." Having persuaded themselves that slavery made it possible for them to enjoy unprecedented freedom and equality, white southerners took great pride in their homeland. They bitterly dismissed Republican portrayals of the South as a region of arrogant planters and degraded white common folk. Submission to the Republicans, declared the Democratic senator Jefferson Davis of Mississippi, "would be intolerable to a proud people."

Nevertheless, as long as the pliant James Buchanan occupied the White House, southerners did no more than *talk* about secession. Once aware that Buchanan had declined to seek reelection, however, they anxiously awaited the election of 1860.

The Election of 1860

As a single-issue, free-soil party, the Republicans had done well in the election of 1856. To win in 1860, however, they would have to broaden their appeal in the North, particularly in states like Pennsylvania and Illinois, which they had lost in 1856. To do so, Republican leaders had concluded, they needed to forge an economic program to complement their advocacy of free soil.

A severe economic slump following the so-called Panic of 1857 furnished the Republicans a fitting opening. The depression shattered more than a decade of American prosperity and thrust economic concerns to the fore. In response, in the late 1850s, the Republicans developed an economic program based on support for a protective tariff (popular in Pennsylvania) and on two issues favored in the Midwest, federal aid for internal improvements and the granting of free 160-acre homesteads to settlers out of publicly owned land. By proposing to make these homesteads available to immigrants who were not yet citizens, the Republicans went far to shed their nativist image that lingered from their early association with the Know-Nothings. Carl Schurz, an 1848 German political refugee who had campaigned for Lincoln against Douglas in 1858, now labored mightily to bring his antislavery countrymen over to the Republican party.

The Republicans' desire to broaden their appeal also influenced their choice of a candidate. At their convention in Chicago, they nominated Abraham Lincoln over the early front-runner, William H. Seward of New York. Although better known than Lincoln, Seward failed to convince his party that he could carry the key states of Pennsylvania, Illinois, Indiana, and New Jersey. (Rueful Republicans remembered that their presidential candidate John C. Frémont would have won in 1856 if he had carried Pennsylvania and one of the remaining three states.) Lincoln held the advantage not only of hailing from Illinois but also of projecting a more moderate image than Seward on the slavery issue. Seward's penchant for controversial phrases like "irrepressible conflict" and "higher law" had given him a radical image. Lincoln, in contrast, had repeatedly affirmed that Congress had no constitutional right to interfere with slavery in the South and had explicitly rejected the "higher law" doctrine. The Republicans now needed only to widen their northern appeal.

The Democrats, however, who still claimed to be a national party, had to bridge their sectional divisions. The *Dred Scott* decision and the conflict over the Lecompton constitution had weakened the northern Democrats and emboldened the southern Democrats. Whereas Douglas desperately defended popular sovereignty against the free-soil doctrine, southern Democrats increasingly abandoned popular sovereignty for the crisp assurances of the *Dred Scott* decision. Heartened by Chief Justice Taney's ruling that Congress lacked the power to exclude slavery from the territories, many southerners now concluded that Congress had an obligation to safeguard slavery in any territory. In February 1860 Senator Jefferson Davis of Mississippi introduced a set of resolutions calling for the federal government to enforce the *Dred Scott* decision by actively protecting territorial slavery.

The Davis resolutions never stood a chance of adoption by Congress. Nevertheless, they embarrassed the Douglas Democrats. No northern Democrat could win an election on a platform calling for the congressional protection of slavery in the territories. As a Georgia Democrat opposed to the Davis resolutions commented, "Hostility to Douglas is the sole motive of the movers of this mischief. I wish Douglas defeated . . . , but I do not want him and his friends crippled or driven off. Where are we to get as many or as good men in the North to supply their places?"

The Democratic party's internal turmoil boiled over at its Charleston convention in the spring of 1860. Failing to force acceptance of a platform guaranteeing federal protection of slavery in the territories, the delegates from the Lower South stalked out. The convention adjourned to Baltimore, where a new fight broke out over the question of seating hastily elected, pro-Douglas slates of delegates from the Lower South states that had seceded from the Charleston convention. The decision to seat these pro-Douglas slates led to a walkout by delegates from Virginia and other states in the Upper South. The remaining delegates nominated Douglas; the seceders marched off to another hall in Baltimore and nominated Buchanan's vice president, John C. Breckinridge of Kentucky, on a platform calling for the congressional protection of slavery in the territories. Unable to rally behind a single nominee, the divided Democrats thus ran two candidates, Douglas and Breckinridge. The disruption of the Democratic party was now complete.

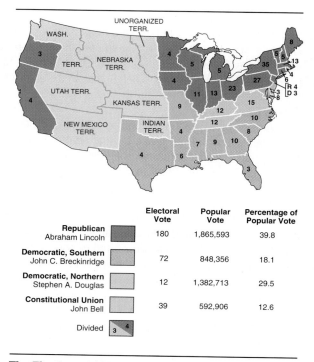

		Electoral Vote	Popular Vote	Percentage of Popular Vote
Republican Abraham Lincoln		180	1,865,593	39.8
Democratic, Southern John C. Breckinridge		72	848,356	18.1
Democratic, Northern Stephen A. Douglas		12	1,382,713	29.5
Constitutional Union John Bell		39	592,906	12.6
Divided				

The Election of 1860

The South still contained an appreciable number of moderates, often former Whigs who had joined with the Know-Nothings behind Fillmore in 1856. In 1860 these moderates, aided by former northern Whigs who opposed both Lincoln and Douglas, forged the new Constitutional Union party and nominated John Bell, a Tennessee slaveholder who had opposed both the Kansas-Nebraska Act and the Lecompton constitution. Calling for the preservation of the Union, the new party took no stand on the divisive issue of slavery extension.

With four candidates in the field, voters faced a relatively clear choice. Lincoln conceded that the South had a constitutional right to preserve slavery but demanded that Congress prohibit its extension. At the other extreme, Breckinridge insisted that Congress had to protect slavery in any territory that contained slaves. This left the middle ground to Bell and Douglas, the latter still committed to popular sovereignty but in search of a verbal formula that might reconcile it with the *Dred Scott* decision. Despite this four-way race, Lincoln won a clear majority of the electoral vote, 180 to 123 for his three opponents combined. Although Lincoln gained only 39 percent of the popular vote, his popular votes were concentrated in the North, the majority section, and were sufficient to carry every free state. Douglas ran a respectable second to Lincoln in the popular vote but a dismal last in the electoral vote. As the only candidate to campaign in both sections, Douglas suffered from the scattered quality of his votes and carried only Missouri. Bell won Virginia, Kentucky, and Tennessee, and Breckinridge captured Maryland and the Lower South.

The Movement for Secession

As the dust from the election settled, southerners faced a disconcerting fact: a man so unpopular among southerners that his name had not even appeared on the ballot in much of their section was now president. Lincoln's election struck most of the white South as a calculated northern insult. The North, a South Carolina planter told a visitor from England, "has got so far toward being abolitionized as to elect a man avowedly hostile to our institutions." Few southerners believed that Lincoln would fulfill his promise to protect slavery in the South, and most feared that he would act as a mere front man for more John Browns. "Now that the black radical Republicans have the power I suppose they will Brown us all," a South Carolinian lamented. An uneducated Mississippian residing in Illinois expressed his reaction to the election more bluntly:

> It seems the north wants the south to raise cotton and sugar rice tobacco for the northern states, also to pay taxes and fight her battles and get territory for the purpose of the north to send her greasy Dutch and free niggers into the territory to get rid of them. At any rate that was what elected old Abe President. Some professed conservative Republicans Think and say that Lincoln will be conservative also but sir my opinion is that Lincoln will deceive them. [He] will undoubtedly please the abolitionists for at his election they nearly all went into fits with Joy.

Some southerners had threatened secession at the prospect of Lincoln's election; now the moment of choice had arrived. On December 20, 1860, a South Carolina convention voted unanimously for secession; and by February 1, 1861, Alabama, Mississippi, Florida, Georgia, Louisiana, and Texas had followed South Carolina's lead (see "A Place in Time"). On February 4 delegates from these seven states met in Montgomery, Al-

Jefferson Davis
Davis brought an abundance of public experience to the Confederate presidency. Wounded in the Mexican War, he had served in the U.S. Senate, become secretary of war under President Franklin Pierce, and negotiated the Gadsden Purchase.

abama, and established the Confederate States of America.

Despite the abruptness of southern withdrawal from the Union, the movement for secession had been, and continued to be, laced with uncertainty. Many southerners had resisted calls for immediate secession. Even after Lincoln's election, fire-eating secessionists had met fierce opposition in the Lower South from so-called cooperationists, who called upon the South to act in unison or not at all. Many cooperationists had hoped to delay secession in order to wring concessions from the North that might remove the need for secession. Jefferson Davis, who was inaugurated in February 1861 as the first president of the Confederacy, was a most reluctant secessionist, and he remained in the United States Senate for two weeks after his own state of Mississippi had seceded. Even zealous advocates of secession had a hard time reconciling themselves to secession and believing that they were

Charleston in the Secession Crisis, 1860–1861

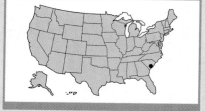

After securing the nomination of Pennsylvania's James Buchanan for the presidency in 1856, northern Democrats made a conciliatory gesture to the South. They agreed to hold their party's 1860 convention in Charleston, South Carolina. Time would give northerners many opportunities to regret that gesture. Long in decline, with only a few overpriced hotels, Charleston offered little as a convention city. The supporters of Stephen A. Douglas had to convert the second floor of a meeting hall into a giant dormitory, where they slept in rows of beds and baked in one-hundred-degree heat. Far more troubling to the delegates who descended on the city in April 1860 was the hysteria that consumed Charleston in reaction to John Brown's raid on Harpers Ferry in Virginia six months earlier. Mounted police, armed with swords and muskets, patrolled the streets, and vigilantes combed the byways in search of abolitionists. Panicked Charlestonians viewed every northerner in the city—whether a politician, a traveling salesman, or a schoolteacher—as "necessarily imbued with doctrines hostile to our institutions."

Suspicion and harassment greeted northern sojourners, but Charleston's blacks endured a virtual reign of terror after "the late outrage at Harpers Ferry." A little under half the city's population in 1860 was black, and 81 percent of the blacks were slaves. White southerners distrusted urban slaves, most of whom lived apart from their rural masters and were hired out to city employers. Indeed, some slaves took advantage of their distance from their masters to hire themselves out for wages, a practice that whites feared would infect slaves with the notion that they were free. In addition, white workingmen resented competition from urban slaves in the skilled trades, and they used the furor over John Brown's raid to pressure the city's mayor into enforcing an old and long-neglected ordinance that slaves working away from their masters wear badges. Those without badges were rounded up and jailed, and their masters fined.

Charleston's enslaved blacks were not the sole targets of the city's increasingly repressive mood. Few southern cities had more visible or well-organized communities of free blacks than Charleston. Composed mainly of mulattos who took pride in their light skin and assembled in the Brown Fellowship Society, Charleston's free people of color formed a brown aristocracy of skilled tailors, carpenters, and small tradesmen. Free blacks like John Marsh Johnson worshiped in the same Episcopal church as such elite whites as Christopher G. Memminger, a prominent lawyer and politician who would soon become the Confederacy's secretary of the treasury. The financial prosperity of these free blacks depended on the white aristocrats who frequented their stores, admired their thrift and sobriety, and took comfort in their apparent loyalty. When a bill calling for the enslavement or expulsion of South Carolina's free blacks came before the state legislature in 1859, Memminger reminded the legislators that a free black had helped to expose Denmark Vesey's planned uprising of slaves back in 1822. Heartened by the support of Memminger and others, John Marsh Johnson congratu-

Slave Badges
The badges that they were forced to wear constantly reminded Charleston's slaves of their bondage.

Saluda Sentinels, Always Ready

Secessionist sentiment also flared in interior areas of South Carolina such as Saluda. This militia flag of the Saluda Sentinels, featuring an officer in Revolutionary War garb, shows how secessionists invoked memories of the American struggle for independence.

First Shots of the Civil War

Stunned Charleston residents crowded the city's rooftops to view the firing on Fort Sumter—a siege that lasted thirty-four hours.

lated himself for predicting "from the onset that nothing would be done affecting our position."

Johnson little realized the extent to which the world of Charleston's free blacks was in danger of falling apart. The city had been a center of southern-rights radicalism since the days of the nullification crisis. Charleston was the home of the fire-eater, Robert Barnwell Rhett; and it always rolled out the welcome carpet for Edmund Ruffin, a Virginia drumbeater for slavery. Furthermore, after John Brown's raid, even moderate citizens, including former Unionists, were embracing secession. The cause of secession demanded, in turn, that elite whites unite with working-class whites in a common front against the North. During the 1850s Charleston's working-class whites had grown increasingly powerful and aggressive; the increase in their numbers gave the city a white majority in 1860, for the first time in its history. Working-class whites feared competition from any blacks but had a special loathing for free blacks, who on Sundays dared "to draw up in fine clothes" and "wear a silk hat and gloves" and who celebrated weddings by drinking champagne and riding to the church in elegant carriages.

Soon free blacks became the victims of the growing cooperation between elite and working-class whites. Indeed, by August 1860 Charleston was in the grip of an "enslavement crisis." The same police dragnets that had snared urban slaves without badges now trapped innumerable free blacks as well. Unenslaved blacks suddenly had to prove that they were free, a tall order inasmuch as South Carolina had long prohibited the freeing of slaves. For decades white masters who wanted to free favored slaves had resorted to complicated legal ruses, with the result that many blacks who had lived for years as free people could not prove that they were free and were forced back into slavery. Abandoning his initial optimism, John Marsh Johnson wrote nervously to his brother-in-law to report "cases of persons who for 30 yrs. have been paying capitation Tax [as free persons of color] & one of 35 yrs. that have to go back to bondage & take out their Badges." Many other free African-Americans fled to the North.

A religious man, Johnson believed that God helped those who helped them-

selves. Rather than "supinely wait for the working of a miracle by having a Chariot let down to convey us away," he resolved in late August 1860 to stay and endure the "present calamity." By then, however, the Democratic party had snapped apart under the pressure of southern demands for the congressional recognition of slavery in all the territories. "The last party pretending to be a national party, is broken up," the secessionist Charleston *Mercury* exulted, "and the antagonism of the sections of the Union has nothing to arrest its fierce collision." In December 1860 another convention meeting in Charleston would proclaim South Carolina's secession from the United States. In April 1861, only a year after the Democratic delegates had assembled in Charleston for their party's convention, shore batteries along Charleston's harbor would open fire on Fort Sumter. This action set in motion a train of events leading to the extinction of slavery itself. Ironically, after the Civil War, the free blacks who had weathered the enslavement crisis of 1860 would emerge as the leaders of the city's black people, all of them now free.

no longer citizens of the United States. "How do you feel now, dear Mother," a Georgian wrote, "that *we* are in a foreign land?"

In the month after the establishment of the Confederate States of America, moreover, secessionists suffered stinging disappointments in the Upper South. Virginia, North Carolina, Tennessee, Arkansas, and the border slave states of Maryland, Kentucky, Delaware, and Missouri all rejected calls for secession. Various factors account for the Upper South's reluctance to embrace the movement. In contrast to the Lower South, which had a guaranteed export market for its cotton, the Upper South depended heavily on economic ties to the North, bonds that would be severed by secession. Furthermore, with proportionately far fewer slaves than the Lower South, the states of the Upper South and the border states doubted the loyalty of their sizable nonslaveholding populations to the idea of secession. Virginia, for example, had every reason to question the allegiance to secession of its nonslaveholding western counties, which would soon break away to form Unionist West Virginia. Few in the Upper South could forget the raw nerve touched by the publication in 1857 of Hinton R. Helper's *The Impending Crisis of the South*. A nonslaveholding North Carolinian, Helper had described slavery as a curse upon poor white southerners and thereby questioned one of the most sacred southern doctrines, the idea that slavery rendered all whites equal. If secession were to spark a war between the states, moreover, the Upper South appeared to be the likeliest battleground. Whatever the exact weight assignable to each of these factors, one point is clear: the secession movement that South Carolina so boldly started in December 1860 seemed to be falling apart by March 1861.

The Search for Compromise

The lack of southern unity confirmed the long-standing belief of Lincoln and most Republicans that the secessionists' talk, and even their actions, contained more bluster than substance. Seward described secession as the work of "a relatively few hotheads," and Lincoln expected that the loyal majority of southerners would soon wrest the initiative from the fire-eating minority.

This perception among the Republicans stiffened their resolve to resist the compromises that some moderates were trying to forge. In the immediate

wake of South Carolina's secession, Senator John J. Crittenden of Kentucky brought forth the most important of the compromises. Crittenden's plan included calls for the compensation of owners of runaway slaves, the repeal of the North's personal-liberty laws, a constitutional amendment to prohibit the federal government from ever interfering with slavery in the southern states, and another constitutional amendment that would restore the Missouri Compromise line for the remaining territories and guarantee federal protection of slavery below the line. This last amendment proved to be the sticking point. Lincoln stood firm against any abandonment of free soil. "On the territorial issue," he wrote to a southerner, "I am inflexible." In the face of steadfast Republican opposition, the Crittenden plan collapsed.

Lincoln's opposition to compromise rested partly on his belief that a loyal majority of southerners would soon overturn secession. The president-elect, however, almost certainly exaggerated the strength and dedication of southern Unionists. In reality, many of the southern opponents of the fire-eating secessionists were sitting on the fence and hoping for major concessions from the North; their allegiance to the Union was conditional, not unconditional. Lincoln can be faulted for his misreading of southern opinion. But even if his assessment had been accurate, it is unlikely that he would have accepted the Crittenden plan. Republicans viewed the plan as a surrender rather than a compromise, because it hinged on the abandonment of free soil, the principle on which the Republican party had been founded. In addition, as Lincoln well knew, some southerners still talked of seizing more territory for slavery in the Caribbean. In proposing to extend the 36°30′ line, the Crittenden plan specifically referred to territories "hereafter acquired," a veiled reference to future Caribbean expansion. If he were to accept the Crittenden compromise, Lincoln feared that it would be only a matter of time "till we shall have to take Cuba as a condition upon which they [the seceding states] will stay in the Union."

Beyond these considerations, the precipitous secession of the Lower South subtly changed the question that Lincoln faced. The issue was no longer slavery extension but secession. The Lower South had left the Union in the face of losing a fair election. For Lincoln to have caved in to such pressure would have violated majority rule, the principle upon which the nation, not just his party, had been founded.

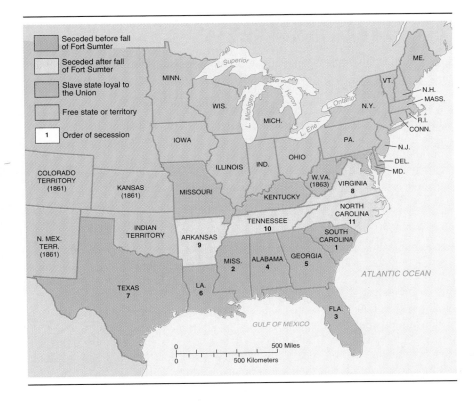

Legend:
- Seceded before fall of Fort Sumter
- Seceded after fall of Fort Sumter
- Slave state loyal to the Union
- Free state or territory
- 1 Order of secession

Secession

Four key states—Virginia, Arkansas, Tennessee, and North Carolina—did not secede until after the fall of Fort Sumter. The border slave states of Maryland, Delaware, Kentucky, and Missouri stayed in the Union.

The Coming of War

By the time Lincoln took office in March 1861, little more than a spark was needed to ignite a war. Lincoln pledged in his inaugural address to "hold, occupy, and possess" federal property in the seven states that had seceded, an assertion that committed him to the defense of Fort Pickens in Florida and Fort Sumter in the harbor of Charleston, South Carolina. William Seward, whom Lincoln had appointed secretary of state, now became obsessed with the idea of conciliating the Lower South in order to hold the Upper South in the Union. In addition to advising the evacuation of federal forces from Fort Sumter, Seward proposed a scheme to reunify the nation by provoking a war with France and Spain. But Lincoln brushed aside Seward's advice. Instead, the president informed the governor of South Carolina of his intention to supply Fort Sumter with much-needed provisions, but not with men and ammunition. To gain the dubious military advantage of attacking Fort Sumter before the arrival of relief ships, Confederate batteries began to bombard the fort shortly before dawn on April 12. The next day, the fort's garrison surrendered.

Proclaiming an insurrection in the Lower South, Lincoln now appealed for seventy-five thousand militiamen from the loyal states to suppress the rebellion. His proclamation pushed citizens of the Upper South off the fence upon which they had perched for three months. "I am a Union man," one southerner wrote, "but when they [the Lincoln administration] send men south it will change my notions. I can do nothing against my own people." In quick succession, Virginia, North Carolina, Arkansas, and Tennessee leagued with the Confederacy. After acknowledging that "I am one of those dull creatures that cannot see the good of secession," Robert E. Lee resigned from the United States Army rather than lead federal troops against his native Virginia.

The North, too, was ready for a fight, less to abolish slavery than to punish secession. Worn out from his efforts to find a peaceable solution to the issue of slavery extension, and with only a short time to live, Stephen Douglas assaulted "the new system of resistance by the sword and bayonet to the results of the ballot-box" and affirmed: "I deprecate war, but if it must come I am with my country, under all circumstances, and in every contingency."

CONCLUSION

During the 1850s the gap widened between northerners and southerners on the vexing issue of slavery extension. Popular sovereignty, which in 1850 struck many Americans as a practical solution to slavery in the territories, foundered in Kansas amid civil strife and turmoil over the Lecompton constitution. As support for popular sovereignty withered, sentiment for free soil gained ground in the North. In the South the *Dred Scott* decision provided judicial support for the position that Congress had to protect slavery in whatever territories it appeared.

Although the differences between northern and southern opinion on the slavery-extension issue sharpened and widened during the tempestuous decade, the two sections stood far apart by 1850. The Compromise of 1850 merely papered over an already considerable gulf. Decades of industrial expansion had convinced northerners of the value of free labor, a view that excluded competition with slaves. Yet decades of agricultural prosperity had persuaded southerners of the economic and moral value of slavery. The success of their system made southerners antagonistic to any suggestion that slave property was inferior to other property.

Despite this clear division by 1850, secession festered for ten years before erupting. More than a broad disagreement over slavery in the territories was needed to push the South into secession. Before the South took that drastic step, it had to convince itself that the North aimed not merely to bar the spread of slavery but also to corrode the moral and political foundations of southern society. Several events persuaded the South that such was indeed the North's intention: northern fury over the Kansas-Nebraska bill, the emergence of the purely sectional Republican party, northern opposition to the *Dred Scott* decision, and John Brown's raid on Harpers Ferry. Once southerners came to believe that northern attacks on slavery's expansion were tactics in a wider campaign to reduce the South to subjection and "slavery," secession became a natural recourse.

As an expression of principled outrage, secession fittingly capped a decade in which each side had clothed itself in principles. The conflicts over principle that marked the 1850s were deeply embedded in the nation's political heritage. Both sides, North and South, laid claim to the ideals of the Constitution, but each understood those ideals differently. For northerners wedded to free soil, liberty meant an individual's freedom to pursue self-interest without competition from slaves. For white southerners, liberty meant their freedom to dispose of their legally acquired property as they saw fit. Similarly, both sides subscribed to the rule of law, which each accused the other of deserting. Northerners found evidence of southern treachery in the voting fraud that culminated in the Lecompton constitution. Southerners pointed to northern defiance of the Fugitive Slave Act and, later, of the *Dred Scott* decision, and to northern complicity in John Brown's raid. In the end, war broke out between siblings who, although they claimed the same inheritance, had become virtual strangers to each other.

CHRONOLOGY

1846   Wilmot Proviso.

1848   Treaty of Guadalupe Hidalgo ends Mexican War.
Free-Soil party formed.
Zachary Taylor elected president.

1849   California seeks admission to the Union as a free state.

1850   Nashville convention assembles to discuss the South's grievances.
Compromise of 1850.

1852   Harriet Beecher Stowe, *Uncle Tom's Cabin*.
Franklin Pierce elected president.

1853   Gadsden Purchase.

1854   Ostend Manifesto.
Kansas-Nebraska Act.
William Walker leads a filibustering expedition into Nicaragua.

1854–1855   Know-Nothing and Republican parties emerge.

1855   Proslavery forces steal the election for a territorial legislature in Kansas.
Proslavery Kansans establish a government in Lecompton.
Free-soil government established in Topeka, Kansas.

1856   The "Sack of Lawrence."

1856 John Brown's Pottawatomie massacre.
James Buchanan elected president.

1857 *Dred Scott* decision.
President Buchanan
endorses the Lecomp-
ton constitution in
Kansas.
Panic of 1857.

Dred Scott

1858 Congress refuses to admit Kansas to the Union under the Lecompton constitution.
Lincoln-Douglas debates.

1859 John Brown's raid on Harpers Ferry.

1860 Abraham Lincoln elected president.
South Carolina secedes from the Union.

1861 The remaining Lower South states secede.
Confederate States of America established.
Crittenden compromise plan collapses.
Lincoln takes office.
Firing on Fort Sumter; Civil War begins.
Upper South secedes.

FOR FURTHER READING

William W. Freehling, *The Road to Disunion: Secessionists at Bay, 1776–1854* (1990). A major study that traces the roots of secession.

Eric Foner, *Free Soil, Free Labor, Free Men: The Ideology of the Republican Party Before the Civil War* (1970). An outstanding analysis of the thought, values, and components of the Republican party.

William E. Gienapp, *The Origins of the Republican Party,* *1852–1856* (1987). A comprehensive account of the birth of a major party.

Michael F. Holt, *The Political Crisis of the 1850s* (1978). A lively reinterpretation of the politics of the 1850s.

Allan Nevins, *The Ordeal of the Union* (vols. 1–2, 1947). A detailed, highly regarded account of the coming of the Civil War.

David Potter, *The Impending Crisis, 1848–1861* (1976). The best one-volume overview of the events leading to the Civil War.

ADDITIONAL BIBLIOGRAPHY

The Compromise of 1850 and Its Aftermath

Stephen W. Campbell, *The Slave Catchers* (1968); Thomas F. Gossett, *Uncle Tom's Cabin and American Culture* (1985); Holman Hamilton, *Prologue to Conflict: The Crisis and Compromise of 1850* (1964); Thelma Jennings, *The Nashville Convention* (1980); Thomas D. Morris, *Free Men All: The Personal Liberty Laws of the North, 1780–1861* (1974); Chaplain W. Morrison, *Democratic Politics and Sectionalism: The Wilmot Proviso Controversy* (1967).

Political Realignment, 1852–1856

Tyler Anbinder, *Nativism and Slavery: The Northern Know Nothings and the Politics of the 1850s* (1992); Eugene Berwanger, *The Frontier Against Slavery: Western Anti-Negro Prejudice in the Slavery Extension Controversy* (1967); Michael F. Holt, *Political Parties and American Political Development from the Age of Jackson to the Age of Lincoln* (1992); James A. Rawley, *Race and Politics: "Bleeding Kansas" and the Coming of the Civil War* (1969); Geoffrey W. Wolff, *The Kansas-Nebraska Bill* (1977).

The South and the Sectional Crisis

Charles H. Brown, *Agents of Manifest Destiny: The Lives and Times of the Filibusters* (1978); John Hope Franklin, *The Militant South, 1800–1861* (1970) and *A Southern Odyssey: Travelers in the Antebellum North* (1976); Michael P. Johnson and James L. Roark, eds., *No Chariot Let Down: Charleston's Free People of Color on the Eve of the Civil War* (1984); John McCardell, *The Idea of a Southern Nation: Southern Nationalists and Southern Nationalism, 1830–1861* (1979); Robert E. May, *The Southern Dream of a Caribbean Empire, 1854–1861* (1973); Rollin G. Os-

terweiss, *Romanticism and Nationalism in the Old South* (1949); Ronald L. Takaki, *A Proslavery Crusade: The Agitation to Reopen the African Slave Trade* (1971); J. Mills Thornton, *Politics and Power in a Slave Society* (1978).

The Disruption of the Union

William L. Barney, *The Road to Secession* (1972); Steven A. Channing, *Crisis of Fear: Secession in South Carolina* (1970); David Donald, *Charles Sumner and the Coming of the Civil War* (1960); Don E. Fehrenbacher, *The Dred Scott Case* (1978) and *Prelude to Greatness: Lincoln in the 1850s* (1962); George B. Forgie, *Patricide in the House Divided: A Psychological Interpretation of Lincoln and His Age* (1979); Henry V. Jaffa, *Crisis of the House Divided: An Interpretation of the Lincoln-Douglas Debates* (1959); Robert W. Johannsen, *Stephen A. Douglas* (1973); Michael Johnson, *Secession and Conservatism in the Lower South: The Social and Ideological Bases of Secession in Georgia, 1860–1861* (1983); Albert J. Kirwan, *John J. Crittenden: The Struggle for the Union* (1962); Milton Klein, *President James Buchanan: A Biography* (1962); Paul C. Nagel, *One Nation Indivisible: The Union in American Thought* (1964); Allan Nevins, *The Emergence of Lincoln* (2 vols., 1950); Roy F. Nichols, *The Disruption of American Democracy* (1948); Stephen B. Oates, *To Purge This Land with Blood: A Biography of John Brown* (1970); David Potter, *Lincoln and His Party in the Secession Crisis* (1942); Elbert B. Smith, *The Presidency of James Buchanan* (1975); Kenneth Stampp, *And the War Came: The North and the Secession Crisis, 1860–1861* (1970); R. A. Wooster, *The Secession Conventions of the South* (1962).

News from Home
by William Ludwell Sheppard

REFORGING THE UNION: CIVIL WAR 1861–1865

With the fall of Fort Sumter in April 1861, northerners and southerners rushed to arms. "They sing and whoop, they laugh: they holler to de people on de ground and sing out 'Good-bye,'" remarked a slave watching rebel troops depart. "All going down to die." Longing for the excitement of battle, the first volunteers enlisted with hopes of adventure and glory. Garish uniforms reflected their expectation of martial romance. Gaudiest of all were the northern Zouave regiments, whose members patterned their dress on that of French troops in North Africa, who, in turn, modeled their uniforms on a notion of what the Turks wore into battle: baggy red pantaloons, spotless white gaiters, and fezzes. Marching to war in dashing attire provided more than an outlet for romantic yearnings: it also gave boys a chance to act like men. A contemplative New Yorker, who sent two teenaged sons to enlist, marveled how the war provided "so much manhood suddenly achieved." In their early letters home, victorious soldiers exulted over their transformation in battle. "With your first shot you become a new man," an Alabama volunteer wrote to his father. Neither volunteers nor politicians expected a long or bloody war. Most northern estimates ranged from one month to a year. Southerners also looked forward to a speedy war. One rebel could lick ten Yankees, southerners liked to think, because "the Yankee army is filled with the scum of creation."

These expectations of military glory and quick fame proved the first of many miscalculations. Actual battlefield experiences scarcely conformed to the early volunteers' rosy visions. For most soldiers, achieving manhood meant surviving in fetid army camps and inuring themselves to the stench of death. "We don't mind the sight of dead men no more than if they were dead hogs," a Union soldier claimed after one engagement. Soldiers rapidly learned the value of caution in battle. When "solid shot is cracking skulls like eggshells," a northern volunteer wrote, "the consuming passion is to get out of the way." You learn, a southerner wrote, to become "cool and deliberate."

These were the reactions of the lucky ones. One out of every five soldiers who fought in the Civil War died in it. The 620,000 American soldiers who lost their lives between 1861 and 1865 nearly equaled the number of American soldiers killed in all the nation's earlier and later wars combined. The war's gruesome destructiveness shattered politicians' expectations as well as soldiers' romantic visions. Once it became clear that the war could not be ended by a few battles, leaders on both sides contemplated strategies once unpalatable and even unthinkable. The South, where the hand of government had always fallen lightly on the citizenry, found that it had to draft men into its army and virtually extort supplies from its civilian population. By the end of the war, the Confederacy was even prepared to arm its slaves in an ironically desperate effort to save a society founded on slavery. The North, which began the war with the restricted objective of overcoming secession, and which explicitly disclaimed any intention of interfering with slavery, found that in order to win, it had to shred the fabric of southern society by destroying slavery. For politicians as well as soldiers, the war turned into a series of surprises.

◆

MOBILIZING FOR WAR

North and South alike were unprepared for war. In April 1861 the Union had only a small army of sixteen thousand men, scattered all over the country, mostly in the West. One-third of the officers of the Union army had resigned to join the Confederacy. The Union seemed to hang by a thread politically. The nation had not had a strong president since James K. Polk in the 1840s. Its new president, Abraham Lincoln, struck many observers as a yokel. That such a government could marshal its people for war seemed a doubtful proposition. The federal government had levied no direct taxes on its citizens for decades, and it had never drafted anyone into its army. The Confederacy was even less prepared, for it had no tax structure, no navy, only two tiny gunpowder factories, and poorly equipped, unconnected railroad lines.

During the first two years of the war, both sides would have to overcome these deficiencies, raise and supply large armies, and finance the heavy costs of war. In each region mobilization for war expanded the powers of the central government to an extent that few had anticipated.

Recruitment and Conscription

The Civil War armies were the largest organizations ever created in America; by the end of the war, over 2 million men would have served in the Union army and 800,000 in the Confederate army. In the first flush of enthusiasm for war, volunteers rushed to the colors. "I go for wiping them out," a Virginian wrote to his governor. A similar zest for enlistment engulfed the North. "War! and volunteers are the only topics of conversation or thought," an Oberlin College student wrote to his brother in April 1861. "I cannot study. I cannot sleep. I cannot work, and I don't know as I can write."

At first, the raising of armies depended on local efforts rather than on national or even state direction. Cit-

izens opened recruiting offices in their hometowns, held rallies, and signed up volunteers. As a consequence, regiments were usually composed of soldiers from the same locale. Localism and voluntarism did not stop with the recruitment of troops. In the South cavalrymen were expected to provide their own horses, and uniforms everywhere were left mainly to local option. In both armies officers up to the rank of colonel were elected by other officers and enlisted men.

This informal and democratic way of raising and organizing soldiers conformed to the nation's political traditions. Americans had argued for generations that the freely given consent of the people, not the dictates of the government, could alone create an army in a republic. Because of its length and gruesome destructiveness, the Civil War would place insupportable stress on this tradition, however. As early as July 1861, the Union instituted examinations for officers, and its practice of electing officers gradually died out. In addition, as casualties mounted, military demand soon exceeded the supply of volunteers. Because nearly half of its 1861 volunteers had enlisted for only a year, the Confederacy felt the pinch first and in April 1862 enacted the first conscription law in American history. All able-bodied white males aged eighteen to thirty-five would be required to serve in the military for three years. Subsequent amendments raised the age limit to forty-five and then to fifty, and lowered it to seventeen.

The Confederacy's Conscription Act aroused little enthusiasm among southerners. Opponents charged that the draft was an assault on state sovereignty by a despotic regime and that the law would "do away with all the patriotism we have." Exemptions applied to many occupations, from religious ministry to shoemaking, and these angered the nonexempt. So did a loophole, closed in 1863, that allowed the well-off to purchase substitutes. Hostility also mounted over an amendment, the so-called 20-Negro law, that exempted an owner or overseer of twenty or more slaves from service. Although southerners widely feared that the slave population could not be controlled if all ablebodied white males were away in the army, the 20-Negro law evoked complaints about "a rich man's war but a poor man's fight."

Despite opposition, the Confederate draft became increasingly hard to evade, and this fact stimulated volunteering. Only one soldier in five was a draftee, but four out of every five eligible white southerners served in the Confederate army. In addition, a new conscription law, passed in 1864, required all soldiers then in the army to stay in for the duration of the war. This requirement ensured that a high proportion of Confederate soldiers would be battle-hardened veterans.

Once the army was raised, the Confederacy faced the challenge of supplying it. At first, the South lacked facilities to produce arms and ammunition and relied on imports from Europe, weapons confiscated from federal arsenals situated in the South, and guns captured on the battlefield. These stopgap measures bought time until an industrial base was established. By 1862 the Confederacy had a competent head of ordnance (weaponry), Josiah Gorgas. Working through Gorgas and other officials, the Confederacy assigned ordnance contracts to privately owned factories like the Tredegar Iron Works in Richmond, provided loans to establish new factories, and created government-owned industries like the giant Augusta Powder Works in Georgia. The South lost few, if any, battles for want of munitions.

The Confederacy was less successful in supplying its troops with clothing and food. Southern soldiers frequently went without shoes; during the South's invasion of Maryland in 1862, thousands of Confederate soldiers had to be left behind because they could not march barefoot on Maryland's gravel-surfaced roads. Late in the war, Robert E. Lee's Army of Northern Virginia ran out of food but never out of ammunition. The South's supply problems had several sources: railroads that fell into disrepair or were captured, an economy that relied more heavily on producing tobacco and cotton than growing food, and Union invasions early in the war that overran the livestock and grain-raising districts of central Tennessee and Virginia. Close to desperation, the Confederate Congress passed the Impressment Act in 1863, which authorized army officers to take food from reluctant farmers at prescribed rates. This law was even more unpopular than the Conscription Act. It also empowered agents to impress slaves into labor for the army, a provision that provoked yet more resentment. Slaveowners were willing to give up their relatives to military service, a Georgia congressman noted, "but let one of their negroes be taken and what a howl you will hear."

The industrial North could more easily supply its troops with arms, clothes, and food than could the South. However, keeping a full army was another matter. When the initial tide of enthusiasm for enlistment passed and the terms of the early recruits ended, Congress followed the Confederacy's example and turned to conscription. The Enrollment Act of March 1863 made every able-bodied white male citizen aged twenty to forty-five eligible for draft into the Union army.

Like the Confederate conscription law of 1862, the Enrollment Act granted exemptions, although only to high government officials, ministers, and men who were the sole support of widows, orphans, or indigent parents. It also offered two means of escaping the draft: substitution, or paying another man who would serve instead; and commutation, paying a $300 fee to the government. To provide draft machinery, the law divided each state into enrollment districts and gave them quotas to meet, first through volunteers and then through the draft. The new system was difficult to administer and chaotic in practice. Enrollment districts often competed for volunteers by offering cash payments (bounties); dishonest "bounty jumpers" repeatedly registered and deserted after collecting their payment. And as in the South, conscription aroused opposition. Democrats denounced it as a violation of individual liberties and states' rights. Ordinary citizens of little means resented the commutation and substitution provision and leveled their own "poor man's fight" charges. Still, as the Confederates had learned, the law stimulated volunteering. Only 8 percent of Union soldiers were draftees or substitutes.

Financing the War

The recruitment and supply of huge armies lay far beyond the capacity of American public finance at the start of the war. During the 1840s and 1850s, annual federal spending had averaged only 2 percent of the gross national product.* With such meager expenditures, the federal government could meet its revenue needs from tariff duties and from income brought in by the sale of public lands. In fact, the government had not imposed any direct taxes on its citizens for thirty years. During the war, however, annual federal expenditures gradually rose to 15 percent of the gross national product, and the need for new sources of revenue became urgent. Yet neither the Union nor the Confederacy initially showed much enthusiasm for imposing taxes. Americans were unaccustomed to paying taxes to their national government, both sides expected the war to be short, and neither wanted the

---

*Gross national product (GNP): the sum, measured in dollars, of all goods and services produced in a given year. By contrast, in the 1980s the federal budgets averaged about 25 percent of the GNP.

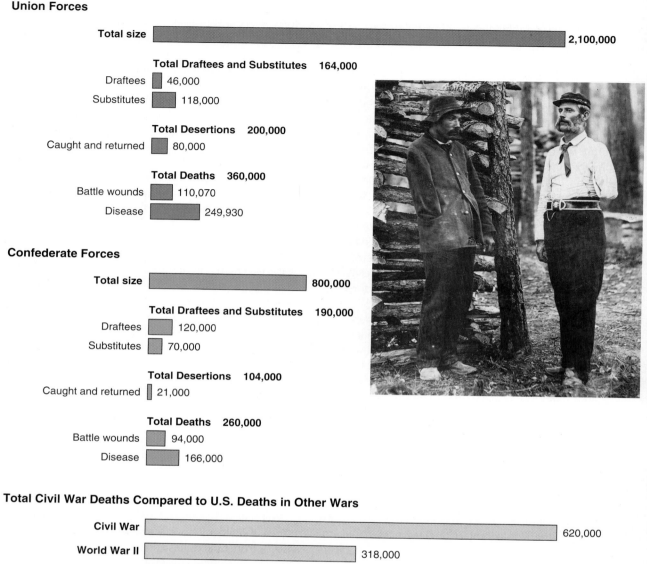

Union Forces

Total size — 2,100,000

Total Draftees and Substitutes 164,000
Draftees — 46,000
Substitutes — 118,000

Total Desertions 200,000
Caught and returned — 80,000

Total Deaths 360,000
Battle wounds — 110,070
Disease — 249,930

Confederate Forces

Total size — 800,000

Total Draftees and Substitutes 190,000
Draftees — 120,000
Substitutes — 70,000

Total Desertions 104,000
Caught and returned — 21,000

Total Deaths 260,000
Battle wounds — 94,000
Disease — 166,000

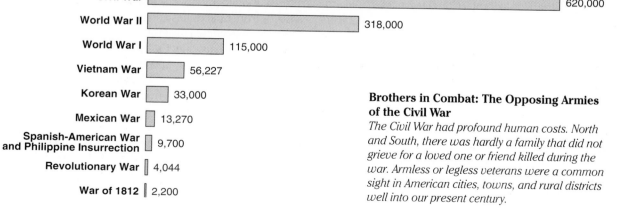

Total Civil War Deaths Compared to U.S. Deaths in Other Wars

Civil War — 620,000
World War II — 318,000
World War I — 115,000
Vietnam War — 56,227
Korean War — 33,000
Mexican War — 13,270
Spanish-American War and Philippine Insurrection — 9,700
Revolutionary War — 4,044
War of 1812 — 2,200

Brothers in Combat: The Opposing Armies of the Civil War
The Civil War had profound human costs. North and South, there was hardly a family that did not grieve for a loved one or friend killed during the war. Armless or legless veterans were a common sight in American cities, towns, and rural districts well into our present century.

knock of the tax collector to dampen patriotic spirit. In August 1861 the Confederacy enacted a small property tax and the Union an income tax, but both measures were halfhearted, and neither raised much revenue. The Union's first income-tax law actually postponed collection until 1863.

Still needing revenue, both sides turned to war bonds; that is, to loans from citizens, to be repaid by future generations. The patriotic fervor of the early war years helped to sell these bonds. Southerners quickly bought up the Confederacy's first bond issue ($15 million) in 1861. That same year, a financial wizard, Philadelphia banker Jay Cooke, led a successful campaign to induce the northern public to subscribe to a much larger bond issue ($150 million). But in themselves bonds did not answer the requirements of wartime finance, because they had to be paid for in gold or silver coin (specie), which was in short supply. Soaking up most of its available specie, the South's first bond issue threatened to be its last. In the North many hoarded their gold rather than spend it on bonds.

Recognizing the limitations of taxation and of bond issues, the Union and the Confederacy began to print paper money. Early in 1862 Lincoln signed into law the Legal Tender Act, which authorized the issue of $150 million of the so-called greenbacks. Christopher Memminger, the Confederacy's treasury secretary, and Salmon P. Chase, his Union counterpart, shared a distrust of paper money, but each came around to the idea because, as Chase bluntly put it, *"The Treasury is nearly empty."* The availability of paper money would make it easier to pay soldiers, to levy and raise taxes, and to sell war bonds. The Legal Tender Act not only authorized the issuance of the greenbacks but also provided for the emission of $500 million of war bonds purchasable with greenbacks.

Yet doubts about paper money lingered. Unlike gold and silver, which had established market values, the value of paper money depended mainly on the public's confidence in the government that issued it. To bolster that confidence, Union officials made the greenbacks legal tender (that is, acceptable in payment of most public and private debts) and overcame their early reservations about taxes by imposing increasingly stiff taxes on everything from income to liquor and billiard tables. The steady flow of tax revenue into the federal treasury strengthened public confidence in the government's ability to meet its obligations and helped check the inflationary tendency inherent in paper money.

In contrast, the Confederacy never made its paper money legal tender. This omission raised the suspicion that the southern government had little confidence in its own paper issues. To compound the problem, the Confederacy raised less than 5 percent of its wartime revenue from taxes. (The comparable figure for the North was 21 percent.) The Confederacy did enact a comprehensive tax measure in 1863, but Union invasions disrupted its ability to collect taxes. In addition, the South's relatively undeveloped system of internal transportation made tax collection a hit-or-miss proposition. For example, the Confederacy's tax measures of 1863 included a tax-in-kind, a sort of tithe. After feeding their families, farmers had to pledge one-tenth of their crops to the government. Because thousands of agents were sent to collect it, the tax-in-kind brought results, but it fell disproportionately on farmers who lived near the railroads traveled by tax collectors. Some of the food collected, moreover, rotted in government warehouses for want of transportation. To many farmers, the Confederacy's tax policies seemed unfair and incompetently administered.

In the face of the Confederacy's sorry performance in collecting taxes, confidence in the South's paper money quickly evaporated, and the value of Confederate paper in relation to gold plunged. The Confederacy responded by printing more paper money, a billion dollars by 1865, but this action merely accelerated southern inflation. Whereas prices in the North rose about 80 percent during the war, the Confederacy suffered an inflation rate of over 9,000 percent. What cost a southerner one dollar in 1861 cost forty-six dollars by 1864.

By raising taxes, floating bonds, and printing paper money, both the Union and the Confederacy broke with the hard-money, minimal-government traditions of American public finance. For the most part, these changes occurred as unanticipated and often reluctant adaptations to wartime conditions. But in the North the Republicans took advantage of the departure of the southern Democrats from Congress to push through one measure that they and their Whig predecessors had long advocated, a system of national banking. In February 1863 Congress passed the National Bank Act over the concerted opposition of the northern Democrats. This law established criteria by which a bank could obtain a federal charter and issue national bank notes (notes backed by the federal government). It also gave private bankers an incentive to purchase war bonds, because once a private bank had obtained a federal charter, it could issue national bank notes up to 90 percent of the value of the war bonds that it held.

The North's ability to revolutionize its system of public finance reflected not only its longer experience with the complex financial transactions required by its industrial and commercial economy but its greater political cohesion during the war.

Political Leadership in Wartime

The Civil War pitted rival political systems as well as armies and economies against each other. The South entered the war with several apparent political advantages. Lincoln's call for militiamen to suppress the rebellion had transformed hesitators in the South into tenacious secessionists. "Never was a people more united or more determined," a New Orleans resident wrote in the spring of 1861. "There is but one mind, one heart, one action." Moreover, since the founding of the United States, the South had produced a disproportionate share of the nation's strong presidents: Washington, Jefferson, Madison, Monroe, Jackson, and Polk. Now President Jefferson Davis of the Confederacy, as a former war secretary and U.S. senator, possessed experience, honesty, courage, and what one officer described as "a jaw sawed in *steel*."

In contrast, the Union's list of political liabilities appeared lengthy. Loyal but contentious, northern Democrats wanted to prosecute the war without conscription, without the financial centralization represented by the National Bank Act, and without the abolition of slavery. Within the rival Republican party, Lincoln had trouble commanding respect. Unlike Davis, he had served in neither the cabinet nor the Senate, and his informal western manners inspired little confidence among eastern Republicans. Northern setbacks early in the war convinced most Republicans in Congress that Lincoln was an ineffectual leader. Vocal criticism of Lincoln sprang from a group of Republicans who became known as the Radicals and who included Secretary of the Treasury Salmon P. Chase, Senator Charles Sumner of Massachusetts, and Representative Thaddeus Stevens of Pennsylvania. The Radicals never formed a tightly knit cadre; on some issues they cooperated with Lincoln. But they did criticize him early in the war for failing to make the emancipation of the slaves a war goal and later for being too eager to readmit the conquered rebel states into the Union.

Abraham Lincoln
When Lincoln became president in March 1861, he faced more severe problems than any predecessor. Washington photographer Mathew Brady captured this image of the solemn President-elect on February 23, 1861, a few weeks after the formation of the Confederacy and shortly before Lincoln's inauguration.

Lincoln's distinctive style of leadership encouraged and simultaneously disarmed opposition within the Republican party. Keeping his counsel to himself until ready to act, he met criticism with homespun anecdotes that caught his opponents off guard. The Radicals frequently concluded that Lincoln was a prisoner of the conservative wing of the party, whereas conservatives complained that Lincoln was too close to the Radicals. But Lincoln's cautious reserve had the dual benefit of leaving open his lines of communication with both wings of the party and fragmenting his opposition. Lincoln shrewdly brought several of his critics into his cabinet, including Chase. Chase not only moderated his criticism of Lincoln but proved a fine administrator.

In contrast, Jefferson Davis had a knack for making enemies. A West Pointer, he would rather have led the army than the government, and he used his sharp tongue to win arguments rather than to win over his foes. Davis's cabinet suffered from frequent resignations; the Confederacy had five secretaries of war in four years, for example. In particular, Davis's relations with his vice president, Alexander Stephens of Georgia, bordered on disastrous. A wisp of a man, Stephens weighed less than a hundred pounds and looked like a boy with a withered face. But he compensated for his slight physique with a tongue as acidic as Davis's. Leaving Richmond, the Confederate capital, in 1862, Stephens spent most of the war in Georgia, where he sniped at Davis as "weak and vacillating, timid, petulant, peevish, obstinate."

The conflict between Davis and Stephens involved not only a clash of personalities but also an ideological division, a rift, in fact, like that at the heart of the Confederacy. Although the Confederate Constitution, drafted in February 1861, resembled the U.S. Constitution in several ways, the southern charter explicitly guaranteed the sovereignty of the Confederate states and prohibited the Confederate Congress from enacting protective tariffs and from supporting internal improvements (measures long opposed by southern voters). For Stephens and other influential Confederate leaders—among them, governors Joseph Brown of Georgia and Zebulon Vance of North Carolina—the Confederacy existed not only to protect slavery but, equally important, to enshrine the doctrine of states' rights. (Brown condemned the Confederate Conscription Act as the most severe blow to constitutional liberty in American history.) In contrast, Davis's main objective was to secure the independence of the entire South from the North, a goal that frequently led him to override the wishes of state governors for the good of the Confederacy as a whole.

This difference between Davis and Stephens bore some resemblance to the discord between Lincoln and the northern Democrats. Like Davis, Lincoln believed that winning the war demanded an enhancement of the central government's power; like Stephens, northern Democrats resisted governmental centralization. But Lincoln could control his opponents more effectively than Davis, not only because, by temperament, he was more suited than Davis to conciliation but also because of the different nature of party politics in the two sections.

In the South the Democrats and the remaining Whigs agreed to suspend party rivalries for the duration of the war. However, this decision, made to pro-mote southern unity, actually encouraged disunity. Without the institutionalization of conflict that party rivalry provided, southern politics tended to disintegrate along personal and factional lines. Lacking a party organization to back him, Davis could not mobilize votes to pass measures that he favored through the Confederate Congress, nor could he depend on the support of party loyalists throughout the slave states. In contrast, in the Union, northern Democrats' organized opposition to Lincoln tended to unify the Republicans. In the 1862 elections, which occurred at a low ebb of Union military fortunes, the Democrats won control of five large states, including Lincoln's own Illinois. Republican leaders learned a lesson: no matter how much they disdained Lincoln, they had to rally behind him or risk being driven from office. Ultimately, the Union would develop more political cohesion than the Confederacy, not because it had fewer divisions but because it managed its divisions more effectively.

Securing the Union's Borders

Even before large-scale fighting began, Lincoln moved to safeguard Washington, which was bordered by two slave states (Virginia and Maryland) and filled with Confederate sympathizers. A week after Fort Sumter, a Baltimore mob attacked a Massachusetts regiment bound for Washington, but enough troops slipped through to protect the capital. Lincoln then dispatched federal troops to Maryland, where he suspended the writ of habeas corpus*; federal troops could now arrest prosecession Marylanders without formally charging them with specific offenses. Mindful that strong Unionist sentiment flourished in the western part of the state, and cowed by Lincoln's bold moves, the Maryland legislature rejected secession. Delaware, another border slave state, followed suit.

Next Lincoln authorized the arming of Union sympathizers in Kentucky, a slave state with a Unionist legislature, a secessionist governor, and a thin chance of staying neutral. Lincoln also stationed troops under General Ulysses S. Grant just across the Ohio River from Kentucky, in Illinois. When a Confederate army invaded Kentucky early in 1862, the state's legislature turned to Grant to drive it out. Officially, at least, Kentucky

---

*Habeas corpus: a court order requiring that the detainer of a prisoner bring the person in custody to court and show cause for his or her detention.

became the third slave state to declare for the Union. The fourth, Missouri, was ravaged by four years of fighting between Union and Confederate troops and between sundry bands of guerrillas and bushwackers, including William Quantrill, a Confederate desperado, and his murderous apprentices, Frank and Jesse James. Despite savage fighting and the divided loyalties of its people, Missouri never left the Union.[*]

By holding these four border slave states—Maryland, Delaware, Kentucky, and Missouri—in the Union, Lincoln kept open his lines to the free states and gained access to the river systems in Kentucky and Missouri that led into the heart of the Confederacy. (In 1862 invasions of the South by river would provide the North with most of its early military successes.) Lincoln's firmness, particularly in the case of Maryland, scotched charges that he was weak-willed, and it demonstrated how the crisis forced the president to exercise long-dormant powers. Although in the case *Ex parte* Merryman (1861), Chief Justice Roger B. Taney ruled that Lincoln had exceeded his authority in suspending the writ of habeas corpus in Maryland, the president, citing the Constitution's authorization of the writ's suspension in "Cases of Rebellion" (Article I, Section 9), insisted that he, rather than Congress, would determine whether a rebellion existed; and he ignored Taney's ruling.

◆

IN BATTLE, 1861–1862

The Civil War was the first war to rely extensively on railroads, the telegraph, mass-produced weapons, joint army-navy tactics, iron-plated warships, rifled guns and artillery, and trench warfare. All of this lends some justification to its description as the first modern war. But to the participants, slogging through muddy swamps and weighed down with equipment, the war hardly seemed modern. In many ways, the soldiers had the more accurate perspective, for the new weapons did not always work, and both sides employed tactics that were more traditional than modern.

---

[*]Admitted to the Union in 1863, West Virginia became the fifth border state. This state originated in the refusal of thirty-five counties in the predominantly nonslaveholding region of Virginia west of the Shenandoah Valley to follow the state's leaders into secession in 1861.

Armies, Weapons, and Strategies

Compared to the Confederacy's 9 million people, of whom over one-third were slaves, the Union had 22 million people in 1861. The North also had 3.5 times as many white men of military age, 90 percent of all U.S. industrial capacity, and two-thirds of its railroad track. Yet the Union faced a daunting challenge. Its goal was to force the South back into the Union, whereas the South was fighting merely for its independence. To subdue the Confederacy, the North would have to sustain offensive operations over an area comparable in size to the part of Russia that the French emperor Napoleon had invaded in 1812 with disastrous results.

Measured against this challenge, the Union's advantages in population and technology shrank. The North had more men, but needing to defend long supply lines and occupy captured areas, it could commit a smaller proportion of them to frontline duty. The South, on the other hand, with black slaves as the basis of its labor force, could assign a higher proportion of its white male population to combat. As for technology, the North required, and possessed, superior railroads. Fighting defensively on so-called interior lines, the South could shift its troops relatively short distances within its defensive arc without relying on railroads, whereas the North had to move its troops and supplies huge distances around the exterior of the arc. Not only could guerrillas easily sabotage northern railroads, but once Union troops moved away from their railroad bases, their supply wagons often bogged down on wretched southern roads, which frequently became watery ditches in bad weather. Even on good roads, horses and mules, which themselves consumed supplies, were needed to pull wagons; an invading army of 100,000 men required 35,000 horses or mules. Finally, southerners had an edge in soldiers' morale, for Confederate troops battled on home ground. "No people ever warred for independence," a southern general acknowledged, "with more relative advantages than the Confederates."

The Civil War witnessed experiments with a variety of newly developed weapons, including the submarine, the repeating rifle, and the multibarreled Gatling gun, the forerunner of the machine gun. Yet these futuristic innovations had less impact on the war than did the perfection in the 1850s of a bullet whose powder would not clog a rifle's spiraled internal grooves after a few shots. Like the smoothbore muskets that both armies had employed at the start of the

	Union		Confederacy
Total population	71%		29%
Free male population, 18 – 20 years	81		19
Industrial workers	92		8
Factory production	91		9
Textile production	93		7
Firearm production	97		3
Railroad mileage	71		29
Iron production	94		6
Coal production	97		3
Livestock	60		40
Farm acreage	75		25
Wheat	81		19
Corn	67		33
Cotton	4		96
Wealth produced	75		25

Union　　　Confederacy

Comparative Population and Economic Resources of the Union and the Confederacy, 1861

At the start of the war, the Union enjoyed huge advantages in population, industry, railroad mileage, and wealth produced.

SOURCE: *The Times Atlas of World History* (New Jersey: Hammond, Inc., 1978).

war, most improved rifles had to be reloaded after each shot. But where the smoothbore musket had an effective range of only eighty yards, the Springfield or Enfield rifles widely employed by 1863 could hit targets accurately at four hundred yards.

The development of the rifle posed a challenge to long-accepted military tactics. The tactical manuals used at West Point in the 1840s and 1850s had identified the mass infantry charge against an opponent's weakest point as the key to victory. These manuals assumed that defenders armed with muskets would be able to fire only a round or two before being overwhelmed. The same assumption led tacticians to disdain trenches; against assaulting infantry, trenches would become mere traps for defenders. Armed with rifles, however, a defending force could fire several rounds before closing with the enemy. Attackers would now have far greater difficulty getting close enough to thrust bayonets; less than 1 percent of the casualties in the Civil War resulted from bayonet wounds.

Thus the rifle produced some changes in tactics during the war. Both sides gradually came to under-

stand the value of trenches, which provided defenders with some protection against the withering fire of attacking forces. By 1865 trenches pockmarked the landscape in Virginia and Georgia. In addition, growing use of the rifle forced generals to rely less on cavalry. Traditionally, the cavalry had ranked among the most prestigious components of an army, in part because cavalry charges were often devastatingly effective and in part because the cavalry helped maintain class distinctions within the army. Indeed, at the start of the war, one of the clearest Confederate advantages lay in the quality of its cavalry. But rifles reduced the effectiveness of cavalry by increasing the firepower of foot soldiers. Bullets that might miss the rider would at least hit the horse. Thus as cavalry charges against infantry became more difficult, both sides relegated cavalry to reconnaissance missions and to raids on supply trains.

Although the rifle exposed traditional tactics to new hazards, it by no means invalidated those tactics. The attacking army still stood an excellent chance of success if it achieved surprise. The South's lush forests provided abundant opportunities for an army to sneak up on its opponent. For example, at the Battle of Shiloh

Life in the Field

*The implements in this Union
army-owned field surgical kit could remove bullets but not stop infection.
The British-made five-shot revolver reached the South despite the Union blockade.
A Confederate officer owned the brass-and-leather-adorned field glass. The bullet-rent trousers
belonged to a Union officer wounded at Peachtree Creek. Although he survived the war, he endured
repeated operations in the remaining forty-five years of his life to remove tissue infected by the bullet.*

in 1862, Confederate attackers surprised and almost defeated a larger Union army despite the rumpus created by green rebel troops en route to the battle, many of whom fired their rifles into the air to see if they would work.

Achieving such complete surprise normally lay beyond the skill or luck of generals. In the absence of any element of surprise, disaster became a likely result for the attacking army. At the Battle of Fredericksburg in December 1862, Confederate troops inflicted appalling casualties on Union forces attacking uphill over open terrain, and at Gettysburg in July 1863, Union riflemen and artillery shredded charging southerners. But generals might still achieve partial surprise by hitting an enemy before it had concentrated its troops; in fact,

this is what the North tried to do at Fredericksburg. Because surprise often proved effective, most generals continued to believe that their best chance of success lay in striking an unwary or weakened enemy with all the troops they could muster rather than in relying on guerrilla or trench warfare.

Much like previous wars, the Civil War was fought basically in a succession of battles during which exposed infantry traded volleys, charged, and countercharged. Whichever side withdrew from the field usually was thought to have lost the battle, but the losing side frequently sustained lighter casualties than the supposed victors. Both sides had trouble exploiting their victories, for neither had airplanes to hammer or tanks to envelop retreating columns. As a rule, the beaten army moved back a few miles from the field to lick its wounds; the winners stayed in place to lick theirs. Politicians on both sides denounced their generals as timorous fools for not pursuing a beaten foe, but these politicians rarely understood how difficult it was for a mangled victor to gather horses, mules, supply trains, and exhausted soldiers for a new attack. Until the end of the war, the only cases of entire armies actually surrendering arose from captured garrisons. Not surprisingly, for much of the war, generals on both sides concluded that the best defense was a good offense.

To the extent that the North had a long-range strategy in 1861, it lay in the so-called Anaconda plan. Devised by the Mexican War hero General Winfield Scott, the plan called for the Union to blockade the southern coastline and to thrust, like a huge snake, down the Mississippi River. Scott expected that this sealing off and severing of the Confederacy would make the South recognize the futility of secession and restore southern Unionists to power. The Anaconda plan promised a relatively bloodless end to the war, but Scott, a southern Unionist, exaggerated the strength of Unionist spirit in the South. Furthermore, although Lincoln ordered a blockade of the southern coast a week after the fall of Fort Sumter, the North hardly had the troops and naval flotillas to seize the Mississippi in 1861. So while the Mississippi was an obvious objective, northern strategy did not unfold according to any blueprint like the Anaconda plan.

Early in the war, the pressing need to secure the border slave states, particularly Kentucky and Missouri, dictated Union strategy west of the Appalachian Mountains. Once in control of Kentucky, northern troops plunged southward into Tennessee. The Appalachians tended to seal this western theater off from the eastern theater, where the Confederacy's decision to move its capital from Montgomery, Alabama, to Richmond, Virginia, shaped the Union strategy. "Forward to Richmond" became the Union's first war cry in 1861.

Stalemate in the East

Before they could reach Richmond, one hundred miles southwest of Washington, Union troops would have to dislodge a Confederate army brazenly encamped at Manassas Junction, only twenty-five miles from the Union capital. Lincoln ordered General Irvin McDowell to attack his former West Point classmate, Confederate general P. G. T. Beauregard. "You are green, it is true," Lincoln told McDowell, "but they are green also; you are all green alike." In the resulting First Battle of Bull Run (or First Manassas),* amateur armies clashed in bloody chaos under a blistering July sun. The engagement was a spectacle that contrasted vividly with the picnicking of the well-dressed Washington dignitaries who had gathered to view the action. Aided by last-minute reinforcements and by the disorganization of the attacking federals, Beauregard routed the larger Union army.

After Bull Run, Lincoln replaced McDowell with General George B. McClellan as commander of the Union's Army of the Potomac. Another West Pointer, McClellan had served with distinction in the Mexican War and mastered the art of administration by managing various midwestern railroads in the 1850s. Few generals could match his ability to turn a ragtag mob into a disciplined fighting force. His soldiers adored him, but Lincoln quickly became disenchanted with his new commander. Lincoln believed that the key to a Union victory lay in simultaneous, coordinated attacks on several fronts. In this way, the North could exploit its advantage in manpower and resources and negate the South's advantage of interior lines. McClellan, a proslavery Democrat, hoped to maneuver the South into a relatively bloodless defeat and then negotiate a peace that would readmit the Confederate states with slavery intact.

McClellan soon got an opportunity to demonstrate the value of his strategy. After Bull Run, the Confederates had pulled back behind the Rappahannock River and awaited the Union onslaught against Richmond. Rather than directly attack the Confederate army, McClellan formulated a plan in the spring of 1862 to move the Army of the Potomac by water to the tip of the peninsula formed by the York and James rivers and then move northwestward up the peninsula to Richmond. McClellan's plan had several advantages. Depending on water transport rather than on railroads (which Confederate cavalry could cut), the McClellan strategy reduced the vulnerability of northern supply lines. By dictating an approach to Richmond from the southeast, it threatened the South's supply lines. By aiming for the capital of the Confederacy rather than for the Confederate army stationed northeast of Richmond, finally, McClellan hoped to maneuver the

---

*Because the North sometimes named battles after local landmarks, often bodies of water, and the South after the nearest town, several Civil War battles are known by two names.

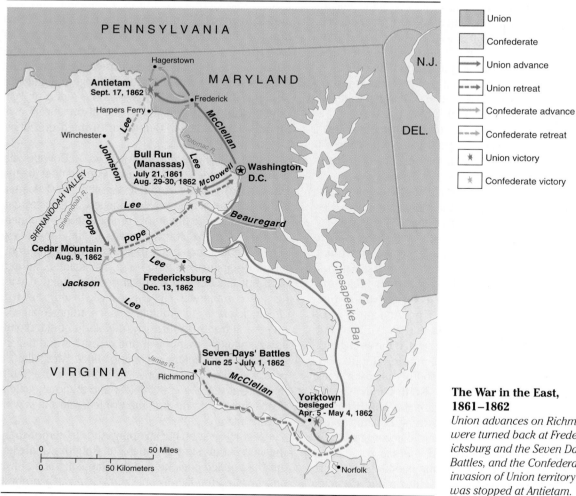

The War in the East, 1861–1862

Union advances on Richmond were turned back at Fredericksburg and the Seven Days' Battles, and the Confederacy's invasion of Union territory was stopped at Antietam.

southern troops into a futile attack on his army in order to avert a destructive siege of Richmond.

By far the most massive military campaign in American history to that date, the Peninsula Campaign at first unfolded smoothly. Three hundred ships transported seventy thousand men and huge stores of supplies to the tip of the peninsula. Reinforcements swelled McClellan's army to one hundred thousand. Although Confederate troops also poured into the peninsula, by late May McClellan was within five miles of Richmond.

If the war had been a chess game, McClellan would have become a grand master. But after luring the Confederacy to the brink of defeat, McClellan hesitated. Overestimating the Confederates' strength, he refused to launch a final attack on Richmond without

the reinforcements that he expected, which were turned back by Confederate general Thomas "Stonewall" Jackson in the Shenandoah Valley. While McClellan delayed, General Robert E. Lee took command of the Confederacy's Army of Northern Virginia. A foe of secession and so courteous that at times he seemed too gentle, Lee nevertheless possessed the qualities that McClellan most lacked, boldness and a willingness to accept casualties. Seizing the initiative, Lee attacked McClellan in late June 1862. The ensuing Seven Days' Battles, fought in the forests east of Richmond, cost the South nearly twice as many men as the North and ended in a virtual slaughter of Confederates at Malvern Hill. But it was his own northern casualties that unnerved McClellan, and he began to send increasingly panicky reports to Washington. Lincoln, who cared little for McClellan's peninsula strategy, ordered McClellan to call off the campaign and return to Washington.

With McClellan out of the picture, Lee and his lieutenant, Stonewall Jackson, now boldly struck north and, at the Second Battle of Bull Run (Second Manassas), routed a Union army under General John Pope that had been held back from the peninsula to guard Washington. Lee's next stroke was even bolder. Crossing the Potomac River in early September 1862, he invaded western Maryland, where the forthcoming fall harvest could provide him with desperately needed supplies. By seizing western Maryland, moreover, Lee could threaten Washington, indirectly relieve pressure on Richmond, improve the prospects of peace candidates in the North's upcoming fall elections, and possibly induce Britain and France to recognize the Confederacy as an independent nation. But McClellan met Lee at the Battle of Antietam (or Sharpsburg) on September 17. Although a tactical draw, Antietam proved a strategic victory for the North, for Lee subsequently called off his invasion and retreated south of the Potomac. Heartened by the apparent success of northern

arms, Lincoln then issued the Emancipation Proclamation, a war measure that freed all slaves under rebel control (see below). The carnage of the twenty-four thousand casualties at Antietam, however, made it the bloodiest day of the entire war. A Union veteran recollected that one part of the battlefield contained so many bodies that a man could have walked through it without stepping on the ground.

Complaining that McClellan had "the slows," Lincoln faulted his commander for not pursuing Lee after the battle and replaced him with General Ambrose Burnside, who thought himself, and soon proved himself, unfit for high command. In December 1862 Burnside led 122,000 federal troops against 78,500 Confederates at the Battle of Fredericksburg. Burnside captured the town of Fredericksburg, northeast of Richmond, but then sacrificed his army in futile charges up the heights west of the town. Even Lee was shaken by the northern casualties. "It is well that war is so terrible—we should grow fond of it," he told an aide during the battle. Richmond remained, in the words of a southern song, "a hard road to travel." The war in the East had become a stalemate.

Dead Soldiers at Antietam
These dead rebel gunners lie next to the wreckage of their battery at Antietam. The building, a Dunker church, was the site of furious fighting.

The War in the West

The Union fared better in the West. Unlike the geographically limited eastern theater, the war in the West shifted over a vast and crucial terrain that provided access to rivers leading directly into the South. The West also spawned new leadership. During the first year of war, an obscure Union general, Ulysses S. Grant, proved his competence. A West Point graduate, Grant had fought in the Mexican War and retired from the army in 1854 with a reputation for heavy drinking. He then had embarked on ventures in farming and in business, all of them dismal failures. When the Civil War began, he had gained an army commission through political pressure.

In 1861–1862 Grant retained control of two border states, Missouri and Kentucky. Moving into Tennessee, he captured two strategic forts, Fort Henry on the Tennessee River and Fort Donelson on the Cumberland. Grant then headed south to attack Corinth, Mississippi.

Corinth was a major railroad junction through which troops and supplies could be transported from the east to Memphis on the Mississippi River. In early April 1862, Confederate forces under generals Albert Sidney Johnston and P. G. T. Beauregard tried to relieve the Union pressure on Corinth by a surprise attack on Grant's army, encamped twenty miles north of the town, in southern Tennessee near a church named Shiloh. Hoping to whip Grant before the imminent arrival of twenty-five thousand Union reinforcements under General Don Carlos Buell, the Confederates exploded from the woods near Shiloh before breakfast and almost drove the federals into the Tennessee River. Beauregard cabled Richmond with news of a splendid Confederate victory. But Grant and his lieutenant, William T. Sherman, steadied the Union line. Buell's reinforcements arrived in the night, and a Union counterattack drove the Confederates from the field the next day. Although Antietam would soon erase the distinction, the Battle of Shiloh was the bloodiest in Ameri-can history to that date. Of the seventy-seven thousand men engaged, twenty-three thousand were killed or wounded, including Confederate general Albert Sidney Johnston, who bled to death from a leg wound. Defeated at Shiloh, the Confederates soon evacuated Corinth.

To attack Grant at Shiloh, the Confederacy had stripped the defenses of New Orleans, leaving only three thousand militia to guard its largest city. A combined Union land-sea force under General

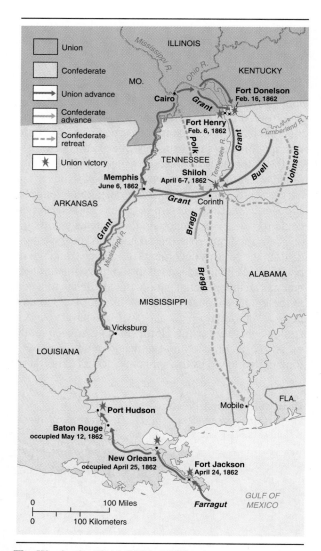

The War in the West, 1861–1862
By the end of 1862, the North held New Orleans and the entire Mississippi River except for the stretch between Vicksburg and Port Hudson.

Benjamin Butler, a Massachusetts politician, and Admiral David G. Farragut, a Tennessean loyal to the Union, quickly capitalized on the opportunity. Blasting his way past two river forts south of New Orleans, Farragut took the city in late April and soon added Baton Rouge and Natchez to his list of conquests. Meanwhile, another Union flotilla moved down the Mississippi and captured Memphis in June. Now the North controlled the entire river, except for a two-hundred-mile stretch between Port Hudson, Louisiana, and Vicksburg, Mississippi.

Union and Confederate forces also clashed in 1862 in the Trans-Mississippi West, the vast region of states and territories stretching from the Midwest to the Pacific coast. On the banks of the Rio Grande, Union volunteers, joined by Mexican-American companies, drove a Confederate army from Texas out of New Mexico. "Fight for your rights and repel the invaders!" the territorial governor had urged the Mexican-American recruits. A thousand miles to the east, in northern Arkansas and western Missouri, opposing armies vied to secure the Missouri River, a crucial waterway that flowed into the Mississippi. In Pea Ridge, Arkansas, in March 1862, forewarned northern troops scattered a Confederate force of sixteen thousand that included three Cherokee regiments. (Indian units fought on *both* sides in Missouri, where guerrilla combat raged until the war's end.)

These Union victories changed the nature of the Trans-Mississippi war. As the rebel threat faded, regiments of western volunteers that had mobilized to crush Confederates turned to fighting Indians. Conflict between the Dakota Sioux and Minnesota volunteers in the fall of 1862 spread to the north and west. Indian wars erupted in Arizona, Nevada, Colorado, and New Mexico, where California volunteers and the New Mexico cavalry, led by Colonel Kit Carson, overwhelmed the Apaches and Navajos. After 1865 federal troops moved west to complete the rout of the Indians that had begun in the Civil War (see Chapter 17).

Ironclads and Cruisers: The Naval War

By plunging its navy into the Confederacy like a dagger, the Union was exploiting one of its clearest advantages. The North began the war with over forty active warships against none for the South, and with the technology and industrial capacity to produce many more. Indeed, by 1865 the United States had the largest navy in the world. Steam-driven ships could penetrate the South's excellent river system from any direction and thereby turn a peacetime advantage into a wartime liability. For example, the Confederacy had stripped New Orleans's defenses in the belief that the real threat to the city would come from the north, only to find Farragut slipping in from the south.

Despite its size, the Union navy faced an extraordinary challenge in its efforts to blockade the South's thirty-five hundred miles of coast. Early in the war, small, sleek Confederate blockade-runners darted in and out of southern harbors and inlets with little

Deck of the *Monitor*
Although much smaller than its famous rival the Merrimac (*C.S.S.* Virginia), *the Union ironclad* Monitor *benefited from its shallow draft, speed, and maneuverability. Its flat, raftlike shape made it hard to hit.*

chance of capture. The North gradually tightened the blockade by outfitting tugs, whalers, excursion steamers, and ferries as well as frigates to patrol southern coasts. The proportion of Confederate blockade-runners that made it through dropped from 90 percent early in the war to 50 percent by 1865. Even more than tightening the blockade, however, northern seizure of rebel ports and coastal areas shrank the South's foreign trade. In daring amphibious assaults during 1861 and 1862, the Union captured the excellent harbor of Port Royal, South Carolina, the coastal islands off South Carolina, and most of North Carolina's river outlets. Naval patrols and amphibious operations contributed to a decline in the South's ocean trade to one-third its prewar level.

Although its resources were meager, the South made impressive efforts to offset the North's naval advantage. Early in the war, the Confederacy raised the scuttled Union frigate *Merrimac,* sheathed its sides with an armor of iron plate, rechristened it *Virginia,* and dispatched it to attack wooden Union ships in Hampton Roads, Virginia. The *Merrimac* quickly destroyed two northern warships but met its match in the hastily built Union ironclad the *Monitor.* In the first engagement of ironclads in history, the two ships fought an indecisive battle on March 9, 1862. The South constructed other ironclads and even the first submarine, which dragged a mine through the water to sink a Union ship off Charleston in 1864. Unfortunately, the "fish" failed to resurface and went down with its victim. But short of mechanics and iron-fabricating shops, the South could never build enough ironclads to overcome the North's supremacy in home waters. The Confederacy had more success on the high seas, where wooden, steam-driven commerce raiders like the *Alabama* and the *Florida* (both built in England) wreaked havoc on the Union's merchant marine. Commerce raiding, however, would not tip the balance of the war in the South's favor, because the North, unlike its opponent, did not depend on imports for war materials. The South would lose the naval war.

The Diplomatic War

While armies and navies clashed in 1861–1862, conflict developed on a third front, diplomacy. At the outbreak of the war, the Confederacy began a campaign to gain European recognition of its status as an independent nation. Southern confidence in a swift diplomatic victory ran high. Planning to establish a colonial empire in Mexico, Napoleon III of France had grounds to welcome the permanent division of the United States. Moreover, the upper classes in France, and also in Britain, were widely viewed as sympathetic to the aristocratic South and eager for the downfall of the brash Yankee republic. Furthermore, for years such influential southerners as South Carolina's senator and governor James Henry Hammond had contended that an embargo of cotton exports would bring Britain to its knees. These southerners reasoned that Britain, dependent on the South for four-fifths of its cotton, would break the Union blockade and provoke a war with the North rather than watch its textile workers sink into revolutionary discontent under the weight of an embargo.

Leaving nothing to chance, the Confederacy in 1861 dispatched emissaries James Mason to Britain and John Slidell to France to lobby for recognition of the South as an independent nation. When a Union ship captain, acting without orders, boarded the British vessel the *Trent,* which was carrying Mason and Slidell, and brought the two men to Boston as prisoners, British tempers exploded. "You may stand for this," Britain's prime minister, Lord Palmerston, roared to his cabinet, "but damned if I will." But cooler heads prevailed. Considering one war at a time enough, President Lincoln released Mason and Slidell.

Settlement of the *Trent* affair did not eliminate friction between the United States and Britain. The construction in British shipyards of two Confederate commerce raiders, the *Florida* and the *Alabama,* evoked protests from Union diplomats. In 1863 the U.S. minister to London, Charles Francis Adams (the son of former president John Quincy Adams), threatened war if two British-built ironclads commissioned by the Confederacy, the so-called Laird rams, were turned over to the South. Armed with long spikes below the water, the powerful rams posed a genuine threat to the Union blockade of the South. Britain, however, capitulated to Adams's protests and purchased the rams for its own navy.

On balance, the South fell far short of its diplomatic objectives. Although recognizing the Confederacy as a belligerent, neither Britain nor France ever recognized it as a nation. Basically, the Confederacy overestimated its hand. For several reasons, the South's vaunted "cotton diplomacy" failed dismally. The Confederate government talked of embargoing cotton exports in order to bring the British to their knees, but in reality, the government never controlled

CAVING IN, OR A REBEL "DEEPLY HUMILIATED".

Lincoln Battles Davis in an 1863 Cartoon
In the first years of war, European nations played a waiting game without commitments to Union or Confederacy. By 1863, the North seemed to gain the advantage in the diplomatic war, as this cartoon suggests. Still, the European leaders watching the contest from behind a rope consider self-interest and avoid involvement.

more than 15 percent of the South's cotton. Planters conducted business as usual by raising cotton and trying to slip it through the blockade. The South ultimately lost its share of the British market anyway; with 77 percent of that market in 1860, it held only 10 percent by 1865. But this loss resulted from forces beyond southern control. Bumper cotton crops in the late 1850s had glutted the British market by the start of the war and weakened British demand for cotton. In addition, Britain had responded to the threat of a cotton embargo by developing new suppliers in Egypt and India, thereby buffering itself from southern pressure. Gradually, too, the North's tightened blockade restricted southern exports.

The South also exaggerated Britain's stake in helping the Confederacy. As a naval power that had frequently blockaded its own enemies, Britain's diplomatic interest lay in supporting the Union blockade in principle; from Britain's standpoint, to help the South break the blockade would set a precedent that could easily boomerang. Finally, although France and Britain often talked of recognizing the Confederacy, the timing never seemed quite right. The Union's success at Antietam in 1862 and Lincoln's subsequent issuance of the Emancipation Proclamation dampened

Europe's enthusiasm for recognition at a crucial juncture. By transforming the war into a struggle to end slavery, the Emancipation Proclamation produced an upsurge of pro-Union feeling in antislavery Britain, particularly among liberals and the working class. Workingmen in Manchester, England, wrote Lincoln to praise his resolve to free the slaves. The proclamation, wrote Henry Adams (diplomat Charles Francis Adams's son) from London, "has done more for us here than all of our former victories and all our diplomacy."

◆

EMANCIPATION TRANSFORMS THE WAR

"I hear old John Brown knocking on the lid of his coffin and shouting 'Let me out! Let me out!'" abolitionist Henry Stanton wrote to his wife after the fall of Fort Sumter. "The Doom of Slavery is at hand." In 1861 this prediction seemed wildly premature. In his inaugural that year, Lincoln had stated bluntly, "I have no purpose, directly or indirectly, to interfere with the institution of slavery in the states where it exists." Yet in two years, the North's priorities underwent a decisive transformation. A mix of practical necessity and ideological conviction thrust the emancipation of the slaves to the forefront of northern war goals.

The rise of emancipation as a Union war goal reflected the changing character of the war itself. As late as July 1862, General George McClellan had written to Lincoln to restate his conviction that "neither confiscation of property . . . or forcible abolition of slavery should be contemplated for a moment." As the struggle dragged on, however, demands for the prosecution of "total war" intensified in the North. Even northerners who saw no moral value in abolishing slavery were starting to recognize the military value of emancipation as a technique to cripple the South's resources.

From Confiscation to Emancipation

Union policy on emancipation developed in stages. As soon as northern troops began to invade the South, questions arose about the disposition of captured rebel property, including slaves. Slaves who fled behind the Union lines were sometimes considered "contra-band"—enemy property liable to seizure— and were put to work for the Union army. Whereas some northern commanders viewed this practice a useful tool of war, others did not, and the Lincoln administration was evasive. To establish an official policy, Congress in August 1861 passed the first Confiscation Act, which authorized the seizure of all property used in military aid of the rebellion, including slaves. By the terms of this act, slaves who had been employed directly by the Confederate armed services and who later fled to freedom became "captives of war." But nothing in the act actually freed these contrabands, nor did the law apply to contrabands who had not worked for the Confederate military.

Several factors underlay the Union's cautious approach to the confiscation of rebel property. Officially maintaining that the South's rebellion lacked any legal basis, Lincoln argued that southerners were thus still entitled to the Constitution's protection of property. The president also had practical reasons to walk softly. The Union not only contained four slave states but also held a sizable body of proslavery Democrats who flatly opposed turning the war into a crusade against slavery. If the North in any way tampered with slavery, these Democrats feared, "two or three million semi-savages" might come north and compete with white workers. Aware of strong northern opposition to turning a limited policy of confiscation into a general program of emancipation, Lincoln assured Congress in December

1861 that the war would not become a "remorseless revolutionary struggle."

From the start of the war, however, Lincoln faced pressure from the loosely knit but determined Radical Republicans to adopt a policy of emancipation. Radicals hailed the war as a second American Revolution, one that would abolish slavery. Pennsylvanian Thaddeus Stevens urged that the Union "free every slave— slay every traitor—burn every Rebel mansion, if these things be necessary to preserve this temple of freedom." Radicals agreed with black abolitionist Frederick Douglass that "to fight against slaveholders without fighting against slavery, is but a half-hearted business."

With every new northern setback, support for the Radicals' point of view grew. Each Union military defeat reminded northerners that the confederacy, with a slave labor force in place to harvest southern crops and run southern factories, could commit a higher proportion of its white men to battle. As a military measure, the idea of emancipation thus gained increasing favor in the North, and in July 1862 Congress passed the second Confiscation Act. This law authorized the seizure of the property of all persons in rebellion and stipulated that slaves who came within Union lines "shall be forever free." Finally, the law opened the door to blacks' military service by authorizing the president to employ blacks as soldiers.

Nevertheless, Lincoln continued to stall, even in the face of rising pressure for emancipation. "My paramount object in this struggle *is* to save the Union, and is *not* either to save or destroy slavery," Lincoln told antislavery journalist Horace Greeley. "If I could save the Union without freeing *any* slave, I would do it, and if I could save it by freeing *all* the slaves, I would do it; and if I could save it by freeing some and leaving others alone, I would also do that." Yet Lincoln had always loathed slavery, and by the spring of 1862, he had come around to the Radical position that the war must lead to its abolition. He hesitated principally because he did not want to be stampeded by Congress into a measure that might disrupt northern unity and because he feared that a public commitment to emancipation in the summer of 1862, on the heels of the northern defeat at Second Manassas and the collapse of the Peninsula Campaign, might be interpreted as an act of frantic desperation. After failing to persuade the Union slave states to emancipate slaves in return for federal compensation, he drafted a proclamation of emancipation, circulated it within his cabinet, and waited for a right moment to issue it. Finally, after the

Union victory in September 1862 at Antietam, Lincoln issued the Preliminary Emancipation Proclamation, which declared all slaves under rebel control free as of January 1, 1863. Announcing the plan in advance softened the surprise, tested public opinion, and gave the states still in rebellion an opportunity to preserve slavery by returning to the Union—an opportunity that none, however, took. The final Emancipation Proclamation, issued on January 1, 1863, declared "forever free" all slaves in areas in rebellion.

The proclamation had limited practical impact. Applying only to rebellious areas, where the Union had no authority, it exempted the Union slave states and those parts of the Confederacy then in Union hands (Tennessee, West Virginia, southern Louisiana, and sections of Virginia). Moreover, it mainly restated what the second Confiscation Act had already stipulated: if rebels' slaves fell into Union hands, those slaves would be free. Yet the proclamation was a brilliant political stroke. By issuing it as a military measure, in his role as commander in chief, Lincoln pacified northern conservatives. Its aim, he stressed, was to injure the Confederacy, threaten its property, heighten its dread, sap its morale, and thus hasten its demise. By issuing the proclamation himself, Lincoln stole the initiative from the Radicals in Congress and mobilized support for the Union among European liberals far more dramatically than could any act of Congress. Furthermore, the declaration pushed the border states toward emancipation: by the end of the war, Maryland and Missouri would abolish slavery. Finally, it increased slaves' incentives to escape as northern troops approached. Fulfilling the worst of Confederate fears, it enabled blacks to join the Union army.

The Emancipation Proclamation did not end slavery everywhere or free "*all* the slaves." But it changed the war. From 1863 on, the war for the Union would also be a war against slavery.

Crossing Union Lines

The attacks and counterattacks of the opposing armies turned many slaves into pawns of war. Some slaves became free when Union troops overran their areas. Others fled their plantations at the approach of federal troops to take refuge behind Union lines. A few were freed by northern assaults, only to be reenslaved by Confederate counterthrusts. One North Carolina slave celebrated liberation on twelve occasions, as many times as Union soldiers marched

through his area. By 1865 about half a million slaves were in Union hands.

In the first year of the war, when the Union had not yet established a policy toward contrabands (fugitive slaves), masters were able to retrieve them from the Union army. After 1862, however, the thousands of slaves who crossed Union lines were considered free. The continual influx of freed slaves created a huge refugee problem for army commanders. "What shall I do about the negroes?" wrote a Union general in Louisiana to army headquarters in 1862:

> You can form no idea of . . . the appearance of my brigade as it marched down the Bayou. . . . Every soldier had a negro marching in the flanks, carrying his knapsack. Plantation carts, filled with negro women and children, with their effects; and of course compelled to pillage for their subsistence, as I have no rations to issue them. I have a great many more negroes in my camp now than I have whites.

As 1862 drew to a close, Union commanders in the South were appointing superintendents of freedmen to supervise large contraband camps. Many freedmen served in army camps as cooks, teamsters, and laborers. Some worked for pay on abandoned plantations or were leased out to planters who swore allegiance to the Union and who paid them wages stipulated by the army. Whether in camps or working outside of them, freedmen had reason to question the value of their liberation. Deductions for clothing, rations, and medicine ate up most, if not all, of their earnings. Labor contracts frequently tied them to their employers for prolonged periods. Moreover, freedmen encountered fierce prejudice among Yankee soldiers, many of whom feared that emancipation would propel blacks north after the war. The best solution to the "question of what to do with the darkies," wrote one northern soldier, "would be to shoot them."

But this was not the whole story. Contrabands who aided the Union army as spies and scouts helped to break down ingrained bigotry. "The sooner we get rid of our foolish prejudice the better for us," a Massachusetts soldier wrote home. Before the end of the war, northern missionary groups and freedmen's aid societies sent agents into the South to work among the freed slaves, distribute relief, and organize schools. In March 1865, just before the hostilities ceased, Congress created the Freedmen's Bureau, which had responsibility for the relief, education, and employment

The Sea Island Experiments, 1861–1865

The Sea Islands

The island chain, famous for the production of what had come to be called sea-island cotton, was the site of unique wartime experiments in new social policies.

In November 1861 a Union fleet sailed into Port Royal Sound, an inlet among the South Carolina Sea Islands, and bombarded the port's defenses. Before Union troops could occupy the islands, the white residents, many of them slaveowning planters, fled to the mainland. Left behind were elegant mansions, sprawling cotton plantations, and ten thousand slaves, who would remember the invasion as the "gun shoot at Bay Point."

Lying just off the southern coast between Charleston and Savannah, the conquered islands—including Port Royal, Hilton Head, and St. Helena—provided an operating base for the Union blockade fleet. They were of potential value to the Treasury Department, too. The Sea Islands were known for their high-grade cotton, which could be used to supply northern textile mills and to bolster the Union economy. But the takeover of the islands presented the Union with a challenge as well as a triumph.

Before the invasion, slaves had composed 83 percent of the Sea Island population. Long isolated from the mainland, they retained a distinctive culture and perpetuated many African customs. Their syntax and vocabulary were West Indian, and their Gullah dialect was almost incomprehensible to outsiders. Since the late eighteenth century, they had endured a harsh slave system similar to that of the West Indies. To the northerners who now arrived on the Sea Islands—army personnel, treasury agents, plantation managers, teachers, and missionaries—the very numbers of the black inhabitants seemed overwhelming. "Negroes, negroes, negroes," wrote Elizabeth Botume, a Boston teacher. "They hovered around like bees in a swarm. . . . Every doorstep, box, or barrel was covered with them." With the war barely under way and victory still a vision on the distant horizon, the Union suddenly had to forge a policy toward these thousands of "contrabands." While warfare occupied the rest of the nation, Sea Island administrators embarked on a series of experiments in emancipation.

These experiments revealed deep divisions in northerners' thinking about the future of blacks. Some northerners on the scene focused on blacks' potential as soldiers. In May 1862 General David Hunter, who commanded the Union forces occupying the Sea Islands, formed a black army regiment; by August Sea Island men were being impressed into the First South Carolina "Volunteers," commanded by Massachusetts minister Thomas Wentworth Higginson. The drafting of blacks infuriated idealistic teachers and missionaries, who saw education as the blacks' primary need. "The negroes . . . will do anything for us, if we will only teach them," another teacher from Boston claimed. "The majority learn with wonderful rapidity," reported the free black Charlotte Forten of Philadelphia, "and they are said to be among the most degraded negroes of the South."

Equally sharp disagreements swirled around the question of economic opportunity for blacks. Edward Philbrick of Boston, an engineer who worked as a plantation superintendent on the islands, embodied one approach to the issue. Philbrick hoped to make the islands a showcase for free labor by turning the freed slaves into wage earners on the large cotton plantations there. For blacks to produce more cotton as wage earners than they had as slaves, Philbrick reasoned, would squelch northern "gabble about the danger of immediate emancipation" and buttress the position of those northerners who wanted emancipation to become the Union's main war goal. But the freedmen themselves had little enthusiasm for working in gangs on plantations, even if for wages. The practice smacked too much of their conditions under slavery. Instead, most Sea Island blacks would have preferred to plant food for themselves rather than cotton for northern factories, and many dreamed of owning their own land. "I should like to buy the very spot on which I live," an elderly freedman wrote to President Abraham Lincoln in a dictated letter. "I had rather work for myself . . . than work for a gentleman for wages."

Union administrators made some concessions to blacks' wishes. When, in the fall of 1863, Sea Island officials sold sixty thousand acres of confiscated rebel

Sea Island Teachers

The teachers and missionaries who arrived in the Sea Islands to work among the freed slaves were known as Gideon's Band. Above, a Gideonite group gathers in front of a stately home in Port Royal.

Sea Island Wage Labor

Free blacks sort cotton on an Edisto Island plantation. Northern managers who ran plantations on the Sea Islands during the war hoped to prove the virtues of free labor by turning freedmen into wage earners.

estates, only sixteen thousand acres were reserved for freedmen. The rest of the land was open to purchase by northern investors and speculators. Protesting the injustice of reserving a mere quarter of the acreage for those who composed the vast majority of the Sea Island residents, General Rufus Saxton, the islands' military governor and a "thoroughgoing Abolitionist, of the radical sort," secured approval in Washington for a plan to allow blacks to claim unsold land merely by squatting on it (a practice called preemption). Pressured by Saxton's rivals, however, the fed-eral government reversed itself early in 1864 and forbade squatter claims.

The policy shifts continued. In December 1864 General William T. Sherman, fresh from his sweep across Georgia, arrived on the Sea Islands in the company of thousands of black camp followers who had gathered around his army during its march to the sea. To provide for these people, Sherman took steps to establish a class of black freeholders. General Sherman's Order No. 15 granted blacks the right to preempt unsold land not only on the Sea Islands but for thirty miles inland, on the mainland. By 1865 the islands had become a haven for black refugees from all over the South.

The new land policy would yet again be reversed: in August 1865 President Andrew Johnson would order all Sea Island lands returned to their original owners, thus dispossessing most of the blacks anew and leaving them no better or worse off than emancipated slaves elsewhere in the South. But during the Civil War, the islands had fulfilled a unique function. They had provided an arena wherein the Union first supervised emancipation and abolitionists first confronted large numbers of slaves. The scene of pioneer ventures in freedmen's education, black wage labor, and land redistribution, the Sea Islands had served as a testing ground for new social policies.

of former slaves. The Freedmen's Bureau law also provided that forty acres of abandoned or confiscated land could be leased to each freedman or southern Unionist, with an option to buy after three years. This was the first and only time that Congress provided for the redistribution of confiscated Confederate property.

Black Soldiers in the Union Army

During the first year of war, the Union had rejected black soldiers. Black applicants at northern recruiting offices were sent home, and black companies that had been formed in the occupied South were disbanded. After the second Confiscation Act, Union generals formed black regiments in occupied New Orleans and on the Sea Islands off the coasts of South Carolina and Georgia. Only after the Emancipation Proclamation did large-scale enlistment begin. Leading blacks such as Frederick Douglass and Harvard-educated physician Martin Delany worked as recruiting agents in northern cities. Douglass voiced the connection between black military service and black claims as citizens. "Once let the black man get upon his person the brass letters, U.S.; let him get an eagle on his button, and a musket on his shoulder and bullets in his pocket, and there is no power on earth which can deny that he has earned the right to citizenship." Union drafts now included blacks, recruiting offices arose in the loyal border

states, and freedmen in refugee camps throughout the occupied South were enlisted. By the end of the war, 186,000 blacks had served in the Union army, one-tenth of all Union soldiers. Fully half came from the Confederate states.

White Union soldiers commonly objected to the new recruits on racial grounds. But some, including Colonel Thomas Wentworth Higginson, a liberal minister and former John Brown supporter who led a black regiment, welcomed the black soldiers. "Nobody knows anything about these men who has not seen them in battle," Higginson exulted after a successful raid in Florida in 1863. "There is a fierce energy about them beyond anything of which I have ever read, except it be the French Zouaves [French troops in North Africa]." Even Union soldiers who held blacks in contempt pragmatically came to approve of "anything that will kill a rebel." Furthermore, black recruitment offered new opportunities for whites to secure commissions, for blacks served in separate regiments under white officers. Colonel Robert Gould Shaw of the Fifty-fourth Massachusetts Infantry, an elite black regiment, died in combat—as did half his troops—in an attack on Fort Wagner in Charleston harbor in July 1863.

Black soldiers suffered a far higher mortality rate than white troops. Typically assigned to labor detachments or garrison duty, blacks were less likely than whites to be killed in action but more likely to die of

Flag of the Second Regiment of U.S. Colored Troops; Black Artillerymen
Black troops, organized after the Emancipation Proclamation, fought under flags such as the Second Regiment colors. The soldiers in the photograph belonged to the Second U.S. Colored Light Artillery, which took part in the Battle of Nashville in 1864.

disease in the bacteria-ridden garrisons. In addition, the Confederacy refused to treat captured black soldiers as prisoners of war, a policy that denied captured blacks the opportunity to be exchanged for Confederate prisoners. Instead, Jefferson Davis ordered all blacks taken in battle to be sent back to the states from which they came, where they were reenslaved or executed. In an especially gruesome incident, when Confederate troops captured Fort Pillow, Tennessee, in 1864, they massacred 262 blacks—an action that provoked outcries but no retaliation from the North.

Well into the war, black soldiers faced inequities in their pay. In contrast to white soldiers, who earned $13.00 a month plus a $3.50 clothing allowance, black privates received only $10.00 a month, with clothing deducted. "We have come out Like men and we Expected to be Treated as men but we have bin Treated more Like Dogs then men," a black soldier complained to Secretary of War Edwin Stanton. In June 1864 Congress belatedly equalized the pay of black and white soldiers.

Although fraught with hardships and inequities, military service was a symbol of citizenship for blacks. It proved that "black men can give blows as well as take them," Frederick Douglass declared. "Liberty won by white men would lose half its lustre." A black private explained: "If we hadn't become sojers, all might have gone back as it was before. But now things can never go back because we have showed our energy and our courage . . . and our natural manhood." Above all, the use of black soldiers, especially former slaves, was seen by northern generals as a major strike at the Confederacy. "They will make good soldiers," General Grant wrote to Lincoln in 1863, "and taking them from the enemy weakens him in the same proportion they strengthen us."

Slavery in Wartime

Anxious white southerners on the home front felt as if they were perched on a volcano. "We should be practically helpless should the negroes rise," declared a Louisiana planter's daughter, "since there are so few men left at home." When Mary Boykin Chesnut of South Carolina learned that her cousin had been murdered in bed by two trusted house slaves, she became almost frantic. "The murder," Chesnut wrote, "has clearly driven us all wild." To maintain control over their 3 million black slaves, white southerners resorted to a variety of measures. They tightened slave patrols,

at times moved entire plantations to relative safety in Texas or in the upland regions of the coastal South, and spread scare stories among the slaves. "The whites would tell the colored people not to go to the Yankees, for they would harness them to carts . . . in place of horses," reported Susie King Taylor, a black fugitive from Savannah.

Wartime developments had a mixed effect on the slaves. Some remained faithful to their owners and helped hide treasured family belongings from marauding Union soldiers. Others were torn between loyalty and lust for freedom: one body servant, for example, accompanied his master to war, rescued him when he was wounded, and then escaped on his master's horse. Given a clear choice between freedom and bondage, slaves usually chose freedom. Few slaves helped the North as dramatically as Robert Smalls, a hired-out slave boatman who turned over a Confederate steamer to the Union navy, but most slaves who had a chance to flee to Union lines did so. The idea of freedom held irresistible appeal. Upon learning from a Union soldier that he was free, a Virginia coachman dressed in his master's clothes, "put on his best watch and chain, took his stick, and . . . told him that he might for the future drive his own coach."

The majority of slaves, however, had no escape and remained on their plantations under the nominal control of their masters. Despite the fears of southern whites, no general uprising of slaves occurred; and the Confederate war effort continued to utilize slave labor. The Confederacy impressed thousands of slaves to work in war plants, to toil as teamsters and cooks in army camps, and to serve as nurses in field hospitals. But wartime conditions reduced the slaves' productivity. With most of the white men off at war, the master-slave relationship weakened. The women and boys who remained on plantations complained of their difficulty in controlling slaves, who commonly refused to work, performed their labors inefficiently, or even destroyed property. A Texas wife contended that her slaves were "trying all they can, it seems to me, to aggravate me" by neglecting the stock, breaking plows, and tearing down fences. "You may give your Negroes away," she finally wrote despairingly to her husband in 1864.

Whether southern slaves fled to freedom or merely stopped working, they effectively undermined the plantation system. Thus southern slavery disintegrated even as the Confederacy fought to preserve it. Hard pressed by Union armies, short of manpower, and unsettled by the erosion of plantation slavery, the

Confederate Congress in 1864 considered the drastic step of impressing slaves into its army as soldiers in exchange for their freedom at the war's end. Robert E. Lee favored the use of slaves as soldiers on the grounds that if the Confederacy did not arm its slaves, the Union would. Others, however, were adamantly opposed. "If slaves will make good soldiers," a Georgia general argued, "our whole theory of slavery is wrong." Originally against arming slaves, Jefferson Davis changed his mind in 1865. In March 1865 the Confederate Congress narrowly passed a bill to arm three hundred thousand slave soldiers, although it omitted any mention of emancipation. As the war ended a few weeks later, however, the plan was never put into effect.

Although the Confederacy's decision to arm the slaves came too late to affect the war, the debate over arming them damaged southern morale by revealing deep internal disagreements concerning war goals. Even before these conflicts had become obvious, the South's military position had started to deteriorate.

The Turning Point of 1863

In the summer and fall of 1863, Union fortunes dramatically improved in every theater of the war. Yet the year began badly for the North. The slide, which had started with Burnside's defeat at Fredericksburg, Virginia, in December 1862, continued into the spring of 1863. Burnside's successor, General Joseph "Fighting Joe" Hooker, a windbag fond of issuing pompous proclamations to his troops, devised a plan to dislodge the Confederates from Fredericksburg by crossing the Rappahannock River north of the town and descending on the rebel rear. But Lee and Stonewall Jackson beat Hooker to the punch by routing him at Chancellorsville, Virginia, early in May 1863. The battle proved costly for the South, because Jackson was accidentally shot by Confederate pickets and died a few days later. Because Hooker had twice as many men as Lee, however, the Union defeat at Chancellorsville was especially humiliating for the North. "What will the country say?" Lincoln moaned. News from the West was no more heartening for the Union. Although repulsed at Shiloh in western Tennessee, the Confederates still had a powerful army in central Tennessee under General Braxton Bragg. Furthermore, despite repeated efforts, Grant was unable to take Vicksburg; the two-hundred-mile stretch of the Mississippi between Vicksburg and Port Hudson remained in rebel hands.

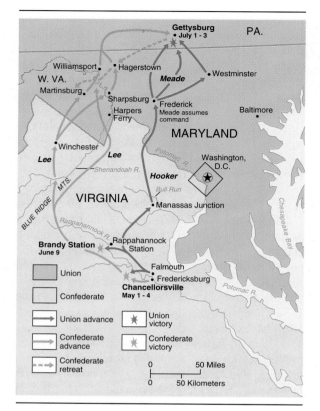

The War in the East, 1863
Victorious at Chancellorsville in May 1863, Lee again invaded Union territory but was decisively stopped at Gettysburg.

The upswing in Union fortunes began with Lee's decision after Chancellorsville to invade the North. The decision provoked dissent within the Confederate government, and Lincoln suspected that Lee was making a big mistake, but Lee had his reasons. He needed supplies that war-wracked Virginia could no longer provide, he hoped to panic Lincoln into moving troops from besieged Vicksburg to the eastern theater, and he thought that a major Confederate victory on northern soil would tip the balance in northern politics to the pro-peace Democrats and gain European recognition of the Confederacy. Moving his seventy-five thousand men down the Shenandoah Valley, Lee crossed the Potomac into Maryland and pressed forward into southern Pennsylvania. At this point, with Lee's army far to the west of Richmond, Hooker recommended a Union stab at the Confederate capital. But Lincoln brushed aside the advice. "Lee's *army*, and not *Richmond*, is

Gettysburg, 1863
The failure of Pickett's charge against the Union center on July 3 was the decisive action in the war's greatest battle.

your true objective," Lincoln shot back, and then he replaced Hooker with the more reliable George G. Meade.

Early in July 1863, Lee's offensive ground to a halt at a Pennsylvania road junction, Gettysburg. Confederates foraging for shoes in the town encountered some Union cavalry. Soon both sides called for reinforcements, and the war's greatest battle commenced. On July 1 Meade's troops installed themselves in hills south of town along a line that resembled a fishhook: the shank ran along Cemetery Ridge and a northern hook encircled Culp's Hill. By the end of the first day of fighting, most of the troops on both sides had arrived: Meade's army outnumbered the Confederates ninety thousand to seventy-five thousand. On July 2 Lee rejected advice to plant the Confederate army in a defensive position between Meade's forces and Washington

and instead attacked the Union flanks, with some success. But because the Confederate assaults were uncoordinated, and some southern generals disregarded orders and struck where they chose, the Union was able to move in reinforcements and regain its earlier losses.

By the afternoon of July 3, believing that the Union flanks had been weakened, Lee attacked Cemetery Ridge in the center of the North's defensive line. After southern cannon shelled the line, a massive infantry force of fifteen thousand Confederates, Pickett's charge, moved in. But as the Confederate cannon sank into the ground and fired a shade too high, and as Union fire wiped out the rebel charge, rifled weapons proved their deadly effectiveness. At the end of the day, Confederate bodies littered the field. "The dead and the dying were lying by the thousands between the two lines," a dazed Louisiana soldier wrote. "The enemy seemed to be launching his cavalry to sweep the remaining handful of men from the face of the earth." A little more than half of Pickett's troops were dead, wounded, or captured in the horrible encounter. When Lee withdrew to Virginia on July 4, he had lost seventeen generals and over one-third of his army. Total Union and Confederate casualties numbered almost fifty thousand. Despite the Confederate defeat, Gettysburg was not a model Union victory, since Meade failed to pursue and destroy the retreating rebels. Still, because he had halted Lee's foray into the North, the Union rejoiced.

Almost simultaneously, the North won a less bloody but more strategic victory in the West, where Grant finally solved the puzzle posed by Vicksburg's defenses. Situated on a bluff on the east bank of the Mississippi, Vicksburg was protected on the west by the river and on the north by hills, forests, and swamps. Vicksburg could be attacked only over a thin strip of dry land to its east and south. Positioned to the north of Vicksburg, Grant had to find a way to get his army south of the city and onto the Mississippi's east bank. His solution lay in moving his troops far to the west of the city and down to a point on the river south of Vicksburg. Meanwhile, Union gunboats and supply ships ran past the Confederate batteries overlooking the river at Vicksburg (not without sustaining considerable damage) to rendezvous with Grant's army and transport it across to the east bank. Grant then swung in a large semicircle, first northeastward to capture Jackson, the capital of Mississippi, and then westward back to Vicksburg. After a six-week siege, during which famished soldiers and civilians in Vicksburg

The War in the West, 1863: Vicksburg
Grant first moved his army west of Vicksburg to a point on the Mississippi south of the town. Then he marched northeast, taking Jackson, and finally west to Vicksburg.

were reduced to eating mules and even rats, General John C. Pemberton surrendered his thirty-thousand-man garrison to Grant on July 4, the day after Pickett's charge at Gettysburg. Port Hudson, the last Confederate holdout on the Mississippi, soon surrendered to another Union army. "The Father of Waters flows unvexed to the sea," Lincoln declared.

Before the year was out, the Union won another crucial victory in the West. General William S. Rosecrans fought and maneuvered Braxton Bragg's Confederate army out of central Tennessee and into Chattanooga, in the southeastern tip of the state, and then forced Bragg to evacuate Chattanooga. Bragg defeated the pursuing Rosecrans at the Battle of Chickamauga (September 19–20, 1863), one of the bloodiest of the war, and drove him back into Chattanooga. But the arrival of Grant and of reinforcements from the Army of the Potomac enabled the North to break Bragg's siege of Chattanooga in November. With Chattanooga secure, the way lay open for a Union strike into Georgia.

Coming on the heels of reverses that had driven northern morale to its lowest point of the war, Union successes in the second half of 1863 stiffened the

North's will to keep fighting and plunged some rebel leaders into despair. Hearing of the fall of Vicksburg, Confederate ordnance chief Josiah Gorgas wrote, "Yesterday we rode the pinnacle of success—today absolute ruin seems our portion. The Confederacy totters to its destruction."

Totter it might, but the South was far from beaten. Although the outcome at Gettysburg quashed southerners' hopes for victory on northern soil, it did not significantly impair Lee's ability to defend Virginia. The loss of Vicksburg and the Mississippi cut the Confederate states west of the river—Arkansas, Louisiana, and Texas—off from those to the east; but these western states could still provide soldiers. Even with the loss of Chattanooga, the Confederacy continued to hold most of the Carolinas, Georgia, Florida, and Mississippi. Few contemporaries thought that the fate of the Confederacy had been sealed.

WAR AND SOCIETY, NORTH AND SOUTH

Extending beyond the battlefields of Gettysburg and Vicksburg, the Civil War engulfed two economies and societies. By 1863 the progress of the war provided stark contrasts: with its superior resources, the Union could meet wartime demands as the imperiled Confederacy could not. But both regions experienced labor shortages and inflation. As the conflict dragged on, both societies confronted problems of disunity and dissent, for war issues opened fissures between social classes. In both regions war encroached on everyday life. Families were disrupted and dislocated, especially in the South. Women on both sides took on new roles at home, in the workplace, and in relief efforts.

The War's Economic Impact: The North

The war had an uneven effect on the Union's economy. Some industries fared poorly. For instance, the loss of southern markets damaged the shoe industry in Massachusetts, where output declined from 45 million pairs in 1855 to 32 million pairs in 1865. A shortage of raw cotton sent the cotton-textile industry into a tailspin that was only partly offset by a rise in the production of woolens. On the other hand, industries directly related to the war effort, such as the manufacture of arms and clothing, benefited from huge government contracts. By 1865, for example, the ready-made clothing industry was receiving orders for more than a million uniforms a year. Military demand also provided abundant business for the railroads. Some privately owned lines, which had overbuilt before the war, doubled the volume of their traffic during the war. In 1862 the federal government itself went into the railroad business by establishing the United States Military Railroads (USMRR) to carry troops and supplies to the front. "The quicker you build the railroad," Union general William T. Sherman told his troops, "the quicker you'll get something to eat." By 1865 the USMRR was the largest railroad in the world.

The Republicans in Congress actively promoted business development during the war. Holding 102 of 146 House seats and 29 of 36 Senate seats in 1861, they overrode Democratic foes and hiked the tariff in 1862 and again in 1864 to protect domestic industries. The Republican-sponsored Pacific Railroad Act of 1862 provided for the development of a transcontinental railroad, an idea that had foundered before the war on disagreements over which route such a railroad should follow. With the South out of the picture and no longer able to demand a southern route from New Orleans across the Southwest, Congress chose a northern route from Omaha to San Francisco. Chartering the Union Pacific and Central Railroad corporations, Congress then gave to each large land grants and generous loans. These two corporations combined received more than 60 million acres in land grants and $20 million in loans from the government. The issuance of greenbacks and the creation of a national banking system, meanwhile, brought a measure of uniformity to the nation's financial system.

By raising the federal government's profile in the North's economy, the Republicans hoped to benefit a variety of social classes. To a degree, they succeeded. Republican measures like the Homestead Act, passed in 1862, embodied the party's ideal of "free soil, free labor, free men" by granting 160 acres of public land to settlers after five years of residence on the land. By 1865 twenty thousand homesteaders occupied new land in the West under the Homestead Act. To bring higher education within the reach of the common people, the Republicans secured passage in 1862 of the Morrill Land Grant Act. This law gave to the states proceeds of public lands—to fund the establishment of universities emphasizing "such branches of learning as

are related to agriculture and mechanic arts." The Morrill Act spurred the growth of large state universities, mainly in the Midwest and West. Michigan State, Iowa State, and Purdue universities, among many others, profited from the law.

Despite the idealistic goals behind some Republican laws, the war benefited the wealthy more than the average citizen. Corrupt contractors grew fat by selling the government substandard merchandise such as the notorious "shoddy," clothing made from compressed rags, which quickly fell apart. Speculators who locked their patriotism in the closet made millions in the gold market. Because the price of gold in relation to greenbacks rose whenever public confidence in the government fell, those who bought gold in the hope that its price would rise actually gained from Union defeats, and even more from Union disasters. Businessmen with access to scarce commodities also reaped astounding profits. For example, manpower shortages stimulated wartime demand for the mechanical reaper that Cyrus McCormick had patented in 1834. McCormick also profited from his distrust of the greenbacks. When paid for reapers in greenbacks, he immediately reinvested them in pig iron and then watched in glee as wartime demand drove the price of pig iron from twenty-three dollars to forty dollars a ton.

The war had a far less happy impact on ordinary workers. Protected from foreign competition by higher tariffs, northern manufacturers hoisted the prices of finished goods. Wartime excise taxes and inflation combined to push prices still higher. At the same time, wages lagged 20 percent or more behind cost increases for most of the war. This lag in wages, common in most periods of rapid inflation, became especially severe during the war because boys and women poured into government offices and factories as replacements for adult male workers who had joined the army. Not only did the new workers draw lower pay than the men whom they had replaced, but employers' mere threats of hiring more youths and females undercut the bargaining power of the men who remained in the work force.

Some workers organized to decry their low wages. "We are unable to sustain life for the price offered by contractors who fatten on their contracts," Cincinnati seamstresses declared in a petition to President Lincoln. Cigar makers and locomotive engineers formed national unions, a process that would accelerate after the war. But organized protests had little impact on wages; employers often denounced worker protests as unpatriotic hindrances to the war effort. In 1864 army troops were diverted from combat to put down protests in war industries from New York to the Midwest.

The War's Economic Impact: The South

Although stimulating some sectors of the North's economy, the war shattered the South's. Indeed, if both regions are considered together, the overall impact of the war was to retard *American* economic growth. For example, the commodity output of the American economy, which had registered huge increases of 51 percent and 62 percent in the 1840s and 1850s, respectively, rose only 22 percent during the 1860s. Even this modest gain depended wholly on the North, for in the 1860s commodity output in the South actually *declined* 39 percent.

Substantial wartime industrial growth by the South was more than offset by other factors. For example, the war wrecked the South's railroads; in 1864 Union troops, marching through Georgia under General William T. Sherman, tore up railroad tracks, heated them in giant fires, and twisted them into "Sherman neckties." Cotton production, once the foundation of the South's prosperity, sank from more than 4 million bales in 1861 to 300,000 bales in 1865 as Union invasions took their toll on production, particularly in Tennessee and Louisiana.

Invading Union troops also occupied the South's food-growing as well as cotton-producing regions. Moreover, in agricultural areas under Confederate control, the drain of manpower into the army decreased the yields per acre of crops like wheat and corn. Even the loss of a few carpenters and blacksmiths could disrupt the economy of rural districts. For example, the drafting of certain of their craftsmen, complained some Alabama petitioners to the federal government in 1863, had left their county "entirely Destitute of any man that is able to keep in order any kind of Farming Tules." Food shortages abounded late in the war. "The people are subsisting on the ungathered crops and nine families out of ten are left without meat," a Mississippi citizen lamented in 1864.

Agricultural shortages worsened the South's already severe inflation. By 1863 salt selling for $1.25 a sack in New York City cost $60.00 in the Confederacy. Food riots erupted in 1863 in Mobile, Atlanta, and Richmond; in Richmond the wives of ironworkers paraded to demand lower food prices.

Part of the blame for the South's food shortages rested with the planter class itself. Although some planters heeded government pleas to shift from cotton to food production, and cotton crops declined sharply

Destroying Railroad Track

As the Union general William T. Sherman invaded Georgia, his troops demolished Confederate property of military value, such as arsenals and railroads. These Union soldiers in Atlanta break up a railroad track before setting forth on their march to the sea. The damaged rails that they left behind, often bent out of shape to form "Sherman neckties," may still be found in parts of the South.

overall, many planters still raised more cotton than they could market abroad. The consequences were far-reaching. Slave labor, which could have been diverted to army camps, where slaves might have relieved soldiers of menial tasks, remained essential on the cotton plantations. This increased the Confederacy's reliance on its unpopular conscription laws. Moreover, cotton continued to sprout from land that could have been used for food production. To feed its hungry armies, the Confederacy had to resort to impressing food from civilians. This policy not only elicited resentment of planters but contributed to the South's mounting military desertions. Food-impressment agents usually concentrated on the easiest targets—farms run by the wives of active soldiers. Soldiers found it hard to resist desperate pleas to return home. The wife of an Alabama soldier wrote to him: "We haven't got nothing in the house to eat but a little bit o meal. I don't want you to stop fighting them Yankees . . . but try and get off and come home and fix us all up some and then you can go back." By the end of 1864, half of the Confederacy's soldiers were absent from their units.

In one respect, the persistence of cotton growing did aid the South, because cotton became the basis for the Confederacy's flourishing trade with the enemy. The U.S. Congress virtually legalized this trade in July 1861 by allowing northern commerce with southerners loyal to the Union. In practice, of course, it proved impossible to tell loyalists from disloyalists, and for most traders it hardly mattered. As long as Union textile mills stood idle for lack of cotton, northern traders happily swapped bacon, salt, blankets, and other necessaries for southern cotton. The Union's penetration of the Confederate heartland eased business dealings between the two sides. By 1864 traffic through the lines was providing the South with enough food daily to feed the entire Army of Northern Virginia. To a northern congressman, it seemed that the Union's policy was "to feed an army and fight it at the same time."

Trading with the enemy alleviated the South's food shortages but intensified its morale problems. The prospect of traffic with the Yankees gave planters an incentive to keep growing cotton, and it fattened merchants and middlemen. "Oh! the extortioners," complained a Confederate war-office clerk in Richmond. "Our patriotism is mainly in the army and among the ladies of the South. The avarice and cupidity of men at home could only be exceeded by ravenous wolves."

Dealing with Dissent

Both wartime governments faced mounting dissent and disloyalty. Within the Confederacy, dissent took two basic forms. First, a vocal group of states' rights activists, notably Vice President Alexander Stephens and governors Zebulon Vance of North Carolina and Joseph Brown of Georgia, spent much of the war attacking Jefferson Davis's government as a despotism. Second, loyalty to the Union flourished among a segment of the Confederacy's common people, particularly those living in the Appalachian Mountain region that ran from western North Carolina through eastern Tennessee and into northern Georgia and Alabama. The nonslaveholding small farmers who predominated here saw the Confederate rebellion as a slaveowners' conspiracy. Resentful of such measures as the 20-Negro exemption from conscription, they were reluctant to fight for what a North Carolinian defined as "an adored trinity, cotton, niggers, and chivalry." "All they want," an Alabama farmer complained of the planters, "is to get you pupt up and to fight for their infurnal negroes and after you do there fighting you may kiss there hine parts for o they care." On the whole, the Confederate government responded mildly to popular disaffection. In 1862 the Confederate Congress gave Jefferson Davis the power to suspend the writ of habeas corpus, but Davis used his power only sparingly, by occasionally and briefly putting areas under martial law, mainly to aid tax collectors.

Lincoln faced similar challenges in the North, where the Democratic minority opposed both emancipation and the wartime growth of centralized power. Although "War Democrats" conceded that war was necessary to preserve the Union, "Peace Democrats" (called Copperheads by their opponents, to suggest a resemblance to a species of easily concealed poisonous snakes) disagreed. Demanding a truce and a peace conference, they charged that administration war policy was intended to "exterminate the South," make reconciliation impossible, and spark "terrible social change and revolution" nationwide.

Strongest in the border states, the Midwest, and the northeastern cities, the Democrats mobilized the support of farmers of southern background in the Ohio Valley and of members of the urban working class, especially recent immigrants, who feared losing their jobs to an influx of free blacks. In 1863 this volatile brew of political, ethnic, racial, and class antagonisms in northern society exploded into antidraft protests in several cities. By far the most violent eruption occurred in July in New York City. Catalyzed by the first drawing of names under the Enrollment Act, and by a long-shoremen's strike in which blacks had been used as strikebreakers, mobs of Irish working-class men and women roamed the streets for four days until suppressed by federal troops. The city's laboring Irish loathed the idea of being drafted to fight a war on behalf of the slaves, who, once emancipated, might migrate north to compete with them for low-paying jobs. Too, they bitterly resented the provision of the draft law that allowed the rich to purchase substitutes. The Irish mobs' targets revealed the scope of their grievances. The rioters lynched at least a dozen blacks, injured hundreds more, and burned draft offices, the homes of wealthy Republicans, and the Colored Orphan Asylum.

President Lincoln's speedy dispatch of federal troops to quash these riots typified his forceful response to dissent. Throughout the war, Lincoln imposed martial law with far less hesitancy than Davis. After suspending the writ of habeas corpus in Maryland in 1861, he barred it nationwide in 1863 and authorized the arrest of rebels, draft resisters, and those engaged in "any disloyal practice." The differing responses of Davis and Lincoln to dissent underscored the differences between the two regions' wartime political systems. As we have seen, Davis lacked the institutionalization of dissent provided by party conflict and thus had to tread warily, lest his opponents brand him a despot. In contrast, Lincoln and other Republicans used dissent to rally patriotic fervor against the Democrats. After the New York City draft riots, for example, the Republicans blamed the violence on New York's antidraft Democratic governor, Horatio Seymour. When Seymour, rushing to the city to quell the disturbances, addressed a crowd of rioters as "my friends," the Republican press had a field day branding the Democrats as disloyal.

Forceful as he was, Lincoln did not unleash a reign of terror against dissent. In general, the North preserved freedom of the press, speech, and assembly. In 1864 the Union became the first warring nation in history to hold a contested national election. Moreover, although some fifteen thousand civilians were arrested during the war, most were quickly released. A few cases, however, aroused widespread concern. In 1864 a military commission sentenced an Indiana man to be hanged for an alleged plot to free Confederate prisoners. The Supreme Court reversed his conviction two years later when it ruled that civilians could not be tried

by military courts when the civil courts were open (*Ex parte* Milligan, 1866). Of more concern were the arrests of politicians, notably Clement L. Vallandigham, an Ohio Peace Democrat. Courting arrest, Vallandigham challenged the administration, denounced the suspension of habeas corpus, proposed an armistice, and in 1863 was sentenced to jail for the rest of the war by a military commission. When Ohio Democrats then nominated him for governor, Lincoln changed the sentence to banishment. Escorted to enemy lines in Tennessee, Vallandigham was left in the hands of bewildered Confederates and eventually escaped to Canada. The Supreme Court refused to review his case.

The Medical War

Despite the discontent and disloyalty of some citizens, both the Union and the Confederacy witnessed a remarkable wartime patriotism that propelled civilians, especially women, to work tirelessly toward alleviating the suffering of soldiers. The United States Sanitary Commission, organized early in the war by civilians to assist the Union's medical bureau, consisted mainly of women volunteers. Described as a "great artery that bears the people's love to the army," the commission raised funds at "sanitary fairs," bought and distributed supplies, ran special kitchens to supplement army rations, tracked down the missing, and inspected army camps. The volunteers' exploits became legendary. One poor widow, Mary Ann "Mother" Bickerdyke, served sick and wounded Union soldiers as both nurse and surrogate mother. When asked by a doctor by what authority she demanded supplies for the wounded, she shot back, "From the Lord God Almighty. Do you have anything that ranks higher than that?"

Women also reached out to aid the battlefront through the nursing corps. Before the war ended, some thirty-two hundred women served the Union and the Confederacy as nurses. Already famed for her tireless campaigns on behalf of the insane, Dorothea Dix became the head of the Union's nursing corps. Clara Barton began the war as a clerk in the U.S. Patent Office, but she, too, greatly aided the medical effort, finding ingenious ways of channeling medicine to the sick and wounded. Catching wind of Union movements before Antietam, Barton showed up at the battlefield on the eve of the clash with a wagonload of supplies. When army surgeons ran out of

Andersonville Prison
Started in early 1864, the overcrowded Andersonville prison in southwest Georgia provided no shel-
ter for its inmates, who built tent-like structures out of blankets, sticks, or whatever they could find.
Exposure, disease, and poor sanitation contributed to a mortality rate almost double that in other
Confederate prison camps, and made Andersonville a scandal that outlived the war.

bandages and started to dress wounds with corn husks, she raced forward with lint and bandages. "With what joy," she wrote, "I laid my precious burden down among them." After the war, in 1881, she would found the American Red Cross. The Confederacy, too, had extraordinary nurses. One, Sally Tompkins, was commissioned a captain for her hospital work; another, Belle Boyd, served the Confederacy as both a nurse and a spy and once dashed through a field, waving her bonnet, to give Stonewall Jackson information. Danger stalked nurses even in hospitals far from the front. Author Louisa May Alcott, a nurse at the Union Hotel Hospital in Washington, D.C., contracted typhoid. Wherever they worked, nurses witnessed haunting, unforgettable sights. "About the amputating table," one reported, "lay large piles of human flesh—legs, arms, feet, and hands . . . the stiffened membrances seemed to be clutching oftentimes at our clothing."

Pioneered by British reformer Florence Nightingale in the 1850s, nursing was a new vocation for women and, in the eyes of many, a brazen departure from women's proper sphere. Male doctors were unsure about how to react to female nurses and sanitary workers. Some saw the potential for mischief in attractive women's roaming around male hospital wards. But other doctors viewed nursing and sanitary work as potentially useful. The miasm theory of disease (see Chapter 11) won wide respect among physicians and stimulated some valuable sanitary measures, particularly in hospitals behind the lines. In partial consequence, the ratio of disease to battle deaths was much lower in the Civil War than in the Mexican War.

Still, for every soldier killed during the Civil War, two died of disease. "These Big Battles is not as Bad as the fever," a North Carolina soldier wrote. The scientific investigations that would lead to the germ theory of disease were only commencing during the 1860s. Arm and leg wounds frequently led to gangrene or tetanus, and typhoid, malaria, diarrhea, and dysentery raged through army camps.

Prison camps posed a special problem. Prisoner exchanges between the North and the South, common early in the war, collapsed by midwar, partly because the South refused to exchange the black prisoners it held and partly because the North gradually concluded that exchanges benefited the manpower-short Confederacy more than the Union. As a result, the two sides had far more prisoners than either could handle. Prisoners on both sides suffered gravely from camp conditions. "This cold weather is not just suited to Southern Constitutions," a Mississippian imprisoned in a Union camp in Illinois wrote home. The worst conditions, however, plagued southern camps. Squalor and insufficient rations turned the Confederate prison camp at Andersonville, Georgia, into a virtual death camp; three thousand prisoners a month (out of a total of thirty-two thousand) were dying there by August 1864. After the war an outraged northern public secured the execution of Andersonville's commandant. Although the commandant was partly to blame, the deterioration of the southern economy had contributed massively to the wretched state of southern prison camps. The Union camps were not much better, but the fatality rate among northerners held by the South exceeded that of southerners imprisoned by the North.

The War and Women's Rights

Female nurses and Sanitary Commission workers were not the only women to serve society in wartime. In both northern and southern government offices and mills, thousands of women took over jobs vacated by men. Moreover, home industry revived at all levels of society. In rural areas, where manpower shortages were most acute, women often did the plowing, planting, and harvesting.

Few women worked more effectively for their region's cause than Philadelphia-born Anna E. Dickinson. After losing her job in the federal mint (for denouncing General George McClellan as a traitor), Dickinson threw herself into hospital volunteer work and public lecturing. Her lecture "Hospital Life," recounting the soldiers' sufferings, won the attention of Republican politicians. In 1863, hard pressed by the Democrats, these politicians invited Dickinson, then

scarcely twenty-one, to campaign on behalf of the Republican tickets in New Hampshire and Connecticut. This decision paid handsome dividends for the party. Articulate and poised, Dickinson captured the hearts and votes of her listeners. Soon Republican candidates who had dismissed the offer of aid from a woman begged her to campaign for them.

Mindful of the contributions of Dickinson and others, northern women's rights advocates hoped that the war would yield equality for women as well as for slaves. Not only should a grateful North reward women for their wartime services, these women reasoned, but it should recognize the link between black rights and women's rights. In 1863 feminists Elizabeth Cady Stanton and Susan B. Anthony organized the National Woman's Loyal League. Although the league's main activity was to gather four hundred thousand signatures on a petition calling for a constitutional amendment to abolish slavery, Stanton and Anthony used the organization to promote woman suffrage as well.

Despite high expectations, the war did not bring women significantly closer to economic or political equality. Women in government offices and factories continued to be paid less than men. Sanitary Commission workers and most wartime nurses, as volunteers, earned nothing. Nor did the war produce a major change in the prevailing definition of woman's sphere. In 1860 that sphere already included charitable and benevolent activities; during the war the scope of benevolence grew to embrace organized care for the wounded. Yet men continued to dominate the medical profession, and for the rest of the nineteenth century, nurses would be classified in the census as domestic help.

The keenest disappointment of women's rights advocates lay in their failure to capitalize on rising sentiment for the abolition of slavery to secure the vote for women. Although the North had compelling reasons to abolish slavery in the rebellious areas of the South, northern politicians could see little practical value in woman suffrage. The *New York Herald*, which supported the Loyal League's attack on slavery, dismissed its call for woman suffrage as "nonsense and tomfoolery." Stanton wrote bitterly, "So long as woman labors to second man's endeavors and exalt his sex above her own, her virtues pass unquestioned; but when she dares to demand rights and privileges for herself, her motives, manners, dress, personal appearance, and character are subjects for ridicule and detraction."

THE UNION VICTORIOUS, 1864–1865

Despite successes at Gettysburg and Vicksburg in 1863, the Union stood no closer to taking Richmond at the start of 1864 than in 1861, and most of the Lower South still remained under Confederate control. The constant press of Union invasion had taken its toll on the South's home front, but the North's persistent inability to destroy the main Confederate armies had eroded the Union's will to keep attacking. Northern war weariness strengthened the Democrats and jeopardized Lincoln's prospects for reelection in 1864.

The year 1864 proved crucial for the North. While Grant occupied Lee in the East, a Union army under William T. Sherman attacked from Tennessee into northwestern Georgia and took Atlanta in early September. The fall of Atlanta not only boosted northern morale but contributed to Lincoln's reelection. Now the curtain rose on the last act of the war. After taking Atlanta, Sherman marched across Georgia to Savannah, devastated the state's resources, and cracked its morale. Pivoting north from Savannah, Sherman then moved into South Carolina. Meanwhile, having backed Lee into trenches around Petersburg and Richmond, Grant forced the evacuation of both cities and brought on the Confederacy's collapse.

The Eastern Theater in 1864

Early in 1864 Lincoln made Grant commander of all Union armies and promoted him to lieutenant general. At first glance, the stony-faced Grant seemed an unlikely candidate for so exalted a rank, held previously only by George Washington. Grant, a contemporary noted, "padlocks his mouth, while his countenance in battle or repose . . . indicates nothing." Grant's only distinguishing characteristics were his ever-present cigars and a penchant for whittling sticks into chips. "There is no glitter, no parade about him." But Grant's success in the West had made him the Union's most popular general, perhaps even the Union's most popular person. With his promotion, Grant moved his headquarters to the Army of the Potomac in the East and mapped a strategy for final victory.

Like Lincoln, Grant believed that the Union had to coordinate its attacks on all fronts in order to exploit its numerical advantage and prevent the South from shifting troops back and forth between the eastern and western theaters. (The South's victory at Chickamauga in September 1863, for example, had rested in part on reinforcements sent by Lee to Braxton Bragg in the West.) Accordingly, Grant planned a sustained offensive against Lee in the East while ordering William T. Sherman to attack the rebel army in Georgia commanded by Bragg's replacement, General Joseph Johnston. Sherman's mission was "to break it [the Confederate army] up, and to get into the interior of the enemy's country . . . inflicting all the damage you can."

In early May 1864, Grant led 118,000 men against Lee's 64,000 in a forested area near Fredericksburg, Virginia, called the Wilderness. After being checked by Lee in a series of bloody engagements (the Battle of the Wilderness, May 5–7), Grant tried to swing around Lee's right flank, only to suffer new reverses at Spotsylvania on May 12 and Cold Harbor on June 3. These engagements were among the war's fiercest; at Cold Harbor, Grant lost 7,000 men in one hour. Oliver Wendell Holmes, Jr., a Union lieutenant and later a Supreme Court justice, wrote home how "immense the butcher's bill has been." But Grant refused to interpret repulses as defeats. Rather, he viewed the engagements at the Wilderness, Spotsylvania, and Cold Harbor merely as less than complete victories. Pressing on, he forced Lee to pull back to the trenches guarding Petersburg and Richmond.

Grant had accomplished a major objective, because once entrenched, Lee could no longer swing around to the Union rear, cut Yankee supply lines, or as at Chancellorsville, surprise the Union's main force. Lee did dispatch General Jubal A. Early on raids down the Shenandoah Valley, which the Confederacy had long used both as a granary and as an indirect way to menace Washington. But Grant countered by ordering General Philip Sheridan to march up the valley from the north and so devastate it that a crow flying over would have to carry its own provisions. The time had come, a Union chaplain wrote, "to peel this land." After defeating Early at Winchester, Virginia, in September 1864, Sheridan controlled the valley.

Sherman in Georgia

While Grant and Lee grappled in the Wilderness, Sherman advanced into Georgia at the head of 98,000 men. Opposing him with 53,000 Confederate troops (soon reinforced to 65,000), General Joseph Johnston

The Election of 1864

Candidates	Parties	Electoral Vote	Popular Vote	Percentage of Popular Vote
ABRAHAM LINCOLN	Republican	212	2,206,938	55.0
George B. McClellan	Democratic	21	1,803,787	45.0

retreated toward Atlanta. Johnston's plan was to conserve strength for a final defense of Atlanta while forcing Sherman to extend his supply lines. But Jefferson Davis, dismayed by Johnston's defensive strategy, replaced him with the adventurous John B. Hood. Hood, who lost the use of an arm at Gettysburg and a leg at Chickamauga, had to be strapped to his saddle; but for all his disabilities, he liked to take risks. In a prewar poker game, he had bet $2,500 with "nary a pair in his hand." Hood gave Davis what he wanted, a series of attacks on Sherman's army. The forays, however, failed to dislodge Sherman and severely depleted Hood's army. No longer able to defend Atlanta's supply lines, Hood evacuated the city, which Sherman took on September 2, 1864.

The Election of 1864

Atlanta's fall came at a timely moment for Lincoln, who was in the thick of a tough reelection campaign. Indeed, Lincoln had secured the Republican renomination with great difficulty. The Radicals, who had earlier flayed Lincoln for delay in adopting emancipation as a war goal, now dismissed his plans to restore the occupied parts of Tennessee, Louisiana, and Arkansas to the Union. The Radicals insisted that Congress, not the president, could alone set the requirements for readmission of conquered states and criticized Lincoln's reconstruction standards as too lenient. Whereas the Radicals rallied around Secretary of the Treasury Salmon P. Chase for the nomination, the Democrats attacked from a different direction. They had never forgiven Lincoln for making emancipation a war goal, and now the Copperheads, or Peace Democrats, demanded an immediate armistice, followed by negotiations between the North and the South to settle outstanding issues.

Although facing formidable challenges, Lincoln benefited from both his own resourcefulness and that of his political enemies. Playing his hand too quickly and openly, Chase turned the early boom for his nomination into a bust. By the time of the Republican convention in July, Lincoln's managers were firmly in control. Moreover, to isolate the Peace Democrats and attract prowar Democrats, the Republicans formed a temporary organization, the National Union party, and replaced Lincoln's vice president, Hannibal Hamlin, with a prowar southern Unionist, Democratic senator Andrew Johnson of Tennessee. This tactic helped exploit the widening division among the Democrats, who nominated George B. McClellan, the former commander of the Army of the Potomac and an advocate of continuing the war until the Confederacy's collapse, and then ran him on a platform written by the Peace Democrats. McClellan spent much of his campaign distancing himself from his party's peace-without-victory platform.

Despite the Democrats' disarray, as late as August 1864, Lincoln seriously doubted that he would be reelected. Leaving little to chance, he arranged for furloughs so that Union soldiers, most of whom supported Lincoln, could vote in states lacking absentee ballots. But in the end it was chance, the timely fall of Atlanta, that aided him. Although Hood's army had escaped from the city, a Richmond newspaper conceded that the "disaster at Atlanta" had punctured the northern antiwar movement and saved Lincoln's presidency. With 55 percent of the popular vote and 212 out of 233 electoral votes, Lincoln swept to victory.

Sherman's March Through Georgia

Meanwhile, Sherman gave the South a new lesson in total war. After evacuating Atlanta, Hood led his Confederate army north toward Tennessee in the hope of luring Sherman out of Georgia. But Sherman did not rise to the bait. The war would never be won, he concluded, by chasing Hood around Tennessee and stretching his own supply lines to the breaking point. Rather, Sherman proposed to abandon his supply lines altogether, march his army across Georgia to Savannah, and live off the countryside as he moved along. He

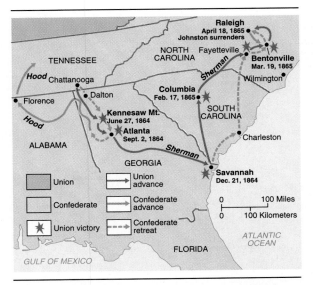

Sherman's March Through the South, 1864–1865

would break the South's will to fight, terrify its people, and "make war so terrible . . . that generations would pass before they could appeal again to it."

Sherman began by burning much of Atlanta and forcing the evacuation of most of its civilian population. This harsh measure relieved him of the need to feed and garrison the city. Then, sending enough troops north to ensure the futility of Hood's campaign in Tennessee, he led the bulk of his army, sixty-two thousand men, out of Atlanta to start the 285-mile trek to Savannah. Soon thousands of slaves were following the army. "Dar's de man dat rules the world," a slave cried on seeing Sherman. Sherman's four columns of infantry, augmented by cavalry screens, moved on a front sixty miles wide and at a pace of ten miles a day. They destroyed everything that could aid southern resistance—arsenals, railroads, munitions plants, cotton gins, cotton stores, crops, and livestock. The ruin far exceeded Sherman's orders. Moreover, although Sherman's troops were told not to destroy civilian property, foragers carried out their own version of total war, ransacking and sometimes demolishing homes. Indeed, the havoc seemed a vital part of Sherman's own strategy. By the time he occupied Savannah and made contact with the Union navy, he estimated that his army had destroyed about a hundred million dollars worth of property. After taking Savannah in December 1864, Sherman's army wheeled north toward South Carolina, the first state

to secede and, in the general's view, one "that deserves all that seems in store for her." Sherman's columns advanced unimpeded to Columbia, South Carolina's capital. After fires set by looters, slaves, soldiers of both sides, and liberated Union prisoners gutted much of the city, Sherman headed for North Carolina. By the spring of 1865, his army had left over four hundred miles of ruin. Other Union armies moved into Alabama and Georgia and took thousands of prisoners. Northern forces had penetrated the entire Confederacy, except for Texas and Florida, and crushed its wealth. "War is cruelty and you cannot refine it," Sherman wrote. "Those who brought war into our country deserve all the curses and maledictions a people can pour out."

Toward Appomattox

While Sherman headed north, Grant renewed his assault on the entrenched Army of Northern Virginia. Grant's main objective was Petersburg, a city south of Richmond through which most of the rail lines to the Confederate capital passed. Although Grant had failed on several occasions to overwhelm the Confederate defenses in front of Petersburg, the fall of Atlanta and Sherman's subsequent march through Georgia and into the Carolinas had taken their toll on Confederate morale. Rebel soldiers were accustomed to shortages of food and clothing, but now they were burdened as well by growing hopelessness. Rebel desertions, proportionately about the same as Union desertions until 1864, reached epidemic proportions in the winter of 1864–1865. Lee reported hundreds of his men deserting every night. Reinforced by Sheridan's army, triumphant from its campaign in the Shenandoah Valley, Grant late in March 1865 swung his forces around the western flank of Petersburg's defenders. Lee could not stop him. On April 2 Sheridan smashed the rebel flank at the Battle of Five Forks. A courier bore the grim news to Jefferson Davis, attending church in Richmond: "General Lee telegraphs that he can hold his position no longer."

Davis left his pew, gathered his government, and fled the city. In the morning of April 3, Union troops entered Richmond, pulled down the Confederate flag, and ran up the Stars and Stripes over the capitol. As white and black regiments entered in triumph, explosions set by retreating Confederates left the city "a sea of flames." "Over all," wrote a Union officer, "hung a canopy of dense smoke lighted up now and then by

The Final Virginia Campaign, 1864–1865
Refusing to abandon his campaign in the face of enormous casualties, Grant finally pushed Lee (below) into defensive fortifications around Petersburg, whose fall doomed Richmond. When Lee tried to escape to the west, Grant cut him off and forced his surrender.

the bursting shells from the numerous arsenals throughout the city." Fires damaged the Tredegar Iron Works. Union troops liberated the town jail, which housed slaves awaiting sale, and its rejoicing inmates poured into the streets. On April 4 Lincoln toured the city and, for a few minutes, sat at Jefferson Davis's desk with a dreamy expression on his face.

Meanwhile, Lee was making a last-ditch effort to escape from Grant and from Sheridan's enveloping movements. Lee's destination was Lynchburg, sixty miles west of Petersburg. He planned to use the rail connections at Lynchburg to join General Joseph Johnston's army, which Sherman had pushed into North Carolina. But Grant and Sheridan swiftly choked off Lee's escape route, and on April 9 Lee bowed to the inevitable. He asked for terms of surrender and met Grant in a private home in the village of Appomattox Courthouse, Virginia, east of Lynchburg. While stunned troops gathered outside, Lee appeared in full dress uniform, with a sword. Grant entered in his customary disarray, smoking a cigar. When Union troops began to fire celebratory salutes, Grant put a stop to it. The final surrender of Lee's army occurred four days later. Lee's troops laid down their arms between federal ranks. "On our part," wrote a Union officer, "not a sound of trumpet . . . nor roll of drum; not a cheer ... but an awed stillness rather." Grant paroled Lee's twenty-six thousand men and sent them home with their horses and mules "to work their little farms." The remnants of Confederate resistance collapsed within a month of Appomattox. Johnston surrendered to Sherman on April 18. While jubilation swept the North, Jefferson Davis was captured in Georgia on May 10.

Grant returned to Washington. On April 14 he turned down a theater date with the Lincolns, because Julia Grant found first lady Mary Lincoln overbearing. That night at Ford's Theater, an unemployed pro-Confederate actor, John Wilkes Booth, entered Lincoln's box and shot him in the head. Waving a knife, Booth leaped onstage shouting the Virginia state motto, *"Sic semper tyrannis"* ("Such is always the fate of tyrants") and then escaped, despite having broken his leg. That same night, a Booth accomplice stabbed Secretary of State Seward, who later recovered, while a third conspirator, assigned to Vice President Johnson, failed to attack. Union troops hunted down Booth and shot him within two weeks, or else he shot himself. Of eight accused accomplices, including a woman boardinghouse keeper, four were hanged and the rest imprisoned. On April 15, when Lincoln died, Andrew Johnson became president. Six days later Lincoln's funeral train departed on a mournful journey from Washington to Springfield, Illinois, with crowds of thousands gathering at stations to weep as it passed.

CONCLUSION

The Civil War took a larger human toll than any other war in American history. The death count stood at 360,000 Union soldiers and 260,000 Confederates. Most families in the nation suffered losses. Vivid reminders of the human toll remained beyond the end of the century. For many years armless and legless veterans gathered at regimental reunions. Citizens erected monuments to the dead in front of town halls and on village greens. Soldiers' widows collected pensions well into the twentieth century.

The economic costs were staggering, but the war did not ruin the national economy, only the southern part of it. The vast Confederate losses, about 60 percent of southern wealth, were offset by northern advances. At the war's end, the North had almost all of the nation's wealth and capacity for production. Spurring economic modernization, the war provided a hospitable climate for industrial development and capital investment. "The truth is," wrote Ohio senator John Sherman to his brother, General William T. Sherman, "the close of the war with our resources unimpaired gives an elevation, a scope to the ideas of leading capitalists, far higher than anything undertaken in this country before." No longer the largest slaveowning power in the world, the United States would now become a major industrial nation.

The war had political as well as economic ramifications. It created a "more perfect Union" in place of the prewar federation of states. The doctrine of states' rights did not disappear, but it was shorn of its extreme features. There would be no further talk of secession, nor would states ever again exercise their antebellum range of powers. The national banking system, created in 1863, gradually supplanted state banks. The greenbacks provided a national currency. The federal government had exercised powers that many in 1860 doubted it possessed. By abolishing slavery and imposing an income tax, it asserted power over kinds of private property once thought untouchable. The war also promoted large-scale organization in both the business world and public life. The giant railroad corporation, with its thousands of employees, and the huge Sanitary Commission, with its thousands of auxiliaries and volunteers, pointed out the road that the nation increasingly would take.

Finally, the Civil War fulfilled abolitionist prophecies as well as Unionist goals. The war produced the very sort of radical upheaval within southern society that Lincoln originally said that it would not induce. Beaten Confederates had no idea of what to expect. Some wondered whether blacks and Yankees would permanently take over the South. The same thought occurred to the freedmen. "Hello, massa," a black Union soldier called out when he spotted his former owner among a group of Confederate prisoners whom he was guarding. "Bottom rail top dis time." The nation now turned its attention to the reconstruction of the conquered South and to the fate of 3.5 million newly freed slaves.

CHRONOLOGY

1861 President Abraham Lincoln calls for volunteers to suppress the rebellion (April).

Virginia, Arkansas, Tennessee, and North Carolina join the Confederacy (April–May).

Lincoln imposes a naval blockade on the South (April).

First Battle of Bull Run (July).

First Confiscation Act (August).

Sheet Music

1862 Legal Tender Act (February).

George B. McClellan's Peninsula Campaign (March–July).

Battle of Shiloh (April).

Confederate Congress passes the Conscription Act (April).

David G. Farragut captures New Orleans (April).

Homestead Act (May).

Seven Days' Battles (June–July).

Pacific Railroad Act (July).

Morrill Land Grant Act (July).

Second Confiscation Act (July).

Second Battle of Bull Run (August).

Battle of Antietam (September).

1862 Preliminary Emancipation Proclamation (September).

Battle of Fredericksburg (December).

1863 Emancipation Proclamation issued (January).

Lincoln suspends writ of habeas corpus nationwide (January).

National Bank Act (February).

Congress passes the Enrollment Act (March).

Battle of Chancellorsville (May).

Battle of Gettysburg (July).

Surrender of Vicksburg (July).

New York City draft riots (July).

Battle of Chickamauga (September).

1864 Ulysses S. Grant given command of all Union armies (March).

Battle of the Wilderness (May).

Battle of Spotsylvania (May).

Battle of Cold Harbor (June).

Surrender of Atlanta (September).

Lincoln reelected (November).

William T. Sherman's march to the sea (November–December).

1865 Sherman moves through South Carolina (January–March).

Grant takes Richmond (April).

Robert E. Lee surrenders at Appomattox (April).

Lincoln dies (April).

Joseph Johnston surrenders to Sherman (April).

FOR FURTHER READING

Iver Bernstein, *The New York Draft Riots: The Significance for American Society and Politics in the Age of the Civil War* (1990). An exploration of the social, economic, and political facets of the riots, and their ramifications.

Catherine Clinton and Nina Silber, eds., *Divided Houses: Gender and the Civil War* (1992). Essays focusing on changes in women's roles and activities.

Leon Litwack, *Been in the Storm So Long: The Aftermath of Slavery* (1979). A prizewinning examination of slaves' responses to the process of emancipation, continuing into the Reconstruction era.

James M. McPherson, *Battle Cry of Freedom: The Civil War Era*

(1988). An award-winning study of the war years, skillfully integrating political, military, and social history.

Phillip Shaw Paludan, *The Presidency of Abraham Lincoln* (1994). An assessment of Lincoln as statesman, party leader, commander-in-chief, and emancipator.

Charles Royster, *The Destructive War: William Tecumseh Sherman, Stonewall Jackson, and the Americans* (1991). An exploration of the meaning of violence and nationality in the Civil War era.

Emory M. Thomas, *The Confederate Nation, 1861–1865* (1979). An engaging narrative history, emphasizing the rise and fall of southern nationalism.

ADDITIONAL BIBLIOGRAPHY

General

Daniel Aaron, *The Unwritten War* (1973); William L. Barney, *Flawed Victory* (1975); David P. Crook, *Diplomacy During the Civil War* (1975); David Donald, ed., *Why the North Won the Civil War* (1960); Eric Foner, *Politics and Ideology in the Age of the Civil War* (1980); Paul G. Gates, *Agriculture and the Civil War* (1965); Harold Hyman, *A More Perfect Union* (1975); James M.

McPherson, *Ordeal by Fire* (1982); Mary Elizabeth Massey, *Bonnet Brigades: American Women and the Civil War* (1966); Allan Nevins, *The War for the Union*, 4 vols. (1959–1971); Lewis P. Simpson, *Mind and the American Civil War* (1989); Maris A. Vinovskis, *Toward a Social History of the American Civil War: Exploratory Essays* (1990); Edmund Wilson, *Patriotic Gore* (1961).

Lincoln

LaWanda Cox, *Lincoln and Black Freedom* (1981); David Donald, *Lincoln Reconsidered: Essays on the Civil War Era*, 2d ed. (1956); James M. McPherson, *Abraham Lincoln and the Second American Revolution* (1990); Mark E. Neely, Jr., *The Last Best Hope on Earth: Abraham Lincoln and the Promise of America* (1993); Stephen B. Oates, *With Malice Toward None: The Life of Abraham Lincoln* (1979); James R. Randall, *Lincoln the President*, 4 vols. (1944–1955); Benjamin Thomas, *Abraham Lincoln* (1952); T. Harry Williams, *Lincoln and the Radicals* (1941) and *Lincoln and His Generals* (1952); Garry Wills, *Lincoln at Gettysburg: The Words That Remade America* (1992).

The Military Experience

Michael Barton, *Good Men: The Character of Civil War Soldiers* (1981); Richard G. Beringer et al., *Why the South Lost the Civil War* (1986); Bruce Catton, *Mr. Lincoln's Army* (1951), *Glory Road* (1952), *A Stillness at Appomattox* (1953); Shelby Foote, *The Civil War: A Narrative*, 3 vols. (1958–1974); Joseph T. Glatthaar, *The March to the Sea and Beyond* (1985) and *Partners in Command: The Relationships Between Leaders in the Civil War* (1994); Edward Hagerman, *The American Civil War and the Origins of Modern Warfare* (1988); Herman Hattaway and Archer Jones, *How the North Won: A Military History of the Civil War* (1984); Alvin M. Josephy, Jr., *The Civil War in the American West* (1991); Gerald F. Linderman, *Embattled Courage: The Experience of Combat in the American Civil War* (1987); James M. McPherson, *What They Fought for, 1861–1865* (1994).

The Black Experience

Dudley Cornish, *The Sable Arm: Negro Troops in the Union Army* (1956); John Hope Franklin, *The Emancipation Proclamation* (1963); Louis S. Gerteis, *From Contraband to Freedman: Federal Policy Toward Southern Blacks, 1861–1865* (1973); Joseph T. Glatthaar, *Forged in Battle: The Civil War Alliance of Black Soldiers and White Officers* (1990); James M. McPherson, ed., *The Negro's Civil War* (1965); Benjamin Quarles, *The Negro in the Civil War* (1953); Willie Lee Rose, *Rehearsal for Reconstruction: The Port Royal Experiment* (1964).

The Southern Experience

Thomas B. Alexander and Richard E. Beringer, *The Anatomy of the Confederate Congress* (1972); Paul D. Escott, *After Secession: Jefferson Davis and the Failure of Southern Nationalism* (1978); Eli N. Evans, *Judah P. Benjamin* (1987); Drew Gilpin Faust, *The Creation of Confederate Nationalism* (1988) and *Southern Stories: Slaveholders in Peace and War* (1992); Douglas Southall Freeman, *R. E. Lee: A Biography*, 4 vols. (1934–1935); Clarence Mohr, *On the Threshold of Freedom: Masters and Slaves in Civil War Georgia* (1986); Robert M. Myers, ed., *The Children of Pride: A True Story of Georgia and the Civil War* (1972); Alan T. Nolan, *Lee Considered: General Robert E. Lee and Civil War History* (1991); George C. Rable, *Women and the Crisis of Southern Nationalism* (1989); James L. Roark, *Masters Without Slaves: Southern Planters in the Civil War and Reconstruction* (1978); Emory M. Thomas, *The Confederacy as a Revolutionary Experience* (1971); Bell I. Wiley, *The Plain People of the Confederacy* (1943) and *Road to Appomattox* (1956).

The Northern Experience

Adrian Cook, *Armies of the Streets: The New York City Draft Riots of 1863* (1974); George M. Fredrickson, *The Inner Civil War: Northern Intellectuals and the Crisis of the Union* (1965); David Gilchrist and W. David Lewis, eds., *Economic Change in the Civil War Era* (1965); Frank L. Klement, *The Copperheads of the Middle West* (1960) and *Dark Lanterns: Secret Political Societies, Conspiracies, and Treason Trials in the Civil War* (1984); William S. McFeely, *Grant: A Biography* (1981); James H. Moorhead, *American Apocalypse: Yankee Protestants and the Civil War* (1978); Philip Shaw Paludan, *"A People's Contest": The Union and the Civil War, 1861–1865* (1988); Joel Silbey, *A Respectable Minority: The Democratic Party in the Civil War Era, 1860–1868* (1977); George W. Smith and Charles Judah, eds., *Life in the North During the Civil War* (1968); Hans L. Trefousse, *The Radical Republicans* (1968).

Personal Narratives

Eliza Frances Andrews, *Wartime Journal of a Georgia Girl* (1908); David Donald, ed., *Inside Lincoln's Cabinet: The Civil War Diaries of Salmon P. Chase* (1959); Ulysses S. Grant, *Memoirs and Selected Letters* (1990); Rupert S. Hallard, ed., *The Letters and Diaries of Laura M. Towne* (1970); T. W. Higginson, *Army Life in a Black Regiment* (1867); Mary Ashton Livermore, *My Story of the War* (1881); W. T. Sherman, *Memoirs* (1990); C. Vann Woodward, ed., *Mary Chesnut's Civil War* (1982).

Freedmen in Jacksonville, Florida
mid–1870s

THE CRISES OF RECONSTRUCTION
1865–1877

When the Civil War ended, parts of the South resembled a wasteland. The landscape "looked for many miles like a broad black streak of ruin and desolation," wrote a Union general. Homes, crops, and railroads had been destroyed; farming and business had come to a standstill; and uprooted southerners wandered about. As the Confederate armies dispersed, remnants of regiments made their way home. White refugees who had fled Union armies and burned-out plantations traveled the roads. So did black refugees. Some former slaves returned to areas where they had once lived, in search of relatives from whom they had been separated. Others moved off plantations to test their free-

dom, to look for work, or to seek relief. "Right off colored folks started on the move," a Texas freedman recalled. "They seemed to want to get closer to freedom—so they'd know what it was—like a place or a city."

The mood of the ex-Confederates was often as grim as the landscape. "The South lies prostrate— their foot is on us—there is no help," a Virginia woman lamented in her diary. Unable to face "southern Yankeedom," some planters considered emigrating to the American West or to Europe, Mexico, or Brazil, and a few thousand did. A large northern presence increased the rebels' dismay: two hundred thousand federal troops occupied the former Confederacy. Northern journalists and officials also

ventured south to investigate conditions and assess rebel attitudes. Their conclusions varied. Chief Justice Salmon P. Chase, on a self-appointed fact-finding mission, insisted that southerners were conciliatory and flexible. "The people are now in a mood to accept almost anything which promises of a definite settlement," he wrote from North Carolina in May 1865. A few days later, a *New York Tribune* reporter, also in North Carolina, offered a harsher view of the ex-Confederates. "They are haughty, exacting, unsubdued, and if possible, *more* devilish than they ever were," he contended. "One would think that we were the subjugated and conquered people and not the rebels."

In previous wars, the mood of the vanquished had rarely, if ever, concerned victors. But the Civil War was a special case, for the Union had sought not merely victory but the return of national unity. The questions the federal government faced in 1865 were therefore unprecedented. First, how could the Union be restored and the defeated South reintegrated into the nation? Would the Confederate states be treated as conquered territories, or would they quickly be readmitted to the Union with the same rights as other states? Who would set requirements for readmission—Congress or the president? Would Confederate leaders be punished for treason? Would their property be confiscated and their political rights curtailed? Most important, what would happen to the more than 3.5 million former slaves? The future of the freedmen constituted *the* crucial issue of the postwar era, for emancipation had set in motion the most profound upheaval in the nation's history. Before the war slavery had been the distinguishing feature of southern society. A labor system and a means of racial control, it had determined the South's social, economic, and political structure. What would replace slavery in the postwar South? The end of the Civil War, in short, posed two problems that had to be solved simultaneously: how to readmit the South to the Union and what status the free blacks would have in American society.

Between 1865 and 1877, the drama of Reconstruction unfolded in several theaters. In Washington a conflict between President Andrew Johnson and Congress led to the enactment of a stringent Republican plan for restoring the South to the Union. In the defeated Confederate states, first readmitted to the Union under presidential directives, state governments were reorganized according to the new congressional plan, and Republicans took power. Throughout the South, the Reconstruction years spawned far-reaching social and economic changes.

Emancipation reshaped black communities, where former slaves sought new identities as free people, and it transformed the southern economy as a new labor system replaced slavery. The North, meanwhile, hurtled headlong into an era of industrial expansion, labor unrest, and financial crises. By the mid-1870s northern politicians were ready to discard the Reconstruction policies that Congress had imposed in the 1860s. Simultaneously, the southern states returned to "home rule," or Democratic control, as Republican regimes toppled one by one. In 1877 Reconstruction collapsed. But the nature and causes of its failure have engaged historians ever since.

RECONSTRUCTION POLITICS

At the end of the Civil War, President Johnson might have exiled, imprisoned, or executed Confederate leaders and imposed martial law indefinitely. Demobilized Confederate soldiers might have continued armed resistance to federal occupation forces. Freed

The Devastated South in 1865

As the Civil War ended, demoralized ex-Confederates confronted bleak prospects—"a joyless future of probable ignominy, poverty, and want," wrote one planter's daughter, "a life robbed of every blessing and already becoming intolerable." Here, a family in Fredericksburg, Virginia, returns to its war-shattered dwelling in a mood of resignation or despair. Significantly, no men of military age remain.

slaves might have taken revenge on former owners and the rest of the white community. But none of these drastic possibilities occurred. Instead, intense *political* conflict dominated the three years immediately after the war. In national politics unparalleled disputes produced new constitutional amendments, a presidential impeachment crisis, and some of the most ambitious domestic legislation ever enacted by Congress, the Reconstruction Acts of 1867–1868. The major outcome of Reconstruction politics was the enfranchisement of black men, a development that few had expected when Lee surrendered.

In 1865 only a small group of politicians supported black suffrage. These advocates were all Radical Republicans, a minority faction that had emerged during the war. Led by Senator Charles Sumner of Massachusetts and Congressman Thaddeus Stevens of Pennsylvania, the Radicals had clamored for the abolition of slavery, just as they supported a demanding reconstruction policy, both in wartime and after. Any valid plan to restore the Union, Stevens contended, must "revolutionize Southern institutions, habits, and manners . . . or all our blood and treasure have been spent in vain." But the Radicals, outnumbered in Congress by moderate and conservative Republicans and opposed by the Democratic minority, seemingly had little chance of success. Nonetheless, in the complex political battles of 1865–1868, the Radicals managed to win broad Republican support for parts of their Reconstruction program, including black male enfranchisement. Just as civil war had led to emancipation, a goal once supported by only a minority of Americans, so Reconstruction policy became bound to black suffrage, a momentous change that originally had only narrow political backing.

Lincoln's Plan

Conflict over Reconstruction began even before the war ended. In December 1863 President Lincoln issued the Proclamation of Amnesty and Reconstruction, which outlined a path by which each southern state could rejoin the Union. Under Lincoln's plan a minority of voters (equal to at least 10 percent of those who had cast ballots in the election of 1860) would have to take an oath of allegiance to the Union and accept emancipation. This minority could then create a loyal state government. But Lincoln's plan excluded some southerners from taking the oath: Confederate government officials, army and naval officers, as well

as those military or civil officers who had resigned from Congress or from U.S. commissions in 1861. All such persons would have to apply for presidential pardons. Also excluded, of course, were blacks, who had not been voters in 1860. Lincoln hoped through his "10 percent plan" to undermine the Confederacy by establishing pro-Union governments within it. Characteristically, Lincoln had partisan goals, too. He wanted to win the allegiance of southern Unionists (those who had opposed secession), especially former Whigs, and to build a southern Republican party.

Radical Republicans in Congress, however, envisioned a slower readmission process that would exclude even more ex-Confederates from political life. Their plan won the backing of almost all Republicans, who agreed that Lincoln's program was too weak. Thus in July 1864 Congress enacted the Wade-Davis bill, which provided that each former Confederate state would be ruled by a military governor. Under the Wade-Davis plan, after at least half the eligible voters took an oath of allegiance to the Union, delegates could be elected to a state convention that would repeal secession and abolish slavery. But to qualify as a voter or delegate, a southerner would have to take a second, "ironclad" oath, swearing that he had never voluntarily supported the Confederacy. Like the 10 percent plan, the congressional plan did not provide for black suffrage, a measure then supported by only some Radicals. Unlike Lincoln's plan, however, the Wade-Davis scheme would have delayed the readmission process almost indefinitely.

Claiming that he did not want to bind himself to any single restoration policy, Lincoln pocket-vetoed* the Wade-Davis bill. The bill's sponsors, Senator Benjamin Wade of Ohio and Congressman Henry Winter Davis of Maryland, blasted Lincoln's act as an outrage. By the end of the war, the president and Congress had reached an impasse. Arkansas, Louisiana, Tennessee, and parts of Virginia under Union army control moved toward readmission under variants of Lincoln's plan. But Congress refused to seat their delegates, as it had a right to do. Lincoln, meanwhile, gave hints that a more rigorous Reconstruction policy might be in store. In his last speech (April 1865), he revealed that he favored some form of black suffrage, perhaps for blacks who had served in the Union army. He also entertained Secretary of War Stanton's proposal for temporary

---

*Pocket veto: failure to sign a bill within ten days of the adjournment of Congress.

military occupation of the South. What Lincoln's ultimate policy would have been remains unknown. But at the time of his death, Radical Republicans turned with hope toward his successor, Andrew Johnson of Tennessee, in whom they felt they had an ally.

Presidential Reconstruction Under Johnson

The only southern senator to remain in Congress when his state seceded, Andrew Johnson had worked amicably with Radical Republicans in wartime and had served as military governor of Tennessee from 1862 to 1864. He had taken a strong anti-Confederate stand, declaring, for example, that "treason is a crime and must be made odious." Above all, Johnson had long sought the destruction of the planter aristocracy, a goal that dominated his political career. A self-educated man of humble North Carolina origins, Johnson had moved to Greenville, Tennessee, in 1826 and become a tailor. His wife, Eliza McCardle, had taught him how to write. An ardent Jacksonian, he had entered politics in the 1830s as a spokesman for nonslaveowning whites and risen rapidly from local official to congressman to governor to senator. Once the owner of eight slaves, Johnson reversed his position on slavery during the war. When emancipation became Union policy, he supported it, and as military governor, he assured Tennessee blacks that he would be their "Moses." But Johnson neither adopted abolitionist ideals nor challenged racist sentiments. He hoped mainly that the fall of slavery would injure southern aristocrats. Andrew Johnson, in short, had his own political agenda, which, as Republicans would soon learn, did not coincide with theirs. Moreover, he was a lifelong Democrat who had been added to the Republican, or National Union, ticket in 1864 to broaden its appeal and who had become president by accident.

Many Republicans voiced shock when Johnson announced a new plan for the restoration of the South in May 1865—with Congress out of session and not due to convene until December. The president presented his program as a continuation of Lincoln's plan, but in fact, it was very much his own. He explained in two proclamations how the seven southern states still without reconstruction governments—Alabama, Florida, Georgia, Mississippi, North Carolina, South Carolina, and Texas—could return to the Union. Almost all southerners who took an oath of allegiance would receive a pardon and amnesty, and all their property except slaves would be restored. Oath takers could elect

Andrew Johnson
When Vice President Johnson became president at Lincoln's death in April 1865, many Republicans expected him to impose "harsh terms" upon the defeated South.

delegates to state conventions, which would provide for regular elections. Each state convention, Johnson later added, would have to proclaim the illegality of secession, repudiate state debts incurred when the state belonged to the Confederacy, and ratify the Thirteenth Amendment, which abolished slavery. (Proposed by an enthusiastic wartime Congress early in 1865, the amendment would be ratified in December of that year.) As under Lincoln's plan, Confederate civil and military officers would be excluded from the oath needed for voting. But Johnson added a new disqualification. All well-off ex-Confederates, those with taxable property worth $20,000 or more, would also be barred from political life. This exclusion, said Johnson, would benefit "humble men, the peasantry and yeomen of the South, who have been decoyed . . . into rebellion." Johnson seemed to be planning a purge of aristocratic leaders. Poorer whites would now be in control.

Presidential Reconstruction took effect in the summer of 1865, supervised by provisional governors. But it had unforeseen consequences. Those southerners disqualified on the basis of wealth or high Confederate position applied for pardons in droves. Either gratified by their supplications or seeking support for reelection in 1868, Johnson handed out pardons liberally—some thirteen thousand of them. He also dropped plans for the punishment of treason. By the end of 1865, all seven states had created new civil governments to replace the imposed military rule, but in other ways the states had almost returned to the status quo ante bellum. Confederate army officers and large planters assumed state offices. Former Confederate congressmen, state officials, and generals were elected to Congress. (Most of these new representatives were former Whigs who had not supported secession; southerners thought that they were electing "Union" men.) Georgia sent Alexander Stephens, the former Confederate vice president and a one-time Unionist, back to Congress as a senator. Some states refused to ratify the Thirteenth Amendment or to repudiate their Confederate debts.

Most important, all states took steps to ensure a landless, dependent black labor force—in one Alabamian's words, to "secure the services of the negroes, teach them their place." This goal was achieved through the "black codes," which replaced the slave codes, the state laws that had regulated slavery. Because the ratification of the Thirteenth Amendment was assured by the terms of Johnson's Reconstruction plan, all states guaranteed the freedmen some basic rights. They could marry, own property, make contracts, and testify in court against other blacks. But the important parts of the black codes were their restrictions, which varied from state to state. Some codes established racial segregation in public places; most prohibited racial intermarriage, jury service by blacks, and court testimony by blacks against whites. All codes included economic restrictions that would prevent former slaves from leaving the plantations. South Carolina required special licenses for blacks who wished to enter nonagricultural employment. Mississippi prohibited blacks from buying and selling farmland. Most states required annual contracts between landowners and black agricultural workers and provided that blacks without lawful employment would be arrested as vagrants and auctioned off to employers who would pay their fines.

The black codes established a halfway status for the southern freedmen, who, though no longer slaves, were not really liberated either. Although "free" to sign labor contracts, for instance, those who failed to sign them would be considered in violation of the law and swept back into involuntary servitude. In practice,

many clauses in the codes never took effect: the Union army and the Freedmen's Bureau swiftly suspended the enforcement of racially discriminatory provisions of the new laws. But the black codes were important indicators of white southern intentions. They showed what "home rule" would have been like without federal interference.

When former abolitionists and Radical Republicans decried the black codes, Johnson defended the codes and his restoration program. Ex-Confederates, he contended, should not be forced back into the Union as "a degraded and debased people." Many northerners, however, perceived signs of southern defiance: voters had elected ex-rebels to public office; southern conventions had been reluctant to repudiate secession or slow to pronounce slavery dead; and new laws had robbed freedmen of basic rights. "What can be hatched from such an egg but another rebellion?" asked a Boston newspaper. Republicans in Congress agreed. When the Thirty-ninth Congress convened in December 1865, it refused to seat the delegates of the ex-Confederate states. Establishing the Joint (House-Senate) Committee on Reconstruction, Republicans prepared to dismantle the black codes and lock ex-Confederates out of power.

Congress Versus Johnson

The status of the southern blacks now became the major issue in Congress. "This is not a 'white man's government,' " exclaimed Republican congressman Thaddeus Stevens. "To say so is political blasphemy." But Radical Republicans like Stevens—who hoped to impose black suffrage on the former Confederacy and delay the readmission of the southern states into the Union—still constituted a congressional minority. Conservative Republicans, who tended to favor the Johnson plan, formed a minority too, as did the Democrats, who also supported the president. Moderate Republicans, the largest congressional bloc, agreed with the Radicals that Johnson's plan was too feeble. But they did not believe that northern voters would support black suffrage, and they wanted to avoid a dispute with the president. Since none of the four congressional blocs even approached the two-thirds majority required to overturn a presidential veto, Johnson's program would stay in place unless the moderates and the Radicals joined forces. The impetus for this alliance came from an unexpected source—Andrew Johnson himself, who soon alienated a majority of moderates and pushed them into the Radicals' arms.

The moderate Republicans supported two proposals drafted by one of their own, Senator Lyman Trumbull of Illinois, to invalidate the black codes. These measures won wide Republican support. In the first, Congress voted to continue the Freedmen's Bureau, established in 1865, whose term was coming to an end. This agency, headed by former Union general O. O. Howard and staffed mainly by army officers, was a major federal arm in the South. It provided relief, rations, and medical care; built schools for the freed blacks; put them to work on abandoned or confiscated lands; and tried to protect their rights as laborers. Congress voted to extend the bureau's life for three years and to give it new power: it could run special military courts to settle labor disputes and could invalidate labor contracts forced on freedmen by the black codes. In February 1866 Johnson vetoed the Freedmen's Bureau bill. The Constitution, he declared, did not sanction military trials of civilians in peacetime, nor did it support a system to care for "indigent persons."

In March 1866 Congress passed a second measure proposed by Trumbull, a bill that made blacks U.S. citizens with the same civil rights as other citizens and gave the federal government the right to intervene in the states to ensure black rights in court. Johnson vetoed the civil rights bill also. He argued that it would "operate in favor of the colored and against the white race." But in April Congress overrode his veto; the Civil Rights Act of 1866 was the first major law ever passed over a presidential veto. Then in July Congress enacted the Supplementary Freedmen's Bureau Act over Johnson's veto as well.

Johnson's vetoes bewildered many Republicans because the new laws did not undercut the basic structure of presidential Reconstruction. The president insisted, however, that both bills were illegitimate because southerners had been shut out of the Congress that passed them. His stance won support not only from the South but from northern Democrats, who were fast becoming Johnson's constituency. But the president had alienated the moderate Republicans, who began to work with the Radicals against him. Johnson had lost "every friend he has," one moderate legislator declared.

Some historians view Andrew Johnson as a political incompetent who, at this crucial turning point, bungled both his readmission scheme and his political future. Others contend that he was merely trying to forge a coalition of the center, made up of Democrats

King Andrew
This Thomas Nast cartoon, published in Harper's Weekly *just before the 1866 congressional elections, conveyed Republican antipathy to Andrew Johnson. The president is depicted as an autocratic tyrant. Radical Republican Thaddeus Stevens, upper right, has his head on the block and is about to lose it. The Republic sits in chains.*

and non-Radical Republicans. In either case, Johnson underestimated the possibility of Republican unity. Once united, the Republicans moved on to a third step: the passage of a constitutional amendment that would prevent the Supreme Court from invalidating the new Civil Rights Act and would block Democrats in Congress from repealing it.

The Fourteenth Amendment

In April 1866 Congress adopted the Fourteenth Amendment, which had been proposed by the Joint Committee on Reconstruction. To protect blacks' rights, the amendment declared in its first clause that all persons born or naturalized in the United States were citizens of the nation and citizens of their states and that no state could abridge their rights without due process of law or deny them equal protection of the law. This section nullified the *Dred Scott* decision of 1857 (see Chapter 14), which had declared that blacks were not citizens. Second, the amendment guaranteed that if a state denied suffrage to any of its male citizens, its representation in Congress would be proportionally reduced. This clause did not guarantee black suffrage, but it threatened to deprive southern states of some legislators if black men were denied the vote. Third, the amendment disqualified from state and national office *all* prewar officeholders—civil and military, state and federal—who had supported the Confederacy, unless Congress removed their disqualifications by a two-thirds vote. In so providing, Congress intended to invalidate Johnson's wholesale distribution of amnesties and pardons. Finally, the amendment repudiated the Confederate debt and maintained the validity of the federal debt.

The Fourteenth Amendment was the most ambitious step that Congress had yet taken. It revealed the growing receptivity among Republican legislators to the Radicals' demands, including black male enfranchisement. It reflected the Republican consensus that southern states would not deal fairly with blacks unless forced to do so. Most important, it was the first national effort to limit state control of civil and political rights. With its passage a huge controversy erupted. Abolitionists decried the second clause as a "swindle" because it did not explicitly ensure black suffrage. Southerners and northern Democrats condemned the third clause as vengeful. Southern legislatures, except for Tennessee's, refused to ratify the amendment, and President Johnson denounced it. His intransigence solidified the new alliance between moderate and Radical Republicans. It also turned the congressional elections of 1866 into a referendum on the Fourteenth Amendment.

Over the summer Johnson set off on a whistle-stop train tour from Washington to St. Louis and Chicago and back, speaking to the public at railroad stations along the way. But this innovative campaign tactic—the "swing around the circle," as Johnson called it—was a debacle. Humorless and defensive, the president argued with his audiences and made fresh enemies. His hope of creating a new National Union party, composed of Democrats and conservative Republicans who opposed the Fourteenth Amendment, thus cap-

sized. Moderate and Radical Republicans, meanwhile, defended the amendment, condemned the president, and branded the Democratic party "a common sewer . . . into which is emptied every element of treason, North and South."

When the votes in the congressional elections were tallied, Republican candidates won in a landslide, often with even greater margins of victory than in 1864. In the Fortieth Congress, which would convene in March 1867, Republicans would outnumber Democrats almost two to one in the House and almost four to one in the Senate. In the interim the Republicans had secured a mandate to overcome southern resistance to the Fourteenth Amendment and to enact their own Reconstruction program, even if the president vetoed every part of it.

Congressional Reconstruction

The congressional debate over how to reconstruct the South began in December 1866 and lasted three months. To stifle a resurgence of Confederate power, Radical Republican leaders called for black suffrage, federal support for public schools, confiscation of Confederate estates, and an extended period of military occupation in the South. Moderate Republicans, who once would have rejected such a plan as too extreme, were now willing to accept parts of it. Legislators debated every ramification, including the constitutional question of whether the southern states had in fact seceded from the Union during the war. In February 1867 after complex legislative maneuvers and many late-night sessions, Congress passed the Reconstruction Act of 1867 and, after Johnson vetoed it, repassed the law on March 2. Later that year and in 1868, Congress passed three further Reconstruction acts, all enacted over presidential vetoes, to refine and enforce the first.

The Reconstruction Act of 1867 invalidated the state governments formed under the Lincoln and Johnson plans and all the legal decisions made by those governments. Only Tennessee, which had ratified the Fourteenth Amendment and had been readmitted to the Union, escaped further reconstruction. The new law divided the other ten former Confederate states into five temporary military districts, each run by a Union general. Voters—all black men, plus those white men who had not been disqualified by the Fourteenth Amendment—could elect delegates to a state convention that would write a new state constitution granting black suffrage. When eligible voters ratified

Major Reconstruction Legislation

Law and Date of Congressional Passage	Provisions	Purpose
Civil Rights Act pf 1866 (April 1866)*	Declared blacks citizens and guaranteed them equal protection of the laws.	To invalidate the black codes.
Supplementary Freedmen's Bureau Act (July 1866)*	Extended the life of the Freedmen's Aid Bureau and expanded its powers.	To invalidate the black codes.
Reconstruction Act of 1867 (March 1867)*	Invalidated state governments formed under Lincoln and Johnson.	To replace presidential Reconstruction with a more stringent plan.
	Divided the former Confederacy into five military districts.	
	Set forth requirements for readmission of ex-Confederate states to the Union.	
Supplementary Reconstruction Acts		To enforce the First Reconstruction Act.
Second Reconstruction Act (March 1867)*	Required military commanders to initiate voter enrollment.	
Third Reconstruction Act (July 1867)*	Expanded military commanders' powers.	
Fourth Reconstruction Act (March 1868)*	Provided that a majority of voters, however few, could put a new state constitution into force.	
Army Appropriations Act (March 1867)*	Declared in a rider that only the general of the army could issue military orders.	To prevent President Johnson from obstructing Reconstruction.
Tenure of Office Act (March 1867)*	Prohibited the president from removing any federal official without the Senate's consent.	To prevent President Johnson from obstructing Reconstruction.
Omnibus Act (June 1868)†	Readmitted seven ex-Confederate states to the Union.	To restore the Union, under the terms of the First Reconstruction Act.
Enforcement Act of 1870 (May 1870)‡	Provided for the protection of black voters.	To enforce the Fifteenth Amendment.
Second Enforcement Act (February 1871)	Provided for federal supervision of southern elections.	To enforce the Fifteenth Amendment.
Third Enforcement Act (Ku Klux Klan Act) (April 1871)	Strengthened sanctions against those who impeded black suffrage.	To combat the Ku Klux Klan and enforce the Fourteenth Amendment.
Amnesty Act (May 1872)	Restored the franchise to almost all ex-Confederates.	Effort by Grant Republicans to deprive Liberal Republicans of a campaign issue.
Civil Rights Act of 1875 (March 1875)§	Outlawed racial segregation in transportation and public accommodations and prevented exclusion of blacks from jury service.	To honor the late senator Charles Sumner.

*Passed over Johnson's veto.

†Georgia was soon returned to military rule. The last four states were readmitted in 1870.

‡Sections of the law declared unconstitutional in 1876.

§Invalidated by the Supreme Court in 1883.

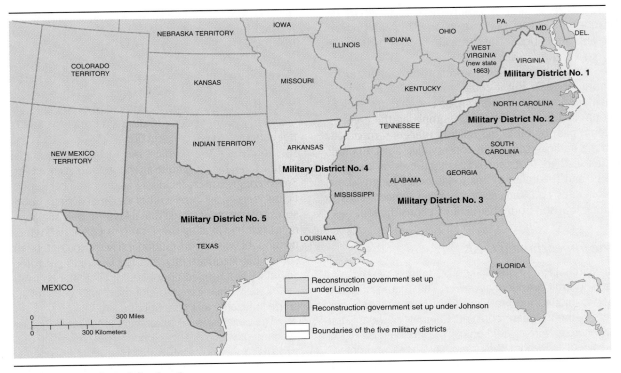

The Reconstruction of the South
The Reconstruction Act of 1867 divided the former Confederate states, except Tennessee, into
five military districts and set forth the steps by which new state governments could be created.

the new constitution, elections could be held for state officers. Once Congress approved the state constitution, once the state legislature ratified the Fourteenth Amendment, and once the amendment became part of the federal Constitution, Congress would readmit the state into the Union—and Reconstruction, in a constitutional sense, would be complete.

The Reconstruction Act of 1867 was far more radical than the Johnson program because it enfranchised blacks and disfranchised many ex-Confederates. It fulfilled a central goal of the Radical Republicans: to delay the readmission of former Confederate states until Republican governments could be established and thereby prevent an immediate rebel resurgence. But the new law was not as harsh toward ex-Confederates as it might have been. It provided for only temporary military rule. It did not prosecute Confederate leaders for treason or permanently exclude them from politics. Finally, it made no provision for the confiscation or redistribution of property.

During the congressional debates, Radical Republican congressman Thaddeus Stevens had argued for the confiscation of large Confederate estates to "humble the proud traitors" and to provide for the former slaves. In March 1867 he had proposed subdividing such confiscated property into forty-acre tracts to be distributed among the freedmen. The remainder of the confiscated land, some 90 percent of it, would be sold to pay off war debts. Stevens wanted to crush the planter aristocracy and create a new class of self-sufficient black yeoman farmers. Political independence rested on economic independence, he contended; land grants would be more valuable to the freedmen than the vote, although both were deserved. Stevens's land-reform bill won the support of other Radicals, but it never made progress, for most Republicans held property rights sacred. Tampering with such rights in the South, they feared, would jeopardize those rights in the North. Moreover, Stevens's proposal would alienate southern ex-Whigs from the Republican cause, antagonize other white southerners, and thereby endanger the rest of Reconstruction. Thus land reform never came about. The "radical" Reconstruction acts were a compromise.

Congressional Reconstruction took effect in the spring of 1867. But it could not be enforced without military power, and Johnson, as commander in chief, controlled the army. When he impeded the congressional plan by replacing military officers sympathetic to the Radical cause with conservative ones, Republicans seethed. More suspicious than ever of the president and frustrated by his roadblocks, congressional moderates and Radicals once again joined forces to block Johnson from obstructing Reconstruction.

The Impeachment Crisis

In March 1867 Republicans in Congress passed two laws to limit presidential power. The Tenure of Office Act prohibited the president from removing civil officers without Senate consent. Cabinet members, the law stated, were to hold office "during the term of the president by whom they may have been appointed" and could be fired only with the Senate's approval. The goal was to bar Johnson from dismissing Secretary of War Stanton, the Radicals' ally, whose support Congress needed to enforce the Reconstruction acts. The other law, a rider to an army appropriations bill, barred the president from issuing military orders except through the commanding general, Ulysses S. Grant, who could not be removed without the Senate's consent.

The Radicals' enmity to Johnson, however, would not die until he was out of office. They began to look for grounds on which to impeach him and convict him and thereby remove all potential obstacles to congressional Reconstruction. The House Judiciary Committee, aided by private detectives, could at first uncover no valid charges against Johnson. On a second try, they produced some charges, but the House found them inadequate. Just as impeachment efforts seemed a lost cause, Johnson again came to his opponents' rescue by providing the charges they needed.

In August 1867, with Congress out of session, Johnson suspended Secretary of War Stanton and replaced him with General Grant. In early 1868 the reconvened Senate refused to approve Stanton's suspension, and Grant, sensing the Republican mood, vacated the office. Johnson then removed Stanton and replaced him with an aged general, Lorenzo Thomas. Johnson's

defiance forced Republican moderates, who had at first resisted impeachment, into yet another alliance with the Radicals: the president had "thrown down the gauntlet," a moderate charged. The House approved eleven charges of impeachment, nine of them based on violation of the Tenure of Office Act. The other charges accused Johnson of being "unmindful of the high duties of office," of seeking to disgrace Congress, and of not enforcing the Reconstruction acts.

Johnson's trial, which began in the Senate in March 1868, riveted public attention for eleven weeks. Seven congressmen, including leading Radical Republicans, served as prosecutors or "managers." Johnson's lawyers maintained that he was merely seeking a court test by violating the Tenure of Office Act, which he thought was unconstitutional. They also contended, somewhat inconsistently, that the law did not protect Secretary Stanton, an appointee of Lincoln, not Johnson. Finally, they asserted, Johnson was guilty of no crime indictable in a regular court.

The congressional "managers" countered that impeachment was a political process, not a criminal trial, and that Johnson's "abuse of discretionary power" constituted an impeachable offense. Although Senate opinion split along party lines and Republicans outnumbered Democrats, some Republicans wavered, fearing that the removal of a president would destroy the balance of power among the three branches of the federal government. They also distrusted Radical Republican Benjamin Wade, the president pro tempore of the Senate, who, because there was no vice president, would accede to the presidency if Johnson were thrown out.

Intense pressure from colleagues and constituents bombarded the wavering Republican senators, whose votes would prove crucial. Late in May 1868, the Senate voted against Johnson 35 to 19, one vote short of the two-thirds majority needed for conviction. Seven Republicans had risked political suicide and sided with the twelve Senate Democrats in voting against removal. In so doing, they set a precedent. Future presidents would not be impeached solely on political grounds or because two-thirds of Congress disagreed with them. But the anti-Johnson forces had also achieved their goal: Andrew Johnson had no future as president. After serving out the rest of his term, he returned to Tennessee, where he was reelected to the Senate five years later. Republicans in Congress, meanwhile, pursued their last major Reconstruction objective: to guarantee black male suffrage.

The Reconstruction Amendments

Amendment and Date of Congressional Passage	Provisions	Ratification
Thirteenth (January 1865)	Prohibited slavery in the United States.	December 1865
Fourteenth (June 1866)	Defined citizenship to include all persons born or naturalized in the United States.	July 1868, after Congress made ratification a prerequisite for readmission of ex-Confederate states to the Union.
	Provided proportional loss of congressional representation for any state that denied suffrage to any of its male citizens.	
	Disqualified prewar officeholders who supported the Confederacy from state or national office.	
	Repudiated the Confederate debt.	
Fifteenth (February 1869)	Prohibited the denial of suffrage because of race, color, or previous condition of servitude.	March 1870; ratification required of Virginia, Texas, Mississippi, and Georgia for readmission to the Union.

The Fifteenth Amendment

Black suffrage was the linchpin of congressional Reconstruction. Only with the support of black voters could Republicans secure control of the ex-Confederate states. The Fourteenth Amendment had promoted black suffrage indirectly, by threatening a penalty where it was denied. The Reconstruction Act of 1867, however, forced every southern state legislature to enfranchise black men as a prerequisite for readmission to the Union. But though black voting had begun in the South, much of the North had rejected it. At the end of the Civil War, only five New England states enfranchised black men; so did New York, on the condition that they owned property. Between 1867 and 1869, nine referenda in northern states defeated proposals for black suffrage. Iowa voters alone extended the franchise to blacks. Congressional Republicans therefore had two aims. They sought to protect black suffrage in the South against future repeal by Congress or the states and to enfranchise northern and border-state blacks, who would presumably vote Republican. To achieve these goals, Congress in 1869 proposed the Fifteenth Amendment, which prohibited the denial of suffrage by the states to any citizen on account of race, color, or previous condition of servitude.

Democrats argued that the proposed amendment violated states' rights by denying each state the power to determine who would vote. But Democrats did not control enough states to defeat the amendment, and it was ratified in 1870. Four votes came from those ex-Confederate states—Mississippi, Virginia, Georgia, and Texas—that had delayed the Reconstruction process and were therefore forced to approve the Fifteenth Amendment, as well as the Fourteenth, in order to rejoin the Union. Some southerners contended that the new amendment's omissions made it acceptable, for it had, as a Richmond newspaper pointed out, "loopholes through which a coach and four horses can be driven." What were these loopholes? The Fifteenth Amendment did not guarantee black officeholding, nor did it prohibit voting restrictions such as property requirements and literacy tests. Such restrictions might be used to deny blacks the vote, and indeed, ultimately they were so used.

The debate over black suffrage not only pervaded national politics but drew new participants into the fray. Since the end of the war, a small group of abolitionists, men and women, had sought to revive the cause of women's rights. In 1866, when Congress adopted the Fourteenth Amendment, women's rights advocates tried to join forces with their old abolitionist allies to promote both black suffrage and woman suffrage. Most Radical Republicans, however, did not want to be saddled with the woman-suffrage plank; they feared it would impede their primary goal, black enfranchisement.

This defection provoked disputes among women's rights advocates. Some, who continued to support black suffrage, contended that it would pave the way for the women's vote and that black men deserved priority. "If the elective franchise is not extended to the Negro, he is dead," explained Frederick Douglass, a longtime women's rights supporter. "Woman has a thousand ways by which she can attach herself to the ruling power of the land that we have not." But the women's rights leaders Elizabeth Cady Stanton and Susan B. Anthony, who repudiated black suffrage without attendant woman suffrage, decried the Fifteenth Amendment and denounced the Republicans for supporting it. The amendment, insisted Stanton, would establish an "aristocracy of sex." Moreover, she argued, if suffrage were extended without including women, their disabilities would merely increase. The battle over black suffrage and the Fifteenth Amendment divided women's rights advocates into two rival suffrage associations, both formed in 1869. It also severed reformers such as Stanton and Anthony from the abolitionist tradition in which they had matured politically and inspired the development of an independent women's rights movement.

By the time the Fifteenth Amendment was ratified in 1870, Congress could look back on five years of momentous achievement. Since the start of 1865, federal legislators had broadened the scope of American democracy by passing three constitutional amendments. The Thirteenth Amendment abolished slavery, the Fourteenth affirmed the rights of federal citizens, and the Fifteenth prohibited the denial of suffrage on the basis of race. Congress had also readmitted the former Confederate states into the Union. But after 1868 congressional momentum slowed. And in 1869, when Ulysses S. Grant became president, the fierce battle between Congress and the chief executive ceased. The theater of action now shifted to the South, where an era of tumultuous change was under way.

RECONSTRUCTION GOVERNMENTS

During the unstable years of presidential Reconstruction, 1865–1867, the southern states had to create new governments, revive the war-torn economy, and face the impact of emancipation. Social and economic problems abounded. War costs had cut into southern wealth, cities and factories lay in rubble, plantation-labor systems disintegrated, and racial tensions flared. Beginning in 1865, freedmen organized black conventions, political meetings at which they protested ill treatment and demanded equal rights. These meetings took place in a climate of violence. Race riots erupted in major southern cities. In Memphis in May 1866, white crowds attacked black veterans, charged through black neighborhoods, and killed forty-six people; in New Orleans two months later, a white mob and police assaulted black delegates on their way to a political convention and left forty people dead. Even when Congress reimposed military rule in 1867, ex-Confederates did not feel defeated. "Having reached bottom, there is hope now that we may rise again to the surface in the course of time," a South Carolina planter wrote in his diary.

Congressional Reconstruction, supervised by federal troops, took effect in the spring of 1867. Despite efforts to stall it—many southern whites preferred military rule to the prospect of new civil governments based on black suffrage—the process moved forward. The Johnson regimes were dismantled, state constitutional conventions met, and voters elected new state governments, which Republicans dominated. In 1868 a majority of the former Confederate states rejoined the Union, and two years later, the last four states—Virginia, Mississippi, Georgia, and Texas—followed.

Readmission to the Union did not end the *process* of Reconstruction, for Republicans still held power in the South. Republican rule was very brief, lasting less than a decade in all southern states, far less in most of them, and on average under five years. Opposition from southern Democrats, the landowning elite, thousands of vigilantes, and indeed, most white voters proved insurmountable. Still, the governments formed under congressional Reconstruction were unique, because black men, including ex-slaves, participated in them. In no other society where slaves had been liberated—neither Haiti, where slaves had revolted in the 1790s, nor the British Caribbean islands, where Parliament had ended slavery in 1833—had freedmen gained democratic political rights.

A New Electorate

The Reconstruction laws of 1867–1868 transformed the southern electorate by temporarily disfranchising 10 percent to 15 percent of potential white voters and by enfranchising more than seven hundred thousand freedmen. Outnumbering registered white voters by

The Carpetbaggers
Southern Democrats disparaged carpetbaggers as interlopers who hoped to "fatten on our misfortunes." In reality, most were Union army officers, businessmen, and professionals with capital and energy to invest in the South. This 1869 sheet-music cover caricatures the carpetbaggers by depicting a predatory northern migrant casting a greedy eye upon the defeated Confederacy.

one hundred thousand, blacks gained voting majorities in five states.

The new electorate provided a base for the Republican party, which had never existed in the South. To their Democratic opponents, southern Republicans comprised three types of scoundrels: northern "carpetbaggers," who had allegedly come south seeking wealth and power (with so few possessions that they could be stuffed into traveling bags made of carpet material); southern "scalawags," predominantly poor and ignorant, who sought to profit from Republican rule; and hordes of uneducated freedmen, who were ready prey for Republican manipulators. Although the "carpetbag" and "scalawag" labels were derogatory and the stereotypes that they conveyed inaccurate, they remain in use as a form of shorthand. Crossing class and racial lines, the hastily established Republican party

was in fact a loose coalition of factions with varied and often contradictory goals.

To northerners who moved south after the Civil War, the former Confederacy was an undeveloped region, ripe with possibility. The carpetbaggers' ranks included many former Union soldiers who hoped to buy land, open factories, build railroads, or simply enjoy the warmer southern climate. Albion Tourgee, a young lawyer who had served with the New York and Ohio volunteers, for example, relocated in North Carolina after the war to improve his health. There he worked as a journalist, politician, and Republican judge, until Republican rule collapsed. Perhaps no more than twenty thousand northern migrants like Tourgee—including veterans, missionaries, teachers, and Freedmen's Bureau agents—headed south immediately after the war, and many returned north by 1867. But those who remained played a disproportionate part in Reconstruction politics, for they held almost one out of three state offices. Carpetbaggers recruited black support through a patriotic society called the Union League, which held meetings and rallies, urged blacks to vote, and escorted them to the polls.

Scalawags, white southerners who supported the Republicans, included some entrepreneurs who applauded party policies such as the national banking system and high protective tariffs as well as some prosperous planters, former Whigs who had opposed the South's secession. They also comprised a few prominent politicians, among them James Orr of South Carolina and Mississippi's governor James Alcorn, who became Republicans for practical reasons: they wanted to retain influence and limit Republican radicalism. Republicans appreciated such important recruits and hoped to attract more of them. Most scalawags, however, were small farmers from the mountain regions of North Carolina, Georgia, Alabama, and Arkansas. Former Unionists who had owned no slaves and had no allegiance to the landowning elite, they sought to improve their economic position. Unlike carpetbaggers, they lacked commitment to black rights and black suffrage; most came from regions with small black populations and cared little whether blacks voted or not. Scalawags held the most political offices during Reconstruction, but they proved the least stable element of the southern Republican coalition: eventually, many drifted back to the Democratic fold.

Freedmen, the backbone of southern Republicanism, provided eight out of ten Republican votes. Republican rule lasted longest in states with the largest

RADICAL · MEMBERS
OF THE Sº. CA. LEGISLATURE.

Republicans in the South Carolina Legislature, *c. 1868*
Only in South Carolina did blacks comprise a majority in the legislature and dominate the legislative process during Reconstruction. This photographic collage of "Radical" legislators, black and white, suggests the extent of black representation. In 1874, blacks won the majority of seats in South Carolina's state senate as well.

black populations, such as South Carolina, Mississippi, Alabama, and Louisiana. Introduced to politics in the black conventions of 1865–1867, the freedmen sought land, education, civil rights, and political equality. Even when land was not forthcoming, they continued to vote Republican. As an elderly freedman announced at a Georgia political convention in 1867, "We know our friends."

Although Reconstruction governments would have collapsed without black votes, freedmen held at most one in five political offices. Blacks served in all southern legislatures and filled many high posts in Louisiana, Mississippi, and South Carolina. They constituted a majority, however, only in the legislature of South Carolina, a state in which more than 60 percent of the population was black. No blacks won the office of governor, and only two served in the U.S. Senate, Hiram Revels and Blanche K. Bruce, both of Mississippi.

In the House of Representatives, a mere 6 percent of southern members were black, and almost half of these came from South Carolina.

Black officeholders on the state level formed a political elite. They often differed from their black constituents in background, education, wealth, and complexion. A disproportionate number were literate blacks who had been free before the Civil War. (Many more former slaves held office on the local level than on the state level.) South Carolina's roster of elected officials illustrates some distinctions between high-level black officeholders and the freedmen who voted for them. Among those blacks sent to Congress, almost all claimed some secondary education, and some held advanced degrees. In South Carolina's state legislature, most black members, unlike the majority of their constituents, came from large towns and cities; many had spent time in the North; and some were well-off property owners or even former slaveowners. Color differences were evident, too: 43 percent of South Carolina's black state legislators were mulattos, as were only 7 percent of the state's black population.

The status gap between high-level black officials and black voters was significant. Most freedmen cared mainly about their economic future, especially about acquiring land, whereas black officeholders cared most about attaining equal rights. Still, both groups shared high expectations, and both prized enfranchisement. "We are not prepared for this suffrage," averred William Beverly Nash, an uneducated former slave, at the South Carolina constitutional convention. "But we can learn. Give a man tools and let him commence to use them and in time he will learn a trade. So it is with voting. We may not understand it at the start, but in time we shall learn to do our duty."

Republican Rule

Large numbers of blacks participated in American government for the first time in the state constitutional conventions of 1867–1868. The South Carolina convention had a black majority, and in Louisiana half the delegates were freedmen. The conventions forged democratic changes in their state constitutions. Delegates abolished property qualifications for officeholding, made many appointive offices elective, and redistricted state legislatures more equitably. All states established universal manhood suffrage, and some conventions offered further innovations: the new constitutions of Louisiana and South Carolina opened public schools to both races. These provisions integrated the New Orleans public schools as well as the University of South Carolina, from which whites withdrew. But most states did not provide for integrated schools, and no state instituted land reform. When proposals for land confiscation and redistribution arose at the state conventions, they fell to defeat, as they had in Congress. Hoping to attract northern investment to the reconstructed South, southern Republicans hesitated to threaten property rights or to adopt land-reform measures that northern Republicans had rejected. South Carolina did set up a commission to buy land and make it available to freedmen, and several states changed their tax structures to force uncultivated land onto the market, but in no case was ex-Confederate land confiscated.

Once civil power shifted from the federal army to the newly formed state governments, the Republican administrations began ambitious programs of public works. They built roads, bridges, and public buildings; promoted railroad development by endorsing railroad bonds; and funded institutions to care for orphans, the insane, and the disabled. The Republican regimes also expanded state bureaucracies, raised salaries for government employees, and formed state militia, in which blacks were often heavily represented. Finally, they created public-school systems, almost nonexistent in the South until then.

Because rebuilding the devastated South and expanding the state governments cost millions, state debts and taxes skyrocketed. During the 1860s the southern tax burden rose 400 percent. State legislatures increased poll taxes or "head" taxes (levies on individuals); enacted luxury, sales, and occupation taxes; and imposed new property taxes. Before the war southern states had taxed property in slaves but had barely taxed landed property at all. Now for the first time, state governments assessed even small farmers' holdings, and big planters paid what they considered an excessive burden. Although northern tax rates still exceeded southern rates, southern landowners resented the new levies. In their view, Reconstruction strained the pocketbooks of the propertied, who were already beset by labor problems and falling land values, in order to finance the vast expenditures of Republican legislators, or what one Alabamian called the "no property herd."

To Reconstruction's opponents, moreover, Republican rule was wasteful and corrupt, if not the "most stupendous system of organized robbery in history." A state like Mississippi, which had an honest government, provided little basis for such charges. But critics could justifiably point to Louisiana, where the governor pocketed thousands of dollars of state funds and corruption permeated all government transactions (as indeed it had before the war). Or they could cite South Carolina, where bribery ran rampant. The main postwar profiteers, besides the government officials who took bribes, were the railroad promoters who doled them out, and these were not necessarily Republicans. Nor did the Republican regimes in the South hold a monopoly on big spending or corruption. After the war bribery pervaded government transactions North and South, and far more money changed hands in the North. But Reconstruction's critics assailed Republican rule for additional reasons.

Counterattacks

Vexed as they were by northern interference, scalawag "treachery," and high taxes, ex-Confederates especially chafed at black enfranchisement and spoke with dread about the "horror of Negro domination." As soon as congressional Reconstruction took effect, a clamorous campaign began to undermine it. When the state constitutional conventions met, the Democratic press stood ready. Newspapers assailed North Carolina's delegates as an "Ethiopian minstrelsy . . . baboons, monkeys, mules . . . and other jackasses." They demeaned Louisiana's constitution as "the work of ignorant Negroes cooperating with a gang of white adventurers." A Little Rock newspaper denigrated the Arkansas convention as "a foul gathering whose putridity stinks in the nostrils of all decency."

The Democrats delayed political mobilization until the southern states were readmitted to the Union. After readmission, however, the Democrats swung into action, calling themselves Conservatives so as not to repel those former Whigs who might join them. At first they sought to win the votes of blacks; but when that effort failed, they tried other tactics. In 1868–1869 Georgia Democrats challenged the eligibility of black legislators and expelled them from office. In response, the federal government reestablished military rule in Georgia, but determined Democrats still undercut Republican power. In every southern state, they contested elections, backed dissident Republican factions, and were able to elect some

The Ku Klux Klan

The menacing symbol and hooded disguise characterized the Ku Klux Klan's campaign of intimidation during Reconstruction. A Klan flag of 1866 (below) features a fierce emblem and a threatening Latin motto ("Because it always is, because it is everywhere, because it is abominable"). Hooded Klansmen, like this Tennessee nightrider (right), wore colored robes with astrological symbols, such as the moon and stars. The Klan strove to end Republican rule, restore white supremacy, and obliterate, in a southern editor's words, "the preposterous and wicked dogma of negro equality."

Democratic legislators. They also made steady inroads among the scalawags, siphoning some of their votes from the Republicans.

Vigilante efforts to reduce black votes bolstered the Democrats' campaigns to win white ones. Antagonism toward free blacks, long a prominent motif in southern life, resurged after the war. During presidential Reconstruction, when the white South sought to control freedmen's mobility, antiblack violence often erupted. Freedmen's Bureau agents in 1865 itemized a variety of outrages against blacks, including shooting, murder, rape, arson, roasting, and "severe and inhuman beating." Vigilante groups sprang up spontaneously in all parts of the former Confederacy under names like moderators, regulators, and in Louisiana, Knights of the White Camelia. A new group soon rose to dominance. In the spring of 1866, when the Johnson governments were still in power, six young Confederate war veterans in Tennessee formed a social club, the Ku Klux Klan, distinguished by elaborate rituals, hooded costumes, and secret passwords. New Klan dens spread through the state, and within a year

Democratic politicians and former Confederate officers took control of them. By the election of 1868, when black suffrage had become a reality, Klan dens existed in all the southern states, and Klansmen embarked on night raids to intimidate black voters. One of its founders now denounced the Klan as "perverted" and "pernicious," and indeed, it was no longer a social club but a widespread terrorist movement. Reminiscent of the antebellum slave patrols, the Ku Klux Klan became a violent arm of the Democratic party.

The Klan's goals were to suppress black voting, reestablish white supremacy, and topple the Reconstruction governments. Its members attacked Union League officers, Freedmen's Bureau officials, white Republicans, black militia units, economically successful blacks, and black voters. Concentrated in areas where the black and white populations were most evenly balanced and racial tensions greatest, Klan dens adapted their strategies and timing to local conditions. In Mississippi the Klan targeted black schools; in Alabama it concentrated on Republican officeholders. In Arkansas terror reigned in 1868; in Georgia and

Florida Klan strength surged in 1870. Some Democrats denounced Klan members as "cut-throats and riff-raff." But prominent ex-Confederates were also known to be active Klansmen, among them General Nathan Bedford Forrest, the leader of the 1864 Fort Pillow massacre (see Chapter 15). Vigilantism united southern whites of different social classes and drew on the energy of many Confederate veterans. In areas where the Klan was inactive, other vigilante groups took its place.

Republican legislatures outlawed vigilantism through laws providing for fines and imprisonment of offenders. But the state militia could not enforce the laws, and state officials turned to the federal government for help. In May 1870 Congress passed the Enforcement Act to protect black voters. Even this law was unenforceable, because witnesses to violations were afraid to testify against vigilantes, and local juries refused to convict them. The Second Enforcement Act, which provided for federal supervision of southern elections, followed in February 1871. Two months later Congress passed the Third Enforcement Act, or Ku Klux Klan Act, which strengthened the sanctions against those who prevented blacks from voting. It also empowered the president to use federal troops to enforce the law and to suspend the writ of habeas corpus in areas that he declared in insurrection. President Grant suspended the writ in nine South Carolina counties that had been devastated by Klan attacks.

After Congress enacted the three laws, a joint congressional committee launched a full-scale investigation of Klan activities. Victimized blacks and southern politicians of both parties testified. "I have heard of any quantity of horrible deeds," Henry M. Turner, a black minister, politician, and former Union army chaplain told government investigators. "Every man in Georgia who has got any brains must be satisfied, that there are organized bands of night assassins, murderous villains, who have banded themselves together and roam about and kill Republicans, kill any man who has got the name of radical attached to him." While Turner and others testified, the Ku Klux Klan Act generated thousands of arrests; most terrorists, however, escaped conviction.

By 1872 the federal government had effectively suppressed the Klan, but vigilantism had served its purpose. Only a large military presence in the South could have protected black rights, and the government in Washington never provided it. Instead, federal power in the former Confederacy diminished. President Grant steadily reduced troop levels in the South; Congress allowed the Freedmen's Bureau to die in 1869; and the Enforcement acts became dead letters. White southerners, a Georgia politician explained to congressional investigators in 1871, could not discard "a feeling of bitterness, a feeling that the Negro is a sort of instinctual enemy of ours." The battle over Reconstruction was in essence a battle over the implications of emancipation, and it had begun as soon as the war ended.

THE IMPACT OF EMANCIPATION

"The master he says we are all free," a South Carolina slave declared in 1865. "But it don't mean we is white. And it don't mean we is equal." Emancipated slaves faced extreme handicaps. They had no property, tools, or capital and usually possessed meager skills. Only a minority had been trained as artisans, and more than 95 percent were illiterate. Still, the exhilaration of freedom was overwhelming, as slaves realized, "Now I am for myself" and "All that I make is my own." At emancipation they gained the right to their own labor and a new sense of autonomy. Under Reconstruction the freed blacks asserted their independence by seeking to cast off white control and shed the vestiges of slavery.

Confronting Freedom

For the former slaves, mobility was often the first perquisite of liberty. Some moved out of the slave quarters and set up dwellings elsewhere on their plantations; others left their plantations entirely. Landowners found that one freed slave after another vanished, with house servants and artisans leading the way. "I have never in my life met with such ingratitude," one South Carolina mistress exclaimed when a former slave ran off. Field-workers, who had less contact with whites, were more likely to stay behind or more reluctant to leave. Still, flight remained tempting. "The moment they see an opportunity to improve themselves, they will move on," diarist Mary Chesnut observed.

Emancipation stirred waves of migration within the former Confederacy. Some freed slaves left the Upper South for the Deep South and the Southwest—Florida, Mississippi, Arkansas, and Texas—where planters desperately needed labor and paid higher wages. Even more left the countryside for towns and cities, traditional havens of independence for blacks. Urban black populations sometimes doubled or tripled after emancipation. Overall during the 1860s, the urban black population increased by 75 percent, and the number of blacks in small rural towns grew as well. Many migrants eventually returned to their old locales, in search of their families or out of an attachment to the land. But they tended to settle on neighboring plantations rather than with their former owners. Freedom was the major goal. "I's wants to be a free man, cum when I please, and nobody say nuffin to me, nor order me roun'," an Alabama freedman declared to a northern journalist.

Freed blacks' yearnings to find lost family members prompted considerable movement. "They had a passion, not so much for wandering as for getting together," a Freedmen's Bureau official commented. Parents sought children who had been sold; husbands and wives who had been separated by sale, or who lived on different plantations, reunited; and families reclaimed youngsters who were being raised in masters' homes. The Freedmen's Bureau helped former slaves get information about missing relatives and travel to find them. Bureau agents also tried to resolve entanglements over the multiple alliances of spouses who had been separated under slavery.

Reunification efforts often failed. Some fugitive slaves had died during the war or were untraceable. Other ex-slaves had formed new partnerships and could not revive old ones. "I am married," one husband wrote to a former wife (probably in a dictated letter), "and my wife [and I] have two children, and if you and I meet it would make a very dissatisfied family." But there were success stories, too. "I's hunted an' hunted till I track you up here," one freedman told his wife, whom he found in a refugee camp twenty years after their separation by sale.

Once reunited, freed blacks quickly legalized unions formed under slavery, sometimes in mass ceremonies of up to seventy couples. Legal marriage had a tangible impact on family life. Men asserted themselves as household heads; wives and children of able-bodied men often withdrew from the labor force. "When I married my wife, I married her to wait on me and she has got all she can do right here for me and the children," a Tennessee freedman explained. Black women's desire to "play the lady," as southern whites described it, caused planters severe labor shortages.

Before the war at least half of field-workers had been women; in 1866, a southern journal claimed, men performed almost all the field labor. Nevertheless, by the end of Reconstruction, many black women had returned to agricultural work as part of sharecropper families. Others took paid work in cities, as laundresses, cooks, and domestic servants. (Many white women sought employment as well, for the war had incapacitated white breadwinners, reduced the supply of future husbands, and left families destitute or in diminished circumstances.) Still, former slaves continued to view stable, independent domestic life, especially the right to bring up their own children, as a major blessing of freedom. In 1870 eight out of ten black families in the cotton-producing South were two-parent families, about the same proportion as among whites.

Black Institutions

The freed blacks' desire for independence also led to the postwar growth of black churches. During the late 1860s, some freedmen congregated at churches operated by northern missionaries in the South; others withdrew from white-run churches and formed their own. The African Methodist Episcopal church, founded by Philadelphia blacks in the 1790s, gained thousands of new southern members. Negro Baptist churches sprouted everywhere, often growing out of plantation "praise meetings," religious gatherings organized by slaves.

The black churches offered a fervent, participatory experience. They also provided relief, raised funds for schools, and supported Republican policies. From the outset black ministers assumed leading political roles, first in the black conventions of 1865–1866 and later in the Reconstruction governments. After southern Democrats excluded most freedmen from political life at Reconstruction's end, ministers remained the main pillars of authority within black communities.

Black schools played a crucial role for freedmen as well. The ex-slaves eagerly sought literacy for themselves and above all for their children. At emancipation blacks organized their own schools, which the Freedmen's Bureau soon supervised. Northern philanthropic societies paid the wages of instructors, about half of whom were women. These teachers sometimes felt like pioneers in a foreign land. "Our work is just as much missionary work as if we were in

The Freedmen's School
Supported by the Freedmen's Bureau, northern freedmen's aid societies, and black denomina-
tions, freedmen's schools reached about 12 percent of school-age black children in the South by
1870. Here, a northern teacher poses with her students at a school in rural North Carolina.

India or China," a Sea Islands teacher commented. In 1869, just before it expired, the bureau reported more than four thousand black schools in the former Confederacy. Within three years each southern state had a public-school system, at least in principle, generally with separate schools for blacks and whites. Advanced schools for blacks opened as well, to train tradespeople, teachers, and ministers. The Freedmen's Bureau and northern organizations like the American Missionary Association helped to found Howard, Atlanta, and Fisk universities (all started in 1866–1867) and Hampton Institute (1868).

Despite these advances, black education remained limited. Located in towns, most freedmen's schools could not reach the large black rural population. Black public schools, similarly inaccessible to most rural black children, held classes only for very short seasons. Underfunded and inferior, they were sometimes the targets of vigilante attacks. At the end of Reconstruction, more than 80 percent of the black population were illiterate. Still, the proportion of youngsters who could not read and write had declined

and would continue to fall (see table, p. 518). "Perhaps some *will* get an education in a little while. I *knows* de *next generation will*," a freedman told a missionary in 1865. "But . . . we has been kep down *a hundred years* and *I* think it will take *a hundred years to get us back again.*"

School segregation and other forms of racial separation were taken for granted. Some black codes of 1865–1866 had segregated public-transit conveyances and public accommodations. Even after the invalidation of the codes, the custom of segregation had continued on streetcars, steamboats, and trains as well as in churches, theaters, inns, and restaurants. On railroads, for example, whites could ride in the "ladies' car" or first-class car, whereas blacks had to stay in smoking cars or boxcars with benches. In 1870 Senator Charles Sumner began campaigning in Congress for a bill that would desegregate schools, transportation facilities, juries, and public accommodations. After Sumner's death in 1874, Congress honored him by enacting a new law, the Civil Rights Act of 1875, which encompassed many ideas from his program, except

Percentage of Persons Unable to Write, by Age Group, 1870–1890, in South Carolina, Georgia, Alabama, Mississippi, and Louisiana

Age Group	1870	1880	1890
10–14			
Black	78.9	74.1	49.2
White	33.2	34.5	18.7
15–20			
Black	85.3	73.0	54.1
White	24.2	21.0	14.3
Over 20			
Black	90.4	82.3	75.5
White	19.8	17.9	17.1

Source: Roger Ransom and Richard Sutch, *One Kind of Freedom* (Cambridge: Cambridge University Press, 1978), 30.

for the controversial school-integration provision. But the law was rarely enforced, and in 1883, in the *Civil Rights Cases,* the Supreme Court invalidated it. The Fourteenth Amendment did not prohibit discrimination by individuals, the Court ruled, only that perpetrated by the state.

White southerners adamantly rejected the prospect of racial integration, which they insisted would lead to racial amalgamation. "If we have social equality, we shall have intermarriage," one white southerner contended, "and if we have intermarriage, we shall degenerate." Urban blacks, the most likely to be affected by segregation practices, sometimes challenged them, and black legislators promoted bills to desegregate public transit. Some black officeholders decried all forms of racial separatism. "The sooner we as a people forget our sable complexion," said a Mobile official, "the better it will be for us as a race." But most freed blacks were less interested in "social equality," in the sense of interracial mingling, than in black liberty and community. The newly formed postwar elite—teachers, ministers, and politicians— served black constituencies and therefore had a vested interest in separate black institutions. Rural blacks, too, widely preferred all-black institutions. They had little desire to mix with whites. On the contrary, they sought freedom from white control. Above all else, they wanted to secure personal independence by acquiring land.

Land, Labor, and Sharecropping

"The sole ambition of the freedman," a New Englander wrote from South Carolina in 1865, "appears to be to become the owner of a little piece of land, there to erect a humble home, and to dwell in peace and security, at his own free will and pleasure." Indeed, to freed blacks everywhere, "forty acres and a mule" promised emancipation from plantation labor, from white domination, and from cotton, the "slave crop." Just as garden plots provided a measure of autonomy under slavery, so did landownership signify economic independence afterward. "We want to be placed on land until we are able to buy it and make it our own," a black minister had told General Sherman in Georgia during the war. Some freedmen defended their right to the land on which they lived, by pointing out that they and their forebears had worked on it for decades without pay.

But freedmen's visions of landownership failed to materialize, for, as we have seen, large-scale land reform never occurred. Proposals to confiscate or redistribute Confederate property failed in Congress as well as in the southern state legislatures. Some freedmen did obtain land with the help of the Union army or the Freedmen's Bureau, and black soldiers sometimes pooled resources to buy land, as on the Sea Islands (see Chapter 15). The federal government also attempted to provide ex-slaves with land. In 1866 Congress passed the Southern Homestead Act, which set aside 44 million acres of land in five southern states for freedmen and loyal whites. Not only did this acreage contain poor soil, but few former slaves had the resources to survive even until their first harvest. Thus although about four thousand blacks were resettled on homesteads under the law, most were unable to establish farms. (White southern homesteaders fared little better.) By the end of Reconstruction, only a small minority of former slaves in each state owned working farms. In Georgia in 1876, for instance, blacks controlled a mere 1.3 percent of total acreage. Without large-scale land reform, the obstacles to black landownership remained overwhelming.

What were these obstacles? First, most freedmen lacked the capital to buy land and the equipment needed to work it. Furthermore, white southerners on the whole opposed selling land to blacks. Most important, planters sought to preserve a black labor force. They insisted that freedmen would work only under coercion, and not at all if the possibility of landownership arose. As soon as the war ended, the white South took steps to make sure that black labor would remain available where it was needed, on the plantations.

During presidential Reconstruction, southern state legislatures tried to limit black mobility and to preserve a captive labor force through the black codes. Under labor contracts in effect in 1865–1866, freedmen received wages, housing, food, and clothing in exchange for fieldwork. With cash so scarce, wages usually took the form of a very small share of the crop, often one-eighth or less, divided among the entire plantation work force. Serving as mediators between former slaves and landowners, Freedmen's Bureau agents actively promoted the new labor system; they encouraged freedmen to sign labor contracts and tried to ensure adequate wages. Imbued with the northern free-labor ideology, which held that wage workers could rise to the status of self-supporting tradesmen and property owners, bureau officials and agents endorsed black wage labor as an interim arrangement that would lead to economic independence. "You must begin at the bottom of the ladder and climb up," Freedmen's Bureau head O. O. Howard exhorted a group of Louisiana freedmen in 1865.

But the freedmen disliked the new wage system, especially the use of gang labor, which resembled the work pattern under slavery. Planters had complaints, too. In some regions the black labor force had shrunk to half its prewar size or less, due to the migration of freedmen and to black women's withdrawal from fieldwork. Once united in defense of slavery, planters now competed for black workers. Moreover, their labor problems mounted, for the freedmen, whom planters often scorned as lazy and incorrigible, did not intend to work as long or as hard as they had labored under slavery. One planter estimated that workers accomplished only "two-fifths of what they did under the old system"; and as productivity fell, so did land values. Some planters considered importing white immigrant labor, but they doubted that whites would perform black fieldwork for long. To top off the planters' problems, cotton prices plummeted, for during the war northern and foreign buyers had found new sources of cotton in Egypt and India, and the world supply had vastly increased. Finally, the harvests of 1866 and 1867 were extremely poor. By then an agricultural impasse had been reached: landowners lacked labor and freedmen lacked land. But free blacks, unlike slaves, had the right to enter into contracts—or to refuse to do so—and thereby gained some leverage.

Planters and freedmen began experimenting with new labor schemes, including the division of plantations into small tenancies (see "A Place in Time"). Sharecropping, the most widespread arrangement, evolved as a compromise. Under the sharecropping system, landowners subdivided large plantations into farms of thirty to fifty acres, which they rented to freedmen under annual leases for a share of the crop, usually half. Freedmen preferred this system to wage labor because it represented a step toward independence. The decentralized plan enabled heads of households to use the labor of family members. Moreover, a half-share of the crop far exceeded the fraction that freedmen had received as wages under the black codes. Planters often spoke of sharecropping as a capitulation, but they gained as well. Landowners retained power over tenants, because annual leases did not have to be renewed; they could expel undesirable tenants at the end of the year. Planters also shared the risk of planting with tenants: if a crop failed, both suffered the loss. Most important, planters retained control of their land and in some cases extended their holdings. The most productive land, therefore, remained in the hands of a small group of owners, as before the war. Sharecropping forced planters to relinquish day-to-day control over the labor of freedmen, but it helped to preserve the planter elite.

Sharecropping arrangements varied widely and were not universal. On sugar and rice plantations, the wage system continued. Some freedmen remained independent renters. Some landowners leased areas to white tenants who then subcontracted with black labor. But by the end of the 1860s, the plantation tradition had given way to sharecropping in the cotton South, and the new system continued to expand. A severe depression in 1873 drove many black renters into sharecropping. By then thousands of independent white farmers had become sharecroppers as well. Stung by wartime losses and by the dismal postwar economy, they sank into debt and lost their land to creditors. Many backcountry residents, no longer able to get by on subsistence farming, shifted to cash crops like cotton and suffered the same fate. At the end of Reconstruction, one-third of the white farmers in Mississippi, for instance, worked as sharecroppers.

By 1880, 80 percent of the land in the cotton-producing states had been subdivided into tenancies, most of it farmed by sharecroppers, white and black. Indeed, white sharecroppers now outnumbered black ones, although a higher proportion of southern blacks,

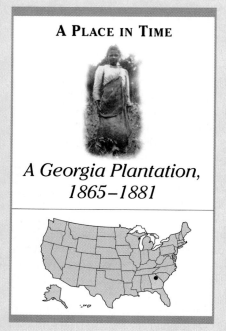

The transformation of the Barrow plantation in Oglethorpe County, Georgia, is a microcosmic illustration of the striking changes that occurred in southern agriculture during Reconstruction. Before the Civil War, David Crenshaw Barrow had been the absentee owner of a two-thousand-acre plantation long known as the Pope Place. He had inherited the land through his first wife, Sarah Elizabeth Pope. The owner of several other plantations as well, Barrow had possessed some 400 slaves, about 135 of whom had lived on the "Pope Place." Assisted by slave foremen, an overseer had run the plantation. The overseer had lived in the main plantation house, from where he had kept a watchful eye on the slave quarters.

After the war the plantation changed in so many ways that by 1881, according to Barrow's son, David Crenshaw Barrow, Jr., "the place would now hardly be recognized." But the changes had occurred in stages.

The critical period immediately followed the war. At emancipation some of Barrow's former slaves had left the plantation, probably for nearby towns or other plantations. Those remaining had signed

annual labor contracts with Barrow. Divided into two competing squads and supervised by a hired foreman, the freedmen grew cotton under the gang system. They received wages in the form of a share of the crop, with a reward going to the squad that worked more efficiently. Barrow liked the new system, but the freedmen did not. Within a few years, they rebelled against the hired foreman, "each man feeling the very natural desire to be his own 'boss' and farm to himself," Barrow's son wrote. The squads split into smaller groups and spread over the plantation. Still working for a small share of the crop, they continued to use the owner's mules and equipment. Now Barrow found the system unsatisfactory. He claimed that the freedmen mistreated the mules and failed to deliver his full share of the crop.

In the late 1860s, life on the Barrow plantation entered a third phase. One of the first planters in his area to subdivide his land, Barrow transformed the plantation into tenant farms of twenty-five to thirty acres. With this change, the freedmen moved their households from the old slave quarters to their own farms. They typically set up their log cabins at springs around

Tenants on the Barrow Plantation
Children pick cotton on the Barrow plantation in the late nineteenth century.

David Crenshaw Barrow, Jr.
The young Barrow posed for this photograph around the time that his article in Scribner's Monthly *appeared.*

The Barrow Plantation, 1860 and 1881
These maps show the changes that transformed the Barrow plantation after the Civil War.

the plantation and then added outhouses, stables, corncribs, and fodderhouses. Each head of family signed an annual contract, agreeing to pay a rent of 500 to 750 pounds of cotton plus varied amounts of other crops. As tenant farmers, the freedmen raised cotton (about half their crop), corn, and vegetables; the men did the plowing, and women and children the hoeing. Using uncultivated land for pasture, the tenants also raised hogs, chickens, and a few cattle. Barrow sold each farmer a mule on credit, and he set aside an acre on the edge of the plantation for a church and a school, which was open three months a year.

In 1881 David Crenshaw Barrow lived in the main house with two family members, probably his second wife (a former New Englander) and an unmarried daughter, Clara. The plantation's tenants numbered 162, at least half of them children. One out of four families was named Barrow. When David Crenshaw Barrow, Jr., summed up plantation life in 1881 for the readers of *Scribner's Monthly*, he emphasized "how completely the relations between the races at the South have changed." For instance, his father's tenants needed little supervision. "Very many negro farmers are capable of directing the working of their own crops," he explained,

"and not a few object to directions." The younger Barrow expressed pride that no tenant on his father's land had joined the "exodus" movement that had drawn blacks out of the South in the late 1870s. He also took pleasure in the fact that the most troublesome slave, Lem Bryant, once beyond the overseer's control, had become the most industrious tenant—a transformation Barrow, Jr., attributed to the impact of freedom.

Claiming satisfaction with the changes that he and his father had seen, planter Barrow's son assured his readers that southern freedmen were content with their lives as tenant farmers. "In Georgia, the negro has adapted himself to his new circumstances, and freedom fits him as if it had been cut out and made for him," he reported. "As a people, they are happy; they have become suited to their new estate and it to them." The younger Barrow's positive view of postwar farming arrangements might well have been challenged by the growing number of southerners, black and white, who had become mired in debt as sharecroppers. His article in *Scribner's*, however, written for a northern audience, was intended to convey a political message. Not only had the one-time slaves adjusted to emancipation, Barrow, Jr., sug-

gested, but so had their former owners. This concession was part of the national celebration of reunion that followed the collapse of Reconstruction.

Few if any of David Crenshaw Barrow's nine offspring, all born on the "Pope Place," found a vocation in southern agriculture. Two sons had died as young men, and another in a Civil War battle. By 1881 the surviving Barrow children, save Clara, had moved away from their father's home and chosen a variety of occupations. Pope Barrow, the oldest, became a lawyer and a judge and would later serve as U.S. senator from Georgia. Thomas Barrow, who had fought with the Confederate army, first turned to business and then became a Baptist minister. Lucy Barrow married the son of a prominent Georgian, Howell Cobb, who had once been considered for the post of president of the Confederacy. Nellie Barrow also married and moved to Sapelo Island off the coast of Georgia. David Crenshaw Barrow, Jr., began his career as a lawyer but in 1879 became a mathematics teacher at the University of Georgia in Athens, not far from the Oglethorpe County plantation. Barrow, Jr., retained an avid interest in farming, which he later practiced in partnership with the son of his father's former overseer.

Southern Share-cropping, 1880

The depressed economy of the late 1870s caused poverty and debt, increased tenancy among white farmers, and forced many renters, black and white, into sharecropping. By 1880 the sharecropping system pervaded most southern counties, with the highest concentrations in the cotton belt from South Carolina to eastern Texas.

SOURCE: U.S. Census Office, Tenth Census, 1880, *Report of the Production of Agriculture* (Washington, D.C.: Government Printing Office, 1883), Table 5.

Percentage of sharecropped farms, by county

- 35% – 80%
- 26% – 34%
- 20% – 25%
- 13% – 19%
- 0% – 12%

about 75 percent, were involved in the system. Changes in marketing and finance, meanwhile, made the sharecroppers' lot increasingly precarious.

Toward a Crop-Lien Economy

Before the Civil War, planters had depended on factors, or middlemen, who sold them supplies, extended credit, and marketed their crops through urban merchants. These long-distance credit arrangements were backed by the high value and liquidity of slave property. When slavery ended, the factorage system collapsed. The postwar South, with hundreds of thousands of tenants and sharecroppers, needed a far more localized network of credit.

Into the gap stepped the rural merchants (often themselves planters), who advanced supplies to tenants and sharecroppers on credit and sold their crops to wholesalers or textile manufacturers. Because renters had no property to use as collateral, the merchants secured their loans with a lien, or claim, on each farmer's next crop. They charged exorbitant interest of 50 percent or more and quickly drew many tenants and sharecroppers into a cycle of indebtedness. Owing part of the crop to a landowner for rent, a sharecropper also owed a rural merchant a large sum (perhaps amounting to the rest of his crop, or more)

for supplies. Often, an illiterate tenant could not keep track of his financial arrangements, and a merchant could easily take advantage of him. "A man that didn't know how to count would always lose," an Arkansas freedman later explained. Once a tenant's debts or alleged debts exceeded the value of his crop, he was tied to the land, to cotton, and to sharecropping.

By the end of Reconstruction, sharecropping and crop liens had transformed southern agriculture. They bound the entire region to staple production and prevented crop diversification, for despite plunging cotton prices, creditors—landowners and merchants—insisted that tenants raise only easily marketable cash crops. Short of capital, planters could no longer invest in new equipment or improve their land by such techniques as crop rotation and contour plowing. Soil depletion, land erosion, and agricultural backwardness soon locked much of the South into a cycle of poverty. Overall, postwar changes in southern agriculture left the region with extremely bleak economic prospects.

But the major victims of the new agricultural arrangements were the indebted tenant farmers, who had been trapped in a system of what has been called debt peonage. Raising cotton for distant markets, for prices over which they had no control, remained the only survival route open to poor farmers, regardless of race. But the low income thus derived often forced them into sharecropping and crop liens, from which escape was difficult. Black tenants, for whom neither landownership nor economic independence ever materialized, suffered further handicaps. Not only were their rights as workers limited, but when Reconstruction ended, their political rights dwindled too. As one southern regime after another returned to Democratic control, freedmen could no longer look to the state governments for protection. Nor could they turn to the federal government, for northern politicians were preoccupied with their own problems.

NEW CONCERNS IN THE NORTH

The nomination of Ulysses S. Grant for president in 1868 launched a chaotic era in national politics. Grant's two terms in office featured political scandals, a party revolt, a massive depression, and a steady retreat from Reconstruction policies. By the mid-1870s, northern voters cared more about the economic climate, unemployment, labor unrest, and currency problems than about the "southern question." Responsive to the shift in popular mood, Republicans became eager to end sectional conflict and consequently turned their backs on the freedmen of the South.

Grantism

Republicans had good reason to pass over longtime party leaders and nominate the popular Grant. A war hero, Grant was endorsed by Union veterans and admired throughout the North. Although identified with Radical Republican views by 1867, he had nonetheless escaped the bitter feuds of Reconstruction politics. At first a Johnson adviser, Grant had broken with Johnson during the tenure-of-office crisis and become his competitor. Even before Grant's nomination, important visitors to Washington called on him as well as Johnson.

To oppose Grant in the 1868 election, the Democrats nominated New York governor Horatio Seymour, arch-critic of the Lincoln administration during the war. Seymour opposed Reconstruction and advocated "sound money," or the withdrawal of greenbacks from circulation, a policy begun by Hugh McCulloch, Johnson's treasury secretary. Grant, who defended Reconstruction, ran on his personal popularity more than on issues. Although he carried all but eight states in the election, the popular vote was very close; in the South, the votes of newly enfranchised freedmen provided the margin of victory. When he was inaugurated, Grant vowed to execute all the laws whether he agreed with them or not, to support sound money, and to follow a humane policy toward the Indians.

A strong leader in war, Grant proved a passive president. Although he lacked Johnson's instinct for disaster, he had little skill at politics. Many of his cabinet appointees—business executives, army men, and family friends—were mediocre if not unscrupulous, and a string of scandals plagued his administration. In 1869 financier Jay Gould and his partner Jim Fisk attempted to corner the gold market with the help of Grant's brother-in-law, a New York speculator. When gold prices tumbled, Gould salvaged his own fortune, but investors were ruined and Grant's reputation was tarnished. Then before the president's first term ended, his vice president, Schuyler Colfax, was found to be linked to the Crédit Mobilier, a fraudulent construction company created to skim off the profits of the Union Pacific Railroad. Using government funds granted to the railroad, the Union Pacific directors awarded padded construction contracts to the Crédit Mobilier, of which they were also the directors. Discredited, Colfax was dropped from the Grant ticket in 1872. More trouble lay ahead. Grant's private secretary, Orville Babcock, was unmasked in 1875 after taking money from the "whiskey ring," a group of distillers who bribed federal agents to avoid paying millions in

The Election of 1868

Candidates	Parties	Electoral Vote	Popular Vote	Percentage of Popular Vote
ULYSSES S. GRANT	Republican	214	3,013,421	52.7
Horatio Seymour	Democratic	80	2,706,829	47.3

Boss Tweed
Thomas Nast's cartoons in Harper's Weekly *helped topple New York Democratic boss William M. Tweed (photo at far left), who, with his associates, embodied corruption on a large scale. The Tweed Ring had granted lucrative franchises to companies they controlled, padded construction bills, practiced graft and extortion, and exploited every opportunity to plunder the city's funds.*

whiskey taxes. And in 1876 voters learned that Grant's secretary of war, William E. Belknap, had taken bribes to sell lucrative Indian trading posts in Oklahoma. Impeached and disgraced, Belknap resigned.

Although Grant was not personally involved in the scandals, he loyally defended his subordinates. To his critics, "Grantism" came to stand for fraud, bribery, and corruption in office. Such evils spread far beyond Washington. In Pennsylvania, for example, the Standard Oil Company and the Pennsylvania Railroad controlled the legislature. Urban politics also provided rich opportunities for graft and swindles. The New York City press revealed in 1872 that Democratic boss William M. Tweed, the "Grand Sachem" of Tammany Hall, led a ring that looted the city treasury and collected an estimated $200 million in kickbacks and payoffs. When Mark Twain and coauthor Charles Dudley Warner published their satiric novel *The Gilded Age** (1873), readers recognized the book's speculators, self-promoters, and maniacal opportunists as familiar types in public life.

Grant had some success in foreign policy. In 1872 his competent secretary of state, Hamilton Fish, engineered the settlement of the *Alabama* claims with

---

*The term "Gilded Age" was subsequently used to refer to the decades from the 1870s to the 1890s.

England. To compensate for damage done by British-built raiders sold to the Confederacy during the war, an international tribunal awarded the United States $15.5 million. But the Grant administration undercut this success with a fiasco when it tried to add nonadjacent territory to the United States, as the Johnson administration had done. In 1867 Johnson's secretary of state, William H. Seward, had negotiated a treaty in which the United States bought Alaska from Russia at the bargain price of $7.2 million. Although the press mocked "Seward's Ice Box," the purchase kindled expansionists' hopes. In 1870 Grant decided to annex the Caribbean island nation of Santo Domingo. Formerly known as Hispaniola and today called the Dominican Republic, Santo Domingo had been passed back and forth since the late eighteenth century among France, Spain, and Haiti. Annexation, Grant believed, would promote Caribbean trade and provide a haven for persecuted southern blacks, who might settle among the Dominicans. American speculators anticipated windfalls from land sales, commerce, and mining in Santo Domingo. But Congress disliked Grant's plan. Senator Charles Sumner denounced the scheme as an imperialist "dance of blood." The Senate rejected the annexation treaty and further diminished Grant's reputation.

The Election of 1872

Candidates	Parties	Electoral Vote	Popular Vote	Percentage of Popular Vote
ULYSSES S. GRANT	Republican	286	3,596,745	55.6
Horace Greeley*	Democratic		2,843,446	43.9

*Upon Greeley's death shortly after the election, the electors supporting him divided their votes among minor candidates.

As the election of 1872 approached, dissident Republicans expressed fears that "Grantism" at home and abroad would ruin the party. Even Grant's new running mate, Henry Wilson, referred to the president privately as a millstone, or burden, on his fellow Republicans. The dissidents took action. Led by a combination of former Radicals—including Sumner (now Grant's enemy), Senator Carl Schurz of Missouri, and Congressman George Julian of Indiana—and Republicans left out of Grant's "Great Barbecue," the president's critics formed their own party, the Liberal Republicans.

The Liberals' Revolt

The Liberal Republican revolt marked a turning point in Reconstruction history. By splitting the Republican party, it undermined support for Republican southern policy. The Liberals attacked the "regular" Republicans on several key issues. Denouncing "Grantism" and "spoilsmen" (political hacks who gained party office), they demanded civil-service reform to bring the "best men" into government. Rejecting the usual Republican high-tariff policy, they espoused free trade. Most important, the Liberals condemned "bayonet rule" in the South. Even some Republicans once known for radicalism did a turnabout, claiming that Reconstruction had achieved its goal: blacks had been enfranchised and could henceforth manage for themselves. Corruption in government, North and South, they asserted, now posed a greater danger than Confederate resurgence. In the South, indeed, corrupt Republican regimes were *kept* in power, the Liberals said, because the "best men"—the most capable politicians—were ex-Confederates who had been barred from officeholding.

For president the new party bypassed Charles Sumner and nominated *New York Tribune* editor Horace Greeley, who had inconsistently supported both a stringent reconstruction policy and leniency toward former rebels. The Democrats endorsed Greeley as well, despite his longtime condemnation of them. Their campaign slogan explained their support: "Anything to Beat Grant." Republican reformers were suddenly allied with the Democratic party that they had recently castigated as a "sewer" of treasonous sentiments.

Horace Greeley proved so diligent a campaigner that he worked himself to death making speeches from the back of a campaign train. He died a few weeks after the election. Grant, who won 56 percent of the popular vote, carried all the northern states as well as a majority of the sixteen southern and border states. But the division among Republicans affected Reconstruction. To deprive the Liberals of a campaign issue, Grant Republicans in Congress, the "regulars," passed an amnesty act that effectively allowed all but a few hundred ex-Confederate officials to hold office. The flood of private amnesty acts that followed convinced white southerners that any ex-Confederate save Jefferson Davis could rise to power. During Grant's second term, Republican desires to discard the "southern question" mounted as a depression of unprecedented scope gripped the whole nation.

The Panic of 1873

With the postwar years came accelerated industrialization, rapid economic expansion, and frantic speculation. Investors rushed to take advantage of rising prices, new markets, high tariffs, and seemingly boundless opportunities. Railroads provided the biggest lure. In May 1869 railroad executives drove a golden spike into the ground at Promontory Point, Utah, joining the Union Pacific and Central Pacific lines (see Chapter 17). The first transcontinental railroad heralded a new era. By 1873 almost four hundred railroad corporations crisscrossed the Northeast, consuming tons of coal and miles of steel rail from the mines and mills of Pennsylvania and neighboring states. Transforming the northern economy, the railroad boom led entrepreneurs to overspeculate, with drastic results.

Philadelphia banker Jay Cooke, who had helped finance the Union effort with his bond campaign during the Civil War, had taken over a new transcontinental line, the Northern Pacific, in 1869. Northern Pacific securities sold briskly for several years, but in 1873 the line's construction costs outran new investments. In September of that year, his vaults full of bonds he could no longer sell, Cooke failed to meet his obligations, and his bank, the largest in the nation, shut down. Smaller firms collapsed, as did the stock market. This Panic of 1873 triggered a five-year depression that wrought widespread devastation. Banks closed, farm prices plummeted, steel furnaces stood idle, and one out of four railroads failed. Within two years, eighteen thousand businesses went bankrupt, and by 1878 3 million employees were out of jobs. Those still at work suffered repeated wage cuts, labor protests mounted, and industrial violence spread (see Chapter 18). The depression of the 1870s revealed the conflicts of a new, industrial America.

The depression also fed a dispute over currency that had begun in 1865. The Civil War had created fiscal chaos. During the war, Americans had used both national bank notes, yellow in color, which would eventually be converted into gold, and greenbacks, a paper currency not "backed" by a particular weight in gold. To stabilize the postwar currency, greenbacks would have to be withdrawn from circulation. This "sound-money" policy, favored by investors, was implemented by Treasury Secretary Hugh McCulloch with the backing of Congress. But those who depended on easy credit, both indebted farmers and manufacturers, wanted an expanding currency; that is, more greenbacks. Once the depression began, demands for such "easy money" rose. The issue divided both major parties and was compounded by another one: how to repay the federal debt.

During the war the Union government had borrowed what were then astronomical sums, on whatever terms it could get, mainly through the sale of war bonds—in effect, short-term federal IOUs—to private citizens. By 1869 the issue of war-debt repayment was straining the Republican party, whose support came from voters with diverse financial interests. To pacify bondholders, Senator John Sherman of Ohio and other Republican leaders obtained passage of the Public Credit Act of 1869, which promised to pay the war debt in "coin." Holders of war bonds expected no less; in fact, they expected payment in coin, although many had bought their bonds with greenbacks!

With investors reassured by the Public Credit Act, Sherman guided legislation through Congress that swapped the old short-term bonds for new ones payable over the next generation. In 1872 another bill in effect defined "coin" as "gold coin" by dropping the traditional silver dollar from the official coinage. Through a feat of ingenious compromise, which placated investors and debtors, Sherman preserved the public credit, the currency, and Republican unity. In 1875 he engineered the Specie Resumption Act, which promised to put the nation effectively on the gold standard in 1879, while tossing a few more immediate but less important bones to Republican voters who wanted "easy money." Grant, no financial theorist, signed this act.

The Republican leadership acted not a moment too soon, because when the Democrats gained control of the House in 1875, with the depression in full force, a verbal storm broke out. Many Democrats and some Republicans passionately demanded that the silver dollar be restored in order to expand the currency and relieve the depression. These "free-silver" advocates secured passage of the Bland-Allison Act of 1878, which partially restored silver coinage. The law required the treasury to buy $2 million to $4 million worth of silver each month and turn it into coin but did not revive the silver standard. In 1876 other expansionists formed the Greenback party, which adopted the debtors' cause and fought to keep greenbacks in circulation. But despite the election of fourteen Greenback congressmen, they did not get even as far as the free-silver people had. As the nation emerged from depression in 1879, the clamor for "easy money" subsided, only to resurge in the 1890s (see Chapter 21). The controversial "money question" of the 1870s, never permanently solved, gave politicians and voters another reason to focus on new northern issues and forget about the South.

Reconstruction and the Constitution

The Supreme Court of the 1870s also played a role in weakening northern support for Reconstruction. In the wartime crisis, few cases of note had come before the Court. After the war, however, constitutional questions surged into prominence.

First, would the Court support congressional laws to protect freedmen's rights? The decision in *Ex parte Milligan* (1866) suggested not. In this case, the Court declared that a military commission established by the president or Congress could not try civilians in areas remote from war where the civil courts were functioning. Thus special military courts to enforce the Supplementary Freedmen's Bureau Act were doomed. Second, would the Court sabotage the congressional Reconstruction plan, as Republicans feared? Their qualms were valid, for if the Union was indissoluble, as the North had claimed during the war, then the concept of *restoring* states to the Union would be meaningless. In *Texas* v. *White* (1869), the Court ruled that although the Union was indissoluble and secession was legally impossible, the process of Reconstruction was still constitutional. It was grounded in Congress's power to ensure each state a republican form of government and to recognize the legitimate government in any state.

The 1869 decision protected the Republicans' Reconstruction plan. But during the 1870s, when cases arose involving the Fourteenth and Fifteenth amendments, the Court backed away from Reconstruction policy. Significantly, most of the justices at this time were Republicans who had been appointed to the Court by Lincoln and Grant.

In the *Slaughterhouse* cases of 1873, the Supreme Court began to chip away at the Fourteenth Amendment. The cases involved a business monopoly rather than freedmen's rights, but they provided an opportunity to interpret the amendment narrowly. In 1869 the Louisiana legislature had granted a monopoly over the New Orleans slaughterhouse business to one firm and had closed down all other slaughterhouses in the interest of public health. The excluded butchers brought suit. The state had deprived them of their lawful occupation without due process of law, they claimed, and such action violated the Fourteenth Amendment, which guaranteed that no state could "abridge the privileges or immunities" of U.S. citizens. The Supreme Court upheld the Louisiana legislature by issuing a doctrine of "dual citizenship." The Fourteenth Amendment, declared the Court, protected only the rights of *national* citizenship, such as the right of interstate travel or the right to federal protection when on the high seas. It did not protect those basic civil rights that fell to citizens by virtue of their *state* citizenship. Therefore, the federal government was not obliged to protect such rights against violation by the states. The

Slaughterhouse decision came close to nullifying the intent of the Fourteenth Amendment—to secure freedmen's rights against state encroachment.

The Supreme Court again backed away from Reconstruction in two cases involving the Enforcement Act of 1870. The case of *U.S.* v. *Reese* (1876) centered on Kentucky officials who, after barring blacks from voting, had been indicted in 1873 by a Kentucky federal court under the First Enforcement Act. In its decision in favor of the officials, the Supreme Court stated that the Fifteenth Amendment did not "confer the right of suffrage upon anyone." It merely prohibited the hindrance of voting on the basis of race, color, or previous condition of servitude. Since the Enforcement Act prohibited the hindrance of *anyone* from voting for *any* reason (that is, since it did not repeat the exact wording of the amendment), the Court declared its crucial sections, and the Kentucky indictment, invalid. Another 1876 case, *U.S.* v. *Cruikshank*, concerned the indictment under the 1870 Enforcement Act of white Louisianians after the Colfax massacre, a battle between armed whites and black state militiamen in which seventy blacks had surrendered, half of whom were then murdered. The Fourteenth Amendment, contended the Court, prohibited only the encroachment on individual rights by a *state*, not by other individuals; "ordinary crime" was not the target of federal law. The decision threw out the indictments and, with them, the effectiveness of the Enforcement Act.

Continuing its retreat from Reconstruction, the Supreme Court in 1883 invalidated both the Civil Rights Act of 1875 and the Ku Klux Klan Act of 1871 and later upheld segregation laws (see Chapter 21). These decisions cumulatively dismantled the Reconstruction policies that Republicans had sponsored after the war. The 1870s rulings that initiated the judicial retreat had a more immediate impact as well. They confirmed rising northern sentiment that Reconstruction's egalitarian goals could not be enforced.

Republicans in Retreat

The Republicans did not reject Reconstruction suddenly but rather disengaged from it gradually. The withdrawal process began with Grant's election to the presidency in 1868. Although not one of the architects of Reconstruction policy, Grant defended that policy and tried to enforce the laws. But he shared with most Americans a belief in decentralized government and a reluctance to assert federal authority in local and state affairs.

During the 1870s, as the northern military presence shrank in the South, Republican idealism waned in the North. The Liberal Republican revolt of 1872 eroded what remained of radicalism. Although the "regular" Republicans, who backed Grant, continued to defend Reconstruction in the 1872 election, many held ambivalent views. Commercial and industrial interests now dominated both wings of the party, and Grant supporters had greater zeal for doing business in and with the South than for rekindling sectional strife. After the Democrats showed renewed strength by winning control of the House in the 1874 elections, in a nationwide sweep, Reconstruction became a political liability.

By 1875 the Radical Republicans, so prominent in the 1860s, had vanished from the political scene. Chase, Stevens, and Sumner were dead. Other Radicals had lost office or had abandoned their former convictions. "Waving the Bloody Shirt," or defaming Democratic opponents by reviving wartime animosity, now struck many Republicans, including former Radicals, as counterproductive. Party leaders reported that voters were "sick of carpet-bag government" and tiring of both the "southern question" and the "Negro question." It now seemed pointless to continue the unpopular and expensive policy of military intervention in the South to prop up Republican regimes that even President Grant found corrupt. Finally, few Republicans shared the egalitarian spirit that had animated Stevens and Sumner. Politics aside, Republican leaders and voters generally agreed with southern Democrats that blacks, although worthy of freedom, were inferior to whites. To insist on black equality would be a thankless, divisive, and politically suicidal undertaking. Moreover, it would quash any hope of reunion between the regions. The Republicans' retreat from Reconstruction set the stage for its demise in 1877.

RECONSTRUCTION ABANDONED

"We are in a very hot political contest just now," a Mississippi planter wrote to his daughter in 1875, "with a good prospect of turning out the carpetbag thieves by whom we have been robbed for the past six to ten years." Similar contests raged through the South in the

The White League
Alabama's White League, formed in 1874, strove to oust Republicans from office by intimidating black voters. To political cartoonist Thomas Nast, such vigilante tactics suggested an alliance between the White League and the outlawed Ku Klux Klan.

1870s, as the resentment of white majorities grew and Democratic influence surged. By the end of 1872, the Democrats had regained power in Tennessee, Virginia, Georgia, and North Carolina. Within three years they won control in Texas, Alabama, Arkansas, and Mississippi. As the 1876 elections approached, Republican rule survived in only three states—South Carolina, Florida, and Louisiana. Democratic victories in the state elections of 1876 and political bargaining in Washington in 1877 abruptly ended what little remained of Reconstruction.

Redeeming the South

After 1872 the Republicans' collapse in the South accelerated. Congressional amnesty enabled almost all ex-Confederate officials to regain office, divisions among the Republicans loosened their party's weak grip on the southern electorate, and attrition diminished Republican ranks. Some carpetbaggers gave up and returned North, whereas others, including supporters of Liberal Republicans in the divisive 1872 election, shifted to the Democratic party. Scalawags de-

The Duration of Republican Rule in the Ex-Confederate States

Former Confederate States	Readmission to the Union Under Congressional Reconstruction	Democrats (Conservatives) Gain Control	Duration of Republican Rule
Alabama	June 25, 1868	November 14, 1874	6½ years
Arkansas	June 22, 1868	November 10, 1874	6½ years
Florida	June 25, 1868	January 2, 1877	8½ years
Georgia	July 15, 1870	November 1, 1871	1 year
Louisiana	June 25, 1868	January 2, 1877	8½ years
Mississippi	February 23, 1870	November 3, 1875	5½ years
North Carolina	June 25, 1868	November 3, 1870	2 years
South Carolina	June 25, 1868	November 12, 1876	8 years
Tennessee	July 24, 1866*	October 4, 1869	3 years
Texas	March 30, 1870	January 14, 1873	3 years
Virginia	January 26, 1870	October 5, 1869[†]	0 years

*Admitted before start of Congressional Reconstruction.
[†]Democrats gained control before readmission.
Source: John Hope Franklin, *Reconstruction After the Civil War* (Chicago: University of Chicago Press, 1962), 231.

serted in even larger numbers. Southerners who had joined the Republicans to moderate rampant radicalism tired of northern interference; once "home rule" by Democrats became a possibility, staying Republican meant going down with a sinking ship. Scalawag defections ruined Republican prospects. In some states, as white southerners fled the Republican party, blacks became more powerful within it, thus polarizing voters into white and black camps. Unable to win new white votes or retain the old ones, the always precarious Republican coalition fell apart.

Meanwhile, the Democrats mobilized grass roots support and overcame the white voter apathy that had plagued the early days of Reconstruction. The resurrected southern Democratic party was not a pillar of unity. Within it, businessmen who envisioned an industrialized "New South" opposed an agrarian faction called the Bourbons, who represented the old planter elite. But all Democrats shared a major goal: to oust the Republicans from office. Their tactics varied from state to state. Alabama Democrats won by promising to cut taxes and by getting out the white vote. In Louisiana the "White League," a vigilante organization formed in 1874, undermined the Republicans' hold. Intimidation also proved effective in Mississippi, where violent incidents—like the 1874 slaughter in Vicksburg of about three hundred blacks by rampaging whites—terrorized black voters. In 1875 the "Mississippi plan" took ef-

fect: local Democratic clubs armed their members, dispersed Republican meetings, patrolled voter-registration places, and marched through black areas. "The Republicans are paralyzed through fear and will not act," the anguished carpetbag governor of Mississippi wrote to his wife. "Why should I fight a hopeless battle . . . when no possible good to the Negro or anybody else would result?" In 1876, South Carolina's "Rifle Clubs" and "Red Shirts," armed groups that threatened Republicans, continued the scare tactics that had worked so well in Mississippi.

New outbursts of intimidation did not completely squelch black voting. Many southern blacks continued to vote until the end of Reconstruction and after. But the Democrats deprived the Republicans of enough black votes to win state elections. In some counties they encouraged freedmen to vote Democratic at supervised polls where voters cast their ballots in public by placing a card with a party label in a box. In other instances employers and landowners impeded black suffrage. Labor contracts included clauses barring attendance at political meetings; planters used the threat of eviction to keep sharecroppers in line. Since the Enforcement acts could not be enforced, intimidation and economic pressure succeeded.

Redemption, the word Democrats used to describe their return to power, meant more than a mere rotation in personnel. When the Democrats took office,

The Exodus to Kansas

Benjamin "Pap" Singleton, once a fugitive slave from Kentucky, returned there to promote the "exodus" movement of the late 1870s. Forming a real-estate company, Singleton traveled the South recruiting parties of freedmen who were disillusioned with the outcome of Reconstruction. These emigrants, boarding a riverboat at Vicksburg, Mississippi, looked forward to political equality, freedom from violence, and homesteads in Kansas.

they made changes as sweeping as those imposed by the Republicans in 1867–1868. Some states called constitutional conventions to reverse Republican policies. All cut back expenses, wiped out social programs, lowered taxes, and revised their tax systems to relieve landowners of large burdens. State courts limited the rights of tenants and sharecroppers. Most important, the Democrats used the law to ensure a stable black labor force. Legislatures restored vagrancy laws and revised crop-lien statutes to make landowners' claims superior to those of merchants. The redeemers extended their inventiveness to criminal law. Local ordinances in heavily black counties might restrict hunting, fishing, gun carrying, and ownership of dogs and thereby curtail the everyday activities of freedmen who lived off the land. States passed severe laws against trespassing and theft; stealing livestock or wrongly taking part of a crop became grand larceny with a penalty of up to five years

at hard labor. By the end of Reconstruction, a large black convict work force had been leased out to private contractors, who profited from their labor.

For the freedmen, whose aspirations had been raised by Republican rule, the impact of redemption was demoralizing. The new laws, Tennessee blacks contended at an 1875 convention, would impose "a condition of servitude scarcely less degrading than that endured before the late civil war." In the late 1870s, as the political climate grew more oppressive, an "exodus" movement spread through Mississippi, Tennessee, Texas, and Louisiana. "We . . . seed that there was no way on earth that we could better our condition," a Louisiana "colonization council" declared in 1877. Seeking a way out of the South, some freed blacks decided to become homesteaders in Kansas. After a major outbreak of "Kansas fever" in 1879, four thousand "exodusters" from Mississippi and Louisiana

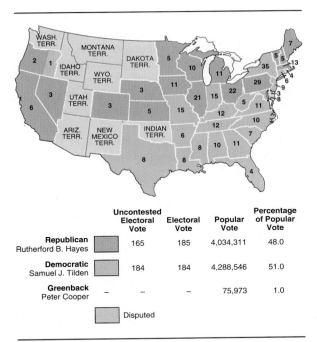

	Uncontested Electoral Vote	Electoral Vote	Popular Vote	Percentage of Popular Vote
Republican Rutherford B. Hayes	165	185	4,034,311	48.0
Democratic Samuel J. Tilden	184	184	4,288,546	51.0
Greenback Peter Cooper	–	–	75,973	1.0
Disputed				

The Disputed Election of 1876

joined about ten thousand who had reached Kansas in smaller groups earlier in the decade. But the vast majority of freedmen, devoid of resources, had no migration options or escape route. Mass movement of southern blacks to the North and Midwest would not gain momentum until the twentieth century.

The Election of 1876

By the autumn of 1876, with redemption almost complete, both parties moved to discard the heritage of animosity left by the war and Reconstruction. The Republicans nominated Rutherford B. Hayes, three times Ohio's governor, for president. Untainted by the scandals of the Grant years and popular with all factions in his party, Hayes presented himself as a "moderate" on southern policy. He favored "home rule" in the South and a guarantee of civil and political rights for all—two planks that were clearly contradictory. The Democrats nominated Governor Samuel J. Tilden of New York, a millionaire corporate lawyer and political reformer. Known for his assaults on the rapacious Tweed Ring that had plundered New York City's treasury, Tilden campaigned against fraud and waste. The candidates had much in common. Fiscal conservatives, both fa-

vored sound money. Both endorsed civil-service reform and decried corruption, an irony since the 1876 election would be extremely corrupt.

Tilden won the popular vote by a small margin and seemed destined to capture the 185 electoral votes needed for victory. But the Republicans challenged the pro-Tilden returns from South Carolina, Florida, and Louisiana. If they could deprive the Democrats of these nineteen electoral votes, Hayes would triumph. The Democrats, who needed only one of the disputed electoral votes for victory, challenged the validity of Oregon's single electoral vote, which the Republicans had won, on a technicality. Twenty electoral votes, therefore, were in contention. Republicans, however, still controlled the electoral machinery in the three unredeemed southern states, where they threw out enough Democratic ballots to declare candidate Hayes the winner.

The nation now faced an unprecedented dilemma: each party claimed victory in the contested states, and each accused the other of fraud. In fact, both sets of southern results had been obtained by fraud: the Republicans had discarded legitimate Democratic ballots, and the Democrats had illegally prevented freedmen from voting. To resolve the conflict, Congress in January 1877 created a special electoral commission to determine which party would get the contested electoral votes. Made up of senators, representatives, and Supreme Court justices, the commission included seven Democrats, seven Republicans, and one independent, Justice David Davis of Illinois. When Davis resigned to run for the Senate, Congress replaced him with a Republican, and the commission gave Hayes the election by an 8 to 7 vote.

Congress now had to certify the new electoral vote. But since the Democrats controlled the House, a new problem loomed. Some Democrats threatened to obstruct debate and delay approval of the electoral vote. Had they carried out their scheme, the nation would have been without a president on inauguration day. But there remained room for compromise, for many southern Democrats accepted Hayes's election. Among them were former scalawags with commercial interests to protect, who still favored Republican financial policies, and railroad investors, who hoped that a Republican administration would help them build a southern transcontinental line. Other southerners cared mainly about Democratic state victories and did not mind conceding the presidency as long as the new Republican administration would leave the South alone.

Republican leaders, although sure of eventual triumph, were willing to bargain as well, for candidate Hayes desired not merely victory but southern approval.

A series of informal negotiations ensued, at which politicians of both parties exchanged promises. Ohio Republicans and southern Democrats who met at the Wormley House, a Washington hotel, reached an agreement that if Hayes won the election, he would remove federal troops from South Carolina and Louisiana, and Democrats could gain control of those states. In other bargaining sessions, southern politicians asked for federal patronage, federal aid to railroads, and federal support for internal improvements. In return, they promised to drop the filibuster, to accept Hayes as president, and to treat freedmen fairly.

With the threatened filibuster broken, Congress ratified Hayes's election. Once in office, Hayes fulfilled some of the promises his Republican colleagues had made. He appointed a former Confederate as postmaster general and ordered federal troops who guarded the South Carolina and Louisiana statehouses back to their barracks. Although federal soldiers remained in the South after 1877, they no longer served a political function. The Democrats, meanwhile, took control of state governments in Louisiana, South Carolina, and Florida. When Republican rule toppled in these states, the era of Reconstruction finally ended, though more with a whimper than with a resounding crash.

But some of the bargains struck in the Compromise of 1877, such as Democratic promises to treat southern blacks fairly, were forgotten, as were Hayes's pledges to ensure freedmen's rights. "When you turned us loose, you turned us loose to the sky, to the storm, to the whirlwind, and worst of all . . . to the wrath of our infuriated masters," Frederick Douglass had charged at the Republican convention in 1876. "The question now is, do you mean to make good to us the promises in your Constitution?" The answer provided by the 1876 election and the 1877 compromises was "No."

CONCLUSION

The end of Reconstruction brought benefits to both political parties. Although unable to retain a southern constituency, the Republican party was no longer burdened by the unpopular "southern question." And it had firm support in New England, the Middle Atlantic states, and the Great Lakes states. The Democrats, who had regained power in the ex-Confederate states, would remain entrenched there for almost a century. To be sure, the South was now tied to sharecropping and economic backwardness as securely as it had once been tied to slavery. But "home rule," or Democratic control, was firmly in place.

Reconstruction's end also signaled a triumph for nationalism and the spirit of reunion. In the fall of 1877, President Hayes made a rousing goodwill tour of the South to champion reconciliation, and similar celebrations continued through the 1880s and 1890s. When former president Grant died in 1885, veterans of both Civil War armies served as pallbearers. Jefferson Davis, imprisoned for two years after the war but never brought to trial, urged young men to "lay aside all rancor, all bitter sectional feeling." The federal government turned battlefields into national parks where veterans of both armies could gather for reunions. As the nation applauded reconciliation, the reputation of Reconstruction sank. Looking back on the 1860s and 1870s, most late-nineteenth-century Americans dismissed the congressional effort to reconstruct the South as a fiasco—a tragic interlude of "radical rule" or "black reconstruction," fashioned by carpetbaggers, scalawags, and Radical Republicans.

With the hindsight of over a century, historians continue to regard Reconstruction as a failure, though of a different kind. No longer viewed as a misguided scheme that collapsed because of radical excess, Reconstruction is now widely seen as a democratic experiment that did not go far enough. Historians cite two main causes. First, Congress did not promote freedmen's independence through land reform; without property of their own, southern blacks lacked the economic power to defend their interests as free citizens. Property ownership, however, does not necessarily ensure political rights, nor does it invariably provide economic security. Considering the depressed state of southern agriculture in the postwar decades, the freedmen's fate as independent farmers would likely have been perilous. Thus the land-reform question, like much else about Reconstruction, remains a subject of debate. A second cause of Reconstruction's collapse is less open to dispute: the federal government neglected to back congressional Reconstruction with military force. Given the choice between protecting blacks' rights at whatever cost and promoting reunion, the government opted for reunion. Reconstruction's failure, therefore, was the federal government's failure to fulfill its own goals and create a biracial democracy in the South. As a result, the nation's adjustment to the consequences of emancipation would continue into the twentieth century.

The Reconstruction era left some significant legacies, including the Fourteenth and Fifteenth amendments, both products of an extraordinary chain of postwar political crises. Although neither amendment would be used to protect minority rights for almost a century, they remain monuments to the democratic zeal that swept Congress in the 1860s. The Reconstruction years also hold a significant place in black history. During this brief respite between slavery and repression, southern blacks reconstituted their families, created new institutions, took part in the transformation of southern agriculture, and participated in government, for the first time in American history. The aspirations and achievements of the Reconstruction era left an indelible mark on black citizens, as is vividly conveyed in an excerpt from a federal document. In the 1880s a congressional committee investigating southern labor conditions solicited the testimony of James K. Green of Montgomery, Alabama, a black politician during Reconstruction and subsequently a carpenter and contractor. At the end of the war, Green reported,

> *I knew nothing more than to obey my master, and there were thousands of us in the same attitude, that didn't know the Lord's prayer, but the tocsin of freedom sounded and knocked at the door and we walked out like free men and we met the exigencies as they grew up, and shouldered the responsibilities.*

Green's proud memory of blacks' achievements reflected one kind of postwar experience. Consigning the Reconstruction era to history, other Americans of the 1880s turned their energies to their economic futures—to their railroads, factories, and mills, and to the exploitation of the country's bountiful natural resources.

CHRONOLOGY

1863 President Abraham Lincoln issues Proclamation of Amnesty and Reconstruction.

1864 Wade-Davis bill passed by Congress and pocket-vetoed by Lincoln.

1865 Freedmen's Bureau established.
Civil War ends.
Lincoln assassinated.

Lincoln Mourning Shield

Andrew Johnson becomes president.
Johnson issues Proclamation of Amnesty and Reconstruction.

1865 Ex-Confederate states hold constitutional conventions (May–December).
Black conventions begin in the ex-Confederate states.
Thirteenth Amendment added to the Constitution.
Presidential Reconstruction completed.

1866 Congress enacts the Civil Rights Act of 1866 and the Supplementary Freedmen's Bureau Act over Johnson's vetoes.
Ku Klux Klan founded in Tennessee.
Congress proposes the Fourteenth Amendment.
Tennessee readmitted to the Union.
Race riots in southern cities.
Republicans win congressional elections.
Thirty-ninth Congress begins debates over Reconstruction policy.

1867 Reconstruction Act of 1867.
William Seward negotiates the purchase of Alaska.
Constitutional conventions meet in the ex-Confederate states.
Howard University founded.

1868 President Johnson is impeached, tried, and acquitted.

Omnibus Act.

Fourteenth Amendment added to the Constitution.

Ulysses S. Grant elected president.

1869 Transcontinental railroad completed.

1870 Congress readmits the four remaining southern states to the Union.

Fifteenth Amendment added to the Constitution.

Enforcement Act of 1870.

1871 Second Enforcement Act.

Ku Klux Klan Act.

1872 Liberal Republican party formed.

Amnesty Act.

Alabama claims settled.

Grant reelected president.

1873 Panic of 1873 begins (September–October), setting off a five-year depression.

1874 Democrats gain control of the House of Representatives.

1875 Civil Rights Act of 1875.

Specie Resumption Act.

1876 Disputed presidential election: Rutherford B. Hayes versus Samuel J. Tilden.

1877 Electoral commission decides election in favor of Hayes.

The last Republican-controlled governments overthrown in Florida, Louisiana, and South Carolina.

1879 "Exodus" movement spreads through several southern states.

FOR FURTHER READING

Eric Foner, *Reconstruction: America's Unfinished Revolution, 1863–1877* (1988). A thorough exploration of Reconstruction that draws on recent scholarship and stresses the centrality of the black experience.

John Hope Franklin, *Reconstruction After the Civil War* (1961). An overview that dismantles the traditional view of Reconstruction as a disastrous experiment in radical rule.

William Gillette, *Retreat from Reconstruction, 1869–1879* (1979). A survey of the era's national politics, indicting Republican policy makers for vacillation and lack of commitment to racial equality.

Leon Litwack, *Been in the Storm So Long: The Aftermath of Slavery* (1979). A comprehensive study of the black response to emancipation in 1865–1866.

Michael Perman, *Emancipation and Reconstruction, 1862–1879* (1987). A brief, readable interpretive survey of the period.

Roger L. Ransom and Richard Sutch, *One Kind of Freedom: The Economic Consequences of Emancipation* (1977). Two economists' assessment of the impact of free black labor on the South and explanation of the development of sharecropping and the crop-lien system.

Kenneth M. Stampp, *The Era of Reconstruction, 1865–1877* (1965). A classic revisionist interpretation of Reconstruction, focusing on the establishment and fall of Republican governments.

Joel Williamson, *The Negro in South Carolina During Reconstruction, 1861–1877* (1965). A pioneer study of black life and institutions after emancipation.

ADDITIONAL BIBLIOGRAPHY

Reconstruction Politics

Richard H. Abbott, *The Republican Party and the South, 1855–1877* (1986); Herman Belz, *Emancipation and Equal Rights: Politics and Constitutionalism in the Civil War Era* (1978); Michael Les Benedict, *A Compromise of Principle: Congressional Republicans and Reconstruction, 1863–1869* (1974) and *The Impeachment and Trial of Andrew Johnson* (1973); W. R. Brock, *An American Crisis: Congress and Reconstruction, 1865–1867* (1963); Fawn Brodie, *Thaddeus Stevens: Scourge of the South* (1959); Richard O. Curry, ed., *Radicalism, Racism, and Party Realignment: The Border States During Reconstruction* (1969); David Donald, *Charles Sumner and the Rights of Man* (1970) and *The Politics of Reconstruction, 1863–1867* (1965); Ellen Carol DuBois, *Feminism and Suffrage: The Emergence of an Independent Women's Movement in America, 1848–1869* (1978); William Gillette, *The Right to Vote: Politics and Passage of the Fifteenth Amendment* (1969); Harold Hyman, *A More Perfect Union: The Impact of the Civil War and Reconstruction on the Constitution* (1973); Stanley I. Kutler, *Judicial Power and Reconstruction* (1968); Eric McKitrick, *Andrew Johnson and Reconstruction* (1960); James C. Mohr, *Radical Republicans in the North: State Politics During Reconstruction* (1976); William E. Nelson, *The Fourteenth Amendment* (1988); Hans Trefousse, *Andrew Johnson: A Biography* (1989).

The South

Dan C. Carter, *When the War Was Over: Self-Reconstruction in the South, 1865–1867* (1985); Richard Nelson Current, *Those Terrible Carpetbaggers* (1988); Stephen Hahn, *The Roots of Southern Populism* (1983); William C. Harris, *The Day of the Carpetbagger: Republican Reconstruction in Mississippi* (1979); Otto Olsen, ed., *Reconstruction and Redemption in the South* (1980); Michael Perman, *Reunion Without Compromise: The South and Reconstruction, 1865–1868* (1973) and *The Road to*

Redemption: Southern Politics, 1869–1879 (1984); Howard N. Rabinowitz, *Race Relations in the Urban South, 1865–1890* (1978); George C. Rable, *But There Was No Peace: The Role of Violence in the Politics of Reconstruction* (1984); Mark W. Summers, *Railroads, Reconstruction, and the Gospel of Prosperity* (1984); Allen W. Trelease, *White Terror: The Ku Klux Klan Conspiracy and Southern Reconstruction* (1971); Ted Tunnell, *Crucible of Reconstruction: War, Radicalism, and Race in Louisiana, 1862–1877* (1984); Jonathan M. Wiener, *Social Origins of the New South: Alabama, 1860–1885* (1978); Gavin Wright, *Old South, New South: Revolutions in the Southern Economy Since the Civil War* (1986).

Emancipation and the Freedmen

Ira Berlin et al., eds., *Freedom, A Documentary History of Emancipation, 1861–1867* (1982–1993); Carol Rothrock Bleser, *The Promised Land: The History of the South Carolina Land Commission, 1869–1890* (1969); W. E. B. Du Bois, *Black Reconstruction in America, 1860–1880* (1935); Barbara Jeanne Fields, *Slavery and Freedom on the Middle Ground: Maryland During the Nineteenth Century* (1985); Eric Foner, *Nothing but Freedom: Emancipation and Its Legacies* (1983) and *Politics and Ideology in the Age of the Civil War* (1980), Chapters 6–7; Herbert G. Gutman, *The Black Family in Slavery and Freedom, 1750–1925* (1976); Robert Higgs, *Competition and Coercion: Blacks in the American Economy, 1865–1914* (1977); Thomas Holt, *Black over White: Negro Political Leadership in South Carolina During Reconstruction* (1977); Gerald Jaynes, *Branches Without Roots: Genesis of the Black Working Class in the American South, 1862–1882* (1986); Jacqueline Jones, *Soldiers of Light and Love: Northern Teachers and Georgia Blacks, 1865–1873* (1980) and *Labor of Love, Labor of Sorrow: Black Women, Work, and the Family from Slavery to the Present* (1985), Chapter 2; Peter Kolchin, *First Freedom: The Responses of Alabama's Blacks to Emancipation and Reconstruction* (1972); Lawrence W. Levine, *Black Culture and Black Consciousness: Afro-American Folk Thought from Slavery to Freedom* (1977); William S. McFeely, *Yankee Stepfather: General O. O. Howard and the Freedmen* (1966); Nell Irvin Painter, *Exodusters* (1977); James Roark, *Masters Without Slaves: Southern Planters in the Civil War and Reconstruction* (1978); William Preston Vaughan, *Schools for All: The Blacks and Public Education in the South, 1865–1877* (1974); Joel Williamson, *The Crucible of Race: Black-White Relations in the American South Since Emancipation* (1984).

National Trends

Paul H. Buck, *The Road to Reunion, 1865–1900* (1937); Adrian Cook, *The Alabama Claims* (1975); Ari M. Hoogenboom, *Outlawing the Spoils: A History of the Civil Service Reform Movement* (1961); William S. McFeely, *Grant: A Biography* (1981); David Montgomery, *Beyond Equality: Labor and the Radical Republicans, 1862–1872* (1967); Walter T. K. Nugent, *The Money Question During Reconstruction* (1967) and *Money and American Society, 1865–1880* (1968); Keith I. Polakoff, *The Politics of Inertia: The Election of 1876 and the End of Reconstruction* (1973); John C. Sproat, *"The Best Men": Liberal Reformers in the Gilded Age* (1968); Irwin Unger, *The Greenback Era: A Social and Political History of American Finance* (1964); Allen Weinstein, *Prelude to Populism: Origins of the Silver Issue, 1867–1878* (1970); C. Vann Woodward, *Reunion and Reaction: The Compromise of 1877 and the End of Reconstruction* (rev. ed., 1956).

DECLARATION OF INDEPENDENCE

IN CONGRESS, JULY 4, 1776

THE UNANIMOUS DECLARATION OF THE THIRTEEN UNITED STATES OF AMERICA

When, in the course of human events, it becomes necessary for one people to dissolve the political bands which have connected them with another, and to assume, among the powers of the earth, the separate and equal station to which the laws of nature and of nature's God entitle them, a decent respect to the opinions of mankind requires that they should declare the causes which impel them to the separation.

We hold these truths to be self-evident: That all men are created equal; that they are endowed by their Creator with certain unalienable rights; that among these are life, liberty, and the pursuit of happiness; that, to secure these rights, governments are instituted among men, deriving their just powers from the consent of the governed; that whenever any form of government becomes destructive of these ends, it is the right of the people to alter or to abolish it, and to institute new government, laying its foundation on such principles, and organizing its powers in such form, as to them shall seem most likely to effect their safety and happiness. Prudence, indeed, will dictate that governments long established should not be changed for light and transient causes; and accordingly all experience hath shown that mankind are more disposed to suffer, while evils are sufferable, than to right themselves by abolishing the forms to which they are accustomed. But when a long train of abuses and usurpations, pursuing invariably the same object, evinces a design to reduce them under absolute despotism, it is their right, it is their duty, to throw off such government, and to provide new guards for their future security. Such has been the patient sufferance of these colonies; and such is now the necessity which constrains them to alter their former systems of government. The history of the present King of Great Britain is a history of repeated injuries and usurpations, all having in direct object the establishment of an absolute tyranny over these states. To prove this, let facts be submitted to a candid world.

He has refused his assent to laws, the most wholesome and necessary for the public good.

He has forbidden his governors to pass laws of immediate and pressing importance, unless suspended in their operation till his assent should be obtained; and, when so suspended, he has utterly neglected to attend to them.

He has refused to pass other laws for the accommodation of large districts of people, unless those people would relinquish the right of representation in the legislature, a right inestimable to them, and formidable to tyrants only.

He has called together legislative bodies at places unusual, uncomfortable, and distant from the depository of their public records, for the sole purpose of fatiguing them into compliance with his measures.

He has dissolved representative houses repeatedly, for opposing, with manly firmness, his invasions on the rights of the people.

He has refused for a long time, after such dissolutions, to cause others to be elected; whereby the legislative powers, incapable of annihilation, have returned to the people at large for their exercise; the state remaining, in the mean time, exposed to all the dangers of invasions from without and convulsions within.

He has endeavored to prevent the population of these states; for that purpose obstructing the laws of naturalization of foreigners; refusing to pass others to encourage their migration hither, and raising the conditions of new appropriation of lands.

He has obstructed the administration of justice, by refusing his assent to laws for establishing judiciary powers.

He has made judges dependent on his will alone, for the tenure of their offices, and the amount and payment of their salaries.

He has erected a multitude of new offices, and sent hither swarms of officers to harass our people and eat out their substance.

He has kept among us, in times of peace, standing armies, without the consent of our legislatures.

He has affected to render the military independent of, and superior to, the civil power.

He has combined with others to subject us to a jurisdiction foreign to our constitution, and unacknowledged by our laws, giving his assent to their acts of pretended legislation:

For quartering large bodies of armed troops among us;

For protecting them, by a mock trial, from punishment for any murders which they should commit on the inhabitants of these states;

For cutting off our trade with all parts of the world;

For imposing taxes on us without our consent;

For depriving us, in many cases, of the benefits of trial by jury;

For transporting us beyond seas, to be tried for pretended offenses;

For abolishing the free system of English laws in a neighboring province, establishing therein an arbitrary government, and enlarging its boundaries, so as to render it at once an example and fit instrument for introducing the same absolute rule into these colonies;

For taking away our charters, abolishing our most valuable laws, and altering fundamentally the forms of our governments;

For suspending our own legislatures, and declaring themselves invested with power to legislate for us in all cases whatsoever.

He has abdicated government here, by declaring us out of his protection and waging war against us.

He has plundered our seas, ravaged our coasts, burned our towns, and destroyed the lives of our people.

He is at this time transporting large armies of foreign mercenaries to complete the works of death, desolation, and tyranny already begun with circumstances of cruelty and perfidy scarcely paralleled in the most barbarous ages, and totally unworthy of the head of a civilized nation.

He has constrained our fellow-citizens, taken captive on the high seas, to bear arms against their country, to become the executioners of their friends and brethren, or to fall themselves by their hands.

He has excited domestic insurrection among us, and has endeavored to bring on the inhabitants of our frontiers the merciless Indian savages, whose known rule of warfare is an undistinguished destruction of all ages, sexes, and conditions.

In every stage of these oppressions we have petitioned for redress in the most humble terms; our repeated petitions have been answered only by repeated injury. A prince, whose character is thus marked by every act which may define a tyrant, is unfit to be the ruler of a free people.

Nor have we been wanting in our attentions to our British brethren. We have warned them, from time to time, of attempts by their legislature to extend an unwarrantable jurisdiction over us. We have reminded them of the circumstances of our emigration and settlement here. We have appealed to their native justice and magnanimity; and we have conjured them by the ties of our common kindred, to disavow these usurpations, which would inevitably interrupt our connections and correspondence. They, too, have been deaf to the voice of justice and of consanguinity. We must, therefore, acquiesce in the necessity which denounces our separation, and hold them, as we hold the rest of mankind, enemies in war, in peace friends.

We, therefore, the representatives of the United States of America, in General Congress assembled, appealing to the Supreme Judge of the world for the rectitude of our intentions, do, in the name and by the authority of the good people of these colonies, solemnly publish and declare, that these United Colonies are, and of right ought to be, FREE AND INDEPENDENT STATES; that they are absolved from all allegiance to the British crown, and that all political connection between them and the state of Great Britain is, and ought to be, totally dissolved; and that, as free and independent states, they have full power to levy war, conclude peace, contract alliances, establish commerce, and do all other acts and things which independent states may of right do. And for the support of this declaration, with a firm reliance on the protection of Divine Providence, we mutually pledge to each other our lives, our fortunes, and our sacred honor.

JOHN HANCOCK [*President*]
[*and fifty-five others*]

THE ARTICLES OF CONFEDERATION AND PERPETUAL UNION

BETWEEN THE STATES OF NEW HAMPSHIRE, MASSACHUSETTS BAY, RHODE ISLAND AND PROVIDENCE PLANTATIONS, CONNECTICUT, NEW YORK, NEW JERSEY, PENNSYLVANIA, DELAWARE, MARYLAND, VIRGINIA, NORTH CAROLINA, SOUTH CAROLINA, GEORGIA.*

Article 1.

The stile of this confederacy shall be "The United States of America."

Article 2.

Each State retains its sovereignty, freedom and independence, and every power, jurisdiction, and right, which is not by this confederation expressly delegated to the United States, in Congress assembled.

Article 3.

The said states hereby severally enter into a firm league of friendship with each other for their common defence, the security of their liberties and their mutual and general welfare; binding themselves to assist each other against all force offered to, or attacks made upon them, or any of them, on account of religion, sovereignty, trade, or any other pretence whatever.

Article 4.

The better to secure and perpetuate mutual friendship and intercourse among the people of the different states in this union, the free inhabitants of each of these states, paupers, vagabonds, and fugitives from justice excepted, shall be entitled to all privileges and immunities of free citizens in the several states; and the people of each State shall have free ingress and regress to and from any other State, and shall enjoy therein all the privileges of trade and commerce, subject to the same duties, impositions, and restrictions, as the inhabitants thereof respectively; provided, that such restrictions shall not extend so far as to prevent the removal of property, imported into any State, to any other State of which the owner is an inhabitant; provided also, that no imposition, duties, or restriction, shall be laid by any State on the property of the United States, or either of them.

If any person guilty of, or charged with treason, felony, or other high misdemeanor in any State, shall flee from justice and be found in any of the United States, he shall, upon demand of the governor or executive power of the State from which he fled, be delivered up and removed to the State having jurisdiction of his offence.

Full faith and credit shall be given in each of these states to the records, acts, and judicial proceedings of the courts and magistrates of every other State.

Article 5.

For the more convenient management of the general interests of the United States, delegates shall be annually appointed, in such manner as the legislature of each State shall direct, to meet in Congress, on the 1st Monday in November in every year, with a power reserved to each State to recall its delegates, or any of them, at any time within the year, and to send others in their stead for the remainder of the year.

No State shall be represented in Congress by less than two, nor by more than seven members; and no person shall be capable of being a delegate for more than three years in any term of six years; nor shall any person, being a delegate, be capable of holding any office under the United States, for which he, or any other for his benefit, receives any salary, fees, or emolument of any kind.

Each State shall maintain its own delegates in a meeting of the states, and while they act as members of the committee of the states.

---

*This copy of the final draft of the Articles of Confederation is taken from the *Journals,* 9:907–925, November 15, 1777.

In determining questions in the United States, in Congress assembled, each State shall have one vote.

Freedom of speech and debate in Congress shall not be impeached or questioned in any court or place out of Congress: and the members of Congress shall be protected in their persons from arrests and imprisonments, during the time of their going to and from, and attendance on Congress, *except for treason,* felony, or breach of the peace.

Article 6.

No State, without the consent of the United States, in Congress assembled, shall send any embassy to, or receive any embassy from, or enter into any conference, agreement, alliance, or treaty with any king, prince, or state; nor shall any person, holding any office of profit or trust under the United States, or any of them, accept of any present, emolument, office or title, of any kind whatever, from any king, prince, or foreign state; nor shall the United States, in Congress assembled, or any of them, grant any title of nobility.

No two or more states shall enter into any treaty, confederation, or alliance, whatever, between them, without the consent of the United States, in Congress assembled, specifying accurately the purposes for which the same is to be entered into, and how long it shall continue.

No State shall lay any imposts or duties which may interfere with any stipulations in treaties entered into by the United States, in Congress assembled, with any king, prince, or state, in pursuance of any treaties already proposed by Congress to the courts of France and Spain.

No vessels of war shall be kept up in time of peace by any State, except such number only as shall be deemed necessary by the United States, in Congress assembled, for the defence of such State or its trade; nor shall any body of forces be kept up by any State, in time of peace, except such number only as, in the judgment of the United States, in Congress assembled, shall be deemed requisite to garrison the forts necessary for the defence of such State; but every State shall always keep up a well regulated and disciplined militia, sufficiently armed and accoutred, and shall provide, and constantly have ready for use, in public stores, a due number of field pieces and tents, and a proper quantity of arms, ammunition and camp equipage.

No State shall engage in any war without the consent of the United States, in Congress assembled, un-

less such State be actually invaded by enemies, or shall have received certain advice of a resolution being formed by some nation of Indians to invade such State, and the danger is so imminent as not to admit of a delay till the United States, in Congress assembled, can be consulted; nor shall any State grant commissions to any ships or vessels of war, nor letters of marque or reprisal, except it be after a declaration of war by the United States, in Congress assembled, and then only against the kingdom or state, and the subjects thereof, against which war has been so declared, and under such regulations as shall be established by the United States, in Congress assembled, unless such States be infested by pirates, in which case vessels of war may be fitted out for that occasion, and kept so long as the danger shall continue, or until the United States, in Congress assembled, shall determine otherwise.

Article 7.

When land forces are raised by any State for the common defence, all officers of or under the rank of colonel, shall be appointed by the legislature of each State respectively, by whom such forces shall be raised, or in such manner as such State shall direct; and all vacancies shall be filled up by the State which first made the appointment.

Article 8.

All charges of war and all other expences, that shall be incurred for the common defence or general welfare, and allowed by the United States, in Congress assembled, shall be defrayed out of a common treasury, which shall be supplied by the several states, in proportion to the value of all land within each State, granted to or surveyed for any person, as such land and the buildings and improvements thereon shall be estimated according to such mode as the United States, in Congress assembled, shall, from time to time, direct and appoint.

The taxes for paying that proportion shall be laid and levied by the authority and direction of the legislatures of the several states, within the time agreed upon by the United States, in Congress assembled.

Article 9.

The United States, in Congress assembled, shall have the sole and exclusive right and power of determining on peace and war, except in the cases mentioned in the

6th article; of sending and receiving ambassadors; entering into treaties and alliances, provided that no treaty of commerce shall be made, whereby the legislative power of the respective states shall be restrained from imposing such imposts and duties on foreigners as their own people are subjected to, or from prohibiting the exportation or importation of any species of goods or commodities whatsoever; of establishing rules for deciding, in all cases, what captures on land or water shall be legal, and in what manner prizes, taken by land or naval forces in the service of the United States, shall be divided or appropriated; of granting letters of marque and reprisal in times of peace; appointing courts for the trial of piracies and felonies committed on the high seas, and establishing courts for receiving and determining, finally, appeals in all cases of captures; provided, that no member of Congress shall be appointed a judge of any of the said courts.

The United States, in Congress assembled, shall also be the last resort on appeal in all disputes and differences now subsisting, or that hereafter may arise between two or more states concerning boundary, jurisdiction or any other cause whatever; which authority shall always be exercised in the manner following: whenever the legislative or executive authority, or lawful agent of any State, in controversy with another, shall present a petition to Congress, stating the matter in question, and praying for a hearing, notice thereof shall be given, by order of Congress, to the legislative or executive authority of the other State in controversy, and a day assigned for the appearance of the parties by their lawful agents, who shall then be directed to appoint, by joint consent, commissioners or judges to constitute a court for hearing and determining the matter in question; but, if they cannot agree, Congress shall name three persons out of each of the United States, and from the list of such persons each party shall alternately strike out one, in the petitioners beginning, until the number shall be reduced to thirteen; and from that number not less than seven, nor more than nine names, as Congress shall direct, shall, in the presence of Congress, be drawn out by lot; and the persons whose names shall be drawn, or any five of them, shall be commissioners or judges to hear and finally determine the controversy, so always as a major part of the judges who shall hear the cause shall agree in the determination; and if either party shall neglect to attend at the day appointed, without shewing reasons which Congress shall judge sufficient, or, being present, shall refuse to strike, the Congress shall proceed to nominate three persons out of each State, and the secretary of Congress shall strike in behalf of such party absent or refusing; and the judgment and sentence of the court to be appointed, in the manner before prescribed, shall be final and conclusive; and if any of the parties shall refuse to submit to the authority of such court, or to appear or defend their claim or cause, the court shall nevertheless proceed to pronounce sentence or judgment, which shall, in like manner, be final and decisive, the judgment or sentence and other proceedings being, in either case, transmitted to Congress, and lodged among the acts of Congress for the security of the parties concerned: provided, that every commissioner, before he sits in judgment, shall take an oath, to be administered by one of the judges of the supreme or superior court of the State where the cause shall be tried, "well and truly to hear and determine the matter in question, according to the best of his judgment, without favour, affection, or hope of reward": provided, also, that no State shall be deprived of territory for the benefit of the United States.

All controversies concerning the private right of soil, claimed under different grants of two or more states, whose jurisdictions, as they may respect such lands and the states which passed such grants, are adjusted, the said grants, or either of them, being at the same time claimed to have originated antecedent to such settlement of jurisdiction, shall, on the petition of either party to the Congress of the United States, be finally determined, as near as may be, in the same manner as is before prescribed for deciding disputes respecting territorial jurisdiction between different states.

The United States, in Congress assembled, shall also have the sole and exclusive right and power of regulating the alloy and value of coin struck by their own authority, or by that of the respective states; fixing the standard of weights and measures throughout the United States; regulating the trade and managing all affairs with the Indians not members of any of the states; provided that the legislative right of any State within its own limits be not infringed or violated; establishing and regulating post offices from one State to another throughout all the United States, and exacting such postage on the papers passing through the same as may be requisite to defray the expences of the said office; appointing all officers of the land forces in the service of the United States, excepting regimental officers; appointing all the officers of the naval forces, and commissioning all officers whatever in the service of the United States; making rules for the government and regulation of the said land and naval forces, and directing their operations.

The United States, in Congress assembled, shall have authority to appoint a committee to sit in the recess of Congress, to be denominated "a Committee of the States," and to consist of one delegate from each State, and to appoint such other committees and civil officers as may be necessary for managing the general affairs of the United States, under their direction; to appoint one of their number to preside; provided that no person be allowed to serve in the office of president more than one year in any term of three years; to ascertain the necessary sums of money to be raised for the service of the United States, and to appropriate and apply the same for defraying the public expences; to borrow money or emit bills on the credit of the United States, transmitting, every half year, to the respective states, an account of the sums of money so borrowed or emitted; to build and equip a navy; to agree upon the number of land forces, and to make requisitions from each State for its quota, in proportion to the number of white inhabitants in such State; which requisitions shall be binding; and, thereupon, the legislature of each State shall appoint the regimental officers, raise the men, and cloathe, arm, and equip them in a soldier-like manner, at the expence of the United States; and the officers and men so cloathed, armed, and equipped, shall march to the place appointed and within the time agreed on by the United States, in Congress assembled; but if the United States, in Congress assembled, shall, on consideration of circumstances, judge proper that any State should not raise men, or should raise a smaller number than its quota, and that any other State should raise a greater number of men than the quota thereof, such extra number shall be raised, officered, cloathed, armed, and equipped in the same manner as the quota of such State, unless the legislature of such State shall judge that such extra number cannot be safely spared out of the same, in which case they shall raise, officer, cloathe, arm, and equip as many of such extra number as they judge can be safely spared. And the officers and men so cloathed, armed, and equipped, shall march to the place appointed and within the time agreed on by the United States, in Congress assembled.

The United States, in Congress assembled, shall never engage in a war, nor grant letters of marque and reprisal in time of peace, nor enter into any treaties or alliances, nor coin money, nor regulate the value thereof, nor ascertain the sums and expences neces-

sary for the defence and welfare of the United States, or any of them: nor emit bills, nor borrow money on the credit of the United States, nor appropriate money, nor agree upon the number of vessels of war to be built or purchased, or the number of land or sea forces to be raised, nor appoint a commander in chief of the army or navy, unless nine states assent to the same; nor shall a question on any other point, except for adjourning from day to day, be determined, unless by the votes of a majority of the United States, in Congress assembled.

The Congress of the United States shall have power to adjourn to any time within the year, and to any place within the United States, so that no period of adjournment be for a longer duration than the space of six months, and shall publish the journal of their proceedings monthly, except such parts thereof, relating to treaties, alliances or military operations, as, in their judgment, require secrecy; and the yeas and nays of the delegates of each State on any question shall be entered on the journal, when it is desired by any delegate; and the delegates of a State, or any of them, at his, or their request, shall be furnished with a transcript of the said journal, except such parts as are above excepted, to lay before the legislatures of the several states.

Article 10.

The committee of the states, or any nine of them, shall be authorized to execute, in the recess of Congress, such of the powers of Congress as the United States, in Congress assembled, by the consent of nine states, shall, from time to time, think expedient to vest them with; provided, that no power be delegated to the said committee for the exercise of which, by the articles of confederation, the voice of nine states, in the Congress of the United States assembled, is requisite.

Article 11.

Canada acceding to this confederation, and joining in the measures of the United States, shall be admitted into and entitled to all the advantages of this union; but no other colony shall be admitted into the same, unless such admission be agreed to by nine states.

Article 12.

All bills of credit emitted, monies borrowed and debts contracted by, or under the authority of Congress before the assembling of the United States, in pursuance of the present confederation, shall be deemed and considered as a charge against the United States, for payment and satisfaction whereof the said United States and the public faith are hereby solemnly pledged.

Article 13.

Every State shall abide by the determinations of the United States, in Congress assembled, on all questions which, by this confederation, are submitted to them. And the articles of this confederation shall be inviolably observed by every State, and the union shall be perpetual; nor shall any alteration at any time hereafter be made in any of them, unless such alteration be agreed to in a Congress of the United States, and be afterwards confirmed by the legislatures of every State.

These articles shall be proposed to the legislatures of all the United States, to be considered, and if approved of by them, they are advised to authorize their delegates to ratify the same in the Congress of the United States; which being done, the same shall become conclusive.

CONSTITUTION OF THE
UNITED STATES OF AMERICA

PREAMBLE

We the people of the United States, in order to form a more perfect union, establish justice, insure domestic tranquillity, provide for the common defense, promote the general welfare, and secure the blessings of liberty to ourselves and our posterity, do ordain and establish this CONSTITUTION for the United States of America.

Article I

Section 1. All legislative powers herein granted shall be vested in a Congress of the United States, which shall consist of a Senate and a House of Representatives.

Section 2. The House of Representatives shall be composed of members chosen every second year by the people of the several States, and the electors in each State shall have the qualifications requisite for electors of the most numerous branch of the State Legislature.

No person shall be a Representative who shall not have attained to the age of twenty-five years, and been seven years a citizen of the United States, and who shall not, when elected, be an inhabitant of that State in which he shall be chosen.

Representatives and direct taxes shall be apportioned among the several States which may be included within this Union, according to their respective numbers, *which shall be determined by adding to the whole number of free persons, including those bound to service for a term of years and excluding Indians not taxed, three-fifths of all other persons.* The actual enumeration shall be made within three years after the first meeting of the Congress of the United States, and within every subsequent term of ten years, in such manner as they shall by law direct. The number of Representatives shall not exceed one for every thirty thousand, but each State shall have at least one Representa-

tive; *and until such enumeration shall be made, the State of New Hampshire shall be entitled to choose three, Massachusetts eight, Rhode Island and Providence Plantations one, Connecticut five, New York six, New Jersey four, Pennsylvania eight, Delaware one, Maryland six, Virginia ten, North Carolina five, South Carolina five, and Georgia three.*

When vacancies happen in the representation from any State, the Executive authority thereof shall issue writs of election to fill such vacancies.

The House of Representatives shall choose their Speaker and other officers; and shall have the sole power of impeachment.

Section 3. The Senate of the United States shall be composed of two Senators from each State, *chosen by the legislature thereof,* for six years; and each Senator shall have one vote.

Immediately after they shall be assembled in consequence of the first election, they shall be divided as equally as may be into three classes. The seats of the Senators of the first class shall be vacated at the expiration of the second year, of the second class at the expiration of the fourth year, and of the third class at the expiration of the sixth year, so that one-third may be chosen every second year; *and if vacancies happen by resignation or otherwise, during the recess of the legislature of any State, the Executive thereof may make temporary appointments until the next meeting of the legislature, which shall then fill such vacancies.*

No person shall be a Senator who shall not have attained to the age of thirty years, and been nine years

---

Note: Passages that are no longer in effect are printed in italic type.

a citizen of the United States, and who shall not, when elected, be an inhabitant of that State for which he shall be chosen.

The Vice President of the United States shall be President of the Senate, but shall have no vote, unless they be equally divided.

The Senate shall choose their other officers, and also a President *pro tempore,* in the absence of the Vice President, or when he shall exercise the office of the President of the United States.

The Senate shall have the sole power to try all impeachments. When sitting for that purpose, they shall be on oath or affirmation. When the President of the United States is tried, the Chief Justice shall preside: and no person shall be convicted without the concurrence of two-thirds of the members present.

Judgment in cases of impeachment shall not extend further than to removal from the office, and disqualification to hold and enjoy any office of honor, trust or profit under the United States; but the party convicted shall nevertheless be liable and subject to indictment, trial, judgment and punishment, according to law.

Section 4. The times, places and manner of holding elections for Senators and Representatives shall be prescribed in each State by the legislature thereof; but the Congress may at any time by law make or alter such regulations, except as to the places of choosing Senators.

The Congress shall assemble at least once in every year, and such meeting *shall be on the first Monday in December, unless they shall by law appoint a different day.*

Section 5. Each house shall be the judge of the elections, returns and qualifications of its own members, and a majority of each shall constitute a quorum to do business; but a smaller number may adjourn from day to day, and may be authorized to compel the attendance of absent members, in such manner, and under such penalties, as each house may provide.

Each house may determine the rules of its proceedings, punish its members for disorderly behavior, and with the concurrence of two-thirds, expel a member.

Each house shall keep a journal of its proceedings, and from time to time publish the same, excepting such parts as may in their judgment require secrecy; and the yeas and nays of the members of either house on any question shall, at the desire of one-fifth of those present, be entered on the journal.

Neither house, during the session of Congress, shall, without the consent of the other, adjourn for more than three days, nor to any other place than that in which the two houses shall be sitting.

Section 6. The Senators and Representatives shall receive a compensation for their services, to be ascertained by law and paid out of the treasury of the United States. They shall in all cases except treason, felony and breach of the peace, be privileged from arrest during their attendance at the session of their respective houses, and in going to and returning from the same; and for any speech or debate in either house, they shall not be questioned in any other place.

No Senator or Representative shall, during the time for which he was elected, be appointed to any civil office under the authority of the United States, which shall have been created, or the emoluments whereof shall have been increased, during such time; and no person holding any office under the United States shall be a member of either house during his continuance in office.

Section 7. All bills for raising revenue shall originate in the House of Representatives; but the Senate may propose or concur with amendments as on other bills.

Every bill which shall have passed the House of Representatives and the Senate, shall, before it become a law, be presented to the President of the United States; if he approve he shall sign it, but if not he shall return it with objections to that house in which it originated, who shall enter the objections at large on their journal, and proceed to reconsider it. If after such reconsideration two-thirds of that house shall agree to pass the bill, it shall be sent, together with the objections, to the other house, by which it shall likewise be reconsidered, and, if approved by two-thirds of that house, it shall become a law. But in all such cases the votes of both houses shall be determined by yeas and nays, and the names of the persons voting for and against the bill shall be entered on the journal of each house respectively. If any bill shall not be returned by the President within ten days (Sundays excepted) after it shall have been presented to him, the same shall be a law, in like manner as if he had signed it, unless the Congress by their adjournment prevent its return, in which case it shall not be a law.

Every order, resolution, or vote to which the concurrence of the Senate and House of Representatives may be necessary (except on a question of adjournment) shall be presented to the President of the United

States; and before the same shall take effect, shall be approved by him, or being disapproved by him, shall be repassed by two-thirds of the Senate and House of Representatives, according to the rules and limitations prescribed in the case of a bill.

Section 8. The Congress shall have power

To lay and collect taxes, duties, imposts, and excises, to pay the debts and provide for the common defense and general welfare of the United States; but all duties, imposts and excises shall be uniform throughout the United States;

To borrow money on the credit of the United States;

To regulate commerce with foreign nations, and among the several States, and with the Indian tribes;

To establish an uniform rule of naturalization, and uniform laws on the subject of bankruptcies throughout the United States;

To coin money, regulate the value thereof, and of foreign coin, and fix the standard of weights and measures;

To provide for the punishment of counterfeiting the securities and current coin of the United States;

To establish post offices and post roads;

To promote the progress of science and useful arts by securing for limited times to authors and inventors the exclusive right to their respective writings and discoveries;

To constitute tribunals inferior to the Supreme Court;

To define and punish piracies and felonies committed on the high seas and offenses against the law of nations;

To declare war, grant letters of marque and reprisal, and make rules concerning captures on land and water;

To raise and support armies, but no appropriation of money to that use shall be for a longer term than two years;

To provide and maintain a navy;

To make rules for the government and regulation of the land and naval forces;

To provide for calling forth the militia to execute the laws of the Union, suppress insurrections, and repel invasions;

To provide for organizing, arming, and disciplining the militia, and for governing such part of them as may be employed in the service of the United States, reserv-

ing to the States respectively the appointment of the officers, and the authority of training the militia according to the discipline prescribed by Congress;

To exercise exclusive legislation in all cases whatsoever, over such district (not exceeding ten miles square) as may, by cession of particular States, and the acceptance of Congress, become the seat of government of the United States, and to exercise like authority over all places purchased by the consent of the legislature of the State, in which the same shall be, for erection of forts, magazines, arsenals, dock-yards, and other needful buildings;—and

To make all laws which shall be necessary and proper for carrying into execution the foregoing powers, and all other powers vested by this Constitution in the government of the United States, or in any department or officer thereof.

Section 9. *The migration or importation of such persons as any of the States now existing shall think proper to admit shall not be prohibited by the Congress prior to the year 1808; but a tax or duty may be imposed on such importation, not exceeding $10 for each person.*

The privilege of the writ of habeas corpus shall not be suspended, unless when in cases of rebellion or invasion the public safety may require it.

No bill of attainder or ex post facto law shall be passed.

No capitation, or other direct, tax shall be laid, unless in proportion to the census or enumeration herein before directed to be taken.

No tax or duty shall be laid on articles exported from any State.

No preference shall be given by any regulation of commerce or revenue to the ports of one State over those of another; nor shall vessels bound to, or from, one State, be obliged to enter, clear, or pay duties in another.

No money shall be drawn from the treasury, but in consequence of appropriations made by law; and a regular statement and account of the receipts and expenditures of all public money shall be published from time to time.

No title of nobility shall be granted by the United States: and no person holding any office of profit or trust under them, shall, without the consent of the Congress, accept of any present, emolument, office, or title, of any kind whatever, from any king, prince, or foreign state.

Section 10. No State shall enter into any treaty, alliance, or confederation; grant letters of marque and reprisal; coin money; emit bills of credit; make anything but gold and silver coin a tender in payment of debts; pass any bill of attainder, ex post facto law, or law impairing the obligation of contracts, or grant any title of nobility.

No State shall, without the consent of Congress, lay any imposts or duties on imports or exports, except what may be absolutely necessary for executing its inspection laws: and the net produce of all duties and imposts, laid by any State on imports or exports, shall be for the use of the treasury of the United States; and all such laws shall be subject to the revision and control of the Congress.

No State shall, without the consent of Congress, lay any duty of tonnage, keep troops or ships of war in time of peace, enter into any agreement or compact with another State, or with a foreign power, or engage in war, unless actually invaded, or in such imminent danger as will not admit of delay.

Article II

Section 1. The executive power shall be vested in a President of the United States of America. He shall hold his office during the term of four years, and, together with the Vice President, chosen for the same term, be elected as follows:

Each state shall appoint, in such manner as the legislature thereof may direct, a number of electors, equal to the whole number of Senators and Representatives to which the State may be entitled in the Congress; but no Senator or Representative, or person holding an office of trust or profit under the United States, shall be appointed an elector.

The electors shall meet in their respective States, and vote by ballot for two persons, of whom one at least shall not be an inhabitant of the same State with themselves. And they shall make a list of all the persons voted for, and of the number of votes for each; which list they shall sign and certify, and transmit sealed to the seat of government of the United States, directed to the President of the Senate. The President of the Senate shall, in the presence of the Senate and the House of Representatives, open all the certificates, and the votes shall then be counted. The person having the greatest number of votes shall be the President, *if such number be a majority of the whole number of electors appointed; and if there be more than one who have such majority, and have an equal number of votes, then the House of Representatives shall immediately choose by ballot one of them for President; and if no person have a majority, then from the five highest on the list said house shall in like manner choose the President. But in choosing the President the votes shall be taken by States, the representation from each State having one vote; a quorum for this purpose shall consist of a member or members from two-thirds of the States, and a majority of all the States shall be necessary to a choice. In every case, after the choice of the President, the person having the greatest number of votes of the electors shall be the Vice President. But if there should remain two or more who have equal votes, the Senate shall choose from them by ballot the Vice President.*

The Congress may determine the time of choosing the electors and the day on which they shall give their votes; which day shall be the same throughout the United States.

No person except a natural-born citizen, *or a citizen of the United States at the time of the adoption of this Constitution,* shall be eligible to the office of President; neither shall any person be eligible to that office who shall not have attained to the age of thirty-five years, and been fourteen years a resident within the United States.

In case of the removal of the President from office or of his death, resignation, or inability to discharge the powers and duties of the said office, the same shall devolve on the Vice President, and the Congress may by law provide for the case of removal, death, resignation, or inability, both of the President and Vice President, declaring what officer shall then act as President, and such officer shall act accordingly, until the disability be removed, or a President shall be elected.

The President shall, at stated times, receive for his services a compensation, which shall neither be increased nor diminished during the period for which he shall have been elected, and he shall not receive within that period any other emolument from the United States, or any of them.

Before he enter on the execution of his office, he shall take the following oath or affirmation:—"I do solemnly swear (or affirm) that I will faithfully execute the office of the President of the United States, and will to the best of my ability preserve, protect and defend the Constitution of the United States."

Section 2. The President shall be commander in chief of the army and navy of the United States, and of the militia of the several States, when called into the actual service of the United States; he may require the opinion, in writing, of the principal officer in each of the executive departments, upon any subject relating to the duties of their respective offices, and he shall have power to grant reprieves and pardons for offenses against the United States, except in cases of impeachment.

He shall have power, by and with the advice and consent of the Senate, to make treaties, provided two-thirds of the Senators present concur; and he shall nominate, and by and with the advice and consent of the Senate, shall appoint ambassadors, other public ministers and consuls, judges of the Supreme Court, and all other officers of the United States, whose appointments are not herein otherwise provided for, and which shall be established by law: but Congress may by law vest the appointment of such inferior officers, as they think proper, in the President alone, in the courts of law, or in the heads of departments.

The President shall have power to fill up all vacancies that may happen during the recess of the Senate, by granting commissions which shall expire at the end of their next session.

Section 3. He shall from time to time give to the Congress information of the state of the Union, and recommend to their consideration such measures as he shall judge necessary and expedient; he may, on extraordinary occasions, convene both houses, or either of them, and in case of disagreement between them, with respect to the time of adjournment, he may adjourn them to such time as he shall think proper; he shall receive ambassadors and other public ministers; he shall take care that the laws be faithfully executed, and shall commission all the officers of the United States.

Section 4. The President, Vice President and all civil officers of the United States shall be removed from office on impeachment for, and on conviction of, treason, bribery, or other high crimes and misdemeanors.

Article III

Section 1. The judicial power of the United States shall be vested in one Supreme Court, and in such inferior courts as the Congress may from time to time ordain and establish. The judges, both of the Supreme

and inferior courts, shall hold their offices during good behavior, and shall, at stated times, receive for their services a compensation which shall not be diminished during their continuance in office.

Section 2. The judicial power shall extend to all cases, in law and equity, arising under this Constitution, the laws of the United States, and treaties made, or which shall be made, under their authority;—to all cases affecting ambassadors, other public ministers and consuls;—to all cases of admiralty and maritime jurisdiction;—to controversies to which the United States shall be a party;—to controversies between two or more States;—*between a State and citizens of another State;*—between citizens of different States;—between citizens of the same State claiming lands under grants of different States, and between a State, or the citizens thereof, and foreign states, citizens or subjects.

In all cases affecting ambassadors, other public ministers and consuls, and those in which a State shall be party, the Supreme Court shall have original jurisdiction. In all the other cases before mentioned, the Supreme Court shall have appellate jurisdiction, both as to law and fact, with such exceptions, and under such regulations, as the Congress shall make.

The trial of all crimes, except in cases of impeachment, shall be by jury; and such trial shall be held in the State where said crimes shall have been committed; but when not committed within any State, the trial shall be at such place or places as the Congress may by law have directed.

Section 3. Treason against the United States shall consist only in levying war against them, or in adhering to their enemies, giving them aid and comfort. No person shall be convicted of treason unless on the testimony of two witnesses to the same overt act, or on confession in open court.

The Congress shall have power to declare the punishment of treason, but no attainder of treason shall work corruption of blood, or forfeiture except during the life of the person attainted.

Article IV

Section 1. Full faith and credit shall be given in each State to the public acts, records, and judicial proceedings of every other State. And the Congress may by general laws prescribe the manner in which such acts, records, and proceedings shall be proved, and the effect thereof.

Section 2.   The citizens of each State shall be entitled to all privileges and immunities of citizens in the several States.

A person charged in any State with treason, felony, or other crime, who shall flee from justice, and be found in another State, shall on demand of the executive authority of the State from which he fled, be delivered up, to be removed to the State having jurisdiction of the crime.

No person held to service or labor in one State, under the laws thereof, escaping into another, shall, in consequence of any law or regulation therein, be discharged from such service or labor, but shall be delivered up on claim of the party to whom such service or labor may be due.

Section 3.   New States may be admitted by the Congress into this Union; but no new State shall be formed or erected within the jurisdiction of any other State; nor any State be formed by the junction of two or more States, or parts of States, without the consent of the legislatures of the States concerned as well as of the Congress.

The Congress shall have power to dispose of and make all needful rules and regulations respecting the territory or other property belonging to the United States; and nothing in this Constitution shall be so construed as to prejudice any claims of the United States, or of any particular State.

Section 4.   The United States shall guarantee to every State in this Union a republican form of government, and shall protect each of them against invasion; and on application of the legislature, or of the executive (when the legislature cannot be convened), against domestic violence.

Article V

The Congress, whenever two-thirds of both houses shall deem it necessary, shall propose amendments to this Constitution, or, on the application of the legislatures of two-thirds of the several States, shall call a convention for proposing amendments, which, in either case, shall be valid to all intents and purposes, as part of this Constitution, when ratified by the legislatures of three-fourths of the several States, or by conventions in three-fourths thereof, as the one or the other mode of ratification may be proposed by the Congress; provided *that no amendments which may be made prior to the year one thousand eight hundred and eight shall in any manner affect the first and fourth clauses in the ninth section of the first article;* and that no State, without its consent, shall be deprived of its equal suffrage in the Senate.

Article VI

All debts contracted and engagements entered into, before the adoption of this Constitution, shall be as valid against the United States under this Constitution, as under the Confederation.

This Constitution, and the laws of the United States which shall be made in pursuance thereof; and all treaties made, or which shall be made, under the authority of the United States, shall be the supreme law of the land; and the judges in every State shall be bound thereby, anything in the Constitution or laws of any State to the contrary notwithstanding.

The Senators and Representatives before mentioned, and the members of the several State legislatures, and all executive and judicial officers, both of the United States and of the several States, shall be bound by oath or affirmation to support this Constitution; but no religious test shall ever be required as a qualification to any office or public trust under the United States.

Article VII

The ratification of the conventions of nine States shall be sufficient for the establishment of this Constitution between the States so ratifying the same.

Done in Convention by the unanimous consent of the States present, the seventeenth day of September in the year of our Lord one thousand seven hundred and eighty-seven and of the Independence of the United States of America the twelfth. In witness whereof we have hereunto subscribed our names.

[Signed by]
G° WASHINGTON
Presidt and Deputy from Virginia
[*and thirty-eight others*]

AMENDMENTS TO THE CONSTITUTION

Article I*

Congress shall make no law respecting an establishment of religion, or prohibiting the free exercise thereof; or abridging the freedom of speech, or of the press; or the right of the people peaceably to assemble, and to petition the government for a redress of grievances.

Article II

A well-regulated militia being necessary to the security of a free State, the right of the people to keep and bear arms shall not be infringed.

Article III

No soldier shall, in time of peace, be quartered in any house without the consent of the owner, nor in time of war, but in a manner to be prescribed by law.

Article IV

The right of the people to be secure in their persons, houses, papers, and effects, against unreasonable searches and seizures, shall not be violated, and no warrants shall issue but upon probable cause, supported by oath or affirmation, and particularly describing the place to be searched, and the persons or things to be seized.

Article V

No person shall be held to answer for a capital, or otherwise infamous crime, unless on a presentment or indictment of a grand jury, except in cases arising in the land or naval forces, or in the militia, when in actual service in time of war or public danger; nor shall any person be subject for the same offense to be twice put in jeopardy of life or limb; nor shall be compelled in any criminal case to be a witness against himself, nor be deprived of life, liberty, or property, without due process of law; nor shall private property be taken for public use without just compensation.

Article VI

In all criminal prosecutions, the accused shall enjoy the right to a speedy and public trial, by an impartial jury of the State and district wherein the crime shall have been committed, which district shall have been previously ascertained by law, and to be informed of the nature and cause of the accusation; to be confronted with the witnesses against him; to have compulsory process for obtaining witnesses in his favor, and to have the assistance of counsel for his defense.

Article VII

In suits at common law, where the value in controversy shall exceed twenty dollars, the right of trial by jury shall be preserved, and no fact tried by a jury shall be otherwise reexamined in any court of the United States, than according to the rules of the common law.

Article VIII

Excessive bail shall not be required, nor excessive fines imposed, nor cruel and unusual punishments inflicted.

Article IX

The enumeration in the Constitution, of certain rights, shall not be construed to deny or disparage others retained by the people.

Article X

The powers not delegated to the United States by the Constitution, nor prohibited by it to the States, are reserved to the States respectively, or to the people.

Article XI
[*Adopted 1798*]

The judicial power of the United States shall not be construed to extend to any suit in law or equity, commenced or prosecuted against one of the United States by citizens of another State, or by citizens or subjects of any foreign state.

Article XII
[*Adopted 1804*]

The electors shall meet in their respective States, and vote by ballot for President and Vice President, one of whom, at least, shall not be an inhabitant of the same State with themselves; they shall name in their ballots the person voted for as President, and in distinct ballots the person voted for as Vice President, and they shall make distinct lists of all persons voted for as President, and of all per-

---

*The first ten Amendments (Bill of Rights) were adopted in 1791.

sons voted for as Vice President, and of the number of votes for each, which lists they shall sign and certify, and transmit sealed to the seat of government of the United States, directed to the President of the Senate;—the President of the Senate shall, in the presence of the Senate and House of Representatives, open all the certificates and the votes shall then be counted;—the person having the greatest number of votes for President shall be the President, if such number be a majority of the whole number of electors appointed; and if no person have such majority, then from the persons having the highest numbers not exceeding three on the list of those voted for as President, the House of Representatives shall choose immediately, by ballot, the President. But in choosing the President, the votes shall be taken by States, the representation from each State having one vote; a quorum for this purpose shall consist of a member or members from two-thirds of the States, and a majority of all the States shall be necessary to a choice. And if the House of Representatives shall not choose a President whenever the right of choice shall devolve upon them, before *the fourth day of March* next following, then the Vice President shall act as President, as in the case of the death or other constitutional disability of the President.

The person having the greatest number of votes as Vice President shall be the Vice President, if such a number be a majority of the whole number of electors appointed; and if no person have a majority, then from the two highest numbers on the list the Senate shall choose the Vice President; a quorum for the purpose shall consist of two-thirds of the whole number of Senators, and a majority of the whole number shall be necessary to a choice. But no person constitutionally ineligible to the office of President shall be eligible to that of Vice President of the United States.

Article XIII
[*Adopted 1865*]

Section 1.   Neither slavery nor involuntary servitude, except as a punishment for crime whereof the party shall have been duly convicted, shall exist within the United States, or any place subject to their jurisdiction.

Section 2.   Congress shall have power to enforce this article by appropriate legislation.

Article XIV
[*Adopted 1868*]

Section 1.   All persons born or naturalized in the United States, and subject to the jurisdiction thereof, are citizens of the United States and of the State wherein they reside. No State shall make or enforce any law which shall abridge the privileges or immunities of citizens of the United States; nor shall any State deprive any person of life, liberty, or property, without due process of law; nor deny to any person within its jurisdiction the equal protection of the laws.

Section 2.   Representatives shall be apportioned among the several States according to their respective numbers, counting the whole number of persons in each State, excluding Indians not taxed. But when the right to vote at any election for the choice of Electors for President and Vice President of the United States, Representatives in Congress, the executive and judicial officers of a State, or the members of the legislature thereof, is denied to any of the male inhabitants of such State, being twenty-one years of age and citizens of the United States, or in any way abridged, except for participation in rebellion, or other crime, the basis of representation therein shall be reduced in the proportion which the number of such male citizens shall bear to the whole number of male citizens twenty-one years of age in such State.

Section 3.   No person shall be a Senator or Representative in Congress or Elector of President and Vice President, or hold any office, civil or military, under the United States, or under any State, who, having previously taken an oath, as a member of Congress, or as an officer of the United States, or as a member of any State legislature, or as an executive or judicial officer of any State, to support the Constitution of the United States, shall have engaged in insurrection or rebellion against the same, or given aid and comfort to the enemies thereof. Congress may, by a vote of two-thirds of each house, remove such disability.

Section 4.   The validity of the public debt of the United States, authorized by law, including debts incurred for payment of pensions and bounties for services in suppressing insurrection or rebellion, shall not be questioned. But neither the United States nor any State shall assume or pay any debt or obligation incurred in aid of insurrection or rebellion against the United States, or any claim for the loss or emancipation of any slave; but all such debts, obligations, and claims shall be held illegal and void.

Section 5.   The Congress shall have the power to enforce, by appropriate legislation, the provisions of this article.

Article XV
[*Adopted 1870*]

Section 1.   The right of citizens of the United States to vote shall not be denied or abridged by the United States or by any State on account of race, color, or previous condition of servitude.

Section 2.   The Congress shall have power to enforce this article by appropriate legislation.

Article XVI
[*Adopted 1913*]

The Congress shall have power to lay and collect taxes on incomes, from whatever source derived, without apportionment among the several States, and without regard to any census or enumeration.

Article XVII
[*Adopted 1913*]

Section 1.   The Senate of the United States shall be composed of two Senators from each State, elected by the people thereof, for six years; and each Senator shall have one vote. The electors in each State shall have the qualifications requisite for electors of [voters for] the most numerous branch of the State legislatures.

Section 2.   When vacancies happen in the representation of any State in the Senate, the executive authority of such State shall issue writs of election to fill such vacancies: Provided, that the Legislature of any State may empower the executive thereof to make temporary appointments until the people fill the vacancies by election as the Legislature may direct.

Section 3.   This amendment shall not be so construed as to affect the election or term of any Senator chosen before it becomes valid as part of the Constitution.

Article XVIII
[*Adopted 1919; repealed 1933*]

Section 1.   *After one year from the ratification of this article the manufacture, sale, or transportation of intoxicating liquors within, the importation thereof into, or the exportation thereof from the United States and all territory subject to the jurisdiction thereof, for beverage purposes, is hereby prohibited.*

Section 2.   *The Congress and the several States shall have concurrent power to enforce this article by appropriate legislation.*

Section 3.   *This article shall be inoperative unless it shall have been ratified as an amendment to the Constitution by the legislatures of the several States, as provided by the Constitution, within seven years from the date of the submission thereof to the States by the Congress.*

Article XIX
[*Adopted 1920*]

Section 1.   The right of citizens of the United States to vote shall not be denied or abridged by the United States or by any State on account of sex.

Section 2.   The Congress shall have the power to enforce this article by appropriate legislation.

Article XX
[*Adopted 1933*]

Section 1.   The terms of the President and Vice President shall end at noon on the 20th day of January, and the terms of Senators and Representatives at noon on the 3d day of January, of the years in which such terms would have ended if this article had not been ratified; and the terms of their successors shall then begin.

Section 2.   The Congress shall assemble at least once in every year, and such meeting shall begin at noon on the 3d of January, unless they shall by law appoint a different day.

Section 3.   If, at the time fixed for the beginning of the term of the President, the President-elect shall have died, the Vice President-elect shall become President. If a President shall not have been chosen before the time fixed for the beginning of his term, or if the President-elect shall have failed to qualify, then the Vice President-elect shall act as President until a President shall have qualified; and the Congress may by law provide for the case wherein neither a President-elect nor a Vice President-elect shall have qualified, declaring who shall then act as President, or the manner in which one who is to act shall be selected, and such persons shall act accordingly until a President or Vice President shall have qualified.

Section 4. The Congress may by law provide for the case of the death of any of the persons from whom the House of Representatives may choose a President whenever the right of choice shall have devolved upon them, and for the case of the death of any of the persons from whom the Senate may choose a Vice President whenever the right of choice shall have devolved upon them.

Section 5. Sections 1 and 2 shall take effect on the 15th day of October following the ratification of this article.

Section 6. This article shall be inoperative unless it shall have been ratified as an amendment to the Constitution by the Legislatures of three-fourths of the several States within seven years from the date of its submission.

Article XXI
[*Adopted 1933*]

Section 1. The eighteenth article of amendment to the Constitution of the United States is hereby repealed.

Section 2. The transportation or importation into any State, Territory, or Possession of the United States for delivery or use therein of intoxicating liquors, in violation of the laws thereof, is hereby prohibited.

Section 3. This article shall be inoperative unless it shall have been ratified as an amendment to the Constitution by conventions in the several States, as provided in the Constitution, within seven years from the date of submission thereof to the States by the Congress.

Article XXII
[*Adopted 1951*]

Section 1. No person shall be elected to the office of President more than twice, and no person who has held the office of President, or acted as President, for more than two years of a term to which some other person was elected President shall be elected to the office of President more than once. But this article shall not apply to any person holding the office of President when this article was proposed by the Congress, and shall not prevent any person who may be holding the office of President, or acting as President, during the term within which this article becomes operative from holding the office of President or acting as President during the remainder of such term.

Section 2. This article shall be inoperative unless it shall have been ratified as an amendment to the Constitution by the legislatures of three-fourths of the several States within seven years from the date of its submission to the States by the Congress.

Article XXIII
[*Adopted 1961*]

Section 1. The District constituting the seat of Government of the United States shall appoint in such manner as the Congress may direct:

A number of electors of President and Vice President equal to the whole number of Senators and Representatives in Congress to which the District would be entitled if it were a State, but in no event more than the least populous State; they shall be in addition to those appointed by the States, but they shall be considered for the purposes of the election of President and Vice President, to be electors appointed by a State; and they shall meet in the District and perform such duties as provided by the twelfth article of amendment.

Section 2. The Congress shall have the power to enforce this article by appropriate legislation.

Article XXIV
[*Adopted 1964*]

Section 1. The right of citizens of the United States to vote in any primary or other election for President or Vice President, for electors for President or Vice President, or for Senator or Representative in Congress, shall not be denied or abridged by the United States or any State by reason of failure to pay any poll tax or other tax.

Section 2. The Congress shall have the power to enforce this article by appropriate legislation.

Article XXV
[*Adopted 1967*]

Section 1. In case of the removal of the President from office or of his death or resignation, the Vice President shall become President.

Section 2. Whenever there is a vacancy in the office of the Vice President, the President shall nominate a Vice President who shall take office upon confirmation by a majority vote of both Houses of Congress.

Section 3. Whenever the President transmits to the President pro tempore of the Senate and the Speaker of the House of Representatives his written declaration that he is unable to discharge the powers and duties of his office, and until he transmits to them a written declaration to the contrary, such powers and duties shall be discharged by the Vice President as Acting President.

Section 4. Whenever the Vice President and a majority of either the principal officers of the executive departments or of such other body as Congress may by law provide, transmit to the President pro tempore of the Senate and the Speaker of the House of Representatives their written declaration that the President is unable to discharge the powers and duties of his office, the Vice President shall immediately assume the powers and duties of the office as Acting President.

Thereafter, when the President transmits to the President pro tempore of the Senate and the Speaker of the House of Representatives his written declaration that no inability exists, he shall resume the powers and duties of his office unless the Vice President and a majority of either the principal officers of the executive department[s] or of such other body as Congress may by law provide, transmit within four days to the President pro tempore of the Senate and the Speaker of the House of Representatives their written declaration that the President is unable to discharge the powers and duties of his office. Thereupon Congress shall decide the issue, assembling within forty-eight hours for that purpose if not in session. If the Congress, within twenty-one days after receipt of the latter written declaration, or, if Congress is not in session, within twenty-one days after Congress is required to assemble, determines by two-thirds vote of both Houses that the President is unable to discharge the powers and duties of his office, the Vice President shall continue to discharge the same as Acting President; otherwise, the President shall resume the powers and duties of his office.

Article XXVI
[*Adopted 1971*]

Section 1. The right of citizens of the United States, who are eighteen years of age or older, to vote shall not be denied or abridged by the United States or by any State on account of age.

Section 2. The Congress shall have power to enforce this article by appropriate legislation.

Article XXVII*
[*Adopted 1992*]

No law, varying the compensation for services of the Senators and Representatives, shall take effect, until an election of Representatives shall have intervened.

---

*Originally proposed in 1789 by James Madison, this amendment failed to win ratification along with the other parts of what became the Bill of Rights. However, the proposed amendment contained no deadline for ratification, and over the years other state legislatures voted to add it to the Constitution; many such ratifications occurred during the 1980s and early 1990s as public frustration with Congress's performance mounted. In May 1992 the Archivist of the United States certified that, with the Michigan legislature's ratification, the article had been approved by three-fourths of the states and thus automatically became part of the Constitution. But congressional leaders and constitutional specialists questioned whether an amendment that took 202 years to win ratification was valid, and the issue had not been resolved by the time this book went to press.

Growth of U.S. Population and Area

Census	Population	Percentage of Increase over Preceding Census	Land Area Square Miles	Population per Square Mile
1790	3,929,214		867,980	4.5
1800	5,308,483	35.1	867,980	6.1
1810	7,239,881	36.4	1,685,865	4.3
1820	9,638,453	33.1	1,753,588	5.5
1830	12,866,020	33.5	1,753,588	7.3
1840	17,069,453	32.7	1,753,588	9.7
1850	23,191,876	35.9	2,944,337	7.9
1860	31,443,321	35.6	2,973,965	10.6
1870	39,818,449	26.6	2,973,965	13.4
1880	50,155,783	26.0	2,973,965	16.9
1890	62,947,714	25.5	2,973,965	21.2
1900	75,994,575	20.7	2,974,159	25.6
1910	91,972,266	21.0	2,973,890	30.9
1920	105,710,620	14.9	2,973,776	35.5
1930	122,775,046	16.1	2,977,128	41.2
1940	131,669,275	7.2	2,977,128	44.2
1950	150,697,361	14.5	2,974,726*	50.7
1960†	178,464,236	18.4	2,974,726	59.9
1970	204,765,770	14.7	2,974,726	68.8
1980	226,504,825	10.6	2,974,726	76.1
1990	248,709,873	9.8	2,974,726	83.6

*As remeasured in 1940.
†Not including Alaska (pop. 226,167) and Hawaii (632,772).

Admission of States into the Union

State	Date of Admission	State	Date of Admission
1. Delaware	December 7, 1787	26. Michigan	January 26, 1837
2. Pennsylvania	December 12, 1787	27. Florida	March 3, 1845
3. New Jersey	December 18, 1787	28. Texas	December 29, 1845
4. Georgia	January 2, 1788	29. Iowa	December 28, 1846
5. Connecticut	January 9, 1788	30. Wisconsin	May 29, 1848
6. Massachusetts	February 6, 1788	31. California	September 9, 1850
7. Maryland	April 28, 1788	32. Minnesota	May 11, 1858
8. South Carolina	May 23, 1788	33. Oregon	February 14, 1859
9. New Hampshire	June 21, 1788	34. Kansas	January 29, 1861
10. Virginia	June 25, 1788	35. West Virginia	June 20, 1863
11. New York	July 26, 1788	36. Nevada	October 31, 1864
12. North Carolina	November 21, 1789	37. Nebraska	March 1, 1867
13. Rhode Island	May 29, 1790	38. Colorado	August 1, 1876
14. Vermont	March 4, 1791	39. North Dakota	November 2, 1889
15. Kentucky	June 1, 1792	40. South Dakota	November 2, 1889
16. Tennessee	June 1, 1796	41. Montana	November 8, 1889
17. Ohio	March 1, 1803	42. Washington	November 11, 1889
18. Louisiana	April 30, 1812	43. Idaho	July 3, 1890
19. Indiana	December 11, 1816	44. Wyoming	July 10, 1890
20. Mississippi	December 10, 1817	45. Utah	January 4, 1896
21. Illinois	December 3, 1818	46. Oklahoma	November 16, 1907
22. Alabama	December 14, 1819	47. New Mexico	January 6, 1912
23. Maine	March 15, 1820	48. Arizona	February 14, 1912
24. Missouri	August 10, 1821	49. Alaska	January 3, 1959
25. Arkansas	June 15, 1836	50. Hawaii	August 21, 1959

Presidential Elections, 1789–1992

Year	States in the Union	Candidates	Parties	Electoral Vote	Popular Vote	Percentage of Popular Vote
1789	11	GEORGE WASHINGTON	No party designations	69		
		John Adams		34		
		Minor candidates		35		
1792	15	GEORGE WASHINGTON	No party designations	132		
		John Adams		77		
		George Clinton		50		
		Minor candidates		5		
1796	16	JOHN ADAMS	Federalist	71		
		Thomas Jefferson	Democratic-Republican	68		
		Thomas Pinckney	Federalist	59		
		Aaron Burr	Democratic-Republican	30		
		Minor candidates		48		
1800	16	THOMAS JEFFERSON	Democratic-Republican	73		
		Aaron Burr	Democratic-Republican	73		
		John Adams	Federalist	65		
		Charles C. Pinckney	Federalist	64		
		John Jay	Federalist	1		
1804	17	THOMAS JEFFERSON	Democratic-Republican	162		
		Charles C. Pinckney	Federalist	14		
1808	17	JAMES MADISON	Democratic-Republican	122		
		Charles C. Pinckney	Federalist	47		
		George Clinton	Democratic-Republican	6		
1812	18	JAMES MADISON	Democratic-Republican	128		
		DeWitt Clinton	Federalist	89		
1816	19	JAMES MONROE	Democratic-Republican	183		
		Rufus King	Federalist	34		
1820	24	JAMES MONROE	Democratic-Republican	231		
		John Quincy Adams	Independent Republican	1		
1824	24	JOHN QUINCY ADAMS	Democratic-Republican	84	108,740	30.5
		Andrew Jackson	Democratic-Republican	99	153,544	43.1
		William H. Crawford	Democratic-Republican	41	46,618	13.1
		Henry Clay	Democratic-Republican	37	47,136	13.2
1828	24	ANDREW JACKSON	Democratic	178	642,553	56.0
		John Quincy Adams	National Republican	83	500,897	44.0
1832	24	ANDREW JACKSON	Democratic	219	687,502	55.0
		Henry Clay	National Republican	49	530,189	42.4
		William Wirt	Anti-Masonic	7 ⎫	33,108	2.6
		John Floyd	National Republican	11 ⎭		
1836	26	MARTIN VAN BUREN	Democratic	170	765,483	50.9
		William H. Harrison	Whig	73 ⎫		
		Hugh L. White	Whig	26 ⎪	739,795	49.1
		Daniel Webster	Whig	14 ⎪		
		W. P. Mangum	Whig	11 ⎭		
1840	26	WILLIAM H. HARRISON	Whig	234	1,274,624	53.1
		Martin Van Buren	Democratic	60	1,127,781	46.9
1844	26	JAMES K. POLK	Democratic	170	1,338,464	49.6
		Henry Clay	Whig	105	1,300,097	48.1
		James G. Birney	Liberty		62,300	2.3

cont.

Because candidates receiving less than 1 percent of the popular vote are omitted, the percentage of popular vote may not total 100 percent.

Before the Twelfth Amendment was passed in 1804, the electoral college voted for two presidential candidates; the runner-up became vice president.

Presidential Elections, 1789–1992 (cont.)

Year	States in the Union	Candidates	Parties	Electoral Vote	Popular Vote	Percentage of Popular Vote
1848	30	ZACHARY TAYLOR	Whig	163	1,360,967	47.4
		Lewis Cass	Democratic	127	1,222,342	42.5
		Martin Van Buren	Free Soil		291,263	10.1
1852	31	FRANKLIN PIERCE	Democratic	254	1,601,117	50.9
		Winfield Scott	Whig	42	1,385,453	44.1
		John P. Hale	Free Soil		155,825	5.0
1856	31	JAMES BUCHANAN	Democratic	174	1,832,955	45.3
		John C. Frémont	Republican	114	1,339,932	33.1
		Millard Fillmore	American	8	871,731	21.6
1860	33	ABRAHAM LINCOLN	Republican	180	1,865,593	39.8
		Stephen A. Douglas	Democratic	12	1,382,713	29.5
		John C. Breckinridge	Democratic	72	848,356	18.1
		John Bell	Constitutional Union	39	592,906	12.6
1864	36	ABRAHAM LINCOLN	Republican	212	2,206,938	55.0
		George B. McClellan	Democratic	21	1,803,787	45.0
1868	37	ULYSSES S. GRANT	Republican	214	3,013,421	52.7
		Horatio Seymour	Democratic	80	2,706,829	47.3
1872	37	ULYSSES S. GRANT	Republican	286	3,596,745	55.6
		Horace Greeley	Democratic	*	2,843,446	43.9
1876	38	RUTHERFORD B. HAYES	Republican	185	4,034,311	48.0
		Samuel J. Tilden	Democratic	184	4,288,546	51.0
		Peter Cooper	Greenback		75,973	1.0
1880	38	JAMES A. GARFIELD	Republican	214	4,453,295	48.5
		Winfield S. Hancock	Democratic	155	4,414,082	48.1
		James B. Weaver	Greenback-Labor		308,578	3.4
1884	38	GROVER CLEVELAND	Democratic	219	4,879,507	48.5
		James G. Blaine	Republican	182	4,850,293	48.2
		Benjamin F. Butler	Greenback-Labor		175,370	1.8
		John P. St. John	Prohibition		150,369	1.5
1888	38	BENJAMIN HARRISON	Republican	233	5,477,129	47.9
		Grover Cleveland	Democratic	168	5,537,857	48.6
		Clinton B. Fisk	Prohibition		249,506	2.2
		Anson J. Streeter	Union Labor		146,935	1.3
1892	44	GROVER CLEVELAND	Democratic	277	5,555,426	46.1
		Benjamin Harrison	Republican	145	5,182,690	43.0
		James B. Weaver	People's	22	1,029,846	8.5
		John Bidwell	Prohibition		264,133	2.2
1896	45	WILLIAM McKINLEY	Republican	271	7,102,246	51.1
		William J. Bryan	Democratic	176	6,492,559	47.7
1900	45	WILLIAM McKINLEY	Republican	292	7,218,491	51.7
		William J. Bryan	Democratic; Populist	155	6,356,734	45.5
		John C. Wooley	Prohibition		208,914	1.5
1904	45	THEODORE ROOSEVELT	Republican	336	7,628,461	57.4
		Alton B. Parker	Democratic	140	5,084,223	37.6
		Eugene V. Debs	Socialist		402,283	3.0
		Silas C. Swallow	Prohibition		258,536	1.9

*When Greeley died shortly after the election, his supporters divided their votes among the minor candidates.

Because candidates receiving less than 1 percent of the popular vote are omitted, the percentage of popular vote may not total 100 percent.

Presidential Elections, 1789–1992 *(cont.)*

Year	States in the Union	Candidates	Parties	Electoral Vote	Popular Vote	Percentage of Popular Vote
1908	46	WILLIAM H. TAFT	Republican	321	7,675,320	51.6
		William J. Bryan	Democratic	162	6,412,294	43.1
		Eugene V. Debs	Socialist		420,793	2.8
		Eugene W. Chafin	Prohibition		253,840	1.7
1912	48	WOODROW WILSON	Democratic	435	6,296,547	41.9
		Theodore Roosevelt	Progressive	88	4,118,571	27.4
		William H. Taft	Republican	8	3,486,720	23.2
		Eugene V. Debs	Socialist		900,672	6.0
		Eugene W. Chafin	Prohibition		206,275	1.4
1916	48	WOODROW WILSON	Democratic	277	9,127,695	49.4
		Charles E. Hughes	Republican	254	8,533,507	46.2
		A. L. Benson	Socialist		585,113	3.2
		J. Frank Hanly	Prohibition		220,506	1.2
1920	48	WARREN G. HARDING	Republican	404	16,143,407	60.4
		James N. Cox	Democratic	127	9,130,328	34.2
		Eugene V. Debs	Socialist		919,799	3.4
		P. P. Christensen	Farmer-Labor		265,411	1.0
1924	48	CALVIN COOLIDGE	Republican	382	15,718,211	54.0
		John W. Davis	Democratic	136	8,385,283	28.8
		Robert M. La Follette	Progressive	13	4,831,289	16.6
1928	48	HERBERT C. HOOVER	Republican	444	21,391,993	58.2
		Alfred E. Smith	Democratic	87	15,016,169	40.9
1932	48	FRANKLIN D. ROOSEVELT	Democratic	472	22,809,638	57.4
		Herbert C. Hoover	Republican	59	15,758,901	39.7
		Norman Thomas	Socialist		881,951	2.2
1936	48	FRANKLIN D. ROOSEVELT	Democratic	523	27,752,869	60.8
		Alfred M. Landon	Republican	8	16,674,665	36.5
		William Lemke	Union		882,479	1.9
1940	48	FRANKLIN D. ROOSEVELT	Democratic	449	27,307,819	54.8
		Wendell L. Willkie	Republican	82	22,321,018	44.8
1944	48	FRANKLIN D. ROOSEVELT	Democratic	432	25,606,585	53.5
		Thomas E. Dewey	Republican	99	22,014,745	46.0
1948	48	HARRY S TRUMAN	Democratic	303	24,105,812	49.5
		Thomas E. Dewey	Republican	189	21,970,065	45.1
		Strom Thurmond	States' Rights	39	1,169,063	2.4
		Henry A. Wallace	Progressive		1,157,172	2.4
1952	48	DWIGHT D. EISENHOWER	Republican	442	33,936,234	55.1
		Adlai E. Stevenson	Democratic	89	27,314,992	44.4
1956	48	DWIGHT D. EISENHOWER	Republican	457	35,590,472	57.6
		Adlai E. Stevenson	Democratic	73	26,022,752	42.1
1960	50	JOHN F. KENNEDY	Democratic	303	34,227,096	49.7
		Richard M. Nixon	Republican	219	34,108,546	49.5
		Harry F. Byrd	Independent	15	502,363	.7
1964	50	LYNDON B. JOHNSON	Democratic	486	43,126,506	61.1
		Barry M. Goldwater	Republican	52	27,176,799	38.5
1968	50	RICHARD M. NIXON	Republican	301	31,770,237	43.4
		Hubert H. Humphrey	Democratic	191	31,270,533	42.7
		George C. Wallace	American Independent	46	9,906,141	13.5

cont.

Because candidates receiving less than 1 percent of the popular vote are omitted, the percentage of popular vote may not total 100 percent.

Presidential Elections, 1789–1992 *(cont.)*

Year	States in the Union	Candidates	Parties	Electoral Vote	Popular Vote	Percentage of Popular Vote
1972	50	RICHARD M. NIXON	Republican	520	47,169,911	60.7
		George S. McGovern	Democratic	17	29,170,383	37.5
1976	50	JIMMY CARTER	Democratic	297	40,827,394	49.9
		Gerald R. Ford	Republican	240	39,145,977	47.9
1980	50	RONALD W. REAGAN	Republican	489	43,899,248	50.8
		Jimmy Carter	Democratic	49	35,481,435	41.0
		John B. Anderson	Independent		5,719,437	6.6
		Ed Clark	Libertarian		920,859	1.0
1984	50	RONALD W. REAGAN	Republican	525	54,451,521	58.8
		Walter F. Mondale	Democratic	13	37,565,334	40.5
1988	50	GEORGE H. W. BUSH	Republican	426	47,946,422	54.0
		Michael S. Dukakis	Democratic	112	41,016,429	46.0
1992	50	WILLIAM J. CLINTON	Democratic	370	43,728,275	43.2
		George H. W. Bush	Republican	168	38,167,416	37.7
		H. Ross Perot	Independent		19,237,247	19.0

Because candidates receiving less than 1 percent of the popular vote are omitted, the percentage of popular vote may not total 100 percent.

Vice President and Cabinet Members, 1789–1995

The Washington Administration (1789–1797)

Vice President	John Adams	1789–1797
Secretary of State	Thomas Jefferson	1789–1793
	Edmund Randolph	1794–1795
	Timothy Pickering	1795–1797
Secretary of Treasury	Alexander Hamilton	1789–1795
	Oliver Wolcott	1795–1797
Secretary of War	Henry Knox	1789–1794
	Timothy Pickering	1795–1796
	James McHenry	1796–1797
Attorney General	Edmund Randolph	1789–1793
	William Bradford	1794–1795
	Charles Lee	1795–1797
Postmaster General	Samuel Osgood	1789–1791
	Timothy Pickering	1791–1794
	Joseph Habersham	1795–1797

The John Adams Administration (1797–1801)

Vice President	Thomas Jefferson	1797–1801
Secretary of State	Timothy Pickering	1797–1800
	John Marshall	1800–1801
Secretary of Treasury	Oliver Wolcott	1797–1800
	Samuel Dexter	1800–1801
Secretary of War	James McHenry	1797–1800
	Samuel Dexter	1800–1801
Attorney General	Charles Lee	1797–1801
Postmaster General	Joseph Habersham	1797–1801
Secretary of Navy	Benjamin Stoddert	1798–1801

The Jefferson Administration (1801–1809)

Vice President	Aaron Burr	1801–1805
	George Clinton	1805–1809
Secretary of State	James Madison	1801–1809
Secretary of Treasury	Samuel Dexter	1801
	Albert Gallatin	1801–1809
Secretary of War	Henry Dearborn	1801–1809
Attorney General	Levi Lincoln	1801–1805
	Robert Smith	1805
	John Breckinridge	1805–1806
	Caesar Rodney	1807–1809
Postmaster General	Joseph Habersham	1801
	Gideon Granger	1801–1809
Secretary of Navy	Robert Smith	1801–1809

The Madison Administration (1809–1817)

Vice President	George Clinton	1809–1812
	Elbridge Gerry	1813–1814

cont.

The Madison Administration (1809–1817)   (cont.)

Secretary of State	Robert Smith	1809–1811
	James Monroe	1811–1817
Secretary of Treasury	Albert Gallatin	1809–1813
	George Campbell	1814
	Alexander Dallas	1814–1816
	William Crawford	1816–1817
Secretary of War	William Eustis	1809–1812
	John Armstrong	1813–1814
	James Monroe	1814–1815
	William Crawford	1815–1817
Attorney General	Caesar Rodney	1809–1811
	William Pinkney	1811–1814
	Richard Rush	1814–1817
Postmaster General	Gideon Granger	1809–1814
	Return Meigs	1814–1817
Secretary of Navy	Paul Hamilton	1809–1813
	William Jones	1813–1814
	Benjamin Crowninshield	1814–1817

The Monroe Administration (1817–1825)

Vice President	Daniel Tompkins	1817–1825
Secretary of State	John Quincy Adams	1817–1825
Secretary of Treasury	William Crawford	1817–1825
Secretary of War	George Graham	1817
	John C. Calhoun	1817–1825
Attorney General	Richard Rush	1817
	William Wirt	1817–1825
Postmaster General	Return Meigs	1817–1823
	John McLean	1823–1825
Secretary of Navy	Benjamin Crowninshield	1817–1818
	Smith Thompson	1818–1823
	Samuel Southard	1823–1825

The John Quincy Adams Administration (1825–1829)

Vice President	John C. Calhoun	1825–1829
Secretary of State	Henry Clay	1825–1829
Secretary of Treasury	Richard Rush	1825–1829
Secretary of War	James Barbour	1825–1828
	Peter Porter	1828–1829
Attorney General	William Wirt	1825–1829
Postmaster General	John McLean	1825–1829
Secretary of Navy	Samuel Southard	1825–1829

The Jackson Administration (1829–1837)

Vice President	John C. Calhoun	1829–1833
	Martin Van Buren	1833–1837
Secretary of State	Martin Van Buren	1829–1831
	Edward Livingston	1831–1833

The Jackson Administration (1829–1837) (cont.)

	Louis McLane	1833–1834
	John Forsyth	1834–1837
Secretary of Treasury	Samuel Ingham	1829–1831
	Louis McLane	1831–1833
	William Duane	1833
	Roger B. Taney	1833–1834
	Levi Woodbury	1834–1837
Secretary of War	John H. Eaton	1829–1831
	Lewis Cass	1831–1837
	Benjamin Butler	1837
Attorney General	John M. Berrien	1829–1831
	Roger B. Taney	1831–1833
	Benjamin Butler	1833–1837
Postmaster General	William Barry	1829–1835
	Amos Kendall	1835–1837
Secretary of Navy	John Branch	1829–1831
	Levi Woodbury	1831–1834
	Mahlon Dickerson	1834–1837

The Van Buren Administration (1837–1841)

Vice President	Richard M. Johnson	1837–1841
Secretary of State	John Forsyth	1837–1841
Secretary of Treasury	Levi Woodbury	1837–1841
Secretary of War	Joel Poinsett	1837–1841
Attorney General	Benjamin Butler	1837–1838
	Felix Grundy	1838–1840
	Henry D. Gilpin	1840–1841
Postmaster General	Amos Kendall	1837–1840
	John M. Niles	1840–1841
Secretary of Navy	Mahlon Dickerson	1837–1838
	James Paulding	1838–1841

The William Harrison Administration (1841)

Vice President	John Tyler	1841
Secretary of State	Daniel Webster	1841
Secretary of Treasury	Thomas Ewing	1841
Secretary of War	John Bell	1841
Attorney General	John J. Crittenden	1841
Postmaster General	Francis Granger	1841
Secretary of Navy	George Badger	1841

The Tyler Administration (1841–1845)

Vice President	None	
Secretary of State	Daniel Webster	1841–1843
	Hugh S. Legaré	1843
	Abel P. Upshur	1843–1844
	John C. Calhoun	1844–1845

cont.

The Tyler Administration (1841–1845) (cont.)

Secretary of Treasury	Thomas Ewing	1841
	Walter Forward	1841–1843
	John C. Spencer	1843–1844
	George Bibb	1844–1845
Secretary of War	John Bell	1841
	John C. Spencer	1841–1843
	James M. Porter	1843–1844
	William Wilkins	1844–1845
Attorney General	John J. Crittenden	1841
	Hugh S. Legaré	1841–1843
	John Nelson	1843–1845
Postmaster General	Francis Granger	1841
	Charles Wickliffe	1841
Secretary of Navy	George Badger	1841
	Abel P. Upshur	1841
	David Henshaw	1843–1844
	Thomas Gilmer	1844
	John Y. Mason	1844–1845

The Polk Administration (1845–1849)

Vice President	George M. Dallas	1845–1849
Secretary of State	James Buchanan	1845–1849
Secretary of Treasury	Robert J. Walker	1845–1849
Secretary of War	William L. Marcy	1845–1849
Attorney General	John Y. Mason	1845–1846
	Nathan Clifford	1846–1848
	Isaac Toucey	1848–1849
Postmaster General	Cave Johnson	1845–1849
Secretary of Navy	George Bancroft	1845–1846
	John Y. Mason	1846–1849

The Taylor Administration (1849–1850)

Vice President	Millard Fillmore	1849–1850
Secretary of State	John M. Clayton	1849–1850
Secretary of Treasury	William Meredith	1849–1850
Secretary of War	George Crawford	1849–1850
Attorney General	Reverdy Johnson	1849–1850
Postmaster General	Jacob Collamer	1849–1850
Secretary of Navy	William Preston	1849–1850
Secretary of Interior	Thomas Ewing	1849–1850

The Fillmore Administration (1850–1853)

Vice President	None	
Secretary of State	Daniel Webster	1850–1852
	Edward Everett	1852–1853
Secretary of Treasury	Thomas Corwin	1850–1853
Secretary of War	Charles Conrad	1850–1853

The Fillmore Administration (1850–1853) (cont.)

Attorney General	John J. Crittenden	1850–1853
Postmaster General	Nathan Hall	1850–1852
	Sam D. Hubbard	1852–1853
Secretary of Navy	William A. Graham	1850–1852
	John P. Kennedy	1852–1853
Secretary of Interior	Thomas McKennan	1850
	Alexander Stuart	1850–1853

The Pierce Administration (1853–1857)

Vice President	William R. King	1853
Secretary of State	William L. Marcy	1853–1857
Secretary of Treasury	James Guthrie	1853–1857
Secretary of War	Jefferson Davis	1853–1857
Attorney General	Caleb Cushing	1853–1857
Postmaster General	James Campbell	1853–1857
Secretary of Navy	James C. Dobbin	1853–1857
Secretary of Interior	Robert McClelland	1853–1857

The Buchanan Administration (1857–1861)

Vice President	John C. Breckinridge	1857–1861
Secretary of State	Lewis Cass	1857–1860
	Jeremiah S. Black	1860–1861
Secretary of Treasury	Howell Cobb	1857–1860
	Philip Thomas	1860–1861
	John A. Dix	1861
Secretary of War	John B. Floyd	1857–1861
	Joseph Holt	1861
Attorney General	Jeremiah S. Black	1857–1860
	Edwin M. Stanton	1860–1861
Postmaster General	Aaron V. Brown	1857–1859
	Joseph Holt	1859–1861
	Horatio King	1861
Secretary of Navy	Isaac Toucey	1857–1861
Secretary of Interior	Jacob Thompson	1857–1861

The Lincoln Administration (1861–1865)

Vice President	Hannibal Hamlin	1861–1865
	Andrew Johnson	1865
Secretary of State	William H. Seward	1861–1865
Secretary of Treasury	Samuel P. Chase	1861–1864
	William P. Fessenden	1864–1865
	Hugh McCulloch	1865
Secretary of War	Simon Cameron	1861–1862
	Edwin M. Stanton	1862–1865
Attorney General	Edward Bates	1861–1864
	James Speed	1864–1865
Postmaster General	Horatio King	1861

cont.

The Lincoln Administration (1861–1865)   (cont.)

	Montgomery Blair	1861–1864
	William Dennison	1864–1865
Secretary of Navy	Gideon Welles	1861–1865
Secretary of Interior	Caleb B. Smith	1861–1863
	John P. Usher	1863–1865

The Andrew Johnson Administration (1865–1869)

Vice President	None	
Secretary of State	William H. Seward	1865–1869
Secretary of Treasury	Hugh McCulloch	1865–1869
Secretary of War	Edwin M. Stanton	1865–1867
	Ulysses S. Grant	1867–1868
	Lorenzo Thomas	1868
	John M. Schofield	1868–1869
Attorney General	James Speed	1865–1866
	Henry Stanbery	1866–1868
	William M. Evarts	1868–1869
Postmaster General	William Dennison	1865–1866
	Alexander Randall	1866–1869
Secretary of Navy	Gideon Welles	1865–1869
Secretary of Interior	John P. Usher	1865
	James Harlan	1865–1866
	Orville H. Browning	1866–1869

The Grant Administration (1869–1877)

Vice President	Schuyler Colfax	1869–1873
	Henry Wilson	1873–1875
Secretary of State	Elihu B. Washburne	1869
	Hamilton Fish	1869–1877
Secretary of Treasury	George S. Boutwell	1869–1873
	William Richardson	1873–1874
	Benjamin Bristow	1874–1876
	Lot M. Morrill	1876–1877
Secretary of War	John A. Rawlins	1869
	William T. Sherman	1869
	William W. Belknap	1869–1876
	Alphonso Taft	1876
	James D. Cameron	1876–1877
Attorney General	Ebenezer Hoar	1869–1870
	Amos T. Ackerman	1870–1871
	G. H. Williams	1871–1875
	Edwards Pierrepont	1875–1876
	Alphonso Taft	1876–1877
Postmaster General	John A. J. Creswell	1869–1874
	James W. Marshall	1874
	Marshall Jewell	1874–1876
	James N. Tyner	1876–1877

The Grant Administration (1869–1877)   (cont.)

Secretary of Navy	Adolph E. Borie	1869
	George M. Robeson	1869–1877
Secretary of Interior	Jacob D. Cox	1869–1870
	Columbus Delano	1870–1875
	Zachariah Chandler	1875–1877

The Hayes Administration (1877–1881)

Vice President	William A. Wheeler	1877–1881
Secretary of State	William M. Evarts	1877–1881
Secretary of Treasury	John Sherman	1877–1881
Secretary of War	George W. McCrary	1877–1879
	Alex Ramsey	1879–1881
Attorney General	Charles Devens	1877–1881
Postmaster General	David M. Key	1877–1880
	Horace Maynard	1880–1881
Secretary of Navy	Richard W. Thompson	1877–1880
	Nathan Goff, Jr.	1881
Secretary of Interior	Carl Schurz	1877–1881

The Garfield Administration (1881)

Vice President	Chester A. Arthur	1881
Secretary of State	James G. Blaine	1881
Secretary of Treasury	William Windom	1881
Secretary of War	Robert T. Lincoln	1881
Attorney General	Wayne MacVeagh	1881
Postmaster General	Thomas L. James	1881
Secretary of Navy	William H. Hunt	1881
Secretary of Interior	Samuel J. Kirkwood	1881

The Arthur Administration (1881–1885)

Vice President	None	
Secretary of State	F. T. Frelinghuysen	1881–1885
Secretary of Treasury	Charles J. Folger	1881–1884
	Walter Q. Gresham	1884
	Hugh McCulloch	1884–1885
Secretary of War	Robert T. Lincoln	1881–1885
Attorney General	Benjamin H. Brewster	1881–1885
Postmaster General	Timothy O. Howe	1881–1883
	Walter Q. Gresham	1883–1884
	Frank Hatton	1884–1885
Secretary of Navy	William H. Hunt	1881–1882
	William E. Chandler	1882–1885
Secretary of Interior	Samuel J. Kirkwood	1881–1882
	Henry M. Teller	1882–1885

cont.

The Cleveland Administration (1885–1889)

Vice President	Thomas A. Hendricks	1885–1885
Secretary of State	Thomas F. Bayard	1885–1889
Secretary of Treasury	Daniel Manning	1885–1887
	Charles S. Fairchild	1887–1889
Secretary of War	William C. Endicott	1885–1889
Attorney General	Augustus H. Garland	1885–1889
Postmaster General	William F. Vilas	1885–1888
	Don M. Dickinson	1888–1889
Secretary of Navy	William C. Whitney	1885–1889
Secretary of Interior	Lucius Q. C. Lamar	1885–1888
	William F. Vilas	1888–1889
Secretary of Agriculture	Norman J. Colman	1889

The Benjamin Harrison Administration (1889–1893)

Vice President	Levi P. Morton	1889–1893
Secretary of State	James G. Blaine	1889–1892
	John W. Foster	1892–1893
Secretary of Treasury	William Windom	1889–1891
	Charles Foster	1891–1893
Secretary of War	Redfield Proctor	1889–1891
	Stephen B. Elkins	1891–1893
Attorney General	William H. H. Miller	1889–1891
Postmaster General	John Wanamaker	1889–1893
Secretary of Navy	Benjamin F. Tracy	1889–1893
Secretary of Interior	John W. Noble	1889–1893
Secretary of Agriculture	Jeremiah M. Rusk	1889–1893

The Cleveland Administration (1893–1897)

Vice President	Adlai E. Stevenson	1893–1897
Secretary of State	Walter Q. Gresham	1893–1895
	Richard Olney	1895–1897
Secretary of Treasury	John G. Carlisle	1893–1897
Secretary of War	Daniel S. Lamont	1893–1897
Attorney General	Richard Olney	1893–1895
	James Harmon	1895–1897
Postmaster General	Wilson S. Bissell	1893–1895
	William L. Wilson	1895–1897
Secretary of Navy	Hilary A. Herbert	1893–1897
Secretary of Interior	Hoke Smith	1893–1896
	David R. Francis	1896–1897
Secretary of Agriculture	Julius S. Morton	1893–1897

The McKinley Administration (1897–1901)

Vice President	Garret A. Hobart	1897–1899
	Theodore Roosevelt	1901

The McKinley Administration (1897–1901)   (cont.)

Secretary of State	John Sherman	1897–1898
	William R. Day	1898
	John Hay	1898–1901
Secretary of Treasury	Lyman J. Gage	1897–1901
Secretary of War	Russell A. Alger	1897–1899
	Elihu Root	1899–1901
Attorney General	Joseph McKenna	1897–1898
	John W. Griggs	1898–1901
	Philander C. Knox	1901
Postmaster General	James A. Gary	1897–1898
	Charles E. Smith	1898–1901
Secretary of Navy	John D. Long	1897–1901
Secretary of Interior	Cornelius N. Bliss	1897–1899
	Ethan A. Hitchcock	1899–1901
Secretary of Agriculture	James Wilson	1897–1901

The Theodore Roosevelt Administration (1901–1909)

Vice President	Charles Fairbanks	1905–1909
Secretary of State	John Hay	1901–1905
	Elihu Root	1905–1909
	Robert Bacon	1909
Secretary of Treasury	Lyman J. Gage	1901–1902
	Leslie M. Shaw	1902–1907
	George B. Cortelyou	1907–1909
Secretary of War	Elihu Root	1901–1904
	William H. Taft	1904–1908
	Luke E. Wright	1908–1909
Attorney General	Philander C. Knox	1901–1904
	William H. Moody	1904–1906
	Charles J. Bonaparte	1906–1909
Postmaster General	Charles E. Smith	1901–1902
	Henry C. Payne	1902–1904
	Robert J. Wynne	1904–1905
	George B. Cortelyou	1905–1907
	George von L. Meyer	1907–1909
Secretary of Navy	John D. Long	1901–1902
	William H. Moody	1902–1904
	Paul Morton	1904–1905
	Charles J. Bonaparte	1905–1906
	Victor H. Metcalf	1906–1908
	Truman H. Newberry	1908–1909
Secretary of Interior	Ethan A. Hitchcock	1901–1907
	James R. Garfield	1907–1909
Secretary of Agriculture	James Wilson	1901–1909
Secretary of Labor and Commerce	George B. Cortelyou	1903–1904
	Victor H. Metcalf	1904–1906
	Oscar S. Straus	1906–1909
	Charles Nagel	1909

cont.

The Taft Administration (1909–1913)

Vice President	James S. Sherman	1909–1912
Secretary of State	Philander C. Knox	1909–1913
Secretary of Treasury	Franklin MacVeagh	1909–1913
Secretary of War	Jacob M. Dickinson	1909–1911
	Henry L. Stimson	1911–1913
Attorney General	George W. Wickersham	1909–1913
Postmaster General	Frank H. Hitchcock	1909–1913
Secretary of Navy	George von L. Meyer	1909–1913
Secretary of Interior	Richard A. Ballinger	1909–1911
	Walter L. Fisher	1911–1913
Secretary of Agriculture	James Wilson	1909–1913
Secretary of Labor and Commerce	Charles Nagel	1909–1913

The Wilson Administration (1913–1921)

Vice President	Thomas R. Marshall	1913–1921
Secretary of State	William J. Bryan	1913–1915
	Robert Lansing	1915–1920
	Bainbridge Colby	1920–1921
Secretary of Treasury	William G. McAdoo	1913–1918
	Carter Glass	1918–1920
	David F. Houston	1920–1921
Secretary of War	Lindley M. Garrison	1913–1916
	Newton D. Baker	1916–1921
Attorney General	James C. McReynolds	1913–1914
	Thomas W. Gregory	1914–1919
	A. Mitchell Palmer	1919–1921
Postmaster General	Albert S. Burleson	1913–1921
Secretary of Navy	Josephus Daniels	1913–1921
Secretary of Interior	Franklin K. Lane	1913–1920
	John B. Payne	1920–1921
Secretary of Agriculture	David F. Houston	1913–1920
	Edwin T. Meredith	1920–1921
Secretary of Commerce	William C. Redfield	1913–1919
	Joshua W. Alexander	1919–1921
Secretary of Labor	William B. Wilson	1913–1921

The Harding Administration (1921–1923)

Vice President	Calvin Coolidge	1921–1923
Secretary of State	Charles E. Hughes	1921–1923
Secretary of Treasury	Andrew Mellon	1921–1923
Secretary of War	John W. Weeks	1921–1923
Attorney General	Harry M. Daugherty	1921–1923
Postmaster General	Will H. Hays	1921–1922
	Hubert Work	1922–1923
	Harry S. New	1923
Secretary of Navy	Edwin Denby	1921–1923
Secretary of Interior	Albert B. Fall	1921–1923
	Hubert Work	1923

The Harding Administration (1921–1923)   (cont.)

Secretary of Agriculture	Henry C. Wallace	1921–1923
Secretary of Commerce	Herbert C. Hoover	1921–1923
Secretary of Labor	James J. Davis	1921–1923

The Coolidge Administration (1923–1929)

Vice President	Charles G. Dawes	1925–1929
Secretary of State	Charles E. Hughes	1923–1925
	Frank B. Kellogg	1925–1929
Secretary of Treasury	Andrew Mellon	1923–1929
Secretary of War	John W. Weeks	1923–1925
	Dwight F. Davis	1925–1929
Attorney General	Henry M. Daugherty	1923–1924
	Harlan F. Stone	1924–1925
	John G. Sargent	1925–1929
Postmaster General	Harry S. New	1923–1929
Secretary of Navy	Edwin Denby	1923–1924
	Curtis D. Wilbur	1924–1929
Secretary of Interior	Hubert Work	1923–1928
	Roy O. West	1928–1929
Secretary of Agriculture	Henry C. Wallace	1923–1924
	Howard M. Gore	1924–1925
	William M. Jardine	1925–1929
Secretary of Commerce	Herbert C. Hoover	1923–1928
	William F. Whiting	1928–1929
Secretary of Labor	James J. Davis	1923–1929

The Hoover Administration (1929–1933)

Vice President	Charles Curtis	1929–1933
Secretary of State	Henry L. Stimson	1929–1933
Secretary of Treasury	Andrew Mellon	1929–1932
	Ogden L. Mills	1932–1933
Secretary of War	James W. Good	1929
	Patrick J. Hurley	1929–1933
Attorney General	William D. Mitchell	1929–1933
Postmaster General	Walter F. Brown	1929–1933
Secretary of Navy	Charles F. Adams	1929–1933
Secretary of Interior	Ray L. Wilbur	1929–1933
Secretary of Agriculture	Arthur M. Hyde	1929–1933
Secretary of Commerce	Robert P. Lamont	1929–1932
	Roy D. Chapin	1932–1933
Secretary of Labor	James J. Davis	1929–1930
	William N. Doak	1930–1933

The Franklin D. Roosevelt Administration (1933–1945)

Vice President	John Nance Garner	1933–1941
	Henry A. Wallace	1941–1945
	Harry S Truman	1945

cont.

The Franklin D. Roosevelt Administration (1933–1945)   (cont.)

Secretary of State	Cordell Hull	1933–1944
	Edward R. Stettinius, Jr.	1944–1945
Secretary of Treasury	William H. Woodin	1933–1934
	Henry Morgenthau, Jr.	1934–1945
Secretary of War	George H. Dern	1933–1936
	Henry A. Woodring	1936–1940
	Henry L. Stimson	1940–1945
Attorney General	Homer S. Cummings	1933–1939
	Frank Murphy	1939–1940
	Robert H. Jackson	1940–1941
	Francis Biddle	1941–1945
Postmaster General	James A. Farley	1933–1940
	Frank C. Walker	1940–1945
Secretary of Navy	Claude A. Swanson	1933–1940
	Charles Edison	1940
	Frank Knox	1940–1944
	James V. Forrestal	1944–1945
Secretary of Interior	Harold L. Ickes	1933–1945
Secretary of Agriculture	Henry A. Wallace	1933–1940
	Claude R. Wickard	1940–1945
Secretary of Commerce	Daniel C. Roper	1933–1939
	Harry L. Hopkins	1939–1940
	Jesse Jones	1940–1945
	Henry A. Wallace	1945
Secretary of Labor	Frances Perkins	1933–1945

The Truman Administration (1945–1953)

Vice President	Alben W. Barkley	1949–1953
Secretary of State	Edward R. Stettinius, Jr.	1945
	James F. Byrnes	1945–1947
	George C. Marshall	1947–1949
	Dean G. Acheson	1949–1953
Secretary of Treasury	Fred M. Vinson	1945–1946
	John W. Snyder	1946–1953
Secretary of War	Robert P. Patterson	1945–1947
	Kenneth C. Royall	1947
Attorney General	Tom C. Clark	1945–1949
	J. Howard McGrath	1949–1952
	James P. McGranery	1952–1953
Postmaster General	Frank C. Walker	1945
	Robert E. Hannegan	1945–1947
	Jesse M. Donaldson	1947–1953
Secretary of Navy	James V. Forrestal	1945–1947
Secretary of Interior	Harold L. Ickes	1945–1946
	Julius A. Krug	1946–1949
	Oscar L. Chapman	1949–1953
Secretary of Agriculture	Clinton P. Anderson	1945–1948
	Charles F. Brannan	1948–1953

The Truman Administration (1945–1953)   (cont.)

Secretary of Commerce	Henry A. Wallace	1945–1946
	W. Averell Harriman	1946–1948
	Charles W. Sawyer	1948–1953
Secretary of Labor	Lewis B. Schwellenbach	1945–1948
	Maurice J. Tobin	1948–1953
Secretary of Defense	James V. Forrestal	1947–1949
	Louis A. Johnson	1949–1950
	George C. Marshall	1950–1951
	Robert A. Lovett	1951–1953

The Eisenhower Administration (1953–1961)

Vice President	Richard M. Nixon	1953–1961
Secretary of State	John Foster Dulles	1953–1959
	Christian A. Herter	1959–1961
Secretary of Treasury	George M. Humphrey	1953–1957
	Robert B. Anderson	1957–1961
Attorney General	Herbert Brownell, Jr.	1953–1958
	William P. Rogers	1958–1961
Postmaster General	Arthur E. Summerfield	1953–1961
Secretary of Interior	Douglas McKay	1953–1956
	Fred A. Seaton	1956–1961
Secretary of Agriculture	Ezra T. Benson	1953–1961
Secretary of Commerce	Sinclair Weeks	1953–1958
	Lewis L. Strauss	1958–1959
	Frederick H. Mueller	1959–1961
Secretary of Labor	Martin P. Durkin	1953
	James P. Mitchell	1953–1961
Secretary of Defense	Charles E. Wilson	1953–1957
	Neil H. McElroy	1957–1959
	Thomas S. Gates, Jr.	1959–1961
Secretary of Health, Education, and Welfare	Oveta Culp Hobby	1953–1955
	Marion B. Folsom	1955–1958
	Arthur S. Flemming	1958–1961

The Kennedy Administration (1961–1963)

Vice President	Lyndon B. Johnson	1961–1963
Secretary of State	Dean Rusk	1961–1963
Secretary of Treasury	C. Douglas Dillon	1961–1963
Attorney General	Robert F. Kennedy	1961–1963
Postmaster General	J. Edward Day	1961–1963
	John A. Gronouski	1963
Secretary of Interior	Stewart L. Udall	1961–1963
Secretary of Agriculture	Orville L. Freeman	1961–1963
Secretary of Commerce	Luther H. Hodges	1961–1963
Secretary of Labor	Arthur J. Goldberg	1961–1962
	W. Willard Wirtz	1962–1963
Secretary of Defense	Robert S. McNamara	1961–1963

cont.

The Kennedy Administration (1961–1963)   (cont.)

Secretary of Health, Education, and Welfare	Abraham A. Ribicoff	1961–1962
	Anthony J. Celebrezze	1962–1963

The Lyndon Johnson Administration (1963–1969)

Vice President	Hubert H. Humphrey	1965–1969
Secretary of State	Dean Rusk	1963–1969
Secretary of Treasury	C. Douglas Dillon	1963–1965
	Henry H. Fowler	1965–1969
Attorney General	Robert F. Kennedy	1963–1964
	Nicholas Katzenbach	1965–1966
	Ramsey Clark	1967–1969
Postmaster General	John A. Gronouski	1963–1965
	Lawrence F. O'Brien	1965–1968
	Marvin Watson	1968–1969
Secretary of Interior	Stewart L. Udall	1963–1969
Secretary of Agriculture	Orville L. Freeman	1963–1969
Secretary of Commerce	Luther H. Hodges	1963–1964
	John T. Connor	1964–1967
	Alexander B. Trowbridge	1967–1968
	Cyrus R. Smith	1968–1969
Secretary of Labor	W. Willard Wirtz	1963–1969
Secretary of Defense	Robert F. McNamara	1963–1968
	Clark Clifford	1968–1969
Secretary of Health, Education, and Welfare	Anthony J. Celebrezze	1963–1965
	John W. Gardner	1965–1968
	Wilbur J. Cohen	1968–1969
Secretary of Housing and Urban Development	Robert C. Weaver	1966–1969
	Robert C. Wood	1969
Secretary of Transportation	Alan S. Boyd	1967–1969

The Nixon Administration (1969–1974)

Vice President	Spiro T. Agnew	1969–1973
	Gerald R. Ford	1973–1974
Secretary of State	William P. Rogers	1969–1973
	Henry A. Kissinger	1973–1974
Secretary of Treasury	David M. Kennedy	1969–1970
	John B. Connally	1971–1972
	George P. Shultz	1972–1974
	William E. Simon	1974
Attorney General	John N. Mitchell	1969–1972
	Richard G. Kleindienst	1972–1973
	Elliot L. Richardson	1973
	William B. Saxbe	1973–1974
Postmaster General	Winton M. Blount	1969–1971
Secretary of Interior	Walter J. Hickel	1969–1970
	Rogers Morton	1971–1974
Secretary of Agriculture	Clifford M. Hardin	1969–1971
	Earl L. Butz	1971–1974

The Nixon Administration (1969–1974)   *(cont.)*

Secretary of Commerce	Maurice H. Stans	1969–1972
	Peter G. Peterson	1972–1973
	Frederick B. Dent	1973–1974
Secretary of Labor	George P. Shultz	1969–1970
	James D. Hodgson	1970–1973
	Peter J. Brennan	1973–1974
Secretary of Defense	Melvin R. Laird	1969–1973
	Elliot L. Richardson	1973
	James R. Schlesinger	1973–1974
Secretary of Health, Education, and Welfare	Robert H. Finch	1969–1970
	Elliot L. Richardson	1970–1973
	Caspar W. Weinberger	1973–1974
Secretary of Housing and Urban Development	George Romney	1969–1973
	James T. Lynn	1973–1974
Secretary of Transportation	John A. Volpe	1969–1973
	Claude S. Brinegar	1973–1974

The Ford Administration (1974–1977)

Vice President	Nelson A. Rockefeller	1974–1977
Secretary of State	Henry A. Kissinger	1974–1977
Secretary of Treasury	William E. Simon	1974–1977
Attorney General	William Saxbe	1974–1975
	Edward Levi	1975–1977
Secretary of Interior	Rogers Morton	1974–1975
	Stanley K. Hathaway	1975
	Thomas Kleppe	1975–1977
Secretary of Agriculture	Earl L. Butz	1974–1976
	John A. Knebel	1976–1977
Secretary of Commerce	Frederick B. Dent	1974–1975
	Rogers Morton	1975–1976
	Elliott L. Richardson	1976–1977
Secretary of Labor	Peter J. Brennan	1974–1975
	John T. Dunlop	1975–1976
	W. J. Usery	1976–1977
Secretary of Defense	James R. Schlesinger	1974–1975
	Donald Rumsfeld	1975–1977
Secretary of Health, Education, and Welfare	Caspar Weinberger	1974–1975
	Forrest D. Mathews	1975–1977
Secretary of Housing and Urban Development	James T. Lynn	1974–1975
	Carla A. Hills	1975–1977
Secretary of Transportation	Claude Brinegar	1974–1975
	William T. Coleman	1975–1977

The Carter Administration (1977–1981)

Vice President	Walter F. Mondale	1977–1981
Secretary of State	Cyrus R. Vance	1977–1980
	Edmund Muskie	1980–1981

cont.

The Carter Administration (1977–1981)   (cont.)

Secretary of Treasury	W. Michael Blumenthal	1977–1979
	G. William Miller	1979–1981
Attorney General	Griffin Bell	1977–1979
	Benjamin R. Civiletti	1979–1981
Secretary of Interior	Cecil D. Andrus	1977–1981
Secretary of Agriculture	Robert Bergland	1977–1981
Secretary of Commerce	Juanita M. Kreps	1977–1979
	Philip M. Klutznick	1979–1981
Secretary of Labor	Ray F. Marshall	1977–1981
Secretary of Defense	Harold Brown	1977–1981
Secretary of Health, Education, and Welfare	Joseph A. Califano	1977–1979
	Patricia R. Harris	1979
Secretary of Health and Human Services	Patricia R. Harris	1979–1981
Secretary of Education	Shirley M. Hufstedler	1979–1981
Secretary of Housing and Urban Development	Patricia R. Harris	1977–1979
	Moon Landrieu	1979–1981
Secretary of Transportation	Brock Adams	1977–1979
	Neil E. Goldschmidt	1979–1981
Secretary of Energy	James R. Schlesinger	1977–1979
	Charles W. Duncan	1979–1981

The Reagan Administration (1981–1989)

Vice President	George Bush	1981–1989
Secretary of State	Alexander M. Haig	1981–1982
	George P. Shultz	1982–1989
Secretary of Treasury	Donald Regan	1981–1985
	James A. Baker III	1985–1988
	Nicholas Brady	1988–1989
Attorney General	William F. Smith	1981–1985
	Edwin A. Meese III	1985–1988
	Richard Thornburgh	1988–1989
Secretary of Interior	James Watt	1981–1983
	William P. Clark, Jr.	1983–1985
	Donald P. Hodel	1985–1989
Secretary of Agriculture	John Block	1981–1986
	Richard E. Lyng	1986–1989
Secretary of Commerce	Malcolm Baldrige	1981–1987
	C. William Verity, Jr.	1987–1989
Secretary of Labor	Raymond Donovan	1981–1985
	William E. Brock	1985–1988
	Ann Dore McLaughlin	1988–1989
Secretary of Defense	Caspar Weinberger	1981–1988
	Frank Carlucci	1988–1989
Secretary of Health and Human Services	Richard Schweiker	1981–1983
	Margaret Heckler	1983–1985
	Otis R. Bowen	1985–1989
Secretary of Education	Terrel H. Bell	1981–1985
	William J. Bennett	1985–1988
	Lauro F. Cavazos	1988–1989

The Reagan Administration (1981–1989)   (cont.)

Secretary of Housing and Urban Development	Samuel Pierce	1981–1989
Secretary of Transportation	Drew Lewis	1981–1983
	Elizabeth Dole	1983–1987
	James L. Burnley IV	1987–1989
Secretary of Energy	James Edwards	1981–1982
	Donald P. Hodel	1982–1985
	John S. Herrington	1985–1989

The Bush Administration (1989–1993)

Vice President	J. Danforth Quayle III	1989–1993
Secretary of State	James Baker III	1989–1993
Secretary of Treasury	Nicholas Brady	1989–1993
Attorney General	Richard Thornburgh	1989–1991
	William Barr	1991–1993
Secretary of Interior	Manuel Lujan	1989–1993
Secretary of Agriculture	Clayton Yeutter	1989–1991
	Edward Madigan	1991–1993
Secretary of Commerce	Robert Mosbacher	1989–1992
	Barbara Franklin	1992–1993
Secretary of Labor	Elizabeth Dole	1989–1990
	Lynn Martin	1991–1993
Secretary of Defense	Richard Cheney	1989–1993
Secretary of Health and Human Services	Louis Sullivan	1989–1993
Secretary of Education	Lauro Cavazos	1989–1990
	Lamar Alexander	1990–1993
Secretary of Housing and Urban Development	Jack Kemp	1989–1993
Secretary of Transportation	Samuel Skinner	1989–1991
	Andrew Card	1992–1993
Secretary of Energy	James Watkins	1989–1993
Secretary of Veterans' Affairs	Edward Derwinski	1989–1993

The Clinton Administration (1993–   )

Vice President	Albert W. Gore, Jr.	1993–
Secretary of State	Warren Christopher	1993–
Secretary of Treasury	Lloyd Bentsen	1993–1994
	Robert Rubin	1995–
Attorney General	Janet Reno	1993–
Secretary of Interior	Bruce Babbitt	1993–
Secretary of Agriculture	Michael Espy	1993–1994
	Dan Glickman	1994–
Secretary of Commerce	Ronald Brown	1993–
Secretary of Labor	Robert Reich	1993–
Secretary of Defense	Les Aspin	1993–1994
	William Perry	1994–
Secretary of Health and Human Services	Donna Shalala	1993–
Secretary of Education	Richard Reilly	1993–
Secretary of Housing and Urban Development	Henry Cisneros	1993–
Secretary of Transportation	Federico Peña	1993–
Secretary of Energy	Hazel O'Leary	1993–
Secretary of Veterans' Affairs	Jesse Brown	1993–

Supreme Court Justices

Name	Terms of Service	Appointed By
JOHN JAY	1789–1795	Washington
James Wilson	1789–1798	Washington
John Rutledge	1790–1791	Washington
William Cushing	1790–1810	Washington
John Blair	1790–1796	Washington
James Iredell	1790–1799	Washington
Thomas Johnson	1792–1793	Washington
William Paterson	1793–1806	Washington
JOHN RUTLEDGE*	1795	Washington
Samuel Chase	1796–1811	Washington
OLIVER ELLSWORTH	1796–1800	Washington
Bushrod Washington	1799–1829	J. Adams
Alfred Moore	1800–1804	J. Adams
JOHN MARSHALL	1801–1835	J. Adams
William Johnson	1804–1834	Jefferson
Brockholst Livingston	1807–1823	Jefferson
Thomas Todd	1807–1826	Jefferson
Gabriel Duvall	1811–1835	Madison
Joseph Story	1812–1845	Madison
Smith Thompson	1823–1843	Monroe
Robert Trimble	1826–1828	J. Q. Adams
John McLean	1830–1861	Jackson
Henry Baldwin	1830–1844	Jackson
James M. Wayne	1835–1867	Jackson
ROGER B. TANEY	1836–1864	Jackson
Philip P. Barbour	1836–1841	Jackson
John Cartron	1837–1865	Van Buren
John McKinley	1838–1852	Van Buren
Peter V. Daniel	1842–1860	Van Buren
Samuel Nelson	1845–1872	Tyler
Levi Woodbury	1845–1851	Polk
Robert C. Grier	1846–1870	Polk
Benjamin R. Curtis	1851–1857	Fillmore
John A. Campbell	1853–1861	Pierce
Nathan Clifford	1858–1881	Buchanan
Noah H. Swayne	1862–1881	Lincoln
Samuel F. Miller	1862–1890	Lincoln
David Davis	1862–1877	Lincoln
Stephen J. Field	1863–1897	Lincoln
SALMON P. CHASE	1864–1873	Lincoln
William Strong	1870–1880	Grant
Joseph P. Bradley	1870–1892	Grant

NOTE: The names of Chief Justices are printed in capital letters.

*Although Rutledge acted as Chief Justice, the Senate refused to confirm his appointment.

Supreme Court Justices *(cont.)*

Name	Terms of Service	Appointed By
Ward Hunt	1873–1882	Grant
MORRISON R. WAITE	1874–1888	Grant
John M. Harlan	1877–1911	Hayes
William B. Woods	1881–1887	Hayes
Stanley Matthews	1881–1889	Garfield
Horace Gray	1882–1902	Arthur
Samuel Blatchford	1882–1893	Arthur
Lucious Q. C. Lamar	1888–1893	Cleveland
MELVILLE W. FULLER	1888–1910	Cleveland
David J. Brewer	1890–1910	B. Harrison
Henry B. Brown	1891–1906	B. Harrison
George Shiras, Jr.	1892–1903	B. Harrison
Howell E. Jackson	1893–1895	B. Harrison
Edward D. White	1894–1910	Cleveland
Rufus W. Peckham	1896–1909	Cleveland
Joseph McKenna	1898–1925	McKinley
Oliver W. Holmes	1902–1932	T. Roosevelt
William R. Day	1903–1922	T. Roosevelt
William H. Moody	1906–1910	T. Roosevelt
Horace H. Lurton	1910–1914	Taft
Charles E. Hughes	1910–1916	Taft
EDWARD D. WHITE	1910–1921	Taft
Willis Van Devanter	1911–1937	Taft
Joseph R. Lamar	1911–1916	Taft
Mahlon Pitney	1912–1922	Taft
James C. McReynolds	1914–1941	Wilson
Louis D. Brandeis	1916–1939	Wilson
John H. Clarke	1916–1922	Wilson
WILLIAM H. TAFT	1921–1930	Harding
George Sutherland	1922–1938	Harding
Pierce Butler	1923–1939	Harding
Edward T. Sanford	1923–1930	Harding
Harlan F. Stone	1925–1941	Coolidge
CHARLES E. HUGHES	1930–1941	Hoover
Owen J. Roberts	1930–1945	Hoover
Benjamin N. Cardozo	1932–1938	Hoover
Hugo L. Black	1937–1971	F. Roosevelt
Stanley F. Reed	1938–1957	F. Roosevelt
Felix Frankfurter	1939–1962	F. Roosevelt
William O. Douglas	1939–1975	F. Roosevelt
Frank Murphy	1940–1949	F. Roosevelt
HARLAN F. STONE	1941–1946	F. Roosevelt
James F. Byrnes	1941–1942	F. Roosevelt
Robert H. Jackson	1941–1954	F. Roosevelt
Wiley B. Rutledge	1943–1949	F. Roosevelt
Harold H. Burton	1945–1958	Truman

cont.

Supreme Court Justices *(cont.)*

Name	Terms of Service	Appointed By
FREDERICK M. VINSON	1946–1953	Truman
Tom C. Clark	1949–1967	Truman
Sherman Minton	1949–1956	Truman
EARL WARREN	1953–1969	Eisenhower
John Marshall Harlan	1955–1971	Eisenhower
William J. Brennan, Jr.	1956–1990	Eisenhower
Charles E. Whittaker	1957–1962	Eisenhower
Potter Stewart	1958–1981	Eisenhower
Byron R. White	1962–1993	Kennedy
Arthur J. Goldberg	1962–1965	Kennedy
Abe Fortas	1965–1970	L. Johnson
Thurgood Marshall	1967–1991	L. Johnson
WARREN E. BURGER	1969–1986	Nixon
Harry A. Blackmun	1970–1994	Nixon
Lewis F. Powell, Jr.	1971–1987	Nixon
William H. Rehnquist	1971–1986	Nixon
John Paul Stevens	1975–	Ford
Sandra Day O'Connor	1981–	Reagan
WILLIAM H. REHNQUIST	1986–	Reagan
Antonin Scalia	1986–	Reagan
Anthony Kennedy	1988–	Reagan
David Souter	1990–	Bush
Clarence Thomas	1991–	Bush
Ruth Bader Ginsburg	1993–	Clinton
Stephen Breyer	1994–	Clinton

PHOTOGRAPH CREDITS

Chapter 5

p. 126, (Detail) Courtesy, Winterthur Museum. Bequest of Henry Francis du Pont; p. 127, The Granger Collection; p. 129, Library of Congress; p. 131, Courtesy, Winterthur Museum; p. 132, Indianapolis Museum of Art, The James E. Roberts Fund; p. 137, Manuscripts & Archives Division, New York Public Library; p. 139, Library of Congress; p. 142, "British Officials Doing the Devil's Work" from *Boston Gazette*. American Antiquarian Society; p. 145, Courtesy, Museum of Fine Arts, Boston, Deposited by the City of Boston; p. 146, Colonial Williamsburg Foundation; p. 148, Historical Society of Pennsylvania; p. 150, Library of Congress; p. 154, American Antiquarian Society; p. 156, Courtesy of the Decorative & Industrial Arts Department of the Chicago Historical Society; p. 157a(vignette), Photograph courtesy of the Concord Museum, Concord, MA #Pi414; p. 157a(bottom), American Antiquarian Society; p. 157b(top), Photograph courtesy of the Concord Museum, Concord, MA #Pi414; p. 157b(bottom), John Carter Brown Library at Brown University; p. 159, Peabody Essex Museum, Salem, Massachusetts.

Chapter 6

p. 162, West Point Museum Collections, United States Military Academy; p. 163, (Detail) Courtesy, Museum of Fine Arts, Boston, Deposited by City of Boston; p. 164, Print Collection, Miriam & Ira D. Wallach Division of Art, Prints and Photographs, The New York Public Library, Astor, Lenox and Tilden Foundations; p. 167, (Detail) Collection of the New-York Historical Society; p. 168, Visual Materials Division, Department of Rare Books & Special Collections, Princeton University Libraries; p. 172, (Detail) Independence National Historical Park; p. 175, Anne S.K. Brown Military Collection, Brown University Library; p. 178, Collection of Alexander A. McBurney; p. 179, (Detail) Boston Athenaeum; p. 180, New York State Office of Parks, Recreation and Historic Preservation, John Jay Homestead State Historic Site; p. 183a(vignette), Rochester Museum & Science Center, Rochester, New York; p. 183a(bottom), The New-York Historical Society; p. 183b, Courtesy of the National Museum of the American Indian, Smithsonian Institution #S3499; p. 189, National Gallery of Canada, Ottawa; p. 191, Henry Groskinsky, LIFE MAGAZINE © Time Warner Inc.; p. 192, (Detail) Colonial Williamsburg Foundation; p. 197, (Detail) National Portrait Gallery/Art Resource, NY.

Chapter 7

p. 200, National Museum of American History, Smithsonian Institution; p. 201, Chicago Historical Society; p. 205, Museum of the City of New York; p. 205a(vignette), "High Street, from Ninth Street, Philadelphia," © 1799 by William Birch. Monticello/Thomas Jefferson Memorial Foundation, Inc.; p. 205a(bottom), Rare Book Department, The Free Library of Philadelphia; p. 205b, (Detail) Delaware Art Museum, Wilmington. Gift of Absalom Jones School, Wilmington; p. 209, Collection of the New-York Historical Society; p. 210, Courtesy, Donaldson Lufkin & Jenrette Collection of Americana; p. 215, Smithsonian Institution Photo #BAE 1169-L-3; p. 218, (Detail) Chicago Historical Society; p. 220, The Brooklyn Museum, #39.536.1. Gift of the Crescent Hamilton Athletic Club; p. 221, Colonial Williamsburg Foundation; p. 224(left), Adams National Historic Site, Photo by Jeffrey Dunn; p. 224(right), National Museum of American Art, Washington, DC/Art Resource, N.Y.; p. 228, Monticello/Thomas Jefferson Memorial Foundation,

Inc.; p. 231, Monticello/Thomas Jefferson Memorial Foundation, Inc.; p. 232(left), Museum of American Political Life/University of Hartford. Photograph by Sally Anderson-Bruce; p. 232(right), Courtesy of Atwater Kent Museum.

Chapter 8

p. 234, (Detail) The Minneapolis Institute of Arts, William Hood Dunwoody Fund; p. 235, The Huntington Museum, San Marino, California; p. 237(left), Courtesy, Robert M. Hinkln Jr., Inc. Spartanburg, South Carolina; p. 237(right), Monticello/Thomas Jefferson Memorial Foundation; p. 238, Franklin D. Roosevelt Library; p. 240, Boston Athenaeum; p. 244(both top), Courtesy, Independence National Historical Park; p. 244(bottom), Peabody Museum, Harvard University. Photo by Hillel Burger; p. 248, The Print and Picture Collection, The Free Library of Philadelphia; p. 251, The Granger Collection; p. 254, The New Haven Colony Historical Society, Gift of Mrs. Philip Galpin; p. 256, Copyrighted by White House Historical Association; p. 257, Visual Materials Division, Department of Rare Books and Special Collections, Princeton University Libraries; p. 257a(vignette), "View of Boston and the South Boston Bridge, 1828." Boston Athenaeum; p. 257a(bottom), Courtesy of The Harvard University Portrait Collection. Gift of Francis V. Bulfinch 1933; p. 257b(top), Print Collection, Miriam & Ira D. Wallach Division of Art, Prints and Photographs, New York Public Library. Astor, Lenox and Tilden Foundations; p. 257b(bottom), Courtesy of Museum of Fine Arts, Boston. Gift of Mrs. Horatio A. Lamb in memory of Mr. & Mrs. Winthrop Sargent; p. 258, Bettmann; p. 264(left), (Detail) Courtesy, Independence National Historical Park; p. 264(right), Anne S K Brown Military Collection, Brown University Library.

Chapter 9

p. 266, (Detail) The Saint Louis Art Museum. Purchase: Ezra H. Lilly Fund; p. 267, Hudson Bay Company Archives/Provincial Archives of Manitoba; p. 269(left), The Walters Art Gallery, Baltimore; p. 269(top right), Buffalo Bill Historical Center, Cody, Wyoming; As a Memorial to Jeanette J. Leonard, on behalf of her husband Dr. Kenneth O. Leonard; p. 269(bottom right), Missouri Historical Society, St. Louis; p. 270, Metropolitan Museum of Art, Rogers Fund 1942 (42.95.12); p. 272, William L. Clements Library, University of Michigan, Ann Arbor; p. 273a(vignette), National Museum of American Art, Washington, DC/Art Resource, NY; p. 273a(left), Collection of The New-York Historical Society; p. 273a(right), National Portrait Gallery, Washington, DC/Art Resource, NY; p. 273b(top), National Museum of American Art, Washington, DC/Art Resource, NY; p. 273b(bottom), State Historical Society of Wisconsin; p. 277, Museum d'Histoire Naturelle, No. 62003-2; p. 278, Collection of The New-York Historical Society; p. 284, University of Massachusetts Lowell; p. 287, The Saint Louis Art Museum. Loan from the collection of Arthur Ziern, Jr.; p. 289, Witt Library/Courtauld Institute of Art; p. 293, Giampietro Gallery, 50 East 78th, New York, NY 10021; p. 296, Yale University Art Gallery. Gift of George Hoadley, B.A. 1801.

Chapter 10

p. 298, (Detail) The Walters Art Gallery, Baltimore; p. 299, Special Collections, Skillman Library, Lafayette College, Easton, PA; p. 302, The Metropolitan Museum of Art, Gift of I.N. Phelps Stokes, Edward S. Hawes, Alice Mary Hawes, Marion Augusta Hawes,

Chapter 16
p. 498, William Gladstone Collection; p. 499, Library of Congress; p. 500, "The Return to Fredericksburg After the Battle," by David English Henderson. Gettysburg National Military Park; p. 502, National Portrait Gallery, Washington, DC/Art Resource, NY; p. 504, *Harpers Weekly,* 1866; p. 511, The Granger Collection; p. 512, The Museum of the Confederacy, Richmond, Virginia. Photograph by Katherine Wetzel; p. 514(below), Decorative and Industrial Arts/Chicago Historical Society; p. 514(right), Tennessee State Museum Collection. Photograph by June Dorman; p. 517, William Gladstone Collection; p. 519a(vignette), Courtesy, Georgia Department of Archives and History; p. 519a, Courtesy, Georgia Department of Archives and History; p. 519b, Hargrett Rare Book and Manuscript Library, The University of Georgia; p. 522(left), *Harpers Weekly,* 1871; p. 522(right), Brown Brothers; p. 526, *Harpers Weekly,* October 24, 1874; p. 528(all), Kansas State Historical Society; p. 531, Museum of American Political Life/University of Hartford. Photo by Steve Laschever.

INDEX

Abenakis people, 49

Abolition movement, 323–325; and American Revolutionary War, 178–180; impact of slave revolts on, 231; and John Brown's raid, 451–452; and *Uncle Tom's Cabin*, 436–437

Acadia, 43, 98

Acadians, 130–131

Act for Religious Toleration (1649), 70

Adams, Abigail, 171, 180; description of Washington by, 206

Adams, Charles Francis, 476 Adams, Henry, 477

Adams, John, 299; and Alien and Sedition Acts, 225–227; and American Revolution, 171; and Articles of Confederation, 185–186; and Boston Massacre, 150; as colonial leader, 111, 142, 151, 157, 158; as delegate to First Continental Congress, 155, 156; in election of 1796, 223–224; in election of 1800, 227; foreign policy under, 224–225, 227; on ideal government, 184; and Peace of Paris, 176; political role of, 235; presidential style of, 235; relations between Jefferson and, 238–239; as vice president, 206, 220–221; and women's rights, 180

Adams, John Quincy: cabinet of, 302; in election of 1824, 301–302; in election of 1828, 303–304; and expansionism, 418; foreign policy of, 302; as man of learning, 360; opposition to gag rule, 325; political role of, 300; as secretary of state, 262; and slavery, 415; and tariff issue, 305

Adams, Samuel: circular letter of, 145; and citizenship, 183; and

colonial resistance, 142, 146, 151, 153; as delegate to First Continental Congress, 155

Adams Family Farm (Stuart), *224*

Adams-Onís Treaty (1819), 262, 406

Adena culture, 10

Administration of Justice Act, 154–155

Africa: people in West, 22, 24–25; reform proposal to ship blacks to, 323; slave trade in West, 33–35

African-Americans: in American Revolutionary War, 178–180; and black codes, 503; in Chesapeake, 75; in Civil War, 478–482; and colonization movement, 323; and Constitution, 193; in early Republic, 229–231; education of, 231, 323, 516–518; and Fifteenth Amendment, 509–510; and Fourteenth Amendment, 504–505; impact of Emancipation on, 515–521; land ownership by, 518–520; language of, 390; and minstrel shows, 350; music of, 393–394; northern migration of, 516; in political office, 512–513; post–Civil War, 499–500, 518–521; protests of, 165–166; religion of, 179, 390–393; sickle-cell trait in, 81; suffrage for, 288, 509–510, 527; survival of West African culture, 79; and Thirteenth Amendment, 502, 503. *See also* Free blacks

African Methodist Episcopal church, 179, 388, 516

Agriculture: cash crops in, 370–371; during Civil War, 486–487; colonial, 103–104; commercial, 274; corn culture in, 368–369; cotton culture in, 336, 366–372; crop-lien system in, 520–521; and immigrants, 400; impact of railroads on, 338; in Jamestown,

47; migrant workers in, P-xxxiv; of Native Americans, 8, 11, 13; in New England, 62, 104; plantation, 373–375, 519a–519b; rice culture in, 80–81, 366; role of yeoman in, 376–377; sharecropping in, 520; slash-and-burn method of, 13; in South, 231, 274; subsistence, 274; sugar culture in, 77–79; technological advances in, 333, 335–336, 520; tobacco culture in, 47, 71, 72–73, 111, 366; in West Africa, 24; and western settlement, 273–274; wheat in, 335. *See also* Farmers

Aix-la-Chapelle, Treaty of (1748), 128

Alabama: admission to Union, 366; agriculture in, 270, 274, 367, 374; economy in, 369; growth of, 268; Ku Klux Klan in, 514; and return to Union, 502; and Yazoo land scandal, 246

Alabama, 476; settlement of claims, 522

Alamance Creek, Battle of, 152

Alamo, 412

Alaska: Eskimo culture in, 5–7; geography of, P-xxxvi–xxxvii; purchase of, 522

Albany Congress (1754), 140

Albany Plan, 129

Albany Regency, 303

Alcorn, James, 511

Alcott, Louisa May, 352, 489

Alcott, William, 292

Aleuts, 2, 5–6

Algiers, 238

Algonquian people, 82–83

Alien and Sedition Act(s) (1798), 225–227, 237, 239

Alien Enemies Act, 225

Alien Friends Act, 225, 226

Allen, Ethan, 157

Allen, William, 104

Alternative of Williamsburg (Dawe), *146*

xlix